GO!
Premium Media Site

Improve your grade with hands-on tools and resources!

- Master *Key Terms* to expand your vocabulary.
- Assess your knowledge with fun *Crossword Puzzles* and *Flipboards*, which let you flip through the definitions of the key terms and match them with the correct term.
- Prepare for exams by taking practice quizzes in the *Online Chapter Review*.
- Download *Student Data Files* for the application projects in each chapter.
- Answer matching and multiple choice questions to test what you learned in each chapter.

And for even more tools, you can access the following Premium Resources using your Access Code. Register now to get the most out of *GO!*.

- *Student Training Videos* for each Objective have been created by the author - a real instructor teaching the same types of courses that you take.*
- *GO! to Work* videos are short interviews with workers showing how they use Office in their job.*
- *GO! for Job Success* videos related to the projects in the chapter cover such important topics as Dressing for Success, Time Management, and Making Ethical Choices.*

*Access code required for these premium resources

Your Access Code is:

Note: If there is no silver foil covering the access code, it may already have been redeemed, and therefore may no longer be valid. In that case, you can purchase online access using a major credit card or PayPal account. To do so, go to **www.pearsonhighered.com/go**, select your book cover, click on "Buy Access" and follow the on-screen instructions.

To Register:

- To start you will need a valid email address and this access code.
- Go to **www.pearsonhighered.com/go** and scroll to find your text book.
- Once you've selected your text, on the Home Page for the book, click the link to access the Student Premium Content.
- Click the Register button and follow the on-screen instructions.
- After you register, you can sign in any time via the log-in area on the same screen.

System Requirements

Windows 7 Ultimate Edition; IE 8
Windows Vista Ultimate Edition SP1; IE 8
Windows XP Professional SP3; IE 7
Windows XP Professional SP3; Firefox 3.6.4
Mac OS 10.5.7; Firefox 3.6.4
Mac OS 10.6; Safari 5

Technical Support

http://247pearsoned.custhelp.com

GO!
with Microsoft®

Office 2013
Volume 1

Shelley Gaskin, Alicia Vargas, and Carolyn McLellan

PEARSON

Boston   Columbus   Indianapolis   New York   San Francisco   Upper Saddle River
Amsterdam   Cape Town   Dubai   London   Madrid   Milan   Munich   Paris   Montréal   Toronto
Delhi   Mexico City   São Paulo   Sydney   Hong Kong   Seoul   Singapore   Taipei   Tokyo

Editor in Chief: Michael Payne
Executive Acquisitions Editor: Jenifer Niles
Editorial Project Manager: Carly Prakapas
Product Development Manager: Laura Burgess
Development Editor: Ginny Munroe
Editorial Assistant: Andra Skaalrud
Director of Marketing: Maggie Leen
Marketing Manager: Brad Forrester
Marketing Coordinator: Susan Osterlitz
Marketing Assistant: Darshika Vyas
Managing Editor: Camille Trentacoste
Senior Production Project Manager: Rhonda Aversa

Operations Specialist: Maura Zaldivar-Garcia
Senior Art Director: Jonathan Boylan
Cover Photo: © photobar/Fotolia
Associate Director of Design: Blair Brown
Director of Media Development: Taylor Ragan
Media Project Manager, Production: John Cassar
Full-Service Project Management: PreMediaGlobal
Composition: PreMediaGlobal
Printer/Binder: Webcrafters, Inc.
Cover Printer: Lehigh-Phoenix Color/Hagerstown
Text Font: MinionPro

ISBN 10: 0-13-314266-3
ISBN 13: 978-0-13-314266-2

Brief Contents

Table of Contents

Office

Word Introduction to Microsoft Word 2013

Chapter 1 Creating Documents with Microsoft Word 2013

Using Tables and Templates to Create Resumes and Cover Letters **179**

Access Introduction to Microsoft Access 2013

Chapter 1   Getting Started with Microsoft Access 2013 487

About the Authors

Shelley Gaskin, Series Editor, is a professor in the Business and Computer Technology Division at Pasadena City College in Pasadena, California. She holds a bachelor's degree in Business Administration from Robert Morris College (Pennsylvania), a master's degree in Business from Northern Illinois University, and a doctorate in Adult and Community Education from Ball State University (Indiana). Before joining Pasadena City College, she spent 12 years in the computer industry, where she was a systems analyst, sales representative, and director of Customer Education with Unisys Corporation. She also worked for Ernst & Young on the development of large systems applications for their clients. She has written and developed training materials for custom systems applications in both the public and private sector, and has also written and edited numerous computer application textbooks.

This book is dedicated to my students, who inspire me every day.

Alicia Vargas is a faculty member in Business Information Technology at Pasadena City College. She holds a master's and a bachelor's degree in business education from California State University, Los Angeles, and has authored several textbooks and training manuals on Microsoft Word, Microsoft Excel, and Microsoft PowerPoint.

This book is dedicated with all my love to my husband Vic, who makes everything possible; and to my children Victor, Phil, and Emmy, who are an unending source of inspiration and who make everything worthwhile.

Carolyn McLellan is the dean of the Division of Information Technology and Business at Tidewater Community College in Virginia Beach, Virginia. She has a master's degree in Secondary Education from Regent University and a bachelor's degree in Business Education from Old Dominion University. She taught for Norfolk Public Schools for 17 years in Business Education and served as a faculty member at Tidewater Community College for eight years teaching networking, where she developed over 23 new courses and earned the Microsoft Certified Trainer and Microsoft Certified System Engineer industry certifications. In addition to teaching, Carolyn loves to play volleyball, boogie board at the beach, bicycle, crochet, cook, and read.

This book is dedicated to my daughters, Megan and Mandy, who have my eternal love; to my mother, Jean, who always believes in me and encouraged me to become a teacher; to my sister Debbie, who was my first student and who inspires me with her strength in overcoming hardships; to my niece Jenna, for her bravery, composure, and beauty; to my grandsons, Jordan and Dexter, who bring me happiness and a renewed joie de vivre; and to the students and IT faculty at Tidewater Community College.

GO! with Office 2013

GO! with Office 2013 is the right solution for you and your students in today's fast-moving, mobile environment. The GO! Series content focuses on the real-world job skills students need to succeed in the workforce. They learn Office by working step-by-step through practical job-related projects that put the core functionality of Office in context. And as has always been true of the GO! Series, students learn the important concepts when they need them, and they never get lost in instruction, because the GO! Series uses Microsoft procedural syntax. Students learn how and learn why—at the teachable moment.

After completing the instructional projects, students are ready to apply the skills in a wide variety of progressively challenging projects that require them to solve problems, think critically, and create projects on their own. *GO! with Office 2013* focuses on today's mobile worker wherever, whenever, and from whatever device. Students engage in hands-on projects covering Office Online (formerly Web Apps), Office 365, collaborative tasks, and touch devices, so students are prepared to work in any environment. And, for those who want to go beyond the classroom and become certified, GO! provides clear MOS preparation guidelines so students know what is needed to ace the Core exam!

What's New

New design reflects the look of Windows 8 and Office 2013 and enhances readability.

Enhanced chapter opener now includes a deeper introduction to the A & B instructional projects and more highly-defined chapter Objectives and Learning Outcomes.

New Application Introductions provide a brief overview of the application and put the chapters in context for students.

Coverage of new features of Office 2013 ensures that students are learning the skills they need to work in today's job market.

New chapter on Windows 8 added because Windows is so integral to teaching Office.

New Office Online versions of Projects A and B and Office 365 Online Collaboration projects using Outlook, SharePoint, and Lync make it easy to teach these tools in your course and help students learn to use touchscreens as well as traditional devices so they know how to get things done from anywhere on any Windows 8 device.

New Application Capstone Projects for each application ensure that students are ready to move on to the next application. Each Application Capstone Project can be found on the Instructor Resource Center and is also a Grader project in MyITLab.

More Grader Projects based on the E, F, and G mastering-level projects, both home-work and assessment versions! These projects are written by our GO! authors, who are all instructors in colleges like yours!

New Training & Assessment Simulations are now written by the authors to match the book one-to-one!

New book Capstone project that you can use as a course final, a test-out exam, or any other way you choose. This can be found on the Instructor Resource Site.

New MOS Map on the Instructor Resource Site and in the Annotated Instructor's Edition indicates clearly where each required MOS Objective is covered.

Three Types of Videos help students understand and succeed in the real world:

- *Student Training Videos* are broken down by Objective and created by the author—a real instructor teaching the same types of courses that you do. Real personal instruction.
- *GO! to Work* videos are short interviews with workers showing how they use Office in their jobs.
- *GO! for Job Success* videos relate to the projects in the chapter and cover important career topics such as *Dressing for Success*, *Time Management*, and *Making Ethical Choices*.

New GO! Learn it Online section at the end of the chapter indicates where various student learning activities can be found, including multiple choice and matching activities.

New styles for in-text boxed content: Another Way, Notes, More Knowledge, Alerts, and **new *By Touch* instructions** are included in line with the instruction and not in the margins so that the student is more likely to read this information.

Clearly indicated Build from Scratch projects: GO! has always had many projects that begin "from scratch," and now we have an icon to really call them out!

New Visual Summary focuses on the four key concepts to remember from each chapter.

New Review and Assessment Guide summarizes the end-of-chapter assessments for a quick overview of the different types and levels of assignments and assessments for each chapter.

New Skills and Procedures Summary chart (online at the Instructor Resource Center) summarizes all of the shortcuts and commands covered in the chapter.

New End-of-Chapter Key Term Glossary with definitions for each chapter, plus a comprehensive end-of-book glossary.

New Flipboards and Crossword Puzzles enable students to review the concepts and key terms learned in each chapter by completing online challenges.

Teach the Course You Want in Less Time

A Microsoft® Office textbook designed for student success!

- **Project-Based** – Students learn by creating projects that they will use in the real world.

- **Microsoft Procedural Syntax** – Steps are written to put students in the right place at the right time.

- **Teachable Moment** – Expository text is woven into the steps—at the moment students need to know it—not chunked together in a block of text that will go unread.

- **Sequential Pagination** – Students have actual page numbers instead of confusing letters and abbreviations.

New Feature

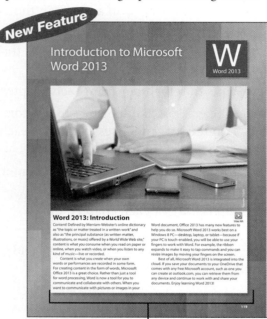

Student Outcomes and Learning Objectives – Objectives are clustered around projects that result in student outcomes.

New Design – Provides a more visually appealing and concise display of important content.

New Application Introductions – provide an overview of the application to prepare students for the upcoming chapters.

Simulation Training and Assessment – Give your students the most realistic Office 2013 experience with open, realistic, high-fidelity simulations.

Project Activities – A project summary stated clearly and quickly.

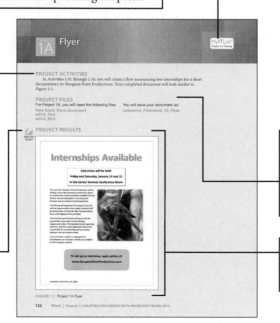

Scenario – Each chapter opens with a job-related scenario that sets the stage for the projects the student will create.

Project Files – Clearly shows students which files are needed for the project and the names they will use to save their documents.

New Build from Scratch icons – enable you to easily see all the projects that the student builds from scratch.

Project Results – Shows students what successful completion looks like.

In-text Features
Another Way, Notes, More Knowledge, Alerts, and By Touch Instructions

Microsoft Procedural Syntax – Steps are written to put the student at the right place at the right time.

Color Coding – Each chapter has two instructional projects, which is less overwhelming for students than one large chapter project. The two projects are differentiated by different colored numbering and headings.

Sequential Pagination – Students are given actual page numbers to navigate through the textbook instead of confusing letters and abbreviations.

Teachable Moment – Expository text is woven into the steps—at the moment students need to know it—not chunked together in a block of text that will go unread.

End-of-Chapter
Content-Based Assessments – Assessments with defined solutions.

Objective List – Every end-of-chapter project includes a listing of covered objectives from Projects A and B.

Review and Assessment Chart – Displays a comprehensive list of each chapter assessment with a description and location to make planning easier.

End-of-Chapter Glossary – Gives students an easy way to review key terms.

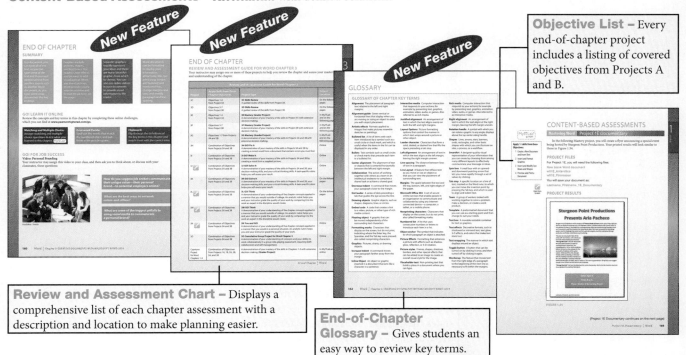

End-of-Chapter

Content-Based Assessments – Assessments with defined solutions. (continued)

Grader projects – Each chapter has six MyITLab Grader projects—three homework and three assessment—clearly indicated by the MyITLab logo.

Task-Specific Rubric – A matrix specific to the GO! Solve It projects that states the criteria and standards for grading these defined-solution projects.

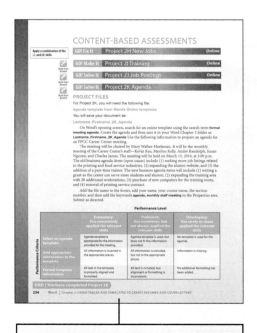

End-of-chapter

Outcomes-Based Assessments – Assessments with open-ended solutions.

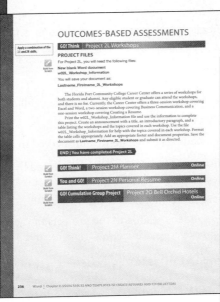

Sample Solution – Outcomes-based assessments include a sample solution so the instructor can compare student work with an example of expert work.

Outcomes Rubric – A matrix specific to the GO! Think projects that states the criteria and standards for grading these open-ended assessments.

Office Online (formerly Web Apps) – For each instructional project, students can create the same or similar result in the corresponding Office Online application - 24 projects in all!

GO! with Microsoft Office 365 – A collaboration project for each chapter teaches students how to use the cloud-based tools of Office 365 to communicate and collaborate from any device, anywhere.

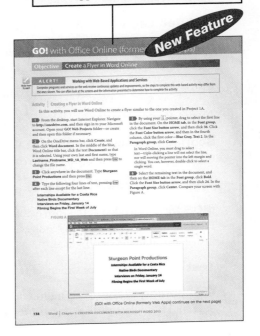

GO! with MyITLab
Gives you a completely integrated solution
Instruction ■ Training ■ Assessment

All of the content in the book and MyITLab is written by the authors, who are instructors, so the instruction works seamlessly with the simulation trainings and grader projects — true 1:1. eText, Training & Assessment Simulations, and Grader Projects

Student Materials

Student Data Files – All student data files are available to all on the Companion Website: www.pearsonhighered.com/go

3 Types of Videos help students understand and succeed in the real world:

- **Student Training Videos** are by Objective and created by the author—a real instructor teaching the same types of courses that you teach.
- *GO! to Work* videos are short interviews with workers showing how they use Office in their job.
- *GO! for Job Success* videos related to the projects in the chapter cover important career topics such as *Dressing for Success, Time Management,* and *Making Ethical Choices.*

Flipboards and crossword puzzles provide a variety of review options for content in each chapter.
Available on the Companion Website using the access code included with your book.
pearsonhighered.com/go

All Instructor and Student materials available at pearsonhighered. com/go

Instructor Materials

Annotated Instructor Edition – An instructor tool includes a full copy of the student textbook and a guide to implementing your course in three different ways, depending on the emphasis you want to place on digital engagement. Also included are teaching tips, discussion topics, and other useful pieces for teaching each chapter.

Assignment Sheets – Lists all the assignments for the chapter. Just add the course information, due dates, and points. Providing these to students ensures they will know what is due and when.

Scripted Lectures – A script to guide your classroom lecture of each instructional project.

Annotated Solution Files – Coupled with the scorecards, these create a grading and scoring system that makes grading easy and efficient.

PowerPoint Lectures – PowerPoint presentations for each chapter.

Audio PowerPoints – Audio versions of the PowerPoint presentations for each chapter.

Scoring Rubrics – Can be used either by students to check their work or by you as a quick check-off for the items that need to be corrected.

Syllabus Templates – For 8-week, 12-week, and 16-week courses.

MOS Map provided at the Instructor Resource Center site and in the Annotated Instructor's Edition, showing where each required MOS Objective is covered either in the book or via additional instructional material provided.

Test Bank – Includes a variety of test questions for each chapter.

Companion Website – Online content such as the Online Chapter Review, Glossary, and Student Data Files are all at www.pearsonhighered.com/go.

Reviewers

GO! Focus Group Participants

Kenneth Mayer	Heald College
Carolyn Borne	Louisiana State University
Toribio Matamoros	Miami Dade College
Lynn Keane	University of South Carolina
Terri Hayes	Broward College
Michelle Carter	Paradise Valley Community College

GO! Reviewers

Abul Sheikh	Abraham Baldwin Agricultural College
John Percy	Atlantic Cape Community College
Janette Hicks	Binghamton University
Shannon Ogden	Black River Technical College
Karen May	Blinn College
Susan Fry	Boise State University
Chigurupati Rani	Borough of Manhattan Community College / CUNY
Ellen Glazer	Broward College
Kate LeGrand	Broward College
Mike Puopolo	Bunker Hill Community College
Nicole Lytle-Kosola	California State University, San Bernardino
Nisheeth Agrawal	Calhoun Community College
Pedro Diaz-Gomez	Cameron
Linda Friedel	Central Arizona College
Gregg Smith	Central Community College
Norm Cregger	Central Michigan University
Lisa LaCaria	Central Piedmont Community College
Steve Siedschlag	Chaffey College
Terri Helfand	Chaffey College
Susan Mills	Chambersburg
Mandy Reininger	Chemeketa Community College
Connie Crossley	Cincinnati State Technical and Community College
Marjorie Deutsch	City University of New York - Queensborough Community College
Mary Ann Zlotow	College of Dupage
Christine Bohnsak	College of Lake County
Gertrude Brier	College of Staten Island
Sharon Brown	College of The Albemarle
Terry Rigsby	Columbia College
Vicki Brooks	Columbia College
Donald Hames	Delgado Community College
Kristen King	Eastern Kentucky University
Kathie Richer	Edmonds Community College
Gary Smith	Elmhurst College
Wendi Kappersw	Embry-Riddle Aeronautical University
Nancy Woolridge	Fullerton College
Abigail Miller	Gateway Community & Technical College
Deep Ramanayake	Gateway Community & Technical College
Gwen White	Gateway Community & Technical College
Debbie Glinert	Gloria K School
Dana Smith	Golf Academy of America
Mary Locke	Greenville Technical College
Diane Marie Roselli	Harrisburg Area Community College
Linda Arnold	Harrisburg Area Community College - Lebanon
Daniel Schoedel	Harrisburg Area Community College - York Campus
Ken Mayer	Heald College
Xiaodong Qiao	Heald College
Donna Lamprecht	Hopkinsville Community College
Kristen Lancaster	Hopkinsville Community College
Johnny Hurley	Iowa Lakes Community College
Linda Halverson	Iowa Lakes Community College
Sarah Kilgo	Isothermal Community College
Chris DeGeare	Jefferson College
David McNair	Jefferson College
Diane San	
Roland S	
Ram R	
Edua	
Ker	
Gle	
Gene Car	
Betty Pearman	
Diane Kosharek	
Peter Meggison	
George Gabb	Mia
Lennie Alice Cooper	Miami D
Richard Mabjish	Miami Dade
Victor Giol	Miami Dade College
John Meir	Midlands Technical Colle
Greg Pauley	Moberly Area Community Co
Catherine Glod	Mohawk Valley Community College
Robert Huyck	Mohawk Valley Community College
Kevin Engellant	Montana Western
Philip Lee	Nashville State Community College
Ruth Neal	Navarro College
Sharron Jordan	Navarro College
Richard Dale	New Mexico State University
Lori Townsend	Niagara County Community College
Judson Curry	North Park University
Mary Zegarski	Northampton Community College
Neal Stenlund	Northern Virginia Community Colege
Michael Goeken	Northwest Vista College
Mary Beth Tarver	Northwestern State University
Amy Rutledge	Oakland University
Marcia Braddock	Okefenokee Technical College
Richard Stocke	Oklahoma State University - OKC
Jane Stam	Onondaga Community College
Mike Michaelson	Palomar College
Kungwen (Dave) Chu	Purdue University Calumet
Wendy Ford	City University of New York - Queensborough Community College
Lewis Hall	Riverside City College
Karen Acree	San Juan College
Tim Ellis	Schoolcraft College
Dan Combellick	Scottsdale Community College
Pat Serrano	Scottsdale Community College
Rose Hendrickson	Sheridan College
Kit Carson	South Georgia College
Rebecca Futch	South Georgia State College
Brad Hagy	Southern Illinois University Carbondale
Mimi Spain	Southern Maine Community College
David Parker	Southern Oregon University
Madeline Baugher	Southwestern Oklahoma State University
Brian Holbert	St. Johns River State College
Bunny Howard	St. Johns River State College
Stephanie Cook	State College of Florida
Sharon Wavle	Tompkins Cortland Community College
George Fiori	Tri-County Technical College
Steve St. John	Tulsa Community College
Karen Thessing	University of Central Arkansas
Richard McMahon	University of Houston-Downtown
Shohreh Hashemi	University of Houston-Downtown
Donna Petty	Wallace Community College
Julia Bell	Walters State Community College
Ruby Kowaney	West Los Angeles College
Casey Thompson	Wiregrass Georgia Technical College
DeAnnia Clements	Wiregrass Georgia Technical College

Getting Started with Windows 8

PROJECT

1A

OUTCOMES
Sign in and out of Windows 8, identify the features of an operating system, create a folder and save a file, use Windows Store apps, and manage your user accounts.

OBJECTIVES
1. Use File Explorer and Desktop Apps to Create a New Folder and Save a File on a Removable Storage Device
2. Identify the Functions of the Windows 8 Operating System and Windows Store Apps
3. Use Windows Store Apps
4. Sign Out of Windows 8 and Turn Off Your Computer
5. Manage User Accounts

PROJECT

1B

OUTCOMES
Personalize your Windows 8 Start screen, manage files and folders, copy and move files and folders, and use the Recycle Bin.

OBJECTIVES
6. Use File Explorer to Display Libraries, Folders, and Files
7. Start Programs and Open Data Files
8. Personalize Your Windows 8 Start Screen
9. Create, Rename, and Copy Files and Folders
10. Move and Delete Files and Folders

violetkaipa/Fotolia

In This Chapter

In this chapter, you will use Microsoft Windows 8, which is software that manages your computer's hardware, software, and data files. Windows 8 also helps you create a personal dashboard to connect you to the things that matter to you. You will use the taskbar and desktop features to get your work done with ease and use Windows Store apps to get your latest personal information and to find information and entertainment. You will sign in to your computer, explore the features of Windows 8, create folders and save files, use Windows Store apps, manage multiple windows, sign out of your computer, and examine user accounts.

The projects in this chapter relate to the **Bell Orchid Hotels**, headquartered in Boston, and which own and operate resorts and business-oriented hotels. Resort properties are located in popular destinations, including Honolulu, Orlando, San Diego, and Santa Barbara. The resorts offer deluxe accommodations and a wide array of dining options. Other Bell Orchid hotels are located in major business centers and offer the latest technology in their meeting facilities. Bell Orchid offers extensive educational opportunities for employees. The company plans to open new properties and update existing properties over the next decade.

Getting to Know Windows 8

PROJECT ACTIVITIES

In Activities 1.01 through 1.10, you will participate in training along with Steven Ramos and Barbara Hewitt, both of whom work for the Information Technology Department at the Boston headquarters office of the Bell Orchid Hotels. After completing this part of the training, you will be able to sign in and sign out of your computer, create folders and save files on a removable storage device, use Windows Store apps, and manage your user account. You will capture two screens that will look similar to Figure 1.1.

PROJECT FILES

For Project 1A, you will need the following files:

A new Snip file and a new Windows 8 screen capture that you will initiate when prompted to do so

You will save your files as:

Lastname_Firstname_1A_Zoom_Snip
Lastname_Firstname_1A_Graph_Snip

PROJECT RESULTS

FIGURE 1.1 Project 1A Getting to Know Windows 8

A *program* is a set of instructions that a computer uses to accomplish a task. A program is also referred to as an *application* or simply as an *app*—the shortened version of the word *application*. Apps help you perform tasks for a specific purpose; for example, to create a document using word processing software, to play a game, to view the latest weather report, or to manage information.

Windows 8 is an *operating system* developed by Microsoft Corporation that works with mobile computing devices of all types and also with traditional PCs. An operating system is a specific type of computer program that manages the other programs on a computer, and that includes computer devices such as desktop computers, laptop computers, smartphones, tablet computers, and game consoles. You need an operating system to:

- use apps
- coordinate the use of your computer hardware such as a keyboard, mouse, touchpad, touchscreen, game controller, or printer
- organize data that you store on your computer or access data that you store in other locations

The term *desktop app* commonly refers to a computer program that is installed on the hard drive of your computer and requires a computer operating system like Microsoft Windows or Apple OS to run. The programs in Microsoft Office such as Word and Excel are popular desktop apps. Adobe's Photoshop is a popular desktop app. Desktop apps typically have hundreds of features that take time to learn and use efficiently.

Apps installed on your computer's hard drive are referred to as *desktop apps* and apps that run from the device software or the browser software on PCs, tablet computers, game consoles, or smartphones are referred to simply as *apps*.

An app is usually a smaller application designed for a single purpose. You might already be familiar with apps that run on an Apple iPhone or an Android phone or a Windows phone; for example, games like Angry Birds and Words with Friends; information apps like The Weather Channel and ESPN ScoreCenter; apps provided by your bank to enable you to conduct transactions on your smartphone; and services like Skype or Google Search.

Similarly, *Windows Store apps* are built for specific purposes; for example, to view your photos, read sports information, play games, organize your list of contacts, or read updates to your social networks like Facebook and Twitter.

ALERT!   **Variations in Screen Organization, Colors, and Functionality Are Common in Windows 8**

Individuals and organizations can determine how Windows 8 displays; therefore, the colors and the organization of various elements on the screen can vary. Your college or organization may customize Windows 8 to display a college picture or logo, or restrict access to certain features. The basic functions and structure of Windows 8 are not changed by such variations. You can be confident that the skills you will practice in this textbook apply to Windows 8 regardless of available functionality or differences between the figures in the book and your screen.

Activity 1.01 | **Understanding User Accounts in Windows 8**

NOTE   **Comparing Your Screen with the Figures in This Textbook**

Your screen will more closely match the figures shown in this textbook if you set your screen resolution to 1280 × 768. At other resolutions, your screen will closely resemble, but not match, the figures shown. To view your screen's resolution, on the desktop, right-click in a blank area, click *Screen resolution*, and then click the Resolution arrow. To adjust the resolution, move the slider to the desired setting, and then click OK.

On a single computer, Windows 8 can have multiple user accounts. You can share a computer with other people in your family or organization and each person can have his or her own information and settings—none of which others can see. Each user on a single computer is referred to as a **local account**.

But what if you have or use more than one computer? Perhaps you have a computer at home and also a laptop computer that you use at school or when traveling. Maybe you have, or are thinking about getting, a tablet computer. The frustration of working on multiple computers is that they do not look the same. Settings and favorite websites that you have on one PC do not automatically appear on other PCs that you use. Additionally, if you get a new PC, you must try to set it up all over again to look like your old PC.

With Windows 8, you can create a **Microsoft account**, and then use that account to sign in to *any* Windows 8 system. Signing in with a Microsoft account is recommended because you can:

- download apps from the Windows Store.
- get your online content—email, social network updates, updated news—automatically displayed in an app when you sign in.
- sync settings online to make every Windows 8 computer you use look and feel the same.

To use a Windows 8 computer, you must establish and then sign in with either a local account or a Microsoft account. Regardless of which one you select, you should provide an email address to associate with the user account name.

If you create and then sign in with a local account, you can still connect to the Internet, but you will not have the advantage of having your personal arrangement of apps displayed to you every time you sign in to a Windows 8 PC. As shown in Figure 1.2, a new user added to a Windows 8 PC can provide an email address to associate with the account. You can use any email address to create a local account—similar to other online services where an email address is your user ID.

FIGURE 1.2

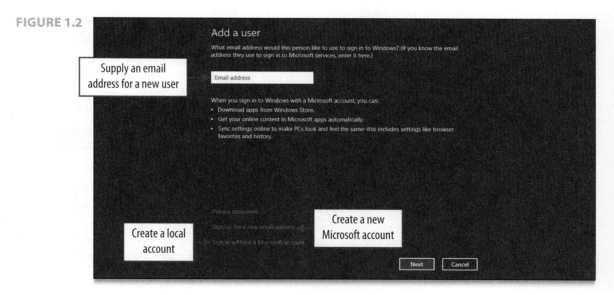

To create a Microsoft account, supply a *hotmail.com*, a *live.com*, or an *outlook.com* email address—or create one from the link at the bottom of the screen to display the form for a new Microsoft account. After you create a Microsoft account, you *do not* have to use it for your email or for any purpose other than to use the Windows 8 interface and to **roam** all of your computing devices. To roam means that you can set up one computer, for example your desktop computer, and then synchronize—roam—all the same settings to your laptop, to your tablet PC, to your Windows phone—to any other device you have that uses Windows 8.

By signing in with a Microsoft account, your computer becomes your connected device where you—not your files—are the center of activity.

To check how well you understand user accounts in Windows 8, take a moment to answer the following questions:

1 On a single Windows 8 computer, multiple people can have a user account with their own information and _____.

2 On a Windows 8 computer, it is recommended that you create a Microsoft account—if you do not have one—and then use that account to sign in because you can sync settings online to make every Windows 8 computer you sign in to _____ and feel the same.

3 To use a Windows 8 computer, you must establish and then sign in with either a _____ account or a Microsoft account.

4 After you create a Microsoft account, you do not have to use it for your _____ or for any other purpose.

5 To _____ means that you can set up one computer and then sync (synchronize) all the same settings to any other device you have that uses Windows 8.

Activity 1.02 | **Turning On Your Computer, Signing In to a Windows 8 User Account, and Exploring the Windows 8 Environment**

Before you begin any computer activity, you must, if necessary, turn on your computer. This process is commonly referred to as *booting the computer*. Because Windows 8 does not require you to completely shut down your computer except to install or repair a hardware device, in most instances moving the mouse or pressing a key will wake your computer in a few seconds. So most of the time you will skip the lengthier boot process.

In this activity, you will turn on your computer and sign in to Windows 8. Within an organization, the sign-in process may differ from that of your own computer.

ALERT! **You Must Have a User Account—Preferably a Microsoft Account—on the Computer at Which You Are Working**

On a Windows 8 PC, you must have a user account in order to sign in. On your own computer, you created your user account when you installed Windows 8 or when you set up your new computer that came with Windows 8. In a classroom or lab, check with your instructor to see how you will sign in to Windows 8. Recall that signing in with a Microsoft account, as described in the previous activity, will enable you to use apps with updated data.

---

1 If necessary, turn on your computer, and then compare your screen with Figure 1.3.

The Windows 8 *Lock screen* displays a picture—this might be a default picture, or a picture that you selected if you have personalized your system already. The Lock screen displays the time, day, and date, and one or more icons—sometimes referred to as *badges*—representing the status of your Internet connection, your battery if you are using a tablet or laptop, and any *Lock screen apps* you might have selected.

Your organization might have a custom sign-in screen with a logo or sign-in instructions, which will differ from the one shown.

FIGURE 1.3

Lock screen picture
(yours may differ)

Time/Day/Date
(yours will differ)

Icons can display under date indicating Internet
and battery status (none shown here)

2 Determine whether you are working with a mouse and keyboard system or with a touchscreen system. If you are working with a touchscreen, determine whether you will use a stylus pen or the touch of your fingers.

Windows 8 is optimized for touchscreen computers and also works with a mouse and keyboard in the way you are probably most accustomed. If your device has a touchscreen, you can use the following gestures with your fingers in place of mouse and keyboard commands:

- Tap an item to click it.
- Press and hold an item for a few seconds and then release to right-click it.
- Touch the screen or an item with two or more fingers and then pinch together to zoom in or stretch your fingers apart to zoom out.
- Slide your finger on the screen to scroll—slide left to scroll right and slide right to scroll left.
- Slide to rearrange—similar to dragging with a mouse.
- Swipe from edge—from right to expose charms; from left to expose open apps, snap apps, or close apps; from top or bottom to show commands or close an app.
- Swipe—slide an item a short distance with a quick movement—to select an item and bring up app commands, if any.

NOTE **This Book Assumes You Are Using a Mouse and Keyboard but You Can Also Use Touch**

The instruction in this textbook uses terminology that assumes you are using a mouse and keyboard, but you need only substitute the gestures listed above to move through the instruction easily using touch. If a touch gesture needs more clarification, a *By Touch* box will assist you in using the correct gesture. Because more precision is needed, for desktop operations touching with a stylus pen may be preferable to touch using your fingers. When working with Windows Store apps, finger gestures are precise.

3 Press Enter to display the Windows 8 sign-in screen.

BY TOUCH   On the Lock screen, swipe upward to display the sign-in screen. Tap your user image if necessary to display the Password box.

4 If you are the displayed user, type your password (if you have established one) and press [Enter]. If you are not the displayed user, click your user image if it displays or click the *Switch user* arrow ⊖ and then click your user image. Type your password, and then compare your screen with Figure 1.4.

⟳ **BY TOUCH**   Tap the Password box to display the on-screen keyboard, type your password, and then at the right end of the Password box, tap the arrow.

The Windows 8 *Start scsreen* displays with square and rectangular boxes—referred to as *tiles*—from which you can access apps, websites, programs, and tools for using your computer by simply clicking or tapping them.

Think of the Start screen as your connected *dashboard*—a one-screen view of links to information and programs that matter to *you*—through which you can connect with the people, activities, places, and apps that you care about. Some tiles are referred to as *live tiles*, meaning they are constantly updated with fresh information relevant to you—the number of new email messages you have, new sports scores that you are interested in, or new updates to social networks such as Facebook or Twitter. Live tiles are at the center of your Windows 8 experience.

As you progress in your study of Windows 8, you will learn to customize the Start screen and add, delete, and organize tiles into meaningful groups. Your Start screen will not look like anyone else's; you will customize it to suit your own information needs.

FIGURE 1.4

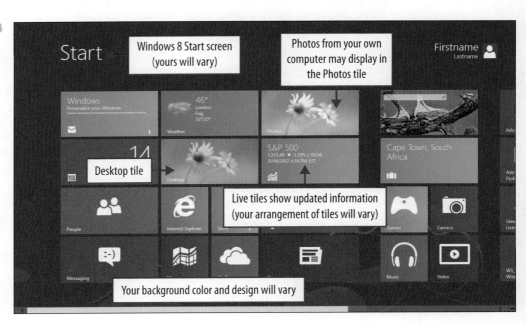

NOTE   **Differing Sign-In Procedures and Passwords**

Depending on whether you are working on your own computer, in a college lab, or in an organization, your sign-in process may differ. If you have a different sign-in screen, sign in as directed and move to Step 5 of this activity. If you are working in a classroom or lab, ask your instructor or lab assistant about the user account name and password to use. On your own computer, use your own user account name and password if you established a password.

---

5 On your **Start screen**, locate and then move the mouse pointer over—*point to*—the **Desktop tile**, and then *click*—press the left button on your mouse pointing device—to display the **Windows desktop**.

The *mouse pointer* is any symbol that displays on your screen in response to moving your mouse.

⟳ **BY TOUCH**   Tap the Windows desktop tile. On a touchscreen, a stylus pen will display a mouse pointer; if you use your fingers, you have no mouse pointer.

6 Compare your screen with Figure 1.5, and then take a moment to study the parts of the Windows desktop as shown in the table in Figure 1.6.

FIGURE 1.5

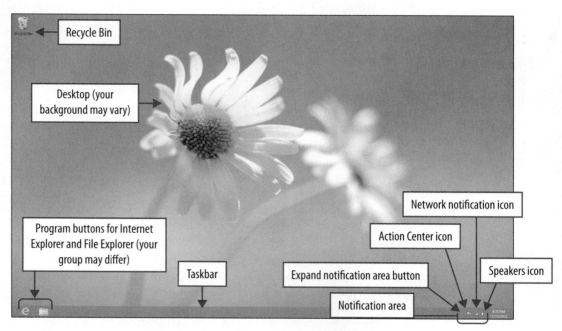

Recycle Bin

Desktop (your background may vary)

Network notification icon

Action Center icon

Speakers icon

Program buttons for Internet Explorer and File Explorer (your group may differ)

Taskbar

Expand notification area button

Notification area

FIGURE 1.6

PARTS OF THE WINDOWS 8 DESKTOP	
Action Center icon in the notification area	Displays the **Action Center**—a central place to view alerts and take actions related to things that need your attention.
Desktop	Serves as a surface for your work, like the top of an actual desk. Here you can arrange **icons**—small pictures that represent a file, folder, program, or other object—on the desktop such as shortcuts to programs, files, folders, and various types of documents in the same manner you would arrange physical objects on top of a desk.
Desktop background	Displays the colors and graphics of your desktop; you can change the **desktop background** to look the way you want it, such as using a picture or a solid color. Also referred to as **wallpaper**.
Expand notification area button	Displays additional icons related to your notifications.
Network notification icon	Displays the status of your network.
Notification area	Displays notification icons and the system clock and calendar; sometimes referred to as the **system tray**.
Program buttons	Launch **Internet Explorer**, the web browser program developed by Microsoft that is included with Windows 8, and **File Explorer**, the program that displays the contents of libraries, folders, and files on your computer, and also enables you to perform tasks related to your files and folders such as copying, moving, and renaming.
Recycle Bin	Contains files and folders that you delete. When you delete a file or folder, it is not actually deleted; it stays in the Recycle Bin if you want it back, until you take an action to empty the Recycle Bin.
Speakers icon	Displays the status of your computer's speakers (if any).
Taskbar	Contains program buttons to launch programs and buttons for all open programs; by default, it is located at the bottom of the desktop, but you can move it. You can customize the number and arrangement of buttons.

Activity 1.03 | Pinning a Program to the Taskbar

Snipping Tool is a program within Windows 8 that captures an image of all or part of your computer's screen within desktop apps. A *snip*, as the captured image is called, can be annotated, saved, copied, or shared via email. This is also referred to as a *screen capture* or a *screenshot*.

1 Point to the lower left corner of your screen to display the **Start screen** icon ▨ and then click one time to display the **Start screen**. Although you will not immediately see your typing, begin to type **snipping** and then compare your screen with Figure 1.7.

The easiest and fastest way to search for an app is to use the *Start search* feature—from the Start screen, just start to type. By default, Windows 8 searches for apps, but you can easily change to search for settings or files.

The Start search feature searches for all apps—both desktop apps and Windows Store apps.

⟳ BY TOUCH   On a touchscreen, swipe in from right edge of the screen, and then tap Search. Tap in the Search box to display the on-screen keyboard, and then begin to type *snipping*.

FIGURE 1.7

2 On the left, with **Snipping Tool** bordered in white—referred to as the *focus* of the search—press Enter one time.

The desktop redisplays, the Snipping Tool dialog box displays on the desktop, and on the taskbar, the Snipping Tool program button displays framed in a lighter shade to indicate that the program is open.

A *dialog box* is a small window that displays options for completing a task.

⟳ BY TOUCH   Tap the Snipping Tool app.

3 On the taskbar, point to the **Snipping Tool program button** ✂ and then *right-click*—click the right mouse button one time. On the displayed **Jump List**, click **Pin this program to taskbar**.

A *Jump List* displays destinations and tasks from a program's taskbar button.

⟳ BY TOUCH   On the taskbar, use the *Swipe to select* technique—swipe upward with a short quick movement—to display the Jump List. On the list, tap *Pin this program to taskbar*.

4 Point to the upper right corner of the **Snipping Tool** dialog box, and then click **Close** ☒.

Because you will use Snipping Tool frequently while completing the projects in this textbook, it is recommended that you leave Snipping Tool pinned to your taskbar.

A *file* is a collection of information stored on a computer under a single name. Examples of a file include a Word document, an Excel workbook, a picture, a song, or a program. A *folder* is a container in which you can store files. Windows 8 organizes and keeps track of your electronic files by letting you create and label electronic folders into which you can place your files.

In this activity, you will create a new folder on a *removable storage device*. Removable storage devices, such as a USB flash drive, are commonly used to transfer information from one computer to another. Such devices are also useful when you want to work with your files on different computers. For example, you probably have files that you work with at your college, at home, and possibly at your workplace.

A *drive* is an area of storage that is formatted with a file system compatible with your operating system and is identified by a drive letter. For example, your computer's *hard disk drive*—the primary storage device located inside your computer where some of your files and programs are typically stored—is usually designated as drive C. Removable storage devices that you insert into your computer will be designated with a drive letter—the letter designation varies from one computer to another.

As you progress in your study of Windows 8, you will also learn to use *cloud storage*—storage space on an Internet site that can also display as a drive on your computer. When you create a Microsoft account, free cloud storage called *OneDrive* (formerly SkyDrive) is provided to you.

> **ALERT!** | You will need a USB flash drive to complete this activity.

1 Be sure your Windows desktop is still displayed. Insert a USB flash drive into your computer.

If this is the first time you have used this device in the computer, in the upper right portion of your screen, a message might indicate *Tap to choose what happens with removable drives*.

You might also hear a sound and see a message in the taskbar that the device software is being installed.

2 If necessary, click the message in the upper right corner, and then click *Take no action*. If a window opens displaying the contents of your USB device, in the upper right corner click **Close** ⊠.

3 On the taskbar, click **File Explorer** 🗎. Compare your screen with Figure 1.8.

The *folder window* for *Libraries* displays. A folder window displays the contents of the current location—folder, library, or drive—and contains helpful parts so that you can *navigate*—explore within the file organizing structure of Windows.

A *library* is a collection of items, such as files and folders, assembled from various locations. A *location* is any disk drive, folder, or other place in which you can store files and folders.

FIGURE 1.8

4 ▷ On the left, in the **navigation pane**, click **Computer**, and then compare your screen to Figure 1.9.

The *navigation pane* is the area on the left side of a folder or library window; it displays favorites, libraries, and an expandable list of drives and folders. If you are connected to a network, the name of the network, such as *Homegroup*, displays.

In the Computer window, you have access to all the storage areas inside and connected to your computer such as your hard disk drive, DVD or CD drives, removable storage devices, and network drive locations if you are connected to a network and have storage space there.

FIGURE 1.9

5 ▷ Under **Hard Disk Drives**, locate **OS (C:)**, point to the device name to display the ⬚ pointer, and then right-click to display a shortcut menu. Compare your screen with Figure 1.10.

A *shortcut menu* is a context-sensitive menu that displays commands and options relevant to the active object.

Your hard disk drive may be referred to by another name such as Local Disk (C:).

🗘 **BY TOUCH**   Press and hold briefly to display a shaded square and then release.

FIGURE 1.10

6 ▷ On the shortcut menu, click **Open** to display the *file list* for this drive.

A file list displays the contents of the current folder or library. Here, in the C: drive, Windows 8 stores various files related to your operating system. The Windows logo on the C: drive indicates this is where the Windows 8 operating system is stored.

🗘 **ANOTHER WAY**   Point to the device name and double-click to display the file list for the device.

7 To the left of the **address bar**, click the **Up** button ↑ to move up one level in the drive hierarchy and close the file list.

The ***address bar*** displays your current location in the folder structure as a series of links separated by arrows.

8 Under **Devices with Removable Storage**, click your **USB flash drive** to select it, and notice that the drive is highlighted in blue, indicating it is selected. At the top of the window, on the ribbon, click the **Computer tab**, and then in the **Location group**, click **Open**. Compare your screen with Figure 1.11.

N O T E | **Does Your Ribbon Show Only the Tab Names?**

By default, the ribbon is minimized and appears as a menu bar, displaying only the ribbon tabs. If only the tabs of your ribbon are displayed, click the Expand the Ribbon arrow ⌄ on the right side to display the full ribbon.

The file list for your USB flash drive displays. If this is a new USB flash drive, there may be no files or only a few files related to the USB device itself.

The ***ribbon*** is a user interface in Windows 8 that groups the commands for performing related tasks on tabs across the upper portion of a window.

FIGURE 1.11

9 On the ribbon, notice that a tab for **Drive Tools** displays above the **Manage tab**.

This is a ***contextual tab***, which is a tab added to the ribbon automatically when a specific object is selected and that contains commands relevant to the selected object.

10 On the ribbon, in the **New group**, click **New folder**.

11 With the text *New folder* highlighted in blue, type **Windows 8 Chapter 1** and press Enter to confirm the folder name and select—highlight in blue—the new folder. With the folder selected, press Enter again to open the folder window. Compare your screen with Figure 1.12.

To ***select*** means to specify, by highlighting, a block of data or text on the screen with the intent of performing some action on the selection.

A new folder is created on your removable storage device. The address bar indicates the ***path*** from Computer to your device to your folder. A path is a sequence of folders that leads to a specific file or folder.

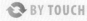 **BY TOUCH** | You may have to tap the keyboard icon in the lower right corner of the taskbar to display the on-screen keyboard.

FIGURE 1.12

Activity 1.05 | Creating and Saving a File

1 In the upper right corner of the folder window, click **Help** 🔘, and then under the **Search** box, click **Help home**. Click **Get started**, and then click **Touch: swipe, tap, and beyond**. Compare your screen with Figure 1.13.

A vertical *scroll bar* displays on the right side of this window. A scroll bar displays when the contents of a window are not completely visible. A scroll bar can be vertical as shown or horizontal and displayed at the bottom of a window.

Within the scroll bar, you can move the *scroll box* to bring the contents of the window into view. The position of the scroll box within the scroll bar indicates your relative position within the window's contents. You can click the *scroll arrow* at either end of the scroll bar to move within the window in small increments.

Each computer manufacturer has some control over the Windows Help and Support opening screen. At the top of this screen, the manufacturer may place links to its own support and information about your computer's hardware.

FIGURE 1.13

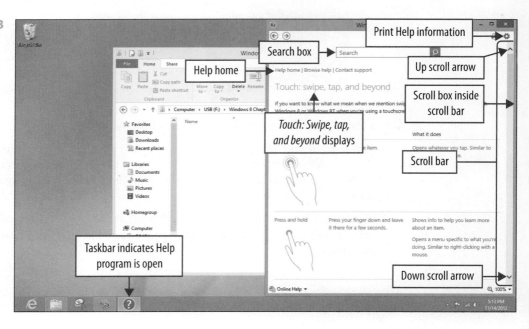

2 Click the **down scroll arrow** as necessary—or drag the scroll box down—until the information and diagram for **Pinch or stretch to zoom** displays in the center of the window, as shown in Figure 1.14.

FIGURE 1.14

3 On the taskbar, click **Snipping Tool** 🔲 to display the small **Snipping Tool** window.

4 On the **menu bar** of the **Snipping Tool**, click the **arrow** to the right of *New*—referred to as the **New arrow**—and then compare your screen with Figure 1.15.

An arrow attached to a button will display a menu when clicked. Such a button is referred to as a *split button*—clicking the main part of the button performs a command and clicking the arrow opens a menu with choices. A *menu* is a list of commands within a category, and a group of menus at the top of a program window is referred to as a *menu bar*.

FIGURE 1.15

5 On the menu, notice that there are four types of snips.

A *free-form snip* lets you draw an irregular line, such as a circle, around an area of the screen. A *rectangular snip* lets you draw a precise box by dragging the mouse pointer around an area of the screen to form a rectangle. A *window snip* captures the entire displayed window. A *full-screen snip* captures the entire screen.

To *drag* is to move something from one location on the screen to another while holding down the left mouse button; the action of dragging includes releasing the mouse button at the desired time or location.

BY TOUCH   Slide your finger to drag and then lift your finger to release.

6 On the menu, click **Window Snip**. Then, move your mouse pointer over the open **Windows Help and Support** window, and notice that a red rectangle surrounds the window; the remainder of your screen dims.

7 With the 🖑 pointer positioned anywhere over the surrounded window, click the left mouse button one time. Use the scroll bar to position the snip near the top of the window, and then compare your screen with Figure 1.16.

Your snip is copied to the Snipping Tool mark-up window. Here you can annotate—mark or make notes on—save, copy, or share the snip.

FIGURE 1.16

8 On the toolbar of the **Snipping Tool** mark-up window, click the **Pen button arrow** [/], and then click **Red Pen**. Notice that your mouse pointer displays as a red dot.

9 In the illustration for *Pinch or stretch to zoom*, point to the end of one of the blue arrows, and then while holding down the left mouse button, draw a red free-form circle around the illustration. If you are not satisfied with your circle, on the toolbar, click **Eraser** [✐], point anywhere on the red circle, click to erase, and then begin again with Step 8.

10 On the toolbar of the **Snipping Tool** mark-up window, click **Highlighter** [✐]. Notice that your mouse pointer displays as a small yellow rectangle.

11 Point to the text *Pinch or stretch to zoom*, hold down the left mouse button, and then drag over the text to highlight it in yellow. If you are not satisfied with your yellow highlight, on the toolbar, click **Eraser** [✐], point anywhere on the yellow highlight, click to erase, and then begin again with Step 10. Compare your screen with Figure 1.17.

 BY TOUCH   Use your finger to draw the circle and to highlight text.

FIGURE 1.17

12 On the **Snipping Tool** mark-up window's toolbar, click **Save Snip** [🖫] to display the **Save As** dialog box.

13 In the **Save As** dialog box, in the **navigation pane** on the left, drag the scroll bar down as necessary to view **Computer**. If necessary, to the left of **Computer**, click ▷ to expand the list, and then click the name of your **USB flash drive**.

14 In the **file list**, scroll as necessary, locate and *double-click*—press the left mouse button two times in rapid succession while holding the mouse still—your **Windows 8 Chapter 1** folder. Compare your screen with Figure 1.18.

ANOTHER WAY   Right-click the folder name and click Open.

FIGURE 1.18

NOTE   Successful Double-Clicking Requires a Steady Hand

Double-clicking needs a steady hand. The speed of the two clicks is not as important as holding the mouse still between the two clicks. If you are not satisfied with your result, try again.

---

15 At the bottom of the **Save As** dialog box, locate **Save as type**, click anywhere in the box to display a list, and then on the displayed list click, **JPEG file**.

> *JPEG*, which is commonly pronounced *JAY-peg* and stands for Joint Photographic Experts Group, is a common file type used by digital cameras and computers to store digital pictures. JPEG is popular because it can store a high-quality picture in a relatively small file.

16 At the bottom of the **Save As** dialog box, click in the **File name** box to select the text *Capture*, and then using your own name, type **Lastname_Firstname_1A_Zoom_Snip**

> Within any Windows-based program, text highlighted in blue—selected—in this manner will be replaced by your typing.

NOTE   File Naming in This Textbook

Windows 8 recognizes file names with spaces. You can use spaces in file names, however, some programs, especially when transferring files over the Internet, may insert the extra characters %20 in place of a space. In this textbook you will be instructed to save files using an underscore instead of a space. The underscore key is the shift of the ⎡ - ⎤ key—on most keyboards located two or three keys to the left of ⎡Backspace⎤.

---

17 In the lower right corner of the window, click the **Save** button.

18 **Close** ⊠ the **Snipping Tool** mark-up window, the **Windows Help and Support** window, and your **USB folder** window. Hold this file until you finish Project 1A, and then submit as directed by your instructor.

> You have successfully created a folder on a removable storage device and saved a file within that folder.

Traditionally, the three major tasks of an operating system are to:

- Manage your computer's hardware—the printers, scanners, disk drives, monitors, and other hardware attached to it.
- Manage the application software installed on your computer—programs like those in Microsoft Office and other programs you might install to manage your money, edit photos, play games, and so on.
- Manage the *data* generated from your application software. Data refers to the documents, worksheets, pictures, songs, and so on that you create and store during the day-to-day use of your computer.

The Windows 8 operating system continues to perform these three tasks, and additionally is optimized for touchscreens; for example, tablets of all sizes and convertible laptop computers. Windows 8 works equally well with any input device, including a mouse, keyboard, touchscreen, and pen—a pen-shaped stylus that you tap on a computer screen.

The apps you use from the Start screen are referred to as *immersive*—they have no borders, no menus, and they behave differently from the traditional Windows desktop programs you just practiced. Because there is no taskbar, these apps cannot be minimized, nor can they be dragged around the screen as smaller windows. This look and behavior of apps is called *Microsoft Design Language*, which refers to the design principles in Windows 8 that include tiles with white text on deeply colored backgrounds, consistent fonts, simpler navigation, and the use of the entire screen. The idea is that you are immersed in the app with no screen distractions.

In most instances, when you purchase a computer, the operating system software is already installed. The operating system consists of many smaller programs, stored as system files, which transfer data to and from the disk and transfer data in and out of your computer's memory. Other functions performed by the operating system include hardware-specific tasks such as checking to see if a key has been pressed on the keyboard and, if it has, displaying the appropriate letter or character on the screen.

When using a Windows 8 computer, you can write and create using traditional desktop apps, and you can also read and socialize and communicate by using the Windows Store apps. With Windows 8, as compared to earlier versions of Windows, your PC behaves like a smartphone or tablet—it is connected, it is mobile, and it is centered on people and activities. If, as Microsoft predicts, the laptop and tablet will ultimately merge into one device—like the Microsoft Surface shown in Figure 1.19—then you will be well prepared by learning to use Windows 8 and the Windows Store apps.

FIGURE 1.19

Surface with Windows RT   Surface with Windows 8 Pro

Windows 8, in the same manner as other operating systems and earlier versions of the Windows operating system, has a desktop that uses a *graphical user interface*—abbreviated as *GUI* and pronounced *GOO-ee*. A GUI uses graphics such as an image of a file folder or wastebasket that you click to activate the item represented. A GUI commonly incorporates the following:

- A *pointer*—any symbol that displays on your screen in response to moving your mouse and with which you can select objects and commands.
- A *pointing device*, such as a mouse or touchpad, to control the pointer.
- *Icons*—small images that represent commands, files, applications, or other windows. By selecting an icon and pressing a mouse button, you can start a program or move objects to different locations on your screen.
- A *desktop*—a simulation of a real desk that represents your work area; here you can arrange icons such as shortcuts to programs, files, folders, and various types of documents in the same manner you would arrange physical objects on top of a desk.

In Windows 8, you now also have the Start screen, organized by tiles, that serves as a connected dashboard to all of your important sites and services. On the Start screen, your view is tailored to your information and activities; for example, pictures display as *thumbnails*—reduced images of graphics—email messages say who they are from, and videos include their length.

The physical parts of your computer such as the central processing unit (CPU), memory, and any attached devices such as a printer, are collectively known as *resources*. The operating system keeps track of the status of each resource and decides when a resource needs attention and for how long.

There will be times when you want and need to interact with the functions of the operating system; for example, when you want to install a new hardware device like a color printer. Windows 8 provides tools with which you can inform the operating system of new hardware that you attach to your computer.

Software application programs are the programs that enable you to do work on, and be entertained by, your computer—programs such as Word and Excel found in the Microsoft Office suite of products, Adobe Photoshop, and computer games. An application program, however, cannot run on its own—it must run under the direction of the operating system.

For the everyday use of your computer, the most important and most often used function of the operating system is managing your files and folders—referred to as *data management*. In the same manner that you strive to keep your paper documents and file folders organized so that you can find information when you need it, your goal when organizing your computer files and folders is to group your files so that you can find information easily. Managing your data files so that you can find your information when you need it is an important computing skill.

To check how well you can identify operating system functions, take a moment to answer the following questions:

1. Of the three major functions of the operating system, the first is to manage your computer's _____ such as disk drives, monitors, and printers.

2. The second major function of the operating system is to manage the application _____ such as Microsoft Word, Microsoft Excel, and video games.

3. The third major function of the operating system is to manage the _____ generated from your applications—the files such as Word documents, Excel workbooks, pictures, and songs.

4. The Start screen, which displays live tiles with your updated information, is your connected _____ to all of your important sites and services.

5. One of the most important computing skills you can learn is how to manage your _____ _____ so that you can find your information quickly.

According to Microsoft, a billion people in the world use Windows and 93% of PCs in the world run some version of Windows. Increasingly people want to use Windows in a format that runs easily on mobile computing devices such as laptops, tablets, and convertibles; research shows this is where people now spend more time.

With only desktop apps to choose from, Windows is centered around files—typing and creating things—and that will continue to be an important part of what you do on your computer. Additionally, you are doing different kinds of things on your PC, and you probably expect your PC to be more like a smartphone—connected all the time, mobile, to have long battery life, and be centered on the people and activities that are important to you. It is for those activities that the Windows Store apps will become important to you.

Think of Windows 8 as a way to do work on your desktop or laptop computer, and then to read and be entertained on your laptop, tablet, or Xbox game console. Microsoft promotes Windows 8 as both serious for work and fun for entertainment and social networking.

Activity 1.07 | Using Windows Store Apps

An array of Windows Store apps displays on the Start screen immediately after you sign in to a Windows 8 computer. On a new computer, the apps might be preselected by your computer manufacturer and by Microsoft. You can use these right away, and later you can add, delete, and rearrange the apps so that your Start screen becomes your own personal dashboard. Recall that some apps are represented by live tiles that will update with your personal information, such as Mail, after you set them to do so.

1 With your **desktop** still displayed, point to the lower left corner of your screen to display and then click one time to display the **Start screen**.

You can use this technique to return to the Start screen from any other screen—including the desktop.

2 On your **Start screen**, locate and point to the **Sports** app tile that comes with Windows 8. If necessary, drag the scroll bar at the bottom of the screen to the right to locate the app. If you cannot locate the Sports app, select some other news app. Compare your screen with Figure 1.20.

⟳ BY TOUCH   To display the Start screen, always swipe in from the right and tap Start. To scroll, slide your finger to the left to scroll to the right.

FIGURE 1.20

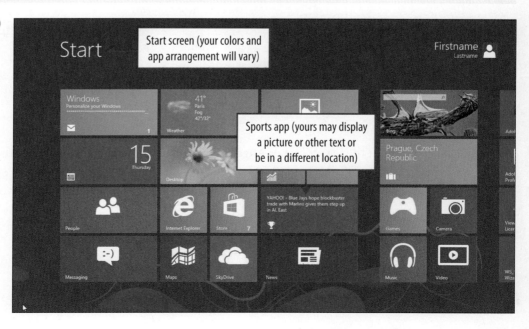

3 Click the **Sports** app tile, if necessary wait a moment if this is the first time you have used this app, point anywhere on the screen, and then right-click to display the app bar. Compare your screen with Figure 1.21.

> Here you can navigate directly to categories such as the NBA (National Basketball Association) or MLB (Major League Baseball). This feature is the **app bar**—an area at the top or bottom of a Windows Store app containing various controls pertaining to the app.

BY TOUCH On a touchscreen, from the bottom or top of the screen, swipe slightly upward or downward to display the app bar.

ANOTHER WAY Press [⊞] + [Z] to display the app bar in an app.

FIGURE 1.21

4 At the top of the screen, click the **Favorite Teams** tile, and then click ⊕ to add another Favorite Team. With the **insertion point** blinking in the **Enter team name** box, type **Los** and then compare your screen with Figure 1.22.

> The **insertion point** is a blinking vertical line that indicates where text will be inserted when you type.

FIGURE 1.22

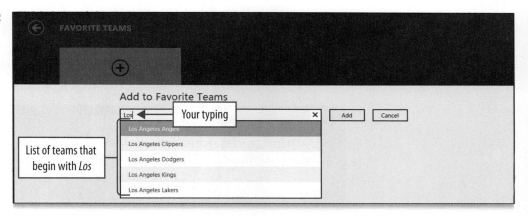

5 On the list, click **Los Angeles Dodgers**, and then compare your screen with Figure 1.23.

> Depending on the time of year and the team's standing, the information will vary.

FIGURE 1.23

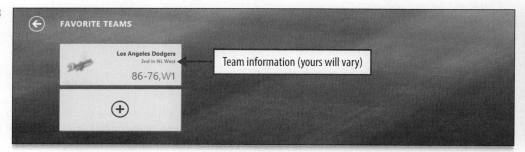

6 On your keyboard, in the lower left corner, locate and then press the [⊞] to display the **Start screen**.

This is the keyboard technique to display the Start screen.

7 On the **Start screen**, click the **Sports** app tile again.

The Favorite Teams screen with your selected team information displays because this was the last screen displayed before you returned to the Start screen.

8 On the **Favorite Teams** screen, click the **Los Angeles Dodgers** tile to see the latest *Top Story* regarding this team. Move your mouse slightly to display the gray scroll bar at the bottom of the screen, and then drag the scroll box to the right to see additional news stories related to the Los Angeles Dodgers.

BY TOUCH   Slide your finger to the left to scroll to the right to view more articles.

9 Point to the top of the screen to display the [✋] pointer, hold down the left mouse button, and then drag the pointer to the bottom of the screen to close the app and redisplay the **Start screen**.

Use this technique to close an app. Leaving an app, for example by redisplaying the Start screen, does not close it.

BY TOUCH   Swipe from the top of the screen to the bottom of the screen to close the app.

10 Locate and click the **Maps** app tile; click Allow if prompted to use your location. Then press [⊞] to return to the **Start screen**.

11 Locate and then click the **Finance** app tile. Right-click anywhere on the screen, and then at the top, click the **Watchlist** tile. Click [⊕], and then in the **Company name/Symbol** box, type **Microsoft** Click **Add** to add the NASDAQ stock listing for Microsoft. If Microsoft is already on your **Watchlist**, click **Cancel**.

A Watchlist tile for Microsoft Corporation, displaying their stock symbol MSFT, displays the latest information about Microsoft's stock price. Other companies might also display on your Watchlist.

12 Click the **MSFT tile** to see a graph of the day's stock price. At the bottom, click **1 Year** to see a graph representing one year.

13 With your Microsoft graph displayed, hold down ⊞ and press ⌊PrintScrn⌋ and then release the two keys. Notice that your screen dims momentarily; you will view the screenshot at the end of this activity.

A ***keyboard shortcut*** is a combination of two or more keyboard keys used to perform a task that would otherwise require a mouse.

On the Start screen or in a Windows Store app, use this technique to create a screenshot. Snipping Tool is not available for the Start screen or Windows Store apps. The screenshot file is automatically stored in your Pictures library.

 BY TOUCH   Use or attach a keyboard; or, enable the on-screen keyboard, tap ⊞ to display it in white, and then tap the key labeled *PrtScn*. The keyboard will display in the picture.

14 Move the mouse slightly to display the gray scroll bar at the bottom of the screen, and then drag the scroll box to the right to read the latest news stories about Microsoft.

15 Press ⊞ to redisplay the **Start screen**.

From any screen, recall that you can redisplay the Start screen by pointing to the lower left corner and clicking ▣ or by pressing ⊞.

16 Locate and then click the **Travel** app tile. Move your mouse slightly to display the gray scroll bar at the bottom of the screen, and then drag the scroll box to the right to display pictures of featured travel sites.

17 Use one of the techniques you have practiced to redisplay the **Start screen**, and then point to the upper left corner of your screen. Notice a thumbnail of the last app you used—the Travel app. Compare your screen with Figure 1.24.

This corner is referred to as the ***Back tip***—it displays a thumbnail image of the last screen you were on, and you can use it to *go back* to your previous screen.

FIGURE 1.24

18 With the Back tip thumbnail displayed, notice faint vertical lines directly below and along the left edge of the screen. Without holding down any mouse buttons, move your mouse down slightly along the left edge of your screen. Compare your screen with Figure 1.25.

This is the ***app switcher***—the thumbnail view of open apps that displays when you move your mouse down from the Back tip in the upper left corner. To switch to an app that is still open, you can click any of the thumbnails. This feature is also referred to as simply ***switcher***.

FIGURE 1.25

Swipe in slightly from the left edge of the screen and when the thumbnail of the previous app thumbnail appears, swipe slightly back to the left. Also, switcher stays docked on the side of the screen until you select something else. To close an app from switcher, drag it out of switcher and to the bottom of the screen.

19 ▸ Move your mouse out of the app switcher to close its view, and then point to the lower left corner of the screen; notice that a thumbnail of the last open app also displays here.

Because you already have the Start screen displayed, pointing to the lower left corner will display the last screen you were on that is still open. This corner is referred to as the *Start tip*.

20 ▸ Move the mouse slightly upward to display app switcher—thumbnails of all open apps.

To display app switcher, you must first point to either the upper left corner or the lower left corner, and then move the mouse upward or downward along the left edge of the screen.

21 ▸ In the app switcher, point to the **Finance** app, right-click, and then click **Close**.

Use this technique to close an app without redisplaying it.

22 ▸ Use the same technique to close the **Maps** app and the **Travel** app.

More **Knowledge** | **Use 🪟 + Tab to Display Switcher**

Hold down 🪟 and press Tab to display switcher. Continue to hold down 🪟 to keep the display open. Click any displayed app in the switcher to move to it.

Activity 1.08 | **Moving Between the Start Screen and Desktop and Saving a Windows Store App Screenshot as a File**

In the day-to-day use of your computer, depending on what you need to do, you will move between desktop apps and Windows Store apps, and it is easy to do so.

1 ▸ On your **Start screen**, locate the **Desktop** tile and click it one time.

If you move frequently from the Start screen to the desktop, you will want to keep your desktop tile easily visible.

ANOTHER WAY

From any Windows Store app or the Start screen, point to the lower left corner of the screen, right-click, and then on the shortcut menu, click Desktop.

---

2 ▸ From the taskbar, open **File Explorer** 🗎 to display the **Libraries** window. In the **file list**, double-click **Pictures**, and then double-click **Screenshots**—this navigation is typically indicated as **Libraries ▸ Pictures ▸ Screenshots**. Compare your screen with Figure 1.26.

Your view might be the Large Icons view.

FIGURE 1.26

3 In the **file list**, click one time to select the **Screenshot (1)** file; if more than one Screenshot file displays, click to select the file that has the highest number.

A screenshot captured in this manner from a Windows Store app is saved as a *.png* file, which is commonly pronounced *PING*, and stands for Portable Network Graphic. This is an image file type that can be transferred over the Internet.

4 On the ribbon, on the **Home tab**, in the **Organize group**, click **Rename**, and then using your own name, type **Lastname_Firstname_1A_Graph_Snip** Press Enter.

5 With the renamed file selected, on the ribbon, in the **Organize group**, click **Move to**, and then click **Choose location**. In the **Move Items** dialog box, scroll down, click **Computer** to expand it, click your **USB** drive, and then click your **Windows 8 Chapter 1** folder. In the lower right corner, click **Move**.

Save this file until you complete Project 1A.

6 **Close** X the **Screenshots** window.

Objective 4   Sign Out of Windows 8 and Turn Off Your Computer

On your own computer, when you are done working, sign out from Windows 8, and then set your computer properly so that your data is saved, you save energy, and your computer remains secure.

When you turn off your computer by using the *Sleep* command, Windows 8 automatically saves your work, the screen goes dark, the computer's fan stops, and your computer goes to sleep. You need not close your programs or files because your work is saved. When you wake your computer by pressing a key, moving the mouse, or using whatever method is appropriate for your device, you need only to dismiss the Lock screen and then enter your password; your screen will display exactly like it did when you turned off your computer.

When you *shut down* your computer, all open programs and files close, network connections close, and the hard disk stops. No power is used. According to Microsoft, about half of all Windows users like to shut down so that they get a "fresh start" each time they turn on the computer. The other half use sleep.

Activity 1.09   Locking, Signing Out of, and Shutting Down Your Computer

In an organization, there might be a specific process for signing out from Windows 8 and turning off the computer.

1 Use any of the techniques you have practiced to display the **Start screen**. In the upper right corner, click your user name.

Here you can sign out or lock your computer, in addition to changing your account picture. If you click Sign out, the Lock screen will display, and when you press Enter, all the user accounts on this computer will display and are able to sign in.

If you click Lock, the Lock screen will display, and when you press Enter, only you will be able to sign in again—unless no passwords have been set.

2 Click **Lock**, and then with the Lock screen displayed, click one time or press Enter, and then sign in to your computer again if necessary.

3 On the **Start screen**, point to the upper right corner of the screen to display the **charms** in a transparent view, and then move the mouse downward slightly into the displayed symbols along the right edge of the screen to display the **charms** in an opaque overlay. Compare your screen with Figure 1.27.

Charms are a specific and consistent set of buttons that you can use in every app, whether a Windows Store app or a desktop app, and they enable you to search, share, access devices, or adjust your PC settings. Specifically you can:

- Use the Search charm to search for an app or search for content located in the active app or in another app.
- Use the Share charm to share content from the active app with people or services.
- Use the Start charm to go directly to the Start screen.
- Use the Devices charm to connect to devices and send content, stream media, and print.
- Use the Settings charm to configure the active app to your preferences and access help.

FIGURE 1.27

ANOTHER WAY You can also display the charms from the *lower* right corner, but because this corner is also used to peek at the desktop when a desktop app is open or to zoom in on the Start screen, use the upper right corner to assure a consistent result.

4 Click the **Settings charm**, and then compare your screen with Figure 1.28.

FIGURE 1.28

5 At the bottom of the **Settings pane**, click **Power**, and then click **Shut down**.

Objective 5 | Manage User Accounts

Windows 8 supports multiple local account users on a single computer, and at least one user is the administrator—the initial administrator that was established when the system was purchased or when Windows 8 was installed.

As the administrator of your own computer, you can restrict access to your computer so that only people you authorize can use your computer or view its files. This access is managed through a local *user account*, which is a collection of information that tells Windows 8 what files and folders the account holder can access, what changes the account holder can make to the computer system, and what the account holder's personal preferences are. Each person accesses his or her user account with a user name and password, and each user has his or her own desktop, files, and folders. Users with a local account should also establish a Microsoft account so that their Start screen arrangement—personal dashboard of tiles—roams with them when they sign on to other Windows 8 computers.

An *administrator account* allows complete access to the computer. Administrators can make changes that affect other users, change security settings, install software and hardware, access all files on the computer, and make changes to other user accounts.

Activity 1.10 | Using PC Settings and Managing Your User Account

1 If necessary, turn on or wake your computer, and then sign in. Display the **Start screen**.

2 Point to the upper right corner to display the **charms**, move your mouse pointer down, and then click the **Settings charm**.

3 At the bottom of the **Settings pane**, click **Change PC settings**. On the left, be sure that **Personalize** is selected, and then compare your screen with Figure 1.29.

⟳ ANOTHER WAY   In the upper right corner, click your name, and then click *Change account picture* to display PC settings.

Here, in *PC settings*, you can control almost everything about how Windows looks and works. You can change colors and backgrounds, the picture on your Lock screen, and your account picture. Here you can also add other users, connect devices like printers, or set up a network.

FIGURE 1.29

4 In the upper right corner, click **Account picture**. Click **Browse**, and then if the Photos app does not display, to the right of **Files**, click ☑ to display all the file locations on your computer. At the bottom, scroll down if necessary, and then click **Photos** to open the **Photos app**. Compare your screen with Figure 1.30.

Assuming that you have signed in with a Microsoft account and that you have connected some of your services, you can get a photo from your Facebook account, your Flickr account, or any pictures you have stored on your OneDrive—in addition to those in your Pictures library on your computer.

FIGURE 1.30

5 Click one of your locations, for example your Pictures library, select any picture, and then click **Choose image**. Compare your screen with Figure 1.31.

Your new image displays, and your previous image remains in case you want to choose it again. Here you can also create an account picture instantly from a camera on your computer if one is available.

FIGURE 1.31

6 Point to the upper right corner of your screen to display the **charms**, click the **Settings charm**, click **Power**, and then click **Shut down** to close all apps and turn off your computer.

7 If you want to do so, turn your computer on, and then using the techniques you just practiced, change your account picture back to its previous picture.

END | You have completed Project 1A

Managing Files and Folders

PROJECT
1B

PROJECT ACTIVITIES

In Activities 1.11 through 1.21, you will assist Barbara Hewitt and Steven Ramos, who work for the Information Technology Department at the Boston headquarters office of the Bell Orchid Hotels. Barbara and Steven have been asked to organize some of the files and folders that comprise the corporation's computer data. You will capture screens that will look similar to Figure 1.32.

PROJECT FILES

For Project 1B, you will need the following files:

The student data files that accompany this textbook stored on a USB flash drive

You will save your files as:

Lastname_Firstname_1B_WordPad_Snip
Lastname_Firstname_1B_Europe_Folders_Snip
Lastname_Firstname_1B_HR_Snip

PROJECT RESULTS

FIGURE 1.32 Project 1B Managing Files and Folders

A file is the fundamental unit of storage that enables Windows 8 to distinguish one set of information from another. A folder is the basic organizing tool for files. In a folder, you can store files that are related to one another. You can also put a folder inside of another folder, which is referred to as a subfolder.

Windows 8 arranges folders in a structure that resembles a *hierarchy*—an arrangement where items are ranked and where each level is lower in rank than the item above it. The hierarchy of folders is referred to as the ***folder structure***. A sequence of folders in the folder structure that leads to a specific file or folder is a path.

A library is a collection of items, such as files and folders, assembled from various locations; the locations might be on your computer, on an external hard drive connected to your computer, or on another computer in your network. A library does not actually store your items; rather, a library provides a single access point from which you can open folders and files from different locations.

ALERT!

For the remainder of this textbook, you will need two of the folders that accompany this textbook. You will download these files in the following activity. Alternatively, your instructor might provide these files, or you can download the files from the Pearson website associated with this textbook. You will also need Microsoft Office 2013 (only Word, Excel, and PowerPoint) installed on the computer you are using. A trial version of Microsoft Office 2013 is sufficient for these projects.

Activity 1.11 | Downloading Files from a Website

To complete the chapters and end-of-chapter exercises in this textbook, you will need the Bell_Orchid folder and Chapter_Files folder from this book's companion website. Follow the steps in this activity to download these folders. Alternatively, your instructor might provide these folders to you, for example in your learning management system.

NOTE Using a Touchscreen

If you are using a touchscreen computer to complete this project, continue to use the tap and swipe gestures that you practiced in Project 1A. The remainder of this textbook will assume a mouse and keyboard setup, but all the projects can be completed using a touchscreen without a mouse or keyboard.

1 Sign in to your computer, and then from the **Start screen**, display the **desktop**.

There are several ways to display the desktop from the Start screen when using a mouse and keyboard. You can click the desktop tile on the Start screen, press [⊞] + [D], or point to the lower left corner, right-click, and then at the bottom of the menu click desktop.

2 If necessary, insert your **USB flash drive**.

3 On the taskbar, click **Internet Explorer** [e], click in the **address bar**, type **www.pearsonhighered.com/go** and then press [Enter].

Recall that Internet Explorer is Microsoft's ***web browser***—software with which you display webpages and navigate the Internet.

4 Scroll down the list, locate and click the name of this textbook, and then click the STUDENT DATA FILES tab.

5 Click the link for **Bell_Orchid Files**. In the **Windows Internet Explorer** dialog box, click **Save As**.

Recall that a dialog box is a small window that displays options for completing a task.

6 In the **Save As** dialog box, in the **navigation pane** on the left, scroll down, and if necessary, to the left of **Computer**, click ▷ to expand the list. Then click the name of your **USB flash drive**. Compare your screen with Figure 1.33.

FIGURE 1.33

File list with your chapter folder (your list may differ)

Save As dialog box

Path to your USB flash drive

Computer expanded in navigation pane

File name box indicates name of file to download

Save as type indicates this is a Compressed (zipped) Folder

7 In the lower right corner, click **Save**.

At the bottom of your screen, the ***Notification bar*** displays information about pending downloads, security issues, and add-ons, and other issues related to the operation of your computer.

A ***compressed file*** is a file that has been reduced in size. Compressed files take up less storage space and can be transferred to other computers faster than uncompressed files. You can also combine a group of files into one compressed folder, which makes it easier to share a group of files.

8 In the **Notification bar**, when the download is complete, click **Open folder**, and then compare your screen with Figure 1.34.

FIGURE 1.34

Compressed Folder Tools on the ribbon

Bell_Orchid folder downloaded as a compressed (zip) folder

9 With the compressed folder selected, on the ribbon, click the **Extract tab** to display the **Compressed Folder Tools**, and then click **Extract all**. Compare your screen with Figure 1.35.

Here you ***extract***—decompress, or pull out—files from a compressed form. When you extract a file, an uncompressed copy is placed in the folder that you specify here.

You can navigate to some other location by clicking the Browse button and navigating within your storage locations.

FIGURE 1.35

Select a Destination and Extract Files

Default path to place extracted files

Extract button

10 Click the **Browse** button. In the **Select a destination** dialog box, click **Computer**, click the name of your **USB flash drive**, and then click **OK**.

11 In the lower right corner, click **Extract**, and notice that a progress bar indicates the progress of the extract process, and that when the extract is complete, the **Bell_Orchid** folder displays on the file list of your **USB flash drive**. If you want to do so, you can delete the compressed (zipped) folder from your flash drive because now you have an extracted *copy* of the folder.

> In a dialog box or taskbar button, a ***progress bar*** indicates visually the progress of a task such as a download or file transfer.

12 In the upper right corner of the **USB device** window, click **Close** ☒.

13 Using the techniques you just practiced, return to the website if necessary, and then download and extract the **Chapter_Files** folder to your **USB flash drive**. Then delete the compressed folder if you want to do so. **Close** ☒ all open windows and redisplay your desktop.

Activity 1.12 | Using File Explorer to Display Libraries, Folders, and Files

Recall that File Explorer is the program that displays the contents of libraries, folders, and files on your computer, and also enables you to perform tasks related to your files and folders such as copying, moving, and renaming. When you open a folder or library, a folder window displays to show its contents. The design of the folder window helps you navigate—explore within the folder structure for the purpose of finding files and folders—so that you can save and locate your files and folders efficiently.

In this activity, you will open a folder window and examine its parts.

1 With your desktop displayed, on the taskbar, *point to* but do not click **File Explorer** 🗔, and notice the ScreenTip *File Explorer*.

> A ***ScreenTip*** displays useful information when you perform various mouse actions, such as pointing to screen elements.

2 Click **File Explorer** 🗔 to display the **Libraries** window.

> File Explorer is at work anytime you are viewing the contents of a library, a folder, or a file.

> By default, the File Explorer button on the taskbar opens your Libraries. Within a library, you can organize, view, and share files just like you can in a folder. However, a library differs from a folder in that it can gather saved files from several locations. For example, from the Documents library, you can access documents in both your My Documents and Public Documents folders.

> In addition to the four default libraries—Documents, Music, Pictures, and Videos—you can create new libraries for other file collections you might have.

3 In the **file list**, click **Documents** one time to select it, and then on the ribbon, in the **Open group**, click **Open** 🗔.

> The window for the Documents library displays. You may or may not have files and folders already stored here.

🔄 **ANOTHER WAY** Point to Documents, right-click to display a shortcut menu, and then click Open; or, point to Documents and double-click.

4 Compare your screen with Figure 1.36, and then take a moment to study the parts of the window as described in the table in Figure 1.37.

FIGURE 1.36

FIGURE 1.37

PARTS OF THE DOCUMENTS LIBRARY WINDOW	
WINDOW PART	**FUNCTION**
Address bar	Displays your current location in the file structure as a series of links separated by arrows. Tap or click a part of the path to go to that level or tap or click at the end to select the path for copying.
Back, Forward, Recent locations, and Up buttons	Provides the ability to navigate to other folders you have already opened without closing the current folder window. These buttons work with the address bar; that is, after you use the address bar to change folders, you can use the Back button to return to the original folder. Use the Up button to open the location where the folder you are viewing is saved—also referred to as the *parent folder*.
Column headings	Identify the columns. By clicking the column heading name, you can change how the files in the file list are organized; by clicking the arrow on the right, you can select various sort arrangements in the file list. Right-click a column heading to select other columns to add to the file list.
File list	Displays the contents of the current folder or library. If you type text into the Search box, only the folders and files that match your search will display here—including files in subfolders.
Library Tools contextual tab	Displays additional tools in context with the selected item.
Minimize or expand ribbon button	Changes the display of the ribbon. When minimized, the ribbon shows only the tab names and not the full ribbon.
Navigation pane	Displays locations to which you can navigate in an area on the left side of a folder window; for example, Favorites, Libraries, a Homegroup if you have one, and an expandable list of drives and folders. Use Favorites to open your most commonly used folders and searches; use Libraries to access your libraries. If you have a folder that you use frequently, you can drag it to the Favorites area so that it is always available.
Ribbon	Groups common tasks such as copying and moving, creating new folders, emailing and zipping items, and changing views on related tabs.
Search box	Enables you to type a word or phrase and then searches for a file or subfolder stored in the current folder that contains matching text. The search begins as soon as you begin typing; for example, if you type *G*, all the files that start with the letter *G* display in the file list.

5 Move your ⬚ pointer anywhere into the **navigation pane**, and notice that a **black arrow** (◢) displays to the left of *Favorites*, *Libraries*, and *Computer*, to indicate that these items are expanded, and a **white arrow** (▷) displays to the left of items that are collapsed (hidden).

You can click these arrows to collapse and expand areas in the navigation pane.

6 In the **navigation pane**, under **Computer**, click your **USB flash drive** one time to display its contents in the **file list**. Compare your screen with Figure 1.38.

In the navigation pane, *Computer* displays all of the drive letter locations attached to your computer, including the internal hard drives, CD or DVD drives, and any connected devices such as a USB flash drive.

The ribbon adds a Drive Tools contextual tab to provide commands you might need when working with various drives on your computer.

FIGURE 1.38

7 In the **file list**, double-click the **Bell_Orchid** folder—not the compressed folder—to display the subfolders.

Recall that the corporate office of the Bell Orchid Hotels is in Boston. The corporate office maintains subfolders labeled for each of its large hotels in Honolulu, Orlando, San Diego, and Santa Barbara.

🔄 **ANOTHER WAY**   Right-click the folder, and then click Open; or, select the folder and then on the ribbon click Open.

8 In the **file list**, double-click **Orlando** to display the subfolders, and then look at the **address bar** to view the path. Compare your screen with Figure 1.39.

Within each city's subfolder, there is a structure of subfolders for the Accounting, Engineering, Food and Beverage, Human Resources, Operations, and Sales and Marketing departments.

Because folders can be placed inside of other folders, such an arrangement is common when organizing files on a computer.

In the address bar, the path from the flash drive to the Bell_Orchid folder to the Orlando folder displays as a series of links.

FIGURE 1.39

9 ▶ In the **address bar**, to the right of **Bell_Orchid**, click the ▶ arrow to display a list of the subfolders in the **Bell_Orchid** folder. On the list that displays, notice that **Orlando** displays in bold, indicating it is open in the file list. Then, on the list, click **Honolulu**.

The subfolders within the Honolulu folder display.

10 ▶ In the **address bar**, to the right of **Bell_Orchid**, click the ▶ arrow again to display the subfolders in the **Bell_Orchid** folder. Then, on the **address bar** (not on the list), point to **Honolulu** and notice that the list of subfolders in the **Honolulu** folder displays.

After you display one set of subfolders in the address bar, all of the links are active and you need only point to them to display the list of subfolders.

Clicking an arrow to the right of a folder name in the address bar displays a list of the subfolders in that folder. You can click a subfolder name to display its contents. In this manner, the address bar is not only a path, but it is also an active control with which you can step from the current folder directly to any other folder above it in the folder structure just by clicking on a folder name.

11 ▶ On the list of subfolders for **Honolulu**, click **Sales_Marketing** to display its contents in the file list. Compare your screen with Figure 1.40.

ANOTHER WAY   In the file list, double-click the Sales_Marketing folder.

The files in the Sales_Marketing folder for Honolulu display. To the left of each file name, an icon indicates the program that created each file. Here, there is one PowerPoint file, one Excel file, one Word file, and four JPEG images.

FIGURE 1.40

12 In the upper left corner of the folder window, click the **Back** button ⬅.

> The Back button retraces each of your clicks in the same manner as clicking the Back button when you are browsing the Internet.

13 In the **file list**, point to the **Human_Resources** folder, and double-click to open the folder.

14 In the **file list**, click one time to select the PowerPoint file **HO_HR_New_Employee_Presentation**, and then on the ribbon, click the **View tab**. In the **Panes group**, click **Details pane**, and then compare your screen with Figure 1.41.

> The *Details pane* displays the most common *file properties* associated with the selected file. File properties refer to information about a file, such as the author, the date the file was last changed, and any descriptive *tags*—properties that you create to help you find and organize your files.

> Additionally, a thumbnail of the first slide in the presentation displays.

FIGURE 1.41

Panes group on the View tab

PowerPoint file selected

Details pane displays file properties and thumbnail

15 On the ribbon, in the **Panes group**, click **Preview pane** to replace the **Details pane** with the **Preview pane**. Compare your screen with Figure 1.42.

> In the Preview pane that displays on the right, you can use the scroll bar to scroll through the slides in the presentation; or, you can click the up or down scroll arrow to view the slides.

FIGURE 1.42

Preview pane

16 On the ribbon, click **Preview pane** to close the right pane completely.

Use the Details pane to see a file's properties and the Preview pane when you want to look at a file quickly without actually opening it.

17 **Close** ⊠ the window.

Activity 1.13 | Using the Navigation Pane to Display the Folder Structure

When it is useful to do so, you can use the navigation pane on the left side of a folder window to navigate files and folders and to display the folder structure.

1 If necessary, **Close** ⊠ any open windows, and then on the taskbar, click **File Explorer** ▭ to open the **Libraries** window.

2 On the left side of the window, in the lower portion of the **navigation pane**, if necessary click ▷ to expand **Computer**. Then point to your **USB flash drive** containing the Bell_Orchid files and click the white expand arrow ▷ to display the subfolders immediately below the name of your USB drive.

3 To the left of **Bell_Orchid**, click the expand arrow ▷ to display the subfolders. Scroll down if necessary, and then to the left of **San_Diego**, click the expand arrow ▷ to display the subfolders. Compare your screen with Figure 1.43.

In the navigation pane, the folder structure is shown in a visual hierarchy.

FIGURE 1.43

4 In the **navigation pane**, under **San_Diego**, click **Accounting** to display the files in the **Accounting** subfolder in the **file list**.

When you no longer see any ▷ arrows to expand further, clicking the folder will display the file list for that folder.

Optionally you can hide the display of the navigation pane, but it is recommended that you leave the navigation pane displayed because of its usefulness in displaying the drives on your computer and the folder structure when you want to see the structure in a hierarchical view.

5 In the upper right corner, click **Close** ⊠.

When you are using the software programs installed on your computer, you create and save data files—the documents, workbooks, databases, songs, pictures, and so on that you need for your job or personal use. Therefore, most of your work with Windows 8 desktop apps is concerned with locating and starting your programs and locating and opening your files.

You can start programs from the Start screen or from the desktop by pinning a program to the taskbar. You can open your data files from within the program in which they were created, or you can open a data file from a folder window in File Explorer, which will simultaneously start the program and open your file.

Activity 1.14 | Starting Programs and Opening Data Files

1 With your desktop displayed, use any technique that you have practiced to display the **Start screen**, and then type **paint**

Recall that from the Start screen, you can begin typing and the Start search feature will immediately begin searching for apps.

Paint is a desktop app that comes with Windows 8 with which you can create and edit drawings and display and edit stored photos.

2 With the **Paint** app in focus—bordered in white—as the result of your search, press [Enter] to open the **desktop** app.

3 On the ribbon, with the **Home tab** active, in the **Tools group**, click the **Pencil** icon. Move your mouse pointer into the white drawing area, hold down the left mouse button, and then try writing your first name in the white area of the window.

 BY TOUCH   Use your finger to draw on the screen.

4 In the upper left corner, to the left of the **Home tab**, click the **File tab** to display a menu of commands of things you can do with your picture.

5 On the menu, click **Exit**. In the displayed message, click **Don't Save**.

Messages like this display in most programs to prevent you from forgetting to save your work. A file saved in the Paint program creates a graphic file in the JPEG format.

6 Return to the **Start screen**, type **wordpad** and then open the **WordPad desktop** app. Notice that this program window has characteristics similar to the Paint program window; for example, it has a ribbon of commands.

7 With the insertion point blinking in the document window, type your first and last name.

8 From the taskbar, start **Snipping Tool**, and then create a **Window Snip**. Click anywhere in the WordPad window to display the **Snipping Tool** mark-up window. **Save** 🖫 the snip as a **JPEG** in your **Windows 8 Chapter 1** folder as **Lastname_Firstname_1B_WordPad_Snip** Hold this file until you finish Project 1B, and then submit this file as directed by your instructor.

9 **Close** ⊠ the **Snipping Tool** window. **Close** ⊠ **WordPad**, and then click **Don't Save**.

10 Display the **Start screen**, type **word 2013** and then open **Microsoft Word**. Compare your screen with Figure 1.44.

N O T E   You Need Microsoft Word 2013

For this project you need Microsoft Word 2013; you can use a trial version if necessary.

The Word program window has features that are common to other programs you have opened; for example, commands are arranged on tabs. When you create and save data in Word, you create a Word document file.

FIGURE 1.44

Word opening screen (your list of documents may differ)

11 On the left, click **Open Other Documents**. Under **Open**, click **Computer**, and then click **Browse** to display the **Open** dialog box. Compare your screen with Figure 1.45, and then take a moment to study the table in Figure 1.46.

Recall that a dialog box is a window containing options for completing a task; its layout is similar to that of a folder window. When you are working in a desktop app, use the Open dialog box to locate and open existing files that were created in the desktop app.

By default, the Open dialog box displays the path to the *Documents* library of the user signed in. On your own computer, you can create a folder structure within the Documents library to store your documents. Alternatively, you can use the skills you have practiced to navigate to other locations on your computer, such as your removable USB flash drive.

FIGURE 1.45

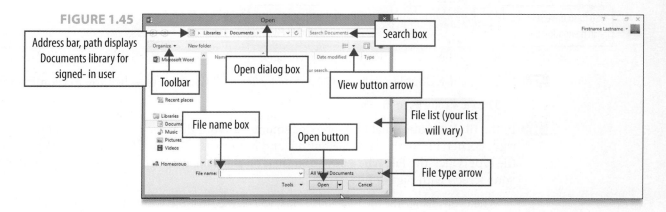

Address bar, path displays Documents library for signed-in user

Toolbar

Open dialog box

File name box

Open button

Search box

View button arrow

File list (your list will vary)

File type arrow

FIGURE 1.46

THE OPEN DIALOG BOX	
DIALOG BOX ELEMENT	**FUNCTION**
Address bar	Displays the path in the library or folder structure; by default, the path displays the Documents library for the signed-in user.
File list	Displays the list of files and folders that are available in the library or folder indicated in the address bar.
File name box	Enables you to type the name of a specific file to locate it.
File type arrow	Enables you to restrict the type of files displayed in the file list; for example, the default All Word Documents restricts the type of files displayed to only Word documents. You can click the arrow and adjust the restrictions to a narrower or wider group of files.
Navigation pane	Enables access to Favorites, Libraries, and Computer.
Search box	Filters the file list based on text that you type; the search is based on text in the file name and in the file itself, and on other properties that you can specify. The search takes place in the current folder or library, as displayed in the address bar, and in any subfolders within that folder.
Toolbar	Displays relevant tasks; for example, creating a new folder.

12 ▸ In the **navigation pane**, scroll down as necessary, and then under **Computer**, click your **USB flash drive**. In the **file list**, double-click the **Bell_Orchid** folder to open it and display its contents. In the upper right portion of the **Open** dialog box, click the **More Options arrow** , and then set the view to **Large icons**. Compare your screen with Figure 1.47.

Notice that the Live Icons feature indicates that each folder contains additional subfolders.

FIGURE 1.47

13 ▸ In the **file list**, double-click the **Corporate** folder, and then double-click the **Accounting** folder.

The view returns to the Details view.

14 ▸ In the **file list**, notice that only one document—a Word document—displays. In the lower right corner, locate the **File type** button, and notice that *All Word Documents* displays as the file type. Click the **File type arrow**, and then on the displayed list, click **All Files**. Compare your screen with Figure 1.48.

When you change the file type to *All Files*, you can see that the Word file is not the only file in this folder. By default, the Open dialog box displays only the files created in the *active program*; however, you can display variations of file types in this manner.

Microsoft Office file types are identified by small icons, which is a convenient way to differentiate one type of file from another. Although you can view all the files in the folder, you can open only the files that were created in the active program, which in this instance is Microsoft Word.

FIGURE 1.48

Excel file type icon →

PowerPoint file type icon →

Folder displays all types of files

Word file type icon

15 ▸ Change the file type back to **All Word Documents**. Then in the **file list**, double-click the **CO_AC_Report_Shareholders** Word file to open the document. Take a moment to scroll through the document. If necessary, **Maximize** ☐ the window.

16 ▸ **Close** ☒ the Word window. On the taskbar, click **File Explorer** ▦. In the **navigation pane**, under **Computer**, click your **USB flash drive** to display its contents in the **file list**.

17 ▸ In the **file list**, use any technique you have practiced to open folders to navigate to **Bell_Orchid** ▸ **Corporate** ▸ **Accounting**.

↻ **ANOTHER WAY**   Expand each folder level in the navigation pane.

18 ▸ In the **file list**, double-click the **CO_AC_Loan_Presentation** file. When the **PowerPoint** window displays (a message regarding comments may display), if necessary **Maximize** ☐ the program window. Compare your screen with Figure 1.49.

FIGURE 1.49

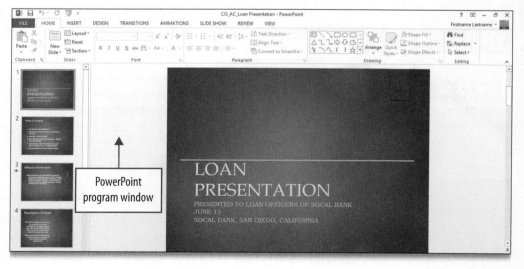

PowerPoint program window

19 ▸ **Close** ☒ the PowerPoint window.

20 ▸ In the **address bar**, to the right of **Bell_Orchid**, click ▸ and then compare your screen with Figure 1.50.

Recall that the address bar is not just a path; rather, it contains active links from which you can click a folder name in the path, and then navigate directly to any displayed subfolders.

FIGURE 1.50

Active links to subfolders

Path in address bar

21▶ On the displayed list, click **Honolulu** to display the contents of the **Honolulu** folder in the **file list**. Open the **Food_Beverage** folder, and then open the **HO_FB_Banquet_Contract** file. Take a moment to view this document in the open Word program. **Close** [**×**] Word, and then **Close** ⊠ the folder window.

More Knowledge   **Storing Files and Creating Desktop Shortcuts for a Program on Your Desktop**

On your desktop, you can add or remove **desktop shortcuts**, which are desktop icons that can link to items accessible on your computer such as a program, file, folder, disk drive, printer, or another computer. In previous versions of Windows, many computer users commonly did this.

Now the Start screen is your personal dashboard for all your programs and online activities, and increasingly you will access programs and your own files in the cloud. So do not clutter your desktop with shortcuts—doing so is more confusing than useful. Placing desktop shortcuts for frequently used programs or folders directly on your desktop may seem convenient, but as you add more icons, your desktop becomes cluttered and the shortcuts are not easy to find. A better organizing method is to use the taskbar for shortcuts to programs. For folders and files, the best organizing structure is to create a logical structure of folders within your Documents library.

You can also drag frequently used folders to the Favorites area in the navigation pane so that they are available any time you open File Explorer. As you progress in your use of Windows 8, you will discover techniques for using the taskbar and the Favorites area of the navigation pane to streamline your work, instead of cluttering your desktop.

Objective 8   Personalize Your Windows 8 Start Screen

Because you will use some tiles on your Start screen more than others, you will want to reposition the tiles to suit your personal needs. To do so, simply drag the tiles with your mouse or your finger if you are using a touch device. You will also want to personalize the live tiles to display the information you want. For example, you can set the weather tile for your location.

Activity 1.15 | Personalizing Your Windows 8 Start Screen

1▶ Display the **Start screen**, and then type **file explorer** On the left, point to the **File Explorer** app bordered in white, and then right-click to display the **app bar**. Compare your screen with Figure 1.51.

Here you can pin the app to the Start screen or to the taskbar on the desktop—or unpin from either of these locations.

FIGURE 1.51

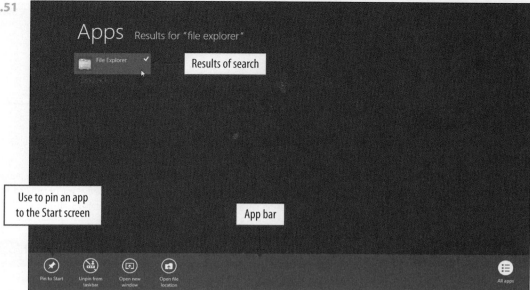

2 On the **app bar**, click **Pin to Start**, and then redisplay the **Start screen**. Point to the bottom of the screen to display the scroll bar, and then drag the scroll box to the right until the **File Explorer** tile comes into view as shown in Figure 1.52.

FIGURE 1.52

🔄 **BY TOUCH**   Drag your finger to the left to scroll to the right.

3 Drag the **File Explorer** tile to the top of the first column of tiles on your **Start screen**, and then drag the **Desktop** tile under it.

   With this tile, you can easily go directly to File Explorer from your Start screen.

4 Click the **Weather** tile, if necessary, follow the prompts to set the app to your location, and then redisplay the **Start screen**.

5 On the **Start screen**, type **store** and press [Enter] to go the Windows Store. Type **twitter** and press [Enter]. If you want to do so, install a **Twitter** app—MetroTwit is one to try—so that you can view your Twitter feed on your **Start screen** as a live tile.

6 Redisplay your **Start screen**, point to an empty area, and then right-click. In the **app bar** at the bottom, click **All apps**.

   Here you can view a small tile for every app—both desktop and Windows Store—in alphabetical order by category.

7 Press ⊞ to redisplay the **Start screen**. In the extreme lower right corner of your screen, click **Minimize** — to shrink the display of tiles.

> This view enables you to see all of your tiles on one screen.

8 Click any empty area of the screen to return to the normal view.

ALERT!	**Allow Time to Complete This Lab in One Session**

If you are working on a computer that is not your own, for example in a college lab, plan your time to complete the remainder of this project in one working session.

Because you will need to store and then delete files on the hard disk drive of the computer at which you are working, it is recommended that you complete this project in one working session—*unless you are working on your own computer or you know that the files will be retained*. In your college lab, it is possible that files you store on the computer's hard drive will not be retained after you log off. Allow approximately 25–40 minutes for the remainder of this project.

Objective 9 Create, Rename, and Copy Files and Folders

File management includes organizing, copying, naming, renaming, moving, and deleting the files and folders you have stored in various locations—both locally and in the cloud.

Activity 1.16 | Copying Files from a Removable Storage Device to the Documents Library on the Hard Disk Drive

Barbara and Steven have the assignment to transfer and then organize some of the corporation's files to a computer that will be connected to the corporate network. Data on such a computer can be accessed by employees at any of the hotel locations through the use of sharing technologies. For example, *SharePoint* is a Microsoft technology that enables employees in an organization to access information across organizational and geographic boundaries.

1 On the Windows 8 **Start screen**, click the **Desktop tile** to display your Windows 8 desktop. If necessary, insert the USB flash drive that contains the student data files that accompany this chapter that you downloaded from the Pearson website. Open **File Explorer** 🗖 and display the folder window for your USB flash drive.

> Recall that in the navigation pane, under Computer, you have access to all the storage areas inside your computer, such as your hard disk drives, and to any devices with removable storage, such as CDs, DVDs, or USB flash drives.

2 In the **file list**, click **Bell_Orchid** to select the folder. Compare your screen with Figure 1.53.

FIGURE 1.53

3 Point to the selected **Bell_Orchid** folder, hold down the left mouse button, and then drag the folder down to the taskbar until the ScreenTip *Pin to File Explorer* displays, and then release the left mouse button. Notice that the **Jump List** for File Explorer displays and that the **Bell_Orchid** folder is pinned to it.

> By pinning the folder to the Jump List, you will be able to access it quickly.

4 Click anywhere on the desktop to close the Jump List. On the ribbon, on the **Home tab**, in the **Organize group**, click **Copy to**, and then on the displayed list, click **Documents**.

> A progress bar displays in a dialog box, and also displays on the File Explorer taskbar button with green shading. A progress bar indicates visually the progress of a task such as a copy process, a download, or a file transfer.

> The Documents library is one of several libraries within your ***personal folder*** stored on the hard disk drive. For each user account—even if there is only one user on the computer—Windows 8 creates a personal folder labeled with the account holder's name.

↻ **ANOTHER WAY**   In the file list, point to the folder name and right-click. On the displayed shortcut menu, point to *Send to*, and then click Documents.

5 When the copy is complete, **Close** ☒ the window.

Activity 1.17 | Creating and Renaming Folders

Barbara and Steven can see that various managers have been placing files related to the new European hotels in the *Future_Hotels* folder. They can also see that the files have not been organized into a logical structure. For example, files that are related to each other are not in separate folders; instead they are mixed in with other files that are not related to the topic.

In this activity, you will create, name, and rename folders to begin a logical structure of folders in which to organize the files related to the European hotels project.

1 On the taskbar, right-click the **File Explorer** button 🗔 to display the **Jump List**, and then under **Pinned**, click **Bell_Orchid**.

↻ **ANOTHER WAY**   If you were not able to pin the folder to the Jump List, click the File Explorer button, and then in the Documents library, navigate to the Bell_Orchid folder.

2 In the **address bar**, to the right of **Bell_Orchid**, click ▶, and then on the list click **Corporate**. To the right of **Corporate**, click ▶, and then click **Information_Technology**. To the right of **Information_Technology**, click ▶, and then click **Future_Hotels**.

> Some computer users prefer to navigate a folder structure using the address bar in this manner. Use whichever method you prefer—double-clicking in the file list, or clicking in the address bar.

↻ **ANOTHER WAY**   In the file list, double-click the Corporate folder, double-click the Information_Technology folder, and then double-click the Future_Hotels folder to display its contents in the file list. Or, in the navigation pane, click Documents, and expand each folder in the navigation pane.

3 Be sure the items are in alphabetical order by **Name**. If the items are not in alphabetical order, recall that by clicking on the column heading name, you can change how the files in the file list are ordered. On the ribbon, click the **View tab**, and then in the **Layout group**, be sure **Details** is selected. If necessary, set the view to **Details**.

> The ***Details view*** displays a list of files or folders and their most common properties.

↻ **ANOTHER WAY**   Right-click in a blank area of the file list, point to View, and then click Details.

4 On the ribbon, click the **Home tab**, and then in the **New group**, click **New folder**. With the text *New folder* selected, type **Paris** and press ⏎. Click **New folder** again, and then type **Venice** and press ⏎.

5 Create a new folder named **Essex** and press ⏎. Click the **Venice** folder, and then on the ribbon, in the **Organize group**, click **Rename**. Notice that the text *Venice* is selected. Type **Rome** and press ⏎.

⟳ ANOTHER WAY   Point to a folder or file name, right-click, and then on the shortcut menu, click Rename.

6 Click the **Essex** folder one time to select it. Point to the selected **Essex** folder, and then click one time again. With the text selected, type **London** and press ⏎ to change the folder name.

You can use either of these techniques to change the name of a folder.

7 From the taskbar, start **Snipping Tool**; if necessary drag the *title bar*—the bar across the top of a window that displays the program name—of Snipping Tool into a blank area of the desktop. Click the **New arrow**, and then click **Window Snip**. Point anywhere in the folder window and click one time. In the **Snipping Tool** mark-up window, click **Save Snip** 🖫.

8 In the **Save As** dialog box, in the **navigation pane**, scroll down as necessary, and then click your **USB flash drive** so that it displays in the **address bar**.

9 In the **file list**, double-click your **Windows 8 Chapter 1** folder to open it. Click in the **File name** box, and then replace the selected text by typing **Lastname_Firstname_1B_Europe_Folders_Snip**

10 Be sure the file type is **JPEG**. Click **Save** or press ⏎. **Close** ☒ the **Snipping Tool** window. Hold this file until you finish Project 1B. Leave the folder window open.

Activity 1.18 | Renaming Files

1 In the **address bar**, click **Information_Technology** to move up one level in the folder structure—or click the **Up button** ⬆.

2 On the ribbon, click the **View tab**, and then in the **Current view group**, click **Size all columns to fit** ⬌ to make it easier to see all the information about the files and folders.

3 Using any of the techniques you practiced to rename a folder, rename the **Dogs** file as **Dogs_1** and then rename the **MoreDogs** file to **Dogs_2** Compare your screen with Figure 1.54.

FIGURE 1.54

Two files renamed

4 **Close** ☒ the folder window.

Activity 1.19 | Copying Files

Copying, moving, renaming, and deleting files and folders comprise the most heavily used features within File Explorer. Probably half or more of the tasks you complete in File Explorer relate to these tasks, so mastering these techniques will increase your efficiency.

When you *copy* a file or a folder, you make a duplicate of the original item and then store the duplicate in another location. In this activity, you will assist Barbara and Steven in making copies of the Staffing_Plan file, and then placing the copies in each of the three folders you created—London, Paris, and Rome.

1 In the taskbar, point to the **File Explorer** button 📁, hold down the left mouse button, and then drag upward slightly into the desktop to display the **Jump List**. Then, on the **Jump List**, under **Pinned**, click **Bell_Orchid**.

> You will increase your efficiency if you make it a habit to work mostly from the taskbar and to display Jump Lists using this technique. After the Jump List displays, you need only move your mouse pointer upward a little more to select the action that you want.

🔄 **BY TOUCH**   Swipe upward with a quick short gesture to display the Jump List.

2 With the **Bell_Orchid** folder window displayed, by double-clicking in the **file list** or following the links in the **address bar**, navigate to **Corporate** ▶ **Information_Technology** ▶ **Future_Hotels**.

3 Maximize 🔲 the folder window. On the **View tab**, if necessary set the **Layout** to **Details**, and then in the **Current view group**, click **Size all columns to fit**.

4 In the **file list**, click the file **Staffing_Plan**, and then on the **Home tab**, in the **Clipboard group**, click **Copy**.

> The Copy command places a copy of your selected file or folder on the *Clipboard* where it will be stored until you use the Paste command to insert the copy somewhere else. The Clipboard is a temporary storage area for information that you have copied or moved from one place and plan to use somewhere else.
>
> In Windows 8, the Clipboard can hold only one piece of information at a time. Whenever something is copied to the Clipboard, it replaces whatever was there before. In Windows 8, you cannot view the contents of the Clipboard nor place multiple items there in the manner that you can in Microsoft Word.

5 At the top of the **file list**, double-click the **London folder** to open it, and then in the **Clipboard group**, click **Paste**. Notice that the copy of the **Staffing_Plan** file displays. Compare your screen with Figure 1.55.

FIGURE 1.55

🔄 **ANOTHER WAY**   Right-click the file you want to copy, and on the menu click Copy. Then right-click the folder into which you want to place the copy, and on the menu click Paste. Or, select the file you want to copy, press Ctrl + C to activate the Copy command, open the folder into which you want to paste the file, and then press Ctrl + V to activate the Paste command.

6 With the **London** folder open, by using any of the techniques you have practiced, rename this copy of the **Staffing_Plan** file to **London_Staffing_Plan**

7 In the **address bar**, click **Future_Hotels** to redisplay this folder window and move up one level in the folder structure.

Click the **Staffing_Plan** file one time to select it, hold down Ctrl, and then drag the file upward over the **Paris** folder until the ScreenTip + *Copy to Paris* displays as shown in Figure 1.56, and then release the mouse button and release Ctrl.

> When dragging a file into a folder, holding down Ctrl engages the Copy command and places a *copy* of the file at the location where you release the mouse button. This is another way to copy a file or copy a folder.

FIGURE 1.56

 Open the **Paris** folder window, and then rename the **Staffing_Plan** file **Paris_Staffing_Plan** Then, move up one level in the folder structure to display the **Future_Hotels** folder window.

 Double-click the **Rome** folder to open it. With your mouse pointer anywhere in the **file list**, right-click, and then from the shortcut menu click **Paste**.

> A copy of the Staffing_Plan file is copied to the folder. Because a copy of the Staffing_Plan file is still on the Clipboard, you can continue to paste the item until you copy another item on the Clipboard to replace it.

 Rename the file **Rome_Staffing_Plan**

 On the **address bar**, click **Future_Hotels** to move up one level and open the **Future_Hotels** folder window. Leave this folder open for the next activity.

Objective 10　Move and Delete Files and Folders

When you *move* a file or folder, you remove it from the original location and store it in a new location. To keep your computer organized, delete files you no longer need.

Activity 1.20　Moving Files

In this activity, you will move items from the Future_Hotels folder into their appropriate folders.

 With the **Future_Hotels** folder open, in the **file list**, click the Excel file **Financials_London** one time to select it. On the **Home tab**, in the **Clipboard group**, click **Cut**.

> The file's Excel icon dims. This action places the item on the Clipboard.

ANOTHER WAY　Right-click the file or folder, and on the shortcut menu, click Cut; or, select the file or folder, and then press Ctrl + X.

 Double-click the **London** folder to open it, and then on the **Home tab**, in the **Clipboard group**, click **Paste**.

ANOTHER WAY   Right-click the folder, and on the shortcut menu, click Paste; or, select the folder, and then press `Ctrl` + `V`.

3 ▶ On the **address bar**, click **Future_Hotels** to move up a level. In the **file list**, point to **Financials_Paris**, hold down the left mouse button, and then drag the file upward over the **Paris** folder until the ScreenTip ➡*Move to Paris* displays, and then release the mouse button.

4 ▶ Open the **Paris** folder, and notice that the file was moved to this folder. On the **address bar**, click **Future_Hotels** to return to that folder.

5 ▶ Using either of the techniques you just practiced, move the **Financials_Rome** file into the **Rome** folder.

6 ▶ Hold down `Ctrl`, and then in the file list, click **Loans_London**, **London**, and **Marketing_London** to select the three files. Release the `Ctrl` key. Compare your screen with Figure 1.57.

> Use this technique to select a group of noncontiguous items in a list.

FIGURE 1.57

7 ▶ Point to any of the selected files, hold down the left mouse button, and then drag upward over the **London** folder until the ScreenTip ➡*Move to London* displays and *3* displays over the files being moved, and then release the mouse button.

ANOTHER WAY   Right-click over any of the selected files, click Cut, right-click over the London folder, and then click Paste.

8 ▶ Using either the select and drag method, or the select and then Cut and Paste method, select the files **France**, **Loans_Paris**, **Marketing_Paris**, and **Paris**, and move these four files into the **Paris** folder.

9 ▶ Select the four files **Italy**, **Loans_Rome**, **Marketing_Rome**, and **Rome**, and move them into the **Rome** folder.

> You can see that by keeping related files together, for example, all the files that relate to the Rome hotel, in folders that have an appropriately descriptive name, it will be easier to locate information later.

ANOTHER WAY   If a group of files to be selected are contiguous, or next to each other in the file list, click the first file to be selected and then press `Shift` and click the left mouse button on the last file to select all of the files between the top and bottom file selections.

10 ▶ Move the **Architects** file into the **London** folder.

11 ▶ In an empty area of the file list, right-click, and then click **Undo Move**. Leave the window open for the next activity.

> Any action that you make in a file list can be undone in this manner.

Press Ctrl + Z to undo an action in the file list.

Activity 1.21 | Copying and Moving Files by Snapping Two Windows

Sometimes you will want to open, in a second window, another instance of a program that you are using; that is, two copies of the program will be running simultaneously. This capability is especially useful in the File Explorer program, because you are frequently moving or copying files from one location to another.

In this activity, you will open two instances of File Explorer, and then use the **Snap** feature to display both instances on your screen.

To copy or move files or folders into a different level of a folder structure, or to a different drive location, the most efficient method is to display two windows side by side and then use drag and drop or copy (or cut) and paste commands.

In this activity, you will assist Barbara and Steven in making copies of the Staffing_Plan files for the corporate office.

1 In the upper right corner, click **Restore Down** ⬜ to restore the **Future_Hotels** folder window to its previous size and not maximized on the screen.

2 On your desk, position your mouse so that you have enough space to drag it on your desk surface to the left about 6 inches. Then, point to the upper edge of the **Future_Hotels** folder window to display the ⬚ pointer and drag the window to the left until the pointer reaches the left edge of the screen and the window snaps into place and occupies the left half of the screen.

3 On the taskbar, drag the **File Explorer** button ⬚ upward slightly into the desktop to display the **Jump List**, and then click **Bell_Orchid** to open a new folder window. Lift your mouse and place it so that you have space to drag to the right, and then snap this window to the right side of the screen.

4 In the folder window on the right, navigate to **Corporate ▶ Human_Resources**. Compare your screen with Figure 1.58.

FIGURE 1.58

5 In the left window, open the **Rome** folder, and then select the file **Rome_Staffing_Plan**.

6 Hold down Ctrl, and then drag the file into the right window, into an empty area of the **Human_Resources file list**, until the ScreenTip + *Copy to Human_Resources* displays, and then release the mouse button and the Ctrl key.

7 In the left window, on the **address bar**, click **Future_Hotels** to redisplay that folder window. Open the **Paris** folder, point to **Paris_Staffing_Plan** and right-click, and then click **Copy**.

8 In the right window, point anywhere in the **file list**, right-click, and then click **Paste**.

9 Use either technique to copy the **London_Staffing_Plan** file on the left to the folder window on the right.

Copies of the three files regarding staffing plans for the three European locations display.

10 Start **Snipping Tool**, click the **New arrow**, and then click **Full-screen Snip**. In the **Snipping Tool** mark-up window, click **Save Snip** 🖫.

11 In the displayed **Save As** dialog box, notice the path in the **address bar**. If necessary, in the **navigation pane**, under **Computer**, click your **USB flash drive**, and then display the folder window for your **Windows 8 Chapter 1** folder.

12 Be sure the file type is **JPEG**. Using your own name, name the file **Lastname_Firstname_1B_HR_Snip** and press ⏎.

13 **Close** ⊠ all open windows. Submit your three snip files from this Project to your instructor as directed.

More **Knowledge**	**Using the Recycle Bin Icon, Permanently Deleting an Item, and Restoring by Dragging**

It is good practice to delete files and folders that you no longer need from your hard disk drive and removable storage devices. Doing so frees up storage space on your devices and makes it easier to keep your data organized.

When you delete a file or folder from any area of your computer's hard disk drive, the file or folder is not immediately deleted. Instead, the deleted item is stored in the **Recycle Bin** and remains there until the Recycle Bin is emptied. Thus, you can recover an item deleted from your computer's hard disk drive so long as the Recycle Bin has not been emptied. Items deleted from removable storage devices like a USB flash drive and from some network drives are immediately deleted and cannot be recovered from the Recycle Bin.

To permanently delete a file without first moving it to the Recycle Bin, click the item, hold down Shift, and then press Delete. A message will display indicating *Are you sure you want to permanently delete this file?* Use caution when using Shift + Delete to permanently delete a file because this action is **not** reversible.

You can restore items by dragging them from the file list of the Recycle Bin window to the file list of the folder window in which you want to restore or you can restore them to the location they were deleted from by right-clicking the items in the file list of the Recycle Bin window and selecting Restore.

END | You have completed Project 1B

END OF CHAPTER

SUMMARY

Windows 8 is optimized for touchscreens and also works with a mouse and keyboard. You will probably use touch when you are reading or communicating on the web and a keyboard when creating files.

The Windows 8 Start screen is your connected dashboard—this is your one-screen view of information that updates continuously with new information and personal communications that are important to you.

The Windows Store apps you use from the Start screen are immersive—they have no borders or screen distractions. Windows Store apps typically have a single purpose; for example, to view Facebook updates.

File Explorer is at work anytime you are viewing the contents of a library, a folder, or a file. Use File Explorer to navigate your Windows 8 structure that stores and organizes the files you create.

GO! LEARN IT ONLINE

Review the concepts and key terms in this chapter by completing these online challenges, which you can find at **www.pearsonhighered.com/go**.

Matching and Multiple Choice: Answer matching and multiple choice questions to test what you learned in this chapter. MyITLab®

Crossword Puzzle: Spell out the words that match the numbered clues, and put them in the puzzle squares.

Flipboard: Flip through the definitions of the key terms in this chapter and match them with the correct term.

GO! FOR JOB SUCCESS

Video: Email Etiquette

Your instructor may assign this video to your class, and then ask you to think about, or discuss with your classmates, these questions:

FotolEdhar / Fotolia

Why do you think it is important to follow specific etiquette when composing email?

Why is it important to include a greeting and sign every email you send?

What are the differences between sending a business email and a personal email, and what are three specific things you should never do in a business email?

END OF CHAPTER

REVIEW AND ASSESSMENT GUIDE FOR WINDOWS 8 CHAPTER 1

Your instructor may assign one or more of these projects to help you review the chapter and assess your mastery and understanding of the chapter.

	Review and Assessment Guide for Windows 8 Chapter 1		
Project	**Apply Skills from These Chapter Objectives**	**Project Type**	**Project Location**
1C	Objectives 1–5 from Project 1A	**1C Skills Review** A guided review of the skills from Project 1A.	On the following pages
1D	Objectives 6–10 from Project 1B	**1D Skills Review** A guided review of the skills from Project 1B.	On the following pages
1E	Objectives 1–5 from Project 1A	**1E Mastery** A demonstration of your mastery of the skills in Project 1A with decision making.	On the following pages
1F	Objectives 6–10 from Project 1B	**1F Mastery** A demonstration of your mastery of the skills in Project 1B with decision making.	On the following pages
1G	Combination of Objectives from Projects 1A and 1B	**1G Mastery** A demonstration of your understanding of the chapter concepts applied in a manner that you would outside of college. An analytic rubric helps you and your instructor grade the quality of your work by comparing it to the work an expert in the discipline would create.	On the following pages
1H	Combination of Objectives from Projects 1A and 1B	**1H GO! Think** A demonstration of your understanding of the chapter concepts applied in a manner that you would outside of college. An analytic rubric helps you and your instructor grade the quality of your work by comparing it to the work an expert in the discipline would create.	On the following pages
1I	Combination of Objectives from Projects 1A and 1B	**1I GO! Think** A demonstration of your understanding of the chapter concepts applied in a manner that you would outside of college. An analytic rubric helps you and your instructor grade the quality of your work by comparing it to the work an expert in the discipline would create.	On the following pages

GLOSSARY

GLOSSARY OF CHAPTER KEY TERMS

.jpg An image file format, commonly pronounced *JPEG*, that stands for Joint Photographic Experts Group; this is a common file type used by digital cameras and computers to store digital pictures; JPEG is popular because it can store a high-quality picture in a relatively small file.

.png An image file format, commonly pronounced *PING*, that stands for Portable Network Graphic; this is an image file type that can be transferred over the Internet.

Action Center Located in the notification area, a central place to view alerts and take actions related to things that need your attention.

Address bar Displays your current location in the folder structure as a series of links separated by arrows.

Administrator account A user account that lets you make changes that will affect other users of the computer; the most powerful of the three types of accounts, because it permits the most control over the computer.

App The shortened version of the word *application*.

App bar An area at the bottom of every Windows Store app containing various controls pertaining to the app.

App switcher The thumbnail view of open apps that displays when you move your mouse down from the Back tip in the upper left corner; to switch to an app that is still open, you can click any of the thumbnails.

Application A set of instructions that a computer uses to accomplish a task; also called a program.

Back tip The upper left corner of the Start screen that when pointed to displays a thumbnail image of the last screen you were on; you can use it to *go back* to your previous screen.

Badge An icon that displays on the Lock screen, below the time, day, and date, that represents the status of your Internet connection, your battery if you are using a tablet or laptop, or any other Lock screen apps you might have selected.

Booting the computer The process of turning on a computer when the computer has been completely shut down.

Charms A set of buttons that display when you point or swipe in from the right side of the screen that you can use in every app—whether a Windows Store app or a desktop app—and that enable you to search, share, access devices, or adjust your PC settings.

Click The action of pressing the left mouse button.

Clipboard A temporary storage area for information that you have copied or moved from one place and plan to use somewhere else.

Cloud storage Storage space on an Internet site that can also display as a drive on your computer.

Compressed file A file that has been reduced in size and that takes up less storage space and can be transferred to other computers faster than uncompressed files.

Contextual tab Context-sensitive commands and options on the ribbon that are relevant to the active object.

Dashboard A descriptive term for the Windows 8 Start screen because it provides a one-screen view of links to information and programs that matter most to the signed-in user.

Data All the files—documents, workbooks, pictures, songs, and so on—that you create and store during the day-to-day use of your computer.

Data management The process of managing your files and folders in an organized manner so that you can find information when you need it.

Desktop The area in Windows 8 where you use desktop apps and that serves as a surface for your work, like the top of an actual desk.

Desktop app A computer program installed on the hard drive of a computer and that requires a computer operating system like Microsoft Windows or Apple OS to run.

Desktop background Displays the colors and graphics of your desktop; you can change the desktop background to look the way you want it.

Desktop shortcuts Desktop icons that link to any item accessible on your computer or on a network, such as a program, file, folder, disk drive, printer, or another computer.

Details pane Displays the most common properties associated with the selected file.

Details view The file list view in File Explorer that displays a list of files or folders and their most common properties.

Dialog box A small window that displays options for completing a task.

Double-click The action of pressing the left mouse button twice in rapid succession while holding the mouse still.

Drag The action of moving something from one location on the screen to another while holding down the left mouse button; the action of dragging includes releasing the mouse button at the desired time or location.

Drive An area of storage that is formatted with a file system compatible with your operating system and is identified by a drive letter.

Extract The action of decompressing—pulling out—files from a compressed form.

File A collection of information that is stored on a computer under a single name, for example a text document, a picture, or a program.

File Explorer The program within Windows 8 that displays the contents of libraries, folders, and files on your computer, and which also enables you to perform tasks related to your files and folders such as copying, moving, and renaming. File Explorer is at work anytime you are viewing the contents of a library, a folder, or a file.

File list Displays the contents of the current folder or library; if you type text into the Search box, only the folders and files that match your search will display here—including files in subfolders.

File properties Information about a file such as its author, the date the file was last changed, and any descriptive tags.

Folder A container in which you store files.

Folder structure The hierarchy of folders in Windows 8.

Folder window Displays the contents of the current folder, library, or device, and contains helpful parts so that you can navigate—explore within the organizing structure of Windows.

Free-form snip When using Snipping Tool, the type of snip that lets you draw an irregular line, such as a circle, around an area of the screen.

Full-screen snip When using Snipping Tool, the type of snip that captures the entire screen.

Graphical user interface The system by which you interact with your computer and which uses graphics such as an image of a file folder or wastebasket that you click to activate the item represented.

GUI The acronym for a graphical user interface, pronounced *GOO-ee*.

Hard disk drive The primary storage device located inside your computer and where most of your files and programs are typically stored; usually labeled as drive C.

Hierarchy An arrangement where items are ranked and where each level is lower in rank than the item above it.

Icons Small images that represent commands, files, applications, or other windows.

Immersive The term that describes the Windows 8 style screens, meaning they have no borders, no menus, and they behave differently from traditional Windows desktop programs because there is no taskbar, an app cannot be minimized like a desktop program, nor can an app be dragged around as a smaller window; the idea is that you are immersed in the app with no screen distractions.

Insertion point A blinking vertical line that indicates where text or graphics will be inserted.

Internet Explorer The web browser program developed by Microsoft that is included with Windows 8.

JPEG An acronym for Joint Photographic Experts Group, and which is a common file type used by digital cameras and computers to store digital pictures; JPEG is popular because it can store a high-quality picture in a relatively small file. A JPEG file has a .jpg file extension.

Jump List A list that displays when you right-click a button on the taskbar, and which displays locations (in the upper portion) and tasks (in the lower portion) from a program's taskbar button.

Keyboard shortcut A combination of two or more keyboard keys, used to perform a task that would otherwise require a mouse.

Library A collection of items, such as files and folders, assembled from various locations.

Live tiles Tiles on the Windows 8 Start screen that are constantly updated with fresh information relevant to the signed-in user; for example, the number of new email messages, new sports scores of interest, or new updates to social networks such as Facebook or Twitter.

Local account A user account in which the information associated with each user is local to a single Windows 8 computer.

Location Any disk drive, folder, or other place in which you can store files and folders.

Lock screen The first screen that displays after turning on a Windows 8 device, which displays the time, day, and date, and one or more icons representing the status of the device's Internet connection, battery status on a tablet or laptop, and any Lock screen apps that are installed such as email notifications.

Lock screen apps Apps that display on a Windows 8 Lock screen and that show quick status and notifications, even if the screen is locked, and include Calendar, Mail, Messaging, and Weather.

Menu A list of commands within a category.

Menu bar A group of menus.

Microsoft account A user account that allows you to set up one Windows 8 computer and then synchronize all the same settings from that computer to any other device you have that uses Windows 8.

Microsoft Design Language The design principles in Windows 8 that include tiles with white text on deeply colored backgrounds, consistent fonts, simpler navigation, and the use of the entire screen; the idea is that you are immersed in the app with no screen distractions.

Mouse pointer Any symbol that displays on your screen in response to moving your mouse.

Navigate (File Explorer) Explore within the file organizing structure of Windows 8.

Navigation pane The area on the left side of a folder window; it displays favorites, libraries, and an expandable list of drives and folders.

Notification area Displays notification icons and the system clock; sometimes referred to as the *system tray*.

Notification bar In Internet Explorer 10, a bar at the bottom of your screen that displays information about pending downloads, security issues, add-ons, and other issues related to the operation of your computer.

OneDrive (formerly **SkyDrive**) A free file storage and file sharing service provided by Microsoft when you sign up for a Microsoft account.

Operating system A specific type of computer program that manages the other programs on a computer—including computer devices such as desktop computers, laptop computers, smartphones, tablet computers, and game consoles.

Paint A program that comes with Windows 8 with which you can create and edit drawings and display and edit stored photos.

Parent folder In the file organizing structure of File Explorer, the location where the folder you are viewing is saved—one level up in the hierarchy.

Path A sequence of folders (directories) that leads to a specific file or folder.

PC settings The area from which you can control almost everything about how Windows 8 looks and works; you can change colors and backgrounds, the picture on your Lock screen, or your account picture, manage other users (if you are the administrator), connect devices like printers, or set up a network.

Personal folder A folder created for each user account on a Windows 8 computer, labeled with the account holder's name, and which contains the subfolders *Documents*, *Pictures*, *Music*, and *Videos*.

PING An acronym for Portable Network Graphic, and which is a common file type that can be transferred over the Internet. A PING file has a .png file extension.

Point to The action of moving the mouse pointer over a specific area.

Pointer Any symbol that displays on your screen in response to moving your mouse and with which you can select objects and commands.

Pointing device A mouse, touchpad, or other device that controls the pointer position on the screen.

Program A set of instructions that a computer uses to accomplish a task; also called an application.

Progress bar In a dialog box or taskbar button, a bar that indicates visually the progress of a task such as a download or file transfer.

Rectangular snip When using Snipping Tool, the type of snip that lets you draw a precise box by dragging the mouse pointer around an area of the screen to form a rectangle.

Recycle Bin A folder that stores anything that you delete from your computer, and from which anything stored can be retrieved until the contents are permanently deleted by activating the Empty Recycle Bin command.

Removable storage device A portable device on which you can store files, such as a USB flash drive, a flash memory card, or an external hard drive, commonly used to transfer information from one computer to another.

Resources A term used to refer collectively to the parts of your computer such as the central processing unit (CPU), memory, and any attached devices such as a printer.

Ribbon The area at the top of a folder window in File Explorer that groups common tasks such as copying and moving, creating new folders, emailing and zipping items, and changing views on related tabs.

Right-click The action of clicking the right mouse button.

Roam The ability to set up one computer, for example a desktop computer, and then synchronize—roam—all the same settings to a laptop, to a tablet PC, to a Windows phone, or to any other device to which one signs in with the same Microsoft account.

Screen capture An image file that contains the contents of a computer screen.

Screenshot Another name for a screen capture.

ScreenTip Useful information that displays in a small box on the screen when you perform various mouse actions, such as pointing to screen elements.

Scroll arrow An arrow at the top and bottom, or left and right, of a scroll bar that when clicked, moves the window in small increments.

Scroll bar A bar that displays on the bottom or right side of a window when the contents of a window are not completely visible; used to move the window up, down, left, or right to bring the contents into view.

Scroll box The box in a vertical or horizontal scroll bar that you drag to reposition the document on the screen.

Select To specify, by highlighting, a block of data or text on the screen with the intent of performing some action on the selection.

SharePoint A Microsoft technology that enables employees in an organization to access information across organizational and geographic boundaries.

Shortcut menu A context-sensitive menu that displays commands and options relevant to the active object.

Shut down Turning off your computer in a manner that closes all open programs and files, closes your network connections, stops the hard disk, and discontinues the use of electrical power.

SkyDrive See **OneDrive**.

Sleep Turning off your computer in a manner that automatically saves your work, stops the fan, and uses a small amount of electrical power to maintain your work in memory.

Snap (desktop apps) A Windows 8 desktop feature that automatically resizes windows when you move— *snap*—them to the edge of the screen.

Snip The image captured using Snipping Tool.

Snipping Tool A program included with Windows 8 with which you can capture an image of all or part of a computer screen, and then annotate, save, copy, or share the image via email.

Speakers icon Displays the status of the computer's speakers (if any).

Split button A button that has two parts—a button and an arrow; clicking the main part of the button performs a command and clicking the arrow opens a menu with choices.

Start screen The first screen that displays after signing in to a Windows 8 device, which displays square and rectangular boxes—referred to as tiles—from which one can access apps, websites, programs, and tools for using the computer by clicking or tapping them.

Start search The search feature in Windows 8 in which, from the Start screen, you can begin to type and by default, Windows 8 searches for apps; you can adjust the search to search for files or settings.

Start tip The thumbnail that displays when you point to the lower left corner of your screen.

Switcher Another name for *app switcher*.

System tray Another name for the notification area on the taskbar.

Tags Properties that you create and add to a file to help you find and organize your files.

Taskbar The area of the desktop that contains program buttons, and buttons for all open programs; by default, it is located at the bottom of the desktop, but you can move it.

Thumbnail A reduced image of a graphic.

Tiles Square and rectangular boxes on the Windows 8 Start screen from which one can access apps, websites, programs, and tools for using the computer by simply clicking or tapping them.

Title bar The bar across the top of the window that displays the program name.

User account A collection of information that tells Windows 8 what files and folders the account holder can access, what changes the account holder can make to the computer system, and what the account holder's personal preferences are.

Wallpaper Another term for the desktop background.

Web browser Software with which you display webpages and navigate the Internet.

Window snip When using Snipping Tool, the type of snip that captures the entire displayed window.

Windows 8 An operating system developed by Microsoft Corporation designed to work with mobile computing devices of all types and also with traditional PCs.

Windows Store apps Apps built for specific purposes; for example, to view photos, read sports information, organize a list of contacts, or read updates to social networks like Facebook and Twitter.

CHAPTER REVIEW

Apply 1A skills from these Objectives:

1 Use File Explorer and Desktop Apps to Create a New Folder and Save a File on a Removable Storage Device

2 Identify the Functions of the Windows 8 Operating System and Windows Store Apps

3 Use Windows Store Apps

4 Sign Out of Windows 8 and Turn Off Your Computer

5 Manage User Accounts

PROJECT FILES

For Project 1C, you will need the following files:

Your USB flash drive containing the student data files
win01_1C_Answer_Sheet (Word document)

You will save your file as:

Lastname_Firstname_1C_Answer_Sheet

1 Display the **Start screen**; point to the upper left corner and drag down slightly to display the app switcher, and then if necessary, close any open apps. Display the **desktop**. **Close** ☒ any open desktop windows. On the taskbar, click **File Explorer**. In the **navigation pane**, click your **USB drive** that contains the student files for this chapter, and then navigate to **Chapter_Files ▶ Chapter_01**. Double-click the Word file **win01_1C_Answer_Sheet** to open Word and display the document. If necessary, at the top click Enable editing; be sure the window is maximized. In the upper left corner, click **FILE**, click **Save As**, click **Computer**, and then click **Browse** to display the **Save As** dialog box. In the **navigation pane**, click your **USB drive** and then double-click to open your **Windows 8 Chapter 1** folder. Using your own name, save the document as **Lastname_Firstname_1C_Answer_Sheet** Click **Save**.

On the taskbar, click the **Word** button to minimize the window and leave your Word document accessible from the taskbar. **Close** the **Chapter_01** folder window. As you complete each step in this project, write the letter of your answer on a piece of paper; you will fill in your Answer Sheet after you complete all the steps in this project.

Display the **Start screen** and type **paint** Which of the following is true?

A.   Applications that begin with the text *paint* display in the search results.

B.   The Paint program opens on the desktop.

C.   From this screen, you can remove the Paint program from your computer.

2 If necessary, press an arrow key on your computer to surround the name of the *Paint* program with a white border, and then press Enter. What is your result?

A.   The Paint program tile displays on the Start screen.

B.   The Paint program opens on the desktop.

C.   File Explorer displays files created in the Paint program.

3 On the taskbar, point to the **Paint** button, right-click, and click **Pin this program to taskbar**. Then **Close** ☒ the **Paint** window. Which of the following is true?

A.   Both B. and C. are true.

B.   The Paint program closes.

C.   The Paint program button displays on the taskbar because it is pinned there.

4 On the taskbar, click **File Explorer**. What is your result?

A.   The window for your USB flash drive displays.

B.   The Libraries window displays.

C.   The Documents window displays.

(Project 1C Getting to Know Windows 8 continues on the next page)

CHAPTER REVIEW

5 In the **file list**, double-click **Documents**. What is your result?

A. The first document in the library opens in its application.

B. The contents of the Documents library display in the file list.

C. The contents of the Documents library display in the address bar.

6 In the **navigation pane**, click **Computer**. What is your result?

A. The storage devices attached to your computer display in the file list.

B. All of the files on the hard drive display in the file list.

C. Your computer restarts.

7 **Close** ☒ the **Computer** window. On the taskbar, point to the **Paint** button, right-click, and then click **Unpin this program from taskbar**. Display the **Start screen**. Type **store** and press Enter. What is your result?

A. All the storage devices attached to your computer display on the Start screen.

B. The Store app displays.

C. A list of games that you can download displays.

8 Display the **Start screen**, type **maps** and press Enter; if necessary, enable your current location. Display the **Start screen** again, type **weather** and then press Enter. Display the **Start screen** again, point to the upper left corner of the screen, and then move the mouse pointer down along the left edge of the screen to display all open apps. This display of all open apps is called what?

A. app navigator

B. app map

C. app switcher

9 Which of the following best describes the group of apps that display as open?

A. Weather, Desktop

B. Maps, Store, Weather

C. Weather, Maps, Store, Desktop

10 On the left side of the screen, point to each open app, right-click, and then click **Close** so that all apps are closed. What is your result?

A. The desktop redisplays.

B. The search results for *store* redisplay.

C. The Start screen displays.

To complete this project: Display the **desktop**, on the taskbar click the **Word** button, and type your answers into the correct boxes. Save and close your Word document, and submit as directed by your instructor. **Close** ☒ all open windows.

END | You have completed Project 1C

CHAPTER REVIEW

PROJECT FILES

For Project 1D, you will need the following files:

Your USB flash drive containing the student data files
win01_1D_Answer_Sheet (Word document)

You will save your file as:

Lastname_Firstname_1D_Answer_Sheet

1 Display the **Start screen**; point to the upper left corner and drag down slightly to display the app switcher, and then if necessary, close any open apps. Display the **desktop**. **Close** ⊠ any open desktop windows. On the taskbar, click **File Explorer**. In the **navigation pane**, click your **USB drive** that contains the student files for this chapter, and then navigate to **Chapter_Files ▶ Chapter_01**. Double-click the Word file **win01_1D_Answer_Sheet** to open Word and display the document. If necessary, at the top click Enable editing; be sure the window is maximized. In the upper left corner, click **FILE**, click **Save As**, click **Computer**, and then click **Browse** to display the **Save As** dialog box. In the **navigation pane**, click your **USB drive** and then double-click to open your **Windows 8 Chapter 1** folder. Using your own name, save the document as **Lastname_Firstname_1D_Answer_Sheet** Click **Save**.

On the taskbar, click the **Word** button to minimize the window and leave your Word document accessible from the taskbar. **Close** the **Chapter_01** folder window. As you complete each step in this project, write the letter of your answer on a piece of paper; you will fill in your Answer Sheet after you complete all the steps in this project.

Open **File Explorer**, navigate to your **USB flash drive**, and then click to select the **Bell_Orchid** folder. On the ribbon, on the **Home tab**, in the **Organize group**, click **Copy to**, and then on the displayed list, click **Documents**. *You will need a new copy of the files for this Project.* If a message indicates **Replace or Skip Files**, click **Replace the files in the destination** so that you have a new copy of the original files from your USB drive.

From the **navigation pane**, double-click your **Documents** folder to open its folder window, and then double-click the **Bell_Orchid** folder. In the **file list**, how many *folders* display?

A. Four

B. Five

C. Six

2 Navigate to **Bell_Orchid ▶ Corporate ▶ Food_Beverage**. How many *folders* are in the **Food_Beverage** folder?

A. Three

B. Two

C. One

3 Open the **Restaurants** folder, and then click one time to select the file **Breakfast_Continental**. On the ribbon, click the **Home tab**. In which group of commands can you change the name of this file?

A. New

B. Select

C. Organize

(Project 1D Managing Files and Folders continues on the next page)

CHAPTER REVIEW

4 With the **Breakfast_Continental** file still selected, point to the file name and right-click. Which of the following is *not* true?

A. From this menu, you can rename the file.

B. From this menu, you can print the file.

C. From this menu, you can move the file to another folder within Bell_Orchid.

5 Click on the desktop to close the shortcut menu, and then click the **Up** button to move up one level in the hierarchy and display the file list for the **Food_Beverage** folder. On the ribbon, click the **View tab**. In the **Layout group**, click **Large icons**. What is your result?

A. The folder window fills the entire screen.

B. Files that are pictures are visible as pictures.

C. Only picture files display in the file list.

6 On the **View tab**, return the **Layout** to **Details view**. In the **file list**, click one time to select the file **CO_FB_Menu_Presentation**. In the **Panes group**, click the **Details pane** button. (*Hint*: you can point to a button to see its ScreenTip). By looking at the displayed details about this file on the right, which of the following is an information item you can determine about this file?

A. The number of words on each slide.

B. The number of slides in the presentation.

C. The number of people who edited this presentation.

7 In the **Panes group**, click the **Preview pane**. In the **Preview pane**, *slowly* drag the scroll box to the bottom of the scroll bar. Which of the following is *not* true?

A. The slide name displays as you drag the scroll box.

B. The PowerPoint program opens as you drag the scroll box.

C. The slide number displays as you drag the scroll box.

8 In the **Panes group**, click the **Preview pane** button again to close the pane. **Close** ☒ the folder window. Display the **Start screen**, type **paint** and then press Enter to display the **Paint** program on your desktop. On the taskbar, point to the **Paint** button and right-click. Which of the following is *not* true?

A. From the displayed menu, you can pin this program to the taskbar.

B. From the displayed menu, you can pin this program to the Start screen.

C. From the displayed menu, you can close the Paint program.

9 Click **Close window**, and then display the **Start screen**. Type **paint** and then in the Apps screen, right-click **Paint** to display the **app bar** at the bottom of the screen. Click **Pin to Start** and then redisplay the **Start screen**. Which of the following is true?

A. Windows 8 creates a tile for the Paint program on the Start screen.

B. The Paint program opens on your desktop.

C. A tile for the Paint program flashes on the Start screen.

(Project 1D Managing Files and Folders continues on the next page)

CHAPTER REVIEW

10 On the **Start screen**, locate and point to the **Paint** tile, and then right-click. Click **Unpin from Start**. Click the **Desktop** tile. Open **File Explorer**, display your **Documents** folder, and then click the **Bell_Orchid** folder one time to select it. On the **Home tab**, in the **Organize group**, locate **Delete**, and then click the **Delete button arrow**. What is your result?

A. The folder window for the Recycle Bin displays.

B. The folder is deleted and the Documents window closes.

C. A list of Delete options displays.

On the list, click **Permanently delete** (or Recycle if you prefer). Recall that you still have the original Bell_Orchid file on your USB flash drive. In the **Delete Folder** dialog box, click **Yes**. In the upper right corner of the folder window, click **Close** ⊠.

To complete this project: On the taskbar, click the **Word** button, and then type your answers into the correct boxes. Save and close your Word document, and submit as directed by your instructor. **Close** ⊠ all open windows.

END | You have completed Project 1D

CONTENT-BASED ASSESSMENTS

Mastering Windows 8 | Project 1E Windows Help and Support

Apply 1A skills from these Objectives:

1 Use File Explorer and Desktop Apps to Create a New Folder and Save a File on a Removable Storage Device

2 Identify the Functions of the Windows 8 Operating System and Windows Store Apps

3 Use Windows Store Apps

4 Sign Out of Windows 8 and Turn Off Your Computer

5 Manage User Accounts

In the following Mastering Windows 8 project, you will capture and save a snip that will look similar to Figure 1.59.

PROJECT FILES

For Project 1E, you will need the following file:

Your USB flash drive containing the student data files
New Snip file

You will save your file as:

Lastname_Firstname_1E_Close_App_Snip

PROJECT RESULTS

FIGURE 1.59

(Project 1E Windows Help and Support continues on the next page)

CONTENT-BASED ASSESSMENTS

1 On the **Start screen**, type **help and support** and press Enter to display the **Windows Help and Support** window. Search for **close an app** Click **How do I close an app? Maximize** ☐ the window.

2 On the taskbar, click **Snipping Tool**, click the **New button arrow**, and then click **Window Snip**. Click anywhere in the **Windows Help and Support** window to capture it.

3 On the toolbar of the **Snipping Tool** mark-up window, click the **Highlighter** and then highlight the text *How do I close an app?* Click the **Save Snip** button.

4 In the displayed **Save As** dialog box, in the **navigation pane**, scroll down, and then under

Computer, click your **USB flash drive**. In the **file list**, open your **Windows 8 Chapter 1** folder so that its name displays in the **address bar**, and then as the **File name**, and using your own name, save the snip as **Lastname_Firstname_1E_Close_App_Snip**

5 **Close** ☒ the **Snipping Tool** window. Take a moment to click the circled play button ▷ to watch the short video about how to close an app.

6 **Close** ☒ the **Windows Help and Support** window. Submit your snip file as directed by your instructor.

END | You have completed Project 1E

CONTENT-BASED ASSESSMENTS

Apply 1B skills from these Objectives:

6 Use File Explorer to Display Libraries, Folders, and Files

7 Start Programs and Open Data Files

8 Personalize Your Windows 8 Start Screen

9 Create, Rename, and Copy Files and Folders

10 Move and Delete Files and Folders

In the following Mastering Windows 8 project, you will capture and save a snip that will look similar to Figure 1.60.

PROJECT FILES

For Project 1F, you will need the following files:

Your USB flash drive containing the student data files
New Snip file

You will save your file as:

Lastname_Firstname_1F_San_Diego_Snip

PROJECT RESULTS

FIGURE 1.60

(Project 1F Managing Files and Folders continues on the next page)

CONTENT-BASED ASSESSMENTS

1 Display the **desktop**, and then on the taskbar, click **File Explorer**. Display the folder window for your **USB flash drive**, and then navigate to **Bell_Orchid** ▶ **San_Diego** ▶ **Sales_Marketing** ▶ **Media**.

2 On the **file list**, click one time to select the file **SanDiego1**.

3 Display the **Preview pane** for this file.

4 Start **Snipping Tool**, create a **Window Snip**, click anywhere in the **Media** folder window to capture it, and then click the **Save Snip** button.

5 In the displayed **Save As** dialog box, in the **navigation pane**, scroll down, and then under **Computer**, click your **USB flash drive**. In the **file list**, open your **Windows 8 Chapter 1** folder so that its name displays in the **address bar**, and then as the **File name**, and using your own name, save the snip as **Lastname_Firstname_1F_San_Diego_Snip**

6 Close ☒ the **Snipping Tool** window. Turn off the display of the **Preview pane**. **Close** ☒ the folder window. Submit your snip file as directed by your instructor.

END | You have completed Project 1F

OUTCOMES-BASED ASSESSMENTS

RUBRIC

The following outcomes-based assessments are *open-ended assessments*. That is, there is no specific correct result; your result will depend on your approach to the information provided. Make *Professional Quality* your goal. Use the following scoring rubric to guide you in *how* to approach the problem, and then to evaluate *how well* your approach solves the problem.

The *criteria*—Software Mastery, Content, Format and Layout, and Process—represent the knowledge and skills you have gained that you can apply to solving the problem. The *levels of performance*—Professional Quality, Approaching Professional Quality, or Needs Quality Improvements—help you and your instructor evaluate your result.

	Your completed project is of Professional Quality if you:	Your completed project is Approaching Professional Quality if you:	Your completed project Needs Quality Improvements if you:
1-Software Mastery	Choose and apply the most appropriate skills, tools, and features and identify efficient methods to solve the problem.	Choose and apply some appropriate skills, tools, and features, but not in the most efficient manner.	Choose inappropriate skills, tools, or features, or are inefficient in solving the problem.
2-Content	Construct a solution that is clear and well organized, contains content that is accurate, appropriate to the audience and purpose, and is complete. Provide a solution that contains no errors in spelling, grammar, or style.	Construct a solution in which some components are unclear, poorly organized, inconsistent, or incomplete. Misjudge the needs of the audience. Have some errors in spelling, grammar, or style, but the errors do not detract from comprehension.	Construct a solution that is unclear, incomplete, or poorly organized; contains some inaccurate or inappropriate content; and contains many errors in spelling, grammar, or style. Do not solve the problem.
3-Format & Layout	Format and arrange all elements to communicate information and ideas, clarify function, illustrate relationships, and indicate relative importance.	Apply appropriate format and layout features to some elements, but not others. Overuse features, causing minor distraction.	Apply format and layout that does not communicate information or ideas clearly. Do not use format and layout features to clarify function, illustrate relationships, or indicate relative importance. Use available features excessively, causing distraction.
4-Process	Use an organized approach that integrates planning, development, self-assessment, revision, and reflection.	Demonstrate an organized approach in some areas, but not others; or, use an insufficient process of organization throughout.	Do not use an organized approach to solve the problem.

OUTCOMES-BASED ASSESSMENTS

In this project, you will construct a solution by applying any combination of the skills you practiced from the Objectives in Projects 1A and 1B.

PROJECT FILES

For Project 1G, you will need the following file:

win01_1G_Help_Desk

You will save your document as:

Lastname_Firstname_1G_Help_Desk

From the student files that accompany this chapter, open the **Chapter_Files** folder, and then in the **Chapter_01** folder, locate and open the Word document **win01_1G_Help_Desk**. Save the document in your **Windows 8 Chapter 1** folder as **Lastname_Firstname_1G_Help_Desk**

The following email question arrived at the Help Desk from an employee at the Bell Orchid Hotel's corporate office. In the Word document, construct a response based on your knowledge of Windows 8. Although an email response is not as formal as a letter, you should still use good grammar, good sentence structure, professional language, and a polite tone. Save your document and submit the response as directed by your instructor.

To: Help Desk

We have a new employee in our department, and as her user picture, she wants to use a picture of her dog. I know that Corporate Policy says it is ok to use an acceptable personal picture on a user account. Can she change the picture herself within her standard user account, or does she need an administrator account to do that?

END | You have completed Project 1G

OUTCOMES-BASED ASSESSMENTS

GO! Think   Project 1H Help Desk

In this project, you will construct a solution by applying any combination of the skills you practiced from the Objectives in Projects 1A and 1B.

PROJECT FILES

For Project 1H, you will need the following file:

win01_1H_Help_Desk

You will save your document as:

Lastname_Firstname_1H_Help_Desk

From the student files that accompany this chapter, open the **Chapter_Files** folder, and then in the **Chapter_01** folder, locate and open **win01_1H_Help_Desk**. Save the document in your **Windows 8 Chapter 1** folder as **Lastname_Firstname_1H_Help_Desk**

The following email question arrived at the Help Desk from an employee at the Bell Orchid Hotel's corporate office. In the Word document, construct a response based on your knowledge of Windows 8. Although an email response is not as formal as a letter, you should still use good grammar, good sentence structure, professional language, and a polite tone. Save your document and submit the response as directed by your instructor.

To: Help Desk

When I'm done using my computer at the end of the day, should I use the Sleep option or the Shut down option, and what's the difference between the two?

END | You have completed Project 1H

OUTCOMES-BASED ASSESSMENTS

GO Think! Project 1I Help Desk

In this project, you will construct a solution by applying any combination of the skills you practiced from the Objectives in Projects 1A and 1B.

For Project 1I, you will need the following file:

win01_1I_Help_Desk

You will save your document as:

Lastname_Firstname_1I_Help_Desk

From the student files that accompany this chapter, open the **Chapter_Files** folder, and then in the **Chapter_01** folder, locate and open **win01_1I_Help_Desk**. Save the document in your **Windows 8 Chapter 1** folder as **Lastname_Firstname_1I_Help_Desk**

The following email question has arrived at the Help Desk from an employee at the Bell Orchid Hotel's corporate office. In the Word document, construct a response based on your knowledge of Windows 8. Although an email response is not as formal as a letter, you should still use good grammar, good sentence structure, professional language, and a polite tone. Save your document and submit the response as directed by your instructor.

To: Help Desk

I am not sure about the differences between copying and moving files and folders. When is it best to copy a file or a folder and when is it best to move a file or folder? Can you also describe some techniques that I can use for copying or moving files and folders? Which do you think is the easiest way to copy or move files and folders?

END | You have completed Project 1I

Introduction to Microsoft Office 2013 Features

PROJECT 1A

OUTCOMES
Create, save, and print a Microsoft Office 2013 document.

PROJECT 1B

OUTCOMES
Use the ribbon and dialog boxes to perform commands in Microsoft Office 2013.

OBJECTIVES

1. Use File Explorer to Download, Extract, and Locate Files and Folders
2. Use Start Search to Locate and Start a Microsoft Office 2013 Desktop App
3. Enter, Edit, and Check the Spelling of Text in an Office 2013 Program
4. Perform Commands from a Dialog Box
5. Create a Folder and Name and Save a File
6. Insert a Footer, Add Document Properties, Print a File, and Close a Desktop App

OBJECTIVES

7. Open an Existing File and Save It with a New Name
8. Sign In to Office and Explore Options for a Microsoft Office Desktop App
9. Perform Commands from the Ribbon and Quick Access Toolbar
10. Apply Formatting in Office Programs
11. Compress Files and Use the Microsoft Office 2013 Help System
12. Install Apps for Office and Create a Microsoft Account

etse1112/Fotolia

In This Chapter

In this chapter, you will use File Explorer to navigate the Windows folder structure, create a folder, and save files in Microsoft Office 2013 programs. You will also practice using features in Microsoft Office 2013 that work similarly across Word, Excel, Access, and PowerPoint. These features include managing files, performing commands, adding document properties, signing in to Office, applying formatting, and using Help. You will also practice compressing files and installing Apps for Office from the Office Store. In this chapter, you will also learn how to set up a free Microsoft account so that you can use OneDrive.

The projects in this chapter relate to **Skyline Metro Grill**, which is a chain of 25 casual, full-service restaurants based in Boston. The Skyline Metro Grill owners are planning an aggressive expansion program. To expand by 15 additional restaurants in Chicago, San Francisco, and Los Angeles by 2018, the company must attract new investors, develop new menus, develop new marketing strategies, and recruit new employees, all while adhering to the company's quality guidelines and maintaining its reputation for excellent service. To succeed, the company plans to build on its past success and maintain its quality elements.

Note Form

PROJECT ACTIVITIES

In Activities 1.01 through 1.09, you will create a note form using Microsoft Word, save it in a folder that you create by using File Explorer, and then print the note form or submit it electronically as directed by your instructor. Your completed note form will look similar to Figure 1.1.

PROJECT FILES

For Project 1A, you will need the following file:

New blank Word document

You will save your file as:

Lastname_Firstname_1A_Note_Form

PROJECT RESULTS

Build from
Scratch

Skyline Metro Grill, Chef's Notes
Executive Chef, Sarah Jackson

On your screen, diagonal shading
will display; shading does not
display on a printed document
as pictured here

Lastname_Firstname_1A_Note_Form

FIGURE 1.1 Project 1A Note Form

Objective 1 | Use File Explorer to Download, Extract, and Locate Files and Folders

Video OF1-1

A *file* is a collection of information stored on a computer under a single name, for example, a Word document or a PowerPoint presentation. A file is stored in a *folder*—a container in which you store files—or a *subfolder*, which is a folder within a folder. The Windows operating system stores and organizes your files and folders, which is a primary task of an operating system.

You *navigate*—explore within the organizing structure of Windows—to create, save, and find your files and folders by using the *File Explorer* program. File Explorer displays the files and folders on your computer and is at work anytime you are viewing the contents of files and folders in a *window*. A window is a rectangular area on a computer screen in which programs and content appear; a window can be moved, resized, minimized, or closed.

Activity 1.01 | Using File Explorer to Download, Extract, and Locate Files and Folders

> **ALERT!** | **You Will Need a USB Flash Drive**
>
> You will need a USB flash drive for this activity to download the Student Data Files for this chapter. If your instructor is providing the files to you, for example by placing the files at your learning management system, be sure you have downloaded them to a location where you can access the files and then skip to Activity 1.02.

> **NOTE** | **Creating a Microsoft Account**
>
> Use a free Microsoft account to sign in to Windows 8 and Office 2013 so that you can work on different PCs and use your OneDrive. You need not use the Microsoft account as your primary email address unless you want to do so. To create a Microsoft account, go to **www.outlook.com**.

1 Sign in to Windows 8 with your Microsoft account—or the account provided by your instructor—to display the Windows 8 **Start screen**, and then click the **Desktop** tile. Insert a **USB flash drive** in your computer; **Close** ☒ any messages or windows that display.

The *desktop* is the screen in Windows that simulates your work area. A *USB flash drive* is a small data storage device that plugs into a computer USB port.

2 On the taskbar, click **Internet Explorer** 🌐. Click in the **address bar** to select the existing text, type **www.pearsonhighered.com/go** and press Enter. Locate and click the name of this textbook, and then click the **STUDENT DATA FILES tab**.

The *taskbar* is the area along the lower edge of the desktop that displays buttons representing programs—also referred to as desktop apps. In the desktop version of Internet Explorer 10, the *address bar* is the area at the top of the Internet Explorer window that displays, and where you can type, a *URL—Uniform Resource Locator*—which is an address that uniquely identifies a location on the Internet.

3 On the list of files, move your mouse pointer over—*point* to—**Office Features Chapter 1** and then *click*—press the left button on your mouse pointing device one time.

4 In the **Windows Internet Explorer** dialog box, click **Save As**.

A *dialog box* is a small window that contains options for completing a task.

5 In the **Save As** dialog box, on the left, locate the **navigation pane**, and point to the vertical **scroll bar**.

The Save As dialog box is an example of a *common dialog box*; that is, this dialog box looks the same in Excel and in PowerPoint and in most other Windows-based desktop applications—also referred to as programs.

Use the *navigation pane* on the left side of the Save As dialog box to navigate to, open, and display favorites, libraries, folders, saved searches, and an expandable list of drives. A *pane* is a separate area of a window.

A *scroll bar* displays when a window, or a pane within a window, has information that is not in view. You can click the up or down scroll arrows—or the left and right scroll arrows in a horizontal scroll bar—to scroll the contents up and down or left and right in small increments.

You can also drag the *scroll box*—the box within the scroll bar—to scroll the window or pane in either direction.

This is a *compressed folder*—also called a *zipped folder*—which is a folder containing one or more files that have been reduced in size. A compressed folder takes up less storage space and can be transferred to other computers faster.

NOTE | **Comparing Your Screen with the Figures in This Textbook**

Your screen will match the figures shown in this textbook if you set your screen resolution to 1280 × 768. At other resolutions, your screen will closely resemble, but not match, the figures shown. To view your screen's resolution, on the desktop, right-click in a blank area, and then click Screen resolution.

---

6 In the **navigation pane**, if necessary, on the scroll bar click ⌄ to scroll down. If necessary, to the left of **Computer**, click ▷ to expand the list. Then click the name of your **USB flash drive**.

7 With *Office_Features* displayed in the **File name** box, in the lower right corner click **Save**.

At the bottom of your screen, the *Notification bar* displays information about pending downloads, security issues, add-ons, and other issues related to the operation of your computer.

8 In the **Notification bar**, when the download is complete, click **Open folder** to display the folder window for your **USB flash drive**.

A *folder window* displays the contents of the current location—folder, library, or drive—and contains helpful parts so that you can navigate within the file organizing structure of Windows.

9 With the compressed **Office_Features** folder selected, on the ribbon, click the **Extract tab** to display the **Compressed Folder Tools**, and then click **Extract all**.

The *ribbon* is a user interface in both Office 2013 and Windows 8 that groups the commands for performing related tasks on tabs across the upper portion of a window.

In the dialog box, you can *extract*—decompress or pull out—files from a compressed folder.

You can navigate to some other location by clicking the Browse button and navigating within your storage locations.

10 In the **Extract Compressed (Zipped) Folders** dialog box, click to the right of the selected text, and then press [Backspace] until only the drive letter of your USB and the colon following it display—for example G:—and then click **Extract**. Notice that a progress bar indicates the progress of the extract process, and that when the extract is complete, the **Office_Features** folder displays on the file list of your **USB flash drive**.

> In a dialog box or taskbar button, a *progress bar* indicates visually the progress of a task such as a download or file transfer.

> The *address bar* in File Explorer displays your current location in the folder structure as a series of links separated by arrows, which is referred to as the *path*—a sequence of folders that leads to a specific file or folder.

> By pressing [Backspace] in the Extract dialog box, you avoid creating an unneeded folder level.

11 Because you no longer need the compressed (zipped) version of the folder, be sure it is selected, click the **Home tab**, and then click **Delete**. In the upper right corner of the **USB drive** folder window, click **Close** ☒. **Close** ☒ the **Internet Explorer** window and in the Internet Explorer message, click **Close all tabs**.

> Your desktop redisplays.

Objective 2   Use Start Search to Locate and Start a Microsoft Office 2013 Desktop App

Video OF1-2

The term *desktop app* commonly refers to a computer program that is installed on your computer and requires a computer operating system such as Microsoft Windows or Apple OS to run. The programs in Microsoft Office 2013 are considered to be desktop apps. Apps that run from the *device software* on a smartphone or a tablet computer—for example, iOS, Android, or Windows Phone—or apps that run from *browser software* such as Internet Explorer, Safari, Firefox, or Chrome on a desktop PC or laptop PC are referred to simply as *apps*.

Activity 1.02 | Using Start Search to Locate and Start a Microsoft Office 2013 Desktop App

The easiest and fastest way to search for an app is to use the *Start search* feature—simply display the Windows 8 Start screen and start typing. By default, Windows 8 searches for apps; you can change it to search for files or settings.

1 With your desktop displayed, press [⊞] to display the Windows 8 **Start screen**, and then type **word 2013** With *word 2013* bordered in white in the search results, press [Enter] to return to the desktop and open Word. If you want to do so, in the upper right corner, sign in with your Microsoft account, and then compare your screen with Figure 1.2.

> Documents that you have recently opened, if any, display on the left. On the right, you can select either a blank document or a *template*—a preformatted document that you can use as a starting point and then change to suit your needs.

 BY TOUCH

Swipe from the right edge of the screen to display the charms, and then tap Search. Tap in the Apps box, and then use the onscreen keyboard that displays to type *word 2013*. Tap the selected Word 2013 app name to open Word.

FIGURE 1.2

Recently opened documents, if any, display here

Start a blank document here

User signed in; this is optional

Templates to start different types of documents

2 ▷ Click **Blank document**. Compare your screen with Figure 1.3, and then take a moment to study the description of these screen elements in the table in Figure 1.4.

NOTE | **Displaying the Full Ribbon**

If your full ribbon does not display, click any tab, and then at the right end of the ribbon, click 📌 to pin the ribbon to keep it open while you work.

FIGURE 1.3

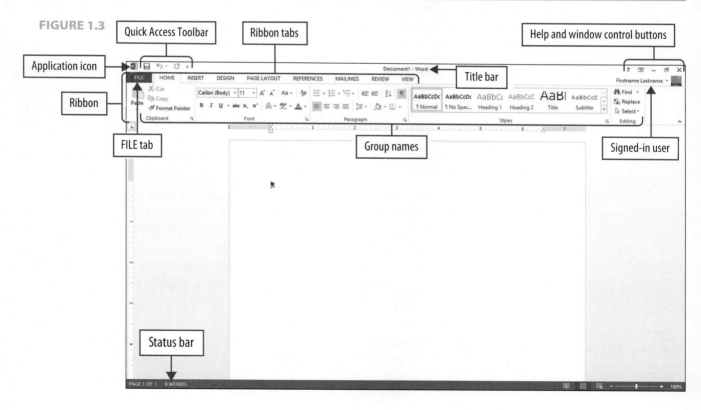

Quick Access Toolbar

Ribbon tabs

Help and window control buttons

Application icon

Title bar

Ribbon

FILE tab

Group names

Signed-in user

Status bar

FIGURE 1.4

MICROSOFT OFFICE SCREEN ELEMENTS	
SCREEN ELEMENT	**DESCRIPTION**
FILE tab	Displays Microsoft Office Backstage view, which is a centralized space for all of your file management tasks such as opening, saving, printing, publishing, or sharing a file—all the things you can do *with* a file.
Group names	Indicate the names of the groups of related commands on the displayed tab.
Help and window control buttons	Display Word Help and Full Screen Mode and enable you to Minimize, Restore Down, or Close the window.
Application icon	When clicked, displays a menu of window control commands including Restore, Minimize, and Close.
Quick Access Toolbar	Displays buttons to perform frequently used commands and use resources with a single click. The default commands include Save, Undo, and Redo. You can add and delete buttons to customize the Quick Access Toolbar for your convenience.
Ribbon	Displays a group of task-oriented tabs that contain the commands, styles, and resources you need to work in an Office 2013 desktop app. The look of your ribbon depends on your screen resolution. A high resolution will display more individual items and button names on the ribbon.
Ribbon tabs	Display the names of the task-oriented tabs relevant to the open program.
Status bar	Displays file information on the left; on the right displays buttons for Read Mode, Print Layout, and Web Layout views; on the far right displays Zoom controls.
Title bar	Displays the name of the file and the name of the program. The Help and window control buttons are grouped on the right side of the title bar.
Signed-in user	Name of the Windows 8 signed-in user.

Objective 3 | Enter, Edit, and Check the Spelling of Text in an Office 2013 Program

Video OF1-3

All of the programs in Office 2013 require some typed text. Your keyboard is still the primary method of entering information into your computer. Techniques to enter text and to **edit**—make changes to—text are similar among all of the Office 2013 programs.

Activity 1.03 | Entering and Editing Text in an Office 2013 Program

1 On the ribbon, on the HOME tab, in the Paragraph group, if necessary, click Show/Hide ¶ so that it is active—shaded. If necessary, on the VIEW tab, in the Show group, select the Ruler check box so that rulers display below the ribbon and on the left side of your window.

The **insertion point**—a blinking vertical line that indicates where text or graphics will be inserted—displays. In Office 2013 programs, the mouse **pointer**—any symbol that displays on your screen in response to moving your mouse device—displays in different shapes depending on the task you are performing and the area of the screen to which you are pointing.

When you press Enter, Spacebar, or Tab on your keyboard, characters display to represent these keystrokes. These screen characters do not print and are referred to as **formatting marks** or **nonprinting characters**.

2 ▶ Type **Skyline Grille Info** and notice how the insertion point moves to the right as you type. Point slightly to the right of the letter *e* in *Grille* and click to place the insertion point there. Compare your screen with Figure 1.5.

A *paragraph symbol* (¶) indicates the end of a paragraph and displays each time you press Enter. This is a type of formatting mark and does not print.

FIGURE 1.5

3 ▶ On your keyboard, locate and then press the Backspace key to delete the letter *e*.

Pressing Backspace removes a character to the left of the insertion point.

4 ▶ Press → one time to place the insertion point to the left of the *I* in *Info*. Type **Chef's** and then press Spacebar one time.

By *default*, when you type text in an Office program, existing text moves to the right to make space for new typing. Default refers to the current selection or setting that is automatically used by a program unless you specify otherwise.

5 ▶ Press Del four times to delete *Info* and then type **Notes**

Pressing Del removes a character to the right of the insertion point.

6 ▶ With your insertion point blinking after the word *Notes*, on your keyboard, hold down the Ctrl key. While holding down Ctrl, press ← three times to move the insertion point to the beginning of the word *Grill*.

This is a *keyboard shortcut*—a key or combination of keys that performs a task that would otherwise require a mouse. This keyboard shortcut moves the insertion point to the beginning of the previous word.

A keyboard shortcut is commonly indicated as Ctrl + ← (or some other combination of keys) to indicate that you hold down the first key while pressing the second key. A keyboard shortcut can also include three keys, in which case you hold down the first two and then press the third. For example, Ctrl + Shift + ← selects one word to the left.

7 ▶ With the insertion point blinking at the beginning of the word *Grill*, type **Metro** and press Spacebar.

8 ▶ Press Ctrl + End to place the insertion point after the letter *s* in *Notes*, and then press Enter one time. With the insertion point blinking, type the following and include the spelling error:
Exective Chef, Madison Dunham

9 With your mouse, point slightly to the left of the *M* in *Madison*, hold down the left mouse button, and then **drag**—hold down the left mouse button while moving your mouse—to the right to select the text *Madison Dunham* but not the paragraph mark following it, and then release the mouse button. Compare your screen with Figure 1.6.

The *mini toolbar* displays commands that are commonly used with the selected object, which places common commands close to your pointer. When you move the pointer away from the mini toolbar, it fades from view.

Selecting refers to highlighting, by dragging or clicking with your mouse, areas of text or data or graphics so that the selection can be edited, formatted, copied, or moved. The action of dragging includes releasing the left mouse button at the end of the area you want to select.

The Office programs recognize a selected area as one unit to which you can make changes. Selecting text may require some practice. If you are not satisfied with your result, click anywhere outside of the selection, and then begin again.

 BY TOUCH Tap once on *Madison* to display the gripper—small circle that acts as a handle—directly below the word. This establishes the start gripper. If necessary, with your finger, drag the gripper to the beginning of the word. Then drag the gripper to the end of Dunham to select the text and display the end gripper.

FIGURE 1.6

Mini toolbar

Misspelled word shows red underline

Selected text

10 With the text *Madison Dunham* selected, type **Sarah Jackson**

In any Windows-based program, such as the Microsoft Office 2013 programs, selected text is deleted and then replaced when you begin to type new text. You will save time by developing good techniques for selecting and then editing or replacing selected text, which is easier than pressing the [Del] key numerous times to delete text.

Activity 1.04 | Checking Spelling

Office 2013 has a dictionary of words against which all entered text is checked. In Word and PowerPoint, words that are not in the dictionary display a wavy red line, indicating a possible misspelled word or a proper name or an unusual word—none of which are in the Office 2013 dictionary.

In Excel and Access, you can initiate a check of the spelling, but red underlines do not display.

1 Notice that the misspelled word *Exective* displays with a wavy red underline.

2 Point to *Exective* and then **right-click**—click your right mouse button one time.

A *shortcut menu* displays, which displays commands and options relevant to the selected text or object. These are *context-sensitive commands* because they relate to the item you right-clicked. These types of menus are also referred to as *context menus*. Here, the shortcut menu displays commands related to the misspelled word.

 BY TOUCH Tap and hold a moment to select the misspelled word, then release your finger to display the shortcut menu.

> **3** Press [Esc] to cancel the shortcut menu, and then in the lower left corner of your screen, on the **status bar**, click the **Proofing** icon ▨, which displays an *X* because some errors are detected. Compare your screen with Figure 1.7.

> The Spelling pane displays on the right. Here you have many more options for checking spelling than you have on the shortcut menu. The suggested correct word, *Executive*, is highlighted.

> You can click the speaker icon to hear the pronunciation of the selected word. You can also see some synonyms for *Executive*. Finally, if you have not already installed a dictionary, you can click *Get a Dictionary*—if you are signed in to Office with a Microsoft account—to find and install one from the online Office store; or if you have a dictionary app installed, it will display here and you can search it for more information.

> In the Spelling pane, you can ignore the word one time or in all occurrences, change the word to the suggested word, select a different suggestion, or add a word to the dictionary against which Word checks.

FIGURE 1.7

 ANOTHER WAY   Press [F7] to display the Spelling pane; or, on the Review tab, in the Proofing group, click Spelling & Grammar.

> **4** In the **Spelling** pane, click **Change** to change the spelling to *Executive*. In the message box that displays, click **OK**.

Objective 4 | Perform Commands from a Dialog Box

Video OF1-4

In a dialog box, you make decisions about an individual object or topic. In some dialog boxes, you can make multiple decisions in one place.

Activity 1.05 | Performing Commands from a Dialog Box

> **1** On the ribbon, click the **DESIGN tab**, and then in the **Page Background group**, click **Page Color**.

> **2** At the bottom of the menu, notice the command **Fill Effects** followed by an **ellipsis** (…). Compare your screen with Figure 1.8.

> An *ellipsis* is a set of three dots indicating incompleteness. An ellipsis following a command name indicates that a dialog box will display when you click the command.

FIGURE 1.8

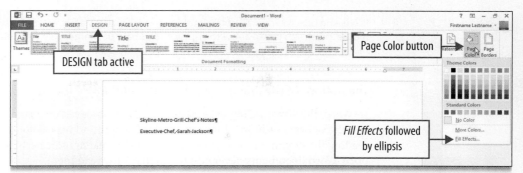

DESIGN tab active

Page Color button

Fill Effects followed by ellipsis

3 Click **Fill Effects** to display the **Fill Effects** dialog box. Compare your screen with Figure 1.9.

Fill is the inside color of a page or object. The Gradient tab is active. In a *gradient fill*, one color fades into another. Here, the dialog box displays a set of tabs across the top from which you can display different sets of options. Some dialog boxes display the option group names on the left.

FIGURE 1.9

Fill Effects dialog box

Tabs within a dialog box

4 Under **Colors**, click the **One color** option button.

The dialog box displays settings related to the One color option. An *option button* is a round button that enables you to make one choice among two or more options.

5 Click the **Color 1 arrow**—the arrow under the text *Color 1*—and then in the third column, point to the second color to display the ScreenTip *Gray-25%, Background 2, Darker 10%*.

A *ScreenTip* displays useful information about mouse actions, such as pointing to screen elements or dragging.

6 Click **Gray-25%, Background 2, Darker 10%**, and then notice that the fill color displays in the **Color 1** box. In the **Dark Light** bar, click the **Light arrow** as many times as necessary until the scroll box is all the way to right. Under **Shading styles**, click the **Diagonal down** option button. Under **Variants**, click the upper right variant. Compare your screen with Figure 1.10.

FIGURE 1.10

One color option button

Gray-25%, Background 2, Darker 10%

Scroll box at Light end

Upper right variant selected

Diagonal down option button

Sample box shows effects

7 > At the bottom of the dialog box, click **OK**, and notice the subtle page color.

In Word, the gray shading page color will not print—even on a color printer—unless you set specific options to do so. However a subtle background page color is effective if people will be reading the document on a screen. Microsoft's research indicates that two-thirds of people who open Word documents never edit them; they only read them.

Activity 1.06 | Using Undo

1 > Point to the *S* in *Skyline*, and then drag down and to the right to select both paragraphs of text and include the paragraph marks. On the mini toolbar, click **Styles,** and then *point to* but do not click **Title**. Compare your screen with Figure 1.11.

A *style* is a group of *formatting* commands, such as font, font size, font color, paragraph alignment, and line spacing that can be applied to a paragraph with one command. Formatting is the process of establishing the overall appearance of text, graphics, and pages in an Office file—for example, in a Word document.

Live Preview is a technology that shows the result of applying an editing or formatting change as you point to possible results—before you actually apply it.

FIGURE 1.11

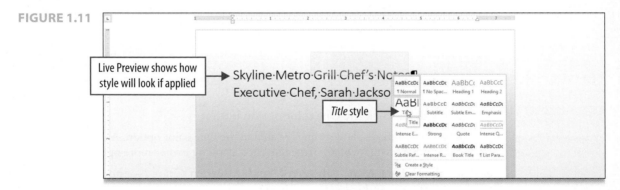

2 > In the **Styles** gallery, click **Title**.

A *gallery* is an Office feature that displays a list of potential results.

3 > On the ribbon, on the **HOME tab**, in the **Paragraph group**, click **Center** ☰ to center the two paragraphs.

Alignment refers to the placement of paragraph text relative to the left and right margins. *Center alignment* refers to text that is centered horizontally between the left and right margins. You can also align text at the left margin, which is the default alignment for text in Word, or at the right.

ANOTHER WAY   Press Ctrl + E to use the Center command.

4 > With the two paragraphs still selected, on the **HOME tab**, in the **Font Group**, click **Text Effects and Typography** [A ▾] to display a gallery.

5 > In the second row, click the first effect—**Gradient Fill – Gray**. Click anywhere to *deselect*—cancel the selection—the text and notice the text effect.

6 Because this effect might be difficult to read, in the upper left corner of your screen, on the **Quick Access Toolbar**, click **Undo** ↻.

The **Undo** command reverses your last action.

🔄 **ANOTHER WAY**   Press Ctrl + Z as the keyboard shortcut for the Undo command.

7 Display the **Text Effects and Typography** gallery again, and then in the second row, click the second effect—**Gradient Fill – Blue, Accent 1, Reflection**. Click anywhere to deselect the text and notice the text effect. Compare your screen with Figure 1.12.

As you progress in your study of Microsoft Office, you will practice using many dialog boxes and applying interesting effects such as this to your Word documents, Excel worksheets, Access database objects, and PowerPoint slides.

FIGURE 1.12

Text formatted with blue reflective text effect

Skyline·Metro·Grill·Chef's·Notes¶
Executive·Chef,·Sarah·Jackson¶

Gray page fill effects

Objective 5   Create a Folder and Name and Save a File

Video OF1-5

A ***location*** is any disk drive, folder, or other place in which you can store files and folders. Where you store your files depends on how and where you use your data. For example, for your college classes, you might decide to store on a removable USB flash drive so that you can carry your files to different locations and access your files on different computers.

If you do most of your work on a single computer, for example your home desktop system or your laptop computer that you take with you to school or work, then you can store your files in one of the Libraries—Documents, Music, Pictures, or Videos—that the Windows 8 operating system creates on your hard drive.

The best place to store files if you want them to be available anytime, anywhere, from almost any device is on your ***OneDrive***, which is Microsoft's free ***cloud storage*** for anyone with a free Microsoft account. Cloud storage refers to online storage of data so that you can access your data from different places and devices. ***Cloud computing*** refers to applications and services that are accessed over the Internet, rather than to applications that are installed on your local computer.

Because many people now have multiple computing devices—desktop, laptop, tablet, smartphone—it is common to store data *in the cloud* so that it is always available. ***Synchronization***, also called ***syncing***—pronounced SINK-ing—is the process of updating computer files that are in two or more locations according to specific rules. So if you create and save a Word document on your OneDrive using your laptop, you can open and edit that document on your tablet. And then when you close the document again, the file is properly updated to reflect your changes.

You need not be connected to the Internet to access documents stored on OneDrive because an up-to-date version of your content is synched to your local system and available on OneDrive. You must, however, be connected to the Internet for the syncing to occur. Saving to OneDrive will keep the local copy on your computer and the copy in the cloud synchronized for as long as you need it. If you open and edit on a different computer, log into the OneDrive website, and then edit using Office 2013, Office 2010, or **Office Online**, you can save any changes back to OneDrive. Office Online is the free online companion to Microsoft Word, Excel, PowerPoint, Access, and OneNote. These changes will be synchronized back to any of your computers that run the OneDrive for Windows application, which you get for free simply by logging in with your Microsoft account at onedrive.com.

The Windows operating system helps you to create and maintain a logical folder structure, so always take the time to name your files and folders consistently.

Activity 1.07 | Creating a Folder and Naming and Saving a File

A Word document is an example of a file. In this activity, you will create a folder on your USB flash drive in which to store your files. If you prefer to store on your OneDrive or in the Documents library on your hard drive, you can use similar steps.

1 If necessary, insert your **USB flash drive** into your computer.

As the first step in saving a file, determine where you want to save the file, and if necessary, insert a storage device.

2 At the top of your screen, in the title bar, notice that *Document1 – Word* displays.

The Blank option on the opening screen of an Office 2013 program displays a new unsaved file with a default name—*Document1, Presentation1*, and so on. As you create your file, your work is temporarily stored in the computer's memory until you initiate a Save command, at which time you must choose a file name and a location in which to save your file.

3 In the upper left corner of your screen, click the **FILE tab** to display **Backstage** view. Compare your screen with Figure 1.13.

Backstage view is a centralized space that groups commands related to *file* management; that is why the tab is labeled *FILE*. File management commands include opening, saving, printing, publishing, or sharing a file. The **Backstage tabs**—*Info, New, Open, Save, Save As, Print, Share, Export*, and *Close*—display along the left side. The tabs group file-related tasks together.

Here, the **Info tab** displays information—*info*—about the current file, and file management commands display under Info. For example, if you click the Protect Document button, a list of options that you can set for this file that relate to who can open or edit the document displays.

On the right, you can also examine the **document properties**. Document properties, also known as **metadata**, are details about a file that describe or identify it, such as the title, author name, subject, and keywords that identify the document's topic or contents. To close Backstage view and return to the document, you can click ⬅ in the upper left corner or press Esc.

FIGURE 1.13

4 > On the left, click **Save As**, and notice that the default location for storing Office files is your **OneDrive**—if you are signed in. Compare your screen with Figure 1.14.

> When you are saving something for the first time, for example a new Word document, the Save and Save As commands are identical. That is, the Save As commands will display if you click Save or if you click Save As.

FIGURE 1.14

N O T E   **Saving after Your File Is Named**

After you name and save a file, the Save command on the Quick Access Toolbar saves any changes you make to the file without displaying Backstage view. The Save As command enables you to name and save a *new* file based on the current one—in a location that you choose. After you name and save the new document, the original document closes, and the new document—based on the original one—displays.

---

5 > To store your Word file on your **USB flash drive**—instead of your OneDrive—click the **Browse** button to display the **Save As** dialog box. On the left, in the navigation pane, scroll down, and then under **Computer**, click the name of your **USB flash drive**. Compare your screen with Figure 1.15.

> In the Save As dialog box, you must indicate the name you want for the file and the location where you want to save the file. When working with your own data, it is good practice to pause at this point and determine the logical name and location for your file.

> In the Save As dialog box, a *toolbar* displays. This is a row, column, or block of buttons or icons, that usually displays across the top of a window and that contains commands for tasks you perform with a single click.

FIGURE 1.15

6 On the toolbar, click **New folder**.

In the file list, Word creates a new folder, and the text *New folder* is selected.

7 Type **Office Features Chapter 1** and press Enter. Compare your screen with Figure 1.16.

In Windows-based programs, the Enter key confirms an action.

8 In the **file list**, double-click the name of your new folder to open it and display its name in the **address bar**.

9 In the lower portion of the dialog box, click in the **File name** box to select the existing text. Notice that Office inserts the text at the beginning of the document as a suggested file name.

10 On your keyboard, locate the hyphen – key. Notice that the Shift of this key produces the underscore character. With the text still selected and using your own name, type **Lastname_Firstname_1A_Note_Form** and then compare your screen with Figure 1.17.

You can use spaces in file names, however, some people prefer not to use spaces. Some programs, especially when transferring files over the Internet, may insert the extra characters *%20* in place of a space. This can happen in *SharePoint*, so using underscores instead of spaces can be a good habit to adopt. SharePoint is Microsoft's collaboration software with which people in an organization can set up team sites to share information, manage documents, and publish reports for others to see. In general, however, unless you encounter a problem, it is OK to use spaces. In this textbook, underscores are used instead of spaces in file names.

11 In the lower right corner, click **Save** or press Enter. Compare your screen with Figure 1.18.

The Word window redisplays and your new file name displays in the title bar, indicating that the file has been saved to a location that you have specified.

12 In the first paragraph, click to place the insertion point after the word *Grill* and type ,
(a comma). In the upper left corner of your screen, on the **Quick Access Toolbar**, click **Save** 🖫.

> After a document is named and saved in a location, you can save any changes you have made since
> the last Save operation by using the Save command on the Quick Access Toolbar. When working
> on a document, it is good practice to save your changes from time to time.

Objective 6 | Insert a Footer, Add Document Properties, Print a File, and Close a Desktop App

Video OF1-6

For most of your files, especially in a workplace setting, it is useful to add identifying
information to help in finding files later. You might also want to print your file on paper or create
an electronic printout. The process of printing a file is similar in all of the Office applications.

Activity 1.08 | Inserting a Footer, Inserting Document Info, and Adding Document Properties

> **N O T E**   **Are You Printing or Submitting Your Files Electronically?**
> In this activity, you can either produce a paper printout or create an electronic file to submit to your instructor if required.

1 On the ribbon, click the **INSERT tab**, and then in the **Header & Footer group**, click **Footer**.

2 At the bottom of the list, click **Edit Footer**. On the ribbon, notice that the **HEADER &
FOOTER TOOLS** display.

> The *Header & Footer Tools Design* tab displays on the ribbon. The ribbon adapts to your work and
> will display additional tabs like this one—referred to as ***contextual tabs***—when you need them.
>
> A ***footer*** is a reserved area for text or graphics that displays at the bottom of each page in a
> document. Likewise, a ***header*** is a reserved area for text or graphics that displays at the top of each
> page in a document. When the footer (or header) area is active, the document area is dimmed,
> indicating it is unavailable.

3 On the ribbon, under **HEADER & FOOTER TOOLS**, on the **DESIGN tab**, in the **Insert group**,
click **Document Info**, and then click **File Name** to insert the name of your file in the footer,
which is a common business practice. Compare your screen with Figure 1.19.

> Ribbon commands that display ▼ will, when clicked, display a list of options for the command.

FIGURE 1.19

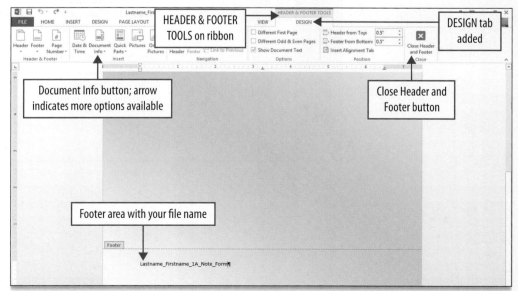

4 At the right end of the ribbon, click **Close Header and Footer**.

ANOTHER WAY   Double-click anywhere in the dimmed document to close the footer.

5 Click the **FILE tab** to display **Backstage** view. On the right, at the bottom of the **Properties** list, click **Show All Properties**.

ANOTHER WAY   Click the arrow to the right of Properties, and then click Show Document Panel to show and edit properties at the top of your document window.

6 On the list of **Properties**, click to the right of **Tags** to display an empty box, and then type **chef, notes, form**

Tags, also referred to as *keywords*, are custom file properties in the form of words that you associate with a document to give an indication of the document's content. Adding tags to your documents makes it easier to search for and locate files in File Explorer and in systems such as Microsoft SharePoint document libraries.

BY TOUCH   Tap to the right of Tags to display the Tags box and the onscreen keyboard.

7 Click to the right of **Subject** to display an empty box, and then type your course name and section #; for example *CIS 10, #5543*.

8 Under **Related People**, be sure that your name displays as the author. If necessary, right-click the author name, click Edit Property, type your name, click outside of the Edit person dialog box, and then click OK. Compare your screen with Figure 1.20.

FIGURE 1.20

Activity 1.09 | Printing a File and Closing a Desktop App

1 On the left, click **Print**, and then compare your screen with Figure 1.21.

Here you can select any printer connected to your system and adjust the settings related to how you want to print. On the right, the ***Print Preview*** displays, which is a view of a document as it will appear on paper when you print it.

At the bottom of the Print Preview area, in the center, the number of pages and page navigation arrows with which you can move among the pages in Print Preview display. On the right, the Zoom slider enables you to shrink or enlarge the Print Preview. ***Zoom*** is the action of increasing or decreasing the viewing area of the screen.

ANOTHER WAY   From the document screen, press Ctrl + P or Ctrl + F2 to display Print in Backstage view.

FIGURE 1.21

2 To submit your file electronically, skip this step and continue to Step 3. To print your document on paper using the default printer on your system, in the upper left portion of the screen, click the **Print** button.

The document will print on your default printer; if you do not have a color printer, the blue text will print in shades of gray. The gray page color you applied to the document does not display in Print Preview nor does it print unless you specifically adjust some of Word's options. Backstage view closes and your file redisplays in the Word window.

3 To create an electronic file, on the left click **Export**. On the right, click the **Create PDF/XPS** button to display the **Publish as PDF or XPS** dialog box.

PDF stands for ***Portable Document Format***, which is a technology that creates an image that preserves the look of your file. This is a popular format for sending documents electronically, because the document will display on most computers.

XPS stands for ***XML Paper Specification***—a Microsoft file format that also creates an image of your document and that opens in the XPS viewer.

4 ▸ On the left in the **navigation pane**, if necessary expand ▷ Computer, and then navigate to your **Office Features Chapter 1** folder on your **USB flash drive**. Compare your screen with Figure 1.22.

FIGURE 1.22

5 ▸ In the lower right corner of the dialog box, click **Publish**; if your Adobe Acrobat or Adobe Reader program displays your PDF, in the upper right corner, click Close ⊠. Notice that your document redisplays in Word.

ANOTHER WAY   In Backstage view, click Save As, navigate to the location of your Chapter folder, click the Save as type arrow, on the list click PDF, and then click Save.

6 ▸ Click the **FILE tab** to redisplay **Backstage** view. On the left, click **Close**, if necessary click Save, and then compare your screen with Figure 1.23.

FIGURE 1.23

7 ▸ In the upper right corner of the Word window, click **Close** ⊠. If directed by your instructor to do so, submit your paper or electronic file.

END | You have completed Project 1A

Memo

PROJECT ACTIVITIES

In Activities 1.10 through 1.21, you will open, edit, and then compress a Word file. You will also use the Office Help system and install an app for Office. Your completed document will look similar to Figure 1.24.

PROJECT FILES

For Project 1B, you will need the following file:

of01B_Rehearsal_Dinner

You will save your file as:

Lastname_Firstname_1B_Rehearsal_Dinner

PROJECT RESULTS

Skyline Metro Grill

TO:	Sarah Jackson, Executive Chef
FROM:	Laura Mabry Hernandez, General Manager
DATE:	February 17, 2016
SUBJECT:	Wedding Rehearsal Dinners

In the spring and summer months, wedding rehearsal dinners provide a new marketing opportunity for Skyline Metro Grill at all of our locations. A rehearsal dinner is an informal meal following a wedding rehearsal at which the bride and groom typically thank those who have helped them make their wedding a special event.

Our smaller private dining rooms with sweeping city views are an ideal location for a rehearsal dinner. At each of our locations, I have directed the Sales and Marketing Coordinator to partner with local wedding planners to promote Skyline Metro Grill as a relaxed yet sophisticated venue for rehearsal dinners. The typical rehearsal dinner includes the wedding party, the immediate family of the bride and groom, and out-of-town guests.

Please develop six menus—in varying price ranges—to present to local wedding planners so that they can easily promote Skyline Metro Grill to couples who are planning a rehearsal dinner. In addition to a traditional dinner, we should also include options for a buffet-style dinner and a family-style dinner.

This marketing effort will require extensive communication with our Sales and Marketing Coordinators and with local wedding planners. Let's meet to discuss the details and the marketing challenges, and to create a promotional piece that begins something like this:

Skyline Metro Grill for Your Rehearsal Dinner

Lastname_Firstname_1B_Rehearsal_Dinner

FIGURE 1.24 Project 1B Memo

Video OF1-7

In any Office program, you can display the **Open dialog box**, from which you can navigate to and then open an existing file that was created in that same program.

The Open dialog box, along with the Save and Save As dialog boxes, is a common dialog box. These dialog boxes, which are provided by the Windows programming interface, display in all Office programs in the same manner. So the Open, Save, and Save As dialog boxes will all look and perform the same regardless of the Office program in which you are working.

Activity 1.10 | Opening an Existing File and Saving It with a New Name

In this activity, you will display the Open dialog box, open an existing Word document, and then save it in your storage location with a new name.

1 Sign in to your computer, and then on the Windows 8 Start screen, type **word 2013** Press Enter to open Word on your desktop. If you want to do so, on the taskbar, right-click the **Word icon**, and then click **Pin this program to taskbar** to keep the Word program available from your desktop.

2 On Word's opening screen, on the left, click **Open Other Documents**. Under **Open**, click **Computer**, and then on the right click **Browse**.

3 In the **Open** dialog box, on the left in the **navigation pane**, scroll down, if necessary expand ▷ Computer, and then click the name of your **USB flash drive**. In the **file list**, double-click the **Office_Features** folder that you downloaded.

4 Double-click **of01B_Rehearsal_Dinner**. If **PROTECTED VIEW** displays at the top of your screen, in the center click **Enable Editing**.

In Office 2013, a file will open in **Protected View** if the file appears to be from a potentially risky location, such as the Internet. Protected View is a security feature in Office 2013 that protects your computer from malicious files by opening them in a restricted environment until you enable them. **Trusted Documents** is another security feature that remembers which files you have already enabled.

You might encounter these security features if you open a file from an email or download files from the Internet; for example, from your college's learning management system or from the Pearson website. So long as you trust the source of the file, click Enable Editing or Enable Content— depending on the type of file you receive—and then go ahead and work with the file.

5 With the document displayed in the Word window, be sure that **Show/Hide** is active; if necessary, on the HOME tab, in the Paragraph group, click Show/Hide to activate it. Compare your screen with Figure 1.25.

FIGURE 1.25

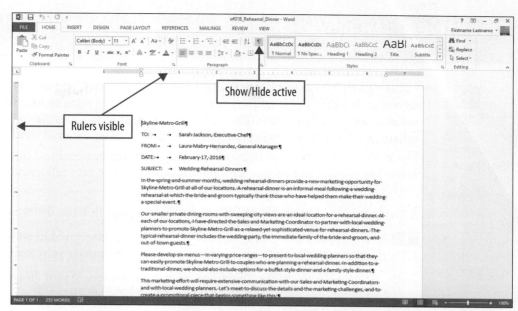

6 ▸ Click the **FILE tab** to display **Backstage** view, and then on the left, click **Save As**. On the right, click the folder under **Current Folder** to open the **Save As** dialog box. Notice that the current folder is the **Office_Features** folder you downloaded.

 ANOTHER WAY   Press F12 to display the Save As dialog box.

7 ▸ In the upper left corner of the **Save As** dialog box, click the **Up** button ↑ to move up one level in the File Explorer hierarchy. In the **file list**, double-click your **Office Features Chapter 1** folder to open it.

8 ▸ Click in the **File name** box to select the existing text, and then, using your own name, type **Lastname_Firstname_1B_Rehearsal_Dinner** Compare your screen with Figure 1.26.

FIGURE 1.26

9 ▸ Click **Save** or press Enter; notice that your new file name displays in the title bar.

The original document closes, and your new document, based on the original, displays with the name in the title bar.

More Knowledge	**Read-Only**

Some files might display **Read-Only** in the title bar, which is a property assigned to a file that prevents the file from being modified or deleted; it indicates that you cannot save any changes to the displayed document unless you first save it with a new name.

Video OF1-8

If you sign in to Windows 8 with a Microsoft account, you may notice that you are also signed in to Office. This enables you to save files to and retrieve files from your OneDrive and to **collaborate** with others on Office files when you want to do so. To collaborate means to work with others as a team in an intellectual endeavor to complete a shared task or to achieve a shared goal.

Within each Office application, an **Options dialog box** enables you to select program settings and other options and preferences. For example, you can set preferences for viewing and editing files.

Activity 1.11 | Signing In to Office and Viewing Application Options

1 In the upper right corner of your screen, if you are signed in with a Microsoft account, click the arrow to the right of your name, and then compare your screen with Figure 1.27.

Here you can change your photo, go to About me to edit your profile, examine your Account settings, or switch accounts to sign in with a different Microsoft account.

FIGURE 1.27

2 Click the **FILE tab** to display **Backstage** view. On the left, click the last tab—**Options**.

3 In the **Word Options** dialog box, on the left, click **Display**, and then on the right, locate the information under **Always show these formatting marks on the screen**.

4 Under **Always show these formatting marks on the screen**, be sure the last check box, **Show all formatting marks**, is selected—select it if necessary. Compare your screen with Figure 1.28.

FIGURE 1.28

5 In the lower right corner of the dialog box, click **OK**.

Objective 9 Perform Commands from the Ribbon and Quick Access Toolbar

Video OF1-9

The ribbon that displays across the top of the program window groups commands in a manner that you would most logically use them. The ribbon in each Office program is slightly different, but all contain the same three elements: *tabs*, *groups*, and *commands*.

Tabs display across the top of the ribbon, and each tab relates to a type of activity; for example, laying out a page. Groups are sets of related commands for specific tasks. Commands—instructions to computer programs—are arranged in groups and might display as a button, a menu, or a box in which you type information.

You can also minimize the ribbon so only the tab names display, which is useful when working on a smaller screen such as a tablet computer where you want to maximize your screen viewing area.

Activity 1.12 | Performing Commands from and Customizing the Ribbon and the Quick Access Toolbar

1 Take a moment to examine the document on your screen. If necessary, on the ribbon, click the VIEW tab, and then in the Show group, click to place a check mark in the Ruler check box. Compare your screen with Figure 1.29.

This document is a memo from the General Manager to the Executive Chef regarding a new restaurant promotion for wedding rehearsal dinners.

When working in Word, display the rulers so that you can see how margin settings affect your document and how text and objects align. Additionally, if you set a tab stop or an indent, its location is visible on the ruler.

FIGURE 1.29

2 In the upper left corner of your screen, above the ribbon, locate the **Quick Access Toolbar**.

Recall that the Quick Access Toolbar contains commands that you use frequently. By default, only the commands Save, Undo, and Redo display, but you can add and delete commands to suit your needs. Possibly the computer at which you are working already has additional commands added to the Quick Access Toolbar.

3 At the end of the **Quick Access Toolbar**, click the **Customize Quick Access Toolbar** button ⟨⇥⟩, and then compare your screen with Figure 1.30.

A list of commands that Office users commonly add to their Quick Access Toolbar displays, including New, Open, Email, Quick Print, and Print Preview and Print. Commands already on the Quick Access Toolbar display a check mark. Commands that you add to the Quick Access Toolbar are always just one click away.

Here you can also display the More Commands dialog box, from which you can select any command from any tab on the ribbon to add to the Quick Access Toolbar.

 BY TOUCH　　Tap once on Quick Access Toolbar commands.

FIGURE 1.30

Customize Quick Access Toolbar button

Commands commonly added to the Quick Access Toolbar

More Commands—use this to add any additional ribbon commands to your Quick Access Toolbar

4 On the list, click **Print Preview and Print**, and then notice that the icon is added to the **Quick Access Toolbar**. Compare your screen with Figure 1.31.

The icon that represents the Print Preview command displays on the Quick Access Toolbar. Because this is a command that you will use frequently while building Office documents, you might decide to have this command remain on your Quick Access Toolbar.

ANOTHER WAY   Right-click any command on the ribbon, and then on the shortcut menu, click Add to Quick Access Toolbar.

FIGURE 1.31

Icon for Print Preview and Print added to Quick Access Toolbar

5 In the first line of the document, if necessary, click to the left of the *S* in *Skyline* to position the insertion point there, and then press Enter one time to insert a blank paragraph. Press ↑ one time to position the insertion point in the new blank paragraph. Compare your screen with Figure 1.32.

FIGURE 1.32

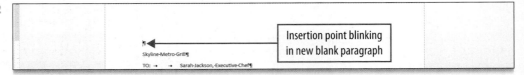

Insertion point blinking in new blank paragraph

6 On the ribbon, click the **INSERT tab**. In the **Illustrations group**, *point* to the **Online Pictures** button to display its ScreenTip.

Many buttons on the ribbon have this type of *enhanced ScreenTip*, which displays useful descriptive information about the command.

7 Click **Online Pictures**, and then compare your screen with Figure 1.33.

In the Insert Pictures dialog box you can search for online pictures using Microsoft's Clip Art collection. *Clip art* refers to royalty-free photos and illustrations you can download from Microsoft's Office.com site.

Here you can also search for images using the Bing search engine, and if you are signed in with your Microsoft account, you can also find images on your OneDrive or on your computer by clicking Browse. At the bottom, you can click the Flickr logo and download pictures from your Flickr account if you have one.

FIGURE 1.33

FIGURE 1.34

8 Click **Office.com Clip Art** and in the box that displays to the right, type **salad in a bowl** and press **Enter**. As shown in Figure 1.34, point to the illustration of the salad bowl to display its keywords.

> You can use various keywords to find clip art that is appropriate for your documents.

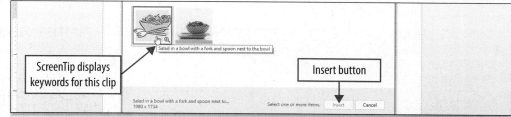

9 Click the illustration of the salad to select it, and then in the lower right corner, click **Insert**. In the upper right corner of the picture, point to the **Layout Options** button to display its ScreenTip, and then compare your screen with Figure 1.35. If you cannot find the image, select a similar image, and then drag one of the corner sizing handles to match the approximate size shown in the figure.

> Inserted pictures anchor—attach to—the paragraph at the insertion point location—as indicated by the anchor symbol. *Layout Options* enable you to choose how the *object*—in this instance an inserted picture—interacts with the surrounding text. An object is a picture or other graphic such as a chart or table that you can select and then move and resize.

> When a picture is selected, the PICTURE TOOLS become available on the ribbon. Additionally, *sizing handles*—small squares that indicate an object is selected—surround the selected picture.

FIGURE 1.35

10 With the image selected, click **Layout Options** ⬛, and then under **With Text Wrapping**, in the second row, click the first layout—**Top and Bottom**.

11 Point to the image to display the ⬛ pointer, hold down the left mouse button to display a green line at the left margin, and then drag the image to the right and slightly upward until a green line displays in the center of the image and at the top of the image, as shown in Figure 1.36, and then release the left mouse button. If you are not satisfied with your result, on the Quick Access Toolbar, click Undo ⬛ and begin again.

> *Alignment Guides* are green lines that display to help you align objects with margins or at the center of a page.

FIGURE 1.36

12 On the ribbon, in the **Picture Styles group**, point to the first style to display the ScreenTip *Simple Frame, White,* and notice that the image displays with a white frame.

13 Watch the image as you point to the second picture style, and then to the third, and then to the fourth.

> Recall that Live Preview shows the result of applying an editing or formatting change as you point to possible results—*before* you actually apply it.

14 In the **Picture Styles group**, click the second style—**Beveled Matte, White**—and then click anywhere outside of the image to deselect it. Notice that the *PICTURE TOOLS* no longer display on the ribbon. Compare your screen with Figure 1.37.

Contextual tabs on the ribbon display only when you need them.

FIGURE 1.37

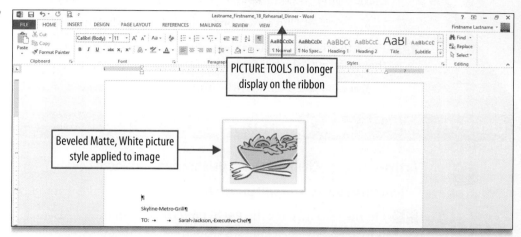

15 On the **Quick Access Toolbar**, click **Save** to save the changes you have made.

Activity 1.13 | Minimizing and Using the Keyboard to Control the Ribbon

Instead of a mouse, some individuals prefer to navigate the ribbon by using keys on the keyboard.

1 On your keyboard, press Alt, and then on the ribbon, notice that small labels display. Press N to activate the commands on the **INSERT tab**, and then compare your screen with Figure 1.38.

Each label represents a *KeyTip*—an indication of the key that you can press to activate the command. For example, on the INSERT tab, you can press F to open the Online Pictures dialog box.

FIGURE 1.38

2 Press Esc to redisplay the KeyTips for the tabs. Then, press Alt or Esc again to turn off keyboard control of the ribbon.

3 Point to any tab on the ribbon and right-click to display a shortcut menu.

Here you can choose to display the Quick Access Toolbar below the ribbon or collapse the ribbon to maximize screen space. You can also customize the ribbon by adding, removing, renaming, or reordering tabs, groups, and commands, although this is not recommended until you become an expert Office user.

4 Click **Collapse the Ribbon**. Notice that only the ribbon tabs display. Click the **HOME tab** to display the commands. Click anywhere in the document, and notice that the ribbon goes back to the collapsed display.

5 Right-click any ribbon tab, and then click **Collapse the Ribbon** again to remove the check mark from this command.

Many expert Office users prefer the full ribbon display.

6 Point to any tab on the ribbon, and then on your mouse device, roll the mouse wheel. Notice that different tabs become active as you roll the mouse wheel.

You can make a tab active by using this technique instead of clicking the tab.

Objective 10 Apply Formatting in Office Programs

Video OF1-10

Activity 1.14 │ **Changing Page Orientation and Zoom Level**

In this activity, you will practice common formatting techniques used in Office applications.

1 On the ribbon, click the **PAGE LAYOUT tab**. In the **Page Setup group**, click **Orientation**, and notice that two orientations display—*Portrait* and *Landscape*. Click **Landscape**.

In ***portrait orientation***, the paper is taller than it is wide. In ***landscape orientation***, the paper is wider than it is tall.

2 In the lower right corner of the screen, locate the **Zoom slider**.

Recall that to zoom means to increase or decrease the viewing area. You can zoom in to look closely at a section of a document, and then zoom out to see an entire page on the screen. You can also zoom to view multiple pages on the screen.

3 Drag the **Zoom slider** to the left until you have zoomed to approximately 60%. Compare your screen with Figure 1.39.

FIGURE 1.39

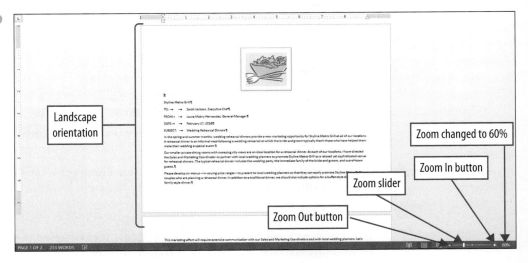

BY TOUCH   Drag the Zoom slider with your finger.

4 Use the technique you just practiced to change the **Orientation** back to **Portrait**.

The default orientation in Word is Portrait, which is commonly used for business documents such as letters and memos.

5 In the lower right corner, click the **Zoom In** button ➕ as many times as necessary to return to the **100%** zoom setting.

> Use the zoom feature to adjust the view of your document for editing and for your viewing comfort.

ANOTHER WAY   You can also control Zoom from the ribbon. On the VIEW tab, in the Zoom group, you can control the Zoom level and also zoom to view multiple pages.

6 On the **Quick Access Toolbar**, click **Save** 🖫.

More Knowledge   **Zooming to Page Width**

Some Office users prefer Page Width, which zooms the document so that the width of the page matches the width of the window. Find this command on the VIEW tab, in the Zoom group.

Activity 1.15 │ Formatting Text by Using Fonts, Alignment, Font Colors, and Font Styles

1 If necessary, on the right side of your screen, drag the vertical scroll box to the top of the scroll bar. To the left of *Skyline Metro Grill*, point in the margin area to display the �Ⓐ pointer and click one time to select the entire paragraph. Compare your screen with Figure 1.40.

> Use this technique to select complete paragraphs from the margin area—drag downward to select multiple-line paragraphs—which is faster and more efficient than dragging through text.

FIGURE 1.40

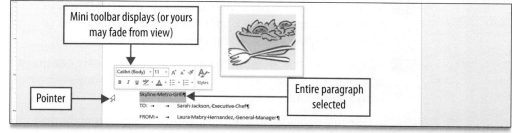

2 On the ribbon, click the **HOME tab**, and then in the **Paragraph group**, click **Center** ☰ to center the paragraph.

3 On the **HOME tab**, in the **Font group**, click the **Font button arrow** Calibri (Body) ▾. On the alphabetical list of font names, scroll down and then locate and *point to* **Cambria**.

> A *font* is a set of characters with the same design and shape. The default font in a Word document is Calibri, which is a *sans serif* font—a font design with no lines or extensions on the ends of characters.

> The Cambria font is a *serif font*—a font design that includes small line extensions on the ends of the letters to guide the eye in reading from left to right.

> The list of fonts displays as a gallery showing potential results. For example, in the Font gallery, you can point to see the actual design and format of each font as it would look if applied to text.

4 Point to several other fonts and observe the effect on the selected text. Then, scroll back to the top of the **Font** gallery. Under **Theme Fonts**, click **Calibri Light**.

> A *theme* is a predesigned combination of colors, fonts, line, and fill effects that look good together and is applied to an entire document by a single selection. A theme combines two sets of fonts—one for text and one for headings. In the default Office theme, Calibri Light is the suggested font for headings.

5 With the paragraph *Skyline Metro Grill* still selected, on the **HOME tab**, in the **Font group**, click the **Font Size button arrow** ![11], point to **36**, and then notice how Live Preview displays the text in the font size to which you are pointing. Compare your screen with Figure 1.41.

FIGURE 1.41

6 On the list of font sizes, click **20**.

Fonts are measured in *points*, with one point equal to 1/72 of an inch. A higher point size indicates a larger font size. Headings and titles are often formatted by using a larger font size. The word *point* is abbreviated as *pt*.

7 With *Skyline Metro Grill* still selected, on the **HOME tab**, in the **Font group**, click the **Font Color button arrow** ![A▼]. Under **Theme Colors**, in the last column, click the last color—**Green, Accent 6, Darker 50%**. Click anywhere to deselect the text.

8 To the left of *TO:*, point in the left margin area to display the ![pointer] pointer, hold down the left mouse button, and then drag down to select the four memo headings. Compare your screen with Figure 1.42.

Use this technique to select complete paragraphs from the margin area—drag downward to select multiple paragraphs—which is faster and more efficient than dragging through text.

 BY TOUCH   Tap once on TO: to display the gripper, then with your finger, drag to the right and down to select the four paragraphs.

FIGURE 1.42

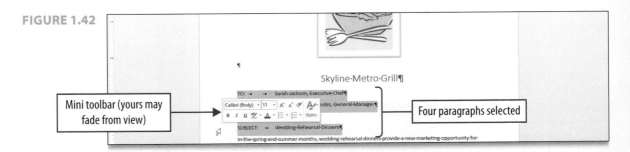

9 With the four paragraphs selected, on the mini toolbar, click the **Font Color** button ![A▾], and notice that the text color of the four paragraphs changes.

> The font color button retains its most recently used color—Green, Accent 6, Darker 50%. As you progress in your study of Microsoft Office, you will use other buttons that behave in this manner; that is, they retain their most recently used format. This is commonly referred to as *MRU*—most recently used.

> Recall that the mini toolbar places commands that are commonly used for the selected text or object close by so that you reduce the distance that you must move your mouse to access a command. If you are using a touchscreen device, most commands that you need are close and easy to touch.

10 On the right, drag the vertical scroll box down slightly to position more of the text on the screen. Click anywhere in the paragraph that begins *In the spring*, and then **triple-click**—click the left mouse button three times—to select the entire paragraph. If the entire paragraph is not selected, click in the paragraph and begin again.

11 With the entire paragraph selected, on the mini toolbar, click the **Font Color button arrow** ![A▾], and then under **Theme Colors**, in the sixth column, click the last color—**Orange, Accent 2, Darker 50%**.

12 In the memo headings, select the guide word *TO:* and then on the mini toolbar, click **Bold** ![B] and **Italic** ![I].

> *Font styles* include bold, italic, and underline. Font styles emphasize text and are a visual cue to draw the reader's eye to important text.

13 On the mini toolbar, click **Italic** ![I] again to turn off the Italic formatting.

> A *toggle button* is a button that can be turned on by clicking it once, and then turned off by clicking it again.

Activity 1.16 | Using Format Painter

Use the Format Painter to copy the formatting of specific text or of a paragraph and then apply it in other locations in your document.

1 With *TO:* still selected, on the mini toolbar, click **Format Painter** ![icon]. Then, move your mouse under the word *Sarah*, and notice the ![icon] mouse pointer. Compare your screen with Figure 1.43.

> The pointer takes the shape of a paintbrush, and contains the formatting information from the paragraph where the insertion point is positioned. Information about the Format Painter and how to turn it off displays in the status bar.

FIGURE 1.43

2 With the ⬚ pointer, drag to select the guide word *FROM:* and notice that Bold formatting is applied. Then, point to the selected text *FROM:* and on the mini toolbar, *double-click* **Format Painter** ✶.

3 Select the guide word *DATE:* to copy the Bold formatting, and notice that the pointer retains the ⬚ shape.

> When you *double-click* the Format Painter button, the Format Painter feature remains active until you either click the Format Painter button again, or press ⎋ to cancel it—as indicated on the status bar.

4 With Format Painter still active, select the guide word *SUBJECT:*, and then on the ribbon, on the **HOME tab**, in the **Clipboard group**, notice that **Format Painter** ✶ is selected, indicating that it is active. Compare your screen with Figure 1.44.

FIGURE 1.44

5 On the ribbon, click **Format Painter** ✶ to turn the command off.

🔁 **ANOTHER WAY**   Press ⎋ to turn off Format Painter.

6 In the paragraph that begins *In the spring*, triple-click again to select the entire paragraph. On the mini toolbar, click **Bold** `B` and **Italic** `I`. Click anywhere to deselect.

7 On the **Quick Access Toolbar**, click **Save** `💾` to save the changes you have made to your document.

Activity 1.17 | Using Keyboard Shortcuts and Using the Clipboard to Copy, Cut, and Paste

The ***Clipboard*** is a temporary storage area that holds text or graphics that you select and then cut or copy. When you ***copy*** text or graphics, a copy is placed on the Clipboard and the original text or graphic remains in place. When you ***cut*** text or graphics, a copy is placed on the Clipboard, and the original text or graphic is removed—cut—from the document.

After copying or cutting, the contents of the Clipboard are available for you to ***paste***—insert—in a new location in the current document, or into another Office file.

1 Hold down `Ctrl` and press `Home` to move to the beginning of your document, and then take a moment to study the table in Figure 1.45, which describes similar keyboard shortcuts with which you can navigate quickly in a document.

FIGURE 1.45

KEYBOARD SHORTCUTS TO NAVIGATE IN A DOCUMENT	
TO MOVE	**PRESS**
To the beginning of a document	`Ctrl` + `Home`
To the end of a document	`Ctrl` + `End`
To the beginning of a line	`Home`
To the end of a line	`End`
To the beginning of the previous word	`Ctrl` + `←`
To the beginning of the next word	`Ctrl` + `→`
To the beginning of the current word (if insertion point is in the middle of a word)	`Ctrl` + `←`
To the beginning of the previous paragraph	`Ctrl` + `↑`
To the beginning of the next paragraph	`Ctrl` + `↓`
To the beginning of the current paragraph (if insertion point is in the middle of a paragraph)	`Ctrl` + `↑`
Up one screen	`PgUp`
Down one screen	`PgDn`

2 To the left of *Skyline Metro Grill*, point in the left margin area to display the `⇗` pointer, and then click one time to select the entire paragraph. On the **HOME tab**, in the **Clipboard group**, click **Copy** `📋`.

> Because anything that you select and then copy—or cut—is placed on the Clipboard, the Copy command and the Cut command display in the Clipboard group of commands on the ribbon. There is no visible indication that your copied selection has been placed on the Clipboard.

◆ ANOTHER WAY   Right-click the selection, and then click Copy on the shortcut menu; or, use the keyboard shortcut `Ctrl` + `C`.

3 On the **HOME tab**, in the **Clipboard group**, to the right of the group name *Clipboard*, click the **Dialog Box Launcher** button, and then compare your screen with Figure 1.46.

The Clipboard pane displays with your copied text. In any ribbon group, the ***Dialog Box Launcher*** displays either a dialog box or a pane related to the group of commands. It is not necessary to display the Clipboard in this manner, although sometimes it is useful to do so.

FIGURE 1.46

4 In the upper right corner of the **Clipboard** pane, click **Close** ☒.

5 Press Ctrl + End to move to the end of your document. Press Enter one time to create a new blank paragraph. On the **HOME tab**, in the **Clipboard group**, point to **Paste**, and then click the *upper* portion of this split button.

The Paste command pastes the most recently copied item on the Clipboard at the insertion point location. If you click the lower portion of the Paste button, a gallery of Paste Options displays. A ***split button*** is divided into two parts; clicking the main part of the button performs a command, and clicking the arrow displays a list or gallery with choices.

ANOTHER WAY   Right-click, on the shortcut menu under Paste Options, click the desired option button; or, press Ctrl + V.

6 Below the pasted text, click **Paste Options** as shown in Figure 1.47.

Here you can view and apply various formatting options for pasting your copied or cut text. Typically you will click Paste on the ribbon and paste the item in its original format. If you want some other format for the pasted item, you can choose another format from the ***Paste Options gallery***.

The Paste Options gallery provides a Live Preview of the various options for changing the format of the pasted item with a single click. The Paste Options gallery is available in three places: on the ribbon by clicking the lower portion of the Paste button—the Paste button arrow; from the Paste Options button that displays below the pasted item following the paste operation; or on the shortcut menu if you right-click the pasted item.

FIGURE 1.47

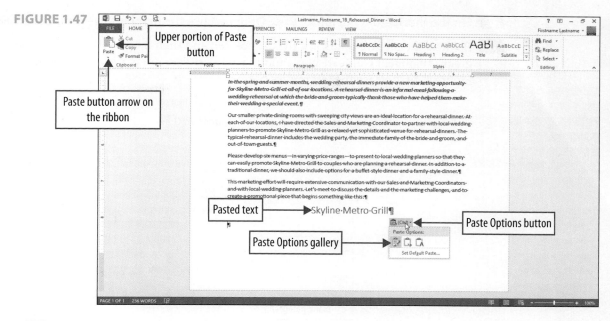

7 ▶ In the **Paste Options** gallery, *point* to each option to see the Live Preview of the format that would be applied if you clicked the button.

The contents of the Paste Options gallery are contextual; that is, they change based on what you copied and where you are pasting.

8 ▶ Press [Esc] to close the gallery; the button will remain displayed until you take some other screen action.

9 ▶ Press [Ctrl] + [Home] to move to the top of the document, and then click the **salad image** one time to select it. While pointing to the selected image, right-click, and then on the shortcut menu, click **Cut**.

Recall that the Cut command cuts—removes—the selection from the document and places it on the Clipboard.

⟳ ANOTHER WAY   On the HOME tab, in the Clipboard group, click the Cut button; or, use the keyboard shortcut [Ctrl] + [X].

10 ▶ Press [Del] one time to remove the blank paragraph from the top of the document, and then press [Ctrl] + [End] to move to the end of the document.

11 ▶ With the insertion point blinking in the blank paragraph at the end of the document, right-click, and notice that the **Paste Options** gallery displays on the shortcut menu. Compare your screen with Figure 1.48.

FIGURE 1.48

12 On the shortcut menu, under **Paste Options**, click the first button—**Keep Source Formatting**.

13 Point to the picture to display the ⟨pointer⟩ pointer, and then drag to the right until the center green **Alignment Guide** displays and the blank paragraph is above the picture, as shown in Figure 1.49. Release the left mouse button.

FIGURE 1.49

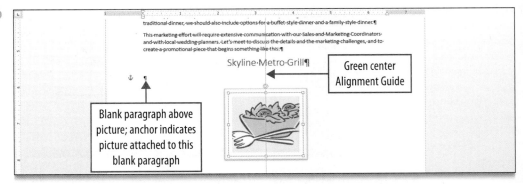

14 Above the picture, click to position the insertion point at the end of the word *Grill*, press [Spacebar] one time, type **for Your Rehearsal Dinner** and then **Save** 🖫 your document. Compare your screen with Figure 1.50.

FIGURE 1.50

15 On the **INSERT tab**, in the **Header & Footer group**, click **Footer**. At the bottom of the list, click **Edit Footer**, and then with the **HEADER & FOOTER Design tab** active, in the **Insert group**, click **Document Info**. Click **File Name** to add the file name to the footer.

16 On the right end of the ribbon, click **Close Header and Footer**.

17 On the **Quick Access Toolbar**, point to the **Print Preview and Print icon** 🔍 you placed there, right-click, and then click **Remove from Quick Access Toolbar**.

If you are working on your own computer and you want to do so, you can leave the icon on the toolbar; in a lab setting, you should return the software to its original settings.

18 Click **Save** 🖫 and then click the **FILE tab** to display **Backstage** view. With the **Info tab** active, in the lower right corner click **Show All Properties**. As **Tags**, type **weddings, rehearsal dinners, marketing**

19 As the **Subject**, type your course name and number—for example *CIS 10, #5543*. Under **Related People**, be sure your name displays as the author (edit it if necessary), and then on the left, click **Print** to display the Print Preview. Compare your screen with Figure 1.51.

FIGURE 1.51

20 On the left side of **Backstage** view, click **Save**. As directed by your instructor, print or submit your file electronically as described in Project 1A, and then in the upper right corner of the Word window, click **Close** [×].

21 If a message indicates *Would you like to keep the last item you copied?* click **No**.

> This message displays if you have copied some type of image to the Clipboard. If you click Yes, the items on the Clipboard will remain for you to use in another program or document.

Objective 11 Compress Files and Use the Microsoft Office 2013 Help System

Video OF1-11

A ***compressed file*** is a file that has been reduced in size. Compressed files take up less storage space and can be transferred to other computers faster than uncompressed files. You can also combine a group of files into one compressed folder, which makes it easier to share a group of files.

Within each Office program, the Help feature provides information about all of the program's features and displays step-by-step instructions for performing many tasks.

Activity 1.18 | Compressing Files

In this activity, you will combine the two files you created in this chapter into one compressed file.

1 On the Windows taskbar, click **File Explorer** [icon]. On the left, in the **navigation pane**, navigate to your **USB flash drive**, and then open your **Office Features Chapter 1** folder. Compare your screen with Figure 1.52.

FIGURE 1.52

2 In the **file list**, click your **Lastname_Firstname_1A_Note_Form** Word file one time to select it. Then, hold down Ctrl, and click your **Lastname_Firstname_1B_Rehearsal_Dinner** file to select the files in the list.

In any Windows-based program, holding down Ctrl while selecting enables you to select multiple items.

3 On the **File Explorer** ribbon, click **Share**, and then in the **Send group**, click **Zip**. Compare your screen with Figure 1.53.

Windows creates a compressed folder containing a *copy* of each of the selected files. The folder name is selected—highlighted in blue—so that you can rename it.

BY TOUCH   Tap the ribbon commands.

FIGURE 1.53

ANOTHER WAY   Point to the selected files in the File List, right-click, point to Send to, and then click Compressed (zipped) folder.

4 Using your own name, type **Lastname_Firstname_Office_Features_Chapter_1** and press Enter.

The compressed folder is ready to attach to an email or share in some other format.

5 In the upper right corner of the folder window, click **Close** ⊠.

Activity 1.19 │ Using the Microsoft Office 2013 Help System in Excel

In this activity, you will use the Microsoft Help feature to find information about formatting numbers in Excel.

1 Press ⊞ to display the Windows 8 **Start screen**, and then type **excel 2013** Press Enter to open the Excel desktop app.

2 On Excel's opening screen, click **Blank workbook**, and then in the upper right corner, click **Microsoft Excel Help** ⍰.

ANOTHER WAY   Press F1 to display Help in any Office program.

3 In the **Excel Help** window, click in the **Search online help** box, type **formatting numbers** and then press Enter.

4 On the list of results, click **Format numbers as currency**. Compare your screen with Figure 1.54.

FIGURE 1.54

5 If you want to do so, at the top of the **Excel Help** window, click Print 🖶 to print a copy of this information for your reference.

6 In the upper right corner of the Help window, click **Close** ✕ .

7 Leave Excel open for the next activity.

Objective 12 Install Apps for Office and Create a Microsoft Account

ALERT! **Working with Web-Based Applications and Services**

Computer programs and services on the web receive continuous updates and improvements. Thus, the steps to complete the following web-based activities may differ from the ones shown. You can often look at the screens and the information presented to determine how to complete the activity.

Video OF1-12

Apps for Office 2013 and SharePoint 2013 are a collection of downloadable apps that enable you to create and view information within your familiar Office programs. Some of these apps are developed by Microsoft, but many more are developed by specialists in different fields. As new apps are developed, they will be available from the online Office Store.

An ***app for Office*** is a webpage that works within one of the Office applications, such as Excel, that you download from the Office Store. Office apps combine cloud services and web technologies within the user interface of Office and SharePoint. For example, in Excel, you can use an app to look up and gather search results for a new apartment by placing the information in an Excel worksheet, and then use maps to determine the distance of each apartment to work and to family members.

Activity 1.20 | Installing Apps for Office

ALERT! **You Must Be Signed In to Office with a Microsoft Account to Complete This Activity**

To download an Office app, you must be signed in to Office with a free Microsoft account. If you do not have a Microsoft account, refer to the next activity to create one by using Microsoft's outlook.com email service, which includes free OneDrive cloud storage.

1 On the Excel ribbon, click the **INSERT tab**. In the **Apps group**, click the **Apps for Office** arrow, and then click **See All**.

2 Click **FEATURED APPS**, and then on the right, click in the **Search for apps on the Office Store** box, type **Bing Maps** and press Enter.

3 Click the **Bing logo**, and then click the **Add** button, and then if necessary, click Continue.

4 **Close** ✕ Internet Explorer, and then **Close** ✕ the **Apps for Office** box.

5 On the **INSERT tab**, in the **Apps group**, click **Apps for Office**, click **See All**, click **MY APPS**, click the **Bing Maps** app, and then in the lower right corner, click **Insert**.

6 On the Welcome message, click **Insert Sample Data**.

Here, the Bing map displays information related to the sample data. Each state in the sample data displays a small pie chart that represents the two sets of data. Compare your screen with Figure 1.55.

This is just one example of many apps downloadable from the Office store.

FIGURE 1.55

7 **Close** ☒ Excel without saving.

Activity 1.21 | Creating a Microsoft Account

> **ALERT!** **This Is an Optional Activity**
>
> You will find both Windows 8 and Office 2013 to be much more useful if you sign in with a Microsoft account. If you already have an email account from msn.com, hotmail.com, live.com, or outlook.com, then you already have a Microsoft account. If you do not, you can create a free Microsoft account by following the steps in this activity.

In Windows 8, you can create a Microsoft account, and then use that account to sign in to *any* Windows 8 PC. Signing in with a Microsoft account is recommended because you can:

- Download Windows 8 apps from the Windows Store.
- Get your online content—email, social network updates, updated news—automatically displayed in an app on the Windows 8 Start screen when you sign in.
- Synch settings online to make every Windows 8 computer you use look and feel the same.
- Sign in to Office so that you can store documents on your OneDrive and download Office apps.

1 Open Internet Explorer 🅴, and then go to **www.outlook.com**

2 Locate and click **Sign up now** to display a screen similar to Figure 1.56. Complete the form to create your account.

FIGURE 1.56

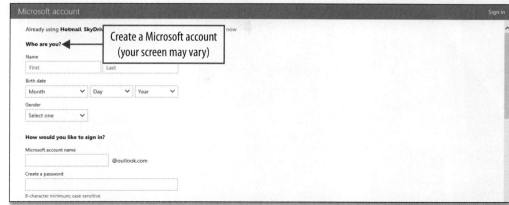

3 **Close** ☒ Internet Explorer.

END | You have completed Project 1B

END OF CHAPTER

SUMMARY

Many Office features and commands, such as the Open and Save As dialog boxes, performing commands from the ribbon and from dialog boxes, and using the Clipboard are the same in all Office desktop apps.

A desktop app is installed on your computer and requires a computer operating system such as Microsoft Windows or Apple OS to run. The programs in Microsoft Office 2013 are considered to be desktop apps.

Apps that run on a smartphone or tablet computer—for example, iOS, Android, or Windows Phone—or apps that run from browser software such as Internet Explorer or Chrome on a PC, are referred to as apps.

Within each Office app, you can install additional Apps for Office from the Office Store. You must have a Microsoft account, which includes free OneDrive storage, to download Windows 8 or Office apps.

GO! LEARN IT ONLINE

Review the concepts and key terms in this chapter by completing these online challenges, which you can find at **www.pearsonhighered.com/go**.

Matching and Multiple Choice:
Answer matching and multiple choice questions to test what you learned in this chapter. MyITLab®

Crossword Puzzle:
Spell out the words that match the numbered clues, and put them in the puzzle squares.

Flipboard:
Flip through the definitions of the key terms in this chapter and match them with the correct term.

GLOSSARY

GLOSSARY OF CHAPTER KEY TERMS

Address bar (Internet Explorer) The area at the top of the Internet Explorer window that displays, and where you can type, a URL—Uniform Resource Locator—which is an address that uniquely identifies a location on the Internet.

Address bar (Windows) The bar at the top of a folder window with which you can navigate to a different folder or library, or go back to a previous one.

Alignment The placement of text or objects relative to the left and right margins.

Alignment guides Green lines that display when you move an object to assist in alignment.

App The term that commonly refers to computer programs that run from the device software on a smartphone or a tablet computer—for example, iOS, Android, or Windows Phone—or computer programs that run from the browser software on a desktop PC or laptop PC—for example Internet Explorer, Safari, Firefox, or Chrome.

App for Office A webpage that works within one of the Office applications, such as Excel, and that you download from the Office Store.

Apps for Office 2013 and SharePoint 2013 A collection of downloadable apps that enable you to create and view information within your familiar Office programs.

Backstage tabs The area along the left side of Backstage view with tabs to display screens with related groups of commands.

Backstage view A centralized space for file management tasks; for example, opening, saving, printing, publishing, or sharing a file. A navigation pane displays along the left side with tabs that group file-related tasks together.

Center alignment The alignment of text or objects that is centered horizontally between the left and right margins.

Click The action of pressing and releasing the left button on a mouse pointing device one time.

Clip art Downloadable predefined graphics available online from Office.com and other sites.

Clipboard A temporary storage area that holds text or graphics that you select and then cut or copy.

Cloud computing Refers to applications and services that are accessed over the Internet, rather than to applications that are installed on your local computer.

Cloud storage Online storage of data so that you can access your data from different places and devices.

Collaborate To work with others as a team in an intellectual endeavor to complete a shared task or to achieve a shared goal.

Commands An instruction to a computer program that causes an action to be carried out.

Common dialog boxes The set of dialog boxes that includes Open, Save, and Save As, which are provided by the Windows programming interface, and which display and operate in all of the Office programs in the same manner.

Compressed file A file that has been reduced in size and thus takes up less storage space and can be transferred to other computers quickly.

Compressed folder A folder that has been reduced in size and thus takes up less storage space and can be transferred to other computers quickly; also called a *zipped* folder.

Context menus Menus that display commands and options relevant to the selected text or object; also called *shortcut menus.*

Context-sensitive commands Commands that display on a shortcut menu that relate to the object or text that you right-clicked.

Contextual tabs Tabs that are added to the ribbon automatically when a specific object, such as a picture, is selected, and that contain commands relevant to the selected object.

Copy A command that duplicates a selection and places it on the Clipboard.

Cut A command that removes a selection and places it on the Clipboard.

Default The term that refers to the current selection or setting that is automatically used by a computer program unless you specify otherwise.

Deselect The action of canceling the selection of an object or block of text by clicking outside of the selection.

Desktop In Windows, the screen that simulates your work area.

Desktop app The term that commonly refers to a computer program that is installed on your computer and requires a computer operating system like Microsoft Windows or Apple OS to run.

Dialog box A small window that contains options for completing a task.

Dialog Box Launcher A small icon that displays to the right of some group names on the ribbon, and which opens a related dialog box or pane providing additional options and commands related to that group.

Document properties Details about a file that describe or identify it, including the title, author name, subject, and keywords that identify the document's topic or contents; also known as *metadata.*

Drag The action of holding down the left mouse button while moving your mouse.

Edit The process of making changes to text or graphics in an Office file.

Ellipsis A set of three dots indicating incompleteness; an ellipsis following a command name indicates that a dialog box will display if you click the command.

Enhanced ScreenTip A ScreenTip that displays more descriptive text than a normal ScreenTip.

Extract To decompress, or pull out, files from a compressed form.

File A collection of information stored on a computer under a single name, for example, a Word document or a PowerPoint presentation.

File Explorer The program that displays the files and folders on your computer, and which is at work anytime you are viewing the contents of files and folders in a window.

Fill The inside color of an object.

Folder A container in which you store files.

Folder window In Windows, a window that displays the contents of the current folder, library, or device, and contains helpful parts so that you can navigate the Windows file structure.

Font A set of characters with the same design and shape.

Font styles Formatting emphasis such as bold, italic, and underline.

Footer A reserved area for text or graphics that displays at the bottom of each page in a document.

Formatting The process of establishing the overall appearance of text, graphics, and pages in an Office file—for example, in a Word document.

Formatting marks Characters that display on the screen, but do not print, indicating where the Enter key, the Spacebar, and the Tab key were pressed; also called *nonprinting characters*.

Gallery An Office feature that displays a list of potential results instead of just the command name.

Gradient fill A fill effect in which one color fades into another.

Groups On the Office ribbon, the sets of related commands that you might need for a specific type of task.

Header A reserved area for text or graphics that displays at the top of each page in a document.

Info tab The tab in Backstage view that displays information about the current file.

Insertion point A blinking vertical line that indicates where text or graphics will be inserted.

Keyboard shortcut A combination of two or more keyboard keys, used to perform a task that would otherwise require a mouse.

KeyTip The letter that displays on a command in the ribbon and that indicates the key you can press to activate the command when keyboard control of the ribbon is activated.

Keywords Custom file properties in the form of words that you associate with a document to give an indication of the document's content; used to help find and organize files. Also called *tags*.

Landscape orientation A page orientation in which the paper is wider than it is tall.

Layout Options A button that displays when an object is selected and that has commands to choose how the object interacts with surrounding text.

Live Preview A technology that shows the result of applying an editing or formatting change as you point to possible results—*before* you actually apply it.

Location Any disk drive, folder, or other place in which you can store files and folders.

Metadata Details about a file that describe or identify it, including the title, author name, subject, and keywords that identify the document's topic or contents; also known as *document properties*.

Mini toolbar A small toolbar containing frequently used formatting commands that displays as a result of selecting text or objects.

MRU Acronym for *most recently used*, which refers to the state of some commands that retain the characteristic most recently applied; for example, the Font Color button retains the most recently used color until a new color is chosen.

Navigate The process of exploring within the organizing structure of Windows.

Navigation pane In a folder window, the area on the left in which you can navigate to, open, and display favorites, libraries, folders, saved searches, and an expandable list of drives.

Nonprinting characters Characters that display on the screen, but do not print, indicating where the Enter key, the Spacebar, and the Tab key were pressed; also called *formatting marks*.

Notification bar An area at the bottom of an Internet Explorer window that displays information about pending downloads, security issues, add-ons, and other issues related to the operation of your computer.

Object A text box, picture, table, or shape that you can select and then move and resize.

Office Online The free online companion to Microsoft Word, Excel, PowerPoint, Access, and OneNote.

OneDrive Microsoft's free cloud storage for anyone with a free Microsoft account.

Open dialog box A dialog box from which you can navigate to, and then open on your screen, an existing file that was created in that same program.

Option button In a dialog box, a round button that enables you to make one choice among two or more options.

Options dialog box A dialog box within each Office application where you can select program settings and other options and preferences.

Pane A separate area of a window.

Paragraph symbol The symbol ¶ that represents the end of a paragraph.

Paste The action of placing text or objects that have been copied or cut from one location to another location.

Paste Options gallery A gallery of buttons that provides a Live Preview of all the Paste options available in the current context.

Path A sequence of folders that leads to a specific file or folder.

PDF The acronym for Portable Document Format, which is a file format that creates an image that preserves the look of your file; this is a popular format for sending documents electronically because the document will display on most computers.

Point The action of moving your mouse pointer over something on your screen.

Pointer Any symbol that displays on your screen in response to moving your mouse.

Points A measurement of the size of a font; there are 72 points in an inch.

Portable Document Format A file format that creates an image that preserves the look of your file, but that cannot be easily changed; a popular format for sending documents electronically, because the document will display on most computers.

Portrait orientation A page orientation in which the paper is taller than it is wide.

Print Preview A view of a document as it will appear when you print it.

Progress bar In a dialog box or taskbar button, a bar that indicates visually the progress of a task such as a download or file transfer.

Protected View A security feature in Office 2013 that protects your computer from malicious files by opening them in a restricted environment until you enable them; you might encounter this feature if you open a file from an email or download files from the Internet.

pt The abbreviation for *point*; for example, when referring to a font size.

Quick Access Toolbar In an Office program window, the small row of buttons in the upper left corner of the screen from which you can perform frequently used commands.

Read-Only A property assigned to a file that prevents the file from being modified or deleted; it indicates that you cannot save any changes to the displayed document unless you first save it with a new name.

Ribbon A user interface in both Office 2013 and File Explorer that groups the commands for performing related tasks on tabs across the upper portion of the program window.

Right-click The action of clicking the right mouse button one time.

Sans serif font A font design with no lines or extensions on the ends of characters.

ScreenTip A small box that that displays useful information when you perform various mouse actions such as pointing to screen elements or dragging.

Scroll bar A vertical or horizontal bar in a window or a pane to assist in bringing an area into view, and which contains a scroll box and scroll arrows.

Scroll box The box in the vertical and horizontal scroll bars that can be dragged to reposition the contents of a window or pane on the screen.

Selecting Highlighting, by dragging with your mouse, areas of text or data or graphics, so that the selection can be edited, formatted, copied, or moved.

Serif font A font design that includes small line extensions on the ends of the letters to guide the eye in reading from left to right.

SharePoint Collaboration software with which people in an organization can set up team sites to share information, manage documents, and publish reports for others to see.

Shortcut menu A menu that displays commands and options relevant to the selected text or object; also called a *context menu*.

Sizing handles Small squares that indicate a picture or object is selected.

Split button A button divided into two parts and in which clicking the main part of the button performs a command and clicking the arrow opens a menu with choices.

Start search The search feature in Windows 8 in which, from the Start screen, you can begin to type and by default, Windows 8 searches for apps; you can adjust the search to search for files or settings.

Status bar The area along the lower edge of an Office program window that displays file information on the left and buttons to control how the window looks on the right.

Style A group of formatting commands, such as font, font size, font color, paragraph alignment, and line spacing that can be applied to a paragraph with one command.

Subfolder A folder within a folder.

Synchronization The process of updating computer files that are in two or more locations according to specific rules—also called *syncing*.

Syncing The process of updating computer files that are in two or more locations according to specific rules—also called *synchronization*.

Tabs (ribbon) On the Office ribbon, the name of each activity area.

Tags Custom file properties in the form of words that you associate with a document to give an indication of the document's content; used to help find and organize files. Also called *keywords*.

Taskbar The area along the lower edge of the desktop that displays buttons representing programs.

Template A preformatted document that you can use as a starting point and then change to suit your needs.

Theme A predesigned combination of colors, fonts, and effects that look good together and is applied to an entire document by a single selection.

Title bar The bar at the top edge of the program window that indicates the name of the current file and the program name.

Toggle button A button that can be turned on by clicking it once, and then turned off by clicking it again.

Toolbar In a folder window, a row of buttons with which you can perform common tasks, such as changing the view of your files and folders or burning files to a CD.

Triple-click The action of clicking the left mouse button three times in rapid succession.

Trusted Documents A security feature in Office that remembers which files you have already enabled; you might encounter this feature if you open a file from an email or download files from the Internet.

Uniform Resource Locator An address that uniquely identifies a location on the Internet.

URL The acronym for Uniform Resource Locator, which is an address that uniquely identifies a location on the Internet.

USB flash drive A small data storage device that plugs into a computer USB port.

Window A rectangular area on a computer screen in which programs and content appear, and which can be moved, resized, minimized, or closed.

XML Paper Specification A Microsoft file format that creates an image of your document and that opens in the XPS viewer.

XPS The acronym for XML Paper Specification—a Microsoft file format that creates an image of your document and that opens in the XPS viewer.

Zipped folder A folder that has been reduced in size and thus takes up less storage space and can be transferred to other computers quickly; also called a *compressed* folder.

Zoom The action of increasing or decreasing the size of the viewing area on the screen.

Introduction to Microsoft Word 2013

W Word 2013

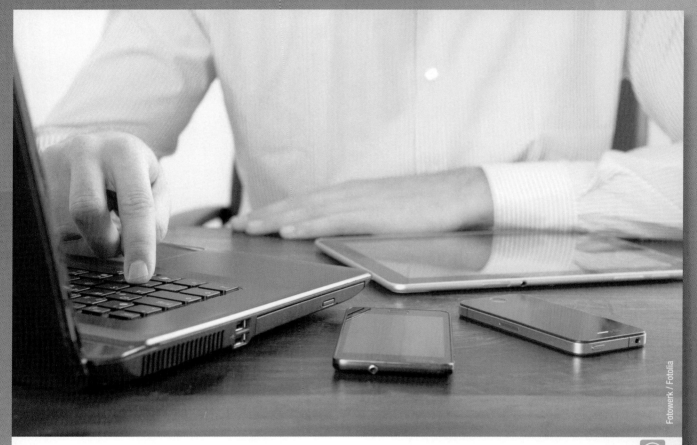

Fotowerk / Fotolia

Word 2013: Introduction

Video WA

Content! Defined by Merriam-Webster's online dictionary as "the topic or matter treated in a written work" and also as "the principal substance (as written matter, illustrations, or music) offered by a World Wide Web site," content is what you consume when you read on paper or online, when you watch video, or when you listen to any kind of music—live or recorded.

Content is what you *create* when your own words or performances are recorded in some form. For creating content in the form of words, Microsoft Office 2013 is a great choice. Rather than just a tool for word processing, Word is now a tool for you to communicate and collaborate with others. When you want to communicate with pictures or images in your Word document, Office 2013 has many new features to help you do so. Microsoft Word 2013 works best on a Windows 8 PC—desktop, laptop, or tablet—because if your PC is touch-enabled, you will be able to use your fingers to work with Word. For example, the ribbon expands to make it easy to tap commands and you can resize images by moving your fingers on the screen.

Best of all, Microsoft Word 2013 is integrated into the cloud. If you save your documents to your OneDrive that comes with any free Microsoft account, such as one you can create at outlook.com, you can retrieve them from any device and continue to work with and share your documents. Enjoy learning Word 2013!

Creating Documents with Microsoft Word 2013

GO! to Work
Video W1

PROJECT **1A**

OUTCOMES
Create a flyer with a picture.

PROJECT **1B**

OUTCOMES
Format text, paragraphs, and documents.

OBJECTIVES

1. Create a New Document and Insert Text
2. Insert and Format Graphics
3. Insert and Modify Text Boxes and Shapes
4. Preview and Print a Document

OBJECTIVES

5. Change Document and Paragraph Layout
6. Create and Modify Lists
7. Set and Modify Tab Stops
8. Insert a SmartArt Graphic and an Online Video

A_ya / Fotolia

In This Chapter

In this chapter, you will begin your study of Microsoft Word, which is one of the most popular computer programs and one that almost everyone has a reason to use. You will use many of the new tools in Word 2013 such as applying attractive styles to your documents. You can use Microsoft Word to perform basic word processing tasks such as writing a memo, a report, or a letter. You can also use Word to complete complex tasks, such as creating sophisticated tables, embedding graphics, writing blogs, and creating publications. Word is a program that you can learn gradually, and then add more advanced skills, one at a time.

The projects in this chapter relate to **Sturgeon Point Productions**, which is an independent film company based in Miami and with offices in Detroit and Milwaukee. The film professionals produce effective broadcast and branded content for many industries, and provide a wide array of film and video production services. Sturgeon Point Productions has won awards for broadcast advertising, business media, music videos, and social media. The mission of the company is to help clients tell their stories—whether the story is about a social issue, a new product, a geographical location, a new company, or a person.

PROJECT ACTIVITIES

In Activities 1.01 through 1.16, you will create a flyer announcing two internships for a short documentary by Sturgeon Point Productions. Your completed document will look similar to Figure 1.1.

PROJECT FILES

For Project 1A, you will need the following files:

New blank Word document
w01A_Text
w01A_Bird

You will save your document as:

Lastname_Firstname_1A_Flyer

PROJECT RESULTS

Build from
Scratch

FIGURE 1.1 Project 1A Flyer

- Tap an item to click it.
- Press and hold for a few seconds to right-click; release when the information or commands display.
- Touch the screen with two or more fingers and then pinch together to zoom in or stretch your fingers apart to zoom out.
- Slide your finger on the screen to scroll—slide left to scroll right and slide right to scroll left.
- Slide to rearrange—similar to dragging with a mouse.
- Swipe from edge: from right to display charms; from left to expose open apps, snap apps, or close apps; from top or bottom to show commands or close an app.
- Swipe to select—slide an item a short distance with a quick movement—to select an item and bring up commands, if any.

Objective 1 Create a New Document and Insert Text

Video W1-1

When you start Word, documents you have recently opened, if any, display on the left. On the right, you can select either a blank document or a ***template***—a preformatted document that you can use as a starting point and then change to suit your needs. When you create a new document, you can type all of the text or you can type some of the text and then insert additional text from another source.

Activity 1.01 │ Starting a New Word Document

1 ▶ **Start** Word, and then click **Blank document**. On the **HOME tab**, in the **Paragraph group**, if necessary, click **Show/Hide** ¶ so that it is active and the formatting marks display. If the rulers do not display, click the **VIEW tab**, and then in the **Show group**, select the **Ruler** check box.

2 ▶ Type **Internships Available** and then press Enter two times. As you type the following text, press the Spacebar only one time at the end of a sentence: **This summer, Sturgeon Point Productions will be filming a short documentary in Costa Rica about its native birds and has positions available for two interns. We are looking for a First Assistant Director and an Assistant Script Supervisor.**

As you type, the insertion point moves to the right, and when it approaches the right margin, Word determines whether the next word in the line will fit within the established right margin. If the word does not fit, Word moves the entire word down to the next line. This is ***wordwrap*** and means that you press Enter *only* when you reach the end of a paragraph—it is not necessary to press Enter at the end of each line of text.

| N O T E | **Spacing between Sentences** |

Although you might have learned to add two spaces following end-of-sentence punctuation, the common practice now is to space only one time at the end of a sentence.

3 ▶ Press Enter. Take a moment to study the table in Figure 1.2 to become familiar with the default document settings in Microsoft Word, and then compare your screen with Figure 1.3.

When you press Enter, Spacebar, or Tab on your keyboard, characters display in your document to represent these keystrokes. These characters do not print and are referred to as ***formatting marks*** or ***nonprinting characters***. These marks will display throughout this instruction.

FIGURE 1.2

DEFAULT DOCUMENT SETTINGS IN A NEW WORD DOCUMENT	
SETTING	**DEFAULT FORMAT**
Font and font size	The default font is Calibri and the default font size is 11 points.
Margins	The default left, right, top, and bottom page margins are 1 inch.
Line spacing	The default line spacing is 1.08, which provides slightly more space between lines than single spacing does.
Paragraph spacing	The default spacing after a paragraph is 8 points, which is slightly less than the height of one blank line of text.
View	The default view is Print Layout view, which displays the page borders and displays the document as it will appear when printed.

FIGURE 1.3

More Knowledge | **Word's Default Settings Are Easier to Read Online**

Until just a few years ago, word processing programs used single spacing, an extra blank paragraph to separate paragraphs, and 12 pt Times New Roman as the default formats. Now, studies show that individuals find the Word default formats described in Figure 1.2 to be easier to read online, where many documents are now viewed and read.

Activity 1.02 | **Inserting Text from Another Document**

1 ▷ On the ribbon, click the **INSERT tab**. In the **Text group**, click the **Object button arrow**, and then click **Text from File**.

ALERT! | **Does the Object Dialog Box Display?**

If the Object dialog box displays, you probably clicked the Object *button* instead of the Object *button arrow*. Close the Object dialog box, and then in the Text group, click the Object button arrow, as shown in Figure 1.4. Click *Text from File*, and then continue with Step 2.

---

2 ▷ In the **Insert File** dialog box, navigate to the student files that accompany this textbook, locate and select **w01A_Text**, and then click **Insert**. Compare your screen with Figure 1.4.

A *copy* of the text from the w01A_Text file displays at the insertion point location; the text is not removed from the original file.

FIGURE 1.4

Object button arrow

Internships Available¶

This summer, Sturgeon Point Productions will be filming a short documentary in Costa Rica about its native birds and has positions available for two interns. We are looking for a first Assistant Director and an Assistant Script Supervisor.¶

The filming will begin the first week of July and will last approximately two weeks. Payment will be by Day Rate of $100 per day. Transportation, food, and lodging will be provided.¶

Text inserted from file →

The First Assistant Director will work with the second film crew, which will be filming background video. The Assistant Script Supervisor will work with the Script Supervisor and will be responsible for coordinating communication between the two camera crews.¶

You must have a valid U.S. passport; no inoculations are necessary. Details are available on the company website.¶

¶

ANOTHER WAY   Open the file, copy the required text, close the file, and then paste the text into the current document.

3 On the **Quick Access Toolbar**, click **Save** 🔲. Under **Save As**, click **Computer**, and then click **Browse**. Navigate to the location where you are saving your files for this chapter, and then create and open a new folder named **Word Chapter 1**. In the **File name** box, using your own name, replace the existing text with **Lastname_Firstname_1A_Flyer** and then click **Save**.

Objective 2   Insert and Format Graphics

Video W1-2

To add visual interest to a document, insert *graphics*. Graphics include pictures, online pictures, charts, and *drawing objects*—shapes, diagrams, lines, and so on. For additional visual interest, you can apply an attractive graphic format to text; add, resize, move, and format pictures; and add a page border.

Activity 1.03   Formatting Text by Using Text Effects

Text effects are decorative formats, such as shadowed or mirrored text, text glow, 3-D effects, and colors that make text stand out.

1 Including the paragraph mark, select the first paragraph of text—*Internships Available*. On the **HOME tab**, in the **Font group**, click **Text Effects and Typography** Ⓐ.

2 In the **Text Effects** gallery, in the third row, point to the first effect to display the ScreenTip *Fill – Black, Text 1, Outline – Background 1, Hard Shadow – Background 1*, and then click this effect.

3 With the text still selected, in the **Font group**, click in the **Font Size** box ⌴ to select the existing font size. Type **52** and then press ⏎.

When you want to change the font size of selected text to a size that does not display in the Font Size list, type the number in the Font Size box and press ⏎ to confirm the new font size.

4 With the text still selected, in the **Paragraph group**, click **Center** 🗉 to center the text. Compare your screen with Figure 1.5.

FIGURE 1.5

Center button selected

Text Effects and Typography button

Text effects applied to title → **Internships·Available¶**

> 5 ▶ With the text still selected, in the **Font group**, click **Text Effects and Typography** 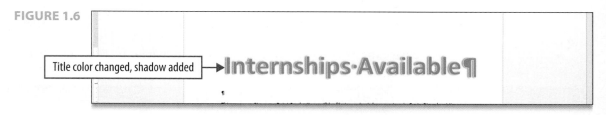. Point to **Shadow**, and then under **Outer**, in the second row, click the third style—**Offset Left**.

> 6 ▶ With the text still selected, in the **Font group**, click the **Font Color button arrow** ◢. Under **Theme Colors**, in the sixth column, click the first color—**Orange, Accent 2**.

> 7 ▶ Click anywhere in the document to deselect the text, click **Save** 🖫, and then compare your screen with Figure 1.6.

FIGURE 1.6

Title color changed, shadow added → **Internships·Available¶**

More Knowledge │ **Clear Existing Formatting**

If you do not like your text effect, you can remove all formatting from any selected text. To do so, on the HOME tab, in the Font group, click Clear All Formatting ⧉.

Activity 1.04 │ Inserting Pictures

> 1 ▶ In the paragraph that begins *This summer*, click to position the insertion point at the beginning of the paragraph.

> 2 ▶ On the **INSERT tab**, in the **Illustrations group**, click **Pictures**. In the **Insert Picture** dialog box, navigate to your student data files, locate and click **w01A_Bird**, and then click **Insert**.

> Word inserts the picture as an ***inline object***; that is, the picture is positioned directly in the text at the insertion point, just like a character in a sentence. The Layout Options button displays to the right of the picture. You can change the ***Layout Options*** to control the manner in which text wraps around a picture or other object. Sizing handles surround the picture indicating it is selected.

> 3 ▶ Notice the square sizing handles around the border of the selected picture, as shown in Figure 1.7.

> The corner sizing handles resize the graphic proportionally. The center sizing handles resize a graphic vertically or horizontally only; however, sizing with these will distort the graphic. A ***rotation handle***, with which you can rotate the graphic to any angle, displays above the top center sizing handle.

FIGURE 1.7

Activity 1.05 | Wrapping Text around a Picture Using Layout Options

Recall that Layout Options enable you to control **text wrapping**—the manner in which text displays around an object.

1 Be sure the picture is selected—you know it is selected if the sizing handles display.

2 To the right of the picture, click **Layout Options** to display a gallery of text wrapping arrangements. Point to each layout option icon to view its ScreenTip.

Each icon visually depicts how text will wrap around an object.

ANOTHER WAY   On the FORMAT tab, in the Arrange group, click Wrap Text.

3 From the gallery, under **With Text Wrapping**, click the first layout—**Square**. Compare your screen with Figure 1.8.

Select Square text wrapping when you want to wrap the text to the left or right of an image. To the left of the picture, an **object anchor** displays indicating that the selected object is anchored to the text at this location in the document.

FIGURE 1.8

4 **Close** ☒ the **Layout Options**, and then **Save** 🖫 your document.

When you move or size a picture, *Live Layout* reflows text as you move or size an object so that you can view the placement of surrounding text.

1 If necessary, scroll your document so the entire picture displays on the screen. At the lower right corner of the picture, point to the sizing handle until the ⬉ pointer displays. Drag slightly upward and to the left and notice that as you drag, a green alignment guide displays at the left margin. Compare your screen with Figure 1.9.

> *Alignment guides* display when you are moving or sizing a picture to help you with object placement, and Live Layout shows you how the document text will flow and display on the page.

FIGURE 1.9

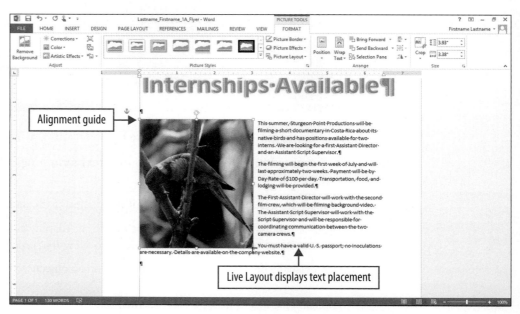

2 Continue to drag up and to the left until the bottom of the graphic is aligned at approximately **4 inches on the vertical ruler** and notice that the graphic is proportionally resized.

3 On the **Quick Access Toolbar**, click **Undo** 🔄 to restore the picture to its original size.

ANOTHER WAY   On the FORMAT tab, in the Adjust group, click Reset Picture.

4 On the ribbon, under **PICTURE TOOLS**, on the **FORMAT tab**, in the **Size group**, click the **Shape Height spin box arrows** ↕ Height: 0.19" ⬍ as necessary to change the height of the picture to **3.8"**. If necessary, scroll down to view the entire picture on your screen, and then compare your screen with Figure 1.10.

> A *spin box* is a small box with an upward- and downward-pointing arrow that lets you move rapidly through a set of values by clicking. When you use the Shape Height and Shape Width spin boxes to change the size of a graphic, the graphic will always resize proportionally; that is, the width adjusts as you change the height and vice versa.

FIGURE 1.10

Height changed to 3.8

Width adjusted proportionally

Picture resized

5 Save your document.

Activity 1.07 | Moving a Picture

There are two ways to move a picture in a document. You can point to the picture and then drag it to a new position. You can also change the picture settings in a dialog box, which gives you more precise control over the picture location.

1 Be sure the picture is selected. On the ribbon, click the **FORMAT tab**. In the **Arrange group**, click **Position**, and then click **More Layout Options**.

2 In the **Layout** dialog box, be sure the **Position tab** is selected. Under **Horizontal**, click the **Alignment** option button. To the right of **Alignment**, click the **arrow**, and then click **Right**. To the right of **relative to**, click the **arrow**, and then click **Margin**.

3 Under **Vertical**, click the **Alignment** option button. Change the **Alignment** options to **Top relative to Line**. Compare your screen with Figure 1.11.

With these alignment settings, the picture will move to the right margin of the page and the top edge will align with the top of the first line of the paragraph to which it is anchored.

FIGURE 1.11

Layout dialog box

Relative to Margin selected

Right Alignment selected

Vertical Alignment set to Top relative to Line

4 At the bottom of the **Layout** dialog box, click **OK**, and then on the **Quick Access Toolbar**, click **Save** 🔲. Notice that the picture moves to the right margin, and the text wraps on the left side of the picture. Compare your screen with Figure 1.12.

FIGURE 1.12

Activity 1.08 | Applying Picture Effects

Picture styles include shapes, shadows, frames, borders, and other special effects with which you can stylize an image. *Picture Effects* enhance a picture with effects such as shadow, glow, reflection, or 3-D rotation.

1 Be sure the picture is selected. On the **FORMAT tab**, in the **Picture Styles group**, click **Picture Effects**.

2 Point to **Soft Edges**, and then click **5 Point**.

The Soft Edges feature fades the edges of the picture. The number of points you choose determines how far the fade goes inward from the edges of the picture.

3 Compare your screen with Figure 1.13, and then **Save** 🔲 your document.

FIGURE 1.13

Activity 1.09 | Applying Artistic Effects

Artistic effects are formats that make pictures look more like sketches or paintings.

1 Be sure the picture is selected. On the **FORMAT tab**, in the **Adjust group**, click **Artistic Effects**.

2 In the first row of the gallery, point to, but do not click, the third effect—**Pencil Grayscale**.

Live Preview displays the picture with the *Pencil Grayscale* effect added.

3 In the second row of the gallery, click the third effect—**Paint Brush**. **Save** 🖫 your document, and then notice that the picture looks more like a painting than a photograph. Compare your screen with Figure 1.14.

FIGURE 1.14

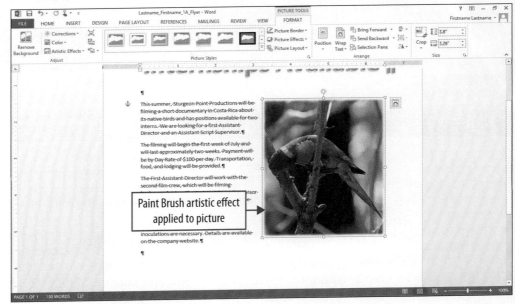

Paint Brush artistic effect applied to picture

Activity 1.10 | Adding a Page Border

Page borders frame a page and help to focus the information on the page.

1 Click anywhere outside the picture to deselect it. On the **DESIGN tab**, in the **Page Background group**, click **Page Borders**.

2 In the **Borders and Shading** dialog box, on the **Page Border tab**, under **Setting**, click **Box**. Under **Style**, scroll the list and click the seventh style—double lines.

3 Click the **Color arrow**, and then in the sixth column, click the first color—**Orange, Accent 2**.

4 Under **Apply to**, be sure **Whole document** is selected, and then compare your screen with Figure 1.15.

FIGURE 1.15

Borders and Shading dialog box

Box setting

Double line style

Border color

5 At the bottom of the **Borders and Shading** dialog box, click **OK**.

6 Press Ctrl + Home to move to the top of the document, click **Save** 🖫, and then compare your screen with Figure 1.16.

FIGURE 1.16

Page border applied to document

Internships·Available¶

Objective 3 | Insert and Modify Text Boxes and Shapes

Video W1-3

Word has predefined **shapes** and **text boxes** that you can add to your documents. A shape is an object such as a line, arrow, box, callout, or banner. A text box is a movable, resizable container for text or graphics. Use these objects to add visual interest to your document.

Activity 1.11 | Inserting, Sizing, and Positioning a Shape

1 Press ↓ one time to move to the blank paragraph below the title. Press Enter four times to create additional space for a text box, and notice that the picture anchored to the paragraph moves with the text.

2 Press Ctrl + End to move to the bottom of the document, and notice that your insertion point is positioned in the empty paragraph at the end of the document. Press Delete to remove the blank paragraph.

3 Click the **INSERT tab**, and then in the **Illustrations group**, click **Shapes** to display the gallery. Compare your screen with Figure 1.17.

FIGURE 1.17

Shapes button

Shapes gallery

Rounded Rectangle shape

4 Under **Rectangles,** click the second shape—**Rounded Rectangle**, and then move your pointer. Notice that the ⊞ pointer displays.

5 Position the ⊞ pointer anywhere in the blank area at the bottom of the document. Click one time to insert a 1-inch by 1-inch rounded rectangle. The exact location is not important.

A blue rectangle with rounded edges displays.

6 To the right of the rectangle object, click **Layout Options** 🖾, and then at the bottom of the gallery, click **See more** to display the **Layout** dialog box.

ANOTHER WAY   On the FORMAT tab, in the Arrange group, click Position.

7 In the **Layout** dialog box, under **Horizontal**, click **Alignment**. To the right of **Alignment**, click the **arrow**, and then click **Centered**. To the right of **relative to**, click the **arrow**, and then click **Page**. Under **Vertical**, click in the **Absolute position** box to select the existing number, and then type **1** To the right of **below**, be sure that **Paragraph** displays. Click **OK**.

> This action centers the rectangle on the page and positions the rectangle one inch below the last paragraph.

8 On the **FORMAT tab**, click in the **Shape Height** box ⬍☐ Height: 0.19" ⬍ to select the existing text. Type **1.5** and then click in the **Shape Width** box ↔ Width: 6.49" ⬍. Type **4.5** and then press Enter.

9 Compare your screen with Figure 1.18, and then **Save** 💾 your document.

FIGURE 1.18

Inserted, sized, and positioned rounded rectangle

✂ **Activity 1.12** | **Typing Text in a Shape and Formatting a Shape**

1 If necessary, select the rectangle shape. Type **To set up an interview, apply online at:** and then press Enter. Type **www.SturgeonPointProductions.com**

2 Press Ctrl + A to select the text you just typed. Right-click over the selected text to display the mini toolbar, and then click **Bold** B. With the text still selected, click **Increase Font Size** A˄ three times to increase the font size to **16 pt**.

> The keyboard shortcut Ctrl + A is convenient to select all of the text in a text box.

3 With the text still selected, on the mini toolbar, click the **Font Color button arrow**. Under **Theme Colors**, click **Black, Text 1**.

4 Click outside the shape to deselect the text. Click the border of the shape to select the shape but not the text. On the **FORMAT tab**, in the **Shape Styles group**, click **Shape Fill**. In the sixth column, click the fourth color—**Orange, Accent 2, Lighter 40%**.

5 With the shape still selected, in the **Shape Styles group**, click **Shape Outline**. In the sixth column, click the first color—**Orange, Accent 2**. Compare your screen with Figure 1.19, and then **Save** 💾 your document.

FIGURE 1.19

Text typed and formatted, shape fill and outline applied

A text box is useful to differentiate portions of text from other text on the page. Because it is a *floating object*—a graphic that can be moved independently of the surrounding text characters—you can place a text box anywhere on the page.

1 Press Ctrl + Home to move to the top of the document.

2 On the **INSERT tab**, in the **Text group**, click **Text Box**. At the bottom of the gallery, click **Draw Text Box**.

3 Position the ⊞ pointer over the first blank paragraph—aligned with the left margin and at approximately **1 inch on the vertical ruler**. Drag down and to the right to create a text box approximately **1.5 inches** high and **4 inches** wide—the exact size and location need not be precise.

4 With the insertion point blinking in the text box, type the following, pressing Enter after each line *except* the last line to create a new paragraph:

> **Interviews will be held:**
>
> **Friday and Saturday, January 14 and 15**
>
> **In the Career Services Conference Room**

5 Compare your screen with Figure 1.20, and then **Save** 💾 your document

FIGURE 1.20

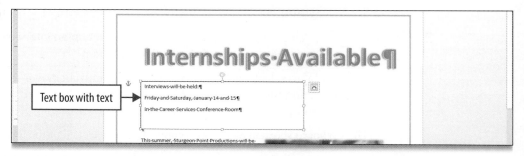

1 Point to the text box border to display the 🔖 pointer. In the space below the *Internships Available* title, by dragging, move the text box until a horizontal green alignment guide displays above the first blank paragraph mark and a vertical green alignment guide displays in the center of the page as shown in Figure 1.21.

FIGURE 1.21

2 To precisely place the text box, on the **FORMAT tab**, in the **Arrange group**, click **Position**, and then click **More Layout Options**.

In the **Layout** dialog box, under **Horizontal**, click **Alignment**. To the right of **Alignment**, click the **arrow**, and then click **Centered**. To the right of **relative to**, click the **arrow**, and then click **Page**.

4 Under **Vertical**, click in the **Absolute position** box, select the existing number, and then type **1.25** To the right of **below**, click the **arrow**, and then click **Margin**.

5 In the **Layout** dialog box, click the **Size tab**. Under **Height**, select the number in the **Absolute** box. Type **1.25** and then under **Width**, select the number in the **Absolute** box. Type **4** and then click **OK**.

> The text box is sized correctly, centered horizontally, and the top edge is positioned 1.25 inches below the top margin of the document.

6 Click in the text box, and then press Ctrl + A to select all of the text. Right-click over the selected text to display the mini toolbar, change the **Font Size** to **16** and apply **Bold** B . Press Ctrl + E to center the text.

> Ctrl + E is the keyboard shortcut to center text in a document or object.

7 On the ribbon, under **DRAWING TOOLS**, click the **FORMAT tab**. In the **Shape Styles group**, click **More** ⤓, and then in the first row, click the third style—**Colored Outline – Orange, Accent 2**.

8 On the **FORMAT tab**, in the **Shape Styles group**, click **Shape Effects**. Point to **Shadow**, and then under **Outer**, in the first row, click the first effect—**Offset Diagonal Bottom Right**.

9 Click anywhere in the document to deselect the text box. Compare your screen with Figure 1.22, and then **Save** 🖫 your document.

FIGURE 1.22

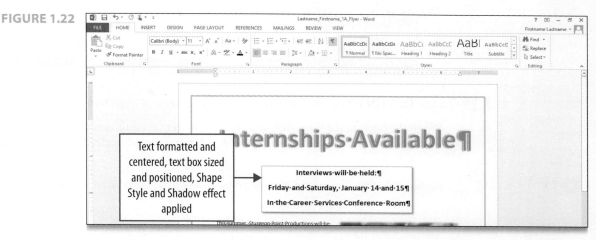

Text formatted and centered, text box sized and positioned, Shape Style and Shadow effect applied

---

Objective 4 Preview and Print a Document

Video W1-4

While you are creating your document, it is useful to preview your document periodically to be sure that you are getting the result you want. Then, before printing, make a final preview to be sure the document layout is what you intend.

Activity 1.15 | Adding a File Name to the Footer by Inserting a Field

Information in headers and footers helps to identify a document when it is printed or displayed electronically. Recall that a header is information that prints at the top of every page; a footer is information that prints at the bottom of every page. In this textbook, you will insert the file name in the footer of every Word document.

> **1** Click the **INSERT tab**, and then in the **Header & Footer group**, click **Footer**.

> **2** At the bottom of the gallery, click **Edit Footer**.

The footer area displays with the insertion point blinking at the left edge, and on the ribbon, the Header & Footer Tools display.

⟳ **ANOTHER WAY**   At the bottom edge of the page, right-click, and then on the shortcut menu, click Edit Footer.

> **3** On the ribbon, under the **HEADER & FOOTER TOOLS**, on the **DESIGN tab**, in the **Insert group**, click **Document Info**, and then click **File Name**. Compare your screen with Figure 1.23.

FIGURE 1.23

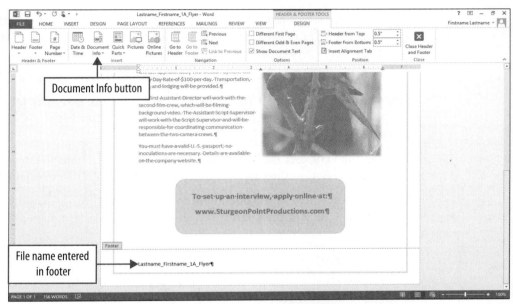

Document Info button

File name entered in footer

> **4** On the **DESIGN tab**, click **Close Header and Footer**, and then **Save** 🔲 your document.

When the body of the document is active, the footer text is dimmed—displays in gray. Conversely, when the footer area is active, the footer text is not dimmed; instead, the document text is dimmed.

⟳ **ANOTHER WAY**   Double-click in the document outside of the footer area to close the footer and return to the document.

Activity 1.16 | Adding Document Properties and Previewing and Printing a Document

> **1** Press [Ctrl] + [Home] to move the insertion point to the top of the document. In the upper left corner of your screen, click the **FILE tab** to display **Backstage** view. On the right, at the bottom of the **Properties** list, click **Show All Properties**.

> **2** On the list of **Properties**, click to the right of **Tags** to display an empty box, and then type **internship, documentary**

> **3** Click to the right of **Subject** to display an empty box, and then type your course name and section number. Under **Related People**, be sure that your name displays as the author. If necessary, right-click the author name, click **Edit Property**, type your name, press [Enter] and click **OK**.

4 On the left, click **Print** to display the **Print Preview**. Compare your screen with Figure 1.24.

Here you can select any printer connected to your system and adjust the settings related to how you want to print. On the right, Print Preview displays your document exactly as it will print; the formatting marks do not display. At the bottom of the Print Preview area, in the center, the number of pages and arrows with which you can move among the pages in Print Preview display. On the right, Zoom settings enable you to shrink or enlarge the Print Preview.

FIGURE 1.24

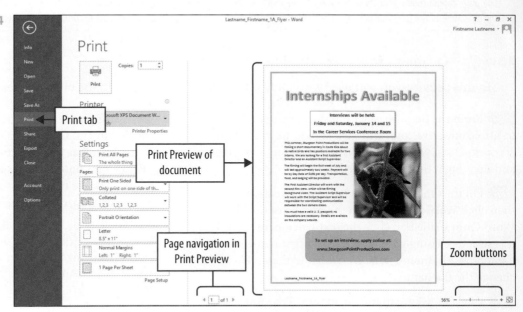

5 In the lower right corner of the window, click **Zoom In** ⊕ several times to view the document at a larger size, and notice that a larger preview is easier to read. Click **Zoom to Page** ▣ to view the entire page.

6 To submit your file electronically, skip this step and move to Step 7. To print your document on paper using the default printer on your system, in the upper left portion of the screen, click **Print**.

The document will print on your default printer; if you do not have a color printer, colors will print in shades of gray. Backstage view closes and your file redisplays in the Word window.

7 To create an electronic printout, on the left, click **Export**. On the right, click **Create PDF/XPS**. In the **Publish as PDF or XPS** dialog box, navigate to your **Word Chapter 1** folder, and then click **Publish**. If your Adobe Acrobat or Adobe Reader program displays your PDF, in the upper right corner, click **Close** ☒.

8 **Save** 🖫 your document. In the upper right corner of the Word window, click **Close** ☒. If directed by your instructor to do so, submit your paper or electronic printout or your Word file.

END | You have completed Project 1A

GO! with Office Online (formerly Web Apps)

Objective | Create a Flyer in Word Online

Build from Scratch

A L E R T ! **Working with Web-Based Applications and Services**

Computer programs and services on the web receive continuous updates and improvements, so the steps to complete this web-based activity may differ from the ones shown. You can often look at the screens and the information presented to determine how to complete the activity.

Activity | Creating a Flyer in Word Online

In this activity, you will use Word Online to create a flyer similar to the one you created in Project 1A.

1 From the desktop, start Internet Explorer. Navigate to **http://onedrive.com**, and then sign in to your Microsoft account. Open your **GO! Web Projects** folder—or create and then open this folder if necessary.

2 On the OneDrive menu bar, click **Create**, and then click **Word document**. In the middle of the blue, Word Online title bar, click the text **Document1** so that it is selected. Using your own last and first name, type **Lastname_Firstname_WD_1A_Web** and then press [Enter] to change the file name.

3 Click anywhere in the document. Type **Sturgeon Point Productions** and then press [Enter].

4 Type the following four lines of text, pressing [Enter] after each line *except* for the last line:

Internships Available for a Costa Rica
Native Birds Documentary
Interviews on Friday, January 14
Filming Begins the First Week of July

5 By using your [I] pointer, drag to select the first line in the document. On the **HOME tab**, in the **Font group**, click the **Font Size button arrow**, and then click **36**. Click the **Font Color button arrow**, and then in the fourth column, click the first color—**Blue Gray, Text 2**. In the **Paragraph group**, click **Center**.

In Word Online, you must drag to select text—triple-clicking a line will not select the line, nor will moving the pointer into the left margin and clicking. You can, however, double-click to select a single word.

6 Select the remaining text in the document, and then on the **HOME tab** in the **Font group**, click **Bold**. Click the **Font Size button arrow**, and then click **24**. In the **Paragraph group**, click **Center**. Compare your screen with Figure A.

FIGURE A

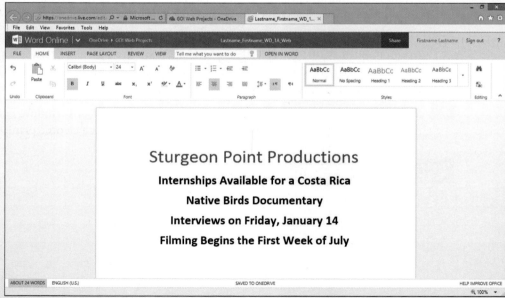

(GO! with Office Online (formerly Web Apps) continues on the next page)

7 Click at the end of the line *Interviews on Friday, January 14*, and then press Enter to insert a blank line.

8 On the **INSERT tab**, in the **Pictures group**, click **Picture**. Navigate to the location where your student data files are stored, and then click **w01A_Bird**. Click **Open**. Notice that the picture is dimmed, indicating that it is selected.

9 Under **PICTURE TOOLS**, click the **FORMAT tab**, and then in the **Image Size group**, click **Shrink** several times until the **Scale** box displays **40.48%**. If the box does not display this exact number, select the number in the **Scale** box, type **40.48%** and then press Enter.

10 With the picture still selected, on the **FORMAT tab**, in the **Picture Styles group**, click the sixth style—**Soft Edge Rectangle**.

11 Click anywhere in a blank area of the document so that the picture is not selected, and then compare your screen with Figure B.

12 Submit your file as directed by your instructor. If you are instructed to submit an electronic printout of your file, create a PDF as indicated in the Note box that follows. Sign out of your OneDrive and close Internet Explorer.

NOTE | **Creating a PDF from Word Online**

Click the FILE tab, click Save As, and then click Download as PDF. In the Microsoft Word Online message box, click Click here to view the PDF of your document. In the message bar at the bottom of your screen, click the Save arrow, and then click Save as. In the Save As dialog box, navigate to your Word Chapter 1 folder, and then save the file.

FIGURE B

PROJECT ACTIVITIES

In Activities 1.17 through 1.29, you will format an information handout from Sturgeon Point Productions that describes internships available to students. Your completed document will look similar to Figure 1.25.

PROJECT FILES

For Project 1B, you will need the following files:

w01B_Programs
w01B_Web

You will save your document as:

Lastname_Firstname_1B_Programs

PROJECT RESULTS

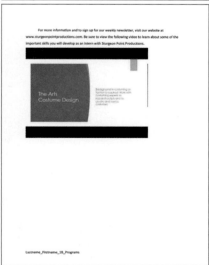

FIGURE 1.25 Project 1B Information Handout

Video W1-5

Document layout includes *margins*—the space between the text and the top, bottom, left, and right edges of the paper. Paragraph layout includes line spacing, indents, and tabs. In Word, the information about paragraph formats is stored in the paragraph mark at the end of a paragraph. When you press Enter, the new paragraph mark contains the formatting of the previous paragraph, unless you take steps to change it.

Activity 1.17 | Setting Margins

1 Start Word, and then click **Open Other Documents**. Navigate to the student files that accompany this textbook, and then open the document **w01B_Programs**. On the **HOME tab**, in the **Paragraph group**, be sure **Show/Hide** ¶ is active so that you can view the formatting marks.

2 Click the **FILE tab**, and then click **Save As**. Navigate to your **Word Chapter 1** folder, and then using your own name, **Save** the document as **Lastname_Firstname_1B_Programs**

3 Click the **PAGE LAYOUT tab**. In the **Page Setup group**, click **Margins**, and then take a moment to study the settings in the Margins gallery.

> If you have recently used custom margins settings, they will display at the top of this gallery. Other commonly used settings also display.

4 At the bottom of the **Margins** gallery, click the command followed by an ellipsis—**Custom Margins** to display the **Page Setup** dialog box.

5 In the **Page Setup** dialog box, under **Margins**, press Tab as necessary to select the value in the **Left** box, and then, with *1.25"* selected, type **1**

> This action will change the left margin to 1 inch on all pages of the document. You do not need to type the inch (") mark.

6 Press Tab to select the margin in the **Right** box, and then type **1** At the bottom of the dialog box, notice that the new margins will apply to the **Whole document**. Compare your screen with Figure 1.26.

FIGURE 1.26

Margins button

Left and Right margins changed

Margins will be applied to entire document

7 ▶ Click **OK** to apply the new margins and close the dialog box. If the ruler below the ribbon is not displayed, on the **VIEW** tab, in the **Show group**, select the **Ruler** check box.

8 ▶ Scroll to position the bottom of **Page 1** and the top of **Page 2** on your screen. Notice that the page edges display, and the page number and total number of pages display on the left side of the status bar.

9 ▶ Near the bottom edge of **Page 1**, point anywhere in the bottom margin area, right-click, and then click **Edit Footer** to display the footer area.

10 ▶ On the ribbon, under the **HEADER & FOOTER TOOLS**, on the **DESIGN tab**, in the **Insert group**, click **Document Info**, and then click **File Name**.

11 ▶ Double-click anywhere in the document to close the footer area, and then **Save** 🖫 your document.

Activity 1.18 | Aligning Text

Alignment refers to the placement of paragraph text relative to the left and right margins. Most paragraph text uses *left alignment*—aligned at the left margin, leaving the right margin uneven. Three other types of paragraph alignment are: *center alignment*—centered between the left and right margins; *right alignment*—aligned at the right margin with an uneven left margin; and *justified alignment*—text aligned evenly at both the left and right margins. The table in Figure 1.27 shows examples of these alignment types.

FIGURE 1.27

TYPES OF PARAGRAPH ALIGNMENT		
ALIGNMENT	**BUTTON**	**DESCRIPTION AND EXAMPLE**
Align Left	📄	Align Left is the default paragraph alignment in Word. Text in the paragraph aligns at the left margin, and the right margin is uneven.
Center	📄	Center alignment aligns text in the paragraph so that it is centered between the left and right margins.
Align Right	📄	Align Right aligns text at the right margin. Using Align Right, the left margin, which is normally even, is uneven.
Justify	📄	The Justify alignment option adds additional space between words so that both the left and right margins are even. Justify is often used when formatting newspaper-style columns.

1 ▶ Scroll to position the middle of **Page 2** on your screen, look at the left and right margins, and notice that the text is justified—both the right and left margins of multiple-line paragraphs are aligned evenly at the margins. On the **HOME tab**, in the **Paragraph group**, notice that **Justify** 📄 is active.

To achieve a justified right margin, Word adjusts the size of spaces between words, which can result in unattractive spacing in a document that spans the width of a page. Many individuals find such spacing difficult to read.

2 ▶ Press Ctrl + A to select all of the text in the document, and then on the **HOME tab**, in the **Paragraph group**, click **Align Left** 📄.

🔄 ANOTHER WAY   On the HOME tab, in the Editing group, click Select, and then click Select All.

3 Press `Ctrl` + `Home` to move to the beginning of the document. In the left margin area, point to the left of the first paragraph—*Sturgeon Point Productions*—until the pointer displays, and then click one time to select the paragraph.

Use this technique to select entire lines of text.

4 On the mini toolbar, in the **Font Size** box, select the existing number, type **40** and then press `Enter`.

Use this technique to change the font size to a size that is not available on the Font Size list.

5 Select the second paragraph—*Internship Guide*—and then on the mini toolbar, change the **Font Size** to **26 pt**. Point to the left of the first paragraph—*Sturgeon Point Productions*—to display the pointer again, and then drag down to select the first two paragraphs, which form the title and subtitle of the document.

6 On the **HOME tab**, in the **Paragraph group**, click **Center** to center the title and subtitle between the left and right margins, and then compare your screen with Figure 1.28.

FIGURE 1.28

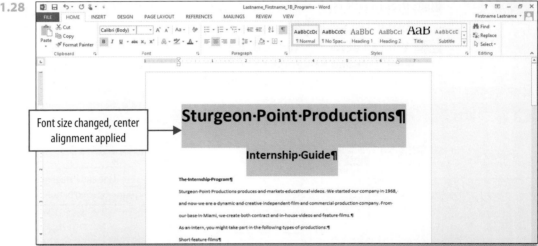

Font size changed, center alignment applied

7 Near the top of **Page 1**, locate the first bold subheading—*The Internship Program*. Point to the left of the paragraph to display the pointer, and then click one time to select this text.

8 With *The Internship Program* selected, use your mouse wheel or the vertical scroll bar to bring the bottom portion of **Page 1** into view. Locate the subheading *Requirements*. Move the pointer to the left of the paragraph to display the pointer, hold down `Ctrl`, and then click one time. Scroll to the middle of **Page 2**, and then use the same technique to select the third subheading—*Introduction to Upcoming Internships*.

Three subheadings are selected; in Windows-based programs, you can hold down `Ctrl` to select multiple items.

9 Click **Center** to center all three subheadings, and then click **Save**.

Activity 1.19 | Changing Line Spacing

Line spacing is the distance between lines of text in a paragraph. Three of the most commonly used line spacing options are shown in the table in Figure 1.29.

FIGURE 1.29

LINE SPACING OPTIONS	
ALIGNMENT	**DESCRIPTION, EXAMPLE, AND INFORMATION**
Single spacing	**This text in this example uses single spacing**. Single spacing was once the most commonly used spacing in business documents. Now, because so many documents are read on a computer screen rather than on paper, single spacing is becoming less popular.
Multiple 1.08 spacing	**This text in this example uses multiple 1.08 spacing**. The default line spacing in Microsoft Word 2013 is 1.08, which is slightly more than single spacing to make the text easier to read on a computer screen. Many individuals now prefer this spacing, even on paper, because the lines of text appear less crowded.
Double spacing	**This text in this example uses double spacing**. College research papers and draft documents that need space for notes are commonly double-spaced; there is space for a full line of text between each document line.

1 Press Ctrl + Home to move to the beginning of the document. Press Ctrl + A to select all of the text in the document.

2 With all of the text in the document selected, on the **HOME tab**, in the **Paragraph group**, click **Line and Paragraph Spacing** [icon], and notice that the text in the document is double spaced—**2.0** is checked. Compare your screen with Figure 1.30.

↻ BY TOUCH   Tap the ribbon commands.

FIGURE 1.30

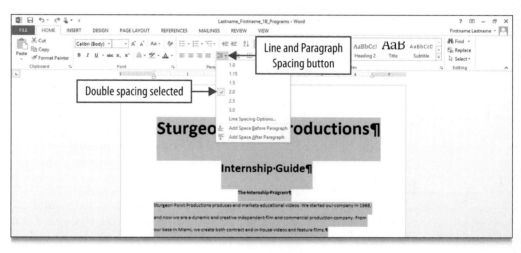

3 On the **Line Spacing** menu, click the *third* setting—**1.5**—and then click anywhere in the document to deselect the text. Compare your screen with Figure 1.31, and then **Save** [icon] your document.

FIGURE 1.31

Activity 1.20 | Indenting Text

Indenting the first line of each paragraph is a common technique to distinguish paragraphs.

1 Below the title and subtitle of the document, click anywhere in the paragraph that begins *Sturgeon Point Productions produces.*

2 On the **HOME tab**, in the **Paragraph group**, click the **Dialog Box Launcher** 🔲.

3 In the **Paragraph** dialog box, on the **Indents and Spacing tab**, under **Indentation**, click the **Special arrow**, and then click **First line** to indent the first line by 0.5", which is the default indent setting. Compare your screen with Figure 1.32.

FIGURE 1.32

4 Click **OK**, and then click anywhere in the next paragraph, which begins *As an intern.* On the ruler under the ribbon, drag the **First Line Indent** marker ▽ to **0.5 inches on the horizontal ruler**, and then compare your screen with Figure 1.33.

FIGURE 1.33

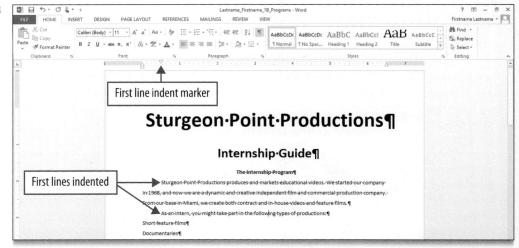

5 By using either of the techniques you just practiced, or by using the **Format Painter**, apply a first line indent of **0.5"** in the paragraph that begins *Here is a partial* to match the indent of the remaining paragraphs in the document.

6 Save 🔲 your document.

Activity 1.21 | Adding Space Before and After Paragraphs

Adding space after each paragraph is another technique to differentiate paragraphs.

 1 Press Ctrl + A to select all of the text in the document. Click the **PAGE LAYOUT tab**, and then in the **Paragraph group**, under **Spacing**, click the **After spin box up arrow** one time to change the value to **6 pt**.

> To change the value in the box, you can also select the existing number, type a new number, and then press Enter. This document will use 6 pt spacing after paragraphs to add space.

 On either the HOME tab or the PAGE LAYOUT tab, display the Paragraph dialog box from the Paragraph group, and then under Spacing, click the spin box arrows as necessary.

2 Press Ctrl + Home, and then compare your screen with Figure 1.34.

FIGURE 1.34

Spacing After set to 6 pt

Sturgeon·Point·Productions¶

Internship·Guide¶

The·Internship·Program¶

Sturgeon·Point·Productions·produces·and·markets·educational·videos.·We·started·our·company·

3 Near the top of **Page 1**, select the subheading *The Internship Program*, including the paragraph mark following it, scroll down, hold down Ctrl, and then select the subheadings *Requirements* and *Introduction to Upcoming Internships*.

4 With all three subheadings selected, in the **Paragraph group**, under **Spacing**, click the **Before up spin box arrow** two times to set the **Spacing Before** to **12 pt**. Compare your screen with Figure 1.35, and then **Save** your document.

> This action increases the amount of space above each of the subheadings, which will make them easy to distinguish in the document. The formatting is applied only to the selected paragraphs.

FIGURE 1.35

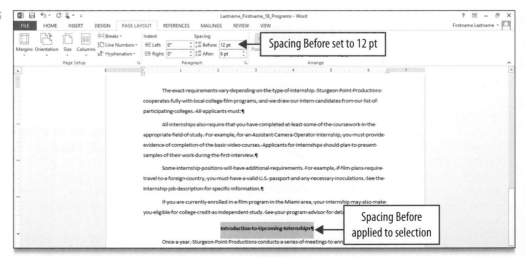

Spacing Before set to 12 pt

The·exact·requirements·vary·depending·on·the·type·of·internship.·Sturgeon·Point·Productions· cooperates·fully·with·local·college·film·programs,·and·we·draw·our·intern·candidates·from·our·list·of· participating·colleges.·All·applicants·must:¶

All·internships·also·require·that·you·have·completed·at·least·some·of·the·coursework·in·the· appropriate·field·of·study.·For·example,·for·an·Assistant·Camera·Operator·internship,·you·must·provide· evidence·of·completion·of·the·basic·video·courses.·Applicants·for·internships·should·plan·to·present· samples·of·their·work·during·the·first·interview.¶

Some·internship·positions·will·have·additional·requirements.·For·example,·if·film·plans·require· travel·to·a·foreign·country,·you·must·have·a·valid·U.S.·passport·and·any·necessary·inoculations.·See·the· internship·job·description·for·specific·information.¶

If·you·are·currently·enrolled·in·a·film·program·in·the·Miami·area,·your·internship·may·also·make· you·eligible·for·college·credit·as·independent·study.·See·your·program·advisor·for·deta

Introduction·to·Upcoming·Internships¶

Spacing Before applied to selection

Once·a·year,·Sturgeon·Point·Productions·conducts·a·series·of·meetings·to·ann

Video W1-6

To display a list of information, you can choose a **bulleted list**, which uses **bullets**—text symbols such as small circles or check marks—to introduce each item in a list. You can also choose a **numbered list**, which uses consecutive numbers or letters to introduce each item in a list.

Use a bulleted list if the items in the list can be introduced in any order; use a numbered list for items that have definite steps, a sequence of actions, or are in chronological order.

Activity 1.22 │ Creating a Bulleted List

1 In the upper portion of **Page 1**, locate the paragraph *Short feature films*, and then point to this paragraph from the left margin area to display the ⟋ pointer. Drag down to select this paragraph and the next five paragraphs.

2 On the **HOME tab**, in the **Paragraph group**, click **Bullets** ☷ ▾ to change the selected text to a bulleted list.

> The spacing between each of the bulleted points changes to the spacing between lines in a paragraph—in this instance, 1.5 line spacing. The 6 pt. spacing after each paragraph is eliminated with the exception of the last item in the list. Each bulleted item is automatically indented.

3 On the ruler, point to **First Line Indent** ▽ and read the ScreenTip, and then point to **Hanging Indent** ⌂. Compare your screen with Figure 1.36.

> By default, Word formats bulleted items with a first line indent of 0.25" and adds a Hanging Indent at 0.5". The hanging indent maintains the alignment of text when a bulleted item is more than one line.

> You can modify the list indentation by using Decrease Indent ⬅ or Increase Indent ➡. **Decrease Indent** moves your paragraph closer to the margin. **Increase Indent** moves your paragraph farther away from the margin.

FIGURE 1.36

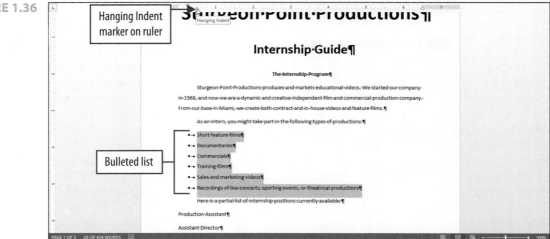

4 Scroll down slightly, and then by using the ⟋ pointer from the left margin area, select the five internship positions, beginning with *Production Assistant* and ending with *Assistant Set Designer*. In the **Paragraph group**, click **Bullets** ☷ ▾.

5 Scroll down to view **Page 2**. Apply bullets to all of the paragraphs that indicate the September meetings and meeting dates, beginning with *Technical* and ending with *Music*. **Save** 🖫 your document.

Activity 1.23 | Creating a Numbered List

1 Under the subheading *Requirements*, in the paragraph that begins *The exact requirements*, click to position the insertion point at the *end* of the paragraph, following the colon. Press [Enter] to create a blank paragraph. Notice that the paragraph is indented, because the First Line Indent from the previous paragraph carried over to the new paragraph.

2 To change the indent formatting for this paragraph, on the ruler, drag the **First Line Indent** marker ▽ to the left so that it is positioned directly above the lower button.

3 Being sure to include the period, type **1.** and press [Spacebar]. Compare your screen with Figure 1.37.

> Word determines that this paragraph is the first item in a numbered list and formats the new paragraph accordingly, indenting the list in the same manner as the bulleted list. The space after the number changes to a tab, and the AutoCorrect Options button displays to the left of the list item. The tab is indicated by a right arrow formatting mark.

FIGURE 1.37

ALERT!   **Activating Automatic Numbered Lists**

If a numbered list does not begin automatically, click the FILE tab, and then click the Options tab. On the left side of the Word Options dialog box, click Proofing. Under AutoCorrect options, click the AutoCorrect Options button. In the AutoCorrect dialog box, click the AutoFormat As You Type tab. Under *Apply as you type*, select the *Automatic numbered lists* check box, and then click OK two times to close both dialog boxes.

4 Click **AutoCorrect Options** 🛫▾, and then compare your screen with Figure 1.38.

> From the displayed list, you can remove the automatic formatting here, or stop using the automatic numbered lists option in this document. You also have the option to open the AutoCorrect dialog box to *Control AutoFormat Options*.

FIGURE 1.38

5 Click **AutoCorrect Options** 🛫▾ again to close the menu without selecting any of the commands. Type **Be enrolled in an accredited film program** and press [Enter]. Notice that the second number and a tab are added to the next line.

6 Type **Be available during the entire production schedule** and press Enter. Type **Submit two faculty recommendation letters** Compare your screen with Figure 1.39, and then **Save** 🖫 your document.

FIGURE 1.39

Numbered list

More Knowledge | **To End a List**

To turn a list off, you can press Backspace, click the Numbering or Bullets button, or press Enter two times. Both list buttons—Numbering and Bullets—act as **toggle buttons**; that is, clicking the button one time turns the feature on, and clicking the button again turns the feature off.

Activity 1.24 | Customizing Bullets

You can use any symbol from any font for your bullet characters.

1 Press Ctrl + End to move to the end of the document, and then scroll up as necessary to display the bulleted list containing the list of meetings.

2 Point to the left of the first list item to display the 🖈 pointer, and then drag down to select all six meetings in the list—the bullet symbols are not highlighted.

3 On the mini toolbar, click the **Bullets button arrow** ☰▾ to display the **Bullet Library**, and then compare your screen with Figure 1.40.

FIGURE 1.40

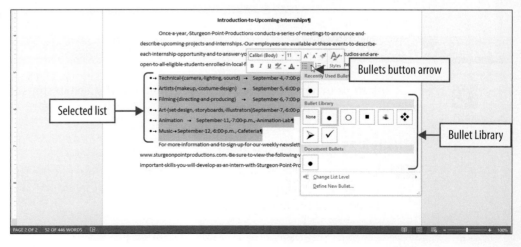

Selected list

Bullets button arrow

Bullet Library

ALERT! | **Did Your Bullet Symbols Disappear?**

If the bullet symbols no longer display, then you clicked the Bullets button. The Bullets button is a toggle button that turns the bullet symbols on and off. Click Undo to reapply the bullets, and then repeat Step 3, making sure that you click the Bullets button arrow.

4 Under **Bullet Library**, click the **check mark** symbol. If the check mark is not available, choose another bullet symbol.

5 With the bulleted list still selected, right-click over the list, and then on the mini toolbar, double-click **Format Painter** .

 ANOTHER WAY   On the HOME tab, in the Clipboard group, click Format Painter.

6 Use the vertical scroll bar or your mouse wheel to scroll to view **Page 1**. Move the pointer to the left of the first item in the first bulleted list to display the pointer, and then drag down to select all six items in the list and to apply the format of the third bulleted list—the check mark bullets—to this list. Repeat this procedure to change the bullets in the second list to check marks. Press Esc to turn off **Format Painter**, and then **Save** your document. Compare your screen with Figure 1.41.

FIGURE 1.41

Objective 7   Set and Modify Tab Stops

Tab stops mark specific locations on a line of text. Use tab stops to indent and align text, and use the Tab key to move to tab stops.

Video W1-7

Activity 1.25 | Setting Tab Stops

1 Scroll to view **Page 2**, and then by using the pointer at the left of the first item, select all of the items in the bulleted list of meetings and dates. Notice that there is a tab mark between the name of the meeting and the date.

The arrow that indicates a tab is a nonprinting formatting mark.

2 To the left of the horizontal ruler, point to **Tab Alignment** to display the *Left Tab* ScreenTip, and then compare your screen with Figure 1.42.

FIGURE 1.42

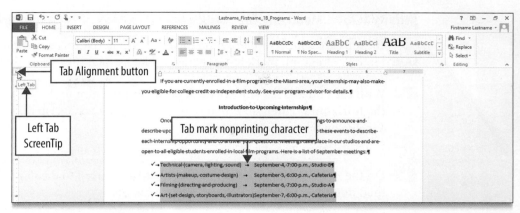

3 Click **Tab Alignment** ⬜ several times to view the tab alignment options shown in the table in Figure 1.43.

FIGURE 1.43

TAB ALIGNMENT OPTIONS		
TYPE	TAB ALIGNMENT BUTTON DISPLAYS THIS MARKER	RESULT OF TAB ALIGNMENT
Left	⬜	Text is left aligned at the tab stop and extends to the right.
Center	⬜	Text is centered around the tab stop.
Right	⬜	Text is right aligned at the tab stop and extends to the left.
Decimal	⬜	The decimal point aligns at the tab stop.
Bar	⬜	A vertical bar displays at the tab stop.
First Line Indent	▽	Text in the first line of a paragraph indents.
Hanging Indent	⬠	Text in all lines except the first line in the paragraph indents.

4 Display **Left Tab** ⬜. Along the lower edge of the horizontal ruler, point to and then click at **3.5 inches on the horizontal ruler**. Notice that all of the dates left align at the new tab stop location, and the right edge of the column is uneven.

5 Compare your screen with Figure 1.44, and then **Save** 🖫 your document.

FIGURE 1.44

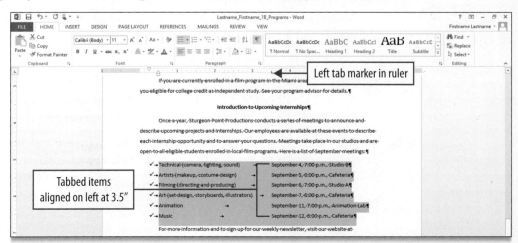

Activity 1.26 | Modifying Tab Stops

Tab stops are a form of paragraph formatting. Therefore, the information about tab stops is stored in the paragraph mark in the paragraphs to which they were applied.

1 With the bulleted list still selected, on the ruler, point to the new tab marker at **3.5 inches on the horizontal ruler**, and then when the *Left Tab* ScreenTip displays, drag the tab marker to **4 inches on the horizontal ruler**.

In all of the selected lines, the text at the tab stop left aligns at 4 inches.

2 On the ruler, point to the tab marker that you moved to display the *Left Tab* ScreenTip, and then double-click to display the **Tabs** dialog box.

 ANOTHER WAY   On the HOME tab, in the Paragraph group, click the Dialog Box Launcher. At the bottom of the Paragraph dialog box, click the Tabs button.

3 In the **Tabs** dialog box, under **Tab stop position**, if necessary, select *4″* and then type **6**

4 Under **Alignment**, click the **Right** option button. Under **Leader**, click the **2** option button. Near the bottom of the **Tabs** dialog box, click **Set**.

Because the Right tab will be used to align the items in the list, the tab stop at 4″ is no longer necessary.

5 In the **Tabs** dialog box, in the **Tab stop position** box, click **4″** to select this tab stop, and then in the lower portion of the **Tabs** dialog box, click the **Clear** button to delete this tab stop, which is no longer necessary. Compare your screen with Figure 1.45.

FIGURE 1.45

6 Click **OK**. On the ruler, notice that the left tab marker at *4″* no longer displays, a right tab marker displays at *6″*, and a series of dots—a ***dot leader***—displays between the columns of the list. Notice also that the right edge of the column is even. Compare your screen with Figure 1.46.

A ***leader character*** creates a solid, dotted, or dashed line that fills the space to the left of a tab character and draws the reader's eyes across the page from one item to the next. When the character used for the leader is a dot, it is commonly referred to as a dot leader.

FIGURE 1.46

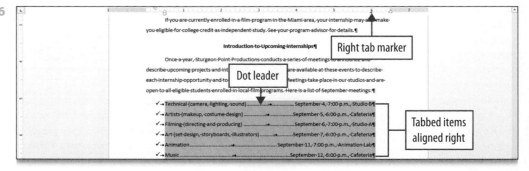

7 In the bulleted list that uses dot leaders, locate the *Art* meeting, and then click to position the insertion point at the end of that line, after the word *Cafeteria*. Press Enter to create a new blank bullet item.

8 Type **Video Editing** and press Tab. Notice that a dot leader fills the space to the tab marker location.

9 Type **September 10, 7:00 p.m., Cafeteria** and notice that the text moves to the left to maintain the right alignment of the tab stop.

10 Save 🖫 your document.

Objective 8 Insert a SmartArt Graphic and an Online Video

Video W1-8

SmartArt graphics are designer-quality visual representations of information, and Word provides many different layouts from which you can choose. You can also insert a link to an online video from a variety of online sources, thus enabling the reader to view the video when connected to the Internet. SmartArt graphics and videos can communicate your messages or ideas more effectively than plain text and these objects add visual interest to a document or webpage.

Activity 1.27 | Inserting a SmartArt Graphic

1 Press Ctrl + Home to move to the top of the document, and then click to the right of the subtitle *Internship Guide*.

2 Click the **INSERT tab**, and then in the **Illustrations group**, point to **SmartArt** to display its ScreenTip. Read the ScreenTip, and then click **SmartArt**.

3 In the center portion of the **Choose a SmartArt Graphic** dialog box, scroll down and examine the numerous types of SmartArt graphics available.

4 On the left, click **Process**, and then by using the ScreenTips, locate and click **Basic Chevron Process**. Compare your screen with Figure 1.47.

At the right of the dialog box, a preview and description of the SmartArt displays.

FIGURE 1.47

5 Click **OK** to insert the SmartArt graphic.

To the left of the inserted SmartArt graphic the text pane may display. The text pane provides one method for entering text into your SmartArt graphic. If you choose not to use the text pane to enter text, you can close it.

6 ▶ On the ribbon under **SMARTART TOOLS**, on the **DESIGN tab**, in the **Create Graphic group**, notice the **Text Pane** button. If the Text Pane button is selected, click **Text Pane** to close the pane.

7 ▶ In the SmartArt graphic, in the first blue arrow, click *[Text]*, and notice that *[Text]* is replaced by a blinking insertion point.

> The word *[Text]* is called ***placeholder text***, which is non-printing text that indicates where you can type.

8 ▶ Type **Apply Online**

9 ▶ Click the placeholder text in the middle arrow. Type **Interview** and then click the placeholder text in the third arrow. Type **Train on the Job** and then compare your screen with Figure 1.48.

FIGURE 1.48

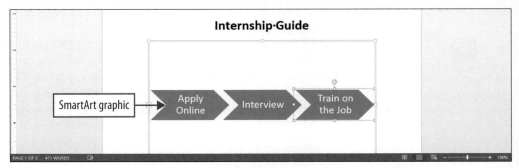

10 ▶ **Save** 🖫 your document.

Activity 1.28 | Sizing and Formatting a SmartArt Graphic

1 ▶ Click the SmartArt graphic border to select it. Be sure that none of the arrows have sizing handles around their border, which would indicate the arrow was selected, not the entire graphic.

2 ▶ Click the **FORMAT tab**, and then in the **Size group**, if necessary, click **Size** to display the **Shape Height** and **Shape Width** boxes.

3 ▶ Set the **Height** to **1.75"** and the **Width** to **6.5"**, and then compare your screen with Figure 1.49.

FIGURE 1.49

4 With the SmartArt graphic still selected, click the **SMARTART TOOLS DESIGN tab**, and then in the **SmartArt Styles group**, click **Change Colors**. Under **Colorful**, click the fourth style— **Colorful Range–Accent Colors 4 to 5**.

5 On the **SMARTART TOOLS DESIGN tab**, in the **SmartArt Styles group**, click **More** ⊟. Under **3-D**, click the second style—**Inset**. Click **Save** 🖫, and then compare your screen with Figure 1.50.

FIGURE 1.50

Activity 1.29 | Inserting an Online Video

> **NOTE** **This is an Optional Activity**
>
> To complete this activity, you must be signed into Office 2013 with your Microsoft Account. If you are using Office 2013 in a college classroom or lab, you may need to sign in with an organizational account. Once you are signed in, verify that YouTube is available by clicking **FILE**, and then on the left click **Account**. Under Connected Services, if YouTube does not display, click **Add a Service**, point to Images & Videos, and then click **YouTube**. If you cannot activate YouTube, skip Steps 1-6 and complete Project 1B.

Microsoft's research indicates that two-thirds of people who open Word documents never edit them; they only read them. So with more and more documents being read online—and not on paper—it makes sense that you may want to include videos in your Word documents.

1 Press Ctrl + End to move to the end of the document.

2 On the **INSERT tab**, in the **Media group**, click **Online Video**. If the YouTube search box does not display, in the lower left corner of the Insert Video window, under Also insert from: click YouTube.

Here you can search the web for an online video, search YouTube, or enter an ***embed code*** to insert a link to a video from a website. An embed code is a code that creates a link to a video, picture, or other type of ***rich media*** content. Rich media, also called ***interactive media***, refers to computer interaction that responds to your actions; for example by presenting text, graphics, animation, video, audio, or games.

3 In the **Search YouTube** box, being sure to include the quotation marks, type **"Go 2013 1B Video"** and then press Enter.

4 Point to the displayed thumbnail and notice the ScreenTip. Click the **1B video**, and then click **Insert**. Compare your screen with Figure 1.51.

FIGURE 1.51

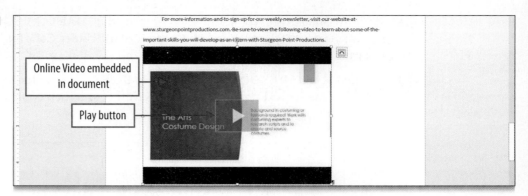

5 In the center of the video, point to the **Play** button ▶ to display the 👆 pointer, and then click. If a black screen displays, double-click one or more times until you see text on the screen, then point to the lower edge of the screen and click the Play button.

> A new window opens that contains the video and a play button. You can click the play button to view the video. When you insert an online video, the embed code is stored with the document and a link is created to the online content. In this manner, you can easily share video content that is relevant to the document without increasing the file size of the document.

6 View a few seconds of the video—more if you want—and then press Esc to return to your document.

7 Click **Save** 🖫 , and then press Ctrl + Home to move to the top of your document.

8 Click the **FILE tab**, and then in the lower right portion of the screen, click **Show All Properties**. In the **Tags** box, type **internship** and in the **Subject** box, type your course name and section number. In the **Author** box, be sure your name displays; edit if necessary.

9 On the left, click **Print** to display **Print Preview**. At the bottom of the preview, click the **Previous Page** ◀ and **Next Page** ▶ buttons to move between pages. If necessary, return to the document and make any necessary changes.

10 As directed by your instructor, print your document or submit it electronically. **Save** 🖫 your document and **Close** ✕ Word.

END | You have completed Project 1B

Objective | Create a Handout in Word Online

You can use Word Online to edit your document if you are not at a computer on which Word 2013 is installed. You can change fonts and font sizes, modify paragraph alignment, and apply bullets and numbering.

ALERT! | **Working with Web-Based Applications and Services**

Computer programs and services on the web receive continuous updates and improvements, so the steps to complete this web-based activity may differ from the ones shown. You can often look at the screens and the information presented to determine how to complete the activity.

Activity | Creating a Handout in Word Online

In this activity, you will use Word Online to edit a flyer similar to the one you edited in Project 1B.

1 Start Word, and then below the **Recent** list, click **Open Other Documents**. Navigate to your student data files, and then open **w01_1B_Web**. If necessary, in the upper right corner, log into Office with your Microsoft account. On the **FILE tab**, click **Save As**, and then on the right, double-click the name of your OneDrive.

2 In the **Save As** dialog box, click your **GO! Web Projects** folder, and then click **Open**. In the **File name** box, type **Lastname_Firstname_WD_1B_Web** and then click **Save**.

3 Close Word, launch **Internet Explorer**, go to http://onedrive.com, sign in, open your **GO! Web Projects** folder, and then click the file you just saved there.

4 In the upper left, click **EDIT DOCUMENT**, and then click **Edit in Word Online**.

5 Press Ctrl + A to select all the text in the document. On the **HOME tab**, in the **Paragraph group**, click **Align Text Left**.

6 Drag to select the first three lines in the document. On the **HOME tab**, in the **Paragraph group**, click **Center**. Compare your screen with Figure A.

7 Click at the beginning of the paragraph that begins *Sturgeon Point Productions produces*, and then press Tab. Click at the beginning of the paragraph that begins *As an intern*, and then press Tab.

8 Scroll the document and click at the beginning of the paragraph that begins *Here is a partial*, and then press Tab.

FIGURE A

(GO! with Office Online (formerly Web Apps) continues on the next page)

9 Click anywhere in the subheading *Introduction to Upcoming Internships*, and then on the **HOME tab**, in the **Paragraph group**, click **Center** ☰. Click at the beginning of the paragraph that begins *Once a year*, and then press Tab.

10 Select the six paragraphs that begin with *Short feature films* and that end with *Recordings of live concerts*. On the **HOME tab**, in the **Paragraph group**, click **Bullets** ☷ ▾ to apply round, filled bullets to the selection.

11 Select the list that begins with *Production Assistant* and ends with *Assistant Set Designer*, and then click **Bullets** ☷ ▾ to apply bullets to the selection.

12 Select the first list to which you applied bullets. On the **HOME tab**, in the **Paragraph group**, click the **Bullets button arrow**, and then click **Square Bullet**. Notice that the same bullet style is applied to the second list.

13 Scroll the document and then select the list that begins with *Artists* and ends with *Music*. On the **HOME tab**, in the **Paragraph group**, click **Numbering** ☷ ▾ to apply numbers to the list.

14 Press Ctrl + A to select the entire document. On the **HOME tab**, in the **Paragraph group**, click **Line Spacing** ☷ ▾, and then click **1.5** to change the line spacing for the entire document. Press Ctrl + Home to move to the top of the document and then compare your screen with Figure B.

15 Submit your file as directed by your instructor. Sign out of your OneDrive and close Internet Explorer.

FIGURE B

GO! with Microsoft Office 365

Andrew Rodriguez / Fotolia; FotolEdhar/ Fotolia; apops/ Fotolia; Yuri Arcurs/ Fotolia

In every job, you must work and communicate with other people. A group of workers tasked with working together to solve a problem, make a decision, or create a work product is referred to as a **team**. For a team to succeed, the team members must be able to communicate with one another easily.

If all the team members work at the same location and work the same hours, communication is easy. You schedule face-to-face meetings and exchange documents and information among yourselves. But that is a rare arrangement in today's organizations. Rather, it is more likely that the members of your team work in different locations—even different countries— and work different hours or travel extensively away from the headquarters location. Also, for specific projects, teams are frequently organized across different departments of an organization or even across different organizations entirely. Then when the project is complete, the team disbands.

Collaboration is when you work together with others as a team in an intellectual endeavor to complete a shared task or achieve a shared goal; for example, when you and one or more of your classmates work together on a class project. Collaboration involves giving feedback to and receiving feedback from others on the team, and then revising the strategies to achieve the goal or produce the work product based on the feedback.

Microsoft Office 365 is a set of secure online services that enable people in an organization to communicate and collaborate by using any Internet-connected device—a computer, a tablet, or a mobile phone. Because Office 365 offers access from anywhere to email, Web conferencing, documents, and calendars, everyone on a team can work together easily. Office 365 is intended for use by multiple users in an organization.

Activity | **Using the Exchange Online Outlook Meeting Tool to Collaborate**

This group project relates to the **Bell Orchid Hotels**. If your instructor assigns this project to your class, you can expect to use the **Outlook Meeting tool** in **Office 365 Exchange Online** to collaborate on the following tasks for this chapter:

- If you are in the **Accounting Group**, you and your teammates will meet virtually to compose, format, proofread, and prepare a letter to send to shareholders.

- If you are in the **Engineering Group**, you and your teammates will meet virtually to compose, format, proofread, and prepare a letter to the three insurance companies that cover the hotel properties.

- If you are in the **Food and Beverage Group**, you and your teammates will meet virtually to compose, format, proofread, and finalize a letter to a customer planning a banquet.

- If you are in the **Human Resources Group**, you and your teammates will meet virtually to compose, format, proofread, and finalize a memo for employees regarding the new employee newsletter.

- If you are in the **Operations Group**, you and your teammates will meet virtually to compose, format, proofread, and finalize letters to three job applicants.

- If you are in the **Sales and Marketing Group**, you and your teammates will meet virtually to compose, edit, and finalize a letter to 20 groups of professional associations.

FIGURE A

END OF CHAPTER

SUMMARY

In a document, you can type all of the text, or you can type some of the text and then insert additional text from another source such as another Word document. As you type, word wrap determines the line endings.

Graphics include pictures, shapes, and text boxes. Use graphics, text effects, and pictures to add visual appeal. When you insert pictures, Word provides many ways to position and format the pictures on the page.

SmartArt graphics visually represent your ideas and there are many SmartArt graphics from which to choose. You can also use online videos in your documents to provide visual information to the reader.

Word documents can be formatted to display your information attractively. You can add a page border, add bulleted and numbered lists, change margins and tabs, and modify paragraph and line spacing.

GO! LEARN IT ONLINE

Review the concepts and key terms in this chapter by completing these online challenges, which you can find at **www.pearsonhighered.com/go.**

Matching and Multiple Choice:
Answer matching and multiple choice questions to test what you learned in this chapter. MyITLab®

Crossword Puzzle:
Spell out the words that match the numbered clues, and put them in the puzzle squares.

Flipboard:
Flip through the definitions of the key terms in this chapter and match them with the correct term.

GO! FOR JOB SUCCESS

Video: Personal Branding

Your instructor may assign this video to your class, and then ask you to think about, or discuss with your classmates, these questions:

FotolEdhar / Fotolia

How do you suggest job seekers communicate their unique value—their *personal brand*—to potential employers online?

What are the best ways to network online and offline?

What are some of the biggest pitfalls in using social media to communicate a personal brand?

END OF CHAPTER

REVIEW AND ASSESSMENT GUIDE FOR WORD CHAPTER 1

Your instructor may assign one or more of these projects to help you review the chapter and assess your mastery and understanding of the chapter.

	Review and Assessment Guide for Word Chapter 1		
Project	**Apply Skills from These Chapter Objectives**	**Project Type**	**Project Location**
1C	Objectives 1-4 from Project 1A	**1C Skills Review** A guided review of the skills from Project 1A.	On the following pages
1D	Objectives 5-8 from Project 1B	**1D Skills Review** A guided review of the skills from Project 1B.	On the following pages
1E	Objectives 1-4 from Project 1A	**1E Mastery (Grader Project)** A demonstration of your mastery of the skills in Project 1A with extensive decision making.	In MyITLab and on the following pages
1F	Objectives 5-8 from Project 1B	**1F Mastery (Grader Project)** A demonstration of your mastery of the skills in Project 1B with extensive decision making.	In MyITLab and on the following pages
1G	Objectives 1-8 from Projects 1A and 1B	**1G Mastery (Grader Project)** A demonstration of your mastery of the skills in Projects 1A and 1B with extensive decision making.	In MyITLab and on the following pages
1H	Combination of Objectives from Projects 1A and 1B	**1H GO! Fix It** A demonstration of your mastery of the skills in Projects 1A and 1B by creating a correct result from a document that contains errors you must find.	Online
1I	Combination of Objectives from Projects 1A and 1B	**1I GO! Make It** A demonstration of your mastery of the skills in Projects 1A and 1B by creating a result from a supplied picture.	Online
1J	Combination of Objectives from Projects 1A and 1B	**1J GO! Solve It** A demonstration of your mastery of the skills in Projects 1A and 1B, your decision-making skills, and your critical thinking skills. A task-specific rubric helps you self-assess your result.	Online
1K	Combination of Objectives from Projects 1A and 1B	**1K GO! Solve It** A demonstration of your mastery of the skills in Projects 1A and 1B, your decision-making skills, and your critical thinking skills. A task-specific rubric helps you self-assess your result.	On the following pages
1L	Combination of Objectives from Projects 1A and 1B	**1L GO! Think** A demonstration of your understanding of the chapter concepts applied in a manner that you would outside of college. An analytic rubric helps you and your instructor grade the quality of your work by comparing it to the work an expert in the discipline would create.	On the following pages
1M	Combination of Objectives from Projects 1A and 1B	**1M GO! Think** A demonstration of your understanding of the chapter concepts applied in a manner that you would outside of college. An analytic rubric helps you and your instructor grade the quality of your work by comparing it to the work an expert in the discipline would create.	Online
1N	Combination of Objectives from Projects 1A and 1B	**1N You and GO!** A demonstration of your understanding of the chapter concepts applied in a manner that you would in a personal situation. An analytic rubric helps you and your instructor grade the quality of your work.	Online
1O	Combination of Objectives from Projects 1A and 1B	**1O Cumulative Group Project for Word Chapter 1** A demonstration of your understanding of concepts and your ability to work collaboratively in a group role-playing assessment, requiring both collaboration and self-management.	Online

GLOSSARY

GLOSSARY OF CHAPTER KEY TERMS

Alignment The placement of paragraph text relative to the left and right margins.

Alignment guide Green vertical or horizontal lines that display when you are moving or sizing an object to assist you with object placement.

Artistic effects Formats applied to images that make pictures resemble sketches or paintings.

Bulleted list A list of items with each item introduced by a symbol such as a small circle or check mark, and which is useful when the items in the list can be displayed in any order.

Bullets Text symbols such as small circles or check marks that precede each item in a bulleted list.

Center alignment The alignment of text or objects that is centered horizontally between the left and right margin.

Collaboration The action of working together with others as a team in an intellectual endeavor to complete a shared task or achieve a shared goal.

Decrease Indent A command that moves your paragraph closer to the margin.

Dot leader A series of dots preceding a tab that guides the eye across the line.

Drawing objects Graphic objects, such as shapes, diagrams, lines, or circles.

Embed code A code that creates a link to a video, picture, or other type of rich media content.

Floating object A graphic that can be moved independently of the surrounding text characters.

Formatting marks Characters that display on the screen, but do not print, indicating where the Enter key, the Spacebar, and the Tab key were pressed; also called nonprinting characters.

Graphics Pictures, charts, or drawing objects.

Increase Indent A command moves your paragraph farther away from the margin.

Inline Object An object or graphic inserted in a document that acts like a character in a sentence.

Interactive media Computer interaction that responds to your actions; for example by presenting text, graphics, animation, video, audio, or games. Also referred to as rich media.

Justified alignment An arrangement of text in which the text aligns evenly on both the left and right margins.

Layout Options Picture formatting options that control the manner in which text wraps around a picture or other object.

Leader character Characters that form a solid, dotted, or dashed line that fills the space preceding a tab stop.

Left alignment An arrangement of text in which the text aligns at the left margin, leaving the right margin uneven.

Line spacing The distance between lines of text in a paragraph.

Live Layout A feature that reflows text as you move or size an object so that you can view the placement of surrounding text.

Margins The space between the text and the top, bottom, left, and right edges of the paper.

Microsoft Office 365 A set of secure online services that enable people in an organization to communicate and collaborate by using any Internet-connected device—a computer, a tablet, or a mobile phone.

Nonprinting characters Characters that display on the screen, but do not print; also called formatting marks.

Numbered list A list that uses consecutive numbers or letters to introduce each item in a list.

Object anchor The symbol that indicates to which paragraph an object is attached.

Picture Effects Formatting that enhances a picture with effects such as shadow, glow, reflection, or 3-D rotation.

Picture styles Frames, shapes, shadows, borders, and other special effects that can be added to an image to create an overall visual style for the image.

Placeholder text Non-printing text that holds a place in a document where you can type.

Rich media Computer interaction that responds to your actions; for example by presenting text, graphics, animation, video, audio, or games. Also referred to as interactive media.

Right alignment An arrangement of text in which the text aligns at the right margin, leaving the left margin uneven.

Rotation handle A symbol with which you can rotate a graphic to any angle; displays above the top center sizing handle.

Shapes Lines, arrows, stars, banners, ovals, rectangles, and other basic shapes with which you can illustrate an idea, a process, or a workflow.

SmartArt A designer-quality visual representation of your information that you can create by choosing from among many different layouts to effectively communicate your message or ideas.

Spin box A small box with an upward- and downward-pointing arrow that lets you move rapidly through a set of values by clicking.

Tab stop A specific location on a line of text, marked on the Word ruler, to which you can move the insertion point by pressing the Tab key, and which is used to align and indent text.

Team A group of workers tasked with working together to solve a problem, make a decision, or create a work product.

Template A preformatted document that you can use as a starting point and then change to suit your needs.

Text box A movable resizable container for text or graphics.

Text effects Decorative formats, such as shadowed or mirrored text, text glow, 3-D effects, and colors that make text stand out.

Text wrapping The manner in which text displays around an object.

Toggle button A button that can be turned on by clicking it once, and then turned off by clicking it again.

Wordwrap The feature that moves text from the right edge of a paragraph to the beginning of the next line as necessary to fit within the margins.

CHAPTER REVIEW

Apply 1A skills from these Objectives:

1 Create a New Document and Insert Text

2 Insert and Format Graphics

3 Insert and Modify Text Boxes and Shapes

4 Preview and Print a Document

Build from Scratch

In the following Skills Review, you will create a flyer announcing a photography internship with Sturgeon Point Productions. Your completed document will look similar to Figure 1.52.

PROJECT FILES

For Project 1C, you will need the following files:

New blank Word document

w01C_Building

w01C_Photographer

You will save your document as:

Lastname_Firstname_1C_Photography

PROJECT RESULTS

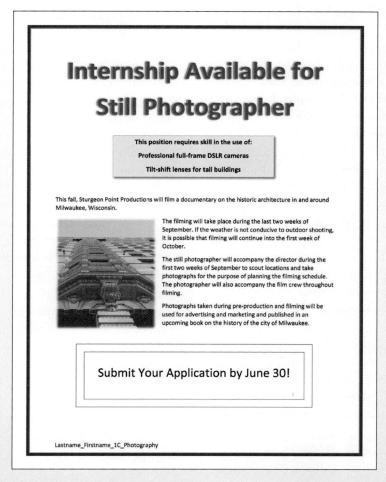

FIGURE 1.52

(Project 1C Photography continues on the next page)

CHAPTER REVIEW

1 Start Word and then click **Blank document**. On the **HOME tab**, in the **Paragraph group**, if necessary, click **Show/Hide** to display the formatting marks. If the rulers do not display, click the **VIEW tab**, and then in the **Show group**, select the **Ruler** check box.

a. Type **Internship Available for Still Photographer** and then press Enter two times. Type the following text: **This fall, Sturgeon Point Productions will film a documentary on the historic architecture in and around Milwaukee, Wisconsin.** Press Enter.

b. On the ribbon, click the **INSERT tab**. In the **Text group**, click the **Object button arrow**, and then click **Text from File**. In the **Insert File** dialog box, navigate to the student files that accompany this textbook, locate and select **w01C_Photographer**, and then click **Insert**. Delete the blank paragraph at the end of the document.

c. Including the paragraph mark, select the first paragraph of text—*Internship Available for Still Photographer*. On the **HOME tab**, in the **Font group**, click **Text Effects and Typography**. In the **Text Effects** gallery, in the first row, click the fourth effect—**Fill – White, Outline – Accent 1, Shadow**.

d. With the text still selected, in the **Font group**, click in the **Font Size** box to select the existing font size. Type **44** and then press Enter. In the **Font group**, click the **Font Color button arrow**. Under **Theme Colors**, in the fourth column, click the first color—**Blue-Gray, Text 2**.

e. With the text still selected, in the **Font group**, click **Text Effects and Typography**. Point to **Shadow**, and then under **Outer**, in the second row, click the third style—**Offset Left**. In the **Paragraph group**, click **Center**.

f. On the **Quick Access Toolbar**, click **Save**. Under **Places**, click **Computer**, and then click **Browse**. Navigate to your **Word Chapter 1** folder. In the **File name** box, replace the existing text with **Lastname_Firstname_1C_Photography** and then click **Save**.

2 In the paragraph that begins *The filming*, click to position the insertion point at the beginning of the paragraph. On the **INSERT tab**, in the **Illustrations group**, click **Pictures**. In the **Insert Picture** dialog box, navigate to your student data files, locate and click **w01C_Building**, and then click **Insert**.

a. To the right of the selected picture, click the **Layout Options** button, and then under **With Text Wrapping**, click the first option—**Square**. **Close** the **Layout Options**.

b. On the **FORMAT tab**, in the **Size group**, click the **Shape Height spin box down arrow** as necessary to change the height of the picture to **2.7"**.

c. With the picture selected, on the **FORMAT tab**, in the **Arrange group**, click **Position**, and then click **More Layout Options**. In the **Layout** dialog box, on the **Position tab**, in the middle of the dialog box, under **Vertical**, click the **Alignment** option button. To the right of **Alignment**, click the arrow, and then click **Top**. To the right of **relative to**, click the arrow, and then click **Line**. Click **OK**.

d. On the **FORMAT tab**, in the **Picture Styles group**, click **Picture Effects**. Point to **Soft Edges**, and then click **5 Point**. On the **FORMAT tab**, in the **Adjust group**, click **Artistic Effects**. In the fourth row, click the third effect—**Crisscross Etching**.

e. Click anywhere outside the picture to deselect it. On the **DESIGN tab**, in the **Page Background group**, click **Page Borders**. In the **Borders and Shading** dialog box, on the **Page Border tab**, under **Setting**, click **Box**. Under **Style**, scroll the list and then click the third style from the bottom—a black line that fades to gray.

f. Click the **Color arrow**, and then in the next to last column, click the first color—**Blue, Accent 5**. Under **Apply to**, be sure **Whole document** is selected, and then click **OK**. Click **Save**.

3 Click the **INSERT tab**, and then in the **Illustrations group**, click **Shapes** to display the gallery. Under **Basic Shapes**, in the second row, click the fifth shape—**Frame**.

a. Position the ⊞ pointer anywhere in the blank area at the bottom of the document. Click one time to insert a 1" by 1" frame. The exact location need not be precise. To the right of the shape, click the **Layout Options** button, and at the bottom click **See more**.

b. In the **Layout** dialog box, under **Horizontal**, click the **Alignment** option button. To the right of **Alignment**, click the arrow, and then click **Centered**. To the right of **relative to**, click the arrow, and then click **Page**. Under **Vertical**, click the **Absolute position**

(Project 1C Photography continues on the next page)

CHAPTER REVIEW

option button. In the **Absolute position** box, select the existing number, and then type **1** To the right of **below**, click the arrow, and then click **Paragraph**. Click **OK**.

c. On the **FORMAT tab**, click in the **Shape Height** box. Type **1.5** and then click in the **Shape Width** box. Type **5.5** and then press Enter.

d. If necessary, select the frame shape. On the **FORMAT tab**, in the **Shape Styles group**, click **More**. In the **Shape Styles** gallery, in the first row, click the sixth style—**Colored Outline - Blue, Accent 5**. Type **Submit Your Application by June 30!** Select the text you just typed, and then on the mini toolbar, change the **Font Size** to **22**.

4 Click outside of the frame to deselect, and then press Ctrl + Home to move to the top of the document. Press ↓ two times to move to the blank paragraph below the title. Press Enter four times to make space for a text box.

a. On the **INSERT tab**, in the **Text group**, click **Text Box**. At the bottom of the gallery, click **Draw Text Box**. Position the + pointer over the first blank paragraph at the left margin. Drag down and to the right to create a text box approximately 1.5 inches high and 4 inches wide—the exact size and location need not be precise.

b. With the insertion point blinking in the text box, type the following, pressing Enter after the first two lines to create a new paragraph; do *not* press Enter after the last line:

This position requires skill in the use of:

Professional full-frame DSLR cameras

Tilt-shift lenses for tall buildings

c. To precisely place the text box, on the **FORMAT tab**, in the **Arrange group**, click **Position**, and then click **More Layout Options**. In the **Layout** dialog box, under **Horizontal**, click the **Alignment** button. To the right of **Alignment**, click the arrow, and then click **Centered**. To the right of *relative to*, click the arrow, and then click **Page**.

d. Under **Vertical**, click the **Absolute position** button. In the **Absolute position** box, select the existing number. Type **2** To the right of **below**, click the arrow, and then click **Margin**.

e. In the **Layout** dialog box, click the **Size tab**. Under **Height**, select the number in the **Absolute** box. Type **1** and then under **Width**, select the number in the **Absolute** box. Type **3.75** and then click **OK**.

f. In the text box, select all of the text. If necessary, right-click over the selected text to display the mini toolbar. Change the **Font Size** to **12**, apply **Bold**, and then press Ctrl + E to **Center** the text.

g. On the **FORMAT tab**, in the **Shape Styles group**, click **Shape Effects**. Point to **Shadow**, and then under **Outer**, in the first row, click the first style—**Offset Diagonal Bottom Right**.

h. In the **Shape Styles group**, click **Shape Outline**. In the fifth column, click the first color—**Blue, Accent 1** to change the color of the text box border. Click **Shape Fill**, and then in the fifth column, click the second color—**Blue, Accent 1, Lighter 80%**. Click **Save**.

5 Click the **INSERT tab**, and then in the **Header & Footer group**, click **Footer**. At the bottom of the menu, click **Edit Footer**. On the **HEADER & FOOTER TOOLS DESIGN tab**, in the **Insert group**, click **Document Info**, and then click **File Name**. Double-click in the document outside of the footer area to close the footer and return to the document.

a. Press Ctrl + Home to move the insertion point to the top of the document. In the upper left corner of your screen, click the **FILE tab** to display **Backstage** view. On the right, at the bottom of the **Properties list**, click **Show All Properties**.

b. On the list of Properties, click to the right of **Tags** to display an empty box, and then type **internship, photographer** Click to the right of **Subject** to display an empty box, and then type your course name and section #. Under **Related People**, be sure that your name displays as the author. If necessary, edit the author name.

c. **Save** your file and submit as directed by your instructor. **Close** Word.

END | You have completed Project 1C

CHAPTER REVIEW

Apply 1B skills from these Objectives:

5 Change Document and Paragraph Layout

6 Create and Modify Lists

7 Set and Modify Tab Stops

8 Insert a SmartArt Graphic and an Online Video

Skills Review Project 1D Internships

In the following Skills Review, you will edit an information handout regarding production and development internships with Sturgeon Point Productions. Your completed document will look similar to Figure 1.53.

PROJECT FILES

For Project 1D, you will need the following file:

w01D_Internship

You will save your document as:

Lastname_Firstname_1D_Internship

PROJECT RESULTS

STURGEON POINT PRODUCTIONS

Sturgeon Point Productions is a full service film and video production facility located in Miami, Florida. Celebrating over 45 years of producing top quality commercial and independent film, our projects range from award winning documentaries and live action short features, to live concert and sporting events, to popular educational and training series of videos for schools, businesses, trade shows and multi-media presentations. We currently offer internships to film students in participating local colleges and universities, in both our development and production departments.

In-House Office Internships

Sturgeon Point Productions is looking for story analysts, research, post production and production assistants to work in our offices. We offer college credit as independent study at participating schools for one semester, which can be repeated for up to one year from the start date of the internship. To receive credit, interns must:

1. Be enrolled as a film major at a participating local college or university
2. Maintain a 3.0 GPA
3. Receive satisfactory monthly progress reports from their direct supervisor

Lastname_Firstname_1D_Internship

Following is a list of departments in our Miami office, currently seeking development and production interns:

✓ Development Department.. Researcher
✓ Development Department...Asst. to Producer
✓ Development Department..Writer's Assistant
✓ Post Production...Asst. Editor
✓ Post Production...Asst. Sound Editor
✓ Production..Asst. Office Manager

Additional Information

For more information and to sign up for our weekly newsletter, visit our website at www.sturgeonpointproductions.com. Be sure to view the following video to learn about some of the important skills you will develop as an intern with Sturgeon Point Productions.

Lastname_Firstname_1D_Internship

FIGURE 1.53

(Project 1D Internships continues on the next page)

CHAPTER REVIEW

1 Start Word, and then click **Open Other Documents**. Click **Computer**, and then click **Browse**. Navigate to your student files, and then open **w01D_Internship**. On the **HOME tab**, in the **Paragraph group**, be sure **Show/Hide** is active. Click the **FILE tab**, and then click **Save As**. Navigate to your **Word Chapter 1** folder, and then **Save** the document as **Lastname_Firstname_1D_Internship**

a. Click the **PAGE LAYOUT tab**. In the **Page Setup group**, click **Margins**, and then click **Custom Margins**. In the **Page Setup** dialog box, press Tab as necessary to select the value in the **Left** box. Type **1** and then press Tab to select the value in the **Right** box. Type **1** and then click **OK**.

b. Scroll down to view the bottom of **Page 1**, point anywhere in the bottom margin area, right-click, and then click **Edit Footer** to display the footer area. On the **HEADER & FOOTER TOOLS DESIGN tab**, in the **Insert group**, click **Document Info**, and then click **File Name**. Double-click anywhere in the document to close the footer area.

c. Press Ctrl + A to select all of the text in the document, and then on the **HOME tab**, in the **Paragraph group**, click **Align Left**.

d. Press Ctrl + Home. Select the document title, and then on the **HOME tab**, in the **Paragraph group**, click **Center**.

e. Locate the first bold subheading—*In-House Office Internships*. Point to the left of the paragraph to display the ⟋ pointer, and then click one time to select the text. With *In-House Office Internships* selected, locate the subheading *Additional Information*. Move the pointer to the left of the paragraph to display the ⟋ pointer, hold down Ctrl, and then click one time to select both paragraphs. In the **Paragraph group**, click **Center**.

f. Press Ctrl + A to select all of the text in the document. On the **HOME tab**, in the **Paragraph group**, click **Line and Paragraph Spacing**, and then click **1.5**.

2 Below the title of the document, click anywhere in the paragraph that begins *Sturgeon Point Productions is a full service*. On the **HOME tab**, in the **Paragraph group**, click the **Dialog Box Launcher** ⌸.

a. In the **Paragraph** dialog box, on the **Indents and Spacing tab**, under **Indentation**, click the **Special**

arrow, and then click **First line** to indent the first line by 0.5". Click **OK**, and then click anywhere in the paragraph that begins *Sturgeon Point Productions is looking for*. On the ruler under the ribbon, drag the **First Line Indent** marker to **0.5 inches on the horizontal ruler**.

b. Press Ctrl + A to select all of the text in the document. Click the **PAGE LAYOUT tab**, and then in the **Paragraph group**, under **Spacing**, click the **After spin box up arrow** one time to change the value to **6 pt**.

c. Select the subheading *In-House Office Internships*, including the paragraph mark following it. Scroll down, hold down Ctrl, and then select the subheading *Additional Information*. With both subheadings selected, in the **Paragraph group**, under **Spacing**, click the **Before up spin box arrow** two times to set the **Spacing Before** to **12 pt**. **Save** your document.

3 Locate the first paragraph that begins *Development Department*, and then point to this paragraph from the left margin area to display the ⟋ pointer. Drag down to select this paragraph and the next five paragraphs so that six paragraphs are selected. On the **HOME tab**, in the **Paragraph group**, click **Bullets** to change the selected text to a bulleted list.

a. Under the subheading *In-House Office Internships*, in the paragraph that begins *Sturgeon Point Productions*, click to position the insertion point at the *end* of the paragraph, following the colon. Press Enter to create a blank paragraph. On the ruler, drag the **First Line Indent** marker to the left so that it is positioned directly above the lower button. Being sure to include the period, type **1.** and then press Spacebar to create the first item in a numbered list.

b. Type **Be enrolled as a film major at a participating local college or university** and then press Enter. Type **Maintain a 3.0 GPA** and then press Enter. Type **Receive satisfactory monthly progress reports from their direct supervisor**

c. Scroll down to view the bulleted list of departments, and then select all six bulleted items in the list. On the mini toolbar, click the **Bullets button arrow**, and then under **Bullet Library**, click the **check mark** symbol. If the check mark is not available, choose another bullet symbol.

(Project 1D Internships continues on the next page)

CHAPTER REVIEW

4 With the list selected, move the pointer to the horizontal ruler, and then point to and click at **3.5 inches on the horizontal ruler** to insert a tab and align the job titles at the tab mark.

a. With the bulleted list still selected, on the ruler, point to the new tab marker at **3.5 inches on the horizontal ruler**, and then when the *Left Tab* ScreenTip displays, drag the tab marker to **4 inches on the horizontal ruler**.

b. On the ruler, point to the tab marker that you moved to display the *Left Tab* ScreenTip, and then double-click to display the **Tabs** dialog box.

c. In the **Tabs** dialog box, under **Tab stop position**, if necessary select *4"*, and then type **6** Under **Alignment**, click the **Right** option button. Under **Leader**, click the **2** option button. Near the bottom of the **Tabs** dialog box, click **Set**.

d. Under **Tab stop position**, select **4"**, and then click **Clear** to delete the tab stop. Click **OK**. **Save** your document.

5 Press Ctrl + Home to move to the top of the document, and then in the title, click to the right of the *S* in *PRODUCTIONS*.

a. Click the **INSERT tab**, and then in the **Illustrations group**, click **SmartArt**. On the left, click **Relationship**, and then scroll the list to the bottom. Locate and then click **Basic Venn**. Click **OK** to insert the SmartArt graphic. If necessary, close the Text Pane.

b. In the SmartArt graphic, click on *[Text]* in the top circle shape. Type **Film** and then click on the placeholder *[Text]* in the lower left shape. Type **Video** In the third circle, type **Internet**

c. Click the SmartArt graphic border to select it. Click the **FORMAT tab**, and then in the **Size group**, if necessary click **Size** to display the **Shape Height** and **Shape Width** boxes. Set the **Height** to 3" and the **Width** to 6.5".

d. With the SmartArt graphic still selected, on the ribbon, under **SMARTART TOOLS**, click the **DESIGN tab**, and then in the **SmartArt Styles group**, click **Change Colors**. Under **Colorful**, click the third style—**Colorful Range–Accent Colors 3 to 4**. On the **DESIGN tab**, in the **SmartArt Styles group**, click **More**. Under **3-D**, in the first row, click the third style—**Cartoon**. Click **Save**.

6 Hold down Ctrl and then press End to move to the end of the document. On the **INSERT tab**, in the **Media group**, click **Online Video**. If necessary, in the lower left corner of the Insert Video window, click YouTube. Click in the **Search YouTube** box. Including the quotation marks, type **"Go 2013 1B video"** and then press Enter. In the first row, click the first video, and then click **Insert**.

a. Click the **FILE tab**, and then on the right, click **Show All Properties**. In the **Tags** box, type **internship** and in the **Subject** box, type your course name and section number. Be sure that your name displays as the author. Click **Save**.

b. Click the **FILE tab** to display **Backstage** view. Click **Print** to display **Print Preview**. At the bottom of the preview, click the **Next Page** and **Previous Page** buttons to move between pages. If necessary, return to the document and make any necessary changes.

c. As directed by your instructor, print your document or submit it electronically. **Close** Word.

END | You have completed Project 1D

CONTENT-BASED ASSESSMENTS

Mastering Word   Project 1E Documentary

In the following Mastery project, you will create a flyer announcing a special event being hosted by Sturgeon Point Productions. Your printed results will look similar to those in Figure 1.54.

Apply 1A skills from these Objectives:

1 Create a New Document and Insert Text

2 Insert and Format Graphics

3 Insert and Modify Text Boxes and Shapes

4 Preview and Print a Document

Build from Scratch

PROJECT FILES

For Project 1E, you will need the following files:

New blank Word document

w01E_Antarctica

w01E_Filmmaker

You will save your document as:

Lastname_Firstname_1E_Documentary

PROJECT RESULTS

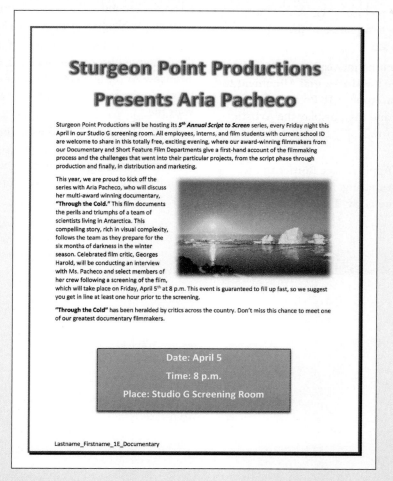

FIGURE 1.54

(Project 1E Documentary continues on the next page)

CONTENT-BASED ASSESSMENTS

1 **Start** Word and display a **Blank document** with the ruler and formatting marks displayed. Type **Sturgeon Point Productions Presents Aria Pacheco** and then press Enter. From your student data files, insert the text file **w01E_Filmmaker**. Using your own name, **Save** the document in your **Word Chapter 1** folder as **Lastname_Firstname_1E_Documentary**

2 To the document title, apply the **Fill – White, Outline – Accent 1, Glow – Accent 1** text effect, and then change the **Font Size** to **36**. Change the **Font Color** to **Blue-Gray, Text 2**—in the fourth column, the first color. Apply an **Outer Shadow** using **Offset Left**—in the second row, the third style. **Center** the title.

3 Position the insertion point at the beginning of the paragraph that begins with *This year*, and then from your student data files, insert the picture **w01E_Antarctica**. Change the **Layout Options** to **Square** and then change the **Height** of the picture to **2.5**

4 Using the **Position** command, display the **Layout** dialog box, and then change the **Horizontal Alignment** to **Right relative to** the **Margin**. Apply a **10 Point Soft Edges** picture effect to the image, and then display the **Artistic Effects** gallery. In the third row, apply the fourth effect—**Mosaic Bubbles**.

5 Deselect the picture. Apply a **Page Border** to the document using the **Shadow** setting. Select the first style, and change the **Color** to **Blue-Gray, Text 2**. Change the **Width** to **3 pt**.

6 Below the last paragraph, draw a **Text Box** that is approximately 1.5 inches high and 4 inches wide—the exact size and location need not be precise. In the text box, type the following text:

> **Date: April 5**
>
> **Time: 8 p.m.**
>
> **Place: Studio G Screening Room**

7 Change the **Height** of the text box to **1.5** and the **Width** to **4.5** and then change the font size to **18**. Apply **Bold** and **Center**. To precisely place the text box, display the **Layout** dialog box. Change the **Horizontal Alignment** to **Centered**, **relative to** the **Page**, and then change the **Vertical Absolute position** to **0.5** below the **Paragraph**.

8 Apply a **Shape Style** to the text box—in the last row, select the second style—**Intense Effect – Blue, Accent 1**. Change the **Shape Outline** to **Black, Text 1**.

9 Insert the **File Name** in the footer, and then display the document properties. As the **Tags**, type **documentary, interview** As the **Subject**, type your course and section #. Be sure your name is indicated as the **Author**. **Save** your file.

10 Display the **Print Preview** and if necessary, return to the document and make any necessary changes. As directed by your instructor, print your document or submit it electronically. **Close** Word.

END | You have completed Project 1E

CONTENT-BASED ASSESSMENTS

In the following Mastery project, you will edit a document with information regarding an event that Sturgeon Point Productions is holding for college students. Your printed results will look similar to those in Figure 1.55.

Apply 1B skills from these Objectives:

5 Change Document and Paragraph Layout

6 Create and Modify Lists

7 Set and Modify Tab Stops

8 Insert a SmartArt Graphic and an Online Video

PROJECT FILES

For Project 1F, you will need the following file:

w01F_Pitch_Festival

You will save your document as:

Lastname_Firstname_1F_Pitch_Festival

PROJECT RESULTS

Pitch Festival!

Do you have a story that must be told? Pitch us your project during the Sturgeon Point Productions annual Pitch Festival! We're setting up several days of conference video calls for college students that are currently enrolled in an accredited film production program anywhere in the United States. If your idea is selected, you will be flown to our studios in Miami, Florida to pitch your idea to our staff of producers and development executives. The following video provides additional information:

Sturgeon Point Productions is one of the leading independent film and video companies in the Miami area. We are currently looking for new, fresh, exciting ideas for short and full-length feature films and documentaries. We like character driven stories that can be shot on an independent budget within one or two locations, preferably either in our studios or in the Miami area. We are currently looking for scripts, ideas, and concepts that are in one of the following categories:

1. Human interest or educational
2. Political or journalistic
3. Biographical or documentary

The Pitch Festival will take place at our secure website on the following dates and times. There are no entry fees to pitch; this unique opportunity to pitch to our staff of professional filmmakers is absolutely free for college film students. Sign up now at www.sturgeonpointproductions.com/pitchfest for one of the following pitch sessions:

- September 12, 11 a.m...Short and Feature Film Pitches
- September 13, 8 p.m. ....Biographical and Documentary Film Pitches
- September 14, 7 p.m. ....Educational Series Pitches

Lastname_Firstname_1F_Pitch_Festival

FIGURE 1.55

(Project 1F Pitch Festival continues on the next page)

1 Start Word, and then from your student files, open **w01F_Pitch_Festival**. Display formatting marks, and then **Save** the file in your **Word Chapter 1** folder as **Lastname_Firstname_1F_Pitch_Festival**

2 Insert the **File Name** in the footer. Select all the document text, and then change the **Line Spacing** for the entire document to **1.5**. **Center** the document title, and then change the title font size to **24**. Change the **Top** and **Bottom** margins to **0.5**

3 Select the three paragraphs below the title, and then apply a **First line** indent of 0.5". Select the entire document, and then change the **Spacing Before** to **6 pt** and the **Spacing After** to **6 pt**.

4 Select the last three paragraphs containing the dates, and then apply filled square bullets. If the bullets are not available, choose another bullet style. With the bulleted list selected, set a **Right** tab with **dot leaders** at **6"**.

5 Locate the paragraph that begins *Sturgeon Point Productions*, and then click at the end of the paragraph, after the colon. Press Enter. Create a numbered list with the following three numbered items; be sure to remove the first line indent before creating the numbered list:

Human interest or educational

Political or journalistic

Biographical or documentary

6 Position the insertion point at the end of the document after the word *Pitches*. Do *not* insert a blank line. Insert a **SmartArt** graphic from the **Process** category. Toward the bottom of the gallery, select the **Equation** SmartArt. Select the outside border of the SmartArt, and then change the **Height** of the SmartArt to **1** and the **Width** to **6.5**

7 With the SmartArt selected, change the layout to **Square**, and change the **Horizontal Alignment** to **Centered relative to** the **Page**. Change the **Vertical Alignment** to **Bottom relative to** the **Margin**.

8 In the first circle type **Your Ideas** and in the second circle type **Our Experts** In the third circle type **Pitch Festival!** Change the SmartArt color to **Colorful Range – Accent Colors 4 to 5**. Apply the **3-D Polished** style.

9 Click at the end of the paragraph below the title. Press Enter, remove the first line indent, and then center the blank line. Insert an **Online Video**. In the **Search YouTube** box, type, including the quotations marks, **"Go 2013 1F Video"** and then insert the video with the cube on a black background. Change the height of the video to **1.5**.

10 Display the document properties. In the **Tags** box, type **pitch festival** and in the **Subject** box, type your course name and section number. Be sure your name displays as the author.

11 Display the **Print Preview** and if necessary, return to the document and make any necessary changes. As directed by your instructor, print your document or submit it electronically. **Close** Word.

END | You have completed Project 1F

CONTENT-BASED ASSESSMENTS

Mastering Word Project 1G Educational Website

In the following Mastery project, you will create a flyer that details a new educational website that Sturgeon Point Productions has developed for instructors. Your printed results will look similar to those in Figure 1.56.

Apply 1A and 1B skills from these Objectives:

1 Create a New Document and Insert Text

2 Insert and Format Graphics

3 Insert and Modify Text Boxes and Shapes

4 Preview and Print a Document

5 Change Document and Paragraph Layout

6 Create and Modify Lists

7 Set and Modify Tab Stops

8 Insert a SmartArt Graphic and an Online Video

Build from Scratch

PROJECT FILES

For Project 1G, you will need the following files:

New blank Word document
w01G_Education
w01G_Media

You will save your document as:

Lastname_Firstname_1G_Educational_Website

PROJECT RESULTS

FIGURE 1.56

(Project 1G Educational Website continues on the next page)

CONTENT-BASED ASSESSMENTS

1 Start Word and display a blank document. Display formatting marks and the ruler. Type **Educational Websites** and then press Enter. Type **Sturgeon Point Productions is offering website tie-ins with every educational video title in our catalog, at no additional cost.** Press Spacebar, and then **Save** the document in your **Word Chapter 1** folder as **Lastname_Firstname_1G_Educational_Website**

2 With the insertion point positioned at the end of the sentence that you typed, insert the text from your student data file **w01G_Education**. Change the **Line Spacing** for the entire document to **1.5** and the spacing **After** to **6 pt**. To each of the four paragraphs that begin *Sturgeon Point Productions*, *As educators*, *When submitting*, and *The video*, apply a **First Line** indent of **0.5"**.

3 Change the font size of the title to **50** and then display the **Text Effects and Typography** gallery. Apply the second effect to the title—**Fill – Blue, Accent 1, Shadow**, and then **Center** the title. With only the title selected, change the **Line Spacing** to **1.0**.

4 Click at the beginning of the paragraph below the title, and then from your student data files, insert the picture **w01G_Media**. Change the picture **Height** to **2** and the **Layout Options** to **Square**. Format the picture with **Soft Edges** in **10 Point**, and then use the **Position** command to display the **Layout** dialog box. Change the picture position so that the **Horizontal Alignment** is **Right relative to** the **Margin**. Change the **Vertical Alignment** to **Top relative to** the **Line**.

5 Select the five paragraphs beginning with *Historic interactive timelines* and ending with *Quizzes and essay exams*, and then apply checkmark bullets. In the paragraph below the bulleted list, click after the colon. Press Enter and remove the first line indent. Type a numbered list with the following three numbered items:

The title in which you are interested

The name of the class and subject

Online tools you would like to see created

6 With the insertion point located at the end of the numbered list, insert a **SmartArt** graphic. In the **Process** category, locate and select the **Basic Chevron Process**. In the first shape type **View** In the second shape type **Interact** and in the third shape type **Assess**

7 Change the SmartArt color to **Colorful Range – Accent Colors 4 to 5**, and then apply the **3-D Flat Scene** style. Change the **Height** of the SmartArt to **1** and the **Width** to **6.5** Change the **Layout Options** to **Square**, the **Horizontal Alignment** to **Centered relative to** the **Page**, and the **Vertical Alignment** to **Bottom relative to** the **Margin**.

8 Select the days and times at the end of the document, and then set a **Right** tab with **dot leaders** at **6"**. Click in the blank line below the tabbed list, and **Center** the line. Insert an **Online Video**. In the **Search YouTube** box, type **Pearson Higher Education Learning**, and then insert the first video that displays. Change the video **Height** to **1.5**

9 In the space below the video, insert a **Rounded Rectangle** shape. The exact location need not be precise. Change the **Shape Height** to **1.5** and the **Shape Width** to **6.5** Display the **Shape Styles** gallery, and then in the fourth row, apply the second style—**Subtle Effect - Blue, Accent 1**. Use the **Position** command to display the **Layout** dialog box, and then change the position so that both the **Horizontal** and **Vertical Alignment** are **Centered relative to** the **Margin**.

10 In the rectangle, type **Sturgeon Point Productions** and then press Enter. Type **Partnering with Educators to Produce Rich Media Content** and then change the font size to **16**.

11 Move to the top of the document and insert a **Text Box** above the title. The exact location need not be precise. Change the **Height** of the text box to **0.5** and the width to **3.7** Type **Sturgeon Point Productions** and then change the font size to **22 Center** the text.

12 Use the **Position** command to display the **Layout** dialog box, and then position the text box so that the **Horizontal Alignment** is **Centered relative to** the **Page** and the **Vertical Absolute position** is **0.5 below** the **Page**.

13 With the text box selected, display the **Shape Fill** gallery, and then in the next to last column, select the second color—**Blue, Accent 5, Lighter 80%**. Change the **Shape Outline** to the same color—**Blue, Accent 5, Lighter 80%**.

14 Deselect the text box. Apply a **Page Border** to the document. Use the **Box** setting, and choose the first style. Change the **Color** to **Blue, Accent 5**. Change the **Top** margin to **1.25** and insert the **File Name** in the footer.

15 Display the document properties. As the **Tags** type **website** and as the **Subject** type your course and section #. Be sure your name displays in the **Author** box, and then **Save** your file. Submit your document as directed.

END | You have completed Project 1G

Apply a combination of the 1A and 1B skills.

Build from Scratch

GO! Fix It	Project 1H Casting Call	Online
GO! Make It	Project 1I Development Team	Online
GO! Solve It	Project 1J Softball	Online
GO! Solve It	Project 1K Production	

PROJECT FILES

For Project 1K, you will need the following files:

w01K_Production
w01K_Studio

You will save your document as:

Lastname_Firstname_1K_Production

The Marketing Director for Sturgeon Point Productions is developing marketing materials aimed at filmmakers. Use the following information to format a flyer that uses text effects, an appropriately placed picture with an artistic effect and text wrapping applied, and an appropriately formatted SmartArt graphic.

From the student files that accompany this textbook, locate and open the file w01K_Production. Format the document using techniques you learned in this chapter. From your student data files, insert the picture w01K_Studio, and then format the picture with an artistic effect. Insert a **SmartArt** graphic that illustrates two or three important points about the company. Be sure the flyer is easy to read and understand and has an attractive design. Save the file in your **Word Chapter 1** folder as **Lastname_Firstname_1K_Production** and submit it as directed.

(Project 1K Production continues on the next page)

CONTENT-BASED ASSESSMENTS

Performance Level

<table>
<tr><th rowspan="2">Performance Criteria</th><th></th><th>Exemplary</th><th>Proficient</th><th>Developing</th></tr>
<tr><td>Use text effects</td><td>Text effects applied to text in an attractive and appropriate manner.</td><td>Text effects applied but do not appropriately display text.</td><td>Text effects not used.</td></tr>
<tr><td></td><td>Insert and format a picture</td><td>The picture is inserted and positioned correctly; text wrapping and an artistic effect are applied.</td><td>The picture is inserted but not formatted properly.</td><td>No picture is inserted in the document.</td></tr>
<tr><td></td><td>Insert and format SmartArt</td><td>The SmartArt is inserted and appropriately formatted.</td><td>The SmartArt is inserted but no formatting is applied.</td><td>No SmartArt is inserted in the document.</td></tr>
</table>

END | You have completed Project 1K

OUTCOMES-BASED ASSESSMENTS

RUBRIC

The following outcomes-based assessments are *open-ended assessments*. That is, there is no specific correct result; your result will depend on your approach to the information provided. Make *Professional Quality* your goal. Use the following scoring rubric to guide you in *how* to approach the problem and then to evaluate *how well* your approach solves the problem.

The *criteria*—Software Mastery, Content, Format and Layout, and Process—represent the knowledge and skills you have gained that you can apply to solving the problem. The *levels of performance*—Professional Quality, Approaching Professional Quality, or Needs Quality Improvements—help you and your instructor evaluate your result.

	Your completed project is of Professional Quality if you:	Your completed project is Approaching Professional Quality if you:	Your completed project Needs Quality Improvements if you:
1-Software Mastery	Choose and apply the most appropriate skills, tools, and features and identify efficient methods to solve the problem.	Choose and apply some appropriate skills, tools, and features, but not in the most efficient manner.	Choose inappropriate skills, tools, or features, or are inefficient in solving the problem.
2-Content	Construct a solution that is clear and well organized, contains content that is accurate, appropriate to the audience and purpose, and is complete. Provide a solution that contains no errors in spelling, grammar, or style.	Construct a solution in which some components are unclear, poorly organized, inconsistent, or incomplete. Misjudge the needs of the audience. Have some errors in spelling, grammar, or style, but the errors do not detract from comprehension.	Construct a solution that is unclear, incomplete, or poorly organized; contains some inaccurate or inappropriate content; and contains many errors in spelling, grammar, or style. Do not solve the problem.
3-Format & Layout	Format and arrange all elements to communicate information and ideas, clarify function, illustrate relationships, and indicate relative importance.	Apply appropriate format and layout features to some elements, but not others. Overuse features, causing minor distraction.	Apply format and layout that does not communicate information or ideas clearly. Do not use format and layout features to clarify function, illustrate relationships, or indicate relative importance. Use available features excessively, causing distraction.
4-Process	Use an organized approach that integrates planning, development, self-assessment, revision, and reflection.	Demonstrate an organized approach in some areas, but not others; or, use an insufficient process of organization throughout.	Do not use an organized approach to solve the problem.

OUTCOMES-BASED ASSESSMENTS

Apply a combination of the 1A and 1B skills.

Build from Scratch

GO! Think   Project 1L Classes

PROJECT FILES

For Project 1L, you will need the following file:

New blank Word document

You will save your document as:

Lastname_Firstname_1L_Classes

The Human Resources Director at Sturgeon Point Productions needs to create a flyer to inform full-time employees of educational opportunities beginning in September. The courses are taught each year by industry professionals and are designed to improve skills in motion picture and television development and production. Employees who have been with Sturgeon Point Productions for at least two years are eligible to take the courses free of cost. The classes provide employees with opportunities to advance their careers, gain valuable skills, and achieve technical certification. All courses take place in Studio G and interested employees should contact Elana Springs in Human Resources to sign up. Information meetings are being held at 5:30 p.m. according to the following schedule: television development on June 15; motion picture production on June 17; and recording services on June 21.

Create a flyer with basic information about the courses and information meetings. Be sure the flyer is easy to read and understand and has an attractive design. Save the document as **Lastname_Firstname_1L_Classes** and submit it as directed.

> **END | You have completed Project 1L**

Build from Scratch

GO! Think   Project 1M Store   Online

Build from Scratch

You and GO!   Project 1N Family Flyer   Online

Build from Scratch

GO! Cumulative Group Project   Project 1O Bell Orchid Hotels
                                                                   Online

Using Tables and Templates to Create Resumes and Cover Letters

GO! to Work
Video W2

PROJECT 2A

OUTCOMES
Write a resume by using a Word table.

PROJECT 2B

OUTCOMES
Write a cover letter and use a template to create a cover sheet.

OBJECTIVES

1. Create a Table
2. Format a Table
3. Present a Word Document Online

OBJECTIVES

4. Create a Custom Word Template
5. Correct and Reorganize Text
6. Use the Proofing Options and Print an Envelope
7. Create a Document Using a Predesigned Microsoft Template

onewordphoto / Fotolia

In This Chapter

Tables are useful for organizing and presenting data. Because a table is so easy to use, many individuals prefer to arrange tabular information in a Word table rather than setting a series of tabs. For example, you can use a table when you want to present rows and columns of information or to create a format for a document such as a resume.

When using Word to write business or personal letters, use a commonly approved letter format, and always use a clear writing style. You will make a good impression on prospective employers if you use a standard business letter style when you are writing a cover letter for a resume.

The projects in this chapter relate to the **College Career Center at Florida Port Community College** in St. Petersburg, Florida, a coastal port city near the Florida High Tech Corridor. With 60 percent of Florida's high tech companies and a third of the state's manufacturing companies located in the St. Petersburg and Tampa Bay areas, the college partners with businesses to play a vital role in providing a skilled workforce. The College Career Center assists students in exploring careers, finding internships, and applying for jobs. The Center offers workshops for resume and cover letter writing and for practice interviews.

PROJECT ACTIVITIES

In Activities 2.01 through 2.11, you will create a table to use as the format for a resume. The director of the Career Center, Mary Walker-Huelsman, will use this model when assisting students with building their resumes. Your completed document will look similar to Figure 2.1.

PROJECT FILES

For Project 2A, you will need the following files:

New blank Word document
w02A_Experience

You will save your document as:

Lastname_Firstname_2A_Resume

PROJECT RESULTS

Build from
Scratch

Josh Hayes
1541 Dearborn Lane, St. Petersburg, FL 33713   (727) 555-0313
                                                                jhayes@alcona.net

OBJECTIVE   Technology writing and editing position in the robotics industry, using
                    research and advanced editing skills to communicate with customers.

SUMMARY OF   • Two years' experience in robotics lab for Aerospace Instruction Team
QUALIFICATIONS   • Excellent interpersonal and communication skills
                    • Proficiency using Microsoft Office
                    • Proficiency using page layout and design software
                    • Fluency in spoken and written Spanish

EXPERIENCE   **Instructional Lab Assistant**, Florida Port Community College, St. Petersburg, FL
                    July 2013 to present
                    • Assist robotics professors with sophisticated experiments
                    • Set up robotics practice sessions for Aerospace Instruction Team

                    Assistant Executive Editor, Tech Today Newsletter, St. Petersburg, FL
                    September 2012 to June 2013
                    • Wrote and edited articles for popular college technology newsletter
                    • Responsible for photo editing, cropping, and resizing photos for newsletter
                    • Received Top College Technology Publication Award

                    Teacher's Assistant, Florida Port Community College, Aerospace Department,
                    St. Petersburg, FL July 2011 to June 2012
                    • Helped students with homework, explained assignments, organized
                      materials for professor
                    • Set up robotics lab assignments for students

EDUCATION   **University of South Florida**, Tampa, FL
                    Bachelor of Science, Mechanical Engineering, June 2015

                    Florida Port Community College, St. Petersburg, FL
                    Associate of Arts, Journalism, June 2013

HONORS AND   • Elected to Pi Tau Sigma, honor society for mechanical engineers
ACTIVITIES   • Qualified for Dean's List six semesters
                    • Student Mentor, help other students in engineering program

---

Lastname_Firstname_2A_Resume

FIGURE 2.1 Project 2A Resume

Video W2-1

A *table* is an arrangement of information organized into rows and columns. The intersection of a row and a column in a table creates a box called a *cell* into which you can type. Tables are useful to present information in a logical and orderly format.

Activity 2.01 | Creating a Table by Defining Table Dimensions

1 **Start** Word and then click **Blank document**. On the **HOME tab**, in the **Paragraph group**, if necessary click **Show/Hide** to display the formatting marks. If the rulers do not display, click the **VIEW tab**, and then in the **Show group**, select the **Ruler check box**.

2 Click the **FILE tab**, and then in **Backstage** view, click **Save As**. In the **Save As** dialog box, navigate to the location where you are storing your projects for this chapter. Create a new folder named **Word Chapter 2**

3 **Save** the file in the **Word Chapter 2** folder as **Lastname_Firstname_2A_Resume**

4 On the **INSERT tab**, in the **Header & Footer group**, click **Footer**, and then at the bottom of the list, click **Edit Footer**. On the ribbon, in the **Insert group**, click **Document Info**, click **File Name**, and then at the right end of the ribbon, click **Close Header and Footer**.

5 On the **INSERT tab**, in the **Tables group**, click **Table**. In the **Insert Table** grid, in the fourth row, point to the second square, and notice that the cells are bordered in orange and *2x4 Table* displays at the top of the grid. Compare your screen with Figure 2.2.

FIGURE 2.2

6 Click one time to create the table. Notice that formatting marks in each cell indicate the end of the contents of each cell; the mark to the right of each *row* indicates the row end. **Save** 🖫 your document, and then compare your screen with Figure 2.3.

A table with four rows and two columns displays at the insertion point location, and the insertion point displays in the upper left cell. The table fills the width of the page, from the left margin to the right margin. On the ribbon, TABLE TOOLS and two additional tabs—*DESIGN* and *LAYOUT*—display. Borders display around each cell in the table.

FIGURE 2.3

In a Word table, each cell behaves similarly to a document. For example, as you type in a cell, when you reach the right border of the cell, wordwrap moves the text to the next line. When you press [Enter], the insertion point moves down to a new paragraph in the same cell. You can also insert text from another document into a table cell.

There are numerous acceptable formats for resumes, many of which can be found in Business Communications textbooks. The layout used in this project is suitable for a recent college graduate and places topics in the left column and details in the right column.

1 With the insertion point blinking in the first cell in the first row, type **OBJECTIVE** and then press [Tab].

> Pressing [Tab] moves the insertion point to the next cell in the row, or, if the insertion point is already in the last cell in the row, pressing [Tab] moves the insertion point to the first cell in the next row.

2 Type **Technology writing and editing position in the robotics industry, using research and advanced editing skills to communicate with customers.** Notice that the text wraps in the cell and the height of the row adjusts to fit the text.

3 Press [Tab] to move to the first cell in the second row. Type **SUMMARY OF QUALIFICATIONS** and then press [Tab]. Type the following, pressing [Enter] at the end of each line *except* the last line:

Two years' experience in robotics lab for Aerospace Instruction Team

Excellent interpersonal and communication skills

Proficiency using Microsoft Office

Proficiency using page layout and design software

Fluency in spoken and written Spanish

> The default font and font size in a table are the same as for a document—Calibri 11 pt. The default line spacing in a table is single spacing with no space before or after paragraphs, which differs from the defaults for a document.

4 **Save** 💾 your document, and then compare your screen with Figure 2.4.

FIGURE 2.4

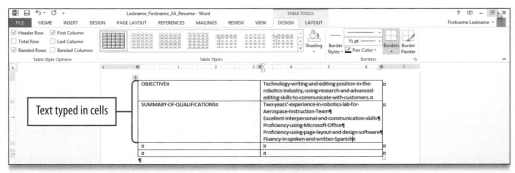

1 Press [Tab] to move to the first cell in the third row. Type **EXPERIENCE** and then press [Tab].

2 Type the following, pressing [Enter] after each item, including the last item:

Instructional Lab Assistant, Florida Port Community College, St. Petersburg, FL July 2013 to present

Assist robotics professors with sophisticated experiments

Set up robotics practice sessions for Aerospace Instruction Team

3 Be sure your insertion point is positioned in the second column to the left of the cell marker below *Instruction Team*. Compare your screen with Figure 2.5.

FIGURE 2.5

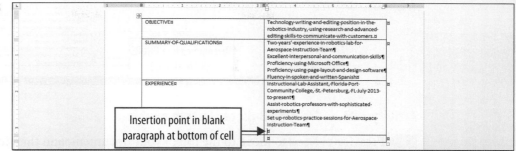

Insertion point in blank paragraph at bottom of cell

4 On the **INSERT tab**, in the **Text group**, click the **Object button arrow**, and then click **Text from File**. Navigate to your student files, select **w02A_Experience**, and then click **Insert**.

All of the text from the w02A_Experience document is added to the document at the insertion point.

ANOTHER WAY   Open the second document and select the text you want. Copy the text, and then paste at the desired location.

5 Press Backspace one time to remove the blank paragraph at the end of the inserted text, and then compare your screen with Figure 2.6.

FIGURE 2.6

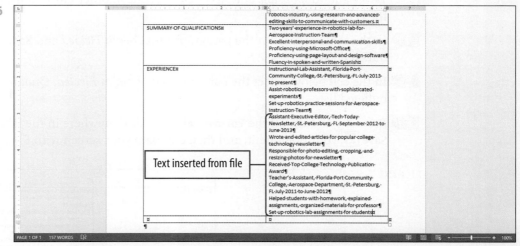

Text inserted from file

PAGE 1 OF 1   157 WORDS

6 Press Tab to move to the first cell in the fourth row. Type **HONORS AND ACTIVITIES** and then press Tab.

7 Type the following, pressing Enter at the end of each item *except* the last one:

Elected to Pi Tau Sigma, honor society for mechanical engineers

Qualified for Dean's List, six semesters

Student Mentor, help other students in engineering program

8 **Save** 💾 your document, and then compare your screen with Figure 2.7.

FIGURE 2.7

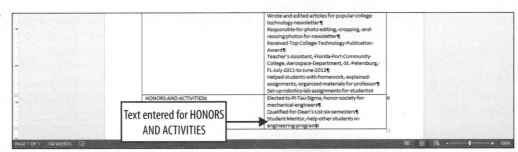

Text entered for HONORS AND ACTIVITIES

Activity 2.04 | Creating Bulleted Lists in a Table

1 Press Ctrl + Home to move to the top of your document, and then in the cell to the right of *SUMMARY OF QUALIFICATIONS*, select all of the text.

2 On the **HOME tab**, in the **Paragraph group**, click **Bullets** ☰ ▾.

The selected text displays as a bulleted list to make each qualification more distinctive.

3 In the **Paragraph group**, click **Decrease Indent** ⇤ one time to align the bullets at the left edge of the cell.

4 Scroll as necessary so that you can view the entire *EXPERIENCE* and *HONORS AND ACTIVITIES* sections on your screen. With the bulleted text still selected, in the **Clipboard group**, double-click **Format Painter**.

5 In the cell to the right of EXPERIENCE, select the second and third paragraphs—beginning *Assist* and *Set up*—to create the same style of bulleted list as you did in the previous step.

6 In the same cell, under *Assistant Executive Editor*, select the three paragraphs that begin *Wrote* and *Responsible* and *Received* to create another bulleted list aligned at the left edge of the cell.

7 In the same cell, select the paragraphs that begin *Helped* and *Set up* to create the same type of bulleted list.

8 In the cell below, select the paragraphs that begin *Elected*, *Qualified*, and *Student* to create a bulleted list.

9 Press Esc to turn off the **Format Painter**. Click anywhere in the table to deselect the text, **Save** 🖫 your document, and then compare your screen with Figure 2.8.

FIGURE 2.8

Bullets added to text

Video W2-2

Use Word's formatting tools to make your tables attractive and easy to read. Types of formatting you can add to a table include changing the row height and the column width, removing or adding borders, increasing or decreasing the paragraph or line spacing, and enhancing the text.

Activity 2.05 | Changing the Width of Table Columns and Using AutoFit

When you create a table, all of the columns are of equal width. In this activity, you will change the width of the columns.

1 Press Ctrl + Home. Click anywhere in the first column, and then on the ribbon, under **TABLE TOOLS**, click the **LAYOUT tab**. In the **Cell Size group**, notice the **Width** box, which displays the width of the active column.

2 Look at the horizontal ruler and locate the **1.5-inch mark**. Then, in the table, in any row, point to the vertical border between the two columns to display the ⟨+⟩ pointer.

3 Hold down the left mouse button and drag the column border to the left until the white arrow on the ruler is at approximately **1.5 inches on the horizontal ruler** and then release the left mouse button.

4 In the **Cell Size group**, click the **Width box down spin arrow** as necessary to set the column width to **1.4"** and notice that the right border of the table moves to the right.

> Adjusting column width by dragging a column border adjusts only the width of the column; adjusting column width with the Width box simultaneously adjusts the right border of the table.

5 In the **Cell Size group**, click **AutoFit**, and then click **AutoFit Window** to stretch the table across the page within the margins so that the right border of the table is at the right margin. **Save** 🖫 and then compare your screen with Figure 2.9.

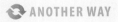 **ANOTHER WAY**   You can adjust column widths by dragging the Move Table Column markers on the ruler. To maintain the right border of the table at the right margin, hold down Shift while dragging. To display measurements on the ruler, hold down Alt while dragging the marker.

FIGURE 2.9

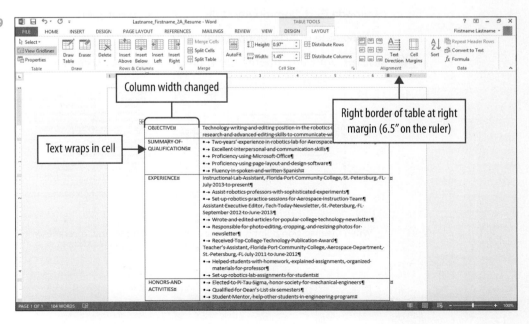

Activity 2.06 | **Using One-Click Row/Column Insertion to Modify Table Dimensions**

One of the most common actions you will take in a table is adding another row or another column. By using *One-click Row/Column Insertion* you can do so in context by pointing to the left or top edge where you want the row or column to appear and then clicking the ⊕ button to add it.

1 Scroll to view the lower portion of the table. On the left border of the table, *point* to the upper left corner of the cell containing the text *HONORS AND ACTIVITIES* to display the **One-click Row/Column Insertion** button ⊕. Compare your screen with Figure 2.10.

FIGURE 2.10

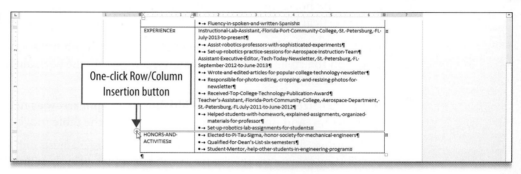

2 Click ⊕ one time to insert a new row above the HONORS AND ACTIVITIES row.

3 Click in the left cell of the new row, type **EDUCATION** and then press Tab.

4 Type the following, pressing Enter at the end of each item *except* the last one:

University of South Florida, Tampa, FL

Bachelor of Science, Mechanical Engineering, June 2015

Florida Port Community College, St. Petersburg, FL

Associate of Arts, Journalism, June 2013

5 **Save** 🖫 your document, and then compare your screen with Figure 2.11.

FIGURE 2.11

 ANOTHER WAY   When the insertion point is in the last cell in the bottom row of a table, you can add a row by pressing the Tab key; the insertion point will display in the first cell of the new row.

Activity 2.07 | Merging Table Cells

The title of a table typically spans all of the columns. In this activity, you will merge cells so that you can position the personal information across both columns.

1 Press [Ctrl] + [Home] to move to the top of your document, and then click anywhere in the top row of the table.

2 On the **LAYOUT tab**, in the **Rows & Columns group**, click **Insert Above**.

A new row displays above the row that contained the insertion point, and the new row is selected. This is another method to insert rows and columns in a table; use this method to insert a new row at the top of a table.

ANOTHER WAY   Right-click in the top row, point to Insert, and then click Insert Rows Above.

3 Be sure the two cells in the top row are selected; if necessary, drag across both cells to select them.

4 On the **LAYOUT tab**, in the **Merge group**, click **Merge Cells**.

The cell border between the two cells no longer displays.

ANOTHER WAY   Right-click the selected row and click Merge Cells on the shortcut menu.

Activity 2.08 | Setting Tabs in a Table

1 With the merged cell still selected, on the **HOME tab**, in the **Paragraph group**, click the **Dialog Box Launcher** to display the **Paragraph** dialog box.

2 On the **Indents and Spacing tab**, in the lower left corner, click **Tabs** to display the **Tabs** dialog box.

3 Under **Tab stop position**, type **6.5** and then under **Alignment**, click the **Right** option button. Click **Set**, and then click **OK** to close the dialog box.

4 Type **Josh Hayes** Hold down [Ctrl] and then press [Tab]. Notice that the insertion point moves to the right-aligned tab stop at 6.5".

In a Word table, you must use [Ctrl] + [Tab] to move to a tab stop, because pressing [Tab] is reserved for moving the insertion point from cell to cell.

5 Type **(727) 555-0313** and then press [Enter].

6 Type **1541 Dearborn Lane, St. Petersburg, FL 33713** Hold down [Ctrl] and then press [Tab].

7 Type **jhayes@alcona.net** Save your document, and then compare your screen with Figure 2.12.

FIGURE 2.12

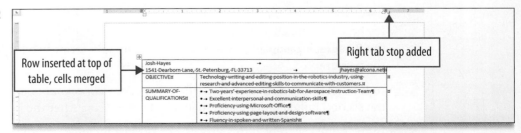

1 In the first row of the table, select the name *Josh Hayes*, and then on the mini toolbar, apply **Bold** [B] and change the **Font Size** to **16**.

2 Under *Josh Hayes*, click anywhere in the second line of text, which contains the address and email address.

3 On the **PAGE LAYOUT tab**, in the **Paragraph group**, click the **Spacing After up spin arrow** three times to add **18 pt** spacing between the first row of the table and the second row. Compare your screen with Figure 2.13.

> This action separates the personal information from the body of the resume and adds focus to the name.

FIGURE 2.13

4 Using the technique you just practiced, in the second column, click in the last paragraph of *every cell* and add **18 pt Spacing After** including the last row; a border will be added to the bottom of the table, and spacing will be needed between the last row and the border.

5 In the second row, point to the word *OBJECTIVE*, hold down the left mouse button, and then drag downward in the first column to select all the headings in uppercase letters. On the mini toolbar, click **Bold** [B].

NOTE | **Selecting Only One Column**

When you drag downward to select the first column, a fast mouse might also begin to select the second column when you reach the bottom. If this happens, drag upward slightly to deselect the second column and select only the first column.

---

6 In the cell to the right of *EXPERIENCE*, without selecting the following comma, select *Instructional Lab Assistant* and then on the mini toolbar, click **Bold** [B].

7 In the same cell, apply **Bold** [B] to the other job titles—*Assistant Executive Editor* and *Teacher's Assistant*.

8 In the cell to the right of *EDUCATION*, apply **Bold** [B] to *University of South Florida, Tampa, FL* and *Florida Port Community College, St. Petersburg, FL*.

9 In the same cell, click anywhere in the line beginning *Bachelor*. On the **PAGE LAYOUT tab**, in the **Paragraph group**, click the **Spacing After up spin arrow** two times to add **12 pt** spacing after the paragraph.

10 In the cell to the right of *EXPERIENCE*, under *Instructional Lab Assistant*, click anywhere in the second bulleted item, and then add **12 pt Spacing After** the item.

11 In the same cell, repeat this process for the last bulleted item under *Assistant Executive Editor*.

12 ▶ Scroll to view the top of your document, **Save** 🖫 your document, and then compare your screen with Figure 2.14.

FIGURE 2.14

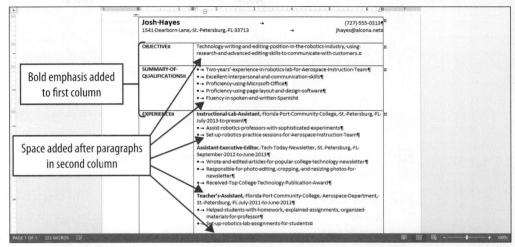

Activity 2.10 | Modifying Table Borders and Using Spacing Before

When you create a table, all of the cells have black 1/2-point, single-line, solid-line borders that print unless you remove them. Most resumes do not display any cell borders. A border at the top and bottom of the resume, however, is attractive and adds a professional look to the document.

1 ▶ Scroll as necessary to view the top margin area above the table, and then point slightly outside of the upper left corner of the table to display the **table move handle** ⊞.

2 ▶ With the 🕂 pointer, click one time to select the entire table, and notice that the row markers at the end of each row are also selected.

> Shaded row markers indicate that the entire row is selected. Use this technique to select the entire table.

3 ▶ On the ribbon, under **TABLE TOOLS**, click the **DESIGN tab**. In the **Borders group**, click the **Borders button arrow**, and then click **No Border**.

> The black borders no longer display.

4 ▶ Press `Ctrl` + `P`, which is the keyboard shortcut to view the Print Preview, and notice that no borders display in the preview. Then, press **Back** ⬅ to return to your document.

5 ▶ With the table still selected, on the **DESIGN tab**, in the **Borders group**, click the **Borders button arrow**, and then at the bottom of the **Borders** gallery, click **Borders and Shading**.

6 ▶ In the **Borders and Shading** dialog box, on the **Borders tab**, under **Setting**, click **Custom**. Under **Style**, scroll down about one-third of the way, and then click the style with a **thick upper line and a thin lower line**.

7 ▶ In the **Preview** box at the right, point to the *top* border of the small preview and click one time.

🔄 **ANOTHER WAY** Click the top border button, which is one of the buttons that surround the Preview.

8 ▶ Under **Style**, scroll down if necessary, click the opposite style—with the **thin upper line and the thick lower line**, and then in the **Preview** box, click the *bottom* border of the preview. Compare your screen with Figure 2.15.

FIGURE 2.15

Thick upper, thin lower border

Borders display in Preview

Thin upper, thick lower border

9 ▸ Click **OK**, click anywhere to cancel the selection, and then notice that there is only a small amount of space between the upper border and the first line of text.

10 ▸ Click anywhere in the text *Josh Hayes*, and then on the **PAGE LAYOUT tab**, in the **Paragraph group**, click the **Spacing Before up spin arrow** as necessary to add **18 pt** spacing before the first paragraph.

11 ▸ Press Ctrl + P to display **Print Preview**. Compare your screen with Figure 2.16.

FIGURE 2.16

Spacing added above paragraph

Top border

Bottom border

12 ▸ Press **Back** ← to return to your document, and then on the Quick Access Toolbar, click **Save** 🖫.

More Knowledge **View Gridlines in a Table**

After you remove borders from a table, you can still view nonprinting gridlines, which show the cell boundaries of a table whenever the table does not have borders applied. Some people find this a useful visual aid. If you cannot see the gridlines, on the ribbon, under TABLE TOOLS, on the DESIGN tab, in the Borders group, click the Borders button arrow, and then click View Gridlines.

More Knowledge **Convert Text to a Table**

To convert paragraphs or lists to a table, insert separator characters such as commas or tabs to show where to divide the text into columns. Then insert paragraph marks (press ENTER) to show where to begin the rows. Select the text, and then on the INSERT tab, in the Table group, click Convert Text to Table. In the Convert Text to Table dialog box, choose the options you want, and then click OK.

Video W2-3

Office Presentation Service enables you to present your Word document to others who can watch in a web browser. No preliminary setup is necessary; Word creates a link to your document that you can share with others via email or instant message. Anyone to whom you send the link can see your document while you are presenting online.

Individuals watching your presentation can navigate within the document independently of you or others in the presentation, so they can use a mouse, keyboard, or touch input to move around in the document while you are presenting it. If an individual is viewing a different portion of the document than the presenter, an alert displays on his or her screen. To return to the portion of the document that the presenter is showing, a Follow Presenter button displays.

While you are presenting, you can make minor edits to the document. If you want to share a copy of the document to the presentation attendees, you can select *Enable remote viewers to download the document* when you start the presentation. You can also share any meeting notes that you or others created in OneNote.

Activity 2.11   Presenting a Word Document Online

If you are creating your own resume, it will be valuable to get feedback from your friends, instructors, or Career Center advisors before you submit your resume for a job application. In this Activity, you will present the resume document online for others to look at.

> **NOTE**   **You May Be Asked to Sign in with Your Microsoft Account**
>
> You may be asked to sign in with your Microsoft account, even if you are already signed in, to present your document online.

1 With your resume document displayed, click **Save** 🖫.

2 Click the **FILE tab**, on the left click **Share**, and then under **Share**, click **Present Online**.

3 On the right, under **Present Online**, be sure **Office Presentation Service** displays; if necessary, click the arrow on the right to select it. Click the **Present Online** button. Wait a moment for the service to connect, and then compare your screen with Figure 2.17.

> There are several methods to send your meeting invitation to others. You can click Copy Link to copy and paste the hyperlink; for example, you could copy the link into a **Skype** window. Skype is a Microsoft product with which you can make voice calls, make video calls, transfer files, or send messages—including instant messages and text messages—over the Internet.

> You can also select Send in Email, which will open your Outlook email window if you use Outlook as your mail client.

> **NOTE**   **Other Presentation Services May Display**
>
> Under Present Online, you might have other services displayed. For example, if you are using Office 365, Microsoft Lync may display as the default presentation service.

FIGURE 2.17

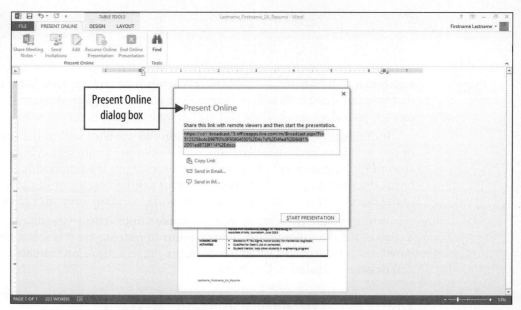

4 If you want to do so, identify a classmate or friend who is at a computer and available to view your presentation, select one of the methods to share, click **START PRESENTATION**, and when you are finished, on the ribbon, click **End Online Presentation**. Otherwise, **Close** ☒ the **Present Online** dialog box.

> If you present online, you will need to initiate voice communication using Skype or by simply phoning the other person.

5 Be sure you have closed the **Present Online** dialog box. On the ribbon, on the **PRESENT ONLINE tab**, click **End Online Presentation**, and then in the message, click **End Online Presentation**.

6 Press Ctrl + Home to move to the top of your document. In the lower right corner, click **Zoom In** ➕ as necessary to set the Zoom level to **100%**. If necessary, on the **HOME tab**, redisplay the formatting marks by clicking **Show/Hide**.

7 Click the **FILE tab**, and then in the lower right portion of the screen, click **Show All Properties**. In the **Tags** box, type **resume, Word table** and in the **Subject** box, type your course name and section number. In the **Author** box, be sure your name is indicated and edit if necessary.

8 On the left, click **Print** to display **Print Preview**. If necessary, return to the document and make any necessary changes.

9 As directed by your instructor, print your document or submit it electronically. **Save** 🖫 your document and **Close** ☒ Word.

More **Knowledge** | **Convert a Table to Text**

To convert a table to text, select the rows or table you want to convert to paragraphs, and then on the LAYOUT tab, in the Data group, click Convert to Text. In the Convert to Text dialog box, under Separate text at, click the separator character to use in place of the column boundaries, and then click OK.

END | You have completed Project 2A

Objective | Edit a Resume in Word Online

You can create and edit tables in Word Online if you are not at a computer on which Word 2013 is installed.

Activity | Editing a Resume in Word Online

In this activity, you will use Word Online to edit a Word table containing a resume similar to the resume you created in Project 1A.

1 From the desktop, start Internet Explorer. Navigate to **http://onedrive.com** and then sign in to your Microsoft account. Click your **GO! Web Projects** folder to open it—or create and then open this folder if necessary.

2 On the OneDrive menu bar, click **Upload**. In the **Choose File to Upload** dialog box, navigate to your student data files, click **w02_2A_Web**, and then click **Open**.

3 Point to the uploaded file **w02_2A_Web**, and then right-click. On the shortcut menu, scroll down as necessary and then click **Rename**. Using your own last name and first name, type **Lastname_Firstname_WD_2A_Web** and then press Enter to rename the file.

4 Click the file that you just renamed, and then in the upper left, click **EDIT DOCUMENT**. On the list, click **Edit in Word Online**.

5 If necessary, click to place the insertion point in the cell *OBJECTIVE*. On the ribbon, under **TABLE TOOLS**, click the **LAYOUT tab**, and then in the **Insert group**, click **Insert Above**.

6 In the first cell of the new row, type **Daniela Frank** press Enter, select the text you just typed, and then on the **HOME tab**, in the **Styles group**, click the **More Styles arrow**, and then click **Title**. With the text selected, change the **Font** to **Calibri (Body)**.

7 Click in the second cell of the new row, and then type **1343 Siena Lane, Deerfield, WI 53531** and press Enter. Type **(608) 555-0588** and press Enter. Type **dfrank@alcona.net** and press Enter. Right-click the email address, and then click **Remove Link**. Select all the text in the second cell that you just typed, and then on the **HOME tab**, in the **Paragraph group**, click **Align Text Right** ☰. Click anywhere to deselect, and then compare your screen with Figure A.

FIGURE A

(GO! with Office Online (formerly Web Apps) continues on the next page)

8 Scroll down and click anywhere in the *EXPERIENCE* cell. On the ribbon, under **TABLE TOOLS**, click the **LAYOUT tab**, and then in the **Insert group**, click **Insert Below**. In the first cell of the new row, press [Backspace] one time to move the insertion point to the left edge of the cell. Type **EDUCATION** Select the text you just typed, and then if necessary, from the **HOME tab**, apply **Bold** [B].

9 Press [Tab] to move to the second cell in the new row, press [Backspace] one time to move to the left edge of the cell, and then type **Madison Area Technical College, Madison, WI** and press [Enter].

10 Type **Associate of Arts in Information Systems, June 2014** and press [Enter]. Select the line of text you just typed, and then press [Ctrl] + [B] to remove **Bold**. Click anywhere to deselect, and then compare your screen with Figure B.

11 Submit the file as directed by your instructor. Sign out of your OneDrive and close Internet Explorer.

FIGURE B

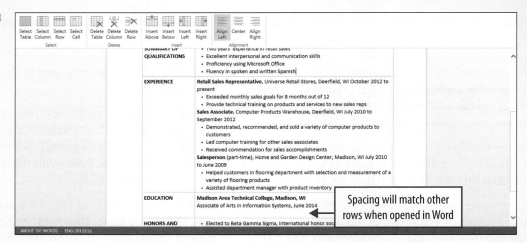

Cover Letter, Reference List, and Envelope

PROJECT ACTIVITIES

In Activities 2.12 through 2.24, you will create a letterhead, save the letterhead as a custom Word template, and then use the letterhead to create a cover letter to accompany a resume. You will also create a list of references from a Microsoft predesigned template and, if you have an envelope and printer available, format and print an envelope. Your completed documents will look similar to Figure 2.18.

PROJECT FILES

For Project 2B, you will need the following files:

New blank Word document
w02B_Cover_Letter_Text

You will save your documents as:

Lastname_Firstname_2B_Cover_Letter
Lastname_Firstname_2B_Reference_List

PROJECT RESULTS

Build from scratch

Jennifer Garcia

1776 Bay Cliff Drive, Tampa, FL 33602
(727) 555-0347 jgarcia@alcona.net

January 8, 2013

Ms. Mary Walker-Huelsman, Director
Florida Port Community College Career Center
2745 Oakland Avenue
St. Petersburg, FL 33713

Dear Ms. Walker-Huelsman:

I am seeking a position in which I can use my computer and communications skills. My education and experience, outlined on the enclosed resume, includes a Business Software Applications Specialist certificate from Florida Port Community College.

With a permanent position as my ultimate goal, I hope to use the Florida Port Community College Career Center to secure a temporary job. I can be available for a flexible number of hours or days and am willing to work in a variety of businesses or organizations.

As my resume illustrates, I have excellent computer skills. I am an honor student at Florida Port Community College and have outstanding references. In addition, I have part-time work experience as a software tester, where I perform the following computer activities:

Microsoft Access	Test database queries
Microsoft Excel	Enter software test data
Microsoft Word	Create and mail form letters

You can contact me by email at jgarcia@alcona.net or by telephone at (727) 555-0347. I am available for an interview at your convenience.

Sincerely,

Jennifer Garcia

Enclosure

Lastname_Firstname_2B_Cover_Letter

Jennifer Garcia
1776 Bay Cliff Drive
Tampa, FL 33602
(727) 555-0347
jgarcia@alcona.net

REFERENCES:

Dr. Tracey Scott
Professor
Florida Port Community College
2745 Oakland Avenue
St. Petersburg, FL 33713
(727) 555-0974
tscott@fpcc-science.edu

Relationship: Professor at Florida Port Community College from July 2012 to July 2013

Mr. James Johnson
Systems Manager
Tampa Tech Group
Two Tech Plaza
Tampa, FL 33602
(727) 555-0144
jjohnson@tech-pro.net

Relationship: Supervisor at Tampa Tech Group from July 2013 to present

Lastname_Firstname_2B_Reference_List

FIGURE 2.18 Project 2B Cover Letter and Reference List

Video W2-4

A *template* is a file you use as a starting point for a *new* document. A template has a predefined document structure and defined settings, such as font, margins, and available styles. On Word's opening screen, you can select from among many different templates—or you can create your own custom template.

When you open a template as the starting point for a new document, the template file opens a copy of itself, unnamed, and then you use the structure—and possibly some content, such as headings—as the starting point for a new document.

All documents are based on a template. When you create a new blank document, it is based on Word's *Normal template*, which serves as the starting point for all blank Word documents.

Activity 2.12 | Changing the Document Style Set for Paragraph Spacing and Applying a Bottom Border to a Paragraph

A *letterhead* is the personal or company information that displays at the top of a letter, and which commonly includes a name, address, and contact information. The term also refers to a piece of paper imprinted with such information at the top. In this activity, you will create a custom template for a personal letterhead.

1 Start Word and display a blank document; be sure that formatting marks and rulers display.

2 On the **DESIGN tab**, in the **Document Formatting group**, click **Paragraph Spacing**.

The Paragraph Spacing command offers various options for setting the line and paragraph spacing of your entire document. A gallery of predefined values displays; or you can create your own custom paragraph spacing.

3 On the list *point* to **Default** and notice the settings in the ScreenTip.

Recall that the default spacing for a new Word document is 0 points of blank space before a paragraph, 8 points of blank space following a paragraph, and line spacing of 1.08.

4 Point to **No Paragraph Space** and notice the settings in the ScreenTip.

The *No Paragraph Space* style inserts *no* extra space before or after a paragraph and uses line spacing of 1. This is the same format used for the line spacing commonly referred to as *single spacing*.

5 Click **No Paragraph Space**.

By using the No Paragraph Space style, you will be able to follow the prescribed format of a letter, which Business Communications texts commonly describe in terms of single spacing.

ANOTHER WAY On Word's opening screen, select the Single spaced (blank) document; or, in a blank document, select the entire document, and then on the HOME tab, in the Styles group, click No Spacing. Also, so long as you leave an appropriate amount of space between the elements of the letter, you can use Word's default spacing. Finally, you could use one of Word's predesigned templates for a cover letter and observe all spacing requirements for a letter.

6 Type **Jennifer Garcia** and then press Enter.

7 Type **1776 Bay Cliff Drive, Tampa, FL 33602** and then press Enter.

8 Type **(727) 555-0347 jgarcia@alcona.net** and then press Enter. If the web address changes to blue text, right-click the web address, and then, click **Remove Hyperlink**.

9 Select the first paragraph—*Jennifer Garcia*—and then on the mini toolbar, apply **Bold** B and change the **Font Size** to **16**.

10 Select the second and third paragraphs. On the mini toolbar, apply **Bold** B and change the **Font Size** to **12**.

11 With the two paragraphs still selected, on the **HOME tab**, in the **Paragraph group**, click **Align Right** ▤.

↻ **ANOTHER WAY**   Press Ctrl + R to align text to the right.

12 Click anywhere in the first paragraph—*Jennifer Garcia*. In the **Paragraph group**, click the **Borders button arrow** ▦ ▾, and then at the bottom, click **Borders and Shading**.

13 In the **Borders and Shading** dialog box, on the **Borders tab**, under **Style**, be sure the first style—a single solid line—is selected.

14 Click the **Width arrow**, and then click **3 pt**. To the right, under **Preview**, click the bottom border of the diagram. Under **Apply to**, be sure *Paragraph* displays. Compare your screen with Figure 2.19.

FIGURE 2.19

↻ **ANOTHER WAY**   Alternatively, under Preview, click the bottom border button ▦ ▾.

15 Click **OK** to display a 3 pt line below *Jennifer Garcia*, which extends from the left margin to the right margin.

The border is a paragraph command and uses the same margins of the paragraph to which it is applied.

Activity 2.13 │ Saving a Document as a Custom Word Template

After you create a document format that you like and will use again, for example, a letterhead for personal letters during a job search, you can save it as a template and then use it as the starting point for any letter.

1 Press F12 to display the **Save As** dialog box. In the lower portion of the dialog box, in the **Save as type** box, at the right edge, click the arrow, and then click **Word Template**.

ALERT!   **Are You Using a Laptop Computer?**

On some laptop computers, you might have to hold down the key labeled FN while pressing the F12 key in order to display the Save As dialog box.

---

2 At the top of the **Save As** dialog box, notice the path, and then compare your screen with Figure 2.20.

By default, Word stores template files on your hard drive in your user folder, in a folder named Custom Word Templates. By doing so, the template is available to you from the Word opening screen.

FIGURE 2.20

3 Click in the **File name** box, using your own name, type **Lastname_Firstname_2B_Letterhead_Template** and then click **Save**.

<table>
<tr><td>**ALERT!**</td><td>**Are You Unable to Save in the Custom Word Templates Folder?**</td></tr>
</table>

Some college computer labs block you from saving on the hard drive. If you are unable to save your template in the Custom Word Templates folder, navigate to your Word Chapter 2 folder on your USB flash drive and save there. If you want to open a template that you stored in a location other than Word's default path, you must open the template directly from File Explorer—not from within Word—for it to open a new unnamed document based on the template.

4 Click the **FILE tab** to display **Backstage** view, and then click **Close** to close the file but leave Word open.

Activity 2.14 | Creating a Cover Letter from a Custom Word Template

A *cover letter* is a document that you send with your resume to provide additional information about your skills and experience. An effective cover letter includes specific information about why you are qualified for the job for which you are applying. Use the cover letter to explain your interest in the position and the organization.

<table>
<tr><td>**ALERT!**</td><td>**Were You Unable to Save in the Custom Word Templates Folder?**</td></tr>
</table>

If you saved your template file on your USB flash drive because you were blocked from saving in the default folder on the hard drive, open your saved document, press [F12] to display the Save As dialog box, and then in your storage location, save the document—using your own name—as Lastname_Firstname_2B_Cover_Letter. Then move to Activity 2.15.

1 With Word open but no documents displayed, click the **FILE tab** to display **Backstage** view, and then click **New** to display the new document options. Compare your screen with Figure 2.21.

Here you can create a new document from a blank document or from one of Word's many built-in or online templates.

FIGURE 2.21

2 Under **Suggested searches**, click **PERSONAL**, *point* to the name of your letterhead template, and then compare your screen with Figure 2.22.

Custom templates that you create and that are stored in the Custom Word Templates folder on your hard drive are accessible to you here whenever you want to create a new document from your stored template.

FIGURE 2.22

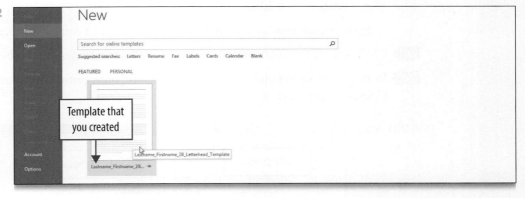

3 Click your letterhead template.

Word opens a copy of your 2B_Letterhead_Template in the form of a new Word document—the title bar indicates *Document* followed by a number. You are not opening the original template file, and changes that you make to this new document will not affect the contents of your 2B_Letterhead_Template file.

4 Press F12 to display the **Save As** dialog box, and then navigate to your **Word Chapter 2** folder. **Save** the file as **Lastname_Firstname_2B_Cover_Letter**

5 On the **INSERT tab**, in the **Header & Footer** group, click **Footer**, click **Edit Footer**, and then in the **Insert group**, click **Document Info**. Click **File Name**, and then click **Close Header and Footer**.

6 Save your document.

Video W2-5

Business letters follow a standard format and contain the following parts: the current date, referred to as the **dateline**; the name and address of the person receiving the letter, referred to as the **inside address**; a greeting, referred to as the **salutation**; the text of the letter, usually referred to as the **body** of the letter; a closing line, referred to as the **complimentary closing**; and the **writer's identification**, which includes the name or job title (or both) of the writer and which is also referred to as the **writer's signature block**.

Some letters also include the initials of the person who prepared the letter, an optional **subject line** that describes the purpose of the letter, or a list of **enclosures**—documents included with the letter.

Activity 2.15 | Adding AutoCorrect Entries

Word's **AutoCorrect** feature corrects commonly misspelled words automatically; for example *teh* instead of *the*. If you have words that you frequently misspell, you can add them to the list for automatic correction.

1 Click the **FILE tab** to display **Backstage** view. On the left, click **Options** to display the **Word Options** dialog box.

2 On the left side of the **Word Options** dialog box, click **Proofing**, and then under **AutoCorrect options**, click the **AutoCorrect Options** button.

3 In the **AutoCorrect** dialog box, click the **AutoCorrect tab**. Under **Replace**, type **resumee** and under **With**, type **resume**

If another student has already added this AutoCorrect entry, a Replace button will display.

4 Click **Add**. If the entry already exists, click **Replace** instead, and then click **Yes**.

5 In the **AutoCorrect** dialog box, under **Replace**, type **computr** and under **With**, type **computer** Compare your screen with Figure 2.23.

FIGURE 2.23

6 Click **Add** (or **Replace**) and then click **OK** two times to close the dialog boxes.

Activity 2.16 | Inserting the Current Date and Creating a Cover Letter

By using the *Date & Time* command, you can select from a variety of formats to insert the current date and time in a document.

For cover letters, there are a variety of accepted letter formats that you will see in reference manuals and Business Communications texts. The one used in this chapter is a block style cover letter following the style in Courtland Bovee and John Thill, *Business Communication Today*, Eleventh Edition, Pearson Prentice Hall, 2012, p. A-2.

1 Press Ctrl + End to move the insertion point to the blank line below the letterhead, and then press Enter three times.

2 On the **INSERT tab**, in the **Text group**, click **Date & Time**, and then click the third date format. Click **OK** to create the dateline.

> Most Business Communication texts recommend that the dateline be positioned at least 0.5 inch (3 blank lines) below the letterhead; or, position the dateline approximately 2 inches from the top edge of the paper.

3 Press Enter four times, which leaves three blank lines. Type the following inside address on four lines, but do *not* press Enter following the last line:

Ms. Mary Walker-Huelsman, Director

Florida Port Community College Career Center

2745 Oakland Avenue

St. Petersburg, FL 33713

The recommended space between the dateline and inside address varies slightly among experts in Business Communication texts and office reference manuals. However, all indicate that the space can be from 1 to 10 blank lines depending on the length of your letter.

4 Press Enter two times to leave one blank line, and then compare your screen with Figure 2.24.

FIGURE 2.24

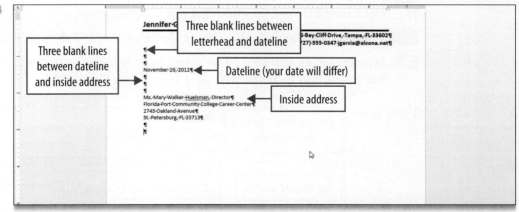

5 Type the salutation **Dear Ms. Walker-Huelsman:** and then press Enter two times.

> Always leave one blank line above and below the salutation.

6 Type, exactly as shown, the following opening paragraph that includes an intentional word usage error: **I am seeking a position in witch I can use my** and press Spacebar. Type, exactly as shown, **computr** and then watch *computr* as you press Spacebar.

> The AutoCorrect feature recognizes the misspelled word, and then changes *computr* to *computer* when you press Spacebar, Enter, or a punctuation mark.

7 Type the following, including the misspelled last word: **and communication skills. My education and experience, outlined on the enclosed resumee** and then type **,** (a comma). Notice that when you type the comma, AutoCorrect replaces *resumee* with *resume*.

8 Press Spacebar, and then complete the paragraph by typing **includes a Business Software Applications Specialist certificate from FPCC.** Compare your screen with Figure 2.25.

FIGURE 2.25

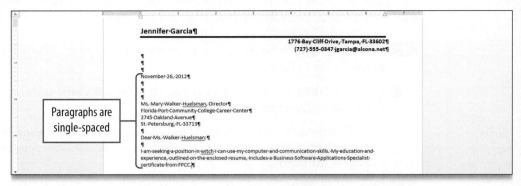

9 Press Enter two times. On the **INSERT tab**, in the **Text group**, click the **Object button arrow**, and then click **Text from File**. From your student files, locate and **Insert** the file **w02B_Cover_Letter_Text**.

Some of the words in the cover letter text display red or blue wavy underlines. These indicate potential spelling, grammar, or word usage errors, and will be addressed before the end of this project.

10 Scroll as necessary to display the lower half of the letter on your screen, and be sure your insertion point is positioned in the blank paragraph at the end of the document.

11 Press Enter one time to leave one blank line between the last paragraph of the letter and the complimentary closing.

12 Type **Sincerely,** as the complimentary closing, and then press Enter four times to leave three blank lines between the complimentary closing and the writer's identification.

13 Type **Jennifer Garcia** as the writer's identification, and then press Enter two times.

14 Type **Enclosure** to indicate that a document is included with the letter. **Save** 🖫 your document, and then compare your screen with Figure 2.26.

FIGURE 2.26

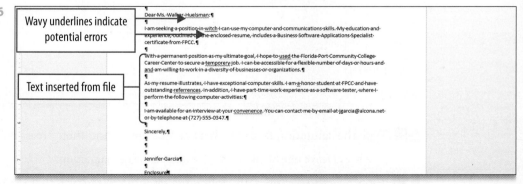

Activity 2.17 | Finding and Replacing Text

Use the Find command to locate text in a document quickly. Use the Find and Replace command to make the same change, or to make more than one change at a time, in a document.

1 ▸ Press [Ctrl] + [Home] to position the insertion point at the beginning of the document.

Because a find operation—or a find and replace operation—begins from the location of the insertion point and proceeds to the end of the document, it is good practice to position the insertion point at the beginning of the document before initiating the command.

2 ▸ On the **HOME tab**, in the **Editing group**, click **Find**.

The navigation pane displays on the left side of the screen with a search box at the top of the pane.

 ANOTHER WAY   Hold down [Ctrl] and press [F].

3 ▸ In the **navigation** pane, in the search box, type **ac** If necessary, scroll down slightly in your document to view the entire body text of the letter, and then compare your screen with Figure 2.27.

In the document, the search letters *ac* are selected and highlighted in yellow for both words that begin with the letters *ac* and also for the word *contact* which contains this letter combination. In the navigation pane, the three instances are shown in context—*ac* displays in bold.

FIGURE 2.27

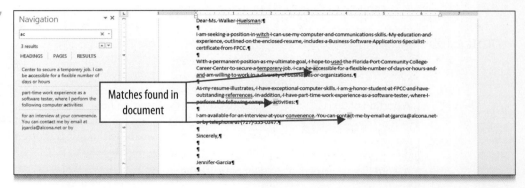

4 ▸ Click in the search box again, and type as necessary to display the word *accessible* in the search box.

One match for the search term displays in context in the navigation pane and is highlighted in the document.

5 ▸ In the document, double-click the yellow highlighted word *accessible*, and then type **available** to replace the word.

6 ▸ **Close** [×] the **navigation** pane, and then on the **HOME tab**, in the **Editing group**, click **Replace**.

7 ▸ In the **Find and Replace** dialog box, in the **Find what** box, replace the existing text by typing **FPCC** and in the **Replace with** box, type **Florida Port Community College** and then compare your screen with Figure 2.28.

FIGURE 2.28

8 In the lower left corner of the dialog box, click **More** to expand the dialog box, and then under **Search Options**, select the **Match case** check box.

The acronym *FPCC* appears in the document two times. In a formal letter, the reader may not know what the acronym means, so you should include the full text instead of an acronym. In this instance, you must select the *Match case* check box so that the replaced text will match the case you typed in the Replace with box, and *not* display in all uppercase letters in the manner of *FPCC*.

9 In the **Find and Replace** dialog box, click **Replace All** to replace both instances of *FPCC*. Click **OK** to close the message box.

10 In the **Find and Replace** dialog box, clear the **Match case** check box, click **Less**, and then **Close** the dialog box. **Save** 🖫 your document.

The Find and Replace dialog box opens with the settings used the last time it was open. Therefore, it is good practice to reset this dialog box to its default settings each time you use it.

Activity 2.18 | Selecting and Moving Text to a New Location

By using Word's **drag-and-drop** feature, you can use the mouse to drag selected text from one location to another. This method is most useful when the text you are moving is on the same screen as the destination location.

1 Take a moment to study the table in Figure 2.29 to become familiar with the techniques you can use to select text in a document quickly.

FIGURE 2.29

SELECTING TEXT IN A DOCUMENT	
TO SELECT THIS:	**DO THIS:**
A portion of text	Click to position the insertion point at the beginning of the text you want to select, hold down Shift, and then click at the end of the text you want to select. Alternatively, hold down the left mouse button and drag from the beginning to the end of the text you want to select.
A word	Double-click the word.
A sentence	Hold down Ctrl and click anywhere in the sentence.
A paragraph	Triple-click anywhere in the paragraph; or, move the pointer to the left of the line, into the margin area. When the ⚟ pointer displays, double-click.
A line	Point to the left of the line. When the ⚟ pointer displays, click one time.
One character at a time	Position the insertion point to the left of the first character, hold down Shift, and press ← or → as many times as desired.
A string of words	Position the insertion point to the left of the first word, hold down Shift and Ctrl, and then press ← or → as many times as desired.
Consecutive lines	Position the insertion point to the left of the first word, hold down Shift and press ↑ or ↓.
Consecutive paragraphs	Position the insertion point to the left of the first word, hold down Shift and Ctrl and press ↑ or ↓.
The entire document	Hold down Ctrl and press A. Alternatively, move the pointer to the left of any line in the document. When the ⚟ pointer displays, triple-click.

2 Be sure you can view the entire body of the letter on your screen. In the paragraph that begins *With a permanent position*, in the second line, locate and double-click *days*.

3 Point to the selected word to display the ▧ pointer.

4 Drag to the right until the dotted vertical line that floats next to the pointer is positioned to the right of the word *hours* in the same line, as shown in Figure 2.30.

FIGURE 2.30

5 Release the mouse button to move the text. Select *hours* and drag it to the left of the word *or*—the previous location of the word *days*. Click anywhere to deselect the text.

6 Examine the text that you moved, and add or remove spaces as necessary.

7 Hold down Ctrl, and then in the paragraph that begins *I am available*, click anywhere in the first sentence to select the entire sentence.

8 Drag the selected sentence to the end of the paragraph by positioning the small vertical line that floats with the pointer to the left of the paragraph mark. **Save** 🖫 your document, and then compare your screen with Figure 2.31.

FIGURE 2.31

Activity 2.19 | Inserting a Table into a Document and Applying a Table Style

1 Locate the paragraph that begins *You can contact me*, and then click to position the insertion point in the blank line above that paragraph. Press Enter one time.

2 On the **INSERT tab**, in the **Tables group**, click **Table**. In the **Table** grid, in the third row, click the second square to insert a 2 × 3 table.

3 In the first cell of the table, type **Microsoft Access** and then press Tab. Type **Test database queries** and then press Tab. Complete the table using the following information:

Microsoft Excel	Enter software test data
Microsoft Word	Create and mail form letters

4 Point slightly outside of the upper left corner of the table to display the **table move handle** button ⊞. With the ⊹ pointer, click one time to select the entire table.

5 On the **LAYOUT tab**, in the **Cell Size group**, click **AutoFit**, and then click **AutoFit Contents** to have Word choose the best column widths for the two columns based on the text you entered.

6 ▶ With the table still selected, on the **DESIGN tab**, in the **Table Styles group**, click **More** ▼. Under **Plain Tables**, click the second style—**Table Grid Light**.

Use Table Styles to change the visual style of a table.

7 ▶ With the table still selected, on the **HOME tab**, in the **Paragraph group**, click **Center** ▤ to center the table between the left and right margins. Click anywhere to deselect the table.

8 ▶ Save ▤ and then compare your screen with Figure 2.32.

FIGURE 2.32

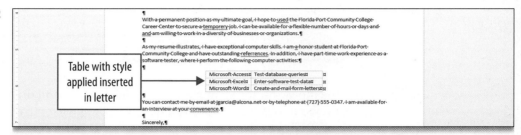

Table with style applied inserted in letter

More Knowledge **Configure Cell Margins in a Table**

You can modify the margins of a cell to increase or decrease the distance between the cell border and the text in the cell. To do so, on the LAYOUT tab, in the Alignment group, click Cell Margins, and then enter the new margins.

Objective 6 | Use the Proofing Options and Print an Envelope

Video W2-6

Word compares your typing to words in the Office dictionary and compares your phrases and punctuation to a list of grammar rules. This automatic proofing is set by default. Words that are not in the dictionary and words, phrases, and punctuation that differ from the grammar rules are marked with wavy underlines; for example, the misuse of *their*, *there*, and *they're*.

Word will not flag the word *sign* as misspelled even though you intended to type *sing a song* rather than *sign a song*, because both are words contained within Word's dictionary. Your own knowledge and proofreading skills are still required, even when using a sophisticated word processing program like Word.

Activity 2.20 | Checking for Spelling and Grammar Errors

There are two ways to respond to spelling and grammar errors flagged by Word. You can right-click a flagged word or phrase, and then from the shortcut menu choose a correction or action. Or, you can initiate the Spelling & Grammar command to display the Spelling and Grammar pane, which provides more options than the shortcut menus.

ALERT! **Activating Spelling and Grammar Checking**

If you do not see any wavy red or blue lines under words, the automatic spelling or grammar checking has been turned off on your system. To activate the spelling and grammar checking, display Backstage view, click Options, click Proofing, and then under *When correcting spelling in Microsoft Office programs*, select the first four check boxes. Under *When correcting spelling and grammar in Word*, select the first four check boxes, and then click the Writing Style arrow and click Grammar Only. Under *Exceptions for*, clear both check boxes. To display the flagged spelling and grammar errors, click the Recheck Document button, and then close the dialog box.

---

1 Position the body of the letter on your screen, and then examine the text to locate wavy underlines.

A list of grammar rules applied by a computer program like Word can never be exact, and a computer dictionary cannot contain all known words and proper names. Therefore, you will need to check any words flagged by Word with wavy underlines, and you will also need to proofread for content errors.

2 In the lower left corner of your screen, in the status bar, locate and point to the ▢ icon to display the ScreenTip *Proofing errors were found. Click to correct.* Compare your screen with Figure 2.33.

If this button displays, you know there are potential errors identified in the document.

FIGURE 2.33

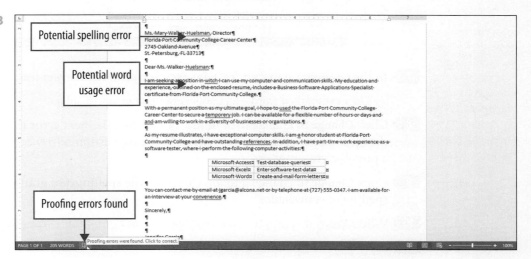

3 In the paragraph that begins *With a permanent*, in the second line, locate the word *temporery* with the wavy red underline. Point to the word and right-click, and then click **temporary** to correct the spelling error.

4 In the next line, locate the word *and* that displays with a wavy red underline, point to the word and right-click, and then on the shortcut menu, click **Delete Repeated Word** to delete the duplicate word.

5 Press Ctrl + Home to move the insertion point to the beginning of the document. Click the **REVIEW tab**, and then in the **Proofing group**, click **Spelling & Grammar** to check the spelling and grammar of the text in the document.

The Spelling pane displays on the right, and the proper name *Huelsman* is flagged. Word's dictionary contains only very common proper names—unusual names like this one will typically be flagged as a potential spelling error. If this is a name that you frequently type, consider adding it to the dictionary.

 ANOTHER WAY   Press F7 to start the Spelling & Grammar command.

6 In the **Spelling** pane, click **Ignore All**. Compare your screen with Figure 2.34.

The word *witch* is highlighted as a grammar error, and in the Grammar pane, *which* is suggested.

FIGURE 2.34

7 In the **Grammar** pane, click **Change** to change to the correct usage *which*.

The next marked word—a possible grammar error—displays.

8 Click **Change** to change *used* to *use*. Notice that the next error is a potential spelling error. In the **Spelling** pane, change *referrences* to the suggestion *references*. Notice that the next error is a possible grammar error.

9 Click **Change** to change *a* to *an*. Continue the spelling and grammar check and correct the spelling of *convenence*.

10 When Word displays the message *Spelling and grammar check complete*, click **OK**.

11 **Save** your document.

Activity 2.21 | Using the Thesaurus

A *thesaurus* is a research tool that lists *synonyms*—words that have the same or similar meaning to the word you selected.

1 Scroll so that you can view the body of the letter. In the paragraph that begins *With a permanent*, double-click to select the word *diversity*, and then in the **Proofing** group, click **Thesaurus**.

The Thesaurus pane displays on the right a list of synonyms; the list will vary in length depending on the selected word.

ANOTHER WAY   Right-click the word, on the shortcut menu, point to Synonyms, and then click Thesaurus.

2 In the **Thesaurus** pane, point to the word *variety*, and then click the arrow that displays. Click **Insert** to change *diversity* to *variety*.

3 In the paragraph that begins *As my resume*, double-click the word *exceptional*, and then on the ribbon, click **Thesaurus** again.

4 In the **Thesaurus** pane, point to *excellent*, click the **arrow**, and then click **Insert**. Compare your screen with Figure 2.35.

FIGURE 2.35

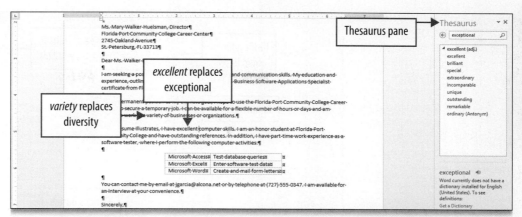

5 Close ☒ the **Thesaurus** pane.

6 Click the **FILE tab** to display **Backstage** view, and then on the **Info tab**, in the lower right portion of the screen, click **Show All Properties**. If you used your template, notice that it is indicated to the right of *Template*.

7 In the **Tags** box, type **cover letter** and in the **Subject** box, type your course name and section number. In the **Author** box, be sure your name is indicated and edit if necessary.

8 On the left, click **Print** to display **Print Preview**. If necessary, return to the document and make any necessary changes.

9 As directed by your instructor, print your document or submit it electronically. **Save** 🖫 your document and **Close** [×] Word.

Activity 2.22 | Addressing and Printing an Envelope

Use Word's Envelopes command on the Mailings label to format and print an envelope.

> **NOTE** | **This Is an Optional Activity**
>
> This activity is optional. If you do not have an envelope and printer, or do not want to complete the activity at this time, move to Activity 2.23.

1 Display your **2B_Cover_Letter**, and then select the four lines that comprise the inside address.

2 On the **MAILINGS tab**, in the **Create group**, click **Envelopes**. Notice that the **Delivery address** contains the selected inside address.

3 Click in the **Return address** box, and then type **Jennifer Garcia** and press ⏎. Type **1776 Bay Cliff Drive** and then press ⏎. Type **Tampa, FL 33602**

4 In the lower portion of the **Envelopes and Labels** dialog box, click **Options**, and then compare your screen with Figure 2.36.

The default envelope size is a standard business envelope referred to as a Size 10.

FIGURE 2.36

5 ▶ Click **OK** to close the **Envelope Options** dialog box. As shown under **Feed**, insert an envelope in your printer and then click **Print**.

Depending on the type and brand of printer you are using, your feed area may vary.

6 ▶ Close your **2B_Cover_Letter**, and then **Close** Word.

Objective 7 Create a Document Using a Predesigned Microsoft Template

Video W2-7

Microsoft provides predesigned templates for letters, calendars, invoices, and other types of documents. Recall that when you open a template, it opens unnamed so that you can reuse it as often as you need to do so.

Activity 2.23 | Locating and Opening a Template

In this activity, you will use a predesigned template to create a list of references to accompany a resume. References are not included on a resume, because you want to use the resume space for personal information. Most employers do not check references until after the first interview and when they have decided to consider you for a position. Be sure that you have already notified these individuals, asked their permission to use their name as a reference, and then contact them to tell them that a specific employer may be contacting them.

1 ▶ **Start** Word, and then on the opening screen, in the **Search for online templates** box, type **resume references** and press Enter.

2 ▶ Locate the reference list that contains three left-aligned reference items as shown in Figure 2.37.

FIGURE 2.37

3 ▸ Click the three-item reference template, and then click **Create**. Compare your screen with Figure 2.38.

> The template opens a copy of itself in the form of a new Word document—the title bar indicates *Document* followed by a number. Recall that you are not opening the template itself, and that changes you make to this new document will not affect the contents of the template file.

FIGURE 2.38

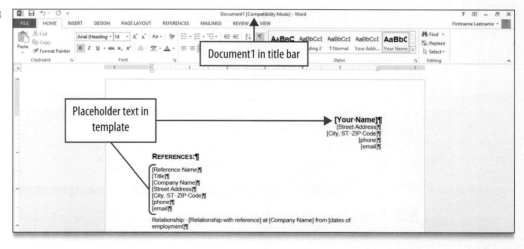

4 ▸ Press F12 to display the **Save As** dialog box. **Save** the document in your **Word Chapter 2** folder as **Lastname_Firstname_2B_Reference_List** and click **Save**. If a message indicates that you will be upgraded to the newest file format, click **OK**.

5 ▸ Add the file name to the footer, and then **Save** 🖫 your document.

Activity 2.24 | Replacing Template Placeholder Text and Removing Controls

After you save the template file as a Word document, you can begin to substitute your own information in the indicated locations. *Placeholder text* is text that indicates the type of information to be entered. Text surrounded by brackets is called a *content control*. There are several different types of content controls, including date, picture, and *text controls*. All of the controls in this template are text controls.

1 In the upper right, click in the placeholder text *[Your Name]* and type **Jennifer Garcia** Click *[Street Address]* and type **1776 Bay Cliff Drive**

2 Click *[City, ST ZIP Code]* and type **Tampa, FL 33602** Click *[phone]* and type **(727) 555-0347** Click *[email]* and type **jgarcia@alcona.net**

3 Under **References**, enter two references using the following information, and then compare your screen with Figure 2.39.

TEMPLATE FIELD	REFERENCE 1	REFERENCE 2
Reference Name	Dr. Tracey Scott	Mr. James Johnson
Title	Professor	Systems Manager
Company Name	Florida Port Community College	Tampa Tech Group
Street Address	2745 Oakland Avenue	Two Tech Plaza
City, ST ZIP Code	St. Petersburg, FL 33713	Tampa, FL 33602
phone	(727) 555-0974	(727) 555-0144
email	tscott@fpcc-science.edu	jjohnson@tech-pro.net
Relationship with reference	Professor	Supervisor
Company Name	Florida Port Community College	Tampa Tech Group
dates of employment	July 2012 to July 2013	July 2013 to present

FIGURE 2.39

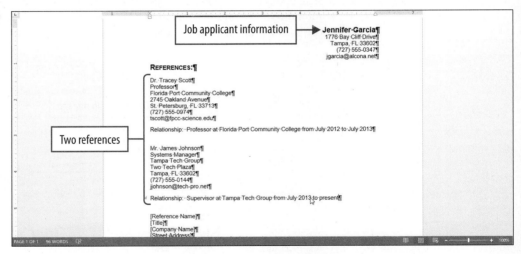

4 Scroll down to the third reference block. Select all the paragraphs of placeholder text, and then press [Del] to delete these unneeded controls; this list will contain only two references.

🔄 **ANOTHER WAY**   Point to a content control, right-click, and then on the shortcut menu, click Remove Content Control.

5 Click **Save** 🔲. Click the **FILE tab**, and then in the lower right portion of the screen, click **Show All Properties**. In the **Tags** box, type **reference list** and in the **Subject** box, type your course name and section number. In the **Author** box, be sure your name is indicated and edit if necessary.

6 On the left, click **Print** to display **Print Preview**. If necessary, return to the document and make any necessary changes.

7 As directed by your instructor, print your document or submit it electronically. **Save** 🔲 your document and **Close** ✕ Word.

END | You have completed Project 2B

Objective   Create a Table in Word Online

You can create and edit tables in Word Online if you are not at a computer on which Word 2013 is installed.

ALERT!	Working with Web-Based Applications and Services

Computer programs and services on the web receive continuous updates and improvements, so the steps to complete this web-based activity may differ from the ones shown. You can often look at the screens and the information presented to determine how to complete the activity.

Activity | Creating a Table in Word Online

In this activity, you will use Word Online to create a Word table within a document similar to Project 2B.

1 From the desktop, start Internet Explorer. Navigate to **http://onedrive.com** and then sign in to your Microsoft account. Open your **GO! Web Projects** folder—or create and then open this folder if necessary.

2 On the OneDrive menu bar, click **Upload**. In the **Choose File to Upload** dialog box, navigate to your student data files, click **w02_2B_Web**, and then click **Open**.

3 Point to the uploaded file **w02_2B_Web**, and then right-click. On the shortcut menu, scroll down as necessary and then click **Rename**. Using your own last name and first name, type **Lastname_Firstname_WD_2B_Web** and then press Enter to rename the file.

4 Click the file that you just renamed, and then in the upper left, click **EDIT DOCUMENT**. On the list, click **Edit in Word Online**.

5 Press Ctrl + End to move to the end of the document, and then press Enter.

6 On the **INSERT tab**, in the **Tables group**, click **Table**, and then insert a **3 × 4 Table**.

7 Type **Position** and press Tab. Type **Type** and press Tab. Type **Location** and press Tab.

8 In the second row type **Paralegal** and press Tab. Type **Part-time** and press Tab. Type **Tampa** and press Tab. Compare your screen with Figure A.

FIGURE A

(GO! with Office Online continues on the next page)

9 Type **Legal Records Clerk** and press `Tab`. Type **Full-time, 2 months** and press `Tab`. Type **North Tampa** and press `Tab`.

10 On the ribbon, under **TABLE TOOLS**, click the **LAYOUT tab**, and then in the **Delete group**, click **Delete Row**.

11 Drag to select all the cells in the first row, and then on the **HOME tab**, in the **Styles group**, click **Heading 1**.

With the three column titles still selected, in the **Paragraph group**, click **Center** ☰. In the **Font group**, change the **Font Color** to **Black, Text 1**. Compare your screen with Figure B.

12 Submit the file as directed by your instructor. Sign out of your OneDrive and close Internet Explorer.

FIGURE B

Office 365 combines tools for collaboration and productivity and delivers them to multiple users in an organization by using *cloud computing*—applications and services that are accessed over the Internet with multiple devices. For example, one cloud service with which you might be familiar is *OneDrive*, a free web-based application with which you can save, store, organize, and share files online. This cloud service is available for anyone that has a free Microsoft account.

Another cloud service from Microsoft is *Office Online*. These are the online companions to the desktop versions of Microsoft Office Word, Excel, PowerPoint, and OneNote that enable you to create, access, share, and perform light editing on Microsoft Office documents from any device that connects to the Internet and uses a supported *web browser*. A web browser is software, such as Internet Explorer, Firefox, Safari, or Chrome, that displays web pages.

For an organization, cloud computing enables the addition of services without investing in additional hardware and software. For you as a team member, you can simply use your web browser to access, edit, store, and share files. You do not need to have a full version of Office installed on your computer to do this. You have all the tools and security that large organizations have!

When you use using Office 365, your email and storage servers are hosted by Microsoft. Your organization gets business-class security from Microsoft—a large, well-established company. Sophisticated security and data management features are built into Office 365 so that you can control *permissions*—access rights that define the ability of an individual or group to view or make changes to documents—and provide secure email and communications.

Activity | Using Lync to Collaborate by Using a Video Call

This group project relates to the **Bell Orchid Hotels**. If your instructor assigns this project to your class, you can expect to use **Lync** in **Office 365** to collaborate on the following tasks for this chapter:

- If you are in the **Accounting Group**, you and your teammates will conduct a video call to discuss and agree on the letter that will be sent to shareholders.
- If you are in the **Engineering Group**, you and your teammates will conduct a video call to discuss and agree on the letter that will be sent to the three insurance companies that cover the hotel properties.
- If you are in the **Food and Beverage Group**, you and your teammates will conduct a video call to discuss and agree on the letter that will be sent to a customer planning a banquet.
- If you are in the **Human Resources Group**, you and your teammates will conduct a video call to discuss and agree on the memo for employees regarding the new employee newsletter.
- If you are in the **Operations Group**, you and your teammates will conduct a video call to discuss and agree on the letter that will be sent to three job applicants.
- If you are in the **Sales and Marking Group**, you and your teammates will conduct a video call to discuss and agree on the letter that will be sent to 20 groups of professional associations.

FIGURE A

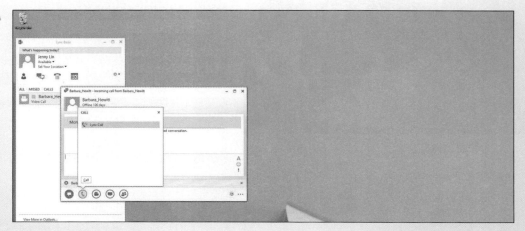

END OF CHAPTER

SUMMARY

Word tables enable you to present information in a logical and orderly format. Each cell in a Word table behaves like a document; as you type in a cell, wordwrap moves text to the next line.

A good source of information for resume formats is a business communications textbook. A simple two-column table created in Word is suitable to create an appropriate resume for a recent college graduate.

Use Word's Office Presentation Service to present a Word document to others who can watch in a web browser. Word automatically creates a link to your document that you can share with others via email.

A template is useful because it has a predefined document structure and defined settings such as font, margins, and available styles. On Word's opening screen, you can select from thousands of templates.

GO! LEARN IT ONLINE

Review the concepts and key terms in this chapter by completing these online challenges, which you can find at **www.pearsonhighered.com/go**.

Matching and Multiple Choice:
Answer matching and multiple choice questions to test what you learned in this chapter. MyITLab®

Crossword Puzzle:
Spell out the words that match the numbered clues, and put them in the puzzle squares.

Flipboard:
Flip through the definitions of the key terms in this chapter and match them with the correct term.

GO! FOR JOB SUCCESS

Video: Cover Letter and Resume Tips

Your instructor may assign this video to your class, and then ask you to think about, or discuss with your classmates, these questions:

FotolEdhar / Fotolia

A cover letter should contain different but complimentary information than the facts on your resume and be tailored to the specific job you are applying for. Name two different things that you could mention in a cover letter.

What type of information belongs in the Career Objective portion of your resume?

When is it best to use a chronological resume layout, and when is it appropriate to use a functional resume layout?

END OF CHAPTER
REVIEW AND ASSESSMENT GUIDE FOR WORD CHAPTER 2

Your instructor may assign one or more of these projects to help you review the chapter and assess your mastery and understanding of the chapter.

	Review and Assessment Guide for Word Chapter 2		
Project	**Apply Skills from These Chapter Objectives**	**Project Type**	**Project Location**
2C	Objectives 1-3 from Project 2A	**2C Skills Review** A guided review of the skills from Project 2A.	On the following pages
2D	Objectives 4-7 from Project 2B	**2D Skills Review** A guided review of the skills from Project 2B.	On the following pages
2E	Objectives 1-3 from Project 2A	**2E Mastery (Grader Project)** A demonstration of your mastery of the skills in Project 2A with extensive decision making.	In MyITLab and on the following pages
2F	Objectives 4-7 from Project 2B	**2F Mastery (Grader Project)** A demonstration of your mastery of the skills in Project 2B with extensive decision making.	In MyITLab and on the following pages
2G	Objectives 1-7 from Projects 2A and 2B	**2G Mastery (Grader Project)** A demonstration of your mastery of the skills in Projects 2A and 2B with extensive decision making.	In MyITLab and on the following pages
2H	Combination of Objectives from Projects 2A and 2B	**2H GO! Fix It** A demonstration of your mastery of the skills in Projects 2A and 2B by creating a correct result from a document that contains errors you must find.	Online
2I	Combination of Objectives from Projects 2A and 2B	**2I GO! Make It** A demonstration of your mastery of the skills in Projects 2A and 2B by creating a result from a supplied picture.	Online
2J	Combination of Objectives from Projects 2A and 2B	**2J GO! Solve It** A demonstration of your mastery of the skills in Projects 2A and 2B, your decision-making skills, and your critical thinking skills. A task-specific rubric helps you self-assess your result.	Online
2K	Combination of Objectives from Projects 2A and 2B	**2K GO! Solve It** A demonstration of your mastery of the skills in Projects 2A and 2B, your decision-making skills, and your critical thinking skills. A task-specific rubric helps you self-assess your result.	On the following pages
2L	Combination of Objectives from Projects 2A and 2B	**2L GO! Think** A demonstration of your understanding of the chapter concepts applied in a manner that you would outside of college. An analytic rubric helps you and your instructor grade the quality of your work by comparing it to the work an expert in the discipline would create.	On the following pages
2M	Combination of Objectives from Projects 2A and 2B	**2M GO! Think** A demonstration of your understanding of the chapter concepts applied in a manner that you would outside of college. An analytic rubric helps you and your instructor grade the quality of your work by comparing it to the work an expert in the discipline would create.	Online
2N	Combination of Objectives from Projects 2A and 2B	**2N You and GO!** A demonstration of your understanding of the chapter concepts applied in a manner that you would in a personal situation. An analytic rubric helps you and your instructor grade the quality of your work.	Online
2O	Combination of Objectives from Projects 2A and 2B	**2O Cumulative Group Project for Word Chapter 2** A demonstration of your understanding of concepts and your ability to work collaboratively in a group role-playing assessment, requiring both collaboration and self-management.	Online

GLOSSARY

GLOSSARY OF CHAPTER KEY TERMS

AutoCorrect A feature that corrects common typing and spelling errors as you type, for example changing *teh* to *the*.

Body The text of a letter.

Cell The box at the intersection of a row and column in a Word table.

Cloud computing Applications and services that are accessed over the Internet with multiple devices.

Complimentary closing A parting farewell in a business letter.

Content control In a template, an area indicated by placeholder text that can be used to add text, pictures, dates, or lists.

Cover letter A document that you send with your resume to provide additional information about your skills and experience.

Date & Time A command with which you can automatically insert the current date and time into a document in a variety of formats.

Dateline The first line in a business letter that contains the current date and which is positioned just below the letterhead if a letterhead is used.

Drag-and-drop A technique by which you can move, by dragging, selected text from one location in a document to another.

Enclosures Additional documents included with a business letter.

Inside address The name and address of the person receiving the letter and positioned below the date line.

Letterhead The personal or company information that displays at the top of a letter.

No Paragraph Style The built-in paragraph style—available from the Paragraph Spacing command—that inserts *no* extra space before or after a paragraph and uses line spacing of 1.

Normal template The template that serves as a basis for all Word documents.

Office Presentation Service A Word feature to present your Word document to others who can watch in a web browser.

One-click Row/Column Insertion A Word table feature with which you can insert a new row or column by pointing to the desired location and then clicking.

Placeholder text The text in a content control that indicates the type of information to be entered in a specific location.

Salutation The greeting line of a business letter.

Single spacing The common name for line spacing in which there is *no* extra space before or after a paragraph and that uses line spacing of 1.

Skype A Microsoft product with which you can make voice calls, make video calls, transfer files, or send messages—including instant message and text messages—over the Internet.

Subject line The optional line following the inside address in a business letter that states the purpose of the letter.

Synonyms Words with the same or similar meaning.

Table An arrangement of information organized into rows and columns.

Template An existing document that you use as a starting point for a new document; it opens a copy of itself, unnamed, and then you use the structure—and possibly some content, such as headings—as the starting point for a new document.

Text control A content control that accepts only a text entry.

Thesaurus A research tool that provides a list of synonyms.

Writer's identification The name and title of the author of a letter, placed near the bottom of the letter under the complimentary closing—also referred to as the *writer's signature block*.

Writer's signature block The name and title of the author of a letter, placed near the bottom of the letter, under the complimentary closing—also referred to as the *writer's identification*.

CHAPTER REVIEW

Skills Review | Project 2C Student Resume

In the following Skills Review, you will use a table to create a resume for Ashley Kent. Your completed resume will look similar to the one shown in Figure 2.40.

PROJECT FILES

For Project 2C, you will need the following files:

New blank Word document
w02C_Skills
w02C_Experience

You will save your document as:

Lastname_Firstname_2C_Student_Resume

PROJECT RESULTS

Ashley Kent

2212 Bramble Road
St. Petersburg, FL 33713
(727) 555-0237
ashleykent@alcona.net

OBJECTIVE A computer programmer position in a small startup company that requires excellent computer programming skills, systems analysis experience, and knowledge of database design.

SKILLS **Computer Programming**
- Advanced C/C++
- Java
- Ruby on Rails
- SQL

Leadership
- Secretary, Florida Port Community College Computer Club
- Vice President, Associated Students, Bay Hills High School

Additional Skills
- Microsoft Office
- Adobe Creative Suite
- Adobe Acrobat Pro

EXPERIENCE **Database Designer** (part-time), Admissions and Records
Florida Port Community College, St. Petersburg, FL
September 2014 to present

Software Tester (part-time), Macro Games Inc., Tampa, FL
September 2011 to September 2014

EDUCATION **Florida Port Community College**, Computer Science major
September 2014 to present

Graduate of Bay Hills High School
June 2014

Lastname_Firstname_2C_Student_Resume

FIGURE 2.40

(Project 2C Student Resume continues on the next page)

CHAPTER REVIEW

1 **Start** Word and display a blank document. Be sure that formatting marks and rulers display. **Save** the document in your **Word Chapter 2** folder as **Lastname_Firstname_2C_Student_Resume**

a. Add the file name to the footer, and then close the footer area. Click the **INSERT tab**, and then in the **Tables group**, click **Table**. In the **Table** grid, in the fourth row, click the second square to insert a **2 × 4** table.

b. In the first cell of the table, type **Ashley Kent** and then press Enter. Type the following text, pressing Enter after each line *except* the last line:

2212 Bramble Road

St. Petersburg, FL 33713

(727) 555-0237

ashleykent@alcona.net

c. Press ↓ to move to the first cell in the second row. Type **SKILLS** and then press ↓ to move to the first cell in the third row.

d. Type **EXPERIENCE** and then press ↓. Type **EDUCATION**

e. In the first cell, if the email address displays in blue, right-click the email address, and then on the shortcut menu, click **Remove Hyperlink**. **Save** your document.

2 Click in the cell to the right of *SKILLS*, and then type the following, pressing Enter after each line including the last line:

Computer Programming

Advanced C/C++

Java

Ruby on Rails

SQL

a. With the insertion point in the new line at the end of the cell, click the **INSERT tab**. In the **Text group**, click the **Object button arrow**, and then click **Text from File**.

b. Navigate to your student files, select **w02C_Skills**, and then click **Insert**. Press Backspace one time to remove the blank paragraph.

c. Click in the cell to the right of *EXPERIENCE*, and then insert the file **w02C_Experience**. Press Backspace one time to remove the blank line.

d. Click in the cell to the right of *EDUCATION*, and then type the following, pressing Enter after all lines *except* the last line:

Florida Port Community College, Computer Science major

September 2014 to present

Graduate of Bay Hills High School

June 2014

3 Point to the upper left corner of the *SKILLS* cell, and then click the **Row Insertion** button. In the first cell of the new row, type **OBJECTIVE** and then press Tab.

a. Type **A computer programmer position in a small startup company that requires excellent computer programming skills, systems analysis experience, and knowledge of database design.**

b. In any row, point to the vertical border between the two columns to display the ✛ pointer. Drag the column border to the left to approximately **1.5 inches on the horizontal ruler**.

c. Under **TABLE TOOLS**, on the **LAYOUT tab**, in the **Cell Size group**, click **AutoFit**, and then click **AutoFit Window** to be sure that your table stretches across the page within the margins.

d. In the first row of the table, drag across both cells to select them. On the **LAYOUT tab**, in the **Merge group**, click **Merge Cells**. Right-click over the selected cell, and then on the mini toolbar, click **Center**.

e. In the top row, select the first paragraph of text—*Ashley Kent*. On the mini toolbar, increase the **Font Size** to **20** and apply **Bold**.

f. In the second row, point to the word *OBJECTIVE*, hold down the left mouse button, and then drag down to select the row headings in uppercase letters. On the mini toolbar, click **Bold**. **Save** your document.

4 Click in the cell to the right of *OBJECTIVE*. On the **PAGE LAYOUT tab**, in the **Paragraph group**, click the **Spacing After up spin arrow** three times to change the spacing to **18 pt**.

a. In the cell to the right of *SKILLS*, apply **Bold** to the words *Computer Programming*, *Leadership*, and *Additional Skills*. Then, under each bold heading in

(Project 2C Student Resume continues on the next page)

CHAPTER REVIEW

the cell, select the lines of text, and create a bulleted list.

b. In the first two bulleted lists, click in the last bullet item, and then on the **PAGE LAYOUT tab**, in the **Paragraph group**, set the **Spacing After** to **12 pt**.

c. In the last bulleted list, click in the last bullet item, and then set the **Spacing After** to **18 pt**.

d. In the cell to the right of *EXPERIENCE*, apply **Bold** to *Database Designer* and *Software Tester*. Click in the line *September 2014 to present* and apply **Spacing After** of **12 pt**. Click in the line *September 2011 to September 2014* and apply **Spacing After** of **18 pt**.

e. In the cell to the right of *EDUCATION*, apply **Bold** to *Florida Port Community College* and *Graduate of Bay Hills High School*.

f. In the same cell, click in the line *September 2014 to present* and apply **Spacing After** of **12 pt**.

g. In the first row, click in the last line—*ashleykent@alcona.net*—and then change the **Spacing After** to **18 pt**. Click in the first line—*Ashley Kent*—and set the **Spacing Before** to **30 pt** and the **Spacing After** to **6 pt**.

5 Point to the upper left corner of the table, and then click the **table move handle** ⊞ to select the entire table. Under **TABLE TOOLS**, on the **DESIGN tab**, in the **Table**

Styles group, click the **Borders button arrow**, and then click **No Border**.

a. In the **Table Styles group**, click the **Borders button arrow** again, and then at the bottom of the gallery, click **Borders and Shading**. In the **Borders and Shading** dialog box, under **Setting**, click **Custom**. Under **Style**, scroll down slightly, and then click the style with two equal lines.

b. Click the **Width arrow**, and then click **1 1/2 pt**. Under **Preview**, click the top border of the preview box, and then click **OK**.

c. Click the **FILE tab** to display **Backstage** view, and then in the lower right portion of the screen, click **Show All Properties**. In the **Tags** box, type **resume, table** and in the **Subject** box, type your course name and section number. In the **Author** box, be sure your name is indicated and edit if necessary.

d. On the left, click **Print** to display **Print Preview**. If necessary, return to the document and make any necessary changes.

e. **Save** 🖫 your document, and then if you want to do so, present your document online to a fellow classmate. Then as directed by your instructor, print your document or submit it electronically. **Close** Word.

END | You have completed Project 2C

CHAPTER REVIEW

Skills Review Project 2D Cover Letter and Reference List

In the following Skills Review, you will create a letterhead, save the letterhead as a custom Word template, and then use the letterhead to create a cover letter to accompany a resume. You will also create a list of references from a Microsoft predesigned template and, if you have an envelope and printer available, format and print an envelope. Your completed documents will look similar to Figure 2.41.

Build from Scratch

PROJECT FILES

For Project 2D, you will need the following files:

New blank Word document
w02D_Cover_Letter_Text

You will save your documents as:

Lastname_Firstname_2D_Cover_Letter
Lastname_Firstname_2D_Reference_List

PROJECT RESULTS

Sarah Villmosky
7279 Rambling Brook Way, St. Petersburg, FL 33713
(727) 555-0117 svillmosky@alcona.net

October 20, 2016

Ms. Mary Walker-Huelsman, Director
Florida Port Community College Career Center
2745 Oakland Avenue
St. Petersburg, FL 33713

Dear Ms. Walker-Huelsman:

I am seeking the assistance of the Career Center in my job search.

Having recently graduated from Florida Port Community College with an Associate of Arts in Media Studies, I am interested in working for a newspaper, a magazine, or a publishing company.

I have previous work experience in the publishing industry as a writer and section editor for the local activities section of the St. Petersburg News and Times. I have the following skills that I developed while working at the St. Petersburg News and Times. I believe these skills would be a good fit with a local or national newspaper or publication:

Editorial experience:	Writing, editing, interviewing
Computer proficiency:	CS In Design, QuarkXPress, Microsoft Publisher
Education focus:	Media Studies and Journalism

I am willing to consider temporary positions that might lead to a permanent position. Please contact me at sarahvillmosky@alcona.net or by phone at (727) 555-0117. I am available immediately for an interview or for further training at the Career Center that you think would be beneficial in my job search.

Sincerely,

Sarah Villmosky

Enclosure

Lastname_Firstname_2D_Cover_Letter

Sarah Villmosky
7279 Rambling Brook Way
St. Petersburg, FL 33713
(727) 555-0177
svillmosky@alcona.net

REFERENCES:

Dr. Thomas Robins
Professor
Florida Port Community College
2745 Oakland Avenue
St. Petersburg, FL 33713
(727) 555-0902
trobins@fpcc-english.edu

Relationship: Professor at Florida Port Community College from July 2012 to July 2013

Ms. Janice Nguyen
Editor
St. Petersburg News and Times
One Gateway Center
St. Petersburg, FL 33713
(727) 555-0932
jnguyen@spnt-editorial.net

Relationship: Editor at St. Petersburg News and Times from July 2013 to present

Lastname_Firstname_2D_Reference_List

FIGURE 2.41

(Project 2D Cover Letter and Reference List continues on the next page)

CHAPTER REVIEW

1 **Start** Word and display a blank document; be sure that formatting marks and rulers display. On the **DESIGN tab**, in the **Document Formatting group**, click **Paragraph Spacing**, and then click **No Paragraph Space**.

a. Type **Sarah Villmosky** and then press Enter. Type **7279 Rambling Brook Way, St. Petersburg, FL 33713** and then press Enter.

b. Type **(727) 555-0117 svillmosky@alcona.net** and then press Enter. If the web address changes to blue text, right-click the web address, and then click **Remove Hyperlink**.

c. Select the first paragraph—*Sarah Villmosky*—and then on the mini toolbar, apply **Bold**, and change the **Font Size** to **16**.

d. Select the second and third paragraphs, and then on the mini toolbar, apply **Bold**, and change the **Font Size** to **12**.

e. Click anywhere in the first paragraph—*Sarah Villmosky*. On the **HOME tab**, in the **Paragraph group**, click the **Borders button arrow**, and then click **Borders and Shading**. Under **Style**, click the first style—a single solid line. Click the **Width arrow**, and then click **3 pt**. In the **Preview** area, click the bottom border, and then click **OK**.

f. Press F12 to display the **Save As** dialog box. In the lower portion of the dialog box, in the **Save as type** box, click the arrow, and then click **Word Template**. In the **File name** box, type **Lastname_Firstname_2D_Letterhead_Template** and then click **Save** to save the custom Word template in the default path, which is the Templates folder on the hard drive of your computer.

g. Click the **FILE tab** to display **Backstage** view, and then click **Close** to close the file but leave Word open.

h. With Word open but no documents displayed, click the **FILE tab**, and then click **New**. Under **Suggested searches**, click **PERSONAL**, and then locate and click the letterhead template that you just created.

i. Press F12 to display the **Save As** dialog box, navigate to your **Word Chapter 2** folder, and then **Save** the file as **Lastname_Firstname_2D_Cover_Letter**

j. On the **INSERT tab**, in the **Header & Footer group**, click **Footer**, click **Edit Footer**, and then in the **Insert**

group, click **Document Info**. Click **File Name**, and then click **Close Header and Footer**. Click **Save**.

2 Click the **FILE tab**. On the left, click **Options**. On the left side of the **Word Options** dialog box, click **Proofing**, and then under **AutoCorrect options**, click the **AutoCorrect Options** button.

a. In the **AutoCorrect** dialog box, click the **AutoCorrect tab**. Under **Replace**, type the misspelled word **assistence** and under **With**, type **assistance** Click **Add**. If the entry already exists, click **Replace instead**, and then click **Yes**. Click **OK** two times to close the dialog boxes.

b. Press Ctrl + End, and then press Enter three times. On the **INSERT tab**, in the **Text group**, click **Date & Time**, and then click the third date format. Click **OK**.

c. Press Enter four times. Type the following inside address using four lines, but do *not* press Enter after the last line:

Ms. Mary Walker-Huelsman, Director

Florida Port Community College Career Center

2745 Oakland Avenue

St. Petersburg, FL 33713

d. Press Enter two times, type **Dear Ms. Walker-Huelsman:** and then press Enter two times. Type, exactly as shown with the intentional misspelling, and then watch *assistence* as you press Spacebar: **I am seeking the assistence**

e. Type **of the Career Center in my job search.** Press Enter two times.

f. On the **INSERT tab**, in the **Text Group**, click the **Object button arrow**, and then click **Text from File**. From your student files, locate and insert the file **w02D_Cover_Letter_Text**.

g. Scroll to view the lower portion of the page, and be sure your insertion point is in the empty paragraph mark at the end. Press Enter, type **Sincerely,** and then press Enter four times. Type **Sarah Villmosky** and press Enter two times. Type **Enclosure** and then **Save** your document.

h. Press Ctrl + Home. On the **HOME tab**, in the **Editing group**, click **Find**. In the **navigation** pane, click in the search box, and then type **journalism** In the letter,

(Project 2D Cover Letter and Reference List continues on the next page)

CHAPTER REVIEW

double-click the yellow highlighted word *Journalism* and type **Media Studies**

i. **Close** the **navigation** pane, and then on the **HOME tab**, in the **Editing group**, click **Replace**. In the **Find and Replace** dialog box, in the **Find what** box, replace the existing text by typing **SPNT** In the **Replace with** box, type **St. Petersburg News and Times** Click **More** to expand the dialog box, select the **Match case** check box, click **Replace All**, and then click **OK**. **Close** the **Find and Replace** dialog box.

j. In the paragraph that begins *I am available*, hold down [Ctrl], and then click anywhere in the first sentence. Drag the selected sentence to the end of the paragraph by positioning the small vertical line that floats with the point to the left of the paragraph mark.

3 Below the paragraph that begins *I have previous*, click to position the insertion point in the blank paragraph, and then press [Enter] one time. On the **INSERT tab**, in the **Tables group**, click **Table**. In the **Table grid**, in the third row, click the second square to insert a 2 × 3 table. Type the following information in the table:

Editorial experience:	Writing, editing, interviewing
Computer proficiency:	CS In Design, QuarkXPress, Microsoft Publisher
Education focus:	Media Studies and Journalism

a. Point outside of the upper left corner of the table and click the **table move handle** button to select the entire table. On the **LAYOUT tab**, in the **Cell Size group**, click **AutoFit**, and then click **AutoFit Contents**.

b. With the table selected, on the **DESIGN tab**, in the **Table Styles group**, click **More** ⬇. Under **Plain Tables**, click the second style—**Table Grid Light**.

c. With the table still selected, on the **HOME tab**, in the **Paragraphs group**, click **Center**. **Save** your document.

4 Press [Ctrl] + [Home]. On the **REVIEW tab**, in the **Proofing group**, click **Spelling & Grammar**. For the spelling of *Villmosky*, in the **Spelling** pane, click **Ignore All**. For the spelling of *Huelsman*, click **Ignore All**.

a. For the grammar error *a*, click **Change**. Click **Change** to correct the misspelling of *intrested*. Click **Delete** to delete the duplicated word *for*. Change *activitys* to *activities*. Change *benificial* to *beneficial*. Click **OK** when the Spelling & Grammar check is complete.

b. In the paragraph that begins *I am willing*, in the third line, double-click the word *preparation*. In the **Proofing group**, click **Thesaurus**.

c. In the **Thesaurus** pane, point to *training*, click the arrow, and then click **Insert**. **Close** the **Thesaurus** pane.

d. Click **FILE tab**, and then in the lower right portion of the screen, click **Show All Properties**. In the **Tags** box, type **cover letter** and in the **Subject** box, type your course name and section number.

e. In the **Author** box, be sure your name is indicated and edit if necessary. On the left, click **Print**. If necessary, return to the document and make any necessary changes. **Save** your document, and then **Close** Word.

5 **Start** Word, and then on the opening screen, in the **Search online templates** box, type **resume references** and press [Enter]. Click the reference list that contains three left-aligned reference items, and then click **Create**.

a. Press [F12] to display the **Save As** dialog box. **Save** the document in your **Word Chapter 2** folder as **Lastname_Firstname_2D_Reference_List** A message may indicate that the file will be upgraded to the newest file format.

b. Add the file name to the footer.

c. In the upper right, click in the placeholder text *[Your Name]* and type **Sarah Villmosky** Click *[Street Address]* and type **7279 Rambling Brook Way**

d. Click *[City, ST ZIP Code]* and type **St. Petersburg, FL 33713** Click *[phone]* and type **(727) 555-0177** Click *[email]* and type **svillmosky@alcona.net**

(Project 2D Cover Letter and Reference List continues on the next page)

CHAPTER REVIEW

6 Under **References**, enter two references using the information in Table 1:

a. Delete the remaining template controls.

b. Click the **FILE tab**, click **Show All Properties**, and then in the **Tags** box, type **reference list** and in the **Subject** box type your course name and section number. In the **Author** box, be sure your name is indicated and edit if necessary.

c. On the left, click **Print**. If necessary, return to the document and make any changes. Click **Save**. As directed by your instructor, print or submit electronically the two documents that are the results of this project. **Close** Word.

TABLE 1

Template Field	Reference 1	Reference 2
Reference Name	Dr. Thomas Robins	Ms. Janice Nguyen
Title	Professor	Editor
Company Name	Florida Port Community College	St. Petersburg News and Times
Street Address	2745 Oakland Avenue	One Gateway Center
City, ST ZIP Code	St. Petersburg, FL 33713	St. Petersburg, FL 33713
phone	(727) 555-0902	(727) 555-0932
email	trobins@fpcc-english.edu	jnguyen@spnt-editorial.net
Relationship with reference	Professor	Editor
Company Name	Florida Port Community College	St. Petersburg News and Times
dates of employment	July 2012 to July 2013	July 2013 to present

END | You have completed Project 2D

Return to Step 6a

CONTENT-BASED ASSESSMENTS

In the following Mastering Word project, you will create an announcement for new job postings at the Career Center. Your completed document will look similar to Figure 2.42.

Apply 2A skills from these Objectives:

1 Create a Table

2 Format a Table

3 Present a Word Document Online

Build from Scratch

PROJECT FILES

For Project 2E, you will need the following files:

New blank Word document
w02E_New_Jobs

You will save your document as:

Lastname_Firstname_2E_Job_Listings

PROJECT RESULTS

Florida Port Community College Career Center

Job Alert! New Positions for Computer Science Majors!

April 11

Florida Port Community College Career Center has new jobs available for both part-time and full-time positions in Computer Science. Some of these jobs are temporary, some are for a specific project with a defined beginning and ending date, and some are open-ended with the potential for permanent employment. The following jobs were posted in the past week. These listings are just in, so apply now to be one of the first candidates considered!

For further information about any of these new jobs, or a complete listing of jobs that are available through the Career Center, please call Mary Walker-Huelsman at (727) 555-0030 or visit our website at www.fpcc.pro/careers.

New Computer Science Listings for the Week of April 11		
Position	**Type**	**Location**
Computer Engineer	Full-time, two months	Clearwater
Project Assistant	Full-time, three months	Coral Springs
Software Developer	Full-time, open-ended	Tampa
UI Designer	Part-time, two months	St. Petersburg

To help prepare yourself before applying for these jobs, we recommend that you review the following articles on our website at www.fpcc.pro/careers.

Topic	**Article Title**
Research	Working in Computer Science Fields
Interviewing	Interviewing in Startup Companies

Lastname_Firstname_2E_Job_Listings

FIGURE 2.42

(Project 2E Table of Job Listings continues on the next page)

CONTENT-BASED ASSESSMENTS

1 **Start** Word and display a blank document; display formatting marks and rulers. **Save** the document in your **Word Chapter 2** folder as **Lastname_Firstname_2E_Job_Listings** and then add the file name to the footer.

2 Type **Florida Port Community College Career Center** and press [Enter]. Type **Job Alert! New Positions for Computer Science Majors!** and press [Enter]. Type **April 11** and press [Enter]. **Insert** the file **w02E_New_Jobs**.

3 At the top of the document, select and **Center** the three title lines. Select the title *Florida Port Community College Career Center*, change the **Font Size** to **20 pt** and apply **Bold**. Apply **Bold** to the second and third title lines. Locate the paragraph that begins *For further*, and then below that paragraph, position the insertion point in the second blank paragraph. **Insert** a **3 × 4** table. Enter the following in the table:

Position	Type	Location
Computer Engineer	Full-time, two months	Clearwater
Software Developer	Full-time, open-ended	Tampa
UI Designer	Part-time, two months	St. Petersburg

4 In the table, point to upper left corner of the cell *Software Developer* to display the **Row Insertion** button, and then click to insert a new row. In the new row, type the following information so that the job titles remain in alphabetic order:

Project Assistant	Full-time, three months	Coral Springs

5 Select the entire table. On the **LAYOUT tab**, in the **Cell Size group**, click **AutoFit**, and then click **AutoFit Contents**. With the table still selected, on the **HOME tab**, **Center** the table. With the table still selected, on the **PAGE LAYOUT tab**, add **6 pt Spacing Before** and **6 pt Spacing After**.

6 With the table still selected, remove all table borders, and then add a **Custom 1 pt** solid line top border and bottom border. Select all three cells in the first row, apply **Bold**, and then **Center** the text. Click anywhere in the first row, and then on the **LAYOUT tab**, in the **Rows & Columns group**, insert a row above. Merge the three cells in the new top row, and then type **New Computer Science Listings for the Week of April 11** Notice that the new row keeps the formatting of the row from which it was created.

7 At the bottom of the document, **Insert** a **2 × 3** table. Enter the following:

Topic	Article Title
Research	Working in Computer Science Fields
Interviewing	Interviewing in Startup Companies

8 Select the entire table. On the **LAYOUT tab**, in the **Cell Size group**, use the **AutoFit** button to **AutoFit Contents**. On the **HOME tab**, **Center** the table. On the **PAGE LAYOUT tab**, add **6 pt Spacing Before** and **6 pt Spacing After**. With the table still selected, remove all table borders, and then add a **Custom 1 pt** solid line top border and bottom border. Select the cells in the first row, apply **Bold**, and then **Center** the text.

9 Click the **FILE tab** to display **Backstage** view, and then in the lower right portion of the screen, click **Show All Properties**. In the **Tags** box, type **new listings, computer science** and in the **Subject** box, type your course name and section number. In the **Author** box, be sure your name is indicated and edit if necessary.

10 On the left, click **Print** to display **Print Preview**. If necessary, return to the document and make any necessary changes. **Save** your document, and then if you want to do so, present your document online to a fellow classmate. Then as directed by your instructor, print your document or submit it electronically. **Close** Word.

END | You have completed Project 2E

CONTENT-BASED ASSESSMENTS

Mastering Word	Project 2F Career Tips Memo and Fax Cover Sheet

In the following Mastering Word project, you will create a memo and fax cover sheet that includes job tips for students and graduates using the services of the Florida Port Community College Career Center. Your completed documents will look similar to Figure 2.43.

Apply 2B skills from these Objectives:

4 Create a Custom Word Template

5 Correct and Reorganize Text

6 Use the Proofing Options and Print an Envelope

7 Create a Document Using a Predesigned Microsoft Template

PROJECT FILES

For Project 2F, you will need the following files:

w02F_Memo_Template
w02F_Memo_Text
Equity Fax template from Microsoft's installed templates

You will save your documents as:

Lastname_Firstname_2F_Career_Tips
Lastname_Firstname_2F_Fax

PROJECT RESULTS

Florida Port Community College Career Center

Memo

DATE: January 12, 2016

TO: Florida Port Community College Students and Graduates

FROM: Mary Huelsman-Walker, Director

SUBJECT: Using the Career Center

Tips for Students and Recent Graduates of Florida Port Community College

It is no surprise that after you leave college, you will be entering one of the most competitive job markets on record. That doesn't mean it's impossible to get your dream job. It does, however, mean that it's critical that you know how to put your best self forward to job interviewers and that you highlight all of your academic, personal, and professional achievements in a way that will help you stand out from the crowd. An Associate degree from Florida Port Community College is just the first step on your journey to getting the professional career that you want.

Give 100 Percent to Every Job

Treat every job as a career. Be willing to go beyond your assignment and complete tasks not delegated to you. Take the initiative to see ways to contribute to the company. Be willing to stay if there is unfinished work. You never know who you will meet on any job. Making a positive impression every time will give you a network of people who may help you down the road. Networking is an established means professionals use to further their careers. You can always benefit from networking. You will distinguish yourself from potential competitors if you truly give 100 percent to each job. Always remember these job basics:

Job Item	Tip for Success
Time Management	Show up on time and don't hurry to leave
Attire	Dress appropriately for the job
Work Area	Keep your work area neat and organized

Use the Career Center

Here at the Career Center and on our website, we offer tips on how to write a stellar resume and a cover letter that puts your hard work up front and center. Have you volunteered somewhere? Have you participated at a club at school? Were you a TA or a tutor? Did you make the Dean's list or graduate with honors? These are the kinds of achievements interviewers want to see. Meet with your career guidance counselor and together, come up with a plan to find the jobs that you want and get the important interview.

Lastname_Firstname_2F_Career_Tips

FAX

To:	Jane Westerfield		From:	Mary Huelsman-Walker
Fax:	(727) 555-0048		Pages:	1
Phone:	(727) 555-0047		Date:	1.12.2016
Re:	Career Tips for Students and Graduates		CC:	President Schultz

☐ Urgent   ☐ For Review   ☐ Please Comment   ☐ Please Reply   ☐ Please Recycle

Comments:

Jane: I know you are on leave, so I thought I would fax this Job Tips memo to you. We look forward to your return.

1.12.2016

Lastname_Firstname_2F_Fax

FIGURE 2.43

(Project 2F Career Tips Memo and Fax Cover Sheet continues on the next page)

CONTENT-BASED ASSESSMENTS

1 Be sure that Word is *closed*. On the taskbar, click **File Explorer**. Navigate to your student files and open **w02F_Memo_Template**. Notice that *Document1* displays in the title bar. (Recall that custom templates stored in a location other than the Templates folder on your hard drive must be opened directly from File Explorer in order for you to create and open a new document based on the template.)

2 Press F12. Navigate to your **Word Chapter 2** folder, and then in the **File name** box, using your own name, type **Lastname_Firstname_2F_Career_Tips**

3 Add the file name to the footer. At the top of your document, in the *DATE* paragraph, click to the right of the tab formatting mark, and then type **January 12, 2016** Use a similar technique to add the following information:

TO:	**Florida Port Community College Students and Graduates**
FROM:	**Mary Huelsman-Walker, Director**
SUBJECT:	**Using the CC**

4 Position the insertion point in the blank paragraph below the memo heading. **Insert** the file **w02F_Memo_Text**, and then press Backspace one time to remove the blank line at the end of the inserted text.

5 Select and **Center** the title *Tips for Students and Recent Graduates of Florida Port Community College*. By using either the **Spelling & Grammar** command on the **REVIEW** tab or by right-clicking words that display blue or red wavy underlines, correct or ignore words flagged as spelling, grammar, or word usage errors. Note: If you are checking an entire document, it is usually preferable to move to the top of the document, and then use the **Spelling & Grammar** command so that you do not overlook any flagged words.

6 In the paragraph that begins *Treat every job*, in the second line of the paragraph, locate and double-click *donate*. On the **REVIEW tab**, in the **Proofing group**, click **Thesaurus**, and then from the **Thesaurus** pane, change the word to *contribute*. In the last line of the same paragraph, point to *fundamentals*, right-click, point to **Synonyms**, and then click *basics*.

7 Using Match Case, replace all instances of *CC* with *Career Center*, and then in the paragraph that begins *An Associate degree*, move the first sentence to the end of the paragraph.

8 At the end of the paragraph that begins *Treat every job*, create a blank paragraph. **Insert** a 2 × 4 table, and then type the following information:

Job Item	Tip for Success
Time Management	Show up on time and don't hurry to leave
Attire	Dress appropriately for the job
Work Area	Keep your work area neat and organized

9 Select the entire table. **AutoFit Contents**, and then apply the **Grid Table 1 Light – Accent 1** table style—under **Grid Tables**, in the first row, the second style. **Center** the table.

10 Click the **FILE tab**, and then click **Show All Properties**. As the **Tags**, type **memo, job tips** and as the **Subject**, type your course name and section number. Be sure your name is indicated as the **Author**, and edit if necessary. **Save** and **Close** the document but leave Word open. Hold this file until you complete this project.

11 With Word open but no documents displayed, click the **FILE tab**, and then click **New**. In the **Search for online templates** box, type **fax (equity)** and press Enter, and then click the first **Fax (Equity theme)** template. Click **Create**. Press F12. Save the document in your **Word Chapter 2** folder, using your own name, as **Lastname_Firstname_2F_Fax** and then insert the file name in the footer. You may see a message indicating that the file will be upgraded to the newest format.

12 Use the following information to type in each control:

To:	**Jane Westerfield**
From:	**Mary Huelsman-Walker**
Fax:	**(727) 555-0048**
Pages:	**1**
Phone:	**(727) 555-0047**
Date:	**1/12/2016**
Re:	**Career Tips for Students and Graduates**
CC:	**President Schultz**
COMMENTS:	**Jane: I know you are on leave, so I thought I would fax this Job Tips memo to you. We look forward to your return.**

(Project 2F Career Tips Memo and Fax Cover Sheet continues on the next page)

CONTENT-BASED ASSESSMENTS

13 ▸ Click the **FILE tab**, and then click **Show All Properties**. As the **Tags**, type **memo, job tips** and as the **Subject**, type your course name and section number. The author will indicate *Mary Huelsman-Walker*. **Save** and **Close** the document. As directed by your instructor, print or submit electronically the two files that are the results of this project. **Close** Word.

END | You have completed Project 2F

CONTENT-BASED ASSESSMENTS

Mastering Word | Project 2G Application Letter, Resume, and Fax Cover Sheet

Apply 2A and 2B skills from these Objectives:

1 Create a Table
2 Format a Table
3 Present a Word Document Online
4 Create a Custom Word Template
5 Correct and Reorganize Text
6 Use the Proofing Options and Print an Envelope
7 Create a Document Using a Predesigned Microsoft Template

In the following Mastering Word project, you will create a letter from a custom template, a resume, and a fax cover sheet from a Microsoft predesigned template. Your completed documents will look similar to Figure 2.44.

PROJECT FILES

For Project 2G, you will need the following files:

w02G_Letter_Text
w02G_Letterhead_Template
w02G_Resume
Equity Fax template from Microsoft's installed templates

You will save your documents as:

Lastname_Firstname_2G_Letter
Lastname_Firstname_2G_Resume
Lastname_Firstname_2G_Fax

PROJECT RESULTS

FIGURE 2.44

(Project 2G Application Letter, Resume, and Fax Cover Sheet continues on the next page)

CONTENT-BASED ASSESSMENTS

1 Be sure that Word is *closed*. On the taskbar, click **File Explorer**. Navigate to your student files and open **w02G_Letterhead_Template**. Notice that *Document1* displays in the title bar. (Recall that custom templates stored in a location other than the Templates folder on your hard drive must be opened directly from File Explorer in order for you to create and open a new document based on the template.)

2 Press F12. Navigate to your **Word Chapter 2** folder, and then in the **File name** box, using your own name, type **Lastname_Firstname_2G_Letter**

3 Add the file name to the footer. Be sure that rulers and formatting marks display. Move to the end of the document, and then press Enter three times. Use the **Date & Time** command to insert the current date using the third format, and then press Enter four times. Type the following:

Ms. Mary Walker-Huelsman, Director

Florida Port Community College Career Center

2745 Oakland Avenue

St. Petersburg, FL 33713

4 Press Enter two times, type **Dear Ms. Walker-Huelsman:** and press Enter two times. **Insert** the text from the file **w02G_Letter_Text** and press Backspace one time to remove the blank paragraph at the bottom of the selected text.

5 By using either the **Spelling & Grammar** command on the **REVIEW tab** or by right-clicking words that display blue or red wavy underlines, correct or ignore words flagged as spelling, grammar, or word usage errors. Hint: If you are checking an entire document, it is usually preferable to move to the top of the document, and then use the **Spelling & Grammar** command so that you do not overlook any flagged words.

6 Replace all instances of **posting** with **listing**. In the paragraph that begins *The job description*, use the **Thesaurus** pane or the **Synonyms** command on the shortcut menu to change *specific* to *explicit* and *credentials* to *qualifications*.

7 In the paragraph that begins *I currently live in Tampa*, select the first sentence of the paragraph and drag it to the end of the same paragraph. Click in the blank paragraph below the paragraph that begins *The job*

description, and then press Enter one time. **Insert** a **2 × 3** table, and then type the text shown in Table 1.

TABLE 1

Education	Bachelor of Science, Business Management
Experience	Two years Computer Support experience at a major university
Required Certifications	MCITP, MCDST

8 Select the entire table. **AutoFit Contents**, and then apply the **Table Grid Light** table style—under **Plain Tables**, in the first row, the first style. **Center** the table.

9 Click the **FILE tab**, and then click **Show All Properties**. As the **Tags**, type **letter, alumni website** and as the **Subject**, type your course name and section number. Be sure your name is indicated as the **Author**, and edit if necessary. **Save** and **Close** the document but leave Word open. Hold this file until you complete this project.

10 From your student files, open **w02G_Resume**. Press F12, and then **Save** the document in your **Word Chapter 2** folder as **Lastname_Firstname_2G_Resume** Add the file name to the footer.

11 **Insert** a new second row in the table. In the first cell of the new row, type **OBJECTIVE** and then press Tab. Type **To obtain a Business Programmer Analyst position that will use my technical and communication skills and computer support experience.** In the same cell, add **12 pt Spacing After**.

12 Select the entire table. On the **LAYOUT tab**, **AutoFit Contents**. Remove the table borders, and then display the **Borders and Shading** dialog box. With the table selected, create a **Custom** single solid line **1 1/2 pt** top border.

13 In the first row of the table, select both cells and then **Merge Cells**. **Center** the five lines and apply **Bold**. In the first row, select *William Franklin* and change the **Font Size** to **20 pt** and add **24 pt Spacing Before**. In the email address at the bottom of the first row, add **24 pt Spacing After**.

14 In the first column, apply **Bold** to the four headings. In the cell to the right of *EDUCATION*, apply **Bold** to the

(Project 2G Application Letter, Resume, and Fax Cover Sheet continues on the next page)

CONTENT-BASED ASSESSMENTS

name and address of the two colleges. Add **12 pt Spacing After** to the two lines that begin *September*. In the cell to the right of *RELEVANT EXPERIENCE*, apply **Bold** to the names of the two jobs—*IT Analyst* and *Computer Technician*. In the same cell, below the line that begins *January 2014*, apply bullets to the six lines that comprise the job duties. Create a similar bulleted list for the duties as a Computer Technician. Add **12 pt Spacing After** to the last line of each of the bulleted lists.

15 In the cell to the right of *CERTIFICATIONS*, select all four lines and create a bulleted list. Click the **FILE tab**, and then click **Show All Properties**. As the **Tags**, type **resume, business programmer analyst** and as the **Subject**, type your course name and section number. Be sure your name is indicated as the **Author**, and edit if necessary. **Save** and **Close** the document but leave Word open. Hold this file until you complete this project.

16 In Word's templates, search for **personal fax** and then select the second (shorter) template named **Fax cover sheet (informal)**. Click **Create**. **Save** the document in your **Word Chapter 2** folder as **Lastname_Firstname_2G_Fax** and then add the file name to the footer.

17 Type the text shown in Table 2 for the content controls.

TABLE 2

Subject:	**Application for Job Listing on Alumni Website**
Date:	**March 6, 2016**
To:	**Mary Walker-Huelsman**
From:	**William Franklin**
Phone number:	**(727) 555-0056**
Phone number:	**(813) 555-0122**
Fax number:	**(727) 555-0057**
No. of Pages	1
Comments:	**Two pages to follow that include my resume and a cover letter for the position of Business Programmer Analyst.**

18 Click the **FILE tab**, and then click **Show All Properties**. As the **Tags**, type **fax cover page** and as the **Subject**, type your course name and section number. Be sure your name is indicated as the **Author**, and edit if necessary. Click **Save**. As directed by your instructor, print or submit electronically the three files that are the results of this project. **Close** Word.

END | You have completed Project 2G

CONTENT-BASED ASSESSMENTS

Apply a combination of the 2A and 2B skills.

Build from Scratch

Build from Scratch

Build from Scratch

GO! Fix It	Project 2H New Jobs	Online

GO! Make It	Project 2I Training	Online

GO! Solve It	Project 2J Job Postings	Online

GO! Solve It	Project 2K Agenda	

PROJECT FILES

For Project 2K, you will need the following file:

Agenda template from Word's Online templates

You will save your document as:

Lastname_Firstname_2K_Agenda

On Word's opening screen, search for an online template using the search term **formal meeting agenda**. Create the agenda and then save it in your Word Chapter 2 folder as **Lastname_Firstname_2K_Agenda** Use the following information to prepare an agenda for an FPCC Career Center meeting.

The meeting will be chaired by Mary Walker-Huelsman. It will be the monthly meeting of the Career Center's staff—Kevin Rau, Marilyn Kelly, André Randolph, Susan Nguyen, and Charles James. The meeting will be held on March 15, 2016, at 3:00 p.m. The old business agenda items (open issues) include (1) seeking more job listings related to the printing and food service industries, (2) expanding the alumni website, and (3) the addition of a part-time trainer. The new business agenda items will include (1) writing a grant so the center can serve more students and alumni, (2) expanding the training area with 20 additional workstations, (3) purchase of new computers for the training room, and (4) renewal of printing service contract.

Add the file name to the footer, add your name, your course name, the section number, and then add the keywords **agenda, monthly staff meeting** to the Properties area. Submit as directed.

Performance Level

Performance Criteria		Exemplary: You consistently applied the relevant skills	Proficient: You sometimes, but not always, applied the relevant skills	Developing: You rarely or never applied the relevant skills
	Select an agenda template	Agenda template is appropriate for the information provided for the meeting.	Agenda template is used, but does not fit the information provided.	No template is used for the agenda.
	Add appropriate information to the template	All information is inserted in the appropriate places.	All information is included, but not in the appropriate places.	Information is missing.
	Format template information	All text in the template is properly aligned and formatted.	All text is included, but alignment or formatting is inconsistent.	No additional formatting has been added.

END | You have completed Project 2K

OUTCOMES-BASED ASSESSMENTS

RUBRIC

The following outcomes-based assessments are *open-ended assessments*. That is, there is no specific correct result; your result will depend on your approach to the information provided. Make *Professional Quality* your goal. Use the following scoring rubric to guide you in *how* to approach the problem and then to evaluate *how well* your approach solves the problem.

The *criteria*—Software Mastery, Content, Format and Layout, and Process—represent the knowledge and skills you have gained that you can apply to solving the problem. The *levels of performance*—Professional Quality, Approaching Professional Quality, or Needs Quality Improvements—help you and your instructor evaluate your result.

	Your completed project is of Professional Quality if you:	Your completed project is Approaching Professional Quality if you:	Your completed project Needs Quality Improvements if you:
1-Software Mastery	Choose and apply the most appropriate skills, tools, and features and identify efficient methods to solve the problem.	Choose and apply some appropriate skills, tools, and features, but not in the most efficient manner.	Choose inappropriate skills, tools, or features, or are inefficient in solving the problem.
2-Content	Construct a solution that is clear and well organized, contains content that is accurate, appropriate to the audience and purpose, and is complete. Provide a solution that contains no errors in spelling, grammar, or style.	Construct a solution in which some components are unclear, poorly organized, inconsistent, or incomplete. Misjudge the needs of the audience. Have some errors in spelling, grammar, or style, but the errors do not detract from comprehension.	Construct a solution that is unclear, incomplete, or poorly organized; contains some inaccurate or inappropriate content; and contains many errors in spelling, grammar, or style. Do not solve the problem.
3-Format & Layout	Format and arrange all elements to communicate information and ideas, clarify function, illustrate relationships, and indicate relative importance.	Apply appropriate format and layout features to some elements, but not others. Overuse features, causing minor distraction.	Apply format and layout that does not communicate information or ideas clearly. Do not use format and layout features to clarify function, illustrate relationships, or indicate relative importance. Use available features excessively, causing distraction.
4-Process	Use an organized approach that integrates planning, development, self-assessment, revision, and reflection.	Demonstrate an organized approach in some areas, but not others; or, use an insufficient process of organization throughout.	Do not use an organized approach to solve the problem.

OUTCOMES-BASED ASSESSMENTS

Apply a combination of the 2A and 2B skills.

Build from
Scratch

GO! Think Project 2L Workshops

PROJECT FILES

For Project 2L, you will need the following files:

New blank Word document
w02L_Workshop_Information

You will save your document as:

Lastname_Firstname_2L_Workshops

The Florida Port Community College Career Center offers a series of workshops for both students and alumni. Any eligible student or graduate can attend the workshops, and there is no fee. Currently, the Career Center offers a three-session workshop covering Excel and Word, a two-session workshop covering Business Communication, and a one-session workshop covering Creating a Resume.

Print the w02L_Workshop_Information file and use the information to complete this project. Create an announcement with a title, an introductory paragraph, and a table listing the workshops and the topics covered in each workshop. Use the file w02L_Workshop_Information for help with the topics covered in each workshop. Format the table cells appropriately. Add an appropriate footer and document properties. Save the document as **Lastname_Firstname_2L_Workshops** and submit it as directed.

END | You have completed Project 2L

Build from
Scratch

GO! Think! Project 2M Planner Online

Build from
Scratch

You and GO! Project 2N Personal Resume Online

Build from
Scratch

GO! Cumulative Group Project Project 2O Bell Orchid Hotels Online

Creating Research Papers, Newsletters, and Merged Mailing Labels

GO! to Work
Video W3

PROJECT 3A	OUTCOMES
	Create a research paper that includes citations and a bibliography.

OBJECTIVES

1. Create a Research Paper
2. Insert Footnotes in a Research Paper
3. Create Citations and a Bibliography in a Research Paper
4. Use Read Mode and PDF Reflow

PROJECT 3B	OUTCOMES
	Create a multiple-column newsletter and merged mailing labels.

OBJECTIVES

5. Format a Multiple-Column Newsletter
6. Use Special Character and Paragraph Formatting
7. Create Mailing Labels Using Mail Merge

Luis Louro / Fotolia

In This Chapter

Microsoft Word provides many tools for creating complex documents. For example, Word has tools that enable you to create a research paper that includes citations, footnotes, and a bibliography. You can also create multiple-column newsletters, format the nameplate at the top of the newsletter, use special character formatting to create distinctive title text, and add borders and shading to paragraphs to highlight important information.

In this chapter, you will edit and format a research paper, create a two-column newsletter, and then create a set of mailing labels to mail the newsletter to multiple recipients.

The projects in this chapter relate to **University Medical Center**, which is a patient-care and research institution serving the metropolitan area of Memphis, Tennessee. Because of its outstanding reputation in the medical community and around the world, University Medical Center is able to attract top physicians, scientists, and researchers in all fields of medicine and achieve a level of funding that allows it to build and operate state-of-the-art facilities. A program in biomedical research was recently added. Individuals throughout the eastern United States travel to University Medical Center for diagnosis and care.

Research Paper

PROJECT
3A

MyITLab®
Project 3A Training

PROJECT ACTIVITIES

In Activities 3.01 through 3.14, you will edit and format a research paper that contains an overview of a new area of study. This paper was created by Gerard Foster, a medical intern at University Medical Center, for distribution to his classmates studying various physiologic monitoring devices. Your completed document will look similar to Figure 3.1.

PROJECT FILES

For Project 3A, you will need the following file:

w03A_Quantitative_Technology

You will save your document as:

Lastname_Firstname_3A_Quantitative_Technology

PROJECT RESULTS

FIGURE 3.1 Project 3A Research Paper

Video W3-1

When you write a research paper or a report for college or business, follow a format prescribed by one of the standard *style guides*—a manual that contains standards for the design and writing of documents. The two most commonly used styles for research papers are those created by the *Modern Language Association (MLA)* and the *American Psychological Association (APA)*; there are several others.

NOTE   If You Are Using a Touchscreen

- Tap an item to click it.
- Press and hold for a few seconds to right-click; release when the information or commands displays.
- Touch the screen with two or more fingers and then pinch together to zoom in or stretch your fingers apart to zoom out.
- Slide your finger on the screen to scroll—slide left to scroll right and slide right to scroll left.
- Slide to rearrange—similar to dragging with a mouse.
- Swipe from edge: from right to display charms; from left to expose open apps, snap apps, or close apps; from top or bottom to show commands or close an app.
- Swipe to select—slide an item a short distance with a quick movement—to select an item and bring up commands, if any.

Activity 3.01 │ Formatting the Spacing and First-Page Information for a Research Paper

When formatting the text for your research paper, refer to the standards for the style guide that you have chosen. In this activity, you will create a research paper using the MLA style. The MLA style uses 1-inch margins, a 0.5" first line indent, and double spacing throughout the body of the document with no extra space above or below paragraphs.

1 Start Word. From your student files, locate and **Open** the document **w03A_Quantitative_Technology**. If necessary, display the formatting marks and rulers. In the location where you are storing your projects for this chapter, create a new folder named **Word Chapter 3** and then **Save** the file in the folder as **Lastname_Firstname_3A_Quantitative_Technology**

2 Press Ctrl + A to select the entire document. On the **HOME tab**, in the **Paragraph group**, click **Line and Paragraph Spacing**, and then change the line spacing to **2.0**. On the **PAGE LAYOUT tab**, in the **Paragraph group**, change the **Spacing After** to **0 pt**.

3 Press Ctrl + Home to deselect and move to the top of the document. Press Enter one time to create a blank line at the top of the document, and then click to position the insertion point in the blank line. Type **Gerard Foster** and press Enter.

4 Type **Dr. Hillary Kim** and press Enter. Type **Biomedical Research 617** and press Enter. Type **February 15, 2016** and press Enter.

5 Type **Quantified Self Movement Gains Momentum** and then press Ctrl + E, which is the keyboard shortcut to center a paragraph of text. Click **Save**, and then compare your screen with Figure 3.2.

More Knowledge   Creating a Document Heading for a Research Paper

On the first page of an MLA-style research paper, on the first line, type the report author. On the second line, type the person for whom the report is prepared—for example, your professor or supervisor. On the third line, type the name of the class or business. On the fourth line, type the date. On the fifth line, type the report title and center it.

FIGURE 3.2

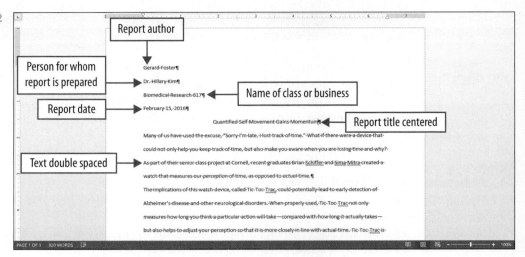

Report author

Person for whom report is prepared

Name of class or business

Report date

Report title centered

Text double spaced

Gerard·Foster¶
Dr.·Hillary·Kim¶
Biomedical·Research·617¶
February·15,·2016¶
Quantified·Self·Movement·Gains·Momentum¶

Many·of·us·have·used·the·excuse,·"Sorry·I'm·late,·I·lost·track·of·time."·What·if·there·were·a·device·that·
could·not·only·help·you·keep·track·of·time,·but·also·make·you·aware·when·you·are·losing·time·and·why?·

As·part·of·their·senior·class·project·at·Cornell,·recent·graduates·Brian·Schiffer·and·Sima·Mitra·created·a·
watch·that·measures·our·*perception*·of·time,·as·opposed·to·*actual*·time.¶

The·implications·of·this·watch·device,·called·Tic-Toc·Trac,·could·potentially·lead·to·early·detection·of·
Alzheimer's·disease·and·other·neurological·disorders.·When·properly·used,·Tic-Toc·Trac·not·only·
measures·how·long·you·think·a·particular·action·will·take—compared·with·how·long·it·actually·takes—
but·also·helps·to·adjust·your·perception·so·that·it·is·more·closely·in·line·with·actual·time.·Tic-Toc·Trac·is·

PAGE 1 OF 3   820 WORDS   100%

More Knowledge   **Creating a Bookmark**

In a document, you can mark a place you want to find again easily. Select the content to which you want to assign the bookmark. On the INSERT tab, in the Links group, click Bookmark, and assign a name. To go to the bookmark, press CTRL + G, select Bookmark, and then click the bookmark name.

Activity 3.02 | **Formatting the Page Numbering and Paragraph Indents for a Research Paper**

1 On the **INSERT tab**, in the **Header & Footer group**, click **Header**, and then at the bottom of the list, click **Edit Header**.

2 Type **Foster** and then press Spacebar.

Recall that the text you insert into a header or footer displays on every page of a document. Within a header or footer, you can insert many different types of information; for example, automatic page numbers, the date, the time, the file name, or pictures.

3 Under **HEADER & FOOTER TOOLS**, on the **DESIGN tab**, in the **Header & Footer group**, click **Page Number**, and then point to **Current Position**. In the gallery, under **Simple**, click **Plain Number**. Compare your screen with Figure 3.3.

Word will automatically number the pages using this number format.

FIGURE 3.3

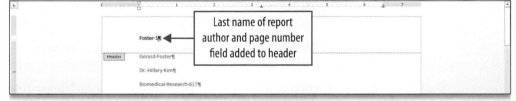

Foster·1¶

Last name of report author and page number field added to header

Header   Gerard·Foster¶
Dr.·Hillary·Kim¶
Biomedical·Research·617¶

---

4 On the **HOME tab**, in the **Paragraph group**, click **Align Right**. Double-click anywhere in the document to close the Header area.

5 Near the top of **Page 1**, locate the paragraph beginning *Many of us*, and then click to position the insertion point at the beginning of the paragraph. By moving the vertical scroll bar, scroll to the end of the document, hold down Shift, and then click to the right of the last paragraph mark to select all of the text from the insertion point to the end of the document. Release Shift.

6 With the text selected, in the **Paragraph group**, click the **Dialog Box Launcher** button to display the **Paragraph** dialog box.

7 On the **INDENTS and SPACING tab**, under **Indentation**, click the **Special arrow**, and then click **First line**. In the **By** box, be sure **0.5"** displays. Click **OK**. Compare your screen with Figure 3.4.

> The MLA style uses 0.5-inch indents at the beginning of the first line of every paragraph. *Indenting*—moving the beginning of the first line of a paragraph to the right or left of the rest of the paragraph—provides visual cues to the reader to help divide the document text and make it easier to read.

FIGURE 3.4

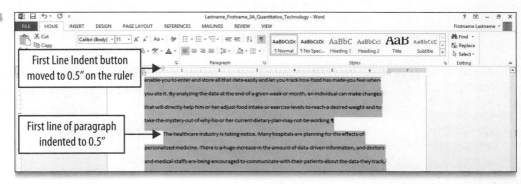

First Line Indent button moved to 0.5" on the ruler

First line of paragraph indented to 0.5"

ANOTHER WAY On the ruler, point to the First Line Indent button 🔽, and then drag the button to 0.5" on the horizontal ruler.

8 Press Ctrl + Home to deselect and move to the top of the document. On the **INSERT tab**, in the **Header & Footer group**, click **Footer**, and then at the bottom of the list click **Edit Footer**.

9 In the **Insert group**, click **Document Info**, and then click **File Name**. On the ribbon, click **Close Header and Footer**.

> The file name in the footer is *not* part of the research report format, but it is included in projects in this textbook so that you and your instructor can identify your work.

10 Save 💾 your document.

More Knowledge | **Suppressing the Page Number on the First Page of a Document**

Some style guidelines require that the page number and other header and footer information on the first page be hidden from view—*suppressed*. To hide the information contained in the header and footer areas on Page 1 of a document, double-click in the header or footer area. Then, under HEADER & FOOTER TOOLS, on the DESIGN tab, in the Options group, select the Different First Page check box.

Objective 2 | Insert Footnotes in a Research Paper

Video W3-2

Reports and research papers typically include information that you find in other sources, and these must be credited. Within report text, numbers mark the location of *notes*—information that expands on the topic being discussed but that does not fit well in the document text. The numbers refer to *footnotes*—notes placed at the bottom of the page containing the note, or to *endnotes*—notes placed at the end of a document or chapter.

You can add footnotes as you type your document or after your document is complete. Word renumbers the footnotes automatically, so footnotes need not be entered in order, and if one footnote is removed, the remaining footnotes automatically renumber.

1 ▸ Scroll to view the upper portion of **Page 2**, and then locate the paragraph that begins *Accurate records*. In the third line of the paragraph, click to position the insertion point to the right of the period after *infancy*.

2 ▸ On the **REFERENCES tab**, in the **Footnotes group**, click **Insert Footnote**.

Word creates space for a footnote in the footnote area at the bottom of the page and adds a footnote number to the text at the insertion point location. Footnote *1* displays in the footnote area, and the insertion point moves to the right of the number. A short black line is added just above the footnote area. You do not need to type the footnote number.

3 ▸ Type **The U.S. Department of Health & Human Services indicates that the widespread use of Health Information Technology will improve the quality of health care and prevent medical errors.**

This is an explanatory footnote; the footnote provides additional information that does not fit well in the body of the report.

4 ▸ Click the **HOME tab**, and then examine the font size and line spacing settings. Notice that the new footnote displays in 10 pt font size and is single-spaced, even though the font size of the document text is 11 pt and the text is double-spaced, as shown in Figure 3.5.

FIGURE 3.5

5 ▸ Scroll to view the top of **Page 1**, and then locate the paragraph that begins *Many of us*. At the end of the paragraph, click to position the insertion point to the right of the period following *time*.

6 ▸ On the **REFERENCES tab**, in the **Footnotes group**, click **Insert Footnote**. Type **Organizations such as airlines and the military could benefit because many employees are involved in time-sensitive operations, where errors can have catastrophic consequences.** Notice that the footnote you just added becomes the new footnote *1*. Click **Save** 🖫, and then compare your screen with Figure 3.6.

The first footnote that you typed, which is on Page 2 and begins *The U.S. Department of Health*, is renumbered as footnote *2*.

FIGURE 3.6

Activity 3.04 | Modifying a Footnote Style

Microsoft Word contains built-in paragraph formats called *styles*—groups of formatting commands, such as font, font size, font color, paragraph alignment, and line spacing—that can be applied to a paragraph with one command.

The default style for footnote text is a single-spaced paragraph that uses a 10-point Calibri font and no paragraph indents. MLA style specifies double-spaced text in all areas of a research paper—including footnotes. According to the MLA style, first lines of footnotes must also be indented 0.5 inch and use the same font size as the report text.

1 At the bottom of **Page 1**, point anywhere in the footnote text you just typed, right-click, and then on the shortcut menu, click **Style**. Compare your screen with Figure 3.7.

The Style dialog box displays, listing the styles currently in use in the document, in addition to some of the word processing elements that come with special built-in styles. Because you right-clicked on the footnote text, the selected style is the Footnote Text style.

FIGURE 3.7

2 In the **Style** dialog box, click **Modify**, and then in the **Modify Style** dialog box, locate the small **Formatting** toolbar in the center of the dialog box. Click the **Font Size button arrow**, click **11**, and then compare your screen with Figure 3.8.

FIGURE 3.8

3 In the lower left corner of the dialog box, click **Format**, and then click **Paragraph**. In the **Paragraph** dialog box, on the **Indents and Spacing tab**, under **Indentation**, click the **Special arrow**, and then click **First line**.

4 Under **Spacing**, click the **Line spacing arrow**, and then click **Double**. Compare your dialog box with Figure 3.9.

FIGURE 3.9

5 Click **OK** to close the **Paragraph** dialog box, click **OK** to close the **Modify Style** dialog box, and then click **Apply** to apply the new style and **close** the dialog box. Compare your screen with Figure 3.10.

Your inserted footnotes are formatted with the modified Footnote Text paragraph style; any new footnotes that you insert will also use this format.

FIGURE 3.10

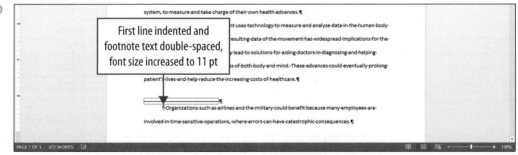

6 Scroll to view the bottom of **Page 2** to confirm that the new format was also applied to the second footnote, and then **Save** 💾 your document.

Objective 3 Create Citations and a Bibliography in a Research Paper

Video W3-3

When you use quotations from or detailed summaries of other people's work, you must specify the source of the information. A **citation** is a note inserted into the text of a report or research paper that refers the reader to a source in the bibliography. Create a **bibliography** at the end of a research paper to list the sources you have referenced. Such a list is typically titled **Works Cited** (in MLA style), *Bibliography*, *Sources*, or *References*.

Activity 3.05 | Adding Citations for a Book

When writing a long research paper, you will likely reference numerous books, articles, and websites. Some of your research sources may be referenced many times, others only one time.

References to sources within the text of your research paper are indicated in an *abbreviated* manner. However, as you enter a citation for the first time, you can also enter the *complete* information about the source. Then, when you have finished your paper, you will be able to automatically generate the list of sources that must be included at the end of your research paper.

1 Scroll to view the middle of **Page 2**. In the paragraph that begins *Accurate records*, at the end of the paragraph, click to position the insertion point to the right of the quotation mark.

The citation in the document points to the full source information in the bibliography, which typically includes the name of the author, the full title of the work, the year of publication, and other publication information.

2 On the **REFERENCES tab**, in the **Citations & Bibliography group**, click the **Style button arrow**, and then click **MLA** to insert a reference using MLA bibliography style.

3 Click **Insert Citation**, and then click **Add New Source**. Click the **Type of Source arrow**, and then click **Book**. Add the following information, and then compare your screen with Figure 3.11:

Author:	**Sopol, Eric J.**
Title:	**The Creative Destruction of Medicine**
Year:	**2012**
City:	**New York**
Publisher:	**Basic Books**
Medium	**Print**

FIGURE 3.11

4 Click **OK** to insert the citation. Point to *(Sopol)* and click one time to select the citation.

In the MLA style, citations that refer to items on the *Works Cited* page are placed in parentheses and are referred to as **parenthetical references**—references that include the last name of the author or authors and the page number in the referenced source, which you add to the reference. No year is indicated, and there is no comma between the name and the page number.

5 Save 🖫 the document.

1 In the lower right corner of the box that surrounds the reference, point to the small arrow to display the ScreenTip *Citation Options*. Click this **Citation Options arrow**, and then on the list of options, click **Edit Citation**.

2 In the **Edit Citation** dialog box, under **Add**, in the **Pages** box, type **5** to indicate that you are citing from Page 5 of this source. Compare your screen with Figure 3.12.

FIGURE 3.12

3 Click **OK** to display the page number of the citation. Click outside of the citation box to deselect it. Then type a period to the right of the citation, and delete the period to the left of the quotation mark.

In the MLA style, if the reference occurs at the end of a sentence, the parenthetical reference always displays to the left of the punctuation mark that ends the sentence.

4 Press Ctrl + End to move to the end of the document, and then click to position the insertion point after the letter *e* in *disease* and to the left of the period.

5 In the **Citations & Bibliography group**, click **Insert Citation**, and then click **Add New Source**. Click the **Type of Source arrow**, if necessary scroll to the top of the list, click **Book**, and then add the following information:

Author:	**Glaser, John P. and Claudia Salzberg**
Title:	**The Strategic Application of Information Technology in Health Care Organizations**
Year:	**2011**
City:	**San Francisco**
Publisher:	**Jossey-Bass**
Medium:	**Print**

6 Click **OK**. Click the inserted citation to select it, click the **Citation Options arrow**, and then click **Edit Citation**.

7 In the **Edit Citation** dialog box, under **Add**, in the **Pages** box, type **28** to indicate that you are citing from page 28 of this source. Click **OK**.

8 On the **REFERENCES tab**, in the **Citations & Bibliography group**, click **Manage Sources**, and then compare your screen with Figure 3.13.

The Source Manager dialog box displays. Other citations on your computer display in the Master List box. The citations for the current document display in the Current List box. Word maintains the Master List so that if you use the same sources regularly, you can copy sources from your Master List to the current document. A preview of the bibliography entry also displays at the bottom of the dialog box.

FIGURE 3.13

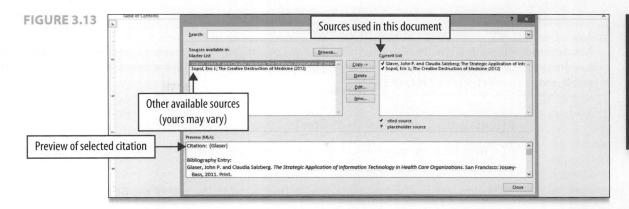

9 At the bottom of the **Source Manager** dialog box, click **Close**. Click anywhere in the document to deselect the parenthetical reference, and then **Save** 🖫 your document.

Activity 3.07 | Adding Citations for a Website

1 In the lower portion of **Page 2**, in the paragraph that begins *Doctors have long*, in the third line, click to position the insertion point after the s in *States* and to the left of the period.

2 In the **Citations & Bibliography group**, click **Insert Citation**, and then click **Add New Source**. Click the **Type of Source arrow**, scroll down as necessary, and then click **Web site**. Type the following information:

Author:	Ogden, Cynthia L., Margaret D. Carroll, Brian K. Kit, and Katherine M. Flegal.
Name of Web Page:	NCHS Data Brief Number 82
Year:	2012
Month:	January
Day:	15
Year Accessed:	2016
Month Accessed:	January
Day Accessed:	17
Medium	Web

3 Click **OK**. **Save** 🖫, and then compare your screen with Figure 3.14.

A parenthetical reference is added. Because the cited web page has no page numbers, only the author name is used in the parenthetical reference.

FIGURE 3.14

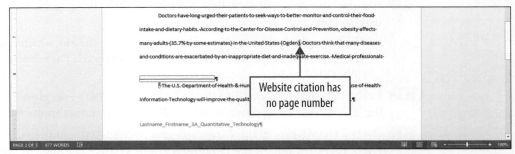

Activity 3.08 | **Inserting Page Breaks**

Your bibliography must begin on a new page, so at the bottom of the last page of your report, you must insert a manual page break.

1 Press Ctrl + End to move the insertion point to the end of the document.

> If there is a footnote on the last page, the insertion point will display at the end of the final paragraph, but above the footnote—a footnote is always associated with the page that contains the citation.

2 Press Ctrl + Enter to insert a manual page break.

> A **manual page break** forces a page to end at the insertion point location, and then places any subsequent text at the top of the next page. Recall that the new paragraph retains the formatting of the previous paragraph, so in this instance the first line is indented.

> A **page break indicator**, which shows where a manual page break was inserted, displays at the bottom of Page 3.

3 On the **HOME tab**, in the **Paragraph group**, click the **Dialog Box Launcher** button to display the **Paragraph** dialog box.

4 On the **Indents and Spacing tab**, under **Indentation**, click the **Special arrow**, and then click **(none)**. Click **OK**, and then **Save** your document.

ANOTHER WAY   On the ruler, point to the First Line Indent button, and then drag the button to 0" on the horizontal ruler.

Activity 3.09 | **Creating a Reference Page**

At the end of a report or research paper, include a list of each source referenced. *Works Cited* is the reference page heading used in the MLA style guidelines. Other styles may refer to this page as a *Bibliography* (Business Style) or *References* (APA Style). Always display this information on a separate page.

1 With the insertion point blinking in the first line of **Page 4**, type **Works Cited** and then press Enter. On the **REFERENCES tab**, in the **Citations & Bibliography group**, in the **Style** box, be sure *MLA* displays.

2 In the **Citations & Bibliography group**, click **Bibliography**, and then near the bottom of the list, click **Insert Bibliography**.

3 Scroll as necessary to view the entire list of three references, and then click anywhere in the inserted text.

> The bibliography entries that you created display as a field, which is indicated by the gray shading. This field links to the Source Manager for the citations. The references display alphabetically by the author's last name.

4 In the bibliography, point to the left of the first entry—beginning *Glaser, John P.*—to display the pointer. Drag down to select all three references in the field.

5 On the **HOME tab**, in the **Paragraph group**, change the **Line spacing** to **2.0**, and then on the **PAGE LAYOUT tab**, in the **Paragraph group**, change the **Spacing After** to **0 pt**.

> The entries display according to MLA guidelines; the text is double-spaced, the extra space between paragraphs has been removed, and each entry uses a **hanging indent**—the first line of each entry extends 0.5 inch to the left of the remaining lines of the entry.

🔄 ANOTHER WAY   Display the Paragraph dialog box. Under Spacing, click the Line spacing arrow, and then click Double. Under Spacing, in the After box, type 0.

6 At the top of **Page 4**, click anywhere in the title text *Works Cited*, and then press Ctrl + E to center the title. Compare your screen with Figure 3.15, and then **Save** 🖫 your document.

In MLA style, the *Works Cited* title is centered.

FIGURE 3.15

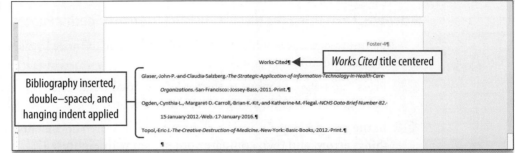

Activity 3.10 | Managing and Modifying Sources for a Document

Use the Source Manager to organize the sources cited in your document. For example, in the Source Manager dialog box, you can copy sources from the master list to the current list, delete a source, edit a source, or search for a source. You can also display a preview of how your citations will appear in your document.

1 On the **REFERENCES tab**, in the **Citations & Bibliography group**, click **Manage Sources**.

2 On the left, in the **Master List**, click the entry for *Sopol, Eric J.* and then between the **Master List** and the **Current List**, click **Edit**.

The name of this source should be *Topol* instead of *Sopol*.

3 In the **Edit Source** dialog box, in the **Author** box, delete *S* and type **T**

4 Click **OK**. When the message box indicates *This source exists in your master list and current document. Do you want to update both lists with these changes?* click **Yes**. Compare your screen with Figure 3.16.

In the lower portion of the Source Manager dialog box, a preview of the corrected entry displays.

FIGURE 3.16

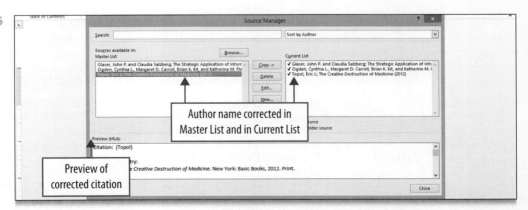

5 In the lower right corner, click **Close**. On your **Works Cited page**, notice that the author name is *not* corrected. Scroll to view the lower portion of **Page 2**, and notice that the author name *is* corrected and the citation is selected.

6 On the selected citation *(Topol 5)*, click the **Citation Options arrow**, and then click **Update Citations and Bibliography**. Press Ctrl + End, and notice that this action updates the **Works Cited page** with the corrected name.

> Editing a source in Source Manager updates only the sources in the document; to update the Works Cited page, use the Update Citations and Bibliography command on the citation.

7 Drag to select all the lines for the three references. On the **HOME tab**, in the **Paragraph group**, click **Line and Paragraph Spacing**, and then click **2.0**. Click **Save**.

Activity 3.11 | Using the Navigation Pane to Go to a Specific Page

In a multipage document, use the navigation pane to move to a specific page or to find specific objects in the document.

1 Press Ctrl + Home to move to the top of the document. Click the **VIEW tab**, and then in the **Show group**, select the **navigation pane** check box.

2 In the **navigation pane**, on the right end of the **Search document** box, click the **Search for more things arrow**, and then compare your screen with Figure 3.17.

FIGURE 3.17

3 Under **Find**, click **Footnotes/Endnotes**. Notice that the first numbered footnote is selected.

4 In the **navigation pane**, to the right of *Result 1 of 2*, click the down arrow to move to the next numbered footnote.

5 Click the **Search for more things arrow** again, and then click **Go To**. In the **Find and Replace** dialog box, under **Go to what**, be sure **Page** is selected, and then in the **Enter page number** box, type **4**

6 Click **Go To**, and then click **Close**. Notice that **Page 4** displays. **Close** the **navigation pane**.

> The navigation pane is useful when you need to navigate to find various elements, especially in a lengthy document.

Activity 3.12 | Managing Document Properties

For a research paper, you may want to add additional document properties.

1 Press Ctrl + Home to return to the top of your document. Click the **FILE tab** to display **Backstage** view, and then in the lower right corner of the screen, click **Show All Properties**.

2 As the document **Title**, type **Quantified Self Movement Gains Momentum** and then as the **Tags**, type **quantified self, physiologic monitoring, research paper**

3 ▸ Click in the **Comments** box and type **Draft copy of a research report that will be distributed to class members** and then in the **Categories** box, type **Biomedical Research**

4 ▸ In the **Subject** box, type your course name and section number. In the **Company** box, select and delete any existing text, and then type **University Medical Center**

5 ▸ Click in the **Manager** box and type **Dr. Hillary Kim** Be sure your name displays as the **Author** and edit if necessary.

6 ▸ At the top of the **Properties** list, click the text *Properties*, and then click **Advanced Properties**. In the dialog box, click the **Summary tab**, and then compare your screen with Figure 3.18.

In the Advanced Properties dialog box, you can view and modify additional document properties.

FIGURE 3.18

7 ▸ Click the **Statistics tab**.

The document statistics show the number of revisions made to the document, the last time the document was edited, and the number of paragraphs, lines, words, and characters in the document. Additional information categories are available by clicking the Custom tab.

8 ▸ **Close** ☒ the dialog box, and then on the left, click **Save** to save and return to your document.

Objective 4 ▏ Use Read Mode and PDF Reflow

Video W3-4

Read Mode optimizes the view of the Word screen for the times when you are *reading* Word documents on the screen and not creating or editing them. Microsoft's research indicates that two-thirds of user sessions in Word contain no editing—meaning that people are simply reading the Word document on the screen. The Column Layout feature of Read Mode reflows the document to fit the size of the device you are reading so that the text is as easy to read on a tablet device as on a 24-inch screen. The Object Zoom feature of Read Mode resizes graphics to fit the screen you are using, but you can click or tap to zoom in on the graphic.

PDF Reflow provides the ability to import PDF files into Word so that you can transform a PDF back into a fully editable Word document. This is useful if you have lost the original Word file or if someone sends you a PDF that you would like to modify. PDF Reflow is not intended to act as a viewer for PDF files—for that you will still want to use the desktop app known as Adobe Reader or the *Windows Reader app*, with which you can open a PDF or XPS file, zoom, find words or phrases, take notes, save changes, and then print or share the file.

Activity 3.13 ▏ Using Read Mode

1 ▸ If necessary, press Ctrl + Home to move to the top of your document. On the **VIEW tab**, in the **Views group**, click **Read Mode**, and notice that **Read Mode** keeps footnotes displayed on the page associated with the footnote.

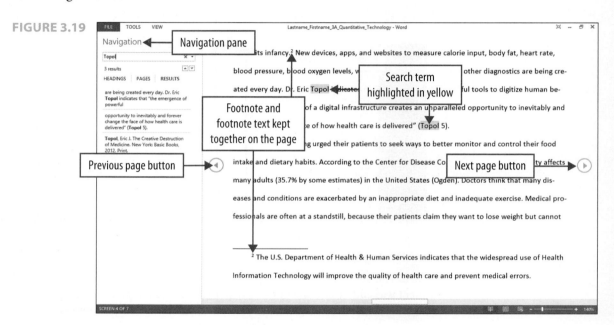
▶ **2** In the upper left corner, click **TOOLS**.

> You can use these tools to find something within the document or jump out to Bing to conduct an Internet search.

▶ **3** Click **Find**, and then in the **Search** box, type **Topol** Notice that Word displays the first page where the search term displays and highlights the term in yellow. Compare your screen with Figure 3.19.

FIGURE 3.19

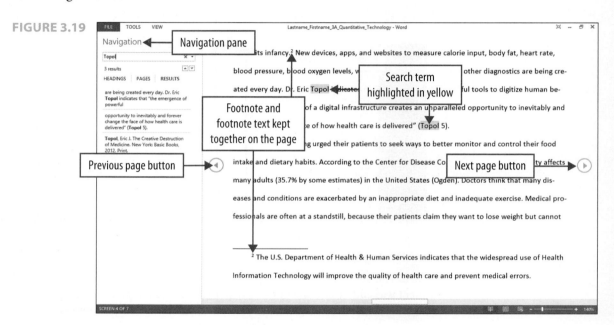

▶ **4** In the upper left corner, click **VIEW**, and then take a moment to study the table in Figure 3.20.

FIGURE 3.20

VIEW COMMANDS IN READ MODE	
VIEW COMMAND	**ACTION**
Edit Document	Return to Print Layout view to continue editing the document.
Navigation Pane	Search for specific text or click a heading or page to move to that location.
Show Comments	See comments, if any, within the document.
Column Width	Change the display of the document to fit more or less text on each line.
Page Color	Change the colors used to show the document to make it easier to read. Some readers prefer a sepia (brownish-gray) shading as the background or a black background with white text.
Layout	Read in different layouts. Select Column Layout, which is the default, or Paper Layout, which mimics the 8.5 × 11 format but without the ribbon.

▶ **5** On the **VIEW** menu, click **Edit Document** to return to **Print Layout** view. **Close** ☒ the **navigation pane**.

🔄 **ANOTHER WAY** On the status bar on the right, click the Print Layout button 📄.

Activity 3.14 | Using PDF Reflow

1 Save 🖫 your document. Click the **FILE tab**, and then on the left, click **Close** to close your document but leave Word open.

2 Press Ctrl + F12 to display the **Open** dialog box, navigate to your student data files, and then click **w03A_PDF**. In the lower right corner, click **Open**. If a message indicates that *Word will now convert the PDF to an editable Word document…*, click **OK**.

3 If necessary, on the right side of the status bar, click **Print Layout** 🖹.

4 In the newsletter heading, change the **Volume** number to **3** Insert a footer, and then, using your own name, type **Lastname_Firstname_3A_PDF_Reflow** as shown in Figure 3.21.

FIGURE 3.21

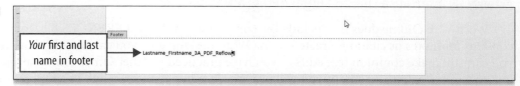

Your first and last name in footer → Footer — Lastname_Firstname_3A_PDF_Reflow¶

5 Close the footer area. Press F12 to display the **Save As** dialog box, and then navigate to your **Word Chapter 3** folder. In the lower portion of the dialog box, click the **Save as type arrow**, and then click **PDF**.

6 In the **File name** box, type **Lastname_Firstname_3A_PDF_Reflow** and then in the lower right corner, click **Save** or press Enter.

This action re-saves the document as a PDF file.

🔄 **ANOTHER WAY** Click the FILE tab, on the left click Export, click Create PDF/XPS, navigate to the desired folder, and then click Publish.

7 **Close** the **w03A_PDF** document without saving. **Close** ⎡ × ⎤ Word. Print or submit electronically the two files that are the result of this project.

More **Knowledge**	**Inserting Watermarks**

You can add ghost text such as *Draft* or *Confidential* behind the content of a page. To do so, on the DESIGN tab, in the Page Background group, click Watermark, and select or create the watermark you want to use.

END | You have completed Project 3A

GO! with Office Online (formerly Web Apps)

Objective | Insert a Link and Highlight Text in a Word Online Document

You can use Word Online to insert a link to a website.

> **ALERT!** **Working with Web-Based Applications and Services**
>
> Computer programs and services on the web receive continuous updates and improvements, so the steps to complete this web-based activity may differ from the ones shown. You can often look at the screens and the information presented to determine how to complete the activity.

Activity | Inserting a Link and Highlighting a Text Selection

Word Web Online does not include the commands on the REFERENCES tab, so if you open a report that contains footnotes or citations created in the Word desktop app, you cannot edit them in Word Online. However, you can still make common text edits as you have practiced in other Office Online projects. You can also insert a link to a website. In this activity, you will use Word Online to insert a link in a report, which you might want to do before sharing the report electronically for review by others.

1 From the desktop, start Internet Explorer. Navigate to **http://onedrive.com**, and then sign in to your Microsoft account. Open your **GO! Web Projects** folder; or create this folder if you have not done so.

2 In the OneDrive menu bar, click **Upload**. Navigate to your student data files, click **w03_3A_Web**, and then click **Open**.

3 Point to the uploaded file **w03_3A_Web**, and then right-click. On the shortcut menu, scroll as necessary, and then click **Rename**. Using your own last name and first name, type **Lastname_Firstname_WD_3A_Web** and then press Enter to rename the file.

4 Click the file that you just renamed, and then click **EDIT DOCUMENT**. On the list, click **Edit in Word Online**.

5 In the paragraph that begins *The implications*, drag to select *Tic-Toc-Trac*, and then on the **HOME tab**, in the

Font group, click **Text Highlight Color** . Click the **Yellow** block to highlight this text in yellow.

6 Press Ctrl + End to move to the end of the document, and then press Enter.

7 On the **INSERT tab**, in the **Links group**, click **Link**. In the **Display text** box, type **See how Tic-Toc-Trac works!**

8 In the **Address** box, type **www.tictoctrac.com** and then click **Insert**. Compare your screen with Figure A.

9 To test the link, point to it, hold down Ctrl and then click one time. The site opens on a new tab.

10 In your browser, close the **TicTocTrac** tab.

11 Submit as directed by your instructor. Sign out of your OneDrive.

FIGURE A

Newsletter with Mailing Labels

PROJECT ACTIVITIES

In Activities 3.15 through 3.29, you will edit a newsletter that University Medical Center is sending to the board of directors and create the necessary mailing labels. Your completed documents will look similar to Figure 3.22.

PROJECT FILES

For Project 3B, you will need the following files:

New blank Word document
w03B_Environment_Newsletter
w03B_Addresses
w03B_Recycling

You will save your documents as:

Lastname_Firstname_3B_Mailing_Labels
Lastname_Firstname_3B_Addresses
Lastname_Firstname_3B_Environment_Newsletter

PROJECT RESULTS

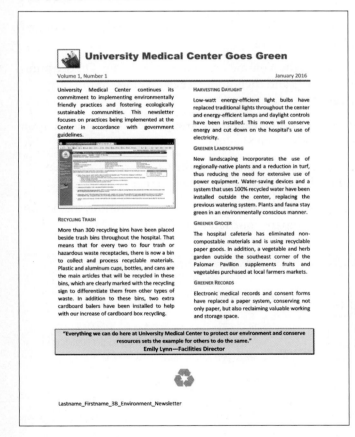

FIGURE 3.22 Project 3B Newsletter with Mailing Labels

Video W3-5

A *newsletter* is a periodical that communicates news and information to a specific group. Newsletters, as well as all newspapers and most magazines, use multiple columns for articles because text in narrower columns is easier to read than text that stretches across a page. You can create a newsletter in Word by changing a single column of text into two or more columns. If a column does not end where you want it to, you can end the column at a location of your choice by inserting a *manual column break*—an artificial end to a column to balance columns or to provide space for the insertion of other objects.

Activity 3.15 │ Changing One Column of Text to Two Columns

Newsletters are usually two or three columns wide. When using 8.5 × 11-inch paper in portrait orientation, avoid creating four or more columns because they are so narrow that word spacing looks awkward, often resulting in one long word on a line by itself.

1 Start Word. On Word's opening screen, in the lower left, click **Open Other Documents**. Navigate to your student files, and then locate and open the document **w03B_Environment_Newsletter**. If necessary, display the formatting marks and rulers. **Save** the file in your **Word Chapter 3** folder as **Lastname_Firstname_3B_Environment_Newsletter** and then add the file name to the footer.

2 Select the first paragraph of text—*University Medical Center Goes Green*. On the mini toolbar, change the **Font** to **Arial Black** and the **Font Size** to **18**.

3 Select the first two paragraphs—the title and the Volume information and date. On the mini toolbar, click the **Font Color button arrow** ![A]▾, and then under **Theme Colors**, in the fifth column, click the last color—**Blue, Accent 1, Darker 50%**.

4 With the text still selected, on the **HOME tab**, in the **Paragraph group**, click the **Borders button arrow** ![]▾, and then at the bottom, click **Borders and Shading**.

5 In the **Borders and Shading** dialog box, on the **Borders tab**, click the **Color arrow**, and then under **Theme Colors**, in the fifth column, click the last color—**Blue, Accent 1, Darker 50%**.

6 Click the **Width arrow**, and then click **3 pt**. In the **Preview** box at the right, point to the *bottom* border of the preview and click one time. Compare your screen with Figure 3.23.

FIGURE 3.23

  ANOTHER WAY   In the Preview area, click the Bottom Border button ![].

7 In the **Borders and Shading** dialog box, click **OK**.

The line visually defines the newsletter's *nameplate*—the banner on the front page of a newsletter that identifies the publication.

8 ▶ Below the Volume information, click at the beginning of the paragraph that begins *University Medical Center continues*. By using the vertical scroll box, scroll to view the lower portion of the document, hold down ⟨Shift⟩, and then click after the paragraph mark at the end of the paragraph that begins *Electronic medical records* to select all of the text between the insertion point and the sentence ending with the word *space*. Be sure that the paragraph mark is included in the selection. Compare your screen with Figure 3.24.

Use ⟨Shift⟩ to define a selection that may be difficult to select by dragging.

FIGURE 3.24

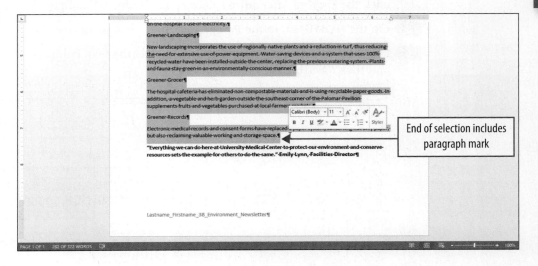

9 ▶ On the **PAGE LAYOUT tab**, in the **Page Setup group**, click **Columns**, and then click **Two**. Compare your screen with Figure 3.25, and then **Save** 🔲 your newsletter.

Word divides the text into two columns and inserts a ***section break*** at the end of the selection, dividing the one-column section of the document from the two-column section of the document. A ***section*** is a portion of a document that can be formatted differently from the rest of the document. A section break marks the end of one section and the beginning of another section.

FIGURE 3.25

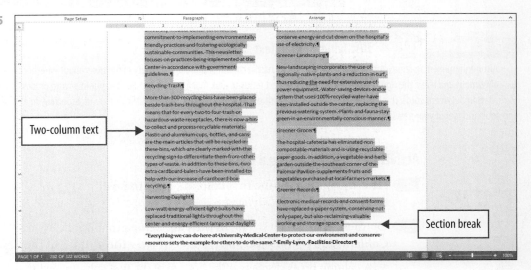

Activity 3.16 | Formatting Multiple Columns

The uneven right margin of a single page-width column is easy to read. When you create narrow columns, justified text is sometimes preferable. Depending on the design and layout of your newsletter, you might decide to reduce extra space between paragraphs and between columns to improve the readability of the document.

1 With the two columns of text still selected, on the **PAGE LAYOUT tab**, in the **Paragraph group**, click the **Spacing After down spin arrow** one time to change the spacing after to **6 pt**.

2 On the **HOME tab**, in the **Paragraph group**, click **Justify** ▤.

3 Click anywhere in the document to deselect the text, compare your screen with Figure 3.26, and then **Save** 🖫.

FIGURE 3.26

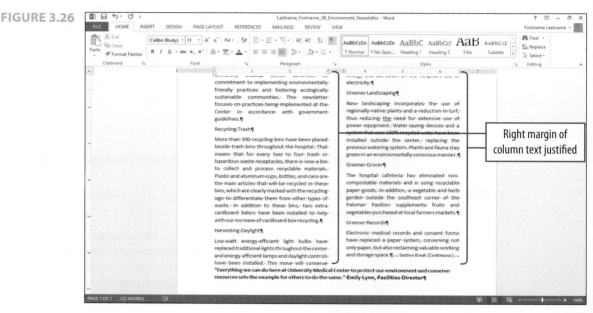

Right margin of column text justified

Activity 3.17 | Inserting a Column Break

1 Near the bottom of the first column, click to position the insertion point at the beginning of the line *Harvesting Daylight*.

2 On the **PAGE LAYOUT tab**, in the **Page Setup group**, click **Breaks**. Under **Page Breaks**, click **Column**, and then if necessary, scroll to view the bottom of the first column.

A column break displays at the bottom of the first column; text to the right of the column break moves to the top of the next column.

3 Compare your screen with Figure 3.27, and then **Save** 🖫.

A *column break indicator*—a dotted line containing the words *Column Break*—displays at the bottom of the column.

FIGURE 3.27

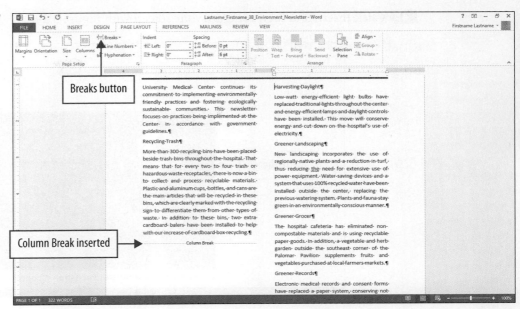

University Medical Center continues its commitment to implementing environmentally-friendly practices and fostering ecologically-sustainable communities. This newsletter focuses on practices being implemented at the Center in accordance with government guidelines.¶

Recycling Trash¶

More than 300 recycling bins have been placed beside trash bins throughout the hospital. That means that for every two to four trash or hazardous waste receptacles, there is now a bin to collect and process recyclable materials. Plastic and aluminum cups, bottles, and cans are the main articles that will be recycled in these bins, which are clearly marked with the recycling sign to differentiate them from other types of waste. In addition to these bins, two extra cardboard balers have been installed to help with our increase of cardboard box recycling.¶

Harvesting Daylight¶

Low-watt energy-efficient light bulbs have replaced traditional lights throughout the center and energy-efficient lamps and daylight controls have been installed. This move will conserve energy and cut down on the hospital's use of electricity.¶

Greener Landscaping¶

New landscaping incorporates the use of regionally-native plants and a reduction in turf, thus reducing the need for extensive use of power equipment. Water-saving devices and a system that uses 100% recycled water have been installed outside the center, replacing the previous watering system. Plants and fauna stay green in an environmentally-conscious manner.¶

Greener Grocer¶

The hospital cafeteria has eliminated non-compostable materials and is using recyclable paper goods. In addition, a vegetable and herb garden outside the southeast corner of the Palomar Pavilion supplements fruits and vegetables purchased at local farmers markets.¶

Greener Records¶

Electronic medical records and consent forms have replaced a paper system, conserving not

Breaks button

Column Break inserted

Column Break

PAGE 1 OF 1   322 WORDS

Activity 3.18 | Inserting an Online Picture

You can search for and insert online pictures in your document without saving the images to your computer. Pictures can make your document visually appealing and more interesting.

1 ▶ Press Ctrl + Home. On the **INSERT tab**, in the **Illustrations group**, click **Online Pictures**.

2 ▶ In the **Office.com Clip Art** search box, type **recycling bottles** so that Word can search for images that contain the keywords *recycling* and *bottles*. Press Enter.

3 ▶ Click the image of the recycle bin on a black background. Compare your screen with Figure 3.28. If the image does not display, close the Insert Pictures dialog box. Then, on the **INSERT tab**, in the **Illustrations group**, click **Pictures**, navigate to your student data files, and then double-click **w03B_Recycling**.

FIGURE 3.28

Online Pictures button

Keywords

Selected image

4 Click **Insert**, and then compare your screen with Figure 3.29.

FIGURE 3.29

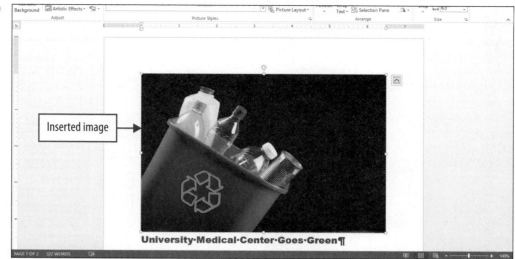

Inserted image

University·Medical·Center·Goes·Green¶

5 Press Ctrl + End to move to the end of the document. On the **INSERT tab**, in the **Illustrations group**, click **Online Pictures**. In the **Office.com Clip Art** search box, type **green recycling symbol** and then press Enter.

6 Click the first recycling symbol and then compare your screen with Figure 3.30. If the picture is not available, choose a similar picture.

FIGURE 3.30

Selected image

‹ BACK TO SITES

Office.com Clip Art
81 search results for green recycling symbol

green recycling symbol

Green recycle symbol
1402 x 1319 - PresentationPro

1 item selected.   Insert   Cancel

7 Click **Insert**. With the picture selected, on the **FORMAT tab**, in the **Size group**, click in the **Height** box. Type **0.5** and then press Enter. To the right of the picture, click **Layout Options**, and then click **Square**. At the bottom of the **Layout Options gallery**, click **See more**.

8 On the **Position tab**, under **Horizontal**, click the **Alignment** option button. Click the **Alignment arrow**, and then click **Centered**. Click the **relative to arrow** and then click **Page**. Under **Vertical**, click the **Alignment** option button. Click the **Alignment arrow**, and then click **Bottom**. Click the **relative to arrow**, and then click **Margin**. Compare your screen with Figure 3.31.

FIGURE 3.31

Horizontal alignment

Vertical alignment

9 Click **OK**, scroll to the bottom of the page, and then notice that the recycle image displays at the bottom of the second page. **Save** 🖫 the document.

🔄 ANOTHER WAY   Drag the image to visually position the image.

Activity 3.19 │ Cropping a Picture and Resizing a Picture by Scaling

In this activity, you will edit the recycle bin image by cropping and scaling the picture. When you *crop* a picture, you remove unwanted or unnecessary areas of the picture. When you *scale* a picture, you resize it to a percentage of its size.

1 Press Ctrl + Home to move to the top of the document, and then click the recycle bin picture to select it. On the **FORMAT tab**, in the **Size group**, click the upper portion of the **Crop** button to display crop handles around the picture. Compare your screen with Figure 3.32.

Crop handles are used like sizing handles to define unwanted areas of the picture.

FIGURE 3.32

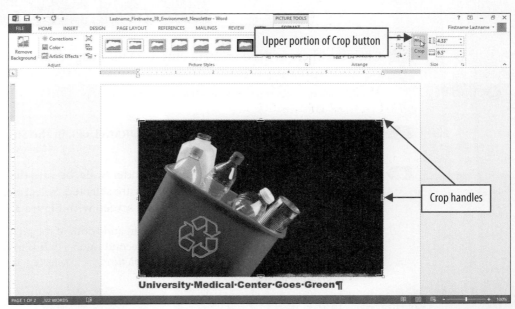

2 Point to the center right crop handle to display the 🯄 pointer. Compare your screen with Figure 3.33.

Use the *crop pointer* to crop areas of a picture.

FIGURE 3.33

3 With the crop pointer displayed, hold down the left mouse button and drag to the left to approximately **5 inches on the horizontal ruler**, and then release the mouse button. Compare your screen with Figure 3.34.

> The portion of the image to be removed displays in gray.

FIGURE 3.34

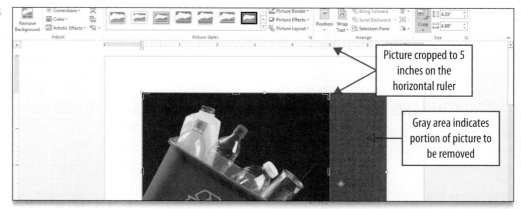

Picture cropped to 5 inches on the horizontal ruler

Gray area indicates portion of picture to be removed

4 Click anywhere in the document outside of the image to apply the crop.

ANOTHER WAY   Click the upper portion of the Crop button to apply the crop.

5 Click to select the picture again. On the **FORMAT tab**, in the **Size group**, click the **Dialog Box Launcher** button 🔲.

6 In the **Layout dialog box**, on the **Size tab**, under **Scale**, be sure that the **Lock aspect ratio** and **Relative to original picture size** check boxes are selected. Select the number in the **Height box**, type **10** and then press Tab. Compare your screen with Figure 3.35.

> When *Lock aspect ratio* is selected, the height and width of the picture are sized proportionately and only one scale value is necessary. The second value—in this instance Width—adjusts proportionately. When *Relative to original picture size* is selected, the scale is applied as a percentage of the original picture size.

FIGURE 3.35

Dialog Box Launcher

Height value

Width value

Check boxes selected

7 In the **Layout** dialog box, click the **Text Wrapping tab**. Under **Wrapping style**, click **Square**.

8 Click the **Position tab**, and then under **Horizontal**, click the **Alignment** option button. Be sure that the **Alignment** indicates **Left** and **relative to Column**. Under **Vertical**, click the **Alignment** option button, and then change the alignment to **Top relative to Margin**. Click **OK**, and then compare your screen with Figure 3.36.

FIGURE 3.36

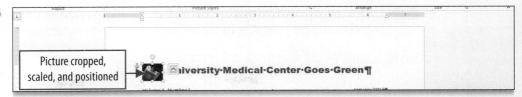

Picture cropped, scaled, and positioned

niversity·Medical·Center·Goes·Green¶

Activity 3.20 | Setting Transparent Color and Recoloring a Picture

You can make one color in a picture transparent using the Set Transparent Color command. When you *recolor* a picture, you change all the colors in the picture to shades of a single color.

1 On the **VIEW tab**, in the **Zoom group**, click **Zoom**, and then click **200%**. Click **OK**. Drag the scroll bars as necessary so that you can view the recycle bin picture at the top of the document.

2 If necessary, select the recycle bin picture. On the **FORMAT tab**, in the **Adjust group**, click **Color**, and then below the gallery, click **Set Transparent Color**. Move the pointer into the document to display the pointer.

3 Point anywhere in the black background of the recycle bin picture, and then click to apply the transparent color to the background. Compare your screen with Figure 3.37.

FIGURE 3.37

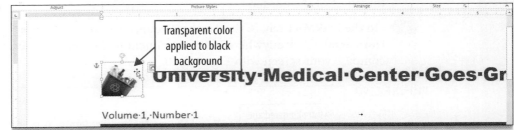

Transparent color applied to black background

University·Medical·Center·Goes·Gr

Volume·1,·Number·1

4 Press Ctrl + End to move to the end of your document, and then select the picture of the recycle symbol. On the **FORMAT tab**, in the **Adjust group**, click **Color** to display a gallery of recoloring options. Under **Recolor**, in the last row, click the fourth option— **Olive Green, Accent color 3 Light**. Compare your screen with Figure 3.38, and then **Save** 🖫 the document.

FIGURE 3.38

Picture recolored

Lastname_Firstname_3B_Environment_Newsletter¶

Activity 3.21 | Adjusting the Brightness and Contrast of a Picture

Brightness is the relative lightness of a picture. *Contrast* is the difference between the darkest and lightest area of a picture.

1 If necessary, select the recycle symbol. On the **FORMAT tab**, in the **Adjust group**, click **Corrections**. Under **Brightness/Contrast**, point to several of the options to view the effect that the settings have on the picture.

2 Under **Brightness/Contrast**, in the last row, click the first setting—**Brightness: –40% Contrast: +40%**. Compare your screen with Figure 3.39.

3 On the **VIEW tab**, in the **Zoom group**, click **100%**, and then **Save** ☐ the document.

Activity 3.22 | Applying a Border to a Picture and Flipping a Picture

The *flip* commands create a reverse image of a picture or object.

1 Press ⌃Ctrl + ⌂Home to move to the top of the document, and then select the picture of the recycle bin. On the **FORMAT tab**, in the **Picture Styles group**, click the **Picture Border button arrow**. Under **Theme Colors**, in the fourth column, click the first color—**Dark Blue, Text 2**.

2 Click the **Picture Border arrow** again, and then point to **Weight**. Click **1 1/2 pt** to change the thickness of the border.

3 On the **FORMAT tab**, in the **Arrange group**, click **Rotate Objects** ⬜, and then click **Flip Horizontal**. Click anywhere in the document to deselect the picture. **Save** ☐, and then compare your screen with Figure 3.40.

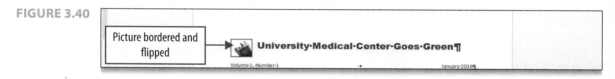

Activity 3.23 | Inserting a Screenshot

A *screenshot* is an image of an active window on your computer that you can paste into a document. Screenshots are especially useful when you want to insert an image of a website into your Word document. You can insert a screenshot of any open window on your computer.

1 In the paragraph that begins *University Medical Center continues*, click after the period at the end of the paragraph. Start Internet Explorer, and then navigate to **www.epa.gov/osw/conserve** and press ⌂Enter.

2 From the taskbar, redisplay your **3B_Environment_Newletter** document.

3 With the insertion point positioned at the end of the paragraph, on the **INSERT tab**, in the **Illustrations group**, click **Screenshot**.

All of your open windows display in the Available Windows gallery and are available to paste into the document.

4 In the **Screenshot** gallery, click the browser window that contains the EPA site to insert the screenshot at the insertion point. If a message box displays asking if you want to hyperlink the screenshot, click No, and then notice that the image is inserted and is sized to fit between the margins of the first column. Compare your screen with Figure 3.41.

By selecting No in the message box, you are inserting a screenshot without links to the actual website. Choose Yes, if you want to link the image to the website.

FIGURE 3.41

5 With the inserted screenshot selected, on the **FORMAT tab**, in the **Picture Styles group**, click the **Picture Border button arrow**, and then under **Theme Colors**, in the second column, click the first color—**Black, Text 1**.

6 Save the document.

Objective 6 | Use Special Character and Paragraph Formatting

Video W3-6

Special text and paragraph formatting is useful to emphasize text, and it makes your newsletter look more professional. For example, you can place a border around one or more paragraphs or add shading to a paragraph. When adding shading, use light colors; dark shading can make the text difficult to read.

Activity 3.24 | Applying the Small Caps Font Effect

For headlines and titles, *small caps* is an attractive font effect. The effect changes lowercase letters to uppercase letters, but with the height of lowercase letters.

1 Under the screenshot, select the paragraph *Recycling Trash* including the paragraph mark.

2 Right-click the selected text, and then on the shortcut menu, click **Font** to display the **Font** dialog box. Click the **Font color arrow**, and then change the color to **Blue, Accent 1, Darker 50%**—in the fifth column, the last color.

3 Under **Font style**, click **Bold**. Under **Effects**, select the **Small caps** check box. Compare your screen with Figure 3.42.

The Font dialog box provides more options than are available on the ribbon and enables you to make several changes at the same time. In the Preview box, the text displays with the selected formatting options applied.

FIGURE 3.42

4 ▸ Click **OK**. With the text still selected, right-click, and then on the mini toolbar, double-click **Format Painter** 🖌. Then, in the second column, with the 🅰I pointer, select each of the heading paragraphs—*Harvesting Daylight*, *Greener Landscaping*, *Greener Grocer*, and *Greener Records*—to apply the same formats. Press Esc to turn off **Format Painter**.

5 ▸ In the first column below the screenshot, notice that the space between the *Recycling Trash* subheading and the screenshot is fairly small. Click anywhere in the *Recycling Trash* subheading, and then on the **PAGE LAYOUT tab**, in the **Paragraph group**, click the **Before up spin arrow** two times to set the spacing to **12 pt**.

6 ▸ Compare your screen with Figure 3.43, and then **Save** 💾 your document.

FIGURE 3.43

Activity 3.25 | Inserting Symbols and Special Characters

You can insert symbols and special characters in a Word document, including copyright symbols, trademark symbols, and em dashes. An ***em dash*** is a punctuation symbol used to indicate an explanation or emphasis.

1 ▸ Press Ctrl + End to move to the end of the document, and then after the name *Emily Lynn* delete the comma and the space that separates her name from her job title—*Facilities Director*.

2 ▸ With the insertion point positioned before the *F* in *Facilities*, on the **INSERT tab**, in the **Symbols group**, click **Symbol**. Below the gallery, click **More Symbols** to display the **Symbol** dialog box.

   Here you can choose the symbol that you want to insert in your document.

3 ▸ In the **Symbol** dialog box, click the **Special Characters tab**. Scroll the list to view the types of special characters that you can insert; notice that some of the characters can be inserted using a Shortcut key.

4 ▸ Click **Em Dash**, and then in the lower right portion of the dialog box, click **Insert**. Compare your screen with Figure 3.44.

   An em dash displays between the name *Lynn* and the word *Facilities*.

FIGURE 3.44

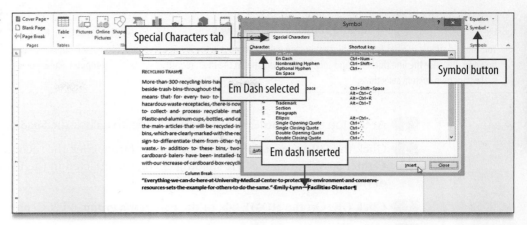

5 In the **Symbol** dialog box, click **Close**, and then **Save** 🖫 your document.

Activity 3.26 | Adding Borders and Shading to a Paragraph and Inserting a Manual Line Break

Paragraph borders provide strong visual cues to the reader. You can use paragraph shading with or without borders; however, combined with a border, light shading can be very effective in drawing the reader's eye to the text.

1 At the end of the document, select the two lines of bold text that begin *"Everything we can do.*"

The recycle picture may also be selected because it is anchored to the paragraph.

2 On the **HOME tab**, in the **Paragraph group**, click the **Borders button arrow** ⊞ ▾, and then click **Borders and Shading**.

3 In the **Borders and Shading** dialog box, be sure the **Borders tab** is selected. Under **Setting**, click **Shadow**. Click the **Color arrow**, and then in the fifth column, click the last color—**Blue, Accent 1, Darker 50%**. Click the **Width arrow**, and then click **1 pt**. Compare your screen with Figure 3.45.

In the lower right portion of the Borders and Shading dialog box, the *Apply to* box indicates *Paragraph*. The *Apply to* box directs where the border will be applied—in this instance, the border will be applied only to the selected paragraph.

FIGURE 3.45

4 At the top of the **Borders and Shading** dialog box, click the **Shading tab**.

5 Click the **Fill arrow**, and then in the fifth column, click the second color—**Blue, Accent 1, Lighter 80%**. Notice that the shading change is reflected in the **Preview area** on the right side of the dialog box.

6 Click **OK**. On the **HOME tab**, in the **Paragraph group**, click **Center** ▤.

7 Click anywhere in the document to deselect, and then compare your screen with Figure 3.46.

FIGURE 3.46

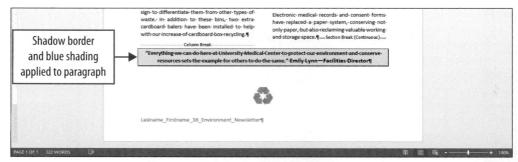

8 In the shaded paragraph, in the second line, click in front of the *E* in the name *Emily*. Hold down Shift and then press Enter.

> Holding down Shift while pressing Enter inserts a ***manual line break***, which moves the text to the right of the insertion point to a new line while keeping the text in the same paragraph. A ***line break indicator***, in the shape of a bent arrow, indicates a manual line break.

9 Press Ctrl + Home to move the insertion point to the top of the document. Click the **FILE tab** to display **Backstage** view. On the right, at the bottom of the **Properties** list, click **Show All Properties**.

10 On the list of **Properties**, click to the right of **Tags**, and then type **newsletter, January**

11 Click to the right of **Subject**, and then type your course name and section number. Under **Related People**, be sure that your name displays as the author. If necessary, right-click the author name, click **Edit Property**, type your name, and click **OK**.

12 On the left, click **Print** to display the **Print Preview**, make any necessary corrections, and then **Save** the document. **Close** Word; hold this file until you complete this project. If necessary, close Internet Explorer.

Objective 7 | Create Mailing Labels Using Mail Merge

Video W3-7

Word's ***mail merge*** feature joins a ***main document*** and a ***data source*** to create customized letters or labels. The main document contains the text or formatting that remains constant. For labels, the main document contains the formatting for a specific label size. The data source contains information including the names and addresses of the individuals for whom the labels are being created. Names and addresses in a data source might come from a Word table, an Excel worksheet, or an Access database.

The easiest way to perform a mail merge is to use the Mail Merge Wizard, which asks you questions and, based on your answers, walks you step by step through the mail merge process.

Activity 3.27 | Starting the Mail Merge Wizard Template

In this activity, you will open the data source for the mail merge, which is a Word table containing names and addresses.

1 Start Word and display a new blank document. Display formatting marks and rulers. **Save** the document in your **Word Chapter 3** folder as **Lastname_Firstname_3B_Mailing_Labels**

2 With your new document open on the screen, from your student files, **Open** the file **w03B_Addresses**. **Save** the address file in your **Word Chapter 3** folder as **Lastname_Firstname_ 3B_Addresses** and then add the file name to the footer.

This document contains a table of addresses. The first row contains the column names. The remaining rows contain the names and addresses.

3 Click to position the insertion point in the last cell in the table, and then press Tab to create a new row. Enter the following information, and then compare your table with Figure 3.47.

FIRST NAME	LAST NAME	ADDRESS 1	UNIT	CITY	STATE	ZIP CODE
Monica	Warren	5626 Summer Road	#234	Lakeland	TN	38002

FIGURE 3.47

4 **Save**, and then **Close** the table of addresses. Be sure that your blank **Lastname_Firstname_3B_Mailing_Labels** document displays.

5 Click the **MAILINGS tab**. In the **Start Mail Merge group**, click **Start Mail Merge**, and then click **Step-by-Step Mail Merge Wizard** to display the **Mail Merge** pane on the right.

6 In the **Mail Merge** pane, under **Select document type**, click **Labels**. At the bottom of the **Mail Merge** pane, click **Next: Starting document** to display Step 2 of 6.

7 Under **Select starting document**, be sure **Change document layout** is selected, and then under **Change document layout**, click **Label options**.

8 In the **Label Options** dialog box, under **Printer information**, click the **Tray arrow**, and then if necessary, click **Default tray** (Automatically Select)—the exact wording may vary depending on your printer, but select the *Default* or *Automatic* option so that you can print the labels on regular paper rather than manually inserting labels in the printer.

9 Under **Label information**, click the **Label vendors arrow**, and then click **Avery US Letter**. Under **Product number**, scroll about halfway down the list, and then click **5160 Easy Peel Address Labels**. Compare your screen with Figure 3.48.

The Avery 5160 address label is a commonly used label. The precut sheets contain three columns of 10 labels each—for a total of 30 labels per sheet.

FIGURE 3.48

10 At the bottom of the **Label Options** dialog box, click **OK**. If a message box displays, click **OK** to set up the labels. If the gridlines do not display, on the **Layout tab**, in the **Table** group, click **View Gridlines**. At the bottom of the **Mail Merge** pane, click **Next: Select recipients**.

The label page is set up with three columns and ten rows. Here, in Step 3 of the Mail Merge Wizard, you must identify the recipients—the data source. For your recipient data source, you can choose to use an existing list—for example, a list of names and addresses that you have in an Access database, an Excel worksheet, a Word table, or your Outlook contacts list. If you do not have an existing data source, you can type a new list at this point in the wizard.

11 In the **Mail Merge** pane, under **Select recipients**, be sure the **Use an existing list** option button is selected. Under **Use an existing list**, click **Browse**.

12 Navigate to your **Word Chapter 3** folder, select your **Lastname_Firstname_3B_Addresses** file, and then click **Open** to display the **Mail Merge Recipients** dialog box. Compare your screen with Figure 3.49.

In the Mail Merge Recipients dialog box, the column headings are formed from the text in the first row of your Word table of addresses. Each row of information that contains data for one person is referred to as a **record**. The column headings—for example, *Last_Name* and *First_Name*—are referred to as **fields**. An underscore replaces the spaces between words in the field name headings.

FIGURE 3.49

13 In the lower left portion of the **Mail Merge Recipients** dialog box, in the **Data Source** box, click the path that contains your file name. Then, at the bottom of the **Mail Merge Recipients** dialog box, click **Edit**.

14 In the upper right corner of the **Data Form** dialog box, click **Add New**. In the blank record, type the following, pressing Tab to move from field to field, and then compare your **Data Form** dialog box with Figure 3.50.

FIRST_NAME	LAST_NAME	ADDRESS_1	UNIT	CITY	STATE	ZIP CODE
Sharon	Williams	1251 Parker Road	#843	Memphis	TN	38123

FIGURE 3.50

15 In the lower right corner of the **Data Form** dialog box, click **Close**. Scroll to the end of the recipient list to confirm that the record for *Sharon Williams* that you just added is in the list. At the bottom of the **Mail Merge Recipients** dialog box, click **OK**.

Activity 3.28 | Completing the Mail Merge Wizard

You can add or edit names and addresses while completing the Mail Merge. You can also match your column names with preset names used in Mail Merge.

1 At the bottom of the **Mail Merge** pane, click **Next: Arrange your labels**.

2 Under **Arrange your labels**, click **Address block**. In the **Insert Address Block** dialog box, under **Specify address elements**, examine the various formats for names. If necessary, under *Insert recipient's name in this format*, select the *Joshua Randall Jr.* format. Compare your dialog box with Figure 3.51.

FIGURE 3.51

3 In the lower right corner of the **Insert Address Block** dialog box, click **Match Fields**, and then compare your screen with Figure 3.52.

> If your field names are descriptive, the Mail Merge program will identify them correctly, as is the case with most of the information in the *Required for Address Block* section. However, the Address 2 field is unmatched—in the source file, this column is named *Unit*.

FIGURE 3.52

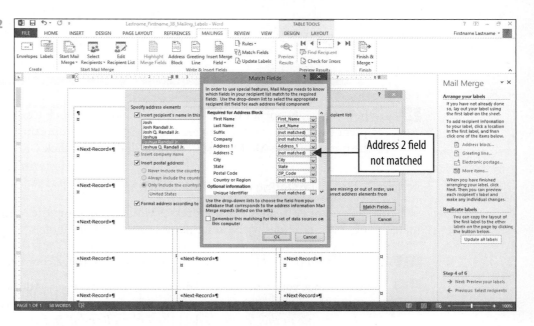

4 Click the **Address 2 arrow**, and then from the list of available fields, click **Unit** to match the Mail Merge field with the field in your data source.

5 At the bottom of the **Match Fields** dialog box, click **OK**. At the bottom of the **Insert Address Block** dialog box, click **OK**.

> Word inserts the Address block in the first label space surrounded by double angle brackets. The *AddressBlock* field name displays, which represents the address block you saw in the Preview area of the Insert Address Block dialog box.

6 In the **Mail Merge** pane, under **Replicate labels**, click **Update all labels** to insert an address block in each label space for each subsequent record.

7 At the bottom of the **Mail Merge** pane, click **Next: Preview your labels**. Notice that for addresses with four lines, the last line of the address is cut off.

8 Press Ctrl + A to select all of the label text, click the **PAGE LAYOUT tab**, and then in the **Paragraph group**, click in the **Spacing Before** box. Type **3** and press Enter.

9 Click in any label to deselect, and notice that 4-line addresses are no longer cut off. Compare your screen with Figure 3.53.

FIGURE 3.53

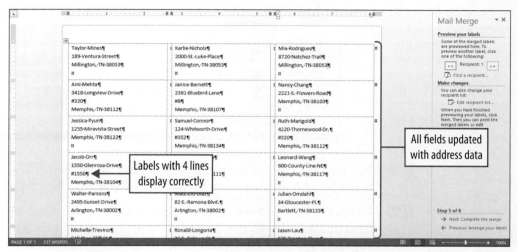

10 At the bottom of the **Mail Merge** pane, click **Next: Complete the merge**.

Step 6 of the Mail Merge displays. At this point you can print or edit your labels, although this is done more easily in the document window.

11 Save 🖫 your labels, and then on the right, **Close** ✖ the **Mail Merge** pane.

Activity 3.29 | Sorting Mail Merge Results

If you discover that you need to make further changes to your labels, you can still make them even though the Mail Merge task pane is closed.

1 Add the file name to the footer, close the footer area, and then move to the top of Page 2. Click anywhere in the empty table row, and then click the **LAYOUT tab**. In the **Rows & Columns group**, click **Delete**, and then click **Delete Rows**.

Adding footer text to a label sheet replaces the last row of labels on a page with the footer text, and moves the last row of labels to the top of the next page. In this instance, a blank second page is created, which you can delete by deleting the blank row.

2 Notice that the labels do not display in alphabetical order. Click the **MAILINGS tab**, and then in the **Start Mail Merge group**, click **Edit Recipient List** to display the list of names and addresses.

3 In the **Mail Merge Recipients** dialog box, click the **Last_Name** field heading, and notice that the names are sorted alphabetically by the recipient's last name.

Mailing labels are often sorted by either last name or by ZIP Code.

4 Click the **Last_Name** field heading again, and notice that the last names are sorted in descending order. Click the **Last_Name** field one more time to return to ascending order, and then click **OK**. Press Ctrl + Home, and then compare your screen with Figure 3.54.

FIGURE 3.54

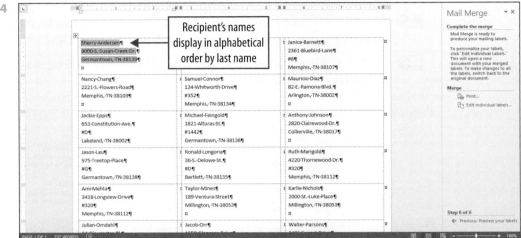

5 Click the **FILE tab**. On the right, at the bottom of the **Properties** list, click **Show All Properties**. On the list of **Properties**, click to the right of **Tags**, and then type **labels**

6 Click to the right of **Subject**, and then type your course name and section number. Be sure that your name displays as the author. If necessary, right-click the author name, click **Edit Property**, type your name, and click **OK**. **Save** 🖫 the file. **Close** the document, and click **Yes** to save the data source.

7 As directed by your instructor, print or submit electronically.

If you print, the labels will print on whatever paper is in the printer; unless you have preformatted labels available, the labels will print on a sheet of paper. Printing the labels on plain paper enables you to proofread the labels before you print them on more expensive label sheets.

8 In addition to your labels and address document, print or submit your **Lastname_Firstname_3B_Environment_Newsletter** document as directed. **Close** Word.

END | You have completed Project 3B

GO! with Office Online (formerly Web Apps)

Objective   Format a Single-Column Newsletter in Word Online

You can use Word Online to insert clip art and to format text. You can change fonts and font color, and modify paragraph spacing.

> **ALERT!**   **Working with Web-Based Applications and Services**
>
> Computer programs and services on the web receive continuous updates and improvements, so the steps to complete this web-based activity may differ from the ones shown. You can often look at the screens and the information presented to determine how to complete the activity.

Activity | Formatting a Single-Column Newsletter

In this activity, you will use Word Online to edit a single-column newsletter similar to the one you edited in Project 3B.

1 From the desktop, start Internet Explorer. Navigate to **http://onedrive.com**, and then sign in to your Microsoft account. Open your **GO! Web Projects** folder; or create this folder if necessary.

2 In the OneDrive menu bar, click **Upload**. Navigate to your student data files, click **w03_3B_Web**, and then click **Open**.

3 Point to the uploaded file **w03_3B_Web**, and then right-click. On the shortcut menu, scroll as necessary, and then click **Rename**. Using your own last name and first name, type **Lastname_Firstname_WD_3B_Web** and then press [Enter] to rename the file.

4 Click the file that you just renamed, and then click **EDIT DOCUMENT**. On the list, click **Edit in Word Online**.

5 Drag to select the newsletter title—*University Medical Center Goes Green*. On the **HOME tab**, in the

Font group, locate and click the **Grow Font button** two times to change the font size to **18**. With the newsletter title still selected, on the **HOME tab**, in the **Font group**, click **Font Color**, and then in the fifth column, click the last color—**Blue Gray, Accent 1, Darker 50%**. Apply the same **Font Color** to the five subheadings—*Recycling Trash*, *Harvesting Daylight*, *Greener Landscaping*, *Greener Grocer*, and *Greener Records*.

6 Drag to select the first subheading—*Recycling Trash*. On the **PAGE LAYOUT tab**, in the **Paragraph group**, click in the **After box**. Type **12** and then press [Enter]—or click the arrow as necessary. Apply the same **Spacing After** to the remaining four subheadings—*Harvesting Daylight*, *Greener Landscaping*, *Greener Grocer*, and *Greener Records*. Click anywhere in the document, and then press [Ctrl] + [Home] to move to the top of the document. Compare your screen with Figure A.

FIGURE A

University Medical Center Goes Green

University Medical Center continues its commitment to implementing environmentally friendly practices and fostering ecologically sustainable communities. This newsletter focuses on practices being implemented at the Center in accordance with government guidelines.

Recycling Trash

More than 300 recycling bins have been placed beside trash bins throughout the hospital. That means that for every two to four trash or hazardous waste receptacles, there is now a bin to collect and process recyclable materials. Plastic and aluminum cups, bottles, and cans are the main articles that will be recycled in these bins, which are clearly marked with the recycling sign to differentiate them from other types of waste. In addition to these bins, two extra cardboard balers have been installed to help with our increase of cardboard box recycling.

Harvesting Daylight

Low-watt energy-efficient light bulbs have replaced traditional lights throughout the center and energy-efficient lamps and daylight controls have been installed. This move will conserve energy and cut down on the hospital's use of electricity.

(GO! with Office Online (formerly Web Apps) continues on the next page)

7 Be sure the insertion point is positioned at the top of the document. On the **PAGE LAYOUT tab**, in the **Page Setup group**, click **Margins**, and then click **Custom Margins**. Click in the **Top** box and type **0.5** and then click in the **Bottom** box. Type **0.5** and then click **OK**.

8 On the **INSERT tab**, in the **Pictures group**, click **Picture**. Navigate to your student data files, and then click **w03B_Recycling**. Click **Insert**.

9 On the **FORMAT tab**, in the **Image Size group**, click in the **Scale** box. Type **5** to replace the existing number, and then press [Enter]. On the **FORMAT tab**, in the **Picture Styles group**, use the ScreenTips to locate and then click **Reflected Rounded Rectangle**.

10 Deselect the picture. Press [Ctrl] + [End] to move to the end of the document, and then press [Enter]. On the **INSERT tab**, in the **Pictures group**, click **Clip Art**. In the **Search** box, type **green recycle symbol** and then press [Enter]. Click

the image of the green recycle symbol that you used in Project 3B. If the image is not available, choose a similar picture. Click **Insert**.

11 On the **FORMAT tab**, in the **Image Size group**, click in the **Scale** box. Type **5** to replace the existing number, and then press [Enter]. On the **HOME tab**, in the **Paragraph group**, click **Center**.

12 In the last paragraph of the newsletter, click to position the insertion point between the second quotation mark and the letter *E* in *Emily*. Hold down [Shift] and then press [Enter] to insert a manual line break. On the **HOME tab**, in the **Paragraph group**, click **Center** to center the three lines of text in the last paragraph. Deselect the picture and then compare your screen with Figure B.

13 Submit your file as directed by your instructor. Sign out of your OneDrive and close Internet Explorer.

FIGURE B

Andrew Rodriguez / Fotolia; FotolEdhar/ Fotolia; apops/ Fotolia; Yuri Arcurs/ Fotolia

The advantage of using Office 365 is that your organization does not have to purchase and install server hardware and software for sophisticated business applications and does not need a full-time IT person or staff just to manage the technology your teams need.

By using Office 365, you are able to have business-class services for your employees without investing in expensive hardware, software, and personnel. However, at least one person in an organization must be designated as the *Office 365 Administrator*—the person who creates and manages the account, adds new users, sets up the services your organization wants to use, sets permission levels, and manages the SharePoint team sites. You can have more than one Administrator if you want to share these tasks with others.

Microsoft provides easy-to-use instructions and videos to get you started, and you might also have contact with a Microsoft representative. You will probably find, however, that subscribing to and setting up the account, adding users, and activating services is a straightforward process that requires little or no assistance.

After purchasing the required number of licenses, you will add each team member as a user that includes his or her email address.

The Admin Overview page, as shown in the Figure below, assists the Office 365 Administrator. On the left, there are links to manage the users and domains in your Office 365 account. This is where you can add new users, delete users, set permission levels, enter and change passwords, and update the user properties and the licenses.

In the center, you can see the various services available to you in Office 365. In the site shown in Figure A, Outlook, Lync, SharePoint (team sites), and a public-facing website are all part of the services.

Activity | Using a Team Site to Collaborate

This group project relates to the **Bell Orchid Hotels**. If your instructor assigns this project to your class, you can expect to use a SharePoint team site in **Office 365** to collaborate on the following tasks for this chapter:

- If you are in the **Accounting Group**, you and your teammates will finalize the report to shareholders, merge the letter with the labels, and post the final report on the SharePoint team site.

- If you are in the **Engineering Group**, you and your teammates will finalize the report to the three insurance companies, merge the letter with the labels, and post the final report on the SharePoint team site.

- If you are in the **Food and Beverage Group**, you and your teammates will finalize the letter to customers planning a banquet, merge the letter with the labels, and post the final letter on the SharePoint team site.

- If you are in the **Human Resources Group**, you and your teammates will finalize the memo to employees, merge the memo with the labels, and post the final memo on the SharePoint team site.

- If you are in the **Operations Group**, you and your teammates will finalize the letter to job applicants, merge the letter with the labels, and post the final letter on the SharePoint team site.

- If you are in the **Sales and Marketing Group**, you and your teammates will finalize the letter to the 20 professional associations, merge the letter with the labels, and post the final letter on the SharePoint team site.

FIGURE A

END OF CHAPTER

SUMMARY

Word assists you in formatting a research paper for college or business by providing built-in styles and applies the most commonly used footnote and citation styles for research papers—MLA and APA.

Word helps you create the bibliography for your research paper by recording all of your citations in the Source Manager, and then generating the bibliography—in MLA, called Works Cited—for you.

Newsletters are often used by organizations to communicate information to a specific group. A newsletter can be formatted in two columns with a nameplate at the top that identifies the publication.

The Mail Merge Wizard enables you to easily merge a main document and a data source to create customized letters or labels. The data source can be a Word table, Excel spreadsheet, or Access database.

GO! LEARN IT ONLINE

Review the concepts and key terms in this chapter by completing these online challenges, which you can find at **www.pearsonhighered.com/go**.

Matching and Multiple Choice: Answer matching and multiple choice questions to test what you learned in this chapter. MyITLab®

Crossword Puzzle: Spell out the words that match the numbered clues, and put them in the puzzle squares.

Flipboard: Flip through the definitions of the key terms in this chapter and match them with the correct term.

GO! FOR JOB SUCCESS

Video: Email Etiquette

Your instructor may assign this video to your class, and then ask you to think about, or discuss with your classmates, these questions:

FotolEdhar / Fotolia

Why do you think it is important to follow specific etiquette when composing email?

Why is it important to include a greeting and sign every email that you send?

What are the differences between sending a business email and a personal email, and what are three specific things you should never do in a business email?

END OF CHAPTER

REVIEW AND ASSESSMENT GUIDE FOR WORD CHAPTER 3

Your instructor may assign one or more of these projects to help you review the chapter and assess your mastery and understanding of the chapter.

		Review and Assessment Guide for Word Chapter 3	
Project	**Apply Skills from These Chapter Objectives**	**Project Type**	**Project Location**
3C	Objectives 1-4 from Project 3A	**3C Skills Review** A guided review of the skills from Project 3A.	On the following pages
3D	Objectives 5-7 from Project 3B	**3D Skills Review** A guided review of the skills from Project 3B.	On the following pages
3E	Objectives 1-4 from Project 3A	**3E Mastery (Grader Project)** A demonstration of your mastery of the skills in Project 3A with extensive decision making.	In MyITLab and on the following pages
3F	Objectives 5-7 from Project 3B	**3F Mastery (Grader Project)** A demonstration of your mastery of the skills in Project 3B with extensive decision making.	In MyITLab and on the following pages
3G	Objectives 1-7 from Projects 3A and 3B	**3G Mastery (Grader Project)** A demonstration of your mastery of the skills in Projects 3A and 3B with extensive decision making.	In MyITLab and on the following pages
3H	Combination of Objectives from Projects 3A and 3B	**3H GO! Fix It** A demonstration of your mastery of the skills in Projects 3A and 3B by creating a correct result from a document that contains errors you must find.	Online
3I	Combination of Objectives from Projects 3A and 3B	**3I GO! Make It** A demonstration of your mastery of the skills in Projects 3A and 3B by creating a result from a supplied picture.	Online
3J	Combination of Objectives from Projects 3A and 3B	**3J GO! Solve It** A demonstration of your mastery of the skills in Projects 3A and 3B, your decision-making skills, and your critical thinking skills. A task-specific rubric helps you self-assess your result.	Online
3K	Combination of Objectives from Projects 3A and 3B	**3K GO! Solve It** A demonstration of your mastery of the skills in Projects 3A and 3B, your decision-making skills, and your critical thinking skills. A task-specific rubric helps you self-assess your result.	On the following pages
3L	Combination of Objectives from Projects 3A and 3B	**3L GO! Think** A demonstration of your understanding of the chapter concepts applied in a manner that you would outside of college. An analytic rubric helps you and your instructor grade the quality of your work by comparing it to the work an expert in the discipline would create.	On the following pages
3M	Combination of Objectives from Projects 3A and 3B	**3M GO! Think** A demonstration of your understanding of the chapter concepts applied in a manner that you would outside of college. An analytic rubric helps you and your instructor grade the quality of your work by comparing it to the work an expert in the discipline would create.	Online
3N	Combination of Objectives from Projects 3A and 3B	**3N You and GO!** A demonstration of your understanding of the chapter concepts applied in a manner that you would in a personal situation. An analytic rubric helps you and your instructor grade the quality of your work.	Online
3O	Combination of Objectives from Projects 3A and 3B	**3O Cumulative Group Project for Word Chapter 3** A demonstration of your understanding of concepts and your ability to work collaboratively in a group role-playing assessment, requiring both collaboration and self-management.	Online
Capstone Project for Word Chapters 1-3	Combination of Objectives from Projects 1A, 1B, 2A, 2B, 3A, and 3B	A demonstration of your mastery of the skills in Chapters 1-3 with extensive decision making. **(Grader Project)**	In MyITLab and online

GLOSSARY

GLOSSARY OF CHAPTER KEY TERMS

American Psychological Association (APA) One of two commonly used style guides for formatting research papers.

Bibliography A list of cited works in a report or research paper; also referred to as Works Cited, Sources, or References, depending upon the report style.

Brightness The relative lightness of a picture.

Citation A note inserted into the text of a research paper that refers the reader to a source in the bibliography.

Column break indicator A dotted line containing the words *Column Break* that displays at the bottom of the column.

Contrast The difference between the darkest and lightest area of a picture.

Crop A command that removes unwanted or unnecessary areas of a picture.

Crop handles Handles used to define unwanted areas of a picture.

Crop pointer The pointer used to crop areas of a picture.

Data source A document that contains a list of variable information, such as names and addresses, that is merged with a main document to create customized form letters or labels.

Em dash A punctuation symbol used to indicate an explanation or emphasis.

Endnote In a research paper, a note placed at the end of a document or chapter.

Fields In a mail merge, the column headings in the data source.

Flip A command that creates a reverse image of a picture or object.

Footnote In a research paper, a note placed at the bottom of the page.

Hanging indent An indent style in which the first line of a paragraph extends to the left of the remaining lines and that is commonly used for bibliographic entries.

Line break indicator A non-printing character in the shape of a bent arrow that indicates a manual line break.

Mail merge A feature that joins a main document and a data source to create customized letters or labels.

Main document In a mail merge, the document that contains the text or formatting that remains constant.

Manual column break An artificial end to a column to balance columns or to provide space for the insertion of other objects.

Manual line break A break that moves text to the right of the insertion point to a new line while keeping the text in the same paragraph.

Manual page break The action of forcing a page to end and placing subsequent text at the top of the next page.

Modern Language Association (MLA) One of two commonly used style guides for formatting research papers.

Nameplate The banner on the front page of a newsletter that identifies the publication.

Newsletter A periodical that communicates news and information to a specific group.

Note In a research paper, information that expands on the topic, but that does not fit well in the document text.

Office 365 Administrator—the person who creates and manages the account, adds new users, sets up the services your organization wants to use, sets permission levels, and manages the SharePoint team sites.

Page break indicator A dotted line with the text *Page Break* that indicates where a manual page break was inserted.

Parenthetical references References that include the last name of the author or authors, and the page number in the referenced source.

PDF Reflow The ability to import PDF files into Word so that you can transform a PDF back into a fully editable Word document.

Read Mode A view in Word that optimizes the Word screen for the times when you are reading Word documents on the screen and not creating or editing them.

Recolor A feature that enables you to change all colors in the picture to shades of a single color.

Record Each row of information that contains data for one person.

Scale A command that resizes a picture to a percentage of its size.

Screenshot An image of an active window on your computer that you can paste into a document.

Section A portion of a document that can be formatted differently from the rest of the document.

Section break A double dotted line that indicates the end of one section and the beginning of another section.

Small caps A font effect that changes lowercase letters to uppercase letters, but with the height of lowercase letters.

Style A group of formatting commands, such as font, font size, font color, paragraph alignment, and line spacing that can be applied to a paragraph with one command.

Style guide A manual that contains standards for the design and writing of documents.

Suppress A Word feature that hides header and footer information, including the page number, on the first page of a document.

Windows Reader app A Windows Store app with which you can open a PDF or XPS file, zoom, find words or phrases, take notes, save changes, and then print or share the file.

Works Cited In the MLA style, a list of cited works placed at the end of a research paper or report.

CHAPTER REVIEW

Apply 3A skills from these Objectives:

1 Create a Research Paper

2 Insert Footnotes in a Research Paper

3 Create Citations and a Bibliography in a Research Paper

4 Use Read Mode and PDF Reflow

Skills Review — Project 3C Diet and Exercise Report

In the following Skills Review, you will edit and format a research paper that contains information about the effects of diet and exercise. This paper was created by Rachel Holder, a medical intern at University Medical Center, for distribution to her classmates studying physiology. Your completed document will look similar to the one shown in Figure 3.55.

PROJECT FILES

For Project 3C, you will need the following file:

w03C_Diet_Exercise

You will save your document as:

Lastname_Firstname_3C_Diet_Exercise

PROJECT RESULTS

FIGURE 3.55

(Project 3C Diet and Exercise Report continues on the next page)

CHAPTER REVIEW

1 Start Word. From your student files, locate and open the document **w03C_Diet_Exercise**. Display the formatting marks and rulers. **Save** the file in your **Word Chapter 3** folder as **Lastname_Firstname_3C_Diet_Exercise**

a. Press Ctrl + A to select all the text. On the **HOME tab**, in the **Paragraph group**, click **Line and Paragraph Spacing**, and then change the line spacing to **2.0**. On the **PAGE LAYOUT tab**, change the **Spacing After** to **0 pt**.

b. Press Ctrl + Home, press Enter to create a blank line at the top of the document, and then click to position the insertion point in the new blank line. Type **Rachel Holder** and press Enter. Type **Dr. Hillary Kim** and press Enter. Type **Physiology 621** and press Enter. Type **August 31, 2016** and press Enter.

c. Type **Effects of Diet and Exercise** and then press Ctrl + E to center the title you just typed.

2 On the **INSERT tab**, in the **Header & Footer group**, click **Header**, and then at the bottom of the list, click **Edit Header**. Type **Holder** and then press Spacebar.

a. Under **HEADER & FOOTER TOOLS**, on the **DESIGN tab**, in the **Header & Footer group**, click **Page Number**, and then point to **Current Position**. Under **Simple**, click **Plain Number**.

b. On the **HOME tab**, in the **Paragraph group**, click **Align Right**. Double-click anywhere in the document to close the Header area.

c. Near the top of **Page 1**, locate the paragraph beginning *The scientific evidence*, and then click to position the insertion point at the beginning of that paragraph. Scroll to the end of the document, hold down Shift, and then click to the right of the last paragraph mark to select all of the text from the insertion point to the end of the document.

d. On the **HOME tab**, in the **Paragraph group**, click the **Dialog Box Launcher** button. In the **Paragraph** dialog box, on the **Indents and Spacing tab**, under **Indentation**, click the **Special arrow**, and then click **First line**. Click **OK**.

e. On the **INSERT tab**, in the **Header & Footer group**, click **Footer**, and then click **Edit Footer**. In the **Insert group**, click **Document Info**, and then click **File Name**. Click **Close Header and Footer**.

3 Scroll to view the top of **Page 2**, locate the paragraph that begins *Exercise also has*, and then at the end of that paragraph, click to position the insertion point to the right of the period following *Irwin*. On the **REFERENCES tab**, in the **Footnotes group**, click **Insert Footnote**.

a. As the footnote text, type **Physical activity may provide a low-risk method of preventing weight gain. Unlike diet-induced weight loss, exercise-induced weight loss increases cardiorespiratory fitness levels.**

b. In the upper portion of **Page 1**, locate the paragraph that begins *Regular cardiovascular exercise*. Click to position the insertion point at the end of the paragraph and insert a footnote.

c. As the footnote text, type **The objective of the study was to examine the effects of exercise on total and intra-abdominal body fat overall and by level of exercise. Save** your document.

4 At the bottom of **Page 1**, right-click in the footnote you just typed. On the shortcut menu, click **Style**. In the **Style** dialog box, click **Modify**. In the **Modify Style** dialog box, locate the small Formatting toolbar in the center of the dialog box, click the **Font Size button arrow**, and then click **11**.

a. In the lower left corner of the dialog box, click **Format**, and then click **Paragraph**. In the **Paragraph** dialog box, under **Indentation**, click the **Special arrow**, and then click **First line**. Under **Spacing**, click the **Line spacing button arrow**, and then click **Double**.

b. Click **OK** to close the **Paragraph** dialog box, click **OK** to close the **Modify Style** dialog box, and then click **Apply** to apply the new style. **Save** your document.

5 Scroll to view the top of **Page 1**, and then in the paragraph that begins *The scientific evidence*, click to position the insertion point to the left of the period at the end of the paragraph.

a. On the **REFERENCES tab**, in the **Citations & Bibliography group**, click the **Style button arrow**, and then click **MLA** to insert a reference using MLA style. Click **Insert Citation**, and then click **Add New Source**. Click the **Type of Source arrow**, scroll as

(Project 3C Diet and Exercise Report continues on the next page)

necessary to locate and click **Book**, and then add the following information:

Author	Otto, Michael and Jasper A. J. Smits
Title	Exercise for Mood and Anxiety: Proven Strategies for Overcoming Depression and Enhancing Well-Being
Year	2011
City	New York
Publisher	Oxford University Press, USA
Medium	Print

b. Click **OK** to insert the citation. In the paragraph, click to select the citation, click the **Citation Options arrow**, and then click **Edit Citation**. In the **Edit Citation** dialog box, under **Add**, in the **Pages** box, type **3** and then click **OK**.

c. On the upper portion of **Page 2**, in the paragraph that begins *Other positive effects*, in the third line, click to position the insertion point to the left of the period following *substantially*. In the **Citations & Bibliography group**, click **Insert Citation**, and then click **Add New Source**. Click the **Type of Source arrow**, click **Book**, and then add the following information:

Author	Lohrman, David and Lois Heller
Title	Cardiovascular Physiology, Seventh Edition
Year	2010
City	New York
Publisher	McGraw-Hill Professional
Medium	Print

d. Click **OK**. Click to select the citation in the paragraph, click the **Citation Options arrow**, and then click **Edit Citation**. In the **Edit Citation** dialog box, under **Add**, in the **Pages** box, type **195** and then click **OK**.

6 Press Ctrl + End to move to the end of the last paragraph in the document. Click to the left of the period following *loss*. In the **Citations & Bibliography group**,

click **Insert Citation**, and then click **Add New Source**. Click the **Type of Source arrow**, click **Web site**, and then select the **Corporate Author** check box. Add the following information:

Corporate Author	U.S. Department of Health and Human Services
Name of Web Page	NIH News
Year	2012
Month	October
Day	15
Year Accessed	2016
Month Accessed	July
Day Accessed	21
Medium	Web

a. Click **OK**. Press Ctrl + End to move the insertion point to the end of the document. Press Ctrl + Enter to insert a manual page break. On the **HOME tab**, in the **Paragraph group**, click the **Dialog Box Launcher** button. In the **Paragraph** dialog box, on the **Indents and Spacing tab**, under **Indentation**, click the **Special arrow**, and then click **(none)**. Click **OK**.

b. Type **Works Cited** and then press Enter. On the **REFERENCES tab**, in the **Citations & Bibliography group**, be sure **MLA** displays in the **Style** box. In the **Citations & Bibliography group**, click **Bibliography**, and then at the bottom, click **Insert Bibliography**.

c. Click anywhere in the *Works Cited* title, and then press Ctrl + E to center the title. **Save** your document.

7 On the **REFERENCES tab**, in the **Citations & Bibliography group**, click **Manage Sources**. On the left, on the **Master List**, click the entry for *Lohrman, David*, and then click **Edit**. In the **Edit Source** dialog box, in the **Author** box, change the *L* in *Lohrman* to **M** Click **OK**, click **Yes**, and then click **Close**.

a. On **Page 2**, in the paragraph that begins *Other positive effects*, in the third line, on the selected citation, click the **Citation Options arrow**, and then click **Update Citations and Bibliography**.

(Project 3C Diet and Exercise Report continues on the next page)

CHAPTER REVIEW

b. In the bibliography, move the pointer to the left of the first entry—beginning *Mohrman*—to display the ⬉ pointer. Drag down to select all three references in the field. On the **HOME tab**, in the **Paragraph group**, set the **Line spacing** to **2.0**. On the **PAGE LAYOUT tab**, set the **Spacing After** to **0 pt**.

c. Click the **FILE tab**, and then in the lower right corner, click **Show All Properties**. Add the following information:

Title	Diet and Exercise
Tags	weight loss, exercise, diet
Comments	Draft copy of report for class
Categories	biomedical research
Company	University Medical Center
Manager	Dr. Hillary Kim

d. In the **Subject** box, type your course name and section number. Be sure that your name displays as the Author and edit if necessary. On the left, click **Save** to redisplay your document. On the **VIEW tab**, in the **Views group**, click **Read Mode**. In the upper left, click **TOOLS**, click **Find**, and then in the search box, type **Yale** and notice that the text you searched for is highlighted in the document.

e. In the upper left, click **VIEW**, and then click **Edit Document** to return to **Print Layout** view. **Close** the **navigation pane**. **Save** your document, view the **Print Preview**, and then print or submit electronically as directed by your instructor. **Close** Word.

END | You have completed Project 3C

Skills Review   Project 3D Career Newsletter

In the following Skills Review, you will format a newsletter regarding professional development opportunities offered by University Medical Center, and you will create mailing labels for staff interested in these opportunities. Your completed document will look similar to Figure 3.56.

PROJECT FILES

For Project 3D, you will need the following files:

New blank Word document

w03D_Career_Newsletter

w03D_Addresses

You will save your documents as:

Lastname_Firstname_3D_Career_Newsletter

Lastname_Firstname_3D_Addresses

Lastname_Firstname_3D_Mailing_Labels

PROJECT RESULTS

FIGURE 3.56

(Project 3D Career Newsletter continues on the next page)

CHAPTER REVIEW

1 Start Word. On Word's opening screen, in the lower left, click **Open Other Documents**. Navigate to your student files, and then locate and open **w03D_Career_ Newsletter**. **Save** the file in your **Word Chapter 3** folder as **Lastname_Firstname_3D_Career_Newsletter** and then add the file name to the footer.

a. Select the first two lines of the document. On the mini toolbar, change the **Font** to **Arial Black** and the **Font Size** to **18**. Select the first three lines of the document. Click the **Font Color button arrow**, and then under **Theme Colors**, in the fifth column, click the last color—**Blue, Accent 1, Darker 50%**.

b. With the text still selected, on the **HOME tab**, in the **Paragraph group**, click the **Borders button arrow**, and then at the bottom, click **Borders and Shading**. In the **Borders and Shading** dialog box, on the **Borders tab**, click the **Color arrow**, and then under **Theme Colors**, in the fifth column, click the last color—**Blue, Accent 1, Darker 50%**.

c. Click the **Width arrow**, and then click **3 pt**. In the **Preview** box, click the bottom border. Click **OK**.

d. Click at the beginning of the paragraph that begins *Professional Development*. Scroll the document, hold down [Shift], and then click after the paragraph mark at the end of the *Internship Essentials* line. On the **PAGE LAYOUT tab**, in the **Page Setup group**, click **Columns**, and then click **Two**. With the two columns of text selected, on the **HOME tab**, in the **Paragraph group**, click **Justify**.

e. In the first column, click at the beginning of the paragraph that begins *Courses are taught*. On the **PAGE LAYOUT tab**, in the **Page Setup group**, click **Breaks**. Under **Page Breaks**, click **Column**.

2 Press [Ctrl] + [Home]. On the **INSERT tab**, in the **Illustrations group**, click **Online Pictures**. In the **Office.com Clip Art** search box, type **career** and then press [Enter]. Click the image of the sign with the text *Your Career*. If the image does not display, select a similar picture. Click **Insert**.

a. On the **FORMAT tab**, in the **Size group**, click the **Dialog Box Launcher** button. In the **Layout** dialog box, on the **Size tab**, under **Scale**, be sure the **Lock aspect ratio** and **Relative to original picture size** check boxes are selected. Select the number in the **Height** box, type **10** and then press [Tab].

b. In the **Layout** dialog box, click the **Text Wrapping tab**. Under **Wrapping style**, click **Square**.

c. Click the **Position tab**, and then under **Horizontal**, click the **Alignment** option button. Be sure that the **Alignment** indicates **Left** and **relative to Column**. Under **Vertical**, click the **Alignment** option button, and then change the alignment to **Top relative to Margin**. Click **OK**. **Save** your newsletter.

3 Press [Ctrl] + [End] to move to the end of the document. On the **INSERT tab**, in the **Illustrations group**, click **Online Pictures**. In the **Office.com Clip Art** search box, search for **caducei healthcare symbol** and then insert the picture of the gray caducei with a gray shadow. If the image does not display, select a similar picture.

a. On the **FORMAT tab**, in the **Size group**, click the upper portion of the **Crop** button. Point to the center right crop handle, and then drag to the left to approximately **5.5 inches on the horizontal ruler**. Point to the center left crop handle, and then drag to the right to approximately **1.5 inches on the horizontal ruler**. Click the upper portion of the **Crop** button to apply the crop.

b. On the **FORMAT tab**, in the **Adjust group**, click **Color**, and then click **Set Transparent Color**. In the lower left area of the picture, click in the gray shadow to apply the transparent color.

c. With the picture selected, on the **FORMAT tab**, in the **Size group**, click in the **Height** box. Type **1** and then press [Enter]. On the **FORMAT tab**, in the **Arrange group**, click **Position**, and then click **More Layout Options** to display the **Layout** dialog box. Click the **Text Wrapping tab**, and then under **Wrapping Style**, click **Square**.

d. On the **Position tab**, under **Horizontal**, click the **Alignment** option button, and then change the **Alignment** to **Centered relative to Page**. Under **Vertical**, click the **Alignment** option button, and then change the **Alignment** to **Bottom relative to Margin**. Click **OK**.

e. On the **FORMAT tab**, in the **Picture Styles group**, click the **Picture Border button arrow**. Under **Theme Colors**, in the fourth column, click the first color—**Dark Blue, Text 2**. Click the **Picture Border button arrow** again, and then point to **Weight**. Click **1 pt**.

(Project 3D Career Newsletter continues on the next page)

CHAPTER REVIEW

f. On the **FORMAT tab**, in the **Adjust group**, click **Color**. Under **Recolor**, in the first row, click the last option—**Black and White, 75%**. On the **FORMAT tab**, in the **Adjust group**, click **Corrections**. Under **Brightness/Contrast**, in the second row, click the fourth setting—**Brightness: +20% Contrast: –20%**.

4 In the paragraph that begins *University Medical Center is a dynamic*, click after the period at the end of the paragraph, and then press Enter. Start Internet Explorer, maximize the window, and then navigate to **www.ahrq.gov/clinic/**

a. Redisplay your **3D_Career_Newletter** document. With the insertion point positioned in the blank line above the column break, on the **INSERT tab**, in the **Illustrations group**, click **Screenshot**. In the **Screenshot** gallery, click the browser window that contains the website; click **No** in the message that displays.

b. Select the subheading *Professional Development at UMC* including the paragraph mark. Right-click the selected text, and then on the shortcut menu, click **Font**. In the **Font** dialog box, click the **Font color arrow**, and then in the fifth column, click the last color—**Blue, Accent 1, Darker 50%**. Under **Font style**, click **Bold**, and then under **Effects**, select **Small caps**. Click **OK**.

c. With the text still selected, right-click, and then on the mini toolbar, double-click **Format Painter**. In the second column, with the ▲I pointer, select each of the subheadings—*What to Expect from Coursework at UMC* and *Example of Courses at UMC*. Press Esc to turn off **Format Painter**.

5 Press Ctrl + End to move to the end of the document, and then select the two lines of bold text—the graphic will also be selected. On the **HOME tab**, in the **Paragraph group**, click the **Borders button arrow**, and then click **Borders and Shading**.

a. In the **Borders and Shading** dialog box, on the **Borders tab**, under **Setting**, click **Shadow**. Click the **Color arrow**, and then in the fifth column, click the last color—**Blue, Accent 1, Darker 50%**. Click the **Width arrow**, and then click **1 pt**.

b. In the **Borders and Shading** dialog box, click the **Shading tab**. Click the **Fill arrow**, and then in the fifth column, click the second color—**Blue, Accent 1, Lighter 80%**. Click **OK**. On the **HOME tab**, in the **Paragraph group**, click **Center**. In the shaded paragraph, click in front of the *D* in the word *Director*. Hold down Shift and then press Enter.

c. Press Ctrl + Home, and then click the **FILE tab**. At the bottom of the **Properties** list, click **Show All Properties**. Click to the right of **Tags**, and then type **newsletter, careers** Click to the right of **Subject**, and then type your course name and section number. Under **Related People**, if necessary, type your name in the Author box. Display the **Print Preview** and make any necessary corrections. **Save** the document; close Word and close Internet Explorer.

6 Start Word and display a new blank document. **Save** the document in your **Word Chapter 3** folder as **Lastname_Firstname_3D_Mailing_Labels** With your new document open on the screen, from your student files, **Open** the file w03D_Addresses. **Save** the address file in your **Word Chapter 3** folder as **Lastname_Firstname_3D_Addresses** and then add the file name to the footer. **Save** and then **Close** the file. Be sure that your **Lastname_Firstname_3D_Mailing_Labels** document displays.

a. Click the **MAILINGS tab**. In the **Start Mail Merge group**, click **Start Mail Merge**, and then click **Step-by-Step Mail Merge Wizard**. In the **Mail Merge** pane, under **Select document type**, click **Labels**. At the bottom of the **Mail Merge** pane, click **Next: Starting document**.

b. Under **Select starting document**, under **Change document layout**, click **Label options**. In the **Label Options** dialog box, under **Printer information**, be sure that the **Default tray** is selected.

c. Under **Label information**, click the **Label vendors arrow**, and then click **Avery US Letter**. Under **Product number**, scroll about halfway down the list, and then click **5160 Easy Peel Address Labels**. At the bottom of the **Label Options** dialog box, click **OK**. At the bottom of the **Mail Merge** pane, click **Next: Select recipients**.

d. In the **Mail Merge** pane, under **Select recipients**, under **Use an existing list**, click **Browse**. Navigate to your **Word Chapter 3** folder, select your **Lastname_Firstname_3D_Addresses** file, and then click **Open**.

(Project 3D Career Newsletter continues on the next page)

CHAPTER REVIEW

7 In the lower left portion of the **Mail Merge Recipients** dialog box, in the **Data Source** box, click the path that contains your file name. Then, at the bottom of the **Mail Merge Recipients** dialog box, click **Edit**. In the upper right corner of the **Data Form** dialog box, click **Add New**. In the blank record, type the following, pressing Tab to move from field to field:

First_Name:	Mia
Last_Name:	Orr
Address_1:	1378 Lima Ave.
Unit:	#82
City:	Memphis
State:	TN
ZIP_Code:	38123

a.   In the lower right corner of the **Data Form** dialog box, click **Close**. At the bottom of the **Mail Merge Recipients** dialog box, click **OK**.

b.   At the bottom of the **Mail Merge** pane, click **Next: Arrange your labels**. Under **Arrange your labels**, click **Address block**. In the lower right corner of the **Insert Address Block** dialog box, click **Match Fields**.

c.   Click the **Address 2 arrow**, and then from the list of available fields, click **Unit**. Click **OK** two times.

d.   In the **Mail Merge** pane, under **Replicate labels**, click **Update all labels**. At the bottom of the **Mail**

Merge pane, click **Next: Preview your labels**. Press Ctrl + A to select all of the label text, click the **PAGE LAYOUT tab**, and then in the **Paragraph group**, click in the **Spacing Before** box. Type **3** and press Enter. At the bottom of the **Mail Merge** pane, click **Next: Complete the merge**.

e.   Click the **MAILINGS tab**, and then in the **Start Mail Merge group**, click **Edit Recipient List** to display the list of names and addresses. In the **Mail Merge Recipients** dialog box, click the **Last_Name** field heading to sort the names. Click **OK**. **Close** the **Mail Merge** pane.

f.   Scroll the document and then click anywhere in the empty table row at the bottom. Click the **LAYOUT tab**. In the **Rows & Columns group**, click **Delete**, and then click **Delete Rows**. Add the file name to the footer, close the footer area, and then click the **FILE tab**. Click **Show All Properties**. As the **Tags**, type **labels** and as the **Subject**, type your course name and section number. Be sure your name displays as the **Author**, and then **Save** your file.

g.   As directed by your instructor, print or submit electronically. **Close** the document, click **Yes** to save the data source, and then if necessary, click **Save** to save the labels. In addition to your labels and address document, submit your **3D_Career_Newsletter** document as directed. **Close** Word.

END | You have completed Project 3D

CONTENT-BASED ASSESSMENTS

Mastering Word Project 3E Skin Protection Report

In the following Mastering Word project, you will edit and format a research paper that contains information about skin protection and the use of sunblocks and sunscreens. This paper was created by Rachel Holder, a medical intern at University Medical Center, for distribution to her classmates studying dermatology. Your completed document will look similar to the one shown in Figure 3.57.

Apply 3A skills from these Objectives:

1 Create a Research Paper

2 Insert Footnotes in a Research Paper

3 Create Citations and a Bibliography in a Research Paper

4 Use Read Mode and PDF Reflow

PROJECT FILES

For Project 3E, you will need the following file:

w03E_Skin_Protection

You will save your document as:

Lastname_Firstname_3E_Skin_Protection

PROJECT RESULTS

FIGURE 3.57

(Project 3E Skin Protection Report continues on the next page)

CONTENT-BASED ASSESSMENTS

1 Start Word. From your student files, locate and open the document **w03E_Skin_Protection**. Display formatting marks and rulers. Save the file in your **Word Chapter 3** folder as **Lastname_Firstname_3E_Skin_Protection**

2 Select all the text, change the **Line Spacing** to **2.0**, and then change the **Spacing After** to **0 pt**. At the top of the document, insert a new blank paragraph, and then in the new paragraph, type **Rachel Holder** Press Enter. Type **Dr. Hillary Kim** and press Enter. Type **Dermatology 544** and press Enter. Type **August 31, 2016** and press Enter. Type **Skin Protection** and then press Ctrl + E to center the title you just typed.

3 Insert a header, type **Holder** and then press Spacebar. Display the **Page Number gallery**, and then in the **Current Position**, add the **Plain Number** style. Apply **Align Right** formatting to the header. Insert a footer with the file name. Starting with the paragraph that begins *One way to prevent*, select all the text in the document, and then set a **First line** indent of **0.5"**.

4 On **Page 2**, at the end of the paragraph that begins *In the medical field*, insert a footnote with the following text: **The American Academy of Dermatology recommends using a broad spectrum sunscreen with an SPF of 30 or more.**

5 On **Page 2**, at the end of the paragraph that begins *Individuals should protect*, insert a footnote with the following text: **For babies, the American Academy of Dermatology recommends using a sunscreen that contains only inorganic filters, such as zinc oxide and titanium dioxide, to avoid any skin or eye irritation.**

6 Modify the **Footnote Text** style so that the **Font Size** is **11**, there is a **First line indent** of **0.5"**, and the spacing is **Double**, and then apply the style.

7 On **Page 1**, at the end of the paragraph that begins *According to an article*, click to the left of the period, and then using **MLA** format, insert a citation for a **Journal Article** with the following information:

Author	Frash, D. E., A. S. Jonason, and J. A. Simon
Title	Sunlight and Sunburn in Human Skin Cancer
Journal Name	The Journal of Investigative Dermatology

Year	1996
Pages	136-142
Medium	Print

8 In the report, select the citation you just created, display the **Citation Options**, and then edit the citation to include **Pages 136-142** At the end of the last paragraph of the report, click to the left of the period, and then insert a citation for a **Book** with the following information:

Author	Leffell, David
Title	Total Skin: The Definitive Guide to Whole Skin Care for Life
Year	2000
City	New York
Publisher	Hyperion
Medium	Print

9 In the report, select the citation you just created, display the **Citation Options**, and then edit the citation to include **Page 96** At the top of **Page 2**, at the end of the paragraph that begins *According to Dr.*, click to the left of the period, and then insert a citation for a **Web site** with the following information:

Author	Gibson, Lawrence E.
Name of Web Page	Does Sunscreen Expire?
Year	2011
Month	April
Day	01
Year Accessed	2016
Month Accessed	June
Day Accessed	30
Medium	Web

10 Move to the end of the document, and then insert a manual page break to create a new page. Display the **Paragraph** dialog box, and then change the **Indentation** under **Special** to **(none)**. Add a **Works Cited** title, press Enter, and then click **Insert Bibliography**. **Center** the *Works Cited* title.

(Project 3E Skin Protection Report continues on the next page)

CONTENT-BASED ASSESSMENTS

11 By using the **Manage Sources** command, display the **Source Manager**. On the **Master List**, select the entry for **Frash, D. E.**, and then **Edit** this source—the last name should be **Brash** instead of *Frash*. In the message that displays, update both lists. Locate the citation in the text of the report, display the **Citation Options**, and then **Update Citations and Bibliography**. On the Works Cited page, select the references, apply **Double** line spacing, and then set the **Spacing After** paragraphs to **0 pt**.

12 Update the **Document Properties** with the following information:

Title	**Skin Protection**
Tags	**sunscreen, sun exposure**
Comments	**Draft copy of report for class**
Categories	**Dermatology**
Company	**University Medical Center**
Manager	**Dr. Hillary Kim**

13 In the **Subject** box, type your course name and section number. Be sure that your name displays as the **Author** and edit if necessary. On the left, click **Print** to view the **Print Preview**, and then click **Save** to redisplay your document. Print or submit electronically as directed by your instructor. **Close** Word.

END | You have completed Project 3E

Mastering Word | Project 3F Dogs Newsletter and Mailing Labels

In the following Mastering Word project, you will format a newsletter with information about the therapy dogs handled by volunteers at the University Medical Center. You will also create mailing labels so that the newsletter can be sent to the volunteer staff. Your completed documents will look similar to Figure 3.58.

PROJECT FILES

For Project 3F, you will need the following files:

New blank Word document
w03F_Dogs_Newsletter
w03F_Addresses

You will save your documents as:

Lastname_Firstname_3F_Dogs_Newsletter
Lastname_Firstname_3F_Addresses
Lastname_Firstname_3F_Mailing_Labels

PROJECT RESULTS

University Medical Center
Health Improvement Newsletter

Volume 3   Spring 2016

DOGS FOR HEALING

At University Medical Center, therapy dogs have been a welcomed asset to patient care and recovery since 2004. UMC works with several non-profit organizations to bring dedicated volunteers and their canine teams into the hospital to visit children, adults, and seniors. Information regarding service dog regulations, training, and laws is available on the ADA website.

BENEFITS TO PATIENTS

Medical research shows that petting a dog or other domestic animal relaxes patients and helps ease symptoms of stress from illness or from the hospital setting. Studies have shown that such therapies contribute to decreased blood pressure and heart rate, and can help with patient respiratory rate.

CUDDLES

Cuddles, a 4 year-old Labrador, is one of our most popular therapy dogs and is loved by both young and senior patients. You'll see Cuddles in the Children's wing on Mondays with his owner, Jason, who trained him since he was a tiny pup.

BRANDY

Brandy is a 6 year-old Beagle who brings smiles and giggles to everyone she meets. Over the past several years, Brandy has received accolades and awards for her service as a therapy dog. Brandy is owned by Melinda Sparks, a 17-year veteran employee of University Medical Center. Brandy and Melinda can be seen making the rounds on Wednesdays in the Children's wing and on Mondays and Fridays throughout the hospital.

Your picture may differ.

To request a visit from a therapy dog, or to learn how to become involved with therapy dog training, call Carole Yates at extension 2365.

Lastname_Firstname_3F_Dogs_Newsletter

Mary Ackerman 82 E. Roxie Blvd. Arlington, TN 38002	Anthony Borman 2820 Lincoln Ave. Collierville, TN 38017	Jerry Camden 543 Verde Way Memphis, TN 38120
Jacqueline Epps 653 Vista Ave. #D Lakeland, TN 38002	Renee Farnsworth 36 S. Levin St. #D Bartlett, TN 38135	Anita Figueroa 9000 S. Masters Dr. Germantown, TN 38139
Emily Gold 888 Packard Court Lakeland, TN 38002	Abel Heaphy 55 Amigo Lane #4 Collierville, TN 38017	Katie Hughes 34 Sadler Pl. Bartlett, TN 38133
Bin Lee 676 Silver St. Memphis, TN 38120	Anh Ly 1255 Chestnut Street Memphis, TN 38122	Priya Malik 975 Ricardo Place #G Germantown, TN 38138
Leland Marcus 600 Garfield Ave. Memphis, TN 38117	Walter McKidd 2495 Holly Drive Arlington, TN 38002	Sharon Moreno 1330 Golden Ave. Memphis, TN 38120
Thai Nguyen 179 Sierra Court Collierville, TN 38017	Thomas Norris 492 Mahogany Street Bartlett, TN 38135	Daniel Scofield 1518 Price Place Arlington, TN 38002
Erica Scott 124 Susan Drive #352 Memphis, TN 38134	Andrew Sharma 1550 Beverly Drive #1550 Memphis, TN 38104	Sara Thompson 4220 Glendora Dr. #320 Memphis, TN 38112
Simone Thompson 648 Michaela St. Bartlett, TN 38133	David Turnbull 1821 Chelsea St. #1442 Germantown, TN 38138	Jackson Williams 15 Atlantic Rd. Memphis, TN 38111
Miranda Yanos 1256 Loma Ave. #34 Memphis, TN 38123		

Lastname_Firstname_3F_Mailing_Labels

FIGURE 3.58

(Project 3F Dogs Newsletter and Mailing Labels continues on the next page)

CONTENT-BASED ASSESSMENTS

1 Start Word. From your student files, open **w03F_Dogs_Newsletter**. **Save** the file in your **Word Chapter 3** folder as **Lastname_Firstname_3F_Dogs_Newsletter** and then add the file name to the footer. Select the first three lines of the document, and then change the **Font Color** to **Olive Green, Accent 3, Darker 25%**—in the seventh column, the fifth color. With the text selected, display the **Borders and Shading** dialog box. Apply a **3 pt** bottom border in **Black, Text 1**.

2 Click at the beginning of the newsletter title *University Medical Center*. Insert an online picture from **Office.com Clip Art** by searching for **caducei** Insert the picture of the physician symbol on top of the green oval with a blue outline. Use the **Set Transparent Color** command to make the green background transparent. Change the **Brightness/Contrast** to **Brightness: 0% (Normal) Contrast: +40%**.

3 **Scale** the picture to **50%** of its **Height**, and then change the **Text Wrapping** to **Square**. Change the **Horizontal Alignment** to **Left relative** to **Margin** and the **Vertical Alignment** to **Top relative** to **Margin**.

4 Starting with the paragraph that begins *Dogs for Healing*, select all of the text from that point to the end of the document. Change the **Spacing After** to **10 pt**, format the text in two columns, and apply **Justify** alignment. Insert a **Column break** before the subheading *Cuddles*.

5 Click at the beginning of the sentence that begins with *Brandy is a 6 year-old Beagle*. Insert an online picture from **Office.com Clip Art** by searching for **dog sitting up begging** and then insert the picture that displays. Insert the picture of the beagle sitting on the grass. If the picture is not available, from your student data files insert w03F_Dog. Rotate the picture using **Flip Horizontal**. Change the picture **Height** to **1.5** and then apply the **Square** layout option. Change the **Horizontal Alignment** to **Right relative** to **Margin** and the **Vertical Alignment** to **Top relative** to **Line**. Apply a **Black, Text 1 Picture Border** and change the **Weight** to **2 1/4 pt**.

6 Start Internet Explorer, navigate to **www.ada.gov/qasrvc.htm** and then maximize your browser window. In your **3F_Dogs_Newsletter** file, click at the end of the paragraph below the *Dogs for Healing* subheading, and then press Enter. In the blank line, insert a **Screenshot** of the website; do not link to the URL. Apply a **Black, Text 1 Picture Border** and change the **Weight** to **1 pt**.

7 Select the subheading *Dogs for Healing* including the paragraph mark. By using the **Font** dialog box, change the **Size** to **16**, apply **Bold**, apply the **Small caps** effect, and change the **Font color** to **Olive Green, Accent 3, Darker 50%**—in the seventh column, the last color. Apply the same formatting to the subheadings *Benefits to Patients*, *Cuddles*, and *Brandy*.

8 Select the last paragraph in the newsletter, and then apply a **1 pt Shadow** border, in **Black, Text 1**. Shade the paragraph with a **Fill** color of **Olive Green, Accent 3, Lighter 80%**—in the seventh column, the second color. Click the **FILE tab**, and then click **Show All Properties**. As the **Tags**, type **dogs, newsletter** As the **Subject**, type your course name and section number. Under **Related People**, if necessary, type your name in the **Author box**. **Print Preview** the document and make any necessary corrections. **Save** the document and **close** Word.

9 Start Word and display a new blank document. **Save** the document in your **Word Chapter 3** folder as **Lastname_Firstname_3F_Mailing_Labels** From your student files, **Open** the file w03F_Addresses. **Save** the address file in your **Word Chapter 3** folder as **Lastname_Firstname_3F_Addresses** and then add the file name to the footer. **Save** and **Close** the file. Be sure that your **Lastname_Firstname_3F_Mailing_Labels** document displays.

10 Start the **Step-by-Step Mail Merge Wizard** to create **Labels**. Be sure that the **Default tray** is selected and that the label vendor is **Avery US Letter**. The **Product number** is **5160 Easy Peel Address Labels**. Select the **Use an existing list** option, and then from your **Word Chapter 3** folder, open your **Lastname_Firstname_3F_Addresses** file. Add the following record to your file:

First Name	**Miranda**
Last Name	**Yanos**
Address 1	**1256 Loma Ave.**
Unit	**#34**
City	**Memphis**
State	**TN**
ZIP Code	**38123**

(Project 3F Dogs Newsletter and Mailing Labels continues on the next page)

11 Insert an **Address block** and match the fields. Match the **Address 2** field to the **Unit** field, and then update the labels. Preview the labels, and then select the entire document. Change the **Spacing Before** to **3** and then **Complete the merge**. Delete the last row from the bottom of the table, and then add the file name to the footer.

12 Display the document properties. As the **Tags** type **labels** and as the **Subject** type your course name and section number. Be sure your name displays in the **Author box**, and then **Save** your file. As directed by your instructor, print or submit electronically. In addition to your labels and address document, submit your **3F_Dogs_Newsletter** document as directed. **Close** Word and Internet Explorer.

END | You have completed Project 3F

CONTENT-BASED ASSESSMENTS

Mastering Word Project 3G Research Paper, Newsletter, and Mailing Labels

In the following Mastering Word project, you will edit and format a research paper and a newsletter, and you will create mailing labels. Your completed documents will look similar to Figure 3.59.

PROJECT FILES

For Project 3G, you will need the following files:

New blank Word document
w03G_Electronic_Records
w03G_Newsletter
w03G_Addresses

You will save your documents as:

Lastname_Firstname_3G_Electronic_Records
Lastname_Firstname_3G_Newsletter
Lastname_Firstname_3G_Mailing_Labels
Lastname_Firstname_3G_Addresses

PROJECT RESULTS

FIGURE 3.59

(Project 3G Research Paper, Newsletter, and Mailing Labels continues on the next page)

CONTENT-BASED ASSESSMENTS

1 Start Word. From your student files, locate and open the document **w03G_Electronic_Records**, and then **Save** it in your **Word Chapter 3** folder as **Lastname_Firstname_3G_Electronic_Records** Display the header area, type **Eisler** and then press Spacebar. From the **Header & Footer group**, add a **Plain Number** page number from the **Current Position** gallery. Apply **Align Right** formatting to the header. Move to the footer area and add the file name to the footer.

Select all the text in the document, change the **Line Spacing** to **2.0**, and then change the **Spacing After** to **0 pt**. **Center** the title *Electronic Health Records*. Beginning with text below the centered title, select the text from that point to the end of the document, and then set a **First line** indent of **0.5"**.

2 At the top of **Page 1**, at the end of the paragraph that begins *There is often*, insert a footnote with the following text: **Electronic Health Records is an evolving concept that shares records in digital format across different health care settings and might include medical history, test results, and x-rays.**

At the top of **Page 2**, in the second line, at the end of the sentence that ends *if they had it*, insert a footnote with the following text: **The EMR (electronic medical record) is the patient record created in hospitals and ambulatory environments; it serves as a data source for other systems.**

3 On **Page 1**, at the end of the paragraph that begins *Those clinical practices*, click to the left of the period, and then using **MLA** format, insert a citation for a **Web site** with the following information:

Author	Sabriel, Barbara A.
Name of Web Page	Do EMRS Make You a Better Doctor?
Year	2008
Month	July
Day	15
Year Accessed	2016
Month Accessed	June
Day Accessed	30
Medium	Web

On **Page 2**, at the end of the paragraph that begins *Further research*, click to the left of the period, and then

using **MLA** format, insert a citation for a **Book** with the following information:

Author	DeVore, Amy
Title	The Electronic Health Record for the Physician's Office, 1e
Year	2010
City	Maryland Heights
Publisher	Saunders
Medium	Print

In the report, select the citation you just created, display the **Citation Options**, and then edit the citation to include **Pages 253**

4 Insert a manual page break at the end of the document. On the new **Page 3**, display the **Paragraph** dialog box, and then change the **Special** indentation to **(none)**. Type **Works Cited** and then press Enter. On the **REFERENCES tab**, click **Bibliography**, and then click **Insert Bibliography**. **Center** the *Works Cited* title.

Use the **Source Manager** to change the name of the reference *Sabriel* to **Gabriel** and update both lists. Then in the selected citation in the report, display the **Citation Options** and click **Update Citations and Bibliography**. On the Works Cited page, select the references, apply **Double** line spacing, and then set the **Spacing After** paragraphs to **0 pt**.

Update the **Document Properties** with the following information:

Title	Electronic Records
Tags	EMR, health records
Comments	Draft copy of report for class
Categories	Health Administration
Subject	(insert your course name and section number)
Company	University Medical Center
Manager	Dr. Hillary Kim

On the left, click **Print** to display the **Print Preview**, make any necessary corrections, **save** and **close** the document; leave Word open. Hold this file until you complete this project.

(Project 3G Research Paper, Newsletter, and Mailing Labels continues on the next page)

CONTENT-BASED ASSESSMENTS

5 From your student files, open **w03G_ Newsletter**. **Save** the file in your **Word Chapter 3** folder as **Lastname_ Firstname_3G_Newsletter** and then add the file name to the footer. Select the first three lines of the document and apply a **3 pt** bottom border in **Black, Text 1.**

Click at the beginning of the newsletter title *University Medical Center*. Insert an online picture from **Office.com Clip Art** by searching for **microscope** Insert a picture of a black and white microscope. **Recolor** the picture by applying **Blue, Accent color 1 Light**. Apply a **Black, Text 1 Picture Border** and change the **Weight** to **2 1/4 pt.**

Scale the picture to **10**% of its **Height**, and then change the **Text Wrapping** to **Square**. Change the **Horizontal Alignment** to **Left relative to Margin** and the **Vertical Alignment** to **Top relative to Margin.**

6 Starting with the paragraph that begins *Are You Getting a Good Night's Sleep?*, select all of the text from that point to the end of the document. Format the text in two columns, and apply **Justify** alignment. Insert a **Column break** before the subheading *Can Chemistry Help?*

Start and maximize Internet Explorer, and then navigate to **www.nhlbi.nih.gov/health** and then in the middle of the page, click **Sleep Disorders**. In your **3G_Newsletter** file, click at the end of the paragraph below the *Are You Getting a Good Night's Sleep* subheading, and then press Enter. In the blank line, insert a **Screenshot** of the website; do not link to the URL. Apply a **Black, Text 1 Picture Border** and change the **Weight** to **1 pt.**

Select the subheading *Are You Getting a Good Night's Sleep?* including the paragraph mark. From the **Font** dialog box, apply **Bold** and **Small Caps** and change the **Font color** to **Dark Blue, Text 2**—in the fourth column, the first color. Apply the same formatting to the subheadings *Light and Sleep, Can Chemistry Help?* and *Sleep Aid Apps.*

7 Select the last paragraph in the newsletter, and then apply a **1 pt Shadow** border using **Black, Text 1**. Shade the paragraph with the **Fill** color **Dark Blue, Text 2, Lighter 80%**—in the fourth column, the second color. **Center** the text.

Click the **FILE tab**, and then click **Show All Properties**. As the **Tags**, type **sleep, newsletter** As the **Subject**, type your course name and section number. Under **Related People**, if necessary, type your name in the **Author box**. On the left, click **Print** to display the

Print Preview. Make any necessary corrections. **Save** the document and **Exit** Word.

8 Start Word and display a new blank document. **Save** the document in your **Word Chapter 3** folder as **Lastname_Firstname_3G_Mailing_Labels** From your student files, **Open** the file **w03G_Addresses**. **Save** the address file in your **Word Chapter 3** folder as **Lastname_ Firstname_3G_Addresses** and then add the file name to the footer. **Save** and **Close** the file. Be sure that your **Lastname_Firstname_3G_Mailing_Labels** document displays.

9 Start the **Step-by-Step Mail Merge Wizard** to create **Labels**. Be sure that the **Default tray** is selected and that the label vendor is **Avery US Letter**. The **Product number** is **5160 Easy Peel Address Labels**. Select the **Use an existing list option**, and then from your **Word Chapter 3** folder, **Open** your **Lastname_Firstname_3G_Addresses** file. Add the following record to your file:

First Name	**Mason**
Last Name	**Zepeda**
Address 1	**134 Atlantic Ave.**
Unit	**#21**
City	**Memphis**
State	**TN**
ZIP Code	**38123**

10 Insert an **Address block** and match the fields. Match the **Address 2** field to the **Unit** field, and then update the labels. Preview the labels, and then select the entire document. Change the **Spacing Before** to **3** and then **Complete the merge**. Delete the last row from the bottom of the table, and then add the file name to the footer.

Display the document properties. As the **Tags** type **labels** and as the **Subject** type your course name and section number. Be sure your name displays in the **Author box**, and then **Save** your file. As directed by your instructor, print or submit your work electronically. In addition to your labels and address document, submit your **3G_Newsletter** and **3G_Electronic_Records** documents as directed. **Close** Word and Internet Explorer.

END | You have completed Project 3G

CONTENT-BASED ASSESSMENTS

GO! Fix It   Project 3H Hospital Materials   **Online**

GO! Make It   Project 3I Health Newsletter   **Online**

Build from Scratch

GO! Solve It   Project 3J Colds and Flu   **Online**

GO! Solve It   Project 3K Cycling Newsletter

PROJECT FILES

For Project 3K, you will need the following file:

w03K_Cycling_Newsletter

You will save your document as:

Lastname_Firstname_3K_Cycling_Newsletter

    The UMC Emergency Department publishes a newsletter focusing on safety and injury prevention. The topic for the current newsletter is bicycle safety. From your student data files, open w03K_Cycling_Newsletter, add the file name to the footer, and then save the file in your Word Chapter 3 folder as **Lastname_Firstname_3K_Cycling_Newsletter**.

    Using the techniques that you practiced in this chapter, format the document in two-column, newsletter format. Format the nameplate so that it is clearly separate from the body of the newsletter. Insert column breaks as necessary and apply appropriate formatting to subheadings. Insert and format at least one appropriate online picture and insert a screenshot of a relevant website. Apply a border and shading to the last paragraph.

    Add your name, your course name and section number, and the keywords **safety, newsletter** to the Properties area. Submit as directed.

CONTENT-BASED ASSESSMENTS

GO! Solve It Project 3K Cycling Newsletter (continued)

Performance Level

Performance Criteria	Exemplary: You consistently applied the relevant skills	Proficient: You sometimes, but not always, applied the relevant skills	Developing: You rarely or never applied the relevant skills
Format nameplate	The nameplate is formatted attractively and in a manner that clearly indicates that it is the nameplate.	The nameplate includes some formatting but is not clearly separated from the body of the newsletter.	The newsletter does not include a nameplate.
Insert and format at least one online picture	An sized and positioned online picture image is included.	An online picture is inserted but is either inappropriate, or is formatted or positioned poorly.	No online picture is included.
Border and shading added to a paragraph	The last paragraph displays an attractive border with shading.	An appropriate border or shading is displayed but not both.	No border or shading is applied.
Insert a screenshot	A relevant screenshot is inserted in one of the columns.	A screenshot is inserted in the document but does not relate to the content of the article.	No screenshot is inserted.

END | You have completed Project 3K

OUTCOMES-BASED ASSESSMENTS

RUBRIC

The following outcomes-based assessments are *open-ended assessments*. That is, there is no specific correct result; your result will depend on your approach to the information provided. Make *Professional Quality* your goal. Use the following scoring rubric to guide you in *how* to approach the problem and then to evaluate *how well* your approach solves the problem.

The *criteria*—Software Mastery, Content, Format and Layout, and Process—represent the knowledge and skills you have gained that you can apply to solving the problem. The *levels of performance*—Professional Quality, Approaching Professional Quality, or Needs Quality Improvements—help you and your instructor evaluate your result.

	Your completed project is of Professional Quality if you:	Your completed project is Approaching Professional Quality if you:	Your completed project Needs Quality Improvements if you:
1-Software Mastery	Choose and apply the most appropriate skills, tools, and features and identify efficient methods to solve the problem.	Choose and apply some appropriate skills, tools, and features, but not in the most efficient manner.	Choose inappropriate skills, tools, or features, or are inefficient in solving the problem.
2-Content	Construct a solution that is clear and well organized, contains content that is accurate, appropriate to the audience and purpose, and is complete. Provide a solution that contains no errors in spelling, grammar, or style.	Construct a solution in which some components are unclear, poorly organized, inconsistent, or incomplete. Misjudge the needs of the audience. Have some errors in spelling, grammar, or style, but the errors do not detract from comprehension.	Construct a solution that is unclear, incomplete, or poorly organized; contains some inaccurate or inappropriate content; and contains many errors in spelling, grammar, or style. Do not solve the problem.
3-Format & Layout	Format and arrange all elements to communicate information and ideas, clarify function, illustrate relationships, and indicate relative importance.	Apply appropriate format and layout features to some elements, but not others. Overuse features, causing minor distraction.	Apply format and layout that does not communicate information or ideas clearly. Do not use format and layout features to clarify function, illustrate relationships, or indicate relative importance. Use available features excessively, causing distraction.
4-Process	Use an organized approach that integrates planning, development, self-assessment, revision, and reflection.	Demonstrate an organized approach in some areas, but not others; or, use an insufficient process of organization throughout.	Do not use an organized approach to solve the problem.

Build from Scratch

OUTCOMES-BASED ASSESSMENTS

GO! Think   Project 3L Influenza Report

PROJECT FILES

For Project 3L, you will need the following file:

New blank Word document

You will save your document as:

Lastname_Firstname_3L_Influenza

As part of the ongoing research conducted by University Medical Center in the area of community health and contagious diseases, Dr. Hillary Kim has asked Sarah Stanger to create a report on influenza—how it spreads, and how it can be prevented in the community.

Create a new file and save it as **Lastname_Firstname_3L_Influenza** Create the report in MLA format. The report should include at least two footnotes, at least two citations, and should include a *Works Cited* page.

The report should contain an introduction, and then information about what influenza is, how it spreads, and how it can be prevented. A good place to start is at http://health.nih.gov/topic/influenza.

Add the file name to the footer. Add appropriate information to the Document Properties and submit it as directed.

END | You have completed Project 3L

OUTCOMES-BASED ASSESSMENTS

Build from Scratch

| GO! Think | Project 3M Volunteer Newsletter | Online |

Build from Scratch

| You and GO! | Project 3N College Newsletter | Online |

| GO! Cumulative Group Project | Project 3O Bell Orchid Hotels |
| | Online |

Introduction to Microsoft Excel 2013

E

Excel 2013

modern financial analysis / Fotolia

Excel 2013: Introduction

Quantitative information! Defined as a type of information that can be counted or that communicates the quantity of something, quantitative information can be either easy or hard to understand—depending on how it is presented. According to Stephen Few in his book *Show Me the Numbers*: "Quantitative information forms the core of what businesses must know to operate effectively."

Excel 2013 is a tool to communicate quantitative business information effectively. Sometimes you need to communicate quantitative relationships. For example, the number of units sold per geographic region shows a relationship of sales to geography. Sometimes you need to summarize numbers. A list of every student enrolled at

your college with his or her major is not as informative as a summary of the total number of students in each major. In business, the most common quantitative information is some measure of money—costs, sales, payroll, expenses—and so on.

Rather than just a tool for making calculations, Excel is now a tool for you to communicate and collaborate with others. When you want to communicate visually with tables and graphs, Excel 2013 has many new features to help you do so. Microsoft Excel 2013 works best on a Windows 8 PC—desktop, laptop, or tablet—because if your PC is touch-enabled, you will be able to use your fingers to work with Excel.

Video EA

Creating a Worksheet and Charting Data

GO! to Work
Video E1

PROJECT 1A

OUTCOMES
Create a sales report with an embedded column chart and sparklines.

OBJECTIVES

1. Create, Save, and Navigate an Excel Workbook
2. Enter Data in a Worksheet
3. Construct and Copy Formulas and Use the SUM Function
4. Format Cells with Merge & Center, Cell Styles, and Themes
5. Chart Data to Create a Column Chart and Insert Sparklines
6. Print a Worksheet, Display Formulas, and Close Excel

PROJECT 1B

OUTCOMES
Calculate the value of an inventory.

OBJECTIVES

7. Check Spelling in a Worksheet
8. Enter Data by Range
9. Construct Formulas for Mathematical Operations
10. Edit Values in a Worksheet
11. Format a Worksheet

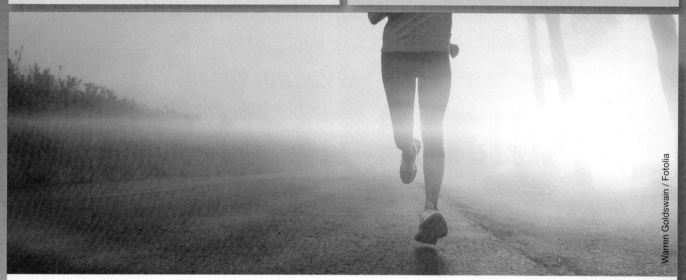

Warren Goldswain / Fotolia

In This Chapter

In this chapter, you will use Microsoft Excel 2013 to create and analyze data organized into columns and rows. After entering data in a worksheet, you can perform complex calculations, analyze the data to make logical decisions, and create informative charts that help readers visualize your data in a way they can understand and that is meaningful. In this chapter, you will create and modify Excel workbooks. You will practice the basics of worksheet design; create a footer; enter and edit data in a worksheet; chart data; and then save, preview, and print workbooks. You will also construct formulas for mathematical operations.

The projects in this chapter relate to **Pro Fit Marietta**, a distributor of fitness equipment and apparel to private gyms, personal trainers, health clubs, corporate wellness centers, hotels, college athletic facilities, physical therapy practices, and multi-unit residential properties. The company's mission is to find, test, and distribute the highest quality fitness products in the world to its customers for the benefit of consumers. Their popular blog provides useful tips on how to use the latest workout and fitness equipment. The company is located in Marietta, Georgia, which is metropolitan Atlanta's largest suburb.

PROJECT
1A

Sales Report with Embedded Column Chart and Sparklines

PROJECT ACTIVITIES

In Activities 1.01 through 1.17, you will create an Excel worksheet for Michelle Barry, the President of Pro Fit Marietta. The worksheet displays the second quarter sales of cardio equipment for the current year and includes a chart to visually represent the data. Your completed worksheet will look similar to Figure 1.1.

PROJECT FILES

For Project 1A, you will need the following file:

New blank Excel workbook

You will save your workbook as:

Lastname_Firstname_1A_Quarterly_Sales

PROJECT RESULTS

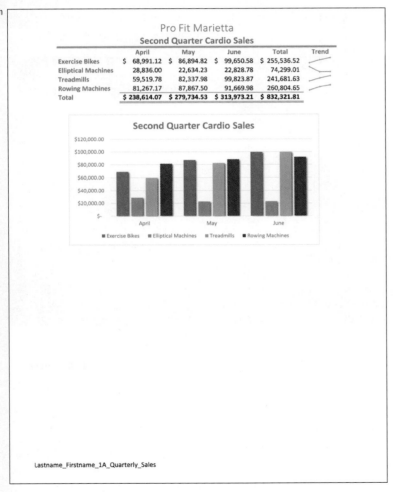

FIGURE 1.1 Project 1A Sales Report with Embedded Column Chart and Sparklines

Objective 1   Create, Save, and Navigate an Excel Workbook

Video E1-1

On startup, Excel displays a new blank *workbook*—the Excel document that stores your data—which contains one or more pages called a *worksheet*. A worksheet—or *spreadsheet*—is stored in a workbook and is formatted as a pattern of uniformly spaced horizontal rows and vertical columns. The intersection of a column and a row forms a box referred to as a *cell*.

Activity 1.01 | Starting Excel, Navigating Excel, and Naming and Saving a Workbook

1 ▷ Start Excel, and then on the opening screen, click **Blank workbook**. In the lower right corner of the window, on the status bar, if necessary, click the Normal button ▦, and then to the right, locate the zoom—magnification—level.

> Your zoom level should be 100%, although some figures in this textbook may be shown at a higher zoom level. The *Normal view* maximizes the number of cells visible on your screen and keeps the column letters and row numbers closer.

 BY TOUCH   On Excel's opening screen, tap Blank workbook.

2 ▷ Press F12 to display the **Save As** dialog box, and then navigate to the location where you will store your workbooks for this chapter.

3 ▷ In your storage location, create a new folder named **Excel Chapter 1** Open the new folder to display its folder window, and then in the **File name** box, notice that *Book1* displays as the default file name.

4 ▷ In the **File name** box, if necessary click *Book1* to select it, and then using your own name, type **Lastname_Firstname_1A_Quarterly_Sales** being sure to include the underscore (_) instead of spaces between words.

5 ▷ In the **Save As** dialog box, click **Save**. Compare your screen with Figure 1.2, and then take a moment to study the Excel window parts in the table in Figure 1.3.

More **Knowledge**   **Creating a New Workbook by Using a Template**

On Excel's opening screen, you can select a professional-look template instead of a blank workbook. Templates have some formatting completed; you just add and modify what you want. You can select or search for a template to match your needs from Excel's opening screen; or, from the Excel window, click FILE, and then click New to search for online templates.

FIGURE 1.2

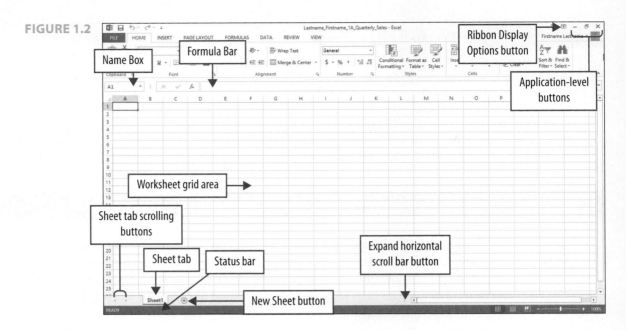

FIGURE 1.3

PARTS OF THE EXCEL WINDOW	
WINDOW PART	**DESCRIPTION**
Expand horizontal scroll bar button	Increases the width of the horizontal scroll bar.
Formula Bar	Displays the value or formula contained in the active cell; also permits entry or editing.
Sheet tab	Identifies the worksheet in the workbook.
New sheet button	Inserts an additional worksheet.
Name Box	Displays the name of the selected cell, table, chart, or object.
Sheet tab scrolling buttons	Display sheet tabs that are not in view when there are numerous sheet tabs.
Status bar	Displays the current cell mode, page number, worksheet information, view and zoom buttons, and for numerical data, common calculations such as Sum and Average.
Application-level buttons	Minimize, close, or restore the previous size of the displayed workbook.
Ribbon Display Options button	Displays various ways you can display the ribbon—the default is Show Tabs and Commands.
Worksheet grid area	Displays the columns and rows that intersect to form the worksheet's cells.

6 ▸ Take a moment to study Figure 1.4 and the table in Figure 1.5 to become familiar with the Excel workbook window.

FIGURE 1.4

FIGURE 1.5

EXCEL WORKBOOK WINDOW ELEMENTS	
WORKBOOK WINDOW ELEMENT	**DESCRIPTION**
Excel pointer	Displays the location of the pointer.
Expand Formula Bar button	Increases the height of the Formula Bar to display lengthy cell content.
Lettered column headings	Indicate the column letter.
Numbered row headings	Indicate the row number.
Select All box	Selects all the cells in a worksheet.

7 In the lower right corner of the screen, in the horizontal scroll bar, click the **right scroll arrow** one time to shift **column A** out of view.

A *column* is a vertical group of cells in a worksheet. Beginning with the first letter of the alphabet, *A*, a unique letter identifies each column—this is called the *column heading*. Clicking one of the horizontal scroll bar arrows shifts the window either left or right one column at a time.

8 Point to the **right scroll arrow**, and then hold down the left mouse button until the columns begin to scroll rapidly to the right; release the mouse button when you begin to see pairs of letters as the column headings.

BY TOUCH   Anywhere on the worksheet, slide your finger to the left to scroll to the right.

9 Slowly drag the horizontal scroll box to the left, and notice that just above the scroll box, ScreenTips with the column letters display as you drag. Drag the horizontal scroll box left or right—or click the **left or right scroll arrow**—as necessary to position **column Z** near the center of your screen.

Column headings after column Z use two letters starting with AA, AB, and so on through ZZ. After that, columns begin with three letters beginning with AAA. This pattern provides 16,384 columns. The last column is XFD.

10 In the vertical scroll bar, click the **down scroll arrow** one time to move **Row 1** out of view.

A *row* is a horizontal group of cells. Beginning with number 1, a unique number identifies each row—this is the *row heading*, located at the left side of the worksheet. A single worksheet can handle 1 million rows of data.

11 Use the skills you just practiced to scroll horizontally to display **column A**, and if necessary, **row 1**.

12 Click **Save** 🖫.

Objective 2   Enter Data in a Worksheet

Video E1-2

Cell content, which is anything you type in a cell, can be one of two things: either a *constant value*—referred to simply as a *value*—or a *formula*. A formula is an equation that performs mathematical calculations on values in your worksheet. The most commonly used values are *text values* and *number values*, but a value can also include a date or a time of day. A text value is also referred to as a *label*.

A text value usually provides information about number values in other worksheet cells. For example, a title such as Second Quarter Cardio Sales gives the reader an indication that the data in the worksheet relates to information about sales of cardio equipment during the three-month period April through June.

1 Point to and then click the cell at the intersection of **column A** and **row 1** to make it the *active cell*—the cell is outlined in black and ready to accept data.

The intersecting column letter and row number form the *cell reference*—also called the *cell address*. When a cell is active, its column letter and row number are highlighted. The cell reference of the selected cell, *A1*, displays in the Name Box.

2 With cell **A1** as the active cell, type the worksheet title **Pro Fit Marietta** and then press Enter. Compare your screen with Figure 1.6.

Text or numbers in a cell are referred to as *data*. You must confirm the data you type in a cell by pressing Enter or by some other keyboard movement, such as pressing Tab or an arrow key. Pressing Enter moves the active cell to the cell below.

FIGURE 1.6

Name Box displays active cell—A2

Worksheet title entered

3 In cell **A1**, notice that the text does not fit; the text extends into cell **B1** to the right.

If text is too long for a cell and cells to the right are empty, the text will display. If the cells to the right contain other data, only the text that will fit in the cell displays.

4 In cell **A2**, type the worksheet subtitle **Second Quarter Cardio Sales** and then press Enter. Compare your screen with Figure 1.7.

FIGURE 1.7

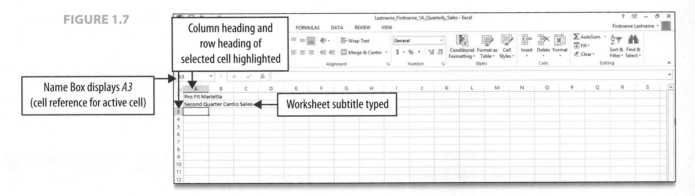

Column heading and row heading of selected cell highlighted

Name Box displays *A3* (cell reference for active cell)

Worksheet subtitle typed

5 Above **column A**, click in the **Name Box** to select the cell reference *A3*, and then type **a4** Press Enter to make cell **A4** the active cell. In cell **A4**, type **Exercise Bikes** to form the first row title, and then press Enter.

The text characters that you typed align at the left edge of the cell—referred to as *left alignment*—and cell A5 becomes the active cell. Left alignment is the default for text values. You can type a cell address in the Name Box and press Enter to move to a specific cell quickly.

6 In cell **A5**, type **E** and notice the text from the previous cell displays.

> If the first characters you type in a cell match an existing entry in the column, Excel fills in the remaining characters for you. This feature, called *AutoComplete*, assists only with alphabetic values.

7 Continue typing the remainder of the row title **lliptical Machines** and press Enter.

> The AutoComplete suggestion is removed when the entry you are typing differs from the previous value.

8 In cell **A6**, type **Treadmills** and press Enter. In cell **A7**, type **Rowing Machines** and press Enter. In cell **A8**, type **Total** and press Enter. On the **Quick Access Toolbar**, click **Save** 🖫.

ANOTHER WAY   Use the keyboard shortcut Ctrl + S to save changes to your workbook.

Activity 1.03 | Using Auto Fill and Keyboard Shortcuts

1 Click cell **B3**. Type **A** and notice that when you begin to type in a cell, on the **Formula Bar**, the **Cancel** and **Enter** buttons become active, as shown in Figure 1.8.

FIGURE 1.8

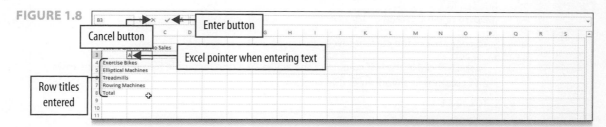

2 Continue to type **pril** On the **Formula Bar**, notice that values you type in a cell also display there. Then, on the **Formula Bar**, click **Enter** ✓ to confirm the entry and keep cell **B3** active.

3 With cell **B3** active, locate the small square in the lower right corner of the selected cell.

> You can drag this *fill handle*—the small square in the lower right corner of a selected cell—to adjacent cells to fill the cells with values based on the first cell.

4 Point to the **fill handle** until the ➕ pointer displays, hold down the left mouse button, drag to the right to cell **D3**, and as you drag, notice the ScreenTips *May* and *June*. Release the mouse button.

5 Under the text that you just filled, click the **Auto Fill Options** button 🖳 that displays, and then compare your screen with Figure 1.9.

> *Auto Fill* generates and extends a *series* of values into adjacent cells based on the value of other cells. A series is a group of things that come one after another in succession; for example, *April, May, June*.

> The Auto Fill Options button displays options to fill the data; options vary depending on the content and program from which you are filling, and the format of the data you are filling.

> *Fill Series* is selected, indicating the action that was taken. Because the options are related to the current task, the button is referred to as being *context sensitive*.

FIGURE 1.9

6 Click in any cell to cancel the display of the list.

The list no longer displays; the button will display until you perform some other screen action.

7 Press Ctrl + Home, which is the keyboard shortcut to make cell **A1** active.

8 On the **Quick Access Toolbar**, click **Save** 🖫 to save the changes you have made to your workbook.

9 Take a moment to study the table in Figure 1.10 to become familiar with keyboard shortcuts with which you can navigate the Excel worksheet.

FIGURE 1.10

KEYBOARD SHORTCUTS TO NAVIGATE THE EXCEL WINDOW	
TO MOVE THE LOCATION OF THE ACTIVE CELL:	**PRESS:**
Up, down, right, or left one cell	↑, ↓, →, ←
Down one cell	Enter
Up one cell	Shift + Enter
Up one full screen	PageUp
Down one full screen	PageDown
To column A of the current row	Home
To the last cell in the last column of the active area (the rectangle formed by all the rows and columns in a worksheet that contain entries)	Ctrl + End
To cell A1	Ctrl + Home
Right one cell	Tab
Left one cell	Shift + Tab
To the cell one worksheet window to the right	Alt + PageDown
To the cell one worksheet window to the left	Alt + PageUp
To the cell containing specific content that you enter in the Find and Replace dialog box	Shift + F5
To the cell that corresponds with the cell reference you enter in the Go To dialog box	F5

Activity 1.04 | Aligning Text and Adjusting the Size of Columns

1 In the **column heading area**, point to the vertical line between **column A** and **column B** to display the ➕ pointer, press and hold down the left mouse button, and then compare your screen with Figure 1.11.

A ScreenTip displays information about the width of the column. The default width of a column is 64 *pixels*. A pixel, short for *picture element*, is a point of light measured in dots per square inch. Sixty-four pixels equal 8.43 characters, which is the average number of characters that will fit in a cell using the default font. The default font in Excel is Calibri and the default font size is 11.

FIGURE 1.11

Column heading area

ScreenTip

Mouse pointer

2 Drag to the right, and when the number of pixels indicated in the ScreenTip reaches **120 pixels**, release the mouse button. If you are not satisfied with your result, click Undo ⟲ on the Quick Access Toolbar and begin again.

This width accommodates the longest row title in cells A4 through A8—*Elliptical Machines*. The worksheet subtitle in cell A2 spans more than one column and still does not fit in column A.

3 Point to cell **B3** and then drag across to select cells **B3**, **C3**, and **D3**. Compare your screen with Figure 1.12; if you are not satisfied with your result, click anywhere and begin again.

The three cells, B3 through D3, are selected and form a ***range***—two or more cells on a worksheet that are adjacent (next to each other) or nonadjacent (not next to each other). This range of cells is referred to as *B3:D3*. When you see a colon (:) between two cell references, the range includes all the cells between the two cell references.

A range of cells you select this way is indicated by a dark border, and Excel treats the range as a single unit so you can make the same changes to more than one cell at a time. The selected cells in the range are highlighted except for the first cell in the range, which displays in the Name Box.

When you select a range of data, the ***Quick Analysis tool*** displays in the lower right corner of the selected range with which you can analyze your data by using Excel tools such as charts, color-coding, and formulas.

FIGURE 1.12

Column A widened to 120 pixels

First cell in selected range—B3—displays in Name Box

Quick Analysis tool

Range B3:D3 selected

🔄 **BY TOUCH**

To select a range, tap and hold the first cell, and then when the circular gripper displays, drag it to the right, or to the right and down, to define the beginning and end of a range.

4 With the range **B3:D3** selected, point anywhere over the selected range, right-click, and then on the mini toolbar, click **Center** ≡. On the **Quick Access Toolbar**, click **Save** 🖫.

The column titles *April*, *May*, *June* align in the center of each cell.

Activity 1.05 | Entering Numbers

To type number values, use either the number keys across the top of your keyboard or the numeric keypad if you have one—laptop computers may not have a numeric keypad.

1 Under *April*, click cell **B4**, type **68991.12** and then on the **Formula Bar**, click **Enter** ☑ to maintain cell **B4** as the active cell. Compare your screen with Figure 1.13.

By default, *number* values align at the right edge of the cell. The default *number format*—a specific way in which Excel displays numbers—is the *general format*. In the default general format, whatever you type in the cell will display, with the exception of trailing zeros to the right of a decimal point. For example, in the number 237.50 the *0* following the *5* is a trailing zero and will not display.

Data that displays in a cell is the *displayed value*. Data that displays in the Formula Bar is the *underlying value*. The number of digits or characters that display in a cell—the displayed value—depends on the width of the column. Calculations on numbers will always be based on the underlying value, not the displayed value.

FIGURE 1.13

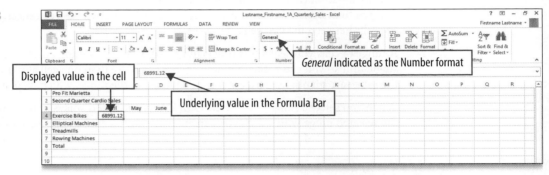

2 Press [Tab] to make cell **C4** active. Type **86894.82** and then press [Tab] to move to cell **D4**. Type **99650.58** and then press [Enter] to move to cell **B5** in the next row. Then, by using the same technique, enter the remaining sales numbers as shown:

	APRIL	MAY	JUNE
Elliptical Machines	28836	22634.23	22828.78
Treadmills	59519.78	82337.98	99823.87
Rowing Machines	81267.17	87867.50	91669.98

3 Compare the numbers you entered with Figure 1.14, and then **Save** 🖫 your workbook.

In the default General format, trailing zeros to the right of a decimal point will not display. For example, when you type *87867.50*, the cell displays 87867.5 instead.

FIGURE 1.14

Video E1-3

A cell contains either a constant value (text or numbers) or a formula. A formula is an equation that performs mathematical calculations on values in other cells, and then places the result in the cell containing the formula. You can create formulas or use a ***function***—a prewritten formula that looks at one or more values, performs an operation, and then returns a value.

Activity 1.06 | Constructing a Formula and Using the SUM Function

In this activity, you will practice three different ways to sum a group of numbers in Excel.

1 Click cell **B8** to make it the active cell and type **=**

The equal sign (=) displays in the cell with the insertion point blinking, ready to accept more data.

All formulas begin with the = sign, which signals Excel to begin a calculation. The Formula Bar displays the = sign, and the Formula Bar Cancel and Enter buttons display.

2 At the insertion point, type **b4** and then compare your screen with Figure 1.15.

A list of Excel functions that begin with the letter *B* may briefly display—as you progress in your study of Excel, you will use functions of this type. A blue border with small corner boxes surrounds cell B4, which indicates that the cell is part of an active formula. The color used in the box matches the color of the cell reference in the formula.

FIGURE 1.15

Cell B8 displays the beginning of the formula, with B4 in blue to match outlined cell

Cell B4 outlined in blue to show it is part of an active formula

3 At the insertion point, type **+** and then type **b5**

A border of another color surrounds cell B5, and the color matches the color of the cell reference in the active formula. When typing cell references, it is not necessary to use uppercase letters.

4 At the insertion point, type **+b6+b7** and then press Enter.

The result of the formula calculation—*238614.1*—displays in the cell. Recall that in the default General format, trailing zeros do not display.

5 Click cell **B8** again, look at the **Formula Bar**, and then compare your screen with Figure 1.16.

The formula adds the values in cells B4 through B7, and the result displays in cell B8. In this manner, you can construct a formula by typing. Although cell B8 displays the *result* of the formula, the formula itself displays in the Formula Bar. This is referred to as the ***underlying formula***.

Always view the Formula Bar to be sure of the exact content of a cell—*a displayed number may actually be a formula*.

FIGURE 1.16

Formula displays in Formula Bar

Total of values in cells B4:B7 displays in cell B8

> **6** Click cell **C8** and type **=** to signal the beginning of a formula. Then, point to cell **C4** and click one time.

> The reference to the cell C4 is added to the active formula. A moving border surrounds the referenced cell, and the border color and the color of the cell reference in the formula are color coded to match.

> **7** At the insertion point, type **+** and then click cell **C5**. Repeat this process to complete the formula to add cells **C6** and **C7**, and then press **Enter**.

> The result of the formula calculation—*279734.5*—displays in the cell. This method of constructing a formula is the ***point and click method***.

> **8** Click cell **D8**. On the **HOME tab**, in the **Editing group**, click **AutoSum** Σ AutoSum ▾ , and then compare your screen with Figure 1.17.

> ***SUM*** is an Excel function—a prewritten formula. A moving border surrounds the range D4:D7 and *=SUM(D4:D7)* displays in cell D8.

> The = sign signals the beginning of a formula, *SUM* indicates the type of calculation that will take place (addition), and *(D4:D7)* indicates the range of cells on which the sum calculation will be performed. A ScreenTip provides additional information about the action.

FIGURE 1.17

ANOTHER WAY   Use the keyboard shortcut **Alt** + **=** ; or, on the Formulas tab, in the Function Library group, click the AutoSum button.

> **9** Look at the **Formula Bar**, and notice that the formula also displays there. Then, look again at the cells surrounded by the moving border.

> When you activate the ***Sum function***, Excel first looks *above* the active cell for a range of cells to sum. If no range is above the active cell, Excel will look to the *left* for a range of cells to sum. If the proposed range is not what you want to calculate, you can select a different group of cells.

> **10** Press **Enter** to construct a formula by using the prewritten SUM function.

> Your total is *313973.2*. Because the Sum function is frequently used, it has its own button in the Editing group on the Home tab of the ribbon. A larger version of the button also displays on the FORMULAS tab in the Function Library group. This button is also referred to as ***AutoSum***.

> **11** Notice that the totals in the range **B8:D8** display only one decimal place. Click **Save** 🖫 .

> Number values that are too long to fit in the cell do *not* spill over into the unoccupied cell to the right in the same manner as text values. Rather, Excel rounds the number to fit the space.

> ***Rounding*** is a procedure that determines which digit at the right of the number will be the last digit displayed and then increases it by one if the next digit to its right is 5, 6, 7, 8, or 9.

Activity 1.07 | Copying a Formula by Using the Fill Handle

You have practiced three ways to create a formula—by typing, by using the point-and-click technique, and by using a Function button from the ribbon. You can also copy formulas. When you copy a formula from one cell to another, Excel adjusts the cell references to fit the new location of the formula.

1 Click cell **E3**, type **Total** and then press Enter.

The text in cell E3 is centered because the centered format continues from the adjacent cell.

2 With cell **E4** as the active cell, hold down Alt, and then press =. Compare your screen with Figure 1.18.

Alt + = is the keyboard shortcut for the Sum function. Recall that Excel first looks above the selected cell for a proposed range of cells to sum, and if no data is detected, Excel looks to the left and proposes a range of cells to sum.

FIGURE 1.18

3 On the **Formula Bar**, click **Enter** ✓ to display the result and keep cell **E4** active.

The total dollar amount of *Exercise Bikes* sold in the quarter is *255536.5*. In cells E5:E8, you can see that you need a formula similar to the one in E4, but formulas that refer to the cells in row 5, row 6, and so on.

4 With cell **E4** active, point to the **fill handle** in the lower right corner of the cell until the + pointer displays. Then, drag down through cell **E8**; if you are not satisfied with your result, on the Quick Access Toolbar, click Undo ↶ and begin again. Compare your screen with Figure 1.19.

FIGURE 1.19

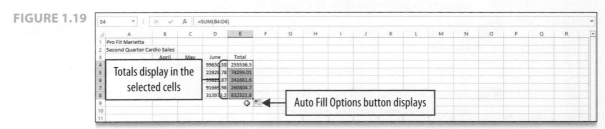

5 Click cell **E5**, look at the **Formula Bar**, and notice the formula *=SUM(B5:D5)*. Click cell **E6**, look at the **Formula Bar**, and then notice the formula *=SUM(B6:D6)*.

In each row, Excel copied the formula but adjusted the cell references *relative to* the row number. This is called a ***relative cell reference***—a cell reference based on the relative position of the cell that contains the formula and the cells referred to in the formula.

The calculation is the same, but it is performed on the cells in that particular row. Use this method to insert numerous formulas into spreadsheets quickly.

6 Click cell **F3**, type **Trend** and then press Enter. **Save** 🖫 your workbook.

Video E1-4

Format—change the appearance of—cells to make your worksheet attractive and easy to read.

Activity 1.08 | Using Merge & Center and Applying Cell Styles

1 Select the range **A1:F1**, and then in the **Alignment group**, click **Merge & Center**. Then, select the range **A2:F2** and click **Merge & Center**.

The *Merge & Center* command joins selected cells into one larger cell and centers the contents in the merged cell; individual cells in the range B1:F1 and B2:F2 can no longer be selected—they are merged into cell A1 and A2 respectively.

🔄 **ANOTHER WAY** Select the range, right-click over the selection, and then on the mini toolbar, click the Merge & Center button.

2 Click cell **A1**. In the **Styles group**, click **Cell Styles**, and then compare your screen with Figure 1.20.

A *cell style* is a defined set of formatting characteristics, such as font, font size, font color, cell borders, and cell shading.

FIGURE 1.20

3 In the displayed gallery, under **Titles and Headings**, click **Title** and notice that the row height adjusts to accommodate the larger font size.

4 Click cell **A2**, display the **Cell Styles** gallery, and then under **Titles and Headings**, click **Heading 1**.

Use cell styles to maintain a consistent look in a worksheet and across worksheets in a workbook.

5 Select the horizontal range **B3:F3**, hold down Ctrl, and then select the vertical range **A4:A8** to select the column titles and the row titles.

Use this technique to select two or more ranges that are nonadjacent—not next to each other.

6 Display the **Cell Styles** gallery, click **Heading 4** to apply this cell style to the column titles and row titles, and then **Save** 🖫 your workbook.

1 Select the range **B4:E4**, hold down Ctrl, and then select the range **B8:E8**.

This range is referred to as *b4:e4,b8:e8* with a comma separating the references to the two nonadjacent ranges.

> **ANOTHER WAY** In the Name Box type b4:e4,b8:e8 and then press Enter.

2 On the **HOME tab**, in the **Number group**, click **Accounting Number Format** $ ▾. Compare your screen with Figure 1.21.

The *Accounting Number Format* applies a thousand comma separator where appropriate, inserts a fixed U.S. dollar sign aligned at the left edge of the cell, applies two decimal places, and leaves a small amount of space at the right edge of the cell to accommodate a parenthesis when negative numbers are present. Excel widens the columns to accommodate the formatted numbers.

At the bottom of your screen, in the status bar, Excel displays the results for some common calculations that might be made on the range; for example, the Average of the numbers selected and the Count—the number of items selected.

FIGURE 1.21

> **ANOTHER WAY** Display the Cell Styles gallery, and under Number Format, click Currency.

3 Select the range **B5:E7**, and then in the **Number group**, click **Comma Style** ▾.

The *Comma Style* inserts a thousand comma separator where appropriate and applies two decimal places. Comma Style also leaves space at the right to accommodate a parenthesis when negative numbers are present.

When preparing worksheets with financial information, the first row of dollar amounts and the total row of dollar amounts are formatted in the Accounting Number Format; that is, with thousand comma separators, dollar signs, two decimal places, and space at the right to accommodate a parenthesis for negative numbers, if any. Rows that are *not* the first row or the total row should be formatted with the Comma Style.

4 Select the range **B8:E8**. In the **Styles group**, display the **Cell Styles** gallery, and then under **Titles and Headings**, click **Total**. Click any blank cell to cancel the selection, and then compare your screen with Figure 1.22.

This is a common way to apply borders to financial information. The single border indicates that calculations were performed on the numbers above, and the double border indicates that the information is complete. Sometimes financial documents do not display values with cents; rather, the values are rounded up. You can do this by selecting the cells, and then clicking the Decrease Decimal button two times.

FIGURE 1.22

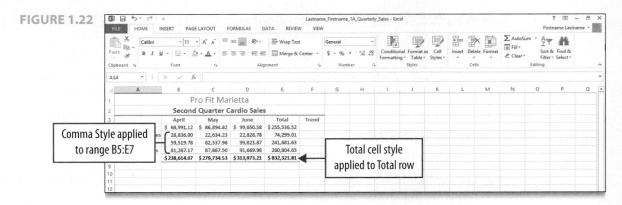

Comma Style applied to range B5:E7

Total cell style applied to Total row

Activity 1.10 | Changing the Workbook Theme

A *theme* is a predefined set of colors, fonts, lines, and fill effects that coordinate for an attractive look.

> **1** Click the **PAGE LAYOUT tab**, and then in the **Themes group**, click **Themes**.

> **2** Click the **Retrospect** theme, and notice that the cell styles change to match the new theme. Click **Save** 📄.

More Knowledge | **Formatting a Cell's Font, Style, Size, or Color with Individual Commands**

Instead of using Cell Styles, you could use a combination of individual commands to format a cell. For example, on the HOME tab, in the Font group, you can change a cell's font by clicking the Font arrow and selecting a different font. You can change the font size by clicking the Font Size arrow and selecting a size. From the same group, you can apply various styles to the cell—such as Bold or Italic or Underline. To change a cell's font color, in the Font Group, click the Font Color arrow and select a different color.

Objective 5 | Chart Data to Create a Column Chart and Insert Sparklines

Video E1-5

A *chart* is a graphic representation of data in a worksheet. Data in a chart is easier to understand than a table of numbers. *Sparklines* are tiny charts embedded in a cell that give a visual trend summary alongside your data. A sparkline makes a pattern more obvious to the eye.

Activity 1.11 | Charting Data and Using Recommended Charts to Select and Insert a Column Chart

Recommended Charts is an Excel feature that displays a customized set of charts that, according to Excel's calculations, will best fit your data based on the range of data that you select. In this activity, you will create a *column chart* showing the monthly sales of cardio equipment by category during the second quarter. A column chart is useful for illustrating comparisons among related numbers. The chart will enable the company president, Michelle Barry, to see a pattern of overall monthly sales.

> **1** Select the range **A3:D7**.

> When charting data, typically you should *not* include totals—include only the data you want to compare.

2 With the data that you want to compare selected, click the **INSERT tab**, and then in the **Charts group**, click **Recommended Charts**. Compare your screen with Figure 1.23.

The Insert Chart dialog box displays a list of recommended charts on the left and a preview of the first chart, which is selected, on the right. The second tab of the Insert Chart dialog box includes all chart types—even those that are not recommended by Excel for this type of data.

By using different *chart types*, you can display data in a way that is meaningful to the reader—common examples are column charts, pie charts, and line charts.

FIGURE 1.23

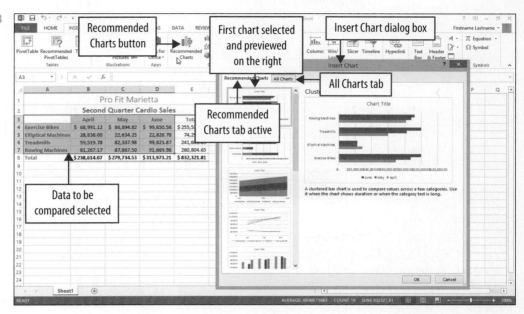

3 In the **Insert Chart** dialog box, use the scroll bar to scroll down about one-third of the way, and then click the second Clustered Column chart. Compare your screen with Figure 1.24.

Here, *each type of cardio equipment* displays its *sales for each month*. A clustered column chart is useful to compare values across a few categories, especially if the order of categories is not important.

FIGURE 1.24

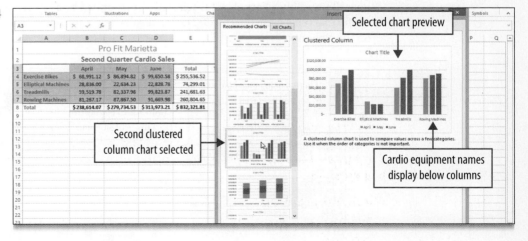

4 In the **Insert Chart** dialog box, click the chart directly above the selected chart—the first clustered column chart. Compare your screen with Figure 1.25.

In this clustered column chart, *each month* displays its *sales for each type of cardio equipment*. When constructing a chart, you can switch the row and column data in this manner to display the data in a way that is most useful to the reader. Here, the president of Pro Fit Marietta wants to compare sales of each type of equipment by month to detect patterns.

The comparison of data—either by month or by type of equipment—depends on the type of analysis you want to perform. You can select either chart, or, after your chart is complete, you can use the *Switch/Row Column* command on the ribbon to swap the data over the axis; that is, data being charted on the vertical axis will move to the horizontal axis and vice versa.

FIGURE 1.25

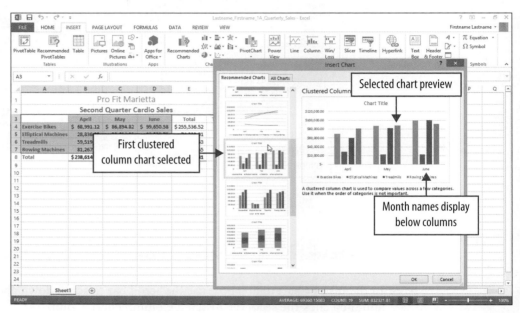

5 In the lower right corner of the **Insert Chart** dialog box, click **OK** to insert the selected chart into the worksheet. Compare your screen with Figure 1.26.

Your selected column chart displays in the worksheet, and the charted data is bordered by colored lines. Because the chart object is selected—surrounded by a border and displaying sizing handles—contextual tools named *CHART TOOLS* display and add contextual tabs next to the standard tabs on the ribbon.

FIGURE 1.26

1 ▷ On the ribbon, locate the contextual tabs under **CHART TOOLS—DESIGN** and **FORMAT**.

When a chart is selected, CHART TOOLS become available and these two tabs provide commands for working with the chart.

Based on the data you selected in your worksheet and the chart you selected in the Insert Chart dialog box, Excel constructs a column chart and adds *category labels*—the labels that display along the bottom of the chart to identify the category of data. This area is referred to as the *category axis* or the *x-axis*.

Depending on which arrangement of row and column data you select in the Insert Chart dialog box, Excel arranges either the row titles or the column titles as the category names. Here, based on your selection, the column titles that form the category labels are bordered in purple, indicating the cells that contain the category names.

On the left side of the chart, Excel includes a numerical scale on which the charted data is based; this is the *value axis* or the *y-axis*. Along the lower edge of the chart, a *legend*, which is a chart element that identifies the patterns or colors that are assigned to the categories in the chart, displays. Here, the row titles are bordered in red, indicating the cells containing the legend text.

2 ▷ To the right of the chart, notice the three buttons, and then point to each button to display its ScreenTip, as shown in Figure 1.27.

The *Chart Elements button* enables you to add, remove, or change chart elements such as the title, legend, gridlines, and data labels.

The *Chart Styles button* enables you to set a style and color scheme for your chart.

The *Chart Filters button* enables you to change which data displays in the chart—for example, to see only the data for *May* and *June* or only the data for *Treadmills* and *Rowing Machines*.

FIGURE 1.27

3 ▷ In the worksheet data, locate the group of cells bordered in blue.

Each of the twelve cells bordered in blue is referred to as a *data point*—a value that originates in a worksheet cell. Each data point is represented in the chart by a *data marker*—a column, bar, area, dot, pie slice, or other symbol in a chart that represents a single data point.

Related data points form a *data series*; for example, there is a data series for *April*, for *May*, and for *June*. Each data series has a unique color or pattern represented in the chart legend.

4 ▷ On the **DESIGN tab**, in the **Chart Layouts group**, click **Quick Layout**, and then compare your screen with Figure 1.28.

In the Quick Layout gallery, you can change the overall layout of the chart by selecting a predesigned *chart layout*—a combination of chart elements, which can include a title, legend, labels for the columns, and the table of charted cells.

FIGURE 1.28

5 *Point* to several different layouts to see how Live Preview displays the effect on your chart, and then click the **Quick Layout** button again *without* changing the layout.

6 In the chart, click anywhere in the text *Chart Title* to select the title box, watch the **Formula Bar** as you begin to type **Second** and notice that AutoComplete fills in the subtitle for you. Press [Enter] at any point to insert the subtitle as the chart title.

7 Click in a white area just slightly *inside* the chart border to deselect the chart title but keep the chart selected. To the right of the chart, click **Chart Styles** , and then at the top of the **Chart Styles** gallery, be sure that **Style** is selected. Compare your screen with Figure 1.29.

> The *Chart Styles gallery* displays an array of pre-defined *chart styles*—the overall visual look of the chart in terms of its colors, backgrounds, and graphic effects such as flat or shaded columns. You can also select Chart Styles from the Chart Styles group on the ribbon, but having the gallery closer to the chart makes it easier to use a touch gesture on a touch device to format a chart.

FIGURE 1.29

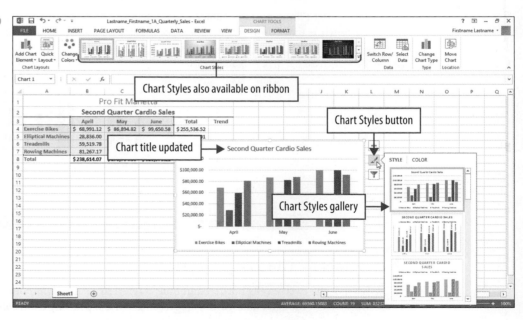

8 On the right side of the **Style** gallery, scroll down about halfway, and then by using the ScreenTips as your guide, locate and click **Style 6**.

> This style uses a white background, formats the columns with theme colors, and applies a slight shadowed effect to the columns. With this clear visual representation of the data, the president can see the sales of all product categories in each month, and can see that the sale of exercise bikes and treadmills has risen markedly during the quarter.

9 At the top of the gallery, click **COLOR**. Under **Colorful**, point to the third row of colors to display the ScreenTip *Color 3*, and then click to apply the **Color 3** variation of the theme colors.

10 Point to the top border of the chart to display the pointer, and then drag the upper left corner of the chart just inside the upper left corner of cell **A10**, approximately as shown in Figure 1.30.

FIGURE 1.30

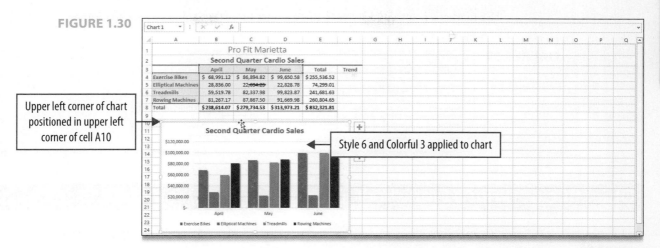

Upper left corner of chart positioned in upper left corner of cell A10

Style 6 and Colorful 3 applied to chart

11 Click any cell to deselect the chart, and notice that the chart buttons no longer display to the right of the chart and the CHART TOOLS no longer display on the ribbon. Click **Save** 🖫.

Contextual tabs display when an object is selected and then are removed from view when the object is deselected.

Activity 1.13 | Creating and Formatting Sparklines

By creating sparklines, you provide a context for your numbers. Your readers will be able to see the relationship between a sparkline and its underlying data quickly.

1 Select the range **B4:D7**, which represents the monthly sales figures for each product and for each month. Click the **INSERT tab**, and then in the **Sparklines group**, click **Line**. In the displayed **Create Sparklines** dialog box, notice that the selected range *B4:D7* displays as the Data Range.

2 With the insertion point blinking in the **Location Range** box, type **f4:f7** which is the range of cells where you want the sparklines to display. Compare your screen with Figure 1.31.

FIGURE 1.31

Data range selected

Create Sparklines dialog box

Selected data range in Data Range box

Location Range typed

🔄 **ANOTHER WAY**   In the worksheet, select the range F4:F7 to insert it into the Location Range box.

3 Click **OK** to insert the sparklines in the range **F4:F7**, and then on the **DESIGN tab**, in the **Show group**, click the **Markers** check box to select it.

Alongside each row of data, the sparkline provides a quick visual trend summary for sales of each cardio item over the three-month period. For example, you can see instantly that of the four items, only Elliptical Machines had declining sales for the period.

4 On the **DESIGN tab**, in the **Style group**, click **More** ⬇. In the second row, click the fourth style—**Sparkline Style Accent 4, Darker 25%**. Press Ctrl + Home to deselect the range and make cell **A1** the active cell. Click **Save** 🖫, and then compare your screen with Figure 1.32.

Use markers, colors, and styles in this manner to further enhance your sparklines.

FIGURE 1.32

Video E1-6

Use the Show Formulas command to display the formula in each cell instead of the resulting value. Use the commands on the PAGE LAYOUT tab to prepare for printing.

Activity 1.14 | Creating a Footer and Centering a Worksheet

For each Excel project in this textbook, you will create a footer containing the file name, which includes your name and the project name. You will also center the data horizontally on the page to create an attractive result if your worksheet is printed.

1 If necessary, click cell **A1** to deselect the chart. Click the **PAGE LAYOUT tab**, and then in the **Page Setup group**, click **Margins**. At the bottom of the **Margins** gallery, click **Custom Margins**, to display the **Page Setup** dialog box. Compare your screen with Figure 1.33.

FIGURE 1.33

2 On the **Margins tab**, under **Center on page**, select the **Horizontally** check box.

This action will center the data and chart horizontally on the page, as shown in the Preview area.

3 Click the **Header/Footer tab**, and then in the center of the dialog box, click **Custom Footer**. In the **Footer** dialog box, with your insertion point blinking in the **Left section**, on the row of buttons, click **Insert File Name** 🗐. Compare your screen with Figure 1.34.

&[File] displays in the Left section. Here you can type or insert information from the row of buttons into the left, middle, or right section of the footer. The Custom Header button displays a similar screen to enter information in the header of the worksheet.

FIGURE 1.34

FIGURE 1.34

Footer dialog box

&[File] in Left section

4 Click **OK** two times.

The vertical dotted line between columns indicates that as currently arranged, only the columns to the left of the dotted line will print on the first page. The exact position of the vertical line may depend on your default printer setting.

ANOTHER WAY
Deselect the chart. On the INSERT tab, in the Text group, click Header & Footer to display Page Layout view. Click in the Left section of the displayed footer, and then in the Header & Footer Elements group, click File Name. Click any cell in the workbook to deselect the footer area, and then on the status bar, click the Normal button to return to Normal view.

Activity 1.15 | Adding Document Properties and Printing a Workbook

1 In the upper left corner of your screen, click the **FILE tab** to display **Backstage** view. In the lower right corner, click **Show All Properties**.

2 As the **Tags**, type **cardio sales** In the **Subject** box, type your course name and section number. Be sure your name displays as the author and edit if necessary.

3 On the left, click **Print** to view the **Print Preview**. Compare your screen with Figure 1.35.

FIGURE 1.35

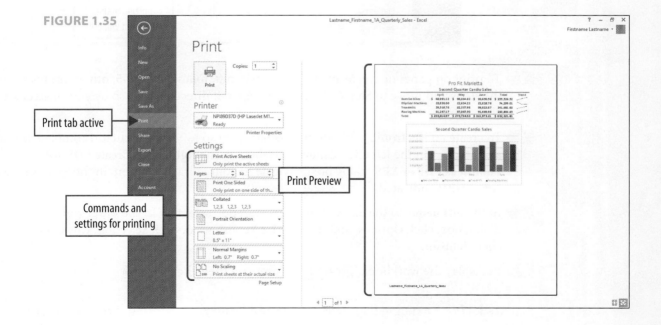

Print tab active

Print Preview

Commands and settings for printing

> **4** Note any adjustments that need to be made, and then on the left, click **Save** to save and return to the workbook.

> **5** If you are directed to print on paper, be sure that a printer is available to your system. Press Ctrl + F2, which is the keyboard shortcut to display the **Print Preview**, and then under **Print**, click the **Print** button.

> **6** If you are directed to create an electronic printout, click the **FILE tab**, on the left click **Export**, and then on the right, click **Create PDF/XPS**. In the **Publish as PDF or XPS** dialog box, navigate to your storage location, in the **Save as type** box, be sure **PDF** is indicated, and then click **Publish** to create the PDF file.

Activity 1.16 | Printing a Section of the Worksheet

From Backstage view, you can print only the portion of the worksheet that you select, and there are times you might want to do this.

> **1** Select the range **A2:F5** to select only the subtitle and the data for *Exercise Bikes* and *Elliptical Machines* and the column titles

> **2** Press Ctrl + F2 to display **Print Preview**, and then under **Settings**, click the first arrow, which currently displays *Print Active Sheets*. On the list that displays, click **Print Selection**, and then compare your screen with Figure 1.36.

FIGURE 1.36

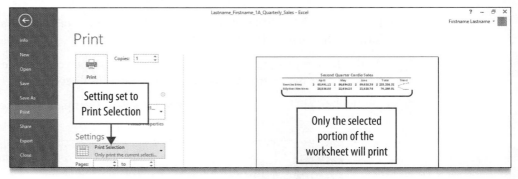

> **3** To print on paper or create an electronic printout, follow Steps 3-5; otherwise read through the steps and move to Step 6. To print on paper, if directed to do so by your instructor, click **Print**.

> **4** To create an electronic printout, if directed to do so by your instructor, complete this step and Step 5. On the left click **Export**, and then on the right, click **Create PDF/XPS**. In the **Publish as PDF or XPS** dialog box, navigate to your storage location, in the **Save as type** box, be sure **PDF** is indicated.

> **5** In the **File name**, to the end of the file name, add **_selection** In the lower right corner of the dialog box, click **Options**, and then under **Publish what**, click **Selection**. Click **OK**, and then click **Publish**.

> **6** Redisplay the workbook, press Ctrl + Home, and then click **Save** 🖫.

Activity 1.17 | Changing Page Orientation and Displaying, Printing, and Hiding Formulas

When you type a formula in a cell, the cell displays the *results* of the formula calculation. Recall that this value is called the displayed value. You can view and print the underlying formulas in the cells. When you do so, a formula often takes more horizontal space to display than the result of the calculation.

1 If necessary, redisplay your worksheet. Because you will make some temporary changes to your workbook, on the **Quick Access Toolbar**, click **Save 🖫** to be sure your work is saved up to this point.

2 On the **FORMULAS tab**, in the **Formula Auditing group**, click **Show Formulas**.

ANOTHER WAY   Hold down [Ctrl], and then press [~] (usually located below [Esc]).

3 In the **column heading area**, point to the **column A** heading to display the ⬇ pointer, hold down the left mouse button, and then drag to the right to select columns **A:F**. Compare your screen with Figure 1.37.

FIGURE 1.37

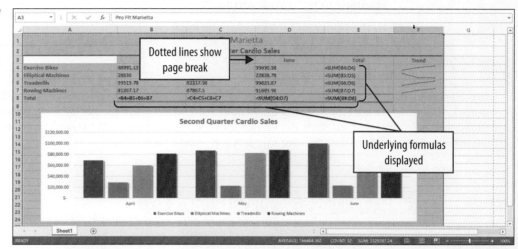

NOTE   **Turning the Display of Formulas On and Off**

The Show Formulas button is a toggle button. Clicking it once turns the display of formulas on—the button will be shaded. Clicking the button again turns the display of formulas off.

---

4 Point to the column heading boundary between any two of the selected columns to display the ✛ pointer, and then double-click to AutoFit the selected columns.

  AutoFit adjusts the width of a column to fit the cell content of the *widest* cell in the column.

ANOTHER WAY   With the columns selected, on the HOME tab, in the Cells group, click Format, and then click AutoFit Column Width.

5 On the **PAGE LAYOUT tab**, in the **Page Setup group**, click **Orientation**, and then click **Landscape**. In the **Scale to Fit** group, click the **Width arrow**, and then click **1 page** to scale the data to fit onto one page.

  Scaling shrinks the width or height of the printed worksheet to fit a maximum number of pages, and is convenient for printing formulas. Although it is not always the case, formulas frequently take up more space than the actual data.

ANOTHER WAY   In the Scale to Fit group, click the Dialog Box Launcher button to display the Page tab of the Page Setup dialog box. Then, under Scaling, click the Fit to option button.

---

6 ▸ In the **Page Setup group**, click **Margins**, click **Custom Margins**, and then on the **Margins tab**, under **Center on page**, be sure the **Horizontally** check box is selected—select it if necessary.

7 ▸ Click **OK** to close the dialog box. Check to be sure your chart is centered below the data and the left and right edges are slightly inside column A and column F—use the ⟦↸⟧ pointer to drag a chart edge and then deselect the chart if necessary.

8 ▸ Click any cell so that the chart is not selected, and then press ⟦Ctrl⟧ + ⟦F2⟧ to display the **Print Preview**. Under **Settings**, if necessary switch back to the option to **Print Active Sheets**. If directed to do so by your instructor, print on paper or click Save As and name the worksheet **Lastname_Firstname_1A_Quarterly_Sales_fomulas**

9 ▸ On the left, click **Close**, and when prompted, click **Don't Save** so that you do *not* save the changes you made—displaying formulas, changing column widths and orientation, and scaling—to print your formulas.

10 ▸ In the upper right corner of your screen, click **Close** ⟦ x ⟧ to close Excel.

More Knowledge | **Inserting a Watermark**

Excel does not have a watermark feature like the watermark in Word, but there are two ways you can achieve the same effect. To use WordArt to mimic a watermark, on the INSERT tab, in the Text group, click Insert WordArt, and then click the style you want to use. Type the text and resize as necessary. Then, right-click the WordArt, click Format Text Effects, click Text Fill & Outline, and then drag one or both transparency sliders to the percentage you want. Or, simply create an image of a watermark and insert the image in the worksheet header or footer.

END | You have completed Project 1A

Objective   Create a Sales Report with an Embedded Column Chart Using Excel Online

If you are working on a computer that does not have Microsoft Office installed, you can still create new workbooks in your web browser by using Excel Office Online.

> **ALERT!**   **Working with Web-Based Applications and Services**
>
> Computer programs and services on the web receive continuous updates and improvements, so the steps to complete this web-based activity may differ from the ones shown. You can often look at the screens and the information presented to determine how to complete the activity.

Activity | Creating a Sales Report with Embedded Column Chart Using Excel Online

In this activity, you will use Excel Online to create a sales report and chart similar to the one you created in Project 1A.

1 Start Excel, open a new blank workbook, and then if necessary, in the upper right corner, log into Office with your Microsoft account. In cell **A1**, type **Pro Fit Marietta** press Enter, and then click the **FILE tab**. On the left, click **Save As**, and then on the right, click the name of your OneDrive— the path to your GO! Web Projects folder on the OneDrive may display under Recent Folders and if so, you can click there.

2 In the **Save As** dialog box for your OneDrive, if necessary open your **GO! Web Projects** folder, and then save the file as **Lastname_Firstname_EX_1A_ Web** Close Excel, launch Internet Explorer, go to http://onedrive.com, sign in, and then from your **GO! Web Projects** folder, open the file you just saved there.

3 To help you create this project quickly and to eliminate extra typing, you will import the data from a Word table. From the taskbar, open **File Explorer**, navigate to the student data files that accompany this textbook, and then open the Word document **e01_1A_Web**. Press Ctrl + A to select all of the text, right-click anywhere over the

selection, and then click **Copy**. **Close** ⌧ Word and **Close** ⌧ File Explorer.

4 Click cell **A2**, on the Excel Online ribbon, in the **Clipboard group**, click the upper portion of the **Paste** button; if necessary click **Allow access**. Notice that number symbols display when numeric data is too wide for the cell.

5 Select column headings **A:E**, point to the border between any two selected column headings to display the ⟷ pointer, and then double-click to resize all the columns to display all data.

6 Drag to select the range **A1:E1**, and then in the **Alignment group**, click **Merge & Center** ▤▾. Merge and center the worksheet's subtitle in the same manner. Select the range **A1:A2**, and then in the **Font group**, apply **Bold** B and change the **Font Color** A ▾ to **Dark Blue**.

7 Select the range **B4:E4**. In the **Number group**, click the **Number Format arrow**, and then click **Currency**. Apply the same format to the range **B8:E8**.

FIGURE A

	A	B	C	D	E	F	G	H	I	J	K	L	M	N	O	P
1			Pro Fit Marietta													
2			Second Quarter Cardio Sales													
3																
4	Exercise Bikes	$68,991.12	$86,894.82	$99,650.58	$255,536.52											
5	Elliptical Machines	28,836.00	22,634.23	22,828.78	74,299.01											
6	Treadmills	59,519.78	82,337.98	99,823.87	241,681.63											
7	Rowing Machines	81,267.17	87,867.50	91,669.98	260,804.65											
8	Total	$238,614.07	$279,734.53	$313,973.21	$832,321.81											

(GO! with Office Online (formerly Web Apps) continues on the next page)

8 Select the range **B7:E7**, and then in the **Font group**, click **Underline** [U ▾]. Select the range **B8:E8**, and then in the **Font group** click **Double Underline** [D]. Click any empty cell, and then compare your screen with Figure A.

9 Click cell **B3**, type **April** and press [Enter], and then click the cell **B3** again. Drag the fill handle to select cells **C3:D3** to complete the series. In cell **E3** type **Total** Select these four column titles and apply **Center** [≡] and **Bold** [B].

10 Select the range **A3:D7**—the data without the totals. On the **INSERT tab**, in the **Charts group**, click **Column**, and then click the first chart type—**Clustered Column**. In the **Data group**, click **Switch Row/Column**.

11 Drag the chart so that the upper left corner of the chart is inside the upper left portion of cell **A9**. From

the **Labels group**, add a **Chart Title** in the **Above Chart** position with the text **2nd Quarter Cardio Sales**

12 Click cell **A1**, and then compare your screen with Figure B.

In Excel Online, you do not have the same set of features available that you have in the full version of Office; for example, you do not have Cell Styles, sparklines, and chart styles. But you can still create the data and chart in a meaningful way.

13 If you are instructed to submit your file, use one of the methods outlined in the Note box below. In Excel Online, there is no Save button because your workbook is being saved automatically. Sign out of your OneDrive and close Internet Explorer.

FIGURE B

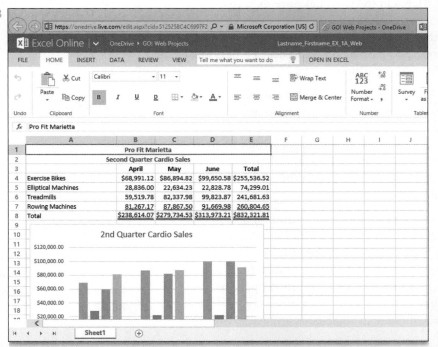

Inventory Valuation

PROJECT ACTIVITIES

In Activities 1.18 through 1.27 you will create a workbook for Josh Feingold, Operations Manager, which calculates the retail value of an inventory of plyometric training products. Your completed worksheet will look similar to Figure 1.38.

PROJECT FILES

For Project 1B, you will need the following file:

New blank Excel workbook

You will save your workbook as:

Lastname_Firstname_1B_Plyo_Products

PROJECT RESULTS

Pro Fit Marietta
Plyometric Products Inventory Valuation
As of September 30

	Warehouse Location	Quantity in Stock	Retail Price	Total Retail Value	Percent of Total Retail Value
Power Hurdle	Atlanta	125	$ 32.95	$ 4,118.75	1.41%
Speed Hurdle	Atlanta	995	59.95	59,650.25	20.37%
Stackable Steps	Marietta	450	251.59	113,215.50	38.65%
Pro Jump Rope	Marietta	1,105	49.95	55,194.75	18.84%
Plyometric Box Set	Marietta	255	158.05	40,302.75	13.76%
Plyometric Mat	Atlanta	215	94.99	20,422.85	6.97%
Total Retail Value for All Products				$ 292,904.85	

Lastname_Firstname_1B_Plyo_Products

FIGURE 1.38 Project 1B Inventory Valuation

Video E1-7

In Excel, the spelling checker performs similarly to the other Microsoft Office programs.

Activity 1.18 | Checking Spelling in a Worksheet

1 **Start** Excel and display a new blank workbook. In cell **A1**, type **Pro Fit Marietta** and press Enter. In cell **A2**, type **Plyometric Products Inventory** and press Enter.

2 Press F12 to display the **Save As** dialog box, and then navigate to your **Excel Chapter 1** folder. As the **File name**, using your own name, type **Lastname_Firstname_1B_Plyo_Products** and then click **Save**.

3 Press Tab to move to cell **B3**, type **Quantity** and press Tab. In cell **C3**, type **Average Cost** and press Tab. In cell **D3**, type **Retail Price** and press Tab.

4 Click cell **C3**, and then look at the **Formula Bar**. Notice that in the cell, the displayed value is cut off; however, in the **Formula Bar**, the entire text value—the underlying value—displays. Compare your screen with Figure 1.39.

> Text that is too long to fit in a cell extends into cells on the right only if they are empty. If the cell to the right contains data, the text in the cell to the left is truncated—cut off. The entire value continues to exist, but is not completely visible.

FIGURE 1.39

Entire contents of C3 display in Formula Bar

Cell C3 active; text cut off

5 Click cell **E3**, type **Total Retail Value** and press Tab. In cell **F3**, type **Percent of Total Retail Value** and press Enter.

6 Click cell **A4**. *Without* correcting the spelling error, type **Powr Hurdle** and then press Enter. In the range **A5:A10**, type the remaining row titles shown below. Then compare your screen with Figure 1.40.

Speed Hurdle
Stackable Steps
Pro Jump Rope
Plyometric Box Set
Plyometric Mat
Total Retail Value for All Products

FIGURE 1.40

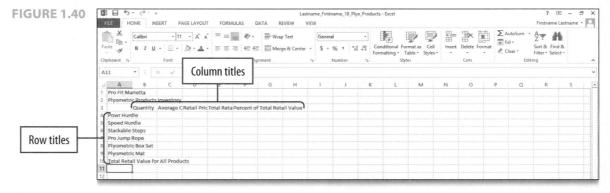

Column titles

Row titles

7 In the **column heading area**, point to the right boundary of **column A** to display the ⊞ pointer, and then drag to the right to widen **column A** to **215** pixels.

8 Select the range **A1:F1**, **Merge & Center** the text, and then from the **Cell Styles** gallery, apply the **Title** style.

9 Select the range **A2:F2**, **Merge & Center** the text, and then from the **Cell Styles** gallery, apply the **Heading 1** style. Press Ctrl + Home to move to the top of your worksheet.

10 With cell **A1** as the active cell, click the **REVIEW tab**, and then in the **Proofing group**, click **Spelling**. Compare your screen with Figure 1.41.

FIGURE 1.41

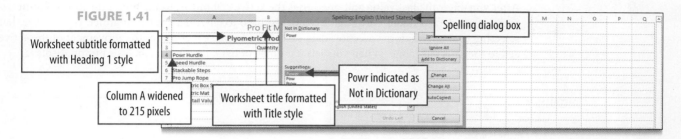

Worksheet subtitle formatted with Heading 1 style

Spelling dialog box

Powr indicated as Not in Dictionary

Column A widened to 215 pixels

Worksheet title formatted with Title style

ALERT! **Does a Message Display Asking if You Want to Continue Checking at the Beginning of the Sheet?**

If a message displays asking if you want to continue checking at the beginning of the sheet, click Yes. The Spelling command begins its checking process with the currently selected cell and moves to the right and down. If your active cell was a cell after A1, this message may display.

ANOTHER WAY Press F7, which is the keyboard shortcut for the Spelling command.

11 In the **Spelling** dialog box, under **Not in Dictionary**, notice the word *Powr*.

The spelling tool does not have this word in its dictionary. Under *Suggestions*, Excel provides a list of suggested spellings.

12 Under **Suggestions**, click **Power**, and then click **Change**.

Powr, a typing error, is changed to *Power*. A message box displays *Spell check complete. You're good to go!*—unless you have additional unrecognized words. Because the spelling check begins its checking process starting with the currently selected cell, it is good practice to return to cell A1 before starting the Spelling command.

13 Correct any other errors you may have made. When the message displays, *Spell check complete. You're good to go!*, click **OK**. **Save** 💾 your workbook.

Objective 8 Enter Data by Range

Video E1-8

You can enter data by first selecting a range of cells. This is a time-saving technique, especially if you use the numeric keypad to enter the numbers.

Activity 1.19 | Entering Data by Range

1 Select the range **B4:D9**, type **125** and then press Enter.

The value displays in cell B4, and cell B5 becomes the active cell.

2 With cell **B5** active in the range, and pressing Enter after each entry, type the following, and then compare your screen with Figure 1.42:

1125
450
1105
255
215

After you enter the last value and press Enter, the active cell moves to the top of the next column within the selected range. Although it is not required to enter data in this manner, you can see that selecting the range before you enter data saves time because it confines the movement of the active cell to the selected range. When you select a range of data, the Quick Analysis button displays.

FIGURE 1.42

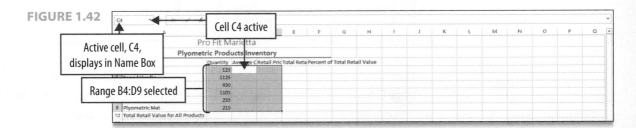

3 With the selected range still active, from the following table, beginning in cell **C4** and pressing Enter after each entry, enter the data for the **Average Cost** column and then the **Retail Price** column. If you prefer, deselect the range to enter the values—typing in a selected range is optional.

AVERAGE COST	RETAIL PRICE
15.50	32.95
29.55	59.95
125.95	251.59
18.75	49.95
85.25	159.05
49.95	94.99

Recall that the default number format for cells is the *General* number format, in which numbers display exactly as you type them and trailing zeros do not display, even if you type them.

4 Click any blank cell, and then compare your screen with Figure 1.43. Correct any errors you may have made while entering data, and then click **Save** 🖫.

FIGURE 1.43

Objective 9 | Construct Formulas for Mathematical Operations

Video E1-9

Operators are symbols with which you can specify the type of calculation you want to perform in a formula.

Activity 1.20 | Using Arithmetic Operators

1 Click cell **E4**, type **=b4*d4** and notice that the two cells are outlined as part of an active formula. Then press Enter.

The *Total Retail Value* of all *Power Hurdle* items in inventory—*4118.75*—equals the *Quantity* (125) times the *Retail Price* (selling price) of 32.95. In Excel, the asterisk (*) indicates multiplication.

2 Take a moment to study the symbols you will use to perform basic mathematical operations in Excel as shown in the table in Figure 1.44, which are referred to as ***arithmetic operators***.

FIGURE 1.44

SYMBOLS USED IN EXCEL FOR ARITHMETIC OPERATORS	
OPERATOR SYMBOL	**OPERATION**
+	Addition
–	Subtraction (also negation)
*	Multiplication
/	Division
%	Percent
^	Exponentiation

3 Click cell **E4**.

You can see that in cells E5:E9, you need a formula similar to the one in E4, but one that refers to the cells in row 5, row 6, and so forth. Recall that you can copy formulas and the cell references will change *relative to* the row number.

4 With cell **E4** selected, position your pointer over the fill handle in the lower right corner of the cell until the ⊞ pointer displays. Then, drag down through cell **E9** to copy the formula.

5 Select the range **B4:B9**, and then on the **HOME tab**, in the **Number group**, click **Comma Style** ⌄. In the **Number group**, click **Decrease Decimal** two times to remove the decimal places from these values.

Comma Style formats a number with two decimal places; because these are whole numbers referring to quantities, no decimal places are necessary.

ANOTHER WAY Select the range, display the Cell Styles gallery, and then under Number Format, click Comma [0].

6 Select the range **E4:E9**, and then at the bottom of your screen, in the status bar, notice the displayed values for **Average**, **Count**, and **Sum**—*50158.89167, 6* and *300953.35*.

When you select a range of numerical data, Excel's ***AutoCalculate*** feature displays three calculations in the status bar by default—Average, Count, and Sum. Here, Excel indicates that if you averaged the selected values, the result would be *50158.89167*, there are *6* cells in the selection that contain values, and that if you added the values the result would be *300953.35*.

You can display three additional calculations to this area by right-clicking the status bar and selecting them—Numerical Count, Minimum, and Maximum.

Activity 1.21 | Using the Quick Analysis Tool

Recall that the Quick Analysis button displays when you select a range of data. Quick Analysis is convenient because it keeps common commands close to your mouse pointer and also displays commands in a format that is easy to touch with your finger if you are using a touchscreen device.

1 ▶ In the lower right corner of the selected range, click **Quick Analysis** , and then in the displayed gallery, click **TOTALS**. *Point to*, but do not click, the first **Sum** button, which shows blue cells at the bottom. Compare your screen with Figure 1.45.

Here, the shaded cells on the button indicate what will be summed and where the result will display, and a preview of the result displays in the cell bordered with a gray shadow.

FIGURE 1.45

2 ▶ Click the first **Sum** button to display the column total *300953.4* formatted in Bold.

Sums calculated using the Quick Analysis tool are formatted in Bold.

3 ▶ Select the range **C5:E9** and apply the **Comma Style** ; notice that Excel widens the columns to accommodate the data.

4 ▶ Select the range **C4:E4**, hold down Ctrl, and then click cell **E10**. Release Ctrl, and then apply the **Accounting Number Format** $ ▾. Notice that Excel widens the columns as necessary.

5 ▶ Click cell **E10**, and then in the **Cell Styles** gallery, apply the **Total** style. Click any blank cell, **Save** your workbook, and then compare your screen with Figure 1.46.

FIGURE 1.46

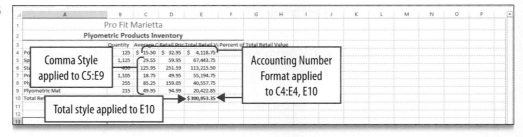

Activity 1.22 | Copying Formulas Containing Absolute Cell References

In a formula, a relative cell reference refers to a cell by its position *relative to* the cell that contains the formula. An ***absolute cell reference***, on the other hand, refers to a cell by its *fixed* position in the worksheet, for example, the total in cell E10.

A relative cell reference automatically adjusts when a formula is copied. In some calculations, you do *not* want the cell reference to adjust; rather, you want the cell reference to remain the same when the formula is copied.

1 ▸ Click cell **F4**, type **=** and then click cell **E4**. Type **/** and then click cell **E10**.

> The formula *=E4/E10* indicates that the value in cell E4 will be *divided* by the value in cell E10. Why? Because Mr. Feingold wants to know the percentage by which each product's Total Retail Value makes up the Total Retail Value for All Products.
>
> Arithmetically, the percentage is computed by dividing the *Total Retail Value* for each product by the *Total Retail Value for All Products*. The result will be a percentage expressed as a decimal.

2 ▸ Press Enter. Click cell **F4** and notice that the formula displays in the **Formula Bar**. Then, point to cell **F4** and double-click.

> The formula, with the two referenced cells displayed in color and bordered with the same color, displays in the cell. This feature, called the **range finder**, is useful for verifying formulas because it visually indicates which workbook cells are included in a formula calculation.

3 ▸ Press Enter to redisplay the result of the calculation in the cell, and notice that .013686, which is approximately 1% of the total retail value of the inventory, is made up of Power Hurdles.

4 ▸ Click cell **F4** again, and then drag the fill handle down through cell **F9**. Compare your screen with Figure 1.47.

> Each cell displays an error message—*#DIV/0!* and a green triangle in the upper left corner of each cell indicates that Excel detects an error.
>
> Like a grammar checker, Excel uses rules to check for formula errors and flags errors in this manner. Additionally, the Auto Fill Options button displays, from which you can select formatting options for the copied cells.

FIGURE 1.47

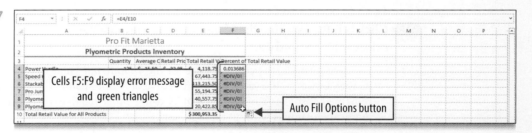

5 ▸ Click cell **F5**, and to the left of the cell, point to the **Error Checking** button ◈ ▾ to display its ScreenTip—*The formula or function used is dividing by zero or empty cells.*

> In this manner, Excel suggests the cause of an error.

6 ▸ Look at the **Formula Bar** and examine the formula.

> The formula is =E5/E11. The cell reference to E5 is correct, but the cell reference following the division operator (/) is *E11*, and E11 is an *empty* cell.

7 ▸ Click cell **F6**, point to the **Error Checking** button ◈ ▾, and in the **Formula Bar** examine the formula.

> Because the cell references are relative, Excel builds the formulas by increasing the row number for each equation. But in this calculation, the divisor must always be the value in cell E10—the *Total Retail Value for All Products.*

8 ▸ Point to cell **F4**, and then double-click to place the insertion point within the cell.

9 ▸ Within the cell, use the arrow keys as necessary to position the insertion point to the left of *E10*, and then press F4. Compare your screen with Figure 1.48.

> Dollar signs ($) display, which changes the reference to cell E10 to an absolute cell reference. The use of the dollar sign to denote an absolute reference is not related in any way to whether or not the values you are working with are currency values. It is simply the symbol that Excel uses to denote an absolute cell reference.

FIGURE 1.48

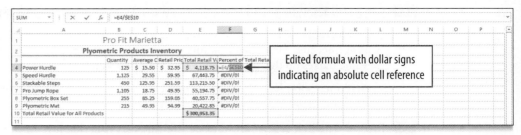

Edited formula with dollar signs indicating an absolute cell reference

ANOTHER WAY   Edit the formula so that it indicates =E4/$E$10.

10 On the **Formula Bar**, click **Enter** ✓ so that **F4** remains the active cell. Then, drag the fill handle to copy the new formula down through cell **F9**. Compare your screen with Figure 1.49.

FIGURE 1.49

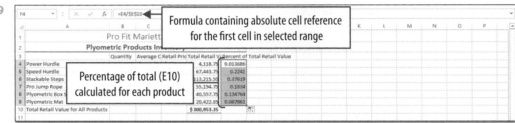

Formula containing absolute cell reference for the first cell in selected range

Percentage of total (E10) calculated for each product

11 Click cell **F5**, examine the formula in the **Formula Bar**, and then examine the formulas for cells **F6**, **F7**, **F8**, and **F9**.

For each formula, the cell reference for the *Total Retail Value* of each product changed relative to its row; however, the value used as the divisor—*Total Retail Value for All Products* in cell E10—remained absolute. You can see that by using either relative or absolute cell references, it is easy to duplicate formulas without typing them.

12 Save 💾 your workbook.

More Knowledge	**Calculate a Percentage if You Know the Total and the Amount**

Using the equation *amount/total = percentage*, you can calculate the percentage by which a part makes up a total—with the percentage formatted as a decimal. For example, if on a test you score 42 points correctly out of 50, your percentage of correct answers is 42/50 = 0.84 or 84%.

Objective 10   Edit Values in a Worksheet

Video E1-10

Excel performs calculations on numbers; that is why you use Excel. If you make changes to the numbers, Excel automatically *re*-calculates the results. This is one of the most powerful and valuable features of Excel.

Activity 1.23 | Editing Values in a Worksheet

You can edit text and number values directly within a cell or in the Formula Bar.

1 In cell **E10**, notice the column total *$300,953.35*. Then, click cell **B5**, and to change its value type **995** Watch cell **E5** and press ⎆Enter.

Excel formulas *re-calculate* if you change the value in a cell that is referenced in a formula. It is not necessary to delete the old value in a cell; selecting the cell and typing a new value replaces the old value with your new typing.

The *Total Retail Value* of all *Speed Hurdle* items recalculates to *59,650.25* and the total in cell E10 recalculates to *$293,159.85*. Additionally, all of the percentages in column F recalculate.

2 Point to cell **D8**, and then double-click to place the insertion point within the cell. Use the arrow keys to move the insertion point to left or right of 9, and use either ⎈Del or ⎈Backspace to delete 9 and then type **8** so that the new Retail Price is *158.05*.

3 Watch cell **E8** and **E10** as you press ⎆Enter, and then notice the recalculation of the formulas in those two cells.

Excel recalculates the value in cell E8 to *40,302.75* and the value in cell E10 to *$292,904.85*. Additionally, all of the percentages in column F recalculate because the *Total Retail Value for All Products* recalculated.

4 Point to cell **A2** so that the ⊕ pointer is positioned slightly to the right of the word *Inventory*, and then double-click to place the insertion point in the cell. Edit the text to add the word **Valuation** pressing ⎵Spacebar as necessary, and then press ⎆Enter.

5 Click cell **B3**, and then in the **Formula Bar**, click to place the insertion point after the letter *y*. Press ⎵Spacebar one time, type **in Stock** and then on the **Formula Bar**, click **Enter** ✓. Click **Save** 🖫, and then compare your screen with Figure 1.50.

Recall that if text is too long to fit in the cell and the cell to the right contains data, the text is truncated—cut off—but the entire value still exists as the underlying value.

FIGURE 1.50

Activity 1.24 | Formatting Cells with the Percent Style

A percentage is part of a whole expressed in hundredths. For example, 75 cents is the same as 75 percent of one dollar. The Percent Style button formats the selected cell as a percentage rounded to the nearest hundredth.

1 Click cell **F4**, and then in the **Number group**, click **Percent Style** %.

Your result is 1%, which is *0.014062* rounded to the nearest hundredth and expressed as a percentage. Percent Style displays the value of a cell as a percentage.

2 Select the range **F4:F9**, right-click over the selection, and then on the mini toolbar, click **Percent Style** %, click **Increase Decimal** two times, and then click **Center** ≡.

Percent Style may not offer a percentage precise enough to analyze important financial information—adding additional decimal places to a percentage makes data more precise.

3 Click any cell to cancel the selection, **Save** your workbook, and then compare your screen with Figure 1.51.

FIGURE 1.51

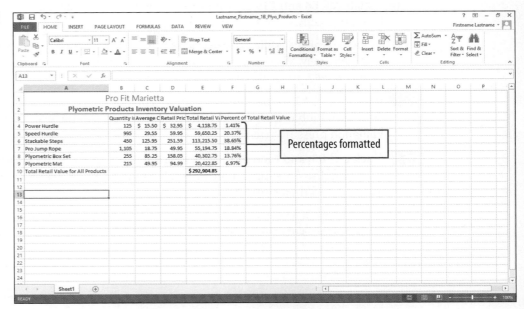

Objective 11 | Format a Worksheet

Video E1-11

Formatting refers to the process of specifying the appearance of cells and the overall layout of your worksheet. Formatting is accomplished through various commands on the ribbon, for example, applying Cell Styles, and also from commands on shortcut menus, using keyboard shortcuts, and in the Format Cells dialog box.

Activity 1.25 | Inserting and Deleting Rows and Columns

1 In the **row heading area** on the left side of your screen, point to the row heading for **row 3** to display the ➡ pointer, and then right-click to simultaneously select the row and display a shortcut menu.

2 On the shortcut menu, click **Insert** to insert a new **row 3** above the selected row.

The rows below the new row 3 move down one row, and the Insert Options button displays. By default, the new row uses the formatting of the row *above*.

 ANOTHER WAY   Select the row, on the Home tab, in the Cells group, click the Insert button arrow, and then click Insert Sheet Rows. Or, select the row and click the Insert button—the default setting of the button inserts a new sheet row above the selected row.

3 Click cell **E11**. On the **Formula Bar**, notice that the range changed to sum the new range **E5:E10**. Compare your screen with Figure 1.52.

If you move formulas by inserting additional rows or columns in your worksheet, Excel automatically adjusts the formulas. Excel adjusted all of the formulas in the worksheet that were affected by inserting this new row.

FIGURE 1.52

4 Click cell **A3**, type **As of September 30** and then on the **Formula Bar**, click **Enter** ☑ to maintain **A3** as the active cell. **Merge & Center** the text across the range **A3:F3**, and then apply the **Heading 2** cell style.

5 In the **column heading area**, point to **column B** to display the ⬇ pointer, right-click, and then click **Insert**.

A column is inserted to the left of column B. By default, the new column uses the formatting of the column to the *left*.

 ANOTHER WAY Select the column, on the Home tab, in the Cells group, click the Insert button arrow, and then click Insert Sheet Columns. Or, select the column and click the Insert button—the default setting of the button inserts a new sheet column to the right of the selected column.

6 Click cell **B4**, type **Warehouse Location** and then press Enter.

7 In cell **B5**, type **Atlanta** and then type **Atlanta** again in cells **B6** and **B10**. Use AutoComplete to speed your typing by pressing Enter as soon as the AutoComplete suggestion displays. In cells **B7**, **B8**, and **B9**, type **Marietta**

8 In the **column heading area**, point to **column D**, right-click, and then click **Delete**.

The remaining columns shift to the left, and Excel adjusts all the formulas in the worksheet accordingly. You can use a similar technique to delete a row in a worksheet.

9 Compare your screen with Figure 1.53, and then **Save** 🖫 your workbook.

FIGURE 1.53

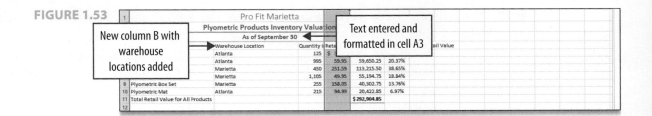

Hiding Rows and Columns

To hide a row or column from view, select the row or column, right-click, and then click Hide. A border displays to indicate that data is hidden from view. To unhide, select the rows above and below—or the adjacent columns—right-click, and then click Unhide.

Activity 1.26 | Adjusting Column Widths and Wrapping Text

Use the Wrap Text command to display the contents of a cell on multiple lines.

1 In the **column heading area**, point to the **column B** heading to display the ⬇ pointer, and then drag to the right to select **columns B:F**.

2 With the columns selected, in the **column heading area**, point to the right boundary of any of the selected columns to display the ⬌ pointer, and then drag to set the width to **95 pixels**.

Use this technique to format multiple columns or rows simultaneously.

3 Select the range **B4:F4** that comprises the column titles, and then on the **HOME tab**, in the **Alignment group**, click **Wrap Text** 📑. Notice that the row height adjusts to display the titles on multiple lines.

4 With the range **B4:F4** still selected, in the **Alignment group**, click **Center** ☰ and **Middle Align** ☰. With the range **B4:F4** still selected, apply the **Heading 4** cell style.

The Middle Align command aligns text so that it is centered between the top and bottom of the cell.

5 Select the range **B5:B10**, right-click, and then on the mini toolbar, click **Center** ☰. Click cell **A11**, and then from the **Cell Styles** gallery, under **Themed Cell Styles**, click **40% - Accent1**. **Save** 💾 your workbook.

Activity 1.27 | Changing Theme Colors

You can change only the Theme colors of a workbook—without changing the theme fonts or effects.

1 On the **PAGE LAYOUT tab**, in the **Themes group**, click the **Colors arrow**, and then click **Green** to change the theme color. Click any blank cell, and then compare your screen with Figure 1.54.

FIGURE 1.54

2 ▶ On the **PAGE LAYOUT tab**, in the **Page Setup group**, click **Margins**, and then click **Custom Margins**.

3 ▶ In the **Page Setup** dialog box, on the **Margins tab**, under **Center on page**, select the **Horizontally** check box.

> This action will center the data and chart horizontally on the page, as shown in the Preview area.

4 ▶ In the displayed **Page Setup** dialog box, click the **Header/Footer tab**, and then in the center of the dialog box, click **Custom Footer**. In the **Footer** dialog box, with your insertion point blinking in the **Left section**, on the row of buttons, click **Insert File Name** 📄.

> &[File] displays in the Left section. Here you can type or insert information from the row of buttons into the left, middle, or right section of the footer. The Custom Header button displays a similar screen to enter information in the header of the worksheet.

5 ▶ Click **OK** two times.

6 ▶ Click the **FILE tab** to display **Backstage** view, and then in the lower right corner, click **Show All Properties**.

7 ▶ As the **Tags**, type **plyo products, inventory** and as the **Subject**, type your course name and section number. Be sure your name displays as the author.

8 ▶ On the left, click **Print** to view the **Print Preview**. At the bottom of the **Print Preview**, click **Next Page** ▶, and notice that as currently formatted, the worksheet occupies two pages.

9 ▶ Under **Settings**, click **Portrait Orientation**, and then click **Landscape Orientation**. Compare your screen with Figure 1.55.

> You can change the orientation on the Page Layout tab, or here, in Print Preview. Because it is in the Print Preview that you will often see adjustments that need to be made, commonly used settings display on the Print tab in Backstage view.

FIGURE 1.55

10 By using the techniques you practiced in Project 1A, print or submit electronically as directed by your instructor. If required by your instructor, print or create an electronic version of your worksheet with formulas displayed.

11 Close your workbook and Close Excel.

END | You have completed Project 1B

Objective Calculate the Value of an Inventory in Excel Online

If you are working on a computer that does not have Microsoft Office installed, you can still create new workbooks in your web browser by using Excel Online.

ALERT! **Working with Web-Based Applications and Services**

Computer programs and services on the web receive continuous updates and improvements, so the steps to complete this web-based activity may differ from the ones shown. You can often look at the screens and the information presented to determine how to complete the activity.

Activity | **Creating an Inventory Valuation Report in Excel Online**

In this activity, you will use Excel Online to create an inventory valuation similar to the one you created in Project 1B.

1 From the desktop, start Internet Explorer. Navigate to **http://onedrive.com**, and then sign in to your Microsoft account. Open your **GO! Web Projects** folder—or create and then open this folder if necessary.

2 Near the top of the screen, click **Create**, and then click **Excel workbook**. Above the ribbon, click Book1 to select the text. Using your own name, as the file name type **Lastname_Firstname_EX_1B_Web** Click cell **1A**.

3 To help you create this project quickly and to eliminate extra typing, you will import the data from a Word table. From the taskbar, open **File Explorer**, navigate to the student data files that accompany this textbook, and then open the Word document **e01_1B_Web**. Press [Ctrl] + [A] to select all of the text, right-click anywhere over the selection, and then click **Copy**. **Close** Word and File Explorer.

4 With cell **A1** selected, on the Excel Online ribbon, in the **Clipboard group**, click the upper portion of the **Paste** button; if necessary click **Allow access**.

5 Select column headings **A:D**, point to the border between any two selected column headings to display the ⊹⊢ pointer, and then double-click to resize the selected columns to display all the data.

6 In cell **E3** type **Total Retail Value** and press [Enter]. Select the range **B3:E3**, and then in the **Alignment group**, click **Center** ≡, **Middle Align** ≡, and **Wrap Text** ≡. Widen **column E** so that *Total Retail* is on one line and *Value* is on the second line.

7 Click cell **E4** and type **=c4*d4** to create the formula and press [Enter]; your result is *4118.75*. Click cell **E4** again, and then drag the fill handle down through cell **E9** to calculate each row. Compare your screen with Figure A.

FIGURE A

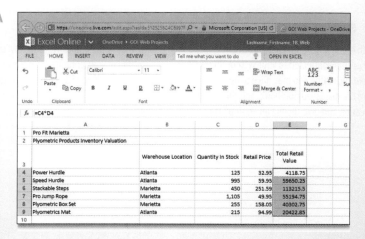

(GO! with Office Online (formerly Web Apps) continues on the next page)

8 Click cell **E10**, and then in the **Editing group**, click **AutoSum** and press Enter to total the column.

9 In cell **F3** type **Percent of Total Retail Value** and then apply **Center** ☰, **Middle Align** ☰, and **Wrap Text** ☲. Widen the column to display the column title on three lines. In cell **F4** type the formula to calculate the percent of total value **=e4/e10** and press Enter, and then copy the formula down through cell **F9**. With the range **F4:F9** still selected, from the **Number Format arrow**, click **Percentage**.

10 Select the range **E4:E10** and then from the **Number Format arrow**, apply **Currency** format. Click cell **E9**, and then in the **Font group**, click **Underline**. Click cell **E10**, and then in the **Font group**, click **Double Underline**.

11 Select the range **A1:F1**, and then in the **Alignment group**, click **Merge & Center**. Merge and center the worksheet's subtitle in the same manner. Select the range **A1:A2**, and then in the **Font group**, apply **Bold** B and change the **Font Color** A to **Orange, Darker 50%**.

12 Click cell **B3**, and then adjust the width of **column B** so that the column title displays on two lines. Click cell **C3** and adjust in the same manner.

13 In cell **A10** type **Total Retail Value for All Products** and then AutoFit **column A**.

14 Click cell **A1**, and then compare your screen with Figure B.

15 If you are instructed to submit your file, use one of the methods outlined in the Note box below. Recall that in Excel Online, there is no Save button because your workbook is being saved automatically. Sign out and close Internet Explorer.

FIGURE B

NOTE   **Printing or Creating an Electronic File from Excel Online**

To print on paper, click the FILE tab, click Print, click the Print button, and then click Print. In the Print Preview display, click Print. In the displayed Print dialog box, click Print to print on the printer connected to your system. To create an electronic file of your printout, from the Print dialog box, click the printer labeled *Send to OneNote 2013*, and then click Print. You may have to open and then close OneNote first if you have never opened it before. When OneNote opens, click the Quick Notes section of the displayed notebook, and then click OK. On the ribbon, click the FILE tab, click Export, and then create a PDF of the page. Navigate to an appropriate location and give the file an appropriate name. Close OneNote.

Andrew Rodriguez / Fotolia; FotolEdhar/ Fotolia; apops/ Fotolia; Yuri Arcurs/ Fotolia

In every job, you must work and communicate with other people. A group of workers tasked with working together to solve a problem, make a decision, or create a work product is referred to as a *team*. For a team to succeed, the team members must be able to communicate with one another easily.

If all the team members work at the same location and work the same hours, communication is easy. You schedule face-to-face meetings and exchange documents and information among yourselves. But that is a rare arrangement in today's organizations. Rather, it is more likely that the members of your team work in different locations—even different countries—and work different hours or travel extensively away from the headquarters location. Also, for specific projects, teams are frequently organized across different departments of an organization or even across different organizations entirely. Then when the project is complete, the team disbands.

Collaboration is when you work together with others as a team in an intellectual endeavor to complete a shared task or achieve a shared goal; for example, when you and one or more of your classmates work together on a class project. Collaboration involves giving feedback to and receiving feedback from others on the team, and then revising the strategies to achieve the goal or produce the work product based on the feedback.

Microsoft Office 365 is a set of secure online services that enable people in an organization to communicate and collaborate by using any Internet-connected device—a computer, a tablet, or a mobile phone. Because Office 365 offers access from anywhere to email, Web conferencing, documents, and calendars, everyone on a team can work together easily. Office 365 is intended for use by multiple users in an organization and is offered on a monthly subscription basis to organizations starting as low as $6 per month per user.

Activity | **Using the Exchange Online Outlook Meeting Tool to Collaborate**

This team project relates to the **Bell Orchid Hotels**. If your instructor assigns this project to your class, in this chapter you can expect to use the **Outlook Meeting tool** in **Office 365 Exchange Online** to collaborate on the following tasks for this chapter:

- If you are in the **Accounting Group**, you and your teammates will meet virtually to plan a workbook to summarize hotel rooms sold over a four-week period in April.

- If you are in the **Engineering Group**, you and your teammates will meet virtually to plan a workbook summarizing Maintenance Expenses for the first quarter.

- If you are in the **Food and Beverage Group**, you and your teammates will meet virtually to plan a Menu Analysis workbook to analyze the profitability of the ten most popular entrees in the hotel's restaurant.

- If you are in the **Human Resources Group**, you and your teammates will meet virtually to plan a Salary Analysis workbook summarizing the pay of salaried employees over the first six months of operation.

- If you are in the **Operations Group**, you and your teammates will meet virtually to plan a workbook for Rooms and Housekeeping Service Analysis that will be used to determine ongoing needs for housekeeping service.

- If you are in the **Sales and Marking Group**, you and your teammates will meet virtually to plan a Rooms Sold Analysis workbook summarizing rooms sold by four salespersons during January-June that will be used to develop a marketing plan for the rest of the year.

FIGURE A

END OF CHAPTER

SUMMARY

In Excel, you work with worksheets that are contained in a workbook. A worksheet is formatted as a pattern of uniformly spaced horizontal rows and vertical columns, the intersection of which forms a cell.

A cell can contain a constant value—referred to as a value—or a formula, which is an equation that performs mathematical calculations on the values in your worksheet. Common values are text and numbers.

You can insert sparklines in an Excel worksheet, which are tiny charts embedded in a cell that give a visual trend summary alongside your data. A sparkline makes a pattern more obvious to the eye.

Charts provide a graphic representation of data in a worksheet. Use the Recommended Charts feature to display customized charts that, according to Excel's calculations, will best represent your data.

GO! LEARN IT ONLINE

Review the concepts and key terms in this chapter by completing these online challenges, which you can find at **www.pearsonhighered.com/go**.

Matching and Multiple Choice:
Answer matching and multiple choice questions to test what you learned in this chapter. **MyITLab**

Crossword Puzzle:
Spell out the words that match the numbered clues, and put them in the puzzle squares.

Flipboard:
Flip through the definitions of the key terms in this chapter and match them with the correct term.

GO! FOR JOB SUCCESS

Video: Dress to Impress

Your instructor may assign this video to your class, and then ask you to think about, or discuss with your classmates, these questions:

FotolEdhar / Fotolia

If you were interviewing people for your company, what would you look for in terms of their dress and personal presentation?

What might you want to change about your personal dress for work or for an interview?

Do you feel that it's right to "judge a book by its cover"? Why or why not?

REVIEW AND ASSESSMENT GUIDE FOR EXCEL CHAPTER 1

Your instructor may assign one or more of these projects to help you review the chapter and assess your mastery and understanding of the chapter.

	Review and Assessment Guide for Excel Chapter 1		
Project	**Apply Skills from These Chapter Objectives**	**Project Type**	**Project Location**
1C	Objectives 1–6 from Project 1A	**1C Skills Review** A guided review of the skills from Project 1A.	On the following pages
1D	Objectives 7–11 from Project 1B	**1D Skills Review** A guided review of the skills from Project 1B.	On the following pages
1E	Objectives 1–6 from Project 1A	**1E Mastery (Grader Project)** A demonstration of your mastery of the skills in Project 2A with extensive decision making.	In MyITLab and on the following pages
1F	Objectives 7–11 from Project 1B	**1F Mastery (Grader Project)** A demonstration of your mastery of the skills in Project 1B with extensive decision making.	In MyITLab and on the following pages
1G	Objectives 1–11 from Projects 1A and 1B	**1G Mastery (Grader Project)** A demonstration of your mastery of the skills in Projects 1A and 1B with extensive decision making.	In MyITLab and on the following pages
1H	Combination of Objectives from Projects 1A and 1B	**1H GO! Fix It** A demonstration of your mastery of the skills in Projects 1A and 1B by creating a correct result from a document that contains errors you must find.	Online
1I	Combination of Objectives from Projects 1A and 1B	**1I GO! Make It** A demonstration of your mastery of the skills in Projects 1A and 1B by creating a result from a supplied picture.	Online
1J	Combination of Objectives from Projects 1A and 1B	**1J GO! Solve It** A demonstration of your mastery of the skills in Projects 1A and 1B, your decision-making skills, and your critical thinking skills. A task-specific rubric helps you self-assess your result.	Online
1K	Combination of Objectives from Projects 1A and 1B	**1K GO! Solve It** A demonstration of your mastery of the skills in Projects 1A and 1B, your decision-making skills, and your critical thinking skills. A task-specific rubric helps you self-assess your result.	On the following pages
1L	Combination of Objectives from Projects 1A and 1B	**1L GO! Think** A demonstration of your understanding of the chapter concepts applied in a manner that you would outside of college. An analytic rubric helps you and your instructor grade the quality of your work by comparing it to the work an expert in the discipline would create.	On the following pages
1M	Combination of Objectives from Projects 1A and 1B	**1M GO! Think** A demonstration of your understanding of the chapter concepts applied in a manner that you would outside of college. An analytic rubric helps you and your instructor grade the quality of your work by comparing it to the work an expert in the discipline would create.	Online
1N	Combination of Objectives from Projects 1A and 1B	**1N You and GO!** A demonstration of your understanding of the chapter concepts applied in a manner that you would in a personal situation. An analytic rubric helps you and your instructor grade the quality of your work.	Online
1O	Combination of Objectives from Projects 1A and 1B	**1O Cumulative Group Project for Excel Chapter 1** A demonstration of your understanding of concepts and your ability to work collaboratively in a group role-playing assessment, requiring both collaboration and self-management.	Online

GLOSSARY

GLOSSARY OF CHAPTER KEY TERMS

Absolute cell reference A cell reference that refers to cells by their fixed position in a worksheet; an absolute cell reference remains the same when the formula is copied.

Accounting Number Format The Excel number format that applies a thousand comma separator where appropriate, inserts a fixed U.S. dollar sign aligned at the left edge of the cell, applies two decimal places, and leaves a small amount of space at the right edge of the cell to accommodate a parenthesis for negative numbers.

Active cell The cell, surrounded by a black border, ready to receive data or be affected by the next Excel command.

Arithmetic operators The symbols +, −, *, /, %, and ^ used to denote addition, subtraction (or negation), multiplication, division, percentage, and exponentiation in an Excel formula.

Auto Fill An Excel feature that generates and extends values into adjacent cells based on the values of selected cells.

AutoCalculate A feature that displays three calculations in the status bar by default— Average, Count, and Sum—when you select a range of numerical data.

AutoComplete A feature that speeds your typing and lessens the likelihood of errors; if the first few characters you type in a cell match an existing entry in the column, Excel fills in the remaining characters for you.

AutoFit An Excel feature that adjusts the width of a column to fit the cell content of the widest cell in the column.

AutoSum A button that provides quick access to the SUM function.

Category axis The area along the bottom of a chart that identifies the categories of data; also referred to as the x-axis.

Category labels The labels that display along the bottom of a chart to identify the categories of data; Excel uses the row titles as the category names.

Cell The intersection of a column and a row.

Cell address Another name for a cell reference.

Cell content Anything typed into a cell.

Cell reference The identification of a specific cell by its intersecting column letter and row number.

Cell style A defined set of formatting characteristics, such as font, font size, font color, cell borders, and cell shading.

Chart The graphic representation of data in a worksheet; data presented as a chart is usually easier to understand than a table of numbers.

Chart Elements button A button that enables you to add, remove, or change chart elements such as the title, legend, gridlines, and data labels.

Chart Filters button A button that enables you to change which data displays in the chart.

Chart layout The combination of chart elements that can be displayed in a chart such as a title, legend, labels for the columns, and the table of charted cells.

Chart style The overall visual look of a chart in terms of its graphic effects, colors, and backgrounds; for example, you can have flat or beveled columns, colors that are solid or transparent, and backgrounds that are dark or light.

Chart Styles button A button that enables you to set a style and color scheme for your chart.

Chart Styles gallery A group of predesigned chart styles that you can apply to an Excel chart.

Chart types Various chart formats used in a way that is meaningful to the reader; common examples are column charts, pie charts, and line charts.

Column A vertical group of cells in a worksheet.

Column chart A chart in which the data is arranged in columns and that is useful for showing how data changes over a period of time or for illustrating comparisons among items.

Column heading The letter that displays at the top of a vertical group of cells in a worksheet; beginning with the first letter of the alphabet, a unique letter or combination of letters identifies each column.

Comma Style The Excel number format that inserts thousand comma separators where appropriate and applies two decimal places; Comma Style also leaves space at the right to accommodate a parenthesis when negative numbers are present.

Constant value Numbers, text, dates, or times of day that you type into a cell.

Context sensitive A command associated with the currently selected or active object; often activated by right-clicking a screen item.

Data Text or numbers in a cell.

Data marker A column, bar, area, dot, pie slice, or other symbol in a chart that represents a single data point; related data points form a data series.

Data point A value that originates in a worksheet cell and that is represented in a chart by a data marker.

Data series Related data points represented by data markers; each data series has a unique color or pattern represented in the chart legend.

Displayed value The data that displays in a cell.

Excel pointer An Excel window element with which you can display the location of the pointer.

Expand Formula Bar button An Excel window element with which you can increase the height of the Formula Bar to display lengthy cell content.

Expand horizontal scroll bar button An Excel window element with which you can increase the width of the horizontal scroll bar.

Fill handle The small black square in the lower right corner of a selected cell.

Format Changing the appearance of cells and worksheet elements to make a worksheet attractive and easy to read.

Formula An equation that performs mathematical calculations on values in a worksheet.

Formula Bar An element in the Excel window that displays the value or formula contained in the active cell; here you can also enter or edit values or formulas.

Function A predefined formula—a formula that Excel has already built for you—that performs calculations by using specific values in a particular order.

General format The default format that Excel applies to numbers; this format has no specific characteristics—whatever you type in the cell will display, with the exception that trailing zeros to the right of a decimal point will not display.

Label Another name for a text value, and which usually provides information about number values.

Left alignment The cell format in which characters align at the left edge of the cell; this is the default for text entries and is an example of formatting information stored in a cell.

Legend A chart element that identifies the patterns or colors that are assigned to the categories in the chart.

Lettered column headings The area along the top edge of a worksheet that identifies each column with a unique letter or combination of letters.

Merge & Center A command that joins selected cells in an Excel worksheet into one larger cell and centers the contents in the merged cell.

Name Box An element of the Excel window that displays the name of the selected cell, table, chart, or object.

Normal view A screen view that maximizes the number of cells visible on your screen and keeps the column letters and row numbers close to the columns and rows.

Number format A specific way in which Excel displays numbers in a cell.

Number values Constant values consisting of only numbers.

Numbered row headings The area along the left edge of a worksheet that identifies each row with a unique number.

Operators The symbols with which you can specify the type of calculation you want to perform in an Excel formula.

Page Layout view A screen view in which you can use the rulers to measure the width and height of data, set margins for printing, hide or display the numbered row headings and the lettered column headings, and change the page orientation; this view is useful for preparing your worksheet for printing.

Picture element A point of light measured in dots per square inch on a screen; 64 pixels equals 8.43 characters, which is the average number of characters that will fit in a cell in an Excel worksheet using the default font.

Pixel The abbreviated name for a picture element.

Point and click method The technique of constructing a formula by pointing to and then clicking cells; this method

is convenient when the referenced cells are not adjacent to one another.

Quick Analysis tool A tool that displays in the lower right corner of a selected range with which you can analyze your data by using Excel tools such as charts, color-coding, and formulas.

Range Two or more selected cells on a worksheet that are adjacent or nonadjacent; because the range is treated as a single unit, you can make the same changes or combination of changes to more than one cell at a time.

Range finder An Excel feature that outlines cells in color to indicate which cells are used in a formula; useful for verifying which cells are referenced in a formula.

Recommended Charts An Excel feature that displays a customized set of charts that, according to Excel's calculations, will best fit your data based on the range of data that you select.

Relative cell reference In a formula, the address of a cell based on the relative positions of the cell that contains the formula and the cell referred to in the formula.

Rounding A procedure in which you determine which digit at the right of the number will be the last digit displayed and then increase it by one if the next digit to its right is 5, 6, 7, 8, or 9.

Row A horizontal group of cells in a worksheet.

Row heading The numbers along the left side of an Excel worksheet that designate the row numbers.

Scaling The process of shrinking the width and/or height of printed output to fit a maximum number of pages.

Select All box A box in the upper left corner of the worksheet grid that, when clicked, selects all the cells in a worksheet.

Series A group of things that come one after another in succession; for example, January, February, March, and so on.

Sheet tab scrolling buttons Buttons to the left of the sheet tabs used to display Excel sheet tabs that are not in view; used when there are more sheet tabs than will display in the space provided.

Sheet tabs The labels along the lower border of the Excel window that identify each worksheet.

Show Formulas A command that displays the formula in each cell instead of the resulting value.

Sparkline A tiny chart in the background of a cell that gives a visual trend summary alongside your data; makes a pattern more obvious.

Spreadsheet Another name for a worksheet.

Status bar The area along the lower edge of the Excel window that displays, on the left side, the current cell mode, page number, and worksheet information; on the right side, when numerical data is selected, common calculations such as Sum and Average display.

SUM function A predefined formula that adds all the numbers in a selected range of cells.

Switch Row/Column A charting command to swap the data over the axis—data being charted on the vertical axis will move to the horizontal axis and vice versa.

Text values Constant values consisting of only text, and which usually provide information about number values; also referred to as labels.

Theme A predefined set of colors, fonts, lines, and fill effects that coordinate with each other.

Underlying formula The formula entered in a cell and visible only on the Formula Bar.

Underlying value The data that displays in the Formula Bar.

Value Another name for a constant value.

Value axis A numerical scale on the left side of a chart that shows the range of numbers for the data points; also referred to as the Y-axis.

Workbook An Excel file that contains one or more worksheets.

Workbook-level buttons Buttons at the far right of the ribbon tabs that minimize or restore a displayed workbook.

Worksheet The primary document that you use in Excel to work with and store data, and which is formatted as a pattern of uniformly spaced horizontal and vertical lines.

Worksheet grid area A part of the Excel window that displays the columns and rows that intersect to form the worksheet's cells.

X-axis Another name for the horizontal (category) axis.

Y-axis Another name for the vertical (value) axis.

CHAPTER REVIEW

Apply 1A skills from these Objectives:

1 Create, Save, and Navigate an Excel Workbook

2 Enter Data in a Worksheet

3 Construct and Copy Formulas and Use the SUM Function

4 Format Cells with Merge & Center, Cell Styles, and Themes

5 Chart Data to Create a Column Chart and Insert Sparklines

6 Print a Worksheet, Display Formulas, and Close Excel

Build from Scratch

In the following Skills Review, you will create a new Excel worksheet with a chart that summarizes the first quarter sales of fitness equipment for step training. Your completed worksheet will look similar to Figure 1.56.

PROJECT FILES

For Project 1C, you will need the following file:

New blank Excel workbook

You will save your workbook as:

Lastname_Firstname_1C_Step_Sales

PROJECT RESULTS

FIGURE 1.56

(Project 1C Step Sales continues on the next page)

CHAPTER REVIEW

1 **Start** Excel and open a new blank workbook. Click the **FILE tab** to display **Backstage** view, click **Save As**, and then navigate to your **Excel Chapter 1** folder. In the **File name** box, using your own name, type **Lastname_Firstname_1C_Step_Sales** and then press Enter.

a. With cell **A1** as the active cell, type the worksheet title **Pro Fit Marietta** and then press Enter. In cell **A2**, type the worksheet subtitle **First Quarter Step Sales** and then press Enter.

b. Leave row 3 blank, click in cell **A4**, type **Basic Step Box** and then press Enter. In cell **A5**, type **Step Storage Box** and then press Enter. In cell **A6**, type **Stackable Steps** and then press Enter. In cell **A7**, type **Step Mats** and then press Enter. In cell **A8**, type **Total** and then press Enter.

c. Click cell **B3**. Type **January** and then in the **Formula Bar**, click **Enter** to keep cell **B3** the active cell. With **B3** as the active cell, point to the **fill handle** in the lower right corner of the selected cell, drag to the right to cell **D3**, and then release the mouse button to enter the text *February* and *March*.

d. Press Ctrl + Home to make cell **A1** the active cell. In the **column heading area**, point to the vertical line between **column A** and **column B** to display the ⊞ pointer, hold down the left mouse button, and drag to the right to increase the column width to **130 pixels**.

e. Point to cell **B3**, and then drag across to select cells **B3** and **C3** and **D3**. With the range **B3:D3** selected, point anywhere over the selected range, right-click, and then on the mini toolbar, click **Center**.

f. Click cell **B4**, type **75826.99** and press Tab to make cell **C4** active. Enter the remaining values, as shown below in **Table 1**, pressing Tab to move across the rows and Enter to move down the columns.

TABLE 1

	January	February	March
Basic Step Box	75826.99	81657.32	72431.22
Step Storage Rack	85245.90	92618.95	88337.68
Stackable Steps	68751.64	71997.48	78951.23
Step Mats	63255.10	58742.67	67995.20

2 Click cell **B8** to make it the active cell and type =

a. At the insertion point, type **b4** and then type **+** Type **b5** and then type **+b6+b7** Press Enter. Your result is *293079.6*.

b. Click in cell **C8**. Type **=** and then click cell **C4**. Type **+** and then click cell **C5**. Repeat this process to complete the formula to add cells **C6** and **C7** to the formula, and then press Enter. Your result is *305016.4*.

c. Click cell **D8**. On the **HOME tab**, in the **Editing group**, click **AutoSum**, and then press Enter to construct a formula by using the SUM function. Your result is *307715.3*.

d. In cell **E3** type **Total** and press Enter. With cell **E4** as the active cell, hold down Alt, and then press =. On the **Formula Bar**, click **Enter** to display the result and keep cell **E4** active.

e. With cell **E4** active, point to the **fill handle** in the lower right corner of the cell. Drag down through cell **E8**, and then release the mouse button to copy the formula with relative cell references down to sum each row.

3 Click cell **F3**. Type **Trend** and then press Enter.

a. Select the range **A1:F1**, and then on the **HOME tab**, in the **Alignment group**, click **Merge & Center**. Select the range **A2:F2** and **Merge & Center** the selection.

b. Click cell **A1**. In the **Styles group**, click **Cell Styles**. Under **Titles and Headings**, click **Title**. Click cell **A2**, display the **Cell Styles** gallery, and then click **Heading 1**.

c. Select the range **B3:F3**, hold down Ctrl, and then select the range **A4:A8**. From the **Cell Styles** gallery, click **Heading 4** to apply this cell style to the column and row titles.

d. Select the range **B4:E4**, hold down Ctrl, and then select the range **B8:E8**. On the **HOME tab**, in the **Number group**, click **Accounting Number Format**. Select the range **B5:E7**, and then in the **Number group**, click **Comma Style**. Select the range **B8:E8**. From the **Styles group**, display the **Cell Styles** gallery, and then under **Titles and Headings**, click **Total**.

e. On the ribbon, click the **PAGE LAYOUT tab**, and then in the **Themes group**, click **Themes** to display the **Themes** gallery. Click the **Basis** theme. (This theme widens the columns slightly). On the **Quick Access Toolbar**, click **Save**.

(Project 1C Step Sales continues on the next page)

CHAPTER REVIEW

4 Select the range **A3:D7**, which includes the row titles, the column titles and the data without the totals. Click the **INSERT tab**, and then in the **Charts group**, click **Recommended Charts**. In the **Insert Chart** dialog box, scroll down and click the fifth recommended chart—a **Clustered Column** chart in which *each month* displays its *sales for each type of step training equipment*. Click **OK**.

   a. In the chart, click anywhere in the text *Chart Title* to select the text box. Watch the **Formula Bar** as you type **First** and then let AutoComplete complete the title by pressing Enter.

   b. Click in a white area just slightly *inside* the chart border to deselect the chart title but keep the chart selected. To the right of the chart, click the second button—the **Chart Styles** button. Be sure the **STYLE** tab is selected. Use the scroll bar to scroll down, and then by using the ScreenTips, locate and click **Style 6**.

   c. At the top of the gallery, click **COLOR**. Under **Colorful**, point to the fourth row of colors to display the ScreenTip *Color 4*, and then click to apply the **Color 4** variation of the theme colors.

   d. Point to the top border of the chart to display the pointer, and then drag the upper left corner of the chart just to the center of cell **A10** to visually center it below the data.

5 Select the range **B4:D7**. Click the **INSERT tab**, and then in the **Sparklines group**, click **Line**. In the **Create Sparklines** dialog box, in the **Location Range** box, type **f4:f7** and then click **OK** to insert the sparklines.

   a. On the **DESIGN tab**, in the **Show group**, select the **Markers** check box to display markers in the sparklines.

   b. On the **DESIGN tab**, in the **Style group**, click **More** and then in the second row, click the fourth style—**Sparkline Style Accent 4, Darker 25%**.

6 Click cell **A1** to deselect the chart. Click the **PAGE LAYOUT tab**, and then in the **Page Setup group**, click **Margins**. At the bottom, click **Custom Margins** to display the **Page Setup** dialog box, and then on the **Margins tab**, under **Center on page**, select the **Horizontally** check box.

   a. In the dialog box, click the **Header/Footer tab**, and then click **Custom Footer**. With your insertion point in the **Left section**, click **Insert File Name**. Click **OK** two times.

   b. Click the **FILE tab** to display **Backstage** view. In the lower right corner, click **Show All Properties**. As the **Tags**, type **step sales, 1st quarter** In the **Subject** box, type your course name and section number. Be sure your name displays as the Author—edit if necessary.

   c. On the left, click **Save**.

   d. Print or submit your workbook electronically as directed by your instructor. If required by your instructor, print or create an electronic version of your worksheet with formulas displayed by using the instructions in Project 1A. **Close** Excel without saving so that you do not save the changes you made to print formulas.

END | You have completed Project 1C

CHAPTER REVIEW

Skills Review Project 1D Band and Tubing Inventory

In the following Skills Review, you will create a worksheet that summarizes the inventory of band and tubing exercise equipment. Your completed worksheet will look similar to Figure 1.57.

PROJECT FILES

For Project 1D, you will need the following file:

New blank Excel workbook

You will save your workbook as:

Lastname_Firstname_1D_Band_Inventory

Build from Scratch

PROJECT RESULTS

Pro Fit Marietta
Band and Tubing Inventory
As of June 30

	Material	Quantity in Stock	Retail Price	Total Retail Value	Percent of Total Retail Value
Super Strength Bands	Latex	225	$ 48.98	$ 11,020.50	25.16%
Medium Tubing	Rubber	198	27.95	5,534.10	12.64%
Resistance Band, Average	Latex	165	42.95	7,086.75	16.18%
Mini Bands, Medium	Latex	245	25.95	6,357.75	14.52%
Mini Bands, Heavy	Rubber	175	32.95	5,766.25	13.17%
Heavy Tubing	Latex	187	42.95	8,031.65	18.34%
Total Retail Value for All Products				$ 43,797.00	

Lastname_Firstname_1D_Band_Inventory

FIGURE 1.57

(Project 1D Band and Tubing Inventory continues on the next page)

CHAPTER REVIEW

1 **Start** Excel and display a new blank workbook. **Save** the workbook in your **Excel Chapter 1** folder as **Lastname_Firstname_1D_Band_Inventory** In cell **A1** type **Pro Fit Marietta** and in cell **A2** type **Band and Tubing Inventory**

a. Click cell **B3**, type **Quantity in Stock** and press [Tab]. In cell **C3** type **Average Cost** and press [Tab]. In cell **D3**, type **Retail Price** and press [Tab]. In cell **E3**, type **Total Retail Value** and press [Tab]. In cell **F3** type **Percent of Total Retail Value** and press [Enter].

b. Click cell **A4**, type **Super Strength Bands** and press [Enter]. In the range **A5:A10**, type the remaining row titles as shown below, including any misspelled words.

   Medium Tubing

   Resistnce Band, Average

   Mini Bands, Medium

   Mini Bands, Heavy

   Heavy Tubing

   Total Retail Value for All Products

c. Press [Ctrl] + [Home] to move to the top of your worksheet. On the **REVIEW tab**, in the **Proofing group**, click **Spelling**. Correct *Resistnce* to **Resistance** and any other spelling errors you may have made, and then when the message displays, *Spell check complete. You're good to go!* click **OK**.

d. In the **column heading area**, point to the right boundary of **column A** to display the [+] pointer, and then drag to the right to widen **column A** to **225 pixels**.

e. In the **column heading area**, point to the **column B** heading to display the [↓] pointer, and then drag to the right to select **columns B:F**. With the columns selected, in the **column heading area**, point to the right boundary of any of the selected columns, and then drag to the right to set the width to **100 pixels**.

f. Select the range **A1:F1**. On the **HOME tab**, in the **Alignment group**, click **Merge & Center**, and then in the **Cell Styles** gallery, apply the **Title** style. Select the range **A2:F2**. **Merge & Center** the text across the selection, and then in the **Cell Styles** gallery, apply the **Heading 1** style.

2 On the **PAGE LAYOUT tab**, in the **Themes group**, change the **Colors** to **Blue Green**. Select the empty range **B4:D9**. With cell **B4** active in the range, type **225** and then press [Enter].

a. With cell **B5** active in the range, and pressing [Enter] after each entry, type the following data in the *Quantity in Stock* column:

   198
   265
   245
   175
   187

b. With the selected range still active, from the following table, beginning in cell **C4** and pressing [Enter] after each entry, enter the following data for the **Average Cost** column and then the **Retail Price** column. If you prefer, type without selecting the range first; recall that this is optional.

Average Cost	Retail Price
22.75	48.98
15.95	27.95
26.90	42.95
12.95	25.95
18.75	32.95
26.90	42.95

3 In cell **E4**, type **=b4*d4** and then press [Enter] to construct a formula that calculates the *Total Retail Value* of the *Super Strength Bands* (Quantity in Stock × Retail Price).

a. Click cell **E4**, position your pointer over the fill handle, and then drag down through cell **E9** to copy the formula with relative cell references.

b. Select the range **B4:B9**, and then on the **HOME tab**, in the **Number group**, click **Comma Style**. Then, in the **Number group**, click **Decrease Decimal** two times to remove the decimal places from these non-currency values.

c. To calculate the *Total Retail Value for All Products*, select the range **E4:E9**, and then in the lower right corner of the selected range, click the **Quick Analysis** button [📊].

(Project 1D Band and Tubing Inventory continues on the next page)

CHAPTER REVIEW

d. In the gallery, click **TOTALS**, and then click the *first* **Sum** button, which visually indicates that the column will be summed with a result at the bottom of the column.

e. Select the range **C5:E9** and apply the **Comma Style**. Select the range **C4:E4**, hold down Ctrl, and then click cell **E10**. With the nonadjacent cells selected, apply the **Accounting Number Format**. Click cell **E10**, and then from the **Cell Styles** gallery, apply the **Total** style.

f. Click cell **F4**, type = and then click cell **E4**. Type / and then click cell **E10**. Press F4 to make the reference to cell *E10* absolute, and then on the **Formula Bar**, click ✓ so that cell **F4** remains the active cell. Drag the **fill handle** to copy the formula down through cell **F9**.

g. Point to cell **B6**, and then double-click to place the insertion point within the cell. Use the arrow keys to move the insertion point to the left or right of *2*, and use either Delete or Backspace to delete *2*, and then type **1** and press Enter so that the new *Quantity in Stock* is *165*. Notice the recalculations in the worksheet.

4 Select the range **F4:F9**, right-click over the selection, and then on the mini toolbar, click **Percent Style**. Click **Increase Decimal** two times, and then **Center** the selection.

a. In the **row heading area** on the left side of your screen, point to **row 3** to display the ➡ pointer, and then right-click to simultaneously select the row and display a shortcut menu. On the shortcut menu, click **Insert** to insert a new **row 3**.

b. Click cell **A3**, type **As of June 30** and then on the **Formula Bar**, click ✓ to keep cell **A3** as the active cell. **Merge & Center** the text across the range **A3:F3**, and then apply the **Heading 2** cell style.

5 In the **column heading area**, point to **column B**. When the ⬇ pointer displays, right-click, and then click **Insert** to insert a new column.

a. Click cell **B4**, type **Material** and then press Enter. In cell **B5**, type **Latex** and then press Enter. In cell **B6**, type **Rubber** and then press Enter.

b. Using AutoComplete to speed your typing by pressing Enter as soon as the AutoComplete suggestion displays, in cells **B7**, **B8**, and **B10** type **Latex** and in cell **B9** type **Rubber**

c. In the **column heading area**, point to the right boundary of **column B**, and then drag to the left and set the width to **90 pixels**. In the **column heading area**, point to **column D**, right-click, and then click **Delete**.

d. Select the column titles in the range **B4:F4**, and then on the **HOME tab**, in the **Alignment group**, click **Wrap Text**, **Center**, and **Middle Align**. With the range still selected, apply the **Heading 4** cell style.

e. Click cell **A11**, and then in the **Cell Styles** gallery, under **Themed Cell Styles**, click **40% - Accent1**.

6 Click the **PAGE LAYOUT tab**, in the **Page Setup group**, click **Margins**, and then click **Custom Margins**. In the **Page Setup** dialog box, on the **Margins tab**, under **Center on page**, select the **Horizontally** check box.

a. Click the **Header/Footer tab**, and then click **Custom Footer**. With your insertion point in the **Left section**, click **Insert File Name**. Click **OK** two times.

b. In the **Page Setup group**, click **Orientation**, and then click **Landscape**.

c. Click the **FILE tab** to display **Backstage** view. In the lower right corner, click **Show All Properties**. As the **Tags**, type **bands, tubing, inventory** In the **Subject** box, type your course name and section number. Be sure your name displays as the author—edit if necessary.

d. On the left, click **Save** to be sure that you have saved your work up to this point.

e. Print or submit your workbook electronically as directed by your instructor. If required by your instructor, print or create an electronic version of your worksheet with formulas displayed by using the instructions in Project 1A. **Close** Excel without saving so that you do not save the changes you made to print formulas.

END | You have completed Project 1D

CONTENT-BASED ASSESSMENTS

Mastering Excel   Project 1E Gym Sales

In the following Mastering Excel project, you will create a worksheet comparing the sales of different types of home gym equipment sold in the second quarter. Your completed worksheet will look similar to Figure 1.58.

Apply 1A skills from these Objectives:

1 Create, Save, and Navigate an Excel Workbook

2 Enter Data in a Worksheet

3 Construct and Copy Formulas and Use the SUM Function

4 Format Cells with Merge & Center, Cell Styles, and Themes

5 Chart Data to Create a Column Chart and Insert Sparklines

6 Print a Worksheet, Display Formulas, and Close Excel

PROJECT FILES

For Project 1E, you will need the following files:

New blank Excel workbook

You will save your workbook as:

Lastname_Firstname_1E_Gym_Sales

PROJECT RESULTS

Build from Scratch

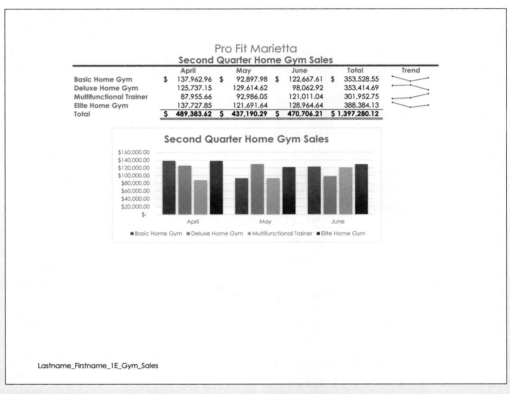

FIGURE 1.58

(Project 1E Gym Sales continues on the next page)

CONTENT-BASED ASSESSMENTS

1 Start Excel and display a new blank workbook. In cell **A1**, type **Pro Fit Marietta** and in cell **A2**, type **Second Quarter Home Gym Sales** Change the **Theme** to **Wisp**, and then **Save** the workbook in your **Excel Chapter 1** folder as **Lastname_Firstname_1E_Gym_Sales**

2 In cell **B3**, type **April** and then fill the months *May* and *June* in the range **C3:D3**. In cell **E3**, type **Total** and in cell **F3**, type **Trend**

3 Center the column titles in the range **B3:F3**. **Merge & Center** the title across the range **A1:F1**, and apply the **Title** cell style. **Merge & Center** the subtitle across the range **A2:F2**, and then apply the **Heading 1** cell style.

4 Widen **column A to 180 pixels**, and then in the range **A4:A8**, type the following row titles:

Basic Home Gym

Deluxe Home Gym

Multifunctional Trainer

Elite Home Gym

Total

5 Widen columns **B:F** to **115 pixels**, and then in the range **B4:D7**, enter the monthly sales figures for each type of gym, as shown in the table below:

	April	May	June
Basic Home Gym	137962.96	92897.98	122667.61
Deluxe Home Gym	125737.15	129614.62	98062.92
Multifunctional Trainer	87955.66	92986.05	121011.04
Elite Home Gym	137727.85	121691.64	128964.64

6 Select the range that represents April sales, and then on the **HOME tab**, in the **Editing group**, click **AutoSum**. Copy the formula across to cells **C8:D8**. Select the range that represents the sales of the *Basic Home Gym*, and then on the **HOME tab**, in the **Editing group**, click **AutoSum**. Copy the formula down to cells **E5:E8**.

7 Apply the **Heading 4** cell style to the row titles and the column titles. Apply the **Total** cell style to the totals in the range **B8:E8**. Apply the **Accounting Number Format** to the first row of sales figures and to the total row. Apply the **Comma Style** to the remaining sales figures.

8 To compare the monthly sales of each product visually, select the range that represents the sales figures for the three months, including the month names and the product names—do not include any totals in the range. With this data selected, use **Recommended Charts** to insert a **Clustered Column** chart with the month names displayed on the category axis and the product names displayed in the legend.

9 Drag the center right sizing handle to widen the chart slightly so that all the legend items display on one line, and then position the chart so that it is visually centered below the data with its top edge aligned with the top edge of row 10 approximately as shown in Figure 1.58. Apply **Chart Style 6** and **Color 2** under **Colorful**. Change the **Chart Title** to **Second Quarter Home Gym Sales**

10 In the range **F4:F7**, insert **Line** sparklines that compare the monthly data. Do not include the totals. Show the sparkline **Markers** and apply **Sparkline Style Accent 2, Darker 50%**.

11 Center the worksheet **Horizontally** on the page, and then insert a **Footer** with the **File Name** in the **Left section**. Change the **Orientation** to **Landscape**. Display the document properties, and then as the **Tags** type **home gym, sales** As the **Subject**, type your course name and section number. Be sure your name displays as the author. Check your worksheet by previewing it in **Print Preview**, and then make any necessary corrections.

12 Save your workbook, and then print or submit electronically as directed. If required by your instructor, print or create an electronic version of your worksheet with formulas displayed by using the instructions in Project 1A. **Close** Excel without saving so that you do not save the changes you made to print formulas.

END | You have completed Project 1E

CONTENT-BASED ASSESSMENTS

In the following Mastering Excel project, you will create a worksheet that summarizes the sales of balance and stabilization equipment that Pro Fit Marietta is marketing. Your completed worksheet will look similar to Figure 1.59.

Apply 1B skills from these Objectives:

7 Check Spelling in a Worksheet

8 Enter Data by Range

9 Construct Formulas for Mathematical Operations

10 Edit Values in a Worksheet

11 Format a Worksheet

PROJECT FILES

For Project 1F, you will need the following file:

New blank Excel workbook

You will save your workbook as:

Lastname_Firstname_1F_Balance_Sales

PROJECT RESULTS

Build from Scratch

Pro Fit Marietta
Balance and Stabilization Sales

Month Ending March 31				
	Quantity Sold	Retail Price	Total Sales	Percent of Total Sales
Balance Pillow	275	$ 22.95	$ 6,311.25	5.43%
Slide Board	382	75.50	28,841.00	24.82%
Foam Roller	251	39.50	9,914.50	8.53%
Rebounder	162	139.95	22,671.90	19.51%
Stability Ball	380	51.50	19,570.00	16.84%
Balance Board	206	84.95	17,499.70	15.06%
Balance Pad	150	75.99	11,398.50	9.81%
Total Sales for All Products			$ 116,206.85	

Lastname_Firstname_1F_Balance_Sales

FIGURE 1.59

(Project 1F Balance Sales continues on the next page)

CONTENT-BASED ASSESSMENTS

1 Start Excel and display a new blank workbook. **Save** the workbook in your **Excel Chapter 1** folder as **Lastname_Firstname_1F_Balance_Sales** In cell **A1**, type **Pro Fit Marietta** In cell **A2**, type **Balance and Stabilization Sales** and then **Merge & Center** the title and the subtitle across **columns A:F**. Apply the **Title** and **Heading 1** cell styles respectively.

2 Beginning in cell **B3**, type the following column titles: **Product Number** and **Quantity Sold** and **Retail Price** and **Total Sales** and **Percent of Total Sales**

3 Beginning in cell **A4**, type the following row titles, including misspelled words:

Balance Pillow
Silde Board
Foam Roller
Rebounder
Stability Ball
Balance Board
Balance Pad
Total Sales for All Products

4 Make cell **A1** the active cell, and then check spelling in your worksheet. Correct *Silde* to **Slide**, and make any other necessary corrections. Widen **column A** to **180 pixels** and **columns B:F** to **95 pixels**.

5 In the range **B4:D10**, type the following data:

	Product Number	Quantity Sold	Retail Price
Balance Pillow	BP-3	275	22.95
Slide Board	SB-8	382	99.95
Foam Roller	FR-2	251	39.50
Rebounder	RB-4	162	139.95
Stability Ball	SB-5	380	51.50
Balance Board	BB-6	206	84.95
Balance Pad	BP-8	220	75.99

6 In cell **E4**, construct a formula to calculate the *Total Sales* of the *Balance Pillow* by multiplying the *Quantity Sold* times the *Retail Price*. Copy the formula down for the remaining products. Select the range **E4:E10**, and then use the **Quick Analysis tool** to **Sum** the *Total Sales for All Products*, which will be formatted in **Bold**. To the total in cell **E11**, apply the **Total** cell style.

7 Using absolute cell references as necessary so that you can copy the formula, in cell **F4**, construct a formula to calculate the *Percent of Total Sales* for the first product. Copy the formula down for the remaining products. To the computed percentages, apply **Percent Style** with two decimal places, and then **Center** the percentages.

8 Apply the **Comma Style** with no decimal places to the *Quantity Sold* figures. To cells **D4**, **E4**, and **E11** apply the **Accounting Number Format**. To the range **D5:E10**, apply the **Comma Style**.

9 Change the *Retail Price* of the *Slide Board* to **75.50** and the *Quantity Sold* of the *Balance Pad* to **150** Delete **column B**, and then **Insert** a new **row 3**. In cell **A3**, type **Month Ending March 31** and then **Merge & Center** the text across the range **A3:E3**. Apply the **Heading 2** cell style. To cell **A12**, apply the **20%-Accent1** cell style. Select the four column titles, apply **Wrap Text**, **Middle Align**, and **Center** formatting, and then apply the **Heading 3** cell style.

10 Center the worksheet **Horizontally** on the page, and then insert a **Footer** with the **File Name** in the **Left** section. Display the document properties, and then as the **Tags**, type **balance, stability, sales** In the **Subject** box, add your course name and section number. Be sure your name displays as the author.

11 **Save** your workbook, and then print or submit electronically as directed. If required by your instructor, print or create an electronic version of your worksheet with formulas displayed by using the instructions in Project 1A. **Close** Excel without saving so that you do not save the changes you made to print formulas.

END | You have completed Project 1F

CONTENT-BASED ASSESSMENTS

In the following Mastering Excel project, you will create a new worksheet that compares annual sales by region. Your completed worksheet will look similar to Figure 1.60.

Apply a combination of 1A and 1B skills:

1. Create, Save, and Navigate an Excel Workbook
2. Enter Data in a Worksheet
3. Construct and Copy Formulas and Use the SUM Function
4. Format Cells with Merge & Center, Cell Styles, and Themes
5. Chart Data to Create a Column Chart and Insert Sparklines
6. Print a Worksheet, Display Formulas, and Close Excel
7. Check Spelling in a Worksheet
8. Enter Data by Range
9. Construct Formulas for Mathematical Operations
10. Edit Values in a Worksheet
11. Format a Worksheet

Build from Scratch

PROJECT FILES

For Project 1G, you will need the following file:

New blank Excel workbook

You will save your workbook as:

Lastname_Firstname_1G_Regional_Sales

PROJECT RESULTS

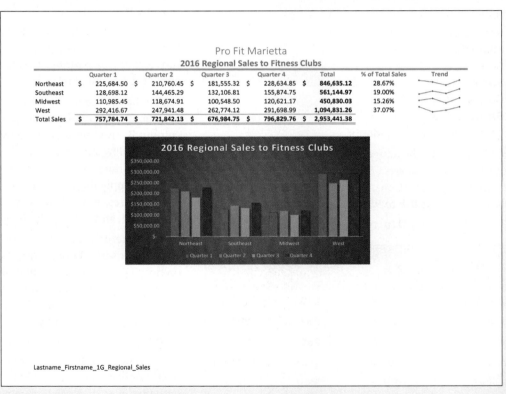

FIGURE 1.60

(Project 1G Regional Sales continues on the next page)

CONTENT-BASED ASSESSMENTS

1 ▶ Start Excel and display a new blank workbook. Change the **Theme** to **Retrospect**. In cell **A1**, type **Pro Fit Marietta** In cell **A2**, type **2016 Regional Sales to Fitness Clubs** and then **Save** the workbook in your **Excel Chapter 1** folder as **Lastname_Firstname_1G_Regional_Sales**

2 ▶ In cell **B3**, type **Quarter 1** and fill *Quarter 2*, *Quarter 3*, and *Quarter 4* in the range **C3:E3**. In cell **F3**, type **Total** In cell **G3**, type **% of Total Sales** and in cell **H3**, type **Trend**

3 ▶ In the range **A4:A7**, type the following row titles: **Northeast** and **Southeast** and **West** and **Total Sales**

4 ▶ Set the width of **column A** to **80 pixels** and the width of columns **B:H** to **110 pixels**. **Merge & Center** the title across the range **A1:H1**, and then apply the **Title** cell style. **Merge & Center** the subtitle across the range **A2:H2**, and then apply the **Heading 1** cell style. Select the seven column titles, apply **Center** formatting, and then apply the **Heading 4** cell style.

5 ▶ In the range **B4:E6**, enter the sales values for each Quarter as shown below.

	Quarter 1	Quarter 2	Quarter 3	Quarter 4
Northeast	225684.50	210760.45	181555.32	228634.85
Southeast	128698.12	144465.29	132106.81	155874.75
West	292416.67	247941.48	262774.12	291698.99

6 ▶ By using the **Quick Analysis tool**, **Sum** the *Quarter 1* sales, and then copy the formula across for the remaining Quarters. By using the **Quick Analysis tool**, **Sum** the sales for the *Northeast* region, and then copy the formula down through cell **F7**. Recall that the **Quick Analysis tool** formats sums in **Bold**. Apply the **Accounting Number Format** to the first row of sales figures and to the total row, and apply the **Comma Style** to the remaining sales figures. Format the totals in **row 7** with the **Total** cell style.

7 ▶ **Insert** a new **row 6** with the row title **Midwest** and the following sales figures for each quarter: **110985.45**

and **118674.91** and **100548.50** and **120621.17** Copy the formula in cell **F5** down to cell **F6** to sum the new row.

8 ▶ Using absolute cell references as necessary so that you can copy the formula, in cell **G4** construct a formula to calculate the *Percent of Total Sales* for the first region. Copy the formula down for the remaining regions. To the computed percentages, apply **Percent Style** with two decimal places, and then **Center** the percentages.

9 ▶ Insert **Line** sparklines in the range **H4:H7** that compare the quarterly data. Do not include the totals. Show the sparkline **Markers** and apply the second style in the second row—**Sparkline Style Accent 2, Darker 25%**.

10 ▶ **Save** your workbook. To compare the quarterly sales of each region visually, select the range that represents the sales figures for the four quarters, including the quarter names and each region—do not include any totals in the range. With this data selected, by using **Recommended Charts**, insert a **Clustered Column** with the regions as the category axis and the Quarters as the legend.

11 ▶ Apply **Chart Style 8** and **Color 3** under **Colorful**. Position the top edge of the chart in **row 10** and visually center it below the worksheet data. Change the **Chart Title** to **2016 Regional Sales to Fitness Clubs**

12 ▶ Deselect the chart. Change the page **Orientation** to **Landscape**, center the worksheet **Horizontally** on the page, and then insert a footer with the file name in the Left section.

13 ▶ Show the document properties. As the **Tags**, type **fitness clubs, sales** In the **Subject** box, type your course name and section number. Be sure your name displays as the author.

14 ▶ **Save** your workbook, and then print or submit electronically as directed. If required by your instructor, print or create an electronic version of your worksheet with formulas displayed by using the instructions in Project 1A. **Close** Excel without saving so that you do not save the changes you made to print formulas.

END | You have completed Project 1G

CONTENT-BASED ASSESSMENTS

| GO! Fix It | Project 1H Team Sales | Online |

| GO! Make It | Project 1I Agility Sales | Online |

| GO! Solve It | Project 1J Kettlebell Sales | Online |

| GO! Solve It | Project 1K Commission | |

PROJECT FILES

For Project 1K, you will need the following file:

e01K_Commission

You will save your workbook as:

Lastname_Firstname_1K_Commission

Open the file **e01K_Commission** and save it as **Lastname_Firstname_1K_Commission** Complete the worksheet by using Auto Fill to complete the month headings, and then calculating the Total Commission for each month and for each region. Insert and format appropriate sparklines in the Trend column. Format the worksheet attractively with a title and subtitle, check spelling, adjust column width, and apply appropriate financial formatting. Insert a chart that compares the total sales commission for each region with the months displaying as the categories, and format the chart attractively. Include the file name in the footer, add appropriate properties, and submit as directed.

Performance Level

		Exemplary: You consistently applied the relevant skills	Proficient: You sometimes, but not always, applied the relevant skills	Developing: You rarely or never applied the relevant skills
Performance Criteria	**Create formulas**	All formulas are correct and are efficiently constructed.	Formulas are correct but not always constructed in the most efficient manner.	One or more formulas are missing or incorrect, or only numbers were entered.
	Create a chart	Chart created properly.	Chart was created but incorrect data was selected.	No chart was created.
	Insert and format sparklines	Sparklines inserted and formatted properly.	Sparklines were inserted but incorrect data was selected or sparklines were not formatted.	No sparklines were inserted.
	Format attractively and appropriately	Formatting is attractive and appropriate.	Adequately formatted but difficult to read or unattractive.	Inadequate or no formatting.

END | You have completed Project 1K

OUTCOMES-BASED ASSESSMENTS

RUBRIC

The following outcomes-based assessments are *open-ended assessments*. That is, there is no specific correct result; your result will depend on your approach to the information provided. Make *Professional Quality* your goal. Use the following scoring rubric to guide you in *how* to approach the problem and then to evaluate *how well* your approach solves the problem.

The *criteria*—Software Mastery, Content, Format and Layout, and Process—represent the knowledge and skills you have gained that you can apply to solving the problem. The *levels of performance*—Professional Quality, Approaching Professional Quality, or Needs Quality Improvements—help you and your instructor evaluate your result.

	Your completed project is of Professional Quality if you:	Your completed project is Approaching Professional Quality if you:	Your completed project Needs Quality Improvements if you:
1-Software Mastery	Choose and apply the most appropriate skills, tools, and features and identify efficient methods to solve the problem.	Choose and apply some appropriate skills, tools, and features, but not in the most efficient manner.	Choose inappropriate skills, tools, or features, or are inefficient in solving the problem.
2-Content	Construct a solution that is clear and well organized, contains content that is accurate, appropriate to the audience and purpose, and is complete. Provide a solution that contains no errors in spelling, grammar, or style.	Construct a solution in which some components are unclear, poorly organized, inconsistent, or incomplete. Misjudge the needs of the audience. Have some errors in spelling, grammar, or style, but the errors do not detract from comprehension.	Construct a solution that is unclear, incomplete, or poorly organized; contains some inaccurate or inappropriate content; and contains many errors in spelling, grammar, or style. Do not solve the problem.
3-Format & Layout	Format and arrange all elements to communicate information and ideas, clarify function, illustrate relationships, and indicate relative importance.	Apply appropriate format and layout features to some elements, but not others. Overuse features, causing minor distraction.	Apply format and layout that does not communicate information or ideas clearly. Do not use format and layout features to clarify function, illustrate relationships, or indicate relative importance. Use available features excessively, causing distraction.
4-Process	Use an organized approach that integrates planning, development, self-assessment, revision, and reflection.	Demonstrate an organized approach in some areas, but not others; or, use an insufficient process of organization throughout.	Do not use an organized approach to solve the problem.

OUTCOMES-BASED ASSESSMENTS

Apply a combination of the 1A and 1B skills.

Build from Scratch

GO! Think | Project 1L Video Sales

PROJECT FILES

For Project 1L, you will need the following file:

New blank Excel workbook

You will save your workbook as:

Lastname_Firstname_1L_Video_Sales

Michelle Barry, President of Pro Fit Marietta, needs a worksheet that summarizes the following data regarding the first quarter sales of training videos. Michelle would like the worksheet to include a calculation of the total sales for each type of video and a total of the sales of all of the videos. She would also like to know each type of video's percentage of total sales.

	Number Sold	Price
Pilates	156	29.99
Step	392	14.99
Weight Training	147	54.99
Kickboxing	282	29.99
Yoga	165	34.99

Create a worksheet that provides Michelle with the information needed. Include appropriate worksheet, column, and row titles. Using the formatting skills that you practiced in this chapter, format the worksheet in a manner that is professional and easy to read and understand. Insert a footer with the file name and add appropriate document properties. Save the file as **Lastname_Firstname_1L_Video_Sales** and print or submit as directed by your instructor.

END | You have completed Project 1L

Build from Scratch

GO! Think | Project 1M Planner | Online

You and GO! | Project 1N Personal Expenses | Online

GO! Cumulative Group Project | Project 1O Bell Orchid Hotels | Online

Using Functions, Creating Tables, and Managing Large Workbooks

GO! to Work
Video E2

PROJECT 2A

OUTCOMES
Analyze inventory by applying statistical and logical calculations to data and by sorting and filtering data.

OBJECTIVES

1. Use Flash Fill and the SUM, AVERAGE, MEDIAN, MIN, and MAX Functions
2. Move Data, Resolve Error Messages, and Rotate Text
3. Use COUNTIF and IF Functions and Apply Conditional Formatting
4. Use Date & Time Functions and Freeze Panes
5. Create, Sort, and Filter an Excel Table
6. View, Format, and Print a Large Worksheet

PROJECT 2B

OUTCOMES
Summarize the data on multiple worksheets.

OBJECTIVES

7. Navigate a Workbook and Rename Worksheets
8. Enter Dates, Clear Contents, and Clear Formats
9. Copy and Paste by Using the Paste Options Gallery
10. Edit and Format Multiple Worksheets at the Same Time
11. Create a Summary Sheet with Column Sparklines
12. Format and Print Multiple Worksheets in a Workbook

In This Chapter

In this chapter, you will use the Statistical functions to calculate the average of a group of numbers and use other Logical and Date & Time functions. Excel's statistical functions are useful for common calculations that you probably encounter frequently. You will also use Excel's new Flash Fill to automatically fill in values, use the counting functions, and apply different types of conditional formatting to make data easy to visualize. You will create a table to organize related information and analyze the table's information by sorting and filtering. You will summarize a workbook that contains multiple worksheets.

The projects in this chapter relate to **Rosedale Landscape and Garden**, which grows and sells trees and plants suitable for all areas of North America. Throughout its 75 year history, the company has introduced many new plants for the enjoyment of home gardeners. The company has nurseries and stores in the major metropolitan areas in the United States and Canada. In addition to high-quality plants and trees, Rosedale sells garden tools and outdoor furniture. Rosedale also offers professional landscape design and installation for both commercial and residential clients. The company headquarters is in Pasadena, California.

PROJECT 2A Inventory Status Report

MyITLab®
Project 2A Training

PROJECT ACTIVITIES

In Activities 2.01 through 2.20 you will edit a worksheet for Holman Hill, President, detailing the current inventory of trees at the Pasadena nursery. Your completed worksheet will look similar to Figure 2.1.

PROJECT FILES

For Project 2A, you will need the following file:

e02A_Tree_Inventory

You will save your workbook as:

Lastname_Firstname_2A_Tree_Inventory

PROJECT RESULTS

Quantity in Stock	Item #	Tree Name	Retail Price	Light	Landscape Use	Category	Stock Level
93	38700	Pacific Fire	103.75	Full Shade	Erosion Control	Oak	OK
45	38744	Cheals Weeping	104.99	Partial Shade	Erosion Control	Cherry	Order
58	39704	Embers	105.99	Partial Sun	Erosion Control	Oak	Order
90	42599	Beurre	109.98	Partial Sun	Border	Pear	OK
350	43153	Bradford	104.99	Full Shade	Border	Pear	OK

Edited by Maria Acuna
11/11/2012 5:08

Pasadena Tree Nursery
As of December 31

Tree Statistics

Total Items in Stock	3,022
Average Price	$ 107.89
Median Price	$ 107.99
Lowest Price	$ 102.99
Highest Price	$ 117.98

Oak Trees   13
Maple Trees   6 (571 total items in stock)

Quantity in Stock	Item #	Tree Name	Retail Price	Light	Landscape Use	Category	Stock Level
78	13129	Golden Oak	108.99	Partial Sun	Erosion Control	Oak	OK
35	13358	Columnar English	106.95	Full Shade	Border	Oak	Order
60	15688	Coral Bark	106.25	Partial Shade	Erosion Control	Oak	Order
20	16555	Crimson King	105.50	Full Shade	Border	Oak	Order
75	21683	Japanese Blooming	103.99	Partial Shade	Erosion Control	Cherry	OK
60	22189	Crimson Queen	109.95	Filtered Sun	Erosion Control	Oak	Order
68	23677	Black Japanese	107.99	Partial Sun	Border	Maple	Order
71	23688	Artist Flowering	109.95	Partial Sun	Erosion Control	Pear	Order
159	24896	Bing Small Sweet	105.99	Partial Shade	Border	Cherry	OK
60	25678	Bartlett	109.75	Partial Sun	Erosion Control	Pear	Order
179	25844	Bloodgood	110.99	Partial Shade	Border	Maple	OK
90	26787	Sentry	108.50	Partial Sun	Border	Oak	OK
81	32544	Burgundy Bell	110.95	Partial Sun	Border	Maple	OK
81	34266	Lace Maple	109.99	Partial Sun	Border	Maple	OK
113	34793	Emerald Elf	103.98	Full Shade	Erosion Control	Oak	OK
191	34878	Ginger Pear	107.78	Partial Sun	Border	Pear	OK
102	34982	Fernleaf	105.99	Partial Shade	Border	Oak	OK
170	35677	Flamingo	109.99	Partial Sun	Border	Oak	OK
170	35690	Bing Sweet	107.99	Partial Sun	Erosion Control	Cherry	OK
70	35988	Butterfly Japanese	111.75	Partial Sun	Border	Maple	Order
92	36820	Ever Red	110.95	Partial Sun	Border	Maple	OK
173	37803	Osakazuki	103.88	Full Shade	Erosion Control	Oak	OK
113	37845	Anna	117.98	Partial Sun	Woodland Garden	Magnolia	OK
75	38675	Palo Alto	102.99	Partial Shade	Erosion Control	Oak	OK

Lastname_Firstname_2A_Tree_Inventory

FIGURE 2.1 Project 2A Inventory Status Report

Video E2-1

Flash Fill recognizes a pattern in your data, and then automatically fills in values when you enter examples of the output that you want. Use Flash Fill to split data from two or more cells or to combine data from two cells.

A *function* is the name given to a predefined formula—a formula that Excel has already built for you—that performs calculations by using specific values that you insert in a particular order or structure. *Statistical functions*, which include the AVERAGE, MEDIAN, MIN, and MAX functions, are useful to analyze a group of measurements.

Activity 2.01 │ Using Flash Fill

1 Start Excel, and then in the lower left corner of Excel's opening screen, click **Open Other Workbooks**.

ANOTHER WAY   Press Ctrl + F12 to display the Open dialog box.

2 Navigate to the student files that accompany this textbook, and then locate and open **e02A_Tree_Inventory**. Press F12 to display the **Save As** dialog box, and then navigate to the location where you are storing your projects for this chapter.

3 Create a new folder named **Excel Chapter 2** and open the new folder. In the **File name** box, using your own name, type **Lastname_Firstname_2A_Tree_Inventory** and click **Save** or press Enter.

4 Scroll down. Notice that the worksheet contains data related to types of trees in inventory, including information about the *Quantity in Stock*, *Item #/Category*, *Tree Name*, *Retail Price*, *Light*, and *Landscape Use*.

5 In the **column heading area**, point to **column C** to display the ⬇ pointer, and then drag to the right to select **columns C:D**. On the **HOME tab**, in the **Cells group**, click the **Insert button arrow**, and then click **Insert Sheet Columns**.

New columns for C and D display and the remaining columns move to the right.

ANOTHER WAY   Select the columns, right-click anywhere over the selected columns, and then on the shortcut menu, click Insert.

6 Click cell **C11**, type **13129** and then on the **Formula Bar**, click ✔ to confirm the entry and keep **C11** as the active cell.

7 On the **HOME tab**, in the **Editing group**, click **Fill**, and then click **Flash Fill**. Compare your screen with Figure 2.2.

Use this technique to split a column of data based on what you type. Flash Fill looks to the left and sees the pattern you have established, and then fills the remaining cells in the column with only the Item #. The Flash Fill Options button displays.

FIGURE 2.2

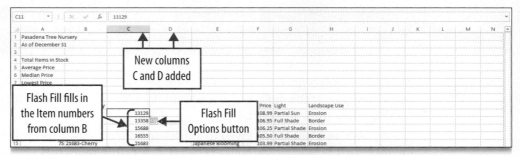

8 ▶ Near the lower right corner of cell **C11**, click the **Flash Fill Options** button, and notice that here you can *Undo Flash Fill*, *Accept suggestions*, or *Select all 28 changed cells*, for example, to apply specific formatting. Click the button again to close it.

> If Excel is not sure what pattern to use, it suggests a pattern by filling with pale gray characters, and then you can use the Accept suggestions command to accept or start again.

9 ▶ Click cell **D11**, type **Oak** On the **Formula Bar**, click ☑ to confirm the entry and keep **D11** as the active cell, and then press Ctrl + E, which is the keyboard shortcut for Flash Fill.

> Flash Fill extracts the text from the *Item#/Category* column and also inserts *Category* as the column name. Now that *Item #* and *Category* are in two separate columns, Mr. Hill can sort and filter by both Item # and Category.

10 ▶ Select **column B**, and then in the **Cells group**, click the **Delete button arrow**. Click **Delete Sheet Columns**. On the Quick Access Toolbar, click **Save** 🖫.

🔄 **ANOTHER WAY**   Select the column, right-click anywhere over the selected column, and then on the shortcut menu, click Delete.

Activity 2.02 │ Moving a Column

1 ▶ In cell **B10** type **Item #** and press Enter. Select **column C**, and then on the **HOME tab**, in the **Clipboard group**, click **Cut** ✂. Notice that the column is surrounded by a moving border. Click cell **H1**, and then in the **Clipboard group**, click the upper portion of the **Paste** button.

🔄 **ANOTHER WAY**   Press Ctrl + X to cut and Ctrl + V to paste.

2 ▶ Select and then delete **column C**. Select **columns A:G**. In the **Cells group**, click **Format**, and then click **AutoFit Column Width**.

🔄 **ANOTHER WAY**   Select the columns, in the column heading area point to any of the column borders to display the ➕ pointer, and then double-click to AutoFit the columns.

3 ▶ Press Ctrl + Home to deselect and make cell **A1** the active cell.

4 ▶ **Merge & Center** cell **A1** across the range **A1:H1**, and then apply the **Title** cell style. **Merge & Center** cell **A2** across the range **A2:H2**, and apply the **Heading 1** cell style. Compare your screen with Figure 2.3. **Save** 🖫 your workbook.

FIGURE 2.3

Activity 2.03 | Using the SUM and AVERAGE Functions

Mr. Hill has a worksheet with information about the inventory of trees currently in stock at the Pasadena nursery. In this activity, you will use the SUM and AVERAGE functions to gather information about the product inventory.

1 Click cell **B4**. Click the **FORMULAS tab**, and then in the **Function Library group**, click the upper portion of the **AutoSum** button. Compare your screen with Figure 2.4.

The **SUM function** that you have used is a predefined formula that adds all the numbers in a selected range of cells. Because it is frequently used, there are several ways to insert the function. For example, you can insert the function from the HOME tab's Editing group, or by using the keyboard shortcut Alt + =, or from the Function Library group on the Formulas tab, or from the Math & Trig button in that group.

FIGURE 2.4

2 With the insertion point blinking in the function, type the cell range **a11:a39** to sum all the values in the **Quantity in Stock** column, and then press Enter; your result is *3022*.

3 Click cell **B4**, look at the **Formula Bar**, and then compare your screen with Figure 2.5.

SUM is the name of the function. The values in parentheses are the *arguments*—the values that an Excel function uses to perform calculations or operations. In this instance, the argument consists of the values in the range A11:A39.

FIGURE 2.5

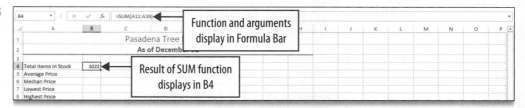

4 Click cell **B5**. In the **Function Library group**, click **More Functions**, point to **Statistical**, point to **AVERAGE**, and notice the ScreenTip. Compare your screen with Figure 2.6.

The ScreenTip describes how the AVERAGE function will compute the calculation.

FIGURE 2.6

5 Click **AVERAGE**, and then if necessary, drag the title bar of the **Function Arguments** dialog box down and to the right so you can view the **Formula Bar** and cell **B5**.

The *AVERAGE function* adds a group of values, and then divides the result by the number of values in the group. In the cell, the Formula Bar, and the dialog box, Excel proposes to average the value in cell B4. Recall that Excel functions will propose a range if there is data above or to the left of a selected cell.

6 In the **Function Arguments** dialog box, notice that *B4* is highlighted. Press ⟨Del⟩ to delete the existing text, type **d11:d39** and then compare your screen with Figure 2.7.

Because you want to average the values in the range D11:D39—and not cell B4—you must edit the proposed range.

FIGURE 2.7

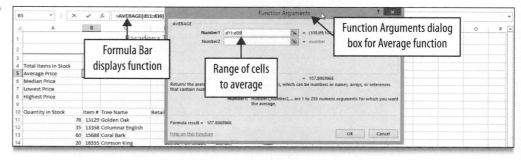

7 In the **Function Arguments** dialog box, click **OK**, and then click **Save** 🔲.

The result indicates that the average Retail Price of all products is *107.89*.

Activity 2.04 | Using the MEDIAN Function

The *MEDIAN function* is a statistical function that describes a group of data—it is commonly used to describe the price of houses in a particular geographical area. The MEDIAN function finds the middle value that has as many values above it in the group as are below it. It differs from

AVERAGE in that the result is not affected as much by a single value that is greatly different from the others.

1️⃣ Click cell **B6**. In the **Function Library group**, click **More Functions**, display the list of **Statistical** functions, scroll down as necessary, and then click **MEDIAN**.

2️⃣ Press Del to delete the text in the **Number1** box, and then type **d11:d39** Compare your screen with Figure 2.8.

> When indicating which cells you want to use in the function's calculation—known as *defining the arguments*—you can either select the values with your mouse or type the range of values, whichever you prefer.

FIGURE 2.8

3️⃣ Click **OK** to display *107.99* in cell **B6**. Click **Save** 🖫, and then compare your screen with Figure 2.9.

> In the range of prices, 107.99 is the middle value. Half of all trees in inventory are priced *above* 107.99 and half are priced *below* 107.99.

FIGURE 2.9

Activity 2.05 | Using the MIN and MAX Functions

The statistical *MIN function* determines the smallest value in a selected range of values. The statistical *MAX function* determines the largest value in a selected range of values.

1️⃣ Click cell **B7**. On the **FORMULAS tab**, in the **Function Library group**, click **More Functions**, display the list of **Statistical** functions, scroll as necessary, and then click **MIN**.

2️⃣ Press Del, and then in the **Number1** box, type **d11:d39** Click **OK**.

> The lowest Retail Price is *102.99*.

3️⃣ Click cell **B8**, and then by using a similar technique, insert the **MAX** function to determine the highest **Retail Price**, then check to see that your result is *117.98*.

4️⃣ Press Ctrl + Home. Point to cell **B4**, right-click, and then on the mini toolbar, click **Comma Style** ▾ one time and **Decrease Decimal** ▾ two times.

5️⃣ Select the range **B5:B8**, apply the **Accounting Number Format** $ ▾, click **Save** 🖫, and then compare your screen with Figure 2.10.

FIGURE 2.10

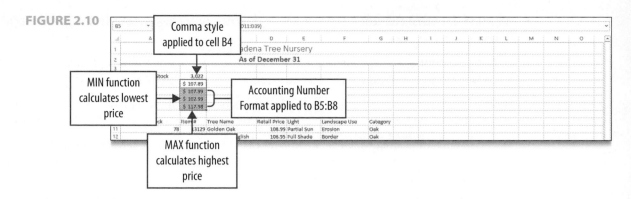

Comma style applied to cell B4

MIN function calculates lowest price

Accounting Number Format applied to B5:B8

MAX function calculates highest price

Objective 2 | Move Data, Resolve Error Messages, and Rotate Text

Video E2-2

When you move a formula, the cell references within the formula do not change, no matter what type of cell reference you use.

If you move cells into a column that is not wide enough to display number values, Excel will display a message so that you can adjust as necessary.

You can reposition data within a cell at an angle by rotating the text.

Activity 2.06 | Moving Data and Resolving a # # # # # Error Message

1 Select **column E** and set the width to **50 pixels**. Select the range **A4:B8**. Point to the right edge of the selected range to display the pointer, and then compare your screen with Figure 2.11.

FIGURE 2.11

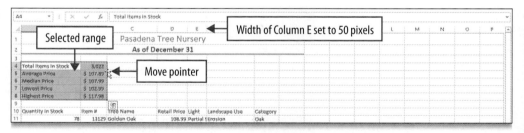

Selected range

Width of Column E set to 50 pixels

Move pointer

2 Drag the selected range to the right until the ScreenTip displays *D4:E8*, release the mouse button, and then notice that a series of # symbols displays in **column E**. Point to any of the cells that display # symbols, and then compare your screen with Figure 2.12.

Using this technique, cell contents can be moved from one location to another; this is referred to as *drag and drop*.

If a cell width is too narrow to display the entire number, Excel displays the ##### message, because displaying only a portion of a number would be misleading. The underlying values remain unchanged and are displayed in the Formula Bar for the selected cell. An underlying value also displays in the ScreenTip if you point to a cell containing # symbols.

FIGURE 2.12

Range moved to D4:E8

symbols display

ScreenTip indicates underlying value

3 Select **column E** and widen it to **60** pixels, and notice that four cells are still not wide enough to display the cell contents.

4 Select **columns D:E**, and then in the **column heading area**, point to the right boundary of **column E** to display the ⊞ pointer. Double-click to AutoFit the column to accommodate the widest entry.

5 Select the range **D4:E8**. On the **HOME tab**, in the **Styles group**, display the **Cell Styles** gallery. Under **Themed Cell Styles**, click **20%-Accent1**. Click **Save** 🖫.

Activity 2.07 | Rotating Text

1 In cell **C6**, type **Tree Statistics** Select the range **C4:C8**, right-click over the selection, and then on the shortcut menu, click **Format Cells**.

2 In the **Format Cells** dialog box, click the **Alignment tab**. Under **Text control**, select the **Merge cells** check box.

3 Under **Orientation**, click in the **Degrees** box, select the existing text, type **30** and then compare your screen with Figure 2.13.

🔄 **ANOTHER WAY**   In the upper right portion of the dialog box, under Orientation, point to the red diamond, and then drag the diamond upward until the Degrees box indicates 30.

FIGURE 2.13

4 In the lower right corner of the **Format Cells** dialog box, click **OK**.

5 With the merged cell still selected, on the **HOME tab**, in the **Font group**, change the **Font Size** 11 ▾ to **14**, and then apply **Bold** 🅱 and **Italic** 𝐼. Click the **Font Color arrow** 🅰 ▾, and then in the fifth column, click the first color—**Blue, Accent 1**.

6 In the **Alignment group**, apply **Align Right** ≣. Press Ctrl + Home, **Save** 🖫 your workbook, and then compare your screen with Figure 2.14.

FIGURE 2.14

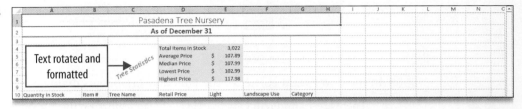

7 In the **row heading area**, point to **row 9** and right-click to select the row and display the shortcut menu. Click **Insert**, and then press F4 two times to repeat the last action and insert three blank rows.

F4 is useful to repeat commands in Microsoft Office programs. Most commands can be repeated in this manner.

8 From the **row heading area**, select **rows 9:11**. On the **HOME tab**, in the **Editing group**, click **Clear** ✎ and then click **Clear Formats** to remove the blue accent color in columns D and E from the new rows. Click **Save** 🖫.

When you insert rows or columns, formatting from adjacent rows or columns repeats in the new cells.

Objective 3 Use COUNTIF and IF Functions and Apply Conditional Formatting

Video E2-3

Recall that statistical functions analyze a group of measurements. Another group of Excel functions, referred to as *logical functions*, test for specific conditions. Logical functions typically use conditional tests to determine whether specified conditions—called *criteria*—are true or false.

Activity 2.08 | Using the COUNT and COUNTIF Functions

The **Count function** counts the number of cells in a range that contain numbers. The **COUNTIF function** is a statistical function that counts the number of cells within a range that meet the given condition—the criteria that you provide. The COUNTIF function has two arguments—the range of cells to check and the criteria.

The trees of Rosedale Landscape and Garden will be featured on an upcoming segment of a TV gardening show. In this activity, you will use the COUNTIF function to determine the number of *Oak* trees currently available in inventory that can be featured in the TV show.

1 Click cell **E4**, look at the **Formula Bar**, and then notice that the arguments of the **SUM** function adjusted and refer to the appropriate cells in rows 14:42.

The referenced range updates to *A14:A42* after you insert the three new rows. In this manner, Excel adjusts the cell references in a formula relative to their new locations.

2 Click cell **A10**, type **Oak Trees** and then press Tab.

3 With cell **B10** as the active cell, on the **FORMULAS tab**, in the **Function Library group**, click **More Functions**, and then display the list of **Statistical** functions. Click **COUNTIF**.

The COUNTIF function counts the number of cells within a range that meet the given condition.

4 In the **Range** box, type **g14:g42** Click in the **Criteria** box, type **Oak** and then compare your screen with Figure 2.15.

FIGURE 2.15

5 In the lower right corner of the **Function Arguments** dialog box, click **OK**.

There are *13* different *Oak* trees available to feature on the TV show.

6 On the **HOME tab**, in the **Alignment group**, click **Align Left** 🖹 to place the result closer to the row title. **Save** 🖫 your workbook.

Activity 2.09 | Using the IF Function

A *logical test* is any value or expression that you can evaluate as being true or false. The *IF function* uses a logical test to check whether a condition is met, and then returns one value if true, and another value if false.

For example, *C14=228* is an expression that can be evaluated as true or false. If the value in cell C14 is equal to 228, the expression is true. If the value in cell C14 is not 228, the expression is false.

In this activity, you will use the IF function to determine the inventory levels and determine if more products should be ordered.

1 Click cell **H13**, type **Stock Level** and then press Enter.

2 In cell **H14**, on the **FORMULAS tab**, in the **Function Library group**, click **Logical**, and then in the list, click **IF**. Drag the title bar of the **Function Arguments** dialog box up or down to view **row 14** on your screen.

3 With the insertion point in the **Logical_test** box, type **a14 < 75**

This logical test will look at the value in cell A14, which is *78*, and then determine if the number is less than 75. The expression *<75* includes the < *comparison operator*, which means *less than*. Comparison operators compare values.

4 Examine the table in Figure 2.16 for a list of comparison operator symbols and their definitions.

FIGURE 2.16

COMPARISON OPERATORS	
COMPARISON OPERATORS	**SYMBOL DEFINITION**
=	Equal to
>	Greater than
<	Less than
>=	Greater than or equal to
<=	Less than or equal to
<>	Not equal to

5 Press Tab to move the insertion point to the **Value_if_true** box, and then type **Order**

If the result of the logical test is true—the Quantity in Stock is less than 75—cell H14 will display the text *Order* indicating that additional trees must be ordered.

6 Press Tab to move to the **Value_if_false** box, type **OK** and then compare your screen with Figure 2.17.

If the result of the logical test is false—the Quantity in Stock is *not* less than 75—then Excel will display *OK* in the cell.

FIGURE 2.17

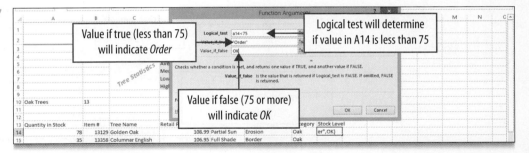

7 ▶ Click **OK** to display the result *OK* in cell **H14**.

8 ▶ Using the fill handle, copy the function in cell **H14** down through cell **H42**. Then scroll as necessary to view cell **A18**, which contains the value *75*. Look at cell **H18** and notice that the **Stock Level** is indicated as *OK*. **Save** 🖫 your workbook. Compare your screen with Figure 2.18.

> The comparison operator indicated <75 (less than 75) and therefore a value of *exactly* 75 is indicated as OK.

FIGURE 2.18

Activity 2.10 | Applying Conditional Formatting by Using Highlight Cells Rules and Data Bars

A ***conditional format*** changes the appearance of a cell based on a condition—a criteria. If the condition is true, the cell is formatted based on that condition; if the condition is false, the cell is *not* formatted. In this activity, you will use conditional formatting as another way to draw attention to the Stock Level of trees.

1 ▶ Be sure the range **H14:H42** is selected. On the **HOME tab**, in the **Styles group**, click **Conditional Formatting**. In the list, point to **Highlight Cells Rules**, and then click **Text that Contains**.

2 ▶ In the **Text That Contains** dialog box, with the insertion point blinking in the first box, type **Order** and notice that in the selected range, the text *Order* displays with the default format—Light Red Fill with Dark Red Text.

3 ▶ In the second box, click the **arrow**, and then in the list, click **Custom Format**.

> Here, in the Format Cells dialog box, you can select any combination of formats to apply to the cell if the condition is true. The custom format you specify will be applied to any cell in the selected range if it contains the text *Order*.

4 ▶ On the **Font tab**, under **Font style**, click **Bold Italic**. Click the **Color arrow**, and then under **Theme Colors**, in the last column, click the first color—**Green, Accent 6**. Click **OK**. Compare your screen with Figure 2.19.

> In the range, if the cell meets the condition of containing *Order*, the font color will change to Bold Italic, Green, Accent 6.

FIGURE 2.19

5 In the **Text That Contains** dialog box, click **OK**.

6 Select the range **A14:A42**. In the **Styles group**, click **Conditional Formatting**. Point to **Data Bars**, and then under **Gradient Fill**, click **Orange Data Bar**. Click anywhere to cancel the selection, click **Save** 🖫, and then compare your screen with Figure 2.20.

A ***data bar*** provides a visual cue to the reader about the value of a cell relative to other cells. The length of the data bar represents the value in the cell. A longer bar represents a higher value and a shorter bar represents a lower value. Data bars are useful for identifying higher and lower numbers quickly within a large group of data, such as very high or very low levels of inventory.

FIGURE 2.20

Activity 2.11 | Using Find and Replace

The ***Find and Replace*** feature searches the cells in a worksheet—or in a selected range—for matches, and then replaces each match with a replacement value of your choice.

Comments from customers on the company's blog indicate that using the term *Erosion Control* would be clearer than *Erosion* when describing the best landscape use for specific trees. Therefore, all products of this type will be re-labeled accordingly. In this activity, you will replace all occurrences of *Erosion* with *Erosion Control*.

1 Select the range **F14:F42**.

Restrict the find and replace operation to a specific range in this manner, especially if there is a possibility that the name occurs elsewhere.

2 On the **HOME tab**, in the **Editing group**, click **Find & Select**, and then click **Replace**.

3 Type **Erosion** to fill in the **Find what** box. In the **Replace with** box, type **Erosion Control** and then compare your screen with Figure 2.21.

FIGURE 2.21

4 Click **Replace All**. In the message box, notice that 13 replacements were made, and then click **OK**. In the lower right corner of the **Find and Replace** dialog box, click **Close**. Click **Save** 🖫.

Video E2-4

Excel can obtain the date and time from your computer's calendar and clock and display this information on your worksheet.

By freezing or splitting panes, you can view two areas of a worksheet and lock rows and columns in one area. When you freeze panes, you select the specific rows or columns that you want to remain visible when scrolling in your worksheet.

Activity 2.12 | Using the NOW Function to Display a System Date

The **NOW function** retrieves the date and time from your computer's calendar and clock and inserts the information into the selected cell. The result is formatted as a date and time.

1 To the left of the **Formula Bar**, click in the **Name Box**, type **a44** and then press Enter. Notice that cell **A44** is the active cell. In cell **A44**, type **Edited by Maria Acuna** and then press Enter.

2 With cell **A45** as the active cell, on the **FORMULAS tab**, in the **Function Library group**, click **Date & Time**. In the list of functions, click **NOW**. Compare your screen with Figure 2.22.

FIGURE 2.22

3 Read the description in the **Function Arguments** dialog box, and notice that this result is *Volatile*.

The Function Arguments dialog box displays a message indicating that this function does not require an argument. It also states that this function is *volatile*, meaning the date and time will not remain as entered, but rather the date and time will automatically update each time you open this workbook.

4 In the **Function Arguments** dialog box, click **OK** to close the dialog box and display the current date and time in cell **A45**. **Save** your workbook.

More Knowledge | **NOW Function Recalculates Each Time a Workbook Opens**

The NOW function updates each time the workbook is opened. With the workbook open, you can force the NOW function to update by pressing F9, for example, to update the time.

Activity 2.13 | Freezing and Unfreezing Panes

In a large worksheet, if you scroll down more than 25 rows or scroll beyond column O (the exact row number and column letter varies, depending on your screen resolution), you will no longer see the top rows or first column of your worksheet where identifying information about the data is usually placed. You will find it easier to work with your data if you can always view the identifying row or column titles.

The **Freeze Panes** command enables you to select one or more rows or columns and then freeze (lock) them into place. The locked rows and columns become separate panes. A **pane** is a portion of a worksheet window bounded by and separated from other portions by vertical or horizontal bars.

1 ▸ Press `Ctrl` + `Home` to make cell **A1** the active cell. Scroll down until **row 21** displays at the top of your Excel window, and notice that all of the identifying information in the column titles is out of view.

2 ▸ Press `Ctrl` + `Home` again, and then from the **row heading area**, select **row 14**. Click the **VIEW tab**, and then in the **Window group**, click **Freeze Panes**. In the list, click **Freeze Panes**. Click any cell to deselect the row, and then notice that a line displays along the upper border of **row 14**.

By selecting row 14, the rows above—rows 1–13—are frozen in place and will not move as you scroll down.

3 ▸ Watch the row numbers below **row 13**, and then begin to scroll down to bring **row 21** into view again. Notice that rows 1:13 are frozen in place. Compare your screen with Figure 2.23.

The remaining rows of data continue to scroll. Use this feature when you have long or wide worksheets.

FIGURE 2.23

4 ▸ In the **Window group**, click **Freeze Panes**, and then click **Unfreeze Panes** to unlock all rows and columns. **Save** 🖫 your workbook.

More **Knowledge** │ **Freeze Columns or Freeze Both Rows and Columns**

You can freeze columns that you want to remain in view on the left. Select the column to the right of the column(s) that you want to remain in view while scrolling to the right, and then click the Freeze Panes command. You can also use the command to freeze both rows and columns; click a *cell* to freeze the rows *above* the cell and the columns to the *left* of the cell.

Objective 5 │ Create, Sort, and Filter an Excel Table

Video E2-5

To analyze a group of related data, you can convert a range of cells to an ***Excel table***. An Excel table is a series of rows and columns that contains related data that is managed independently from the data in other rows and columns in the worksheet.

Activity 2.14 │ **Creating an Excel Table and Applying a Table Style**

1 ▸ Be sure that you have applied the Unfreeze Panes command—no rows on your worksheet are locked.

2 Click any cell in the data below row 13. Click the **INSERT tab**. In the **Tables group**, click **Table**. In the **Create Table** dialog box, if necessary, click to select the My table has headers check box, and then compare your screen with Figure 2.24.

The column titles in row 13 will form the table headers. By clicking in a range of contiguous data, Excel will suggest the range as the data for the table. You can adjust the range if necessary.

FIGURE 2.24

 ANOTHER WAY   Select the range of cells that make up the table, including the header row, and then click the Table button.

3 Click **OK**. With the range still selected, on the ribbon notice that the **TABLE TOOLS** are active.

4 On the **DESIGN tab**, in the **Table Styles group**, click **More** ⌄, and then under **Light**, locate and click **Table Style Light 16**.

5 Press Ctrl + Home. Click **Save** 🔲, and then compare your screen with Figure 2.25.

Sorting and filtering arrows display in the table's header row.

FIGURE 2.25

Activity 2.15 | Sorting an Excel Table

You can *sort* tables—arrange all the data in a specific order—in ascending or descending order.

1 In the header row of the table, click the **Retail Price arrow**, and then on the menu, click **Sort Smallest to Largest**. Next to the arrow, notice the small **up arrow** indicating an ascending (smallest to largest) sort.

This action sorts the rows in the table from the lowest retail price to highest retail price.

2 In the table's header row, click the **Category arrow**. On the menu, click **Sort A to Z**. Next to the arrow, notice the small **up arrow** indicating an ascending (A to Z) sort.

This action sorts the rows in the table alphabetically by Category, and within a Category, sorts the rows from smallest to largest by Retail Price.

3 Click the **Category arrow** again, and then sort from **Z to A**.

This action sorts the rows in the table in reverse alphabetic order by Category name, and the small arrow points downward, indicating a descending (Z to A) sort. The Retail Price continues to be sorted from smallest to largest within each category.

Activity 2.16 │ Filtering an Excel Table and Displaying a Total Row

You can *filter* tables—display only a portion of the data based on matching a specific value—to show only the data that meets the criteria that you specify.

1 Click the **Category arrow** again. On the menu, click the **(Select All)** check box to clear all the check boxes. Click to select only the **Maple** check box, and then click **OK**. Compare your screen with Figure 2.26.

Only the rows containing *Maple* in the Category column display—the remaining rows are hidden from view. A small funnel—the filter icon—indicates that a filter is applied to the data in the table. Additionally, the row numbers display in blue to indicate that some rows are hidden from view. A filter hides entire rows in the worksheet.

FIGURE 2.26

2 Point to the funnel icon to the right of *Category*, and notice that *Equals "Maple"* displays to indicate the filter criteria.

3 Click any cell in the table so that the table is selected. On the ribbon, click the **DESIGN tab**, and then in the **Table Style Options group**, select the **Total Row** check box.

Total displays in cell A43. In cell H43, the number *6* indicates that six rows currently display.

4 Click cell **A43**, click the **arrow** that displays to the right of cell **A43**, and then in the list, click **Sum**.

Excel sums only the visible rows in Column A, and indicates that 571 products in the Maple category are in stock. In this manner, you can use an Excel table to quickly find information about a group of data.

5 Click cell **A11**, type **Maple Trees** and press Tab. In cell **B11**, type **6 (571 total items in stock)** and then press Enter.

6 In the table header row, click the **Category arrow**, and then on the menu, click **Clear Filter From "Category"**.

All the rows in the table redisplay. The Z to A sort on Category remains in effect.

More Knowledge │ **Band Rows and Columns in a Table**

You can band rows to format even rows differently from odd rows making them easier to read. To band rows or columns, on the DESIGN tab, in the Table Style Options group, select the Banded Rows or Banded Columns check box.

> **7** Click the **Landscape Use arrow**, click the **(Select All)** check box to clear all the check boxes, and then click to select the **Erosion Control** check box. Click **OK**.

> **8** Click the **Category arrow**, click the **(Select All)** check box to clear all the check boxes, and then click the **Oak** check box. Click **OK**, Save your workbook, and then compare your screen with Figure 2.27.

> By applying multiple filters, Mr. Hill can determine quickly that eight tree names identified with a *Landscape Use* of *Erosion Control* are in the *Oak* tree category with a total of 710 such trees in stock.

FIGURE 2.27

Activity 2.17 | Clearing Filters and Converting a Table to a Range of Data

When you are finished answering questions about the data in a table by sorting, filtering, and totaling, you can convert the table into a normal range. Doing so is useful if you want to use the Table feature only to apply a Table Style to a range. For example, you can insert a table, apply a Table Style, and then convert the table to a normal range of data but keep the formatting.

> **1** Click the **Category arrow**, and then click **Clear Filter From "Category"**. Use the same technique to remove the filter from the **Landscape Use** column.

> **2** In the table header row, click the **Item # arrow**, and then click **Sort Smallest to Largest**, which will apply an ascending sort to the data using the *Item #* column.

> **3** Click anywhere in the table to activate the table and display the **TABLE TOOLS** on the ribbon. Click the **DESIGN tab**, and then in the **Table Style Options group**, click the **Total Row** check box to clear the check mark and remove the Total row from the table.

> **4** On the **DESIGN tab**, in the **Tools group**, click **Convert to Range**. In the message box, click **Yes**. Click **Save** , and then compare your screen with Figure 2.28.

FIGURE 2.28

 ANOTHER WAY   With any table cell selected, right-click, point to Table, and then click Convert to Range.

Objective 6   View, Format, and Print a Large Worksheet

Video E2-6

You can magnify or shrink the view of a worksheet on your screen to either zoom in to view specific data or zoom out to see the entire worksheet. You can also split a worksheet window into panes to view different parts of a worksheet at the same time.

A worksheet might be too wide, too long—or both—to print on a single page. Use Excel's *Print Titles* and *Scale to Fit* commands to create pages that are attractive and easy to read.

The Print Titles command enables you to specify rows and columns to repeat on each printed page. Scale to Fit commands enable you to stretch or shrink the width, height, or both, of printed output to fit a maximum number of pages.

Activity 2.18 | Modifying and Shrinking the Worksheet View

1 Press [Ctrl] + [Home] to display the top of your worksheet. On the **VIEW tab**, in the **Zoom group**, click **Zoom**.

2 In the **Zoom** dialog box, click the **75%** option button, and then click **OK**. Notice that by zooming out in this manner, you can see additional rows of your worksheet on the screen.

3 In the lower right corner of your worksheet, in the status bar, click the **Zoom In** button until the worksheet redisplays at 100%.

Activity 2.19 | Splitting a Worksheet Window into Panes

The *Split* command splits the window into multiple resizable panes that contain views of your worksheet. This is useful to view multiple distant parts of your worksheet at one time.

1 Click cell **F9**. On the **VIEW tab**, in the **Window group**, click **Split**.

Horizontal and vertical split bars display. You can drag the split bars to view any four portions of the worksheet.

2 Notice on the right that separate vertical scroll bars display for the upper and lower panes and at the bottom, separate horizontal scroll bars display for the left and right panes.

3 Drag the lower vertical scroll box down to the bottom of the scroll bar to view **line 44**. Compare your screen with Figure 2.29.

Here it could be useful to isolate the Tree Statistics at the top and then scroll to the bottom to browse the inventory items or to make a note about who edited the original worksheet.

FIGURE 2.29

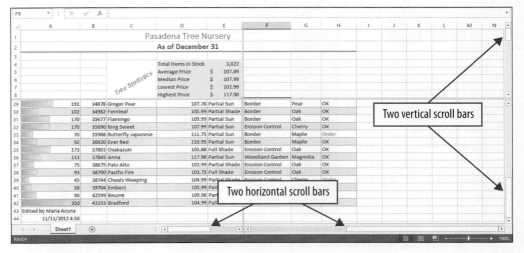

4 On the **VIEW tab**, click **Split** again to remove the split bars.

5 Press [Ctrl] + [Home] to display the top of your worksheet. On the **PAGE LAYOUT tab**, in the **Themes group**, click **Themes**, and then click **Slice**.

6 Select the range **A13:H13**. On the **HOME tab**, from the **Styles group**, apply the **Heading 4** cell style, and then apply **Center** ☰. Click cell **A1**.

1 Click the **PAGE LAYOUT tab**, and then in the **Page Setup group**, click **Margins**. At the bottom of the gallery, click **Custom Margins** to display the **Page Setup** dialog box. Under **Center on page**, select the **Horizontally** check box.

2 Click the **Header/Footer tab**, and then in the center of the dialog box, click **Custom Footer**. In the **Footer** dialog box, with your insertion point blinking in the **Left section**, on the row of buttons, click **Insert File Name** 🗐. Click **OK** two times.

3 In the **Page Setup group**, click **Orientation**, and then click **Landscape**.

The dotted line indicates that as currently formatted, column H will not fit on one page.

4 Press Ctrl + F2 to display the **Print Preview**. At the bottom of the **Print Preview**, click **Next Page** ▶.

As currently formatted, the worksheet will print on four pages, and the columns will span multiple pages. Additionally, after Page 1, no column titles are visible to identify the data in the columns.

5 Click **Next Page** ▶ two times to display **Page 4**, and notice that one column moves to an additional page.

6 In the upper left corner of **Backstage** view, click **Back** ⬅ to return to the worksheet. In the **Page Setup group**, click **Print Titles**. Under **Print titles**, click in the **Rows to repeat at top** box, and then at the right, click **Collapse Dialog** 🖼.

7 From the **row heading area**, select **row 13**, and then in the **Page Setup - Rows to repeat at top** dialog box, click **Expand Dialog** 🖼. Click **OK** to print the column titles in row 13 at the top of every page.

You can collapse and then expand dialog boxes on your screen to enable a better view of your data.

8 Press Ctrl + F2 to display the **Print Preview** again. At the bottom of the **Settings group**, click the **No Scaling arrow**, and then on the displayed list, point to **Fit All Columns on One Page**. Compare your screen with Figure 2.30.

This action will shrink the width of the printed output to fit all the columns on one page. You can make adjustments like this on the Page Layout tab, or here, in the Print Preview.

FIGURE 2.30

9 Click **Fit All Columns on One Page**. Notice in the **Print Preview** that all the columns display on one page.

 ANOTHER WAY   With the worksheet displayed, on the Page Layout tab, in the Scale to Fit group, click the Width button arrow, and then click 1 page.

10 At the bottom of the **Print Preview**, click **Next Page** ▶ one time. Notice that the output will now print on two pages and that the column titles display at the top of **Page 2**. Compare your screen with Figure 2.31.

FIGURE 2.31

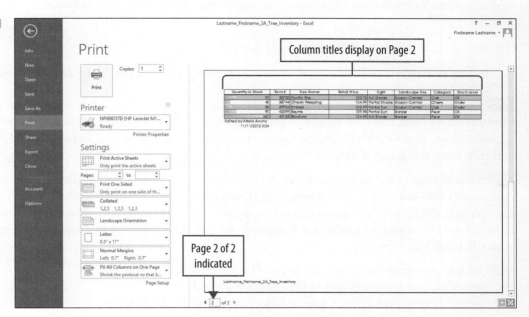

11 On the left, click **Info**, and then click **Show All Properties**. As the **Tags**, type **tree inventory, Pasadena** As the **Subject**, type your course name and section number. Be sure your name displays as the author; edit if necessary.

12 On the left, click **Save**. By using the techniques you practiced in Project 1A, print or submit electronically as directed by your instructor. If required by your instructor, print or create an electronic version of your worksheet with formulas displayed.

13 Close your workbook and close Excel.

More **Knowledge**   **Scaling for Data That Is Slightly Larger Than the Printed Page**

For data just a little too large to fit on a page, you can scale the worksheet to make it fit. Scaling reduces the width and height of the printed data to a percentage of its original size or by the number of pages that you specify. On the Page Layout tab, in the Scale to Fit group, click the Scale arrows to select a percentage.

END | You have completed Project 2A

GO! with Office Online (formerly Web Apps)

Objective | Sort, Filter, and Use Functions in a Table in Excel Online

If you are working on a computer that does not have Microsoft Office installed, you can still create new workbooks with tables in your web browser by using Excel Office Online.

> **ALERT!** **Working with Web-Based Applications and Services**
>
> Computer programs and services on the web receive continuous updates and improvements, so the steps to complete this web-based activity may differ from the ones shown. You can often look at the screens and the information presented to determine how to complete the activity.

Activity | Sort, Filter, and Use Functions in a Table

In this activity, you will use Excel Online to create a table similar to the one you created in Project 2A.

1 Launch your web browser, navigate to **http://onedrive.com**, and then sign in to your Microsoft account. Open your **GO! Web Projects** folder—or create and then open this folder if necessary.

2 Near the top of the screen, click **Create**, and then click **Excel workbook**. Above the ribbon, click Book1 (the number may differ) to select the text. Using your own name, as the file name type **Lastname_Firstname_EX_2A_Web** Click cell **1A**.

3 To help you create this project quickly and to eliminate extra typing, you will import the data from a Word document. From the taskbar, open **File Explorer**, navigate to the student data files that accompany this textbook, and then open the Word document **e02_2A_Web**. Press **Ctrl** + **A** to select all of the text, right-click anywhere over the selection, and then click **Copy**. **Close** [**×**] Word and if necessary **Close** [×] the folder window.

4 With cell **A1** selected, on the Excel Online ribbon, in the **Clipboard group**, click **Paste**; if necessary click Allow access.

5 Select column headings **A:H**, point to the border between any two selected column headings to display the [↔] pointer, and then double-click to resize all the columns to display all data.

6 Click cell **A1**, type **Pasadena Nursery: Tree Inventory** Press **Enter** and then **Merge & Center** the text

across the range **A1:H1**. In cell **A2**, type **As of December 31** and **Merge & Center** across the range **A2:H2**. Select the range **A1:A2** and apply **Bold** [**B**].

7 Click cell **B4**. On the **HOME tab**, in the **Editing group**, click the **AutoSum arrow** and then click **Sum**. Within the formula's parentheses, type **a13:a67** and press **Enter** for a result of *7085*. In cell **B5**, click the **AutoSum arrow** again, and then click **Average**. With *B4* selected, press **Backspace** one time, and then within the parentheses type **d13:d67** and press **Enter**. Your result is *108.09*.

8 With cell **B6** selected, click the **INSERT tab**, and then click **Function**. Click the **Pick a category arrow**, click **Statistical**, and then scroll down and click **MEDIAN**. Click **OK**. Type **d13:d67)** and press **Enter** for a result of *106.98*.

9 In cell **B7**, click **Function**, from the **Commonly Used** group click **MIN**, click **OK**, type **d13:d67)** and press **Enter** for a result of *79.99*. In cell **B8**, use the same technique to compute the Highest Price for a result of *131.78*.

10 In cell **B9**, display the list of **Commonly Used** functions, scroll down, click **COUNTIF**, and then click **OK**. Type **g13:g67,"Oak")** and press **Enter**. Compare your screen with Figure A.

FIGURE A

1	Pasadena Nursery: Tree Inventory	
2	As of December 31	
3		
4	Total Items in Stock	7085
5	Average Price	108.09
6	Median Price	106.98
7	Lowest Price	79.99
8	Highest Price	131.78
9	Oak Trees:	20
10	Magnolia Trees:	
11		

(GO! with Office Online (formerly Web Apps) continues on the next page)

11 Click cell **H13**. From the **Commonly Used** list of functions, insert **IF**, and then type **a13<75,"Order","OK")** and press Enter. Copy this formula down through cell **H67**, which you will have to do in sections due to the way Excel Online scrolls on your screen.

12 Scroll up and click cell **A12**, hold down Shift, drag the vertical scroll box down to view **row 67**, and then click cell **H67** to select the entire range of the table data. On the **INSERT tab**, click **Table**, and then click **OK**. Drag the scroll box back to the top of the vertical scroll bar.

13 Sort the **Retail Price** column in **Ascending** order. Click the **Category arrow**, click **Filter**, and then filter on **Magnolia**.

14 Scroll as necessary to view all the rows in the filtered table, click the **HOME tab**, and then in the **Tables**

group, click the **Format as Table arrow**. On the list, click **Toggle Total Row**. Notice that a total row displays and indicates *8* different types of Magnolia trees. In cell **B10** type **8 types** and press Enter.

15 Click any cell in the table. Click the **Format as Table arrow** again, and then click **Toggle Total Row** to turn it off. In the table, click the **Category arrow**, and then clear the filter. Press Ctrl + Home, and then compare your screen with Figure B.

16 If you are instructed to submit your file, use one of the methods outlined in the Note box below. Sign out of your OneDrive and close Internet Explorer.

N O T E   **Printing or Creating an Electronic File from Excel Online**

To print on paper, click the FILE tab, click Print, click the Print button, and then click Print. In the Print preview display, click Print. In the displayed Print dialog box, click Print to print on the printer connected to your system. To create an electronic file of your printout, from the Print dialog box, click the printer labeled *Send to OneNote 2013*, and then click Print. You may have to open and then close OneNote first if you have never opened it before. When OneNote opens, click the Quick Notes section of the displayed notebook, and then click OK. On the ribbon, click the FILE tab, click Export, and then create a PDF of the page. Navigate to an appropriate location and give the file an appropriate name. Close OneNote.

FIGURE B

	Quantity in Stock	Item #	Tree Name	Retail Price	Light	Landscape Use	Category	Stock Level
1	Pasadena Nursery: Tree Inventory							
2	As of December 31							
4	Total Items in Stock	7085						
5	Average Price	108.0944						
6	Median Price	106.98						
7	Lowest Price	79.99						
8	Highest Price	131.78						
9	Oak Trees:	20						
10	Magnolia Trees:	8 types						
13	20	43625	Petite Red	79.99	Partial Shade	Hedge	Oak	Order
14	120	55255	Canadian Boxwood	89.99	Partial Sun	Hedge	Oak	OK
15	190	46532	Bold Box	100.95	Partial Sun	Erosion	Maple	OK
16	140	78655	Honey Oak	102.78	Filtered Sun	Erosion	Oak	OK
17	75	38675	Palo Alto	102.99	Partial Shade	Erosion	Oak	OK
18	250	54635	Kagiri	102.99	Partial Shade	Border	Maple	OK

Sheet1

Weekly Sales Summary

MyITLab®
Project 2B Training

PROJECT ACTIVITIES

In Activities 2.21 through 2.35, you will edit an existing workbook for the Sales Director, Mariam Daly. The workbook summarizes the online and in-store sales of products during a one-week period in April. The worksheets of your completed workbook will look similar to Figure 2.32.

PROJECT FILES

For Project 2B, you will need the following file:

e02B_Weekly_Sales

You will save your workbook as:

Lastname_Firstname_2B_Weekly_Sales

PROJECT RESULTS

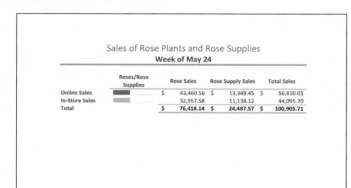

Sales of Rose Plants and Rose Supplies
Week of May 24

	Roses/Rose Supplies	Rose Sales	Rose Supply Sales	Total Sales
Online Sales		$ 43,460.56	$ 13,349.45	$ 56,810.01
In-Store Sales		32,957.58	11,138.12	44,095.70
Total		$ 76,418.14	$ 24,487.57	$ 100,905.71

Rose Plants and Rose Supplies: Weekly Online Sales
Week of May 24

Day	Climbing Roses	Patio Roses	Tea Roses	Total Rose Sales	Rose Supply Sales	Total Sales
Sun	$ 1,911.51	$ 2,026.46	$ 2,033.47	$ 5,971.44	$ 1,926.49	$ 7,897.93
Mon	2,310.49	2,313.85	1,782.64	6,406.98	1,526.03	7,933.01
Tue	1,942.37	2,402.99	2,030.08	6,375.44	1,853.82	8,229.26
Wed	2,185.89	1,992.29	2,253.98	6,432.16	1,922.36	8,354.52
Thu	2,003.53	1,825.79	2,340.34	6,169.66	1,973.73	8,143.39
Fri	1,931.46	1,946.92	1,966.92	5,845.30	2,121.47	7,966.77
Sat	2,047.23	1,978.23	2,234.12	6,259.58	2,025.55	8,285.13
Total	$ 14,332.48	$ 14,486.53	$ 14,641.55	$ 43,460.56	$ 13,349.45	$ 56,810.01

Recorded on:
6/3/16

Reviewed on:
6/7/16

Rose Plants and Rose Supplies: Weekly In-Store Sales
Week of May 24

Day	Climbing Roses	Patio Roses	Tea Roses	Total Rose Sales	Rose Supply Sales	Total Sales
Sun	$ 1,493.21	$ 1,681.92	$ 1,594.22	$ 4,769.35	$ 1,626.59	$ 6,395.94
Mon	1,689.37	1,552.58	1,624.44	4,866.39	1,483.69	6,350.08
Tue	1,271.12	1,709.58	1,386.26	4,366.96	1,693.82	6,060.78
Wed	1,410.88	1,584.02	1,596.72	4,591.62	1,778.94	6,370.56
Thu	1,558.58	1,526.63	1,735.51	4,820.72	1,416.37	6,237.09
Fri	1,483.62	1,486.91	1,656.56	4,627.09	1,645.24	6,272.33
Sat	1,605.58	1,783.64	1,526.23	4,915.45	1,493.47	6,408.92
Total	$ 10,512.36	$ 11,325.28	$ 11,119.94	$ 32,957.58	$ 11,138.12	$ 44,095.70

Recorded on:
6/3/16

Reviewed on:
6/7/16

FIGURE 2.32 Project 2B Weekly Sales Summary

Video E2-7

Use multiple worksheets in a workbook to organize data in a logical arrangement. When you have more than one worksheet in a workbook, you can *navigate* (move) among worksheets by clicking the *sheet tabs*. Sheet tabs identify each worksheet in a workbook and display along the lower left edge of the window. When you have more worksheets than can display in the sheet tab area, use the sheet tab scrolling buttons to move sheet tabs into and out of view.

Activity 2.21 | Navigating Among Worksheets, Renaming Worksheets, and Changing the Tab Color of Worksheets

Excel names the first worksheet in a workbook *Sheet1* and each additional worksheet that you add in order—*Sheet2*, *Sheet3*, and so on. Most Excel users rename their worksheets with meaningful names. In this activity, you will navigate among worksheets, rename worksheets, and change the tab color of sheet tabs.

1 Start Excel, and then in the lower left corner of Excel's opening screen, click **Open Other Workbooks**.

♻ ANOTHER WAY   Press Ctrl + F12 to display the Open dialog box.

2 Navigate to the student files that accompany this textbook, and then locate and open **e02B_Weekly_Sales**. Press F12 to display the **Save As** dialog box, and then navigate to your **Excel Chapter 2** folder. In the **File name** box, using your own name, type **Lastname_Firstname_2B_Weekly_Sales** and click **Save** or press Enter

In this workbook, two worksheets display into which some data has already been entered. For example, on the first worksheet, the days of the week and sales data for the one-week period displays.

3 Along the bottom of the Excel window, point to and then click the **Sheet2 tab**.

The second worksheet in the workbook displays and becomes the active worksheet. *Sheet2* displays in bold.

4 In cell **A1**, notice the text *In-Store*—this worksheet will contain data for in-store sales.

5 Click the **Sheet1 tab**. Then, point to the **Sheet1 tab**, and double-click to select the sheet tab name. Type **Online Sales** and press Enter.

The first worksheet becomes the active worksheet, and the sheet tab displays *Online Sales*.

6 Point to the **Sheet2 tab**, right-click, and then from the shortcut menu, click **Rename**. Type **In-Store Sales** and press Enter. Compare your screen with Figure 2.33.

You can use either of these methods to rename a sheet tab.

More Knowledge	Copying a Worksheet

To copy a worksheet to the same workbook, right-click the sheet tab, on the shortcut menu click Move or Copy, click the sheet before which you want to insert the copied sheet, select the Create a copy check box, and then click OK. To copy to a different workbook, in the Move or Copy dialog box, click the To book arrow, and then select the workbook into which you want to insert the copy.

FIGURE 2.33

7 Point to the **In-Store Sales sheet tab** and right-click. Point to **Tab Color**, and then in the last column, click the first color—**Green, Accent 6**.

 ANOTHER WAY   On the Home tab, in the Cells group, click the Format button, and then on the displayed list, point to Tab Color.

8 Using the technique you just practiced, change the tab color of the **Online Sales sheet tab** to **Blue, Accent 5**—in the next to last column, the first color. **Save** your workbook.

Objective 8 | Enter Dates, Clear Contents, and Clear Formats

Video E2-8

Dates represent a type of value that you can enter in a cell. When you enter a date, Excel assigns a serial value—a number—to the date. This makes it possible to treat dates like other numbers. For example, if two cells contain dates, you can find the number of days between the two dates by subtracting the older date from the more recent date.

Activity 2.22 | Entering and Formatting Dates

In this activity, you will examine the various ways that Excel can format dates in a cell. Date values entered in any of the following formats will be recognized by Excel as a date:

Format	Example
m/d/yy	7/4/2016
d-mmm	4-Jul
d-mmm-yy	4-Jul-16
mmm-yy	Jul-12

On your keyboard, - (the hyphen key) and / (the forward slash key) function identically in any of these formats and can be used interchangeably. You can abbreviate the month name to three characters or spell it out. You can enter the year as two digits, four digits, or even leave it off. When left off, the current year is assumed but does not display in the cell.

A two-digit year value of 30 through 99 is interpreted by the Windows operating system as the four-digit years of 1930 through 1999. All other two-digit year values are assumed to be in the 21st century. If you always type year values as four digits, even though only two digits may display in the cell, you can be sure that Excel interprets the year value as you intended. Examples are shown in Figure 2.34.

FIGURE 2.34

HOW EXCEL INTERPRETS DATES	
DATE TYPED AS:	**COMPLETED BY EXCEL AS:**
7/4/15	7/4/2015
7/4/98	7/4/1998
7/4	4-Jul (current year assumed)
7-4	4-Jul (current year assumed)
July 4	4-Jul (current year assumed)
Jul 4	4-Jul (current year assumed)
Jul/4	4-Jul (current year assumed)
Jul-4	4-Jul (current year assumed)
July 4, 1998	4-Jul-98
July 2012	Jul-12 (first day of month assumed)
July 1998	Jul-98 (first day of month assumed)

1 On the **Online Sales** sheet, click cell **A16** and notice that the cell displays *6/3*. In the **Formula Bar**, notice that the full date of June 3, 2016 displays in the format *6/3/2016*.

2 With cell **A16** selected, on the **HOME tab**, in the **Number group**, click the **Number Format arrow**. At the bottom, click **More Number Formats** to display the **Number tab** of the **Format Cells** dialog box.

Under Category, *Date* is selected, and under Type, *3/14* is selected. Cell A16 uses this format type; that is, only the month and day display in the cell.

3 In the displayed dialog box, under **Type**, click several other date types and watch the **Sample** area to see how applying the selected date format will format your cell. When you are finished, click the **3/14/12** type, and then compare your screen with Figure 2.35.

FIGURE 2.35

4 At the bottom of the dialog box, click **OK**. Click cell **A19**, type **6-7-16** and then press Enter.

Cell A19 has no special date formatting applied, and displays in the default date format *6/7/2016*.

ALERT! **The Date Does Not Display as 6/7/2016?**

Settings in your Windows operating system determine the default format for dates. If your result is different, it is likely that the formatting of the default date was adjusted on the computer at which you are working.

5 Click cell **A19** again. Hold down Ctrl and press [;] (semicolon) on your keyboard. Press Enter to confirm the entry.

> Excel enters the current date, obtained from your computer's internal calendar, in the selected cell using the default date format. Ctrl + [;] is a quick method to enter the current date.

6 Click cell **A19** again, type **6/7/16** and then press Enter.

> Because the year *16* is less than 30, Excel assumes a 21st century date and changes *16* to *2016* to complete the four-digit year. Typing *98* would result in *1998*. For two-digit years that you type that are between 30 and 99, Excel assumes a 20th century date.

7 Click cell **A16**, and then on the **HOME tab**, in the **Clipboard group**, click **Format Painter**. Click cell **A19**, and notice that the date format from cell **A16** is copied to cell **A19**. **Save** your workbook.

Activity 2.23 | Clearing Cell Contents and Formats

A cell has *contents*—a value or a formula—and a cell may also have one or more *formats* applied, for example bold and italic font styles, fill color, font color, and so on. You can choose to clear—delete—the *contents* of a cell, the *formatting* of a cell, or both.

Clearing the contents of a cell deletes the value or formula typed there, but it does *not* clear formatting applied to a cell. In this activity, you will clear the contents of a cell and then clear the formatting of a cell that contains a date to see its underlying content.

1 In the **Online Sales** worksheet, click cell **A1**. In the **Editing group**, click **Clear**, and then click **Clear Contents**. Notice that the text is cleared, but the green formatting remains.

2 Click cell **A2**, and then press Delete.

> You can use either of these two methods to delete the *contents* of a cell. Deleting the contents does not, however, delete the formatting of the cell; you can see that the green fill color format applied to the two cells still displays.

3 In cell **A1**, type **Online Sales** and then on the **Formula Bar**, click **Enter** so that cell **A1** remains the active cell.

> In addition to the green fill color, the bold italic text formatting remains with the cell.

4 In the **Editing group**, click **Clear**, and then click **Clear Formats**.

> Clearing the formats deletes formatting from the cell—the green fill color and the bold and italic font styles—but does not delete the cell's contents.

5 Use the same technique to clear the green fill color from cell **A2**. Click cell **A16**, click **Clear**, and then click **Clear Formats**. In the **Number group**, notice that *General* displays as the number format of the cell.

> The box in the Number group indicates the current Number format of the selected cell. Clearing the date formatting from the cell displays the date's serial number. The date, June 3, 2016, is stored as a serial number that indicates the number of days since January 1, 1900. This date is the 42,524th day since the reference date of January 1, 1900.

6 On the Quick Access Toolbar, click **Undo** to restore the date format. **Save** your workbook, and then compare your screen with Figure 2.36.

FIGURE 2.36

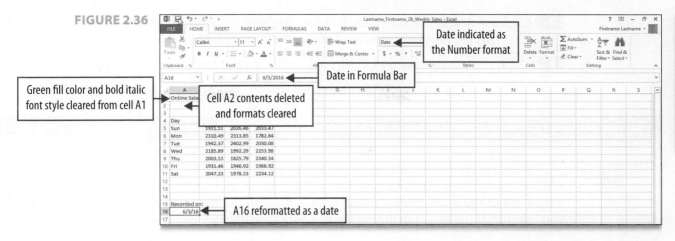

Green fill color and bold italic font style cleared from cell A1

Cell A2 contents deleted and formats cleared

Date indicated as the Number format

Date in Formula Bar

A16 reformatted as a date

More Knowledge | **Clearing an Entire Worksheet**

To clear an entire worksheet, in the upper left corner of the worksheet, click the Select All button, and then on the Home tab, in the Editing group, click Clear, and then click Clear All.

Objective 9 | Copy and Paste by Using the Paste Options Gallery

Video E2-9

Data in cells can be copied to other cells in the same worksheet, to other sheets in the same workbook, or to sheets in another workbook. The action of placing cell contents that have been copied or moved to the Clipboard into another location is called **paste**.

Activity 2.24 | Copying and Pasting by Using the Paste Options Gallery

Recall that the Clipboard is a temporary storage area maintained by your Windows operating system. When you select one or more cells, and then perform the Copy command or the Cut command, the selected data is placed on the Clipboard. From the Clipboard storage area, the data is available for pasting into other cells, other worksheets, other workbooks, and even into other Office programs. When you paste, the **Paste Options gallery** displays, which includes Live Preview to preview the Paste formatting that you want.

1 With the **Online Sales** worksheet active, select the range **A4:A19**.

A range of cells identical to this one is required for the *In-Store Sales* worksheet.

2 Right-click over the selection, and then click **Copy** to place a copy of the cells on the Clipboard. Notice that the copied cells display a moving border.

3 At the bottom of the workbook window, click the **In-Store Sales sheet tab** to make it the active worksheet. Point to cell **A4**, right-click, and then on the shortcut menu, under **Paste Options**, *point* to the first button—**Paste**. Compare your screen with Figure 2.37.

Live Preview displays how the copied cells will be placed in the worksheet if you click the Paste button. In this manner, you can experiment with different paste options, and then be sure you are selecting the paste operation that you want. When pasting a range of cells, you need only point to or select the cell in the upper left corner of the **paste area**—the target destination for data that has been cut or copied using the Clipboard.

FIGURE 2.37

Paste Options (6 option buttons)

4 ❯ Click the first button, **Paste**. In the status bar, notice the message that displays, indicating that your selected range remains available on the Office Clipboard.

5 ❯ Display the **Online Sales** worksheet. Press (Esc) to cancel the moving border. **Save** your workbook.

The status bar no longer displays the message.

Objective 10   Edit and Format Multiple Worksheets at the Same Time

Video E2-10

You can enter or edit data on several worksheets at the same time by selecting and grouping multiple worksheets. Data that you enter or edit on the active sheet is reflected in all selected sheets. If you apply color to the sheet tabs, the name of the sheet tab will be underlined in the color you selected. If the sheet tab displays with a background color, you know the sheet is not selected.

Activity 2.25 | Grouping Worksheets for Editing

1 ❯ With the **Online Sales** sheet active, press (Ctrl) + (Home) to make cell **A1** the active cell. Point to the **Online Sales sheet tab**, right-click, and then click **Select All Sheets**.

2 ❯ At the top of your screen, notice that *[Group]* displays in the title bar. Compare your screen with Figure 2.38.

Both worksheets are selected, as indicated by *[Group]* in the title bar and the sheet tab names underlined. Data that you enter or edit on the active sheet will also be entered or edited in the same manner on all the selected sheets in the same cells.

FIGURE 2.38

3 ❯ Select **columns A:G**, and then set their width to **85 pixels**.

4 ❯ Click cell **A2**, type **Week of May 24** and then on the **Formula Bar**, click **Enter** ✓ to keep cell **A2** as the active cell. **Merge & Center** the text across the range **A2:G2**, and then apply the **Heading 1** cell style.

5 ❯ Click cell **E4**, type **Total Rose Sales** and then press (Tab). In cell **F4**, type **Rose Supply Sales** and then press (Tab). In cell **G4**, type **Total Sales** and then press (Enter).

6 ❯ Select the range **A4:G4**, and then apply the **Heading 3** cell style. In the **Alignment group**, click **Center**, **Middle Align**, and **Wrap Text**. **Save** your workbook.

7 ❯ Display the **In-Store Sales** worksheet to cancel the grouping, and then compare your screen with Figure 2.39.

As soon as you select a single sheet, the grouping of the sheets is canceled and *[Group]* no longer displays in the title bar. Because the sheets were grouped, the same new text and formatting were applied to both sheets. In this manner, you can make the same changes to all the sheets in a workbook at one time.

More Knowledge   **Hide Worksheets**

You can hide any worksheet in a workbook to remove it from view using this technique:
Select the sheet tabs of the worksheets you want to hide, right-click any of the selected sheet tabs, and then click Hide.

FIGURE 2.39

ANOTHER WAY   Right-click any sheet tab, and then click Ungroup Sheets.

Activity 2.26 | Formatting and Constructing Formulas on Grouped Worksheets

Recall that formulas are equations that perform calculations on values in your worksheet and that a formula starts with an equal sign (=). Operators are the symbols with which you specify the type of calculation that you want to perform on the elements of a formula. In this activity, you will enter and calculate sales for Rose Supply items from both Online and In-Store sales.

1 Display the **Online Sales** worksheet. Verify that the sheets are not grouped—*[Group]* does *not* display in the title bar.

2 Click cell **A1**, replace *Online Sales* by typing **Rose Plants and Rose Supplies: Weekly Online Sales** and then on the **Formula Bar**, click **Enter** ✓ to keep cell **A1** as the active cell. **Merge & Center** the text across the range **A1:G1**, and then apply the **Title** cell style.

3 In the column titled *Rose Supply Sales*, click cell **F5**, in the range **F5:F11**, type the following data for Rose Supply Sales, and then compare your screen with Figure 2.40.

	ROSE SUPPLY SALES
Sun	1926.49
Mon	1526.03
Tue	1853.82
Wed	1922.36
Thu	1973.73
Fri	2121.47
Sat	2025.55

FIGURE 2.40

Worksheet title entered and formatted for Online Sales sheet

Rose Supply Sales data entered

4 ▶ Display the **In-Store Sales** sheet. In cell **A1**, replace *In-Store* by typing **Rose Plants and Rose Supplies: Weekly In-Store Sales** and then on the **Formula Bar**, click **Enter** ✓ to keep cell **A1** as the active cell. **Merge & Center** the text across the range **A1:G1**, and then apply the **Title** cell style.

5 ▶ In the column titled *Rose Supply Sales*, click cell **F5**, in the range **F5:F11**, type the following data for Rose Supply Sales, and then compare your screen with Figure 2.41.

ROSE SUPPLY SALES	
Sun	1626.59
Mon	1483.69
Tue	1693.82
Wed	1778.94
Thu	1416.37
Fri	1645.24
Sat	1493.47

FIGURE 2.41

Worksheet title entered and formatted for In-Store Sales sheet

Rose Supply Sales data entered

6 ▶ **Save** 🖫 your workbook. Right-click the **Online Sales sheet tab**, and then click **Select All Sheets**.

The first worksheet becomes the active sheet, and the worksheets are grouped. *[Group]* displays in the title bar, and the sheet tabs are underlined in the tab color to indicate they are selected as part of the group. Recall that when grouped, any action that you perform on the active worksheet is *also* performed on any other selected worksheets.

7 ▶ With the sheets *grouped* and the **Online Sales** sheet active, click cell **E5**. On the **HOME tab**, in the **Editing group**, click **AutoSum**. Compare your screen with Figure 2.42.

Recall that when you enter the SUM function, Excel looks first above and then left for a proposed range of cells to sum.

FIGURE 2.42

8 Press Enter to display Total Rose Sales for Sunday, which is *5971.44*.

9 Click cell **E5**, and then drag the fill handle down to copy the formula through cell **E11**.

10 Click cell **G5**, type **=** click cell **E5**, type **+** click cell **F5**, and then compare your screen with Figure 2.43.

> Using the point-and-click technique to construct this formula is only one of several techniques you can use. Alternatively, you could use any other method to enter the SUM function to add the values in these two cells.

FIGURE 2.43

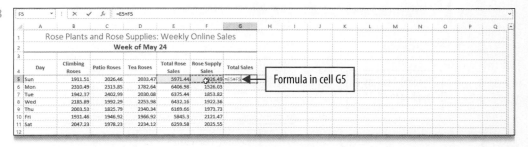

11 Press Enter to display the result *7897.93*, and then copy the formula down through cell **G11**.

Activity 2.27 | Determining Multiple Totals at the Same Time

You can select a contiguous range of cells adjacent to rows or columns of numbers and then click the Sum button—or use Alt + =—to enter the a SUM function for each row or column.

1 **Save** 🖫 your workbook. With the two worksheets still grouped, in cell **A12**, type **Total** and then select the range **B5:G12**, which is all of the sales data and the empty cells at the bottom of each column of sales data.

2 With the range **B5:G12** selected, hold down Alt and press = to enter the **SUM** function in each empty cell. Click **Save** 🖫.

> Selecting a range in this manner and then clicking the SUM button, or entering the SUM function with the keyboard shortcut Alt = =, places the Sum function in the empty cells at the bottom of each column.

Activity 2.28 | Formatting Grouped Worksheets

1 With the two worksheets still grouped, select the range **A5:A12**, and then apply the **Heading 4** cell style.

2 To apply financial formatting to the worksheets, select the range **B5:G5**, hold down Ctrl, and then select the range **B12:G12**. With the nonadjacent ranges selected, apply the **Accounting Number Format** $ ▾.

3 ▸ Select the range **B6:G11** and apply **Comma Style** ⎇. Select the range **B12:G12** and apply the **Total** cell style.

4 ▸ Press ⎘Ctrl + ⎘Home to move to the top of the worksheet; compare your screen with Figure 2.44.

FIGURE 2.44

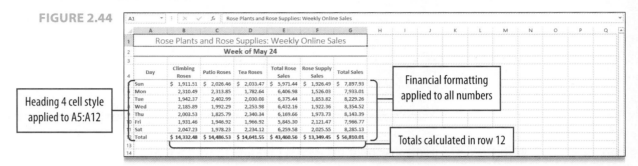

Heading 4 cell style applied to A5:A12

Financial formatting applied to all numbers

Totals calculated in row 12

Activity 2.29 | Ungrouping Worksheets

1 ▸ Click the **In-Store Sales sheet tab** to cancel the grouping and display the second worksheet. Click Save 🖫, and then compare your screen with Figure 2.45.

With your worksheets grouped, the calculations and formatting on the first worksheet were also added on the second worksheet. As soon as you click a single sheet tab, the grouping is canceled.

FIGURE 2.45

Heading 4 cell style applied to A5:A12

Financial formatting applied to all numbers

Totals calculated in row 12

Objective 11   Create a Summary Sheet with Column Sparklines

Video E2-11

A *summary sheet* is a worksheet where totals from other worksheets are displayed and summarized. Recall that sparklines are tiny charts within a single cell that show a data trend.

Activity 2.30 | Inserting a Worksheet

1 ▸ To the right of the **In-Store Sales** sheet tab, click **New sheet** ⊕.

2 ▸ Rename the new worksheet tab **Summary** and change its **Tab Color** to **Gold, Accent 4**.

3 ▸ Widen **columns A:E** to **110** pixels. In cell **A1**, type **Sales of Rose Plants and Rose Supplies** Merge & Center the title across the range **A1:E1**, and then apply the **Title** cell style.

4 ▸ In cell **A2**, type **Week of May 24** and then **Merge & Center** across **A2:E2**; apply the **Heading 1** cell style.

5 ▸ Leave **row 3** blank. To form column titles, in cell **B4**, type **Roses/Rose Supplies** and press ⎘Tab. In cell **C4**, type **Rose Sales** and press ⎘Tab. In cell **D4**, type **Rose Supply Sales** and press ⎘Tab. In cell **E4**, type **Total Sales** Press ⎘Enter.

6 Select the range **B4:E4**. Apply the **Heading 3** cell style. In the **Alignment group**, click **Center** ▤, **Middle Align** ▤, and **Wrap Text**.

7 To form row titles, in cell **A5**, type **Online Sales** In cell **A6**, type **In-Store Sales** Save 🖫, and then compare your screen with Figure 2.46.

FIGURE 2.46

FIGURE 2.46

Activity 2.31 | Constructing Formulas That Refer to Cells in Another Worksheet

In this activity, you will construct formulas in the Summary worksheet to display the total sales for both online sales and in-store sales that will update the Summary worksheet whenever changes are made to the other worksheet totals.

1 Click cell **C5**. Type **=** Click the **Online Sales sheet tab**. On the **Online Sales** worksheet, click cell **E12**, and then press Enter to redisplay the **Summary** worksheet and insert the total **Rose Sales** amount of *$43,460.56*.

2 Click cell **C5** to select it again. Look at the **Formula Bar**, and notice that instead of a value, the cell contains a formula that is equal to the value in another cell in another worksheet. Compare your screen with Figure 2.47.

The value in this cell is equal to the value in cell E12 of the *Online Sales* worksheet. The Accounting Number Format applied to the referenced cell is carried over. By using a formula of this type, changes in cell E12 on the *Online Sales* worksheet will be automatically updated in this *Summary* worksheet.

FIGURE 2.47

3 Click cell **D5**. Type **=** and then click the **Online Sales sheet tab**. Click cell **F12**, and then press Enter to redisplay the **Summary** worksheet and insert the total **Rose Supply Sales** amount of *$13,349.45*.

4 By using the techniques you just practiced, in cells **C6** and **D6** insert the total **Rose Sales** and **Rose Supply Sales** data from the **In-Store Sales** worksheet. Click **Save** 🖫, and then compare your screen with Figure 2.48.

FIGURE 2.48

Activity 2.32 | Changing Values in a Detail Worksheet to Update a Summary Worksheet

The formulas in cells C5:D6 display the totals from the other two worksheets. Changes made to any of the other two worksheets—sometimes referred to as **detail sheets** because the details of the information are contained there—that affect their totals will display on this Summary worksheet. In this manner, the Summary worksheet accurately displays the current totals from the other worksheets.

1 In cell **A7**, type **Total** Select the range **C5:E6**, and then on the **HOME tab**, in the **Editing group**, click **AutoSum** to total the two rows.

> This technique is similar to selecting the empty cells at the bottom of columns and then inserting the SUM function for each column. Alternatively, you could use any other method to sum the rows. Recall that cell formatting carries over to adjacent cells unless two cells are left blank.

2 Select the range **C5:E7**, and then click **AutoSum** to total the three columns. Compare your screen with Figure 2.49.

FIGURE 2.49

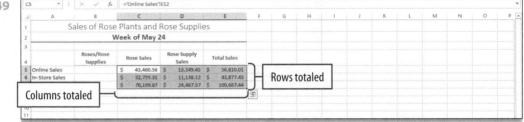

3 In cell **C6**, notice that total **Rose Sales** for **In-Store** Sales is *$32,739.31*, and in cell **C7**, notice the total of *$76,199.87*.

4 Display the **In-Store Sales** worksheet, click cell **B8**, type **1410.88** and then press Enter. Notice that the formulas in the worksheet recalculate.

5 Display the **Summary** worksheet, and notice that in the **Rose Sales** column, both the total for the *In-Store Sales* and the *Total* were recalculated.

> In this manner, a Summary sheet recalculates any changes made in the other worksheets.

6 On the **Summary** worksheet, select the range **C6:E6** and change the format to **Comma Style**. Select the range **C7:E7**, and then apply the **Total** cell style. Select the range **A5:A7** and apply the **Heading 4** cell style. Save your workbook. Click cell **A1**, and then compare your screen with Figure 2.50.

FIGURE 2.50

Activity 2.33 | Inserting Column Sparklines

In this activity, you will insert column sparklines to visualize the ratio of Rose sales to Rose Supply sales for both Online and In-Store.

1 On the **Summary** worksheet, click cell **B5**. On the **INSERT tab**, in the **Sparklines group**, click **Column**. In the **Create Sparklines** dialog box, with the insertion point blinking in the **Data Range** box, type **c5:d5** and then compare your screen with Figure 2.51.

FIGURE 2.51

 Video E2-12

2 ▶ Click **OK**. Click cell **B6**, and then **INSERT** a **Column Sparkline** for the range **c6:d6** In the **Style group**, apply **Sparkline Style Accent 4, (no dark or light)**—in the third row, the fourth style. Press [Ctrl] + [Home], click **Save** 🗖, and then compare your screen with Figure 2.52.

You can see, at a glance, that for both Online and In-Store sales, Rose sales are much greater than Rose Supply sales.

FIGURE 2.52

Column sparklines compare sales of Roses to Rose Supplies in both Online and In-Store

---

Objective 12 | Format and Print Multiple Worksheets in a Workbook

Each worksheet within a workbook can have different formatting, for example different headers or footers. If all the worksheets in the workbook will have the same header or footer, you can select all the worksheets and apply formatting common to all of the worksheets; for example, you can set the same footer in all of the worksheets.

Activity 2.34 | Moving a Worksheet, Repeating Footers, and Formatting Multiple Worksheets in a Workbook

In this activity, you will move the Summary sheet to become the first worksheet in the workbook. Then you will format and prepare your workbook for printing. The three worksheets containing data can be formatted simultaneously.

1 ▶ Point to the **Summary sheet tab**, hold down the left mouse button to display a small black triangle—a caret—and then notice that a small paper icon attaches to the mouse pointer.

2 ▶ Drag to the left until the caret and mouse pointer are to the left of the **Online Sales sheet tab**, as shown in Figure 2.53, and then release the left mouse button.

Use this technique to rearrange the order of worksheets within a workbook.

FIGURE 2.53

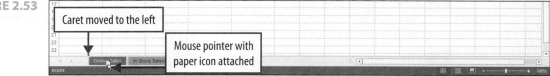

Caret moved to the left

Mouse pointer with paper icon attached

3 ▶ Be sure the **Summary** worksheet is the active sheet, point to its sheet tab, right-click, and then click **Select All Sheets** to display *[Group]* in the title bar.

4 ▶ Click the **PAGE LAYOUT tab**. In the **Page Setup group**, click **Margins**, and then at the bottom of the gallery, click **Custom Margins** to display the **Page Setup** dialog box.

5 In the **Page Setup** dialog box, on the **Margins tab**, under **Center on page**, select the **Horizontally** check box.

6 Click the **Header/Footer tab**, and then in the center of the dialog box, click **Custom Footer**. In the **Footer** dialog box, with your insertion point blinking in the **Left section**, on the row of buttons, click **Insert File Name** 📄.

7 Click **OK** two times.

The dotted line indicates the page break as currently formatted.

8 Press Ctrl + Home; verify that *[Group]* still displays in the title bar.

By selecting all sheets, you can apply the same formatting to all the worksheets at the same time, for example to repeat headers or footers.

9 Click the **FILE tab** to display **Backstage** view, and then click **Show All Properties**. As the **Tags**, type **weekly sales, online, in-store, rose plants, rose supplies** In the **Subject** box, type your course name and section number. Be sure your name displays as the author.

10 On the left, click **Print** to display the **Print Preview**, and then compare your screen with Figure 2.54.

By grouping, you can view all sheets in Print Preview. If you do not see *1 of 3* at the bottom of the Preview, redisplay the workbook, select all the sheets again, and then redisplay Print Preview.

FIGURE 2.54

11 At the bottom of the **Print Preview**, click **Next Page** ▶ as necessary and take a moment to view each page of your workbook.

Activity 2.35 | Printing All or Individual Worksheets in a Workbook

1 In **Backstage** view, click **Save** to save your workbook before printing. In the displayed workbook, right-click the **Summary sheet tab**, and then click **Ungroup Sheets**.

2 Press Ctrl + F2 to display **Print Preview**, and then at the bottom of the window, notice that *1 of 1* is indicated.

Because the worksheets are no longer grouped, only the active sheet is available for printing.

3 On the left, under **Settings**, click **Print Active Sheets**, and then click **Print Entire Workbook**.

At the bottom of the window, *1 of 3* is indicated. By default, Excel prints only the active worksheet; however, you can use this command to print an entire workbook.

4 By using the techniques you practiced in Project 1A, print or submit electronically as directed by your instructor. If required by your instructor, print or create an electronic version of your worksheet with formulas displayed.

5 Close your workbook and close Excel.

END | You have completed Project 2B

Objective | Summarize the Data on Multiple Worksheets in Excel Online

If you are working on a computer that does not have Microsoft Office installed, you can still create new workbooks in your web browser by using Excel Online.

> **A L E R T !** | **Working with Web-Based Applications and Services**
>
> Computer programs and services on the web receive continuous updates and improvements, so the steps to complete this web-based activity may differ from the ones shown. You can often look at the screens and the information presented to determine how to complete the activity.

Activity | Creating an Inventory Valuation Report in Excel Online

In this activity, you will use Excel Online to add a worksheet to a workbook created in Excel.

1 Launch your web browser, navigate to **http://onedrive.com**, and then sign in to your Microsoft account. Open your **GO! Web Projects** folder—or create and then open this folder if necessary.

2 In the OneDrive menu bar, click **Upload**. In the **Choose File to Upload** dialog box, navigate to your student data files, click the Excel file **e02_2B_Web**, and then click **Open**.

3 Point to the uploaded file **e02_2B_Web**, and then right-click. On the shortcut menu, scroll as necessary, and then click **Rename**. Using your own name, type **Lastname_Firstname_EX_2B_Web** and then press Enter to rename the file.

4 Click the file you just renamed to open it in Excel Online.

5 At the bottom of the workbook, at the right end of the sheet tabs, click **New sheet** ⊕. Double-click the **Sheet4 tab**, and then name the worksheet tab **TV Sales**

6 To help you create this project quickly and to eliminate extra typing, you will import the data from

a Word table. From the taskbar, open **File Explorer**, navigate to the student data files that accompany this textbook, and then open the Word document **e02_2B_TV_Sales**. Press Ctrl + A to select all of the text, right-click anywhere over the selection, and then click **Copy**. **Close** Word and the File Explorer window.

7 With cell **A1** selected, on the ribbon, in the **Clipboard group**, click **Paste**; if necessary click Allow access. Notice that # symbols display when numeric data is too wide for the cell.

8 Select the range **A1:G1**, and then in the **Alignment group**, click **Merge & Center**. Merge and center the worksheet's subtitle in the same manner. Select the range **A1:A2**, and then in the **Font group**, apply **Bold**.

9 Select column headings **A:G**, point to the border between any two selected column headings to display the ⇪ pointer, and then double-click to resize all the columns to display all data.

10 Select the range **B5:G12**, and then in the **Editing group**, click **AutoSum** to total all the columns. Compare your screen with Figure A.

FIGURE A

(GO! with Office Online (formerly Web Apps) continues on the next page)

11 ▶ Display the **Summary** worksheet, and then click cell **A7**. In the **Cells group**, click the **Insert button arrow**, and then click **Insert Rows**. In the new cell **A7**, type **TV Sales** and then press Tab two times to make cell **C7** active.

12 ▶ Type **='TV Sales'!E12** and press Enter for a result of *$10,460.56*. Notice that you cannot use the = plus Enter method in Excel Online, but you can simply type the command.

13 ▶ Click cell **C7** and drag the fill handle to the right to cell **E7**. Compare your screen with Figure B. Notice that

Excel copies the formula and adjusts the cell references to record the Rose Supply Sales and the Total Sales from the TV Sales worksheet. Also, the sparkline is filled in. The TV Sales had higher sales of Rose Supplies than Rose plants.

14 ▶ If you are instructed to submit your file, use one of the methods outlined in the Note box below. Sign out of your OneDrive and close Internet Explorer.

NOTE   **Printing or Creating an Electronic File from Excel Online**

To print on paper, click the FILE tab, click Print, click the Print button, and then click Print. In the Print preview display, click Print. In the displayed Print dialog box, click Print to print on the printer connected to your system. To create an electronic file of your printout, from the Print dialog box, click the printer labeled *Send to OneNote 2013*, and then click Print. You may have to open and then close OneNote first if you have never opened it before. When OneNote opens, click the Quick Notes section of the displayed notebook, and then click OK. On the ribbon, click the FILE tab, click Export, and then create a PDF of the page. Navigate to an appropriate location and give the file an appropriate name. Close OneNote.

FIGURE B

Andrew Rodriguez / Fotolia; FotolEdhar/ Fotolia; apops/ Fotolia; Yuri Arcurs/ Fotolia

Office 365 includes business-class security and is backed by Microsoft. For an organization, what does that mean?

When you and a few classmates work together on a class project, you are not concerned about the security of your data. You probably use free personal email services such as Hotmail, Gmail, or Yahoo Mail to exchange documents, or perhaps you post your documents to free services such as Google Docs.

Organizations, on the other hand—even small ones with only two or three employees—must be concerned with the privacy and security of their data. Organizations cannot entrust their data and confidential communications to free services that may change frequently or that have no legal responsibility for the security of the data.

Organizations must provide each employee with a company email address rather than having each employee use his or her own personal free email address for business communications. Organizations must provide a central storage location for its data rather than having employees store data on flash drives or local hard drives with no control or oversight.

An organization must have a *secure environment*, which is a system that uses controlled *servers*—computers that provide services on a network such as an email server or a file server—to ensure the security and privacy of email, to control the storage and use of information, and to protect against the loss of confidential data.

Most small organizations cannot afford to hire the people with the skills necessary to install and maintain servers. So to establish and maintain a secure environment, many small organizations contract with and rely on small IT—the acronym for *Information Technology*—hosting companies to host their email communications and to provide secure storage.

Activity | **Using Lync to Collaborate by Using a Video Call**

This group project relates to the **Bell Orchid Hotels**. If your instructor assigns this project to your class, you can expect to use **Lync** in **Office 365** to collaborate on the following tasks for this chapter:

- If you are in the **Accounting Group**, you and your teammates will conduct a video call to discuss and agree on a workbook to summarize hotel rooms sold over a four-week period in April.

- If you are in the **Engineering Group**, you and your teammates will conduct a video call to discuss and agree on a workbook summarizing Maintenance Expenses for the first quarter.

- If you are in the **Food and Beverage Group**, you and your teammates will conduct a video call to discuss and agree on a Menu Analysis workbook to analyze the profitability of the ten most popular entrees in the hotel's restaurant.

- If you are in the **Human Resources Group**, you and your teammates will conduct a video call to discuss and agree on a Salary Analysis workbook summarizing the pay of salaried employees over the first six months of operation.

- If you are in the **Operations Group**, you and your teammates will conduct a video call to discuss and agree on a workbook for Rooms and Housekeeping Service Analysis that will be used to determine ongoing needs for housekeeping service.

- If you are in the **Sales and Marking Group**, you and your teammates will conduct a video call to discuss and agree on a Rooms Sold Analysis workbook summarizing rooms sold by four salespersons during January-June that will be used to develop a marketing plan for the rest of the year.

FIGURE A

END OF CHAPTER

SUMMARY

Use Flash Fill to recognize a pattern in data and automatically fill in values when you enter examples of desired output. Flash Fill can split data from two or more cells or combine data from two cells.

Functions are formulas that Excel provides and that perform calculations by using specific values in a particular order or structure. Statistical functions are useful to analyze a group of measurements.

You can navigate among worksheets in a workbook by clicking the sheet tabs, which identify each worksheet in a workbook. Use multiple worksheets in a workbook to organize data in a logical arrangement.

Dates are a value you can enter in a cell to which Excel assigns a serial value—a number—so that you can treat dates like other numbers. For example, you can find the number of days between two dates.

GO! LEARN IT ONLINE

Review the concepts and key terms in this chapter by completing these online challenges, which you can find at **www.pearsonhighered.com/go**.

Matching and Multiple Choice:
Answer matching and multiple choice questions to test what you learned in this chapter. MyITLab®

Crossword Puzzle:
Spell out the words that match the numbered clues, and put them in the puzzle squares.

Flipboard:
Flip through the definitions of the key terms in this chapter and match them with the correct term.

GO! FOR JOB SUCCESS

Video: Customer Service

Your instructor may assign this video to your class, and then ask you to think about, or discuss with your classmates, these questions:

FotolEdhar / Fotolia

How could Lee have been more helpful to the customer?

What did the supervisor, Christine, do to calm the customer?

What might SunTel do on a company-wide basis to create a better customer service experience?

END OF CHAPTER

REVIEW AND ASSESSMENT GUIDE FOR EXCEL CHAPTER 2

Your instructor may assign one or more of these projects to help you review the chapter and assess your mastery and understanding of the chapter.

	Review and Assessment Guide for Excel Chapter 2		
Project	**Apply Skills from These Chapter Objectives**	**Project Type**	**Project Location**
2C	Objectives 1-6 from Project 2A	**2C Skills Review** A guided review of the skills from Project 2A.	On the following pages
2D	Objectives 7-12 from Project 2B	**2D Skills Review** A guided review of the skills from Project 2B.	On the following pages
2E	Objectives 1-6 from Project 2A	**2E Mastery (Grader Project)** A demonstration of your mastery of the skills in Project 2A with extensive decision making.	In MyITLab and on the following pages
2F	Objectives 7-12 from Project 2B	**2F Mastery (Grader Project)** A demonstration of your mastery of the skills in Project 2B with extensive decision making.	In MyITLab and on the following pages
2G	Objectives 1-12 from Projects 2A and 2B	**2G Mastery (Grader Project)** A demonstration of your mastery of the skills in Projects 2A and 2B with extensive decision making.	In MyITLab and on the following pages
2H	Combination of Objectives from Projects 2A and 2B	**2H GO! Fix It** A demonstration of your mastery of the skills in Projects 2A and 2B by creating a correct result from a document that contains errors you must find.	Online
2I	Combination of Objectives from Projects 2A and 2B	**2I GO! Make It** A demonstration of your mastery of the skills in Projects 2A and 2B by creating a result from a supplied picture.	Online
2J	Combination of Objectives from Projects 2A and 2B	**2J GO! Solve It** A demonstration of your mastery of the skills in Projects 2A and 2B, your decision-making skills, and your critical thinking skills. A task-specific rubric helps you self-assess your result.	Online
2K	Combination of Objectives from Projects 2A and 2B	**2K GO! Solve It** A demonstration of your mastery of the skills in Projects 2A and 2B, your decision-making skills, and your critical thinking skills. A task-specific rubric helps you self-assess your result.	On the following pages
2L	Combination of Objectives from Projects 2A and 2B	**2L GO! Think** A demonstration of your understanding of the Chapter concepts applied in a manner that you would outside of college. An analytic rubric helps you and your instructor grade the quality of your work by comparing it to the work an expert in the discipline would create.	On the following pages
2M	Combination of Objectives from Projects 2A and 2B	**2M GO! Think** A demonstration of your understanding of the Chapter concepts applied in a manner that you would outside of college. An analytic rubric helps you and your instructor grade the quality of your work by comparing it to the work an expert in the discipline would create.	Online
2N	Combination of Objectives from Projects 2A and 2B	**2N You and GO!** A demonstration of your understanding of the Chapter concepts applied in a manner that you would in a personal situation. An analytic rubric helps you and your instructor grade the quality of your work.	Online
2O	Combination of Objectives from Projects 2A and 2B	**2O Cumulative Group Project for Excel Chapter 2** A demonstration of your understanding of concepts and your ability to work collaboratively in a group role-playing assessment, requiring both collaboration and self-management.	Online

GLOSSARY

GLOSSARY OF CHAPTER KEY TERMS

Arguments The values that an Excel function uses to perform calculations or operations.

AVERAGE function An Excel function that adds a group of values, and then divides the result by the number of values in the group.

Comparison operators Symbols that evaluate each value to determine if it is the same (=), greater than (>), less than (<), or in between a range of values as specified by the criteria.

Conditional format A format that changes the appearance of a cell—for example, by adding cell shading or font color—based on a condition; if the condition is true, the cell is formatted based on that condition, and if the condition is false, the cell is *not* formatted.

COUNT A statistical function that counts the number of cells in a range that contain numbers.

COUNTIF function A statistical function that counts the number of cells within a range that meet the given condition and that has two arguments—the range of cells to check and the criteria.

Criteria Conditions that you specify in a logical function.

Data bar A cell format consisting of a shaded bar that provides a visual cue to the reader about the value of a cell relative to other cells; the length of the bar represents the value in the cell—a longer bar represents a higher value and a shorter bar represents s lower value.

Detail sheets The worksheets that contain the details of the information summarized on a summary sheet.

Drag and drop The action of moving a selection by dragging it to a new location.

Excel table A series of rows and columns that contains related data that is managed independently from the data in other rows and columns in the worksheet.

Filter The process of displaying only a portion of the data based on matching a specific value to show only the data that meets the criteria that you specify.

Find and replace A command that searches the cells in a worksheet—or in a selected range—for matches and then replaces each match with a replacement value of your choice.

Flash Fill Recognizes a pattern in your data, and then automatically fills in values when you enter examples of the output that you want. Use it to split data from two or more cells or to combine data from two cells.

Formula AutoComplete An Excel feature that, after typing an = (equal sign) and the beginning letter or letters of a function name, displays a list of function names that match the typed letter(s), and from which you can insert the function by pointing to its name and pressing the Tab key or double-clicking.

Freeze Panes A command that enables you to select one or more rows or columns and freeze (lock) them into place; the locked rows and columns become separate panes.

Function A predefined formula—a formula that Excel has already built for you—that performs calculations by using specific values in a particular order or structure.

IF function A function that uses a logical test to check whether a condition is met, and then returns one value if true, and another value if false.

Logical functions A group of functions that test for specific conditions and that typically use conditional tests to determine whether specified conditions are true or false.

Logical test Any value or expression that can be evaluated as being true or false.

MAX function An Excel function that determines the largest value in a selected range of values.

MEDIAN function An Excel function that finds the middle value that has as many values above it in the group as are below it; it differs from AVERAGE in that the result is not affected as much by a single value that is greatly different from the others.

MIN function An Excel function that determines the smallest value in a selected range of values.

Navigate The process of moving within a worksheet or workbook.

NOW function An Excel function that retrieves the date and time from your computer's calendar and clock and inserts the information into the selected cell.

Pane A portion of a worksheet window bounded by and separated from other portions by vertical and horizontal bars.

Paste The action of placing cell contents that have been copied or moved to the Clipboard into another location.

Paste area The target destination for data that has been cut or copied using the Office Clipboard.

Paste Options gallery A gallery of buttons that provides a Live Preview of all the Paste options available in the current context.

Print Titles An Excel command that enables you to specify rows and columns to repeat on each printed page.

Scale to Fit Excel commands that enable you to stretch or shrink the width, height, or both, of printed output to fit a maximum number of pages.

Sheet tabs The labels along the lower border of the workbook window that identify each worksheet.

Sort The process of arranging data in a specific order based on the value in each field.

Split Splits the window into multiple resizable panes that contain views of your worksheet. This is useful to view multiple distant parts of your worksheet at one time.

Statistical functions Excel functions, including the AVERAGE, MEDIAN, MIN, and MAX functions, which are useful to analyze a group of measurements.

SUM function A predefined formula that adds all the numbers in a selected range of cells.

Summary sheet A worksheet where totals from other worksheets are displayed and summarized.

Volatile A term used to describe an Excel function that is subject to change each time the workbook is reopened; for example the NOW function updates itself to the current date and time each time the workbook is opened.

CHAPTER REVIEW

Skills Review Project 2C Roses

In the following Skills Review, you will edit a worksheet detailing the current inventory of Roses at the Pasadena nursery. Your completed workbook will look similar to Figure 2.55.

PROJECT FILES

For Project 2C, you will need the following file:

e02C_Roses

You will save your workbook as:

Lastname_Firstname_2C_Roses

PROJECT RESULTS

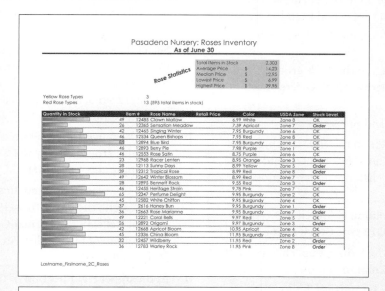

FIGURE 2.55

(Project 2C Roses continues on the next page)

CHAPTER REVIEW

1 Start Excel. From your student files, locate and open **e02C_Roses**. Save the file in your **Excel Chapter 2** folder as **Lastname_Firstname_2C_Roses**

a. In the **column heading area**, point to **column C** to display the ↓ pointer, and then drag to the right to select **columns C:D**. On the **HOME tab**, in the **Cells group**, click the **Insert button arrow**, and then click Insert **Sheet Columns**.

b. Click cell **C14**, type **12113** and then on the **Formula Bar**, click **Enter** to confirm the entry and keep cell **C14** as the active cell. On the **HOME tab**, in the **Editing group**, click **Fill**, and then click **Flash Fill**.

c. Click cell **D14**, type **Zone 5** On the **Formula Bar**, click **Enter** to confirm the entry and keep the cell active. Press [Ctrl] + [E], which is the keyboard shortcut for Flash Fill.

d. Select **column B**, and then in the **Cells group**, click the **Delete button arrow**. Click **Delete Sheet Columns**.

2 In cell **B13** type **Item #** and press [Enter].

a. Select **column C**, and then on the **HOME tab**, in the **Clipboard group**, click **Cut**. Click cell **G1**, and then in the **Clipboard group**, click the upper portion of the **Paste** button.

b. Select and then delete **column C**. In cell **F13** type **USDA Zone** and in cell **G13** type **Stock Level**

c. Select columns **A:G**. In the **Cells group**, click **Format**, and then click **AutoFit Column Width**.

d. Press [Ctrl] + [Home]. **Merge & Center** cell **A1** across the range **A1:G1**, and then apply the **Title** cell style. **Merge & Center** cell **A2** across the range **A2:G2**, and then apply the **Heading 1** cell style. Click **Save**.

3 Click cell **B4**. On the **FORMULAS tab**, in the **Function Library group**, click **AutoSum**, and then within the parentheses, type **a14:a68** which is the range containing the quantities for each item.

a. Click cell **B5**, in the **Function Library group**, click **More Functions**. Point to **Statistical**, click **AVERAGE**, and then in the **Number1** box, type **d14:d68** which is the range containing the *Retail Price* for each item. Click **OK**.

b. Click cell **B6**. In the **Function Library group**, click **More Functions**, point to **Statistical**, and then click

MEDIAN. In the **Function Arguments** dialog box, to the right of the **Number1** box, click **Collapse Dialog** ⬚, and then select the range **D14:D68**. Click **Expand Dialog** ⬚, and then click **OK**. Recall that you can select or type a range and that you can collapse the dialog box to make it easier to view your selection.

c. Click cell **B7**, and then by typing or selecting, insert the **MIN** function to determine the lowest **Retail Price**. Click cell **B8**, and then insert the **MAX** function to determine the highest **Retail Price**.

4 Select cell **B4**. On the **HOME tab**, apply **Comma Style**, and then click **Decrease Decimal** two times. Select the range **B5:B8**, and then apply the **Accounting Number Format**.

a. Select the range **A4:B8**. Point to the right edge of the selected range to display the ⬚ pointer. Drag the selected range to the right until the ScreenTip displays *D4:E8*, and then release the mouse button. AutoFit **column D**.

b. With the range **D4:E8** selected, on the **HOME tab**, in the **Styles group**, display the **Cell Styles** gallery, and then apply **20%—Accent1**.

c. In cell **C6**, type **Rose Statistics** Select the range **C4:C8**, right-click over the selection, and then click **Format Cells**. In the **Format Cells** dialog box, click the **Alignment tab**. Under **Text control**, select the **Merge cells** check box.

d. In the upper right portion of the dialog box, under **Orientation**, point to the **red diamond**, and then drag the diamond upward until the **Degrees** box indicates *20*. Click **OK**.

e. With the merged cell still selected, change the **Font Size** to 14, and then apply **Bold** and **Italic**. Click the **Font Color button arrow**, and then in the fifth column, click the first color—**Blue, Accent 1**. Apply **Middle Align** and **Center** to the cell.

5 Click cell **B10**. On the **FORMULAS tab**, in the **Function Library group**, click **More Functions**, and then display the list of **Statistical** functions. Click **COUNTIF**.

a. As the range, type **e14:e68** which is the range with the color of each item. Click in the **Criteria** box, type **Yellow** and then click **OK** to calculate the number of yellow rose types.

(Project 2C Roses continues on the next page)

b. Click cell **G14**. On the **FORMULAS tab**, in the **Function Library group**, click **Logical**, and then on the list, click **IF**. If necessary, drag the title bar of the **Function Arguments** dialog box up or down so that you can view **row 14** on your screen.

c. With the insertion point in the **Logical_test** box, click cell **A14**, and then type **<40** Press [Tab] to move the insertion point to the **Value_if_true** box, and then type **Order** Press [Tab] to move the insertion point to the **Value_if_false** box, type **OK** and then click **OK**. Using the fill handle, copy the function in cell **G14** down through cell **G68**.

6 With the range **G14:G68** selected, on the **HOME tab**, in the **Styles group**, click **Conditional Formatting**. In the list, point to **Highlight Cells Rules**, and then click **Text that Contains**.

a. In the **Text That Contains** dialog box, with the insertion point blinking in the first box, type **Order** and then in the second box, click the arrow. On the list, click **Custom Format**.

b. In the **Format Cells** dialog box, on the **Font tab**, under **Font style**, click **Bold Italic**. Click the **Color arrow**, and then under **Theme Colors**, in the fourth column, click the first color—**Blue-Gray, Text 2**. Click **OK** two times to apply the font color, bold, and italic to the cells that contain the word *Order*.

c. Select the range **A14:A68**. In the **Styles group**, click **Conditional Formatting**. In the list, point to **Data Bars**, and then under **Gradient Fill**, click **Red Data Bar**. Click anywhere to cancel the selection.

d. Select the range **E14:E68**. On the **HOME tab**, in the **Editing group**, click **Find & Select**, and then click **Replace**. In the **Find and Replace** dialog box, in the **Find what** box, type **Deep Burgundy** and then in the **Replace with** box type **Burgundy** Click **Replace All** and then click **OK**. In the lower right corner of the **Find and Replace** dialog box, click **Close**.

e. Scroll down as necessary, and then click cell **A70**. Type **Edited by Maria Rios** and then press [Enter]. With cell **A71** as the active cell, on the **FORMULAS tab**, in the **Function Library group**, click **Date & Time**. In the list of functions, click **NOW**, and then click **OK** to enter the current date and time. **Save** your workbook.

7 Click any cell in the data below row 13. Click the **INSERT tab**, and then in the **Tables group**, click **Table**. In the **Create Table** dialog box, be sure the **My table has headers** check box is selected, and then click **OK**. On the **DESIGN tab**, in the **Table Styles group**, click **More** ⏷ and then under **Light**, locate and click **Table Style Light 9**.

a. In the header row of the table, click the **Retail Price arrow**, and then from the menu, click **Sort Smallest to Largest**. Click the **Color arrow**. On the menu, click the **(Select All)** check box to clear all the check boxes. Scroll as necessary and then select only the **Red** check box. Click **OK**.

b. Click anywhere in the table. On the **DESIGN tab**, in the **Table Style Options group**, select the **Total Row** check box. Click cell **A69**, click the arrow that displays to the right of cell **A69**, and then click **Sum**. In cell **B11**, type the result **13** and then press [Tab]. In cell **C11**, type **(595 total items in stock)** and then press [Enter].

c. In the header row of the table, click the **Color arrow** and then click **Clear Filter From "Color"** to redisplay all of the data. Click anywhere in the table. Click the **DESIGN tab**, in the **Table Style Options group**, clear the **Total Row** check box, and then in the **Tools group**, click **Convert to Range**. Click **Yes**.

8 On the **PAGE LAYOUT tab**, in the **Themes group**, click **Themes** and then click the **Ion** theme. Change the **Orientation** to **Landscape**.

a. In the **Page Setup group**, click **Margins**, and then click **Custom Margins** to display the **Page Setup** dialog box.

b. On the **Margins tab**, under **Center on page**, select the **Horizontally** check box. On the **Header/Footer tab**, display the **Custom Footer**, and then in the **Left section**, insert the file name. Click **OK** two times.

c. In the **Page Setup** group, click **Print Titles** to redisplay the **Page Setup** dialog box. Under **Print titles**, click in the **Rows to repeat at top** box, and then at the right, click **Collapse Dialog**. From the **row heading area**, select **row 13**, and then click **Expand Dialog**. Click **OK** to print the column titles in row 13 at the top of every page.

d. Press [Ctrl] + [F2] to display the **Print Preview**. At the bottom of the **Settings group**, click **No Scaling**, and

(Project 2C Roses continues on the next page)

CHAPTER REVIEW

then on the displayed list, point to **Fit All Columns on One Page**.

e. On the left, click **Info**, and then in the lower right corner, click **Show All Properties**. As the **Tags**, type **inventory, Pasadena, roses** In the **Subject** box, type your course name and section number. Be sure your name displays as the author.

9 ▶ **Save** your workbook. Print or submit electronically as directed by your instructor. If required by your instructor, print or create an electronic version of your worksheets with formulas displayed by using the instructions in Excel Project 1A, and then Close Excel without saving so that you do not save the changes you made to print formulas.

END | You have completed Project 2C

CHAPTER REVIEW

In the following Skills Review, you will edit a workbook that summarizes sales in the Eastern and Western region of Canada. Your completed workbook will look similar to Figure 2.56.

PROJECT FILES

For Project 2D, you will need the following file:

e02D_Canada

You will save your workbook as:

Lastname_Firstname_2D_Canada

PROJECT RESULTS

FIGURE 2.56

(Project 2D Canada continues on the next page)

CHAPTER REVIEW

1 Start Excel. From your student files, locate and open **e02D_Canada**. Save the file in your **Excel Chapter 2** folder as **Lastname_Firstname_2D_Canada**

a. Point to the **Sheet1 tab**, and then double-click to select the sheet tab name. Type **Western Sales** and then press Enter.

b. Point to the **Sheet2 tab**, right-click, and then from the shortcut menu, click **Rename**. Type **Eastern Sales** and press Enter.

c. Point to the **Western Sales sheet tab** and right-click. On the shortcut menu, point to **Tab Color**, and then in the last column, click the first color—**Green, Accent 6**. Change the **Tab Color** of the **Eastern Sales sheet tab** to **Blue, Accent 5**.

d. Click the **Western Sales sheet tab**, and then click cell **A13**. On the **HOME tab**, in the **Number group**, click the **Number Format arrow**. At the bottom of the list, click **More Number Formats** to display the **Number tab** of the **Format Cells** dialog box. Click the **3/14/12** type, and then click **OK**.

e. Click cell **A16**, type **4/5/16** and then press Enter. Click cell **A13**, and then on the **HOME tab**, in the **Clipboard group**, click **Format Painter**. Click cell **A16** to copy the date format from cell **A13** to cell **A16**.

f. Click cell **A1**. In the **Editing group**, click **Clear**, and then click **Clear Formats**.

g. Select the range **A5:A16**. On the **HOME tab**, in the **Clipboard group**, click **Copy**. At the bottom of the workbook window, click the **Eastern Sales sheet tab** to make it the active worksheet. Right-click cell **A5**, and then under **Paste Options**, click the first button—**Paste**. Display the **Western Sales** sheet. Press Esc to cancel the moving border.

2 With the **Western Sales** sheet active, make cell **A1** the active cell. Point to the sheet tab, right-click, and then on the shortcut menu, click **Select All Sheets**. Verify that *[Group]* displays in the title bar.

a. **Merge & Center** the text in cell **A1** across the range **A1:G1**, and then apply the **Title** cell style. Select **columns A:G**, and then set their widths to **100 pixels**.

b. Click cell **A2**, type **Week Ending March 31** and then on the **Formula Bar**, click the **Enter** button to keep cell **A2** as the active cell. **Merge & Center**

the text across the range **A2:G2**, and then apply the **Heading 1** cell style.

c. Select the range **B4:G4**, and then apply the **Heading 3** cell style. In the **Alignment group**, click **Center**, **Middle Align**, and **Wrap Text**.

d. With the sheets still grouped and the **Western Sales** sheet active, click cell **E5**. On the **HOME tab**, in the **Editing group**, click **AutoSum**, and then press Enter. Click cell **E5**, and then drag the fill handle down to copy the formula through cell **E8**.

e. Click cell **G5**, type = click cell **E5**, type + click cell **F5**, and then press Enter. Copy the formula down through cell **G8**. In cell **A9**, type **Total** Select the range **B5:G9**, and then hold down Alt and press = to enter the SUM function for all the columns. Select the range **A5:A9**, and then apply the **Heading 4** cell style.

f. Select the range **B5:G5**, hold down Ctrl, and then select the range **B9:G9**. Apply the **Accounting Number Format** and decrease the decimal places to zero. Select the range **B6:G8**, and then apply **Comma Style** with zero decimal places. Select the range **B9:G9**, and then apply the **Total** cell style.

3 Click the **Eastern Sales sheet tab** to cancel the grouping and display the second worksheet.

a. To the right of the **Eastern Sales sheet tab**, click the **New sheet** button. **Rename** the new worksheet tab **Summary** and then change the **Tab Color** to **Gold, Accent 4**.

b. Widen **columns A:E** to **150** pixels. In cell **A1**, type **Canadian Sales** and then **Merge & Center** the title across the range **A1:E1**. Apply the **Title** cell style. In cell **A2**, type **Week Ending March 31** and then **Merge & Center** the text across the range **A2:E2**. Apply the **Heading 1** cell style. In cell **A5**, type **Western Sales** and in cell **A6**, type **Eastern Sales**

c. In cell **B4**, type **In-Store/Online Sales** and in cell **C4**, type **In-Store Sales** In cell **D4**, type **Online Sales** and in cell **E4**, type **Total Sales** Select the range **B4:E4**, apply the **Heading 3** cell style, and then **Center** these column titles.

d. Click cell **C5**. Type = and then click the **Western Sales sheet tab**. In the **Western Sales** worksheet, click cell **E9**, and then press Enter. Click cell **D5**. Type = and

(Project 2D Canada continues on the next page)

then click the **Western Sales sheet tab**. Click cell **F9**, and then press ⏎.

e.   By using the same technique, in cells **C6** and **D6**, insert the total **In-Store Sales** and **Online Sales** data from the **Eastern Sales** worksheet.

f.   Select the range **C5:E6**, and then click **AutoSum** to total the two rows. In cell **A7**, type **Total** Select the range **C5:E6** again. In the lower right corner of the selection, click the **Quick Analysis** button, click **Totals**, and then click the first **Sum** button. Recall there are many ways to sum a group of cells.

g.   Select the nonadjacent ranges **C5:E5** and **C7:E7**, and then apply **Accounting Number Format** with zero decimal places. Select the range **C6:E6**, and then apply **Comma Style** with zero decimal places. Select the range **C7:E7**, and then apply the **Total** cell style. Select the range **A5:A7** and apply the **Heading 4** cell style.

h.   Click cell **B5**. On the **INSERT tab**, in the **Sparklines group**, click **Column**. In the **Create Sparklines** dialog box, with the insertion point blinking in the **Data Range** box, select the range **C5:D5** and then click **OK**.

i.   Click cell **B6**, and then insert a **Column Sparkline** for the range **C6:D6**. With the **Eastern Sales** sparkline selected, in the **Style group**, click More ⏷. Apply the second style in the third row—**Sparkline Style Accent 2, (no dark or light)**.

4   Point to the **Summary sheet tab**, hold down the left mouse button to display a small black triangle, and drag

to the left until the triangle and mouse pointer are to the left of the **Western Sales sheet tab**, and then release the left mouse button to move the sheet to the first position in the workbook.

a.   Be sure the **Summary** worksheet is the active sheet, and then press Ctrl + Home to move to cell **A1**. Point to the **Summary sheet tab**, right-click, and then click **Select All Sheets** to display [Group] in the title bar. On the **PAGE LAYOUT tab**, in the **Page Setup group**, click **Margins**, and then click **Custom Margins** to display the **Page Setup** dialog box. On the **Margins tab**, center the worksheets **Horizontally**. On the **Header/Footer tab**, insert the file name in the **left section** of the footer.

b.   Display the **Print Preview** of the worksheets. Under **Settings**, click **No Scaling**, and then click **Fit All Columns on One Page**. Use the **Next** button to view all three worksheets.

c.   On the left, click **Info**, and then in the lower right corner of the screen, click **Show All Properties**. As the **Tags**, type **Canada, sales** In the **Subject** box, type your course name and section number. Be sure your name displays as the author.

d.   On the left, click **Save**. Print or submit electronically as directed by your instructor. If required by your instructor, print or create an electronic version of your worksheets with formulas displayed by using the instructions in Excel Project 1A, and then **Close** Excel without saving so that you do not save the changes you made to print formulas.

END | You have completed Project 2D

CONTENT-BASED ASSESSMENTS

Apply 2A skills from these Objectives:

1 Use Flash Fill and the SUM, AVERAGE, MEDIAN, MIN, and MAX Functions

2 Move Data, Resolve Error Messages, and Rotate Text

3 Use COUNTIF and IF Functions and Apply Conditional Formatting

4 Use Date & Time Functions and Freeze Panes

5 Create, Sort, and Filter an Excel Table

6 View, Format, and Print a Large Worksheet

In the following project, you will edit a worksheet detailing the current inventory of plants at the Pasadena facility. Your completed worksheet will look similar to Figure 2.57.

PROJECT FILES

For Project 2E, you will need the following file:

e02E_Plants

You will save your workbook as:

Lastname_Firstname_2E_Plants

PROJECT RESULTS

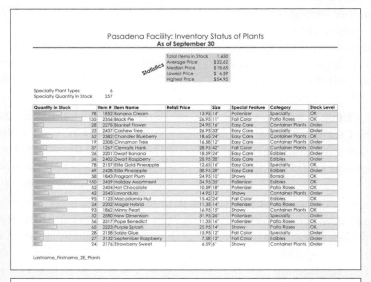

FIGURE 2.57

(Project 2E Plants continues on the next page)

1 Start Excel. From your student files, locate and open **e02E_Plants**, and then **Save** the file in your **Excel Chapter 2** folder as **Lastname_Firstname_2E_Plants**

2 To the right of **column B**, insert two new columns to create **new blank columns C and D**. By using **Flash Fill** in the two new columns, split the data in **column B** into a column for *Item #* in **column C** and *Category* in **column D**. As necessary, type **Item #** as the column title in **column C** and **Category** as the column title in **column D**.

3 Delete **column B**. By using the **Cut** and **Paste** commands, cut **column C**—*Category*—and paste it to **column H**, and then delete the empty **column C**. Apply **AutoFit** to **columns A:G**.

4 In cell **B4**, insert a function to calculate the **Total Items in Stock** by summing the **Quantity in Stock** data, and then apply **Comma Style** with zero decimal places to the result. In each cell in the range **B5:B8**, insert functions to calculate the Average, Median, Lowest, and Highest retail prices, and then apply the **Accounting Number Format** to each result.

5 Move the range **A4:B8** to the range **D4:E8**, apply the **40%—Accent4** cell style to the range, and then select **columns D:E** and **AutoFit**. In cell **C6**, type **Statistics** and then select the range **C4:C8**. In the **Format Cells** dialog box, merge the selected cells, and change the text **Orientation** to **25 Degrees**. Format the cell with **Bold**, a **Font Size** of **14 pt**, and then change the **Font Color** to **Blue-Gray, Text 2**. Apply **Middle Align** and **Align Right**.

6 In the **Category** column, **Replace All** occurrences of **Vine Roses** with **Patio Roses** In cell **B10**, use the **COUNTIF** function to count the number of **Specialty** plant types in the **Category** column.

7 In cell **H13**, type **Stock Level** In cell **H14**, enter an **IF** function to determine the items that must be ordered. If the **Quantity in Stock** is less than **50** the **Value_if_true**

is **Order** Otherwise the **Value_if_false** is **OK** Fill the formula down through cell **H42**. Apply **Conditional Formatting** to the **Stock Level** column so that cells that contain the text *Order* are formatted with **Bold Italic** and with a **Color** of **Green, Accent 6**. Apply conditional formatting to the **Quantity in Stock** column by applying a **Gradient Fill Green Data Bar**.

8 Format the range **A13:H42** as a **Table** with headers, and apply the style **Table Style Light 20**. Sort the table from A to Z by **Item Name**, and then filter on the **Category** column to display the **Specialty** types. Display a **Total Row** in the table, and then in cell **A43**, **Sum** the **Quantity in Stock** for the **Specialty** items. Type the result in cell **B11**. Click in the table, and then on the **DESIGN tab**, remove the total row from the table. Clear the **Category** filter, and convert the table to a range.

9 **Merge & Center** the title and subtitle across **columns A:H**, and apply **Title** and **Heading 1** styles respectively. Change the theme to **Mesh**, and then select and **AutoFit** all the columns. Set the orientation to **Landscape**. In the **Page Setup** dialog box, center the worksheet **Horizontally**, insert a custom footer in the **left section** with the file name, and set **row 13** to repeat at the top of each page. Display the **Print Preview**. Apply the **Fit All Columns on One Page** setting.

10 As the **Tags**, type **plants inventory, Pasadena** As the **Subject**, type your course name and section number. Be sure your name displays as the **Author**. In **Backstage** view, on the left click **Save**, and then print or submit electronically as directed. If required by your instructor, print or create an electronic version of your worksheet with formulas displayed by using the instructions in Project 1A, and then close Excel without saving so that you do not save the changes you made to print formulas.

END | You have completed Project 2E

CONTENT-BASED ASSESSMENTS

In the following project, you will edit a workbook that summarizes the compensation for the commercial salespersons who qualified for bonuses in the Western and Eastern Canadian regions. Your completed worksheets will look similar to Figure 2.58.

PROJECT FILES

Apply 2B skills from these Objectives:

7 Navigate a Workbook and Rename Worksheets

8 Enter Dates, Clear Contents, and Clear Formats

9 Copy and Paste by Using the Paste Options Gallery

10 Edit and Format Multiple Worksheets at the Same Time

11 Create a Summary Sheet with Column Sparklines

12 Format and Print Multiple Worksheets in a Workbook

For Project 2F, you will need the following file:

e02F_Bonus

You will save your workbook as:

Lastname_Firstname_2F_Bonus

PROJECT RESULTS

FIGURE 2.58

(Project 2F Bonus continues on the next page)

CONTENT-BASED ASSESSMENTS

1 **Start** Excel. From your student files, open **e02F_Bonus**, and then save the file in your **Excel Chapter 2** folder as **Lastname_Firstname_2F_Bonus**

2 Rename **Sheet1** as **Western** and change the **Tab Color** to **Brown, Accent 2**. Rename **Sheet2** as **Eastern** and change the **Tab Color** to **Orange, Accent 1**.

3 Click the **Western sheet tab** to make it the active sheet, and then group the worksheets. In cell **A1**, type **Rosedale Landscape and Garden** and then **Merge & Center** the text across the range **A1:F1**. Apply the **Title** cell style. **Merge & Center** the text in cell **A2** across the range **A2:F2**, and then apply the **Heading 3** cell style.

4 With the sheets still grouped, in cell **D5** calculate the **Bonus** for *Reid* by multiplying the **Sales Eligible for Bonus** times the **Bonus Rate**. Copy the formula down through cell **D8**. In cell **F5**, calculate **Total Compensation** by summing the **Bonus** and **Base Salary** for *Reid*. Copy the formula down through the cell **F8**.

5 In **row 9**, sum the columns for **Sales Eligible for Bonus, Bonus, Base Salary**, and **Total Compensation**. Apply the **Accounting Number Format** with two decimal places to the appropriate cells in **row 5** and **row 9** (do not include the percentages). Apply the **Comma Style** with two decimal places to the appropriate cells in **rows 6:8** (do not include the percentages). Apply the **Total** cell style to the appropriate cells in the Total row.

6 Click the **Eastern** sheet tab to ungroup the sheets, and then insert a new worksheet. Change the sheet name to **Summary** and then change the **Tab Color** to **Brown, Text 2**. Widen **column A** to **210** pixels, widen **columns B:E** to **155** pixels, and then move the **Summary** sheet so that it is the first sheet in the workbook. In cell **A1** of the **Summary** sheet, type **Rosedale Landscape and Garden** and then **Merge & Center** the title across the range **A1:E1**. Apply the **Title** cell style. In cell **A2**, type **June Commercial Salesperson Bonus Summary: Canada** and then **Merge & Center** the text across the range **A2:E2**. Apply the **Heading 1** cell style.

7 In the range **A5:A7**, type the following row titles and then apply the **Heading 4** cell style:

Bonus

Base Salary

Total Compensation

8 In the range **B4:E4**, type the following column titles, and then **Center** and apply the **Heading 3** cell style.

Western/Eastern

Western

Eastern

Total

9 In cell **C5**, enter a formula that references cell **D9** in the **Western** worksheet so that the total bonus amount for the Western region displays in **C5**. Create similar formulas to enter the total **Base Salary** for the Western region in cell **C6**. Using the same technique, enter formulas in the range **D5:D6** so that the **Eastern** totals display.

10 Sum the **Bonus** and **Base Salary** rows, and then calculate **Total Compensation** for the **Western, Eastern,** and **Total** columns.

11 In cell **B5**, insert a **Column Sparkline** for the range **C5:D5**. In cells **B6** and **B7**, insert **Column** sparklines for the appropriate ranges to compare Western totals with Eastern totals. To the sparkline in cell **B5**, apply the second style in the third row—**Sparkline Style Accent 2**, (**no dark or light**). To the sparkline in cell **B6**, apply the first style in the fifth row—**Sparkline Style Dark #1**. To the sparkline in cell **B7**, apply the first style in the fourth row—**Sparkline Style Accent 1, Lighter 40%**.

12 **Group** the three worksheets, and then in the **Page Setup** dialog box, center the worksheets **Horizontally** on the page, and insert a **Custom Footer** in the **left section** with the file name. Change the **Orientation** to **Landscape**.

13 As the **Tags**, type **June, bonus, compensation** As the **Subject**, type your course name and section number. Be sure your name displays as the **Author**. Click **Save**, and then print or submit your workbook electronically as directed. If required by your instructor, print or create an electronic version of your worksheets with formulas displayed by using the instructions in Project 1A, and then close Excel without saving so that you do not save the changes you made to print formulas.

END | You have completed Project 2F

CONTENT-BASED ASSESSMENTS

Mastering Excel   Project 2G Inventory

In the following project, you will edit a worksheet that summarizes the inventory of bulbs and trees at the Pasadena facility. Your completed workbook will look similar to Figure 2.59.

Apply a combination of 2A and 2B skills:

1 Use Flash Fill and the SUM, AVERAGE, MEDIAN, MIN, and MAX Functions

2 Move Data, Resolve Error Messages, and Rotate Text

3 Use COUNTIF and IF Functions and Apply Conditional Formatting

4 Use Date & Time Functions and Freeze Panes

5 Create, Sort, and Filter an Excel Table

6 View, Format and Print a Large Worksheet

7 Navigate a Workbook and Rename Worksheets

8 Enter Dates, Clear Contents, and Clear Formats

9 Copy and Paste by Using the Paste Options Gallery

10 Edit and Format Multiple Worksheets at the Same Time

11 Create a Summary Sheet with Column Sparklines

12 Format and Print Multiple Worksheets in a Workbook

PROJECT FILES

For Project 2G, you will need the following file:

e02G_Inventory

You will save your workbook as

Lastname_Firstname_2G_Inventory

PROJECT RESULTS

FIGURE 2.59

(Project 2G Inventory continues on the next page)

CONTENT-BASED ASSESSMENTS

1 Start Excel. From your student files, open **e02G_ Inventory**. Save the file in your **Excel Chapter 2** folder as **Lastname_Firstname_2G_Inventory.**

2 Change the **Theme** to **Slice**. Rename **Sheet1** as **Bulbs** and **Sheet2** as **Trees** Click the **Bulbs sheet tab** to make it the active sheet.

3 To the right of **column B**, insert two new columns to create **new blank columns C and D**. By using **Flash Fill** in the two new columns, split the data in **column B** into a column for *Item #* in **column C** and *Category* in **column D**. As necessary, type **Item #** as the column title in **column C** and **Category** as the column title in **column D**.

4 Delete **column B**. By using the **Cut** and **Paste** commands, cut **column C**—*Category*—and paste it to **column G**, and then delete the empty **column C**. Apply **AutoFit** to **columns A:F**.

5 Display the **Trees** worksheet, and then repeat Steps 3 and 4 on this worksheet.

6 Make the following calculations in each of the two worksheets *without* grouping the sheets:

- In cell **B4**, enter a function to sum the **Quantity in Stock** data, and then apply **Comma Style** with zero decimal places to the result.

- In cells **B5:B8**, enter formulas to calculate the Average, Median, Lowest, and Highest retail prices, and then apply the **Accounting Number Format**.

7 In each of the two worksheets, make the following calculations *without* grouping the sheets:

- In cell **B10**, enter a COUNTIF function to determine how many different types of **Tulips** are in stock on the **Bulbs** sheet and how many different types of **Evergreens** are in stock on the **Trees** worksheet.

- In cell **G14** type **Stock Level** In cell **G15**, enter an **IF** function to determine the items that must be ordered. If the **Quantity in Stock** is less than **75** the **Value_if_true** is **Order** Otherwise the **Value_ if_false** is **OK** Fill the formula down through all the rows.

- Apply **Conditional Formatting** to the **Stock Level** column so that cells that contain the text *Order* are formatted with **Bold Italic** with a **Font Color** of **Dark Blue, Text 2**. Apply **Gradient Fill Blue Data Bars** to the **Quantity in Stock** column.

8 In the **Bulbs** sheet, format the range **A14:G42** as a table with headers and apply **Table Style Light 20**. Insert a **Total Row**, filter by **Category** for **Tulips**, and then **Sum** the **Quantity in Stock** column. Record the result in cell **B11**.

9 Select the table, clear the filter, **Sort** the table on the **Item Name** column from **A to Z**, remove the **Total Row**, and then convert the table to a range. On the **Page Layout tab**, set **Print Titles** so that **row 14** repeats at the top of each page.

10 In the **Trees** sheet, format the range **A14:G42** as a table with headers and apply **Table Style Light 19**. Insert a **Total Row**, filter by **Category** for **Evergreens**, and then **Sum** the **Quantity in Stock** column. Record the result in cell **B11**.

11 Select the table, clear the filter, **Sort** the table on the **Item Name** column from **A to Z**, remove the **Total Row**, and then convert the table to a range.

12 On the **Page Layout tab**, set **Print Titles** so that **row 14** repeats at the top of each page, and then **Save** your workbook. **Group** the two worksheets. Center the title in cell **A1** across the range **A1:G1** and apply the **Title** cell style. Center the subtitle in cell **A2** across the range **A2:G2** and apply the **Heading 1** cell style. **Center** the worksheets **Horizontally**, change the **Orientation** to **Landscape**, display the **Print Preview**, and then change the **Settings** to **Fit All Columns on One Page**.

13 In **Backstage** view, on the left click **Save**, and then click the **Trees sheet tab** to cancel the grouping. Insert a new worksheet. Change the sheet name to **Summary** and then widen **columns A:D** to **170** pixels. Move the **Summary** sheet so that it is the first sheet in the workbook. In cell **A1**, type **Pasadena Inventory Summary** and then **Merge & Center** the title across **A1:D1**. Apply the **Title** cell style. In cell **A2**, type **As of December 31** and then **Merge & Center** the text across the range **A2:D2**. Apply the **Heading 1** cell style.

14 On the **Bulbs sheet**, **Copy** the range **A4:A8**. Display the **Summary sheet** and **Paste** the selection to cell **A5**. Apply the **Heading 4** cell style to the selection. In the **Summary sheet**, in cell **B4**, type **Bulbs** In cell **C4** type **Trees** In cell **D4** type **Bulbs/Trees** and then **Center** the column titles. Apply the **Heading 3** cell style.

(Project 2G Inventory continues on the next page)

CONTENT-BASED ASSESSMENTS

Mastering Excel | **Project 2G Inventory** (continued)

15 In cell **B5**, enter a formula that references cell **B4** in the **Bulbs sheet** so that the **Bulbs Total Items in Stock** displays in **B5**. Create similar formulas to enter the **Average Price**, **Median Price**, **Lowest Price**, and **Highest Price** from the **Bulbs sheet** into the **Summary** sheet in the range **B6:B9**. Enter formulas in the range **C5:C9** that reference the appropriate cells in the **Trees** worksheet.

16 To the range **B5:C5**, apply **Comma Style** with zero decimal places, and to the range **B6:C9**, apply **Accounting Number Format**. In cells **D5, D6, D7, D8**, and **D9**, insert **Column** sparklines using the values in the *Bulbs* and *Trees* columns. Format each sparkline using the first five Sparkline styles in the first row.

17 Center the **Summary** worksheet **Horizontally** and change the **Orientation** to **Landscape**. **Group** the worksheets and insert a footer in the left section with the **File Name**. As the **Tags**, type **Pasadena inventory** As the **Subject**, type your course name and section number. Be sure your name displays as the **Author**.

18 In **Backstage** view, on the left click **Save**, and then print or submit electronically as directed. If required by your instructor, print or create an electronic version of your worksheet with formulas displayed by using the instructions in Project 1A, and then close Excel without saving so that you do not save the changes you made to print formulas.

END | You have completed Project 2G

CONTENT-BASED ASSESSMENTS

Apply a combination of the 2A and 2B skills.

GO! Fix It	Project 2H Planters	Online
GO! Make It	Project 2I Salary	Online
GO! Solve It	Project 2J Sod	Online
GO! Solve It	Project 2K Products	

PROJECT FILES

For Project 2K, you will need the following file:

e02K_Products

You will save your workbook as:

Lastname_Firstname_2K_Products

From your student data files, open the file e02K_Products and save it as **Lastname_Firstname_2K_Products** This workbook contains two worksheets: one for U.S. sales data by product and one for Canadian sales data by product. Complete the two worksheets by calculating totals by product and by month. Then calculate the Percent of Total for all products by dividing the Product Total by the Monthly Total, using absolute cell references as necessary. Format the percentages with two decimal places and center in the cells. Format the worksheets attractively and apply financial formatting. Insert a new worksheet that summarizes the monthly totals for the U.S. and Canada. Enter the months as the column titles and the countries as the row titles. Include a Product Total column and a column for sparklines titled **April/May/June** Format the Summary worksheet attractively with a title and subtitle, insert column sparklines that compare the months, and apply financial formatting. Include the file name in the footer, add appropriate document properties, and submit as directed.

(Project 2K Products continues on the next page)

CONTENT-BASED ASSESSMENTS

Performance Level

Performance Criteria		Exemplary: You consistently applied the relevant skills	Proficient: You sometimes, but not always, applied the relevant skills	Developing: You rarely or never applied the relevant skills
	Create formulas	All formulas are correct and are efficiently constructed.	Formulas are correct but not always constructed in the most efficient manner.	One or more formulas are missing or incorrect; or only numbers were entered.
	Create Summary worksheet	Summary worksheet created properly.	Summary worksheet was created but the data, sparklines, or formulas were incorrect.	No Summary worksheet was created.
	Format attractively and appropriately	Formatting is attractive and appropriate.	Adequately formatted but difficult to read or unattractive.	Inadequate or no formatting.

END | You have completed Project 2K

OUTCOMES-BASED ASSESSMENTS

RUBRIC

The following outcomes-based assessments are open-ended assessments. That is, there is no specific correct result; your result will depend on your approach to the information provided. Make Professional Quality your goal. Use the following scoring rubric to guide you in how to approach the problem and then to evaluate how well your approach solves the problem.

The *criteria*—Software Mastery, Content, Format and Layout, and Process—represent the knowledge and skills you have gained that you can apply to solving the problem. The *levels of performance*—Professional Quality, Approaching Professional Quality, or Needs Quality Improvements—help you and your instructor evaluate your result.

	Your completed project is of Professional Quality if you:	Your completed project is Approaching Professional Quality if you:	Your completed project Needs Quality Improvements if you:
1-Software Mastery	Choose and apply the most appropriate skills, tools, and features and identify efficient methods to solve the problem.	Choose and apply some appropriate skills, tools, and features, but not in the most efficient manner.	Choose inappropriate skills, tools, or features, or are inefficient in solving the problem.
2-Content	Construct a solution that is clear and well organized, contains content that is accurate, appropriate to the audience and purpose, and is complete. Provide a solution that contains no errors in spelling, grammar, or style.	Construct a solution in which some components are unclear, poorly organized, inconsistent, or incomplete. Misjudge the needs of the audience. Have some errors in spelling, grammar, or style, but the errors do not detract from comprehension.	Construct a solution that is unclear, incomplete, or poorly organized; contains some inaccurate or inappropriate content; and contains many errors in spelling, grammar, or style. Do not solve the problem.
3-Format & Layout	Format and arrange all elements to communicate information and ideas, clarify function, illustrate relationships, and indicate relative importance.	Apply appropriate format and layout features to some elements, but not others. Overuse features, causing minor distraction.	Apply format and layout that does not communicate information or ideas clearly. Do not use format and layout features to clarify function, illustrate relationships, or indicate relative importance. Use available features excessively, causing distraction.
4-Process	Use an organized approach that integrates planning, development, self-assessment, revision, and reflection.	Demonstrate an organized approach in some areas, but not others; or, use an insufficient process of organization throughout.	Do not use an organized approach to solve the problem.

OUTCOMES-BASED ASSESSMENTS

Apply a combination of the 2A and 2B skills.

GO! Think | Project 2L Palms

PROJECT FILES

For Project 2L, you will need the following file:

e02L_Palms

You will save your workbook as:

Lastname_Firstname_2L_Palms

Melanie Castillo, Product Manager for Rosedale Landscape and Garden, has requested a worksheet that summarizes the palm tree inventory data for the month of March. Melanie would like the worksheet to include the total Quantity in Stock and Number of Items for each of the four categories of palm trees, and she would like the items to be sorted from lowest to highest retail price. She would also like a separate column for Item # and for Category.

Edit the workbook to provide Melanie with the information requested, and use the Table feature to find the data requested. Format the worksheet titles and data and include an appropriately formatted table so that the worksheet is professional and easy to read and understand. Insert a footer with the file name and add appropriate document properties. Save the file as **Lastname_Firstname_2L_Palms** and print or submit as directed by your instructor.

END | You have completed Project 2L

GO! Think | Project 2M Contracts | Online

You and GO! | Project 2N Annual Expenses | Online

Build from Scratch

GO! Cumulative Group Project | Project 2O Bell Orchid Hotels | Online

Analyzing Data with Pie Charts, Line Charts, and What-If Analysis Tools

3

GO! to Work
Video E3

PROJECT 3A

OUTCOMES
Present fund data in a pie chart.

PROJECT 3B

OUTCOMES
Make projections by using what-if analysis and present projections in a line chart.

OBJECTIVES

1. Chart Data with a Pie Chart
2. Format a Pie Chart
3. Edit a Workbook and Update a Chart
4. Use Goal Seek to Perform What-If Analysis

OBJECTIVES

5. Design a Worksheet for What-If Analysis
6. Answer What-If Questions by Changing Values in a Worksheet
7. Chart Data with a Line Chart

In This Chapter

In this chapter, you will work with two different types of commonly used charts that make it easy to visualize data. You will create a pie chart in a separate chart sheet to show how the parts of a fund contribute to a total fund. Pie charts are one type of chart you can use to show part-to-whole relationships. You will also practice by using parentheses in a formula, calculate the percentage rate of an increase, answer what-if questions, and then chart data in a line chart to show the flow of data over time and the flow of one value to the next. In this chapter, you will also practice formatting the axes in a line chart.

The projects in this chapter relate to the city of **Pacifica Bay**, a coastal city south of San Francisco. The city's access to major transportation provides both residents and businesses an opportunity to compete in the global marketplace. The city's mission is to create a more beautiful and more economically viable community for its residents. Each year the city welcomes a large number of tourists who enjoy exploring the rocky coastline and seeing the famous landmarks in San Francisco. The city encourages best environmental practices and partners with cities in other countries to promote sound government at the local level.

PROJECT ACTIVITIES

In Activities 3.01 through 3.12, you will edit a worksheet for Michael Larsen, City Manager, that reports the adjusted figures for Enterprise Fund Expenditures for the next fiscal year, and then present the data in a pie chart. Your completed worksheets will look similar to Figure 3.1.

PROJECT FILES

For Project 3A, you will need the following file:

e03A_Enterprise_Fund

You will save your workbook as:

Lastname_Firstname_3A_Enterprise_Fund

PROJECT RESULTS

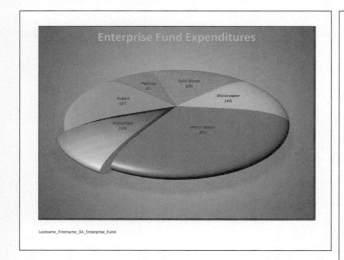

Pacifica Bay				
Enterprise Fund Expenditures				
Recommended Adjustments				
	Originally Proposed		Adjusted	% of Total Fund Expenditures
Airport	$	17,610,810	$ 18,121,067	18%
Parking		6,824,865	7,897,526	8%
Solid Waste		18,695,222	17,845,287	18%
Wastewater		12,657,765	13,985,695	14%
Water Usage		30,457,903	32,356,236	32%
Waterfront		10,976,843	10,945,369	11%
Total	$	97,223,408	$ 101,151,180	

Goal: To Reduce Waterfront Expenditures from 11% to 9% of Total Expenditures

Goal Amount:	$	9,103,606	9%

Lastname_Firstname_3A_Enterprise_Fund

FIGURE 3.1 Project 3A Enterprise Fund Pie Chart

A **pie chart** shows the relationship of each part to a whole. The size of each pie slice is equal to its value compared to the total value of all the slices. The pie chart style charts data that is arranged in a single column or single row, and shows the size of items in a single data series proportional to the sum of the items. Whereas a column or bar chart can have two or more data series in the chart, a pie chart can have only one data series.

Consider using a pie chart when you have only one data series to plot, you do not have more than seven categories, and the categories represent parts of a total value.

Activity 3.01 | Calculating Values for a Pie Chart

A **fund** is a sum of money set aside for a specific purpose. In a municipal government like the city of Pacifica Bay, the **general fund** is money set aside for the normal operating activities of the city, such as police, fire, and administering the everyday functions of the city.

Municipal governments also commonly establish an **enterprise fund** to report income and expenditures related to municipal services for which a fee is charged in exchange for goods or services. For example, Pacifica Bay receives income from airport landing fees, parking fees, water usage fees, and rental fees along public beaches, but there are costs—expenditures—related to building and maintaining these facilities and services from which income is received.

1 Start Excel. From the student files that accompany this textbook, open **e03A_Enterprise_Fund**. From **Backstage** view, display the **Save As** dialog box. Navigate to the location where you are storing your projects for this chapter.

2 Create a new folder named **Excel Chapter 3** and open the new folder. In the **File name** box, using your name, type **Lastname_Firstname_3A_Enterprise_Fund** Click **Save** or press Enter.

The worksheet indicates the originally proposed and adjusted expenditures from the Enterprise Fund for the next fiscal year.

3 Click cell **D5**, and then type **=** to begin a formula.

4 Click cell **C5**, which is the first value that is part of the total Fund Expenditures, to insert it into the formula. Type **/** to indicate division, and then click cell **C11**, which is the total adjusted expenditures.

Recall that to determine the percentage by which a value makes up a total, you must divide the value by the total. The result will be a percentage expressed as a decimal.

5 Press F4 to make the reference to the value in cell **C11** absolute, which will enable you to copy the formula. Compare your screen with Figure 3.2.

Recall that an **absolute cell reference** refers to a cell by its fixed position in the worksheet—the cell reference will not change when you copy the formula. The reference to cell C5 is a *relative cell reference*, because when you copy the formula, you want the reference to change *relative* to its row. Recall also that dollar signs display to indicate that a cell reference is absolute. A **mixed cell** reference occurs when only the column or row reference must be absolute, and the other is relative—such as $A10 or A$10. When the cell is copied, only the relative reference changes.

FIGURE 3.2

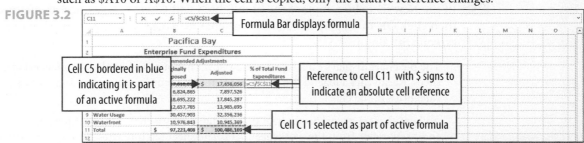

6 On the **Formula Bar**, click **Enter** ☑ to confirm the entry and to keep cell **D5** the active cell. Copy the formula down through cell **D10**, and then compare your screen with Figure 3.3.

FIGURE 3.3

7 With the range **D5:D10** still selected, right-click over the selection, and then on the mini toolbar, click **Percent Style** % and **Center** ☰. Click cell **A1** to cancel the selection, and then **Save** 🖫 your workbook. Compare your screen with Figure 3.4.

FIGURE 3.4

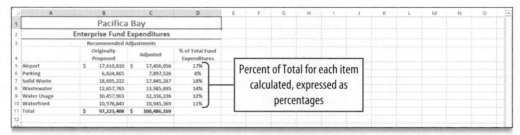

Activity 3.02 | Creating a Pie Chart in a Chart Sheet

1 Select the range **A5:A10**, hold down Ctrl, and then select the range **C5:C10** to select the nonadjacent ranges with the item names and the adjusted expenditure for each item.

> To create a pie chart, you must select two ranges. One range contains the labels for each slice of the pie chart, and the other range contains the values that add up to a total. The two ranges must have the same number of cells and the range with the values should *not* include the cell with the total.

> The item names (Airport, Parking, and so on) are the category names and will identify the slices of the pie chart. Each projected expenditure is a *data point*—a value that originates in a worksheet cell and that is represented in a chart by a *data marker*. In a pie chart, each pie slice is a data marker. Together, the data points form the *data series*—related data points represented by data markers—and determine the size of each pie slice.

2 With the nonadjacent ranges selected, click the **INSERT tab**, and then in the **Charts group**, click **Insert Pie or Doughnut Chart** 🔵▾. Under **3-D Pie**, click the chart **3-D Pie** to create the chart on your worksheet and to display the **CHART TOOLS** on the ribbon.

3 On the **DESIGN tab**, at the right end of the ribbon in the **Location group**, click **Move Chart**. In the **Move Chart** dialog box, click the **New sheet** option button.

4 In the **New sheet** box, replace the highlighted text *Chart1* by typing **Expenditures Chart** and then click **OK** to display the chart on a separate worksheet in your workbook. Compare your screen with Figure 3.5.

> The pie chart displays on a separate new sheet in your workbook, and a *legend* identifies the pie slices. Recall that a legend is a chart element that identifies the patterns or colors assigned to the categories in the chart.

> A *chart sheet* is a workbook sheet that contains only a chart; it is useful when you want to view a chart separately from the worksheet data. The sheet tab indicates *Expenditures Chart*.

FIGURE 3.5

Chart displays on a separate new worksheet

Legend at bottom identifies pie slices

Chart Elements button

Chart Filters button

Chart Styles button

CHART TOOLS active on ribbon

Move Chart button on DESIGN tab

Objective 2 | Format a Pie Chart

Video E3-2

Activity 3.03 | Formatting a Chart Title by Applying a WordArt Style and Changing Font Size

1 Click the text *Chart Title* to surround it with selection handles, and then watch the **Formula Bar** as you type **Enterprise Fund Expenditures** Press Enter to create the new chart title in the box.

2 Click the **FORMAT tab**, and then in the **WordArt Styles group**, click **More** ▽. In the first row, click the last style—**Fill – Gold, Accent 4, Soft Bevel**.

3 With the I pointer, drag to select the chart title text, and then on the mini toolbar, change the **Font Size** to **32**. Click the edge of the chart to deselect the title, and then compare your screen with Figure 3.6.

FIGURE 3.6

Chart Title text typed, WordArt Style applied, Font Size 32 → **Enterprise Fund Expenditures**

Activity 3.04 | Formatting Chart Elements by Removing a Legend and Adding and Formatting Data Labels

In your worksheet, for each budget item, you calculated the percent of the total in column D. These percentages can also be calculated by the Chart feature and added to the pie slices as labels.

1 If necessary, click the edge of the chart to display the three chart buttons on the right, and then click **Chart Elements** ✛. Compare your screen with Figure 3.7.

> Use the Chart Elements button to add, remove, or change chart elements such as the chart title, the legend, and the data labels.

FIGURE 3.7

2 Click the **Legend** check box to deselect it and remove the legend from the bottom of the chart.

3 *Point* to **Data Labels**, and then click the ▶ arrow to display a menu. At the bottom of the menu, click **More Options** to display the **Format Data Labels** pane on the right.

> The Format Data Labels pane displays and data labels representing the values display on each pie slice.

4 In the **Format Data Labels** pane, under **LABEL OPTIONS**, click as necessary to select the **Category Name** and **Percentage** check boxes. Click to *clear* any other check boxes in this group. Under **Label Position**, click the **Center** option button. Compare your screen with Figure 3.8.

> All of the data labels are selected and display both the category name and the percentage. In the worksheet, you calculated the percent of the total in column D. Here, the percentage will be calculated by the Chart feature and added to the chart as a label.

FIGURE 3.8

5 Point to any of the selected data labels, right-click to display a shortcut menu, and then click **Font** to display the **Font** dialog box.

6 In the **Font** dialog box, on the **Font tab**, click the **Font style arrow**, and then click **Bold Italic**. In the **Size** box, drag to select *9* and type **11** Compare your screen with Figure 3.9.

FIGURE 3.9

7 ▸ Click **OK** to close the dialog box and apply the formatting to the data labels. In the upper right corner of the **Format Data Labels** pane, click **Close** ☒.

Activity 3.05 | Formatting a Data Series with 3-D Effects

3-D, which is short for *three-dimensional*, refers to an image that appears to have all three spatial dimensions—length, width, and depth.

1 ▸ In any pie slice, point anywhere outside of the selected label, and then double-click to display the **Format Data Series** pane on the right.

🔄 **ANOTHER WAY**   Right-click outside the label of any pie slice, and then click Format Data Series to display the Format Data Series pane. Or, on the FORMAT tab, in the Current Selection group, click the Chart Elements arrow, click Series 1, and then click Format Selection.

2 ▸ In the **Format Data Series** pane, under **SERIES OPTIONS**, click **Effects** ⬠, and then click **3-D FORMAT**. Compare your screen with Figure 3.10.

FIGURE 3.10

3 ▸ Click the **Top bevel arrow**, and then in the gallery, under **Bevel**, click the first bevel—**Circle**—as shown in Figure 3.11.

Bevel is a shape effect that uses shading and shadows to make the edges of a shape appear to be curved or angled.

FIGURE 3.11

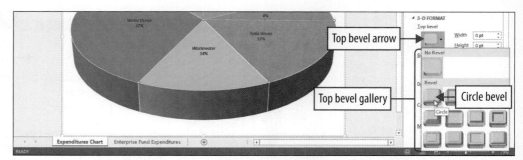

> **4** Under **Top bevel**, in the **Width** box, select the existing text and type **512 pt** Use the same technique to change the **Height** to **512 pt**

> **5** Under **Bottom bevel**, use the technique you just practiced to apply a **Circle** bevel with **Width** of **512 pt** and **Height** of **512 pt** Compare your screen with Figure 3.12.

FIGURE 3.12

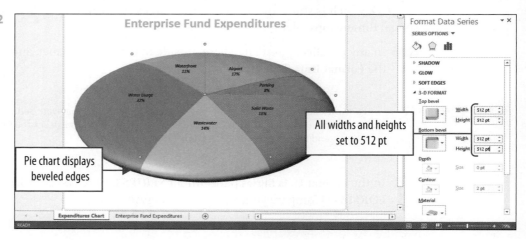

> **6** In the **Format Data Series** pane, scroll down as necessary, and then click the **Material arrow**. Under **Standard**, click the third material—**Plastic**.

Activity 3.06 | Formatting a Data Series with a Shadow Effect

> **1** If necessary, in the **Format Data Series** pane, scroll back to the top of the pane, and then click **SHADOW** to expand the options for this effect.

> **2** Under **SHADOW**, click the **Presets arrow**, use the scroll bar to move to the bottom of the gallery, and then under **Perspective**, in the first row, point to the third effect to display the ScreenTip *Below*. Compare your screen with Figure 3.13.

FIGURE 3.13

> **3** Click **Below** to apply the shadow to the chart.

Activity 3.07 | Rotating a Pie Chart by Changing the Angle of the First Slice

The order in which the data series in pie charts are plotted in Excel is determined by the order of the data on the worksheet. To gain a different view of the chart, you can rotate the chart within the 360 degrees of the circle of the pie shape to present a different visual perspective of the chart.

1 Notice the position of the **Water Usage** and **Waterfront** slices in the chart. Then, with the pie chart still selected—sizing handles surround the pie—in the **Format Data Series** pane, under **SERIES OPTIONS**, click **Series Options** [icon].

2 Under **Angle of first slice**, in the box to the right, drag to select **0°**, type **250** and then press [Enter] to rotate the chart 250 degrees to the right.

ANOTHER WAY   Drag the slider to 250°, or click the spin box up arrow as many times as necessary.

3 Click **Save** [icon], and then compare your screen with Figure 3.14.

Rotating the chart can provide a better perspective to the chart. Here, rotating the chart in this manner emphasizes that Water Usage is the largest enterprise fund expenditure.

FIGURE 3.14

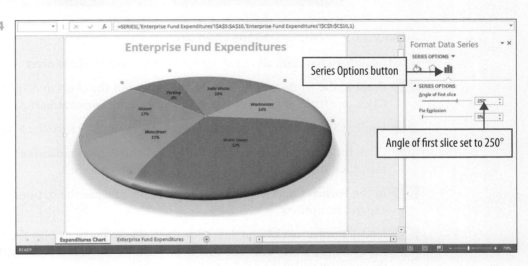

Activity 3.08 | Exploding and Coloring a Pie Slice

You can pull out—**explode**—one or more slices of a pie chart to emphasize a specific slice or slices.

1 In the **Format Data Series** pane, under **SERIES OPTIONS**, notice the slider and box for *Pie Explosion*.

When all the pie slices are selected, as they currently are, you can use this command to explode *all* of the pie pieces away from the center by varying degrees to emphasize all the individual slices of the pie chart. An exploded pie chart visualizes the contribution of each value to the total, while at the same time emphasizing individual values.

2 On the pie chart, click the green **Waterfront** slice to select only that slice, and then on the right, notice that the **Format Data Point** pane displays.

Excel adjusts the pane, depending on what you have selected, so that the commands you need are available.

3 In the **Format Data Point** pane, in the **Point Explosion** box, select the existing text, type **10%** and then press [Enter].

4 With the **Waterfront** slice still selected, in the **Format Data Point** pane, under **SERIES OPTIONS**, click **Fill & Line** [icon], and then click **FILL** to expand its options.

5 Click the **Gradient fill** option button, click the **Preset gradients arrow**, and then in the fourth row, click the last gradient—**Bottom Spotlight – Accent 6**. Click **Save** 🔲, and then compare your screen with Figure 3.15.

FIGURE 3.15

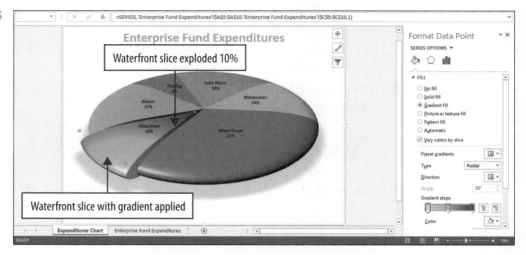

Activity 3.09 | Formatting the Chart Area

The entire chart and all of its elements comprise the ***chart area***.

1 Point to the white area just inside the border of the chart to display the ScreenTip *Chart Area*. Click one time, and notice that on the right, the **Format Chart Area** pane displays.

2 Under **CHART OPTIONS**, click **Fill & Line** 🖌, and be sure the **FILL** options are still displayed.

3 Click the **Gradient fill** option button, click the **Preset gradients arrow**, and then in the fourth row, click the first gradient—**Bottom Spotlight – Accent 1**.

4 In the **Format Chart Area** pane, click **FILL** to collapse the options, and then click **BORDER** to expand its options.

5 Under **Border**, click **Solid line**, click the **Color arrow** to display the Outline colors, and then in the fourth column, click the first color—**Blue – Gray, Text 2**. In the **Width** box, drag to select the existing width, and then type **5 pt**

6 **Close** ❌ the **Format Chart Area** pane, and then click outside of the Chart Area to deselect the chart. Click **Save** 🔲, and then compare your screen with Figure 3.16.

FIGURE 3.16

Activity 3.10 | **Editing a Workbook and Updating a Chart**

Video E3-3

If you edit the data in your worksheet, the chart data markers—in this instance the pie slices—will adjust automatically to accurately represent the new values.

1 On the pie chart, notice that *Airport* represents 17% of the total projected expenses.

2 In the sheet tab area at the bottom of the workbook, click the **Enterprise Fund Expenditures tab** to redisplay the worksheet.

3 Click cell **C5**, type **18121067** and then press Enter. Notice that the Accounting Number Format is retained in the cell.

ANOTHER WAY Double-click the cell to position the insertion point in the cell and edit.

4 Notice that the total in cell **C11** is recalculated to *$101,151,180* and the percentages in **column D** are also recalculated.

5 Display the **Expenditures Chart** sheet. Notice that the pie slices adjust to show the recalculation—*Airport* is now *18%* of the adjusted expenditures. Click **Save** 🖫, and then compare your screen with Figure 3.17.

FIGURE 3.17

Activity 3.11 | **Using Goal Seek to Perform What-If Analysis**

Video E3-4

The process of changing the values in cells to see how those changes affect the outcome of formulas in your worksheet is referred to as *what-if analysis*. One what-if analysis tool in Excel is *Goal Seek*, which finds the input needed in one cell to arrive at the desired result in another cell.

1 Click the **Enterprise Fund Expenditures sheet tab** to redisplay the worksheet. In cell **A13**, type **Goal: To Reduce Waterfront Expenditures from 11% to 9% of Total Expenditures** **Merge & Center** the text across the range **A13:D13**, and then apply the **Heading 3** Cell Style.

2 In cell **A14**, type **Goal Amount:** and press Enter.

3 Select the range **C10:D10**, right-click over the selection, and then click **Copy**. Point to cell **B14**, right-click, and then under **Paste Options**, click **Paste** 📋.

4 Press [Esc] to cancel the moving border, click cell **C14**, and then compare your screen with Figure 3.18.

FIGURE 3.18

5 Be sure cell **C14** is the active cell. On the **DATA tab**, in the **Data Tools group**, click **What-If Analysis**, and then click **Goal Seek**.

6 In the **Goal Seek** dialog box, notice that the active cell, **C14**, is indicated in the **Set cell** box. Press [Tab] to move to the **To value** box, and then type **9%**

C14 is the cell in which you want to set a specific value; 9% is the percentage of the total expenditures that is your goal for the Waterfront Expenditure. The Set cell box contains the formula that calculates the information you seek.

7 Press [Tab] to move the insertion point to the **By changing cell** box, and then click cell **B14**. Compare your screen with Figure 3.19.

Cell B14 contains the value that Excel changes to reach the goal. Excel formats this cell as an absolute cell reference.

FIGURE 3.19

8 Click **OK**. In the displayed **Goal Seek Status** dialog box, click **OK**.

9 Select the range **A14:C14**. On the **HOME tab**, display the **Cell Styles** gallery. Under **Themed Cell Styles**, apply **20% - Accent1**.

10 Click cell **B14**, display the **Cell Styles** gallery again, and then at the bottom, under **Number Format**, click **Currency [0]**.

Use this cell style when you want to apply currency formatting with no decimal places quickly.

11 ▸ Press Ctrl + Home, click **Save** 🖫, and then compare your screen with Figure 3.20.

Excel calculates that the city must budget for *$9,103,606* in Waterfront expenditures in order for this item to become 9% of the total projected budget.

FIGURE 3.20

Activity 3.12 | Preparing and Printing a Workbook with a Chart Sheet

1 ▸ Click the **PAGE LAYOUT tab**. In the **Page Setup group**, click **Margins**, and then click **Custom Margins**.

2 ▸ In the **Page Setup** dialog box, on the **Margins tab**, under **Center on page**, select the **Horizontally** check box.

3 ▸ Click the **Header/Footer tab**, and then in the center of the dialog box, click **Custom Footer**. In the **Footer** dialog box, with your insertion point blinking in the **Left section**, on the row of buttons, click **Insert File Name** 🗐.

4 ▸ Click **OK** two times.

The dotted line indicates the page break as currently formatted.

5 ▸ Display the **Expenditures Chart**, which must have its footer formatted separately. In the **Page Setup group**, click the **Dialog Box Launcher** 🖫.

Chart sheets are automatically centered on the page.

6 ▸ Click the **Header/Footer tab**, and then in the center of the dialog box, click **Custom Footer**. In the **Footer** dialog box, with your insertion point blinking in the **Left section**, on the row of buttons, click **Insert File Name** 🗐.

7 ▸ Click **OK** two times. Click the **FILE tab**, and then click **Show All Properties**. As the **Tags**, type **enterprise fund, expenditures** As the **Subject**, type your course name and section number. Be sure your name displays as the author.

8 ▸ On the left, click **Save**. Right-click the **Expenditures Chart sheet tab**, and then click **Select All Sheets**. Verify that *[Group]* displays in the title bar.

Recall that by selecting all sheets, you can view all of the workbook pages in Print Preview.

9 ▸ Press Ctrl + F2 to display the **Print Preview**. Examine the first page, and then at the bottom of the **Print Preview**, click **Next Page** ▸ to view the second page of your workbook.

NOTE	**Printing a Chart Sheet Uses More Toner**

Printing a chart that displays on a chart sheet will use more toner or ink than a small chart that is part of a worksheet. If you are printing your work, check with your instructor to verify whether or not you should print the chart sheet.

10 On the left, click **Save** to redisplay the workbook.

11 By using the techniques you practiced in Project 1A, print or submit electronically as directed by your instructor. If required by your instructor, print or create an electronic version of your worksheet with formulas displayed.

12 **Close** your workbook and close **Excel**.

END | You have completed Project 3A

Recall that **OneNote** is a Microsoft application with which you can create a digital notebook that gives you a single location where you can gather and organize information in the form of notes. OneNote Online enables you to share your OneNote notebooks on the web.

> **ALERT!** | **Working with Web-Based Applications and Services**
>
> Computer programs and services on the web receive continuous updates and improvements, so the steps to complete this web-based activity may differ from the ones shown. You can often look at the screens and the information presented to determine how to complete the activity.

Activity | Creating a JPEG Photo of a Chart and Uploading It to a OneNote Online Notebook

In this activity, you will create a JPEG image of a chart, and then upload the image to a OneNote Online notebook.

1 From File Explorer, navigate to your **Excel Chapter 3** folder, and then open your file **Lastname_Firstname_3A_ Enterprise_Fund** workbook. Display the **Expenditures Chart** worksheet.

2 Display the **Start** screen and type **snipping** Click the **Snipping Tool** program to start it.

3 In the Snipping Tool dialog box, click the **New arrow**, and then click **Rectangular Snip**. With the ➕ pointer, point to the upper left corner of the chart, hold down the left mouse button, and then drag down to the lower right corner of the chart to create a red rectangle around the chart. Release the mouse button. Compare your screen with Figure A.

4 On the **Snipping Tool** mark-up window toolbar, click **Save Snip** 🖫. In the **Save As** dialog box, navigate to your **Excel Chapter 3** folder. Be sure the **Save as type** box displays **JPEG file**. In the **File name** box, type **Lastname_Firstname_EX_3A_Web** and then click **Save**. **Close** ☒ the **Snipping Tool** window and **Close** ☒ Excel.

5 Launch Internet Explorer, navigate to **http://onedrive.com** and then sign in to your **Microsoft** account. Click your **GO! Web Projects** folder to open it; if necessary, create this folder.

FIGURE A

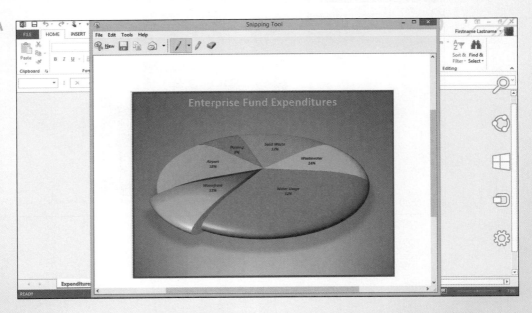

(GO! with Office Online (formerly Web Apps) continues on the next page)

6 In the OneDrive menu bar, click **Create**, and then click **OneNote notebook** to create a new notebook. In the **New Microsoft OneNote notebook** box, using your own name, type **Lastname_Firstname_EX_3A_Web** and then click **Create**.

7 Point to the text *Untitled Section*, right-click, and then click **New Section**. As the **Section Name**, type **Fund Reports** and then click **OK**.

8 With the insertion point blinking at the top of the notebook page, type **Chart of Enterprise Fund Expenditures** and press Enter. With the insertion point in the blank page, on the ribbon, click the **INSERT tab**, and then in the **Pictures group**, click **Picture**.

9 In the **Choose File to Upload** dialog box, navigate to your **Excel Chapter 3** folder, and then click the **EX_3A_Web** JPEG file that you created with the Snipping Tool. Click **Open**.

Use this technique to insert a picture to store in a OneNote notebook.

10 With the insertion point blinking below the inserted picture, click the **HOME tab**, and then in the **Tags group**,

click **Tag** to display a list of tags. Click **Important**. Below the picture, click to the right of the tag—a gold star—to position the insertion point there. Type **Attention Council Members: The expenditures from the Enterprise Fund will be discussed at the August City Council meeting.** Compare your screen with Figure B.

A note tag can help you locate specific information quickly. A note tag is both a descriptive term representing a category, such as *Important* or *To Do*, and a related icon that can be associated with a specific note. When this notebook on your OneDrive is shared with all of the City Council members, each will be able to view the chart and see that it is important.

11 If you are instructed to submit your file, use one of the methods outlined in the Note box below. In OneNote Online, there is no Save button because your notebook is being saved automatically.

12 Sign out of your Microsoft account, and then close all windows.

NOTE **Printing or Creating an Electronic File of a Online OneNote Page**

You can use Snipping Tool to create an electronic file or to paste the snip into a document to save and print. In the OneNote Online, in which you can open this page, you can print pages directly to a printer.

FIGURE B

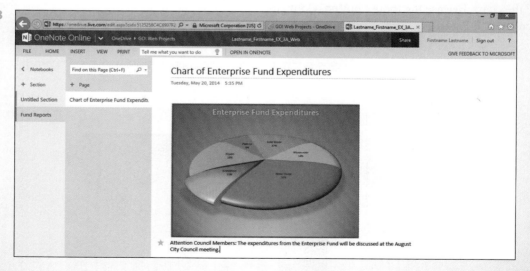

Tourism Spending Projection with Line Chart

PROJECT ACTIVITIES

In Activities 3.13 through 3.20, you will assist Michael Larsen, City Manager, in creating a worksheet to estimate future tourism spending based on two possible growth rates. You will also create a line chart to display past visitor spending. Your resulting worksheet and chart will look similar to Figure 3.21.

PROJECT FILES

uild from
Scratch

For Project 3B, you will need the following files:

New blank Excel file
e03B_Surfers

You will save your workbook as:

Lastname_Firstname_3B_Tourism

PROJECT RESULTS

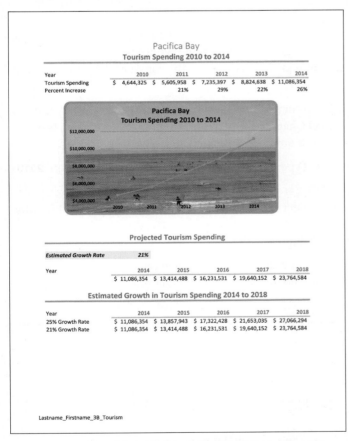

FIGURE 3.21 Project 3B Tourism Spending Projection with Line Chart

Video E3-5

If you change the value in a cell referenced in a formula, Excel automatically recalculates the result of the formula. This means that you can change cell values to see *what* would happen *if* you tried different values. Recall that this process of changing the values in cells to see how those changes affect the outcome of formulas in your worksheet is referred to as what-if analysis.

Activity 3.13 | Using Parentheses in a Formula to Calculate a Percentage Rate of Increase

Mr. Larsen has the city's tourism spending figures for the recent 5-year period. In each year, tourism spending has increased. In this activity, you will construct a formula to calculate the **percentage rate of increase**—the percent by which one number increases over another number—for each year since 2010. From this information, future tourism spending growth can be estimated.

Excel follows a set of mathematical rules called the **order of operations**, which has four basic parts:

- Expressions within parentheses are processed first.
- Exponentiation, if present, is performed before multiplication and division.
- Multiplication and division are performed before addition and subtraction.
- Consecutive operators with the same level of precedence are calculated from left to right.

1 Start Excel and open a new blank workbook. In cell **A1**, type **Pacifica Bay** and in cell **A2**, type **Tourism Spending 2010 to 2014** and then **Merge & Center** ⊞▾ cell A1 across the range **A1:F1** and apply the **Title** cell style. **Merge & Center** ⊞▾ cell A2 across the range **A2:F2** and apply the **Heading 1** cell style.

2 Widen **column A** to **150 pixels** and widen **columns B:F** to **90 pixels**. Press F12 to display the **Save As** dialog box. Navigate to your **Excel Chapter 3** folder, and then in the **File name** box, using your own name, type **Lastname_Firstname_3B_Tourism** Click **Save** or press Enter.

3 Leave **row 3** blank, and then click cell **A4**. Type **Year** and then press Tab. In cell **B4**, type **2010** and then press Tab.

4 In cell **C4**, type **2011** and then press Tab. Select the range **B4:C4**, and then drag the fill handle to the right through cell **F4** to extend the series to *2014*. Apply the **Heading 3** cell style to the selected range. Compare your screen with Figure 3.22.

By establishing a pattern of 1-year intervals with the first two cells, you can use the fill handle to continue the series. The AutoFill feature will do this for any pattern that you establish with two or more cells.

FIGURE 3.22

5 In cell **A5**, type **Tourism Spending** and press Enter. In cell **A6**, type **Percent Increase** and press Enter.

6 Click cell **B5**, and then beginning in cell **B5** and pressing `Tab` to move across the row, enter the following values for tourism spending in the years listed:

2010	2011	2012	2013	2014
4644325	5605958	7235397	8824638	11086354

7 Click cell **C6**. Being sure to include the parentheses, type **=(c5-b5)/b5** and then on the **Formula Bar**, click **Enter** ☑ to keep cell **C6** active; your result is *0.207055492*. Compare your screen with Figure 3.23.

> Recall that as you type, a list of Excel functions that begin with the letter *C* and *B* may briefly display. This is *Formula AutoComplete*, an Excel feature which, after typing an = (equal sign) and the beginning letter or letters of a function name, displays a list of function names that match the typed letter(s). In this instance, the letters represent cell references, *not* the beginning of a function name.

FIGURE 3.23

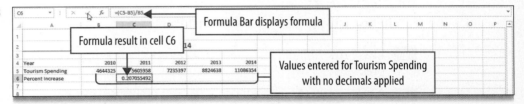

8 With cell **C6** selected, drag the fill handle to the right to copy the formula through cell **F6**.

> Because this formula uses relative cell references—that is, for each year, the formula is the same but the values used are relative to the formula's location—you can copy the formula in this manner. For example, the result for 2012 uses the 2011 value as the base, the result for 2013 uses the 2012 value as the base, and the result for 2014 uses the 2013 value as the base.

9 Select the range **B5:F5**, right-click, on the mini toolbar, click **Accounting Number Format** $ ▾, and then click **Decrease Decimal** two times. Select the range **C6:F6**, right-click, and then apply **Percent Style** %. Click cell **C6** and look at the **Formula Bar**.

> The mathematical formula ***rate = amount of increase/base*** is used to calculated the percentage rate of tourism spending increase from 2010 to 2011. The formula is applied as follows:

> First, determine the *amount of increase* by subtracting the *base*—the starting point represented by the 2010 tourism spending—from the 2011 tourism spending. Therefore, the *amount of increase* = $5,605,958 – $4,644,325 or $961,633. Between 2010 and 2011 tourism spending increased by $961,633. In the formula, this calculation is represented by *C5-B5*.

> Second, calculate the *rate*—what the amount of increase ($961,633) represents as a percentage of the base (2010's tourism spending of $4,644,325). Determine this by dividing the amount of increase ($961,633) by the base ($4,644,325). Therefore $961,633 divided by $4,644,325 is equal to *0.207055492* or, when formatted as a percent and rounded up, 21%.

10 In the **Formula Bar**, locate the parentheses enclosing *C5-B5*.

> Recall that Excel follows a set of mathematical rules called the order of operations, in which expressions within parentheses are processed first, multiplication and division are performed before addition and subtraction, and consecutive operators with the same level of precedence are calculated from left to right.

11 **Save** 🖫 your workbook, and then compare your screen with Figure 3.24.

FIGURE 3.24

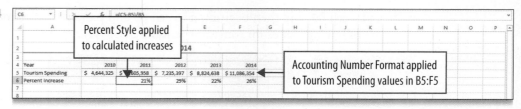

Percent Style applied to calculated increases

Accounting Number Format applied to Tourism Spending values in B5:F5

More Knowledge | **Use of Parentheses in a Formula**

When writing a formula in Excel, use parentheses to specify the order in which the operations should occur. For example, to average three test scores of 100, 50, and 90 that you scored on three different tests, you would add the test scores and then divide by the number of test scores in the list. If you write this formula as =100+50+90/3, the result would be 180, because Excel would first divide 90 by 3 and then add 100+50+30. Excel would do so because the order of operations states that multiplication and division are calculated *before* addition and subtraction.

The correct way to write this formula is =(100+50+90)/3. Excel will add the three values, and then divide the result by 3, or 240/3 resulting in a correct average of 80. Parentheses play an important role in ensuring that you get the correct result in your formulas.

Activity 3.14 | Using Format Painter

In this activity, you will use Format Painter to copy text (non-numeric) formats.

1 Leave **row 7** blank, and then click cell **A8**. Type **Projected Tourism Spending** and then press Enter.

2 Point to cell **A2**, right-click, on the mini toolbar, click **Format Painter** , and then click cell **A8** to copy the format.

The format of cell **A2** is *painted*—applied to—cell **A8**, including the merging and centering of the text across the range **A8:F8**.

 BY TOUCH   On the Home tab, in the Clipboard group, tap the Format Painter button.

---

3 Leave **row 9** blank, and then click cell **A10**. Type **Estimated Growth Rate** and then press Tab.

4 In cell **B10**, type **25%** and press Enter. Select the range **A10:B10**, right-click over the selection, and then from the mini toolbar, apply **Bold** B and **Italic** I.

5 Leave **row 11** blank. Click cell **A12**, type **Year** and then press Tab. In cell **B12**, type **2014** and press Tab. In cell **C12**, type **2015** and press Tab.

6 Select the range **B12:C12**, and then drag the fill handle through cell **F12** to extend the pattern of years to *2018*. Apply the **Heading 3** cell style to the selected range.

7 Point to cell **F5**, right-click, and then click **Copy**. Point to cell **B13**, right-click, and then click **Paste** . Compare your screen with Figure 3.25, and then **Save** your workbook.

FIGURE 3.25

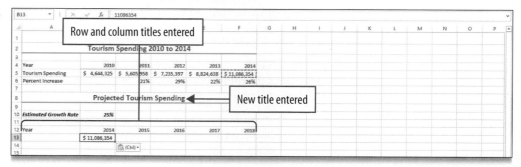

Row and column titles entered

New title entered

Activity 3.15 | Calculating a Value After an Increase

A growth in tourism spending means that the city can plan for additional revenues and also plan more hotel and conference space to accommodate the increasing number of visitors. Therefore, city planners in Pacifica Bay want to estimate how much tourism spending will increase in the future. The calculations you made in the previous activity show that tourism spending has increased at varying rates during each year from 2010 to 2014, ranging from a low of 21% to a high of 29% per year.

Economic data suggests that future growth will trend close to that of the recent past. To plan for the future, Mr. Larsen wants to prepare a forecast of tourism spending based on the percentage increase halfway between the high of 29% and the low of 21%; that is, for 25%. In this activity, you will calculate the tourism spending that would result from a 25% increase.

1 Click cell **C13**. Type **=b13*(100%+b10)** and then on the **Formula Bar**, click **Enter** ✓ to display a result of *13857942.5*. Point to cell **B13**, right-click, click **Format Painter** 🖌, and then click cell **C13** to copy the format. Compare your screen with Figure 3.26.

This formula calculates what tourism spending will be in the year 2015 assuming an increase of 25% over 2014's tourism spending. Use the mathematical formula *value after increase = base × percent for new value* to calculate a value after an increase as follows:

First, establish the *percent for new value*. The **percent for new value = base percent + percent of increase**. The *base percent* of 100% represents the base tourism spending and the *percent of increase*—in this instance is 25%. Therefore, the tourism spending will equal 100% of the base year plus 25% of the base year. This can be expressed as 125% or 1.25. In this formula, you will use 100% + the rate in cell **B10**, which is 25%, to equal 125%.

Second, enter a reference to the cell that contains the *base*—the tourism spending in 2014. The base value resides in cell **B13**—*$11,086,354*.

Third, calculate the *value after increase*. Because in each future year the increase will be based on 25%—an absolute value located in cell **B10**—this cell reference can be formatted as absolute by typing dollar signs.

FIGURE 3.26

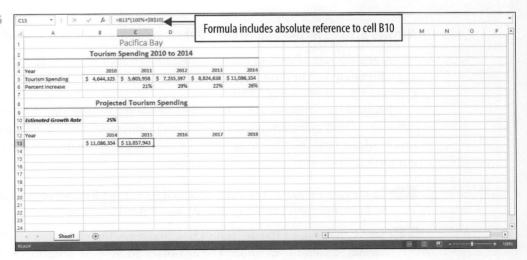

2 With cell **C13** as the active cell, drag the fill handle to copy the formula to the range **D13:F13**. Click an empty cell to cancel the selection, click **Save** 🖫 and then compare your screen with Figure 3.27.

This formula uses a relative cell address—B13—for the *base*; the tourism spending in the year is used in each of the formulas in cells D13:F13 as the *base* value. Because the reference to the *percent of increase* in cell B10 is an absolute reference, each *value after increase* is calculated with the value from cell B10.

The tourism spending projected for 2015—*$13,857,943*—is an increase of 25% over the spending in 2014. The projected spending in 2016—*$17,322,428*—is an increase of 25% over the spending in 2015, and so on.

FIGURE 3.27

More Knowledge   **Percent Increase or Decrease**

The basic formula for calculating an increase or decrease can be done in two parts. First determine the percent by which the base value will be increased or decreased, and then add or subtract the results to the base. The formula can be simplified by using (1+amount of increase) or (1−amount of decrease), where 1, rather than 100%, represents the whole. Therefore, the formula used in Step 1 of Activity 3.15 could also be written =b13*(1+b10), or =(b13*b10)+b13.

Objective 6   Answer What-If Questions by Changing Values in a Worksheet

Video E3-6

If a formula depends on the value in a cell, you can see what effect it will have if you change the value in that cell. Then, you can copy the value computed by the formula and paste it into another part of the worksheet where you can compare it to other values.

Activity 3.16   Answering What-If Questions and Using Paste Special

A growth rate of 25% in tourism spending in each year will result in tourism spending of approximately $27 million by 2018. The city planners will likely ask: *What if* tourism spending grows at the lowest rate of 21%?

Because the formulas are constructed to use the growth rate displayed in cell **B10**, Mr. Larsen can answer that question quickly by entering a different percentage into that cell. To keep the results of the new calculation so it can be compared, you will paste the results of the what-if question into another area of the worksheet.

1 Leave **row 14** blank, and then click cell **A15**. Type **Estimated Growth in Tourism Spending 2014 to 2018** and then press Enter. Use **Format Painter** 🖌 to copy the format from cell **A8** to cell **A15**.

2 Select the range **A10:B10**, right-click to display the mini toolbar, click the **Fill Color button arrow** 🖜 ▾, and then under **Theme Colors**, in the first column, click the third color—**White, Background 1, Darker 15%**.

3 Leave **row 16** blank, and then in the range **A17:A19**, type the following row titles:

Year

25% Growth Rate

21% Growth Rate

4 Select the range **B12:F12**, right-click over the selection, and then on the shortcut menu, click **Copy**.

🔄 ANOTHER WAY   Press Ctrl + C; or, on the Home tab, in the Clipboard group, click the Copy button.

5 Point to cell **B17**, right-click, and then on the shortcut menu, under **Paste Options**, click **Paste** 📋.

Recall that when pasting a group of copied cells to a target range, you need only point to or select the first cell of the range.

6 Select and **Copy** the range **B13:F13**, and then **Paste** it beginning in cell **B18**.

7 Click cell **C18**. On the **Formula Bar**, notice that the *formula* was pasted into the cell, as shown in Figure 3.28.

This is *not* the desired result. The actual *calculated values*—not the formulas—are needed in the range.

FIGURE 3.28

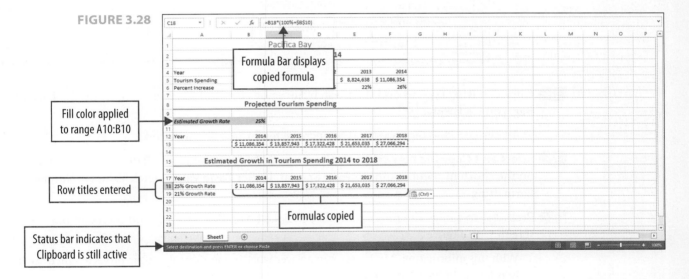

8 On the **Quick Access Toolbar**, click **Undo** ↺. With the range **B13:F13** still copied to the Clipboard—as indicated by the message in the status bar and the moving border—point to cell **B18**, and then right-click to display the shortcut menu.

9 Under **Paste Options**, point to **Paste Special** to display another gallery, and then under **Paste Values**, point to **Values & Number Formatting** 📋 to display the ScreenTip as shown in Figure 3.29.

The ScreenTip *Values & Number Formatting (A)* indicates that you can paste the calculated values that result from the calculation of formulas along with the formatting applied to the copied cells. *(A)* is the keyboard shortcut for this command.

FIGURE 3.29

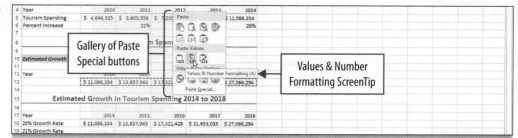

10 Click **Values & Number Formatting**, click cell **C18** and notice on the **Formula Bar** that the cell contains a *value*, not a formula. Press Esc to cancel the moving border. Compare your screen with Figure 3.30.

The calculated estimates based on a 25% growth rate are pasted along with their formatting.

FIGURE 3.30

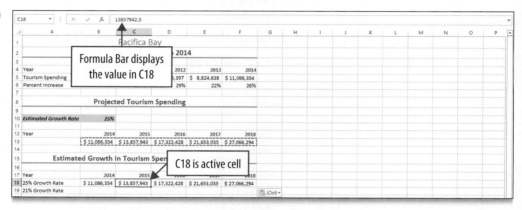

11 Click cell **B10**. Type **21** and then watch the values in **C13:F13** *recalculate* as, on the **Formula Bar**, you click **Enter**.

The value *21%* is the lowest percent increase for the past 5-year period.

12 Select and **Copy** the new values in the range **B13:F13**. Point to cell **B19**, right-click, and then on the shortcut menu, point to **Paste Special**. Under **Paste Values**, click **Values & Number Formatting**.

13 Press Esc to cancel the moving border, click cell **A1**, click **Save**, and then compare your screen with Figure 3.31.

With this information, Mr. Larsen can answer what-if questions about the projected increase in tourism spending based on the rates of increase over the past 5 years.

FIGURE 3.31

Video E3-7

A *line chart* displays trends over time. Time is displayed along the bottom axis and the data point values connect with a line. The curve and direction of the line make trends obvious to the reader.

The columns in a column chart and the pie slices in a pie chart emphasize the distinct values of each data point. A line chart, on the other hand, emphasizes the flow from one data point value to the next.

Activity 3.17 | Inserting Multiple Rows and Creating a Line Chart

So that City Council members can see how tourism spending has increased over the past five years, in this activity, you will chart the actual tourism spending from 2010 to 2014 in a line chart.

1 ▶ Click the **PAGE LAYOUT tab**. In the **Themes group**, click the **Colors arrow**, and then change the **Theme Colors** to **Orange**.

2 ▶ In the **row header area**, point to **row 8** to display the ➡ pointer, and then drag down to select **rows 8:24**. Right-click over the selection, and then click **Insert** to insert the same number of blank rows as you selected. Compare your screen with Figure 3.32.

Use this technique to insert multiple rows quickly.

FIGURE 3.32

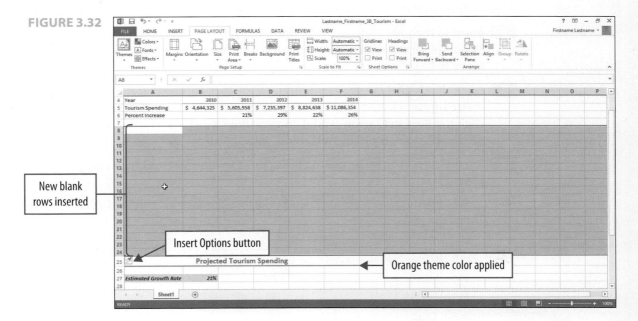

3 ▶ Near **row 25**, click **Insert Options** 🖌, and then click the **Clear Formatting** option button to clear any formatting from these rows.

You will use this blank area to position your line chart.

4 ▶ Press Ctrl + Home to deselect the rows and move to the top of your worksheet. Select the range **A5:F5**. On the **INSERT tab**, in the **Charts group**, click **Insert Line Chart** ᙁᙁ ▾.

5 ▶ In the gallery of line charts, in the second row, point to the first chart type to display the ScreenTip *Line with Markers*. Compare your screen with Figure 3.33.

FIGURE 3.33

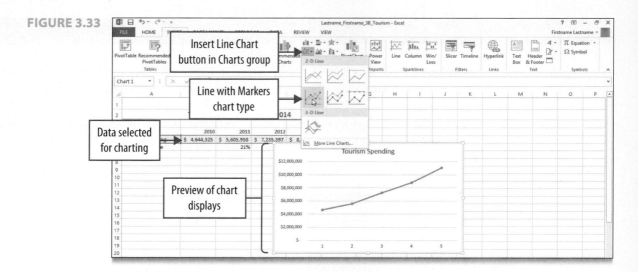

6 Click the **Line with Markers** chart type to create the chart as an embedded chart in the worksheet.

7 Point to the border of the chart to display the 🔲 pointer, and then drag the chart so that its upper left corner is positioned in cell **A8**, aligned approximately under the *t* in the word *Percent* above.

> Excel uses the label in cell A5—*Tourism Spending*—as the suggested chart title.

8 Point to the **Chart Title** *Tourism Spending* and right-click. On the shortcut menu, click **Edit Text** to place the insertion point in the title. Type **Pacifica Bay** and press Enter. Press End to move to the end of *Spending*, press Spacebar, and then type **2010 to 2014**

9 Click the dashed border surrounding the **Chart Title** so that it is a solid line, indicating the entire title is selected. Right-click over the title, and then click **Font**. In the **Font** dialog box, click the **Font style arrow**, and then click **Bold**. Click the **Font color arrow**, and then in the second column, click the first color—**Black, Text 1**. Click **OK**.

10 On the right side of the chart, click **Chart Elements** ➕, and then compare your screen with Figure 3.34.

> Three of the available chart elements are included for this chart by default—the axes, the chart title, and the gridlines.

FIGURE 3.34

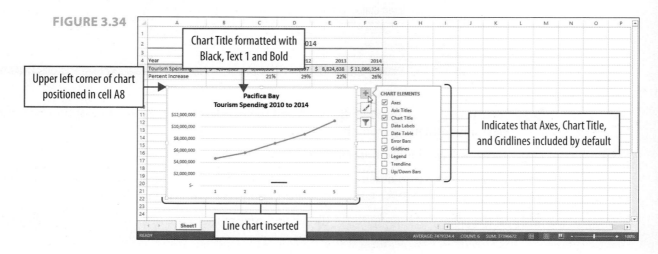

Activity 3.18 | Formatting Axes in a Line Chart

An *axis* is a line that serves as a frame of reference for measurement; it borders the chart *plot area*. The plot area is the area bounded by the axes, including all the data series. Recall that the area along the bottom of a chart that identifies the categories of data is referred to as the *category axis* or the *x-axis*. Recall also that the area along the left side of a chart that shows the range of numbers for the data points is referred to as the *value axis* or the *y-axis*.

In this activity, you will change the category axis to include the years 2010 to 2014 and adjust the numeric scale of the value axis.

1 Be sure the chart is still selected. At the bottom of the chart, point to any of the numbers *1* through *5* to display the ScreenTip *Horizontal (Category) Axis*, and then right-click. On the shortcut menu, click **Select Data**.

BY TOUCH   On the ribbon, tap the DESIGN tab, and then in the Data group, tap Select Data.

2 On the right side of the **Select Data Source** dialog box, under **Horizontal (Category) Axis Labels**, locate **Edit**, as shown in Figure 3.35.

Here you can change the labels on the category axis to the years that are represented in the chart.

FIGURE 3.35

3 In the right column, click **Edit**. If necessary, drag the title bar of the **Axis Labels** dialog box to the right of the chart so that it is not blocking your view of the data, and then select the years in the range **B4:F4**. Compare your screen with Figure 3.36.

FIGURE 3.36

4 In the **Axis Labels** dialog box, click **OK**, and notice that in the right column of the **Select Data Source** dialog box, the years display as the category labels. Click **OK** to close the **Select Data Source** dialog box. Compare your screen with Figure 3.37.

FIGURE 3.37

Lower portion of chart unused by the data series

Years display as the category labels on the category axis (axis selected)

5 ▷ With the **Horizontal (Category) Axis** still selected, click the **Chart Elements** button ⊞, point to **Axes**, click the ▶ **arrow**, and then click **More Options** to display the **Format Axis** pane.

6 ▷ Under **AXIS OPTIONS**, click **Fill & Line** ◇, if necessary click **LINE** to expand the options, and then click the **No line** option button so that the line can become a gridline at the bottom of the chart when you format the plot area. **Close** ✕ the **Format Axis** pane.

7 ▷ On the chart, notice that the orange line—the data series—does not display in the lower portion of the chart. On the left side of the chart, point to any of the dollar values to display the ScreenTip *Vertical (Value) Axis*, and then right-click. On the shortcut menu, click **Format Axis** to display the **Format Axis** pane again on the right. Compare your screen to Figure 3.38.

FIGURE 3.38

Vertical (Value) Axis selected in the chart

Format Axis pane

⟳ ANOTHER WAY   On the FORMAT tab, in the Current Selection group, click the Chart Elements arrow, click Vertical (Value) Axis, and then click Format Selection. Or, click the Chart Elements button, point to Axes, click the arrow, click More Options, and then in the Format Axis pane, click the AXIS OPTIONS arrow. On the displayed list, click Vertical (Value) Axis.

8 ▷ In the **Format Axis** pane, under **Bounds**, click in the **Minimum** box, select the existing text *0.0*, and then type **4000000**

Because none of the spending figures are under $4,000,000, changing the Minimum number to $4,000,000 will enable the data series to occupy more of the plot area.

9 Under **Units**, in the **Major** box, select the text *2.0E6*, type **2000000** and press Enter. Click **Save** 🔲, and then compare your screen with Figure 3.39.

The *Major unit* value determines the spacing between the gridlines in the plot area. By default, Excel started the values at zero and increased in increments of $2,000,000. By setting the Minimum value on the value axis to $4,000,000 and changing the Major unit to $2,000,000, the line chart shows a clearer and more pronounced trend in tourism spending.

Numbers that display E + a number are expressed by Excel in the Scientific format, which displays a number in exponential notation.

FIGURE 3.39

On Value Axis, values increase in increments of $2,000,000 and values begin with $4,000,000 (Minimum)

Line representing data series displays in lower portion of the chart

Activity 3.19 | Formatting the Chart Area in a Line Chart

An Excel chart has two background elements—the plot area and the chart area—which, by default display a single fill color. To add visual appeal to a chart, you can insert a graphic image as the background.

1 Near the top of the **Format Axis** pane, click the **AXIS OPTIONS arrow**, and then click **Chart Area** to display the **Format Chart Area** pane. Then click **Fill & Line** 🔲.

When formatting chart elements, Excel provides multiple ways to display the panes that you need. You can right-click the area you want to format and choose a command on the shortcut menu. You can use an existing pane to move to a different pane. And you can use the FORMAT tab on the ribbon to navigate among various chart elements in the Current Selection group. Use whatever method is easiest for you.

🔄 **ANOTHER WAY**   On the FORMAT tab, in the Current Selection group, click the Chart Elements arrow, click Chart Area, and then click Format Selection. Or, right-click slightly inside the chart to display the shortcut menu, and then click Format Chart Area.

2 In the **Format Chart Area** pane, click **FILL** to expand the options, and then click the **Picture or texture fill** option button.

A default texture displays in the chart area.

3 In the **Format Chart Area** pane, under **Insert picture from**, click **File**. In the **Insert Picture** dialog box, navigate to the student data files that accompany this textbook, and then click **e03B_Surfers**. Click **Insert**. Compare your screen with Figure 3.40.

FIGURE 3.40

Picture or texture fill option selected

File command to search for a picture from your files

Picture inserted as fill for Chart Area

4 ▶ In the **Format Chart Area** pane, click **FILL** to collapse the options, and then click **BORDER** to expand the options. Click the **Solid line** option button, click the **Color arrow**, and then under **Theme Colors**, in the fifth column, notice that the first color—**Orange, Accent 1**—is already selected by default.

5 ▶ Click the **Color arrow** again to accept the default color and close the color palette.

6 ▶ Set the **Width** to **4 pt** either by selecting the existing text in the Width box and typing or by clicking the up spin box arrow as necessary.

7 ▶ Use the scroll bar on the right side of the **Format Chart Area** pane if necessary to scroll to the bottom of the pane, and then select the **Rounded corners** check box. On the **Quick Access Toolbar**, click Save 🖫, and then compare your screen with Figure 3.41.

FIGURE 3.41

Width of border set to 4 pt

Rounded corners selected

Activity 3.20 │ Formatting the Plot Area Gridlines and Axis Fonts in a Line Chart

1 ▶ To the right of the chart, if necessary click **Chart Elements** ➕ to display the list of elements, point to **Gridlines**, click the **arrow**, and then click **More Options** to display the **Format Major Gridlines** pane. Compare your screen with Figure 3.42.

FIGURE 3.42

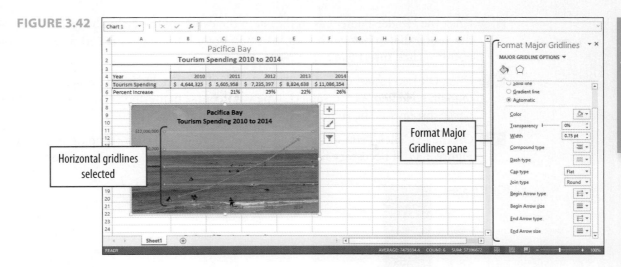

Horizontal gridlines selected

Format Major Gridlines pane

2 If necessary, in the pane, scroll to the top and click to expand **LINE**. Click the **Solid line** option button. Click the **Color arrow**, and be sure that **Orange, Accent 1**—in the fifth column, the first color—is selected.

3 Set the **Width** to **1 pt**.

4 In the chart, point to any of the dollar values on the **Vertical (Value) Axis**, right-click, and then click **Font**.

5 In the **Font** dialog box, change the **Font style** to **Bold**, and then change the **Font color** to **Black, Text 1**—in the second column, the first color. Click **OK**.

6 Use the same technique to format the font of the **Horizontal (Category) Axis** to **Bold** with **Black, Text 1**.

7 **Close** ☒ the **Format Axis** pane. Click cell **A1** to deselect the chart. Click **Save** 🔲, and then compare your screen with Figure 3.43.

FIGURE 3.43

Vertical (Value) Axis font changed to Bold and Black, Text 1

Plot Area gridlines set to 1 pt

Horizontal (Category) Axis changed to Bold and Black, Text 1

8 Click the **PAGE LAYOUT tab**. In the **Page Setup group**, click **Margins**, and then click **Custom Margins**.

9 In the **Page Setup** dialog box, on the **Margins tab**, under **Center on page**, select the **Horizontally** check box.

10 Click the **Header/Footer tab**, and then in the center of the dialog box, click **Custom Footer**. In the **Footer** dialog box, with your insertion point blinking in the **Left section**, on the row of buttons, click **Insert File Name** 📄.

11 Click **OK** two times. Click the **FILE tab**, and then click **Show All Properties**. As the **Tags**, type **tourism spending** As the **Subject**, type your course name and section number. Be sure your name displays as the author.

12 On the left, click **Print** to display the **Print Preview**, and then compare your screen with Figure 3.44. If necessary return to the worksheet and make any corrections.

FIGURE 3.44

13 On the left, click **Save** to redisplay the workbook.

14 Using the techniques you practiced in Project 1A, print or submit electronically as directed by your instructor. If required by your instructor, print or create an electronic version of your worksheet with formulas displayed.

15 Close your workbook and close Excel.

More **Knowledge**   **Resizing a Chart**

To resize a chart, on the CHART TOOLS FORMAT tab, in the Size group, type the dimensions in the Shape Height or Shape Width box. Or:

- To change the width of a chart, drag a left or right sizing handle.
- To change the height of a chart, drag a top or bottom sizing handle.
- To size a chart proportionately, drag a corner sizing handle.

END | You have completed Project 3B

Objective   Convert an Excel Worksheet to a Google Docs Spreadsheet with a Chart

Google Docs is Google's free, web-based word processor, spreadsheet, slide show, and form service that, along with free data storage, is known as *Google Drive*. You can convert an Excel worksheet to a Google Docs spreadsheet. Google Drive and Google Docs are similar to OneDrive and Office Online—both are free, cloud-based productivity tools.

ALERT!   **Working with Web-Based Applications and Services**

Computer programs and services on the web receive continuous updates and improvements, so the steps to complete this web-based activity may differ from the ones shown. You can often look at the screens and the information presented to determine how to complete the activity.

Activity | **Converting an Excel Worksheet to a Google Docs Spreadsheet with a Chart**

In this activity, you will convert an Excel worksheet to a Google Docs spreadsheet and create a column chart.

1 If you do *not* have a Google account, skip to Step 2. If you already have a Google account, start Internet Explorer, in the address bar, type **http://docs.google.com** and then press Enter. Sign in to your Google account your Google Drive. Now skip to Step 3.

2 From the desktop, start Internet Explorer. In the address bar, type **http://docs.google.com** and then press Enter. Locate and click the button to sign up for a new account, and then complete the information. As your email address, you can use your Microsoft account or other email address. Sign in to your new Google account.

3 Locate and click **CREATE**, and then click **Spreadsheet**. Under **Untitled spreadsheet**, click **File**, and then click **Import**. Click **Upload**, and then click **Select a file from your computer**. In the **Choose File to Upload**

dialog box, navigate to your student data files and click **e03_3B_Web**. In the lower right corner of the dialog box, click **Open**, and then click **Import**.

4 When the screen indicates that the file was imported successfully, click **Open now**. Compare your screen with Figure A.

5 Drag to select the years and values in the range **A4:F5**, and then on the menu bar, click **Insert**. On the menu, click **Chart**.

6 On the **Chart Editor** screen, under **Recommended charts**, click the second chart—the **Column chart**. On the left above **Recommended charts**, click to select the first check box—**Switch rows/columns**, and then the second check box **Use column A as headers**, and then the third check box, **Use row 4 as labels**.

FIGURE A

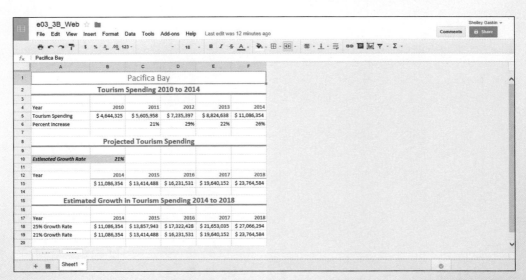

(GO! with Office Online (formerly Web Apps) continues on the next page)

7 In the lower left corner, click **Insert**. In the upper right corner, click the down arrow and then click **Move to own sheet**.

8 On the displayed chart, click the text *Chart title*. In the box that displays, with the text selected, and then using your own name, type **2010 – 2014 Tourism Spending Prepared by Firstname Lastname** Press Enter.

9 In the upper right corner of the chart, click the small square labeled *Tourism Spending*, and then click one time to edit the legend. In the toolbar that displays above, click **Right**, and then on the displayed list, click **None**. Compare your screen with Figure B.

10 In the upper right, click **Save image**, and then in the **Notification bar** at the bottom, click the **Save arrow**. Click **Save as**, and then in the **Save As** dialog box, navigate to

your **Excel Chapter 3** folder. In the **File name** box, using your own name, type **Lastname_Firstname_EX_3B_Web** and then press Enter.

11 In the upper right corner, click your Google name, and then click **Sign out**. Close Internet Explorer.

It is not necessary to save your spreadsheet, because Google Drive saves your work automatically. Your image is saved as a *.png* file, which is the file extension for an image in the *Portable Network Graphics* format. This format, like JPEG, is commonly used for graphics on the web.

12 Submit your .png image file to your instructor as directed.

FIGURE B

Andrew Rodriguez / Fotolia; FotolEdhar/ Fotolia; apops/ Fotolia; Yuri Arcurs/ Fotolia

The advantage of using Office 365 is that your organization does not have to purchase and install server hardware and software for sophisticated business applications and does not need a full-time IT person or staff just to manage the technology your teams need.

By using Office 365, you are able to have business-class services for your employees without investing in expensive hardware, software, and personnel. However, at least one person in an organization must be designated as the *Office 365 Administrator*—the person who creates and manages the account, adds new users, sets up the services your organization wants to use, sets permission levels, and manages the SharePoint team sites. You can have more than one Administrator if you want to share these tasks with others.

Microsoft provides easy-to-use instructions and videos to get you started, and you might also have contact with a Microsoft representative. You will probably find, however, that subscribing to and setting up the account, adding users, and activating services is a straightforward process that requires little or no assistance.

After purchasing the required number of licenses, you will add each team member as a user that includes his or her email address.

The Office 365 Administrator can manage the team sites, as shown in Figure A. On the left there are links to manage the site pages in the Office 365 account. Here the administrator can manage permissions, specifying which users can access and edit which team sites. The administrator can also manage and modify the look and feel of the team site.

Activity | Using a Team Site to Collaborate

This group project relates to the **Bell Orchid Hotels**. If your instructor assigns this project to your class, you can expect to use **Lync** in **Office 365** to collaborate on the following tasks for this chapter:

- If you are in the **Accounting Group**, you and your teammates will finalize the workbook to summarize hotel rooms sold over a four-week period in April and post it to your team site.

- If you are in the **Engineering Group**, you and your teammates will finalize your workbook summarizing Maintenance Expenses for the first quarter and post it to your team site.

- If you are in the **Food and Beverage Group**, you and your teammates will finalize your workbook to analyze the profitability of the ten most popular entrees in the hotel's restaurant and post it to your team site.

- If you are in the **Human Resources Group**, you and your teammates will finalize your workbook summarizing the pay of salaried employees over the first six months of operation and post it to your team site.

- If you are in the **Operations Group**, you and your teammates will finalize your workbook for Rooms and Housekeeping Service Analysis that will be used to determine ongoing needs for housekeeping service and post it to your team site.

- If you are in the **Sales and Marketing Group**, you and your teammates will finalize your Rooms Sold Analysis workbook summarizing rooms sold by four salespersons during January-June that will be used to develop a marketing plan for the rest of the year and post it to your team site.

FIGURE A

END OF CHAPTER

SUMMARY

Use pie charts when you want to show the relationship of each part to a whole. Consider using a pie chart when you have only one data series to plot and you do not have more than seven categories.

To create a pie chart, you must select two ranges. One range contains the labels for each pie slice; the other contains the values that add up to a total. Both ranges must have the same number of cells.

In formulas, Excel follows rules called the order of operations; expressions within parentheses are processed first, and multiplication and division are performed before addition and subtraction.

Use a line chart when you want to show trends over time. Time displays along the bottom axis and the data point values connect with a line. The curve and direction of the line make trends obvious.

GO! LEARN IT ONLINE

Review the concepts and key terms in this chapter by completing these online challenges, which you can find at **www.pearsonhighered.com/go**.

Matching and Multiple Choice: Answer matching and multiple choice questions to test what you learned in this chapter. MyITLab®

Crossword Puzzle: Spell out the words that match the numbered clues, and put them in the puzzle squares.

Flipboard: Flip through the definitions of the key terms in this chapter and match them with the correct term.

GO! FOR JOB SUCCESS

Video: Planning and Managing Your Career
Your instructor may assign this video to your class, and then ask you to think about, or discuss with your classmates, these questions:

FotolEdhar / Fotolia

When did you start career planning and what were the main steps you took to plan your career?

What have been your best sources for networking?

What advice would you give to others about how to stay employable throughout your career?

END OF CHAPTER

REVIEW AND ASSESSMENT GUIDE FOR EXCEL CHAPTER 3

Your instructor may assign one or more of these projects to help you review the chapter and assess your mastery and understanding of the chapter.

Project	Apply Skills from These Chapter Objectives	Project Type	Project Location
		Review and Assessment Guide for Excel Chapter 3	
3C	Objectives 1-4 from Project 3A	**3C Skills Review** A guided review of the skills from Project 3A.	On the following pages
3D	Objectives 5-7 from Project 3B	**3D Skills Review** A guided review of the skills from Project 3B.	On the following pages
3E	Objectives 1-4 from Project 3A	**3E Mastery (Grader Project)** A demonstration of your mastery of the skills in Project 3A with extensive decision making.	In MyITLab and on the following pages
3F	Objectives 5-7 from Project 3B	**3F Mastery (Grader Project)** A demonstration of your mastery of the skills in Project 3B with extensive decision making.	In MyITLab and on the following pages
3G	Objectives 1-7 from Projects 3A and 3B	**3G Mastery (Grader Project)** A demonstration of your mastery of the skills in Projects 3A and 3B with extensive decision making.	In MyITLab and on the following pages
3H	Combination of Objectives from Projects 3A and 3B	**3H GO! Fix It** A demonstration of your mastery of the skills in Projects 3A and 3B by creating a correct result from a document that contains errors you must find.	Online
3I	Combination of Objectives from Projects 3A and 3B	**3I GO! Make It** A demonstration of your mastery of the skills in Projects 3A and 3B by creating a result from a supplied picture.	Online
3J	Combination of Objectives from Projects 3A and 3B	**3J GO! Solve It** A demonstration of your mastery of the skills in Projects 3A and 3B, your decision-making skills, and your critical thinking skills. A task-specific rubric helps you self-assess your result.	Online
3K	Combination of Objectives from Projects 3A and 3B	**3K GO! Solve It** A demonstration of your mastery of the skills in Projects 3A and 3B, your decision-making skills, and your critical thinking skills. A task-specific rubric helps you self-assess your result.	On the following pages
3L	Combination of Objectives from Projects 3A and 3B	**3L GO! Think** A demonstration of your understanding of the Chapter concepts applied in a manner that you would outside of college. An analytic rubric helps you and your instructor grade the quality of your work by comparing it to the work an expert in the discipline would create.	On the following pages
3M	Combination of Objectives from Projects 3A and 3B	**3M GO! Think** A demonstration of your understanding of the Chapter concepts applied in a manner that you would outside of college. An analytic rubric helps you and your instructor grade the quality of your work by comparing it to the work an expert in the discipline would create.	Online
3N	Combination of Objectives from Projects 3A and 3B	**3N You and GO!** A demonstration of your understanding of the Chapter concepts applied in a manner that you would in a personal situation. An analytic rubric helps you and your instructor grade the quality of your work.	Online
3O	Combination of Objectives from Projects 3A and 3B	**3O Cumulative Group Project for Excel Chapter 3** A demonstration of your understanding of concepts and your ability to work collaboratively in a group role-playing assessment, requiring both collaboration and self-management.	Online
Capstone Project for Excel Chapters 1-3	Combination of Objectives from Projects 1A, 1B, 2A, 2B, 3A, and 3B	A demonstration of your mastery of the skills in Chapters 1-3 with extensive decision making. **(Grader Project)**	In MyITLab and online

GLOSSARY

GLOSSARY OF CHAPTER KEY TERMS

3-D The shortened term for *three-dimensional*, which refers to an image that appears to have all three spatial dimensions—length, width, and depth.

Absolute cell reference A cell reference that refers to cells by their fixed position in a worksheet; an absolute cell reference remains the same when the formula is copied.

Axis A line that serves as a frame of reference for measurement and which borders the chart plot area.

Base The starting point when you divide the amount of increase by it to calculate the rate of increase.

Bevel A shape effect that uses shading and shadows to make the edges of a shape appear to be curved or angled.

Category axis The area along the bottom of a chart that identifies the categories of data; also referred to as the x-axis.

Chart area The entire chart and all of its elements.

Chart sheet A workbook sheet that contains only a chart.

Data marker A column, bar, area, dot, pie slice, or other symbol in a chart that represents a single data point; related data points form a data series.

Data point A value that originates in a worksheet cell and that is represented in a chart by a data marker.

Data series Related data points represented by data markers; each data series has a unique color or pattern represented in the chart legend.

Enterprise fund A municipal government fund that reports income and expenditures related to municipal

services for which a fee is charged in exchange for goods or services.

Explode The action of pulling out one or more pie slices from a pie chart for emphasis.

Formula AutoComplete An Excel feature which, after typing an = (equal sign) and the beginning letter or letters of a function name, displays a list of function names that match the typed letter(s).

Fund A sum of money set aside for a specific purpose.

General fund The term used to describe money set aside for the normal operating activities of a government entity such as a city.

Goal Seek A what-if analysis tool that finds the input needed in one cell to arrive at the desired result in another cell.

Google Docs Google's free, web-based word processor, spreadsheet, slide show, and form service, that along with free data storage, is known as Google Drive.

Google Drive Google's free web-based word processor, spreadsheet, slide show, and form service, that includes free data storage.

Legend A chart element that identifies the patterns or colors that are assigned to the categories in the chart.

Line chart A chart type that displays trends over time; time displays along the bottom axis and the data point values are connected with a line.

Major unit The value in a chart's value axis that determines the spacing between tick marks and between the gridlines in the plot area.

Order of operations The mathematical rules for performing multiple calculations within a formula.

Percent for new value = base percent + percent of increase The formula for calculating a percentage by which a value increases by adding the base percentage—usually 100%—to the percent increase.

Percentage rate of increase The percent by which one number increases over another number.

Pie chart A chart that shows the relationship of each part to a whole.

Plot area The area bounded by the axes of a chart, including all the data series.

Rate = amount of increase/base The mathematical formula to calculate a rate of increase.

Relative cell reference In a formula, the address of a cell based on the relative position of the cell that contains the formula and the cell referred to.

Value after increase = base x percent for new value The formula for calculating the value after an increase by multiplying the original value—the base—by the percent for new value (see the *Percent for new value* formula).

Value axis A numerical scale on the left side of a chart that shows the range of numbers for the data points; also referred to as the Y-axis.

What-if analysis The process of changing the values in cells to see how those changes affect the outcome of formulas in a worksheet.

x-axis Another name for the category axis.

y-axis Another name for the value axis.

CHAPTER REVIEW

Skills Review | Project 3C Parks

Apply 3A skills from these Objectives:

1 Chart Data with a Pie Chart
2 Format a Pie Chart
3 Edit a Workbook and Update a Chart
4 Use Goal Seek to Perform What-If Analysis

In the following Skills Review, you will edit a worksheet for Jerry Silva, City Parks Manager, which details the revenue generated from city parks and structures. Your completed worksheets will look similar to Figure 3.45.

PROJECT FILES

For Project 3C, you will need the following file:

e03C_Parks

You will save your workbook as:

Lastname_Firstname_3C_Parks

PROJECT RESULTS

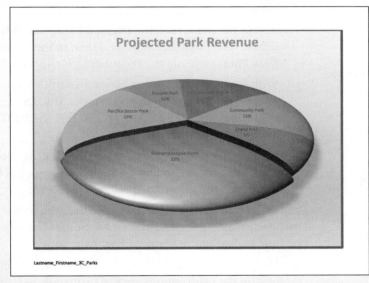

FIGURE 3.45

(Project 3C Parks continues on the next page)

CHAPTER REVIEW

1 Start Excel. From your student data files, open the file **e03C_Parks**. Save the file in your **Excel Chapter 3** folder as **Lastname_Firstname_3C_Parks**

a. Click cell **D5**, and then type **=** to begin a formula. Click cell **C5**, type **/** and then click cell **C11**. Press F4 to make the reference to the value in cell **C11** absolute. On the **Formula Bar**, click **Enter**, and then fill the formula down through cell **D10**.

b. With the range **D5:D10** selected, right-click over the selection, and then on the mini toolbar, click **Percent Style** and **Center**.

2 Select the nonadjacent ranges **A5:A10** and **C5:C10** to select the park names and the projected revenue. Click the **INSERT tab**, and then in the **Charts group**, click **Insert Pie or Doughnut Chart**. Under **3-D Pie**, click the chart type **3-D Pie**.

a. On the **DESIGN tab**, in the **Location group**, click **Move Chart**. In the **Move Chart** dialog box, click the **New sheet** option button. In the **New sheet** box, replace the highlighted text *Chart1* by typing **Projected Park Revenue Chart** and then click **OK**.

b. Click the text *Chart Title*, and then type **Projected Park Revenue** Press Enter to create the new chart title.

c. With the title selected, on the **FORMAT tab**, in the **WordArt Styles group**, click **More** ⊽ to display the gallery. In the second row, select the fifth style— **Fill – Olive Green, Accent 3, Sharp Bevel**. Drag to select the chart title text, and then on the mini toolbar, change the **Font Size** to **32**.

d. Click in a white area of the chart to deselect the chart title. Click **Chart Elements** ⊞, and then click the **Legend** check box to remove the legend.

e. In the list of **CHART ELEMENTS**, point to **Data Labels**, click the **arrow** that displays, and then click **More Options**. In the **Format Data Labels** pane on the right, under **LABEL OPTIONS**, select the **Category Name** and **Percentage** check boxes, and *clear* all other check boxes. Under **Label Position**, click **Center**.

f. Point to any of the selected labels, right-click to display a shortcut menu, and then click **Font**. In the **Font** dialog box, on the **Font tab**, change the **Font style** to **Bold Italic** and change the **Size** to **11** Click **OK**.

3 In any pie slice, point anywhere outside the selected label, and then double-click to display the **Format Data Series** pane. Under **SERIES OPTIONS**, click **Effects** ◻, and then click **3-D FORMAT**.

a. Click the **Top bevel arrow**, and then under **Bevel**, click the first button—**Circle**. Apply the **Circle** bevel to the **Bottom bevel**.

b. Set the **Width** and **Height** of both the **Top bevel** and the **Bottom bevel** to **512 pt**

c. Scroll down, click the **Material arrow**, and then under **Standard**, click the third material—**Plastic**.

d. Scroll to the top of the **Format Data Series** pane, click **SHADOW**, and then click the **Presets arrow**. Scroll down, and then under **Perspective**, in the first row, click the third effect—**Below**.

e. In the **Format Data Series** pane, under **SERIES OPTIONS**, click the third button—**Series Options** ◪. Set the **Angle of first slice** to **50**

f. On the pie chart, click the **Diamond League Fields** slice to select only that slice, and then in the **Format Data Point** pane, set the Point Explosion to **10%**

g. With the **Diamond League Fields** slice still selected, in the **Format Data Point** pane, under **SERIES OPTIONS**, click **Fill & Line** ◇, and then click **FILL** to expand the options.

h. Click the **Gradient fill** option button, click the **Preset gradients arrow**, and then in the fourth row, click the third gradient—**Bottom Spotlight – Accent 3**.

4 Point to the white area just inside the border of the chart to display the ScreenTip *Chart Area*, and then click one time to display the **Format Chart Area** pane.

a. Under **CHART OPTIONS**, click **Fill & Line** ◇, and be sure the **FILL** options are still displayed.

b. Click the **Gradient fill** option button, click the **Preset gradients arrow**, and then in the first row, click the fifth gradient—**Light Gradient – Accent 5**.

c. In the **Format Chart Area** pane, click **FILL** to collapse the options, and then click **BORDER** to expand the options.

d. Click the **Solid line** option button, click the **Color arrow**, and then in the fifth column, click the last color—**Ice Blue, Accent 1, Darker 50%**. Set the **Width** of the border to **5 pt** Close the pane, and then **Save** your workbook.

(Project 3C Parks continues on the next page)

CHAPTER REVIEW

5 In the sheet tab area at the bottom of the workbook, click the **Sheet1 tab**. In cell **A13**, type **Goal: To Increase Revenue at Grand Park from 8% to 10%** and then **Merge & Center** the text across the range **A13:D13**. Apply the **Heading 3** cell style.

a. In cell **A14**, type **Goal Amount:** and press Enter. Select the range **C6:D6**, right-click over the selection, and then click **Copy**. Point to cell **B14**, right-click, and then under **Paste Options**, click **Paste**. Press Esc to cancel the moving border.

b. Click cell **C14**. On the **DATA tab**, in the **Data Tools group**, click **What-If Analysis**, and then click **Goal Seek**. In the **Goal Seek** dialog box, press Tab to move to the **To value** box, and then type **10%**

c. Press Tab to move the insertion point to the **By changing cell** box, and then click cell **B14**. Click **OK**. In the displayed **Goal Seek Status** dialog box, click **OK**.

d. Select the range **A14:C14**. From the **HOME tab**, display the **Cell Styles** gallery. Under **Themed Cell Styles**, apply **20% - Accent6**. Click cell **B14**, and then from the **Cell Styles** gallery, under **Number Format**, apply the **Currency [0]** cell style.

6 With your worksheet displayed, in the sheet tab area, double-click *Sheet1* to select the text, and then type **Projected Park Revenue Data** and press Enter.

a. Click the **PAGE LAYOUT tab**. In the **Page Setup Group**, click **Margins**, click **Custom Margins**, and then in the **Page Setup** dialog box, on the **Margins tab**, under **Center on page**, select the **Horizontally** check box.

b. Click the **Header/Footer tab**, click **Custom Footer**, and then with your insertion point in the **Left section**, on the row of buttons, click **Insert File Name**. Click **OK** two times.

c. Display the **Projected Park Revenue Chart**—recall a chart sheet must have its footer formatted separately. Display the **Page Setup** dialog box.

d. Click the **Header/Footer tab**, click **Custom Footer**, and then in the **Left section**, click the **Insert File Name** button. Click **OK** two times.

e. Click the **FILE tab**, and then click **Show All Properties**. As the **Tags**, type **park revenue** As the **Subject**, type your course name and section number. Be sure your name displays as the **Author**.

f. On the left, click **Save**. Right-click the **Projected Park Revenue Chart sheet tab**, and then click **Select All Sheets**. Print or submit electronically as directed by your instructor. If required by your instructor, print or create an electronic version with formulas displayed by using the instructions in Project 1A. Close Excel without saving so that you do not save the changes you made to print formulas.

END | You have completed Project 3C

CHAPTER REVIEW

Apply 3B skills from these Objectives:

5 Design a Worksheet for What-If Analysis

6 Answer What-If Questions by Changing Values in a Worksheet

7 Chart Data with a Line Chart

Build from Scratch

In the following Skills Review, you will edit a worksheet that forecasts the revenue from new housing permits that the City of Pacifica Bay expects to collect in the five-year period 2014–2018. Your completed worksheet will look similar to Figure 3.46.

PROJECT FILES

For Project 3D, you will need the following files:

New blank workbook
e03D_Housing

You will save your workbook as:

Lastname_Firstname_3D_Housing

PROJECT RESULTS

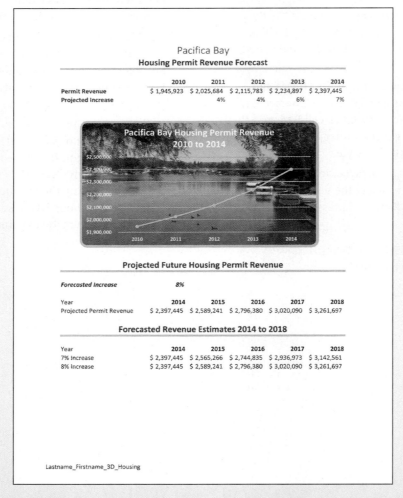

FIGURE 3.46

(Project 3D Housing Permits continues on the next page)

CHAPTER REVIEW

1 ▶ Start Excel and display a new blank workbook. By using your own name, save the file in your **Excel Chapter 3** folder as **Lastname_Firstname_3D_Housing**

a. In cell **A1**, type **Pacifica Bay** and in cell **A2** type **Housing Permit Revenue Forecast**

b. **Merge & Center** the title and subtitle across **columns A:F**. To **A1** apply the **Title** cell style and to **A2** apply the **Heading 1** cell style.

c. Widen **column A** to **175 pixels**, and widen **columns B:F** to **80 pixels**.

d. In cell **A5**, type **Permit Revenue** and in cell **A6** type **Projected Increase** Apply the **Heading 4** cell style to both cells. In cell **B4**, type **2010** Press [Tab], and then in **C4**, type **2011** Use the fill handle to fill the remaining years through **column F** so that the last year that displays is 2014. Apply the **Heading 3** cell style to the years.

e. In the range **B5:F5**, type the values **1945923** and **2025684** and **2115783** and **2234897** and **2397445** Select the values you just typed, display the **Cell Styles** gallery, and then at the bottom, apply the **Currency [0]** cell style.

2 ▶ Click cell **C6**. Being sure to include the parentheses, type **=(c5-b5)/b5** and then press [Enter]. Select cell **C6**, and then apply **Percent Style**.

a. With cell **C6** selected, drag the fill handle to the right through cell **F6**.

b. In cell **A8**, type **Projected Future Housing Permit Revenue** and then press [Enter]. Point to cell **A2**, right-click, on the mini toolbar, click **Format Painter**, and then click cell **A8**. In cell **A10**, type **Forecasted Increase** leave row 11 blank, and then in cell **A12**, type **Year**

c. In cell **A13**, type **Projected Permit Revenue** and then in cell **B12**, type **2014** and press [Tab]. In cell **C12**, type **2015** and then press [Tab]. Select the range **B12:C12**, and then drag the fill handle through cell **F12** to extend the pattern of years to *2018*. Apply **Bold** to the selection.

d. Right-click cell **F5**, and then click **Copy**. Right-click over cell **B13**, and then click **Paste**.

e. In cell **B10**, type **7%** which is the percent of increase from 2013 to 2014. Select the range **A10:B10**, and then from the mini toolbar, apply **Bold** and **Italic**.

3 ▶ Click cell **C13**. Type **=b13*(100%+b10)** and then on the **Formula Bar**, click **Enter** to keep the cell active. With cell **C13** as the active cell, drag the fill handle to copy the formula to the range **D13:F13**.

a. Point to cell **B13**, right-click, click **Format Painter**, and then select the range **C13:F13**.

b. Click cell **A15**. Type **Forecasted Revenue Estimates 2014 to 2018** and then press [Enter]. Use **Format Painter** to copy the format from cell **A8** to cell **A15**.

c. In the range **A17:A19**, type the following row titles:

Year

7% Increase

8% Increase

4 ▶ Select the range **B12:F12**, right-click over the selection, and then on the shortcut menu, click **Copy**. **Paste** the selection to the range **B17:F17**.

a. Select the range **B13:F13**, right-click over the selection, and then on the shortcut menu, click **Copy**. Point to cell **B18**, right-click, and then from the shortcut menu, point to **Paste Special**. Under **Paste Values**, click the second button—**Values & Number Formatting**. Press [Esc] to cancel the moving border.

b. Click cell **B10**. Type **8** and then press [Enter]. Copy the new values in the range **B13:F13**. Point to cell **B19**, right-click, and then point to **Paste Special**. Under **Paste Values**, click **Values & Number Formatting**. **Save** your workbook.

5 ▶ In the **row header area**, point to **row 8** to display the pointer, and then drag down to select **rows 8:24**. Right-click over the selection, and then click **Insert** to insert the same number of blank rows as you selected. Under the selection area near cell **A25**, click **Insert Options**, and then click the **Clear Formatting** option button to clear any formatting from these rows.

a. On the **PAGE LAYOUT tab**, in the **Themes group**, click the **Colors arrow**, and then click **Yellow**. Select the range **A5:F5**. On the **INSERT tab**, in the **Charts group**, click **Insert Line Chart**. In the displayed gallery of line charts, in the second row, click the **Line with Markers** chart type to create the chart as an embedded chart in the worksheet.

b. Point to the border of the chart to display the ⬚ pointer, and then drag the chart so that its upper left corner is positioned in cell **A9**, aligned approximately under the *c* in the word *Projected* above.

(Project 3D Housing Permits continues on the next page)

CHAPTER REVIEW

c. Point to the Chart Title *Permit Revenue* and right-click. On the shortcut menu, click **Edit Text** so that the insertion point is positioned before the word *Permit*. Type **Pacifica Bay Housing** and then press Spacebar. Press End and then press Enter to create a second line. Type **2010 to 2014**

6 At the bottom of the chart, point to any of the numbers *1* through *5*, and then right-click. On the shortcut menu, click **Select Data**. On the right side of the **Select Data Source** dialog box, click **Edit**. In the worksheet, select the years in the range **B4:F4**, and then click **OK** two times to enter the years as the category labels.

a. With the **Horizontal (Category) Axis** still selected, click **Chart Elements** +, point to **Axes**, click the ▶ arrow, and then click **More Options**. In the **Format Axis** pane, under **AXIS OPTIONS**, click **Fill & Line** ◇, if necessary click **LINE** to expand the options, and then click the **No line** option button. **Close** the **Format Axis** pane.

b. On the left side of the chart, point to any of the dollar values, right-click, and then click **Format Axis**. In the **Format Axis** pane, under **Bounds**, select the text in the **Minimum** box, and then type **1900000**

c. Under **Units**, in the **Major** box, select the existing text, and then type **100000**

d. Near the top of the **Format Axis** pane, click the **AXIS OPTIONS arrow**, and then click **Chart Area** to display the **Format Chart Area** pane. Then, click **Fill & Line** ◇.

e. In the **Format Chart Area** pane, click **FILL** to expand the options, and then click the **Picture or texture fill** option button. Under **Insert picture from**, click **File**. In the **Insert Picture** dialog box, navigate to your student data files, and then click **e03D_Housing**. Click **Insert**.

f. In the **Format Chart Area** pane, click **FILL** to collapse the options, and then click **Border** to expand the options. Click the **Solid line** option button, click the **Color arrow**, and then under **Theme Colors**, in the fifth column, click the first color—**Gold Accent 1**. Set the **Width** to **4 pt** Scroll to the bottom of the pane, and then select the **Rounded corners** check box

g. Right-click the chart title, and then on the shortcut menu, click **Font**. In the **Font** dialog box, change the **Font style** to **Bold**, change the **Size** to **16**, and change the **Font color** to **White, Background 1**—in the first column, the first color. Click **OK**.

7 To the right of the chart, click **Chart Elements** +, point to **Gridlines**, click the **arrow**, and then click **More Options** to display the **Format Major Gridlines** pane.

a. Under **LINE**, click the **Solid line** option button. Click the **Color arrow**, and be sure that **Gold, Accent 1** is the selected color. Set the **Width** to **1 pt**

b. In the chart, point to any of the dollar values on the **Vertical (Value) Axis**, right-click, and then click **Font**. In the **Font** dialog box, change the **Font style** to **Bold**, and then change the **Font color** to **White, Background 1**—in the first column, the first color. Click **OK**.

c. By using the same technique, format the **Font** of the **Horizontal (Category) Axis** to **Bold** with **White, Background 1** as the font color.

d. **Close** the **Format Axis** pane, and then click cell **A1** to deselect the chart. Click the **PAGE LAYOUT tab**. In the **Page Setup group**, click **Margins**, and then click **Custom Margins**. In the **Page Setup** dialog box, on the **Margins tab**, select the **Horizontally** check box. Click the **Header/Footer tab**, click **Custom Footer**, and then in the **Left section**, insert the file name. Click **OK** two times.

e. Click the **FILE tab**, and then click **Show All Properties**. As the **Tags**, type **housing permit revenue, forecast** In the **Subject** box, type your course name and section number. Be sure your name displays as the **Author**.

f. View the **Print Preview**, and then **Save** your workbook. Print or submit electronically as directed by your instructor. If required by your instructor, print or create an electronic version of your worksheet with formulas displayed by using the instructions in Project 1A, and then **Close** Excel without saving so that you do not save the changes you made to print formulas.

END | You have completed Project 3D

In the following project, you will edit a worksheet that summarizes the revenue budget for the City of Pacifica Bay. Your completed worksheets will look similar to Figure 3.47.

Apply 3A skills from these Objectives:

1 Chart Data with a Pie Chart

2 Format a Pie Chart

3 Edit a Workbook and Update a Chart

4 Use Goal Seek to Perform What-If Analysis

PROJECT FILES

For Project 3E, you will need the following file:

e03E_Revenue

You will save your workbook as:

Lastname_Firstname_3E_Revenue

PROJECT RESULTS

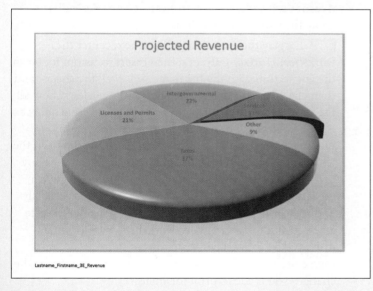

FIGURE 3.47

(Project 3E Revenue continues on the next page)

CONTENT-BASED ASSESSMENTS

1 Start Excel. From your student data files, locate and open **e03E_Revenue**. **Save** the file in your **Excel Chapter 3** folder as **Lastname_Firstname_3E_Revenue**

2 In cells **B10** and **C10**, enter formulas to calculate totals for each column. In cell **D5**, construct a formula to calculate the **% of Total Projected Revenue** from **Taxes** by dividing the **Projected Revenue for Next Fiscal Year** for **Taxes** by the **Total Projected Revenue for Next Fiscal Year**. Use absolute cell references as necessary, format the result in **Percent Style**, and **Center** the percentage. Fill the formula down through cell **D9**.

3 Select the nonadjacent ranges **A5:A9** and **C5:C9** as the data for a pie chart, and then insert a **3-D Pie** chart. Move the chart to a **New sheet** named **Projected Revenue Chart** As the text for the **Chart Title** element, type **Projected Revenue** Format the **Chart Title** by using the **WordArt Style Fill – Aqua, Accent 1, Shadow**—in the first row, the second style and a **Font Size** of **32**.

4 Remove the **Legend** chart element, and then add the **Data Labels** chart element formatted so that only the **Category Name** and **Percentage** display positioned in the **Center**. Format the data labels with a **Font style** of **Bold** and a **Font Size** of **14**.

5 Format the **Data Series** by using a **3-D Format** effect. Change the **Top bevel** and **Bottom bevel** to **Art Deco**. Set the **Top bevel Width** and **Height** to **350 pt** and then set the **Bottom bevel Width** and **Height** to **0 pt** Change the **Material** to the second **Special Effect—Soft Edge**.

6 Display the **Series Options**, and then set the **Angle of first slice** to **115** so that the **Taxes** slice is in the front of the pie. Select the **Services** slice, and then explode the slice **10%**. Change the **Fill Color** of the **Services** slice to a **Solid fill** by using **Gray-50%, Accent 4**—in the eighth column, the first color.

7 Format the **Chart Area** by applying a **Gradient fill** by using the **Preset gradients Light Gradient – Accent 4**.

Format the **Border** of the **Chart Area** by applying a **Solid line** border by using **Gray-50%, Accent 4** and a **5 pt Width**. Close any panes that are open on the right.

8 Display the **Page Setup** dialog box, and then for this chart sheet, insert a **Custom Footer** in the **left section** with the file name.

9 Display **Sheet1** and rename the sheet as **Revenue Sources** Click in any blank cell to cancel any selections. In cell **A12**, type **Goal: Increase Intergovernmental Revenue** and then **Merge & Center** the text across the range **A12:D12**. Apply the **Heading 3** cell style. In cell **A13**, type **Goal Amount**

10 **Copy** the range **C7:D7** to the range **B13:C13**. Click cell **C13**, and then use **Goal Seek** to determine the projected amount of Intergovernmental Revenue in cell **B13** if the value in **C13** is **25%**

11 Select the range **A13:C13**, and then apply the **20% - Accent4** cell style. In **B13**, from the **Cell Styles** gallery, apply the **Currency [0]** cell style.

12 Display the **Page Setup** dialog box, center the worksheet **Horizontally**, and then insert a custom footer in the **left section** with the file name. Select all the sheets, and then click the **FILE tab** to display **Backstage** view. Show all the properties, and then as the **Tags**, type **revenue sources** As the **Subject**, type your course name and section number. Be sure your name displays as the **Author**. On the left, click **Print** to display the **Print Preview**, and note any necessary changes or corrections. In **Backstage** view, on the left click **Save**, and then print or submit electronically as directed. If required by your instructor, print or create an electronic version of your worksheet with formulas displayed by using the instructions in Project 1A, and then close Excel without saving so that you do not save the changes you made to print formulas.

END | You have completed Project 3E

CONTENT-BASED ASSESSMENTS

Mastering Excel | Project 3F Streets

In the following project, you will create a worksheet that the City of Pacifica Bay Facilities Director will use to prepare a five-year forecast of the costs associated with street maintenance. Your completed worksheet will look similar to Figure 3.48.

Apply 3B skills from these Objectives:

5 Design a Worksheet for What-If Analysis

6 Answer What-If Questions by Changing Values in a Worksheet

7 Chart Data with a Line Chart

Build from Scratch

PROJECT FILES

For Project 3F, you will need the following file:

New blank Excel workbook

You will save your workbook as:

Lastname_Firstname_3F_Streets

PROJECT RESULTS

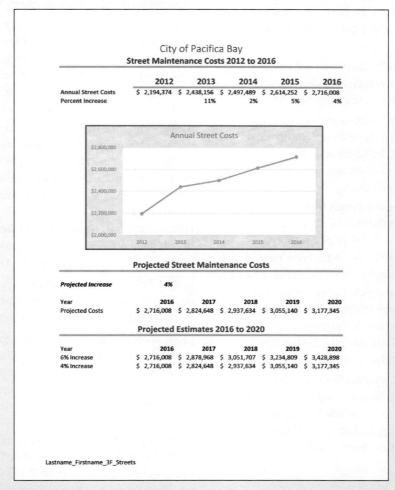

FIGURE 3.48

(Project 3F Streets continues on the next page)

CONTENT-BASED ASSESSMENTS

1 ▶ Start Excel and display a new Blank workbook. Change the **Theme Colors** to **Paper**, and then **Save** the file in your **Excel Chapter 3** folder as **Lastname_Firstname_3F_Streets**

2 ▶ In cell **A1**, type the title **City of Pacifica Bay** and then in cell **A2** type the subtitle **Street Maintenance Costs 2012 to 2016 Merge & Center** both the title and the subtitle across **columns A:F**, and then apply the **Title** and **Heading 1** cell styles respectively.

3 ▶ In the range **B4:F4**, fill the year range with the values 2012 through 2016. In cell **A5** type **Annual Street Costs** and in cell **A6** type **Percent Increase** Change the width of **column A** to **150 pixels**, and then change the width of **columns B:F** to **85 pixels**. In the range **B5:F5** type **2194374** and **2438156** and **2497489** and **2614252** and **2716008**

4 ▶ Apply the **Currency [0]** cell style to the values in **B5:F5**. Apply the **Heading 1** cell style to the years, and apply the **Heading 4** cell style to the range **A5:A6**.

5 ▶ In cell **C6**, construct a formula to calculate the percent of increase in annual street maintenance costs from 2012 to 2013. Format the result with the **Percent Style** and then fill the formula through cell **F6** to calculate the percent of increase in each year.

6 ▶ In cell **A8**, type **Projected Street Maintenance Costs** and then use **Format Painter** to copy the formatting from cell **A2** to cell **A8**. In cell **A10**, type **Projected Increase** and then in cell **A12**, type **Year** In cell **A13**, type **Projected Costs** and then in the range **B12:F12**, use the fill handle to enter the years 2016 through 2020. Apply **Bold** to the years. **Copy** the value in cell **F5** to cell **B13**. In cell **B10**, type **6%** which is the projected increase estimated by the City financial analysts. To the range **A10:B10**, apply **Bold** and **Italic**.

7 ▶ In cell **C13**, construct a formula to calculate the annual projected street maintenance costs for the year 2017 after the projected increase of 6% is applied. Fill the formula through cell **F13**, and then use **Format Painter** to copy the formatting from cell **B13** to the range **C13:F13**.

8 ▶ In cell **A15**, type **Projected Estimates 2016 to 2020** and then use **Format Painter** to copy the format from cell **A8** to cell **A15**. In cells **A17:A19**, type the following row titles:

　Year

　6% Increase

　4% Increase

9 ▶ **Copy** the range **B12:F12**, and then **Paste** the selection to **B17:F17**. Copy the range **B13:F13** and then paste the **Values & Number Formatting** to the range **B18:F18**. Complete the Projected Estimates section of the worksheet by changing the *Projected Increase* in **B10** to **4%** and then copying and pasting the **Values & Number Formatting** to the appropriate range in the worksheet. **Save** your workbook.

10 ▶ Select **rows 8:24**, and then **Insert** the same number of blank rows as you selected. **Clear Formatting** from the inserted rows. By using the data in **A4:F5**, insert a **Line with Markers** chart in the worksheet. Move the chart so that its upper left corner is positioned in cell **A9** and visually centered under the data above.

11 ▶ Format the **Bounds** of the **Vertical (Value) Axis** so that the **Minimum** is **2000000** and the **Major unit** is at **200000** Format the **Fill** of the **Chart Area** with a **Texture fill** by applying the **Parchment** texture—in the third row, the fifth texture. Format the **Plot Area** with a **Solid fill** by using **White, Background 1**—in the first column, the first color. Format the **Chart Area** with a **Border** by applying a **Solid line** by using **Olive Green, Accent 1, Darker 50%**—in the fifth column, the last color. Change the **Width** of the border to **2**

12 ▶ Click cell **A1** to deselect the chart. From the **Page Setup** dialog box, center the worksheet **Horizontally**, and then insert a **Custom Footer** in the **left section** with the file name.

13 ▶ Show all the properties, and then as the **Tags**, type **street maintenance costs** As the **Subject**, type your course name and section number. Be sure your name displays as the **Author**. In **Backstage** view, on the left, click **Print** to view the Print Preview. Print or submit electronically as directed. **Save** your workbook. If required by your instructor, print or create an electronic version of your worksheet with formulas displayed by using the instructions in Project 1A, and then close Excel without saving so that you do not save the changes you made to print formulas.

END | You have completed Project 3F

CONTENT-BASED ASSESSMENTS

Mastering Excel   Project 3G Operations

In the following project, you will edit a workbook for Jennifer Carson, City Finance Manager, that summarizes the operations costs for the Public Works Department. Your completed worksheets will look similar to Figure 3.49.

Apply a combination of 3A and 3B skills:

1. Chart Data with a Pie Chart
2. Format a Pie Chart
3. Edit a Workbook and Update a Chart
4. Use Goal Seek to Perform What-If Analysis
5. Design a Worksheet for What-If Analysis
6. Answer What-If Questions by Changing Values in a Worksheet
7. Chart Data with a Line Chart

PROJECT FILES

For Project 3G, you will need the following file:

e03G_Expenses

You will save your workbook as

Lastname_Firstname_3G_Expenses

PROJECT RESULTS

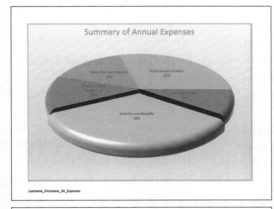

FIGURE 3.49

(Project 3G Operations continues on the next page)

CONTENT-BASED ASSESSMENTS

1 Start Excel. From your student data files, open **e03G_Expenses**. **Save** the file in your **Excel Chapter 3** folder as **Lastname_Firstname_3G_Expenses**

2 In the **Expenses** worksheet, calculate row totals for each expense item in the range **F5:F9**. Format the range **F6:F9** by applying the cell style **Comma [0]**. Calculate column totals for each quarter and for the Annual Total in the range **B10:F10**. In cell **G5**, construct a formula to calculate the **Percent of Total** by dividing the **Annual Total** for **Salaries and Benefits** by the **Annual Total** for all quarters. Use absolute cell references as necessary, format the result in **Percent Style**, and then **Center**. Fill the formula down through cell **G9**.

3 Use a **3-D Pie** chart to chart the **Annual Total** for each item. Move the chart to a **New sheet**; name the sheet **Annual Expenses Chart** As the text for the **Chart Title** element, type **Summary of Annual Expenses** Format the **Chart Title** by using **WordArt Style Fill - Blue, Accent 1, Shadow**—in the first row, the second style and a **Font Size** of **28**.

4 Remove the **Legend** from the chart, and then add **Data Labels** formatted so that only the **Category Name** and **Percentage** display positioned in the **Center**. Format the data labels with **Bold** and **Italic** and a **Font Size** of **12**.

5 Format the **Data Series** by using a **3-D Format** effect. Change the **Top bevel** and **Bottom bevel** to **Circle**. Set the **Top bevel Width** and **Height** to **50 pt** and then set the **Bottom bevel Width** and **Height** to **256 pt** Change the **Material** to the fourth **Standard Effect**—**Metal**.

6 Display the **Series Options**, and then set the **Angle of first slice** to **125** so that the **Salaries and Benefits** slice is in the front of the pie. Select the **Salaries and Benefits** slice, and then explode the slice **10%**. Change the **Fill Color** of the **Salaries and Benefits** slice to a **Solid fill** by using **Green, Accent 6, Lighter 40%**—in the last column, the fourth color.

7 Format the **Chart Area** by applying a **Gradient fill** using the **Preset gradients Light Gradient – Accent 4**. Format the **Border** of the **Chart Area** by adding a **Solid line** border using **Gold, Accent 4** and a **5 pt Width**.

8 Display the **Page Setup** dialog box, and then for this chart sheet, insert a **Custom Footer** in the **left section** with the file name. **Save** your workbook.

9 Display the **Expenses** worksheet, and then by using the Quarter names and the Totals by Quarter, insert a **Line with Markers** chart in the worksheet. Move the chart so that its upper left corner is positioned slightly inside the upper left corner of cell **A12**, and then drag the right sizing handle so that the chart extends slightly inside the right border of **column G**. As the **Chart Title** type **City of Pacifica Bay Annual Expense Summary**

10 Format the **Bounds** of the **Vertical (Value) Axis** so that the **Minimum** is **2100000** and the **Major unit** is at **50000** Format the **Fill** of the **Chart Area** with a **Gradient fill** by applying the preset **Light Gradient - Accent 3**—in the first row, the third gradient. Format the **Plot Area** with a **Solid fill** by using **White, Background 1**—in the first column, the first color. Close any panes on the right, click cell **A1** to deselect the chart, and then **Save** your workbook.

11 Copy the **Annual Total** in cell **F10** and then use **Paste Special** to paste **Values & Number Formatting** in cell **B35**. In cell **C35**, construct a formula to calculate the **Projected Expenses** after the forecasted increase of **3.5%** in cell **B31** is applied. Fill the formula through cell **F35**, and then use **Format Painter** to copy the formatting from cell **B35** to the range **C35:F35**.

12 Change the **Orientation** of this worksheet to **Landscape**, and then use the **Scale to Fit** options to fit the **Height** to **1 page**. In the **Page Setup** dialog box, center this worksheet **Horizontally**, and insert a **Custom Footer** in the **left section** with the file name. **Save** your workbook.

13 Display the **Projected Decrease** worksheet. In cell **C5**, calculate the **Percent of Total** for the first expense, apply **Percent Style**, and then copy the formula down for the remaining expenses.

14 Copy cell **B8**, and then use **Paste Special** to paste the **Values & Number Formatting** to cell **B13**. **Copy** and **Paste** cell **C8** to cell **C13**. With cell **C13** selected, use **Goal Seek** to determine the goal amount of Professional Services expenses in cell **B13** if the value in **C13** is set to **25%**

15 In the **Page Setup** dialog box, center this worksheet **Horizontally**, and insert a **Custom Footer** in the **left section** with the file name.

16 Select all the sheets, and then click the **FILE tab** to display **Backstage** view. Show all the properties, and then as the **Tags**, type **annual expense summary** As the **Subject**, type your course name and section number. Be sure your name displays as the **Author**. On the left, click

(Project 3G Operations continues on the next page)

CONTENT-BASED ASSESSMENTS

Print to display the **Print Preview**, and view all three worksheets. Note any necessary changes or corrections. In **Backstage** view, on the left click **Save**, and then print or submit electronically as directed. If required by your instructor, print or create an electronic version of your worksheet with formulas displayed by using the instructions in Project 1A, and then close Excel without saving so that you do not save the changes you made to print formulas.

END | You have completed Project 3G

CONTENT-BASED ASSESSMENTS

Build from
Scratch

| GO! Fix It | Project 3H Schools | Online |

| GO! Make It | Project 3I Tax | Online |

| GO! Solve It | Project 3J Staffing | Online |

| GO! Solve It | Project 3K Water Usage | |

Build from
Scratch

PROJECT FILES

For Project 3K, you will need the following files:

New blank Excel workbook
e03K_Beach

You will save your workbook as:

Lastname_Firstname_3K_Water_Usage

Pacifica Bay is a growing community and the City Council has requested an analysis of future resource needs. In this project, you will create a worksheet for the Department of Water and Power that illustrates residential water usage over a five-year period. Create a worksheet with the following data:

	2014	2015	2016	2017	2018
Water Use in Acre Feet	62518	65922	71864	76055	82542

Calculate the percent increase for the years 2015 to 2018. Below the Percent Increase, insert a line chart that illustrates the city's water usage from 2014 to 2018. Format the chart and worksheet attractively with a title and subtitle, and apply appropriate formatting. If you choose to format the chart area with a picture, you can use e03K_Beach located with your student files. Include the file name in the footer and enter appropriate document properties. Save the workbook as **Lastname_Firstname_3K_Water_Usage** and submit as directed.

Performance Level

Performance Criteria	Exemplary: You consistently applied the relevant skills	Proficient: You sometimes, but not always, applied the relevant skills	Developing: You rarely or never applied the relevant skills
Create formulas	All formulas are correct and are efficiently constructed.	Formulas are correct but not always constructed in the most efficient manner.	One or more formulas are missing or incorrect or only numbers were entered.
Insert and format a line chart	Line chart created correctly and is attractively formatted.	Line chart was created but the data was incorrect or the chart was not appropriately formatted.	No line chart was created.
Format attractively and appropriately	Formatting is attractive and appropriate.	Adequately formatted but difficult to read or unattractive.	Inadequate or no formatting.

END | You have completed Project 3K

OUTCOMES-BASED ASSESSMENTS

RUBRIC

The following outcomes-based assessments are open-ended assessments. That is, there is no specific correct result; your result will depend on your approach to the information provided. Make Professional Quality your goal. Use the following scoring rubric to guide you in how to approach the problem and then to evaluate how well your approach solves the problem.

The *criteria*—Software Mastery, Content, Format and Layout, and Process—represent the knowledge and skills you have gained that you can apply to solving the problem. The *levels of performance*—Professional Quality, Approaching Professional Quality, or Needs Quality Improvements—help you and your instructor evaluate your result.

	Your completed project is of Professional Quality if you:	Your completed project is Approaching Professional Quality if you:	Your completed project Needs Quality Improvements if you:
1-Software Mastery	Choose and apply the most appropriate skills, tools, and features and identify efficient methods to solve the problem.	Choose and apply some appropriate skills, tools, and features, but not in the most efficient manner.	Choose inappropriate skills, tools, or features, or are inefficient in solving the problem.
2-Content	Construct a solution that is clear and well organized, contains content that is accurate, appropriate to the audience and purpose, and is complete. Provide a solution that contains no errors in spelling, grammar, or style.	Construct a solution in which some components are unclear, poorly organized, inconsistent, or incomplete. Misjudge the needs of the audience. Have some errors in spelling, grammar, or style, but the errors do not detract from comprehension.	Construct a solution that is unclear, incomplete, or poorly organized; contains some inaccurate or inappropriate content; and contains many errors in spelling, grammar, or style. Do not solve the problem.
3-Format & Layout	Format and arrange all elements to communicate information and ideas, clarify function, illustrate relationships, and indicate relative importance.	Apply appropriate format and layout features to some elements, but not others. Overuse features, causing minor distraction.	Apply format and layout that does not communicate information or ideas clearly. Do not use format and layout features to clarify function, illustrate relationships, or indicate relative importance. Use available features excessively, causing distraction.
4-Process	Use an organized approach that integrates planning, development, self-assessment, revision, and reflection.	Demonstrate an organized approach in some areas, but not others; or, use an insufficient process of organization throughout.	Do not use an organized approach to solve the problem.

OUTCOMES-BASED ASSESSMENTS

Apply a combination of the 3A and 3B skills.

Build from Scratch

GO! Think | Project 3L Employment

PROJECT FILES

For Project 3L, you will need the following file:

New blank Excel workbook

You will save your workbook as:

Lastname_Firstname_3L_Employment

Sandy Ingram, the Director of the Employment Development Department for the city of Pacifica Bay, has requested an analysis of employment sectors in the city. Employment data for the previous two years is listed below:

Job Sector	2015 Employment	2016 Employment
Government	1,795	1,524
Healthcare	2,832	2,952
Retail	2,524	2,480
Food Service	3,961	3,753
Industrial	1,477	1,595
Professional	2,515	2,802

Create a workbook to provide Sandy with the employment information for each sector and the total employment for each year. Insert a column to calculate the percent change from 2015 to 2016. Note that some of the results will be negative numbers. Format the percentages with two decimal places. Insert a pie chart in its own sheet that illustrates the 2016 employment figures, and format the chart attractively. Format the worksheet so that it is professional and easy to read and understand. Insert a footer with the file name and add appropriate document properties. Save the file as **Lastname_Firstname_3L_Employment** and print or submit as directed by your instructor.

END | You have completed Project 3L

Build from Scratch

GO! Think | Project 3M Population   Online

Build from Scratch

You and GO! | Project 3N Expense Analysis   Online

Build from Scratch

GO! Cumulative Group Project | Project 3O Bell Orchid Hotels
Online

Introduction to Microsoft Access 2013

A
Access 2013

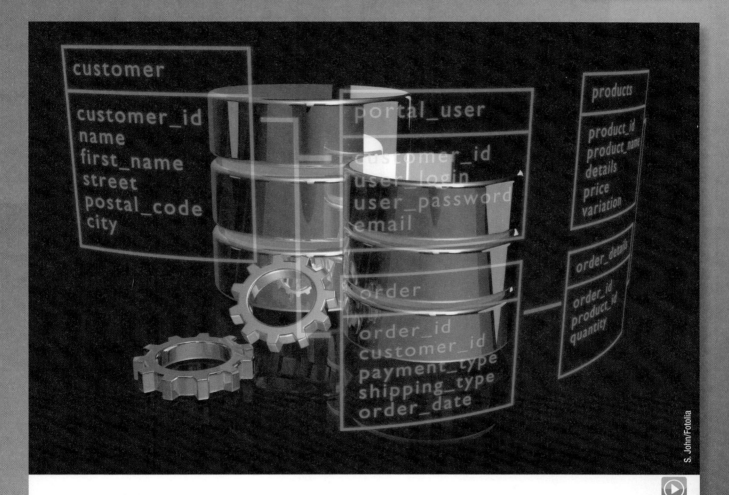

S. John/Fotolia

Access 2013: Introduction

Microsoft Access 2013 provides a convenient way to organize data that makes it easy for you to retrieve information. Access uses tables to store data. Like Excel spreadsheets, data is stored in rows and columns in a table. So why use a database rather than an Excel spreadsheet? By using a database, you can manipulate and work with data in a more robust manner. For example, if you have thousands of records about patients in a hospital, you can easily find all of the records that pertain to the patients who received a specific type of medicine on a particular day. Information from one table can be used to retrieve information from another table.

For example, by knowing a patient's ID number, you can view immunization records or view insurance information or view hospitalization records. Having information stored in an Access database enables you to make bulk changes to data at one time even when it is stored in different tables.

It's easy to get started with Access by using one of the many prebuilt database templates. For example, a nonprofit organization can track events, donors, members, and donations. A small business can use a prebuilt database to track inventory, create invoices, keep track of projects, manage pricing, track competitors, and manage quotes.

Video AA

Getting Started with Microsoft Access 2013

GO! to Work
Video A1

PROJECT 1A

OUTCOMES
Create a new database.

OBJECTIVES

1. Identify Good Database Design
2. Create a Table and Define Fields in a Blank Desktop Database
3. Change the Structure of Tables and Add a Second Table
4. Create a Query, Form, and Report
5. Close a Database and Exit Access

PROJECT 1B

OUTCOMES
Create a database from a template.

OBJECTIVES

6. Use a Template to Create a Database
7. Organize Objects in the Navigation Pane
8. Create a New Table in a Database Created with a Template
9. Print a Report and a Table

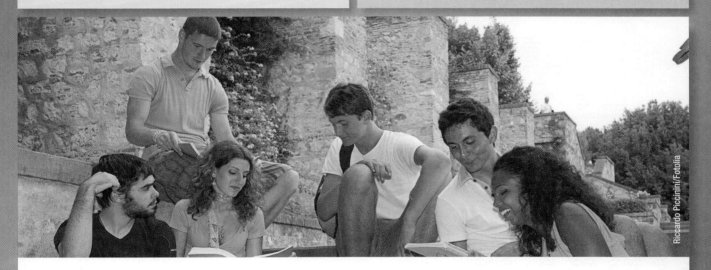

Riccardo Piccinini/Fotolia

In This Chapter

In this chapter, you use Microsoft Access 2013 to organize a collection of related information. You will create new databases, create tables, and enter data into the tables. You will create a query, a form, and a report—all of which are Access objects that make a database useful for finding and analyzing information. You will also create a complete database from a template that you can use as provided, or that you can modify to suit your needs. In this chapter, you will also learn how to apply good database design principles to your Access database and to define the structure of a database.

The projects in this chapter relate to **Texas Lakes Community College**, which is located in the Austin, Texas, area. Its four campuses serve over 30,000 students and offer more than 140 certificate programs and degrees. The college has a highly acclaimed Distance Education program and an extensive Workforce Development program. The college makes positive contributions to the community through cultural and athletic programs and has significant partnerships with businesses and nonprofit organizations. Popular fields of study include nursing and health care, solar technology, computer technology, and graphic design.

Student Advising Database with Two Tables

PROJECT ACTIVITIES

In Activities 1.01 through 1.17, you will assist Dr. Daniel Martinez, vice president of Student Services at Texas Lakes Community College, in creating a new database for tracking students and their faculty advisors. Your completed database objects will look similar to Figure 1.1.

PROJECT FILES

For Project 1A, you will need the following files:

Blank desktop database
a01A_Students (Excel workbook)
a01A_Faculty_Advisors (Excel workbook)

You will save your database as:

Lastname_Firstname_1A_Advising

Build from
Scratch

PROJECT RESULTS

FIGURE 1.1 Project 1A Advising

Objective 1 Identify Good Database Design

Video A1-1

A **database** is an organized collection of **data**—facts about people, events, things, or ideas—related to a specific topic or purpose. **Information** is data that is organized in a useful manner. Your contact list is a type of database because it is a collection of data about one topic—the people with whom you communicate. A simple database of this type is called a **flat database** because it is not related or linked to any other collection of data. Another example of a simple database is a list of your music collection. You do not keep information about your music collection in your contact list because the data is not related to the people in your contact list.

A more sophisticated type of database is a **relational database**, so-called because multiple collections of data in the database are related to one another; for example, data about the students, the courses, and the faculty members at a college. Microsoft Access 2013 is a relational **database management system**—also referred to as a **DBMS**—which is software that controls how related collections of data are stored, organized, retrieved, and secured.

Activity 1.01 | Using Good Design Techniques to Plan a Database

Before creating a new database, the first step is to determine the information you want to keep track of by asking yourself, *What questions should this database be able to answer?* The purpose of a database is to store the data in a manner that makes it easy to get the information you need by asking questions. For example, in a student database for Texas Lakes Community College, the questions to be answered might include:

- How many students are enrolled at the college?
- How many students have not yet been assigned a faculty advisor?
- Which students live in Austin, Texas?
- Which students owe money for tuition?
- Which students are majoring in Information Systems Technology?

Tables are the foundation of an Access database because all of the data is stored in one or more tables. A table is similar in structure to an Excel worksheet because data is organized into rows and columns. Each table row is a **record**—all of the categories of data pertaining to one person, place, event, thing, or idea. Each table column is a **field**—a single piece of information for every record. For example, in a table storing student contact information, each row forms a record for only one student. Each column forms a field for every record; for example, the student ID number or the student last name.

When organizing the fields of information in your table, break each piece of information into its smallest, most useful part. For example, create three fields for the name of a student—one field for the last name, one field for the first name, and one field for the middle name or initial.

The *first principle of good database design* is to organize data in the tables so that *redundant*—duplicate—data does not occur. For example, record the student contact information in only *one* table, so that if a student's address changes, you can change the information in just one place. This conserves space, reduces the likelihood of errors when recording new data, and does not require remembering all of the different places where the student's address is stored.

The *second principle of good database design* is to use techniques that ensure the accuracy and consistency of data as it is entered into the table. Typically, many different people enter data into a database—think of all the people who enter data about students at your college. When entering a state in a student contacts table, one person might enter the state as *Texas*, while another might enter the state as *TX*. Use design techniques to help those who enter data into a database to enter the data more accurately and consistently.

Normalization is the process of applying design rules and principles to ensure that your database performs as expected. Taking the time to plan and create a database that is well designed will ensure that you can retrieve meaningful information from the database.

The tables of information in a relational database are linked or joined to one another by a *common field*—a field in two or more tables that stores the same data. For example, a Students table includes the Student ID, name, and address of every student. The Student Activities table includes the club name and the Student ID of members, but not the name or address, of each student in the club. Because the two tables share a common field—Student ID—you can create a list of names and addresses of all of the students in the Photography Club. The names and addresses are stored in the Students table, and the Student IDs of the Photography Club members are stored in the Student Activities table.

Objective 2 Create a Table and Define Fields in a Blank Desktop Database

Video A1-2

There are three methods to create a new Access database. One method is to create a new database using a *database template*—a preformatted database designed for a specific purpose. A second method is to create a new database from a *blank desktop database*. A blank desktop database is stored on your computer or other storage device. It has no data and has no database tools; you create the data and the tools as you need them. A third method is to create a *custom web app* database from scratch or by using a template that you can publish and share with others over the Internet.

Regardless of the method you use, you must name and save the database before you can create any *objects* in it. Objects are the basic parts of a database; you create objects to store your data, to work with your data, and to display your data. The most common database objects are tables, queries, forms, and reports. Think of an Access database as a container for the objects that you create.

Activity 1.02 | Starting with a Blank Desktop Database

1 Start Access using the same technique you used to locate and open other Office desktop apps. Take a moment to compare your screen with Figure 1.2 and study the parts of the Microsoft Access opening screen described in the table in Figure 1.3.

From this Access opening screen, you can open an existing database, create a custom web app, create a blank desktop database, or create a new web app or desktop database from a template.

FIGURE 1.2

FIGURE 1.3

MICROSOFT ACCESS OPENING SCREEN ELEMENTS	
SCREEN ELEMENT	**DESCRIPTION**
Available templates	Starts a database for a specific purpose that includes built-in objects and tools ready for use.
Blank desktop database	Starts a blank database that is stored on your computer or on a storage device.
Custom web app	Starts a web app database that can be published and shared on the Internet.
Open Other Files	Enables you to open a database file from your computer, a shared location, or other location that you have designated.
Recent files	Displays a list of database files that have been recently opened.
Search box	Enables you to search the Microsoft Office website for templates.
Suggested searches	Enables you to click on a category to start an online search for a template.

2 ▸ In the Access opening screen, click **Blank desktop database**. In the **Blank desktop database** dialog box, to the right of the **File Name** box, click **Browse** 🗀. In the **File New Database** dialog box, navigate to the location where you are saving your databases for this chapter, create a **New folder** named **Access Chapter 1** and then press Enter. With the folder name selected, in the **File New Database** dialog box, click **Open**.

> In the File name box, *Database1* displays as the default file name—the number at the end of your file name might differ if you have saved a database previously with the default name. In the Save as type box, the default database type is *Microsoft Access 2007 – 2013 Databases*, which means that you can open a database created in Access 2013 by using Access 2007, Access 2010, or Access 2013.

3 ▸ Click in the **File name** box. Using your own name, replace the existing text with **Lastname_ Firstname_1A_Advising** and then click **OK** or press Enter. Compare your screen with Figure 1.4.

> In the Blank desktop database dialog box, in the File Name box, the name of your database displays. Under the File Name box, the drive and folder where the database will be stored displays. An Access database has a file extension of *.accdb*.

FIGURE 1.4

4 In the **Blank desktop database** dialog box, click **Create**. Compare your screen with Figure 1.5, and then take a moment to study the screen elements described in the table in Figure 1.6.

Access creates the new database and opens *Table1*. Recall that a table is an Access object that stores data in columns and rows, similar to the format of an Excel worksheet. Table objects are the foundation of a database because tables store the data that is used by other database objects.

FIGURE 1.5

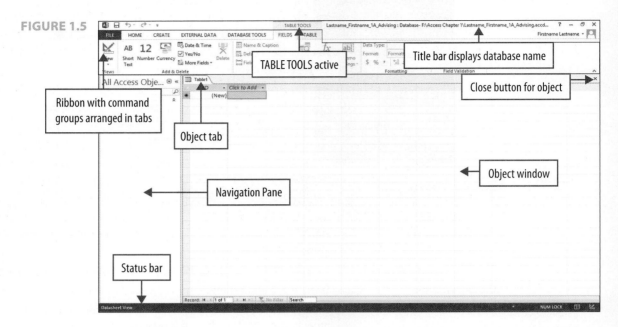

FIGURE 1.6

MICROSOFT ACCESS DATABASE WINDOW ELEMENTS	
ACCESS WINDOW ELEMENT	**DESCRIPTION**
Navigation Pane	Displays the database objects that you can open in the object window.
Object tab	Identifies and enables you to work with the open object.
Object window	Displays the active or open object (table, query, or other object).
Close button for object	Closes the active object (table, query, or other object).
Ribbon with command groups arranged in tabs	Groups the commands for performing related database tasks on tabs.
Status bar	Indicates the active view and the status of action occurring within the database on the left; provides buttons on the right to switch between Datasheet view and Design view.
Table Tools	Provides tools for working with a table object—only available when a table object is active.
Title bar	Displays the database name.

After you have named and saved your database, the next step is to consult your database design plan and then create the tables for your data. Limit the data in each table to *one* subject. For example, in this project, your database will have two tables—one for student information and one for faculty advisor information.

Recall that each column in a table is a field; field names display at the top of each column of the table. Recall also that each row in a table is a record—all of the data pertaining to one person, place, thing, event, or idea. Each record is broken up into its smallest usable parts—the fields. Use meaningful names for fields; for example, *Last Name*.

1 ▶ Notice the new blank table that displays in **Datasheet** view, and then take a moment to study the elements of the table's object window. Compare your screen with Figure 1.7.

> The table displays in ***Datasheet view***, which displays the data in columns and rows similar to the format of an Excel worksheet. Another way to view a table is in ***Design view***, which displays the underlying design—the ***structure***—of the table's fields. The ***object window*** displays the open object—in this instance, the table object.
>
> In a new blank database, there is only one object—a new blank table. Because you have not yet named this table, the object tab displays a default name of *Table1*. Access creates the first field and names it *ID*. In the ID field, Access assigns a unique sequential number—each number incremented by one—to each record as it is entered into the table.

FIGURE 1.7

- Navigation Pane Shutter Bar Open/Close button
- FIELDS tab on the ribbon
- Object tab with default table name
- Field names row
- First field name is ID
- New record row
- Navigation Pane

2 ▶ In the **Navigation Pane**, click **Shutter Bar Open/Close Button** « to collapse the **Navigation Pane** to a narrow bar on the left.

> The ***Navigation Pane*** displays and organizes the names of the objects in a database. From the Navigation Pane, you can open objects. Collapse or close the Navigation Pane to display more of the object—in this case, the table.

 ANOTHER WAY   Press F11 to close or open the Navigation Pane.

3 ▶ In the field names row, click anywhere in the text *Click to Add* to display a list of data types. Compare your screen with Figure 1.8.

> A ***data type*** defines the kind of data that you can store in a field, such as numbers, text, or dates. A field in a table can have only one data type. The data type of each field should be included in your database design. After selecting the data type, you can name the field.

ANOTHER WAY   To the right of *Click to Add*, click the arrow.

FIGURE 1.8

Navigation Pane closed

When clicked, displays list of data types

List of data types

4 On the list of data types, click **Short Text**, and notice that in the second column, *Click to Add* changes to *Field1*, which is selected. Type **Last Name** and then press Enter.

The second column displays *Last Name* as the field name, and, in the third column, the data type list displays. The **Short Text data type** describes text, a combination of text and numbers, or numbers that are not used in calculations, such as the Postal Code. This data type enables you to enter up to 255 characters in the field.

 ANOTHER WAY With the list of data types displayed, type the character that is underscored to select the data type. For example, type *t* to select Short Text or type *u* to select Currency.

5 In the third field name box, type **t** to select *Short Text*, type **First Name** and then press Enter.

6 In the fourth field name box, click **Short Text**, type **Middle Initial** and then press Enter.

7 Create the remaining fields from the table given by first selecting the data type, typing the field name, and then pressing Enter. The field names in the table will display on one line—do not be concerned if the field names do not completely display in the column; you will adjust the column widths later.

Data Type		Short Text	Short Text	Short Text	Short Text	Short Text	Short Text	Short Text	Short Text	Short Text	Short Text	Currency
Field Name	ID	Last Name	First Name	Middle Initial	Address	City	State	Postal Code	Phone	Email	Faculty Advisor ID	Amount Owed

The Postal Code and Phone fields are assigned a data type of Short Text because the numbers are never used in calculations. The Amount Owed field is assigned the **Currency data type**, which describes monetary values and numeric data that can be used in calculations and that have one to four decimal places. A U.S. dollar sign ($) and two decimal places are automatically included for all of the numbers in a field with the Currency data type.

8 If necessary, scroll to bring the first column—**ID**—into view, and then compare your screen with Figure 1.9.

Access automatically created the ID field, and you created 11 additional fields in the table.

FIGURE 1.9

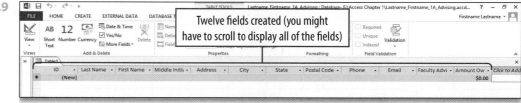

Twelve fields created (you might have to scroll to display all of the fields)

Activity 1.04 | Renaming Fields and Changing Data Types in a Table

1 In the first column, click anywhere in the text *ID*. On the ribbon, under **TABLE TOOLS**, on the **FIELDS tab**, in the **Properties group**, click **Name & Caption**. In the **Enter Field Properties** dialog box, in the **Name** box, change *ID* to **Student ID**

The field name *Student ID* is a clearer and more precise description of this field's data. In the Enter Field Properties dialog box, you have the option to change the ***Caption*** to display a name for a field other than the name that displays in the Name box. Many database designers do not use spaces in field names; instead, they might name a field *LastName* or *LName* and then create a caption for the field so it displays as *Last Name* in tables, forms, or reports. In the Enter Field Properties dialog box, you can also provide a description for the field.

ANOTHER WAY   Right-click the field name to display the shortcut menu, and then click Rename Field; or, double-click the field name to select the existing text, and then type the new field name.

2 Click **OK** to close the **Enter Field Properties** dialog box. On the ribbon, in the **Formatting group**, notice that the **Data Type** for the **Student ID** field is *AutoNumber*. Click the **Data Type arrow**, click **Short Text**, and then compare your screen with Figure 1.10.

In the new record row, the Student ID field is selected. By default, Access creates an ID field for all new tables and sets the data type for the field to AutoNumber. The ***AutoNumber data type*** describes a unique sequential or random number assigned by Access as each record is entered. Changing the data type of this field to Short Text enables you to enter a custom student ID number.

When records in a database have *no* unique value, such as a book ISBN or a license plate number, the AutoNumber data type is a useful way to automatically create a unique number. In this manner, you are sure that every record is different from the others.

FIGURE 1.10

Activity 1.05 | Adding a Record to a Table

A new contact list is not useful until you fill it with names and phone numbers. Likewise, a new database is not useful until you ***populate*** it by filling one or more tables with data. You can populate a table with records by typing data directly into the table.

1 In the new record row, click in the **Student ID** field to display the insertion point, type **1023045** and then press Enter. Compare your screen with Figure 1.11.

The pencil icon 🖉 in the ***record selector box*** indicates that a record is being entered or edited. The record selector box is the small box at the left of a record in Datasheet view. When clicked, the entire record is selected.

🔄 **ANOTHER WAY**   Press Tab to move the insertion point to the next field.

FIGURE 1.11

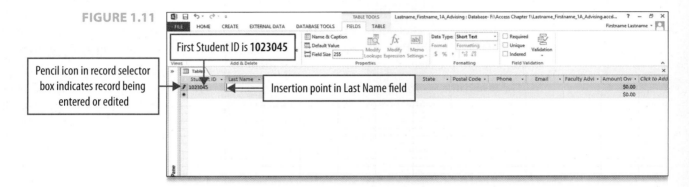

2 With the insertion point positioned in the **Last Name** field, type **Fresch** and then press Enter.

> **NOTE**   **Correcting Typing Errors**
>
> Correct any typing errors you make by using the techniques you have practiced in other Office applications. For example, use Backspace to remove characters to the left of the insertion point. Use Del to remove characters to the right of the insertion point. Or select the text you want to replace and type the correct information. Press Esc to exit out of a record that has not been completely entered.

---

3 In the **First Name** field, type **Jenna** and then press Enter.

4 In the **Middle Initial** field, type **A** and then press Enter.

5 In the **Address** field, type **7550 Douglas Ln** and then press Enter.

Do not be concerned if the data does not completely display in the column. As you progress in your study of Access, you will adjust column widths so that you can view all of the data.

6 Continue entering data in the fields as indicated in the table given, pressing Enter to move to the next field.

City	State	Postal Code	Phone	Email	Faculty Advisor ID
Austin	**TX**	**78749**	**(512) 555-0857**	**jfresch@tlcc.edu**	**FAC-2289**

> **NOTE**   **Format for Typing Telephone Numbers in Access**
>
> Access does not require a specific format for typing telephone numbers in a record. The examples in this textbook use the format of Microsoft Outlook. Using such a format facilitates easy transfer of Outlook information to and from Access.

---

7 In the **Amount Owed** field, type **250** and then press Enter. Compare your screen with Figure 1.12.

Pressing Enter or Tab in the last field moves the insertion point to the next row to begin a new record. Access automatically saves the record as soon as you move to the next row; you do not have to take any specific action to save a record.

FIGURE 1.12

Insertion point blinking in first field of new record row

First record entered and saved

8 To give your table a meaningful name, on the **Quick Access Toolbar**, click **Save** 🖫. In the **Save As** dialog box, in the **Table Name** box, using your own name, replace the selected text by typing **Lastname Firstname 1A Students**

> Save each database object with a name that identifies the data that it contains. When you save objects within a database, it is not necessary to use underscores in place of the spaces between words. Your name is included as part of the object name so that you and your instructor can identify your printouts or electronic files easily.

9 In the **Save As** dialog box, click **OK**. Notice that the object tab—located directly above the **Student ID** field name—displays the new table name that you just entered.

More **Knowledge** | **Renaming or Deleting a Table**

To change the name of a table, close the table, display the Navigation Pane, right-click the table name, and then click Rename. Type the new name or edit as you would any selected text. To delete a table, close the table, display the Navigation Pane, right-click the table name, and then click Delete.

Activity 1.06 | **Adding Additional Records to a Table**

1 In the new record row, click in the **Student ID** field, and then enter the data for two additional students as shown in the table given. Press Enter or Tab to move from field to field. The data in each field will display on one line in the table.

Student ID	Last Name	First Name	Middle Initial	Address	City	State	Postal Code	Phone	Email	Faculty Advisor ID	Amount Owed
2345677	Ingram	Joey	S	621 Hilltop Dr	Leander	TX	78646	(512) 555-0717	jingram@ tlcc.edu	FAC-2377	378.5
3456689	Snyder	Amanda	J	4786 Bluff St	Buda	TX	78610	(512) 555-9120	asnyder@ tlcc.edu	FAC-9005	0

2 Compare your screen with Figure 1.13.

FIGURE 1.13

Some fields may be out of view on your screen

Records for three students entered

Activity 1.07 | **Importing Data from an Excel Workbook into an Existing Access Table**

You can type records directly into a table. You can also ***import*** data from a variety of sources. Importing is the process of copying data from one source or application to another application. For example, you can import data from a Word table or an Excel spreadsheet into an Access database because the data is arranged in columns and rows, similar to a table in Datasheet view.

In this activity, you will **append**—add on—data from an Excel spreadsheet to your *1A Students* table. To append data, the table must already be created, and it must be closed.

1 In the upper right corner of the table, below the ribbon, click **Object Close** ✕ to close your **1A Students** table. Notice that no objects are open.

2 On the ribbon, click the **EXTERNAL DATA tab**. In the **Import & Link group**, click **Excel**. In the **Get External Data – Excel Spreadsheet** dialog box, click **Browse**.

3 In the **File Open** dialog box, navigate to your student files, double-click the Excel file **a01A_Students**, and then compare your screen with Figure 1.14.

> The path to the **source file**—the file being imported—displays in the File name box. There are three options for importing data from an Excel spreadsheet: import the data into a *new* table in the current database, append a copy of the records to an existing table, or link the data from the spreadsheet to a linked table in the database. A **link** is a connection to data in another file. When linking, Access creates a table that maintains a link to the source data, so that changes to the data in one file are automatically made in the other—linked—file.

🔄 **ANOTHER WAY**   Click the file name, and then in the File Open dialog box, click Open.

FIGURE 1.14

4 Click the **Append a copy of the records to the table** option button, and then, in the box to the right, click the **arrow**.

> Currently, your database has only one table, so no other tables display on the list. However, when a database has multiple tables, click the arrow to select the table to which you want to append records. The table into which you import or append data is referred to as the **destination table**.

5 Press [Esc] to cancel the list, and in the dialog box, click **OK**. Compare your screen with Figure 1.15.

> The first screen of the Import Spreadsheet Wizard displays, and the presence of scroll bars indicates that records and fields are out of view in this window. To append records from an Excel workbook to an existing database table, the column headings in the Excel worksheet or spreadsheet must be identical to the field names in the table. The **wizard** identifies the first row of the spreadsheet as column headings, which are equivalent to field names. A wizard is a feature in a Microsoft Office program that walks you step by step through a process.

FIGURE 1.15

First row identified as column headings, which are equivalent to field names

Field names in Excel Spreadsheet exactly match the field names in the Access table

Scroll bars indicate more data

6 In the lower right corner of the wizard, click **Next**. Notice that the name of your table displays under **Import to Table**. In the lower right corner of the wizard, click **Finish**.

7 In the **Get External Data – Excel Spreadsheet** dialog box, click **Close**. Open ⟫ the **Navigation Pane**.

8 Point to the right edge of the **Navigation Pane** to display the ⟷ pointer. Drag to the right to increase the width of the **Navigation Pane** so that the entire table name displays, and then compare your screen with Figure 1.16.

FIGURE 1.16

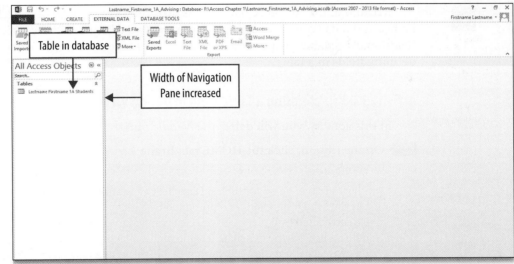

Table in database

Width of Navigation Pane increased

9 In the **Navigation Pane**, double-click your **1A Students** table to open the table in **Datasheet** view, and then **Close** ⟪ the **Navigation Pane**.

🔁 ANOTHER WAY   To open an object from the Navigation Pane, right-click the object name, and then click Open.

10 In the lower left corner of your screen, locate the navigation area, and notice that there are a total of **25** records in the table—you entered three records and imported 22 additional records. Compare your screen with Figure 1.17.

The records that you entered and the records you imported from the Excel spreadsheet display in your table; the first record in the table is selected. The *navigation area* indicates the number of records in the table and has controls in the form of arrows that you click in order to navigate among the records.

FIGURE 1.17

Three records you entered

Navigation area

25 total records

Current view indicated

Objective 3 | Change the Structure of Tables and Add a Second Table

Video A1-3

Recall that the structure of a table is the underlying design of the table and includes field names and data types. You can create or modify a table in Datasheet view. To define and modify fields, many database experts prefer to work in Design view, where you have more options for defining fields in a table.

Activity 1.08 | Deleting a Table Field in Design View

In this activity, you will delete the *Middle Initial* field from the table.

1 On the ribbon, click the **HOME tab**. In the **Views group**, click the **View arrow** to display a list of views.

There are two views for tables: Datasheet view and Design view. Other objects have different views. On the list, Design view is represented by a picture of a pencil, a ruler, and an angle. Datasheet view is represented by a picture of a table arranged in columns and rows. In the Views group, if the View button displays the pencil, ruler, and angle, clicking View will switch your view to Design view. Likewise, clicking the View button that displays as a datasheet will switch your view to Datasheet view.

2 On the list, click **Design View**, and then compare your screen with Figure 1.18.

Design view displays the underlying design—the structure—of the table and its fields. In Design view, the records with the data in the table do not display. You can only view the information about each field's characteristics. Each field name is listed, along with its data type. You can add more descriptive information about a field in the Description column.

You can decide how each field should look and behave in the Field Properties area. For example, you can set a specific field size in the Field Properties area. In the lower right corner, information displays about the active selection—in this case, the Field Name.

FIGURE 1.18

3 In the **Field Name** column, to the left of **Middle Initial**, point to the row selector box to display the ➡ pointer, and then click one time to select the entire row.

4 Under **TABLE TOOLS**, on the **DESIGN tab**, in the **Tools group**, click **Delete Rows**. Read the message in the message box, and then click **Yes**.

Deleting a field deletes both the field and its data. After you save the changes, you cannot undo this action, so Access prompts you to be sure you want to proceed. If you change your mind after deleting a field and saving the changes, you must add the field back into the table and then reenter the data for that field for every record.

🔁 ANOTHER WAY   In Design view, right-click the selected row, and then click Delete Rows; or, in Datasheet view, select the field—column—and on the HOME tab, in the Records group, click Delete.

Activity 1.09 | Changing a Field Size and Adding a Description

Typically, many different individuals in an organization have the ability to enter data into a table. For example, at your college, many registration assistants enter and modify student and course information daily. Two ways to help reduce errors are to restrict what can be typed in a field and to add descriptive information to help the individuals when entering the data.

1 With your table still displayed in **Design** view, in the **Field Name** column, click anywhere in the **Student ID** field name.

2 In the lower area of the screen, under **Field Properties**, click **Field Size** to select *255*, type **7** and then press Enter.

This action limits the size of the Student ID field to no more than seven characters. *Field properties* control how the field displays and how data can be entered into the field. You can define properties for each field in the Field Properties area by first clicking on the field name.

The default field size for a Short Text field is 255. Limiting the Field Size property to seven ensures that no more than seven characters can be entered for each Student ID. However, this does not prevent someone from entering seven characters that are incorrect or entering fewer than seven characters. Setting the proper data type for the field and limiting the field size are two ways to *help* reduce errors during data entry.

🔁 ANOTHER WAY   In Datasheet view, click in the field. On the FIELDS tab, in the Properties group, click in the Field Size box, and then type the number that represents the maximum number of characters for that field.

3 In the **Student ID** row, click in the **Description** box, type **Seven-digit Student ID number** and then press ⏎. Compare your screen with Figure 1.19.

Descriptions for fields in a table are optional. Include a description if the field name does not provide an obvious explanation of the type of data to be entered. If a description is provided for a field, when data is entered in that field in Datasheet view, the text in the Description displays on the left side of the status bar to provide additional information for the individuals who are entering the data.

When you enter a description for a field, a Property Update Options button displays below the text you typed, which enables you to copy the description for the field to all other database objects that use this table as an underlying source.

FIGURE 1.19

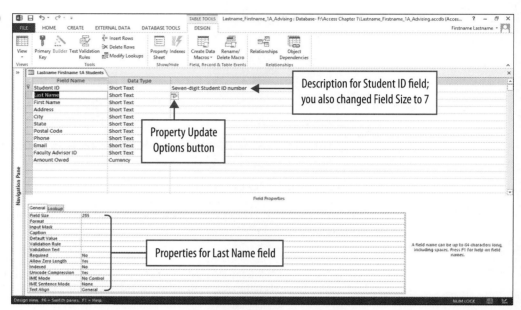

4 Click in the **State** field name box. In the **Field Properties** area, change the **Field Size** to **2** and in the **Description** box for this field, type **Two-character state abbreviation** and then press ⏎.

5 Click in the **Faculty Advisor ID** field name box. In the **Field Properties** area, change the **Field Size** to **8** and in the **Description** box for this field, type **Eight-character ID of instructor assigned as advisor** and then press ⏎.

6 On the **Quick Access Toolbar**, click **Save** 🖫 to save the design changes to your table, and then notice the message.

The message indicates that the field size property of one or more fields has changed to a shorter size. If more characters are currently present in the Student ID, State, or Faculty Advisor ID fields than you have set as the field size, the data will be *truncated*—cut off or shortened—because the fields were not previously restricted to these specific number of characters.

7 In the message box, click **Yes**.

Activity 1.10 | Viewing the Primary Key in Design View

Primary key refers to the field in the table that uniquely identifies a record. For example, in a college registration database, your Student ID number uniquely identifies you—no other student at the college has your exact student number. In the 1A Students table, the Student ID uniquely identifies each student.

When you create a table using the blank desktop database template, Access designates the first field as the primary key field and names the field ID. It is good database design practice to establish a primary key for every table, because doing so ensures that you do not enter the same record more than once. You can imagine the confusion if another student at your college had the same Student ID number as your own.

1 With your table still displayed in **Design** view, in the **Field Name** column, click in the **Student ID** field name box. To the left of the box, notice the small icon of a key, as shown in Figure 1.20.

Access automatically designates the first field as the primary key field, but you can set any field as the primary key by clicking the field name, and then in the Tools group, clicking Primary Key.

FIGURE 1.20

2 On the **DESIGN tab**, in the **Views group**, notice that the **View** button displays a picture of a datasheet, indicating that clicking **View** will switch the view to **Datasheet** view. Click the top of the **View** button.

If you make design changes to a table and switch views without first saving the table, Access prompts you to save the table before changing views.

Activity 1.11 | Adding a Second Table to a Database by Importing an Excel Spreadsheet

Many Microsoft Office users track data in an Excel spreadsheet. The sorting and filtering capabilities of Excel are useful for a simple database where all of the information resides in one large Excel spreadsheet. However, Excel is limited as a database management tool because it cannot *relate* the information in multiple spreadsheets in a way that you can ask a question and get a meaningful result. Because data in an Excel spreadsheet is arranged in columns and rows, the spreadsheet can easily become an Access table by importing the spreadsheet.

1 On the ribbon, click the **EXTERNAL DATA tab**, and then in the **Import & Link group**, click **Excel**. In the **Get External Data – Excel Spreadsheet** dialog box, click **Browse**.

2 In the **File Open** dialog box, navigate to the location where your student data files are stored, and then double-click **a01A_Faculty_Advisors**. Compare your screen with Figure 1.21.

FIGURE 1.21

> **3** Be sure that the **Import the source data into a new table in the current database** option button is selected, click **OK**, and then click **Next**.

The Import Spreadsheet Wizard displays the spreadsheet data.

> **4** In the upper left corner of the wizard, select the **First Row Contains Column Headings** check box.

The Excel data is framed, indicating that the first row of Excel column titles will become the Access table field names, and the remaining rows will become the individual records in the new Access table.

> **5** Click **Next**. Notice that the first column—**Faculty ID**—is selected, and in the upper area of the wizard, the **Field Name** and the **Data Type** display. Compare your screen with Figure 1.22.

Here, under Field Options, you can review and change the name or the data type of each selected field. You can also identify fields in the spreadsheet that you do not want to import into the Access table by selecting the Do not import field (Skip) check box.

FIGURE 1.22

> **6** Click **Next**. In the upper area of the wizard, click the **Choose my own primary key** option button, and then be sure that **Faculty ID** displays in the box to the right.

In the new table, Faculty ID will be the primary key. No two faculty members have the same Faculty ID. By default, Access selects the first field as the primary key, but you can click the arrow to select a different field.

> **7** Click **Next**. In the **Import to Table** box, using your own name, type **Lastname Firstname 1A Faculty Advisors** and then click **Finish**.

> **8** In the **Get External Data – Excel Spreadsheet** dialog box, click **Close. Open** ⟩⟩ the **Navigation Pane**.

9 In the **Navigation Pane**, double-click your **1A Faculty Advisors** table to open it in **Datasheet** view, and then **Close** « the **Navigation Pane**.

Two tables that are identified by their object tabs are open in the object window. Your 1A Faculty Advisors table is the active table and displays the 29 records that you imported from the Excel spreadsheet.

10 In your **1A Faculty Advisors** table, click in the **Postal Code** field in the first record. On the ribbon, under **TABLE TOOLS**, click the **FIELDS tab**. In the **Formatting group**, click the **Data Type arrow**, and then click **Short Text**. Compare your screen with Figure 1.23.

When you import data from an Excel spreadsheet, check the data types of all fields to ensure they are correct. Recall that if a field, such as the Postal Code, contains numbers that are not used in calculations, the data type should be set to Short Text. To change the data type of a field, click in the field in any record.

FIGURE 1.23

Activity 1.12 | **Adjusting Column Widths**

You can adjust the column widths in a table displayed in Datasheet view by using techniques similar to those you use for Excel spreadsheets.

1 In the object window, click the **object tab** for your **1A Students** table to make it the active object and to display it in the object window.

Clicking the object tabs along the top of the object window enables you to display open objects and make them active so that you can work with them. All of the columns in the datasheet are the same width, regardless of the length of the data in the field, the length of the field name, or the field size that was set. If you print the table as currently displayed, some of the data or field names will not print fully, so you will want to adjust the column widths.

2 In the field names row, point to the right edge of the **Address** field to display the ⊞ pointer, and then compare your screen with Figure 1.24.

FIGURE 1.24

3 With the ⊞ pointer positioned as shown in Figure 1.24, double-click the right edge of the **Address** field.

The column width of the Address field widens to display fully the longest entry in the field. In this manner, the width of a column can be increased or decreased to fit its contents in the same manner as a column in an Excel spreadsheet. In Access, adjusting the column width to fit the contents is referred to as *Best Fit*.

4 ▸ Point to the **City** field name to display the ⬇ pointer, right-click to select the entire column, and then click **Field Width**. In the **Column Width** dialog box, click **Best Fit**.

This is a second way to adjust column widths.

5 ▸ If necessary, scroll to the right to view the last three fields. Point to the **Email** field name to display the ⬇ pointer, hold down the left mouse button, and then drag to the right to select this column, the **Faculty Advisor ID** column, and the **Amount Owed** column. Point to the right edge of any of the selected columns to display the ⊹ pointer, and then double-click to apply **Best Fit** to all three columns.

You can select multiple columns and adjust the widths of all of them at one time by using this technique or by right-clicking any of the selected columns, clicking Field Width, and clicking Best Fit in the Column Width dialog box.

6 ▸ If necessary, scroll to the left to view the **Student ID** field. To the left of the **Student ID** field name, click **Select All** ▢. Notice that all of the fields are selected.

7 ▸ On the ribbon, click the **HOME tab**. In the **Records group**, click **More**, and then click **Field Width**. In the **Column Width** dialog box, click **Best Fit**. Click anywhere in the **Student ID** field, and then compare your screen with Figure 1.25.

Using the More command is a third way to adjust column widths. By using Select All, you can adjust the widths of all of the columns at one time. Adjusting the width of columns does not change the data in the table's records; it only changes the *display* of the data.

FIGURE 1.25

NOTE | **Adjusting Column Widths**

After adjusting column widths, scroll horizontally and vertically to be sure that all of the data displays in all of the fields. Access adjusts column widths to fit the screen size based on the displayed data. If data is not displayed on the screen when you adjust column widths—even if you use Select All—the column width might not be adjusted adequately to display all of the data in the field. After adjusting column widths, save the table before performing other tasks. The column width adjustments might not save with the table. When you reopen a table, be sure to readjust the column widths if you plan to print the table or work with the data in the table.

---

8 ▸ On the **Quick Access Toolbar**, click **Save** 🖫 to save the table design changes—changing the column widths.

If you do not save the table after making design changes, Access prompts you to save when you close the table.

Activity 1.13 | Printing a Table

There are times when you will want to print a table, even though a report may look more professional. For example, you may need a quick reference, or you may want to proofread the data that has been entered. Before printing a table, be sure to apply Best Fit to all of the columns in the table.

1 On the ribbon, click the **FILE tab**, click **Print**, and then click **Print Preview**. Compare your screen with Figure 1.26.

The table displays in Print Preview with the default zoom setting of Fit to Window, a view that enables you to see how your table will print on the page. It is a good idea to view any object in Print Preview before printing so that you can make changes to the object if needed before actually printing it. In the navigation area, the Next Page button is darker (available), an indication that more than one page will print.

FIGURE 1.26

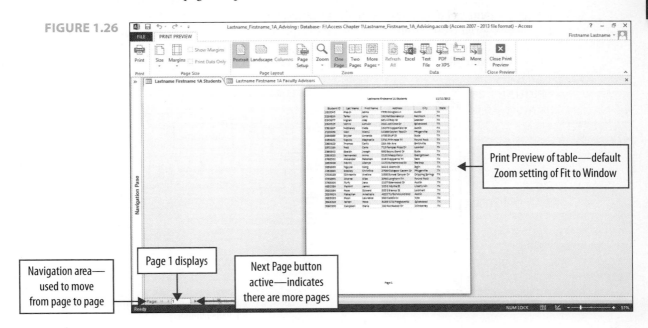

Navigation area— used to move from page to page

Page 1 displays

Next Page button active—indicates there are more pages

Print Preview of table—default Zoom setting of Fit to Window

2 In the navigation area, click **Next Page** ▶ to display Page 2. Point to the top of the page to display the 🔍 pointer, click one time to zoom in, and then compare your screen with Figure 1.27.

The Print Preview display enlarges, and the Zoom Out pointer displays. The second page of the table displays the last five fields. The Next Page button is dimmed, indicating that the button is unavailable because there are no more pages after Page 2. The Previous Page button is available, indicating that a page exists before this page.

FIGURE 1.27

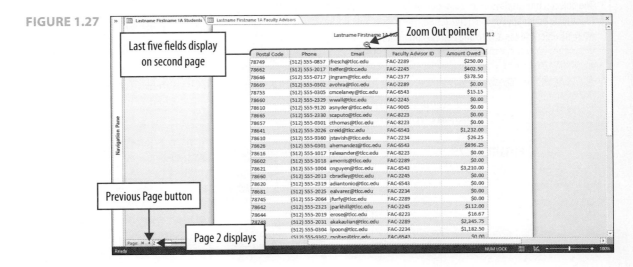

Last five fields display on second page

Zoom Out pointer

Previous Page button

Page 2 displays

3 On the ribbon, on the **PRINT PREVIEW tab**, in the **Zoom group**, click the top portion of the **Zoom** button to change the zoom setting back to the default setting of Fit to Window.

4 In the **Page Layout group**, click **Landscape**, and notice that there are only three fields on Page 2. In the navigation area, click **Previous Page** ◀ to display Page 1, and then compare your screen with Figure 1.28.

The orientation of the page to be printed changes. Included on the page are the table name and current date at the top of the page and the page number at the bottom of the page. The change in orientation from portrait to landscape is not saved with the table. Each time you print, you must check the page orientation, the margins, and any other print parameters so that the object prints as you intend. You should also be sure that Best Fit is applied to each column or to the entire table.

FIGURE 1.28

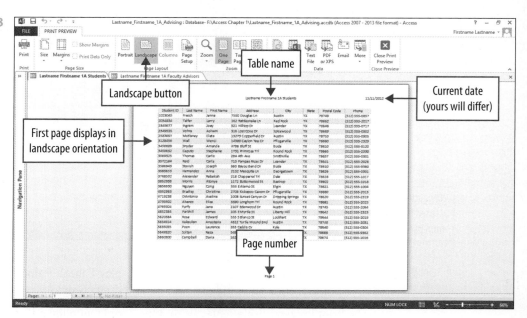

> **NOTE**   **Headers and Footers in Access Objects**
>
> The headers and footers in Access tables and queries are controlled by default settings; you cannot enter additional information or edit the information. The object name displays in the center of the header area, and the current date displays on the right. Adding your name to the object name is helpful in identifying your paper or electronic results. The page number displays in the center of the footer area. The headers and footers in Access forms and reports are more flexible; you can add to and edit the information.

5 On the **PRINT PREVIEW tab**, in the **Print group**, click **Print**. In the **Print** dialog box, under **Print Range**, verify that **All** is selected. Under **Copies**, verify that the **Number of Copies** is **1**. Compare your screen with Figure 1.29.

FIGURE 1.29

6 Determine whether your instructor wants you to submit your work for this project on paper or electronically. If submitting electronically, determine whether, in addition to submitting your Access database, your instructor wants you to create and submit electronic printouts of individual database objects.

7 To print on paper, in the **Print** dialog box, click **OK**; and then on the ribbon, in the **Close Preview group**, click **Close Print Preview**. If you are required to create and submit electronic printouts, in the **Print** dialog box, click **Cancel**, and then follow the steps in the following Note—or follow the specific directions provided by your instructor.

N O T E   **Creating a PDF Electronic Printout of an Access Object**

Display the object (table, query, form, report, and so on) in Print Preview and adjust margins and orientation as needed. On the PRINT PREVIEW tab, in the Data group, click PDF or XPS. In the Publish as PDF or XPS dialog box, navigate to your chapter folder. Use the default file name, or follow your instructor's directions to name the object. If wish to view the PDF file, in the dialog box, select the Open file after publishing check box. In the Publish as PDF or XPS dialog box, click Publish. If necessary, close the Windows 8 Reader, Adobe Reader, or Adobe Acrobat window and the Export – PDF dialog box. On the ribbon, click Close Print Preview; your electronic printout is saved.

---

8 In the upper right corner of the object window, click **Close Object** ⊠ to close your **1A Students** table. Notice that the **1A Faculty Advisors** table is the active object in the object window.

🔁 **ANOTHER WAY**   In the object window, right-click your 1A Students object tab, and then click Close.

9 In your **1A Faculty Advisors** table, to the left of the **Faculty ID** field name, click **Select All** ☐ to select all of the columns. On the **HOME tab**, in the **Records group**, click **More**, and then click **Field Width**. In the **Column Width** dialog box, click **Best Fit** to adjust the widths of all of the columns so that all of the data display. Scroll horizontally and vertically to be sure that all of the data display in each field; if necessary, use the techniques you practiced to apply **Best Fit** to individual columns. **Save** 🖫 the changes you made to the table's column widths, and then click in any record to cancel the selection.

10 On the ribbon, click the **FILE tab**, click **Print**, and then click **Print Preview**. On the **PRINT PREVIEW tab**, in the **Page Layout group**, click **Landscape**. Notice that the table will print on more than one page. In the **Page Size group**, click **Margins**, click **Normal**, and then notice that one more column moved to the first page—your results may differ depending upon your printer's capabilities.

In addition to changing the page orientation to Landscape, you can change the margins to Normal to see if all of the fields will print on one page. In this instance, there are still too many fields to print on one page, although the Postal Code field moved from Page 2 to Page 1.

11 If directed to do so by your instructor, create a paper or electronic printout of your **1A Faculty Advisors** table, and then click **Close Print Preview**.

12 In the object window, **Close** ⊠ your **1A Faculty Advisors** table.

All of your database objects—your *1A Students* table and your *1A Faculty Advisors* table—are closed; the object window is empty.

Video A1-4

Recall that tables are the foundation of an Access database because all of the data is stored in one or more tables. You can display the data stored in tables in other database objects such as queries, forms, and reports.

Activity 1.14 | Creating a Query by Using the Simple Query Wizard

A **query** is a database object that retrieves specific data from one or more database objects—either tables or other queries—and then, in a single datasheet, displays only the data that you specify when you design the query. Because the word *query* means *to ask a question*, think of a query as a question formed in a manner that Access can answer.

A **select query** is one type of Access query. A select query, also called a **simple select query**, retrieves (selects) data from one or more tables or queries and then displays the selected data in a datasheet. A select query creates a subset of the data to answer specific questions; for example, *Which students live in Austin, TX?*

The objects from which a query selects the data are referred to as the query's **data source**. In this activity, you will create a simple select query using a wizard that walks you step by step through the process. The process involves selecting the data source and indicating the fields that you want to include in the query results. The query—the question you want to ask—is *What is the last name, first name, email address, phone number, and Student ID of every student?*

1 On the ribbon, click the **CREATE tab**, and then in the **Queries group**, click **Query Wizard**. In the **New Query** dialog box, be sure **Simple Query Wizard** is selected, and then click **OK**. Compare your screen with Figure 1.30.

FIGURE 1.30

2 In the wizard, click the **Tables/Queries arrow**, and then click **Table: Lastname Firstname 1A Students**.

In the wizard, the displayed table or query name is the object that was last selected on the Navigation Pane. The last object you worked with was your 1A Faculty Advisors table, so that object name displayed in the wizard.

To create a query, first select the data source—the object from which the query is to select the data. The information you need to answer the question is stored in your 1A Students table, so this table is your data source.

3 Under **Available Fields**, click **Last Name**, and then click **Add Field** > to move the field to the **Selected Fields** list on the right. Double-click the **First Name** field to add the field to the **Selected Fields** list.

Use either method to add fields to the Selected Fields list—you can add fields in any order.

4 By using **Add Field** ▶ or by double-clicking the field name, add the following fields to the **Selected Fields** list in the order specified: **Email**, **Phone**, and **Student ID**. Compare your screen with Figure 1.31.

> Selecting these five fields will answer the question, *What is the last name, first name, email address, phone number, and Student ID of every student?*

FIGURE 1.31

5 In the wizard, click **Next**. Click in the **What title do you want for your query?** box. Using your own name, edit as necessary so that the query name is **Lastname Firstname 1A All Students Query** and then compare your screen with Figure 1.32.

FIGURE 1.32

6 In the wizard, click **Finish**. Select all of the columns, apply **Best Fit**, and then **Save** 🖫 the query. In the first record, click in the **Last Name** field to cancel the selection. Compare your screen with Figure 1.33.

> Access *runs* the query—performs the actions indicated in your query design—by searching the records in the specified data source, and then finds the records that match specified criteria. The records that match the criteria display in a datasheet. A select query *selects*—finds and displays—*only* the information from the data source that you request, including the specified fields.

> In the object window, Access displays every student from your 1A Students table—the data source—but displays *only* the five fields that you moved to the Selected Fields list in the Simple Query Wizard.

FIGURE 1.33

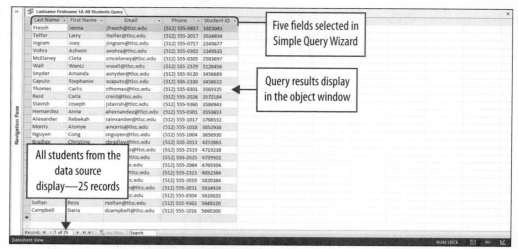

Five fields selected in Simple Query Wizard

Query results display in the object window

All students from the data source display—25 records

7 On the ribbon, click the **FILE tab**, click **Print**, and then click **Print Preview**. Notice that the query results will print on one page. As directed by your instructor, create a paper or electronic printout. Click **Close Print Preview**.

8 In the object window, **Close** ☒ the query.

Activity 1.15 | Creating and Printing a Form

A *form* is an Access object with which you can enter data, edit data, or display data from a table or query. In a form, the fields are laid out in an attractive format on the screen, which makes working with the database easier for those who must enter and look up data.

One type of form displays only one record at a time. Such a form is useful not only to the individual who performs the data entry—typing in the records—but also to anyone who has the job of viewing information in the database. For example, when you visit the Records office at your college to obtain a transcript, someone displays your record on the screen. For the viewer, it is much easier to look at one record at a time, using a form, than to look at all of the student records in the database table.

1 Open ☒ the **Navigation Pane**. Drag the right edge of the **Navigation Pane** to the right to increase the width of the pane so that all object names display fully. Notice that a table name displays with a datasheet icon, and a query name displays an icon of two overlapping datasheets. Right-click your **1A Students** table, and then compare your screen with Figure 1.34.

FIGURE 1.34

Table icon

Query icon

Navigation Pane Close button

Shortcut menu for your 1A Students table

2 On the shortcut menu, click **Open** to display the table in the object window, and then **Close** ☒ the **Navigation Pane** to maximize your object window space.

ANOTHER WAY   On the Navigation Pane, double-click the object name to open it.

3 ▶ Notice that there are 11 fields in the table. On the **CREATE tab**, in the **Forms group**, click **Form**, and then compare your screen with Figure 1.35.

The Form tool creates a form based on the active object—your 1A Students table. The form displays all of the fields from the underlying data source—one record at a time—in a simple top-to-bottom format with all 11 fields lined up in a single column. You can use this new form immediately, or you can modify it. Records that you create or edit in a form are automatically added to or updated in the underlying table or data source.

The new form displays in *Layout view*—the Access view in which you can make changes to an object while the object is open and displaying the data from the data source. Each field in the form displayed in Figure 1.35 displays the data for the first student record—*Jenna Fresch*—from your 1A Students table.

FIGURE 1.35

4 ▶ At the right side of the status bar, notice the three buttons. Point to each button to display its ScreenTip, and notice that **Layout View** ▤ is active, indicating that the form is displayed in Layout view.

5 ▶ In the status bar, click **Form View** ▦.

In *Form view*, you can view the records, create a new record, edit a record, and delete a record. You cannot change the layout or design of the form. Form view is useful for individuals who *access records* in your database. Layout view is useful for individuals who *design* the form.

ANOTHER WAY   On the DESIGN tab, or on the HOME tab, in the Views group, click the top portion of the View button when it displays an icon of a form.

6 ▶ In the navigation area, click **Next record** ▶ two times to display the third record—the record for *Joey Ingram*.

Use the navigation buttons to scroll among the records and to display any single record.

7 ▶ Using your own name, **Save** ▤ the form as **Lastname Firstname 1A Student Form**

8 Be sure that Record 3 displays. On the ribbon, click the **FILE tab**, click **Print**, and then on the right, click **Print**—do *not* click **Print Preview** because you are going to print a *single* record—not all of the records.

9 In the **Print** dialog box, under **Print Range**, click the **Selected Record(s)** option button, and then click **Setup**.

10 In the **Page Setup** dialog box, click the **Columns tab**. Under **Column Size**, double-click in the **Width** box to select the existing value, type **7.5** and then click **OK**.

> Forms are usually not printed, so the default width for a form created with the Form command is larger than most printers can handle to print on one page. If you do not change the width, the form will print on two pages because the last column flows over the margins allowed by the printer. If, after changing the Width to 7.5, your form still prints on two pages, try entering a different Width; for example, 7 or 6.5.

11 If instructed to print your objects, in the **Print** dialog box, click **OK** to print the record for *Joey Ingram* on one page; otherwise, click **Cancel**. If instructed to print an electronic copy, follow the steps in the following Note or the directions provided by your instructor.

> After printing, along the left edge of the record, the narrow bar—the ***record selector bar***—displays in black, indicating that the record is selected.

N O T E	**Printing a Single Form in PDF**

On the FILE tab, click Print, and then on the right, click Print. In the Print dialog box, click Setup. In the Page Setup dialog box, click the Columns tab. Under Column Size, double-click in the Width box, type 7.5 and then click OK. In the Print dialog box, click Cancel. On the left edge of the form, click the record selector bar so that it is black—selected.

On the ribbon, click the EXTERNAL DATA tab. In the Export group, click PDF or XPS. In the Publish as PDF or XPS dialog box, navigate to your chapter folder, and at the lower right corner of the dialog box, click Options. In the Options dialog box, under Range, click the Selected records option button, and then click OK. In the Publish as PDF or XPS dialog box, click Publish. If necessary, close the Window 8 Reader, Adobe Reader, or Adobe Acrobat window.

---

12 Close ⊠ your **1A Student Form** object; leave your **1A Students** table open.

Activity 1.16 │ Creating, Modifying, and Printing a Report

A ***report*** is a database object that displays the fields and records from a table or query in an easy-to-read format suitable for printing. Create professional-looking reports to summarize database information.

1 Open ⟫ the **Navigation Pane**, and then open your **1A Faculty Advisors** table by double-clicking the table name or by right-clicking the table name and clicking **Open**. **Close** ⟪ the **Navigation Pane**.

2 On the ribbon, click the **CREATE tab**. In the **Reports group**, click **Report**.

> The Report tool creates a report in Layout view and includes all of the fields and all of the records in the data source—your 1A Faculty Advisors table. Dotted lines indicate how the report will break across pages if you print it now. In Layout view, you can make quick changes to the report layout while viewing the data from the table.

3 In the report, click the **Faculty ID** field name, and then on the ribbon, under **REPORT LAYOUT TOOLS**, click the **ARRANGE tab**. In the **Rows & Columns group**, click **Select Column**, and then press ⌜Del⌟. Using the same technique, delete the **Rank** field.

> The Faculty ID and Rank fields, along with the data, are deleted from the report. The fields readjust by moving to the left. Deleting the fields from the report does *not* delete the fields and data from the data source—your 1A Faculty Advisors table.

4 ▸ Click the **Address** field name, and then by using the scroll bar at the bottom of the screen, scroll to the right to display the **Cell Phone** field; be careful not to click in the report.

5 ▸ Hold down ⌈Shift⌉, and then click the **Cell Phone** field name to select all of the fields from *Address* through *Cell Phone*. With the six field names selected—surrounded by a colored border—in the **Rows & Columns group**, click **Select Column**, and then press ⌈Del⌉.

Use this method to select and delete multiple columns in Layout view.

6 ▸ Scroll to the left, and notice that the four remaining fields display within the dotted lines—they are within the margins of the report. Click the **Campus** field name. Hold down ⌈Shift⌉, and then click the **First Name** field name to select the first three fields.

7 ▸ On the ribbon, under **REPORT LAYOUT TOOLS**, click the **DESIGN tab**. In the **Tools group**, click **Property Sheet**.

The ***Property Sheet*** for the selected columns displays on the right side of the screen. Every object and every item in an object has an associated Property Sheet where you can make precise changes to the properties—characteristics—of selected items.

8 ▸ In the **Property Sheet**, if necessary, click the **Format tab**. Click **Width**, type **1.5** and then press ⌈Enter⌉. Compare your screen with Figure 1.36.

The width of the three selected field names and the columns changes to 1.5", and the fields readjust by moving to the left. When you change the Width property, you do not need to select the entire column. Change the Width property if you need to move columns within the margins of a report. In this report, the fields already displayed within the margins, but some reports may need this minor adjustment to print on one page.

FIGURE 1.36

9 ▸ **Close** ⌧ the **Property Sheet**. Click the **Last Name** field name. On the ribbon, click the **HOME tab**, and then in the **Sort & Filter group**, click **Ascending**.

Access sorts the report in ascending alphabetical order by the Last Name field. By default, tables are sorted in ascending order by the primary key field—in this instance, the Faculty ID field. Changing the sort order in the report does *not* change the sort order in the underlying table.

10 ▸ At the top of the report, to the right of the green report icon, click anywhere in the title of the report to select the title. On the **HOME tab**, in the **Text Formatting group**, click the **Font Size arrow**, and then click **14**. **Save** 🖫 the report. In the **Save As** dialog box, in the **Report Name** box, add **Report** to the end of *Lastname Firstname 1A Faculty Advisors*, and then click **OK**.

11 On the **FILE tab**, click **Print**, and then click **Print Preview**. On the **PRINT PREVIEW tab**, in the **Zoom group**, click **Two Pages**, and then compare your screen with Figure 1.37.

As currently formatted, the report will print on two pages because the page number at the bottom of the report is positioned beyond the right margin of the report.

FIGURE 1.37

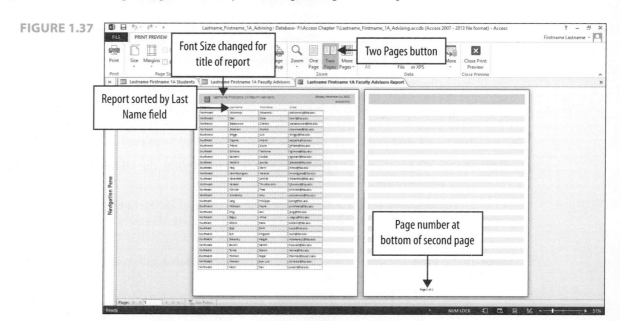

12 In the **Close Preview group**, click **Close Print Preview**. Scroll down to display the bottom of the report, and then, if necessary, scroll to the right to display the page number. Click the page number—**Page 1 of 1**—and then press Del.

Because all of the data will print on one page, the page number is not necessary for this report. If you want the page number to display, you can drag it within the margins of the report.

13 Display the report in **Print Preview**, and notice that the report will now print on one page. In the **Zoom group**, click **One Page**. Click **Save** 🖫 to save the changes to the design of the report, and then create a paper or electronic printout as directed. Click **Close Print Preview**.

When you create a report by using the Report tool, the default margins are 0.25 inch. Some printers require a greater margin, so your printed report may result in two pages. As you progress in your study of Access, you will practice making these adjustments. Also, if a printer is not installed on your system, the electronic PDF printout may result in a two-page report.

14 In the object window, right-click any **object tab**, and then click **Close All** to close all of the open objects. Notice that the object window is empty.

Objective 5   Close a Database and Exit Access

Video A1-5

When you close a table, any changes made to the records are saved automatically. If you make changes to the structure or adjust column widths, you are prompted to save the table when you close the table or when you switch views. Likewise, you are prompted to save queries, forms, and reports if you make changes to the layout or design. If the Navigation Pane is open when you exit Access, it will display when you reopen the database. When you are finished using your database, close the database, and then exit Access.

1 ▶ **Open** ⟨»⟩ the **Navigation Pane**. If necessary, increase the width of the **Navigation Pane** so that all object names display fully. Notice that your report object displays with a green report icon. Compare your screen with Figure 1.38.

FIGURE 1.38

2 ▶ On the ribbon, click the **FILE tab**. Click **Close** to close the database but leave Access open. This action enables you to continue working in Access with another database if you want to do so. In the Access opening screen, in the upper right corner, click **Close** ⟨×⟩ to exit Access. As directed by your instructor, submit your database and the paper or electronic printouts of the five objects—two tables, one query, one form, and one report—that are the results of this project. Specifically, in this project, using your own name, you created the following database and printouts or electronic printouts:

1. Lastname_Firstname_1A_Advising	Database file
2. Lastname Firstname 1A Students	Table (printout or electronic printout – two pages)
3. Lastname Firstname 1A Faculty Advisors	Table (printout or electronic printout – two pages)
4. Lastname Firstname 1A All Students Query	Query (printout or electronic printout)
5. Lastname Firstname 1A Student Form	Form (printout or electronic printout – Record 3)
6. Lastname Firstname 1A Faculty Advisors Report	Report (printout or electronic printout)

 ANOTHER WAY   On the left side of the title bar, click ⟨🔲⟩ and then click Close, or on the right side of the title bar, click ⟨×⟩ to close the database and to exit Access.

END | You have completed Project 1A

Objective | Export an Access Table to an Excel Spreadsheet, Save to OneDrive, Edit a Record, and Save to Your Computer

Access web apps are designed to work with Microsoft's **SharePoint**, an application for setting up websites to share and manage documents. Your college may not have SharePoint installed, so you will use other tools to share objects from your database so that you can work collaboratively with others. Recall that Window's OneDrive is a free file storage and file sharing service. For Access, you can export a database object to an Excel worksheet, a PDF file, or a text file, and then save the file to OneDrive.

> **ALERT!** **Working with Web-Based Applications and Services**
>
> Computer programs and services on the web receive continuous updates and improvements. Therefore, the steps to complete this web-based activity may differ from the ones shown. You can often look at the screens and the information presented to determine how to complete the activity.

Activity | Exporting an Access Table to an Excel Spreadsheet, Saving the Spreadsheet to OneDrive, Editing a Record in OneDrive, and Saving to Your Computer

In this activity, you will *export*—copy data from one file into another file—your 1A Students table to an Excel spreadsheet, upload your Excel file to OneDrive, edit a record in OneDrive, and then download a copy of the edited spreadsheet to your computer.

1 Start Access, navigate to your **Access Chapter 1** folder, and then open your **1A_Advising** database file. If necessary, on the Message Bar, click Enable Content. In the **Navigation Pane**, click your **1A Students** table to select it—do not open it.

2 On the ribbon, click the **EXTERNAL DATA tab**, and then in the **Export group**, click **Excel**. In the **Export – Excel Spreadsheet** dialog box, click **Browse**, and then navigate to your **Access Chapter 1** folder. In the **File Save** dialog box, click in the **File name** box, type **Lastname_Firstname_AC_1A_Web** and then click **Save**.

3 In the **Export – Excel Spreadsheet** dialog box, under **Specify export options**, select the first two check boxes—**Export data with formatting and layout** and **Open the destination file after the export operation is complete**—and then click **OK**. In the **Microsoft Excel**

window, in the column headings row, to the left of column A, click **Select All** ☐. On the **HOME tab**, in the **Cells group**, click **Format**, and then click **AutoFit Column Width**. Click in cell **A1** to cancel the selection, and then compare your screen with Figure A.

4 **Save** the spreadsheet, and then **Close** Excel. In the **Export – Excel Spreadsheet** dialog box, click **Close**, and then **Close** Access.

5 From the desktop, start Internet Explorer. Navigate to **http://onedrive.com**, and then sign in to your Microsoft account. Open your **GO! Web Projects** folder—or create and then open this folder if necessary.

6 On the menu bar, click **Upload**. In the **Choose File to Upload** dialog box, navigate to your **Access Chapter 1** folder, and then double-click your **AC_1A_Web** Excel file to upload it to OneDrive.

FIGURE A

(GO! with Office Online (formerly Web Apps) continues on the next page)

7 When the upload is completed, in your **GO! Web Projects** folder, click your **AC_1A_Web** file to open it in Excel Online.

On the ribbon, notice that you can open this worksheet in Excel instead of using Excel Online. If you are working on a computer that does not have Microsoft Excel installed, you can still create and modify workbooks in your web browser by using Excel Online.

8 In the first record, click in the **Last Name** field. Using your own last name, type **Lastname** and then press Tab to replace *Fresch* with your last name. In the **First Name** field, using your own first name, type **Firstname** to replace *Jenna* with your own first name, and then press ↓ to save the record. Compare your screen with Figure B.

9 On the ribbon, click the **FILE tab**, click **Save As**, and then click **Download a Copy**. In the message box—usually displays at the bottom of your screen—click the **Save arrow**, and then click **Save as**. In the **Save As** dialog box, navigate to your **Access Chapter 1** folder, and then click in the **File name** box. Type **Lastname_Firstname_AC_1A_Web_Download** and then click **Save**. **Close** the message box.

10 In OneDrive, on the title bar, click **OneDrive** to return to your home page. At the top right corner of your screen, click your OneDrive name, and then click **Sign out**. **Close** your browser window.

11 Start Excel. In the Excel opening screen, click **Open Other Workbooks**. Under **Open**, click **Computer**. Under **Computer**, click **Browse**. Navigate to your **Access Chapter 1** folder, and then double-click your **AC_1A_Web** Excel file. Notice that this file is the original file—the first record is not changed. If you are required to print your documents, use one of the methods in the Note box given. **Close** your Excel file, saving the changes to your worksheet, and then **Open** and print your **AC_1A_Web_Download** file by using one of the methods in the following Note. **Close** Excel, saving the changes to your worksheet. As directed by your instructor, submit your two workbooks and the two paper or electronic printouts that are the results of this project.

NOTE | **Adding the File Name to the Footer and Printing or Creating an Electronic Printout of an Excel Spreadsheet on One Page**

Click the FILE tab, click Print, and then click Page Setup. In the Page Setup dialog box, on the Page tab, under Orientation, click Landscape. Under Scaling, click the Fit to option button. In the Page Setup dialog box, click the Header/Footer tab, and then click Custom Footer. With the insertion point blinking in the Left section box, click the Insert File Name button, and then click OK. In the Page Setup dialog box, click OK.

To print on paper, click Print. To create an electronic file of your printout, on the left side of your screen, click Export. Under Export, be sure Create PDF/XPS Document is selected, and then, on the right, click Create PDF/XPS. Navigate to your Access Chapter 1 folder, and then click Publish to save the file with the default name and an extension of pdf.

FIGURE B

PROJECT ACTIVITIES

In Activities 1.18 through 1.25, you will assist Dr. Miriam Yong, director of student activities, in creating a database to store information about student workshops held at Texas Lakes Community College campuses. You will use a database template that tracks event information, add workshop information to the database, and then print the results. Your completed report and table will look similar to Figure 1.39.

PROJECT FILES

For Project 1B, you will need the following files:

Desktop Event Management template
a01B_Workshops (Excel workbook)

You will save your database as:

Lastname_Firstname_1B_Student_Workshops

PROJECT RESULTS

Build from
Scratch

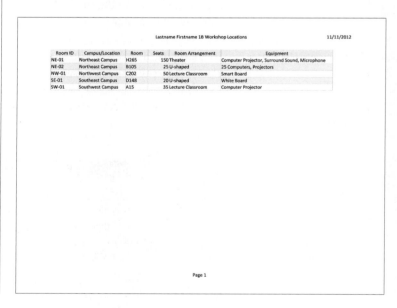

FIGURE 1.39 Project 1B Student Workshops

Video A1-6

A **database template** contains prebuilt tables, queries, forms, and reports that perform a specific task, such as tracking a large number of events. For example, your college may hold events such as athletic contests, plays, lectures, concerts, and club meetings. Using a predefined template, your college's activities director can quickly create a database to manage these events. The advantage of using a template to start a new database is that you do not have to create the objects—all you need to do is enter the data and modify the prebuilt objects to suit your needs.

The purpose of the database in this project is to track the student workshops that are held by Texas Lakes Community College. The questions to be answered might include:

- What workshops will be offered, and when will they be offered?
- In what rooms and on what campuses will the workshops be held?
- Which workshop locations have a computer projector for PowerPoint presentations?

Activity 1.18 | Using a Template to Create a Database

There are two types of database templates—those that will be stored on your desktop and those that are designed to share with others over the Internet. In this activity, you will use a desktop template to create your database.

1 Start Access. In the Access opening screen, scroll down until the last templates display. Notice that there is a **Task management** template and a **Desktop task management** template. Compare your screen with Figure 1.40.

These templates are included with the Access program. To store a database to manage tasks on your desktop, select the *Desktop task management* template. To publish a database to manage tasks and share it with others, select the *Task management* template—the one that displays a globe image. The names of templates designed to create databases stored on your computer start with the word *Desktop*.

You can search the Microsoft Office website for more templates. You can also click on a category under the search box, where templates will be suggested.

FIGURE 1.40

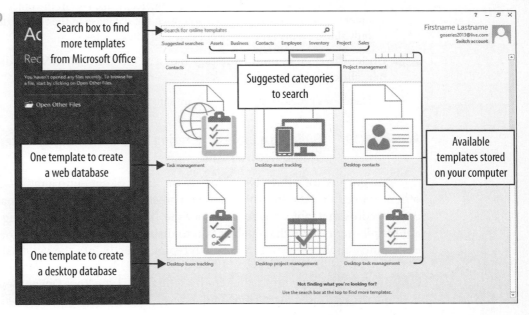

2 At the top of the window, click in the **Search for online templates** box, type **event** and then press Enter. Compare your screen with Figure 1.41.

You must have an Internet connection to search for online templates. Access displays several templates, including the Desktop Event Management template.

FIGURE 1.41

3 Click the **Desktop Event Management** template. In the dialog box, to the right of the **File Name** box, click **Browse** , and then navigate to your **Access Chapter 1** folder.

4 In the **File New Database** dialog box, click in the **File name** box to select the existing text. Using your own name, type **Lastname_Firstname_1B_Student_Workshops** and then press Enter.

5 In the **Desktop Event Management** dialog box, click **Create** to download the template and to save the database.

Access creates the *1B_Student_Workshops* database, and the database name displays in the title bar. A predesigned *form*—Event List—automatically displays in the object window. Although you can enter events for any date, when you open the database in the future, the Event List form will display only those events for the current date and future dates.

6 Under the ribbon, on the **Message Bar**, a *SECURITY WARNING* displays. On the **Message Bar**, click **Enable Content**.

Databases provided by Microsoft are safe to use on your computer.

Activity 1.19 | Building a Table by Entering Records in a Multiple-Items Form and a Single-Record Form

One purpose of a form is to simplify the entry of data into a table—either for you or for others who enter data. In Project 1A, you created a simple form that enabled you to display or enter records in a table, one record at a time. The Desktop Event Management template contains a ***multiple-items form*** that enables you to display or enter *multiple* records in a table, but with an easier and simplified layout rather than typing directly into the table itself.

1 In the new record row, click in the **Title** field. Type **Your Online Reputation** and then press Tab. In the **Start Time** field, type **3/9/18 7p** and then press Tab.

Access formats the date and time. As you enter dates and times, a small calendar displays to the right of the field. You can use the calendar to select a date instead of typing it.

2 In the **End Time** field, type **3/9/18 9p** and then press Tab. In the **Description** field, type **Internet Safety** and then press Tab. In the **Location** field, type **Northeast Campus** and then press Tab three times to move to the **Title** field in the new record row. Compare your screen with Figure 1.42.

> Because the workshops have no unique value, Access uses the AutoNumber data type in the ID field to assign a unique, sequential number to each record.

FIGURE 1.42

Multiple items form named *Event List*

AutoNumber data type creates a unique number for each record

Access formats date and time

First record entered

Total row displays by default

3 In the form, directly above the field names row, click **New Event**.

> A *single-record form* with the name *Event Details* displays, similar to the simple form you created in Project 1A. A single-record form enables you to display or enter one record at a time into a table.

4 Using Tab to move from field to field, enter the following record in the **Event Details** form—press Tab three times to move from the **End Time** field to the **Description** field. Then compare your screen with Figure 1.43.

Title	Location	Start Time	End Time	Description
Writing a Research Paper	**Southwest Campus**	**3/10/18 4p**	**3/10/18 6p**	**Computer Skills**

FIGURE 1.43

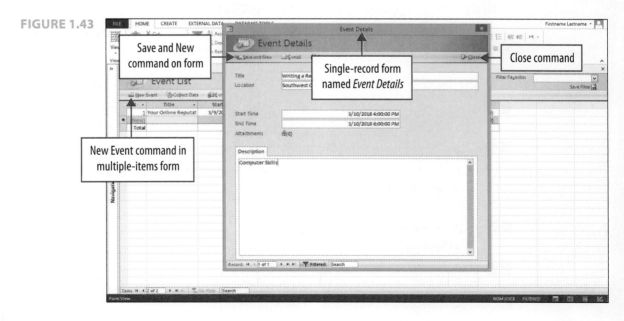

Save and New command on form

Single-record form named *Event Details*

Close command

New Event command in multiple-items form

5 In the **Event Details** single-record form, in the upper right corner, click **Close**, and notice that the new record displays in the multiple-items form—*Event List*.

6 Enter the following records by using either the **Event List** form—the multiple-items form—or the **Event Details** form—the single-record form that is accessed by clicking the *New Event* command on the **Event List** form. The data in the table given is arranged in the same order as the **Event List** form. Be sure the multiple-items form displays, and then compare your screen with Figure 1.44.

ID	Title	Start Time	End Time	Description	Location
3	Resume Writing	3/18/18 2p	3/18/18 4p	Job Skills	Northwest Campus
4	Careers in the Legal Profession	3/19/18 2p	3/19/18 4p	Careers	Southeast Campus

ALERT! **Does a Single-Record Form—***Event Details***–Open?**

In the multiple-items form, pressing ⏎Enter three times at the end of the row to begin a new record will display the single-record form—*Event Details*. If you prefer to use the multiple-items form—Event List—close the single-record form and continue entering records, using the ⎯Tab key to move from field to field.

FIGURE 1.44

Four records entered

7 In the object window, click **Close** ⊠ to close the **Event List** form.

Activity 1.20 | Appending Records by Importing from an Excel Spreadsheet

In this activity, you will append records to the table that stores the data that displays in the Events List form. You will import the records from an Excel spreadsheet.

1 On the ribbon, click the **EXTERNAL DATA tab**. In the **Import & Link group**, click **Excel**.

2 In the **Get External Data – Excel Spreadsheet** dialog box, click **Browse**. Navigate to the location where your student data files are stored, and then double-click **a01B_Workshops**.

3 Click the second option button—**Append a copy of the records to the table**—and then click **OK**.

The table that stores the data is named *Events*. Recall that other objects, such as forms, queries, and reports, display data from tables; so the Event Details form displays data that is stored in the Events table.

4 In the **Import Spreadsheet Wizard**, click **Next**, and then click **Finish**. In the **Get External Data – Excel Spreadsheet** dialog box, click **Close**.

5 **Open** ⟩⟩ the **Navigation Pane**. Double-click **Event List** to open the form that displays data from the **Events** table, and then **Close** ⟪ the **Navigation Pane**. Compare your screen with Figure 1.45.

A total of 12 records display; you entered four records, and you appended eight records from the a01B_Workshops Excel workbook. The data is truncated in several fields because the columns are not wide enough to display all of the data.

FIGURE 1.45

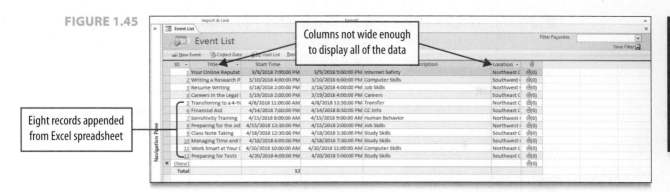

6 To the left of the **ID** field name, click **Select All** [ ] to select all of the columns and rows.

7 In the field names row, point to the right edge of any of the selected columns to display the ⊹ pointer, and then double-click to apply **Best Fit** to all of the columns. **Save** [💾] the form, and then click in any field to cancel the selection.

Objective 7 Organize Objects in the Navigation Pane

Video A1-7

Use the Navigation Pane to open objects, organize database objects, and perform common tasks, such as renaming an object or deleting an object.

Activity 1.21 | Grouping Database Objects in the Navigation Pane

The Navigation Pane groups and displays your database objects and can do so in predefined arrangements. In this activity, you will group your database objects using the ***Tables and Related Views*** category, which groups objects by the table to which the objects are related. This grouping is useful because you can determine easily the table that is the data source of queries, forms, and reports.

1 **Open** [»] the **Navigation Pane**. At the top right side of the **Navigation Pane**, click [⊙]. On the list, under **Navigate To Category**, click **Tables and Related Views**. Compare your screen with Figure 1.46.

In the Navigation Pane, you can see the number of objects that are included in the Desktop Event Management template, including the table named *Events*. Other objects in the database that display data from the Events table include one query, two forms, and five reports. In the Navigation Pane, the Event List form is selected because it is open in the object window and is the active object. Other objects might display on the Navigation Pane; for example, Filters and Unrelated Objects. These filters are objects created for use by the Desktop Event Management template.

FIGURE 1.46

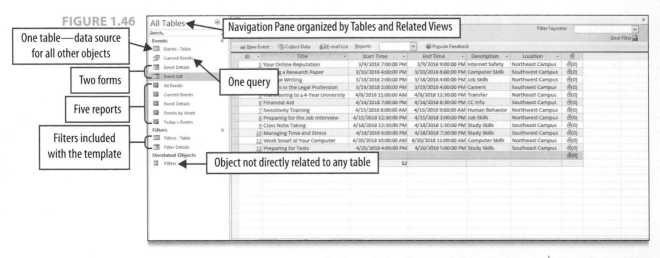

2 In the **Navigation Pane**, point to **Events: Table**, right-click, and then click **Open** to display the records in the underlying table.

The Events table is the active object in the object window. Use the Navigation Pane to open objects for use. The 12 records that display in the Event List multiple-items form are stored in this table. Recall that tables are the foundation of your database because your data must be stored in a table. You can enter records directly into a table or you can use a form to enter records.

ANOTHER WAY   Double-click the table name to open it in the object window.

3 In the object window, click the **Event List tab** to display the form as the active object in the object window.

Recall that a form presents a more user-friendly screen for entering records into a table.

4 In the **Navigation Pane**, double-click the **Current Events** *report* (green icon) to open the report. Compare your screen with Figure 1.47.

An advantage of using a template to create a database is that many objects, such as reports, are already designed for you.

FIGURE 1.47

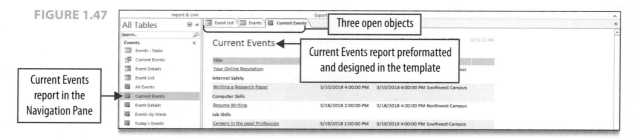

5 In the object window, **Close** ⊠ the **Current Events** report.

6 By double-clicking or right-clicking, from the **Navigation Pane**, open the **Events by Week** report.

In this predesigned report, the events are displayed by week. After entering records in the form or table, the preformatted reports are updated with the records from the table.

7 In the object window, right-click any one of the **object tabs**, and then click **Close All** to close all of the objects. **Close** ⊠ the **Navigation Pane**.

Objective 8   Create a New Table in a Database Created with a Template

Video A1-8

The Desktop Event Management template included only one table—the *Events* table. It is easy to start a database with a template, and then you can add additional objects as needed.

Activity 1.22 │ Using the Table Tool to Create a New Table

Dr. Yong has information about the various locations where workshops are held. For example, on the Northeast Campus, she has information about the room, seating arrangements, number of seats, and multimedia equipment. In the Events table, workshops are scheduled in rooms at each of the four campuses. It would not make sense to store information about the campus rooms multiple times in the same table. It is *not* considered good database design to have duplicate information in a table.

When data becomes redundant, it is usually an indication that you need a new table to store that information. In this activity, you will create a table to track the workshop locations, the equipment, and the seating arrangements in each location.

1 On the ribbon, click the **CREATE tab**, and then in the **Tables group**, click **Table**.

2 In the field names row, click **Click to Add**, click **Short Text**, type **Campus/Location** and then press Enter.

3 In the third column, click **Short Text**, type **Room** and then press Enter. In the fourth column, click **Number**, type **Seats** and then press Enter.

> The *Number data type* describes numbers that may be used in calculations. For the Seats field, you may need to determine the number of seats remaining after reservations are booked for a room. In the new record row, a *0* displays in the field.

4 In the fifth column, type **t** to select *Short Text*, type **Room Arrangement** and then press Enter. In the sixth column, type **t** and then type **Equipment** On your keyboard, press ↓.

> With the data type list displayed, you can select the data type by either clicking it or typing the letter that is underscored for the data type.

> This table has six fields. Access automatically creates the first field in the table—the ID field—to ensure that every record has a unique value. Before naming each field, you must define the data type for the field.

5 Right-click the **ID** field name, and then click **Rename Field**. Type **Room ID** and then press Enter. On the ribbon, under **TABLE TOOLS**, on the **FIELDS tab**, in the **Formatting group**, click the **Data Type arrow**, and then click **Short Text**. On the ribbon, in the **Field Validation group**, notice that **Unique** is selected.

> Recall that, by default, Access creates the ID field with the AutoNumber data type so that the field can be used as the primary key. Here, this field will store a unique room ID that is a combination of letters, symbols, and numbers; therefore, it is appropriate to change the data type to Short Text. In Datasheet view, the primary key field is identified by the selection of the Unique check box.

Activity 1.23 | Entering Records into a New Table

1 If necessary, in the new record row, click in the **Room ID** field. Enter the following record, pressing Enter or Tab to move from one field to the next. Do not be concerned that all of your text does not display; you will adjust the column widths later. After entering the record, compare your screen with Figure 1.48.

> Recall that Access saves a record when you move to another row within the table. You can press either Enter or Tab to move between fields in a table.

Room ID	Campus/ Location	Room	Seats	Room Arrangement	Equipment
NE-01	**Northeast Campus**	**H265**	**150**	**Theater**	**Computer Projector, Surround Sound, Microphone**

FIGURE 1.48

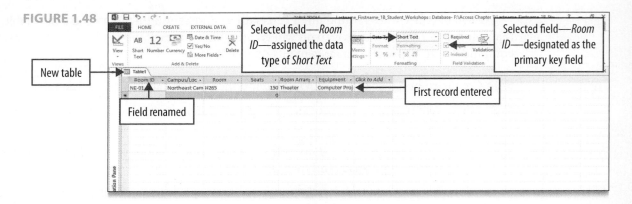

Selected field—*Room ID*—assigned the data type of *Short Text*

Selected field—*Room ID*—designated as the primary key field

New table

Field renamed

First record entered

2 In the **Views group**, click the top of the **View** button to switch to **Design** view. In the **Save As** dialog box, in the **Table Name** box, using your own name, type **Lastname Firstname 1B Workshop Locations** and then click **OK**.

Recall that when you switch views or when you close a table, Access prompts you to save the table if you have not previously saved it.

ANOTHER WAY   On the right side of the status bar, click Design View 🖍 to switch to Design view.

3 In the **Field Name** column, to the left of **Room ID**, notice the key icon.

In Design view, the key icon indicates that the field—Room ID—is the primary key field.

4 In the **Views group**, click the top of the **View** button to switch back to **Datasheet** view.

ANOTHER WAY   On the right side of the status bar, click Datasheet View 🔳 to switch to Datasheet view.

5 In the new record row, click in the **Room ID** field. Enter the following records, pressing Enter or Tab to move from one field to the next.

Room ID	Campus/Location	Room	Seats	Room Arrangement	Equipment
SW-01	Southwest Campus	A15	35	Lecture Classroom	Computer Projector
NW-01	Northwest Campus	C202	50	Lecture Classroom	Smart Board
SE-01	Southeast Campus	D148	20	U-shaped	White Board
NE-02	Northeast Campus	B105	25	U-shaped	25 Computers, Projector

6 To the left of the **Room ID** field name, click **Select All** ☐ to select all of the columns and rows in the table. On the **HOME tab**, in the **Records group,** click **More**, and then click **Field Width**. In the **Column Width** dialog box, click **Best Fit** to display all of the data in each column. **Save** 🖫 the changes to the table, and then click in any field to cancel the selection. In the object window, **Close** ☒ your **1B Workshop Locations** table.

7 **Open** 🔲 the **Navigation Pane**, and notice that your new table name displays in its own group. Point to the right edge of the **Navigation Pane** to display the ⬌ pointer. Drag to the right to increase the width of the **Navigation Pane** so that your entire table name displays. Compare your screen with Figure 1.49.

Recall that by organizing the Navigation Pane by Tables and Related Views, the Navigation Pane groups the objects by each table and displays the related objects under each table name.

FIGURE 1.49

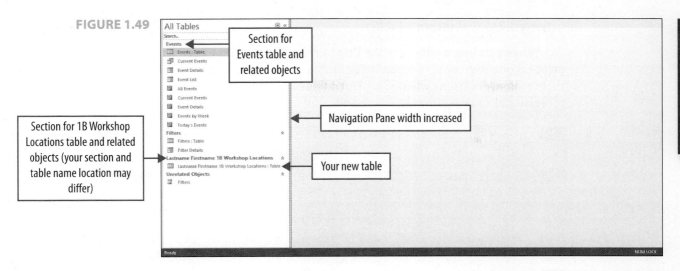

Section for 1B Workshop Locations table and related objects (your section and table name location may differ)

Section for Events table and related objects

Navigation Pane width increased

Your new table

Objective 9 | Print a Report and a Table

Video A1-9

Recall that one advantage to starting a new database with a template, instead of from a blank database, is that many report objects are already created for you.

Activity 1.24 | Viewing Reports and Printing a Report

1 In the **Navigation Pane**, double-click the report (not the form) named **Event Details** to open it in the object window.

This prebuilt Event Details report displays in an attractively arranged format.

2 **Close** ✕ the **Event Details** report. Open the **All Events** report, and then **Close** « the **Navigation Pane**. On the **HOME** tab, in the **Views group**, click the top of the **View** button to switch to **Layout** view.

Recall that Layout view enables you to make changes to an object while viewing the data in the fields. Each prebuilt report displays the records in the table in different useful formats.

ANOTHER WAY On the right side of the status bar, click Layout View 🔲 to switch to Layout view.

3 At the top of the report, click the title—*All Events*—to display a colored border around the title. Click to the left of the letter *A* to place the insertion point there. Using your own name, type **Lastname Firstname 1B** and then press Spacebar. Press Enter, and then **Save** 🖫 the report.

Including your name in the title will help you and your instructor identify any submitted work.

4 On the right side of the status bar, click **Print Preview** 🔍. In the navigation area, notice that the navigation arrows are unavailable, an indication that this report will print on one page.

ANOTHER WAY On the HOME tab, in the Views group, click the View arrow, and then click Print Preview. Or, on the FILE tab, click Print, and then click Print Preview. Or, right-click the object tab, and then click Print Preview.

5 Create a paper or electronic printout as instructed. Click **Close Print Preview**, and then **Close** ✕ the report.

Activity 1.25 | Printing a Table

When printing a table, use the Print Preview command to determine whether the table will print on one page or if you need to adjust column widths, margins, or page orientation. Recall that there will be occasions when you print a table for a quick reference or for proofreading. For a more professional-looking format, create and print a report.

1 Open » the **Navigation Pane**, double-click your **1B Workshop Locations** table to open it in the object window, and then **Close** « the **Navigation Pane**.

2 On the ribbon, click the **FILE tab**, click **Print**, and then click **Print Preview**.

The table displays showing how it will look when printed. Generally, tables are not printed, so there is no Print Preview option on the View button or on the status bar.

The navigation area displays *1* in the Pages box, and the navigation arrows to the right of the box are active, an indication that the table will print on more than one page.

3 In the navigation area, click **Next Page** ▶.

The second page of the table displays the last field. Whenever possible, try to print all of the fields horizontally on one page. Of course, if there are many records, more than one page may be needed to print all of the records and all of the fields.

4 On the **PRINT PREVIEW tab**, in the **Page Layout group**, click **Landscape**, and then compare your screen with Figure 1.50. In landscape orientation, notice that the entire table will print on one page—all of the navigation buttons are unavailable.

FIGURE 1.50

5 Create a paper or electronic printout as instructed, and then click **Close Print Preview**.

6 Close × your **1B Workshop Locations** table. For the convenience of the next individual opening the database, **Open** » the **Navigation Pane**.

7 On the right side of the title bar, click **Close** ☒ to close the database and to exit Access. As directed by your instructor, submit your database and the paper or electronic printouts of the two objects—one report and one table—that are the results of this project. Specifically, in this project, using your own name, you created the following database and printouts or electronic printouts:

1. Lastname_Firstname_1B_Student_Workshops	Database file
2. All Events	Report (printout or electronic printout)
3. Lastname Firstname 1B Workshop Locations	Table (printout or electronic printout)

END | You have completed Project 1B

Objective Export an Access Table to an Excel Spreadsheet, Save to Google Drive, Add a Record, and Save to Your Computer

Access web apps are designed to work with Microsoft's SharePoint, a service for setting up websites to share and manage documents. Your college may not have SharePoint installed, so you will use other tools to share objects from your database so that you can work collaboratively with others. Recall that Google Docs is Google's free, web-based word processor, spreadsheet, slide show, form, and data storage service. Google Drive is Google's free file storage and sharing service. For Access, you can export a database object to an Excel worksheet, a PDF file, or a text file, and then save the file to Google Drive.

> **ALERT!** **Working with Web-Based Applications and Services**
>
> Computer programs and services on the web receive continuous updates and improvements. Therefore, the steps to complete this web-based activity may differ from the ones shown. You can often look at the screens and the information presented to determine how to complete the activity.

Activity | **Exporting an Access Table to an Excel Spreadsheet, Saving the Spreadsheet to Google Drive, Editing a Record in Google Drive, and Saving to Your Computer**

In this activity, you will export your 1B Workshop Locations table to an Excel spreadsheet, upload your Excel file to Google Drive as a Google Doc, add a record in Google Drive, and then download a copy of the edited spreadsheet to your computer.

1 Start Access, navigate to your **Access Chapter 1** folder, and then **Open** your **1B_Student_Workshops** database file. If necessary, on the Message Bar, click Enable Content, and then **Close** the **Event List** form. In the **Navigation Pane**, click your **1B Workshop Locations** table to select it—do not open it.

2 On the ribbon, click the **EXTERNAL DATA tab**, and then in the **Export group**, click **Excel**. In the **Export – Excel Spreadsheet** dialog box, click **Browse**, and then navigate to your **Access Chapter 1** folder. In the **File Save** dialog box, click in the **File name** box, type **Lastname_Firstname_AC_1B_Web** and then click **Save**.

3 In the **Export – Excel Spreadsheet** dialog box, under **Specify export options**, select the first two check boxes—**Export data with formatting and layout** and **Open the destination file after the export operation is complete**—and then click **OK**. Take a moment to examine the data in the file, and then **Close** Excel. In the **Export – Excel Spreadsheet** dialog box, click **Close**, and then **Close** Access.

4 From the desktop, start Internet Explorer, navigate to **http://drive.google.com**, and sign in to your Google account; if necessary, create a new Google account and then sign in. On the right side of the screen, click the **Settings arrow**, and then point to **Upload settings**. Be sure that **Convert uploaded files to Google Docs format** is selected.

If this setting is not selected, your document will upload as a pdf file and cannot be edited without further action.

5 Open your **GO! Web Projects** folder—or create and then open this folder by clicking **New folder**. Under **Drive**, to the right of **Create**, click **Upload**, and then click **Files**. In the **Choose File to Upload** dialog box, navigate to your **Access Chapter 1** folder, and then double-click your **AC_1B_Web** Excel file to upload it to Google Drive. When the title bar of the message box indicates *Upload complete*, **Close** the message box. Compare your screen with Figure A.

FIGURE A

(GO! with Office Online (formerly Web Apps) continues on the next page)

6 Click your **AC_1B_Web** file to open the file in Google Drive. If necessary, maximize the window.

The worksheet displays column letters, row numbers, and data.

7 Click in cell **A7**, type **SW-02** and then press Tab. In cell **B7**, type **Southwest Campus** and then press Tab. In cell **C7**, type **B101** and then press Tab. In cell **D7**, type **25** and then press ↓ to save the record.

The new record might display with a different font than the other records.

8 Above row **1** and to the left of column **A**, click **Select All** ___ . On the menu bar, click **Format**, and then click **Clear formatting** so that the font is the same for all data. Click in cell **A8**, and then compare your screen with Figure B.

9 On the menu, click **File**, point to **Download as**, and then click **Microsoft Excel (.xlsx)**. In the message box—usually displays at the bottom of your screen—click the **Save arrow**, and then click **Save as**. In the **Save As** dialog box, navigate to your **Access Chapter 1** folder, click in the **File name** box, type **Lastname_Firstname_AC_1B_Web_Download** and then click **Save**. **Close** the message box.

10 In Google Drive, at the top right corner of your screen, click your user name, and then click **Sign out**. **Close** your browser window.

11 Start Excel. In the Excel opening screen, click **Open Other Workbooks**. Under **Open**, click **Computer**. On the right, under **Computer**, click **Browse**. Navigate to your **Access Chapter 1** folder, and then double-click your **AC_1B_Web** Excel file. Notice that this file is the original file—the new record is not entered. If you are required to print your documents, use one of the methods in following Note. **Close** your Excel file; and, if prompted, save the changes to your worksheet. Then **Open** and print your **AC_1B_Web_Download** Excel file using one of the methods in the following Note. **Close** Excel; and, if prompted, save the changes to your worksheet. As directed by your instructor, submit your two workbooks and the two paper or electronic printouts that are the results of this project.

N O T E **Adding the File Name to the Footer and Printing or Creating an Electronic Printout of an Excel Spreadsheet on One Page**

Click the FILE tab, click Print, and then click Page Setup. In the Page Setup dialog box, on the Page tab, under Orientation, click Landscape. Under Scaling, click the Fit to option button. In the Page Setup dialog box, click the Header/Footer tab, and then click Custom Footer. With the insertion point blinking in the Left section box, click the Insert File Name button, and then click OK. In the Page Setup dialog box, click OK.

To print on paper, click Print. To create an electronic file of your printout, on the left side of your screen, click Export. Under Export, be sure Create PDF/XPS Document is selected, and then, on the right, click Create PDF/XPS. Navigate to your Access Chapter 1 folder, and then click Publish to save the file with the default name and an extension of pdf.

FIGURE B

Andrew Rodriguez/Fotolia; FotolEdhar/Fotolia; apops/Fotolia; Yuri Arcurs/Fotolia

Office 365 includes business-class security and is backed by Microsoft. For an organization, what does that mean?

When you and a few classmates work together on a class project, you are not concerned about the security of your data. You probably use free personal email services such as Hotmail, Gmail, or Yahoo Mail to exchange documents, or perhaps you post your documents to free services such as Google Docs.

Organizations, on the other hand—even small ones with only two or three employees—must be concerned with the privacy and security of their data. Organizations cannot entrust their data and confidential communications to free services that may change frequently or that have no legal responsibility for the security of the data.

Organizations must provide each employee with a company email address rather than having each employee use his or her own personal free email address for business communications. Organizations must provide a central storage location for its data rather than having employees store data on flash drives or local hard drives with no control or oversight.

An organization must have a *secure environment*, which is a system that uses controlled *servers*—computers that provide services on a network such as an email server or a file server—to ensure the security and privacy of email, to control the storage and use of information, and to protect against the loss of confidential data.

Most small organizations cannot afford to hire the people with the skills necessary to install and maintain servers. So to establish and maintain a secure environment, many small organizations contract with and rely on small IT—the acronym for *Information Technology*—hosting companies to host their email communications and to provide secure storage.

Activity | Using the Exchange Online Outlook Meeting Tool to Collaborate

This group project relates to the **Bell Orchid Hotels**. If your instructor assigns this project to your class, you can expect to use the **Outlook Meeting tool** in **Office 365 Exchange Online** to collaborate on the following tasks for this chapter:

- If you are in the **Accounting Group**, you and your teammates will meet virtually to create a Stockholders Database to track individuals who have purchased stock in the hotel.

- If you are in the **Engineering Group**, you and your teammates will meet virtually to create a Subcontractors Database to track companies used by the Hotel for maintenance and renovation projects.

- If you are in the **Food and Beverage Group**, you and your teammates will meet virtually to create a Banquet Clients Database to track the types of functions taking place in the Hotel's banquet rooms.

- If you are in the **Human Resources Group**, you and your teammates will meet virtually to create an Employee Database for salaried employees.

- If you are in the **Operations Group**, you and your teammates will meet virtually to create a Guests Database to track guest information, as well as room rates and availability.

- If you are in the **Sales and Marketing Group**, you and your teammates will meet virtually to create an Associations Database to track industry and trade associations that book conventions for large groups.

FIGURE A

END OF CHAPTER

SUMMARY

Principles of good database design, also known as normalization, help ensure that the data in your database is accurate and organized in a way that you can retrieve information that is useful.

Databases can be created from scratch by using the blank desktop database template or a custom web app or by using a template that contains prebuilt tables, queries, forms, reports, and other objects.

Before entering records in a table, which is the foundation of a database, you must define data types and name the fields. Common data types are Short Text, Number, Currency, and Date/Time.

Forms are used to enter data into a table or view the data in a table. Queries are used to retrieve information from tables, and reports display information from tables in a professional-looking format.

GO! LEARN IT ONLINE

Review the concepts and key terms in this chapter by completing these online challenges, which you can find at **www.pearsonhighered.com/go.**

Matching and Multiple Choice:
Answer matching and multiple choice questions to test what you learned in this chapter. MyITLab®

Crossword Puzzle:
Spell out the words that match the numbered clues, and put them in the puzzle squares.

Flipboard:
Flip through the definitions of the key terms in this chapter and match them with the correct term.

GO! FOR JOB SUCCESS

Video: Goal Setting

Your instructor may assign this video to your class, and then ask you to think about, or discuss with your classmates, these questions:

FotolEdhar/Fotolia

Is there anything you would change about Theo's behavior at his performance evaluation? Why or why not?

SMART goals are goals that are specific, measurable, achievable, realistic, and time-frame specific. Is Theo's first goal of beating his sales numbers by 10 percent next year a SMART goal?

How important do you think it is to set career development goals for yourself? Why?

END OF CHAPTER
REVIEW AND ASSESSMENT GUIDE FOR ACCESS CHAPTER 1

Your instructor may assign one or more of these projects to help you review the chapter and assess your mastery and understanding of the chapter.

	Review and Assessment Guide for Access Chapter 1		
Project	**Apply Skills from These Chapter Objectives**	**Project Type**	**Project Location**
1C	Objectives 1-5 from Project 1A	**1C Skills Review** A guided review of the skills from Project 1A.	On the following pages
1D	Objectives 6-9 from Project 1B	**1D Skills Review** A guided review of the skills from Project 1B.	On the following pages
1E	Objectives 1-5 from Project 1A	**1E Mastery (Grader Project)** A demonstration of your mastery of the skills in Project 1A with extensive decision making.	In MyITLab and on the following pages
1F	Objectives 6-9 from Project 1B	**1F Mastery (Grader Project)** A demonstration of your mastery of the skills in Project 1B with extensive decision making.	In MyITLab and on the following pages
1G	Objectives 1-9 from Projects 1A and 1B	**1G Mastery (Grader Project)** A demonstration of your mastery of the skills in Projects 1A and 1B with extensive decision making.	In MyITLab and on the following pages
1H	Combination of Objectives from Projects 1A and 1B	**1H GO! Fix It** A demonstration of your mastery of the skills in Projects 1A and 1B by creating a correct result from a document that contains errors you must find.	Online
1I	Combination of Objectives from Projects 1A and 1B	**1I GO! Make It** A demonstration of your mastery of the skills in Projects 1A and 1B by creating a result from a supplied picture.	Online
1J	Combination of Objectives from Projects 1A and 1B	**1J GO! Solve It** A demonstration of your mastery of the skills in Projects 1A and 1B, your decision-making skills, and your critical thinking skills. A task-specific rubric helps you self-assess your result.	Online
1K	Combination of Objectives from Projects 1A and 1B	**1K GO! Solve It** A demonstration of your mastery of the skills in Projects 1A and 1B, your decision-making skills, and your critical thinking skills. A task-specific rubric helps you self-assess your result.	On the following pages
1L	Combination of Objectives from Projects 1A and 1B	**1L GO! Think** A demonstration of your understanding of the chapter concepts applied in a manner that you would outside of college. An analytic rubric helps you and your instructor grade the quality of your work by comparing it to the work an expert in the discipline would create.	On the following pages
1M	Combination of Objectives from Projects 1A and 1B	**1M GO! Think** A demonstration of your understanding of the chapter concepts applied in a manner that you would outside of college. An analytic rubric helps you and your instructor grade the quality of your work by comparing it to the work an expert in the discipline would create.	Online
1N	Combination of Objectives from Projects 1A and 1B	**1N You and GO!** A demonstration of your understanding of the chapter concepts applied in a manner that you would in a personal situation. An analytic rubric helps you and your instructor grade the quality of your work.	Online
1O	Combination of Objectives from Projects 1A and 1B	**1O Cumulative Group Project for Access Chapter 1** A demonstration of your understanding of concepts and your ability to work collaboratively in a group role-playing assessment, requiring both collaboration and self-management.	Online

GLOSSARY

Append To add on to the end of an object; for example, to add records to the end of an existing table.

AutoNumber data type A data type that describes a unique sequential or random number assigned by Access as each record is entered and that is useful for data that has no distinct field that can be considered unique.

Best Fit An Access command that adjusts the width of a column to accommodate the column's longest entry.

Blank desktop database A database that has no data and has no database tools—you must create the data and tools as you need them; the database is stored on your computer or other storage device.

Caption A property setting that displays a name for a field in a table, query, form, or report other than that listed as the field name.

Common field A field in two or more tables that stores the same data.

Currency data type An Access data type that describes monetary values and numeric data that can be used in mathematical calculations involving values with one to four decimal places.

Custom web app A database that you can publish and share with others over the Internet.

Data Facts about people, events, things, or ideas.

Data source The table or tables from which a query, form, or report retrieves its data.

Data type The characteristic that defines the kind of data that can be stored in a field, such as numbers, text, or dates.

Database An organized collection of facts about people, events, things, or ideas related to a specific topic or purpose.

Database management system (DBMS) Database software that controls how related collections of data are stored, organized, retrieved, and secured; also known as a DBMS.

Database template A preformatted database that contains prebuilt tables, queries, forms, and reports that perform a specific task, such as tracking events.

Datasheet view The Access view that displays data organized in columns and rows similar to an Excel worksheet.

DBMS An acronym for database management system.

Design view An Access view that displays the detailed structure of a table, query, form, or report. For forms and reports, may be the view in which some tasks must be performed, and only the controls, and not the data, display in this view.

Destination table The table to which you import or append data.

Export The process of copying data from one file into another file, such as an Access table into an Excel spreadsheet.

Field A single piece of information that is stored in every record; represented by a column in a database table.

Field properties Characteristics of a field that control how the field displays and how data can be entered in the field.

First principle of good database design A principle of good database design stating that data is organized in tables so that there is no redundant data.

Flat database A simple database file that is not related or linked to any other collection of data.

Form An Access object you can use to enter new records into a table, edit or delete existing records in a table, or display existing records.

Form view The Access view in which you can view records, but you cannot change the layout or design of the form.

Import The process of copying data from another file, such as a Word table or an Excel workbook, into a separate file, such as an Access database.

Information Data that is organized in a useful manner.

Layout view The Access view in which you can make changes to a form or report while the object is open—the data from the underlying data source displays.

Link A connection to data in another file.

Multiple-items form A form that enables you to display or enter multiple records in a table.

Navigation area An area at the bottom of the Access window that indicates the number of records in the table and contains controls in the form of arrows that you click to navigate among the records.

Navigation Pane An area of the Access window that displays and organizes the names of the objects in a database; from here, you open objects for use.

Normalization The process of applying design rules and principles to ensure that your database performs as expected.

Number data type An Access data type that describes numbers that might be used in calculations.

Object tab In the object window, a tab that identifies the object and which enables you to make the open object active.

Object window An area of the Access window that displays open objects, such as tables, queries, forms, or reports; by default, each object displays on its own tab.

Objects The basic parts of a database that you create to store your data and to work with your data; for example, tables, queries, forms, and reports.

Populate The action of filling a database table with records.

Primary key The field in a table that uniquely identifies a record; for example, a Student ID number at a college.

Property Sheet A list of characteristics—properties—for fields or controls on a form or report in which you can make precise changes to each property associated with the field or control.

Query A database object that retrieves specific data from one or more database objects—either tables or other queries—and then, in a single datasheet, displays only the data you specify.

Record All of the categories of data pertaining to one person, place, event, thing, or idea; represented by a row in a database table.

Record selector bar The bar at the left edge of a record when it is displayed in a form, and which is used to select an entire record.

Record selector box The small box at the left of a record in Datasheet view that, when clicked, selects the entire record.

Redundant In a database, information that is duplicated in a manner that indicates poor database design.

Relational database A sophisticated type of database that has multiple collections of data within the file that are related to one another.

Report A database object that summarizes the fields and records from a table or query in an easy-to-read format suitable for printing.

Run The process in which Access searches the records in the table(s) included in the query design, finds the records that match the specified criteria, and then displays the records in a datasheet; only the fields that have been included in the query design display.

Second principle of good database design A principle stating that appropriate database techniques are used to ensure the accuracy and consistency of data as it is entered into the table.

Secure environment A system that uses controlled servers to ensure the security and privacy of email, to control the storage and use of information and to protect against the loss of confidential data.

Select query A type of Access query that retrieves (selects) data from one or more tables or queries, displaying the selected data in a datasheet; also known as a simple select query.

Server A computer that provides services on a network such as an email server or a file server.

SharePoint A Microsoft application used for setting up websites to share and manage documents.

Short Text data type An Access data type that describes text, a combination of text and numbers, or numbers that are not used in calculations, such as a Postal Code.

Simple select query Another name for a select query.

Single-record form A form that enables you to display or enter one record at a time in a table.

Source file When importing a file, refers to the file being imported.

Structure In Access, the underlying design of a table, including field names, data types, descriptions, and field properties.

Table A format for information that organizes and presents text and data in columns and rows; the foundation of a database.

Tables and Related Views An arrangement in the Navigation Pane that groups objects by the table to which they are related.

Truncated Refers to data that is cut off or shortened because the field or column is not wide enough to display all of the data or the field size is too small to contain all of the data.

Wizard A feature in Microsoft Office that walks you step by step through a process.

CHAPTER REVIEW

Apply **1A** skills from these Objectives:

1 Identify Good Database Design

2 Create a Table and Define Fields in a Blank Desktop Database

3 Change the Structure of Tables and Add a Second Table

4 Create a Query, Form, and Report

5 Close a Database and Exit Access

Skills Review | Project 1C College Administrators

In the following Skills Review, you will create a database to store information about the administrators of Texas Lakes Community College and their departments. Your completed database objects will look similar to Figure 1.51.

PROJECT FILES

For Project 1C, you will need the following files:

Blank desktop database
a01C_Administrators (Excel workbook)
a01C_Departments (Excel workbook)

You will save your database as:

Lastname_Firstname_1C_College_Administrators

Build from Scratch

PROJECT RESULTS

FIGURE 1.51

(Project 1C College Administrators continues on the next page)

CHAPTER REVIEW

1 Start Access. In the Access opening screen, click **Blank desktop database**. In the **Blank desktop database** dialog box, to the right of the **File Name** box, click **Browse**. In the **File New Database** dialog box, navigate to your **Access Chapter 1** folder. In the **File New Database** dialog box, click in the **File name** box, type **Lastname_Firstname_1C_College_Administrators** and then press Enter. In the **Blank desktop database** dialog box, click **Create**.

   a. Close the **Navigation Pane**. In the field names row, click in the text *Click to Add*, and then click **Short Text**. Type **Title** and then press Enter.

   b. In the third field name box, click **Short Text**, type **Last Name** and then press Enter. In the fourth field name box, click **Short Text**, type **First Name** and then press Enter. Create the remaining fields shown in **Table 1**, pressing Enter after the last field name. All of the data is typed on one line.

   c. If necessary, scroll to bring the first column into view, and then click the **ID** field name. Under **TABLE TOOLS**, on the **FIELDS tab**, in the **Properties group**, click **Name & Caption**. In the **Name** box, change *ID* to **Employee ID** and then click **OK**. On the ribbon, in the **Formatting group**, click the **Data Type arrow**, and then click **Short Text**.

   d. In the new record row, click in the **Employee ID** field, type, **ADM-9200** and press Enter. In the **Title** field, type **Vice President** and press Enter. Continue entering data in the fields shown in **Table 2**, pressing Enter or Tab to move to the next field and to the next row.

   e. On the **Quick Access Toolbar**, click **Save**. In the **Save As** dialog box, in the **Table Name** box, using your own name, replace the selected text by typing **Lastname Firstname 1C Administrators** and then click **OK**.

   f. In the new record row, enter the data for two college administrators shown in **Table 3**, pressing Enter or Tab to move from field to field and to the next row.

TABLE 1

Data Type		Short Text	Short Text	Short Text	Short Text	Short Text	Short Text	Short Text	Short Text	Short Text	Short Text	Currency
Field Name	ID	Title	Last Name	First Name	Middle Initial	Address	City	State	Postal Code	Phone Number	Department ID	Salary

Return to Step 1c

TABLE 2

Last Name	First Name	Middle Initial	Address	City	State	Postal Code	Phone Number	Department ID	Salary
Shaffer	Lonnie	J	489 Ben Ave	Austin	TX	78734	(512) 555-6185	AS	123500

Return to Step 1e

TABLE 3

Employee ID	Title	Last Name	First Name	Middle Initial	Address	City	State	Postal Code	Phone Number	Department ID	Salary
ADM-9201	Associate Vice President	Holtz	Diann	S	8416 Spencer Ln	Georgetown	TX	78627	(512) 555-1069	AS	101524
ADM-9202	Director, Enrollment Services	Fitchette	Sean	H	3245 Deer Trl	Spicewood	TX	78669	(512) 555-9012	SS	45070

Return to Step 1g

(Project 1C College Administrators continues on the next page)

CHAPTER REVIEW

g. **Close** your **1C Administrators** table. On the ribbon, click the **EXTERNAL DATA tab**, in the **Import & Link group**, click **Excel**. In the **Get External Data – Excel Spreadsheet** dialog box, click **Browse**. In the **File Open** dialog box, navigate to your student data files, and then double-click the **a01C_Administrators** Excel file.

h. Click the **Append a copy of the records to the table** option button, and then click **OK**. In the **Import Spreadsheet Wizard**, click **Next**, and then click **Finish**. In the **Get External Data – Excel Spreadsheet** dialog box, click **Close**.

i. **Open** the **Navigation Pane**. Point to the right edge of the **Navigation Pane** to display the ⟷ pointer, and then drag to the right so that the entire table name displays. In the **Navigation Pane**, double-click your **1C Administrators** table to open it, and then **Close** the **Navigation Pane**—there are 30 records in this table.

2 ▸ Click the **HOME tab**, and then in the **Views group**, click the top of the **View** button to switch to **Design** view. In the **Field Name** column, to the left of **Middle Initial**, click the row selector box to select the entire row. Under **TABLE TOOLS, o**n the **DESIGN tab**, in the **Tools group**, click **Delete Rows**. In the message box, click **Yes**.

a. Click in the **Employee ID** field name box. Under **Field Properties**, click **Field Size** to select the existing text. Type **8** and then in the **Employee ID** field row, click in the **Description** box. Type **Eight-character Employee ID** and then press Enter.

b. Click in the **State** field name box. In the **Field Properties** area, click **Field Size**, and then type **2** In the **State Description** box, type **Two-character state abbreviation** and then press Enter.

c. **Save** the design changes to your table, and in the message box, click **Yes**. On the **DESIGN tab**, in the **Views group**, click the top of the **View** button to switch to **Datasheet** view.

d. On the ribbon, click the **EXTERNAL DATA tab**, and then in the **Import & Link group**, click **Excel**. In the **Get External Data – Excel Spreadsheet** dialog box, to the right of the **File name** box, click **Browse**. In the

File Open dialog box, navigate to your student data files, and then double-click **a01C_Departments**. Be sure that the **Import the source data into a new table in the current database** option button is selected, and then click **OK**.

e. In the upper left corner of the wizard, select the **First Row Contains Column Headings** check box, and then click **Next**. Click **Next** again. Click the **Choose my own primary key** option button, be sure that **Department ID** displays, and then click **Next**. In the **Import to Table** box, type **Lastname Firstname 1C Departments** and then click **Finish**. In the **Get External Data – Excel Spreadsheet** dialog box, click **Close**.

f. **Open** the **Navigation Pane**, double-click your **1C Departments** table, and then **Close** the **Navigation Pane**. There are 12 records in your **1C Departments** table.

g. To the left of the **Department** field name, click **Select All**. On the ribbon, click the **HOME tab**. In the **Records group**, click **More**, and then click **Field Width**. In the **Column Width** dialog box, click **Best Fit**. **Save** the table, and then click in any field to cancel the selection. In the object window, click the **object tab** for your **1C Administrators** table. Using the techniques you just practiced, apply **Best Fit** to the columns, **Save** the table, and then cancel the selection.

h. With your **1C Administrators** table displayed, on the ribbon, click the **FILE tab**, click **Print**, and then click **Print Preview**. On the **PRINT PREVIEW tab**, in the **Page Layout group**, click **Landscape**. Create a paper or electronic printout as directed by your instructor—two pages result. On the ribbon, click **Close Print Preview**, and then **Close** your **1C Administrators** table.

i. With your **1C Departments** table displayed, view the table in **Print Preview**. Change the orientation to **Landscape**, and then create a paper or electronic printout as directed by your instructor—one page results. Click **Close Print Preview**, and then **Close** your **1C Departments** table.

(Project 1C College Administrators continues on the next page)

3 On the ribbon, click the **CREATE tab**, and then in the **Queries group**, click **Query Wizard**. In the **New Query** dialog box, be sure **Simple Query Wizard** is selected, and then click **OK**. In the wizard, click the **Tables/Queries arrow**, and then, if necessary, click **Table: Lastname Firstname 1C Administrators**.

a. Under **Available Fields**, click **Last Name**, and then click **Add Field** to move the field to the **Selected Fields** list on the right. Double-click the **First Name** field to move it to the **Selected Fields** list. By using **Add Field** or by double-clicking the field name, add the following fields to the **Selected Fields** list in the order specified: **Title**, **Department ID**, and **Phone Number**. This query will answer the question, *What is the last name, first name, title, Department ID, and phone number of every administrator?*

b. In the wizard, click **Next**. Click in the **What title do you want for your query?** box. Using your own name, edit as necessary so that the query name is **Lastname Firstname 1C All Administrators Query** and then click **Finish**. If necessary, apply **Best Fit** to the columns, and then **Save** the query. Display the query in **Print Preview**, and then create a paper or electronic printout as directed—one page results. Click **Close Print Preview**, and then **Close** the query.

c. **Open** the **Navigation Pane**, right-click your **1C Administrators** table, and then click **Open** to display the table in the object window. **Close** the **Navigation Pane**. Notice that the table has 11 fields. On the ribbon, click the **CREATE tab**, and in the **Forms group**, click **Form**. On the **Quick Access Toolbar**, click **Save**. In the **Save As** dialog box, click in the **Form Name** box, edit to name the form **Lastname Firstname 1C Administrator Form** and then click **OK**.

d. In the navigation area, click **Last record**, and then click **Previous record** two times to display the record for *Diann Holtz*. Using the instructions in Activity 1.15, print or create an electronic printout of only this record on one page. **Close** the form object, saving it if prompted. Your **1C Administrators** table object remains open.

e. **Open** the **Navigation Pane**, open your **1C Departments** table by double-clicking the table name or by right-clicking the table name and clicking **Open**. **Close** the **Navigation Pane**. On the **CREATE tab**, in the **Reports group**, click **Report**.

f. Click the **Department ID** field name, and then on the ribbon, click the **ARRANGE tab**. In the **Rows & Columns group**, click **Select Column**, and then press ⌷Del⌷. Using the same technique, delete the **Department Email** field.

g. Click the **Department Phone** field name. Hold down ⌷Shift⌷, and then click the **Suite Number** field name to select the last three field names. On the ribbon, click the **DESIGN tab**, and then in the **Tools group**, click **Property Sheet**. In the **Property Sheet**, on the **Format tab**, click **Width**, type **1.5** and then press ⌷Enter⌷. **Close** the **Property Sheet**.

h. Click the **Department Name** field name. On the ribbon, click the **HOME tab**. In the **Sort & Filter group**, click **Ascending** to sort the report in alphabetic order by *Department Name*. At the bottom of the report, on the right side, click **Page 1 of 1**, and then press ⌷Del⌷.

i. **Save** the report as **Lastname Firstname 1C Departments Report** and then click **OK**. Display the report in **Print Preview**, and then create a paper or electronic printout of the report as directed. Click **Close Print Preview**. In the object window, right-click any **object tab**, and then click **Close All** to close all open objects, leaving the object window empty.

(Project 1C College Administrators continues on the next page)

CHAPTER REVIEW

4 **Open** the **Navigation Pane**. If necessary, increase the width of the **Navigation Pane** so that all object names display fully. On the right side of the title bar, click **Close** to close the database and to exit Access. As directed by your instructor, submit your database and the paper or electronic printouts of the five objects—two tables, one query, one form, and one report—that are the results of this project. Specifically, in this project, using your own name, you created the following database and printouts or electronic printouts:

1. Lastname_Firstname_1C_College_Administrators	Database file
2. Lastname Firstname 1C Administrators	Table (printout or electronic printout – two pages)
3. Lastname Firstname 1C Departments	Table (printout or electronic printout)
4. Lastname Firstname 1C All Administrators Query	Query (printout or electronic printout)
5. Lastname Firstname 1C Administrator Form	Form (printout or electronic printout – Record 28)
6. Lastname Firstname 1C Departments Report	Report (printout or electronic printout)

END | You have completed Project 1C

CHAPTER REVIEW

Apply 1B skills from these Objectives:

6 Use a Template to Create a Database

7 Organize Objects in the Navigation Pane

8 Create a New Table in a Database Created with a Template

9 Print a Report and a Table

Skills Review | Project 1D Certification Events

In the following Skills Review, you will create a database to store information about certification test preparation events at Texas Lakes Community College. Your completed report and table will look similar to Figure 1.52.

PROJECT FILES

For Project 1D, you will need the following files:

Desktop Event Management template
a01D_Certification_Events (Excel workbook)

You will save your database as:

Lastname_Firstname_1D_Certification_Events

Build from Scratch

PROJECT RESULTS

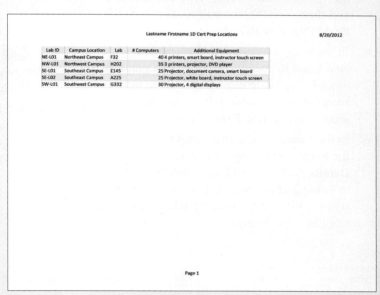

FIGURE 1.52

(Project 1D Certification Events continues on the next page)

CHAPTER REVIEW

1 Start Access. In the Access opening screen, click in the **Search** box, type **event** and then press Enter to search for a template to manage events. Click the **Desktop Event Management** template. In the **Desktop Event Management** dialog box, to the right of the **File Name** box, click **Browse**, and then navigate to your **Access Chapter 1** folder. In the **File New Database** dialog box, click in the **File name** box to select the existing text. Using your own name, type **Lastname_Firstname_1D_ Certification_Events** and then press Enter. In the **Desktop Event Management** dialog box, click **Create** to download the template and to save the database. Under the ribbon, on the **Message Bar**, click **Enable Content**.

a. In the first row, click in the **Title** field, type **Word 2013** and then press Tab. In the **Start Time** field, type **7/9/18 9a** and then press Tab. In the **End Time** field, type **7/9/18 3p** and then press Tab. In the **Description** field, type **Office 2013** and then press Tab. In the **Location** field, type **Southwest Campus** and then press Tab three times to move to the **Title** field in the new record row.

b. In the form, directly above the field names row, click **New Event** to open the **Event Details** single-record form. Using Tab to move from field to field, enter the record shown in **Table 1**. Press Tab three times to move from the **End Time** field to the **Description** field.

c. In the **Events Detail** form, click **Close**. Using either the **Event List** multiple-items form or the **Event Details** single-record form, enter the records shown in **Table 2**. If you use the **Events Detail** form, be sure to close it after entering records to display the records in the **Event List** form.

d. **Close** the **Event List** form. On the ribbon, click the **EXTERNAL DATA tab**, and in the **Import & Link group**, click **Excel**. In the **Get External Data – Excel Spreadsheet** dialog box, click **Browse**. Navigate to your student data files, and then double-click **a01D_Certification_Events**. Click the second option button—**Append a copy of the records to the table**—and then click **OK**.

e. In the **Import Spreadsheet Wizard**, click **Next**, and then click **Finish**. In the **Get External Data – Excel Spreadsheet** dialog box, click **Close**. Open the **Navigation Pane**, and then double-click **Event List** to open the form that displays data stored in the **Events** table—12 total records display. **Close** the **Navigation Pane**.

f. To the left of the **ID** field name, click **Select All**. In the field names row, point to the right edge of any of the selected columns to display the ⊞ pointer, and then double-click to apply **Best Fit** to all of the columns. **Save** the form, and then click in any field to cancel the selection.

2 Open the **Navigation Pane**. At the top of the **Navigation Pane**, click the arrow. On the list, under **Navigate To Category**, click **Tables and Related Views**.

a. In the **Navigation Pane**, point to **Events: Table**, right-click, and then click **Open** to display the records in the underlying table. In the **Navigation Pane**, double-click the **Current Events** *report* (green icon) to view this predesigned report. From the **Navigation Pane**, open the **Events by Week** report to view this predesigned report.

TABLE 1

Title	Location	Start Time	End Time	Description
Excel 2013	**Northeast Campus**	**7/16/18 10a**	**7/16/18 4p**	**Office 2013**

Return to Step 1c

TABLE 2

ID	Title	Start Time	End Time	Description	Location
3	**Access 2013**	**7/23/18 12p**	**7/23/18 6p**	**Office 2013**	**Southeast Campus**
4	**PowerPoint 2013**	**7/30/18 9a**	**7/30/18 3p**	**Office 2013**	**Northwest Campus**

Return to Step 1d

(Project 1D Certification Events continues on the next page)

b. In the object window, right-click any of the **object tabs**, and then click **Close All**. **Close** the **Navigation Pane**.

3 On the ribbon, click the **CREATE tab**, and in the **Tables group**, click **Table**.

a. In the field names row, click **Click to Add**, click **Short Text**, type **Campus Location** and then press [Enter]. In the third column, click **Short Text**, type **Lab** and then press [Enter]. In the fourth column, click **Number**, type **# Computers** and then press [Enter]. In the fifth column, click **Short Text**, type **Additional Equipment** and then press [↓].

b. Right-click the **ID** field name, and then click **Rename Field**. Type **Lab ID** and then press [Enter]. On the **FIELDS tab**, in the **Formatting group**, click the **Data Type arrow**, and then click **Short Text**.

c. In the new record row, click in the **Lab ID** field, and then enter the records shown in **Table 3**, pressing [Enter] or [Tab] to move from one field to the next.

d. In the **Views group**, click the top of the **View** button to switch to **Design** view. In the **Save As** dialog box, in the **Table Name** box, using your own name, type **Lastname Firstname 1D Cert Prep Locations** and then click **OK**. Notice that the **Lab ID** field is the **Primary Key**. On the **DESIGN tab**, in the **Views group**, click the top of the **View** button to switch to **Datasheet** view.

e. To the left of the **Lab ID** field name, click **Select All** to select all of the columns and rows in the table. On the **HOME tab**, in the **Records group**, click **More**, and then click **Field Width**. In the **Column Width** dialog box, click **Best Fit**. **Save** the changes to the table, and then click in any field to cancel the selection. **Close** the table, and then **Open** the **Navigation Pane**. Increase the width of the **Navigation Pane** so that your entire table name displays.

4 In the **Navigation Pane**, double-click the **All Events** report to open it in the object window. **Close** the **Navigation Pane**. On the **HOME tab**, in the **Views group**, click the top of the **View** button to switch to **Layout** view. At the top of the report, click the title—*All Events*—to display a colored border around the title. Click to the left of the letter *A* to place the insertion point there. Using your own name, type **Lastname Firstname 1D** and then press [Spacebar]. Press [Enter], and then **Save** the report.

a. On the right side of the status bar, click **Print Preview**, and notice that the report will print on one page. Create a paper or electronic printout as instructed. Click **Close Print Preview**, and then **Close** the report.

b. **Open** the **Navigation Pane**, double-click your **1D Cert Prep Locations** table, and then **Close** the **Navigation Pane**. On the ribbon, click the **FILE tab**, click **Print**, and then click **Print Preview**. On the **PRINT PREVIEW tab**, in the **Page Layout group**, click **Landscape**. Create a paper or electronic printout as directed, and then click **Close Print Preview**. Close your **1D Cert Prep Locations** table.

TABLE 3

Lab ID	Campus Location	Lab	# Computers	Additional Equipment
NW-L01	Northwest Campus	H202	35	3 printers, projector, DVD player
SE-L01	Southeast Campus	E145	25	Projector, document camera, smart board
NE-L01	Northeast Campus	F32	40	4 printers, smart board, instructor touch screen
SW-L01	Southwest Campus	G332	30	Projector, 4 digital displays
SE-L02	Southeast Campus	A225	25	Projector, white board, instructor touch screen

(Return to Step 3d)

(Project 1D Certification Events continues on the next page)

CHAPTER REVIEW

c. **Open** the **Navigation Pane**. On the right side of the title bar, click **Close** to close the database and to exit Access. As directed by your instructor, submit your database and the paper or electronic printouts of the two objects—one report and one table—that are the results of this project. Specifically, in this project, using your own name, you created the following database and printouts or electronic printouts:

1. Lastname_Firstname_1D_Certification_Events	Database file
2. Lastname Firstname 1D Cert Prep Locations	Table (printout or electronic printout)
3. All Events	Report (printout or electronic printout)

END | You have completed Project 1D

Apply 1A skills from these Objectives:

1 Identify Good Database Design

2 Create a Table and Define Fields in a Blank Desktop Database

3 Change the Structure of Tables and Add a Second Table

4 Create a Query, Form, and Report

5 Close a Database and Exit Access

In the following Mastering Access project, you will create a database to track information about the inventory of items for sale in the kiosk located in the snack bar at the Southeast Campus of Texas Lakes Community College. Your completed database objects will look similar to Figure 1.53.

PROJECT FILES

For Project 1E, you will need the following files:

Blank desktop database
a01E_Inventory (Excel workbook)
a01E_Inventory_Storage (Excel workbook)

You will save your database as:

Lastname_Firstname_1E_Kiosk_Inventory

PROJECT RESULTS

Build from Scratch

FIGURE 1.53

(Project 1E Kiosk Inventory continues on the next page)

CONTENT-BASED ASSESSMENTS

1 Start Access. Create a **Blank desktop database** in your **Access Chapter 1** folder. Name the database **Lastname_Firstname_1E_Kiosk_Inventory** and then **Close** the **Navigation Pane**. Create the fields shown in **Table 1**.

2 For the **ID** field, change the **Data Type** to **Short Text**, rename the field to **Item ID** and then enter the records shown in **Table 2**.

3 Save the table as **Lastname Firstname 1E Inventory** and then **Close** the table. From your student data files, import and then **Append** the data in the Excel file **a01E_Inventory** to your **1E Inventory** table. After importing, open your **1E Inventory** table—17 records display.

4 In **Design** view, delete the **Campus** field, which is redundant data. For the **Category** field, change the **Field Size** to **25** and enter a **Description** of **Enter the category of the item** For the **Item ID** field, change the **Field Size** to **10** and then **Save** the changes to your table. Switch to **Datasheet** view, apply **Best Fit** to all of the fields in the table, and then **Save** your changes. Display the table in **Print Preview**, change the orientation to **Landscape**, and then create a paper or electronic printout as directed by your instructor. **Close Print Preview**, and then **Close** the table.

5 From your student data files, import the **Excel** file **a01E_Inventory_Storage** into the database as a new table; designate the first row as column headings and the **Category** field as the primary key. In the wizard, name the table **Lastname Firstname 1E Inventory Storage** and then open your **1E Inventory Storage** table—five records display. In **Design** view, for the **Location Detail** field, change the **Field Size** to **30** and enter a **Description** of **Room and bin number or alternate location of inventory item Save** the design changes, switch to **Datasheet** view, apply **Best Fit** to all of the fields, and then **Save** your changes. Display the table in **Print Preview**, create a paper or electronic printout as directed, **Close Print Preview**, and then **Close** the table.

6 Use the **Query Wizard** to create a simple query based on your **1E Inventory** table. Include only the three fields that will answer the question, *For all item names, what is the storage location and quantity in stock?* In the wizard, accept the default name for the query. Display the query in **Print Preview**, create a paper or electronic printout as directed, **Close Print Preview**, and then **Close** the query.

TABLE 1

Data Type		Short Text	Short Text	Short Text	Short Text	Currency	Number
Field Name	ID	Item	Category	Campus	Storage Location	Price	Quantity in Stock

(Return to Step 2)

TABLE 2

Item ID	Item	Category	Campus	Storage Location	Price	Quantity in Stock
C-1	Chocolate Bar	Candy	Southeast	SE100A	.89	250
C-2	Lollipop	Candy	Southeast	SE100A	.5	500
T-1	T-shirt, S	Clothing	Southeast	SE100B	17.5	100

(Return to Step 3)

(Project 1E Kiosk Inventory continues on the next page)

CONTENT-BASED ASSESSMENTS

7 Open your **1E Inventory** table, and then create a **Form** for this table. **Save** the form as **Lastname Firstname 1E Inventory Form** and then display and select the fifth record. By using the instructions in Activity 1.15, create a paper or electronic printout of only this record on one page, as directed by your instructor. **Close** the form object, saving changes if prompted.

8 With your **1E Inventory** table open, create a **Report**. Delete the **Category** and **Price** fields, and then sort the **Item ID** field in **Ascending** order. Using the **Property Sheet**, for the **Item ID** field, change the **Width** to **0.75** and then for the **Storage Location** field, change the **Width** to **1.5** Scroll to display the bottom of the report, and then

delete the page number—**Page 1 of 1**. **Save** the report as **Lastname Firstname 1E Inventory Report** and then display the report in **Print Preview**. Create a paper or electronic printout as directed. Click **Close Print Preview**.

9 **Close All** open objects. **Open** the **Navigation Pane** and be sure that all object names display fully. **Close** the database, and then **Close** Access. As directed by your instructor, submit your database and the paper or electronic printouts of the five objects—two tables, one query, one form, and one report—that are the results of this project. Specifically, in this project, using your own name, you created the following database and printouts or electronic printouts:

1. Lastname_Firstname_1E_Kiosk_Inventory	Database file
2. Lastname Firstname 1E Inventory	Table (printout or electronic printout)
3. Lastname Firstname 1E Inventory Storage	Table (printout or electronic printout)
4. Lastname Firstname 1E Inventory Query	Query (printout or electronic printout)
5. Lastname Firstname 1E Inventory Form	Form (printout or electronic printout – Record 5)
6. Lastname Firstname 1E Inventory Report	Report (printout or electronic printout)

END | You have completed Project 1E

CONTENT-BASED ASSESSMENTS

In the following Mastering Access project, you will create a database to store information about the recruiting events that are scheduled to attract new students to Texas Lakes Community College. Your completed report and tables will look similar to Figure 1.54.

Apply 1B skills from these Objectives:

6 Use a Template to Create a Database

7 Organize Objects in the Navigation Pane

8 Create a New Table in a Database Created with a Template

9 Print a Report and a Table

Build from Scratch

PROJECT FILES

For Project 1F, you will need the following files:

Desktop Event Management template
a01F_Recruiting_Events (Excel workbook)

You will save your database as:

Lastname_Firstname_1F_Recruiting_Events

PROJECT RESULTS

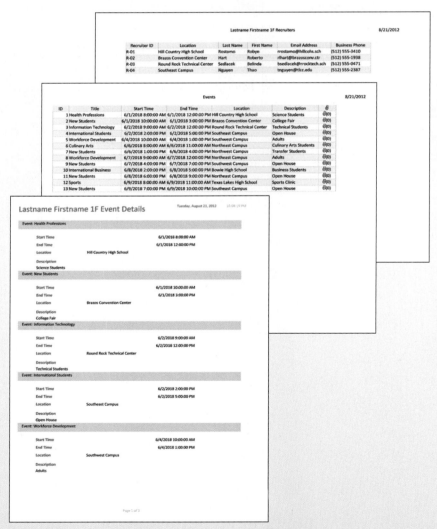

FIGURE 1.54

(Project 1F Recruiting Events continues on the next page)

CONTENT-BASED ASSESSMENTS

1 Start Access. In the Access opening screen, search for **event** and then click the **Desktop Event Management** template. Save the database in your **Access Chapter 1** folder as **Lastname_Firstname_1F_Recruiting_Events** and on the **Message Bar**, click **Enable Content**.

2 In the **Event List** multiple-items form or the **Event Details** single-record form—open by clicking **New Event** on the **Event List** form—enter the records shown in **Table 1**.

3 **Close** the **Event List** form. From your student data files, import and append the data from the **Excel** file **a01F_Recruiting_Events** to the **Events** table. **Open** the **Navigation Pane**, organize the objects by **Tables and Related Views**, and then open the **Events** table to display 13 records. **Close** the table, and then **Close** the **Navigation Pane**.

4 Create a new **Table** defining the new fields shown in **Table 2**.

5 For the **ID** field, change the **Data Type** to **Short Text**, rename the field to **Recruiter ID** and then enter the records shown in **Table 3**.

TABLE 1

ID	Title	Start Time	End Time	Description	Location
1	Health Professions	6/1/18 8a	6/1/18 12p	Science Students	Hill Country High School
2	New Students	6/1/18 10a	6/1/18 3p	College Fair	Brazos Convention Center
3	Information Technology	6/2/18 9a	6/2/18 12p	Technical Students	Round Rock Technical Center
4	International Students	6/2/18 2p	6/2/18 5p	Open House	Southeast Campus

(Return to Step 3)

TABLE 2

Data Type		Short Text	Short Text	Short Text	Short Text	Short Text
Field Name	ID	Location	Last Name	First Name	Email Address	Business Phone

(Return to Step 5)

TABLE 3

Recruiter ID	Location	Last Name	First Name	Email Address	Business Phone
R-01	Hill Country High School	Rostamo	Robyn	rrostamo@hillcohs.sch	(512) 555-3410
R-02	Brazos Convention Center	Hart	Roberto	rlhart@brazosconv.ctr	(512) 555-1938
R-03	Round Rock Technical Center	Sedlacek	Belinda	bsedlacek@rrocktech.sch	(512) 555-0471
R-04	Southeast Campus	Nguyen	Thao	tnguyen@tlcc.edu	(512) 555-2387

(Return to Step 6)

(Project 1F Recruiting Events continues on the next page)

CONTENT-BASED ASSESSMENTS

6 Apply **Best Fit** to all of the columns. **Save** the table as **Lastname Firstname 1F Recruiters** and then **Close** the table.

7 From the **Navigation Pane**, open the **Event Details** *report* (green icon). Switch to **Layout** view. In the report, click in the title—*Event Details*—and then click to position the insertion point to the left of the word *Event*. Using your own name, type **Lastname Firstname 1F** and then press Spacebar and Enter. If necessary, decrease the font size of the title so that the title does not overlap the date on the right side or does not extend to two lines.

Save the report, and then display it in **Print Preview**. If directed to create a paper printout, in the **Print group**, click **Print**. In the **Print** dialog box, under **Print Range**, to the right of **Pages**, click in the **From** box, type **1** and then click in the **To** box and type **1** and then click **OK** to print only the first page. If directed to create an electronic printout, in the **Publish as PDF or XPS** dialog box, click **Options**, and then under **Range**, click the **Pages** option button, and then click **OK**. **Close Print Preview**, and then **Close** the report.

8 From the **Navigation Pane**, open the **Events** table, select all of the columns, and then apply **Best Fit** to all of the columns by double-clicking the right edge of any one of the selected columns. **Save** the table, and then cancel the selection. Display the table in **Print Preview**, change the orientation to **Landscape**, change the **Margins** to **Normal**, and then create a paper or electronic printout as directed. **Close Print Preview**, and then **Close** the table.

9 From the **Navigation Pane**, open your **1F Recruiters** table. Display the table in **Print Preview**, change the orientation to **Landscape**, and then create a paper or electronic printout as directed. **Close Print Preview**, and then **Close** the table.

10 Open the **Navigation Pane**, and be sure that all object names display fully. **Close** Access. As directed by your instructor, submit your database and the paper or electronic printouts of the three objects—one report and two tables—that are the results of this project. Specifically, in this project, using your own name, you created the following database and printouts or electronic printouts:

1. Lastname_Firstname_1F_Recruiting_Events	Database file
2. Event Details	Report (printout or electronic printout – Page 1)
3. Events	Table (printout or electronic printout)
4. Lastname Firstname 1F Recruiters	Table (printout or electronic printout)

END | You have completed Project 1F

CONTENT-BASED ASSESSMENTS

Mastering Access Project 1G College Construction

Apply **1A** and **1B** skills from these Objectives:

1 Identify Good Database Design

2 Create a Table and Define Fields in a Blank Desktop Database

3 Change the Structure of Tables and Add a Second Table

4 Create a Query, Form, and Report

5 Close a Database and Exit Access

6 Use a Template to Create a Database

7 Organize Objects in the Navigation Pane

8 Create a New Table in a Database Created with a Template

9 Print a Report and a Table

In the following Mastering Access project, you will create one database to store information about construction projects for Texas Lakes Community College and a second database to store information about the public events related to the construction projects. Your completed database objects will look similar to Figure 1.55.

PROJECT FILES

For Project 1G, you will need the following files:

Blank desktop database
a01G_Projects (Excel workbook)
a01G_Contractors (Excel workbook)
Desktop Event Management template

You will save your databases as:

Lastname_Firstname_1G_College_Construction
Lastname_Firstname_1G_Public_Events

PROJECT RESULTS

Build from Scratch

FIGURE 1.55

(Project 1G College Construction continues on the next page)

1 Start Access. Create a **Blank desktop database** in your **Access Chapter 1** folder. Name the database **Lastname_ Firstname_1G_College_Construction** and then **Close** the **Navigation Pane**. Create the fields shown in **Table 1**.

2 For the **ID** field, change the **Data Type** to **Short Text**, rename the field to **Project ID** and then enter the three records shown in **Table 2**.

3 Save the table as **Lastname Firstname 1G Projects** and then **Close** the table. From your student data files, import and then append the data in the **Excel** file **a01G_ Projects** to your **1G Projects** table. After importing, open your **1G Projects** table—eight records display.

4 In **Design** view, for the **Project ID** field, change the **Field Size** to **5** and then enter a **Description** of **Enter the Project ID using the format P-### Save** the changes to your table. Switch to **Datasheet** view, apply **Best Fit** to all of the fields in the table, and then **Save** your changes. Display the table in **Print Preview**, change the orientation to **Landscape**, and then create a paper or electronic printout as directed by your instructor. **Close Print Preview**, and then **Close** the table.

5 From your student data files, import the **Excel** file **a01G_Contractors** into the database as a new table; designate the first row as column headings and the **ID** field as the primary key. In the wizard, name the table **Lastname Firstname 1G Contractors** and then open your **1G Contractors** table—four records display. Apply **Best Fit** to all of the fields, and then **Save** your changes. Display the table in **Print Preview**, change the orientation to **Landscape**, and then create a paper or electronic printout as directed. **Close Print Preview**, and then **Close** the table.

6 Use the **Query Wizard** to create a simple query based on your **1G Projects** table. Include only the three fields that will answer the question, *For every site, what is the building project and the budget amount?* In the wizard, accept the default name for the query. Display the query in **Print Preview**, create a paper or electronic printout as directed, **Close Print Preview**, and then **Close** the query.

7 Open your **1G Projects** table, and then create a **Form** for this table. **Save** the form as **Lastname Firstname 1G Project Form** and then display and select the seventh record. By using the instructions in Activity 1.15, create a paper or electronic printout of only this record on one page as directed by your instructor. **Close** the form object, saving changes if prompted.

8 With your **1G Projects** table open, create a **Report**. Delete the **Budget Amount** field, and then sort the **Building Project** field in **Ascending** order. For the **Building Project**, **Site**, and **Contractor** fields, using the **Property Sheet**, change the **Width** of all three fields to **2** At the bottom of the report, delete the page number—**Page 1 of 1**. **Save** the report as **Lastname Firstname 1G Projects Report** and then display the report in **Print Preview**. Create a paper or electronic printout as directed. **Close Print Preview**.

9 **Close All** open objects. **Open** the **Navigation Pane**, arrange the objects by **Tables and Related Views**, and be sure that all object names display fully. **Close** the database, but do *not* close Access.

TABLE 1

Data Type		Short Text	Short Text	Short Text	Currency
Field Name	ID	Building Project	Site	Contractor	Budget Amount

Return to Step 2

TABLE 2

Project ID	Building Project	Site	Contractor	Budget Amount
P-356	Student Center, 3-story	Northeast Campus	RR Construction	61450000
P-823	Student Center, 2-story	Southeast Campus	RR Construction	41960000
P-157	Health Professions Center	Northwest Campus	Marshall Ellis Construction	42630000

Return to Step 3

(Project 1G College Construction continues on the next page)

CONTENT-BASED ASSESSMENTS

10 ▶ In the Access opening screen, search for **event** and then click the **Desktop Event Management** template. Save the database in your **Access Chapter 1** folder as **Lastname_Firstname_1G_Public_Events** and on the **Message Bar**, click **Enable Content**.

11 ▶ In the **Event List** multiple-items form or the **Event Details** single-record form—open by clicking **New Event** on the **Event List** form—enter the three records shown in **Table 3**.

12 ▶ **Close** the **Event List** form. **Open** the **Navigation Pane**, organize the objects by **Tables and Related Views**, and then open the **Current Events** *report* (green icon). Switch to **Layout** view. In the report, click in the title—*Current Events*—and then click to position the insertion point to the left of the letter *C*. Using your own name, type **Lastname Firstname 1G** and then press

Spacebar and Enter. If necessary, decrease the font size of the title so that the title does not overlap the date on the right side or does not extend to two lines. **Save** the report, display it in **Print Preview**, and then create a paper or electronic printout as directed. **Close Print Preview**, and then **Close** the report.

13 ▶ Open the **Navigation Pane**, and be sure that all object names display fully. **Close** Access. As directed by your instructor, submit your database and the paper or electronic printouts of the six objects—two tables, one query, one form, and two reports—that are the results of this project. Specifically, in this project, using your own name, you created the following database and printouts or electronic printouts:

1. Lastname_Firstname_1G_College_Construction	Database file
2. Lastname_Firstname_1G_Public_Events	Database file
3. Lastname Firstname 1G Projects	Table (printout or electronic printout)
4. Lastname Firstname 1G Contractors	Table (printout or electronic printout)
5. Lastname Firstname 1G Projects Query	Query (printout or electronic printout)
6. Lastname Firstname 1G Project Form	Form (printout or electronic printout - Record 7)
7. Lastname Firstname 1G Projects Report	Report (printout or electronic printout)
8. Current Events	Report (printout or electronic printout)

TABLE 3

ID	Title	Start Time	End Time	Description	Location
1	Groundbreaking	6/13/18 10a	6/13/18 11a	Student Center groundbreaking	Northeast Campus
2	Dedication	8/26/18 12:30 p	8/26/18 2p	Gymnasium building dedication	Southwest Campus
3	Community Arts Expo	10/5/18 6p	10/5/18 9p	Book and Art Expo at Library	Southeast Campus

(Return to Step 12)

END | You have completed Project 1G

CONTENT-BASED ASSESSMENTS

Apply a combination of the 1A and 1B skills.

Build from Scratch

Build from Scratch

GO! Fix It	Project 1H Scholarships	Online
GO! Make It	Project 1I Theater Events	Online
GO! Solve It	Project 1J Athletic Scholarships	Online
GO! Solve It	Project 1K Student Activities	

Build from Scratch

PROJECT FILES

For Project 1K, you will need the following files:

Desktop Event Management template
a01K_Student_Activities (Word document)

You will save your database as:

Lastname_Firstname_1K_Student_Activities

Use the Desktop Event Management template to create a database, and save it in your Access Chapter 1 folder as **Lastname_Firstname_1K_Student_Activities** From your student data files, use the information in the Word document a01K_Student_Activities to enter data into the Event List multiple-items form. Each event begins at 6 p.m. and ends at 10 p.m.

After entering the records, close the form, and arrange the Navigation Pane by Tables and Related Views. Open the Event Details *report*, and then add **Lastname Firstname 1K** to the beginning of the report title. If necessary, decrease the font size of the title so that it does not overlap the date and so that it displays on one line. Create a paper or electronic printout as directed—two pages result. As directed, submit your database and the paper or electronic printout of the report that are the results of this project. Specifically, in this project, using your own name, you created the following database and printout or electronic printout:

1. Lastname_Firstname_1K_Student_Activities	Database file
2. Lastname Firstname 1K Event Details	Report (printout or electronic printout)

Performance Level

Performance Criteria		Exemplary	Proficient	Developing
	Create database using Desktop Event Management template and enter data	Database created using the correct template, named correctly, and all data entered correctly.	Database created using the correct template, named correctly, but not all data entered correctly.	Database created using the correct template, but numerous errors in database name and data.
	Modify report	Event Details report title includes name and project on one line.	Event Details report title includes name and project, but not on one line.	Event Details report title does not include name and project.
	Create report printout	Event Details report printout is correct.	Event Details printout is incorrect.	Event Details report printout not created.

END | You have completed Project 1K

OUTCOMES-BASED ASSESSMENTS

RUBRIC

The following outcomes-based assessments are *open-ended assessments*. That is, there is no specific correct result; your result will depend on your approach to the information provided. Make *Professional Quality* your goal. Use the following scoring rubric to guide you in *how* to approach the problem and then to evaluate *how well* your approach solves the problem.

The *criteria*—Software Mastery, Content, Format & Layout, and Process—represent the knowledge and skills you have gained that you can apply to solving the problem. The *levels of performance*—Professional Quality, Approaching Professional Quality, or Needs Quality Improvements—help you and your instructor evaluate your result.

	Your completed project is of Professional Quality if you:	Your completed project is Approaching Professional Quality if you:	Your completed project Needs Quality Improvements if you:
1-Software Mastery	Choose and apply the most appropriate skills, tools, and features and identify efficient methods to solve the problem.	Choose and apply some appropriate skills, tools, and features, but not in the most efficient manner.	Choose inappropriate skills, tools, or features, or are inefficient in solving the problem.
2-Content	Construct a solution that is clear and well organized, contains content that is accurate, appropriate to the audience and purpose, and is complete. Provide a solution that contains no errors in spelling, grammar, or style.	Construct a solution in which some components are unclear, poorly organized, inconsistent, or incomplete. Misjudge the needs of the audience. Have some errors in spelling, grammar, or style, but the errors do not detract from comprehension.	Construct a solution that is unclear, incomplete, or poorly organized; contains some inaccurate or inappropriate content; and contains many errors in spelling, grammar, or style. Do not solve the problem.
3-Format & Layout	Format and arrange all elements to communicate information and ideas, clarify function, illustrate relationships, and indicate relative importance.	Apply appropriate format and layout features to some elements, but not others. Overuse features, causing minor distraction.	Apply format and layout that does not communicate information or ideas clearly. Do not use format and layout features to clarify function, illustrate relationships, or indicate relative importance. Use available features excessively, causing distraction.
4-Process	Use an organized approach that integrates planning, development, self-assessment, revision, and reflection.	Demonstrate an organized approach in some areas, but not others; or, use an insufficient process of organization throughout.	Do not use an organized approach to solve the problem.

OUTCOMES-BASED ASSESSMENTS

Build from Scratch

GO! Think Project 1L Student Clubs

PROJECT FILES

For Project 1L, you will need the following files:

Blank desktop database
a01L_Clubs (Word document)
a01L_Student_Clubs (Excel workbook)
a01L_Club_Presidents (Excel workbook)

You will save your database as

Lastname_Firstname_1L_Student_Clubs

Dr. Daniel Martinez, vice president of Student Services, needs a database that tracks information about student clubs. The database should contain two tables—one for club information and one for contact information for the club presidents.

Create a desktop database, and save the database in your Access Chapter 1 folder as **Lastname_Firstname_1L_Student_Clubs** From your student data files, use the information in the Word document a01L_Clubs to create the first table and to enter two records. Name the table appropriately to include your name and 1L, and then append the 23 records from the Excel workbook a01L_Student_Clubs to your table. For the Club ID and President ID fields, add a description and change the field size.

Create a second table in the database by importing 25 records from the Excel workbook a01L_Club_Presidents, and name the table appropriately to include your name and 1L. For the State and Postal Code fields, add a description and change the field size. Be sure that the field data types are correct—recall that numbers that are not used in calculations should have a data type of Short Text. Be sure all of the data and field names display in each table.

Create a simple query based on the Clubs table that answers the question, *What is the club name, meeting day, meeting time, campus, and Room ID for all of the clubs?* Create a form based on the Clubs table, saving it with an appropriate name that includes your name and 1L. Create a report based on the Presidents table, saving it with an appropriate name that includes your name and 1L, that displays the president's last name (in ascending order), the president's first name, and the phone number of every president. Change the width of the three fields so that there is less space between them, but being sure that each record prints on a single line. Delete the page number from the report.

Create paper or electronic printouts of the two tables, the query, only Record 21 of the form, and the report as directed and being sure that each object prints on one page. Organize the objects on the Navigation Pane by Tables and Related Views, and be sure that all object names display fully. As directed, submit your database and the paper or electronic printouts of the five objects—two tables, one query, one form, and one report—that are the results of this project.

END | You have completed Project 1L

Build from Scratch

GO! Think Project 1M Faculty Training   Online

Build from Scratch

You and GO! Project 1N Personal Contacts   Online

Build from Scratch

GO! Cumulative Group Project Project 1O Bell Orchid Hotels
Online

Sort and Query a Database

GO! to Work
Video A2

PROJECT 2A	OUTCOMES Sort and query a database.

OBJECTIVES

1. Open and Save an Existing Database
2. Create Table Relationships
3. Sort Records in a Table
4. Create a Query in Design View
5. Create a New Query from an Existing Query
6. Sort Query Results
7. Specify Criteria in a Query

PROJECT 2B	OUTCOMES Create complex queries.

OBJECTIVES

8. Specify Numeric Criteria in a Query
9. Use Compound Criteria in a Query
10. Create a Query Based on More Than One Table
11. Use Wildcards in a Query
12. Create Calculated Fields in a Query
13. Calculate Statistics and Group Data in a Query
14. Create a Crosstab Query
15. Create a Parameter Query

In This Chapter

In this chapter, you will sort Access database tables and create and modify queries. To convert data into meaningful information, you must manipulate your data in a way that you can answer questions. One question might be: *Which students have a grade point average of 3.0 or higher?* By having this list of students, you could send information about scholarships or internships to those who meet the grade point average criteria. Queries are one of the most powerful tools in an Access database—a query not only answers questions, but it also provides data for meaningful reports.

The projects in this chapter relate to **Texas Lakes Community College**, which is located in the Austin, Texas, area. Its four campuses serve more than 30,000 students and offer more than 140 certificate programs and degrees. The college has a highly acclaimed Distance Education program and an extensive Workforce Development program. The college makes positive contributions to the community through cultural and athletic programs and has significant partnerships with businesses and nonprofit organizations. Popular fields of study include nursing and health care, solar technology, computer technology, and graphic design.

Instructors and Courses Database

PROJECT ACTIVITIES

In Activities 2.01 through 2.17, you will assist Dr. Carolyn Judkins, dean of the Business Division at the Northeast Campus of Texas Lakes Community College, in locating information about instructors and courses in the division. Your completed database objects will look similar to Figure 2.1.

PROJECT FILES

For Project 2A, you will need the following file:

a02A_Instructors_Courses

You will save your database as:

Lastname_Firstname_2A_Instructors_Courses

PROJECT RESULTS

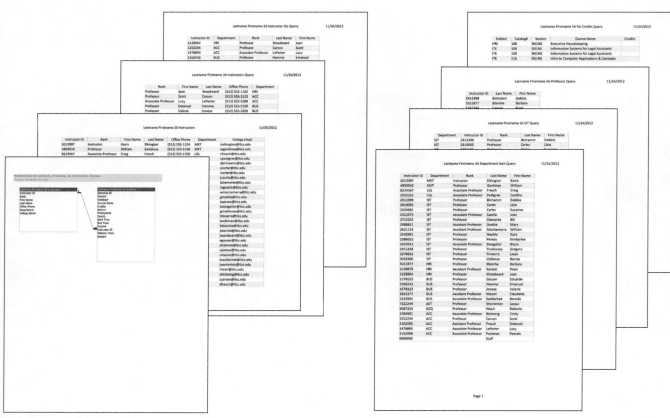

FIGURE 2.1 Project 2A Instructors and Courses

- Tap an item to click it.
- Press and hold for a few seconds to right-click; release when the information or command displays.
- Touch the screen with two or more fingers and then pinch together to zoom in or stretch your fingers apart to zoom out.
- Slide your finger on the screen to scroll—slide left to scroll right and slide right to scroll left.
- Slide to rearrange—similar to dragging with a mouse.
- Swipe from edge: from right to display charms; from left to expose open apps, snap apps, or close apps; from top or bottom to show commands or close an app.
- Swipe to select—slide an item a short distance with a quick movement—to select an item and bring up commands, if any.

Objective 1 Open and Save an Existing Database

Video A2-1

There will be instances when you need to work with a database and still keep the original, unaltered version of the database. Like the other Microsoft Office 2013 applications, you can open a database file and save it with another name.

Activity 2.01 | Opening and Saving an Existing Database

1 **Start** Access. In the Access opening screen, click **Open Other Files**. Under **Open**, click **Computer**, and then on the right, click **Browse**. In the **Open** dialog box, navigate to the location where your student data files for this chapter are stored, and then double-click **a02A_Instructors_Courses** to open the database.

2 On the ribbon, click the **FILE tab**, and then click **Save As**. Under **File Types**, be sure **Save Database As** is selected. On the right, under **Database File Types**, be sure **Access Database** is selected, and then at the bottom of the screen, click **Save As**.

The Access Database file type saves your database in a format that enables the database to be opened with Access 2007, Access 2010, or Access 2013. If you are sharing your database with individuals who have an earlier version of Access, you can save the database in a version that is compatible with that application, although some functionality might be lost if an earlier version of Access does not have the same feature as the later version of Access.

3 In the **Save As** dialog box, navigate to the location where you are saving your databases. Create a **New folder** named **Access Chapter 2**, and then **Open** the folder. Click in the **File name** box, drag to select the existing text, and using your own name, type **Lastname_ Firstname_2A_Instructors_Courses** and then click **Save** or press Enter.

Use this technique when you need to keep a copy of the original database file.

4 On the **Message Bar**, notice the **SECURITY WARNING**. In the **Navigation Pane**, notice that this database contains two table objects. Compare your screen with Figure 2.2.

FIGURE 2.2

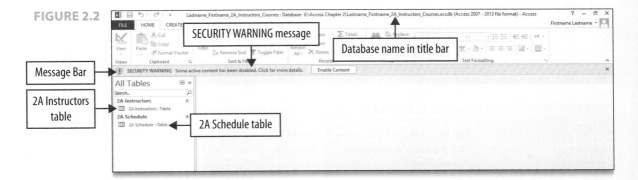

The ***Message Bar*** is the area directly below the ribbon that displays information such as security alerts when there is potentially unsafe, active content in an Office document that you open. Settings that determine the alerts that display on your Message Bar are set in the Access ***Trust Center***, an area in Access where you can view the security and privacy settings for your Access installation.

You may not be able to change the settings in the Trust Center, depending upon decisions made by your organization. To display the Trust Center, click the FILE tab, click Options, and then click Trust Center.

1 On the **Message Bar**, click **Enable Content**.

When working with the student data files that accompany this textbook, repeat this action each time you see the security warning. Databases for this textbook are safe to use on your computer.

2 In the **Navigation Pane**, right-click the **2A Instructors** table, and then click **Rename**. With the table name selected and using your own name, type **Lastname Firstname 2A Instructors** and then press Enter to rename the table. Use the same technique to **Rename** the **2A Schedule** table to **Lastname Firstname 2A Schedule**

Including your name in the table enables you and your instructor to easily identify your work, because Access includes the table name in the header of your paper or electronic printouts.

3 Point to the right edge of the **Navigation Pane** to display the ⟷ pointer. Drag to the right to increase the width of the pane until both table names display fully.

Objective 2 | Create Table Relationships

Video A2-2

Access databases are relational databases because the tables in the database can relate—actually connect—to other tables through common fields. Recall that common fields are fields in two or more tables that store the same data; for example, a Student ID number may be stored in two tables in the same database.

After you have a table for each subject in your database, you must provide a way to connect the data in the tables when you need to obtain meaningful information from the stored data. To do this, create common fields in the related tables, and then define table ***relationships***. A relationship is an association that you establish between two tables based on common fields. After the relationship is established, you can create a query, form, or report that displays information from more than one table.

In this activity, you will select the two tables in the database that you will use to establish the table relationship and identify the common field that will connect the tables.

1 In the **Navigation Pane**, double-click your **2A Instructors** table to open it in the object window. Examine the fields in the table. Double-click your **2A Schedule** table, and examine the fields in the table.

In the 2A Instructors table, *Instructor ID* is the primary key field, which ensures that each instructor has only one record in the table. No two instructors have the same Instructor ID.

In the 2A Schedule table, *Schedule ID* is the primary key field. Every scheduled course section during an academic term has a unique Schedule ID. Some colleges refer to this as the *Section Number.*

2 In the **2A Schedule** table, scroll to display the **Instructor ID** field—third from last column—and then compare your screen with Figure 2.3.

Both the 2A Instructors table and the 2A Schedule table include the *Instructor ID* field, which is the common field of the two tables. Because *one* instructor can teach *many* different courses, *one* Instructor ID can be present *many* times in the 2A Schedule table. When the relationship is established, it will be a ***one-to-many relationship***, which is the most common type of relationship in a relational database.

FIGURE 2.3

3 In the object window, right-click the **2A Schedule object tab**, and then click **Close All** to close both tables. On the ribbon, click the **DATABASE TOOLS tab**, and then in the **Relationships group**, click **Relationships**. Compare your screen with Figure 2.4.

You can close all of the open objects by right-clicking any object tab. The Show Table dialog box displays in the Relationships window. In the Show Table dialog box, the Tables tab displays the two tables that are in this database.

FIGURE 2.4

4 Point to the title bar of the **Show Table** dialog box, and then drag downward and to the right to move the dialog box away from the top of the **Relationships** window.

Moving the Show Table dialog box enables you to see the tables as they are added to the Relationships window.

5 In the **Show Table** dialog box, if necessary, click your **2A Instructors** table, and then click **Add**. In the **Show Table** dialog box, double-click your **2A Schedule** table to add it to the **Relationships** window. In the **Show Table** dialog box, click **Close**, and then compare your screen with Figure 2.5.

You can use either technique to add a table to the Relationships window. A ***field list***—a list of the field names in a table—for each of the two table objects displays, and each table's primary key is identified by the key icon. Although this database has only two tables, larger databases have many tables. Scroll bars in a field list indicate that there are fields that are not currently in view.

FIGURE 2.5

6 In the **2A Schedule** field list—the field list on the right—point to the title bar to display the ☐ pointer. Drag the field list to the right until there are about two inches of space between the field lists.

7 In the **2A Instructors** field list—the field list on the left—point to the lower right corner of the field list to display the ☐ pointer, and then drag downward and to the right to increase the height and width of the field list until the entire name of the table in the title bar displays and all of the field names display.

This action enables you to see all of the available fields and removes the vertical scroll bar.

8 Use the same technique to resize the **2A Schedule** field list so that the table name and all of the field names display as shown in Figure 2.6.

Recall that *one* instructor can teach *many* scheduled courses. The arrangement of field lists in the Relationships window displays the *one table* on the left side and the *many table* on the right side. Recall also that the primary key in each table is the field that contains the data that uniquely identifies each record in the table. In the 2A Instructors table, each instructor is uniquely identified by the Instructor ID. In the 2A Schedule table, each scheduled course section is uniquely identified by the Schedule ID.

FIGURE 2.6

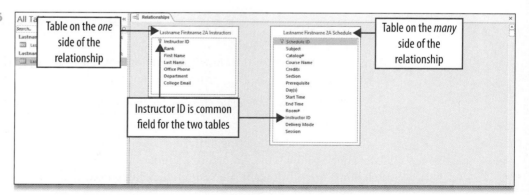

9 In the **2A Instructors** field list, point to **Instructor ID**, and then drag the field name downward and to the right into the **2A Schedule** field list until the ▨ pointer's arrow is on top of **Instructor ID**. Release the mouse button to display the **Edit Relationships** dialog box.

As you drag, a small graphic displays to indicate that you are dragging a field name from one field list to another. A table relationship works by matching data in two fields—the common field. In these two tables, the common field has the same name—*Instructor ID*. Common fields are not required to have the same name; however, they must have the same data type and field size.

ANOTHER WAY   On the DESIGN tab, in the Tools group, click Edit Relationships. In the Edit Relationships dialog box, click Create New. In the Create New dialog box, designate the tables and fields that will create the relationship and click OK.

10 Point to the title bar of the **Edit Relationships** dialog box, and then drag the dialog box downward and to the right below the two field lists as shown in Figure 2.7.

By dragging the common field, you create the *one-to-many* relationship. In the 2A Instructors table, Instructor ID is the primary key. In the 2A Schedule table, Instructor ID is the **foreign key** field. The foreign key is the field in the related table used to connect to the primary key in another table. The field on the *one* side of the relationship is typically the primary key.

FIGURE 2.7

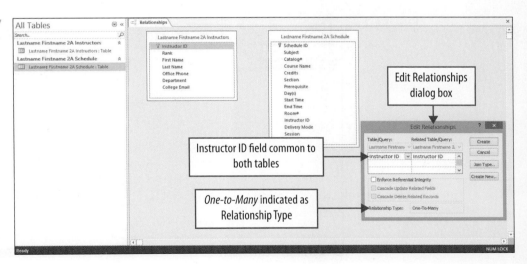

Edit Relationships dialog box

Instructor ID field common to both tables

One-to-Many indicated as Relationship Type

Activity 2.04 | Setting Relationship Options

In this activity, you will set relationship options that enable you to work with records in the two related tables.

1 In the **Edit Relationships** dialog box, click to select the **Enforce Referential Integrity** check box. Notice that the two options under **Enforce Referential Integrity** are now available.

Referential integrity is a set of rules that Access uses to ensure that the data between related tables is valid. Enforcing referential integrity ensures that an Instructor ID cannot be added to a course in the 2A Schedule table if the Instructor ID is *not* included in the 2A Instructors table. Similarly, enforcing referential integrity without selecting a cascade option below ensures that you cannot delete an instructor from the 2A Instructors table if there is a course that has been assigned to that instructor in the 2A Schedule table.

After selecting Enforce Referential Integrity, *cascade options*—relationship options that enable you to update records in related tables when referential integrity is enforced—become available for use.

2 In the **Edit Relationships** dialog box, click to select the **Cascade Update Related Fields** check box.

The ***Cascade Update Related Fields*** option enables you to change the data in the primary key field for the table on the *one* side of the relationship, and updates that change to any fields in the related table that store the same data. For example, in the 2A Instructors table, if you change the data in the Instructor ID field for one instructor, Access automatically finds every scheduled course assigned to that instructor in the 2A Schedule table and changes the data in the common field, in this case, the Instructor ID field. Without this option, if you try to change the Instructor ID number for an instructor, an error message displays if there is a related record in the related table on the *many* side of the relationship.

3 In the **Edit Relationships** dialog box, click to select the **Cascade Delete Related Records** check box, and then compare your screen with Figure 2.8.

The ***Cascade Delete Related Records*** option enables you to delete a record in the table on the *one* side of the relationship and also delete all of the related records in related tables. For example, if an instructor retires or leaves the college and the courses that the instructor teaches must be canceled because no other instructor can be found, you can delete the instructor's record from the 2A Instructors table, and then all of the courses that are assigned to that instructor in the 2A Schedule table are also deleted. Without this option, an error message displays if you try to delete the instructor's record from the 2A Instructors table.

FIGURE 2.8

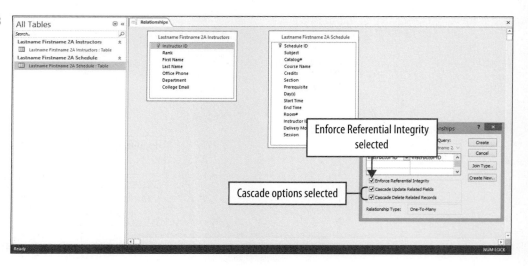

4 In the **Edit Relationships** dialog box, click **Create**, and then compare your screen with Figure 2.9.

The Edit Relationships dialog box closes and a ***join line***—the line connecting or joining the two tables—displays between the two field lists. The join line connects the primary key field—Instructor ID—in the 2A Instructors field list to the common field—Instructor ID—in the 2A Schedule field list. On the join line, *1* indicates the *one* side of the relationship, and the infinity symbol (∞) indicates the *many* side of the relationship. These symbols display when referential integrity is enforced.

FIGURE 2.9

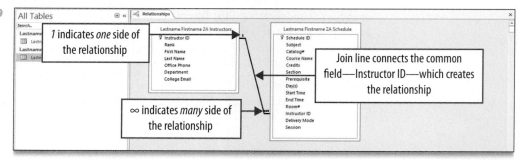

The Relationships window provides a map of how your database tables are related, and you can print and save this information as a report.

1 Under **RELATIONSHIP TOOLS**, on the **DESIGN tab**, in the **Tools group**, click **Relationship Report**.

The report is created and displays in the object window in Print Preview.

2 On the **PRINT PREVIEW tab**, in the **Page Size group**, click **Margins**, and then click **Normal** to increase the margins slightly—some printers cannot print with narrow margins. Compare your screen with Figure 2.10. Create a paper or electronic printout of the relationship report as directed.

FIGURE 2.10

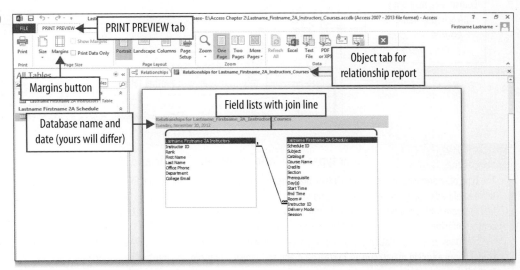

3 On the **Quick Access Toolbar**, click **Save**. In the **Save As** dialog box, click **OK** to accept the default report name.

The report name displays in the Navigation Pane under *Unrelated Objects*. Because the report is just a map of the relationship between the tables, and not a report containing records from a table, it is not associated with or related to any tables.

4 In the object window, click **Close** × to close the report, and then **Close** × the **Relationships** window.

> **NOTE** **Close Print Preview and the Relationship Report**
>
> If you click Close Print Preview when the report is displayed in Print Preview, the Relationship Report displays in Design view in the object window. If this happens, you can Close the object while it is displayed in this view.

Activity 2.06 | Displaying Subdatasheet Records

When you open the table on the *one* side of the relationship, the related records from the table on the *many* side are available for you to view and to modify.

1 In the **Navigation Pane**, double-click your **2A Instructors** table to open it in the object window, and then **Close** « the **Navigation Pane**.

2 On the left side of the first record—*Instructor ID* of *1224567*—click ⊞, and then compare your screen with Figure 2.11.

The ⊞ symbol to the left of a record in a table indicates that *related* records may exist in another table. Click ⊞ to display the related records in a **subdatasheet**. In the first record for *Craig Fresch*, you can see that related records exist in the 2A Schedule table—he is scheduled to teach five LGL (Legal) courses. The ⊞ symbol to the left of each record displays because you created a relationship between the two tables using the Instructor ID field—the common field.

When you click ⊞ to display the subdatasheet, the symbol changes to ⊟, an indication that the subdatasheet is expanded. Click ⊟ to collapse the subdatasheet.

FIGURE 2.11

Course sections from your 2A Schedule table for *Associate Professor Craig Fresch*

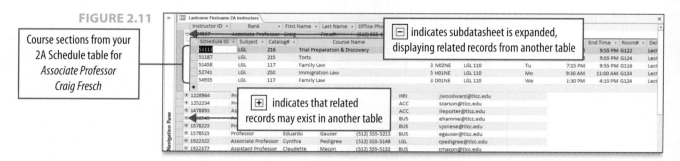

⊟ indicates subdatasheet is expanded, displaying related records from another table

⊞ indicates that related records may exist in another table

Other Types of Relationships: One-to-One and Many-to-Many

The type of relationship is determined by the placement of the primary key field. A one-to-one relationship exists between two tables when a record in one table is related to only one record in a second table. In this case, both tables use the same field as the primary key. This is most often used when data is placed in a separate table because access to that information is restricted; for example, using an Employee ID field as the primary key field, there is one table for contact information and a second table with payroll information.

A many-to-many relationship between tables exists when many records in one table are related to many records in another table. For example, many students can enroll in many courses. To create a many-to-many relationship, you must create a third table that contains the primary key fields from both tables. In the Relationships window, you create a join line from this table to the other two tables. In effect, you create multiple one-to-many relationships.

Activity 2.07 | Testing Cascade Options

Recall that cascade options enable you to make changes to records on the *one* side table of the relationship and update or delete records in the table on the *many* side of the relationship. In this activity, you will change the data in the Instructor ID field—the primary key field—for one instructor, and then delete all of the records associated with another instructor from both tables.

1 In the subdatasheet for the first record—*Instructor ID* of *1224567*—notice that the first course that this instructor is scheduled to teach has a *Schedule ID* of *51113—LGL 216*. In the **2A Instructors** table, to the left of the first record, click ⊟ to collapse the subdatasheet.

2 If necessary, in the first record, in the **Instructor ID** field, select the data—**1224567**. Type **8224567** and then press ↓ to save the record.

Because you enabled Cascade Update Related Fields in the Edit Relationships dialog box, you can change the data in the Instructor ID field—the primary key field—and all records in the 2A Schedule table that store that Instructor ID number are automatically updated. If this option is not enabled, an error message displays.

3 Open » the **Navigation Pane**. In the **Navigation Pane**, double-click your **2A Schedule** table to open it, and then **Close** « the **Navigation Pane**.

🔄 ANOTHER WAY   Press F11 to open or close the Navigation Pane.

4 Scroll to locate the record with a **Schedule ID** of **51113**—*LGL 216*. If necessary, scroll to the right to display the **Instructor ID** field, and notice that for this record, the **Instructor ID** is **8224567**. Compare your screen with Figure 2.12.

The Cascade Update Related Fields option enables you to change the data in the primary key field in your 2A Instructors table, and the five related records for *Craig Fresch* in the 2A Schedule table were updated to store his new Instructor ID of *8224567*.

FIGURE 2.12

Course assigned to *Craig Fresch*

Instructor ID updated by changing Instructor ID in 2A Instructors table

5 **Close** ☒ your **2A Schedule** table. In your **2A Instructors** table, scroll to display the last few records. On the left side of the record for **Instructor ID** of **6145288**—*Professor Ivey Clarke*—click ⊞ to display the subdatasheet. Notice that this instructor is scheduled to teach two courses—*Schedule IDs* of *42837* and *42930*.

6 Click ⊟ to collapse the subdatasheet. For the same record—*Instructor ID* of *6145288*—point to the record selector box to display the ➡ pointer, and then click to select the record. On the **HOME tab**, in the **Records group**, click **Delete**.

A message displays warning you that this record and related records in related tables will be deleted. The record you selected does not display in the table, and the next record is selected. Because you enabled Cascade Delete Related Records, you are able to delete the record for Professor Ivey Clarke and delete the two courses she is scheduled to teach from the 2A Schedule table—with no error message.

🔄 **ANOTHER WAY** With the record selected, press ⌈Del⌉; or with the record selected, right-click within the record, and then click Delete Record.

7 In the message box, click **Yes**.

The record for *Instructor ID* of *6145288* is deleted, and the two courses she was scheduled to teach are deleted from the 2A Schedule table. On the Quick Access Toolbar, Undo is unavailable—if you mistakenly delete a record and its related records, you must enter them again in both tables.

8 **Open** ⟫ the **Navigation Pane**, open your **2A Schedule** table, and then **Close** ⟪ the **Navigation Pane**. Scroll through the records and notice that the records for a **Schedule ID** of **42837** and **42930** have been deleted from the table.

The Cascade Delete Related Records option in the Edit Relationships dialog box enables you to delete a record in the table on the *one* side of the relationship—2A Instructors—and simultaneously delete the records in the table on the *many* side of the relationship—2A Schedule—that are related to the deleted record.

9 In the object window, right-click either **object tab**, and then click **Close All** to close both tables.

Video A2-3

Sorting is the process of arranging data in a specific order based on the value in a field. For example, you can sort the names in your contact list alphabetically by each person's last name, or you can sort your music collection by the artist. Initially, records in an Access table display in the order they are entered into the table. After you close the table and reopen it, the records display in order by the primary key field.

Activity 2.08 | Sorting Records in a Table in Ascending or Descending Order

In this activity, you will determine the departments of the faculty in the Business Division by sorting the data. Data can be sorted in either *ascending order* or *descending order*. Ascending order sorts text alphabetically (A to Z) and sorts numbers from the lowest number to the highest number. Descending order sorts text in reverse alphabetical order (Z to A) and sorts numbers from the highest number to the lowest number.

1 **Open** [»] the **Navigation Pane**, open your **2A Instructors** table, and then **Close** [«] the **Navigation Pane**. Notice that the records in the table are sorted in ascending order by the **Instructor ID** field, which is the primary key field.

2 In the field names row, click the **Department arrow**, click **Sort A to Z**, and then compare your screen with Figure 2.13.

To sort records in a table, click the arrow to the right of the field name in the column on which you want to sort, and then click the sort order. After a field is sorted, a small arrow in the field name box indicates the sort order. For the Department field, the small arrow points upward, indicating an ascending sort; on the ribbon, Ascending is selected.

The records display in alphabetical order by the Department field. Because the department names are now grouped together, you can quickly scroll through the table to see the instructors for each department. The first record in the table has no data in the Department field because the *Instructor ID* of 9999999 is reserved for *Staff*, a designation that is used until a scheduled course has been assigned to a specific instructor.

ANOTHER WAY   Click in the field in any record, and then on the HOME tab, in the Sort & Filter group, click Ascending; or right-click in the field in any record, and then click Sort A to Z.

FIGURE 2.13

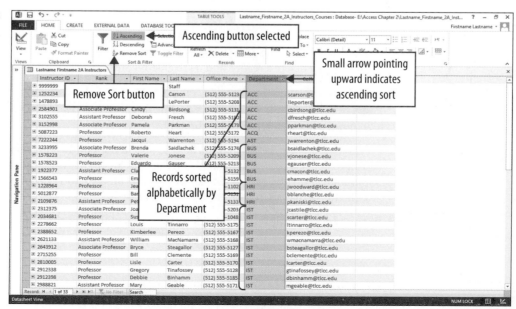

3 On the **HOME tab**, in the **Sort & Filter group**, click **Remove Sort** to clear the sort and to return the records to the default sort order, which is by the primary key field—**Instructor ID**.

4 Click the **Last Name arrow**, and then click **Sort Z to A**.

The records in the table are sorted by the Last Name field in reverse alphabetical order. The small arrow in the field name box points downward, indicating a descending sort. On the ribbon, Descending is selected.

5 In the **Sort & Filter group**, click **Remove Sort** to clear the sort.

Activity 2.09 | Sorting Records in a Table on Multiple Fields

To sort a table on two or more fields, first identify the fields that will act as the ***outermost sort field*** and the ***innermost sort field***. The outermost sort field is the first level of sorting, and the innermost sort field is the second level of sorting. To alphabetize a table by Last Name and then First Name—also called First Name within Last Name—the Last Name field is identified as the outermost sort field. If there are duplicate last names, the records should be further sorted by the First Name field—the innermost sort field. For tables, you sort the *innermost* field *first* and then sort the outermost field.

In this activity, you will sort the records by Last Name—innermost sort field—within the Department—outermost sort field.

1 In the **Last Name** field, click in any record. On the ribbon, on the **HOME tab**, in the **Sort & Filter group**, click **Ascending**.

The records are sorted in ascending order by Last Name—the innermost sort field.

2 In any record, point in the **Department** field, right-click, and then click **Sort Z to A**. Compare your screen with Figure 2.14.

The records are sorted in descending order first by Department—the outermost sort field. Within each Department grouping, the records are sorted in ascending order by Last Name—the innermost sort field. Records can be sorted on multiple fields using both ascending and descending order.

FIGURE 2.14

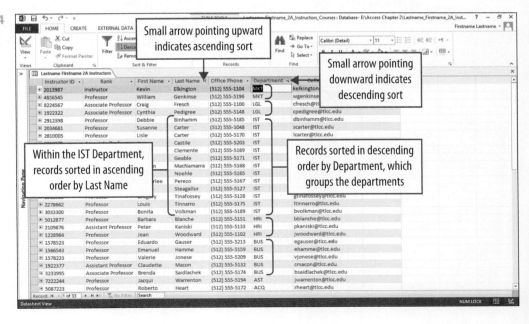

3 On the ribbon, click the **FILE tab**, click **Print**, and then click **Print Preview**. On the **PRINT PREVIEW tab**, in the **Page Layout group**, click **Landscape**. In the **Zoom group**, click **Two Pages**, and notice that the table will print on two pages.

4 In the **Print group**, click **Print**. In the **Print** dialog box, under **Print Range**, click in the **From** box, type **1** and then click in the **To** box. Type **1** to print only the first page. If directed to submit a paper printout, click **OK**. If directed to create an electronic printout, in the **Print** dialog box, click **Cancel**. On the **PRINT PREVIEW tab**, in the **Data group**, click **PDF or XPS**, click **Options**, and then under **Range**, click the **Pages** option button, click **OK**, and then click **Publish**.

5 In the object window, **Close** ☒ the table. In the message box, click **Yes** to save the changes to the sort order.

6 **Open** ☒ the **Navigation Pane**, double-click your **2A Instructors** table to open it, and then **Close** ☒ the **Navigation Pane**. Notice that the table displays the sort order you specified.

7 On the **HOME tab**, in the **Sort & Filter group**, click **Remove Sort**. **Close** ☒ the table, and in the message box, click **Yes** to save the table with the sort removed.

> Generally, tables are not stored with the data sorted. Instead, queries are created that sort the data, and then reports are created to display the sorted data.

Objective 4   Create a Query in Design View

Video A2-4

Recall that a select query is a database object that retrieves (selects) specific data from one or more tables and then displays the specified data in a table in Datasheet view. A query answers a question, such as *Which instructors teach courses in the IST department?* Unless a query has already been designed to ask this question, you must create a new query.

Database users rarely need to see all of the records in all of the tables. That is why a query is so useful; it creates a *subset* of records—a portion of the total records—according to your specifications and then displays only those records.

Activity 2.10   Creating a New Select Query in Design View

Previously, you created a query using the Query Wizard. To create more complex queries, use Query Design view. The table (or tables) from which a query selects its data is referred to as the *data source*.

1 On the ribbon, click the **CREATE tab**, and then in the **Queries group**, click **Query Design**. Compare your screen with Figure 2.15.

> A new query opens in Design view, and the Show Table dialog box displays, which lists both tables in the database.

FIGURE 2.15

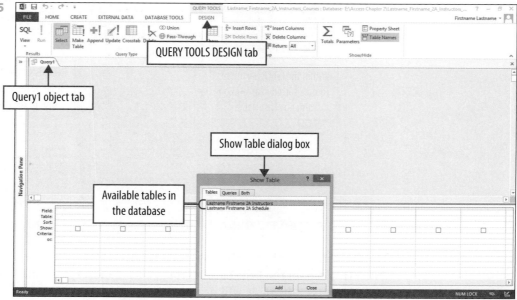

2 In the **Show Table** dialog box, double-click **2A Instructors**, and then, in the dialog box, click **Close**.

> A field list for your 2A Instructors table displays in the upper area of the query window. Instructor ID is the primary key field in this table.

> The query window has two parts: the upper area called the *table area* that displays the field lists for tables that are used in the query, and the lower area called the *design grid* that displays the design of the query.

ALERT! **Is There More Than One Field List in the Table Area?**

If you double-click a table more than one time, a duplicate field list displays in the table area of the query window. To remove a field list from the query window, right-click the title bar of the field list, and then click Remove Table.

3 Point to the lower right corner of the field list to display the pointer, and then drag downward and to the right to resize the field list, displaying all of the field names and the entire table name. In the **2A Instructors** field list, double-click **Rank**, and then look at the design grid.

> The Rank field name displays in the design grid in the Field row. You limit the fields that display in the query results by placing only the desired field names in the design grid.

4 In the **2A Instructors** field list, point to **First Name**, drag the field name down into the design grid until the pointer displays in the **Field** row in the second column, and then release the mouse button. Compare your screen with Figure 2.16.

> This is a second way to add field names to the design grid. As you drag the field, a small rectangular shape attaches to the mouse pointer. When you release the mouse button, the field name displays in the Field row.

FIGURE 2.16

5 In the design grid, in the **Field** row, click in the third column, and then click the **arrow** that displays. From the list, click **Last Name** to add the field to the design grid.

> This is a third way to add field names to the design grid.

6 Using one of the three techniques you just practiced, add the **Office Phone** field to the fourth column and the **Department** field to the fifth column in the design grid.

ALERT! **Is There a Duplicate Field Name or an Incorrect Field Name in the Design Grid?**

If you double-click a field name more than one time, a duplicate field name displays in the design grid. To remove a duplicate field name, in the design grid, in the Field row, right-click the duplicate field name, and then click Cut. Use this same method to delete a field name that you placed in the design grid by mistake. As you progress in your study of query design, you will learn alternate ways to delete field names from the design grid.

Activity 2.11 | Running, Saving, Printing, and Closing a Query

After you design a query, you *run* the query to display the results. When you run a query, Access looks at the records in the table (or tables) you have included in the query, finds the records that match the specified conditions (if any), and displays only those records in a datasheet. Only the fields that you have added to the design grid display in the query results. The query always runs using the current table or tables, presenting the most up-to-date information.

> **1** Under **QUERY TOOLS**, on the **DESIGN tab**, in the **Results group**, click **Run**, and then compare your screen with Figure 2.17.

This query answers the question, *What is the rank, first name, last name, office phone number, and department of all of the instructors in the 2A Instructors table?* A query is a subset of the records in the table, arranged in Datasheet view, using the fields and conditions that you specify in the design grid. The five fields you specified in the design grid display in columns, and the records from the 2A Instructors table display in rows.

 ANOTHER WAY   On the DESIGN tab, in the Results group, click the top portion of the View button, which runs the query by switching to Datasheet view.

FIGURE 2.17

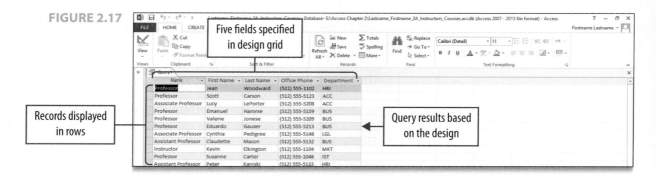

> **2** On the **Quick Access Toolbar**, click **Save** 🖫. In the **Save As** dialog box, type **Lastname Firstname 2A Instructors Query** and then click **OK**.

The query name displays on the object tab in the object window. Save your queries if you are likely to ask the same question again; doing so will save you the effort of creating the query again to answer the same question.

ALERT!   **Does a Message Display After Entering a Query Name?**

Query names are limited to 64 characters. For all projects, if you have a long last name or first name that results in your query name exceeding the 64-character limit, use your first initial instead of your first name.

> **3** On the ribbon, click the **FILE tab**, click **Print**, and then click **Print Preview**. Create a paper or electronic printout as directed, and then click **Close Print Preview**.

Queries answer questions and gather information from the data in tables. Typically, queries are created as a basis for a report, but query results can be printed just like any table of data.

> **4** Close ⊠ the query. Open » the **Navigation Pane**, and then notice that your **2A Instructors Query** object displays under your **2A Instructors** table object.

The new query name displays in the Navigation Pane under the table with which it is related—the 2A Instructors table, which is the data source. Only the design of the query is saved; the records reside in the table object. Each time you open a query, Access runs it again and displays the results based on the data stored in the data source. Thus, the results of the query always reflect the most up-to-date information.

Video A2-5

You can create a new query from scratch, or you can copy an existing query and modify the design to answer another question. Using an existing query saves you time if your new query uses all or some of the same fields and conditions in an existing query.

Activity 2.12 | Copying an Existing Query

1 In the **Navigation Pane**, right-click your **2A Instructors Query**, and then click **Copy**.

> **ANOTHER WAY**   To create a copy of the query, in the Navigation Pane, click the query name to select it. On the HOME tab, in the Clipboard group, click Copy.

2 In the **Navigation Pane**, point to a blank area, right-click, and then click **Paste**.

The Paste As dialog box displays, which enables you to name the copied query.

> **ANOTHER WAY**   On the HOME tab, in the Clipboard group, click Paste.

3 In the **Paste As** dialog box, type **Lastname Firstname 2A Instructor IDs Query** and then click **OK**.

A new query, based on a copy of your 2A Instructors Query is created and displays in the Navigation Pane under its data source—your 2A Instructors table object.

4 In the **Navigation Pane**, double-click your **2A Instructor IDs Query** to run the query and open the query results in **Datasheet** view. **Close** « the **Navigation Pane**.

Activity 2.13 | Modifying the Design of a Query

1 On the **HOME tab**, in the **Views group**, click the top portion of the **View** button to switch to **Design** view.

> **ANOTHER WAY**   On the HOME tab, in the Views group, click the View arrow, and then click Design View; or on the right side of the status bar, click Design View. If the query is not open, in the Navigation Pane, right-click the query name, and then click Design View.

2 In the design grid, point to the thin gray selection bar above the **Office Phone** field name to display the ↓ pointer, and then compare your screen with Figure 2.18.

FIGURE 2.18

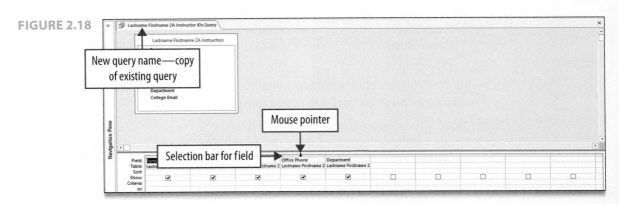

3 With the ⬇ pointer displayed in the selection bar above the **Office Phone** field name, click to select the column, and then press Del.

> This action deletes the field from the query design only—it has no effect on the field in the data source—2A Instructors table. The Department field moves to the left. Similarly, by using the selection bar, you can drag to select multiple fields and delete them at one time.

ANOTHER WAY   In the design grid, click in the field name. On the DESIGN tab, in the Query Setup group, click Delete Columns; or right-click the field name, and then click Cut; or select the column, and on the HOME tab, in the Records group, click Delete.

4 Point to the selection bar above the **First Name** column, and then click to select the column. In the selected column, point to the selection bar, hold down the left mouse button to display the ⬚ pointer, and then drag to the right until a dark vertical line displays on the right side of the **Last Name** column. Release the mouse button to position the **First Name** field in the third column.

> To rearrange fields in a query, first select the field to move, and then drag it to a new position in the design grid.

5 Using the technique you just practiced, move the **Department** field to the left of the **Rank** field.

6 From the field list, drag the **Instructor ID** field down to the first column in the design grid until the ⬚ pointer displays, and then release the mouse button. Compare your screen with Figure 2.19.

> The Instructor ID field displays in the first column, and the remaining four fields move to the right. Use this method to insert a field to the left of a field already displayed in the design grid.

FIGURE 2.19

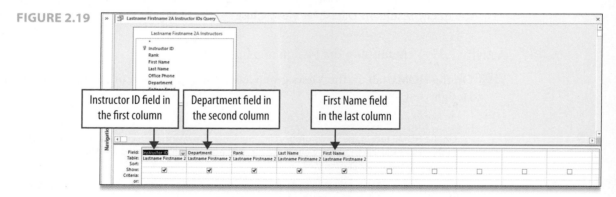

7 On the **DESIGN tab**, in the **Results group**, click **Run**.

> This query answers the question, *What is the instructor ID, department, rank, last name, and first name of every instructor in the 2A Instructors table?* The results of the query are a subset of the records stored in the 2A Instructors table. The records are sorted by the table's primary key field—Instructor ID.

8 On the **FILE tab**, click **Print**, and then click **Print Preview**. Create a paper or electronic printout as directed, and then click **Close Print Preview**.

9 **Close** ✕ the query. In the message box, click **Yes** to save the changes to the query design—deleting a field, moving two fields, and adding a field. **Open** » the **Navigation Pane**.

> The query is saved and closed, and the query name displays in the Navigation Pane under the related table. Recall that only the *design* of the query is saved; the records reside in the related table.

Video A2-6

You can sort the results of a query in ascending or descending order in either Datasheet view or Design view. Use Design view if your query results should always display in a specified sort order or if you intend to use the sorted results in a report.

Activity 2.14 | Sorting Query Results

In this activity, you will copy an existing query and then sort the query results by using the Sort row in Design view.

1 In the **Navigation Pane**, right-click your **2A Instructor IDs Query**, and then click **Copy**. In the **Navigation Pane**, point to a blank area, right-click, and then click **Paste**.

2 In the **Paste As** dialog box, type **Lastname Firstname 2A Department Sort Query** and then click **OK**. Increase the width of the **Navigation Pane** so that the names of all of the objects display fully.

> A new query is created based on a copy of your 2A Instructor IDs Query; that is, the new query includes the same fields in the same order as the query that you copied.

3 In the **Navigation Pane**, right-click your **2A Department Sort Query**, and then click **Design View. Close** « the **Navigation Pane**.

> Use this technique to display the query in Design view if you are redesigning the query. Recall that if you double-click a query name in the Navigation Pane, Access runs the query and displays the query results.

4 In the design grid, in the **Sort** row, under **Last Name**, click to display the insertion point and an arrow. Click the **arrow**, click **Ascending**, and then compare your screen with Figure 2.20.

FIGURE 2.20

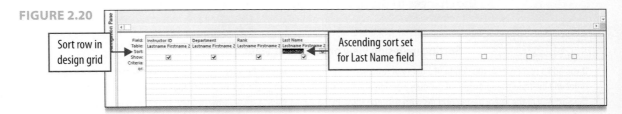

Sort row in design grid

Ascending sort set for Last Name field

5 On the **DESIGN tab**, in the **Results group**, click **Run**.

> In the query results, the records are sorted in ascending order by the Last Name field, and two instructors have the same last name of *Carter*—*Susanne* and *Lisle*.

6 On the **HOME tab**, in the **Views group**, click the top of the **View** button to switch to **Design** view.

7 In the design grid, click in the **Sort** row under **First Name**, click the **arrow**, and then click **Ascending. Run** the query.

> In the query results, the records are sorted first by the Last Name field. If two instructors have the same last name, then those records are sorted by the First Name field. The two instructors with the same last name of *Carter* are sorted by their first names, and the two records with the same last name of *Fresch* are sorted by their first names.

8 Switch to **Design** view. In the design grid, click in the **Sort** row under **Department**, click the **arrow**, and then click **Descending**. **Run** the query, and then compare your screen with Figure 2.21.

In Design view, fields with a Sort setting are sorted from left to right. That is, the sorted field on the left becomes the outermost sort field, and the sorted field on the right becomes the innermost sort field. Thus, the records in this query are sorted first in descending order by the Department field—the leftmost sort field. Then, within each department, the records are sorted in ascending order by the Last Name field. And, finally, within each duplicate last name, the records are sorted in ascending order by the First Name field.

If you run a query and the sorted results are not what you intended, be sure the fields are displayed from left to right according to the groupings that you desire.

FIGURE 2.21

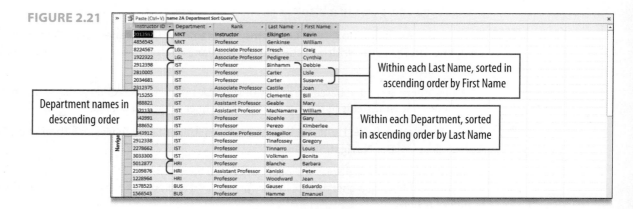

9 Display the query results in **Print Preview**. Create a paper or electronic printout as directed, and then click **Close Print Preview**. **Close** ☒ the query. In the message box, click **Yes** to save the changes to the query design.

More Knowledge | **Sorting in Design View or Datasheet View**

If you add a sort order to the *design* of a query, it remains as a permanent part of the query design. If you use the sort buttons in Datasheet view, the sort order will override the sort order of the query design and can be saved as part of the query. A sort order designated in Datasheet view does not display in the Sort row of the query design grid. As with sorting tables, in Datasheet view, a small arrow displays to the right of the field name to indicate the sort order of the field.

Objective 7 | Specify Criteria in a Query

Video A2-7

Queries locate information in a table based on *criteria* that you specify as part of the query design. Criteria are conditions that identify the specific records that you are looking for. Criteria enable you to ask a more specific question; therefore, you will get a more specific result. For example, to find out how many instructors are in the IST department, limit the results to display only that specific department by entering criteria in the design grid.

Activity 2.15 | Specifying Text Criteria in a Query

In this activity, you will assist Dean Judkins by creating a query to answer the question, *How many instructors are in the IST Department?*

1 On the ribbon, click the **CREATE tab**, and then in the **Queries group**, click **Query Design**.

2 In the **Show Table** dialog box, double-click your **2A Instructors** table to add it to the table area, and then **Close** the **Show Table** dialog box.

3 By dragging the lower right corner downward and to the right, resize the field list to display all of the field names and the table name. Add the following fields to the design grid in the order given: **Department**, **Instructor ID**, **Rank**, **Last Name**, and **First Name**.

4 In the design grid, click in the **Criteria** row under **Department**, type **IST** and then press ⏎. Compare your screen with Figure 2.22.

Access places quotation marks around the criteria to indicate that this is a *text string*—a sequence of characters. Use the Criteria row to specify the criteria that will limit the results of the query to your exact specifications. The criteria is not case sensitive; you can type *ist* instead of *IST*.

FIGURE 2.22

Criteria row in design grid

Access adds quotation marks to text

Five fields added to design grid

NOTE | **Pressing Enter After Adding Criteria**

After adding criteria, when you press ⏎ or click in another column or row in the query design grid, you can see how Access alters the criteria so it can interpret what you have typed. Sometimes there is no change, such as when you add criteria to a field that stores a numeric or currency value. Other times, Access capitalizes a letter or adds quotation marks, words, or other symbols to clarify the criteria. Pressing ⏎ after adding criteria has no effect on the query results; it is used here to help you see how the program behaves.

5 In the design grid, click in the **Sort** row under **Last Name**, click the **arrow**, and then click **Ascending**. Click in the **Sort** row under **First Name**, click the **arrow**, and then click **Ascending**.

6 **Run** the query, and then compare your screen with Figure 2.23.

Thirteen records display. There are 13 instructors in the IST Department; or, more specifically, there are 13 records that have *IST* in the Department field. The records are sorted in ascending order, first by the Last Name field and then by the First Name field.

FIGURE 2.23

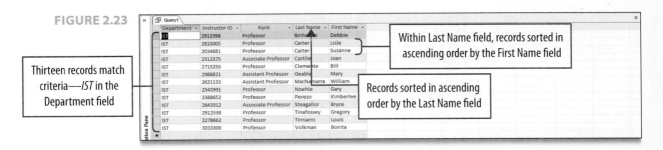

Thirteen records match criteria—*IST* in the Department field

Within Last Name field, records sorted in ascending order by the First Name field

Records sorted in ascending order by the Last Name field

ALERT! | **Do Your Query Results Differ?**

If you mistype the criteria, or enter it under the wrong field, or make some other error, the query results will display no records. This indicates that there are no records in the table that match the criteria as you entered it. If this occurs, return to Design view and examine the query design. Verify that the criteria is entered in the Criteria row, under the correct field, and without typing errors. Then, run the query again.

7 Save 🖫 the query as **Lastname Firstname 2A IST Query** and then display the query results in **Print Preview**. Create a paper or electronic printout as directed, and then click **Close Print Preview**.

8 ▶ **Close** ☒ the query, **Open** ⊠ the **Navigation Pane**, and then notice that your **2A IST Query** object name displays under your **2A Instructors** table—its data source.

> Recall that in the Navigation Pane, queries display an icon of two overlapping datasheets.

Activity 2.16 | Specifying Criteria and Hiding the Field in the Query Results

So far, all of the fields that you included in the query design have also been included in the query results. There are times when you need to use the field in the query design, but you do not need to display that field in the results, usually, when the data in the field is the same for all of the records. In this activity, you will create a query to answer the question, *Which instructors have a rank of professor?*

1 ▶ **Close** ⊠ the **Navigation Pane.** On the ribbon, click the **CREATE tab**, and then in the **Queries group**, click **Query Design**.

2 ▶ In the **Show Table** dialog box, double-click your **2A Instructors** table to add it to the table area, and then **Close** the **Show Table** dialog box.

3 ▶ Resize the field list, and then add the following fields to the design grid in the order given: **Instructor ID**, **Last Name**, **First Name**, and **Rank**.

4 ▶ Click in the **Sort** row under **Last Name**, click the **arrow**, and then click **Ascending**. Click in the **Sort** row under **First Name**, click the **arrow**, and then click **Ascending**.

5 ▶ Click in the **Criteria** row under **Rank**, type **professor** and then press Enter. Compare your screen with Figure 2.24.

> Recall that criteria is not case sensitive. As you start typing *professor*, a list of functions displays, from which you can select if a function is included in your criteria. After pressing Enter, the insertion point moves to the next criteria box, and quotation marks are added around the text string that you entered.

FIGURE 2.24

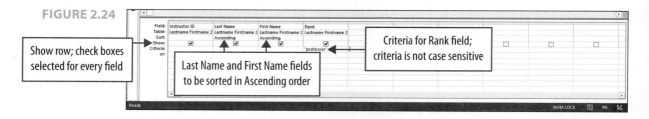

Show row; check boxes selected for every field

Last Name and First Name fields to be sorted in Ascending order

Criteria for Rank field; criteria is not case sensitive

6 ▶ In the design grid, in the **Show** row, notice that a check box is selected for every field. **Run** the query.

> Eighteen records meet the criteria—*professor* in the *Rank* field. In the Rank column, every record displays *Professor*, and the records are sorted in ascending order by the First Name field within the Last Name field.

7 ▶ Switch to **Design** view. In the design grid, in the **Show** row under **Rank**, click to clear the check box.

> Because it is repetitive and not particularly useful to display *Professor* for every record in the query results, clear the Show check box so that the field is hidden and does not display. It is good practice, however, to run the query first before clearing the Show check box to be sure that the correct records display.

8 > **Run** the query, and then notice that the *Rank* field does not display even though it is used to specify criteria in the query.

The same 18 records display, but the *Rank* field is hidden from the query results. Although the Rank field is included in the query design so that you can specify the criteria of *professor*, it is not necessary to display the field in the results. When appropriate, clear the Show check box to avoid cluttering the query results with data that is not useful.

9 > **Save** 🖫 the query as **Lastname Firstname 2A Professor Query** and then display the query results in **Print Preview**. Create a paper or electronic printout as directed, and then click **Close Print Preview. Close** ✕ the query.

Activity 2.17 | Using *Is Null* Criteria to Find Empty Fields

Sometimes you must locate records where data is missing. You can locate such records by using *Is Null* as the criteria in a field. *Is Null* is used to find empty fields. Additionally, you can display only the records where data has been entered in the field by using the criteria of *Is Not Null*, which excludes records where the specified field is empty. In this activity, you will design a query to answer the question, *Which scheduled courses have no credits listed?*

1 > On the ribbon, click the **CREATE tab**, and then in the **Queries group**, click **Query Design**. In the **Show Table** dialog box, double-click your **2A Schedule** table to add it to the table area, and then **Close** the **Show Table** dialog box.

2 > Resize the field list, and then add the following fields to the design grid in the order given: **Subject**, **Catalog#**, **Section**, **Course Name**, and **Credits**.

3 > Click in the **Criteria** row under **Credits**, type **is null** and then press Enter.

Access capitalizes *is null*. The criteria *Is Null* examines the Credits field and locates records that do *not* have any data entered in the field.

4 > Click in the **Sort** row under **Subject**, click the **arrow**, and then click **Ascending**. **Sort** the **Catalog#** field in **Ascending** order, and then **Sort** the **Section** field in **Ascending** order. Compare your screen with Figure 2.25.

FIGURE 2.25

Three fields sorted in Ascending order

Is Null criteria for Credits field

5 > **Run** the query, and then compare your screen with Figure 2.26.

Four scheduled courses do not have credits listed—the Credits field is empty. The records are sorted in ascending order first by the Subject field. Within the Subject field, the records are sorted in ascending order by the Catalog# field. Within the Catalog# field, the records are sorted in ascending order by the Section field. Using the information displayed in the query results, a course scheduler can more easily locate the records in the table and enter the credits for these courses.

FIGURE 2.26

Sorted first by Subject

Credits field empty (null) for four courses

Within Subject, sorted by Catalog#

Within Catalog#, sorted by Section

6 Save ⊞ the query as **Lastname Firstname 2A No Credits Query**, and then display the query results in **Print Preview**. Create a paper or electronic printout as instructed, click **Close Print Preview**, and then **Close** ☒ the query.

7 **Open** » the **Navigation Pane**, and then notice that your **2A No Credits Query** object displays under your **2A Schedule** table object, its data source.

8 On the right side of the title bar, click **Close** ☒ to close the database and to exit Access. As directed by your instructor, submit your database and the paper or electronic printouts of the eight objects—relationship report, sorted table, and six queries—that are the results of this project. Specifically, in this project, using your own name, you created the following database and printouts or electronic printouts:

1. Lastname_Firstname_2A_Instructors_Courses	Database file
2. Relationships for Lastname_Firstname_2A_Instructors_Courses	Relationships Report (printout or electronic printout)
3. Lastname Firstname 2A Instructors table sorted (not saved)	Table sorted (printout or electronic printout - Page 1)
4. Lastname Firstname 2A Instructors Query	Query (printout or electronic printout)
5. Lastname Firstname 2A Instructor IDs Query	Query (printout or electronic printout)
6. Lastname Firstname 2A Department Sort Query	Query (printout or electronic printout)
7. Lastname Firstname 2A IST Query	Query (printout or electronic printout)
8. Lastname Firstname 2A Professor Query	Query (printout or electronic printout)
9. Lastname Firstname 2A No Credits Query	Query (printout or electronic printout)

END | You have completed Project 2A

GO! with Office Online (formerly Web Apps)

Objective	Export an Access Query to a PDF File, Save to OneDrive, and Add a Description to the PDF File

Access web apps are designed to work with Microsoft's SharePoint, an application for setting up websites to share and manage documents. Your college may not have SharePoint installed, so you will use other tools to share objects from your database so that you can work collaboratively with others. When you have information that you want to share with others, you can upload files to OneDrive. Some files can be opened in OneDrive; some can only be downloaded. Because database files are typically large in size, and free storage space on OneDrive is limited, you can export database objects to different formats and then upload those files to OneDrive.

> **ALERT!** **Working with Web-Based Applications and Services**
>
> Computer programs and services on the web receive continuous updates and improvements. Thus, the steps to complete this web-based activity may differ from the ones shown. You can often look at the screens and the information presented to determine how to complete the activity.

Activity | **Exporting an Access Query to a PDF File, Uploading a PDF File to OneDrive, and Adding a Description to a PDF File**

In this activity, you will export your 2A No Credits Query object to a PDF file, upload your PDF file to OneDrive, and then add a description to the PDF File. Recall that PDF stands for Portable Document Format—a file format that creates an image that preserves the look of your file, but that cannot be easily changed. The results of the query will be available for individuals with whom you have shared your OneDrive files or folders.

1 **Start** Access, navigate to your **Access Chapter 2** folder, and then **Open** your **2A_Instructors_Courses** database file. If necessary, on the Message Bar, click Enable Content. In the **Navigation Pane**, click your **2A No Credits Query** object to select it—do not open it.

2 On the ribbon, click the **EXTERNAL DATA tab**, and then in the **Export group**, click **PDF or XPS**. In the **Publish as PDF or XPS** dialog box, navigate to your **Access Chapter 2** folder. Click in the **File name** box, type **Lastname_Firstname_AC_2A_Web** and then be sure the **Open file after publishing** check box is selected, and the **Minimum size (publishing online)** option button is

selected. Click **Publish**, and then compare your screen with Figure A.

> The PDF file is created and opens in the Windows 8 Reader, Adobe Reader, or Adobe Acrobat, depending on the software that is installed on your computer.

3 **Close** your **AC_2A_Web** file. In the **Export – PDF** dialog box, click **Close**, and then **Close** Access.

4 From the desktop, start Internet Explorer, navigate to **http://onedrive.com**, and then sign in to your Microsoft account. Open your **GO! Web Projects** folder—or create and then open this folder if necessary.

FIGURE A

Your 2A No Credits Query exported as a PDF file and opened in Adobe Reader (yours may open in Windows 8 Reader or Adobe Acrobat)

(GO! with Office Online (formerly Web Apps) continues on the next page)

5 On the menu bar, click **Upload**. In the **Choose File to Upload** dialog box, navigate to your **Access Chapter 2** folder, and then double-click your **AC_2A_Web** file to upload it to OneDrive.

6 In your **GO! Web Projects** folder, right-click your **AC_2A_Web** file, and then click **Properties**.

A properties panel displays on the right side of the window.

7 In the properties panel, click **Add a description**. In the box, type **This query displays courses in the schedule that do not have credits assigned to them.** and then press Enter. Compare your screen with Figure B.

8 On your keyboard, press the [⊞] key, type **snip**, and then click **Snipping Tool**. In the **Snipping Tool** dialog box, click the **New arrow**, and then click **Full-screen snip**.

9 On the **Snipping Tool** toolbar, click **Save Snip** [💾]. In the **Save As** dialog box, navigate to your **Access Chapter 2** folder. Click in the **File name** box, type **Lastname_Firstname_AC_2A_Web_Snip** and then click the **Save as type arrow**. Click **JPEG file**, and then click **Save**. **Close** [❌] the **Snipping Tool** window.

10 In OneDrive, on the title bar, click **OneDrive** to return to your home page. At the top right corner of your screen, click your OneDrive name, and then click **Sign out**. **Close** your browser window.

11 If directed to submit a paper printout of your pdf and snip file, follow the directions given in the Note. As directed by your instructor, submit your pdf file and your snip file that are the results of this project.

NOTE | **Printing Your PDF and Snip .jpeg File**

Using Windows Explorer, navigate to your Access Chapter 2 folder. Locate and double-click your AC_2A_Web file. On the toolbar, click the Print file button. Then Close the Windows 8 Reader, Adobe Reader, or Adobe Acrobat window. In your Access Chapter 2 folder, locate and double-click your AC_2A_Web_Snip file. If this is the first time you have tried to open a .jpeg file, you will be asked to identify a program. If you are not sure which program to use, select Windows Photo Viewer. From the ribbon, menu bar, or toolbar, click the Print command, and then Close the program window.

FIGURE B

Athletic Scholarships Database

PROJECT ACTIVITIES

In Activities 2.18 through 2.33, you will assist Roberto Garza, athletic director for Texas Lakes Community College, in creating queries to locate information about athletic scholarships that are awarded to students. Your completed database objects will look similar to Figure 2.27.

PROJECT FILES

For Project 2B, you will need the following files:

a02B_Athletes_Scholarships
a02B_Athletes (Excel workbook)

You will save your database as:

Lastname_Firstname_2B_Athletes_Scholarships

PROJECT RESULTS

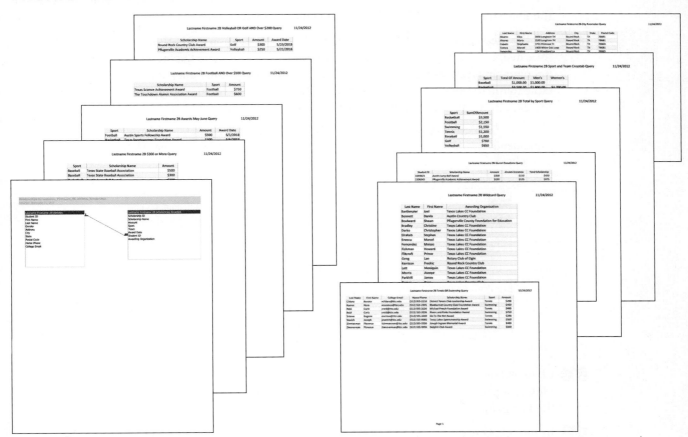

FIGURE 2.27 Project 2B Athletic Scholarships

Video A2-8

Criteria can be set for fields containing numeric data. When you design your table, set the appropriate data type for fields that will contain numbers, currency, or dates so that mathematical calculations can be performed.

Activity 2.18 | Opening, Renaming, and Saving an Existing Database and Importing a Spreadsheet as a New Table

In this activity, you will open, rename, and save an existing database, and then import an Excel spreadsheet as a new table in the database.

1 ▶ **Start** Access. In the Access opening screen, click **Open Other Files**. Under **Open**, click **Computer**. Under **Recent Folders**, if displayed, click the location where your student data files are stored; otherwise, click **Browse** and then navigate to the location where your student data files are stored. Double-click **a02B_Athletes_Scholarships** to open the database.

2 ▶ Click the **FILE tab**, click **Save As**, and then under **File Types**, be sure **Save Database As** is selected. On the right, under **Database File Types**, be sure **Access Database** is selected, and then click **Save As**. In the **Save As** dialog box, navigate to your **Access Chapter 2** folder, click in the **File name** box, type **Lastname_Firstname_2B_Athletes_Scholarships** and then press Enter.

3 ▶ On the **Message Bar**, click **Enable Content**. In the **Navigation Pane**, right-click **2B Scholarships Awarded**, and then click **Rename**. Using your own name, type **Lastname Firstname 2B Scholarships Awarded** and then press Enter. In the **Navigation Pane**, double-click the table name to open it in **Datasheet** view. **Close** « the **Navigation Pane**, and then examine the data in the table. Compare your screen with Figure 2.28.

In this table, Mr. Garza tracks the names and amounts of scholarships awarded to student athletes. Students are identified only by their Student ID numbers, and the primary key is the Scholarship ID field.

FIGURE 2.28

4 ▶ **Close** × the table. On the ribbon, click the **EXTERNAL DATA tab**, and then in the **Import & Link group**, click **Excel**. In the **Get External Data – Excel Spreadsheet** dialog box, to the right of the **File name** box, click **Browse**.

5 ▶ In the **File Open** dialog box, navigate to your student data files, and then double-click **a02B_Athletes**. Be sure that the **Import the source data into a new table in the current database** option button is selected, and then click **OK**.

The Import Spreadsheet Wizard opens and displays the spreadsheet data.

6 ▶ In the wizard, click **Next**. In the upper left area of the wizard, select the **First Row Contains Column Headings** check box, click **Next**, and then click **Next** again.

7 In the wizard, click the **Choose my own primary key** option button, and then be sure that **Student ID** displays in the box.

> In the new table, Student ID will be designated as the primary key. No two students have the same Student ID.

8 Click **Next**. With the text selected in the **Import to Table** box, type **Lastname Firstname 2B Athletes** and then click **Finish**. In the **Get External Data – Excel Spreadsheet** dialog box, click **Close**.

9 Open [»] the **Navigation Pane**, and increase the width of the pane so that the two table names display fully. In the **Navigation Pane**, right-click your **2B Athletes** table, and then click **Design View**. **Close** [«] the **Navigation Pane**.

10 To the right of **Student ID**, click in the **Data Type** box, click the **arrow**, and then click **Short Text**. For the **Postal Code** field, change the **Data Type** to **Short Text**, and in the **Field Properties** area, click **Field Size**, type **5** and then press Enter. In the **Field Name** column, click **State**, set the **Field Size** to **2** and then press Enter. Compare your screen with Figure 2.29.

> Recall that numeric data that is not used in a calculation, such as the Student ID and Postal Code, should be assigned a data type of Short Text.

FIGURE 2.29

11 On the **DESIGN tab**, in the **Views group**, click the top of the **View** button to switch to **Datasheet** view. In the message box, click **Yes** to save the table. In the second message box, click **Yes**—no data will be lost. Take a moment to examine the data in the imported table.

12 In the datasheet, to the left of the **Student ID** field name, click **Select All** [ ]. On the **HOME tab**, in the **Records group**, click **More**, and then click **Field Width**. In the **Column Width** dialog box, click **Best Fit**. Save [ ] the table, click in any record to cancel the selection, and then **Close** [×] the table.

Activity 2.19 | Creating a One-to-Many Table Relationship

In this activity, you will create a one-to-many relationship between your 2B Athletes table and your 2B Scholarships Awarded table by using the common field—*Student ID*.

1 On the ribbon, click the **DATABASE TOOLS tab**, and then in the **Relationships group**, click **Relationships**.

2 In the **Show Table** dialog box, double-click your **2B Athletes** table, and then double-click your **2B Scholarships Awarded** table to add both tables to the **Relationships** window. **Close** the **Show Table** dialog box.

3 ▶ Point to the title bar of the field list on the right, and drag the field list to the right until there are approximately three inches of space between the field lists. By dragging the lower right corner of the field list downward and to the right, resize each field list to display all of the field names and the entire table name.

Repositioning and resizing the field lists are not required, but doing so makes it easier for you to view the field names and the join line when creating relationships.

4 ▶ In the **2B Athletes** field list, point to **Student ID**, and then drag the field name into the **2B Scholarships Awarded** field list on top of **Student ID**. Release the mouse button to display the **Edit Relationships** dialog box.

5 ▶ Point to the title bar of the **Edit Relationships** dialog box, and then drag it downward below the two field lists. In the **Edit Relationships** dialog box, be sure that **Student ID** displays as the common field for both tables.

Repositioning the Edit Relationships dialog is not required, but doing so enables you to see the field lists. The Relationship Type is *One-To-Many*—*one* athlete can have *many* scholarships. The common field in both tables is the *Student ID* field. In the 2B Athletes table, Student ID is the primary key. In the 2B Scholarships Awarded table, Student ID is the foreign key.

6 ▶ In the **Edit Relationships** dialog box, click to select the **Enforce Referential Integrity** check box, the **Cascade Update Related Fields** check box, and the **Cascade Delete Related Records** check box. Click **Create**, and then compare your screen with Figure 2.30.

The one-to-many relationship is established. The *1* and ∞ symbols indicate that referential integrity is enforced, which ensures that a scholarship cannot be awarded to a student whose Student ID is not included in the 2B Athletes table. Recall that the Cascade options enable you to update and delete records automatically on the *many* side of the relationship when changes are made in the table on the *one* side of the relationship.

FIGURE 2.30

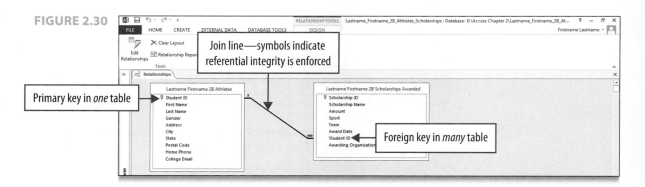

7 ▶ Under **RELATIONSHIP TOOLS**, on the **DESIGN tab**, in the **Tools group**, click **Relationship Report**. On the **PRINT PREVIEW tab**, in the **Page Size group**, click **Margins**, and then click **Normal**. Save ⊟ the report as **Lastname Firstname 2B Relationships** and then create a paper or electronic printout as directed.

8 ▶ In the object window, right-click either **object tab**, and then click **Close All** to close the **Relationship Report** and the **Relationships** window.

9 ▶ Open ⌫ the **Navigation Pane**, double-click your **2B Athletes** table to open it, and then Close ⌦ the **Navigation Pane**. On the left side of the first record, click ⊞ to display the subdatasheet for the record.

In the first record, for *Joel Barthmaier*, one related record exists in the 2B Scholarships Awarded table. Joel has been awarded the *Austin Jump Ball Award* in the amount of *$300*. The subdatasheet displays because you created a relationship between the two tables using Student ID as the common field.

10 Close ⊠ the **2B Athletes** table.

When you close the table, the subdatasheet collapses—you do not need to click ⊟ before closing a table.

Activity 2.20 | Specifying Numeric Criteria in a Query

In this activity, you will create a query to answer the question, *Which scholarships are in the amount of $300, and for which sports?*

1 On the ribbon, click the **CREATE tab**. In the **Queries group**, click **Query Design**.

2 In the **Show Table** dialog box, double-click your **2B Scholarships Awarded** table to add it to the table area, and then **Close** the **Show Table** dialog box. Resize the field list to display all of the fields and the entire table name.

3 Add the following fields to the design grid in the order given: **Sport**, **Scholarship Name**, and **Amount**.

4 Click in the **Sort** row under **Sport**, click the **arrow**, and then click **Ascending**. Click in the **Sort** row under **Scholarship Name**, click the **arrow**, and then click **Ascending**.

The records will be sorted in ascending order by the Scholarship Name field within the Sport field.

5 Click in the **Criteria** row under **Amount**, type **300** and then press Enter. Compare your screen with Figure 2.31.

When you enter currency values as criteria, do not type the dollar sign. Include a decimal point only if you are looking for a specific amount that includes cents; for example, 300.49. Access does not insert quotation marks around the criteria because the data type of the field is Currency, which is a numeric format.

FIGURE 2.31

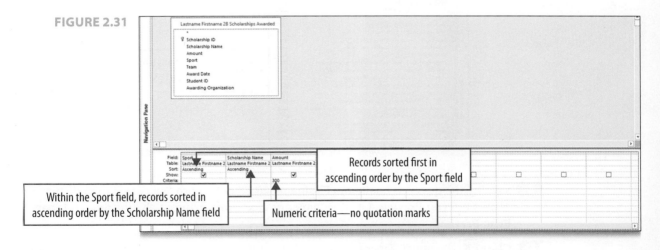

Within the Sport field, records sorted in ascending order by the Scholarship Name field

Records sorted first in ascending order by the Sport field

Numeric criteria—no quotation marks

6 Under **QUERY TOOLS**, on the **DESIGN tab**, in the **Results group**, click **Run** to display the query results.

Five scholarships in the exact amount of $300 were awarded to student athletes. In the navigation area, *1 of 5* displays—1 represents the first record that is selected, and 5 represents the total number of records that meet the criteria.

7 On the **HOME tab**, in the **Views group**, click the top of the **View** button to switch to **Design** view.

Activity 2.21 | Using Comparison Operators in Criteria

Comparison operators are symbols you can use to evaluate data in the field to determine if it is the same (=), greater than (>), less than (<), or in between a range of values as specified by the criteria. If no comparison operator is specified, equal (=) is assumed. For example, in the previous activity, you created a query to display only those records where the *Amount* is *300*. The comparison operator of = was assumed, and the query results displayed only those records that had values in the Amount field equal to 300.

1 In the design grid, in the **Criteria** row under **Amount**, select the existing criteria of *300*. Type **>300** and then press Enter. **Run** the query.

Fourteen records display, and each has a value *greater than* $300 in the Amount field; there are no records for which the Amount is *equal to* $300.

2 Switch to **Design** view. In the **Criteria** row under **Amount**, select the existing criteria of *>300*. Type **<300** and then press Enter. **Run** the query.

Eleven records display, and each has a value *less than* $300 in the Amount field; there are no records for which the Amount is *equal to* $300.

3 Switch to **Design** view. In the **Criteria** row under **Amount**, select the existing criteria of *<300*. Type **>=300** and then press Enter. **Run** the query, and then compare your screen with Figure 2.32.

Nineteen records display, including the records for scholarships in the exact amount of $300. The records include scholarships *greater than* or *equal to* $300. In this manner, comparison operators can be combined. This query answers the question, *Which scholarships have been awarded in the amount of $300 or more, and for which sports, arranged alphabetically by sport?*

FIGURE 2.32

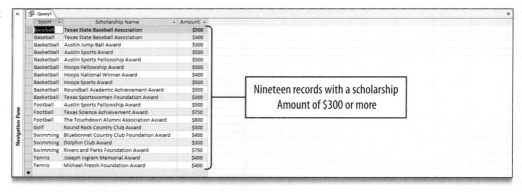

Nineteen records with a scholarship Amount of $300 or more

4 Save 💾 the query as **Lastname Firstname 2B $300 or More Query** and then display the query results in **Print Preview**. Create a paper or electronic printout as directed, and then click **Close Print Preview**.

5 Close ✕ the query. Open » the **Navigation Pane**, and notice that this new query displays under *2B Scholarships Awarded*, its data source.

Activity 2.22 | Using the Between … And Comparison Operator

The *Between … And operator* is a comparison operator that looks for values within a range. It is useful when you need to locate records that are within a range of dates; for example, scholarships awarded between May 1 and June 30.

In this activity, you will create a new query from an existing query, and then add criteria to look for values within a range of dates. The query will answer the question, *Which scholarships were awarded between May 1 and June 30?*

1 In the **Navigation Pane**, right-click your **2B $300 or More Query** object, and then click **Copy**. In the **Navigation Pane**, point to a blank area, right-click, and then click **Paste**.

2 In the **Paste As** dialog box, type **Lastname Firstname 2B Awards May-June Query** and then click **OK**.

> A new query, based on a copy of your 2B $300 or More Query is created and displays in the Navigation Pane under its data source—your 2B Scholarships Awarded table.

3 In the **Navigation Pane**, right-click your **2B Awards May-June Query** object, click **Design View**, and then **Close** «| the **Navigation Pane**.

4 In the **2B Scholarships Awarded** field list, double-click **Award Date** to add it as the fourth column in the design grid.

5 In the **Criteria** row under **Amount**, select the existing criteria of *>=300*, and then press Del so that the query is not restricted by a monetary value.

6 Click in the **Criteria** row under **Award Date**, type **between 5/1/18 and 6/30/18** and then press Enter.

7 Click in the **Sort** row under **Sport**, click the **arrow**, and then click **(not sorted)** to remove the sort from this field. Click in the **Sort** row under **Scholarship Name**, click the **arrow**, and then click **(not sorted)** to remove the sort from this field. Click in the **Sort** row under **Award Date**, click the **arrow**, and then click **Ascending**.

8 In the selection bar of the design grid, point to the right edge of the **Award Date** column to display the ⊞ pointer, and then double-click to apply Best Fit to this column. Compare your screen with Figure 2.33.

> The width of the Award Date column is increased to fit the longest entry in the column, which enables you to see all of the criteria. Access places pound signs (#) around the dates and capitalizes *between* and *and*. This criteria instructs Access to look for values in the Award Date field that begin with 5/1/18 and end with 6/30/18. Both the beginning and ending dates will be included in the query results.

FIGURE 2.33

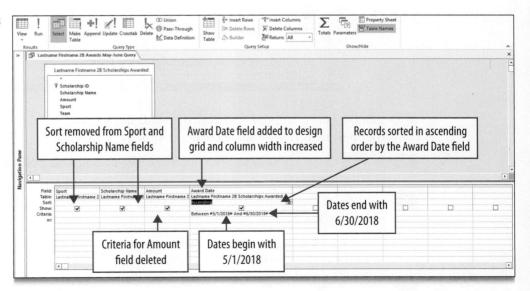

9 **Run** the query, and notice that eight scholarships were awarded between 5/1/2018 and 6/30/2018.

10 Display the query results in **Print Preview**, create a paper or electronic printout as directed, and then click **Close Print Preview**. **Close** ⊠ the query, and in the message box, click **Yes** to save the changes to the query design.

Video A2-9

You can specify more than one condition—criteria—in a query; this is called **compound criteria**. Compound criteria use **logical operators** such as AND and OR. Logical operators evaluate data to determine if a condition is met (true) or not met (false). The AND and OR logical operators enable you to enter multiple criteria for the same field or for different fields.

Activity 2.23 | Using AND Criteria in a Query

The **AND condition** is an example of a compound criteria you can use to display records that match all parts of the specified criteria. In this activity, you will design a query to answer the question, *Which scholarships over $500 were awarded for football?*

1 On the ribbon, click the **CREATE tab**, and in the **Queries group**, click **Query Design**. In the **Show Table** dialog box, double-click your **2B Scholarships Awarded** table to add it to the table area, and then **Close** the **Show Table** dialog box. Resize the field list to display all of the fields and the entire table name.

2 Add the following fields to the design grid in the order given: **Scholarship Name**, **Sport**, and **Amount**.

3 Click in the **Criteria** row under **Sport**, type **football** and then press Enter.

4 In the **Criteria** row under **Amount**, type **>500** and then press Enter. Compare your screen with Figure 2.34.

You create the AND condition by placing the criteria for both fields on the same line in the Criteria row. The criteria indicates that records should be located that contain *Football* in the Sport field AND a value greater than *500* in the Amount field. Both conditions must exist or be true for the records to display in the query results.

FIGURE 2.34

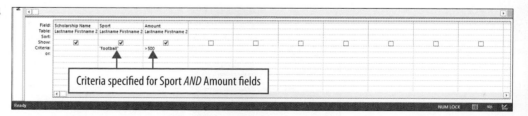

Criteria specified for Sport *AND* Amount fields

5 **Run** the query, and notice that two records display that match both conditions—*Football* in the **Sport** field AND a value greater than *$500* in the **Amount** field.

6 **Save** the query as **Lastname Firstname 2B Football AND Over $500 Query** and then **Close** the query.

7 **Open** the **Navigation Pane**, and then click to select your **2B Football AND Over $500 Query** object. On the ribbon, click the **FILE tab**, click **Print**, and then click **Print Preview**.

You can view an object in Print Preview or print any selected object in the Navigation Pane—the object does not need to be open in the object window to print it.

8 Create a paper or electronic printout as directed, and then click **Close Print Preview**. **Close** the **Navigation Pane**.

Activity 2.24 | Using OR Criteria in a Query

The **OR condition** is an example of a compound criteria you can use to display records that meet one or more parts of the specified criteria. The OR condition can specify criteria in a single field or in different fields. In this activity, you will help Mr. Garza answer the question, *Which scholarships over $200 were awarded for volleyball or golf, and what is the award date of each?*

1 On the ribbon, click the **CREATE tab**. In the **Queries group**, click **Query Design**.

2 In the **Show Table** dialog box, double-click your **2B Scholarships Awarded** table to add it to the table area, and then **Close** the **Show Table** dialog box. Resize the field list, and then add the following fields to the design grid in the order given: **Scholarship Name**, **Sport**, **Amount**, and **Award Date**.

3 In the design grid, click in the **Criteria** row under **Sport**, type **volleyball** and then press ⬇.

The insertion point is blinking in the *or* row under Sport.

4 In the **or** row under **Sport**, type **golf** and then press Enter. **Run** the query.

Six records were located in the 2B Scholarships Awarded table that have either *volleyball* OR *golf* stored in the Sport field. This is an example of using the OR condition to locate records that meet one or more parts of the specified criteria in a single field—*Sport*.

5 Switch to **Design** view. In the **or** row under **Sport**, select *"golf"* and then press Del. In the **Criteria** row under **Sport**, select and delete *"volleyball"*. Type **volleyball or golf** and then press Enter.

6 In the **Criteria** row under **Amount**, type **>200** and then press Enter. Compare your screen with Figure 2.35.

This is an alternative way to enter the OR condition in the Sport field and is a good method to use when you add an AND condition to the criteria. Access will locate records where the Sport field contains *volleyball* OR *golf* AND where the Amount field contains a value greater than *200*.

If you enter *volleyball* in the Criteria row, and *golf* in the or row for the Sport field, then you must enter *>200* in both the Criteria row and the or row for the Amount field so that the correct records are located when you run the query.

FIGURE 2.35

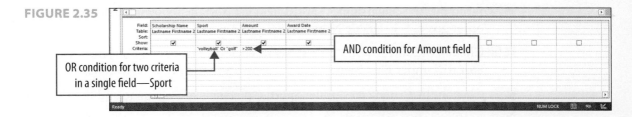

7 **Run** the query.

Two records were located in the 2B Scholarships Awarded table that have either *Volleyball* OR *Golf* stored in the Sport field AND a value greater than $200 stored in the Amount field. This is an example of using the OR condition in combination with an AND condition.

8 Save 🖫 the query as **Lastname Firstname 2B Volleyball OR Golf AND Over $200 Query** and then display the query results in **Print Preview**. Create a paper or electronic printout as directed, click **Close Print Preview**, and then **Close** ☒ the query.

Video A2-10

In a relational database, you can retrieve information from more than one table. Recall that a table in a relational database contains all of the records about a single topic. Tables are joined to one another by relating the primary key in one table to the foreign key in another table. This common field is used to create the relationship and is used to find records from multiple tables when the query is created and run.

For example, the Athletes table stores all of the data about the student athletes—name, address, and so on. The Scholarships Awarded table stores data about the scholarship name, the amount, and so on. When an athlete receives a scholarship, only the Student ID of the athlete is used to identify the athlete in the Scholarships Awarded table. It is not necessary to include any other data about the athlete in the Scholarships Awarded table; doing so would result in redundant data.

Activity 2.25 | Creating a Query Based on More Than One Table

In this activity, you will create a query that selects records from two tables. This is possible because you created a relationship between the two tables in the database. The query will answer the questions, *What is the name, email address, and phone number of athletes who have received a scholarship for tennis or swimming, and what is the name and amount of the scholarship?*

1 On the ribbon, click the **CREATE tab**, and then in the **Queries group**, click **Query Design**. In the **Show Table** dialog box, double-click your **2B Athletes** table, and then double-click your **2B Scholarships Awarded** table to add both tables to the table area. In the **Show Table** dialog box, click **Close**. Drag the **2B Scholarships Awarded** field list—the field list on the right—to the right so that there are approximately three inches of space between the two field lists, and then resize each field list to display all of the field names and the table names.

> The join line displays because you created a one-to-many relationship between the two tables using the common field of Student ID; *one* athlete can receive *many* scholarships.

2 From the **2B Athletes** field list, add the following fields to the design grid in the order given: **Last Name**, **First Name**, **College Email**, and **Home Phone**.

3 From the **2B Scholarships Awarded** field list, add the following fields to the design grid in the order given: **Scholarship Name**, **Sport**, and **Amount**.

4 Click in the **Sort** row under **Last Name**, click the **arrow**, and then click **Ascending**. Click in the **Sort** row under **First Name**, click the **arrow**, and then click **Ascending**.

5 Click in the **Criteria** row under **Sport**, type **tennis or swimming** and then press Enter.

6 In the selection bar of the design grid, point to the right edge of the **Home Phone** column to display the ⊞ pointer, and then double-click to increase the width of the column and to display the entire table name on the **Table** row. Using the same technique, increase the width of the **Scholarship Name** column. If necessary, scroll to the right to display both of these columns in the design grid, and then compare your screen with Figure 2.36.

> When locating data from multiple tables, the information in the Table row is helpful, especially when different tables include the same field name, such as Address. Although the field name is the same, the data may be different; for example, you might have an athlete's address or a coach's address from two different related tables.

FIGURE 2.36

Table row indicates data source

Sorted in ascending order by Last Name and First Name fields

Criteria entered for Sport field

7 **Run** the query, and then compare your screen with Figure 2.37.

Eight records display for athletes who received either a Tennis *or* Swimming scholarship, and the records are sorted in ascending order by the Last Name field, and then the First Name field. Because the common field of Student ID is included in both tables, Access can locate the specified fields in both tables by using one query. Two students—*Carla Reid* and *Florence Zimmerman*— received two scholarships, one for tennis and one for swimming. Recall that *one* student athlete can receive *many* scholarships.

FIGURE 2.37

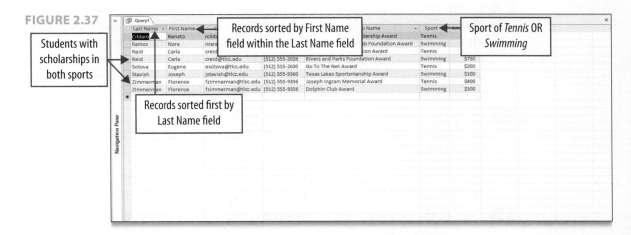

Students with scholarships in both sports

Records sorted by First Name field within the Last Name field

Sport of *Tennis* OR *Swimming*

Records sorted first by Last Name field

8 **Save** 🖫 the query as **Lastname Firstname 2B Tennis OR Swimming Query** and then display the query results in **Print Preview**. Change the orientation to **Landscape**, and the **Margins** to **Normal**. Create a paper or electronic printout as directed, and then click **Close Print Preview**.

9 **Close** ⊠ the query, **Open** » the **Navigation Pane**, increase the width of the **Navigation Pane** to display all object names fully, and then compare your screen with Figure 2.38.

Your *2B Tennis OR Swimming Query* object name displays under both tables from which it selected records.

FIGURE 2.38

Query displays under both of its data sources

10 **Close** « the **Navigation Pane**.

Video A2-11

Wildcard characters serve as a placeholder for one or more unknown characters in criteria. When you are unsure of the specific character or set of characters to include in the criteria, use a wildcard character in place of the character.

Activity 2.26 | Using a Wildcard in a Query

Use the asterisk (*) wildcard character to represent one or more unknown characters. For example, entering Fo* as the criteria in a last name field will result in displaying records containing last names of Foster, Forrester, Fossil, or any other last name that begins with *Fo*. In this activity, you will use the asterisk (*) wildcard character in criteria to answer the question, *Which athletes received scholarships from local rotary clubs, country clubs, or foundations?*

1 On the ribbon, click the **CREATE tab**, and then in the **Queries group**, click **Query Design**. In the **Show Table** dialog box, double-click your **2B Athletes** table, and then double-click your **2B Scholarships Awarded** table to add both tables to the table area. In the **Show Table** dialog box, click **Close**. Drag the **2B Scholarships Awarded** field list to the right so that there are approximately three inches of space between the two field lists, and then resize each field list to display all of the field names and the table names.

2 From the **2B Athletes** field list, add the following fields to the design grid in the order given: **Last Name** and **First Name**. From the **2B Scholarships Awarded** field list, add the **Awarding Organization** field to the design grid.

3 Click in the **Sort** row under **Last Name**, click the **arrow**, and then click **Ascending**. Click in the **Sort** row under **First Name**, click the **arrow**, and then click **Ascending**.

4 Click in the **Criteria** row under **Awarding Organization**, type **rotary*** and then press Enter.

The * wildcard character is a placeholder you can use to match one or more unknown characters. After pressing Enter, Access adds *Like* to the beginning of the criteria and places quotation marks around *rotary*.

5 **Run** the query, and then compare your screen with Figure 2.39.

Three athletes received scholarships from a rotary club from different cities. The results are sorted alphabetically by the Last Name field. If there were two athletes with the same Last Name, the records would be sorted by the First Name field.

FIGURE 2.39

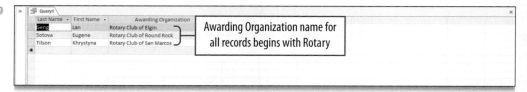

6 Switch to **Design** view. Click in the **or** row under **Awarding Organization**, type ***country club** and then press Enter.

You can use the * wildcard character at the beginning, middle, or end of the criteria. The position of the * determines the location of the unknown characters. By entering *country club, Access will locate records with an Awarding Organization name that ends in *Country Club*.

7 **Run** the query.

Six records display for students receiving scholarships; three from organizations with a name that begins with *Rotary*, and three from organizations with a name that ends with *Country Club*.

8 ▶ Switch to **Design** view. In the design grid under **Awarding Organization** and under **Like** "***country club**", type ***foundation*** and then press Enter. Compare your screen with Figure 2.40.

This query will also display records where the Awarding Organization has *Foundation* anywhere in its name—at the beginning, in the middle, or at the end of the organization name. Three *OR* criteria have been entered for the Awarding Organization field. When run, this query will locate records where the Awarding Organization has a name that begins with *Rotary*, OR ends with *Country Club*, OR has *Foundation* anywhere in its name.

FIGURE 2.40

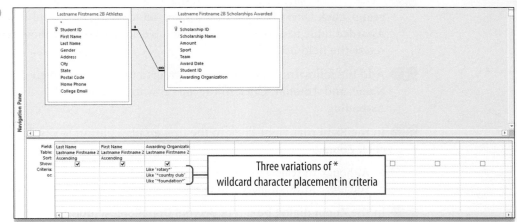

9 ▶ **Run** the query.

Twenty-eight scholarships were awarded from organizations where the name of the organization begins with *Rotary*, ends with *Country Club*, or has *Foundation* anywhere in its name. The records are sorted alphabetically by the Last Name field and then by the First Name field.

10 ▶ Save 🖫 the query as **Lastname Firstname 2B Wildcard Query** and then display the query results in **Print Preview**. Create a paper or electronic printout as directed, and then click **Close Print Preview**.

11 ▶ **Close** ☒ the query, and then **Open** ⏵⏵ the **Navigation Pane**. Notice that your **2B Wildcard Query** displays under both tables because the query selected data from both tables—the data sources.

More Knowledge	Using the ? Wildcard Character to Search for a Single Unknown Character

You can use the question mark (?) wildcard character to search for a single unknown character. For each question mark included in the criteria, the query results can display any character. For example, entering *b?d* as the criteria will result in the display of words such as *bed*, *bid*, or *bud*, or any three-character word that begins with *b* and ends with *d*. Entering *b??d* as the criteria will result in the display of words such as *bard*, *bend*, or *bind*, or any four-character word that begins with *b* and ends with *d*.

Objective 12 | Create Calculated Fields in a Query

Video A2-12

Queries can create calculated values that are stored in a ***calculated field***. A calculated field stores the value of a mathematical operation. For example, you can multiply the value stored in a field named Total Hours Worked by the value stored in a field named Hourly Pay to display the Gross Pay value for each work study student.

There are two steps to create a calculated field in a query. First, name the field that will store the results of the calculation. Second, enter the ***expression***—the formula—that will perform the calculation. When entering the information for the calculated field in the query, the new field name must be followed by a colon (:), and each field name used in the expression must be enclosed within its own pair of brackets.

Activity 2.27 | Creating a Calculated Field in a Query

For each scholarship received by student athletes, the Texas Lakes Community College Alumni Association will donate an amount equal to 50 percent of each scholarship amount. In this activity, you will create a calculated field to determine the amount that the Alumni Association will donate for each scholarship. The query will answer the question, *How much money will the Alumni Association donate for each student athlete who is awarded a scholarship?*

1 ▶ **Close** « the **Navigation Pane**. On the ribbon, click the **CREATE tab**, and then in the **Queries group**, click **Query Design**. In the **Show Table** dialog box, double-click your **2B Scholarships Awarded** table to add the table to the table area, **Close** the **Show Table** dialog box, and then resize the field list.

2 ▶ Add the following fields to the design grid in the order given: **Student ID**, **Scholarship Name**, and **Amount**. Click in the **Sort** row under **Student ID**, click the **arrow**, and then click **Ascending**.

3 ▶ In the **Field** row, right-click in the first empty column to display a shortcut menu, and then click **Zoom**.

Although the calculation can be typed directly in the empty Field box, the Zoom dialog box gives you more working space and enables you to see the entire calculation as you enter it.

4 ▶ In the **Zoom** dialog box, type **Alumni Donation:[Amount]*0.5** and then compare your screen with Figure 2.41.

The first element, *Alumni Donation*, is the new field name that will display the result of the calculation when the query is run. The new field name is followed by a colon (:), which separates the new field name from the expression. *Amount* is enclosed in brackets because it is an existing field name in your 2B Scholarships Awarded table; it contains the numeric data on which the calculation is performed. Following the right square bracket is the asterisk (*), the mathematical operator for multiplication. Finally, the percentage expressed as a decimal—*0.5*—displays.

FIGURE 2.41

5 ▶ In the **Zoom** dialog box, click **OK**, **Run** the query, and then compare your screen with Figure 2.42.

The query results display three fields from your 2B Scholarships Awarded table and a fourth field—*Alumni Donation*—that displays a calculated value. Each calculated value equals the value in the Amount field multiplied by 0.5 or 50%.

FIGURE 2.42

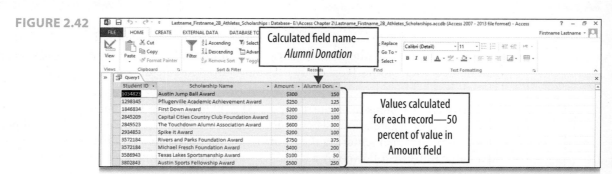

6 Notice the formatting of the values in the **Alumni Donation** field—there are no dollar signs to match the formatting in the **Amount** field; you will adjust the formatting of this field later.

> When using a number, such as 0.5, in an expression, the values that display in the calculated field might not be formatted the same as the existing field that was part of the calculation.

Activity 2.28 | Creating a Second Calculated Field in a Query

In this activity, you will create a calculated field to determine the total value of each scholarship after the Alumni Association donates an additional 50% based on the amount awarded by various organizations. The query will answer the question, *What is the total value of each scholarship after the Alumni Association donates an additional 50%?*

1 Switch to **Design** view. In the **Field** row, right-click in the first empty column to display a shortcut menu, and then click **Zoom**.

2 In the **Zoom** dialog box, type **Total Scholarship:[Amount]+[Alumni Donation]** and then compare your screen with Figure 2.43.

> Each existing field name—*Amount* and *Alumni Donation*—must be enclosed in separate pairs of brackets.

FIGURE 2.43

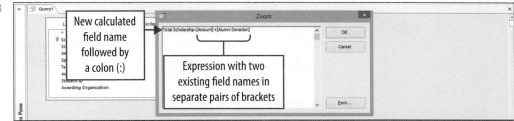

3 In the **Zoom** dialog box, click **OK**, and then **Run** the query.

> The value in the *Total Scholarship* field is calculated by adding together the values in the Amount field and the Alumni Donation field. The values in the Total Scholarship field are formatted with dollar signs, commas, and decimal points, which is carried over from the Currency format in the Amount field.

Activity 2.29 | Formatting Calculated Fields

In this activity, you will format the calculated fields so that the values display in a consistent manner.

1 Switch to **Design** view. In the **Field** row, click in the **Alumni Donation** field name box.

2 Under **QUERY TOOLS**, on the **DESIGN tab**, in the **Show/Hide group**, click **Property Sheet**.

> The Property Sheet displays on the right. Recall that a Property Sheet enables you to make precise changes to the properties—characteristics—of selected items, in this case, a field.

 ANOTHER WAY   In the design grid, on the Field row, right-click in the Alumni Donation field name box, and then click Properties.

3 ▶ In the **Property Sheet**, on the **General tab**, click **Format**. In the property setting box, click the **arrow**, and then compare your screen with Figure 2.44.

A list of available formats for the Alumni Donation field displays.

FIGURE 2.44

4 ▶ On the list, click **Currency**. In the **Property Sheet**, click **Decimal Places**. In the property setting box, click the **arrow**, and then click **0**.

5 ▶ In the design grid, in the **Field** row, click in the **Total Scholarship** field name. In the **Property Sheet**, set the **Decimal Places** property setting to **0**.

You do not need to set the Format setting to Currency as the field already displays with the currency symbol.

6 ▶ Close ☒ the **Property Sheet**, and then **Run** the query.

The Alumni Donation and Total Scholarship fields are formatted as Currency with 0 decimal places.

7 ▶ To the left of the **Student ID** field name, click **Select All** ☐. On the **HOME tab**, in the **Records group**, click **More**, and then click **Field Width**. In the **Column Width** dialog box, click **Best Fit**. **Save** ☐ the query as **Lastname Firstname 2B Alumni Donations Query** and then click in any field to cancel the selection.

The field widths adjust to display fully the calculated field names.

8 ▶ Display the query results in **Print Preview**. On the **PRINT PREVIEW tab**, in the **Page Layout group**, click **Landscape**. Create a paper or electronic printout as directed, and then click **Close Print Preview**. **Close** ☒ the query.

Objective 13 | Calculate Statistics and Group Data in a Query

Video A2-13

You can use queries to perform statistical calculations known as ***aggregate functions*** on a group of records. For example, you can find the total or average amount for a group of records, or you can find the lowest or highest number in a group of records.

Activity 2.30 | Using the Min, Max, Avg, and Sum Functions in a Query

In this activity, you will use aggregate functions to find the lowest and highest scholarship amounts and the average and total scholarship amounts. The last query in this activity will answer the question, *What is the total dollar amount of all scholarships awarded?*

1 ▶ On the ribbon, click the **CREATE tab**, and then in the **Queries group**, click **Query Design**. In the **Show Table** dialog box, double-click your **2B Scholarships Awarded** table to add the table to the table area, **Close** the **Show Table** dialog box, and then resize the field list.

2 ▶ Add the **Amount** field to the design grid.

Include only the field to summarize in the design grid, so that the aggregate function is applied only to that field.

3 ▶ Under **QUERY TOOLS**, on the **DESIGN tab**, in the **Show/Hide group**, click **Totals** to add a **Total** row as the third row in the design grid. Notice that in the design grid, on the **Total** row under **Amount**, *Group By* displays.

Use the Total row to select an aggregate function for the selected field.

4 ▶ In the **Total** row under **Amount**, click in the box that displays *Group By*, and then click the **arrow** to display a list of aggregate functions. Compare your screen with Figure 2.45, and then take a moment to review the available aggregate functions and the purpose of each function as shown in Table 2.46.

FIGURE 2.45

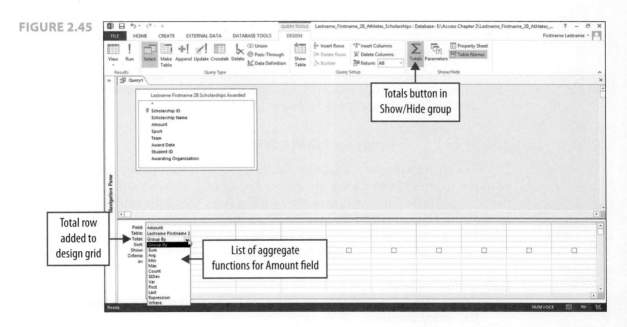

FIGURE 2.46

AGGREGATE FUNCTIONS	
FUNCTION NAME	**PURPOSE**
Group By	Groups the records alphabetically, for example, groups by Sport.
Sum	Totals the values in a field.
Avg	Averages the values in a field.
Min	Locates the smallest value in a field.
Max	Locates the largest value in a field.
Count	Displays the number of records based on a field.
StDev	Calculates the standard deviation for the values in a field.
Var	Calculates the variance for the values in a field.
First	Displays the first value in a field or column.
Last	Displays the last value in a field or column.
Expression	Creates a calculated field that includes an aggregate function.
Where	Limits the records to those that match a condition specified in the Criteria row of a field.

5 In the list of functions, click **Min**, and then **Run** the query. Point to the right edge of the first column to display the ⊕ pointer, and then double-click to apply Best Fit to the field.

Access locates the minimum (smallest) value—*$100*—in the Amount field for all of the records in the 2B Scholarships Awarded table. The field name *MinOfAmount* is automatically created. This query answers the question, *What is the minimum (smallest) scholarship amount awarded to athletes?*

6 Switch to **Design** view. In the **Total** row under **Amount**, click the **arrow**, and then click **Max**. **Run** the query.

The maximum (largest) value for a scholarship award amount is *$750.00*.

7 Switch to **Design** view. In the **Total** row, under **Amount**, click the **arrow**, and then click **Avg**. **Run** the query.

The average scholarship award amount is *$358.33*.

8 Switch to **Design** view. In the **Total** row, under **Amount**, click the **arrow**, and then click **Sum**. **Run** the query.

The values in the Amount field for all records are summed displaying a result of *$10,750.00*. The field name *SumOfAmount* is automatically created. The query answers the question, *What is the total dollar amount of all scholarships awarded?*

Activity 2.31 | Grouping Records in a Query

You can use aggregate functions and then group the records by the data in a field. For example, to group (summarize) the amount of scholarships awarded to each student, you include the Student ID field in addition to the Amount field. Using the Sum aggregate function, the records will be grouped by the Student ID so you can see the total amount of scholarships awarded to each student. Similarly, you can group the records by the Sport field so you can see the total amount of scholarships awarded for each sport.

1 Switch to **Design** view. From the field list, drag the **Student ID** field to the first column of the design grid—the **Amount** field moves to the second column. In the **Total** row, under **Student ID**, notice that *Group By* displays.

This query will group—summarize—the records by Student ID and will calculate a total amount for each student.

2 **Run** the query, and then compare your screen with Figure 2.47.

The query calculates the total amount of all scholarships for each student.

FIGURE 2.47

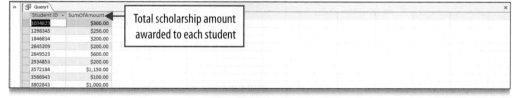

3 Switch to **Design** view. In the design grid, above **Student ID**, point to the selection bar to display the ↓ pointer. Click to select the column, and then press Del to remove the **Student ID** field from the design grid.

4 From the field list, drag the **Sport** field to the first column in the design grid—the **Amount** field moves to the second column. Click in the **Sort** row under **Amount**, click the **arrow**, and then click **Descending**.

5 On the **DESIGN tab**, in the **Show/Hide group**, click **Property Sheet**. In the **Property Sheet**, set the **Decimal Places** property to **0**, and then **Close** ☒ the **Property Sheet**.

6 **Run** the query, and then compare your screen with Figure 2.48.

Access groups—summarizes—the records by each sport and displays the groupings in descending order by the total amount of scholarships awarded for each sport. Basketball scholarships were awarded the largest total amount—*$3,500*—and Volleyball scholarships were awarded the smallest total amount—*$650*.

FIGURE 2.48

Total scholarship amount awarded for each sport

7 **Save** 🖫 the query as **Lastname Firstname 2B Total by Sport Query** and then display the query results in **Print Preview**. Create a paper or electronic printout as directed, click **Close Print Preview**, and then **Close** ☒ the query.

Objective 14 | Create a Crosstab Query

Video A2-14

A **crosstab query** uses an aggregate function for data that can be grouped by two types of information, and then displays the data in a compact, spreadsheet-like format with column headings and row headings. A crosstab query always has at least one row heading, one column heading, and one summary field. Use a crosstab query to summarize a large amount of data in a compact space that is easy to read.

Activity 2.32 | Creating a Crosstab Query Using the Query Wizard

In this activity, you will create a crosstab query that displays the total amount of scholarships awarded for each sport and for each type of team—men's or women's.

1 On the ribbon, click the **CREATE tab**, and then in the **Queries group**, click **Query Wizard**.

2 In the **New Query** dialog box, click **Crosstab Query Wizard**, and then click **OK**.

3 In the **Crosstab Query Wizard**, click your **Table: 2B Scholarships Awarded**, and then click **Next**.

4 In the wizard under **Available Fields**, double-click **Sport** to move the field to the **Selected Fields** list and to group the scholarship amounts by the sports—the sports will display as row headings. Click **Next**, and then compare your screen with Figure 2.49.

The sport names will be grouped and displayed as row headings, and you are prompted to select column headings.

FIGURE 2.49

5 In the wizard, in the field list, click **Team** to select the column headings. Click **Next**, and then compare your screen with Figure 2.50.

The Team types—*Men's* and *Women's*—will display as column headings, and you are prompted to select a field to summarize.

FIGURE 2.50

6 In the wizard under **Fields**, click **Amount**. Under **Functions**, click **Sum**.

The crosstab query will calculate the total scholarship amount for each sport and for each type of team.

7 Click **Next**. In the **What do you want to name your query?** box, select the existing text, type **Lastname Firstname 2B Sport and Team Crosstab Query** and then click **Finish**. Apply **Best Fit** to the datasheet, **Save** the query, click in any field to cancel the selection, and then compare your screen with Figure 2.51.

The field widths adjust to display fully the calculated field names.

FIGURE 2.51

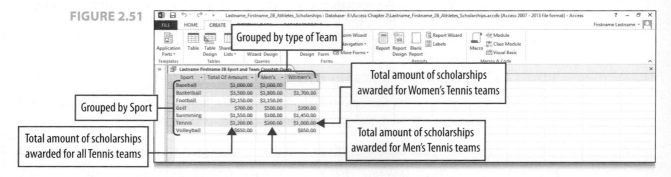

8 Display the query results in **Print Preview**. Create a paper or electronic printout as directed, click **Close Print Preview**, and then **Close** ☒ the query.

More **Knowledge** | **Creating a Crosstab Query Using Data from Two Related Tables**

To create a crosstab query using fields from more than one table, you must first create a select query with the fields from both tables, and then use the query as the data source for the crosstab query.

Video A2-15

A ***parameter query*** prompts you for criteria before running the query. For example, you might need to display the records for students who live in different cities serviced by Texas Lakes Community College. You can create a select query and enter the criteria for a city such as Austin, but when you open the query, only the records for those students who live in Austin will display. To find the students who live in Round Rock, you must open the query in Design view, change the criteria, and then run the query again.

A parameter query eliminates the need to change the design of a select query. You create a single query that prompts you to enter the city; the results are based upon the criteria you enter when prompted.

Activity 2.33 | Creating a Parameter Query with One Criteria

In this activity, you will create a parameter query that displays student athletes from a specified city in the areas serviced by Texas Lakes Community College.

1 On the **CREATE tab**, in the **Queries group**, click **Query Design**.

2 In the **Show Table** dialog box, double-click your **2B Athletes** table to add it to the table area, **Close** the **Show Table** dialog box, and then resize the field list.

3 Add the following fields to the design grid in the order given: **Last Name**, **First Name**, **Address**, **City**, **State**, and **Postal Code**.

4 Click in the **Sort** row under **Last Name**, click the **arrow**, and then click **Ascending**. Click in the **Sort** row under **First Name**, click the **arrow**, and then click **Ascending**.

5 In the **Criteria** row under **City**, type **[Enter a City]** and then press Enter. Compare your screen with Figure 2.52.

The bracketed text indicates a ***parameter***—a value that can be changed—rather than specific criteria.

FIGURE 2.52

6 **Run** the query. In the **Enter Parameter Value** dialog box, type **austin** and then compare your screen with Figure 2.53.

The Enter Parameter Value dialog box prompts you to *Enter a City*, which is the text enclosed in brackets that you entered in the Criteria row under City. The city you enter will be set as the criteria for the query. Because you are prompted for the criteria, you can reuse this query without having to edit the Criteria row in Design view. The value you enter is not case sensitive—you can enter *austin*, *Austin*, or *AUSTIN*.

FIGURE 2.53

ALERT! Did the Enter Parameter Value Dialog Box Not Display?

If the Enter Parameter Value dialog box does not display, you may have typed the parameter incorrectly in the design grid. Common errors include using parentheses or curly braces instead of brackets around the parameter text, which Access interprets as specific criteria, resulting in no records matching the criteria. If you type curly braces instead of brackets, the query will not run. To correct, display the query in Design view and correct the parameter entered in the Criteria row.

7 In the **Enter Parameter Value** dialog box, click **OK**.

Twenty-three students live in the city of Austin, and the records are sorted in alphabetical order by the Last Name field. If students have the same last name, those records will be sorted by the First Name field.

8 Save 🖫 the query as **Lastname Firstname 2B City Parameter Query** and then **Close** ✕ the query.

Recall that only the query design is saved; each time you open a query, it is run using the most up-to-date information from the data source.

9 Open ⟩⟩ the **Navigation Pane**. In the **Navigation Pane**, under your **2B Athletes** table, double-click your **2B City Parameter Query**. In the **Enter Parameter Value** dialog box, type **round rock** and then click **OK**. **Close** ⟨⟨ the **Navigation Pane**. Compare your screen with Figure 2.54.

Nine students live in the city of Round Rock. Every time you open a parameter query, you are prompted to enter criteria. You may have to apply Best Fit to the columns if all of the data in the fields does not display and you wish to print the query results—the length of the data in the fields changes as new records display depending upon the criteria entered.

FIGURE 2.54

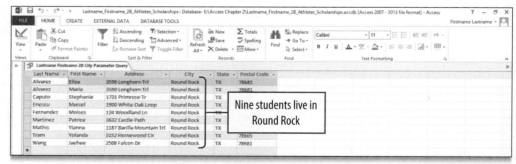

10 Display the query results in **Print Preview**, and change the orientation to **Landscape**. Create a paper or electronic printout as directed, click **Close Print Preview**, and then **Close** ✕ the query.

11 Open ⟩⟩ the **Navigation Pane**, and, if necessary increase the width of the pane so that all object names display fully. On the right side of the title bar, click **Close** ☒ to close the database and to exit Access. As directed by your instructor, submit your database and the paper or electronic printouts of the 11 objects—relationship report and 10 queries—that are the results of this project. Specifically, in this project, using your own name, you created the following database and printouts or electronic printouts:

1. Lastname_Firstname_2B_Athletes_Scholarships	Database file
2. Lastname Firstname 2B Relationships	Relationships Report (printout or electronic printout)
3. Lastname Firstname 2B $300 or More Query	Query (printout or electronic printout)
4. Lastname Firstname 2B Awards May-June Query	Query (printout or electronic printout)
5. Lastname Firstname 2B Football AND Over $500 Query	Query (printout or electronic printout)
6. Lastname Firstname 2B Volleyball OR Golf AND Over $200 Query	Query (printout or electronic printout)
7. Lastname Firstname 2B Tennis OR Swimming Query	Query (printout or electronic printout)
8. Lastname Firstname 2B Wildcard Query	Query (printout or electronic printout)
9. Lastname Firstname 2B Alumni Donations Query	Query (printout or electronic printout)
10. Lastname Firstname 2B Total by Sport Query	Query (printout or electronic printout)
11. Lastname Firstname 2B Sport and Team Crosstab Query	Query (printout or electronic printout)
12. Lastname Firstname 2B City Parameter Query	Query (printout or electronic printout - Round Rock)

More **Knowledge**   **Parameter Query Prompts**

Be sure that the parameter you enter in the Criteria row as a prompt is not the same as the field name. For example, do not use *[City]* as the parameter. Access interprets this as the field name of *City*. Recall that you entered a field name in brackets when creating a calculated field in a query. If you use a field name as the parameter, the Enter Parameter Value dialog box *will not* display, and all of the records *will* display.

The parameter should inform the individual running the query of the data required to display the correct results. If you want to use the field name by itself as the prompt, type a question mark at the end of the text; for example, *[City?]*. You cannot use a period, exclamation mark (!), curly braces ({ }), another set of brackets ([ ]), or the ampersand (&) as part of the parameter.

END | You have completed Project 2B

GO! with Office Online (formerly Web Apps)

Objective | Export an Access Query to a PDF File, Save the PDF File to Google Drive, and Share the File

Access web apps are designed to work with Microsoft's SharePoint, a service for setting up websites to share and manage documents. Your college may not have SharePoint installed, so you will use other tools to share objects from your database so that you can work collaboratively with others. Recall that Google Docs is Google's free, web-based word processor, spreadsheet, slide show, form, and data storage service. Google Drive is Google's free file storage and sharing service. For Access, you can export a database object to an Excel worksheet, a PDF file, or a text file, and then save the file to Google Drive.

Activity | **Exporting an Access Query to a PDF File, Saving the PDF file to Google Drive, and Sharing the File**

In this activity, you will export your 2B Sport and Team Crosstab Query object to a PDF file, upload your PDF file to Google Drive, and then share the file.

1 **Start** Access, navigate to your **Access Chapter 2** folder, and then **Open** your **2B_Athletes_Scholarships** database file. If necessary, on the Message Bar, click **Enable Content**. In the **Navigation Pane**, click your **2B Sport and Team Crosstab Query** object to select it—do not open it.

2 On the ribbon, click the **EXTERNAL DATA tab**, and then in the **Export group**, click **PDF or XPS**. In the **Publish as PDF or XPS** dialog box, navigate to your

Access Chapter 2 folder. Click in the **File name** box. Using your own name, type **Lastname_Firstname_AC_2B_Web** and then be sure that the **Open file after publishing** check box is selected, and the **Minimum size (publishing online)** option button is selected. Click **Publish**, and then compare your screen with Figure A.

The PDF file is created and opens in Windows 8 Reader, Adobe Reader, or Adobe Acrobat, depending on the software that is installed on your computer.

FIGURE A

Your 2B Sport and Team Crosstab Query exported as a PDF file and opened in Adobe Reader (yours may open in Windows Reader 8 or Adobe Acrobat)

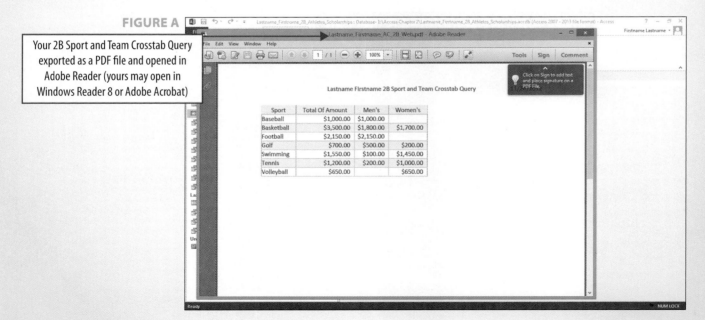

(GO! with Office Online (formerly Web Apps) continues on the next page)

3 **Close** your **AC_2B_Web** file. In the **Export – PDF** dialog box, click **Close**, and then **Close** Access.

4 From the desktop, start Internet Explorer, navigate to **http://drive.google.com**, and sign in to your Google account, or create one.

5 Open your **GO! Web Projects** folder—or create and open this folder if necessary. Under **Drive**, to the right of **Create**, click **Upload** , and then click **Files**. In the **Choose File to Upload** dialog box, navigate to your **Access Chapter 2** folder, and then double-click your **AC_2B_Web** file to upload it to Google Drive. When the title bar of the message box indicates *Upload complete*, **Close** the message box.

6 Click your **AC_2B_Web** file to open the file in Google Drive. Notice that it displays as a PDF file on a separate tab in the browser window.

7 In the browser window, locate the tab for the PDF file, and then **Close** the tab to display your folder in Google Drive.

8 Right-click your **AC_2B_Web** file, point to **Share**, and then click **Share**.

9 In the **Sharing settings** dialog box, click in the **Add people** box, and then type your own email address that you use at your college. Click the **Can edit arrow**, and click **Can comment**. Click **Add message**, type **Please share your comments about the results of this crosstab query.** and then compare your screen with Figure B.

10 On your keyboard, press the ⊞ key, type **snip** and then click **Snipping Tool**. In the **Snipping Tool** dialog box, click the **New arrow**, and then click **Full-screen snip**.

11 On the **Snipping Tool** toolbar, click **Save Snip** 🖫. In the **Save As** dialog box, navigate to your **Access Chapter 2** folder. Click in the **File name** box, type **Lastname_Firstname_AC_2B_Web_Snip** and then be sure that the **Save as type** box displays **JPEG file**. Click **Save**, and then **Close** ✖ the **Snipping Tool** window.

12 In the **Sharing settings** dialog box, click **Share & save**. In the **Sharing settings** dialog box, click **Done**.

You can change who has access to the file in the Sharing settings dialog box. By default, the file is private and is shared only with specific people you have designated. You can grant access to anyone on the web or to anyone who has the link to this file.

13 In Google Drive, click your Google Drive name, and then click **Sign out**. **Close** your browser window.

14 If directed to submit a paper printout of your pdf and snip file, follow the directions given in the Note. As directed by your instructor, submit your pdf file and your snip file that are the results of this project. Your instructor may also request that you submit a copy of the email that was sent to you notifying you of the shared file.

N O T E   **Printing Your PDF and Snip .jpeg File**

Use File Explorer to navigate to your Access Chapter 2 folder. Locate and double-click your AC_2B_Web file. On the toolbar, click the Print file button. Then Close the Windows 8 Reader, Adobe Reader, or Adobe Acrobat window. In your Access Chapter 2 folder, locate and double-click your AC_2B_Web_Snip file. If this is the first time you have tried to open a .jpeg file, you will be asked to identify a program. If you are not sure which program to use, select Windows Photo Viewer. From the ribbon, menu bar, or toolbar, click the Print command, and then Close the program window.

FIGURE B

Sharing Your Calendar in Office 365: With Office 365, you set up your Calendar in Outlook—either in Outlook Web App or on the desktop app—and then you can share your calendar, add appointments and meetings, and see your calendar from anywhere that you have Internet access. Recall that Outlook Web App and the Outlook desktop app work seamlessly together. When you use the desktop app, you have some additional features that are not available in Outlook Web App, but any information you add is available in either app. You will be able to view your calendar—and use email—from your smartphone or from anywhere you have an Internet connection.

In an Office 365 environment, the most important thing to do with your calendar is to share it with others. Recall that Office 365 is specifically designed to help teams work together, and the first step to working together successfully is to share as much information as possible to facilitate good communication.

When you create an appointment in your calendar, Outlook displays one of four indicators associated with your availability for that date and time: Busy, Free, Tentative, or Out of Office. This is referred to as your *free/busy information*. Outlook's default setting for all appointments is Busy. The free/busy indicators also display when others view your calendar on the Office 365 shared Exchange server. Recall that Exchange Server is Microsoft's system for sharing Outlook information among members on a network. Your free/busy schedule is shared automatically with all other users.

In an Exchange Online environment, you can share your calendar with other Exchange Online users in your organization. Additionally, you can publish your calendar to the Internet and other people so they can access it. You could even share your calendar with a customer or client.

Activity | Sharing Calendars

This group project relates to the **Bell Orchid Hotels**. If your instructor assigns this project to your class, you can expect to use your **Outlook Calendar** in **Office 365 Exchange Online** to set meeting times for the following tasks for this chapter:

- If you are in the **Accounting Group**, you and your teammates will set meeting times to sort, filter, and create queries for the Stockholders database you created in Chapter 1.

- If you are in the **Engineering Group**, you and your teammates will set meeting times to sort, filter, and create queries for the Subcontractors database you created in Chapter 1.

- If you are in the **Food and Beverage Group**, you and your teammates will set meeting times to sort, filter, and create queries for the Banquet Clients database you created in Chapter 1.

- If you are in the **Human Resources Group**, you and your teammates will set meeting times to sort, filter, and create queries for the Employee database you created in Chapter 1.

- If you are in the **Operations Group**, you and your teammates will set meeting times to sort, filter, and create queries for the Guests database you created in Chapter 1.

- If you are in the **Sales and Marketing Group**, you and your teammates will set meeting times to sort, filter, and create queries for the Associations database you created in Chapter 1.

FIGURE A

END OF CHAPTER

SUMMARY

Table relationships are created by joining the common fields in tables and provide a means for you to extract information from multiple tables when you create queries, forms, and reports.

Queries are created to answer questions and to extract information from your database tables; saving a query with your database saves you time when you need to answer the question many times.

Queries range from simple queries where you ask a single question to complex queries where you use compound criteria, wildcard characters, logical operators, and create calculated fields.

A crosstab query displays information grouped by two fields that is an easy way to display complex data, and a parameter query prompts you to enter the criteria when you open or run the query.

GO! LEARN IT ONLINE

Review the concepts and key terms in this chapter by completing these online challenges, which you can find at **www.pearsonhighered.com/go**.

Matching and Multiple Choice:
Answer matching and multiple choice questions to test what you learned in this chapter. MyITLab®

Crossword Puzzle:
Spell out the words that match the numbered clues, and put them in the puzzle squares.

Flipboard:
Flip through the definitions of the key terms in this chapter and match them with the correct term.

GO! FOR JOB SUCCESS

Video: Making Ethical Choices

Your instructor may assign this video to your class, and then ask you to think about, or discuss with your classmates, these questions:

FotolEdhar / Fotolia

Which behaviors in this video do you think were unethical?

Is it unethical to "borrow" things from your employer? Why? What would you do if you saw this behavior going on?

What do you think an employer could do to prevent unethical behavior?

END OF CHAPTER

REVIEW AND ASSESSMENT GUIDE FOR ACCESS CHAPTER 2

Your instructor may assign one or more of these projects to help you review the chapter and assess your mastery and understanding of the chapter.

	Review and Assessment Guide for Access Chapter 2		
Project	**Apply Skills from These Chapter Objectives**	**Project Type**	**Project Location**
2C	Objectives 1-7 from Project 2A	**2C Skills Review** A guided review of the skills from Project 2A.	On the following pages
2D	Objectives 8-15 from Project 2B	**2D Skills Review** A guided review of the skills from Project 2B.	On the following pages
2E	Objectives 1-7 from Project 2A	**2E Mastery (Grader Project)** A demonstration of your mastery of the skills in Project 2A with extensive decision making.	In MyITLab and on the following pages
2F	Objectives 8-15 from Project 2B	**2F Mastery (Grader Project)** A demonstration of your mastery of the skills in Project 2B with extensive decision making.	In MyITLab and on the following pages
2G	Objectives 1-15 from Projects 2A and 2B	**2G Mastery (Grader Project)** A demonstration of your mastery of the skills in Projects 2A and 2B with extensive decision making.	In MyITLab and on the following pages
2H	Combination of Objectives from Projects 2A and 2B	**2H GO! Fix It** A demonstration of your mastery of the skills in Projects 2A and 2B by creating a correct result from a document that contains errors you must find.	Online
2I	Combination of Objectives from Projects 2A and 2B	**2I GO! Make It** A demonstration of your mastery of the skills in Projects 2A and 2B by creating a result from a supplied picture.	Online
2J	Combination of Objectives from Projects 2A and 2B	**2J GO! Solve It** A demonstration of your mastery of the skills in Projects 2A and 2B, your decision-making skills, and your critical thinking skills. A task-specific rubric helps you self-assess your result.	Online
2K	Combination of Objectives from Projects 2A and 2B	**2K GO! Solve It** A demonstration of your mastery of the skills in Projects 2A and 2B, your decision-making skills, and your critical thinking skills. A task-specific rubric helps you self-assess your result.	On the following pages
2L	Combination of Objectives from Projects 2A and 2B	**2L GO! Think** A demonstration of your understanding of the chapter concepts applied in a manner that you would outside of college. An analytic rubric helps you and your instructor grade the quality of your work by comparing it to the work an expert in the discipline would create.	On the following pages
2M	Combination of Objectives from Projects 2A and 2B	**2M GO! Think** A demonstration of your understanding of the chapter concepts applied in a manner that you would outside of college. An analytic rubric helps you and your instructor grade the quality of your work by comparing it to the work an expert in the discipline would create.	Online
2N	Combination of Objectives from Projects 2A and 2B	**2N You and GO!** A demonstration of your understanding of the chapter concepts applied in a manner that you would in a personal situation. An analytic rubric helps you and your instructor grade the quality of your work.	Online
2O	Combination of Objectives from Projects 2A and 2B	**2O Cumulative Group Project for Access Chapter 2** A demonstration of your understanding of concepts and your ability to work collaboratively in a group role-playing assessment, requiring both collaboration and self-management.	Online

GLOSSARY

GLOSSARY OF CHAPTER KEY TERMS

Aggregate functions Calculations such as Min, Max, Avg, and Sum that are performed on a group of records.

AND condition A compound criteria used to display records that match all parts of the specified criteria.

Ascending order A sorting order that arranges text alphabetically (A to Z) and numbers from the lowest number to the highest number.

Between … And operator A comparison operator that looks for values within a range.

Calculated field A field that stores the value of a mathematical operation.

Cascade Delete Related Records A cascade option that enables you to delete a record in a table on the *one* side of the relationship and also delete all of the related records in related tables.

Cascade options Relationship options that enable you to update records in related tables when referential integrity is enforced.

Cascade Update Related Fields A cascade option that enables you to change the data in the primary key field in the table on the *one* side of the relationship and update that change to any fields storing that same data in related tables.

Comparison operators Symbols that are used to evaluate data in the field to determine if it is the same (=), greater than (>), less than (<), or in between a range of values as specified by the criteria.

Compound criteria Multiple conditions in a query or filter.

Criteria Conditions in a query that identify the specific records you are looking for.

Crosstab query A query that uses an aggregate function for data that can be grouped by two types of information and displays the data in a compact, spreadsheet-like format with column headings and row headings.

Data source The table or tables from which a form, query, or report retrieves its data.

Descending order A sorting order that arranges text in reverse alphabetical order (Z to A) and numbers from the highest number to the lowest number.

Design grid The lower area of the query window that displays the design of the query.

Expression A formula.

Field list A list of field names in a table.

Foreign key The field that is included in the related table so the field can be joined with the primary key in another table for the purpose of creating a relationship.

Free/Busy information In the Outlook calendar, one of four indicators—Busy, Free, Tentative, or Out of Office—associated with your availability for a specific date and time.

Innermost sort field When sorting on multiple fields in Datasheet view, the field that is used for the second level of sorting.

Is Not Null A criteria that searches for fields that are not empty.

Is Null A criteria that searches for fields that are empty.

Join line In the Relationships window, the line joining two tables that visually indicates the common fields and the type of relationship.

Logical operators Operators that are used to evaluate data to determine if a condition is met (true) or not met (false). With two criteria, AND requires that both conditions be met and OR requires that either condition be met for a record to display in the query results.

Message Bar The area directly below the ribbon that displays information such as security alerts when there is potentially unsafe, active content in an Office document that you open.

One-to-many relationship A relationship between two tables where one record in the first table corresponds to many records in the second table—the most common type of relationship in Access.

OR condition A compound criteria used to display records that match at least one of the specified criteria.

Outermost sort field When sorting on multiple fields in Datasheet view, the field that is used for the first level of sorting.

Parameter A value that can be changed.

Parameter query A query that prompts you for criteria before running the query.

Referential integrity A set of rules that Access uses to ensure that the data between related tables is valid.

Relationship An association that you establish between two tables based on common fields.

Run The process in which Access looks at the records in the table(s) included in the query design, finds the records that match the specified criteria, and then displays the records in a datasheet; only the fields included in the query design display.

Sorting The process of arranging data in a specific order based on the value in a field.

Subdatasheet A format for displaying related records when you click ⊞ next to a record in a table on the *one* side of the relationship.

Subset A portion of the total records available.

Table area The upper area of the query window that displays field lists for the tables that are used in a query.

Text string A sequence of characters.

Trust Center An area of Access where you can view the security and privacy settings for your Access installation.

Wildcard character In a query, a character that serves as a placeholder for one or more unknown characters in criteria; an asterisk (*) represents one or more unknown characters, and a question mark (?) represents a single unknown character.

Apply 2A skills from these Objectives:

1 Open and Save an Existing Database

2 Create Table Relationships

3 Sort Records in a Table

4 Create a Query in Design View

5 Create a New Query from an Existing Query

6 Sort Query Results

7 Specify Criteria in a Query

Skills Review | Project 2C Freshman Orientation

In the following Skills Review, you will assist Dr. Wendy Bowie, the director of counseling at the Southwest Campus, in using her database to answer several questions about the freshman orientation sessions that will be held prior to class registration. Your completed database objects will look similar to Figure 2.55.

PROJECT FILES

For Project 2C, you will need the following file:

a02C_Freshman_Orientation

You will save your database as:

Lastname_Firstname_2C_Freshman_Orientation

PROJECT RESULTS

FIGURE 2.55

(Project 2C Freshman Orientation continues on the next page)

CHAPTER REVIEW

1 Start Access. In the Access opening screen, click **Open Other Files**. Under **Open**, click **Computer**. Under **Recent Folders**, if displayed, click the location where your student data files are stored; otherwise, click **Browse** and then navigate to the location where your student data files are stored. Double-click **a02C_Freshman_Orientation** to open the database.

a. On the ribbon, click the **FILE tab**, and then click **Save As**. Under **File Types**, be sure **Save Database As** is selected. On the right, under **Database File Types**, be sure **Access Database** is selected, and then click **Save As**.

b. In the **Save As** dialog box, navigate to your **Access Chapter 2** folder. Click in the **File name** box, type **Lastname_Firstname_2C_Freshman_Orientation** and then press [Enter]. On the **Message Bar**, click **Enable Content**.

c. In the **Navigation Pane**, right-click **2C New Students**, and then click **Rename**. With the table name selected and using your own name, type **Lastname Firstname 2C New Students** and then press [Enter]. **Rename** the **2C Orientation Sessions** table to **Lastname Firstname 2C Orientation Sessions** and then point to the right edge of the **Navigation Pane** to display the [↔] pointer. Drag to the right to increase the width of the pane until both tables names display fully.

2 In the **Navigation Pane**, double-click your **2C New Students** table to open it in the object window, and examine the fields in the table. Double-click your **2C Orientation Sessions** table, and examine the fields in the table. In the object window, right-click either **object tab**, and then click **Close All** to close both tables. **Close** the **Navigation Pane**.

a. On the ribbon, click the **DATABASE TOOLS tab**, and then in the **Relationships group**, click **Relationships**. Point to the title bar of the **Show Table** dialog box, and then drag downward and slightly to the right to move the dialog box away from the top of the **Relationships** window.

b. In the **Show Table** dialog box, click your **2C Orientation Sessions** table, and then click **Add**. In the **Show Table** dialog box, double-click your **2C New Students** table to add it to the **Relationships** window. In the **Show Table** dialog box, click **Close**.

c. In the **2C New Students** field list—the field list on the right—point to the title bar to display the [↘] pointer, and then drag the field list to the right until there are approximately three inches of space between the field lists. In the **2C New Students** field list, point to the lower right corner of the field list to display the [↘] pointer, and then drag downward and to the right to resize the field list and display all of the field names and the entire table name. Use the same technique to resize the **2C Orientation Sessions** field list—the field list on the left—so that the table name displays fully.

d. In the **2C Orientation Sessions** field list, point to **Orientation ID**, and then drag the field name downward and to the right into the **2C New Students** field list until the [↘] pointer's arrow is on top of **Orientation ID**. Release the mouse button to display the **Edit Relationships** dialog box. Drag the **Edit Relationships** dialog box downward below the two field lists.

e. In the **Edit Relationships** dialog box, click to select the **Enforce Referential Integrity** check box, the **Cascade Update Related Fields** check box, and the **Cascade Delete Related Records** check box. In the **Edit Relationships** dialog box, click **Create** to create a one-to-many relationship—*one* orientation session can be scheduled for *many* new students.

f. Under **RELATIONSHIP TOOLS**, on the **DESIGN tab**, in the **Tools group**, click **Relationship Report**. On the **PRINT PREVIEW tab**, in the **Page Size group**, click **Margins**, and then click **Normal**. Create a paper or electronic printout as directed. On the **Quick Access Toolbar**, click **Save**. In the **Save As** dialog box, click **OK** to accept the default report name. In the object window, **Close** the report, and then **Close** the **Relationships** window.

g. **Open** the **Navigation Pane**, double-click your **2C Orientation Sessions** table to open it in the object window, and then **Close** the **Navigation Pane**. On the left side of the last record—*Orientation ID* of *O-1*—click [+] to display the subdatasheet, and notice that 13 new students are scheduled to attend this orientation session. Click [−] to collapse the subdatasheet.

(Project 2C Freshman Orientation continues on the next page)

CHAPTER REVIEW

h. In the last record, in the **Orientation ID** field, select the existing data—*O-1*—and then type **O-001**—the first character is the letter *O* followed by a hyphen, two zeros, and the number *1*— to make the data consistent with the Orientation IDs of the other sessions. The 13 related records in your 2C New Students table are updated with the new Orientation ID because you selected **Cascade Update Related Fields** in the **Edit Relationships** dialog box.

i. Display the subdatasheet for the record with an **Orientation ID** of **O-010**, and notice that one student—*Student ID* of *8273485*—is scheduled for this orientation session. Collapse the subdatasheet. To the left of the record, point to the record selector box to display the → pointer, and then click to select the record. On the **HOME tab**, in the **Records group**, click **Delete**. In the message box, click **Yes** to delete this record and the related student record in the **2C New Students** table.

3 In the **Date** field, click in any record. On the **HOME tab**, in the **Sort & Filter group**, click **Ascending** to sort the records by the date. In the field names row, click the **Room arrow**, and then click **Sort Z to A** to sort the rooms from Room 203 to Room 201. The records are sorted first by the **Room** field and then by the **Date** field. On the **FILE tab**, click **Print**, and then click **Print Preview**. Create a paper or electronic printout as directed, and then click **Close Print Preview**. On the **HOME tab**, in the **Sort & Filter group**, click **Remove Sort**. **Close** the table, and in the message box, click **No**; you do not need to save any design changes to the table.

4 On the ribbon, click the **CREATE tab**, and then in the **Queries group**, click **Query Design**. In the **Show Table** dialog box, double-click your *2C Orientation Sessions* table, and then **Close** the **Show Table** dialog box. Point to the lower right corner of the field list to display the ⬂ pointer, and then drag downward and to the right to resize the field list, displaying all of the field names and the entire table name.

a. In the field list, double-click **Orientation ID** to add the field to the first column in the design grid. In the field list, point to **Date**, and then drag the field name down into the design grid until the ⬂ pointer displays in the **Field** row in the second

column, and then release the mouse button. In the design grid, in the **Field** row, click in the third column, click the **arrow**, and then click **Day of Week** to add the field to the design grid. Using one of the three techniques you just practiced, add the **Time** field to the fourth column and the **Room** field to the fifth column in the design grid.

b. Under **QUERY TOOLS**, on the **DESIGN tab**, in the **Results group**, click **Run**. This query answers the question, *What is the Orientation ID, date, day of week, time, and room for all of the orientation sessions in the 2C Orientation Sessions table?*

c. On the **Quick Access Toolbar**, click **Save**. In the **Save As** dialog box, type **Lastname Firstname 2C All Sessions Query** and then click **OK**. On the ribbon, click the **FILE tab**, click **Print**, and then click **Print Preview**. Create a paper or electronic printout as directed, and then click **Close Print Preview**. **Close** your **2C All Sessions Query**, and then **Open** the **Navigation Pane**.

5 In the **Navigation Pane**, right-click your **2C All Sessions Query** object, and then click **Copy**. In the **Navigation Pane**, point to a blank area, right-click, and then click **Paste**. In the **Paste As** dialog box, type **Lastname Firstname 2C Day of Week Query** and then click **OK** to create a new query based on an existing query.

a. In the **Navigation Pane**, right click your **2C Day of Week Query** object, and then click **Design View**. **Close** the **Navigation Pane**. In the design grid, point to the thin gray selection bar above the **Orientation ID** field name to display the ⬇ pointer, click to select the column, and then press [Del].

b. Point to the selection bar above the **Day of Week** field name to display the ⬍ pointer, and then drag to the left until a dark vertical line displays on the left side of the **Date** column. Release the mouse button to position the **Day of Week** field in the first column.

c. **Run** the query. The query results display four fields. This query answers the question, *What is the day of week, date, time, and room for every orientation session in the 2C Orientation Sessions table?*

(Project 2C Freshman Orientation continues on the next page)

CHAPTER REVIEW

d. On the **FILE tab**, click **Print**, and then click **Print Preview**. Create a paper or electronic printout as directed, and then click **Close Print Preview**. **Close** the query, and in the message box, click **Yes** to save the changes to the design—you deleted one field and moved another field. **Open** the **Navigation Pane**.

6 In the **Navigation Pane**, right-click your **2C Day of Week Query** object, and then click **Copy**. In the **Navigation Pane**, point to a blank area, right-click, and then click **Paste**. In the **Paste As** dialog box, type **Lastname Firstname 2C Sessions Sort Query** and then click **OK** to create a new query based on an existing query. Increase the width of the **Navigation Pane** so that the names of all of the objects display fully.

a. In the **Navigation Pane**, right-click your **2C Sessions Sort Query** click **Design View**, and then **Close** the **Navigation Pane**. In the design grid, drag the **Room** field to the left of the **Day of Week** field to position it in the first column. In the design grid, click in the **Sort** row under **Room**, click the **arrow**, and then click **Descending**. Click in the **Sort** row under **Date**, click the **arrow**, and then click **Ascending**.

b. **Run** the query. This query answers the question, *For every session, within each room (with the Room field sorted in descending order), what is the day of week, date (with the Date field sorted in ascending order), and time?*

c. Display the query results in **Print Preview**, create a paper or electronic printout as directed, and then click **Close Print Preview**. **Close** the query, and in the message box, click **Yes** to save the changes to the query design.

7 On the ribbon, click the **CREATE tab**, and then in the **Queries group**, click **Query Design**. In the **Show Table** dialog box, double-click your **2C New Students** table to add it to the table area, and then **Close** the **Show Table** dialog box. Resize the field list to display all of the field names and the entire table name. Add the following fields to the design grid in the order given: **Student ID**, **Last Name**, **First Name**, and **Orientation ID**.

a. In the design grid, click in the **Criteria** row under **Orientation ID**, type **O-001**—the first character is the letter *O* followed by a hyphen, two zeros, and the number *1*—and then press [Enter].

b. **Run** the query to display 13 records that meet the specified criteria—records that have *O-001* in the *Orientation ID* field. **Save** the query as **Lastname Firstname 2C First Session Query** and then display the query results in **Print Preview**. Create a paper or electronic printout as directed, click **Close Print Preview**, and then **Close** the query.

c. On the ribbon, click the **CREATE tab**, and then in the **Queries group**, click **Query Design**. In the **Show Table** dialog box, double-click your **2C New Students** table to add it to the table area, and then **Close** the **Show Table** dialog box. Resize the field list, and then add the following fields to the design grid in the order given: **Student ID**, **First Name**, **Last Name**, **Phone Number**, **Email Address**, and **City**. Click in the **Criteria** row under **City**, type **dripping springs** and then press [Enter].

d. **Run** the query to display the five new students who live in *Dripping Springs*. Switch to **Design** view. In the design grid, in the **Show** row under **City**, click to clear the check box. Recall that if all of the results use the same criteria, such as *dripping springs*, it is not necessary to display that field in the query results. **Run** the query again. **Save** the query as **Lastname Firstname 2C Dripping Springs Query** and then display the query results in **Print Preview**. Create a paper or electronic printout as directed, click **Close Print Preview**, and then **Close** the query.

e. On the ribbon, click the **CREATE tab**, and then in the **Queries group**, click **Query Design**. In the **Show Table** dialog box, double-click your **2C New Students** table to add it to the table area, and then **Close** the **Show Table** dialog box. Resize the field list, and then add the following fields to the design grid in the order given: **Student ID**, **Last Name**, **First Name**, **Email Address**, **Phone Number**, and **Orientation ID**. Click in the **Sort** row under **Last Name**, click the **arrow**, and then click **Ascending**. Click in the **Sort** row under **First Name**, click the **arrow**, and then click **Ascending**. Click in the **Criteria** row under **Orientation ID**, type **is null** and then press [Enter].

(Project 2C Freshman Orientation continues on the next page)

CHAPTER REVIEW

f. **Run** the query to display the three new students who have not signed up for an orientation session. **Save** the query as **Lastname Firstname 2C Missing Orientation ID Query** and then display the query results in **Print Preview**. On the **PRINT PREVIEW** tab, in the **Page Size group**, click **Margins**, and then click **Normal**. Create a paper or electronic printout as directed, click **Close Print Preview**, and then **Close** the query.

g. **Open** the **Navigation Pane**. If necessary, increase the width of the pane so that all object names display fully. On the right side of the title bar, click **Close** to close the database and to exit Access. As directed by your instructor, submit your database and the paper or electronic printouts of the eight objects—relationship report, sorted table, and six queries—that are the results of this project. Specifically, in this project, using your own name, you created the following database and printouts or electronic printouts:

1. Lastname_Firstname_2C_Freshman_Orientation	Database file
2. Relationships for Lastname_Firstname_2C_Freshman_Orientation	Relationships Report (printout or electronic printout)
3. Lastname Firstname 2C Orientation Sessions table sorted (not saved)	Table sorted (printout or electronic printout)
4. Lastname Firstname 2C All Sessions Query	Query (printout or electronic printout)
5. Lastname Firstname 2C Day of Week Query	Query (printout or electronic printout)
6. Lastname Firstname 2C Sessions Sort Query	Query (printout or electronic printout)
7. Lastname Firstname 2C First Session Query	Query (printout or electronic printout)
8. Lastname Firstname 2C Dripping Springs Query	Query (printout or electronic printout)
9. Lastname Firstname 2C Missing Orientation ID Query	Query (printout or electronic printout)

END | You have completed Project 2C

CHAPTER REVIEW

Skills Review　Project 2D Club Fundraisers

In the following Skills Review, you will assist Dr. Michael Bransford, the student activities director for Texas Lakes Community College, in answering his questions about fundraisers, clubs, donations, dates of fundraiser events, and fundraiser locations. Your completed database objects will look similar to Figure 2.56.

PROJECT FILES

For Project 2D, you will need the following files:

a02D_Club_Fundraisers

a02D_Clubs (Excel workbook)

You will save your database as:

Lastname_Firstname_2D_Club_Fundraisers

PROJECT RESULTS

FIGURE 2.56

(Project 2D Club Fundraisers continues on the next page)

1 ▶ **Start** Access. In the **Access** opening screen, click **Open Other Files**. Under **Open**, click **Computer**. Under **Recent Folders**, if displayed, click the location where your student data files are stored; otherwise, click **Browse** and then navigate to the location where your student data files are stored. Double-click **a02D_Club_Fundraisers** to open the database.

a. On the ribbon, click the **FILE tab**, and then click **Save As**. Under **File Types**, be sure **Save Database As** is selected. On the right, under **Database File Types**, be sure **Access Database** is selected, and then at the bottom of the screen, click **Save As**. In the **Save As** dialog box, navigate to your **Access Chapter 2** folder. Click in the **File name** box, type **Lastname_Firstname_2D_Club_Fundraisers** and then press Enter. On the **Message Bar**, click **Enable Content**.

b. In the **Navigation Pane**, right-click **2D Fundraisers**, click **Rename**, type **Lastname Firstname 2D Fundraisers** and then press Enter. Increase the width of the **Navigation Pane** to display the entire table name. Double-click the table name to open it, examine the fields in the table, and then **Close** the table.

c. On the ribbon, click the **EXTERNAL DATA tab**, and then in the **Import & Link group**, click **Excel**. In the **Get External Data – Excel Spreadsheet** dialog box, to the right of the **File name** box, click **Browse**. In the **File Open** dialog box, navigate to your student data files, and then double-click **a02D_Clubs**. Be sure that the **Import the source data into a new table in the current database** option button is selected, and then click **OK**.

d. In the upper left area of the wizard, select the **First Row Contains Column Headings** check box, click **Next**, and then click **Next** again. In the wizard, click the **Choose my own primary key** option button, be sure that **Club ID** displays, and then click **Next**. With the text selected in the **Import to Table** box and using your own name, type **Lastname Firstname 2D Clubs**, and then click **Finish**. In the **Get External Data – Excel Spreadsheet** dialog box, click **Close**.

e. In the **Navigation Pane**, right-click your **2D Clubs** table, and then click **Design View**. **Close** the **Navigation Pane**. In the **Field Name** column, click

Club ID. In the **Field Properties** area, click **Field Size**, type **8** and then press Enter. Under **TABLE TOOLS**, on the **DESIGN tab**, in the **Views group**, click the upper portion of the **View** button to switch to **Datasheet** view. In the message box, click **Yes** to save the design changes. In the second message box, click **Yes**—no data will be lost. Examine the fields and data in the table. To the left of the **Club ID** field name, click **Select All**. On the **HOME tab**, in the **Records group**, click **More**, and then click **Field Width**. In the **Column Width** dialog box, click **Best Fit**. **Save** the table, click in any record to cancel the selection, and then **Close** the table.

f. On the ribbon, click the **DATABASE TOOLS tab**, and then in the **Relationships group**, click **Relationships**. In the **Show Table** dialog box, double-click your **2D Clubs** table, and then double-click your **2D Fundraisers** table to add both tables to the **Relationships** window. **Close** the **Show Table** dialog box. Point to the title bar of the field list on the right, and drag the field list to the right until there are approximately two inches of space between the field lists. By dragging the lower right corner of the field list, resize each field list to display all of the field names and the entire table name.

g. In the **2D Clubs** field list, point to **Club ID**, drag the field name into the **2D Fundraisers** table on top of **Club ID**, and then release the mouse button. Point to the title bar of the **Edit Relationships** dialog box, and then drag it downward below the two field lists. In the **Edit Relationships** dialog box, select the **Enforce Referential Integrity** check box, the **Cascade Update Related Fields** check box, the **Cascade Delete Related Records** check box, and then click **Create**. A *one-to-many* relationship is established; *one* student club can raise money for *many* fundraising events.

h. Under **RELATIONSHIP TOOLS**, on the **DESIGN tab**, in the **Tools group**, click **Relationship Report**. On the **PRINT PREVIEW tab**, in the **Page Size group**, click **Margins**, and then click **Normal**. **Save** the report as **Lastname Firstname 2D Relationships** and then create a paper or electronic printout as directed. In the object window, right-click either **object tab**, and then click **Close All**.

(Project 2D Club Fundraisers continues on the next page)

2 ▶ On the ribbon, click the **CREATE tab**. In the **Queries group**, click **Query Design**. In the **Show Table** dialog box, double-click your **2D Fundraisers** table to add it to the table area, and then **Close** the **Show Table** dialog box. Resize the field list. Add the following fields to the design grid in the order given: **Fundraiser Name**, **Donation**, and **Fundraiser Location**.

    a. Click in the **Sort** row under **Fundraiser Name**, click the **arrow**, and then click **Ascending**. Click in the **Criteria** row under **Donation**, type **>=1000** and then press [Enter]. **Run** the query, and notice that seven records match the criteria. This query answers the question, *Where was each fundraiser held (in alphabetical order by the Fundraiser Name field) for fundraisers with a donation greater than or equal to $1,000?*

    b. **Save** the query as **Lastname Firstname 2D $1000 or More Donation Query** and then display the query results in **Print Preview**. Create a paper or electronic printout as directed, click **Close Print preview**, and then **Close** your query object. **Open** the **Navigation Pane**.

    c. In the **Navigation Pane**, right-click your **2D $1000 or More Donation Query** object, and then click **Copy**. In the **Navigation Pane**, point to a blank area, right-click, and then click **Paste**. In the **Paste As** dialog box, type **Lastname Firstname 2D Fundraisers June-July Query** and then click **OK**. In the **Navigation Pane**, right-click your **2D Fundraisers June-July Query** object, and then click **Design View**. **Close** the **Navigation Pane**.

    d. In the **2D Fundraisers** field list, double-click **Date** to add it to the fourth column in the design grid. Click in the **Sort** row under **Fundraiser Name**, click the **arrow**, and then click **(not sorted)**. Click in the **Sort** row under **Date**, click the **arrow**, and then click **Ascending**.

    e. In the **Criteria** row under **Donation**, select the existing criteria of *>=1000*, and then press [Del] so that the query results are not restricted by a monetary value. Click in the **Criteria** row under **Date**, type **between 6/1/18 and 7/31/18** and then press [Enter]. **Run** the query, and notice that four records match the criteria. This query answers the question, *What is the fundraiser name, donation, fundraiser location, and date (in chronological order) for events held between June 1, 2018 and July 31, 2018?*

    f. Display the query results in **Print Preview**, create a paper or electronic printout as directed, and then click **Close Print Preview**. **Close** the query, and in the message box, click **Yes** to save the changes to the query design.

3 ▶ On the ribbon, click the **CREATE tab**, and in the **Queries group**, click **Query Design**. In the **Show Table** dialog box, double-click your **2D Fundraisers** table to add it to the table area, and then **Close** the **Show Table** dialog box. Resize the field list. Add the following fields to the design grid in the order given: **Fundraiser Name**, **Fundraiser Location**, **Donation**, and **Club ID**.

    a. Click in the **Sort** row under **Fundraiser Name**, click the **arrow**, and then click **Ascending**. Click in the **Criteria** row under **Club ID**, type **club-109** and then press [Enter]. Click in the **Criteria** row under **Donation**, type **<=1000** and then press [Enter]. **Run** the query, and notice that two records match the criteria. Switch back to **Design** view, and in the **Show** row under **Club ID**, clear the check box. **Run** the query again. This query answers the question, *Which fundraiser events with their locations listed had donations raised by CLUB-109 of $1,000 or less?*

    b. **Save** the query as **Lastname Firstname 2D CLUB-109 Low Donations Query** and then display the query results in **Print Preview**. Create a paper or electronic printout as directed, click **Close Print Preview**, and then **Close** the query.

    c. On the ribbon, click the **CREATE tab**, and then in the **Queries group**, click **Query Design**. In the **Show Table** dialog box, double-click your **2D Fundraisers** table to add it to the table area, and then **Close** the **Show Table** dialog box. Resize the field list. Add the following fields to the design grid in the order given: **Club ID**, **Fundraiser Name**, **Date**, and **Donation**.

    d. Click in the **Sort** row under **Date**, click the **arrow**, and then click **Ascending**. Click in the **Criteria** row under **Club ID**, type **club-107 or club-115** and then press [Enter]. Click in the **Criteria** row under **Donation**, type **>1000** and then press [Enter]. **Run** the query, and notice that two records match the criteria. This query answers the questions, *Which fundraiser events received donations over $1,000 from either CLUB-107 or CLUB-115, and on what dates (in chronological order) were the fundraiser events held?*

(Project 2D Club Fundraisers continues on the next page)

CHAPTER REVIEW

e. **Save** the query as **Lastname Firstname 2D CLUB 107 OR 115 Over $1000 Query** and then display the query results in **Print Preview**. Create a paper or electronic printout as directed, click **Close Print Preview**, and then **Close** the query.

4 On the ribbon, click the **CREATE tab**, and then in the **Queries group**, click **Query Design**. In the **Show Table** dialog box, double-click your **2D Clubs** table, and then double-click your **2D Fundraisers** table to add both tables to the table area. **Close** the **Show Table** dialog box. Drag the field list on the right side to the right until there are approximately two inches of space between the field lists, and then resize each field list.

a. From the **2D Clubs** field list, add the following fields to the design grid in the order given: **Club Name**, **Campus**, and **Club Email**. From the **2D Fundraisers** field list, add the following fields to the design grid in the order given: **Fundraiser Name**, **Date**, and **Donation**. In the design grid, drag the **Donation** field to the left to position it as the first column.

b. Click in the **Sort** row under **Donation**, click the **arrow**, and then click **Descending**. Click in the **Criteria** row under **Campus**, type **southeast** and then press Enter. Click in the **or** row under **Campus**, type **northeast** and then press Enter. **Run** the query, and notice that 10 records match the criteria. This query answers the question, *For the Southeast and Northeast campuses, what is the donation (in descending order), club name, campus name, club email address, fundraiser name, and date of all fundraising events?*

c. **Save** the query as **Lastname Firstname 2D SE OR NE Donations Query** and then display the query results in **Print Preview**. On the **PRINT PREVIEW tab**, in the **Page Layout group**, click **Landscape**. In the **Page Size group**, click **Margins**, and then click **Normal**. Create a paper or electronic printout as directed, click **Close Print Preview**, and then **Close** the query.

5 On the ribbon, click the **CREATE tab**, and then in the **Queries group**, click **Query Design**. In the **Show Table** dialog box, double-click your **2D Clubs** table, and then double-click your **2D Fundraisers** table to add both tables to the table area. **Close** the **Show Table** dialog box. Drag the field list on the right side to the right until there are approximately two inches of space between the field lists, and then resize each field list. From the **2D Clubs** field

list, add the **Club Name** field to the design grid. From the **2D Fundraisers** field list, add the **Fundraiser Name** field to the design grid.

a. Click in the **Sort** row under **Club Name**, click the **arrow**, and then click **Ascending**. Click in the **Criteria** row under **Club Name**, type **phi*** and then press Enter. In the **Criteria** row under **Fundraiser Name**, type ***walk*** and then press Enter. **Run** the query, and notice that two records match the criteria—Club Name begins with *Phi* and Fundraiser Name has *Walk* anywhere in its name. This query answers the question, *Which clubs (in alphabetical order) that have names starting with Phi have raised money for fundraisers that involve walking?*

b. **Save** the query as **Lastname Firstname 2D Phi Walk Query** and then display the query results in **Print Preview**. Create a paper or electronic printout as directed, click **Close Print Preview**, and then **Close** the query.

6 On the ribbon, click the **CREATE tab**, and then in the **Queries group**, click **Query Design**. In the **Show Table** dialog box, double-click your **2D Clubs** table, and then double-click your **2D Fundraisers** table to add both tables to the table area. **Close** the **Show Table** dialog box. Drag the field list on the right side to the right until there are approximately two inches of space between the field lists, and then resize each field list. From the field lists, add the following fields to the design grid in the order given: **Fundraiser ID**, **Club Name**, and **Donation**.

a. Click in the **Sort** row under **Fundraiser ID**, click the **arrow**, and then click **Ascending**. Alumni will donate an additional 25 percent based on the value in the **Donation** field. In the **Field** row, right-click in the fourth column, and then click **Zoom**. In the **Zoom** dialog box, type **Alumni Donation:[Donation]*0.25** and then click **OK**. **Run** the query to be sure the new field—*Alumni Donation*—displays. In the first record, the *Alumni Donation* displays as *156.25*.

b. Switch to **Design** view. In the **Field** row, right-click in the first empty column, and then click **Zoom**. In the **Zoom** dialog box, type **Total Donation:[Donation]+[Alumni Donation]** and then click **OK**. **Run** the query to be sure that the new field—*Total Donation*—displays. In the first record, the *Total Donation* displays as *$781.25*.

(Project 2D Club Fundraisers continues on the next page)

CHAPTER REVIEW

c. Switch to **Design** view. In the **Field** row, click in the **Alumni Donation** field name box. Under **QUERY TOOLS**, on the **DESIGN tab**, in the **Show/Hide group**, click **Property Sheet**. In the **Property Sheet**, click **Format**. In the property setting box, click the **arrow**, and then click **Currency**. In the **Property Sheet**, click **Decimal Places**. In the property setting box, click the **arrow**, and then click **2**. **Close** the **Property Sheet**, and then **Run** the query. This query answers the question, *In ascending order by Fundraiser ID, what is the club name, donation, alumni donation, and total donation for each fundraising event if the alumni donate an additional 25 percent based on the value in the Donation field?*

d. To the left of the **Fundraiser ID** field name, click **Select All**. On the **HOME tab**, in the **Records group**, click **More**, and then click **Field Width**. In the **Column Width** dialog box, click **Best Fit**. **Save** the query as **Lastname Firstname 2D Alumni Donation Query** and then click in any field to cancel the selection. Display the query results in **Print Preview**. On the **PRINT PREVIEW tab**, in the **Page Layout group**, click **Landscape**. Create a paper or electronic printout as directed, click **Close Print Preview**, and then **Close** the query.

7 On the ribbon, click the **CREATE tab**, and then in the **Queries group**, click **Query Design**. In the **Show Table** dialog box, double-click your **2D Fundraisers** table to add the table to the table area. **Close** the **Show Table** dialog box. Resize the field list, and then add the **Donation** field to the design grid.

a. Under **QUERY TOOLS**, on the **DESIGN tab**, in the **Show/Hide group**, click **Totals** to add a **Total** row as the third row in the design grid. In the **Total** row under **Donation**, click in the box that displays *Group By*, click the **arrow**, and then click **Sum**. In the **Show/Hide group**, click **Property Sheet**. In the **Property Sheet**, set **Decimal Places** to **0**, and then **Close** the **Property Sheet**. **Run** the query. Point to the right edge of the first column to display the ⊞ pointer, and then double-click to apply Best Fit to the field. The sum of the Donation fields is *$20,259.*

b. Switch to **Design** view. From the field list, drag the **Club ID** field to the first column in the design grid—the **Donation** field moves to the second column. **Run** the query. This query answers the question, *For each club ID, what are the total donations?*

c. **Save** the query as **Lastname Firstname 2D Total Donations by Club Query** and then display the query results in **Print Preview**. Create a paper or electronic printout as directed, click **Close Print Preview**, and then **Close** the query.

8 On the ribbon, click the **CREATE tab**, and then in the **Queries group**, click **Query Wizard**. In the **New Query** dialog box, click **Crosstab Query Wizard**, and then click **OK**. In the **Crosstab Query Wizard**, click your **Table: 2D Fundraisers**, and then click **Next**. In the wizard under **Available Fields**, double-click **Fundraiser ID** to group the records by this field and display the Fundraiser IDs as row headings. Click **Next**.

a. In the wizard, in the field list, click **Club ID** to select the column headings, and then click **Next**. Under **Fields**, click **Donation**. Under **Functions**, click **Sum**, and then click **Next**. In the **What do you want to name your query?** box, select the existing text, type **Lastname Firstname 2D Fundraisers and Clubs Crosstab Query** and then click **Finish**.

b. On the ribbon, click the **HOME** tab, and then switch to **Design** view. In the design grid, click in the **[Donation]** column. Under **QUERY TOOLS**, on the **DESIGN tab**, in the **Show/Hide group**, click **Property Sheet**. In the **Property Sheet**, click **Decimal Places**. In the property settings box, click the **arrow**, and then click **0**. In the design grid, click in the **Total Of Donation** column, set the **Decimal Places** to **0**, and then **Close** the **Property Sheet**. **Run** the query. Select all of the columns, apply **Best Fit**, and then **Save** the query. This query answers the question, *Grouped by Fundraiser ID and Club ID, what are the total donations?*

c. Display the query results in **Print Preview**. On the **PRINT PREVIEW tab**, in the **Page Layout group**, click **Landscape**. Create a paper or electronic printout as directed—two pages result. Click **Close Print Preview**, and then **Close** the query.

9 On the ribbon, click the **CREATE tab**, and then in the **Queries group**, click **Query Design**. In the **Show Table** dialog box, double-click your **2D Fundraisers** table to add the table to the table area. **Close** the **Show Table** dialog box, and then resize the field list. Add the following fields to the design grid in the order given: **Club ID**, **Fundraiser Location**, and **Date**.

(Project 2D Club Fundraisers continues on the next page)

a. Click in the **Sort** row under **Date**, click the **arrow**, and then click **Ascending**. In the **Criteria** row under **Club ID**, right-click, and then click **Zoom**. In the **Zoom** dialog box, type **[Enter a Club ID in the format club-###]** and then click **OK**. **Run** the query. In the **Enter Parameter Value** dialog box, type **club-109** and then click **OK**. Three records match the criteria.

b. **Save** the query as **Lastname Firstname 2D Club ID Parameter Query** and then display the query results in **Print Preview**. Create a paper or electronic printout as directed, click **Close Print Preview**, and then **Close** the query.

c. **Open** the **Navigation Pane**, and increase the width of the pane so that all object names display fully. On the right side of the title bar, click **Close** to close the database and to exit Access. As directed by your instructor, submit your database and the paper or electronic printouts of the 11 objects—relationship report and 10 queries, one of which printed on two pages—that are the results of this project. Specifically, in this project, using your own name, you created the following database and printouts or electronic printouts:

1. Lastname_Firstname_2D_Clubs_Fundraisers	Database file
2. Lastname Firstname 2D Relationships	Relationships Report (printout or electronic printout)
3. Lastname Firstname 2D $1000 or More Donation Query	Query (printout or electronic printout)
4. Lastname Firstname 2D Fundraisers June-July Query	Query (printout or electronic printout)
5. Lastname Firstname 2D CLUB-109 Low Donations Query	Query (printout or electronic printout)
6. Lastname Firstname 2D CLUB-107 OR 115 Over $1000 Query	Query (printout or electronic printout)
7. Lastname Firstname 2D SE OR NE Donations Query	Query (printout or electronic printout)
8. Lastname Firstname 2D Phi Walk Query	Query (printout or electronic printout)
9. Lastname Firstname 2D Alumni Donation Query	Query (printout or electronic printout)
10. Lastname Firstname 2D Total Donations by Club Query	Query (printout or electronic printout)
11. Lastname Firstname 2D Fundraisers and Clubs Crosstab Query	Query (printout or electronic printout - two pages)
12. Lastname Firstname 2D Club ID Parameter Query	Query (printout or electronic printout - CLUB-109)

END | You have completed Project 2D

In the following Mastering Access project, you will assist Greg Franklin, chair of the Biology Department at the Southwest Campus, in using his database to answer questions about biology laboratory supplies. Your completed database objects will look similar to Figure 2.57.

Apply 2A skills from these Objectives:

1. Open and Save an Existing Database
2. Create Table Relationships
3. Sort Records in a Table
4. Create a Query in Design View
5. Create a New Query from an Existing Query
6. Sort Query Results
7. Specify Criteria in a Query

PROJECT FILES

For Project 2E, you will need the following file:

a02E_Biology_Supplies

You will save your database as:

Lastname_Firstname_2E_Biology_Supplies

PROJECT RESULTS

FIGURE 2.57

(Project 2E Biology Supplies continues on the next page)

CONTENT-BASED ASSESSMENTS

1 **Start** Access. From your student data files, open **a02E_Biology_Supplies**. Save the database in your **Access Chapter 2** folder as **Lastname_Firstname_2E_Biology_Supplies** and then enable the content. In the **Navigation Pane**, **Rename** each table by adding **Lastname Firstname** to the beginning of the table name. Increase the width of the **Navigation Pane** so that all object names display fully.

2 Open both tables to examine the fields and data, and then **Close** both tables. Create a *one-to-many* relationship between your **2E Vendors** table and your **2E Biology Lab Supplies** table using the common field **Vendor ID**. **Enforce Referential Integrity**, and enable both cascade options. *One* vendor can be the provider of *many* supplies. Create a **Relationship Report** with **Normal Margins**, saving it with the default name. Create a paper or electronic printout as directed, and then **Close All** open objects. Open your **2E Vendors** table. In the last record, in the **Vendor ID** field, select **V-100**, type **V-001** and then press ↓ to save the record. **Close** the table.

3 Open your **2E Biology Lab Supplies** table. Sort the records first in **Descending** order by **Price Per Item** and then in **Ascending** order by **Category**. Using **Landscape** orientation, create a paper or electronic printout as directed. **Close** the table, and do *not* save changes to the table.

4 Create a query in **Query Design** view using your **2E Biology Lab Supplies** table to answer the question, *What is the item ID, item name, room, location, and quantity in stock for all of the items, sorted in ascending order by the Room field and the Location field?* Display the fields in the order listed in the question. **Save** the query as **Lastname Firstname 2E Items by Room Query** and then create a paper or electronic printout as directed. **Close** the query.

5 From the **Navigation Pane**, copy your **2E Items by Room Query** object to create a new query object named **Lastname Firstname 2E Item Categories Query** and then redesign the query to answer the question, *What is the item ID, item name, category, vendor ID, and quantity in stock for all items, sorted in ascending order by the Category field and in ascending order by the Vendor ID field?* Display only the fields necessary to answer the question and in the order listed in the question. Create a paper or electronic printout as directed. **Close** the query, saving the design changes.

6 From the **Navigation Pane**, copy your **2E Items by Room Query** object to create a new query object named **Lastname Firstname 2E Supplies Sort Query** and then redesign the query to answer the question, *What is the item name, category, price per item, and quantity in stock for all supplies, sorted in ascending order by the Category field and then in descending order by the Price Per Item field?* Display only the fields necessary to answer the question and in the order listed in the question. Create a paper or electronic printout as directed. **Close** the query, saving the design changes.

7 From the **Navigation Pane**, copy your **2E Supplies Sort Query** object to create a new query object named **Lastname Firstname 2E Kits Query** and then redesign the query to answer the question, *What is the item name, category, price per item, quantity in stock, and vendor ID for all items that have a category of kits, sorted in ascending order only by the Item Name field?* Do not display the **Category** field in the query results, and display the rest of the fields in the order listed in the question. Six records match the criteria. Create a paper or electronic printout as directed. **Close** the query, saving the design changes.

8 Create a query in **Query Design** view using your **2E Vendors** table to answer the question, *What is the vendor ID and vendor name where the phone number is missing from the table, sorted in ascending order by the Vendor Name field?* Display the fields in the order listed in the question. Two records match the criteria. **Save** the query as **Lastname Firstname 2E Missing Phone Query** and then create a paper or electronic printout as directed. **Close** the query.

(Project 2E Biology Supplies continues on the next page)

CONTENT-BASED ASSESSMENTS

9 ▶ Be sure all objects are closed. **Open** the **Navigation Pane**, be sure that all object names display fully, and then **Close** Access. As directed by your instructor, submit your database and the paper or electronic printouts of the seven objects—relationship report, sorted table, and five queries—that are the results of this project. Specifically, in this project, using your own name, you created the following database and printouts or electronic printouts:

1. Lastname_Firstname_2E_Biology_Supplies	Database file
2. Relationships for Lastname_Firstname_2E_Biology_Supplies	Relationships Report (printout or electronic printout)
3. Lastname Firstname 2E Biology Lab Supplies table sorted (not saved)	Table sorted (printout or electronic printout - one page)
4. Lastname Firstname 2E Items by Room Query	Query (printout or electronic printout)
5. Lastname Firstname 2E Item Categories Query	Query (printout or electronic printout)
6. Lastname Firstname 2E Supplies Sort Query	Query (printout or electronic printout)
7. Lastname Firstname 2E Kits Query	Query (printout or electronic printout)
8. Lastname Firstname 2E Missing Phone Query	Query (printout or electronic printout)

END | You have completed Project 2E

CONTENT-BASED ASSESSMENTS

Mastering Access | Project 2F Student Publications

In the following Mastering Access project, you will assist Siobhan Reiss, the English Writing Lab coordinator, in using her database to answer questions about student publications. Your completed database objects will look similar to Figure 2.58.

Apply 2B skills from these Objectives:

8 Specify Numeric Criteria in a Query

9 Use Compound Criteria in a Query

10 Create a Query Based on More Than One Table

11 Use Wildcards in a Query

12 Create Calculated Fields in a Query

13 Calculate Statistics and Group Data in a Query

14 Create a Crosstab Query

15 Create a Parameter Query

PROJECT FILES

For Project 2F, you will need the following files:

a02F_Student_Publications
a02F_Student_Papers (Excel workbook)

You will save your database as:

Lastname_Firstname_2F_Student_Publications

PROJECT RESULTS

FIGURE 2.58

(Project 2F Student Publications continues on the next page)

1 **Start** Access. From your student data files, open **a02F_Student_Publications**. Save the database in your **Access Chapter 2** folder as **Lastname_Firstname_2F_ Student_Publications** and then enable the content. In the **Navigation Pane**, **Rename** the **2F Publishers** table by adding **Lastname Firstname** to the beginning of the table name. From your student data files, import the **a02F_Student_Papers** Excel file as a new table in the database. Designate the first row of the spreadsheet as column headings, and designate **Paper ID** as the primary key. Name the new table **Lastname Firstname 2F Student Papers** and then increase the width of the **Navigation Pane** so that all object names display fully.

Open your **2F Student Papers** table in **Design** view. For the **Student ID** field, change the **Data Type** to **Short Text**. Switch to **Datasheet** view, saving the change, apply **Best Fit** to all of the columns, and then **Save** the table. Examine the fields and data in this table. Open your **2F Publishers** table, examine the fields and data, and then **Close All** open objects.

Create a *one-to-many* relationship between your **2F Publishers** table and your **2F Student Papers** table using the common field **Publisher ID**. **Enforce Referential Integrity**, and enable both cascade options. *One* publisher can publish *many* student papers. Create a **Relationship Report** with **Normal Margins**, saving it as **Lastname Firstname 2F Relationships** and then create a paper or electronic printout as directed. **Close All** open objects.

2 Create a query in **Query Design** view using your **2F Student Papers** table to answer the question, *What is the student ID, home campus, award paid, and publisher ID for awards greater than or equal to $50, sorted in ascending order by the Student ID field?* Display the fields in the order listed in the question. Five records match the criteria. **Save** the query as **Lastname Firstname 2F Awards $50 or More Query** and then create a paper or electronic printout as directed. **Close** the query.

3 From the **Navigation Pane**, copy your **2F Awards $50 or More Query** object to create a new query object named **Lastname Firstname 2F 2nd Qtr NW Students Query** and then redesign the query to answer the questions, *Which students (Student ID) from the Northwest campus had papers published between 4/1/18 and 6/30/18, and what was the paper name, the award paid, and the category, sorted in ascending order only by the Publication Date field?* Do not restrict the results by **Award Paid**. Do not display the **Home Campus** field in the query results, and display the rest of the fields in the order listed in the question. Three records match the criteria. Using **Landscape** orientation, create a paper or electronic printout as directed. **Close** the query, saving the design changes.

4 Create a query in **Query Design** view using your **2F Student Papers** table to answer the question, *Which paper IDs, paper names, and category for students from the Southeast or Northeast campuses were published that had an award paid greater than $25, sorted in descending order by the Award Paid field?* Display the fields in the order listed in the question. Six records match the criteria. **Save** the query as **Lastname Firstname 2F SE OR NE Over $25 Query** and then using **Normal Margins**, create a paper or electronic printout as directed. **Close** the query.

5 Create a query in **Query Design** view using both tables to answer the questions, *Which paper names were published with a publisher name that has Texas as part of its name, what is the contact name and contact phone number, and what was the award paid, sorted in descending order by the Award Paid field?* (Hint: Use a wildcard character in the **Criteria** row.) Display the fields in the order listed in the question. Eight records match the criteria. **Save** the query as **Lastname Firstname 2F Texas Publishers Query** and then using **Landscape** orientation, create a paper or electronic printout as directed. **Close** the query.

6 The college's Federation of English Faculty will donate money to the English Writing Lab based on 50 percent of the awards paid to the students. Create a query in **Query Design** view using your **2F Student Papers** table to answer the question, *In ascending order by the Paper ID field, what will be the total of each donation to the Writing Lab if the Federation donates an additional 50 percent of each award paid to students?* (Hint: First calculate the amount of the donation, naming the new field **Federation Donation**, and then run the query to be sure the correct results display. Then calculate the total donation, naming the new field **Total Donation**.) Change the property settings of the **Federation Donation** field to display with a **Format** of **Currency** and with **Decimal Places** set to **2**. For the **Publisher ID** of **P-20**, the *Federation Donation* is *$22.50*, and the *Total Donation* is *$67.50*. Apply **Best Fit** to all of the columns, **Save** the query as **Lastname Firstname 2F Federation Donation Query** and then create a paper or electronic printout as directed. **Close** the query.

(Project 2F Student Publications continues on the next page)

CONTENT-BASED ASSESSMENTS

7 Create a query in **Query Design** view using your **2F Student Papers** table and the **Sum** aggregate function to answer the question, *What are the total awards paid for each category, sorted in descending order by the Award Paid field?* Display the fields in the order listed in the question. Change the property settings of the **Award Paid** field to display with **Decimal Places** set to **0**. For the **Category** of **Student Life**, total awards paid are *$265*. Apply **Best Fit** to the **SumOfAward Paid** column. **Save** the query as **Lastname Firstname 2F Awards by Category Query** and then create a paper or electronic printout as directed. **Close** the query.

8 Use the **Query Wizard** to create a crosstab query based on your **2F Student Papers** table. Select **Home Campus** as the row headings and **Category** as the column headings. **Sum** the **Award Paid** field. Name the query **Lastname Firstname 2F Campus and Category Crosstab Query** In **Design** view, change the property settings of the last two fields to display with **Decimal Places** set to **0**. This query answers the question, *What are the total awards paid for student publications by each home campus and by each category?* Apply **Best Fit** to all of the columns, and then **Save** the query. Using **Landscape** orientation and **Normal Margins**, create a paper or electronic printout as directed. **Close** the query.

9 Create a query in **Query Design** view using your **2F Student Papers** table that prompts you to enter the **Home Campus**, and then answers the question, *What is the home campus, student ID, paper name, category, and publication date for student publications, sorted in ascending order by the Publication Date field?* Display the fields in the order listed in the question. **Run** the query, entering **southwest** when prompted for criteria. Seven records match the criteria. **Save** the query as **Lastname Firstname 2F Campus Parameter Query** and then using **Normal Margins**, create a paper or electronic printout as directed. **Close** the query.

10 Open the **Navigation Pane**, and be sure that all object names display fully. **Close** Access. As directed by your instructor, submit your database and the paper or electronic printouts of the nine objects—relationship report and eight queries—that are the results of this project. Specifically, in this project, using your own name, you created the following database and printouts or electronic printouts:

1. Lastname_Firstname_2F_Student_Publications	Database file
2. Lastname Firstname 2F Relationships	Relationships Report (printout or electronic printout)
3. Lastname Firstname 2F Awards $50 or More Query	Query (printout or electronic printout)
4. Lastname Firstname 2F 2nd Qtr NW Students Query	Query (printout or electronic printout)
5. Lastname Firstname 2F SE OR NE Over $25 Query	Query (printout or electronic printout)
6. Lastname Firstname 2F Texas Publishers Query	Query (printout or electronic printout)
7. Lastname Firstname 2F Federation Donation Query	Query (printout or electronic printout)
8. Lastname Firstname 2F Awards by Category Query	Query (printout or electronic printout)
9. Lastname Firstname 2F Campus and Category Crosstab Query	Query (printout or electronic printout)
10. Lastname Firstname 2F Campus Parameter Query	Query (printout or electronic printout - Southwest)

> **END | You have completed Project 2F**

Apply 2A and 2B skills from these Objectives:

1. Open and Save an Existing Database
2. Create Table Relationships
3. Sort Records in a Table
4. Create a Query in Design View
5. Create a New Query from an Existing Query
6. Sort Query Results
7. Specify Criteria in a Query
8. Specify Numeric Criteria in a Query
9. Use Compound Criteria in a Query
10. Create a Query Based on More Than One Table
11. Use Wildcards in a Query
12. Create Calculated Fields in a Query
13. Calculate Statistics and Group Data in a Query
14. Create a Crosstab Query
15. Create a Parameter Query

In the following Mastering Access project, you will assist Kim Ngo, director of Academic Scholarships, in using her database to answer questions about scholarships awarded to students. Your completed database objects will look similar to Figure 2.59.

PROJECT FILES

For Project 2G, you will need the following file:

a02G_Student_Scholarships

You will save your database as:

Lastname_Firstname_2G_Student_Scholarships

PROJECT RESULTS

FIGURE 2.59

(Project 2G Student Scholarships continues on the next page)

CONTENT-BASED ASSESSMENTS

1 **Start** Access. From your student data files, open **a02G_Student_Scholarships**. Save the database in your **Access Chapter 2** folder as **Lastname_Firstname_2G_ Student_Scholarships** and then enable the content. In the **Navigation Pane**, **Rename** each table by adding **Lastname Firstname** to the beginning of the table name. Increase the width of the **Navigation Pane** so that all object names display fully.

2 Open both tables to examine the fields and data, and then **Close** both tables. Create a *one-to-many* relationship between your **2G Students** table and your **2G Scholarships Awarded** table using the common field **Student ID**. **Enforce Referential Integrity**, and enable both cascade options. *One* student can have *many* scholarships. Create a **Relationship Report** with **Normal Margins**, saving it with the default name. Create a paper or electronic printout as directed, and then **Close All** open objects. Open your **2G Students** table. In the last record, in the **Student ID** field, select **9999999**, type **2839403** and then press ↓ to save the record. **Close** the table.

3 Create a query in **Query Design** view using your **2G Scholarships Awarded** table to answer the question, *What is the scholarship name, amount, and major for scholarships greater than or equal to $500, sorted in ascending order by the Scholarship Name field?* Display the fields in the order listed in the question. Eight records match the criteria. **Save** the query as **Lastname Firstname 2G Amount $500 or More Query** and then create a paper or electronic printout as directed. **Close** the query.

4 From the **Navigation Pane**, copy your **2G Amount $500 or More Query** object to create a new query object named **Lastname Firstname 2G Awards 4th Qtr Query** and then redesign the query to answer the question, *Which scholarships (Scholarship Name) were awarded between 10/1/18 and 12/31/18, for what amount, and for which student (Student ID), sorted in ascending order only by the Award Date field?* Display only the fields necessary to answer the question and in the order listed in the question. Do not restrict the results by amount. Five records match the criteria. Create a paper or electronic printout as directed. **Close** the query, saving the design changes.

5 Create a query in **Query Design** view using your **2G Scholarships Awarded** table to answer the question, *Which scholarships (Scholarship Name) were awarded for either Math or Business majors for amounts of more than $200, sorted in descending order by the Amount field?*

Display the fields in the order listed in the question. Four records match the criteria. (Hint: If six records display, switch to **Design** view and combine the majors on one criteria line using OR.) **Save** the query as **Lastname Firstname 2G Math OR Business Over $200 Query** and then create a paper or electronic printout as directed. **Close** the query.

6 Create a query in **Query Design** view using your **2G Students** table and a wildcard character to answer the question, *What is the city, student ID, last name, and first name of students from cities that begin with the letter L, sorted in ascending order by the City field, in ascending order by the Last Name field, and ascending order by the First Name field?* Display the fields in the order listed in the question. Five records match the criteria. **Save** the query as **Lastname Firstname 2G L Cities Query** and then create a paper or electronic printout as directed. **Close** the query.

7 Create a query in **Query Design** view using your **2G Students** table and all of the fields in the same order that they display in the field list to answer the question, *For which students is the Postal Code missing?* Three records match the criteria. **Save** the query as **Lastname Firstname 2G Missing Postal Code Query** and then using **Normal Margins**, create a paper or electronic printout as directed. **Close** the query.

8 The Board of Trustees for the college will donate an amount equal to 50 percent of each scholarship amount. Create a query in **Query Design** view using both tables to answer the question, *In ascending order by the Scholarship Name field, and including the first name and last name of the scholarship recipient, what will be the total value of each scholarship if the Board of Trustees donates an additional 50 percent of each award paid to students?* (Hint: First calculate the amount of the donation, naming the new field **Board Donation**, and then run the query to be sure the correct results display. Then calculate the total donation, naming the new field **Total Donation**.) Change the property settings of the appropriate fields to display with a **Format** of **Currency** and with **Decimal Places** set to **0**. For the **Scholarship Name** of **Amanda Snyder Foundation Scholarship**, the *Board Donation* is *$125*, and the *Total Donation* is *$375*. Apply **Best Fit** to all of the columns, **Save** the query as **Lastname Firstname 2G Board Donation Query** and then using **Landscape** orientation, create a paper or electronic printout as directed. **Close** the query.

(Project 2G Student Scholarships continues on the next page)

CONTENT-BASED ASSESSMENTS

9 Create a query in **Query Design** view using your **2G Scholarships Awarded** table and the **Sum** aggregate function to answer the question, *For each major, what is the total scholarship amount, sorted in descending order by the Amount field?* Display the fields in the order listed in the question. Change the property settings of the **Amount** field to display with **Decimal Places** set to **0**. For the **Major** of **History**, the total scholarship amount is *$1,850*. Apply **Best Fit** to all of the columns. **Save** the query as **Lastname Firstname 2G Amount by Major Query** and then create a paper or electronic printout as directed. **Close** the query.

10 Use the **Query Wizard** to create a crosstab query based on your **2G Scholarships Awarded** table. Select **Student ID** as the row headings and **Major** as the column headings. **Sum** the **Amount** field. Name the query **Lastname Firstname 2G Student ID and Major Crosstab Query** In **Design** view, change the property settings of the last two fields to display with **Decimal Places** set to **0**. This query answers the question, *What are the total scholarship amounts paid by each student ID and by each major?* Apply **Best Fit** to all of the columns, and then **Save** the query. Using **Landscape** orientation, create a paper or electronic printout as directed—two pages result. **Close** the query.

11 Create a query in **Query Design** view using your **2G Scholarships Awarded** table that prompts you to enter the **Major**, and then answers the question, *What is the scholarship name and amount for a major, sorted in ascending order by the Scholarship Name field?* Display the fields in the order listed in the question. **Run** the query, entering **history** when prompted for criteria. Four records match the criteria. **Save** the query as **Lastname Firstname 2G Major Parameter Query** and then create a paper or electronic printout as directed. **Close** the query.

12 Open the **Navigation Pane**, and be sure that all object names display fully. **Close** Access. As directed by your instructor, submit your database and the paper or electronic printouts of the 10 objects—relationship report and nine queries, one of which prints on two pages—that are the results of this project. Specifically, in this project, using your own name, you created the following database and printouts or electronic printouts:

1. Lastname_Firstname_2G_Student_Scholarships	Database file
2. Relationships for Lastname_Firstname_2G_Student_Scholarships	Relationships Report (printout or electronic printout)
3. Lastname Firstname 2G Amount $500 or More Query	Query (printout or electronic printout)
4. Lastname Firstname 2G Awards 4th Qtr Query	Query (printout or electronic printout)
5. Lastname Firstname 2G Math OR Business Over $200 Query	Query (printout or electronic printout)
6. Lastname Firstname 2G L Cities Query	Query (printout or electronic printout)
7. Lastname Firstname 2G Missing Postal Code Query	Query (printout or electronic printout)
8. Lastname Firstname 2G Board Donation Query	Query (printout or electronic printout)
9. Lastname Firstname 2G Amount by Major Query	Query (printout or electronic printout)
10. Lastname Firstname 2G Student ID and Major Crosstab Query	Query (printout or electronic printout - two pages)
11. Lastname Firstname 2G Major Parameter Query (using History)	Query (printout or electronic printout)

END | You have completed Project 2G

CONTENT-BASED ASSESSMENTS

Apply a combination of the **2A** and **2B** skills.

GO! Fix It	Project 2H Social Sciences	Online

GO! Make It	Project 2I Faculty Awards	Online

GO! Solve It	Project 2J Student Refunds	Online

GO! Solve It	Project 2K Leave	

PROJECT FILES

For Project 2K, you will need the following file:

a02K_Leave

You will save your database as:

Lastname_Firstname_2K_Leave

Start Access, navigate to your student data files, open a02K_Leave, and then save the database in your Access Chapter 2 folder as **Lastname_Firstname_2K_Leave** Add **Lastname Firstname** to the beginning of both table names, create a one-to-many relationship with cascade options between the two tables—*one* employee can have *many* leave transactions— and then create a relationship report saving it as **Lastname Firstname 2K Relationships**

Create and save four queries to answer the following questions:

- What is the last name and first name of employees who have used personal leave, sorted in ascending order by the Last Name and First Name fields? Do not display the Leave field in the query results.
- What is the last name, first name, and email address of employees who have no phone number listed, sorted in ascending order by the Last Name and First Name fields?
- Grouped by the Leave Classification field, what is the total of each type of leave used? (Hint: Use the aggregate function Count.)
- What is the total number of leave transactions grouped in rows by the Employee# field and grouped in columns by the Leave Classification field?

As directed, create paper or electronic printouts of the relationship report and the four queries. Be sure that each object prints on one page, and that the object names display fully in the Navigation Pane. As directed, submit your database and the paper or electronic printouts of the five objects that are the results of this project.

(Project 2K Leave continues on the next page)

CONTENT-BASED ASSESSMENTS

Performance Level

		Exemplary	Proficient	Developing
Performance Criteria	**Create relationship and relationship report**	Relationship and relationship report created correctly.	Relationship and relationship report created with one error.	Relationship and relationship report created with two or more errors, or missing entirely.
	Create Personal Leave query	Query created with correct name, fields, sorting, and criteria.	Query created with one element incorrect.	Query created with two or more elements incorrect, or missing entirely.
	Create Missing Phone query	Query created with correct name, fields, sorting, and criteria.	Query created with one element incorrect.	Query created with two or more elements incorrect, or missing entirely.
	Create Type of Leave query	Query created with correct name, fields, and aggregate function.	Query created with one element incorrect.	Query created with two or more elements incorrect, or missing entirely.
	Create Crosstab query	Query created with correct name, row headings, column headings, and aggregate function.	Query created with one element incorrect.	Query created with two or more elements incorrect, or missing entirely.

END | You have completed Project 2K

OUTCOMES-BASED ASSESSMENTS

RUBRIC

The following outcomes-based assessments are *open-ended assessments*. That is, there is no specific correct result; your result will depend on your approach to the information provided. Make *Professional Quality* your goal. Use the following scoring rubric to guide you in *how* to approach the problem and then to evaluate *how well* your approach solves the problem.

The *criteria*—Software Mastery, Content, Format & Layout, and Process—represent the knowledge and skills you have gained that you can apply to solving the problem. The *levels of performance*—Professional Quality, Approaching Professional Quality, or Needs Quality Improvements—help you and your instructor evaluate your result.

	Your completed project is of Professional Quality if you:	Your completed project is Approaching Professional Quality if you:	Your completed project Needs Quality Improvements if you:
1-Software Mastery	Choose and apply the most appropriate skills, tools, and features and identify efficient methods to solve the problem.	Choose and apply some appropriate skills, tools, and features, but not in the most efficient manner.	Choose inappropriate skills, tools, or features, or are inefficient in solving the problem.
2-Content	Construct a solution that is clear and well organized, contains content that is accurate, appropriate to the audience and purpose, and is complete. Provide a solution that contains no errors in spelling, grammar, or style.	Construct a solution in which some components are unclear, poorly organized, inconsistent, or incomplete. Misjudge the needs of the audience. Have some errors in spelling, grammar, or style, but the errors do not detract from comprehension.	Construct a solution that is unclear, incomplete, or poorly organized; contains some inaccurate or inappropriate content; and contains many errors in spelling, grammar, or style. Do not solve the problem.
3-Format & Layout	Format and arrange all elements to communicate information and ideas, clarify function, illustrate relationships, and indicate relative importance.	Apply appropriate format and layout features to some elements, but not others. Overuse features, causing minor distraction.	Apply format and layout that does not communicate information or ideas clearly. Do not use format and layout features to clarify function, illustrate relationships, or indicate relative importance. Use available features excessively, causing distraction.
4-Process	Use an organized approach that integrates planning, development, self-assessment, revision, and reflection.	Demonstrate an organized approach in some areas, but not others; or, use an insufficient process of organization throughout.	Do not use an organized approach to solve the problem.

OUTCOMES-BASED ASSESSMENTS

Apply a combination of the 2A and 2B skills.

GO! Think   Project 2L Coaches

PROJECT FILES

For Project 2L, you will need the following file:

a02L_Coaches

You will save your database as

Lastname_Firstname_2L_Coaches

Start Access, navigate to your student data files, open a02L_Coaches, and then save the database in your Access Chapter 2 folder as **Lastname_Firstname_2L_Coaches** Add **Lastname Firstname** to the beginning of both table names, create a one-to-many relationship with cascade options between the two tables—*one* coach can participate in *many* activities—and then create a relationship report saving it as **Lastname Firstname 2L Relationships**

Create queries to assist Randy Garza, the athletic director, in answering the following questions about the coaches at Texas Lakes Community College:

- What is the last name and first name of every coach involved in *Dive* activities, sorted in ascending order by the Last Name field and First Name fields?
- What is the last name and first name of every coach involved in basketball or football activities, sorted in ascending order first by the Activity Name field and then by the Last Name and First Name fields?
- Grouped by division, what is the total number of activity names, sorted in descending order by the total number? (Hint: Use the Count aggregate function.)
- What is the skill specialty, last name, first name, and phone number for coaches in a specified position that is entered when prompted for the Position, sorted in ascending order first by the Skill Specialty field and then by the Last Name and First Name fields? (When prompted, enter the position of *director* for your paper or electronic printout.)

As directed, create paper or electronic printouts of the relationship report and the four queries. Be sure that each object prints on one page, and that the object names display fully in the Navigation Pane. As directed, submit your database and the paper or electronic printouts of the five objects that are the results of this project.

END | You have completed Project 2L

GO! Think   Project 2M Club Donations   Online

You and GO!   Project 2N Personal Inventory   Online

Build from Scratch

GO! Cumulative Group Project   Project 2O Bell Orchid Hotels   Online

Forms, Filters, and Reports

GO! to Work
Video A3

PROJECT **3A**

OUTCOMES
Create forms to enter and delete records and to display data in a database.

PROJECT **3B**

OUTCOMES
Create reports to display database information.

OBJECTIVES

1. Create and Use a Form to Add and Delete Records
2. Filter Records
3. Create a Form by Using the Form Wizard
4. Modify a Form in Layout View and in Design View

OBJECTIVES

5. Create a Report by Using the Report Tool and Modify the Report in Layout View
6. Create a Report by Using the Report Wizard
7. Modify the Design of a Report
8. Keep Grouped Data Together in a Printed Report

Riccardo Piccinini/Fotolia

In This Chapter

In this chapter, you will create forms to enter and delete data and to view data in database tables. Forms can display one record at a time with fields placed in the same order to match a paper source document. Records in a form or table can be filtered to display a subset of the records based on matching specific values. You will modify forms by adding fields, changing field widths, and adding labels to the forms. You will create professional-looking reports that summarize the data stored in a query or table. You will modify the reports by changing the fields in the report, by changing the layout of the report, by grouping data, and by making sure that groupings of data stay together on the printed page.

The projects in this chapter relate to **Texas Lakes Community College**, which is located in the Austin, Texas, area. Its four campuses serve over 30,000 students and offer more than 140 certificate programs and degrees. The college has a highly acclaimed Distance Education program and an extensive Workforce Development program. The college makes positive contributions to the community through cultural and athletic programs and has significant partnerships with businesses and nonprofit organizations. Popular fields of study include nursing and health care, solar technology, computer technology, and graphic design.

Students and Majors Database

PROJECT ACTIVITIES

In Activities 3.01 through 3.15, you will assist Sean Fitchette, director of Enrollment Services at Texas Lakes Community College, in using his Access database to track new students and their major fields of study. Your completed forms will look similar to Figure 3.1.

PROJECT FILES

For Project 3A, you will need the following file:

a03A_Students_Majors

You will save your database as:

Lastname_Firstname_3A_Students_Majors

PROJECT RESULTS

FIGURE 3.1 Project 3A Students and Majors

Objective 1 Create and Use a Form to Add and Delete Records

Video A3-1

A ***form*** is a database object that you can use to enter new records into a table, or to edit, delete, or display existing records in a table. A form is useful to control access to the data. For example, you can design a form for college registration assistants so that they can see and enter the courses scheduled and fees paid by an individual student. However, they cannot see or enter grades for a student.

Some forms display only one record at a time; other forms display multiple records at the same time. A form that displays only one record at a time is useful not only to the individual who performs the ***data entry***—entering the actual records—but also to anyone who has the job of viewing information in a database. For example, when you request a transcript from your college, someone displays your record on the screen. For the individual viewing your transcript, it is much easier to look at one record at a time, using a form, than to look at all of the student transcripts in the database.

Activity 3.01 | Opening and Saving an Existing Database, Renaming Tables, and Viewing a Table Relationship

1 Start Access. In the Access opening screen, click **Open Other Files**. Under **Open**, click **Computer**, and then on the right, click **Browse**. In the **Open** dialog box, navigate to the location where your student data files for this chapter are stored, and then double-click **a03A_Students_Majors** to open the database.

2 On the ribbon, click the **FILE tab**, and then click **Save As**. Under **File Types**, be sure **Save Database As** is selected. On the right, under **Database File Types**, be sure **Access Database** is selected, and then at the bottom of the screen, click **Save As**.

3 In the **Save As** dialog box, navigate to the location where you are saving your databases. Create a **New folder** named **Access Chapter 3**, and then **Open** the folder. In the **File name** box and using your own name, replace the existing text with **Lastname_Firstname_3A_Students_Majors** and then click **Save** or press Enter.

4 On the **Message Bar**, click **Enable Content**. In the **Navigation Pane**, right-click the **3A Majors** table, and then click **Rename**. With the table name selected and using your own name, type **Lastname Firstname 3A Majors** and then press Enter to rename the table. Use the same technique to **Rename** the **3A New Students** table to **Lastname Firstname 3A New Students**

5 Point to the right edge of the **Navigation Pane** to display the ↔ pointer. Drag to the right to increase the width of the pane until both table names display fully.

6 On the ribbon, click the **DATABASE TOOLS tab**. In the **Relationships group**, click **Relationships**. On the **DESIGN tab**, in the **Relationships group**, click **All Relationships**. If necessary, resize and move the field lists so that the entire table name and fields display for each field list.

Because you renamed the tables, the field lists do not automatically display in the Relationships window.

7 In the **Relationships** window, click the **join line** between the two field lists. In the **Tools group**, click **Edit Relationships**. Point to the title bar of the **Edit Relationships** dialog box, and drag the dialog box downward below the two field lists. Compare your screen with Figure 3.2.

One major is associated with *many* students. A one-to-many relationship is established between your 3A Majors table and your 3A New Students table using the Major ID field as the common field. Recall that Cascade Update Related Fields enables you to change the primary key in the 3A Majors table, and then the data in the foreign key field in the 3A New Students field is automatically updated. Recall that Cascade Delete Related Records enables you to delete a record in the 3A Majors table, and then all related records in the 3A New Students table are automatically deleted.

> **ANOTHER WAY** In the Relationships window, double-click the join line to display the Edit Relationships dialog box.

FIGURE 3.2

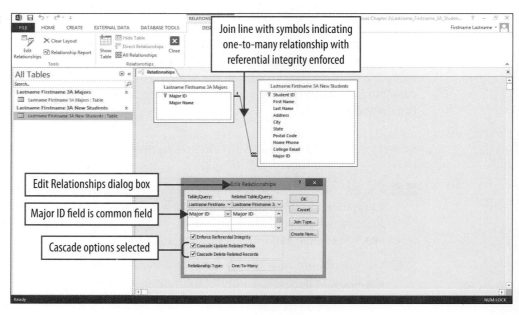

ALERT! **Is Your Edit Relationships Dialog Box Empty?**

The Edit Relationships dialog box does not display any information if you do not first click the join line. If this happens, close the Edit Relationships dialog box, and then be sure that you click the join line—when selected, the join line is darker.

---

8 **Close** ⊠ the **Edit Relationships** dialog box, and then **Close** ⊠ the **Relationships** window. In the message box, click **Yes** to save changes to the layout of the relationships.

Activity 3.02 | Creating a Form and Viewing Records

There are several ways to create a form in Access, but the fastest and easiest way is to use the *Form tool*. With a single mouse click, all fields from the data source are placed on the form. You can use the new form immediately, or you can modify the form in Layout view or in Design view.

The Form tool uses all of the field names and all of the records from an existing table or query. Records that you create or edit using a form are automatically updated in the underlying table or tables. In this activity, you will create a form and then view records from the underlying table—the data source.

1 In the **Navigation Pane**, double-click your **3A New Students** table to open it. Scroll as needed to view all 10 fields—*Student ID, First Name, Last Name, Address, City, State, Postal Code, Home Phone, College Email,* and *Major ID*. **Close** ☒ the table.

2 In the **Navigation Pane**, be sure your **3A New Students** table is selected. On the ribbon, click the **CREATE tab**, and then in the **Forms group**, click **Form**. **Close** ☒ the **Navigation Pane**, and then compare your screen with Figure 3.3.

> The form is created based on the currently selected object—your 3A New Students table—and displays in *Layout view*. In Layout view, you can modify the form with the data displayed in the fields. For example, you can adjust the size of the text boxes to fit the data.
>
> The form is created in a simple top-to-bottom layout, with all 10 fields from your 3A New Students table lined up in a single column. The data for the first record in the data source displays.

FIGURE 3.3

Form displays all 10 fields from your 3A New Students table

Data for Record 1 of 101 displays in form

Dotted lines indicate form is displayed in Layout view

Current record box

New (blank) record button

Layout View button active

Navigation area

3 In the navigation area, click **Next record** ▶ four times to display the fifth record—*Student ID 1298345*. In the navigation area, select the text in the Current record box, type **62** and then press Enter to display the record for *Student ID 5720358*. In the navigation area, click **Last record** ▶I to display the record for *Student ID 9583924*, and then click **First record** I◀ to display the record for *Student ID 1034823*.

> Use the navigation buttons to scroll among the records or the Current record box to display any single record.

4 **Save** 🖫 the form as **Lastname Firstname 3A New Student Form** and then **Close** ☒ the form object.

5 **Open** » the **Navigation Pane**. Notice that your new form displays under the table with which it is related—your **3A New Students** table.

Activity 3.03 | **Creating a Second Form**

In this activity, you will use the Form tool to create a form for your 3A Majors table.

1 In the **Navigation Pane**, click your **3A Majors** table to select it. On the ribbon, click the **CREATE tab**, and then in the **Forms group**, click **Form**. **Close** [«] the **Navigation Pane**, and then compare your screen with Figure 3.4.

Because a one-to-many relationship is established, the form displays related records in the 3A New Students table for each record in the 3A Majors table. Five new students have selected a major of *Diagnostic Medical Sonography—Major ID 105*.

FIGURE 3.4

Form created using your 3A Majors table as the data source

For Major ID of *105*, there are five related records in the 3A New Students table (students selecting this major)

Navigation area for related records

70 records in your 3A Majors table

Navigation area for form

2 **Close** [×] your **3A Majors** form. In the message box, click **Yes**. In the **Save As** dialog box, in the **Form Name** box, type **Lastname Firstname 3A Major Form** and then click **OK**.

Recall that if you do not save an object, you are prompted to do so when you close the object.

3 **Open** [»] the **Navigation Pane**. Notice that your new form displays under the table with which it is related—your **3A Majors** table.

Activity 3.04 | **Adding Records to a Table by Using a Form**

By using a single-record form to add, modify, and delete records, you can reduce the number of data entry errors, because the individual performing the data entry is looking at only one record at a time. Recall that your database is useful only if the information is accurate—just like your contact list is useful only if it contains accurate phone numbers and email addresses.

Forms are based on—also referred to as *bound* to—the table where the records are stored. When a record is entered in a form, the new record is added to the underlying table. The reverse is also true—when a record is added to the table, the new record can be viewed in the related form.

In this activity, you will add a new record to both tables by using the forms that you just created.

1 In the **Navigation Pane**, double-click your **3A New Student Form** object to open it, and then **Close** [«] the **Navigation Pane**. In the navigation area, click **New (blank) record** [▶*] to display a new blank form.

When you open a form, the first record in the underlying table displays in *Form view*, which is used to view, add, modify, and delete records stored in the table.

2 In the **Student ID** field, type **9712345** and then press [Tab].

Use the [Tab] key to move from field to field in a form. *Tab order* is the order in which the insertion point moves from one field to the next when you press the [Tab] key. As you start typing, the pencil icon displays in the *record selector bar* at the left—the bar used to select an entire record. The pencil icon displays when a record is being created or edited.

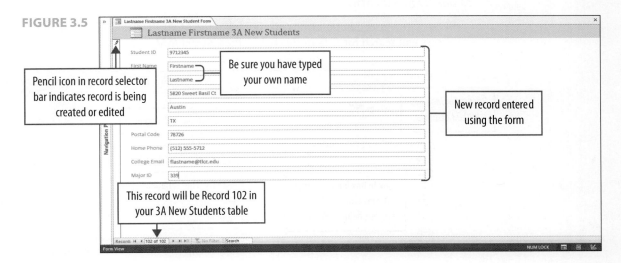

3 Using your own first name and last name and using the first initial of your first name and your last name for the *College Email* field, continue entering the data shown in the following table, and then compare your screen with Figure 3.5.

Student ID	First Name	Last Name	Address	City	State	Postal Code	Home Phone	College Email	Major ID
9712345	First Name	Last Name	5820 Sweet Basil Ct	Austin	TX	78726	(512) 555-5712	flastname@ tlcc.edu	339

FIGURE 3.5

Pencil icon in record selector bar indicates record is being created or edited

Be sure you have typed your own name

New record entered using the form

This record will be Record 102 in your 3A New Students table

4 With the insertion point positioned in the last field, press Tab to save the record and display a new blank record. **Close** ☒ your **3A New Student Form** object.

5 **Open** ☒ the **Navigation Pane**, and then double-click your **3A New Students** table to open it. In the navigation area, click **Last record** ☒ to verify that the record you entered in the form is stored in the underlying table. **Close** ☒ your **3A New Students** table.

6 In the **Navigation Pane**, double-click your **3A Major Form** object to open it. At the bottom of the screen, in the navigation area for the form—*not* the navigation area for the subdatasheet—click **New (blank) record** ☒. In the blank form enter the data shown in the following table:

Major ID	Major Name
339.555.22	Network Security

7 **Close** ☒ your **3A Major Form** object. In the **Navigation Pane**, double-click your **3A Majors** table, and then scroll to verify that the record for *Major ID 339.555.22 Network Security* displays in the table—records are sorted by the *Major ID* field. **Close** ☒ the table.

Activity 3.05 | Deleting Records from a Table by Using a Form

You can delete records from a database table by using a form. In this activity, you will delete the record for *Major ID 800.03* because the program has been discontinued.

1 In the **Navigation Pane**, double-click your **3A Major Form** object to open it, and then **Close** « the **Navigation Pane**. On the **HOME tab**, in the **Find group**, click **Find** to open the **Find and Replace** dialog box.

ANOTHER WAY   Press Ctrl + F to open the Find and Replace dialog box.

---

2 In the **Look In** box, notice that *Current field* displays. In the **Find What** box, type **800.03** and then click **Find Next**. Compare your screen with Figure 3.6, and verify that the record for *Major ID 800.03* displays.

Because the insertion point was positioned in the *Major ID* field before opening the dialog box, Access will search for data in this field—the *Current field*.

FIGURE 3.6

3 **Close** ✖ the **Find and Replace** dialog box. On the **HOME tab**, in the **Records group**, click the **Delete arrow**, and then click **Delete Record**.

The record is removed from the screen, and a message displays alerting you that you are about to delete *1 record(s)*. Once you click *Yes*, you cannot click Undo to reverse this action. If you delete a record by mistake, you must re-create the record by reentering the data. Because no students are associated with this major and the program is being discontinued, you can delete it from the table.

4 In the message box, click **Yes** to delete the record. In the navigation area for the form, notice that the total number of records in the table is *70*. **Close** ✖ your **3A Major Form** object.

5 **Open** » the **Navigation Pane**, and then double-click your **3A Majors** table to open it. Examine the table to verify that the *Major ID 800.03* record has been deleted from the table, and then **Close** ✖ the table.

Adding and deleting records in a form updates the records stored in the underlying table.

Activity 3.06 | Printing a Form

When a form is displayed, clicking Print causes *all* of the records to print in the form layout. In this activity, you will print only *one* record.

1 In the **Navigation Pane**, double-click your **3A New Student Form** object to open it, and then **Close** « the **Navigation Pane**. Press Ctrl + F to open the **Find and Replace** dialog box. In the **Find What** box, type **9712345** and then click **Find Next** to display the record with your name. **Close** ✖ the **Find and Replace** dialog box.

2 On the ribbon, click the **FILE tab**, click **Print**, and then on the right, click **Print**. In the **Print** dialog box, under **Print Range**, click the **Selected Record(s)** option button. In the lower left corner of the dialog box, click **Setup**.

3 In the **Page Setup** dialog box, click the **Columns tab**. Under **Column Size**, double-click in the **Width** box to select the existing value, type **7.5** and then compare your screen with Figure 3.7.

Change the width of the column in this manner so that the form prints on one page. Forms are not typically printed, so the width of the column in a form might be greater than the width of the paper on which you are printing. The maximum column width that you can enter is dependent upon the printer that is installed on your system. This setting is saved when you save or close the form.

FIGURE 3.7

4 In the **Page Setup** dialog box, click **OK**. To create a paper printout, in the **Print** dialog box click **OK**. To create an electronic printout of this single form, click **Cancel** and then follow the instructions in the Note below.

NOTE	**Printing a Single Form in PDF**

To create an electronic printout of a single form in PDF, change the column width to 7.5 as described in Step 3 above, and then in the Print dialog box, click Cancel. On the left side of the form, click the Record Selector bar so that it is black—selected. On the ribbon, click the EXTERNAL DATA tab. In the Export group, click PDF or XPS.

In the Publish as PDF or XPS dialog box, navigate to your chapter folder. In the File name box, the form has the same name as the form. Be sure that the Open file after publishing check box is selected, and that the Minimum size (publishing online) option button is selected. In the Publish as PDF or XPS dialog box, Click Options. In the Options dialog box, under Range, click the Selected records option button, click OK, and then click Publish. Close the Windows 8 Reader, Adobe Reader or Adobe Acrobat window, and then submit the file as directed by your instructor.

---

5 **Close** ☒ your **3A New Student Form** object, **Open** » the **Navigation Pane**, and then double-click your **3A Major Form** object to open it. **Close** « the **Navigation Pane**.

6 Use the techniques you just practiced to **Find** the record for the **Major ID** of **339.555.22**, and then create a paper or electronic printout as directed by your instructor of that record only on one page. After printing, **Close** ☒ your **3A Major Form** object.

If there are no related records in the subdatasheet, the empty subdatasheet does not display in the printed form.

Objective 2   Filter Records

Video A3-2

Filtering records in a form displays only a portion of the total records—a *subset*—based on matching specific values. Filters are commonly used to provide a quick answer, and the result is not generally saved for future use. For example, by filtering records in a form, you can quickly display a subset of records for students majoring in Information Systems Technology, which is identified by the Major ID of 339.

A form provides an interface for the database. For example, because of security reasons, the registration assistants at your college may not have access to the entire student database. Rather, by using a form, they can access and edit only some information—the information necessary for them to do their jobs. Filtering records within a form provides individuals who do not have access to the entire database a way to ask questions of the database without constructing a query. You can save the filter with the form if you are going to use the filter frequently.

Activity 3.07 | Filtering Data by Selection of One Field

In this activity, you will assist a counselor at the college who wants to see records for students majoring in Information Systems Technology. In a form, you can use the *Filter By Selection* command to display only the records that contain the value in the selected field and to hide the records that do *not* contain the value in the selected field.

1 **Open** » the **Navigation Pane**, double-click your **3A New Student Form** object to open it in **Form** view, and then **Close** « the **Navigation Pane**.

2 In the first record, click the **Major ID** field name—or you can click in the field box. Press Ctrl + F to display the **Find and Replace** dialog box. In the **Find What** box, type **339** If necessary, in the Match box, click the arrow, and then click Whole Field. Click **Find Next**, and then compare your screen with Figure 3.8.

This action finds and displays a record with a *Major ID* of *339*—the major of *Information Systems Technology*. You will use this action to filter the records using the value of *339*.

FIGURE 3.8

3 **Close** ⊠ the **Find and Replace** dialog box. On the **HOME tab**, in the **Sort & Filter group**, click **Selection**, and then click **Equals "339"**. Compare your screen with Figure 3.9.

Seven records match the contents of the selected Major ID field—*339*—the Major ID for the Information Systems Technology major. In the navigation area, *Filtered* with a funnel icon displays next to the number of records. *Filtered* also displays on the right side of the status bar to indicate that a filter is applied. On the HOME tab, in the Sort & Filter group, Toggle Filter is active.

ANOTHER WAY   With the data selected in the field, right-click the selection, and then click Equals "339".

FIGURE 3.9

On the **HOME tab**, in the **Sort & Filter group**, click **Toggle Filter** to remove the filter and display all 102 records. Notice *Unfiltered* in the navigation area, which indicates a filter is created but is not active.

ANOTHER WAY   Click Filtered in the navigation area to remove the filter.

NOTE   **The Toggle Filter Button**

On the HOME tab, in the Sort & Filter group, the Toggle Filter button is used to apply or remove a filter. If no filter is created, the button is not available. After a filter is created, the button becomes available. Because it is a toggle button used to apply or remove a filter, the ScreenTip that displays for this button alternates between Apply Filter—when a filter is created but is not currently applied—and Remove Filter—when a filter is applied.

5 Be sure that the first record—for *Jordan Bass*—displays. On the **HOME tab**, in the **Sort & Filter group**, click **Toggle Filter** to reapply the filter. In the navigation area, click **Last record** ▶❙ to display the last of the seven records that match a Major ID of *339*.

The record for *Student ID 9712345* displays—the record with your name. Use Toggle Filter to apply or remove filters as needed.

6 In the navigation area, click **Filtered** to remove the filter and display all of the records.

In the navigation area, *Filtered* changes to *Unfiltered*.

7 In the first record for *Jordan Bass*, in the **Last Name** field, select the first letter—**B**—in *Bass*. In the **Sort & Filter group**, click **Selection**, and then click **Begins with "B"**.

A new filter is applied that displays eight records in which the *Last Name* begins with the letter *B*.

ANOTHER WAY   With the letter *B* selected, right-click the selection, and then click Begins with "B".

8 Use either **Toggle Filter** in the **Sort & Filter group** or **Filtered** in the navigation area to remove the filter and display all of the records.

9 In the **Sort & Filter group**, click **Advanced**, and then click **Clear All Filters**. Notice, that in the navigation area, *Unfiltered* changed to *No Filter*.

> The filter is removed from the form and must be recreated to apply it. If you toggle the filter off and save the form, the filter is saved with the form even though the filter is not currently applied.

Activity 3.08 | Using Filter By Form

Use the *Filter By Form* command to filter the records based on one or more fields, or based on more than one value in the same field. The Filter By Form command offers greater flexibility than the Filter By Selection command and can be used to answer a question that requires matching multiple values. In this activity, you will filter records to help Mr. Fitchette determine how many students live in Dripping Springs or Austin.

1 On the **HOME tab**, in the **Sort & Filter group**, click **Advanced**, and then click **Filter By Form**. Compare your screen with Figure 3.10.

> The Filter by Form window displays all of the field names, but without any data. In the empty text box for each field, you can type a value or select a value from a list. The *Look for* and *Or* tabs display at the bottom.

FIGURE 3.10

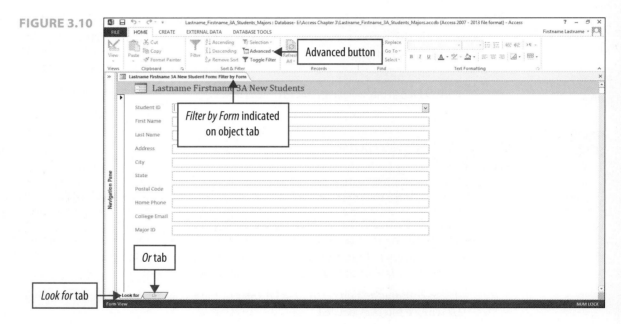

2 In the form, click the **City** field name to position the insertion point in the **City** field box. At the right edge of the **City** field box, click the **arrow**, and then click **Dripping Springs**. In the **Sort & Filter group**, click **Toggle Filter**.

> As displayed in the navigation area, four student records have *Dripping Springs* stored in the City field.

3 In the **Sort & Filter group**, click **Advanced**, and then click **Filter By Form**. In the lower left corner of the form, click the **Or tab**. Click the **City** field box **arrow**, and then click **Austin**. In the **Sort & Filter group**, click **Toggle Filter**, and then compare your screen with Figure 3.11.

> As displayed in the navigation area, 28 student records have either *Dripping Springs* OR *Austin* stored in the City field. You have created an *OR condition*; that is, records display where, in this instance, either of two values—Dripping Springs *or* Austin—is present in the selected field.

🔄 **ANOTHER WAY** Click in the field box, and type the criteria separated by the word *or*. For example, in the City field box, type *Dripping Springs or Austin*.

FIGURE 3.11

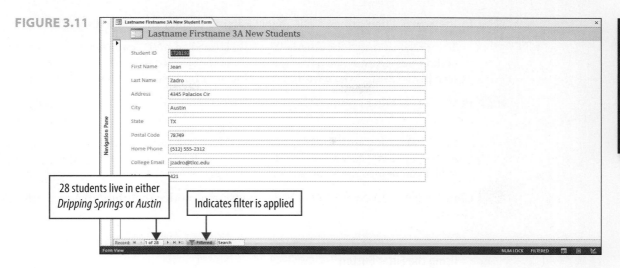

28 students live in either *Dripping Springs* or *Austin*

Indicates filter is applied

4 In the **Sort & Filter group**, click **Advanced**, and then click **Clear All Filters** to display all 102 records.

Activity 3.09 | Using Advanced Filter/Sort

In this activity, you will use the Advanced Filter/Sort command to filter records to locate students who live in Austin with a Major ID of *339*—Information Systems Technology.

1 In the **Sort & Filter group**, click **Advanced**, and then click **Advanced Filter/Sort**.

The Advanced Filter design grid displays, which is similar to the query design grid. A field list for the underlying table of the form displays.

2 In the table area, resize the field list so that the entire table name and all of the field names display.

3 In the **3A New Students** field list, double-click **City**, and then double-click **Major ID** to add both fields to the design grid. In the **Criteria** row under **City**, type **Austin** and then press Enter. In the **Criteria** row under **Major ID**, type **339** and then press Enter. Compare your screen with Figure 3.12.

FIGURE 3.12

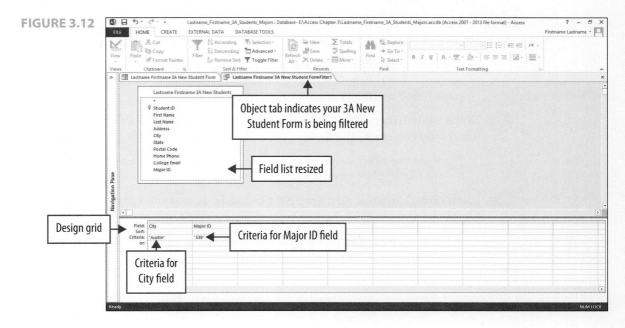

Object tab indicates your 3A New Student Form is being filtered

Field list resized

Design grid

Criteria for Major ID field

Criteria for City field

> **4** In the **Sort & Filter group**, click **Toggle Filter** to display the filtered records.

>> Three records match the criteria. You have created an ***AND condition***; that is, only records where both values—Austin *and* 339—are present in the selected fields display. There are three students who live in Austin who have declared a major of Information Systems Technology.

> **5** In the **Sort & Filter group**, click **Toggle Filter** to remove the filter and to display all of the records.

>> In the navigation area, *Unfiltered* displays, which indicates that a filter has been created for this form. Unless you click Clear All Filters, the filter is saved with the form when the form is closed. When you reopen the form, you can click Toggle Filter or Unfiltered to reapply the filter.

> **6** Close ⌧ your **3A New Student Form** object, and notice that the Advanced Filter grid also closes.

> **More Knowledge** | **Using the Filter Button**
>
> You can filter a form in a manner similar to the way you filter records in a table. Click in the field you wish to use for the filter. On the HOME tab, in the Sort & Filter group, click Filter to display a shortcut menu. Select the (Select All) check box to clear the option, and then select the data by which you want to filter your records by clicking the check boxes preceding the data. To remove the filter, redisplay the menu, and then select the (Select All) check box.

Objective 3   Create a Form by Using the Form Wizard

Video A3-3

The ***Form Wizard*** walks you step by step through the creation of a form and gives you more flexibility in the design, layout, and number of fields in a form than the Form tool. Design a form for the individuals who use the form—either for entering new records or viewing records. For example, when your college counselor displays student information, it may be easier for the counselor to view the information if the fields are arranged in a layout that more closely matches a paper form.

Activity 3.10 | Creating a Form by Using the Form Wizard

In this activity, you will create a form to match the layout of a paper form that a student at Texas Lakes Community College completes when that student changes his or her major. This will make it easier for the individual who changes the data in the database.

> **1** On the ribbon, click the **CREATE tab**, and then in the **Forms group**, click **Form Wizard**.

>> The Form Wizard walks you step by step through the process of creating a form by asking questions. In the first wizard screen, you select the fields to include on the form. The fields can come from more than one table or query.

> **2** In the **Tables/Queries** box, click the **arrow** to display a list of available tables and queries from which you can create the form.

>> There are two tables in the database from which you can create a new form. The selected table is the one that you last worked with.

> **3** Click **Table: Lastname Firstname 3A New Students**, and then compare your screen with Figure 3.13.

>> In the Available Fields list, the field names from your 3A New Students table display.

FIGURE 3.13

4   In the **Available Fields** list, double-click the following field names in the order given to move them to the **Selected Fields** list: **First Name**, **Last Name**, and **Major ID**. Compare your screen with Figure 3.14.

> Three field names from your 3A New Students table display in the Selected Fields list.

↻ **ANOTHER WAY**   Click the field name, and then click One Field > │ to move a field from the Available Fields list to the Selected Fields list.

FIGURE 3.14

5   Click **Next**. In the wizard, be sure **Columnar** is selected as the layout, and then click **Next**. In the **What title do you want for your form?** box, select the existing text, type **Lastname Firstname 3A Student Major Change Form** and then click **Finish** to close the wizard and create the form.

> The three fields and the data from the first record in your 3A New Students table display in Form view.

6   **Open** » the **Navigation Pane**. If necessary, increase the width of the Navigation Pane so that all object names display fully. Compare your screen with Figure 3.15.

> In the Navigation Pane, the form displays under its data source—your 3A New Students table.

FIGURE 3.15

Video A3-4

After you create a form, you can make changes to it. For example, you can group the fields, resize the fields, add more fields to the form, and change the style of the form. Layout view enables you to see the data in the form as you modify the form. Most changes to a form can be made in Layout view.

Activity 3.11 | Grouping Controls in Layout View

In this activity, you will group *controls* in the form so that you can work with them as one unit. Controls are objects on a form that display data or text, perform actions, and let you view and work with information.

▶ 1 **Close** « the **Navigation Pane**, and be sure that your **3A Student Major Change Form** object displays in the object window. On the **HOME tab**, in the **Views group**, click the top portion of the **View** button to switch to **Layout** view. If the Field List pane displays on the right side of your screen, click Close ✕ to close the pane. Compare your screen with Figure 3.16.

The field names and data for the first record in your 3A New Students record display in controls. The data for the first record displays in ***text box controls***. The most commonly used control is the text box control, which typically displays data from a field in the underlying table. A text box control is a ***bound control***—its data comes from a field in a table or query.

The field names—*First Name*, *Last Name*, and *Major ID*—display in ***label controls***. A label control displays to the left of a text box control and contains descriptive information that displays on the form, usually the field name. A control that does not have a data source is an ***unbound control***. Another example of an unbound control is a label control that displays the title of a form.

⟳ **ANOTHER WAY**   On the right side of the status bar, click Layout View ▤ to switch from Form view to Layout view.

FIGURE 3.16

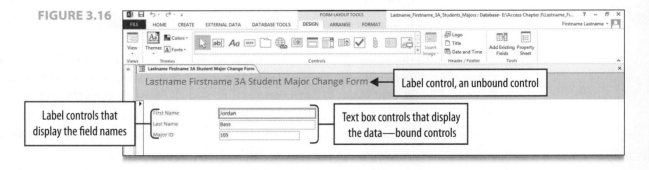

▶ 2 Click the **First Name label control**. Hold down Shift, and then click the **Last Name label control**, the **Major ID label control**, and the three **text box controls** to select all of the label and text box controls on the form.

┌───┐
│ **ALERT!**   **Do Your Controls Change Order When Selecting?**   │
│   │
│ If, when selecting multiple controls, the controls change order, click Undo, and then select the controls again. Be careful not to drag the mouse when you are selecting multiple controls. │
└───┘

3 With all six controls selected—surrounded by a colored border—on the ribbon, under **FORM LAYOUT TOOLS**, click the **ARRANGE tab**. In the **Table group**, click **Stacked**. Click the **First Name label control** to cancel the selection of all of the controls and to surround the **First Name label control** with a colored border. Compare your screen with Figure 3.17.

> This action groups the controls together in the *Stacked layout* format—a layout similar to a paper form, with labels to the left of each field. Because the controls are grouped, you can move and edit the controls more easily as you redesign your form.
>
> A dotted line forms a border around the controls, which indicates that the controls are grouped together. Above and to the left of the first label control that displays *First Name*, the *layout selector* displays. The layout selector is used to select and move or format the entire group of controls.

FIGURE 3.17

Activity 3.12 | Applying a Theme and Formatting a Form in Layout View

In this activity, you will apply a *theme* to the form in Layout view. A theme is a predesigned set of colors, fonts, lines, and fill effects that look good together and that can be applied to all of the objects in the database or to individual objects in the database.

1 On the ribbon, under **FORM LAYOUT TOOLS**, click the **DESIGN tab**. In the **Themes group**, click **Themes**. In the **Themes** gallery, using the ScreenTips, point to the **Retrospect** theme, right-click, and then click **Apply Theme to This Object Only**.

> Right-click a theme so that you can apply the theme to an individual object within the database. Apply a theme before formatting any other controls in your form.

N O T E   **Applying a Theme to an Object and Determining the Applied Theme**

If you click a theme rather than right-clicking it and selecting an option, the theme is applied to all objects in the database. You cannot click Undo to cancel the application of the theme to all objects. To determine the applied theme, in the Themes group, point to Themes. The ScreenTip displays the name of the current theme.

---

2 Click anywhere in the title of the form—*Lastname Firstname 3A Student Major Change Form*—to select the title. On the ribbon, under **FORM LAYOUT TOOLS**, click the **FORMAT tab**. In the **Font group**, click the **Font Size arrow**, and then click **14**. In the **Font group**, click **Bold B**. Click the **Font Color arrow**, and then under **Theme Colors**, in the fourth column, click the last color—**Olive Green, Text 2, Darker 50%**.

In Layout view, you can change the form's **control layout**—the grouped arrangement of controls.

> 1 Be sure that your **3A Student Major Change Form** object displays in **Layout** view. On the ribbon, click the **DESIGN tab**, and in the **Tools group**, click **Add Existing Fields**. Compare your screen with Figure 3.18.

The Field List pane displays, which lists the fields in the underlying table—your 3A New Students table.

FIGURE 3.18

> 2 In the **Field List** pane, click **Student ID**, and then drag the field name to the left until the ⊞ pointer displays above the **First Name label control** and a colored line displays above the control. Release the mouse button, and then compare your screen with Figure 3.19. If you are not satisfied with the result, click Undo, and begin again.

This action adds the Student ID label control and text box control to the form above the First Name controls.

FIGURE 3.19

> 3 **Close** ⊠ the **Field List** pane. Click the **Student ID text box control**, which displays *1034823*, to surround it with a border and to remove the border from the label control.

> 4 On the **DESIGN tab**, in the **Tools group**, click **Property Sheet**.

The Property Sheet for the Student ID text box control displays. Recall that each control has an associated Property Sheet where precise changes to the properties—characteristics—of selected controls can be made. At the top of the Property Sheet, to the right of *Selection type:*, *Text Box* displays because you selected the Student ID text box control.

5 In the **Property Sheet**, click the **Format tab**. Click **Width** to select the property setting, type **1.5** and then press Enter to decrease the width of the text box controls. Compare your screen with Figure 3.20.

All four text box controls are resized simultaneously. Because the controls are grouped together in a stacked layout, you can adjust the width of all of the text box controls at one time without having to select all of the controls. By decreasing the width of the text box controls, you have more space in which to rearrange the form controls. Because you can see the data in Layout view, you can determine visually that the space you have allotted is adequate to display all of the data in every field for every record.

ANOTHER WAY With the text box control selected, point to the right edge of the text box control until the ↔ pointer displays, and then drag left to the desired location.

FIGURE 3.20

6 **Close** ☒ the **Property Sheet**. Click the **Last Name text box control**, which displays *Bass*. On the ribbon, under **FORM LAYOUT TOOLS**, click the **ARRANGE tab**. In the **Rows & Columns group**, click **Select Row** to select the text box control and its associated label control.

7 In the **Move group**, click **Move Up** to move both controls above the **First Name** controls, and then compare your screen with Figure 3.21.

ANOTHER WAY Drag the selected controls to the desired location and then release the mouse button.

FIGURE 3.21

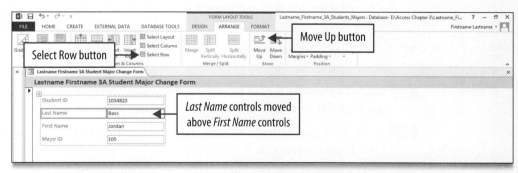

A L E R T ! **Did the Last Name Label Control Not Move with the Last Name Text Box Control?**

Be sure to select both the text box control and the label control before moving the controls; otherwise, only one of the controls will move. If this happens, click Undo, select both controls, and try again. Controls are stacked from top to bottom, not right to left.

8 **Save** 🖫 the changes you have made to the design of your form.

In this activity, you will format and change the property settings for multiple controls.

1 With the form displayed in **Layout** view, click the **Student ID text box control**, which displays *1034823*. On the **ARRANGE tab**, in the **Rows & Columns group**, click **Select Column** to select all four text box controls.

ANOTHER WAY   Click the first text box control, hold down Shift, and then click the last text box control to select all four text box controls.

2 With all four text box controls selected, on the ribbon, click the **FORMAT tab**. In the **Font group**, click the **Background Color arrow** . Under **Theme Colors**, in the last column, click the second color—**Green, Accent 6, Lighter 80%.**

All of the text box controls display a background color of light green. This formatting is not applied to the label controls on the left.

3 Click the **Student ID label control**. On the ribbon, click the **ARRANGE tab**, and then in the **Rows & Columns group**, click **Select Column**. On the ribbon, click the **FORMAT tab**, and then click the **Font Color arrow**—*not* the **Background Color arrow**. Under **Theme Colors**, in the fourth column, click the first color—**Olive Green, Text 2**. Click **Bold** B. Click in a blank area of the form to cancel the selection, and then compare your screen with Figure 3.22.

FIGURE 3.22

Font color and bold applied to label controls

Background color changed for text box controls

4 Click any **label control** to display the **layout selector**, and then click the **layout selector** to select all of the grouped controls.

Recall that the layout selector, which displays to the left and above the Student ID label control, enables you to select and move the entire group of controls in Layout view.

ANOTHER WAY   Click any control, and then on the ARRANGE tab, in the Rows & Columns group, click Select Layout.

5 On the **FORMAT tab**, in the **Font group**, click the **Font Size arrow**, and then click **12** to change the font size of all of the text in all of the controls.

6 With all of the controls still selected, on the ribbon, click the **DESIGN tab**. In the **Tools group**, click **Property Sheet**, and then compare your screen with Figure 3.23.

The Property Sheet for the selected controls displays. At the top of the Property Sheet, to the right of *Selection type:*, *Multiple selection* displays because you have more than one control selected.

FIGURE 3.23

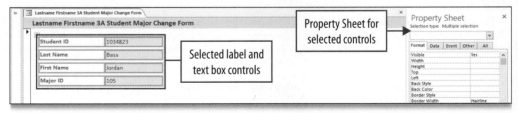

Property Sheet for selected controls

Selected label and text box controls

7 In the **Property Sheet**, click **Height**, type **0.25** and then press Enter to change the height of each selected control.

8 Click the **Student ID label control** to cancel the selection of all of the controls and to select only this label control. In the **Property Sheet**, click **Width**, type **1.25** and then press Enter.

The width of every label control changed to 1.25 inches. Recall that because the label controls are arranged in a stacked layout, you can change the width of all controls by selecting only one control. This is one of the few properties that can be changed without first selecting the column.

9 **Close** X the **Property Sheet**, and then **Save** 🖫 the design changes to your form.

Activity 3.15 | Modifying a Form in Design View

Design view presents a detailed view of the structure of your form. Because the form is not actually running when displayed in Design view, the data does not display in the text box controls. However, some tasks, such as resizing sections, must be completed in Design view.

1 On the status bar, click **Design View** 🗹, and then compare your screen with Figure 3.24.

The form in Design view displays three sections, each designated by a *section bar* at the top of each section. The *Form Header* contains information, such as the form title, that displays at the top of the screen in Form view or Layout view and is printed at the top of the first page when records are printed as forms. The *Detail section* displays the records from the underlying table, and the *Form Footer* displays at the bottom of the screen in Form view or Layout view and is printed after the last detail section on the last page of a printout.

> ⟳ ANOTHER WAY On the HOME tab, in the Views group, click the View arrow, and then click Design view; or right-click the object tab, and then click Design View.

FIGURE 3.24

2 At the bottom of the form, click the **Form Footer section bar** to select it. On the ribbon, click the **DESIGN tab**, and in the **Tools group**, click **Property Sheet**. In the **Property Sheet**, on the **Format tab**, click **Height**, type **0.5** and then press Enter. Compare your screen with Figure 3.25.

In addition to properties for controls, you can make precise changes to sections of the form. Because you selected the Form Footer section bar, the Property Sheet displays a *Selection type* of *Section*, and the section is identified as *Form Footer*.

> ⟳ ANOTHER WAY At the bottom of the form, point to the lower edge of the Form Footer section bar to display the ➕ pointer, and then drag downward approximately 0.5 inch to increase the height of the section.

FIGURE 3.25

On the **DESIGN tab**, in the **Controls group**, click **Label** Aa. Move the ⁺A pointer into the **Form Footer** section and then position the plus sign of the ⁺A pointer at approximately **0.25 inch on the horizontal ruler** and even with the lower edge of the **Form Footer section bar**—the position does not need to be precise. Compare your screen with Figure 3.26.

FIGURE 3.26

Click one time. Type **Texas Lakes Community College** and then press Enter. With the **label control** selected, on the ribbon, click the **FORMAT tab**. In the **Font group**, click **Bold** B. Click the **Font Color arrow**, and then under **Theme Colors**, in the fourth column, click the first color—**Olive Green, Text 2**.

With the **label control** still selected, in the **Property Sheet**, click **Top**, type **0.1** and then press Enter. In the **Property Sheet**, in the **Left** property setting, type **0.6** and then press Enter. **Close** ✕ the **Property Sheet**, and then **Save** 🖫 the design changes to your form.

The top edge of the label control in the Form Footer section displays 0.1 inch from the lower edge of the Form Footer Section bar. The left edge of the label control aligns at 0.6 inch from the left margin of the form. In this manner, you can place a control in a specific location on the form.

On the right side of the status bar, click **Form View** 🔲, and then compare your screen with Figure 3.27.

Form Footer text displays on the screen at the bottom of the form and prints only on the last page if all of the forms are printed. Recall, that in Form view, you can add, modify, or delete records stored in the underlying table.

🔁 **ANOTHER WAY**   On the HOME tab, in the Views group, click the View arrow, and then click Form View; or right-click the object tab, and then click Form View.

FIGURE 3.27

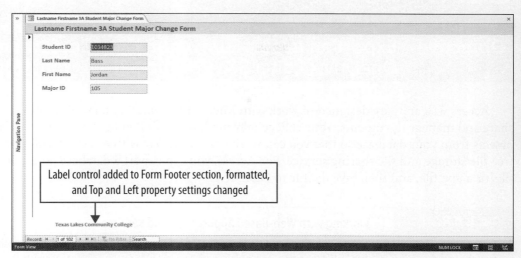

Label control added to Form Footer section, formatted, and Top and Left property settings changed

Texas Lakes Community College

7 In the navigation area, click **Last record** ▶ to display the record containing your name.

8 On the ribbon, click the **FILE tab**, click **Print**, and then on the right, click **Print**. In the **Print** dialog box, under **Print Range**, click the **Selected Records(s)** option button. Create a paper or electronic printout as directed by your instructor. To create an electronic printout, follow the directions given in the Note in Activity 3.06.

Because you decreased the width of the text box controls, you do *not* have to adjust the Column size Width in the Page Setup dialog box as you did with the form you created by using the Form tool.

9 **Close** ✕ all open objects, and then **Open** » the **Navigation Pane**. On the right side of the title bar, click **Close** ✕ to close the database and to exit Access. As directed by your instructor, submit your database and the paper or electronic printouts of the three forms that are the results of this project. Specifically, in this project, using your own name, you created the following database and printouts or electronic printouts:

1. Lastname_Firstname_3A_Students_Majors	Database file
2. Lastname Firstname 3A New Student Form	Form (printout or electronic printout - Record 102)
3. Lastname Firstname 3A Major Form	Form (printout or electronic printout - Record 33)
4. Lastname Firstname 3A Student Major Change Form	Form (printout or electronic printout - Record 102)

END | You have completed Project 3A

Objective | Export an Access Form to an Excel Spreadsheet, Save to OneDrive, Edit a Record, and Save to Your Computer

Access web apps are designed to work with Microsoft's SharePoint, an application for setting up websites to share and manage documents. Your college may not have SharePoint installed, so you will use other tools to share objects from your database so that you can work collaboratively with others. Recall that Window's OneDrive is a free file storage and file sharing service. For Access, you can export a database object to an Excel worksheet, a PDF file, or a text file, and then save the file to OneDrive.

> **A L E R T !** **Working with Web-Based Applications and Services**
>
> Computer programs and services on the web receive continuous updates and improvements. Thus, the steps to complete this web-based activity may differ from the ones shown. You can often look at the screens and the information presented to determine how to complete the activity.

Activity | **Exporting an Access Form to an Excel Spreadsheet, Saving the Spreadsheet to OneDrive, Editing a Record in OneDrive, and Saving to Your Computer**

In this activity, you will export your 3A Student Major Change Form object to an Excel spreadsheet, upload your Excel file to OneDrive, edit a record in OneDrive, and then download a copy of the edited spreadsheet to your computer.

 Start Access, navigate to your **Access Chapter 3** folder, and then **Open** your **3A_Students_Majors** database file. If necessary, on the Message Bar, click Enable Content. In the **Navigation Pane**, click your **3A Student Major Change Form** object to select it.

2 On the ribbon, click the **EXTERNAL DATA tab**, and in the **Export group**, click **Excel**. In the **Export – Excel Spreadsheet** dialog box, click **Browse**, and then navigate to your **Access Chapter 3** folder. In the **File Save** dialog box, click in the **File name** box, type **Lastname_Firstname_AC_3A_Web** and then click **Save**.

3 In the **Export – Excel Spreadsheet** dialog box, under **Specify export options**, select the second check box—**Open the destination file after the export operation is complete**—and then click **OK**.

The records from the underlying table of the form display in Excel. When you export a form to Excel, the formatting and layout are automatically saved. For example, notice the olive green background color of the cells, which was the color that was applied to the text box controls in the form.

4 In the **Microsoft Excel** window, in the column headings row, to the left of column **A**, click **Select All**. On the **HOME tab**, in the **Cells group**, click **Format**, and then click **AutoFit Column Width**. Click in cell **A1** to cancel the selection, and then compare your screen with Figure A.

FIGURE A

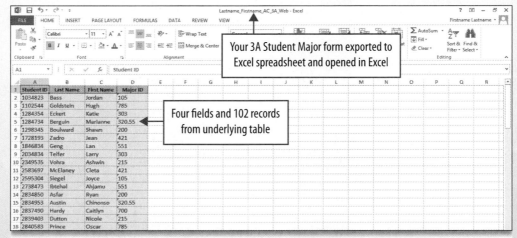

Your 3A Student Major form exported to Excel spreadsheet and opened in Excel

Four fields and 102 records from underlying table

(GO! with Office Online (formerly Web Apps) continues on the next page)

5 **Save** the spreadsheet, and then **Close** Excel. In the **Export – Excel Spreadsheet** dialog box, click **Close**, and then **Close** Access.

6 From the desktop, start Internet Explorer, navigate to **http://onedrive.com**, and then sign in to your Microsoft account. Open your **GO! Web Projects** folder—or create and then open this folder if necessary.

7 On the menu bar, click **Upload**. In the **Choose File to Upload** dialog box, navigate to your **Access Chapter 3** folder, and then double-click your **AC_3A_Web** file to upload it to OneDrive.

8 In your **GO! Web Projects** folder, click your **AC_3A_Web** file to open it in Excel Online.

On the ribbon, notice that you can open this worksheet in Excel instead of using the Excel Online. If you are working on a computer that does not have Microsoft Excel installed, you can still create and modify workbooks in your web browser by using the Excel Online.

9 In the second record, click in the **Last Name** field, using your own last name, type **Lastname** and then press Tab. In the **First Name** field, using your own first name, type **Firstname** and then press ↓ to save the record. Compare your screen with Figure B.

10 On the ribbon, click the **FILE tab**, click **Save As**, and then click **Download a Copy**. In the message box—which usually displays at the bottom of your screen—click the **Save arrow**, and then click **Save as**. In the **Save As** dialog box, navigate to your **Access Chapter 3** folder, click in the **File name** box, and then type **Lastname_Firstname_A3A_Web_ Download** and then click **Save**. **Close** the message box.

11 In OneDrive, on the title bar, click **OneDrive** to return to your home page. At the top right corner of your screen, click your OneDrive name, and then click **Sign out**. **Close** your browser window.

12 Start Excel. In the Excel opening screen, click **Open Other Workbooks**. Under **Open**, click **Computer**, and then on the right, click **Browse**. Navigate to your **Access Chapter 3** folder, and then double-click your **A3A_Web** file. Notice that this file is the original file—the second record is not changed. If you are required to print your documents, use one of the methods in the Note box below. **Close** your Excel file, saving the changes to your worksheet, and then **Open** and print your **A3A_Web_Download** file following one of the methods in the Note box below. **Close** Excel, saving the changes to your worksheet. As directed by your instructor, submit your two workbooks and the two paper or electronic printouts that are the results of this project.

N O T E **Adding the File Name to the Footer and Printing or Creating an Electronic Printout of an Excel Spreadsheet of Only One Page**

Click the FILE tab, click Print, and then click Page Setup. In the Page Setup dialog box, click the Header/Footer tab, and then click Custom Footer. With the insertion point blinking in the Left section box, click the Insert File Name button, and then click OK. In the Page Setup dialog box, click OK. Under Settings, click the *Pages* spin box up arrow to display *1* in the box. Click the *to* spin box up arrow to display *1* in the box.

To print on paper, click Print. To create an electronic file of your printout, on the left side of your screen, click Export. Under Export, be sure Create PDF/ XPS Document is selected, and then click Create PDF/XPS. In the Publish as PDF or XPS dialog box, click Options. In the Options dialog box, under Page range, click Pages, and be sure the From box displays *1* and the To box displays *1*; then click OK. Navigate to your Access Chapter 3 folder, and then click Publish to save the file with the default name and an extension of pdf.

FIGURE B

PROJECT ACTIVITIES

In Activities 3.16 through 3.24, you will assist Jack Woods, director of the Career Center for Texas Lakes Community College, in using his Access database to track the employees and job openings advertised for the annual job fair. Your completed reports will look similar to Figure 3.28.

PROJECT FILES

For Project 3B, you will need the following file:

a03B_Job_Openings

You will save your database as:

Lastname_Firstname_3B_Job_Openings

PROJECT RESULTS

FIGURE 3.28 Project 3B Job Openings

Objective 5 Create a Report by Using the Report Tool and Modify the Report in Layout View

Video A3-5

A *report* is a database object that summarizes the fields and records from a query or from a table in an easy-to-read format suitable for printing. A report consists of information extracted from queries or tables and report design controls, such as labels, headings, and graphics. The queries or tables that provide the underlying data for a report are referred to as the report's *record source*.

Activity 3.16 | Opening and Saving an Existing Database, Renaming Objects, and Viewing a Table Relationship

1 Start Access. In the Access opening screen, click **Open Other Files**. Under **Open**, click **Computer**. Under **Recent Folders**, if displayed, click the location where your student data files are stored; otherwise, click **Browse** and then navigate to the location where your student data files are stored. Double-click **a03B_Job_Openings** to open the database.

2 On the **FILE tab**, click **Save As**. Under **File Types**, be sure **Save Database As** is selected. On the right, under **Database File Types**, be sure **Access Database** is selected, and then click **Save As**. In the **Save As** dialog box, navigate to your **Access Chapter 3** folder. In the **File name** box, replace the existing text with **Lastname_Firstname_3B_Job_Openings** and then press Enter.

3 On the **Message Bar**, click **Enable Content**. In the **Navigation Pane**, right-click the **3B Employers** table, and then click **Rename**. With the table name selected and using your own name, type **Lastname Firstname 3B Employers** and then press Enter to rename the table. Use the same technique to **Rename** the **3B Job Openings** table to **Lastname Firstname 3B Job Openings** and then **Rename** the first **3B Salary $40,000 or More Query** object to **Lastname Firstname 3B Salary $40,000 or More Query**

> Recall that a query that selects data from more than one table displays under both table names in the Navigation Pane. When you rename one of the query objects, the name of the second occurrence automatically changes.

4 Point to the right edge of the **Navigation Pane** to display the ↔ pointer. Drag to the right to increase the width of the pane until all object names display fully.

5 On the ribbon, click the **DATABASE TOOLS tab**. In the **Relationships group**, click **Relationships**. Under **RELATIONSHIP TOOLS**, on the **DESIGN tab**, in the **Relationships group**, click **All Relationships**. Resize and move the field lists so that the entire table name and fields display for each field list.

> Because you renamed the tables, the field lists do not automatically display in the Relationships window.

6 In the **Relationships** window, click the **join line** between the two field lists. In the **Tools group**, click **Edit Relationships**. Point to the title bar of the **Edit Relationships** dialog box, and drag the dialog box downward below the **3B Job Openings** field list. Compare your screen with Figure 3.29.

> *One* employer is associated with *many* job openings. Thus, a one-to-many relationship is established between the 3B Employers table and the 3B Job Openings table by using Employee ID as the common field. Referential integrity is enforced, and cascade options are selected.

FIGURE 3.29

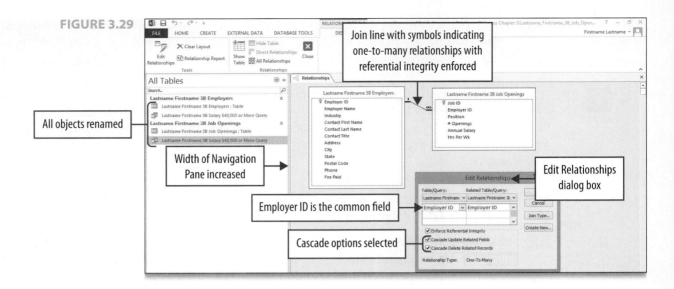

Join line with symbols indicating
one-to-many relationships with
referential integrity enforced

All objects renamed

Width of Navigation
Pane increased

Employer ID is the common field

Cascade options selected

Edit Relationships
dialog box

7 Close ✕ the **Edit Relationships** dialog box, and then **Close** ✕ the **Relationships** window. In the message box, click **Yes** to save changes to the layout of the relationships.

8 In the **Navigation Pane**, double-click each table, and then examine the fields and data in each table. Double-click the query object to run the query and examine the query results, apply **Best Fit** to the query results, and then **Save** the query. Switch to **Design** view to examine the design grid.

Because you renamed the tables that are the underlying source of data for the query, you have to reapply Best Fit to the query results. The query answers the question, *What is the Job ID, position, employer name, number of job openings, and annual salary for job openings that have an annual salary of $40,000 or more, in ascending order by the Employer Name field within the Position field?*

9 In the object window, right-click any **object tab**, and then click **Close All**.

Activity 3.17 | Creating a Report by Using the Report Tool and Applying a Theme to the Report

The ***Report tool*** is the fastest way to create a report. This tool displays all of the fields and records from the record source that you select. You can use the Report tool to look at the underlying data quickly in an easy-to-read format, after which you can save the report and modify it in Layout view or in Design view.

In this activity, you will use the Report tool to create a report from a query that lists all of the job openings with an annual salary of at least $40,000 and apply a theme to the report.

1 In the **Navigation Pane**, if necessary, click to select your **3B Salary $40,000 or More Query** object. On the ribbon, click the **CREATE tab**, and in the **Reports group**, click **Report**. **Close** « the **Navigation Pane**, and then compare your screen with Figure 3.30.

The report is created using the query as the record source and displays in Layout view. The report includes all of the fields and all of the records from the query and the title of the query. In Layout view, the broken lines indicate the page margins in the report.

FIGURE 3.30

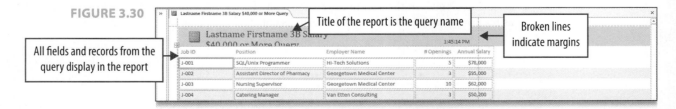

Title of the report is the query name

Broken lines
indicate margins

All fields and records from the
query display in the report

2 Under **REPORT LAYOUT TOOLS**, on the **DESIGN tab**, in the **Themes group**, click **Themes**. In the **Themes** gallery, use the ScreenTips to locate the **Integral** theme, right-click the **Integral** theme, and then click **Apply Theme to This Object Only**.

> Recall that right-clicking a theme enables you to apply a predefined format to the active object only, which is a quick way to apply a professional look to a report. Apply a theme before formatting any other controls on the report.

Activity 3.18 | Modifying a Report in Layout View

After you create a report, you can make changes to it. For example, you can add or delete fields, resize the fields, and change the style of the report. Layout view enables you to see the data in the report as you modify the report. Most changes to a report can be made in Layout view.

1 Click the **Job ID** field name. On the ribbon, under **REPORT LAYOUT TOOLS**, click the **ARRANGE tab**. In the **Rows & Columns group**, click **Select Column** to select the field name and all of the data for each record in the field. Press Del to remove the field from the report.

> The Job ID field is deleted, and the remaining fields move to the left. No fields extend beyond the right margin of the report.

ANOTHER WAY   With the column selected, on the HOME tab, in the Records group, click Delete; or right-click the selected column, and then click Delete or Delete Column.

2 Scroll down, and notice that for the position of *Estimating Manager*, there is an extra blank line in the fields for this record. In the **Employer Name** field, click in the **text box control** that displays *Monroe Heating & Air Conditioning* to select all of the text box controls in this field.

3 On the ribbon, under **REPORT LAYOUT TOOLS**, click the **DESIGN tab**. In the **Tools group**, click **Property Sheet**. In the **Property Sheet**, on the **Format tab**, click **Width**, type **2.5** and then press Enter. Compare your screen with Figure 3.31.

> Recall that you can use the Property Sheet to make precise changes to control properties.

ANOTHER WAY   Point to the right edge of the text box control to display the ↔ pointer. Drag to the right slightly until the data in the text box control displays on one line.

FIGURE 3.31
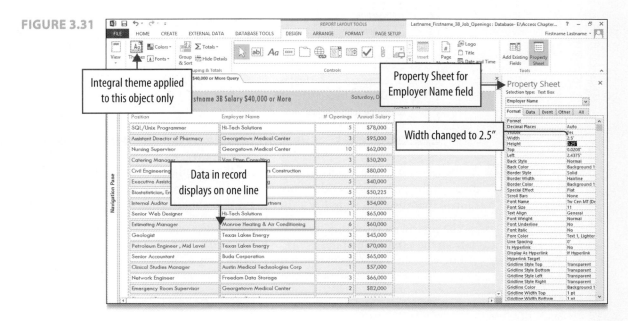

4 **Close** ☒ the **Property Sheet**. Click the **Position** field name, and then on the ribbon, click the **HOME tab**. In the **Sort & Filter group**, click **Ascending** to sort the records in ascending order by the Position field.

⟳ **ANOTHER WAY**   Right-click the selected field name and then click Sort A to Z.

5 Scroll to the bottom of the report, and then click the **calculated control** that displays *$2,157,625*, which is truncated at the bottom. Press ⌊Del⌋ to remove this control.

In a report created by using the Report tool, a ***calculated control*** is automatically created to sum any field that is formatted as currency. A calculated control contains an expression, often a formula or a function. Here, the total is not a useful number and thus can be deleted.

6 Scroll to the bottom of the report again, and then under the last column, click the horizontal line that is the border between the last record and the calculated control that you deleted. Press ⌊Del⌋ to remove this line, and then scroll to the bottom of the report to verify that the line has been deleted.

7 Scroll to the top of the report, and then click the **# Openings** field name. On the ribbon, click the **DESIGN tab**. In the **Grouping & Totals group**, click **Totals**, and then click **Sum**.

8 Scroll to the bottom of the report, and then click the **calculated control** that displays *100*. On the **DESIGN tab**, in the **Tools group**, click **Property Sheet**. In the **Property Sheet**, on the **Format tab**, click **Height**, type **0.25** and then press ⌊Enter⌋. Compare your screen with Figure 3.32.

The total number of job openings for positions with a salary of $40,000 or more is 100.

⟳ **ANOTHER WAY**   Point to the lower edge of the text box control to display the ⌊↕⌋ pointer, and then double-click to resize the control, or drag downward to increase the height of the control.

FIGURE 3.32

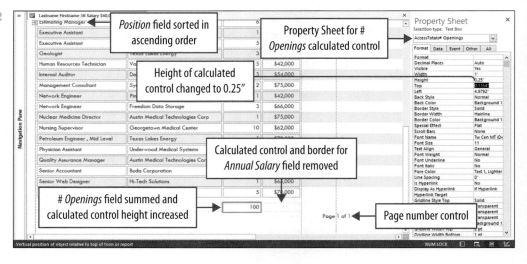

9 At the bottom of the report to the right of the calculated control, notice that the control that displays the page number does not fit entirely within the margins of the report. Click the **control** that displays *Page 1 of 1*. In the **Property Sheet**, click **Left**, type **2.5** and then press ⌊Enter⌋.

The control moves within the margins of the report with the left edge of the control 2.5 inches in from the left margin of the report. When you click on different controls in a report or form, the Property Sheet changes to match the selected control. Before printing, always scroll through the report to be sure that all of the controls display on one page and not outside of the margins.

ANOTHER WAY   Click the control, point to the selected control to display the 🔀 pointer, and then drag the control to the left within the margins of the report.

10 Scroll to the top of the report, and then click the **label control** that displays the title of the report—*Lastname Firstname 3B Salary $40,000 or More Query*. On the ribbon, under **REPORT LAYOUT TOOLS**, click the **FORMAT tab**. In the **Font group**, click the **Font Size arrow**, and then click **14**.

11 With the **label control** for the title still selected, double-click **Query** to select the word, type **Report** and then press [Enter] to change the name of the report to *Lastname Firstname 3B Salary $40,000 or More Report*.

12 Click the **Position** field name. In the **Property Sheet**, click **Left**, type **0.5** and then press [Enter] to move this field 0.5 inch in from the left margin of the report. Compare your screen with Figure 3.33.

> The other fields adjust by moving to the right. The fields are centered approximately within the margins of the report.

ANOTHER WAY   Click the layout selector ⊞ to select all of the controls, and then drag it slightly downward and to the right until the columns are visually centered between the margins of the report. If your columns rearrange, click Undo and begin again.

FIGURE 3.33

13 **Close** ✕ the **Property Sheet**, and then **Save** 🖫 the report as **Lastname Firstname 3B Salary $40,000 or More Report**

Activity 3.19 | Printing a Report

In this activity, you will view your report in Print Preview and display the two pages of the report.

1 On the right side of the status bar, click **Print Preview** 🔍.

ANOTHER WAY   On the DESIGN tab or the HOME tab, in the Views group, click the View arrow, and then click Print Preview; or, in the object window, right-click the object tab, and then click Print Preview.

2 On the **PRINT PREVIEW tab**, in the **Zoom group**, click **Two Pages** to view the two pages of your report. Notice that the page number displays at the bottom of each page.

3 Create a paper or electronic printout as directed—two pages result, and then click **Close Print Preview**. **Close** ☒ the report, and then **Open** ⧉ the **Navigation Pane**.

The report displays under both tables from which the query was created. The report object name displays with a small green notebook icon.

4 **Close** ⧏ the **Navigation Pane**.

Objective 6 | Create a Report by Using the Report Wizard

Video A3-6

Use the ***Report Wizard*** when you need more flexibility in the design of your report. You can group and sort data by using the wizard and use fields from more than one table or query if you have created the relationships between tables. The Report Wizard is similar to the Form Wizard; the wizard walks you step by step through the process of creating the report by asking you questions and then designs the report based on your answers.

Activity 3.20 | Creating a Report by Using the Report Wizard

In this activity, you will prepare a report for Mr. Woods that displays the employers, grouped by industry, and the total fees paid by employers for renting a booth at the Job Fair.

1 On the ribbon, click the **CREATE tab**, and then in the **Reports group**, click **Report Wizard**.

In the first wizard screen, you select the fields to include on the report. The fields can come from more than one table or query.

2 In the **Tables/Queries** box, click the **arrow**, and then click **Table: Lastname Firstname 3B Employers**. In the **Available Fields** list, double-click the following field names in the order given to move them to the **Selected Fields** list: **Industry**, **Employer Name**, and **Fee Paid** (scroll as necessary to locate the *Fee Paid* field). Compare your screen with Figure 3.34.

Three field names from your 3B Employers table display in the Selected Fields list.

 ANOTHER WAY Click the field name, and then click One Field ⎡ > ⎤ to move a field from the Available Fields list to the Selected Fields list.

FIGURE 3.34

3 Click **Next**. In the wizard, notice that you can add grouping levels and that a preview of the grouping level displays on the right.

Grouping data helps to organize and summarize the data in your report.

4 On the left, double-click **Industry**, and then compare your screen with Figure 3.35.

The preview displays how the data will be grouped in the report. Grouping data in a report places all of the records that have the same data in a field together as a group—in this instance, the records will be grouped by *Industry*. Within each Industry name, the Employer Name and Fee Paid will display.

FIGURE 3.35

5 Click **Next**. Click the **1** box **arrow**, click **Employer Name**, and then compare your screen with Figure 3.36.

In this step of the wizard, you indicate how you want to sort the records and summarize the information. You can sort up to four fields. The Summary Options button displays because the data is grouped, and at least one of the fields—*Fee Paid*—contains numerical or currency data. Within each Industry grouping, the records will be sorted alphabetically by the Employer Name. Sorting records in a report presents a more organized view of the records.

FIGURE 3.36

6 In the wizard, click **Summary Options**, and then compare your screen with Figure 3.37.

The Summary Options dialog box displays. The *Fee Paid* field can be summarized by selecting one of the four check boxes for Sum, Avg, Min, or Max. You can also display only summary information or display both the details—each record—and the summary information. The default setting is to display *Detail and Summary*.

FIGURE 3.37

7 In the **Summary Options** dialog box, click to select the **Sum** check box. Under **Show**, be sure that **Detail and Summary** is selected, and then click **OK**. In the wizard, click **Next**.

In this step of the wizard, you select the layout and page orientation. A preview of the layout displays on the left.

8 Click each **Layout** option button, noticing the changes in the preview, and then click **Stepped** to select it as the layout for your report. Under **Orientation**, be sure that **Portrait** is selected. At the bottom of the wizard, be sure that the **Adjust the field width so all fields fit on a page** check box is selected, and then click **Next**.

9 In the **What title do you want for your report?** box, select the existing text, type **Lastname Firstname 3B Booth Fees by Industry Report** and then click **Finish**. Compare your screen with Figure 3.38.

The report is saved and displays in Print Preview using the specifications you defined in the Report Wizard. The records are grouped by Industry. Within each Industry, the records display in ascending order by the Employer Name. Within each Industry grouping, the Fee paid is summed or totaled—the word *Sum* displays at the end of each grouping.

FIGURE 3.38

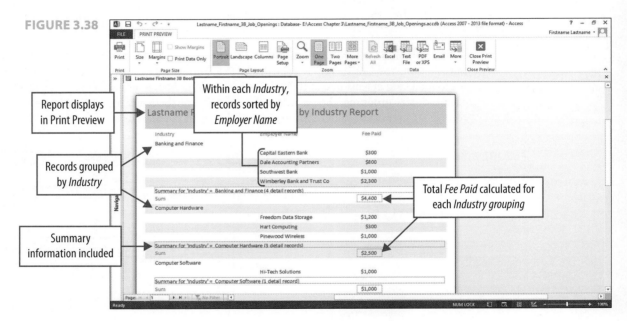

10 In the object window, right-click the **object tab** for the report, and then click **Layout View**.

 ANOTHER WAY   On the status bar, click Layout View ; or click Close Print Preview, and then on the HOME tab or the DESIGN tab, click the View arrow, and then click Layout View.

Objective 7   Modify the Design of a Report

Video A3-7

You can modify the design of a report that is created using the Report Wizard by using the same techniques and tools that you use to modify a report created with the Report tool. Recall that most report modifications can be made in Layout view.

Activity 3.21 | Formatting and Deleting Controls in Layout View

In this activity, you will apply a theme to the report, format the title of the report, and delete the summary information controls.

1 Be sure that your **3B Booth Fees by Industry Report** object is displayed in **Layout** view. Under **REPORT LAYOUT TOOLS**, on the **DESIGN tab**, in the **Themes group**, click **Themes**. In the **Themes** gallery, use the ScreenTips to locate the **Ion Boardroom** theme, right-click the **Ion Boardroom** theme, and then click **Apply Theme to This Object Only**.

Recall that you should apply a theme before applying any other formatting changes. Also, recall that if you click a theme—instead of right-clicking—the theme is applied to all of the objects in the database.

2 At the top of the report, click the title—*Lastname Firstname 3B Booth Fees by Industry*—to display a border around the label control. On the ribbon, under **REPORT LAYOUT TOOLS**, click the **FORMAT tab**. In the **Font group**, click the **Font Size arrow**, and then click **14**. In the **Font group**, click **Bold** **B**.

By changing the font size, the report name is no longer truncated and includes the word *Report*.

3 Within each *Industry* grouping, notice the **Summary for 'Industry'** information.

Because you selected Summary Options, a summary line is included at the end of each grouping that details what is being summarized—in this case, summed—and the number of records that are included in the summary total. Now that Mr. Woods has viewed the report, he has decided that this information is not necessary and can be removed.

4 Click any one of the controls that begins with **Summary for 'Industry'**.

The control that you clicked is surrounded by a border, and all of the other summary information controls are surrounded by paler borders to indicate that all controls are selected.

5 Press Del to remove the controls from the report, and then compare your screen with Figure 3.39.

 ANOTHER WAY   Right-click any of the selected controls, and then click Delete to remove the controls from the report.

FIGURE 3.39

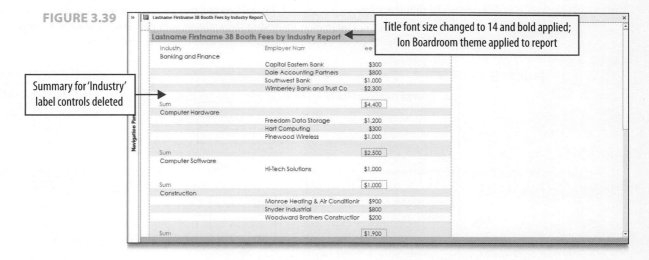

6 **Save** 🖫 the changes you have made to the design of the report.

Activity 3.22 | Modifying Controls in Layout View

In this activity, you will modify the text in controls, move controls, resize controls, and add a control to the report in Layout view.

1 On the left side of the report, click a **Sum label control**, which selects all of the related controls. Double-click the control to select the text—*Sum*. Type **Total Booth Fees by Industry** and then press Enter. Compare your screen with Figure 3.40.

This text states more clearly what is being summed.

FIGURE 3.40

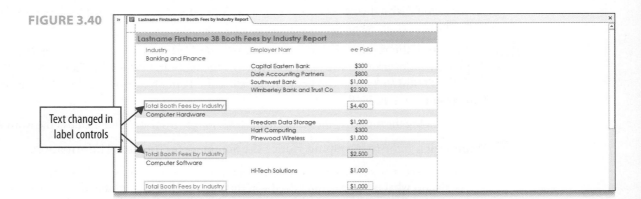

Text changed in label controls

2 At the top of the report, click the **Industry label control** to select it. Hold down Shift, click the **Employer Name label control**, and then click the **Fee Paid label control** to select all three field names. On the **FORMAT tab**, in the **Font group**, click **Bold** **B**.

Clicking Bold also increases the size of the controls so that the text is no longer truncated.

3 At the top of the report, under the **Fee Paid label control**, click the **text box control** that displays *$300* to select the text box controls for all of the records for this field. On the ribbon, click the **DESIGN tab**. In the **Tools group**, click **Property Sheet**. In the **Property Sheet**, on the **Format tab**, click **Left**, type **7** and then press Enter. Compare your screen with Figure 3.41.

All of the Fee Paid text box controls move to the right—7" in from the left margin. Do not be concerned that the summary total and the field name are not aligned with the data; you will correct this in the next activity. The field is moved to the right so that you can increase the width of the Employer Name text box controls so that all of the data for every record displays.

FIGURE 3.41

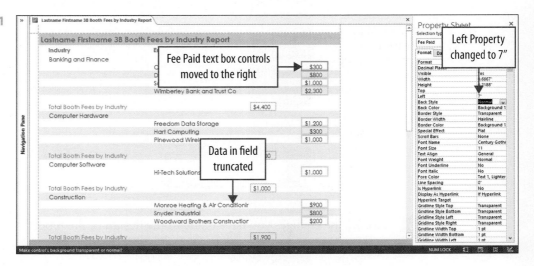

Fee Paid text box controls moved to the right

Data in field truncated

Left Property changed to 7"

4 Scroll to view the bottom of the report. Click to select the **calculated control** for the **Grand Total,** which displays *20,400* and part of the dollar symbol. In the **Property Sheet**, click **Width**, type **0.8** and then press Enter.

> The width of the calculated control increases to display the dollar symbol. Do not be concerned that the right edge of the control no longer aligns with the control above it; you will correct this in the next activity. Recall that a calculated control contains an expression—a formula or function—that displays the result of the expression when the report is displayed in Report view, Print Preview, or Layout view.

🔄 **ANOTHER WAY**   Point to the left edge of the control to display the ↔ pointer. Drag to the left slightly to increase the width of the calculated control.

5 At the bottom of the report, on the left side, click the **Grand Total label control**. In the **Property Sheet**, click **Width**, type **1** and then press Enter. Compare your screen with Figure 3.42.

> The width of the label control is increased so that all of the text displays.

🔄 **ANOTHER WAY**   Point to the right edge of the control to display the ↔ pointer, and then double-click to resize the control.

FIGURE 3.42

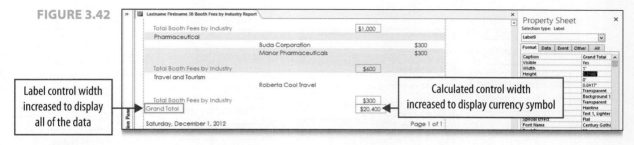

Label control width increased to display all of the data

Calculated control width increased to display currency symbol

6 Scroll to the top to display the Industry grouping of **Construction**, and notice that the first and third records have truncated data in the **Employer Name** field. In the **Construction** grouping, click, the **Employer Name text box control** that starts with *Monroe Heating* to select all of the text box controls for this field.

7 In the **Property Sheet**, click **Width**, type **3** and then press Enter. **Save** 🖫 the design changes to your report, and then compare your screen with Figure 3.43.

> The width of the Employer Name text box controls is increased so that all of the data in this field for every record displays. Recall that you moved the Fee Paid text box controls to the right to make room for the increased width of these controls.

FIGURE 3.43

Width of Employer Name text box control increased to 3"

Text is no longer truncated

Activity 3.23 | Aligning Controls in Design View

Design view gives you a more detailed view of the structure of your report. You can see the header and footer sections for the report, for the page, and for groups. In Design view, your report is not running, so you cannot see the data from the table in the controls. In the same manner as forms, you can add labels to the Page Footer section or increase the height of sections. Some tasks, such as aligning controls, must be completed in Design view.

1 **Close** ☒ the **Property Sheet**. On the status bar, click **Design View** ☑, and then compare your screen with Figure 3.44.

Design view for a report is similar to Design view for a form. You can modify the layout of the report in this view, and use the dotted grid pattern to align controls. This report has several sections. The **Report Header** displays information at the top of the *first page* of a report. The **Page Header** displays information at the top of *every page* of a report. The **Group Header** displays the name of data in the field by which the records are grouped; in this case, the *Industry* name. The **Detail** section displays the data for each record. The **Group Footer** displays the summary information for each grouping; in this case, the Industry name. The **Page Footer** displays information at the bottom of *every page* of the report. The **Report Footer** displays information at the bottom of the *last page* of the report.

If you do not group data in a report, the Group Header section and Group Footer section will not display. If you do not summarize the data, the Group Footer section will not display.

FIGURE 3.44

2 In the **Page Footer** section of the report, examine the two controls in this section. Recall that information in the Page Footer section displays at the bottom of every page in the report.

On the left side, the *date control* displays *=Now( )*, which inserts the current date each time the report is opened. On the right side, the *page number control* displays *="Page " & [Page] & " of " & [Pages]*, which inserts the page number, for example *Page 1 of 2*, when the report is displayed in Print Preview or when printed. Both of these controls contain examples of functions that are used by Access to create controls in a report.

3 In the **Industry Footer** section, click the **Total Booth Fees by Industry label control**. Hold down Shift, and in the **Report Footer** section, click the **Grand Total label control** to select both label controls.

4 On the ribbon, under **REPORT DESIGN TOOLS**, click the **ARRANGE tab**. In the **Sizing & Ordering group**, click **Align**, and then click **Left**.

The left edge of the *Grand Total label control* is aligned with the left edge of the *Total Booth Fees by Industry label control*. When using the Align Left command, the left edges of the selected controls are aligned with the control that is the farthest to the left in the report.

5 In the **Page Header** section, click the **Fee Paid label control**. Hold down Shift while you click the following: in the **Detail** section, click the **Fee Paid text box control**; in the **Industry Footer** section, click the **calculated control** that begins with =*Sum*; and in the **Report Footer** section, click the **calculated control** that begins with =*Sum*.

Four controls are selected.

6 On the **ARRANGE tab**, in the **Sizing & Ordering group**, click **Align**, and then click **Right**. Save 🖫 the design changes to your report, and then compare your screen with Figure 3.45.

The right edges of the four selected controls are aligned with the right edge of the *Fee Paid text box control*. When using the Align Right command, the right edges of the selected controls are aligned with the control that is the farthest to the right in the report.

FIGURE 3.45

7 On the status bar, click **Layout View** 🖽 to display the underlying data in the controls. Scroll to view the bottom of the report. On the left side, notice that the **Total Booth Fees by Industry label control** and the **Grand Total label control** are left aligned. Also, notice the right alignment of the controls in the **Fee Paid** column.

Objective 8 | Keep Grouped Data Together in a Printed Report

Video A3-8

Before you print a report, examine the report in Print Preview to be sure that all of the labels and data display fully and to be sure that all of the data is properly grouped. Sometimes a page break occurs in the middle of a group of data, leaving the labels on one page and the data or summary information on another page.

Activity 3.24 | Keeping Grouped Data Together in a Printed Report

In this activity, you will preview the document and then will keep the data in each group together so a grouping is not split between two pages of the report. This is possible if the data in a grouping does not exceed the length of a page.

1 On the status bar, click **Print Preview** 🔍. On the **PRINT PREVIEW tab**, in the **Zoom group**, click **Two Pages**, and then compare your screen with Figure 3.46.

The report will print on two pages. For the Industry grouping of *Hotel and Food Service*, one record and the summary data display at the top of Page 2 and is separated from the rest of the grouping that displays at the bottom of page 1. Your display may differ depending upon your printer configuration.

In Print Preview, the One Page or Two Pages Zoom view causes the records to be compressed slightly and might display with the bottoms of records truncated. The records, however, will print correctly.

FIGURE 3.46

Top of second page—one record and summary data for *Hotel and Food Service* grouping

Bottom of first page—*Industry* grouping name and two records

2 On the ribbon, click **Close Print Preview** to return to **Layout** view. On the **DESIGN tab**, in the **Grouping & Totals group**, click **Group & Sort**.

At the bottom of the screen, the ***Group, Sort, and Total pane*** displays. This pane is used to control how information is grouped, sorted, or totaled. Layout view is the preferred view in which to accomplish these tasks because you can see how the changes affect the display of the data in the report.

3 In the **Group, Sort, and Total** pane, on the **Group on Industry** bar, click **More**. To the right of **do not keep group together on one page**, click the **arrow**, and then compare your screen with Figure 3.47.

The *keep whole group together on one page* command keeps each industry group together, from the name in the Group Header section through the summary information in the Group Footer section. The default setting is *do not keep group together on one page*. Next to *Group on Industry*, with *A on top* indicates that the industry names are sorted in ascending order.

FIGURE 3.47

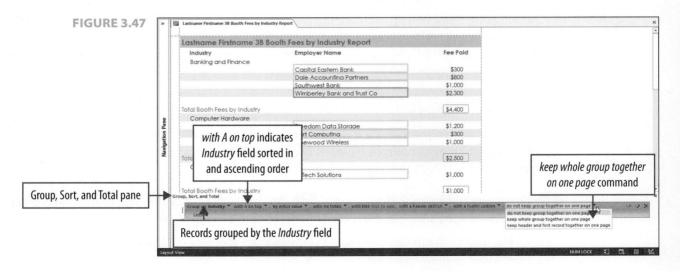

with A on top indicates *Industry* field sorted in and ascending order

keep whole group together on one page command

Group, Sort, and Total pane

Records grouped by the *Industry* field

4 Click **keep whole group together on one page**. On the **DESIGN tab**, in the **Grouping & Totals group**, click **Group & Sort** to close the **Group, Sort, and Total** pane.

5 On the status bar, click **Print Preview** . If necessary, in the Zoom group, click Two Pages. Compare your screen with Figure 3.48.

> The entire grouping for the Industry of *Hotel and Food Service* displays at the top of page 2. The grouping no longer breaks between page 1 and page 2. Recall that even though the bottoms of records display truncated because of the compressed Print Preview setting of Two Pages, the records will print correctly.

FIGURE 3.48

Entire *Hotel and Food Service* grouping kept together at top of second page

6 Save 🖫 the design changes to your report, and then create a paper or electronic printout of the report as directed—two pages result.

7 Close ☒ the report, and then Open ⟫ the **Navigation Pane**. If necessary, increase the width of the Navigation Pane so that all object names display fully.

8 On the right side of the title bar, click **Close** ☒ to close the database and to exit Access. As directed by your instructor, submit your database and the paper or electronic printouts of the two reports—each report is two pages—that are the results of this project. Specifically, in this project, using your own name you created the following database and printouts or electronic printouts:

1. Lastname_Firstname_3B_Job_Openings	Database file
2. Lastname Firstname 3B Salary $40,000 or More Report	Report (printout or electronic printout - two pages)
3. Lastname Firstname 3B Booth Fees by Industry Report	Report (printout or electronic printout - two pages)

END | You have completed Project 3B

Objective	Export an Access Report to a Word File, Save to OneDrive, and Add a Description to the Word File

Access web apps are designed to work with Microsoft's SharePoint, an application for setting up websites to share and manage documents. Your college may not have SharePoint installed, so you will use other tools to share objects from your database so that you can work collaboratively with others. When you have information that you want to share with others, you can upload files to OneDrive. Some files can be opened in OneDrive; some can only be downloaded. Because database files are typically large in size, and free storage space on OneDrive is limited, you can export database objects to different formats and then upload those files to OneDrive.

ALERT!	Working with Web-Based Applications and Services

Computer programs and services on the web receive continuous updates and improvements. Thus, the steps to complete this web-based activity may differ from the ones shown. You can often look at the screens and the information presented to determine how to complete the activity.

Activity | Exporting an Access Report to a Word File, Uploading the Word File to OneDrive, and Adding a Description to the Word File

In this activity, you will export your 3B Salary $40,000 or More Report object to a Word file, upload your Word file to OneDrive, and then add a description to the Word file. The report will be available for individuals with whom you have shared your OneDrive files or folders.

1 Start Access, navigate to your **Access Chapter 3** folder, and then **Open** your **3B_Job_Openings** database file. If necessary, on the Message Bar, click Enable Content. In the **Navigation Pane**, click your **3B Salary $40,000 or More Report** object to select it.

2 On the ribbon, click the **EXTERNAL DATA tab**, and in the **Export group**, click **More**, and then click **Word**.

The report will be exported as a *Rich Text Format (RTF)*—a standard file format that contains text and some formatting such as underline, bold, italic, font sizes, and colors. RTF documents can be opened in many word processing programs and text editors.

3 In the **Export – RTF File** dialog box, navigate to your **Access Chapter 3** folder. In the **File Save** dialog box, click in the **File name** box to select the existing text. Type **Lastname_Firstname_AC_3B_Web** and then click **Save**. In the **Export – RTF File** dialog box, select the **Open the destination file after the export operation is complete** check box, and then click **OK**. Compare your screen with Figure A.

The RTF file is created and opens in Word.

4 Close [X] Word. In the **Export – RTF File** dialog box, click **Close**, and then **Close** [X] Access.

FIGURE A

Your 3B Salary $40,000 or More Report exported as RTF and opened in Word

(GO! with Office Online (formerly Web Apps) continues on the next page)

5 From the desktop, start Internet Explorer, navigate to **http://onedrive.com**, and then sign in to your Microsoft account. Open your **GO! Web Projects** folder—or create and then open this folder if necessary.

6 On the menu bar, click **Upload**. In the **Choose File to Upload** dialog box, navigate to your **Access Chapter 3** folder, and then double-click your **AC_3B_Web** file to upload it to OneDrive.

7 After the file is uploaded, in your **GO! Web Projects** folder, right-click your **AC_3B_Web** file, and then click **Properties**.

A Properties panel displays on the right side of your screen.

8 In the **Properties** panel, click **Add a description**. In the box, type **This report displays job openings in our area that have a salary of $40,000 or more for which our students can apply.** Press Enter, and then compare your screen with Figure B.

9 On your keyboard, press the [⊞] key, type **snip**, and then click **Snipping Tool**. In the **Snipping Tool** dialog box, click the **New arrow**, and then click **Full-screen Snip**.

10 On the **Snipping Tool** toolbar, click **Save Snip** [🖫]. In the **Save As** dialog box, navigate to your **Access Chapter 3** folder. Click in the **File name** box to select the existing text. Type **Lastname_Firstname_AC_3B_Web_Snip** and then, if necessary, click the **Save as type arrow**, and click **JPEG file**. In the **Save As** dialog box, click **Save**, and then **Close** [⊠] the **Snipping Tool** window.

11 In OneDrive, on the title bar, click **OneDrive** to return to your home page. At the top right corner of your screen, click your OneDrive name, and then click **Sign out**. **Close** your browser window.

12 If directed to submit a paper printout of your RTF document and snip file, follow the directions given in the Note below. As directed by your instructor, submit your RTF document, which is two pages, and your snip file that are the results of this project.

NOTE — Printing your RTF Document and Your Snip .JPEG File

Using Windows Explorer, navigate to your Access Chapter 3 folder. Locate and double-click your AC_3B_Web file—it will open in Word. On the ribbon, click the FILE tab, and then click Print. To print on paper, on the right, click Print. To create an electronic file of your printout, on the left side of your screen, click Export. Under Export, be sure Create PDF/XPS Document is selected, and then click Create PDF/XPS. Navigate to your Access Chapter 3 folder, and then click Publish to save the file with the default name and an extension of pdf.

In your Access Chapter 3 folder, locate and double-click your AC_3B_Web_Snip file. If this is the first time you have tried to open a .jpeg file, you will be asked to identify a program. If you are not sure which program to use, select Windows Photo Viewer. From the ribbon, menu bar, or toolbar, click the Print command, and then Close the program window.

FIGURE B

The advantage of using Office 365 is that your organization does not have to purchase and install server hardware and software for sophisticated business applications and does not need a full-time IT person or staff just to manage the technology your teams need.

By using Office 365, you are able to have business-class services for your employees without investing in expensive hardware, software, and personnel. However, at least one person in an organization must be designated as the *Office 365 Administrator*—the person who creates and manages the account, adds new users, sets up the services your organization wants to use, sets permission levels, and manages the SharePoint team sites. You can have more than one administrator if you want to share these tasks with others.

Microsoft provides easy-to-use instructions and videos to get you started, and you might also have contact with a Microsoft representative. You will probably find, however, that subscribing to and setting up the account, adding users, and activating services is a straightforward process that requires little or no assistance.

After purchasing the required number of licenses, you will add each team member as a user that includes his or her email address. The Admin Overview page, as shown in Figure A, assists the Office 365 Administrator. On the left, there are links to manage the users and domains in your Office 365 account. This is where you can add new users, delete users, set permission levels, enter and change passwords, and update the user properties and the licenses.

On this page, you can see the various services available to you in Office 365. In the site shown in Figure A, Outlook, Lync, SharePoint (team sites), and a public-facing website are all part of the services.

Activity | Using a Team Site to Collaborate

This group project relates to the **Bell Orchid Hotels**. If your instructor assigns this project to your class, you will use a SharePoint team site in **Office 365** to collaborate on the following tasks for this chapter:

- If you are in the **Accounting Group**, you and your teammates will finalize the Stockholders database and post it on the SharePoint team site.

- If you are in the **Engineering Group**, you and your teammates will finalize the Subcontractors database and post it on the SharePoint team site.

- If you are in the **Food and Beverage Group**, you and your teammates will finalize Banquet Clients database and post it on the SharePoint team site.

- If you are in the **Human Resources Group**, you and your teammates will finalize the Employees database and post it on the SharePoint team site.

- If you are in the **Operations Group**, you and your teammates will finalize the Guests Database and post it on the SharePoint team site.

- If you are in the **Sales and Marketing Group**, you and your teammates will finalize the Associations database and post it on the SharePoint team site.

FIGURE A

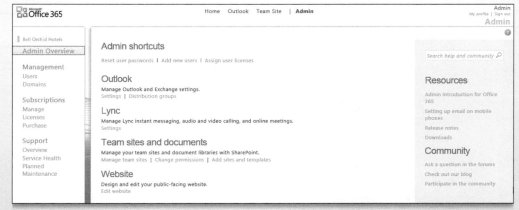

END OF CHAPTER

SUMMARY

A form is a database object that you can use to enter new records into a table, or to edit, delete, or display existing records in a table and can be used to control access to the data in a database.

Filter records in a form to display only a subset of the total records based on matching specific values to provide a quick answer to a question. Filters are generally not saved with a form.

A report is a database object that summarizes the fields and records from a query or from a table, in an easy-to-read format suitable for printing. You can group records and summarize the data in a report.

Most changes to forms and reports can be done in Layout view where the underlying data displays in the controls; however, some modifications, such as aligning controls, must be done in Design view.

GO! LEARN IT ONLINE

Review the concepts and key terms in this chapter by completing these online challenges, which you can find at **www.pearsonhighered.com/go**.

Matching and Multiple Choice: Answer matching and multiple choice questions to test what you learned in this chapter. MyITLab®

Crossword Puzzle: Spell out the words that match the numbered clues, and put them in the puzzle squares.

Flipboard: Flip through the definitions of the key terms in this chapter and match them with the correct term.

GO! FOR JOB SUCCESS

Video: Performance Evaluations

Your instructor may assign this video to your class, and then ask you to think about, or discuss with your classmates, these questions:

FotolEdhar / Fotolia

What kind of message is Sara sending by forgetting to do the self-assessment review she was assigned for her evaluation? Why is it important to do a self-assessment for a review?

How should Sara react to her supervisor's criticisms in her review?

How important is it to follow a company's dress code policy? Do you think Sara's response to not following the dress code is appropriate? Why or why not?

END OF CHAPTER

REVIEW AND ASSESSMENT GUIDE FOR ACCESS CHAPTER 3

Your instructor may assign one or more of these projects to help you review the chapter and assess your mastery and understanding of the chapter.

Project	Apply Skills from These Chapter Objectives	Project Type	Project Location
		Review and Assessment Guide for Access Chapter 3	
3C	Objectives 1-4 from Project 3A	**3C Skills Review** A guided review of the skills from Project 3A.	On the following pages
3D	Objectives 5-8 from Project 3B	**3D Skills Review** A guided review of the skills from Project 3B.	On the following pages
3E	Objectives 1-4 from Project 3A	**3E Mastery (Grader Project)** A demonstration of your mastery of the skills in Project 3A with extensive decision making.	In MyITLab and on the following pages
3F	Objectives 5-8 from Project 3B	**3F Mastery (Grader Project)** A demonstration of your mastery of the skills in Project 3B with extensive decision making.	In MyITLab and on the following pages
3G	Objectives 1-8 from Projects 3A and 3B	**3G Mastery (Grader Project)** A demonstration of your mastery of the skills in Projects 3A and 3B with extensive decision making.	In MyITLab and on the following pages
3H	Combination of Objectives from Projects 3A and 3B	**3H GO! Fix It** A demonstration of your mastery of the skills in Projects 3A and 3B by creating a correct result from a document that contains errors you must find.	Online
3I	Combination of Objectives from Projects 3A and 3B	**3I GO! Make It** A demonstration of your mastery of the skills in Projects 3A and 3B by creating a result from a supplied picture.	Online
3J	Combination of Objectives from Projects 3A and 3B	**3J GO! Solve It** A demonstration of your mastery of the skills in Projects 3A and 3B, your decision-making skills, and your critical thinking skills. A task-specific rubric helps you self-assess your result.	Online
3K	Combination of Objectives from Projects 3A and 3B	**3K GO! Solve It** A demonstration of your mastery of the skills in Projects 3A and 3B, your decision-making skills, and your critical thinking skills. A task-specific rubric helps you self-assess your result.	On the following pages
3L	Combination of Objectives from Projects 3A and 3B	**3L GO! Think** A demonstration of your understanding of the chapter concepts applied in a manner that you would outside of college. An analytic rubric helps you and your instructor grade the quality of your work by comparing it to the work an expert in the discipline would create.	On the following pages
3M	Combination of Objectives from Projects 3A and 3B	**3M GO! Think** A demonstration of your understanding of the chapter concepts applied in a manner that you would outside of college. An analytic rubric helps you and your instructor grade the quality of your work by comparing it to the work an expert in the discipline would create.	Online
3N	Combination of Objectives from Projects 3A and 3B	**3N You and GO!** A demonstration of your understanding of the chapter concepts applied in a manner that you would in a personal situation. An analytic rubric helps you and your instructor grade the quality of your work.	Online
3O	Combination of Objectives from Projects 3A and 3B	**3O Cumulative Group Project for Access Chapter 3** A demonstration of your understanding of concepts and your ability to work collaboratively in a group role-playing assessment, requiring both collaboration and self-management.	Online
Capstone Project for Access Chapters 1-3	Combination of Objectives from Projects 1A, 1B, 2A, 2B, 3A, and 3B	A demonstration of your mastery of the skills in Chapters 1-3 with extensive decision making. **(Grader Project)**	In MyITLab and online

GLOSSARY

GLOSSARY OF CHAPTER KEY TERMS

AND condition A condition in which records display only when all of the values are present in the selected fields.

Bound A term used to describe objects and controls that are based on data that is stored in tables.

Bound control A control that retrieves its data from an underlying table or query; a text box control is an example of a bound control.

Calculated control A control that contains an expression, often a formula or function, that most often summarizes a field that contains numerical data.

Control An object on a form or report that displays data or text, performs actions, and lets you view and work with information.

Control layout The grouped arrangement of controls on a form or report; for example, the Stacked layout.

Data entry The action of entering the data into a record in a database table or form.

Date control A control on a form or report that inserts the current date each time the form or report is opened.

Design view The Access view that displays the detailed structure of a query, form, or report; for forms and reports, may be the view in which some tasks must be performed, and only the controls, and not the data, display.

Detail section The section of a form or report that displays the records from the underlying table or query.

Filter by Form An Access command that filters the records in a form based on one or more fields, or based on more than one value in the field.

Filter by Selection An Access command that displays only the records that contain the value in the selected field and hides the records that do not contain the value.

Filtering The process of displaying only a portion of the total records (a subset) based on matching specific values to provide a quick answer to a question.

Form A database object that you can use to enter new records into a table, or to edit, delete, and display existing records in a table.

Form Footer Information at the bottom of the screen in Form view or Layout view that is printed after the last detail section on the last page of a printout.

Form Header Information such as a form's title that displays at the top of the screen in Form view or Layout view and is printed at the top of the first page when records are printed as forms.

Form tool An Access tool that creates a form with a single mouse click, which includes all of the fields from the underlying data source (table or query).

Form view The Access view in which you can view, modify, delete, or add records in a table; but you cannot change the layout or design of the form.

Form Wizard An Access tool that walks you step by step through the creation of a form and that gives you more flexibility in the design, layout, and number of fields in a form.

Group Footer Information printed at the end of each group of records; used to display summary information for the group.

Group Header Information printed at the beginning of each new group of records; for example, the group name.

Group, Sort, and Total pane A pane that displays at the bottom of the screen in which you can control how information is sorted and grouped in a report; provides the most flexibility for adding or modifying groups, sort orders, or totals options on a report.

Label control A control on a form or report that contains descriptive information, usually a field name or title.

Layout selector A small symbol that displays in the upper left corner of a selected control layout in a form or report that is displayed in Layout view or Design view; used to move or format an entire group of controls.

Layout view The Access view in which you can make changes to a form or report while the object is running—the data from the underlying data source displays.

Office 365 Administrator In Office 365, the person who creates and manages the account, adds new users, sets up the services your organization wants to use, sets permission levels, and manages the SharePoint team sites.

OR condition A condition in which records display that match at least one of the specified values.

Page Footer Information printed at the bottom of every page in a report; most often includes the page number.

Page Header Information printed at the top of every page in a report.

Page number control A control on a form or report that inserts the page numbers when displayed in Print Preview or when printed.

Record selector bar The vertical bar at the left edge of a record when it is displayed in a form that is used to select an entire record.

Record source The tables or queries that provide the underlying data for a form or report.

Report A database object that summarizes the fields and records from a query or table in an easy-to-read format suitable for printing.

Report Footer Information printed at the bottom of the last page of a report.

Report Header Information printed on the first page of a report; used for logos, titles, and dates.

Report tool An Access tool that creates a report with one mouse click and displays all of the fields and records from the record source that you select.

Report Wizard An Access tool that walks you step by step through the creation of a report and that gives you more flexibility in the design, layout, and number of fields in a report.

Rich Text Format (RTF) A standard file format that contains text and some formatting such as underline, bold, italic, font sizes, and colors; RTF documents can be opened in many word processing programs and text editors.

Section bar In Design view, a gray bar in a form or report that identifies and separates one section from another; used to select the section and to change the size of the section.

Stacked layout A control layout format that is similar to a paper form, with label controls placed to the left of each text box control; the controls are grouped together for easy editing.

Subset A portion of the total records available.

Tab order The order in which the insertion point moves from one field to another in a form when you press the Tab key.

Text box control A bound control on a form or report that displays the data from the underlying table or query.

Theme A predesigned set of colors, fonts, lines, and fill effects that look good together and that can be applied to all of the objects in the database or to individual objects in the database.

Unbound control A control that does not have a source of data, such as the title in a form or report.

CHAPTER REVIEW

Apply 3A skills from these Objectives:

1 Create and Use a Form to Add and Delete Records
2 Filter Records
3 Create a Form by Using the Form Wizard
4 Modify a Form in Layout View and in Design View

In the following Skills Review, you will assist Erinique Jerlin, the dean of Business at the Northwest Campus, in using her database to track business students and their internship placements for the current semester. Your completed forms will look similar to Figure 3.49.

PROJECT FILES

For Project 3C, you will need the following file:

a03C_Student_Internships

You will save your database as:

Lastname_Firstname_3C_Student_Internships

PROJECT RESULTS

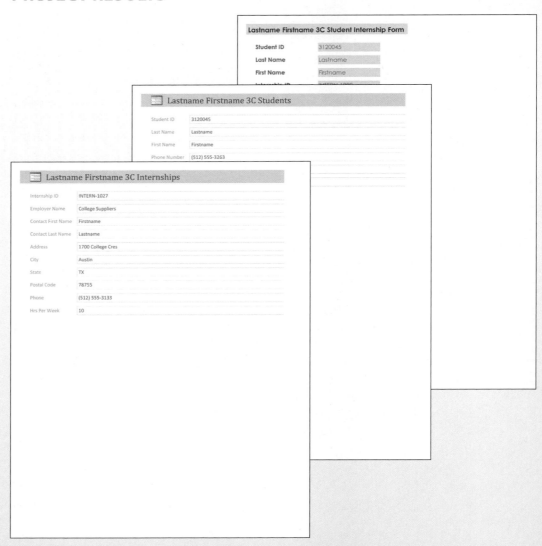

FIGURE 3.49

(Project 3C Student Internships continues on the next page)

CHAPTER REVIEW

1 Start Access. In the Access opening screen, click **Open Other Files**. Under **Open**, click **Computer**. Under **Recent Folders**, if displayed, click the location where your student data files are stored; otherwise, click **Browse** and then navigate to the location where your student data files are stored. Double-click **a03C_Student_Internships** to open the database.

a. On the ribbon, click the **FILE tab**, and then click **Save As**. Under **File Types**, be sure **Save Database As** is selected. On the right, under **Database File Types**, be sure **Access Database** is selected, and then click **Save As**.

b. In the **Save As** dialog box, navigate to your **Access Chapter 3** folder. In the **File name** box, replace the existing text with **Lastname_Firstname_3C_Student_Internships** and then press Enter. On the **Message Bar**, click **Enable Content**.

c. In the **Navigation Pane**, right-click **3C Students**, and then click **Rename**. With the table name selected and using your own name, type **Lastname Firstname 3C Students** and then press Enter. **Rename** the 3C Internships table to **Lastname Firstname 3C Internships** and then point to the right edge of the **Navigation Pane** to display the ⟷ pointer. Drag to the right to increase the width of the pane until both tables names display fully.

d. On the ribbon, click the **DATABASE TOOLS tab**, and then in the **Relationships group**, click **Relationships**. Under **RELATIONSHIP TOOLS**, on the **DESIGN tab**, in the **Relationships group**, click **All Relationships**. Resize and move the field lists so that the entire table name and fields display for each field list. In the **Relationships** window, click the **join line** between the two field lists. In the **Tools group**, click **Edit Relationships**. Point to the title bar of the **Edit Relationships** dialog box, and drag the dialog box downward below the two field lists. Notice that a *one-to-many* relationship is established between

the two tables by using *Internship ID* as the common field. **Close** the **Edit Relationships** dialog box, and then **Close** the **Relationships** window. In the message box, click **Yes** to save changes to the layout of the relationships.

e. In the **Navigation Pane**, click your **3C Students** table to select it. On the ribbon, click the **CREATE tab**, and then in the **Forms group**, click **Form**. **Save** the form as **Lastname Firstname 3C Student Form** and then **Close** the form object.

f. In the **Navigation Pane**, click your **3C Internships** table to select it. On the ribbon, click the **CREATE tab**, and then in the **Forms group**, click **Form**. Notice that for the first record—*Internship ID INTERN-1000* for *Lakes Realty Inc*—there are two student records in the subdatasheet—two students have been assigned internships for this employer. **Close** the form, and in the message box, click **Yes** to save the form. In the **Save As** dialog box, type **Lastname Firstname 3C Internship Company Form** and then press Enter. If necessary, increase the width of the Navigation Pane so that all object names display fully.

g. In the **Navigation Pane**, double-click your **3C Student Form** object to open it, and then **Close** the **Navigation Pane**. In the navigation area, click **New (blank) record** to display a new blank form. In the **Student ID** field, type **3120045** and then press Tab. Using your own last name and first name, continue entering the data as shown in **Table 1**.

h. With the insertion point positioned in the last field, press Tab to save the record and display a new blank record. **Close** your **3C Student Form** object, and then **Open** the **Navigation Pane**. Double-click your **3C Internship Company Form** object to open it, and then **Close** the **Navigation Pane**. Notice that for the first record, in the subdatasheet, the record you just entered displays. Scroll to view the bottom of

TABLE 1

Student ID	Last Name	First Name	Phone Number	Email	Internship ID
3120045	**Lastname**	**Firstname**	**(512) 555-3263**	**ns3120@tlcc.edu**	**INTERN-1000**

⤏ Return to Step 1-h

(Project 3C Student Internships continues on the next page)

CHAPTER REVIEW

the form. In the navigation area for the form—*not* the navigation area for the subdatasheet—click **New (blank) record**. In the blank form, using your own first name and last name, enter the data as shown in **Table 2**.

i. In the navigation area for the form, click **First record**. Click in the **Employer Name** field, and then on the **HOME tab**, in the **Find group**, click **Find**. In the **Find and Replace** dialog box, in the **Find What** box, type **Jones Consulting** and then click **Find Next**. **Close** the **Find and Replace** dialog box. On the **HOME tab**, in the **Records group**, click the **Delete arrow**, and then click **Delete Record**. In the message box, click **Yes** to delete the record. In the navigation area for the form, notice that the total number of records is *27*.

j. Use the technique you just practiced to **Find** the form for the **Internship ID** of INTERN-1027, and then **Close** the **Find and Replace** dialog box. On the ribbon, click the **FILE tab**, click **Print**, and then on the right, click **Print**. In the **Print** dialog box, under **Print Range**, click the **Selected Record(s)** option button. In the lower left corner of the dialog box, click **Setup**. In the **Page Setup** dialog box, click the **Columns tab**. Under **Column Size**, double-click in the **Width** box to select the existing value, type **7.5** and then click **OK**. If directed to print the form, in the **Print** dialog box, click **OK**. If directed to submit an electronic printout of the form, click **Cancel**, and then follow the directions given in the Note in Activity 3.06.

k. **Close** your **3C Internship Company Form** object, and then **Open** the **Navigation Pane**. In the **Navigation Pane**, double-click your **3C Student Form** object to open it, and then **Close** the **Navigation Pane**. Use the **Find** command to display the record where the **Last Name** field contains your last name, and then create a paper or electronic printout of only

that record, being sure to change the **Column Size Width** to **7.5**

2 With your **3C Student Form** object displayed in **Form** view, in the navigation area, click **First record**, and then click the **Internship ID** field name to select the text in the field box. Press Ctrl + F to display the **Find and Replace** dialog box. In the **Find What** box, type **INTERN-1009** and then click **Find Next** to find and display the record for *Michael Fresch*. **Close** the **Find and Replace** dialog box. On the **HOME tab**, in the **Sort & Filter group**, click **Selection**, and then click **Equals "INTERN-1009"**. In the navigation area, notice that two students are assigned internships with the company identified as INTERN-1009.

a. In the **Sort & Filter group**, click **Toggle Filter** to remove the filter and display all 52 records. **Close** the form. If prompted, click **Yes** to save the form.

b. **Open** the **Navigation Pane**, double-click your **3C Internship Company Form** object to open it, and then **Close** the **Navigation Pane**. On the **HOME tab**, in the **Sort & Filter group**, click **Advanced**, and then click **Filter By Form**. In the form, click the **City** field name to position the insertion point in the **City** field box, click the **arrow**, and then click **Georgetown**. In the **Sort & Filter group**, click **Toggle Filter** to display the filtered records. In the navigation area for the form, notice that three internships are located in the *City* of *Georgetown*.

c. In the **Sort & Filter group**, click **Advanced**, and then click **Filter By Form**. In the lower left corner of the form, click the **Or tab**. Click the **City** field box **arrow**, and then click **Elgin**. In the **Sort & Filter group**, click **Toggle Filter**. In the navigation area for the form, notice that five internships are located in either *Georgetown* or *Elgin*. In the **Sort & Filter group**, click **Advanced**, and then click **Clear All Filters** to display all 27 records.

TABLE 2

Internship ID	Employer Name	Contact First Name	Contact Last Name	Address	City	State	Postal Code	Phone	Hrs Per Week
INTERN-1027	**College Suppliers**	**Firstname**	**Lastname**	**1700 College Cres**	**Austin**	**TX**	**78755**	**(512) 555-3133**	**10**

Return to Step 1-i

(Project 3C Student Internships continues on the next page)

d. In the **Sort & Filter group**, click **Advanced**, and then click **Advanced Filter/Sort**. Resize the field list. In the **3C Internships** field list, double-click **City**, and then double-click **Hrs Per Week** to add both fields to the design grid. Click in the **Criteria** row under **City**, type **Austin** and then press Enter. In the **Criteria** row under **Hrs Per Week**, type **>10** and then press Enter. In the **Sort & Filter group**, click **Toggle Filter** to display the filtered records, and notice that that there are five internships in the *City* of *Austin* offering *more than 10* hours per week of work. In the **Sort & Filter group**, click **Toggle Filter** to remove the filter and display all 27 records. **Save** and then **Close** your **3C Internship Company Form** object, which also closes the Advanced Filter grid.

3 ▶ On the ribbon, click the **CREATE tab**, and then in the **Forms group**, click **Form Wizard**. In the **Tables/Queries** box, click the **arrow**, and then click **Table: Lastname Firstname 3C Students**. In the **Available Fields** list, double-click the following field names in the order given to move them to the **Selected Fields** list: **First Name**, **Last Name**, and **Internship ID**. Click **Next**. In the wizard, be sure **Columnar** is selected as the layout, and then click **Next**. In the **What title do you want for your form?** box, select the existing text, type **Lastname Firstname 3C Student Internship Form** and then click **Finish** to close the wizard and create the form.

4 ▶ On the **HOME tab**, in the **Views group**, click the top portion of the **View** button to switch to **Layout** view. If the **Field List** pane displays on the right side of your screen, close the pane. Click the **First Name label control**. Hold down Shift, and then click the **Last Name label control**, the **Internship ID label control**, and the three **text box controls** to select all of the controls. On the ribbon, under **FORM LAYOUT TOOLS**, click the **ARRANGE tab**. In the **Table group**, click **Stacked** to group all of the controls. Click the **First Name label control** to cancel the selection of all of the controls.

a. On the ribbon, under **FORM LAYOUT TOOLS**, click the **DESIGN tab**. In the **Themes group** click **Themes**. In the **Themes** gallery, using the ScreenTips, point to the **Wisp** theme, right-click, and then click **Apply Theme to This Object Only**. Click anywhere in the title—*Lastname Firstname 3C Student Internship*

Form—to select the title. On the ribbon, under **FORM LAYOUT TOOLS**, click the **FORMAT tab**. In the **Font group**, click the **Font Size arrow**, and then click **14**. In the **Font group**, click **Bold**. Click the **Font Color arrow**, and then under **Theme Colors**, in the sixth column, click the last color—**Orange, Accent 2, Darker 50%**.

b. On the ribbon, click the **DESIGN tab**. In the **Tools group**, click **Add Existing Fields**. In the **Field List** pane, click **Student ID**, and then drag the field name to the left until the 🖳 pointer displays above the **First Name label control** and a colored line displays above the control. Release the mouse button to add the *Student ID* controls to the form, and then **Close** the **Field List** pane.

c. Click the **First Name text box control**, which displays *Jordan*, to select it. On the **DESIGN tab**, in the **Tools group**, click **Property Sheet**. In the **Property Sheet**, on the **Format tab**, click **Width**, type **1.75** and then press Enter to decrease the width of the text box controls. **Close** the **Property Sheet**. Be sure that the **First Name text box control** is still selected. On the ribbon, click the **ARRANGE tab**, and in the **Rows & Columns group**, click **Select Row**. In the **Move group**, click **Move Down** to move both controls below the **Last Name** controls. **Save** the changes you have made to the design of your form.

d. Click the **Student ID text box control**, which displays *1010101*. On the **ARRANGE tab**, in the **Rows & Columns group**, click **Select Column** to select all four text box controls. On the ribbon, click the **FORMAT tab**, and in the **Font group**, click the **Background Color arrow**. Under **Theme Colors**, in the fourth column, click the second color—**Brown, Text 2, Lighter 80%**.

e. Click the **Student ID label control**, and then on the ribbon, click the **ARRANGE tab**. In the **Rows & Columns group**, click **Select Column** to select all four label controls. On the ribbon, click the **FORMAT tab**, and then click the **Font Color arrow**—*not* the **Background Color arrow**. Under **Theme Colors**, in the fourth column, click the first color—**Brown, Text 2**. In the **Font group**, click **Bold**.

(Project 3C Student Internships continues on the next page)

f. Click the **layout selector** ⊞ to select all of the controls. In the **Font group**, click the **Font Size arrow**, and then click **12**. With all of the controls still selected, on the ribbon, click the **DESIGN tab**, and in the **Tools group**, click **Property Sheet**. In the **Property Sheet**, on the **Format tab**, click **Height**, type **0.25** and then press [Enter] to change the height of each selected control.

g. Click the **Student ID label control** to select only that control. In the **Property Sheet**, click **Width**, type **1.75** and then press [Enter] to change the width of all of the label controls. **Save** the design changes to your form.

h. On the status bar, click **Design View**. At the bottom of the form, click the **Form Footer section bar** to select it. In the **Property Sheet**, click **Height**, type **0.5** and then press [Enter] to increase the height of the **Form Footer** section.

i. On the ribbon, under **FORM DESIGN TOOLS**, click the **DESIGN tab**. In the **Controls group**, click **Label**. Move the pointer into the **Form Footer** section and then position the plus sign of the pointer at approximately **0.25 inch on the horizontal ruler** and even with the lower edge of the **Form Footer section bar**—the placement does not need to be precise. Click one time, type **Texas Lakes Community College** and then press [Enter].

j. With the **label control** selected, on the ribbon, click the **FORMAT tab**. In the **Font group**, click **Bold**. Click the **Font Color arrow**, and then under **Theme Colors**, in the fourth column, click the first

color—**Brown, Text 2**. If necessary, double-click the right edge of the label control to resize the control so that all of the data displays.

k. With the **label control** still selected, in the **Property Sheet**, click **Top**, type **0.1** and then press [Enter]. In the **Property Sheet**, in the **Left** property setting box, type **0.9** and then press [Enter]. **Close** the **Property Sheet**, and then **Save** the design changes to your form.

l. On the right side of the status bar, click **Form View**. In the navigation area, click **Last record** to display the record containing your name. On the ribbon, click the **FILE tab**, and then click **Print**. In the **Print** dialog box, under **Print Range**, click the **Selected Records(s)** option button. Because you changed the field widths, you do not need to change the Column Size Width in the **Print** dialog box. Create a paper or electronic printout as directed by your instructor. To create an electronic printout, follow the directions given in the Note in Activity 3.06.

m. **Close** all open objects, and then **Open** the **Navigation Pane**. If necessary, increase the width of the pane so that all object names display fully. On the right side of the title bar, click **Close** to close the database and to exit Access. As directed by your instructor, submit your database and the paper or electronic printouts of the three forms that are the results of this project. Specifically, in this project, using your own name, you created the following database and printouts or electronic printouts:

1. Lastname_Firstname_3C_Student_Internships	Database file
2. Lastname Firstname 3C Student Form	Form (printout or electronic printout - Record 52)
3. Lastname Firstname 3C Internship Company Form	Form (printout or electronic printout - Record 27)
4. Lastname Firstname 3C Student Internship Form	Form (printout or electronic printout - Record 52)

END | You have completed Project 3C

CHAPTER REVIEW

Skills Review   Project 3D Student Parking

In the following Skills Review, you will assist Carlos Medina, the chief of security, in using his Access database to track the details about students who have paid for parking in designated lots at the Southeast Campus of Texas Lakes Community College. Your completed reports will look similar to Figure 3.50.

PROJECT FILES

For Project 3D, you will need the following file:

a03D_Student_Parking

You will save your database as:

Lastname_Firstname_3D_Student_Parking

PROJECT RESULTS

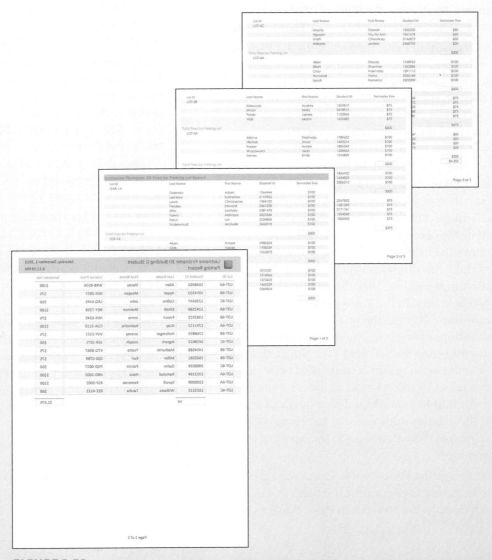

FIGURE 3.50

(Project 3D Student Parking continues on the next page)

CHAPTER REVIEW

1 Start Access. In the Access opening screen, click **Open Other Files**. Under **Open**, click **Computer**. Under **Recent Folders**, if displayed, click the location where your student data files are stored; otherwise, click **Browse** and then navigate to the location where your student data files are stored. Double-click **a03D_Student_Parking** to open the database.

a. On the ribbon, click the **FILE tab**, and then click **Save As**. Under **File Types**, be sure **Save Database As** is selected. On the right, under **Database File Types**, be sure **Access Database** is selected, and then at the bottom of the screen, click **Save As**. In the **Save As** dialog box, navigate to your **Access Chapter 3** folder. In the **File name** box, replace the existing text with **Lastname_Firstname_3D_Student_Parking** and then press Enter. On the **Message Bar**, click **Enable Content**.

b. In the **Navigation Pane**, right-click the **3D Parking Lots** table, and then click **Rename**. Using your own name, type **Lastname Firstname 3D Parking Lots** and then press Enter. Use this same technique to add your last name and first name to the beginning of the names of the two queries and the **3D Students** table. Increase the width of the **Navigation Pane** so that all object names display fully.

c. On the ribbon, click the **DATABASE TOOLS tab**, and then in the **Relationships group**, click **Relationships**. On the **DESIGN tab**, in the **Relationships group**, click **All Relationships**. Resize and move the field lists so that the entire table name and fields display for each field list. In the **Relationships** window, click the **join line** between the two field lists. In the **Tools group**, click **Edit Relationships**. Point to the title bar of the **Edit Relationships** dialog box, and drag the dialog box downward below the two field lists. Notice that a *one-to-many* relationship is established between the two tables by using *Lot ID* as the common field. **Close** the **Edit Relationships** dialog box, and then **Close** the **Relationships** window. In the message box, click **Yes** to save changes to the layout of the relationships.

d. In the **Navigation Pane**, double-click each table to open them, and then examine the fields and data in each table. In the **Navigation Pane**, double-click

your **3D Building G Student Parking Query** object to run the query and view the results. Apply **Best Fit** to the query results, and then **Save** the query. Switch to **Design** view to examine the design grid. This query answers the question, *What is the lot ID, lot location, student ID, student last name, student first name, license plate, and semester fee for students who have paid for parking in front of Building G, in ascending order by the Last Name field?* In the **Navigation Pane**, double-click your **3D Student Parking by Lots Query** object, apply **Best Fit** to the query results, **Save** the query, and then switch to **Design** view to examine the design grid. This query answers the question, *What is the lot ID, student ID, student last name, student first name, license plate, state, and semester fee for all students?* In the object window, right-click any **object tab**, and then click **Close All**.

e. In the **Navigation Pane**, click to select your **3D Building G Student Parking Query** object. On the ribbon, click the **CREATE tab**, and in the **Reports group**, click **Report**. **Close** the **Navigation Pane**. Under **REPORT LAYOUT TOOLS**, on the **DESIGN tab**, in the **Themes group**, click **Themes**. In the **Themes** gallery, use the ScreenTips to locate the **Retrospect** theme, right-click the **Retrospect** theme, and then click **Apply Theme to This Object Only**.

f. Click the **Lot Location** field name. On the ribbon, under **REPORT LAYOUT TOOLS**, click the **ARRANGE tab**. In the **Rows & Columns group**, click **Select Column** to select the field name and all of the data for each record in the field. Press Del to remove the field from the report.

g. Click the **Last Name** field name, hold down Shift, and then click the **First Name** field name. On the ribbon, click the **DESIGN tab**, and in the **Tools group**, click **Property Sheet**. In the **Property Sheet**, on the **Format tab**, click **Width**, type **1.25** and then press Enter to decrease the width of the two fields. **Close** the **Property Sheet**.

h. Click the **Last Name** field name to cancel the selection of both fields and to select only this field. On the ribbon, click the **HOME tab**, and in the **Sort & Filter group**, click **Ascending** to sort the records in ascending order by the Last Name field.

(Project 3D Student Parking continues on the next page)

i. If necessary, scroll to the bottom of the report, and notice that the *Semester Fee* column is automatically totaled. At the top of the report, click the **Student ID** field name. On the ribbon, click the **DESIGN tab**. In the **Grouping & Totals group**, click **Totals**, and then click **Count Records**. If necessary, scroll to the bottom of the report, and notice that *14* students have paid for parking in front of Building G.

j. At the bottom of the report, under **Student ID**, click the **calculated control** that displays *14*. Hold down Ctrl, and then under **Semester Fee**, click the **calculated control** that displays *$1,075*—the two calculated controls are selected. On the **DESIGN tab**, in the **Tools group**, click **Property Sheet**. In the **Property Sheet**, click **Height**, type **0.25** and then press Enter to increase the height of both controls. At the bottom of the report, to the right of the **calculated control** that displays *$1,075*, click the **control** that displays *Page 1 of 1*. In the **Property Sheet**, click **Left**, type **2.5** and then press Enter to move the page number within the margins of the report.

k. At the top of the report, click the **label control** that displays the title of the report—*Lastname Firstname 3D Building G Student Parking Query*. On the ribbon, under **REPORT LAYOUT TOOLS**, click the **FORMAT tab**. In the **Font group**, click the **Font Size arrow**, and then click **14**. With the **label control** still selected, double-click **Query** to select the word, type **Report** and then press Enter to change the title of the report to *Lastname Firstname 3D Building G Student Parking Report*.

l. Click the **Lot ID** field name. In the **Property Sheet**, click **Left**, type **0.25** and then press Enter to move all of the fields slightly to the right from the left margin. **Close** the **Property Sheet**, and then **Save** the report as **Lastname Firstname 3D Building G Student Parking Report**

m. On the right side of the status bar, click **Print Preview**. On the **PRINT PREVIEW tab**, in the **Zoom group**, click **Two Pages**, and notice that the report will print on one page. Create a paper or electronic printout as directed, click **Close Print Preview**, and then **Close** the report.

2 On the ribbon, click the **CREATE tab**, and then in the **Reports group**, click **Report Wizard**. In the **Tables/Queries** box, click the **arrow**, and then click

Query: Lastname Firstname 3D Student Parking by Lots Query. In the **Available Fields** list, double-click the following field names in the order given to move them to the **Selected Fields** list: **Lot ID**, **Last Name**, **First Name**, **Student ID**, and **Semester Fee**.

a. Click **Next**. In the **How do you want to view your data?** box, click **by Lastname Firstname 3D Students**, and then click **Next**. In the list on the left, double-click **Lot ID** to group the records by this field, and then click **Next**. Click the **1** box **arrow**, and then click **Last Name** to sort the records by the student's last name within each Lot ID.

b. In the wizard, click **Summary Options**. In the **Summary Options** dialog box, to the right of **Semester Fee**, click to select the **Sum** check box. Under **Show**, be sure that **Detail and Summary** is selected, and then click **OK**. In the wizard, click **Next**.

c. In the wizard, under **Layout**, be sure that **Stepped** is selected. Under **Orientation**, click **Landscape**. At the bottom of the wizard, be sure that the **Adjust the field width so all fields fit on a page** check box is selected, and then click **Next**. In the **What title do you want for your report?** box, select the existing text, type **Lastname Firstname 3D Fees by Parking Lot Report** and then click **Finish**. In the object window, right-click the **object tab** for the report, and then click **Layout View**.

3 Under **REPORT LAYOUT TOOLS**, on the **DESIGN tab**, in the **Themes group**, click **Themes**. In the **Themes** gallery, use the ScreenTips to locate the **Ion Boardroom** theme, right-click the **Ion Boardroom** theme, and then click **Apply Theme to This Object Only**. In the report, click the title—*Lastname Firstname 3D Fees by Parking Lot*—to display a border around the label control. On the ribbon, under **REPORT LAYOUT TOOLS**, click the **FORMAT tab**. In the **Font group**, click the **Font Size arrow**, and then click **14**. In the **Font group**, click **Bold**. In the body of the report, click any one of the controls that begins with **Summary for 'Lot ID'**, and then press Del. **Save** the design changes to your report.

a. On the left side of the report, click a **Sum label control**, which will select all of the related controls. Double-click the control to select the text—*Sum*. Type **Total Fees by Parking Lot** and then press Enter.

(Project 3D Student Parking continues on the next page)

b. At the top of the report, click the **Lot ID label control** to select it. Hold down Shift, and then click each one of the four other label controls that display the field names to select all five label controls. On the **FORMAT tab**, in the **Font group**, click **Bold**.

c. In the report, under **Last Name**, click the **text box control** that displays *Dolensky*. Hold down Shift, and then under **First Name**, click the **text box control** that displays *Adam*. On the ribbon, click the **DESIGN tab**. In the **Tools group**, click **Property Sheet**. In the **Property Sheet**, click **Width**, type **1.5** and then press Enter.

d. In the report, click the **Student ID label control**. In the **Property Sheet**, click **Left**, type **7.25** and then press Enter. Do not be concerned that the data in the field is not aligned with the field name; you will adjust this later in this project. Scroll to the bottom of the report, and then click the **Grand Total label control**. In the **Property Sheet**, click **Width**, type **1** and then press Enter. **Close** the **Property Sheet**, and then **Save** the design changes to your report.

e. On the status bar, click **Design View**. In the **Lot ID Footer** section, click the **Total Fees by Parking Lot label control**. Hold down Shift, and in the **Report Footer** section, click the **Grand Total label control** to select both controls. On the ribbon, under **REPORT DESIGN TOOLS**, click the **ARRANGE tab**. In the **Sizing & Ordering group**, click **Align**, and then click **Left**.

f. In the report, in the **Page Header** section, click the **Student ID label control**. Hold down Shift, and in the **Detail** section, click the **Student ID text box control**. On the **ARRANGE tab**, in the **Sizing & Ordering group**, click **Align**, and then click **Left**. On the status bar, click **Layout View** and notice the left alignment of the two sets of controls.

4 On the status bar, click **Print Preview**. On the **PRINT PREVIEW tab**, in the **Zoom group**, click **More Pages**, and then click **Four Pages** to view how your report is currently laid out. In the **Zoom group**, click the **Zoom arrow**, and then click **50%**. Notice at the bottom of Page 1 and the top of Page 2, that the grouping for **LOT-2B** breaks across these two pages. Notice at the bottom of Page 2 and the top of Page 3, that the grouping for **LOT-6A** breaks across these two pages. Your pages may display differently depending upon the printer that is installed on your system.

a. On the ribbon, click **Close Print Preview** to return to **Layout** view. On the **DESIGN tab**, in the **Grouping & Totals group**, click **Group & Sort**. In the **Group, Sort, and Total** pane, on the **Group on Lot ID** bar, click **More**. Click the **do not keep group together on one page arrow**, and then click **keep whole group together on one page**. On the **DESIGN tab**, in the **Grouping & Totals group**, click **Group & Sort** to close the **Group, Sort, and Total** pane. **Save** the design changes to your report.

b. On the status bar, click **Print Preview**. Notice that the entire grouping for **LOT-2B** displays at the top of Page 2. Keeping this group together forced the groupings for **LOT-5C** and **LOT-6A** to move to the top of Page 3—your groupings may display differently depending upon the printer that is installed on your system. Create a paper or electronic printout as directed—three pages result.

c. **Close** the report, and then **Open** the **Navigation Pane**. If necessary, increase the width of the pane so that all object names display fully. On the right side of the title bar, click **Close** to close the database and to exit Access. As directed by your instructor, submit your database and the paper or electronic printouts of the two reports—one report is three pages—that are the results of this project. Specifically, in this project, using your own name, you created the following database and printouts or electronic printouts:

1. Lastname_Firstname_3D_Student_Parking	Database file
2. Lastname Firstname 3D Building G Student Parking Report	Report (printout or electronic printout)
3. Lastname Firstname 3D Fees by Parking Lot Report	Report (printout or electronic printout - three pages)

END | You have completed Project 3D

CONTENT-BASED ASSESSMENTS

Mastering Access Project 3E Textbook Publishers

In the following Mastering Access project, you will assist Donna Rider, manager of the bookstore, in using her database to track textbooks and publishers for courses being offered by the Science Department at the Northeast Campus of Texas Lakes Community College. Your completed forms will look similar to Figure 3.51.

Apply 3A skills from these Objectives:

1 Create and Use a Form to Add and Delete Records
2 Filter Records
3 Create a Form by Using the Form Wizard
4 Modify a Form in Layout View and in Design View

PROJECT FILES

For Project 3E, you will need the following file:

a03E_Textbook_Publishers

You will save your database as:

Lastname_Firstname_3E_Textbook_Publishers

PROJECT RESULTS

FIGURE 3.51

(Project 3E Textbook Publishers continues on the next page)

CONTENT-BASED ASSESSMENTS

1 Start Access. From your student data files, open **a03E_Textbook_Publishers**. Save the database in your **Access Chapter 3** folder as **Lastname_Firstname_3E_ Textbook_Publishers** and then enable the content. In the **Navigation Pane, Rename** each table by adding **Lastname Firstname** to the beginning of the table name. Increase the width of the **Navigation Pane** so that all object names display fully. View the relationship between the *3E Publishers* table and the *3E Science Textbooks* table; *one* publisher can provide *many* textbooks for the science courses. Save the changes to the layout of the relationships.

2 Based on your **3E Publishers** table, use the **Form** tool to create a form. **Save** the form as **Lastname Firstname 3E Publisher Form** and then switch to **Form** view. Using the form, add a new record to the underlying table as shown in **Table 1**.

3 Display the first record, and click in the **Publisher ID** field. **Find** the record for the **Publisher ID** of **PUB-1006**, and then **Delete** the record. Display the record you entered for **PUB-1008**, and then, as directed, create a paper or electronic printout of only that record, changing the **Column Size Width** in the **Print** dialog box to **7.5 Save** the design changes to your form.

4 Use the **Filter By Form** tool in your **3E Publisher Form** object to create a filter that displays records with a **State** of **CA** or **TX**. After verifying that three records match this criteria, click **Toggle Filter** to display all seven records. **Save** your form, and then **Close** your form.

5 Use the **Form Wizard** to create a form based on your **3E Science Textbooks** table that includes the following fields in the order given: **Course(s)**, **Textbook Name**, **Publisher ID**, **Price Per Book**, and **# Books**. Apply a **Columnar** layout, and name the form **Lastname Firstname 3E Science Textbook Form.**

6 In **Layout** view, apply the **Stacked** layout to all of the controls, and then apply the **Ion Boardroom** theme to this form only. For the title of the form, change the **Font Size** to **16**, apply **Bold**, and then change the **Font Color** to **Dark Purple, Text 2**—under **Theme Colors**, in the fourth column, the first color. **Save** the design changes to the form.

7 From the **Field List** pane, add the **Textbook ID** field to the form directly above the **Textbook Name** field. Move the **# Books** controls directly above the **Price Per Book** controls. **Close** the **Field List** pane. Display Record 9—this record's textbook name is the longest entry of all records. Click the **Textbook Name text box control**, set the **Width** property to **4** and then **Save** the design changes to your form.

8 Select all six **text box controls**, and change the **Background Color** to **Orange, Accent 4, Lighter 80%**—under **Theme Colors**, in the eighth column, the second color. Select all six **label controls**, and change the **Font Color** to **Orange, Accent 4, Darker 50%**—under **Theme Colors**, in the eighth column, the last color. Apply **Bold** to the **label controls**. With the **label controls** still selected, set the **Width** property to **1.75** and then select all of the **label controls** and all of the **text box controls**. Change the **Font Size** to **12**, set the **Height** property to **0.25** and then **Save** the design changes to your form.

9 In **Design** view, set the **Form Footer** section **Height** property to **0.5** Add a **Label control** to the **Form Footer** section that displays **Texas Lakes Science Books** For this **label control**, change the **Font Color** to **Orange, Accent 4, Darker 50%**—under **Theme Colors**, in the eighth column, the last color—and then apply **Bold**. For this **label control**, set the **Width** property to **2.2** Set the **Top** property to **0.1** and then set the **Left** property to **1.95**.

TABLE 1

Publisher ID	Publisher Name	Address	City	State	Postal Code	Phone Number	Publisher Web Site
PUB-1008	**Hidden Hills Publishing Co**	**5100 Live Oak St**	**Dallas**	**TX**	**75201**	**(214) 555-0857**	**http://www. hhpubco.pub**

(Return to Step 3)

(Project 3E Textbook Publishers continues on the next page)

CONTENT-BASED ASSESSMENTS

10 **Close** the **Property Sheet**, **Save** your form, and then switch to **Form** view. **Find** the record for the **Textbook ID** of **TEXT-0009**, and then, as directed, create a paper or electronic printout of only this record. Because you changed the field widths, you do not need to change the Column Size Width in the **Print** dialog box.

11 **Close** all open objects, and then **Open** the **Navigation Pane**. If necessary, increase the width of the pane so that all object names display fully. **Close** Access. As directed by your instructor, submit your database and the paper or electronic printouts of the two forms that are the results of this project. Specifically, in this project, using your own name, you created the following database and printouts or electronic printouts:

1. Lastname_Firstname_3E_Textbook_Publishers	Database file
2. Lastname Firstname 3E Publisher Form	Form (printout or electronic printout - Record 7)
3. Lastname Firstname 3E Science Textbook Form	Form (printout or electronic printout - Record 9)

END | You have completed Project 3E

CONTENT-BASED ASSESSMENTS

In the following Mastering Access project, you will assist Tom Catogrides, the registrar, in using his database to track degrees and grade point averages for honor students in the health professions program in preparation for graduation. Your completed database objects will look similar to Figure 3.52.

PROJECT FILES

For Project 3F, you will need the following file:

a03F_Degrees_Students

You will save your database as:

Lastname_Firstname_3F_Degrees_Students

PROJECT RESULTS

FIGURE 3.52

(Project 3F Degrees and Students continues on the next page)

CONTENT-BASED ASSESSMENTS

1 Start Access. From your student data files, open **a03F_Degrees_Students**. **Save** the database in your **Access Chapter 3** folder as **Lastname_Firstname_3F_Degrees_ Students** and then enable the content. In the **Navigation Pane**, **Rename** the two tables and two queries by adding **Lastname Firstname** to the beginning of each object name, and then increase the width of the **Navigation Pane** so that all object names display fully. View the relationship that is established between the *3F Degrees* tables and the *3F Students* table—*one* type of degree can be awarded to *many* students. Save the changes to the layout of the relationships. **Run** each query to display the query results, apply **Best Fit**, and then **Save** each query.

Open each query in **Design** view to examine the design grid. The *3F Summa Cum Laude Graduates Query* answers the question, *What is the GPA, student ID, last name, first name, degree, and program for students graduating with a grade point average of 3.8 or higher, in descending order by GPA?* The *3F GPAs by Degree Program Query* answers the question, *What is the program, last name, first name, and GPA for all students, in ascending order by the Last Name field within the Program field?* **Close All** objects.

Based on your **3F Summa Cum Laude Graduates Query** object, use the **Report** tool to create a report. Apply the **Facet** theme to only this report. Delete the **Student ID** field from the report. For the **Last Name**, **First Name**, and **Degree text box controls**, set the **Width** property to **1.25** and then **Sort** the **Last Name** field in **Ascending** order. For the **Program text box controls**, set the **Width** property to **2.5**

At the bottom of the report, for the **calculated control**, which displays 8, set the **Height** to **0.25** and then for the **page number control**, set the **Left** property to **5** For the title of the report, set the **Font Size** to **14** and change the word *Query* to **Report** For the **GPA** field, set the **Left** property to **0.25** to approximately center the fields within the margins of the report. **Save** the report as **Lastname Firstname 3F Summa Cum Laude Graduates Report** and then create a paper or electronic printout as directed. **Close Print Preview**, **Close** the **Property Sheet**, and then **Close** the report.

2 Use the **Report Wizard** to create a report based on your **3F GPAs by Degree Program Query** object that includes the following fields in the order given: **Program**, **GPA**, **Last Name**, and **First Name**. View your data **by 3F Degrees** and do not add any other grouping to the report. Sort first in **Descending** order by **GPA**, and second in **Ascending** order by **Last Name**. Summarize the report by averaging the **GPA** field. Be sure the layout is **Stepped** and the orientation is **Portrait**. For the report title, type **Lastname Firstname 3F GPAs by Program Report** and then switch to **Layout** view.

3 Apply the **Wisp** theme to only this report. For the report title, change the **Font Size** to **16**, and then apply **Bold**. Delete the controls that begin with **Summary for 'Program'**. Under **Program**, for the **text box controls**, set the **Width** property to **2.75** Change the text in the **Avg label control** to **Average GPA by Program** At the top of the report, select the four **label controls** that display the field names, and then apply **Bold**. Select the **GPA label control**, the **GPA text box controls**, and the **calculated controls** for the average GPA, and then set the **Width** property to **1** and the **Left** property to **3 Close** the **Property Sheet**. Display the report in **Design** view. Under **Program Header**, click the **Program text box control**, hold down Shift, and under **Program Footer**, click the **Average GPA by Program label control**. **Align** the controls on the **Right**, and then **Save** the design changes to your report.

4 Switch to **Print Preview**, **Zoom** to display **Two Pages** of the report, and examine how the groupings break across the pages. Switch to **Layout** view, display the **Group, Sort, and Total** pane, select **keep whole group together on one page**, and then close the **Group, Sort, and Total** pane. Switch to **Print Preview**, and notice that the groupings are not split between pages. **Save** the report, and then create a paper or electronic printout as directed—two pages result.

(Project 3F Degrees and Students continues on the next page)

CONTENT-BASED ASSESSMENTS

5 **Close Print Preview**, and then **Close** the report. **Open** the **Navigation Pane**, and, if necessary, increase the width of the pane so that all object names display fully. On the right side of the title bar, click **Close** to close the database and to exit Access. As directed by your instructor, submit your database and the paper or electronic printouts of the two reports—one report is two pages—that are the results of this project. Specifically, in this project, using your own name, you created the following database and printouts or electronic printouts:

1. Lastname_Firstname_3F_Degrees_Students	Database file
2. Lastname Firstname 3F Summa Cum Laude Graduates Report	Report (printout or electronic printout)
3. Lastname Firstname 3F GPAs by Program Report	Report (printout or electronic printout - two pages)

END | You have completed Project 3F

CONTENT-BASED ASSESSMENTS

Mastering Access   Project 3G Career Books

Apply 3A and 3B skills from these Objectives:

1 Create and Use a Form to Add and Delete Records

2 Filter Records

3 Create a Form by Using the Form Wizard

4 Modify a Form in Layout View and in Design View

5 Create a Report by Using the Report Tool and Modify the Report in Layout View

6 Create a Report by Using the Report Wizard

7 Modify the Design of a Report

8 Keep Grouped Data Together in a Printed Report

In the following Mastering Access project, you will assist Rebecca Hennelly, head librarian at the Southwest Campus of Texas Lakes Community College, in using her database to track publishers and book titles that assist students in finding employment. Your completed forms and report will look similar to Figure 3.53.

PROJECT FILES

For Project 3G, you will need the following file:

a03G_Career_Books

You will save your database as:

Lastname_Firstname_3G_Career_Books

PROJECT RESULTS

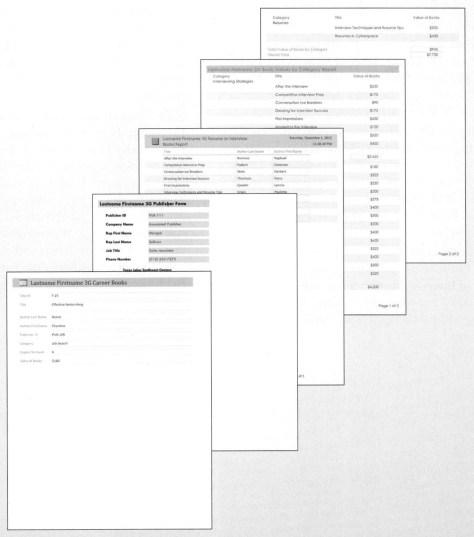

FIGURE 3.53

(Project 3G Career Books continues on the next page)

CONTENT-BASED ASSESSMENTS

1 Start Access. From your student data files, open **a03G_Career_Books**. Save the database in your **Access Chapter 3** folder as **Lastname_Firstname_3G_Career_Books** and then enable the content. In the **Navigation Pane**, **Rename** the two tables and one query by adding **Lastname Firstname** to the beginning of each object name. Increase the width of the **Navigation Pane** so that all object names display fully. View the relationship that is established between the *3G Publishers* tables and the *3G Career Books* table—*one* publisher can publish *many* career books. Save the changes to the layout of the relationships.

Open the **3G Resume or Interview Books Query**, apply **Best Fit**, and then **Save** the query. Switch the query to **Design** view, examine the design of the query, and then **Close** the query object.

2 Based on your **3G Career Books** table, use the **Form** tool to create a form. **Save** the form as **Lastname Firstname 3G Career Book Form** and then switch to **Form** view. Using the form, add a new record to the underlying table as shown in **Table 1**.

3 Display the first record, and click in the **Title ID** field. **Find** the record for the **Title ID** of **T-19**, and then **Delete** the record. Display the record you entered for **T-25**, and then, as directed, create a paper or electronic printout of only that record, changing the **Column Size Width** in the **Print** dialog box to **7.5 Save** the design changes to your form.

4 Use the **Filter By Form** tool in your **3G Career Book Form** object to create a filter that displays records with a **Category** of **Interviewing Strategies** or **Resumes**. After verifying that 10 records match this criteria, click **Toggle Filter** to display all 24 records. **Save** the form, and then **Close** the form.

5 Use the **Form Wizard** to create a form based on your **3G Publishers** table that includes the following fields in the order given: **Company Name**, **Rep Last Name**, **Rep First Name**, **Job Title**, and **Phone Number**. Apply a **Columnar** layout, and name the form **Lastname Firstname 3G Publisher Form**

6 In **Layout** view, apply the **Stacked** layout to all of the controls, and then apply the **Integral** theme to this form only. For the title of the form, change the **Font Size** to **16**, apply **Bold**, and then change the **Font Color** to **Dark Teal, Text 2, Darker 50%**—under **Theme Colors**, in the fourth column, the last color. **Save** the design changes to the form.

7 From the **Field List** pane, add the **Publisher ID** field to the form directly above the **Company Name** field. **Close** the **Field List** pane. Move the **Rep First Name** controls directly above the **Rep Last Name** controls. Click the **Job Title text box control**, set the **Width** property to **2.5** and then **Save** the design changes to your form.

8 Select all six **text box controls**, and change the **Background Color** to **Turquoise, Accent 1, Lighter 80%**—under **Theme Colors**, in the fifth column, the second color. Select all six **label controls**, and change the **Font Color** to **Dark Teal, Text 2, Darker 50%**—under **Theme Colors**, in the fourth column, the last color. Apply **Bold** to the **label controls**. With the **label controls** still selected, set the **Width** property to **1.75** and then select all of the **label controls** and all of the **text box controls**. Change the **Font Size** to **12**, set the **Height** property to **0.25** and then **Save** the design changes to your form.

TABLE 1

Title ID	Title	Author Last Name	Author First Name	Publisher ID	Category	Copies On Hand	Value of Books
T-25	**Effective Networking**	**Nunez**	**Charlene**	**PUB-109**	**Job Search**	6	180

(Return to Step 3)

(Project 3G Career Books continues on the next page)

CONTENT-BASED ASSESSMENTS

9 In **Design** view, set the **Form Footer** section **Height** property to **0.5** Add a **Label** control to the **Form Footer** section that displays **Texas Lakes Southwest Campus** For this **label control**, change the **Font Color** to **Dark Teal, Text 2, Darker 50%**—under **Theme Colors**, in the fourth column, the last color —and then apply **Bold**. For this **label control**, set the **Width** property to **2.2** Set the **Top** property to **0.1** and then set the **Left** property to **1** **Close** the **Property Sheet**, **Save** your form, and then switch to **Form** view. Using the form, add a new record to the underlying table as shown in **Table 2**.

10 Display the record that you just created, and then, as directed, create a paper or electronic printout of only this record. Because you changed the field widths, you do not need to change the Column Size Width in the **Print** dialog box. **Close** the form.

11 Based on your **3G Resume or Interview Books Query** object, use the **Report** tool to create a report. Apply the **Retrospect** theme to only this report. Delete the following fields from the report: **Publisher ID**, **Category**, and **Company Name**. For the **Title text box controls**, set the **Width** property to **3** and then **Sort** the **Title** field in **Ascending** order. For the **Author Last Name text box controls** and the **Author First Name text box controls**, set the **Width** property to **1.5**

12 Click the **Title** field name, and then add a calculated control that counts the number of records. At the bottom of the report, for the **calculated control**, which displays *10*, set the **Height** to **0.25** and then for the **page number control**, set the **Left** property to **5** For the title of the report, set the **Font Size** to **14** and change the word *Query* to **Report** Click the **Title** field name, and then set the **Left** property to **0.75** to move all of the controls to the right. **Save** the report as **Lastname Firstname 3G Resume or Interview Books Report** and then create a paper or electronic printout as directed. **Close Print Preview**, **Close** the **Property Sheet**, and then **Close** the report.

13 Use the **Report Wizard** to create a report based on your **3G Career Books** table that includes the following fields in the order given: **Category**, **Title**, and **Value of Books**. Group your data by **Category**, sort in **Ascending** order by **Title**, and then summarize the report by summing the **Value of Books** field. Be sure the layout is **Stepped** and the orientation is **Portrait**. For the report title, type **Lastname Firstname 3G Book Values by Category Report** and then switch to **Layout** view.

14 Apply the **Ion Boardroom** theme to only this report. For the report title, change the **Font Size** to **14**, and then apply **Bold**. Delete the controls that begin with **Summary for 'Category'**. Select the **Category**, **Title**, and **Value of Books label controls**, and then apply **Bold**. Under **Title**, for the **text box controls**, set the **Width** property to **3.5** For the **Value of Books label control**, set the **Left** property to **6** and then **Save** the design changes to your report.

15 At the bottom of the report in the last column, select the following three controls: **text box control** that displays *$420*, **calculated control** that displays *$945*, and the **calculated control** that displays *7,730*. Set the **Width** property to **1.25** and the **Left** property to **6** For the **Grand Total label control**, set the **Width** property to **1** and then change the text in the **Sum label control** to **Total Value of Books by Category** Click any **Title text box control**, set the **Height** property to **0.35** and then **Save** your report.

16 **Close** the **Property Sheet**, and then display your report in **Design** view. Under **Category Footer**, click the **label control** that displays *Total Value of Books by Category*, hold down Shift, and then under **Report Footer**, click the **Grand Total label control**. **Align** the controls on the **Left**, and then **Save** the design changes to your report.

TABLE 2

Publisher ID	Company Name	Rep First Name	Rep Last Name	Job Title	Phone Number
PUB-111	**Associated Publishers**	**Marquis**	**Sullivan**	**Sales Associate**	**(512) 555-7373**

(Return to Step 10)

(Project 3G Career Books continues on the next page)

CONTENT-BASED ASSESSMENTS

17 Switch to **Print Preview**, **Zoom** to display **Two Pages** of the report, and examine how the groupings break across the pages. Switch to **Layout** view, display the **Group, Sort, and Total** pane, select **keep whole group together on one page**, and then close the **Group, Sort, and Total** pane. Switch to **Print Preview**, and notice that the groupings are no longer split between pages. **Save** the report, and then create a paper or electronic printout as directed—two pages result.

18 **Close Print Preview**, and then **Close** the report. **Open** the **Navigation Pane**, and, if necessary, increase the width of the pane so that all object names display fully. On the right side of the title bar, click **Close** to close the database and to exit Access. As directed by your instructor, submit your database and the paper or electronic printouts of the two forms and two reports—one report is two pages—that are the results of this project. Specifically, in this project, using your own name, you created the following database and printouts or electronic printouts:

1. Lastname_Firstname_3G_Career_Books	Database file
2. Lastname Firstname 3G Career Book Form	Form (printout or electronic printout - Record 24)
3. Lastname Firstname 3G Publisher Form	Form (printout or electronic printout - Record 12)
4. Lastname Firstname 3G Resume or Interview Books Report	Report (printout or electronic printout)
5. Lastname Firstname 3G Book Values by Category Report	Report (printout or electronic printout - two pages)

END | You have completed Project 3G

CONTENT-BASED ASSESSMENTS

Apply a combination of the
3A and 3B skills.

GO! Fix It	Project 3H Resume Workshops	Online

GO! Make It	Project 3I Study Abroad	Online

GO! Solve It	Project 3J Job Offers	Online

GO! Solve It	Project 3K Financial Aid	

PROJECT FILES

For Project 3K, you will need the following file:

a03K_Financial_Aid

You will save your database as:

Lastname_Firstname_3K_Financial_Aid

Start Access, navigate to your student data files, open a03K_Financial_Aid, and then save the database in your **Access Chapter 3** folder as **Lastname_Firstname_3K_Financial_Aid** Using your own name, add **Lastname Firstname** to the beginning of both table names and the query name. Sivia Long, the financial aid director, would like you to create an attractive form and a report for this database, using the following guidelines:

- The form will be used to update student records in the 3K FA Students table. Be sure that the Last Name field displays above the First Name field. After the form is created, enter a new record using your own information with a Student ID of **9091246** and Financial Aid ID of **FA-07** and a Home Phone of **(512) 555-9876** and a College Email of **ns246@tlcc.edu** Create a filter that when toggled on displays the records for those students whose last names begin with the letter *S*. Add a footer to the form that displays **Texas Lakes Community College Financial Aid** Save the form as **Lastname Firstname 3K FA Student Update Form** and then create a paper or electronic printout of your record only.

- The report should use the query and list the Award Name, the Student ID, and the Award Amount for financial aid offered to students, grouped by the Award Name field, and sorted in ascending order by the Student ID field. Include a total for the Award Amount field, save the report as **Lastname Firstname 3K FA Amount by Award Report** and be sure the groupings do not break across pages when the report is printed. Create a paper or electronic printout as directed—multiple pages result.

Open the Navigation Pane, be sure that all object names display fully, and then close Access. As directed, submit your database and the paper or electronic printout of the form and report—the report is multiple pages—that are the results of this project. Specifically, in this project, using your own name, you created the following database and printouts or electronic printouts:

1. Lastname_Firstname_3K_Financial_Aid	Database file
2. Lastname Firstname 3K FA Student Update Form	Form (printout or electronic printout - Record 35)
3. Lastname Firstname 3K FA Amount by Award Report	Report (printout or electronic printout - multiple pages)

(Project 3K Financial Aid continues on the next page)

CONTENT-BASED ASSESSMENTS

Performance Level

Performance Criteria		Exemplary	Proficient	Developing
	Create 3K FA Student Update Form	Form created with correct fields, new record, footer, and filter in an attractive format.	Form created with no more than two missing elements.	Form created with more than two missing elements.
	Create 3K FA Amount by Award Report	Report created with correct fields, grouped, sorted, and summarized correctly, with groupings kept together in an attractive format.	Report created with no more than two missing elements.	Report created with more than two missing elements.

END | You have completed Project 3K

OUTCOMES-BASED ASSESSMENTS

RUBRIC

The following outcomes-based assessments are *open-ended assessments*. That is, there is no specific correct result; your result will depend on your approach to the information provided. Make *Professional Quality* your goal. Use the following scoring rubric to guide you in *how* to approach the problem and then to evaluate *how well* your approach solves the problem.

The *criteria*—Software Mastery, Content, Format & Layout, and Process—represent the knowledge and skills you have gained that you can apply to solving the problem. The *levels of performance*—Professional Quality, Approaching Professional Quality, or Needs Quality Improvements—help you and your instructor evaluate your result.

	Your completed project is of Professional Quality if you:	Your completed project is Approaching Professional Quality if you:	Your completed project Needs Quality Improvements if you:
1-Software Mastery	Choose and apply the most appropriate skills, tools, and features and identify efficient methods to solve the problem.	Choose and apply some appropriate skills, tools, and features, but not in the most efficient manner.	Choose inappropriate skills, tools, or features, or are inefficient in solving the problem.
2-Content	Construct a solution that is clear and well organized, contains content that is accurate, appropriate to the audience and purpose, and is complete. Provide a solution that contains no errors in spelling, grammar, or style.	Construct a solution in which some components are unclear, poorly organized, inconsistent, or incomplete. Misjudge the needs of the audience. Have some errors in spelling, grammar, or style, but the errors do not detract from comprehension.	Construct a solution that is unclear, incomplete, or poorly organized; contains some inaccurate or inappropriate content; and contains many errors in spelling, grammar, or style. Do not solve the problem.
3-Format & Layout	Format and arrange all elements to communicate information and ideas, clarify function, illustrate relationships, and indicate relative importance.	Apply appropriate format and layout features to some elements, but not others. Overuse features, causing minor distraction.	Apply format and layout that does not communicate information or ideas clearly. Do not use format and layout features to clarify function, illustrate relationships, or indicate relative importance. Use available features excessively, causing distraction.
4-Process	Use an organized approach that integrates planning, development, self-assessment, revision, and reflection.	Demonstrate an organized approach in some areas, but not others; or, use an insufficient process of organization throughout.	Do not use an organized approach to solve the problem.

OUTCOMES-BASED ASSESSMENTS

Apply a combination of the 3A and 3B skills.

GO! Think   Project 3L Food Services

PROJECT FILES

For Project 3L, you will need the following file:

a03L_Food_Services

You will save your database as:

Lastname_Firstname_3L_Food_Services

Start Access, navigate to your student data files, open a03L_Food_Services, save the database in your **Access Chapter 3** folder as **Lastname_Firstname_3L_Food_Services** and then enable the content. Using your own name, add **Lastname Firstname** to the beginning of both table names. Luciano Gonzalez, the hospitality director, would like you to create to create an attractive form and a report to assist him with the staff scheduling of food services for a two-day student orientation workshop using the following guidelines:

- The form will be used to update records in the 3L Staff table. Be sure that the Last Name field displays above the First Name field. After the form is created, enter a new record using your own last name and first name with a Staff ID of **STAFF-1119** and a Phone Number of **(512) 555-0845** and a Title of **Server** Create a filter that when toggled on displays the records for staff with a Title of *Server*. Add a footer to the form that displays **Texas Lakes Community College Hospitality Services** Save the form as **Lastname Firstname 3L Staff Update Form** and then create a paper or electronic printout of your record only.

- The report will be used by Mr. Gonzalez to call staff members when the schedule changes. Add a report footer that displays **Texas Lakes Community College Hospitality Services** and then save the report as **Lastname Firstname 3L Staff Phone List** Create a paper or electronic printout as directed.

Open the Navigation Pane, be sure that all object names display fully, and then close Access. As directed, submit your database and the paper or electronic printout of the form and report that are the results of this project. Specifically, in this project, using your own name, you created the following database and printouts or electronic printouts:

1. Lastname_Firstname_3L_Food_Services	Database file
2. Lastname Firstname 3L Staff Update Form	Form (printout or electronic printout - Record 19)
3. Lastname Firstname 3L Staff Phone List	Report (printout or electronic printout)

END | You have completed Project 3L

GO! Think   Project 3M Donor Gifts   Online

You and GO!   Project 3N Personal Inventory   Online

Build from Scratch

Build from Scratch

GO! Cumulative Group Project   Project 3O Bell Orchid Hotels   Online

Introduction to Microsoft PowerPoint 2013

PowerPoint 2013

alexandre zveiger/Fotolia

PowerPoint 2013: Introduction

Video PA

Communication skills are critically important to success in today's business world and when it comes to communicating *your* ideas, presentation is everything! Whether you are planning to deliver your presentation in person or online—to a large audience or to a small group—Microsoft PowerPoint 2013 is a versatile business tool designed to help you create presentations that make a lasting impression. Additionally, collaborating with others to develop a presentation is made easy because you can share the slides you create by using your OneDrive.

New to Microsoft PowerPoint 2013 are a variety of themes that you can apply to a new presentation. Each theme includes several theme variants that coordinate colors, fonts, and effects. The beauty of this approach is that the variations evoke different moods and responses, yet the basic design remains the same. As a result, you can use a similar design within your company to brand your presentations while still changing the colors to make the presentation appropriate to the audience and topic. The best part is that you do not have to determine which colors work well together in the theme you chose. The theme variant does that work for you so that you can concentrate on how best to communicate your message! Focus on creating dynamic, interesting presentations that keep your audience engaged!

Getting Started with Microsoft PowerPoint

PROJECT 1A

OUTCOMES
Creat a company overview presentation.

OBJECTIVES

1. Create a New Presentation
2. Edit a Presentation in Normal View
3. Add Pictures to a Presentation
4. Print and View a Presentation

PROJECT 1B

OUTCOMES
Create a new product announcement presentation.

OBJECTIVES

5. Edit an Existing Presentation
6. Format a Presentation
7. Use Slide Sorter View
8. Apply Slide Transitions

Caleb Foster/Fotolia

In This Chapter

In this chapter you will study presentation skills, which are among the most important skills you will learn. Good presentation skills enhance your communications—written, electronic, and interpersonal. In this technology-enhanced world, communicating ideas clearly and concisely is a critical personal skill. Microsoft PowerPoint 2013 is presentation software with which you create electronic slide presentations. Use PowerPoint to present information to your audience effectively. You can start with a new, blank presentation and add content, pictures, and themes, or you can collaborate with colleagues by inserting slides that have been saved in other presentations.

The projects in this chapter relate to **Kodiak West Travel**, which is a travel agency with offices in Juneau, Anchorage, and Victoria. Kodiak West Travel works closely with local vendors to provide clients with specialized adventure travel itineraries. The company was established in 2001 in Juneau and built a loyal client base that led to the expansion into Anchorage and Victoria. As a full-service travel agency, Kodiak West Travel agents strive to provide their clients with travel opportunities that exceed their expectations. The company works with all major airlines, cruise lines, hotel chains, and vehicle rental companies as well as with small, specialized, boutique hotels.

PROJECT 1A
Company Overview

PROJECT ACTIVITIES

In Activities 1.01 through 1.16, you will create the first five slides of a new presentation that Kodiak West Travel tour manager, Ken Dakano, is developing to introduce the tour services that the company offers. Your completed presentation will look similar to Figure 1.1.

PROJECT FILES

For Project 1A, you will need the following files:

New blank PowerPoint presentation
p01A_Glacier
p01A_Bay

You will save your presentation as:

Lastname_Firstname_1A_KWT_Overview

PROJECT RESULTS

Build from Scratch

FIGURE 1.1 Project 1A Company Overview

Video P1-1

You can edit and format a blank presentation by adding text, a presentation theme, and pictures. When you start PowerPoint, presentations you have recently opened, if any, display on the left. On the right you can select either a blank presentation or a *theme*—a set of unified design elements that provides a look for your presentation by applying colors, fonts, and effects.

N O T E	**If You Are Using a Touch Screen**

- Tap an item to click it.
- Press and hold for a few seconds to right-click; release when the information or commands displays.
- Touch the screen with two or more fingers and then pinch together to zoom in or stretch your fingers apart to zoom out.
- Slide your finger on the screen to scroll—slide left to scroll right and slide right to scroll left.
- Slide to rearrange—similar to dragging with a mouse.
- Swipe from edge: from right to display charms; from left to expose open apps, snap apps, or close apps; from top or bottom to show commands or close an app.
- Swipe to select—slide an item a short distance with a quick movement—to select an item and bring up commands, if any.

Activity 1.01 | Creating a New Presentation and Identifying Parts of the PowerPoint Window

1 Start PowerPoint. On the right, click **Facet** to view a preview of the Facet theme and the color variations associated with this theme. Below the theme preview, click the left and right **More Images** arrows ◀ and ▶ to view the manner in which various types of slides in this theme display. To the right of the preview, click each of the color variations. After you have viewed each color, click the original green color.

2 To the right of the preview window, point to the ⊙ arrow, and then compare your screen with Figure 1.2.

You can use the left and right arrows to scroll through the available themes.

FIGURE 1.2

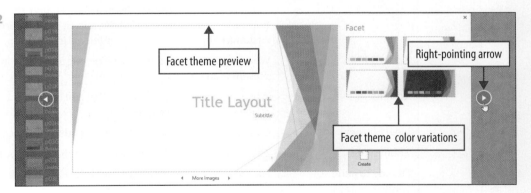

3 Click ⊙ two times to view the next two available themes. Then, to the left of the preview window, click ⊙ two times to return to the **Facet** theme. In the lower right area of the preview window, click **Create** to begin a new presentation using the Facet theme. Compare your screen with Figure 1.3.

The presentation displays in normal view. *Normal view* is the primary editing view in PowerPoint where you write and design your presentations. On the left, a small pane displays miniature images—*thumbnails*—of the slides in your presentation. On the right, the *Slide pane* displays a large image of the active slide.

FIGURE 1.3

4 ▸ Take a moment to study the parts of the PowerPoint window described in the table in Figure 1.4.

FIGURE 1.4

MICROSOFT POWERPOINT SCREEN ELEMENTS	
SCREEN ELEMENT	**DESCRIPTION**
Slide pane	Displays a large image of the active slide.
Slide thumbnails	Miniature images of each slide in the presentation. Clicking a slide thumbnail displays the slide in the Slide pane.
Status bar	Displays, in a horizontal bar at the bottom of the presentation window, the current slide number, number of slides in a presentation, Notes button, Comments button, View buttons, Zoom slider, and Fit slide to current window button; you can customize this area to include additional information.
Notes button	When clicked, displays an area below the Slide pane in which you can type presentation notes.
Comments button	When clicked, displays a Comments pane to the right of the Slide pane, in which reviewers can type comments.
View buttons	Control the look of the presentation window with a set of commands.
Zoom slider	Zooms the slide displayed in the Slide pane, in and out.
Fit slide to current window button	Fits the active slide to the maximum view in the Slide pane.

Activity 1.02 | Entering Presentation Text

When a new presentation is created, PowerPoint displays a new blank presentation with a single slide—a title slide in Normal view. A presentation *slide*—similar to a page in a document—can contain text, pictures, tables, charts, and other multimedia or graphic objects. The *title slide* is most commonly the first slide in a presentation and provides an introduction to the presentation topic.

1 ▸ In the **Slide pane**, click in the text *Click to add title*, which is the title placeholder.

A *placeholder* is a box on a slide with dotted or dashed borders that holds title and body text or other content such as charts, tables, and pictures. This slide contains two placeholders, one for the title and one for the subtitle.

2 Type **Kodiak West** and then click in the subtitle placeholder. Type **Your Travel** and then press **Enter** to create a new line in the subtitle placeholder. Type **Your Way** and then compare your screen with Figure 1.5.

FIGURE 1.5

3 On the **Quick Access Toolbar**, click **Save** 🔲. Under **Save As**, click **Computer**, and then click **Browse**. Navigate to the location where you are saving your files for this chapter, and then create and open a new folder named **PowerPoint Chapter 1** In the **File name** box, using your own name, replace the existing text with **Lastname_Firstname_1A_KWT_Overview** and then click **Save**.

Activity 1.03 | Applying a Presentation Theme

Recall that a theme is a set of unified design elements that provides a look for your presentation by applying colors, fonts, and effects. After you create a presentation, you can change the look of your presentation by applying a different theme.

1 On the ribbon, click the **DESIGN tab**. In the **Themes group**, click **More** to display the **Themes** gallery. Compare your screen with Figure 1.6.

The themes displayed on your system may differ from Figure 1.6.

FIGURE 1.6

2 Under **Office**, point to several of the themes and notice that a ScreenTip displays the name of each theme and the Live Preview feature displays how each theme would look if applied to your presentation.

The first theme that displays is the Office Theme.

3 Use the ScreenTips to locate the **Organic** theme shown in Figure 1.7.

FIGURE 1.7

4 Click **Organic** to change the presentation theme, and then **Save** 🖫 your presentation.

Objective 2 | Edit a Presentation in Normal View

Video P1-2

Editing is the process of modifying a presentation by adding and deleting slides or by changing the contents of individual slides.

Activity 1.04 | Inserting a New Slide

To insert a new slide in a presentation, display the slide that will precede the slide that you want to insert.

1 On the **HOME tab**, in the **Slides group**, point to the **New Slide arrow**—the lower part of the New Slide button. Compare your screen with Figure 1.8.

> The New Slide button is a *split button*—a type of button in which clicking the main part of the button performs a command and clicking the arrow opens a menu, list, or gallery. The upper, main part of the New Slide button, when clicked, inserts a slide without displaying any options. The lower part—the New Slide arrow—when clicked, displays a gallery of slide *layouts*— the arrangement of elements, such as title and subtitle text, lists, pictures, tables, charts, shapes, and movies, on a slide.

FIGURE 1.8

2 In the **Slides group**, click the lower portion of the New Slide button—the **New Slide arrow**—to display the gallery, and then compare your screen with Figure 1.9.

FIGURE 1.9

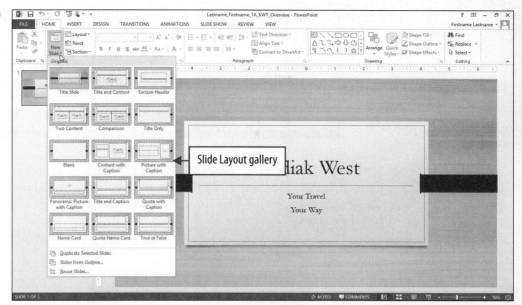

3 In the gallery, in the fourth row, click the first layout—**Panoramic Picture with Caption**—to insert a new slide. Notice that the new blank slide displays in the **Slide pane** and a slide thumbnail displays at the left. Compare your screen with Figure 1.10.

⟳ BY TOUCH In the gallery, tap the desired layout to insert a new slide.

FIGURE 1.10

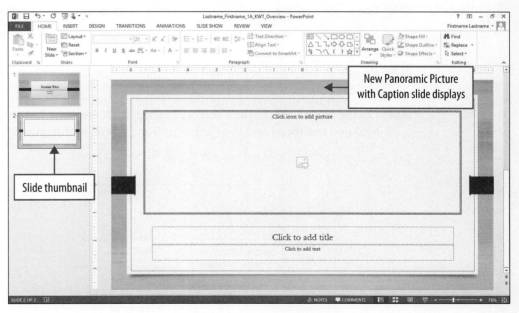

4 On the slide, below the large picture placeholder, click the text *Click to add title*, and then type **Your Dreams**

5 Below the title placeholder, click in the text placeholder. Type **Whether you want to trek on a glacier or spend your time in quiet solitude, Kodiak West Travel can make your dream a reality.** Compare your screen with Figure 1.11.

FIGURE 1.11

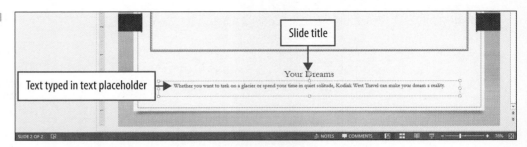

6 ▸ On the **HOME tab**, in the **Slides group**, click the **New Slide arrow** to display the gallery, and then click **Title and Content**. In the title placeholder, type **Our Expertise** and then below the title placeholder, click in the content placeholder. Type **Over 20 years of experience in the travel industry**

7 ▸ **Save** 🖫 your presentation.

Activity 1.05 | Increasing and Decreasing List Levels

Text in a PowerPoint presentation can be organized according to ***list levels***. List levels, each represented by a bullet symbol, are similar to outline levels. On a slide, list levels are identified by the bullet style, indentation, and the size of the text. The first level on an individual slide is the title. Increasing the list level of a bullet point increases its indent and results in a smaller text size. Decreasing the list level of a bullet point decreases its indent and results in a larger text size.

1 ▸ On **Slide 3**, if necessary, click at the end of the last bullet point after the word *industry*, and then press Enter to insert a new bullet point.

2 ▸ Press Tab, and then notice that the bullet is indented. Type **Certified Travel Associates**

> By pressing Tab at the beginning of a bullet point, you can increase the list level and indent the bullet point.

3 ▸ Press Enter, and then notice that a new bullet point displays at the same level as the previous bullet point.

4 ▸ On the **HOME tab**, in the **Paragraph group**, click **Decrease List Level** ◁≣. Type **Specializing in land and sea travel** and then compare your screen with Figure 1.12.

> The indent is removed and the size of the text increases.

FIGURE 1.12

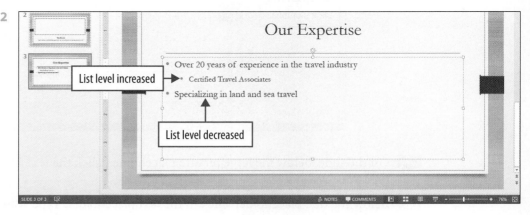

5 ▸ Press Enter, and then on the **HOME tab**, click **Increase List Level** ▷≣. Type **Pacific Northwest including U.S. and Canada**

> You can use the Increase List Level button to indent the bullet point.

6 Compare your screen with Figure 1.13, and then **Save** 🖫 your presentation.

FIGURE 1.13

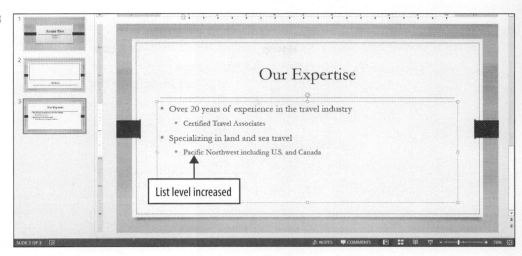

FIGURE 1.13

Activity 1.06 | Adding Speaker's Notes to a Presentation

The ***Notes pane*** is an area of the Normal view window that displays below the Slide pane with space to type notes regarding the active slide. You can refer to these printouts while making a presentation, thus reminding you of the important points that you want to discuss.

1 With **Slide 3** displayed, in the **Status bar**, click **NOTES**, and then notice that below the Slide pane, the Notes pane displays. Click in the **Notes pane**, and then type **Kodiak West Travel has locations in Juneau, Anchorage, and Victoria.**

2 Compare your screen with Figure 1.14, and then **Save** 🖫 your presentation.

FIGURE 1.14

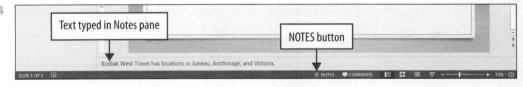

Activity 1.07 | Displaying and Editing Slides in the Slide Pane

1 At the left side of the PowerPoint window, look at the slide thumbnails, and then notice that the presentation contains three slides. At the right side of the PowerPoint window, in the vertical scroll bar, point to the scroll box, and then hold down the left mouse button to display a ScreenTip indicating the slide number and title.

2 Drag the scroll box up until the ScreenTip displays *Slide: 2 of 3 Your Dreams*. Compare your slide with Figure 1.15, and then release the mouse button to display **Slide 2**.

FIGURE 1.15

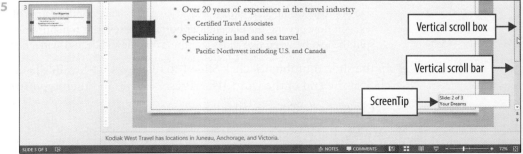

3 At the bottom of the slide, in the content placeholder, click at the end of the sentence, after the period. Press Spacebar, and then type **If you can dream it, we can help you get there.**

4 On the left side of the PowerPoint window, in the slide thumbnails, point to **Slide 3**, and then notice that a ScreenTip displays the slide title. Compare your screen with Figure 1.16.

FIGURE 1.16

5 Click **Slide 3** to display it in the Slide pane. On the **HOME tab**, in the **Slides group**, click the **New Slide arrow** to display the **Slide Layout** gallery, and then click **Section Header**.

A *section header* is a type of slide layout that changes the look and flow of a presentation by providing text placeholders that do not contain bullet points.

6 Click in the title placeholder, and then type **About Our Company**

7 Click in the content placeholder below the title, and then type **Kodiak West Travel was established in May of 2001 by Ken Dakona and Mariam Dorner, two Alaska residents whose sense of adventure and commitment to ecotourism is an inherent aspect of their travel itineraries.** Compare your screen with Figure 1.17.

The placeholder text resizes to fit within the placeholder. The AutoFit Options button displays.

FIGURE 1.17

8 Click **AutoFit Options** ⬍, and then if necessary, click AutoFit Text to Placeholder.

The *AutoFit Text to Placeholder* option keeps the text contained within the placeholder by reducing the size of the text. The *Stop Fitting Text to This Placeholder* option turns off the AutoFit option so that the text can flow beyond the placeholder border; the text size remains unchanged. You can also choose to split the text between two slides, continue on a new slide, or divide the text into two columns.

9 In the slide thumbnails, click **Slide 1** to display it in the **Slide pane**, and then in the slide title, click at the end of the word *West*. Press Spacebar, and then type **Travel**

Clicking a slide thumbnail is the most common method to display a slide in the Slide pane.

10 **Save** 🖫 your presentation.

Video P1-3

Photographic images add impact to a presentation and help the audience visualize your message.

Activity 1.08 | Inserting a Picture from a File

Many slide layouts in PowerPoint accommodate digital picture files so that you can easily add pictures you have stored on your system or on a portable storage device.

1 Display **Slide 2**, and then compare your screen with Figure 1.18.

In the center of the large picture placeholder, the *Pictures* button displays.

FIGURE 1.18

2 In the picture placeholder, click **Pictures** to open the **Insert Picture** dialog box. Navigate to the location in which your student data files are stored, click **p01A_Glacier**, and then click **Insert** to insert the picture in the placeholder. Compare your screen with Figure 1.19.

Small squares—*sizing handles*—surround the inserted picture and indicate that the picture is selected and can be modified or formatted. The *rotation handle*—a circular arrow above the picture—provides a way to rotate a selected image. The PICTURE TOOLS are added to the ribbon, providing picture formatting options.

FIGURE 1.19

3 Display **Slide 3**. On the **HOME tab**, in the **Slides group**, click the **New Slide arrow**, and then click **Title and Content**. In the title placeholder, type **Your Vacation**

4 In the content placeholder, click **Pictures** [image]. Navigate to your student data files, and then click **p01A_Bay**. Click **Insert**, and then compare your screen with Figure 1.20. **Save** [image] the presentation.

FIGURE 1.20

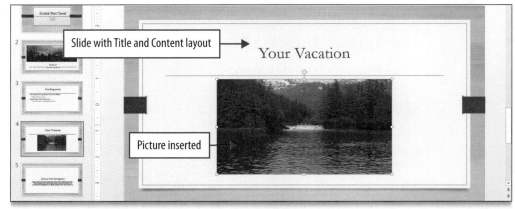

Slide with Title and Content layout

Your Vacation

Picture inserted

Activity 1.09 | Applying a Style to a Picture

When a picture is selected, the PICTURE TOOLS display, adding the Format tab to the ribbon. The Format tab provides numerous styles that you can apply to your pictures. A *style* is a collection of formatting options that you can apply to a picture, text, or an object.

1 With **Slide 4** displayed, if necessary, click the picture to select it. On the ribbon, notice that the *PICTURE TOOLS* are active and the *FORMAT* tab displays.

2 On the **FORMAT tab**, in the **Picture Styles group**, click **More** [▼] to display the **Picture Styles** gallery, and then compare your screen with Figure 1.21.

FIGURE 1.21

Format tab

Picture Styles gallery

3 In the gallery, point to several of the picture styles to display the ScreenTips and to view the effect on your picture. In the second row, click the second style—**Simple Frame, Black**. Click in a blank area of the slide, compare your screen with Figure 1.22, and then **Save** [image] the presentation.

FIGURE 1.22

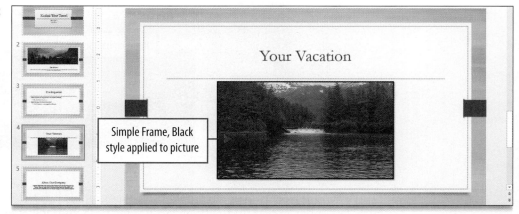

Your Vacation

Simple Frame, Black style applied to picture

Activity 1.10 | Applying and Removing Picture Artistic Effects

Artistic effects are formats applied to images that make pictures resemble sketches or paintings.

1 On **Slide 4**, select the picture. Click the **FORMAT tab**, and then in the **Adjust group**, click **Artistic Effects** to display the **Artistic Effects** gallery. Compare your screen with Figure 1.23.

FIGURE 1.23

2 In the gallery, point to several of the artistic effects to display the ScreenTips and to have Live Preview display the effect on your picture. Then, in the second row, click the **Glow Diffused** effect.

3 With the picture still selected, on the **FORMAT tab**, in the **Adjust group**, click **Artistic Effects** again to display the gallery. In the first row, click the first effect—**None**—to remove the effect from the picture and restore the previous formatting.

4 Save 🖫 the presentation.

Objective 4 | Print and View a Presentation

Video P1-4

There are several print options in PowerPoint. For example, you can print full page images of your slides, presentation handouts to provide your audience with copies of your slides, or Notes pages displaying speaker's notes below an image of the slide.

Activity 1.11 | Viewing a Slide Show

When you view a presentation as an electronic slide show, the entire slide fills the computer screen, and an audience can view your presentation if your computer is connected to a projection system.

1 On the ribbon, click the **SLIDE SHOW tab**. In the **Start Slide Show group**, click **From Beginning**. Compare your screen with Figure 1.24.

The first slide fills the screen, displaying the presentation as the audience would see it if your computer was connected to a projection system.

 ANOTHER WAY   Press F5 to start the slide show from the beginning. Or, display the first slide you want to show and click the Slide Show button on the lower right side of the status bar.

FIGURE 1.24

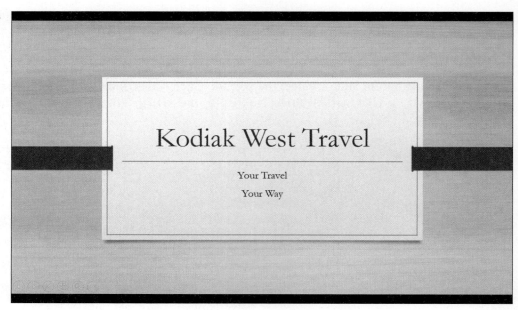

2 Click the left mouse button or press ⟨Spacebar⟩ to advance to the second slide.

3 Continue to click or press ⟨Spacebar⟩ until the last slide displays, and then click or press ⟨Spacebar⟩ one more time to display a ***black slide***—a slide that displays after the last slide in a presentation indicating that the presentation is over.

4 With the black slide displayed, click the left mouse button to exit the slide show and return to the presentation.

Activity 1.12 | Using Presenter View

Presenter View shows the full-screen slide show on one monitor while enabling the presenter to view a preview of the next slide, notes, and a timer on another monitor. Your audience will be able to view only the current slide.

1 On the **SLIDE SHOW tab**, in the **Monitors** group, be sure that the **Use Presenter View** check box is selected. Hold down ⟨Alt⟩ and press ⟨F5⟩. Compare your screen with Figure 1.25.

> If you do not have two monitors, you can practice using Presenter View by pressing ⟨Alt⟩+⟨F5⟩. Above the upper left corner of the slide, a timer displays. Below the timer, the current slide displays. Below the current slide are slide show option buttons. In the upper right corner, the next slide displays. In the lower right corner, any notes that you typed in the notes pane for the current slide display. Below the notes are buttons that enable you to make the notes smaller or larger. Below the current slide, navigation buttons display.

FIGURE 1.25

> 2 Below the current slide, click **Advance to the next slide** ⊙ to display **Slide 2**.

🔁 **BY TOUCH**   Advance to the next slide by swiping the current slide to the left.

> 3 In the upper right corner of the **Presenter View** window, point to the next slide—*Our Expertise*—and then click. Notice that the notes that you typed on **Slide 3** display. Compare your screen with Figure 1.26.

Clicking the image of the next slide advances the presentation.

FIGURE 1.26

> 4 Below the notes, click **Make the text larger** 🅰 one time to increase the font size of the notes in Presenter view, thus increasing readability.

> 5 Below the current slide, click **See all slides** ▦. Compare your screen with Figure 1.27.

A thumbnail view of all of the slides in your presentation displays. Here you can quickly move to another slide; for example, if you want to review a concept or answer a question related to a slide other than the current slide.

FIGURE 1.27

Thumbnail images of all slides display

6 ▶ Click **Slide 4** to make Slide 4 the current slide in Presenter View. Below the current slide, click **Zoom into the slide** 🔍. Move the 🔍 pointer to the middle of the picture on the current slide, and then click to zoom in on the picture. Notice that the ✋ pointer displays. Compare your slide with Figure 1.28.

> With the ✋ pointer displayed, you can move the zoomed image to draw close-up attention to a particular part of your slide.

 BY TOUCH   Touch the current slide with two fingers and then pinch together to zoom in or stretch your fingers apart to zoom out.

FIGURE 1.28

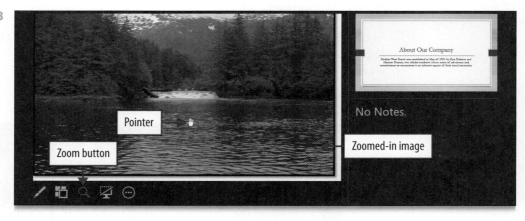

Pointer

Zoom button

No Notes.

Zoomed-in image

7 ▶ Below the current slide, click **Advance to the next slide** ⊙ to display **Slide 5.** At the top of the Presenter View window, click **END SLIDE SHOW** to return to your presentation.

Activity 1.13 | Inserting Headers and Footers on Slide Handouts

A **header** is text that prints at the top of each sheet of **slide handouts** or **notes pages**. Slide handouts are printed images of slides on a sheet of paper. Notes pages are printouts that contain the slide image on the top half of the page and notes that you have created on the Notes pane in the lower half of the page.

In addition to headers, you can insert **footers**—text that displays at the bottom of every slide or that prints at the bottom of a sheet of slide handouts or notes pages.

1 ▶ Click the **INSERT tab**, and then in the **Text group**, click **Header & Footer** to display the **Header and Footer** dialog box.

2 In the **Header and Footer** dialog box, click the **Notes and Handouts tab**. Under **Include on page**, select the **Date and time** check box, and as you do so, watch the Preview box in the upper right corner of the Header and Footer dialog box.

> The Preview box indicates the placeholders on the printed Notes and Handouts pages. The two narrow rectangular boxes at the top of the Preview box indicate placeholders for the header text and date. When you select the Date and time check box, the placeholder in the upper right corner is outlined, indicating the location in which the date will display.

3 Be sure that the **Update automatically** option button is selected so that the current date prints on the notes and handouts each time you print the presentation. If it is not selected, click the Update automatically option button.

4 If necessary, *clear* the Header check box to omit this element. Notice that in the **Preview** box, the corresponding placeholder is not selected.

5 Verify that the **Page number** check box is selected and select it if it is not. Select the **Footer** check box, and then click in the **Footer** box. Using your own name, type **Lastname_Firstname_1A_KWT_Overview** so that the file name displays as a footer, and then compare your dialog box with Figure 1.29.

FIGURE 1.29

6 In the lower right corner of the dialog box, click **Apply to All**. Save 🖫 your presentation.

Activity 1.14 | Inserting Slide Numbers on Slides

In this activity, you will insert the slide numbers on the presentation slides.

1 Display **Slide 1**. On the **INSERT tab**, in the **Text group**, click **Header & Footer** to display the **Header and Footer** dialog box.

2 In the **Header and Footer** dialog box, if necessary, click the **Slide tab**. Under **Include on slide**, select the **Slide number** check box, and then select the **Don't show on title slide** check box. Verify that all other check boxes are cleared, and then compare your screen with Figure 1.30.

> Selecting the *Don't show on title slide* check box omits the slide number from the first slide in a presentation.

FIGURE 1.30

3 ▸ Click **Apply to All**, and then notice that on the first slide, the side number does not display.

4 ▸ Display **Slide 2**, and then notice that the slide number displays in the lower right area of the slide. Display each slide in the presentation and notice the placement of the slide number.

The position of the slide number and other header and footer information is determined by the theme applied to the presentation.

Activity 1.15 | Printing Presentation Handouts

Use Backstage view to preview the arrangement of slides and to print your presentation.

1 ▸ Display **Slide 1**. Click the **FILE tab** to display **Backstage** view, and then click **Print**.

The Print tab in Backstage view displays the tools you need to select your settings and also to view a preview of your presentation. On the right, Print Preview displays your presentation exactly as it will print. If your system is not connected to a color printer, your slide may display in black and white.

2 ▸ Under **Settings**, click **Full Page Slides**, and then compare your screen with Figure 1.31.

The gallery displays either the default print setting—Full Page Slides—or the most recently selected print setting. Thus, on your system, this button might indicate the presentation Notes Pages, Outline, or one of several arrangements of slide handouts—depending on the most recently used setting.

FIGURE 1.31

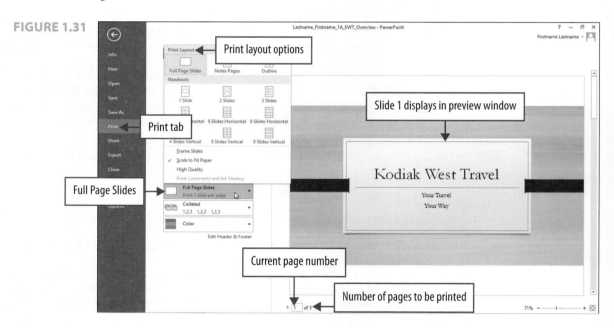

3 ▸ In the gallery, under **Handouts**, click **6 Slides Horizontal**. Notice that the **Print Preview** on the right displays the slide handout, and that the current date, file name, and page number display in the header and footer. Compare your screen with Figure 1.32.

In the Settings group, the Portrait Orientation option displays so that you can change the print orientation from Portrait to Landscape. The Portrait Orientation option does not display when Full Page Slides is chosen.

FIGURE 1.32

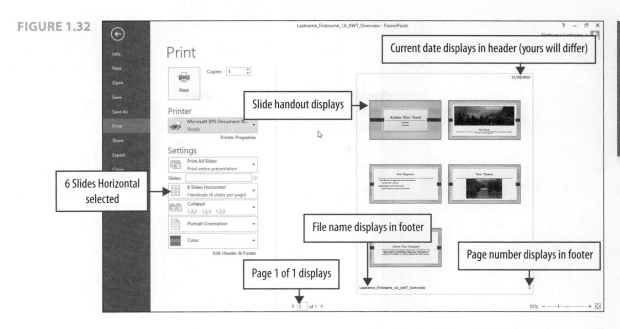

6 Slides Horizontal selected

Current date displays in header (yours will differ)

Slide handout displays

File name displays in footer

Page number displays in footer

Page 1 of 1 displays

4 ▸ To submit your file electronically, skip this step and move to Step 5. To print your document on paper using the default printer on your system, in the upper left portion of the screen, click **Print**.

> The handout will print on your default printer—on a black and white printer, the colors will print in shades of gray. Backstage view closes and your file redisplays in the PowerPoint window.

5 ▸ To create an electronic file, on the left click **Export**. On the right, click **Create PDF/XPS**. In the **Publish as PDF or XPS** dialog box, navigate to your **PowerPoint Chapter 1** folder, and then click **Publish**. If your Adobe Acrobat or Adobe Reader program displays your PDF, close the program.

More **Knowledge**   **Print a Presentation in Grayscale**

To save toner and ink, you can print a presentation in shades of gray using the grayscale setting. To do so, on the FILE tab, click Print. Under Settings, click the Color arrow, and then click Grayscale.

Activity 1.16 │ Printing Speaker Notes

1 ▸ Click the **FILE tab**, and then click **Print**. Under **Settings**, click **6 Slides Horizontal**, and then under **Print Layout**, click **Notes Pages** to view the presentation notes for **Slide 1**; recall that you created notes for **Slide 3**.

> Indicated below the Notes page are the current slide number and the number of pages that will print when Notes Pages is selected. You can use the Next Page and Previous Page arrows to display each Notes page in the presentation.

2 ▸ At the bottom of the **Print Preview**, click **Next Page** ▶ two times so that **Page 3** displays. Notice that the notes you typed for Slide 3 display below the image of the slide. Compare your screen with Figure 1.33.

FIGURE 1.33

3 Under **Settings**, click in the **Slides box**. Type **3** and then click **Notes Pages**. In the lower section, select **Frame Slides**. To print the notes page, click **Print**.

4 Click the **FILE tab** to display **Backstage** view. On the right, at the bottom of the **Properties** list, click **Show All Properties**. On the list of **Properties**, click to the right of **Tags** to display an empty box, and then type **company overview**

5 Click to the right of **Subject** to display an empty box, and then type your course name and section number. Under **Related People**, be sure that your name displays as the author, and edit if necessary.

6 In the lower right corner, scroll down if necessary, click **Show Fewer Properties**, and then on the left, click **Save**. On the right end of the title bar, click **Close** **x** to close the presentation and close PowerPoint.

END | You have completed Project 1A

Objective	Create a Company Overview Presentation in PowerPoint Online

ALERT! **Working with Web-Based Applications and Services**

Computer programs and services on the web receive continuous updates and improvements, so the steps to complete this web-based activity may differ from the ones shown. You can often look at the screens and the information presented to determine how to complete the activity.

Activity | Creating a Company Overview Presentation in PowerPoint Online

In this activity, you will use PowerPoint Online to create a presentation similar to the one you created in Project 1A.

1 From the desktop, start Internet Explorer. Navigate to **http://onedrive.com**, and then sign in to your Microsoft account. Open your **GO! Web Projects** folder—or create and then open this folder if necessary.

2 On the OneDrive menu bar, click **Create**, and then click **PowerPoint presentation**. On the PowerPoint Online title bar, click Presentation1 so that it is selected. Using your own last name and first name, type **Lastname_Firstname_PPT_1A_Web** and then press [Enter] to rename the file.

3 On the **DESIGN tab**, in the **Themes group**, click **Organic** to apply a theme.

4 In the title placeholder, type **Kodiak West Travel** and then in the subtitle placeholder type **Your Travel** and press [Enter]. Type **Your Way** and then click anywhere on the slide outside of the subtitle placeholder to enter the text.

5 On the **HOME Tab**, in the **Slides group**, click **New Slide**. Scroll the **New Slide gallery**, and then click **Panoramic Picture with Caption**. Click **Add Slide**.

6 In the picture placeholder, click **Pictures** , navigate to your student data files, and then click **p01A_Glacier**. Click **Open**.

7 Click in the title placeholder. Type **Your Dreams** and then click in the text placeholder. Type **Let Kodiak West Travel assist you with all of your travel arrangements!** Compare your screen with Figure A.

8 Click outside of the text placeholder. On the **HOME tab**, click **New Slide**, and then click **Title and Content**. Click **Add Slide**. In the title placeholder type **Our Expertise**

9 In the content placeholder, type **Over 20 years of experience in the travel industry** and then press [Enter]. Press [Tab]. Type **Certified Travel Associates** and then press [Enter]. On the **HOME tab**, in the **Paragraph group**, click **Decrease List Level** . Type **Specializing in land and sea travel** and then press [Enter]. Press [Tab] and then type **Pacific Northwest including U.S. and Canada**

FIGURE A

(GO! with Office Online (formerly Web Apps) continues on the next page)

10 Click outside the content placeholder, and then insert a **New Slide** with the **Title and Content** layout. In the title placeholder type **Your Vacation** and then in the content placeholder click **Pictures** 🖼️. From your student data files, insert **p01A_Bay**. On the **PICTURE TOOLS FORMAT** tab, in the **Picture Styles group**, click the **down arrow**, and then in the second row, click the first style **Simple Frame, Black**.

11 Insert a **New Slide** with the **Section Header** layout. In the title placeholder, type **About Our Company** and then click in the text placeholder. Type **Kodiak West Travel was founded in May of 2001 by Ken Dakona and Mariam Dorner.**

12 Click anywhere in a blank area of the slide, and then compare your screen with Figure B.

13 Click **Slide 3**, and then below the slide, click in the Notes pane. Type **Kodiak West Travel has locations in Juneau, Anchorage, and Victoria.**

14 Display **Slide 1**. On the **VIEW tab**, in the **Presentation Views group**, click **Slide Show**. If a Security warning displays at the bottom of your screen, click Allow once. Click the left mouse button to progress through the presentation. When the black slide displays, click the mouse button.

15 If you are instructed to submit your file, create a PDF as indicated in the Note box below. Sign out of OneDrive and close Internet Explorer.

> **NOTE** | **Creating a PDF from the PowerPoint Web App**
>
> Click the **FILE tab**, click **Print**, and then click **Print to PDF**. In the Microsoft PowerPoint Web App message box, click Click here to view the PDF of your document. In the **Print** dialog box, click **Cancel**. Click **File**, and then click **Save As**. In the Save As dialog box, navigate to your PowerPoint Chapter 1 folder, and then save the file as as **Lastname_Firstname_PPT_1A_Web_PDF**.

FIGURE B

Itinerary Presentation

PROJECT ACTIVITIES

In Activities 1.17 through 1.33, you will combine two presentations that the marketing team at Kodiak West Travel developed describing itinerary ideas when visiting Seattle before or after a cruise. You will insert slides from one presentation into another, and then you will rearrange and delete slides. You will also apply font formatting and slide transitions to the presentation. Your completed presentation will look similar to Figure 1.34.

PROJECT FILES

For Project 1B, you will need the following files:

p01B_Seattle
p01B_Slides

You will save your presentation as:

Lastname_Firstname_1B_Seattle

PROJECT RESULTS

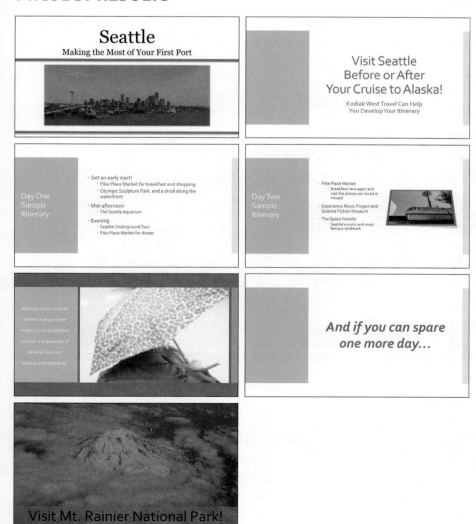

FIGURE 1.34 Project 1B Itinerary Presentation

Video P1-5

Recall that editing refers to the process of adding, deleting, and modifying presentation content. You can edit presentation content in either the Slide pane or in the presentation outline.

Activity 1.17 | Changing Slide Size

Presentations that you create with some of the newer themes in PowerPoint 2013 default to a widescreen format using a 16:9 *aspect ratio*—the ratio of the width of a display to the height of the display. This slide size is similar to most television and computer monitor screens. Previous versions of PowerPoint used a squarer format with a 4:3 aspect ratio. The widescreen format utilizes screen space more effectively.

1 Start PowerPoint. On the left, under the list of recent presentations, click **Open Other Presentations**. Under **Open**, click **Computer** and then click **Browse**. Navigate to your student data files, and then click **p01B_Seattle**. Click **Open**. On the **FILE tab**, click **Save As**, navigate to your **PowerPoint Chapter 1** folder, and then using your own name, save the file as **Lastname_Firstname_1B_Seattle**

2 Notice that **Slide 1** displays in a square format and that in the **Slide pane**, there is white space on the left and right slides of the slide.

3 On the **DESIGN tab**, in the **Customize group**, click **Slide Size**, and then click **Widescreen (16:9)**. Compare your screen with Figure 1.35 and notice that the slide fills the slide pane.

FIGURE 1.35

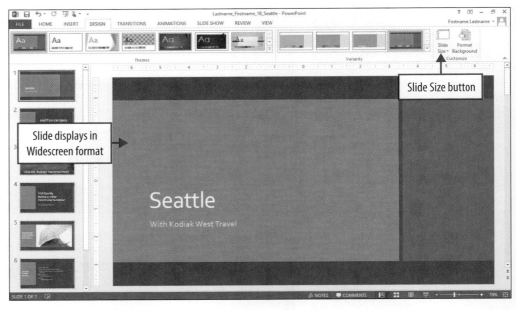

Slide Size button

Slide displays in Widescreen format

4 Save the presentation.

Activity 1.18 | Inserting Slides from an Existing Presentation

Presentation content is commonly shared among group members in an organization. Rather than re-creating slides, you can insert slides from an existing presentation into the current presentation. In this activity, you will insert slides from an existing presentation into your 1B_Seattle presentation.

1 With **Slide 1** displayed, on the **HOME tab**, in the **Slides group**, click the **New Slide arrow** to display the **Slide Layout** gallery and additional commands for inserting slides. Compare your screen with Figure 1.36.

FIGURE 1.36

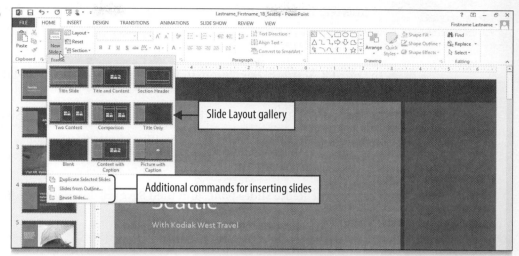

2 Below the gallery, click **Reuse Slides** to open the Reuse Slides pane on the right side of the PowerPoint window.

3 In the **Reuse Slides** pane, click **Browse**, and then click **Browse File**. In the **Browse** dialog box, navigate to the location where your student data files are stored, and then double-click **p01B_Slides** to display the slides from this presentation in the **Reuse Slides** pane.

4 At the bottom of the **Reuse Slides** pane, be sure that the **Keep source formatting** check box is *cleared*, and then compare your screen with Figure 1.37.

When the *Keep source formatting* check box is cleared, the theme formatting of the presentation in which the slides are inserted is applied. When the *Keep source formatting* check box is selected, you retain the formatting applied to the slides when inserted into the existing presentation.

FIGURE 1.37

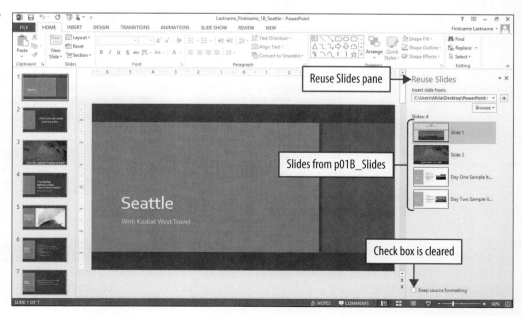

5 In the **Reuse Slides** pane, point to each slide to view a ScreenTip displaying the file name and the slide title.

6 In the **Reuse Slides** pane, click the first slide to insert the slide after Slide 1. Notice that the inserted slide adopts the color of the presentation theme into which the slide was inserted.

N O T E   **Inserting Slides**

You can insert slides into your presentation in any order; remember to display the slide that will precede the slide that you want to insert.

---

7 In your **1B_Seattle** presentation, in the slide thumbnails, click **Slide 7** to display it in the **Slide pane**.

8 In the **Reuse Slides** pane, click the fourth slide to insert it after Slide 7.

Your presentation contains nine slides. When a presentation contains a large number of slides, a scroll box displays to the right of the slide thumbnails so that you can scroll and then select the thumbnails.

9 **Close** ⊠ the **Reuse Slides** pane, and then **Save** 🔲 the presentation.

More **Knowledge**   **Inserting All Slides**

You can insert all of the slides from an existing presentation into the current presentation at one time. In the Reuse Slides pane, right-click one of the slides that you want to insert, and then click Insert All Slides.

Activity 1.19 | Displaying and Editing the Presentation Outline

Outline View displays the presentation outline to the left of the Slide pane. You can use the outline to edit the presentation text. Changes that you make in the outline are immediately displayed in the Slide pane.

1 To the right of the slide thumbnails, drag the scroll box up, and then click **Slide 1** to display it in the Slide pane. On the **VIEW tab**, in the **Presentation Views group**, click **Outline View**. Compare your screen with Figure 1.38.

The outline displays at the left of the PowerPoint window in place of the slide thumbnails. Each slide in the outline displays the slide number, slide icon, and the slide title in bold. Slides that do not display a slide title in the outline use a slide layout that does not include a title, for example, the Blank layout.

FIGURE 1.38

2 In the **Outline**, in **Slide 7**, drag to select the second and third bullet points—*Pike Market for breakfast and shopping*, and *Olympic Sculpture Park and a stroll along the waterfront*. Compare your screen with Figure 1.39.

FIGURE 1.39

Two bullet points selected

3 On the **HOME tab**, in the **Paragraph group**, click **Increase List Level** ⊞ one time to increase the list level of the selected bullet points.

When you type in the outline or change the list level, the changes also display in the Slide pane.

4 In the **Outline**, in **Slide 7**, click at the end of the last bullet point after the word *Tour*. Press Enter to create a new bullet point at the same list level as the previous bullet point. Type **Pike Place Market for dinner** and then compare your screen with Figure 1.40.

FIGURE 1.40

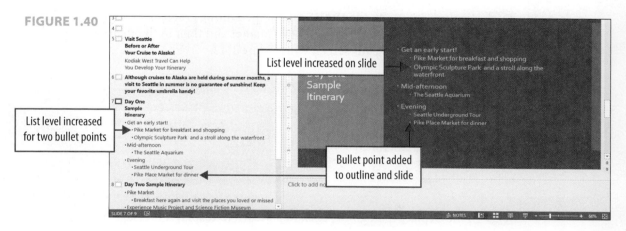

List level increased for two bullet points

List level increased on slide

Bullet point added to outline and slide

5 In the **Status bar**, click **Normal** ▣ to display the slide thumbnails, and then **Save** 🖫 the presentation.

You can type text in the Slide pane or in the Outline. Displaying the Outline enables you to view the entire flow of the presentation.

Activity 1.20 │ Deleting and Moving a Slide

1 To the right of the slide thumbnails, locate the vertical scroll bar and scroll box. If necessary, drag the scroll box down so that **Slide 9** displays in the slide thumbnails. Click **Slide 9** to display it in the Slide pane. Press Del to delete the slide from the presentation.

Your presentation contains eight slides.

2 If necessary, scroll the slide thumbnails so that **Slide 4** displays. Point to **Slide 4**, hold down the left mouse button, and then drag down to position the **Slide 4** thumbnail below the **Slide 8** thumbnail. Release the mouse button and then compare your screen with Figure 1.41.

You can easily rearrange your slides by dragging a slide thumbnail to a new location in the presentation.

 BY TOUCH   Use your finger to drag the slide you want to move to a new location in the presentation.

FIGURE 1.41

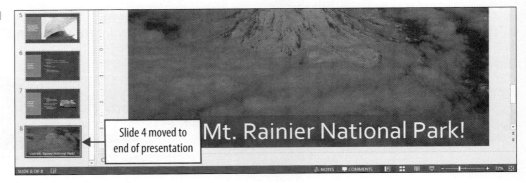

Slide 4 moved to end of presentation

Mt. Rainier National Park!

3 Save 🖫 the presentation.

Activity 1.21 | Finding and Replacing Text

The Replace command enables you to locate all occurrences of specified text and replace it with alternative text.

1 Display **Slide 1**. On the **HOME tab**, in the **Editing group**, click **Replace**. In the **Replace** dialog box, in the **Find what** box, type **Pike Market** and then in the **Replace with** box, type **Pike Place Market** Compare your screen with Figure 1.42.

FIGURE 1.42

Text typed in Replace with box

Text typed in Find what box

Seattle

2 In the **Replace** dialog box, click **Replace All** to display a message box indicating that two replacements were made.

3 In the message box, click **OK**. **Close** the **Replace** dialog box, and then click **Save** 🖫.

Objective 6   Format a Presentation

Video P1-6

Formatting refers to changing the appearance of the text, layout, and design of a slide.

Activity 1.22 | Applying a Theme Variant

Recall that a theme is a set of unified design elements that provides a look for your presentation by applying colors, fonts, and effects. Each PowerPoint theme includes several *variants*—variations on the theme style and color.

1 On the **DESIGN tab**, In the **Variants group**, notice that four variants of the current theme—*Frame*—display.

2 Point to each of the variants to view the change to **Slide 1**.

3 With **Slide 1** displayed, in the **Variants group**, point to the **third variant**, and then right-click. Compare your screen with Figure 1.43.

The shortcut menu displays options for applying the variant.

FIGURE 1.43

> **4** Click **Apply to Selected Slides** to apply the variant to **Slide 1** only.

> **5** In the **Variants group**, right-click the **blue variant**. On the shortcut menu, click **Apply to All Slides** so that the blue color is applied to all of the slides in the presentation. Compare your screen with Figure 1.44.

FIGURE 1.44

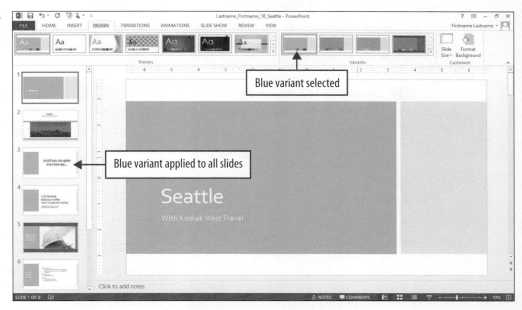

> **6** Save 🖫 your presentation.

Activity 1.23 │ Changing Fonts and Font Sizes

Recall that a font is a set of characters with the same design and shape and that fonts are measured in points. Font styles include bold, italic, and underline, and you can apply any combination of these styles to presentation text. Font styles and font color are useful to provide emphasis and are a visual cue to draw the reader's eye to important text.

> **1** Display **Slide 2**. Select all of the text in the title placeholder, point to the mini toolbar, and then click the **Font button arrow** to display the available fonts. Scroll the font list, and then click **Georgia**.

> **2** Select the first line of the title—*Seattle*. On the mini toolbar, click the **Font Size button arrow** and then click **80**.

> **3** Select the second line of the title—*Making the Most of Your First Port*. On the **HOME tab**, in the **Font group**, click the **Font Size button arrow**, and then click **36**. Click in a blank area of the slide to cancel your selection, and then compare your screen with Figure 1.45. **Save** 🖫 your presentation.

FIGURE 1.45

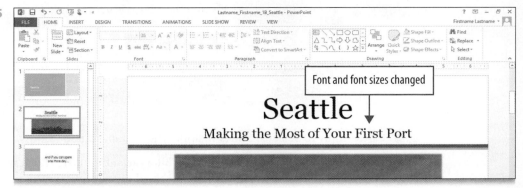

Activity 1.24 | Changing Font Styles and Font Colors

Font styles include bold, italic, and underline, and you can apply any combination of these styles to presentation text. Font styles and font color are useful to provide emphasis and are a visual cue to draw the reader's eye to important text.

1 Display **Slide 3**, and then select both lines of text. On the **HOME tab**, in the **Font group**, click the **Font Color button arrow** and then compare your screen with Figure 1.46.

The colors in the top row of the color gallery are the colors associated with the presentation theme—*Frame*. The colors in the rows below the first row are light and dark variations of the theme colors.

FIGURE 1.46

2 Point to several of the colors and notice that a ScreenTip displays the color name and Live Preview displays the selected text in the color to which you are pointing.

3 In the fifth column of colors, click the last color—**Turquoise, Accent 1, Darker 50%**—to change the font color. Notice that on the **HOME tab**, the lower part of the **Font Color** button displays the most recently applied font color—*Turquoise, Accent 1, Darker 50%*.

When you click the Font Color button instead of the Font Color button arrow, the color displayed in the lower part of the Font Color button is applied to selected text without displaying the color gallery.

4 Display **Slide 4**, and then select the title—*Visit Seattle Before or After Your Cruise to Alaska!* On the mini toolbar, click **Font Color** to apply the font color **Turquoise, Accent 1, Darker 50%** to the selection. Select the subtitle—*Kodiak West Travel Can Help You Develop Your Itinerary*—and then change the **Font Color** to **Turquoise, Accent 1, Darker 50%**. Click anywhere on the slide to cancel the selection, and then compare your screen with Figure 1.47.

FIGURE 1.47

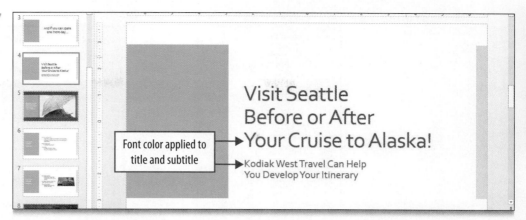

5 Display **Slide 3**, and then select the two lines of text. From the mini toolbar, apply **Bold** $\boxed{B}$ and **Italic** $\boxed{I}$, and then **Save** $\boxed{H}$ your presentation.

Activity 1.25 | Aligning Text

In PowerPoint, *text alignment* refers to the horizontal placement of text within a placeholder. You can align left, centered, right, or justified.

1 Display **Slide 5**, and then on the left side of the slide, click anywhere in the paragraph. On the **HOME tab**, in the **Paragraph group**, click **Center** $\boxed{\equiv}$ to center the text within the placeholder.

2 Display **Slide 4**, and then click anywhere in the slide title. Press Ctrl + E to use the keyboard shortcut to center the text.

3 On **Slide 4**, using one of the methods that you practiced, **Center** the subtitle. Click in a blank area of the slide. Compare your screen with Figure 1.48, and then **Save** $\boxed{H}$ the presentation.

FIGURE 1.48

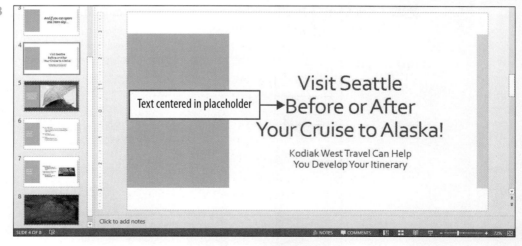

Activity 1.26 | Changing Line Spacing

1 Display **Slide 5**, and then click anywhere in the paragraph. On the **HOME tab**, in the **Paragraph group**, click **Line Spacing** $\boxed{\updownarrow\equiv\cdot}$. On the list, click **2.0** to change from single spacing to double spacing between lines of text. Compare your screen with Figure 1.49.

FIGURE 1.49

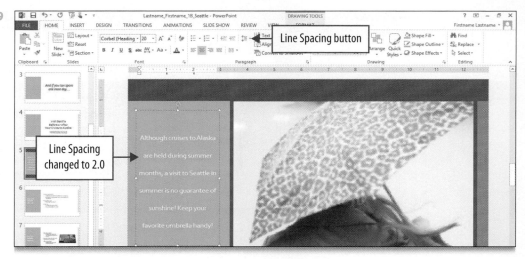

> **2** Save 🔲 your presentation.

Activity 1.27 | Changing the Slide Layout

Recall that the slide layout defines the placement of the content placeholders on a slide. PowerPoint includes predefined layouts that you can apply to your slide for the purpose of arranging slide elements. For example, a Title Slide contains two placeholder elements—the title and the subtitle. When you design your slides, consider the content that you want to include, and then choose a layout with the elements that will display the message you want to convey in the best way.

> **1** Display **Slide 1**. On the **HOME tab**, in the **Slides group**, click **Layout** to display the **Slide Layout** gallery. Notice that *Title Slide* is selected, indicating the layout of the current slide.

> **2** Click **Section Header** to change the slide layout. Compare your screen with Figure 1.50, and then **Save** 🔲 your presentation.

FIGURE 1.50

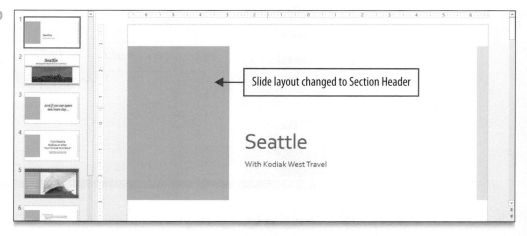

Objective 7 | Use Slide Sorter View

Video P1-7

Slide Sorter view displays thumbnails of all of the slides in a presentation. Use Slide Sorter view to rearrange and delete slides and to apply formatting to multiple slides.

Activity 1.28 | Deleting Slides in Slide Sorter View

1 In the lower right corner of the PowerPoint window, click **Slide Sorter** ⊞ to display all of the slide thumbnails. Compare your screen with Figure 1.51.

> Your slides may display larger or smaller than those shown in Figure 1.51.

ANOTHER WAY   On the VIEW tab, in the Presentation Views group, click Slide Sorter.

FIGURE 1.51

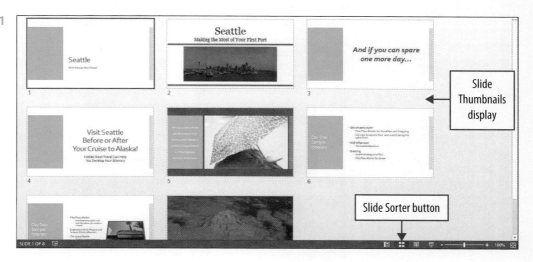

2 Click **Slide 1**, and notice that a thick outline surrounds the slide, indicating that it is selected. On your keyboard, press Delete to delete the slide. Click **Save** 🔲.

Activity 1.29 | Moving a Single Slide in Slide Sorter View

1 With the presentation displayed in Slide Sorter view, point to **Slide 2**. Hold down the left mouse button, and then drag to position the slide to the right of **Slide 6**, as shown in Figure 1.52.

FIGURE 1.52

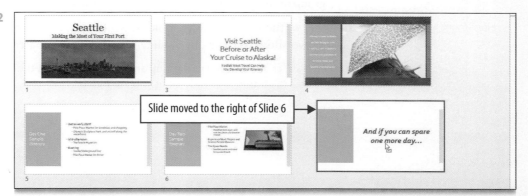

2 Release the mouse button to move the slide to the **Slide 6** position in the presentation. **Save** 🔲 your presentation.

Activity 1.30 | Selecting Contiguous and Noncontiguous Slides and Moving Multiple Slides

Contiguous slides are slides that are adjacent to each other in a presentation. *Noncontiguous slides* are slides that are not adjacent to each other in a presentation.

1 Click **Slide 2**, hold down Ctrl, and then click **Slide 4**. Notice that both slides are selected.

The noncontiguous slides—Slides 2 and 4—are outlined, indicating that both are selected. By holding down Ctrl, you can select noncontiguous slides.

2 Click **Slide 3**, so that only Slide 3 is selected. Hold down Shift, and then click **Slide 5**. Compare your screen with Figure 1.53.

The contiguous slides—Slides 3, 4, and 5—are outlined, indicating that all three slides are selected. By holding down Shift, you can create a group of contiguous selected slides.

FIGURE 1.53

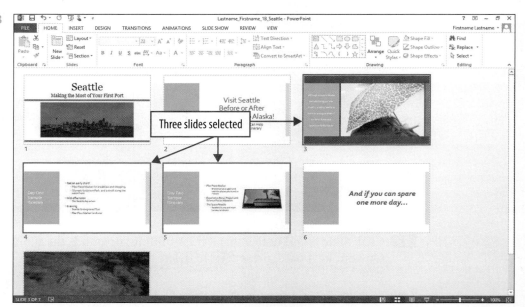

3 With Slides 3, 4, and 5 selected, hold down Ctrl, and then click **Slide 3**. Notice that only slides 4 and 5 are selected.

When a group of slides is selected, you can press Ctrl and then click a selected slide to deselect it.

4 Point to either of the selected slides, hold down the left mouse button, and then drag to position the two slides to the right of **Slide 2**, and then compare your screen with Figure 1.54.

The selected slides are dragged as a group and the number 2 in the upper left area of the selected slides indicates the number of slides that you are moving.

FIGURE 1.54

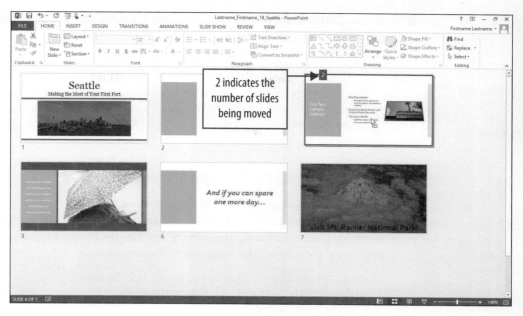

> **5** Release the mouse button to move the two slides. In the status bar, click **Normal** to return to Normal view. **Save** your presentation.

Objective 8 Apply Slide Transitions

Video P1-8

Slide transitions are the motion effects that occur in Slide Show view when you move from one slide to the next during a presentation. You can choose from a variety of transitions, and you can control the speed and method with which the slides advance.

Activity 1.31 │ Applying Slide Transitions to a Presentation

> **1** Display **Slide 1**. On the **TRANSITIONS tab**, in the **Transition to This Slide group**, click **More** to display the **Transitions** gallery. Compare your screen with Figure 1.55.

FIGURE 1.55

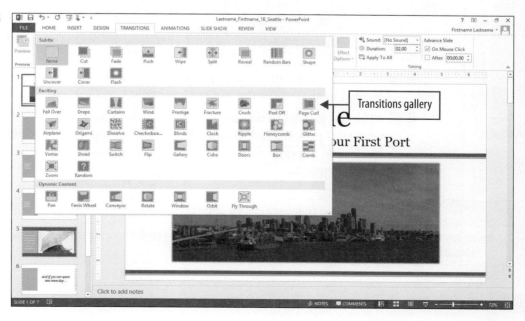

2 Under **Exciting**, click **Doors** to apply and view the transition. In the **Transition to This Slide group**, click **Effect Options** to display the directions from which the slide enters the screen. Click **Horizontal**. In the **Timing group**, click **Apply To All** to apply the *Doors, Horizontal* transition to all of the slides in the presentation. **Save** your presentation 🖫.

> The Effect Options vary depending upon the selected transition and include the direction from which the slide enters the screen or the shape in which the slide displays during the transition. In the slide thumbnails, a star displays below the slide number providing a visual cue that a transition has been applied to the slide.

Activity 1.32 | Setting Slide Transition Timing Options

1 In the **Timing group**, notice that the **Duration** box displays *01.40*, indicating that the transition lasts 1.40 seconds. Click the **Duration up spin arrow** two times so that *01.75* displays. Under **Advance Slide**, verify that the **On Mouse Click** check box is selected; select it if necessary. Compare your screen with Figure 1.56.

> When the On Mouse Click option is selected, the presenter controls when the current slide advances to the next slide by clicking the mouse button or by pressing Spacebar.

FIGURE 1.56

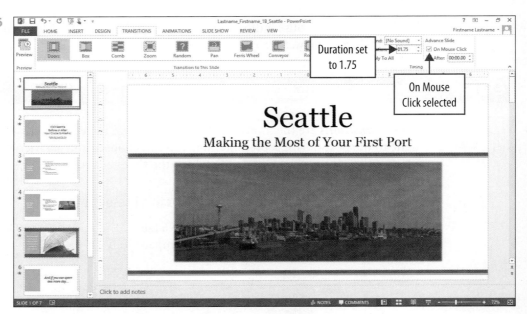

2 In the **Timing group**, click **Apply To All** so that the Duration of *1.75* seconds transition is applied to all of the slides in the presentation.

3 Click the **SLIDE SHOW tab**. In the **Start Slide Show group**, click **From Beginning**, and then view your presentation, clicking the mouse button to advance through the slides. When the black slide displays, click the mouse button one more time to display the presentation in Normal view. **Save** 🖫 your presentation.

More Knowledge   **Applying Multiple Slide Transitions**

You can apply more than one type of transition in your presentation by displaying the slides one at a time, and then clicking the transition that you want to apply instead of clicking Apply To All.

Activity 1.33 | Displaying a Presentation in Reading View

Organizations frequently conduct online meetings when participants are unable to meet in one location. The *Reading view* in PowerPoint displays a presentation in a manner similar to a slide show but the taskbar, title bar, and status bar remain available in the presentation window. This feature enables a presenter to facilitate an online conference easily by switching to another window without closing the slide show.

1 In the lower right corner of the PowerPoint window, click **Reading View** 📖. Compare your screen with Figure 1.57.

In Reading View, the status bar contains the Next and Previous buttons with which you can navigate in the presentation, and the Menu button from which you can print, copy, and edit slides.

ANOTHER WAY   On the VIEW tab, in the Presentation Views group, click Reading View.

FIGURE 1.57

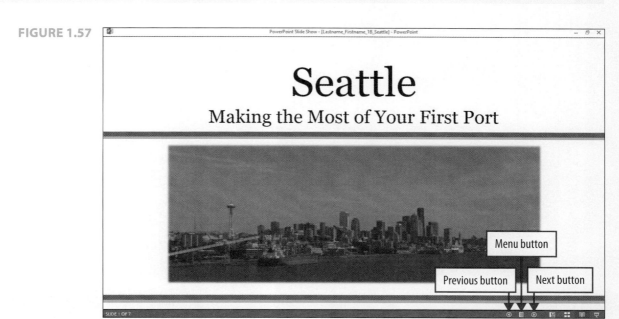

2 Press Spacebar to display **Slide 2**. Click the left mouse button to display **Slide 3**. In the status bar, click **Previous** ◀ to display **Slide 2**.

3 In the status bar, click **Menu** 📄 to display the Reading view menu, and then click **End Show** to return to Normal view.

ANOTHER WAY   Press Esc to exit Reading view and return to Normal view.

4 On the **INSERT tab**, in the **Text group**, click **Header & Footer**, and then click the **Notes and Handouts tab**. Under **Include on page**, select the **Date and time** check box, and if necessary, select **Update automatically**. Clear the **Header** check box if necessary, and then select the **Page number** and **Footer** check boxes. In the **Footer** box, using your own name, type **Lastname_Firstname_1B_Seattle** and then click **Apply to All**.

5 Display **Backstage** view, and then on the right, at the bottom of the **Properties** list, click **Show All Properties**. On the list of properties, click to the right of **Tags**, and type **Seattle** To the right of **Subject**, type your course name and section number. Under **Related People**, be sure that your name displays as the author and edit if necessary.

6 On the left, click **Save**. Submit your presentation electronically or print **Handouts, 4 Slides Horizontal**, as directed by your instructor.

7 Close [**×**] PowerPoint.

More **Knowledge** | **Present a Presentation Online**

You can use the Office Presentation Service to present to people who can watch the presentation in a web browser. You will need a Microsoft account to use this free service. To present online, on the SLIDE SHOW tab, in the Start Slide Show group, click Present Online, and then follow the instructions in the Present Online window.

END | You have completed Project 1B

GO! with Office Online (formerly Web Apps)

Objective   Create an Itinerary Presentation in PowerPoint Online

> **ALERT!**   **Working with Web-Based Applications and Services**
>
> Computer programs and services on the web receive continuous updates and improvements, so the steps to complete this web-based activity may differ from the ones shown. You can often look at the screens and the information presented to determine how to complete the activity.

Activity | Creating an Itinerary Presentation in PowerPoint Online

In this activity, you will use PowerPoint Online to create a presentation similar to the one you created in Project 1B.

1 From the desktop, start Internet Explorer. Navigate to **http://onedrive.com**, and then sign in to your Microsoft account. Open your **GO! Web Projects** folder—or create and then open this folder if necessary.

2 In the OneDrive menu bar, click **Upload**. Navigate to your student data files, click **p01_1B_Web**, and then click **Open**.

3 Point to the uploaded file **p01_1B_Web**, and then right-click. On the shortcut menu, click **Rename**. Using your own last name and first name, type **Lastname_Firstname_PPT_1B_Web** and then press Enter to rename the file.

4 Click the file that you just renamed, and then click **EDIT PRESENTATION**. On the list, click **Edit in PowerPoint Online**.

5 On the **DESIGN tab**, in the **Variants group**, click the variant that includes a light blue background and notice that the variant is applied to all of the slides in the presentation.

6 On **Slide 1**, double-click in the title, and then drag to select the two lines of text. On the **HOME tab**, in the **Font group**, click the **Font button arrow**, and then click **Georgia**.

7 Select the text *Making the Most of Your First Port*. On the **HOME tab**, in the **Font group**, click the **Font Size button arrow**, and then click **28**. Click in a blank area of the slide, and then compare your screen with Figure A.

8 Click **Slide 2**. On the **HOME tab**, in the **Delete group**, Click **Delete** to remove the slide from the presentation.

9 With **Slide 2**—*Seattle Weather*—displayed, press Delete to remove the slide from your presentation. Notice that the Status bar indicates that the presentation contains 7 slides.

10 Display **Slide 3**, and then double-click in the paragraph on the left side of the slide. Drag to select the text, and then on the **HOME tab**, in the **Font group**, click the **Font Color button arrow**. In the first column, click

FIGURE A

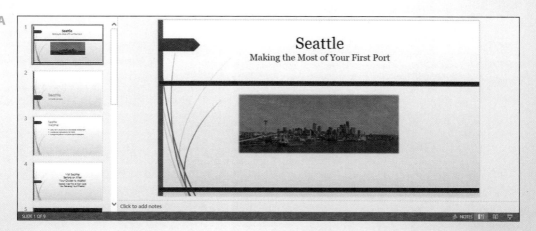

(GO! with Office Online (formerly Web Apps) continues on the next page)

the first color—**White, Background 1**. With the paragraph still selected, in the **Font group**, click **Bold** $\boxed{B}$ and **Italic** $\boxed{I}$. In the **Paragraph group**, click **Center** $\boxed{\equiv}$.

11 Click anywhere in a blank area of the slide to cancel the selection and view your formatting changes. Compare your screen with Figure B.

12 In the slide thumbnails, point to **Slide 4**, hold down the left mouse button, and then drag up slightly. Notice that a black bar displays above Slide 4. Continue to drag up until the black bar displays above **Slide 3**. Release the mouse button to move the slide.

13 Using the technique that you just practiced, move **Slide 5** to position it above **Slide 4**.

14 Display **Slide 6**. Click anywhere in the slide text, and then drag to select all three lines of text. On the **HOME tab**, in the **Paragraph group**, click **Center** $\boxed{\equiv}$. Click anywhere on the slide to cancel the selection.

15 Display **Slide 1**. On the **TRANSITIONS tab**, in the **Transition to This Slide group**, click **Push**. Click **Effect Options**, and then click **From Left**. In the **Transitions group**, click **Apply To All**.

16 Click the **VIEW tab**, and then in the **Presentation Views group**, click **Slide Show**. If a security warning displays at the bottom of your screen, click Allow once. Press $\boxed{\text{Spacebar}}$ or click the left mouse button to advance through the slides in the presentation. When the black slide displays, click one more time to return to the presentation.

17 Submit your file as instructed by your instructor. Sign out of your OneDrive and close Internet Explorer.

FIGURE B

Andrew Rodriguez / Fotolia; FotolEdhar/ Fotolia; apops/ Fotolia; Yuri Arcurs/ Fotolia

In every job, you must work and communicate with other people. A group of workers tasked with working together to solve a problem, make a decision, or create a work product is referred to as a *team*. For a team to succeed, the team members must be able to communicate with one another easily.

If all the team members work at the same location and work the same hours, communication is easy. You schedule face-to-face meetings and exchange documents and information among yourselves. But that is a rare arrangement in today's organizations. Rather, it is more likely that the members of your team work in different locations—even different countries—and work different hours or travel extensively away from the headquarters location. Also, for specific projects, teams are frequently organized across different departments of an organization or even across different organizations entirely. Then when the project is complete, the team disbands.

Collaboration is when you work together with others as a team in an intellectual endeavor to complete a shared task or achieve a shared goal; for example, when you and one or more of your classmates work together on a class project. Collaboration involves giving feedback to and receiving feedback from others on the team, and then revising the strategies to achieve the goal or produce the work product based on the feedback.

Microsoft Office 365 is a set of secure online services that enables people in an organization to communicate and collaborate by using any Internet-connected device—a computer, a tablet, or a mobile phone. Because Office 365 offers access from anywhere to email, web conferencing, documents, and calendars, everyone on a team can work together easily. Office 365 is intended for use by multiple users in an organization.

Activity | Using the Exchange Online Outlook Meeting Tool to Collaborate

This group project relates to the **Bell Orchid Hotels**. If your instructor assigns this project to your class, you can expect to use the **Outlook Meeting tool** in **Office 365 Exchange Online** to collaborate on the following tasks for this chapter:

- If you are in the **Accounting Group**, you and your teammates will meet virtually to create the text and initial formatting for a Loan Presentation to be presented by the Director to the Loan Officers of San Diego's SoCal Bank.

- If you are in the **Engineering Group**, you and your teammates will meet virtually to create the text and initial formatting for a Safety Presentation to be presented to all hotel department heads.

- If you are in the **Food and Beverage Group**, you and your teammates will meet virtually to create the text and initial formatting for a New Menu Item Presentation to be presented by the Director of the F&B Department to restaurant, banquet, and room service managers.

- If you are in the **Human Resources Group**, you and your teammates will meet virtually to create the text and initial formatting for a New Employees Orientation presentation to be presented to new staff hired by the hotel.

- If you are in the **Operations Group**, you and your teammates will meet virtually to create the text and initial formatting for a Front Desk Clerk Training Presentation as part of the hotel's on-the-job training program for Front Desk staff.

- If you are in the **Sales and Marketing Group**, you and your teammates will meet virtually to create the text and initial formatting for a Marketing Plan Presentation to be presented to all department heads and the Executive Office.

FIGURE A

END OF CHAPTER

SUMMARY

When communicating your ideas, PowerPoint is a versatile business tool that will help you create presentations that make a lasting impression. Additionally, you can share slides you create on your OneDrive.

Use a presentation theme to establish a unified presentation design. You can change the color of the presentation theme by applying one of the predefined variants that are supplied with each theme.

Presentations are often organized in a manner similar to how outline levels are organized. List levels represent outline levels and are identified by the bullet style, indentation, and text size.

Slide layout defines the placement of content placeholders on a slide. Each presentation theme includes predefined layouts that you can apply to slides for the purpose of arranging slide elements.

GO! LEARN IT ONLINE

Review the concepts and key terms in this chapter by completing these online challenges, which you can find at **www.pearsonhighered.com/go**.

Matching and Multiple Choice: Answer matching and multiple choice questions to test what you learned in this chapter. MyITLab®

Crossword Puzzle: Spell out the words that match the numbered clues, and put them in the puzzle squares.

Flipboard: Flip through the definitions of the key terms in this chapter and match them with the correct term.

GO! FOR JOB SUCCESS

Video: Managing Priorities and Workspace

Your instructor may assign this video to your class, and then ask you to think about, or discuss with your classmates, these questions:

FotolEdhar / Fotolia

What kind of scheduling tool do you use? Is it on your computer, your cell phone, or other electronic device, or do you write in a notebook or physical calendar? Which kind of scheduling tool will be most effective for you and why?

Name one lifestyle change that you can make today that will help you create more time for your work projects.

What is the *one touch rule* and how do you think it will help you be more efficient?

END OF CHAPTER

REVIEW AND ASSESSMENT GUIDE FOR POWERPOINT CHAPTER 1

Your instructor may assign one or more of these projects to help you review the chapter and assess your mastery and understanding of the chapter.

	Review and Assessment Guide for PowerPoint Chapter 1		
Project	**Apply Skills from These Chapter Objectives**	**Project Type**	**Project Location**
1C	Objectives 1-4 from Project 1A	**1C Skills Review** A guided review of the skills from Project 1A.	On the following pages
1D	Objectives 5-8 from Project 1B	**1D Skills Review** A guided review of the skills from Project 1B.	On the following pages
1E	Objectives 1-4 from Project 1A	**1E Mastery (Grader Project)** A demonstration of your mastery of the skills in Project 1A with extensive decision making.	In MyITlab and on the following pages
1F	Objectives 5-8 from Project 1B	**1F Mastery (Grader Project)** A demonstration of your mastery of the skills in Project 1B with extensive decision making.	In MyITlab and on the following pages
1G	Objectives 1-8 from Projects 1A and lB	**1G Mastery (Grader Project)** A demonstration of your mastery of the skills in Projects 1A and 1B with extensive decision making.	In MyITlab and on the following pages
1H	Combination of Objectives from Projects 1A and 1B	**1H GO! Fix It** A demonstration of your mastery of the skills in Projects 1A and 1B by creating a correct result from a document that contains errors you must find.	Online
1I	Combination of Objectives from Projects 1A and 1B	**1I GO! Make It** A demonstration of your mastery of the skills in Projects 1A and 1B by creating a result from a supplied picture.	Online
1J	Combination of Objectives from Projects 1A and 1B	**1J GO! Solve It** A demonstration of your mastery of the skills in Projects 1A and 1B, your decision-making skills, and your critical thinking skills. A task-specific rubric helps you self-assess your result.	Online
1K	Combination of Objectives from Projects 1A and 1B	**1K GO! Solve It** A demonstration of your mastery of the skills in Projects 1A and 1B, your decision-making skills, and your critical thinking skills. A task-specific rubric helps you self-assess your result.	On the following pages
1L	Combination of Objectives from Projects 1A and 1B	**1L GO! Think** A demonstration of your understanding of the Chapter concepts applied in a manner that you would outside of college. An analytic rubric helps you and your instructor grade the quality of your work by comparing it to the work an expert in the discipline would create.	On the following pages
1M	Combination of Objectives from Projects 1A and 1B	**1M GO! Think** A demonstration of your understanding of the Chapter concepts applied in a manner that you would outside of college. An analytic rubric helps you and your instructor grade the quality of your work by comparing it to the work an expert in the discipline would create.	Online
1N	Combination of Objectives from Projects 1A and 1B	**1N You and GO!** A demonstration of your understanding of the Chapter concepts applied in a manner that you would in a personal situation. An analytic rubric helps you and your instructor grade the quality of your work.	Online
1O	Combination of Objectives from Projects 1A and 1B	**1O Cumulative Group Project for PowerPoint Chapter 1** A demonstration of your understanding of concepts and your ability to work collaboratively in a group role-playing assessment, requiring both collaboration and self-management.	Online

GLOSSARY

GLOSSARY OF CHAPTER KEY TERMS

Artistic effects Formats applied to images that make pictures resemble sketches or paintings.

Aspect ratio The ratio of the width of a display to the height of the display.

Black slide A slide that displays after the last slide in a presentation indicating that the presentation is over.

Collaboration The action of working with others as a team in an intellectual endeavor to complete a shared task or achieve a shared goal.

Contiguous slides Slides that are adjacent to each other in a presentation.

Editing The process of modifying a presentation by adding and deleting slides or by changing the contents of individual slides.

Footer Text that displays at the bottom of every slide or that prints at the bottom of a sheet of slide handouts or notes pages.

Formatting The process of changing the appearance of the text, layout, and design of a slide.

Header Text that prints at the top of each sheet of slide handouts or notes pages.

Layout The arrangement of elements, such as title and subtitle text, lists, pictures, tables, charts, shapes, and movies, on a slide.

List level An outline level in a presentation represented by a bullet symbol and identified in a slide by the indentation and the size of the text.

Microsoft Office 365 A set of secure online services that enable people in an organization to communicate and collaborate by using any Internet-connected device—a computer, a tablet, or a mobile phone.

Noncontiguous slides Slides that are not adjacent to each other in a presentation.

Normal view The primary editing view in PowerPoint where you write and design your presentations.

Notes page A printout that contains the slide image on the top half of the page and notes that you have created on the Notes pane in the lower half of the page.

Notes pane An area of the Normal view window that displays below the Slide pane with space to type notes regarding the active slide.

Outline View A PowerPoint view that displays the presentation outline to the left of the Slide pane.

Placeholder A box on a slide with dotted or dashed borders that holds title and body text or other content such as charts, tables, and pictures.

Reading view A view in PowerPoint that displays a presentation in a manner similar to a slide show but in which the taskbar, title bar, and status bar remain available in the presentation window.

Rotation handle A circular arrow that provides a way to rotate a selected image.

Section header A type of slide layout that changes the look and flow of a presentation by providing text placeholders that do not contain bullet points.

Sizing handles Small squares surrounding a picture that indicate that the picture is selected.

Slide A presentation page that can contain text, pictures, tables, charts, and other multimedia or graphic objects.

Slide handout Printed images of slides on a sheet of paper.

Slide pane A PowerPoint screen element that displays a large image of the active slide.

Slide Sorter view A presentation view that displays thumbnails of all of the slides in a presentation.

Slide transitions Motion effects that occur in Slide Show view when you move from one slide to the next during a presentation.

Split button A type of button in which clicking the main part of the button performs a command and clicking the arrow opens a menu, list, or gallery.

Style A collection of formatting options that you can apply to a picture, text, or an object.

Team A group of workers tasked with working together to solve a problem, make a decision, or create a work product.

Text alignment The horizontal placement of text within a placeholder.

Theme A set of unified design elements that provides a look for your presentation by applying colors, fonts, and effects.

Thumbnails Miniature images of presentation slides.

Title slide A slide layout—most commonly the first slide in a presentation—that provides an introduction to the presentation topic.

Variant A variation on the presentation theme style and color.

CHAPTER REVIEW

Skills Review | Project 1C Glaciers

Build from
Scratch

Apply 1A skills from these Objectives:

1 Create a New Presentation

2 Edit a Presentation in Normal View

3 Add Pictures to a Presentation

4 Print and View a Presentation

In the following Skills Review, you will create a new presentation by inserting content and pictures, adding notes and footers, and applying a presentation theme. Your completed presentation will look similar to Figure 1.58.

PROJECT FILES

For Project 1C, you will need the following files:

New blank PowerPoint presentation
p01C_Glacier_Bay
p01C_Ice
p01C_Ship

You will save your presentation as:

Lastname_Firstname_1C_Glaciers

PROJECT RESULTS

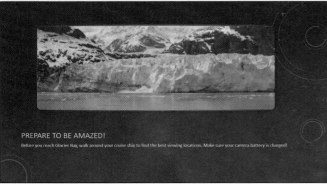

FIGURE 1.58

(Project 1C Glaciers continues on the next page)

CHAPTER REVIEW

1 Start PowerPoint. On the right, click **Celestial**, and then click **Create**. In the **Slide pane**, click in the text *Click to add title*. Type **Glacier Bay** and then click in the subtitle placeholder. Type **Part One in a Series of Alaskan Passage Adventures** Notice that the font uses all uppercase letters.

   a. On the **Quick Access Toolbar**, click **Save** 🖫. Under **Save As**, click **Computer**, and then click **Browse**. Navigate to your **PowerPoint Chapter 1** folder. In the **File name** box, using your own name, replace the existing text with **Lastname_Firstname_1C_Glaciers** and then click **Save**.

   b. On the **HOME tab**, in the **Slides group**, click the **New Slide arrow**, and then in the gallery, click **Two Content**. Click the text *Click to add title*, and then type **About the Park**

2 On the left side of the slide, click in the content placeholder. Type **Located in the Southeast Alaskan Wilderness** and then press Enter. Press Tab. Type **3.3 million acres** and then press Enter. Type **A national park and preserve** and then press Enter

   a. On the **HOME tab**, in the **Paragraph group**, click **Decrease List Level**. Type **Visitor season** and then press Enter. On the **HOME tab**, in the **Paragraph group**, click **Increase List Level**. Type **May to September**

   b. On the **HOME tab**, in the **Slides group**, click the **New Slide arrow**, and then in the gallery, click **Panoramic Picture with Caption**. In the lower portion of the slide, click the text *Click to add title*, and then type **Prepare to be Amazed!**

   c. Click in the text placeholder. Type **Before you reach Glacier Bay, walk around your cruise ship to find the best viewing locations. Make sure your camera battery is charged!**

   d. On the **HOME tab**, in the **Slides group**, click the **New Slide arrow**, and then in the gallery, click **Content with Caption**. In the title placeholder, type **Learn More!**

   e. Click in the text placeholder, and then type **A national park ranger will board your ship during your visit to Glacier Bay. Check your ship's itinerary for presentation information and locations.**

3 With **Slide 4** displayed, in the **Status bar**, click **NOTES**. Click in the **Notes pane**, and then type **Your cruise ship will spend between 6 and 8 hours in Glacier Bay.**

   a. On the left side of the PowerPoint window, in the slide thumbnails, click **Slide 1**. Click in the subtitle placeholder after the *n* in *Alaskan*. Press Spacebar, and then type **Inside**

   b. In the slide thumbnails, click **Slide 2**, and then click at the end of the last bullet point after the word *September*. Press Enter, and then type **Be prepared for rain**

4 With **Slide 2** displayed, in the placeholder on the right side of the slide, click **Pictures**. Navigate to your student data files, and then click **p01C_Glacier_Bay**. Click **Insert**.

   a. With the picture selected, on the **FORMAT tab**, in the **Picture Styles group**, click **More** to display the **Picture Styles** gallery. In the second row, click the third style—**Beveled Oval, Black**.

   b. Display **Slide 3**. In the Picture placeholder, click **Pictures**. Navigate to your student data files, and then click **p01C_Ice**. Click **Insert**.

   c. Display **Slide 4**. In the content placeholder on the right side of the slide, click **Pictures**. Navigate to your student data files, and then insert **p01C_Ship**. On the **FORMAT tab**, in the **Picture Styles group**, click **More** to display the **Picture Styles** gallery. In the third row, click the sixth style—**Soft Edge Oval**.

   d. With the picture still selected, on the **FORMAT tab**, in the **Adjust group**, click **Artistic Effects** to display the gallery. In the fourth row, click the third effect—**Crisscross Etching**.

5 On the ribbon, click the **SLIDE SHOW tab**. In the **Start Slide Show group**, click **From Beginning**.

   a. Click the left mouse button or press Spacebar to advance to the second slide. Continue to click or press Spacebar until the last slide displays, and then click or press Spacebar one more time to display a black slide.

   b. With the black slide displayed, click the left mouse button or press Spacebar to exit the slide show and return to the presentation.

(Project 1C Glaciers continues on the next page)

CHAPTER REVIEW

6 Click the **INSERT tab**, and then in the **Text group**, click **Header & Footer** to display the **Header and Footer** dialog box.

a. In the **Header and Footer** dialog box, click the **Notes and Handouts tab**. Under **Include on page**, select the **Date and time** check box. If necessary, click the Update automatically option button so that the current date prints on the notes and handouts.

b. If necessary, clear the Header check box to omit this element. Select the **Page number** and **Footer** check boxes. In the **Footer** box, using your own name, type **Lastname_Firstname_1C_Glaciers** and then click **Apply to All**.

c. In the upper left corner of your screen, click the **FILE** tab to display **Backstage** view. On the right, at the bottom of the **Properties list**, click **Show All Properties**.

d. On the list of Properties, click to the right of **Tags** to display an empty box, and then type **Glacier Bay** Click to the right of **Subject** to display an empty box, and then type your course name and section number. Under **Related People**, be sure that your name displays as the author; edit if necessary.

e. **Save** your presentation. Submit your presentation electronically or print **Handouts, 4 Slides Horizontal** as directed by your instructor. **Close** PowerPoint.

END | You have completed Project 1C

CHAPTER REVIEW

Apply 1B skills from these Objectives:

5 Edit an Existing Presentation

6 Format a Presentation

7 Use Slide Sorter View

8 Apply Slide Transitions

Skills Review Project 1D Photography

In the following Skills Review, you will edit an existing presentation by inserting slides from another presentation, applying font and slide formatting, and applying slide transitions. Your completed presentation will look similar to Figure 1.59.

PROJECT FILES

For Project 1D, you will need the following files:

p01D_Photography

p01D_Photography_Slides

You will save your presentation as:

Lastname_Firstname_1D_Photography

PROJECT RESULTS

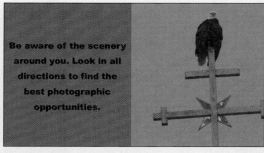

FIGURE 1.59

(Project 1D Photography continues on the next page)

CHAPTER REVIEW

Skills Review Project 1D Photography (continued)

1 Start PowerPoint. On the left, under the list of recent presentations, click **Open Other Presentations**. Under **Open**, click **Computer** and then click **Browse**. Navigate to your student data files, and then click **p01D_Photography**. Click **Open**. On the **FILE tab**, click **Save As**, navigate to your **PowerPoint Chapter 1** folder, and then using your own name, save the file as **Lastname_Firstname_1D_Photography**

a. On the **DESIGN tab**, in the **Customize group**, click **Slide Size**, and then click **Widescreen (16:9)**.

b. With **Slide 1** displayed, on the **HOME tab**, in the **Slides group**, click the **New Slide arrow**, and then click **Reuse Slides**. In the **Reuse Slides** pane, click **Browse**, and then click **Browse File**. In the **Browse** dialog box, navigate to your student data files, and then double-click **p01D_Photography_Slides** to display the slides from this presentation in the Reuse Slides pane.

c. At the bottom of the **Reuse Slides** pane, be sure that the **Keep source formatting** check box is *cleared*. In the **Reuse Slides** pane, click the first slide to insert the slide after Slide 1.

d. At the left of your screen, in the slide thumbnails, click **Slide 6** to display it in the **Slide pane**. In the **Reuse Slides** pane, click the second slide to insert it after Slide 6. **Close** the Reuse Slides pane.

2 Display **Slide 1**. On the **VIEW tab**, in the **Presentation Views group**, click **Outline View**.

a. In the **Outline**, in **Slide 7**, drag to select the second and third bullet points—beginning with *Never approach* and ending with *animal's home*.

b. On the **HOME tab**, in the **Paragraph group**, click **Decrease List Level** one time.

c. In the **Outline**, in the same slide, click at the end of the first bullet point after the word *sense*. Press [Spacebar], and then type **when photographing wildlife**

d. In the **Status bar**, click **Normal** to display the slide thumbnails.

3 Display **Slide 8**, and then press [Delete] to delete the slide from the presentation.

a. Display **Slide 1**. On the **HOME tab**, in the **Editing group**, click **Replace**. In the **Replace** dialog box, in the **Find what** box, type **home** and then in the **Replace with** box, type **habitat**

b. In the **Replace** dialog box, click **Replace All** to display a message box indicating that one replacement was made. In the message box, click **OK**. **Close** the **Replace** dialog box.

c. On the **DESIGN tab**, in the **Variants group**, right-click the green variant. On the shortcut menu, click **Apply to All Slides** so that the green color is applied to all of the slides in the presentation.

4 Display **Slide 5**. Select all of the text in the placeholder. On the **HOME tab**, in the **Font group**, click the **Font button arrow**, scroll the font list, and then click **Arial Black**. Click the **Font Size button arrow**, and then click **32**. In the **Paragraph group**, click **Line Spacing**, and then click **1.5**.

a. Display **Slide 2**. On the **HOME tab**, in the **Slides group**, click **Layout** to display the **Slide Layout** gallery. Click **Title Slide** to change the slide layout.

b. On **Slide 2**, select the title—*Alaskan Wildlife*. On the **HOME tab**, in the **Font group**, click the **Font Color button arrow**. In the fifth column, click the first color—**Dark Teal, Accent 1**.

c. Display **Slide 3**, and then select the title—*Lights, Camera, Action*. On the mini toolbar, click **Font Color** to apply the font color **Dark Teal, Accent 1**.

d. Display **Slide 4**, and then, click anywhere in the text. On the **HOME tab**, in the **Paragraph group**, click **Center** to center the text within the placeholder.

e. Display **Slide 6**, and then select the subtitle. From the mini toolbar, apply **Bold** and **Italic**.

f. In the slide thumbnails, point to **Slide 7**, hold down the left mouse button, and then drag up to position the slide between **Slides 3** and **4**.

5 In the lower right corner of the PowerPoint window, click **Slide Sorter** to display all of the slide thumbnails. Click **Slide 1**, so that it is selected. Press [Delete] to delete the slide.

a. Click **Slide 4**, and then hold down [Ctrl] and click **Slide 5**. With both slides selected, point to either of the selected slides, hold down the left mouse button, and then drag to position the two slides to the right of **Slide 6**. Release the mouse button to move the two slides. In the status bar, click **Normal** to return to Normal view.

(Project 1D Photography continues on the next page)

CHAPTER REVIEW

b. Display **Slide 1**. On the **TRANSITIONS tab**, in the **Transition to This Slide group**, click **More** to display the **Transitions** gallery.

c. Under **Exciting**, click **Gallery** to apply and view the transition. In the **Transition to This Slide group**, click **Effect Options**, and then click **From Left**. In the **Timing group**, click **Apply To All** to apply the *Gallery, From Left* transition to all of the slides in the presentation.

d. In the **Timing group**, click the **Duration up spin arrow** so that *01.75* displays. Under **Advance Slide**, verify that the **On Mouse Click** check box is selected; select it if necessary. In the **Timing group**, click **Apply To All**.

e. Click the **SLIDE SHOW tab**. In the **Start Slide Show group**, click **From Beginning**, and then view your presentation, clicking the mouse button to advance through the slides. When the black slide displays, click the mouse button one more time to display the presentation in Normal view.

6 Click the **INSERT tab**, and then in the **Text group**, click **Header & Footer** to display the **Header and Footer** dialog box.

a. In the **Header and Footer** dialog box, click the **Notes and Handouts tab**. Under **Include on page**, select the **Date and time** check box. If necessary, click the Update automatically option button so that the current date prints on the notes and handouts.

b. If necessary, clear the Header check box to omit this element. Select the **Page number** and **Footer** check boxes. In the **Footer** box, type **Lastname_Firstname_1D_Photography** and then click **Apply to All**.

c. In the upper left corner of your screen, click the **FILE** tab to display **Backstage** view. On the right, at the bottom of the **Properties list**, click **Show All Properties**.

d. On the list of Properties, click to the right of **Tags** to display an empty box, and then type **photography** Click to the right of **Subject** to display an empty box, and then type your course name and section number. Under **Related People**, be sure that your name displays as the author; edit if necessary.

e. **Save** your presentation. Submit your presentation electronically or print **Handouts, 6 Slides Horizontal** as directed by your instructor. **Close** PowerPoint.

END | You have completed Project 1D

CONTENT-BASED ASSESSMENTS

Mastering PowerPoint | Project 1E Juneau

In the following Mastering PowerPoint project, you will create a new presentation that Kodiak West Travel will use in their promotional materials to describe activities in the city of Juneau. Your completed presentation will look similar to Figure 1.60.

PROJECT FILES

For Project 1E, you will need the following files:

New blank PowerPoint presentation
p01E_Aerial_View
p01E_Whale
p01E_Falls

You will save your presentation as:

Lastname_Firstname_1E_Juneau

PROJECT RESULTS

FIGURE 1.60

(Project 1E Juneau continues on the next page)

CONTENT-BASED ASSESSMENTS

1 Start PowerPoint and create a presentation using the **Integral** theme. Use the first color variation. As the title of this presentation type **Juneau Highlights** and as the subtitle type **Kodiak West Travel** Save the presentation in your **PowerPoint Chapter 1** folder as **Lastname_Firstname_1E_Juneau**

2 Insert a **New Slide** using the **Content with Caption** layout. In the title placeholder, type **The View from Above** In the content placeholder on the right side of the slide, from your student data files, insert the picture **p01E_Aerial_View**. Format the picture with the **Bevel Rectangle** picture style and the **Paint Brush** artistic effect.

3 In the text placeholder on the left, type **View a glacial ice field from above by plane or helicopter. If you are more adventurous, try glacier trekking in Juneau where you can land on a glacier and climb an ice wall.**

4 Insert a **New Slide** using the **Two Content** layout. In the title placeholder, type **On Land and Sea** In the content placeholder on the left, type the following text, increasing and decreasing the list level as shown below. In this presentation theme, the first level bullet points do not include a bullet symbol.

> **On the water**
>> **Whale watching**
>> **Kayaking**
> **Mount Roberts tramway**
>> **Spectacular views of Juneau**
>> **Recreational hiking trails**

5 In the content placeholder on the right, from your student data files, insert the picture **p01D_Whale**. Apply the **Rotated, White** picture style.

6 Insert a new slide with the **Picture with Caption** layout. In the title placeholder, type **Mendenhall Glacier** and then in the picture placeholder, from your student data files, insert the picture **p01E_Falls**.

7 In the text placeholder, type **Walk to Mendenhall Glacier from the Visitor Center to get a close-up view of Nugget Falls.**

8 In the **Notes pane**, type **Mendenhall Glacier is the most famous glacier in Juneau and in some years is visited by over 400,000 people.**

9 Insert a **Header & Footer** on the **Notes and Handouts**. Include the **Date and time** updated automatically, the **Page number**, and a **Footer**—using your own name—with the text **Lastname_Firstname_1E_Juneau** and apply to all the slides.

10 Display the **Document Properties**. As the **Tags** type **Juneau** As the **Subject** type your course and section number. Be sure your name is indicated as the author.

11 Save your presentation, and then view the slide show from the beginning. Submit your presentation electronically or print **Handouts, 4 Slides Horizontal** as directed by your instructor. **Close** PowerPoint.

END | You have completed Project 1E

CONTENT-BASED ASSESSMENTS

Mastering PowerPoint   Project 1F Refuge

Apply 1B skills from these Objectives:

5 Edit an Existing Presentation

6 Format a Presentation

7 Use Slide Sorter View

8 Apply Slide Transitions

In the following Mastering PowerPoint project, you will edit a presentation regarding a wildlife refuge where Kodiak West Travel conducts tours. Your completed presentation will look similar to Figure 1.61.

PROJECT FILES

For Project 1F, you will need the following files:

p01F_Refuge
p01F_Excursions

You will save your presentation as:

Lastname_Firstname_1F_Refuge

PROJECT RESULTS

FIGURE 1.61

(Project 1F Refuge continues on the next page)

CONTENT-BASED ASSESSMENTS

1 Start PowerPoint, and then from your student data files, open the file **p01F_Refuge**. In your **PowerPoint Chapter 1** folder, **Save** the file as **Lastname_Firstname_1F_Refuge**

2 Change the **Slide Size** to **Widescreen (16:9),** and then change the **Variant** for all the slides to the option with the orange bar on the right side.

3 Display the presentation **Outline**. In the **Outline**, on **Slide 2**, increase the list level of the third and the fifth bullet points. Click at the end of the last bullet point after the word *roads*, and then type **or facilities**

4 Return the presentation to **Normal view**, and then display **Slide 4**. Display the **Reuse Slides** pane. Browse to your student data files, and then open **p01F_Excursions**. Make sure the **Keep source formatting** check box is *cleared*. With **Slide 4** in your presentation displayed, insert the last two slides from the **Reuse Slides** pane, and then close the pane.

5 Display **Slide 1**, and then change the layout to **Title Slide**. Select the subtitle—*Experience Alaska with Kodiak West Travel*. Change the **Font** to **Arial**, and the **Font Size** to **28**. Change the **Font Color** to **Black, Background 1**. **Center** the title and the subtitle.

6 Display **Slide 5**, and then select the paragraph in the content placeholder. Apply **Bold** and **Italic**, and then change the **Font Size** to **18**. **Center** the text, and then change the **Line Spacing** to **1.5**. **Center** the slide title.

7 In **Slide Sorter** view, delete **Slide 3**. Move **Slide 5** to position it after **Slide 2**. Move **Slide 4** to the end of the presentation.

8 In **Normal** view, display **Slide 1**. Apply the **Split** transition and change the **Effect Options** to **Horizontal Out**. Change the **Duration** to **1.75**, and the apply the transition to all of the slides in the presentation. View the slide show from the beginning.

9 Insert a **Header & Footer** on the **Notes and Handouts**. Include the **Date and time** updated automatically, the **Page number**, and a **Footer** with the text **Lastname_Firstname_1F_Refuge**

10 Display the **Document Properties**. As the **Tags** type **refuge, tours** As the **Subject** type your course and section number. Be sure your name is indicated as the author.

11 **Save** your presentation, and then submit your presentation electronically or print **Handouts, 6 Slides Horizontal** as directed by your instructor. **Close** PowerPoint.

END | You have completed Project 1F

Mastering PowerPoint Project 1G Northern Lights

In the following Mastering PowerPoint project, you will edit an existing presentation that describes the Northern Lights and ideal viewing areas. Your completed presentation will look similar to Figure 1.62.

PROJECT FILES

For Project 1G, you will need the following files:

p01G_Northern_Lights
p01G_Lights
p01G_Slides

You will save your presentation as:

Lastname_Firstname_1G_Northern_Lights

PROJECT RESULTS

Apply 1A and 1B skills from these Objectives:

1 Create a New Presentation
2 Edit a Presentation in Normal View
3 Add Pictures to a Presentation
4 Print and View a Presentation
5 Edit an Existing Presentation
6 Format a Presentation
7 Use Slide Sorter View
8 Apply Slide Transitions

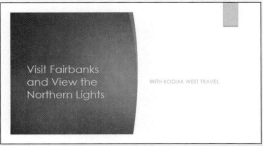

FIGURE 1.62

(Project 1G Northern Lights continues on the next page)

CONTENT-BASED ASSESSMENTS

1 Start PowerPoint, and then from your student data files, open the file **p01G_Northern_Lights**. In your **PowerPoint Chapter 1** folder, **Save** the file as **Lastname_Firstname_1G_Northern_Lights**

2 Replace all occurrences of the text **North** with **Northern** and then change the layout of **Slide 1** to **Title Slide**. Apply the **Ion Boardroom** theme, and then change the **Variant** to the blue variant option. Change the **Slide Size** to **Widescreen (16:9)**.

3 Display **Slide 2**, open the **Reuse Slides** pane, and then from your student data files browse for and open the presentation **p01G_Slides**. If necessary, clear the Keep source formatting check box, and then insert the last two slides from the **p01G_Slides** file.

4 Display **Slide 2**. In either the slide pane or in the slide outline, click at the end of the first bullet point after the word *time*. Add the words **for viewing** and then in the same slide, increase the list level of the second and third bullet points.

5 With **Slide 2** still displayed, select the title and change the **Font Size** to **32**. In the **Notes pane**, type the following notes: **The lights reach their peak in September and March.**

6 Display **Slide 3**. Select the paragraph of text, and then change the **Font Color** to **Green, Accent 6, Lighter 60%**—in the last column, the third color. Change the **Font Size** to **18**, and then apply **Bold**. Change the **Line Spacing** to **1.5**, and then **Center** the paragraph and the slide title.

7 With **Slide 3** still displayed, format the picture with the **Soft Edge Rectangle** picture style and the **Marker** artistic effect.

8 Display **Slide 4**. In the content placeholder on the right, from your student data files, insert the picture **p01G_Lights**. Apply the **Reflected Rounded Rectangle** picture style.

9 Move **Slide 3** between **Slides 1** and **2**, and then display **Slide 4**. Insert a **New Slide** with the **Section Header** layout. In the title placeholder type **Visit Fairbanks and View the Northern Lights!** In the text placeholder type **With Kodiak West Travel**

10 Apply the **Uncover** transition and change the **Effect Options** to **From Top**. Change the **Timing** by increasing the **Duration** to **01.25**. Apply the transition effect to all of the slides. View the slide show from the beginning.

11 Insert a **Header & Footer** on the **Notes and Handouts**. Include the **Date and time** updated automatically, the **Page number**, and a **Footer**, using your own name, with the text **Lastname_Firstname_1G_Northern_Lights**

12 Display the **Document Properties**. As the **Tags** type **northern lights, Fairbanks** As the **Subject** type your course and section number. Be sure your name is indicated as the author.

13 **Save** your presentation, and then submit your presentation electronically or print **Handouts, 6 Slides Horizontal** as directed by your instructor. **Close** PowerPoint.

END | You have completed Project 1G

CONTENT-BASED ASSESSMENTS

Apply a combination of the 1A and 1B skills.

Build from Scratch

GO! Fix It	Project 1H Rain Forest	Online

GO! Make It	Project 1I Eagles	Online

GO! Solve It	Project 1J Packrafting	Online

GO! Solve It	Project 1K Packing	

PROJECT FILES

For Project 1K, you will need the following file:

p01K_Packing

You will save your presentation as:

Lastname_Firstname_1K_Packing

Open the file p01K_Packing and save it as **Lastname_Firstname_1K_Packing** Complete the presentation by applying a theme and changing the variant. Format the presentation attractively by applying appropriate font formatting and by changing text alignment and line spacing. Change the layout of Slide 4 to an appropriate layout. On Slide 2, insert a picture that you have taken yourself, or use one of the pictures in your student data files that you inserted in other projects in this chapter. Apply a style to the picture. Apply slide transitions to all of the slides in the presentation, and then insert a header and footer that includes the date and time updated automatically, the file name in the footer, and the page number. Add your name, your course name and section number, and the tags **packing, weather** to the properties. Save and print or submit as directed by your instructor.

Performance Level

Performance Criteria		Exemplary	Proficient	Developing
	Apply a theme and a variant	An appropriate theme and variant were applied to the presentation.	A theme was applied but the variant was not changed.	Neither a theme nor the variant theme were applied.
	Apply font and slide formatting	Font and slide formatting is attractive and appropriate.	Adequately formatted but difficult to read or unattractive.	Inadequate or no formatting.
	Use appropriate pictures and apply styles attractively	An appropriate picture was inserted and a style is applied attractively.	A picture was inserted but a style was not applied.	Picture was not inserted.
	Apply appropriate slide layout to Slide 4	An appropriate layout was applied to the last slide.	The slide layout was changed but is not appropriate for the type of slide.	The slide layout was not changed.

END | You have completed Project 1K

OUTCOMES-BASED ASSESSMENTS

RUBRIC

The following outcomes-based assessments are open-ended assessments. That is, there is no specific correct result; your result will depend on your approach to the information provided. Make Professional Quality your goal. Use the following scoring rubric to guide you in how to approach the problem and then to evaluate how well your approach solves the problem.

The *criteria*—Software Mastery, Content, Format and Layout, and Process—represent the knowledge and skills you have gained that you can apply to solving the problem. The *levels of performance*—Professional Quality, Approaching Professional Quality, or Needs Quality Improvements—help you and your instructor evaluate your result.

	Your completed project is of Professional Quality if you:	Your completed project is Approaching Professional Quality if you:	Your completed project Needs Quality Improvements if you:
1-Software Mastery	Choose and apply the most appropriate skills, tools, and features and identify efficient methods to solve the problem.	Choose and apply some appropriate skills, tools, and features, but not in the most efficient manner.	Choose inappropriate skills, tools, or features, or are inefficient in solving the problem.
2-Content	Construct a solution that is clear and well organized, contains content that is accurate, appropriate to the audience and purpose, and is complete. Provide a solution that contains no errors in spelling, grammar, or style.	Construct a solution in which some components are unclear, poorly organized, inconsistent, or incomplete. Misjudge the needs of the audience. Have some errors in spelling, grammar, or style, but the errors do not detract from comprehension.	Construct a solution that is unclear, incomplete, or poorly organized; contains some inaccurate or inappropriate content; and contains many errors in spelling, grammar, or style. Do not solve the problem.
3-Format & Layout	Format and arrange all elements to communicate information and ideas, clarify function, illustrate relationships, and indicate relative importance.	Apply appropriate format and layout features to some elements, but not others. Overuse features, causing minor distraction.	Apply format and layout that does not communicate information or ideas clearly. Do not use format and layout features to clarify function, illustrate relationships, or indicate relative importance. Use available features excessively, causing distraction.
4-Process	Use an organized approach that integrates planning, development, self-assessment, revision, and reflection.	Demonstrate an organized approach in some areas, but not others; or, use an insufficient process of organization throughout.	Do not use an organized approach to solve the problem.

OUTCOMES-BASED ASSESSMENTS

Apply a combination of the 1A and 1B skills.

Build from Scratch

GO! Think   Project 1L Bears

PROJECT FILES

For Project 1L, you will need the following files:

New blank PowerPoint presentation
p01L_Bear

You will save your presentation as:

Lastname_Firstname_1L_Bears

Cindy Barrow, Tour Operations Manager for Kodiak West Travel, is developing a presentation describing brown bear viewing travel experiences that the company is developing. In the presentation, Cindy will be describing the brown bear habitat and viewing opportunities.

Kodiak bears are the largest known size of brown bears on record; they can weigh as much as 2,000 pounds and can get as large as polar bears. Kodiak bears are active during the day and are generally solitary creatures. The Kodiak Bear Travel Experience is a small, personalized travel adventure available to only eight participants at a time. It is an opportunity to peer into the life of these majestic mammals.

The adventure takes place on Kodiak Island near a lake with a high concentration of salmon, making it the perfect natural feeding ground for the Kodiak bears. Travelers can view the bears from boats, kayaks, and recently constructed viewing platforms and guides are available.

This is a true wildlife experience because the area is home to deer, fox, and river otter. Accommodations are available at the Kodiak West Breakfast Inn from mid-June to the end of August. Peak season is early August and reservations can be made up to one year in advance. The cost is $1,800 per person for one week, and includes all meals, use of watercraft, and guided tours.

Using the preceding information, create a presentation that Cindy can show at a travel fair. The presentation should include four to six slides describing the travel experience. Apply an appropriate theme and use slide layouts that will effectively present the content. Insert at least one picture and apply appropriate picture formatting. You may use a picture of your choosing or from your student data files, use the file p01L_Bear. Apply font formatting and slide transitions, and modify text alignment and line spacing as necessary.

Save the file as **Lastname_Firstname_1L_Bears** and then insert a header and footer that include the date and time updated automatically, the file name in the footer, and the page number. Add your name, your course name and section number, and the tags **bears, tours** to the properties. Save and print or submit as directed by your instructor.

END | You have completed Project 1L

OUTCOMES-BASED ASSESSMENTS

Build from
Scratch

| GO! Think | Project 1M Sitka | Online |

Build from
Scratch

| You and GO! | Project 1N Travel | Online |

| GO! Cumulative Group Project | Project 1O Bell Orchid Hotels Online |

Formatting PowerPoint Presentations

2

GO! to Work
Video P2

PROJECT 2A

OUTCOMES
Format a presentation to add visual interest and clarity.

OBJECTIVES

1. Format Numbered and Bulleted Lists
2. Insert Online Pictures
3. Insert Text Boxes and Shapes
4. Format Objects

PROJECT 2B

OUTCOMES
Enhance a presentation with WordArt and SmartArt.

OBJECTIVES

5. Remove Picture Backgrounds and Insert WordArt
6. Create and Format a SmartArt Graphic

Spinta / Fotolia

In This Chapter

A PowerPoint presentation is a visual aid in which well-designed slides help the audience understand complex information while keeping them focused on the message. Color is an important element that enhances your slides and draws the audience's interest by creating focus. When designing the background and element colors for your presentation, be sure that the colors you use provide contrast so that the text is visible on the background. Graphic elements such as pictures, SmartArt, and shapes can illustrate important information. Choose elements that work well with the presentation design and colors.

The projects in this chapter relate to **Sensation Park Entertainment Group**, an entertainment company that operates 15 regional theme parks across the United States, Mexico, and Canada. Park types include traditional theme parks, water parks, and animal parks. This year the company will launch three of its new "Sensation Parks" where attractions combine fun and the discovery of math and science information, and where teens and adults enjoy the free Friday night concerts. The company focuses on safe and imaginative attractions that appeal to guests with a variety of entertainment interests, including adventure, science, and the arts.

Employee Training Presentation

PROJECT ACTIVITIES

In Activities 2.01 through 2.21, you will format a presentation for Marc Johnson, Director of Operations for Sensation Park Entertainment Group, that describes important safety guidelines for employees. Your completed presentation will look similar to Figure 2.1.

PROJECT FILES

For Project 2A, you will need the following file:

p02A_Safety

You will save your presentation as:

Lastname_Firstname_2A_Safety

PROJECT RESULTS

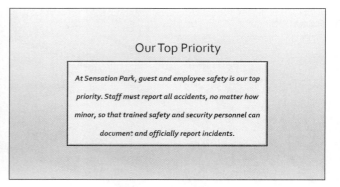

FIGURE 2.1 Project 2A Employee Training Presentation

Video P2-1

The font, color, and style of a numbered or bulleted list are determined by the presentation theme. You can format slide content by changing the bulleted and numbered list styles and colors.

Activity 2.01 | Selecting Placeholder Text

Recall that a placeholder is a box on a slide with dotted or dashed borders that holds title and body text or other content such as charts, tables, and pictures. You can format placeholder contents by selecting text or by selecting the entire placeholder.

1 Start PowerPoint. From the student data files that accompany this textbook, locate and open **p02A_Safety**. Display the **Save As** dialog box, create a **New Folder** with the name **PowerPoint Chapter 2** and then using your own name, save the file in the folder you created as **Lastname_Firstname_2A_Safety**

2 Display **Slide 2**, and then click anywhere in the content placeholder with the single bullet point.

3 Point to the dashed border surrounding the placeholder to display the 🔀 pointer, and then click one time to display the border as a solid line. Compare your screen with Figure 2.2.

When a placeholder's border displays as a solid line, all of the text in the placeholder is selected, and any formatting changes that you make will be applied to *all* of the text in the placeholder.

FIGURE 2.2

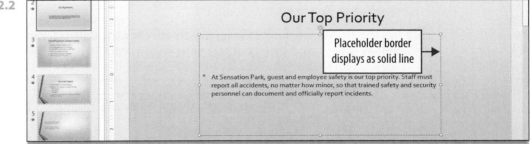

4 With the border of the placeholder displaying as a solid line, change the **Font Size** 20 ▾ to **24**. Notice that the font size of *all* of the placeholder text increases.

5 Save 🖫 your presentation.

Activity 2.02 | Changing a Bulleted List to a Numbered List

1 Display **Slide 3**, and then click anywhere in the bulleted list. Point to the placeholder dashed border to display the 🔀 pointer, and then click one time to display the border as a solid line indicating that all of the text is selected.

2 On the **HOME tab**, in the **Paragraph group**, click **Numbering** 🔢▾, and then compare your slide with Figure 2.3.

All of the bullet symbols are converted to numbers. The color of the numbers is determined by the presentation theme.

FIGURE 2.3

Bullet symbols converted to numbers

Injury Prevention—Protect Guests

1. Complete scheduled equipment checks
2. Enforce boarding restrictions for all rides
3. Verify height requirements for young children
4. Check every seatbelt and harness
5. Assist guests to understand regulations
6. Refer questions to your supervisor

ALERT!   **Did You Display the Numbering Gallery?**

If you clicked the Numbering button arrow instead of the Numbering button, the Numbering gallery displays. Click the Numbering button arrow again to close the gallery, and then click the Numbering button to convert the bullets to numbers.

---

3   **Save** 🖫 your presentation.

Activity 2.03 | Changing the Shape and Color of a Bulleted List Symbol

The presentation theme includes default styles for the bullet points in content placeholders. You can customize a bullet by changing its style, color, and size.

1   Display **Slide 4**, and then select the three second-level bullet points—*Ride entrances*, *Visitor center*, and *Rest areas*.

2   On the **HOME tab**, in the **Paragraph group**, click the **Bullets button arrow** 🗎▾ to display the **Bullets** gallery, and then compare your screen with Figure 2.4.

FIGURE 2.4

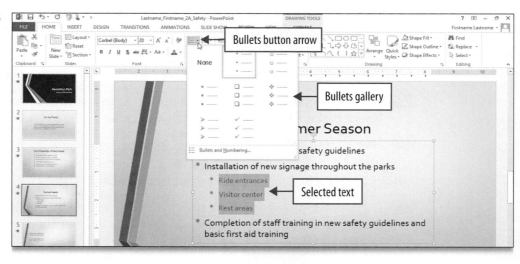

Bullets button arrow

Bullets gallery

Selected text

ALERT!   **Were the Bullets Removed?**

If the bullets were removed, then you clicked the Bullets button instead of the Bullets button arrow. Click the Bullets button arrow, and then continue with Step 3.

---

3   Below the **Bullets** gallery, click **Bullets and Numbering**. In the **Bullets and Numbering** dialog box, point to each bullet style to display its ScreenTip. Then, in the second row, click **Star Bullets**. If the Star Bullets are not available, in the second row of bullets, click the second bullet style, and then click the Reset button.

4 Below the gallery, click the **Color** button. Under **Theme Colors**, in the eighth column, click the last color—**Red, Accent 4, Darker 50%**. In the **Size** box, select the existing number, type **100** and then compare your dialog box with Figure 2.5.

FIGURE 2.5

5 Click **OK** to apply the bullet style, and then **Save** 🖫 your presentation.

More **Knowledge**   **Using Other Symbols as Bullet Characters**

Many bullets styles are available to insert in your presentation. In the Bullets and Numbering dialog box, click Customize to view additional bullet styles.

Activity 2.04 │ Removing a Bullet Symbol from a Bullet Point

The Bullets button is a toggle, enabling you to turn the bullet symbol on and off. A slide that contains a single bullet point can be formatted as a single paragraph *without* a bullet symbol.

1 Display **Slide 2**, and then click in the paragraph. On the **HOME tab**, in the **Paragraph group**, click **Bullets** 📋. Compare your screen with Figure 2.6.

The bullet symbol no longer displays, and the Bullets button is no longer selected. Additionally, the indentation associated with the list level is removed.

FIGURE 2.6

2 **Center** ≡ the paragraph. Click the dashed border to display the solid border and to select all of the text in the paragraph, and then apply **Bold** **B** and **Italic** *I*. On the **HOME tab**, in the **Paragraph group**, click **Line Spacing** 📋, and then click **2.0**.

3 **Save** 🖫 your presentation.

Video P2-2

There are many sources from which you can insert images into a presentation. One type of image that you can insert is a **clip**—a single media file such as art, sound, animation, or a movie.

Activity 2.05 | Inserting Online Pictures in a Content Placeholder

1 Display **Slide 5**. In the placeholder on the right side of the slide, click **Online Pictures** to display the **Insert Pictures** dialog box, and then compare your screen with Figure 2.7.

FIGURE 2.7

2 With the insertion point in the Search Office.com box, type **pouring water** and then press Enter to search for images that contain the keywords *pouring water*. Click the grayish-blue picture of water being poured. Compare your screen with Figure 2.8. If you are unable to locate the picture, choose another image.

FIGURE 2.8

3 With the water picture selected, click **Insert**. Compare your screen with Figure 2.9, and then **Save** your presentation.

On the ribbon, the Picture Tools display, and the water bottle image is surrounded by sizing handles, indicating that the image is selected.

 BY TOUCH   Tap the picture that you want to insert, and then tap Insert.

FIGURE 2.9

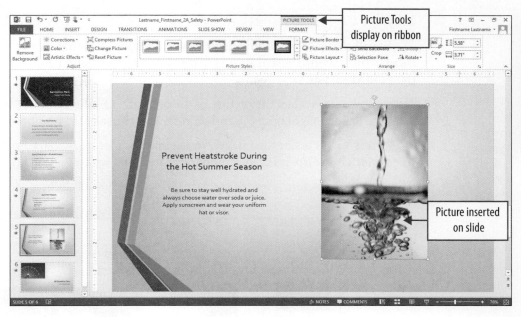

Activity 2.06 | Inserting Online Pictures in Any Location on a Slide

1 Display **Slide 1**. Click the **INSERT tab**, and then in the **Images group**, click **Online Pictures**.

2 In the **Insert Pictures** dialog box, in the **Search Office.com** box, type **red lights** and then press
Enter. Click the picture of the single red warning light, and then click **Insert**. Compare your
screen with Figure 2.10. If you cannot locate the picture, select another image.

When you use the Online Pictures button on the ribbon instead of the Online Pictures button in a
content placeholder, PowerPoint inserts the image in the center of the slide.

FIGURE 2.10

3 **Save** 🖫 your presentation.

Activity 2.07 | Sizing a Picture

Recall that a selected image displays sizing handles that you can drag to resize the image. You can also resize an image using the Shape Height and Shape Width boxes on the FORMAT tab.

1 If necessary, select the picture of the red light. On the **FORMAT tab**, in the **Size group**, click in the **Shape Height** box, and then replace the selected number with **3.5**

2 Press Enter to resize the image. Notice that the picture is resized proportionately, and the **Width** box displays *5.26*. Compare your screen with Figure 2.11.

> When a picture is resized in this manner, the width adjusts in proportion to the picture height.

FIGURE 2.11

BY TOUCH   Drag the corner sizing handle with your finger or mouse to resize the picture proportionately.

3 Save your presentation.

Activity 2.08 | Using Smart Guides and the Ruler to Position a Picture

Smart Guides are dashed lines that display on your slide when you are moving an object to assist you with alignment.

1 On **Slide 1**, on the **VIEW tab**, in the **Show group**, verify that the **Ruler** check box is selected and if necessary, select the check box. On the horizontal and vertical rulers, notice that *0* displays in the center.

> Horizontally, the PowerPoint ruler indicates measurements from the center of the slide *out* to the left and to the right. Vertically, the PowerPoint ruler indicates measurements from the center up and down.

2 Point to the picture to display the pointer. Hold down Shift, and then very slowly, drag the picture to the right and notice that dashed red Smart Guides periodically display along the right edge of the picture. When the dashed red Smart Guide displays on the right edge of the picture at approximately **6 inches to the right of zero on the horizontal ruler**, compare your screen with Figure 2.12, and then release the mouse button.

> Smart Guides display when you move an object and the object is aligned with another object on the slide. Here, the Smart Guide displays because the right edge of the picture is aligned with the right edge of the title placeholder. Pressing Shift while dragging an object constrains object movement in a straight line either vertically or horizontally. Here, pressing Shift maintains the vertical placement of the picture at the top edge of the slide.

FIGURE 2.12

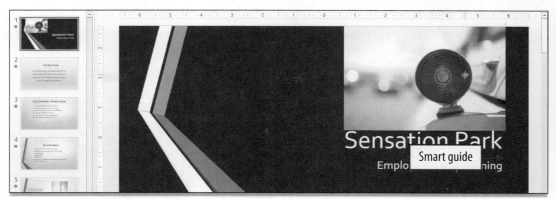

3 ▸ **Save** 🖫 the presentation.

More Knowledge **Moving an Object by Using the Arrow Keys**

You can use the directional arrow keys on your keyboard to move a picture, shape, or other object in small increments. Select the object so that its outside border displays as a solid line. Then, on your keyboard, hold down the Ctrl key and press the directional arrow keys to move the selected object in small, precise increments.

Activity 2.09 │ Cropping a Picture

When you ***crop*** a picture you remove unwanted or unnecessary areas of the picture.

1 ▸ Display **Slide 6**, and then select the ferris wheel picture. On the **FORMAT tab**, in the **Size group**, click the upper portion of the **Crop** button to display the crop handles. Compare your screen with Figure 2.13.

Use the ***crop handles*** like sizing handles to remove unwanted areas of the picture.

FIGURE 2.13

2 ▸ Point to the center right crop handle to display the Crop pointer 📷. Compare your screen with Figure 2.14.

The ***crop pointer*** is the mouse pointer that enables you to crop areas of a picture.

FIGURE 2.14

3 With the crop pointer displayed, hold down the left mouse button and drag to the left to approximately **1.5 inches to the left of 0 on the horizontal ruler**, and then release the mouse button. Compare your screen with Figure 2.15.

The portion of the picture to be removed by the crop displays in gray.

FIGURE 2.15

Picture cropped to 1.5 inches to the left of zero on the horizontal ruler

Portion of picture to be removed

4 Click anywhere on the slide outside of the image to apply the crop, and then **Save** 💾 your presentation.

Activity 2.10 | Using Crop to Shape to Change the Shape of a Picture

An inserted picture is rectangular in shape; however, you can modify a picture by changing its shape.

1 Display **Slide 1**, and then select the picture. On the **FORMAT tab**, in the **Size group**, click the lower portion of the Crop button—the **Crop button arrow**—and then compare your screen with Figure 2.16.

FIGURE 2.16

Crop button arrow

2 Point to **Crop to Shape** to display a gallery of shapes. Compare your screen with Figure 2.17.

FIGURE 2.17

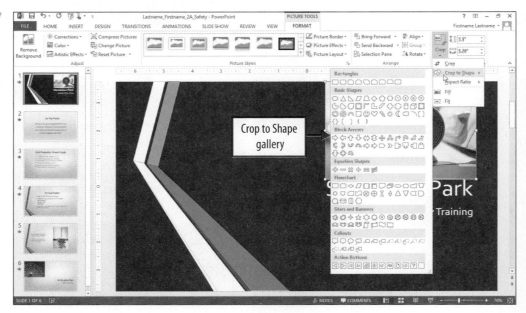

Crop to Shape gallery

3 Under **Basic Shapes**, in the first row, click the first shape—**Oval**—to change the picture's shape to an oval. **Save** 🖫 your presentation.

Objective 3 | Insert Text Boxes and Shapes

Video P2-3

You can use objects, including text boxes and shapes, to draw attention to important information or to serve as containers for slide text. Many shapes, including lines, arrows, ovals, and rectangles, are available to insert and position anywhere on your slides.

Activity 2.11 | Inserting a Text Box

A ***text box*** is an object with which you can position text anywhere on a slide.

1 Display **Slide 3** and verify that the rulers display. Click the **INSERT tab**, and then in the **Text group**, click **Text Box**.

2 Move the ↓ pointer to several different places on the slide, and as you do so, in the horizontal and vertical rulers, notice that ***ruler guides***—dotted red vertical and horizontal lines that display in the rulers indicating the pointer's position—move also.

Use the ruler guides to help you position objects on a slide.

3 Position the pointer so that the ruler guides are positioned on the **left half of the horizontal ruler at 4.5 inches** and on the **lower half of the vertical ruler at 2 inches**, and then compare your screen with Figure 2.18.

FIGURE 2.18

4 Click one time to create a narrow rectangular text box. With the insertion point blinking inside the text box, type **If Safety is Questionable** Notice that as you type, the width of the text box expands to accommodate the text. Compare your screen with Figure 2.19.

Do not be concerned if your text box is not positioned exactly as shown in Figure 2.19.

FIGURE 2.19

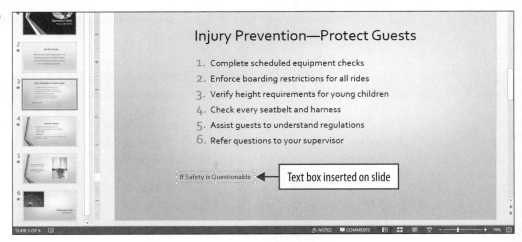

Text box inserted on slide

5   Select the text that you typed, change the **Font Size** to **24** and then **Save** 🖫 your presentation.

You can format the text in a text box by using the same techniques that you use to format text in any other placeholder. For example, you can change the font, font style, font size, and font color.

Activity 2.12 | Inserting and Sizing a Shape

Shapes are slide objects such as lines, arrows, boxes, callouts, and banners. You can size and move shapes using the same techniques that you use to size and move pictures.

1   With **Slide 3** displayed, click the **INSERT tab**, and then in the **Illustrations group**, click **Shapes** to display the **Shapes** gallery. Under **Block Arrows**, click the first shape—**Right Arrow**. Move the pointer into the slide until the ➕ pointer—called the *crosshair pointer*—displays, indicating that you can draw a shape.

2   Move the ➕ pointer to position the ruler guides at approximately **0 on the horizontal ruler** and on the **lower half of the vertical ruler at 2 inches**. Compare your screen with Figure 2.20.

FIGURE 2.20

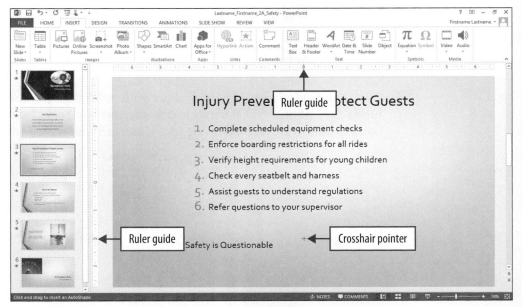

Ruler guide

Ruler guide

Crosshair pointer

3 Click to insert the arrow. On the **FORMAT tab**, in the **Size group**, click in the **Shape Height** box to select the number. Type **0.5** and then click in the **Shape Width** box. Type **2** and then press Enter to resize the arrow. Compare your screen with Figure 2.21.

FIGURE 2.21

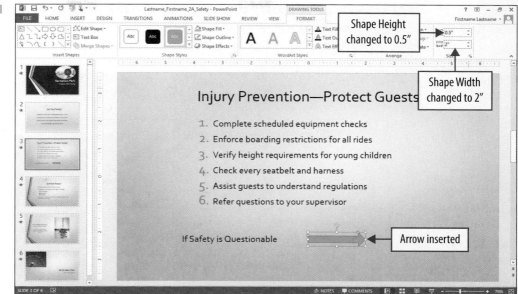

4 On the **FORMAT tab**, in the **Insert Shapes group**, click **More**. In the gallery, under **Basic Shapes**, in the first row, click the second to last shape—**Octagon**.

5 Move the pointer to position the ruler guides on the **right half of the horizontal ruler at 3.5 inches** and on the **lower half of the vertical ruler at 1 inch**, and then click one time to insert an octagon.

6 On the **FORMAT tab**, in the **Size group**, click in the **Shape Height** box to select the number. Type **2** and then click in the **Shape Width** box. Type **2** and then press Enter to resize the octagon. Compare your slide with Figure 2.22. Do not be concerned if your shapes are not positioned exactly as shown in the figure.

FIGURE 2.22

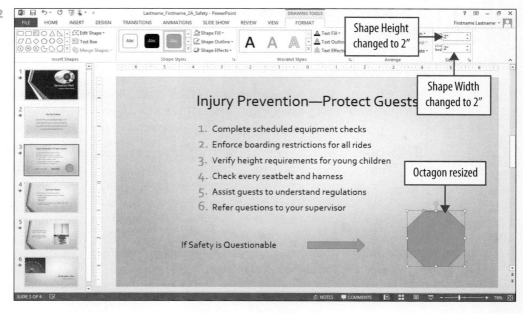

7 Save your presentation.

Activity 2.13 | Adding Text to Shapes

Shapes can serve as a container for text. After you add text to a shape, you can change the font and font size, apply font styles, and change text alignment.

1 On **Slide 3**, if necessary, click the octagon so that it is selected. Type **STOP** and notice that the text is centered within the octagon.

2 Select the text *STOP*, and then on the mini toolbar, change the **Font Size** to **32**.

3 Click in a blank area of the slide to cancel the selection, and then compare your screen with Figure 2.23. **Save** 🖫 your presentation.

FIGURE 2.23

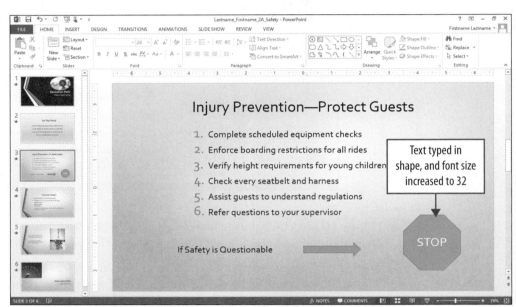

Objective 4 Format Objects

Video P2-4

Apply styles and effects to pictures, shapes, and text boxes to complement slide backgrounds and colors.

Activity 2.14 | Applying Shape Fills and Outlines

Changing the inside *fill color* and the outside line color is a distinctive way to format a shape. A fill color is the inside color of text or of an object. Use the Shape Styles gallery to apply predefined combinations of these fill and line colors and also to apply other effects.

1 Display **Slide 2**, and then click anywhere in the paragraph of text to select the content placeholder.

2 On the **FORMAT tab**, in the **Shape Styles group**, click the **Shape Fill arrow**. Point to several of the theme colors and watch as Live Preview changes the inside color of the text box. In the fifth column, click the second color—**Blue, Accent 1, Lighter 80%**.

3 In the **Shape Styles group**, click the **Shape Outline arrow**. Point to **Weight**, click **3 pt**, and notice that a thick outline surrounds the text placeholder. Click in a blank area of the slide so that nothing is selected, and then compare your slide with Figure 2.24.

You can use combinations of shape fill, outline colors, and weights to format an object.

FIGURE 2.24

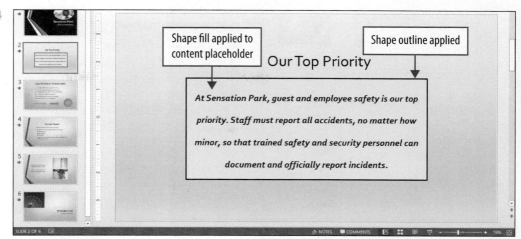

4 **Save** 🖫 your presentation.

Activity 2.15 | Using the Eyedropper to Change Color

The *eyedropper* is a tool that captures the exact color from an object on your screen and then applies the color to any shape, picture, or text. You can use the eyedropper to give your presentation a cohesive look by matching a font color, fill color, border color, or other slide element to any color on any slide.

1 Display **Slide 6**, and then select the title text—*At Sensation Park*.

2 On the **HOME tab**, in the **Font group**, click the **Font Color button arrow**. Below the gallery, click **Eyedropper**, and then move the 🖊 pointer into the upper right corner of the Ferris wheel picture. Compare your screen with Figure 2.25.

A small square displays next to the pointer indicating the exact color to which you are pointing. When you hover over a color, it's *RGB* color coordinates display. RGB is a color model in which the colors red, green, and blue are added together to form another color.

FIGURE 2.25

3 With the 🖊 pointer in the upper right corner of the picture, click one time. Notice that the color is applied to the selected text. Compare your screen with Figure 2.26.

FIGURE 2.26

Color from picture
applied to selected text

At Sensation Park

Safety Is Our Top Priority

4 ▶ Display **Slide 5**, and then select the title. On the mini toolbar, click the **Font Color button arrow**. Under **Recent Colors**, notice that the color you selected with the eyedropper displays. Point to the color to display the ScreenTip—*Dark Blue*. Click **Dark Blue** to apply the color to the selection.

> After a color has been selected with the eyedropper, the color remains available in the presentation each time the color gallery is displayed. When you use the eyedropper in this manner, you can consistently apply the same color throughout your presentation.

5 ▶ **Save** 🖫 your presentation.

Activity 2.16 │ Applying Shape Styles

1 ▶ Display **Slide 3**, and then select the **arrow shape**. On the **FORMAT tab**, in the **Shape Styles group**, click **More** 🔽 to display the **Shape Styles** gallery. In the last row, click the second style— **Intense Effect - Blue, Accent 1**.

2 ▶ Click anywhere in the text *If Safety is Questionable* to select the text box. On the **FORMAT tab**, in the **Shape Styles group**, click **More** 🔽.

3 ▶ In the last row, click the fifth style—**Intense Effect - Red, Accent 4**.

4 ▶ Select the **octagon** shape, and then apply the same style you applied to the text box—**Intense Effect - Red, Accent 4**.

5 ▶ Compare your screen with Figure 2.27, and then **Save** 🖫 your presentation.

FIGURE 2.27

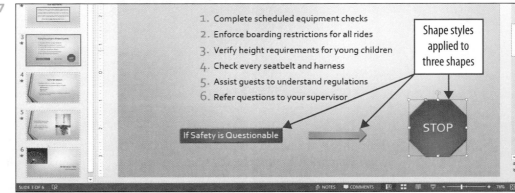

1. Complete scheduled equipment checks
2. Enforce boarding restrictions for all rides
3. Verify height requirements for young children
4. Check every seatbelt and harness
5. Assist guests to understand regulations
6. Refer questions to your supervisor

Shape styles
applied to
three shapes

If Safety is Questionable

STOP

Activity 2.17 | **Applying Shape and Picture Effects**

1 Display **Slide 1**, and then select the picture. On the **FORMAT tab**, in the **Picture Styles group**, click **Picture Effects**.

A list of effects that you can apply to pictures displays. These effects can also be applied to shapes and text boxes.

2 Point to **Soft Edges**, and then in the **Soft Edges** gallery, point to each style to view its effect on the picture. Click the last **Soft Edges** effect—**50 Point**, and then compare your screen with Figure 2.28.

The soft edges effect softens and blurs the outer edge of the picture so that the picture blends into the slide background.

FIGURE 2.28

3 Display **Slide 2**, and then select the light blue content placeholder. On the **FORMAT tab**, in the **Shape Styles group**, click **Shape Effects**. Point to **Bevel** to display the **Bevel** gallery. Point to each bevel to view its ScreenTip and to use Live Preview to examine the effect of each bevel on the content placeholder. In the last row, click the last bevel—**Art Deco**.

4 Click in a blank area of the slide and then compare your screen with Figure 2.29.

FIGURE 2.29

5 Display **Slide 5**, and then select the picture. On the **FORMAT tab**, in the **Picture Styles group**, click **Picture Effects**, and then point to **Glow**.

6 Point to several of the effects to view the effect on the picture, and then under **Glow Variations**, in the second row, click the first glow effect—**Blue, 8 pt glow, Accent color 1**.

The glow effect applies a colored, softly blurred outline to the selected object.

7 **Save** 🔲 your presentation.

Activity 2.18 | Duplicating Objects

1 Display **Slide 6**, and then select the picture.

2 Press and hold down [Ctrl], and then press [D] one time. Release [Ctrl].

[Ctrl] + [D] is the keyboard shortcut to duplicate an object. A duplicate of the picture overlaps the original picture and the duplicated image is selected.

3 Click in a blank area of the slide, and then compare your screen with Figure 2.30. **Save** 🖫 your presentation.

FIGURE 2.30

Original picture behind duplicate

Duplicated picture

At Sensation Park
Safety Is Our Top Priority

Activity 2.19 | Aligning and Distributing Objects Relative to the Slide

You can select multiple slide objects, and then use ribbon commands to align and distribute the objects precisely.

1 With **Slide 6** displayed, position the pointer in the gray area of the Slide pane just outside the upper left corner of the slide to display the 🔓 pointer. Drag down and to the right to draw a transparent, gray, selection rectangle that encloses both pictures. Compare your slide with Figure 2.31.

🔄 **ANOTHER WAY** Hold down [Shift] and then click each object that you want to select.

FIGURE 2.31

Selection rectangle

At Sensation Park

2 Release the mouse button to select the objects, and then compare your screen with Figure 2.32.

Objects completely enclosed by a selection rectangle are selected when the mouse button is released.

FIGURE 2.32

Both pictures selected

At Sensation Park

3 ▸ Click the **FORMAT tab**, and then in the **Arrange group**, click **Align**. Toward the bottom of the menu, click **Align to Slide** to activate this setting. On the **FORMAT tab**, in the **Arrange group**, click **Align** again, and then click **Align Left**.

> The Align to Slide option, in combination with the Align Left option, aligns the left edge of each picture with the left edge of the slide.

4 ▸ With both pictures still selected, on the **FORMAT tab**, in the **Arrange group**, click **Align** again, and then click **Distribute Vertically**. Compare your screen with Figure 2.33.

> The pictures are distributed evenly down the left edge of the slide between the top and bottom edges of the slide.

FIGURE 2.33

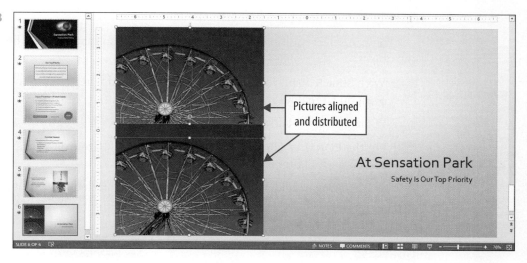

Pictures aligned and distributed

At Sensation Park

Safety Is Our Top Priority

5 ▸ With both pictures selected, on the **FORMAT tab**, in the **Picture Styles group**, click the **Picture Effects** button. Point to **Soft Edges**, and then click **50 Point** to apply the picture effect to both images.

6 ▸ **Save** 🖫 the presentation.

Activity 2.20 | Aligning and Distributing Objects Relative to Each Other

1 ▸ Display **Slide 3**, hold down Shift, and then at the bottom of the slide, click the **text box**, the **arrow**, and the **octagon** to select all three objects.

 BY TOUCH   Tap the text box, hold down Shift, and then tap the arrow and the octagon.

2 With the three objects selected, on the **FORMAT tab**, in the **Arrange group**, click **Align**. Click **Align Selected Objects**.

The *Align Selected Objects* option will cause the objects that you select to align relative to each other, rather than relative to the edges of the slide.

3 On the **FORMAT tab**, in the **Arrange group**, click **Align**, and then click **Align Middle**. Click the **Align** button again, and then click **Distribute Horizontally**.

The midpoint of each object aligns and the three objects are distributed evenly between the left edge of the leftmost object—the text box—and the right edge of the rightmost object—the octagon.

4 Click anywhere on the slide so that none of the objects are selected. Compare your screen with Figure 2.34, and then **Save** the presentation.

FIGURE 2.34

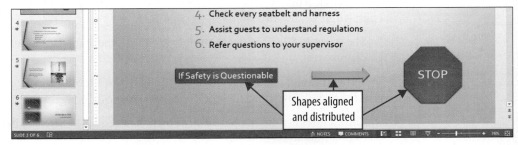

Activity 2.21 | Grouping Objects

You can select multiple objects and group them so that they can be formatted and edited as one object.

1 With **Slide 3** displayed, click the text box, hold down Shift, and then click the arrow and the octagon so that all three objects are selected.

Sizing handles surround each individual object.

2 On the **FORMAT tab**, in the **Arrange group**, click **Group**, and then click **Group**. Compare your screen with Figure 2.35.

The sizing handles surround all three shapes as one, indicating that the three shapes are grouped into one object. The individual objects are not selected. The grouped object can be formatted, aligned, and moved as one object.

FIGURE 2.35

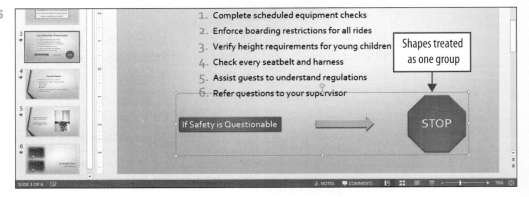

3 On the **FORMAT tab**, in the **Arrange group**, click **Align**, and then click **Align Center**.

The group is centered horizontally on the slide.

4 On the **Slide Show tab**, in the **Start Slide Show group**, click the **From Beginning** button, and then view the slide show. When the black slide displays, press Esc.

5 On the **INSERT tab**, in the **Text group**, click **Header & Footer** to display the **Header and Footer** dialog box. Click the **Notes and Handouts** tab. Under **Include on page**, select the **Date and time** check box, and then select **Update automatically**. If necessary, clear the Header check box. Select the **Page number** and **Footer** check boxes. In the **Footer** box, using your own name, type **Lastname_Firstname_2A_Safety** and then click **Apply to All**.

6 Display the document properties. As the **Tags** type **safety presentation** and as the **Subject** type your course and section number. Be sure your name displays as the author, and then **Save** your file. Print **Handouts 6 Slides Horizontal**, or submit your presentation electronically as directed by your instructor.

7 **Close** PowerPoint.

END | You have completed Project 2A

2
POWERPOINT

GO! with Office Online (formerly Web Apps)

Objective | **Create** an Informational Presentation in PowerPoint Online

> **A L E R T !** | **Working with Web-Based Applications and Services**
>
> Computer programs and services on the web receive continuous updates and improvements, so the steps to complete this web-based activity may differ from the ones shown. You can often look at the screens and the information presented to determine how to complete the activity.

Activity | Creating an Informational Presentation in PowerPoint Online

In this activity, you will use PowerPoint Online to create a presentation similar to the one you created in Project 2A.

1 From the desktop, start Internet Explorer. Navigate to **http://onedrive.com**, and then sign in to your Microsoft account. Open your **GO! Web Projects** folder—or create and then open this folder if necessary.

2 On the OneDrive menu bar, click **Upload**, and then navigate to your student data files and select **p02_2A_Web**. Click **Open**. When the upload is complete, right click **p02_2A_Web**, and then click **Rename**. Using your own name, as the file name type **Lastname_Firstname_PPT_2A_Web** and then press Enter. Click your file, and then click **EDIT PRESENTATION**. Click **Edit in PowerPoint Online**.

3 Display **Slide 5**. In the content placeholder, click the third button—**Online Pictures** 🖼. In the **Search** box, type **pouring water** and then press Enter. Insert the picture that you inserted in Project 2A. If the picture is not available, choose another appropriate image.

4 Display **Slide 2**, and then click the paragraph to activate the content placeholder. Click in the paragraph again so that you can edit the paragraph. On the **HOME**

tab, in the **Paragraph group**, click **Bullets** to remove the bullet symbol from the paragraph.

5 On the **HOME tab**, in the **Paragraph group**, click **Center** and then select the entire paragraph. Change the **Font Size** to **24** and apply **Bold**.

6 With **Slide 2** displayed and the paragraph selected, click outside of the content placeholder and then click the outer edge so that it displays as a solid line. On the **DRAWING TOOLS FORMAT tab**, in the **Shape Styles group**, click the small down arrow. In the last row, click the second style—**Intense Effect – Blue, Accent 1**. In the **Shape Styles group**, click **Shape Outline**, in the second column, click the first color—**Black, Text 1**. Click **Shape Outline** again, point to **Weight**, and then click **4 1/2 pt**.

7 Click outside the content placeholder to apply your changes, and then compare your screen with Figure A.

8 Display **Slide 3**, and then click in the bulleted list, and then drag to select all of the bullet points. On the **HOME tab**, in the **Paragraph group**, click **Numbering** to apply numbers to all of the bullet points.

FIGURE A

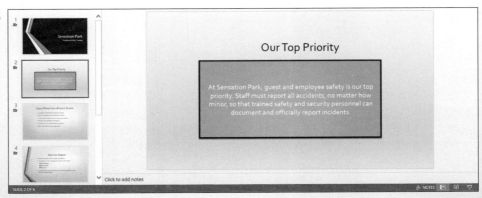

(GO! with Office Online (formerly Web Apps) continues on the next page)

Click outside of the content placeholder to deselect it. With **Slide 3** still displayed, on the **INSERT tab**, in the **Text group**, click **Text Box** to insert a text box in the middle of your slide. Point to the text box border, and then drag down and to the left to position the text box so that the circular rotation handle above the center of the text box is positioned below the number 6.

10 Click in the text box and then drag to select *Click to add text*. Type **If Safety is Questionable** and then click outside the text box. Click the text box border, and then on the **FORMAT tab**, in the **Shape Styles group**, click the small down arrow. In the last row, click the fifth style—**Intense Effect – Red, Accent 4**.

11 On the **INSERT tab**, in the **Illustrations group**, click **Right Arrow** to insert an arrow in the middle of your slide. Drag the arrow so that it is aligned horizontally with the text box and its left edge aligns with the *y* in *your*.

12 Click outside of the arrow to deselect it. On the **INSERT tab**, in the **Illustrations group**, click **Rounded Rectangle** to insert a 1 × 1 rounded rectangle in the middle of your slide. Drag the rectangle so that so that its center sizing handle aligns with the arrow point and its left edge aligns with the *s* in *regulations*. On the **FORMAT tab**, in the **Shape Styles group**, click the small down arrow. In the last row, click the fifth style—**Intense Effect – Red, Accent 4**.

13 Click in the rectangle. Type **STOP** and then click in a blank area of the slide. Compare your screen with Figure B and make adjustments to the position of the shapes as necessary.

14 Submit your file as instructed. Sign out of your OneDrive and then close Internet Explorer.

FIGURE B

Event Announcement

PROJECT ACTIVITIES

In Activities 2.22 through 2.34, you will format slides in a presentation for the Sensation Park Entertainment Group's Marketing Director that informs employees about upcoming events at the company's amusement parks. You will enhance the presentation using SmartArt and WordArt graphics. Your completed presentation will look similar to Figure 2.36.

PROJECT FILES

For Project 2B, you will need the following files:

p02B_Celebrations
p02B_Canada_Contact
p02B_Mexico_Contact
p02B_US_Contact

You will save your presentation as:

Lastname_Firstname_2B_Celebrations

PROJECT RESULTS

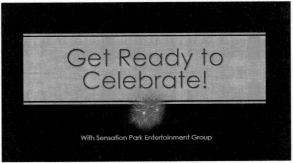

FIGURE 2.36 Project 2B Event Announcement

Video P2-5

To avoid the boxy look that results when you insert an image into a presentation, use **Background Removal** to flow a picture into the content of the presentation. Background Removal removes unwanted portions of a picture so that the picture does not appear as a self-contained rectangle.

WordArt is a gallery of text styles with which you can create decorative effects, such as shadowed or mirrored text. You can choose from the gallery of WordArt styles to insert a new WordArt object or you can customize existing text by applying WordArt formatting.

Activity 2.22 | Removing the Background from a Picture and Applying Soft Edge Options

1 Start PowerPoint. From your student data files, open **p02B_Celebrations**. On the **VIEW tab**, in the **Show group**, if necessary, select the Ruler check box. In your **PowerPoint Chapter 2** folder, **Save** the file as **Lastname_Firstname_2B_Celebrations**

2 Display **Slide 6**. Click the picture to select it, and then on the **FORMAT tab**, in the **Adjust group**, click **Remove Background**. Compare your screen with Figure 2.37.

PowerPoint determines what portion of the picture is the foreground—the portion to keep—and which portion is the background—the portion to remove. The background is overlaid in magenta, leaving the remaining portion of the picture as it will look when the background removal is complete. A rectangular selection area displays that you can move and size to select additional areas of the picture. The Background Removal options display in the Refine group on the ribbon.

FIGURE 2.37

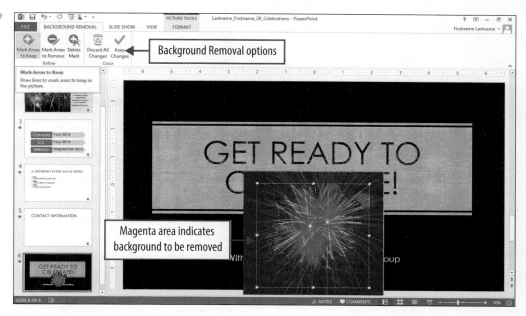

3 On the **Background Removal tab**, in the **Close group**, click **Keep Changes** to remove the background.

4 With the picture selected, on the **FORMAT tab**, in the **Picture Styles group**, click **Picture Effects**, point to **Soft Edges**, and then click **50 Point**. Compare your slide with Figure 2.38, and then **Save** your presentation.

FIGURE 2.38

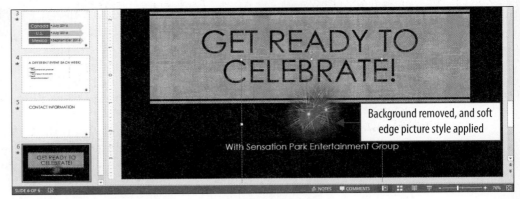

Background removed, and soft edge picture style applied

Activity 2.23 | Applying WordArt Styles to Existing Text

1 On **Slide 6**, click anywhere in the word *Get* to activate the title placeholder, and then select the title—*Get Ready to Celebrate!* Click the **FORMAT tab**, and then in the **WordArt Styles group**, click **More** ⯆ to display the WordArt gallery.

2 Point to several WordArt styles to view the change to the slide title. In the first row, click the first style—**Fill – White, Text 1, Shadow**. Click anywhere on the slide to cancel the selection.

3 Compare your screen with Figure 2.39, and then **Save** 🖫 your presentation.

FIGURE 2.39

WordArt style applied to title

Activity 2.24 | Changing the Text Fill and Text Outline Colors of a WordArt Object

A WordArt object can be modified by changing the text fill and text outline colors.

1 On **Slide 6**, select the title. On the **FORMAT tab**, in the **WordArt Styles group**, click the **Text Fill button arrow**. Under **Theme Colors**, in the sixth column, click the fifth color—**Dark Red, Accent 2, Darker 25%.**

2 With the text still selected, in the **WordArt Styles group**, click the **Text Outline button arrow**. In the second column, click the first color—**White, Text 1**. Click anywhere on the slide to cancel the selection.

3 Compare your screen with Figure 2.40, and then **Save** 🖫 your presentation.

FIGURE 2.40

WordArt text fill and text outline colors changed

Activity 2.25 | Inserting and Aligning a WordArt Object

In addition to formatting existing text using WordArt, you can insert a new WordArt object anywhere on a slide.

1 Display **Slide 3**. On the **INSERT tab**, in the **Text group**, click **WordArt**. In the gallery, in the second row, click the third WordArt style—**Gradient Fill – Brown, Accent 4, Outline – Accent 4**.

> In the center of your slide, a WordArt placeholder displays *Your text here*. Text that you type will replace this text and the placeholder will expand to accommodate the text. The WordArt is surrounded by sizing handles with which you can adjust its size.

2 Type **Schedule of Events** to replace the WordArt placeholder text. Compare your screen with Figure 2.41.

FIGURE 2.41

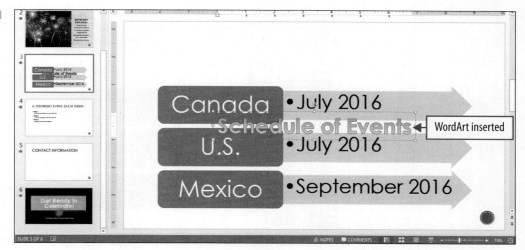

3 With the WordArt selected, on the **FORMAT tab**, in the **Arrange group**, click **Align**, and then click **Align Top** to move the WordArt to the top of the slide.

4 Click in a blank area of the slide, and then compare your screen with Figure 2.42.

FIGURE 2.42

5 **Save** 🖫 your presentation.

Activity 2.26 | Adding Text Effects to a WordArt

Text effects are formats applied to text that include shadows, reflections, glows, bevels, and 3-D rotations.

1 ▶ With **Slide 3** displayed, select the **WordArt** text. On the mini toolbar, change the **Font** to **Arial** and the **Font Size** to **66**.

2 ▶ On the **FORMAT tab**, in the **WordArt Styles group**, click **Text Effects**. Point to **Shadow**, and then compare your screen with Figure 2.43.

FIGURE 2.43

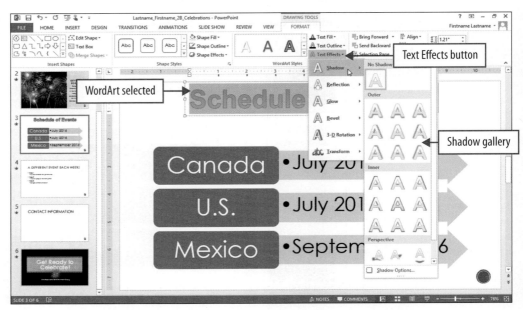

3 ▶ Under **Outer**, in the third row, click the third style—**Offset Diagonal Top Left**. Click in a blank area of the slide, and then compare your screen with Figure 2.44.

FIGURE 2.44

4 ▶ Save 🖫 your presentation.

Objective 6 | Create and Format a SmartArt Graphic

Video P2-6

A *SmartArt graphic* is a visual representation of information that you create by choosing from among various layouts to communicate your message or ideas effectively. SmartArt graphics can illustrate processes, hierarchies, cycles, lists, and relationships. You can include text and pictures in a SmartArt graphic, and you can apply colors, effects, and styles that coordinate with the presentation theme.

Activity 2.27 | Creating a SmartArt Graphic from Bulleted Points

You can convert an existing bulleted list into a SmartArt graphic. When you create a SmartArt graphic, consider the message that you are trying to convey, and then choose an appropriate layout. The table in Figure 2.45 describes types of SmartArt layouts and suggested purposes.

FIGURE 2.45

MICROSOFT POWERPOINT SMARTART GRAPHIC TYPES	
GRAPHIC TYPE	**PURPOSE OF GRAPHIC**
List	Shows non-sequential information
Process	Shows steps in a process or timeline
Cycle	Shows a continual process
Hierarchy	Shows a decision tree or displays an organization chart
Relationship	Illustrates connections
Matrix	Shows how parts relate to a whole
Pyramid	Shows proportional relationships with the largest component on the top or bottom
Picture	Includes pictures in the layout to communicate messages and ideas
Office.com	Additional layouts available from Office.com

1 ▶ Display **Slide 4**, and then click anywhere in the bulleted list placeholder. On the **HOME tab**, in the **Paragraph group**, click **Convert to SmartArt**. Below the gallery, click **More SmartArt Graphics**.

Three sections comprise the Choose a SmartArt Graphic dialog box. The left section lists the SmartArt graphic types. The center section displays the SmartArt layouts according to type. The third section displays the selected SmartArt graphic, its name, and a description of its purpose.

ANOTHER WAY   Right-click in a bulleted list to display the shortcut menu, point to Convert to SmartArt, and then click More SmartArt Graphics.

2 ▶ On the left side of the **Choose a SmartArt Graphic** dialog box, click **List**. Use the ScreenTips to locate and then click **Vertical Box List**. Compare your screen with Figure 2.46.

FIGURE 2.46

3 ▶ In the **Choose a SmartArt Graphic** dialog box, click **OK**. Compare your screen with Figure 2.47, and then **Save** 🖫 your presentation.

It is not necessary to select all of the text in the list. By clicking in the list, PowerPoint converts all of the bullet points to the selected SmartArt graphic. On the ribbon, the SmartArt contextual tools display two tabs—Design and Format. The thick border surrounding the SmartArt graphic indicates that the SmartArt graphic is selected and displays the area that the object will cover on the slide.

FIGURE 2.47

4 Save 🖫 your presentation.

Activity 2.28 | Adding Shapes in a SmartArt Graphic

If a SmartArt graphic does not have enough shapes to illustrate a concept or display the relationships, you can add more shapes.

1 Click in the shape that contains the text *Week 3*. In the **SMARTART TOOLS**, click the **DESIGN tab**. In the **Create Graphic group**, click the **Add Shape arrow**, and then click **Add Shape After** to insert a shape at the same level. Type **Week 4**

The text in each of the SmartArt shapes resizes to accommodate the added shape.

ANOTHER WAY   Right-click the shape, point to Add Shape, and then click Add Shape After.

2 On the **DESIGN tab**, in the **Create Graphic group**, click **Add Bullet** to add a bullet below the *Week 4* shape.

3 Type **25% discount on food and beverages** Compare your slide with Figure 2.48, and then Save 🖫 your presentation.

FIGURE 2.48

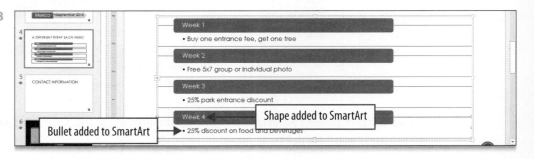

Activity 2.29 | Inserting a SmartArt Graphic Using a Content Layout

1 Display **Slide 5**. In the center of the content placeholder, click **Insert a SmartArt Graphic** 🖼 to open the **Choose a SmartArt Graphic** dialog box.

2 On the left, click **Picture**, and then scroll as necessary and use the ScreenTips to locate **Picture Strips**. Click **Picture Strips** and then compare your screen with Figure 2.49.

FIGURE 2.49

3 Click **OK** to insert the SmartArt graphic.

You can type text directly into the shapes or you can type text in the Text Pane, which may display to the left of your SmartArt graphic. You can display the Text Pane by clicking the Text Pane tab on the left side of the SmartArt graphic border, or by clicking the Text Pane button in the Create Graphic group. Depending on your software settings, the Text Pane may display.

Activity 2.30 | Inserting Pictures and Text in a SmartArt Graphic

1 In the SmartArt graphic, in the upper left text rectangle shape, type **Sophia Ackerman** and then press Enter. Type **United States** and then click in the text rectangle on the right. Type **Joseph Mercado** and then press Enter. Type **Mexico** and then click in the lower text rectangle. Type **Michael Lewis** and then press Enter. Type **Canada**

2 In the top left picture placeholder, click **Insert Picture** 🖼. In the **Insert Pictures** dialog box, to the right of **From a file**, click **Browse**. Navigate to your student data files, click **p02B_US_Contact**, and then click **Insert** to insert the picture.

3 Using the technique you just practiced, in the right picture placeholder, insert **p02B_Mexico_Contact**. In the lower picture placeholder, insert **p02B_Canada_Contact**.

4 Compare your screen with Figure 2.50, and then **Save** 🖫 your presentation.

FIGURE 2.50

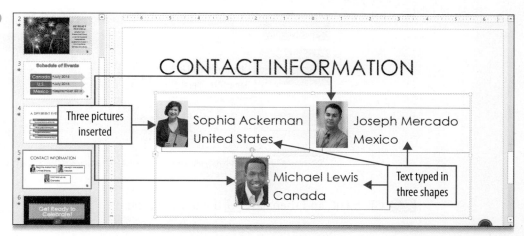

Activity 2.31 | Changing the Size and Shape of SmartArt Elements

You can select individual or groups of shapes in a SmartArt graphic and make them larger or smaller, and you can change selected shapes to another type of shape.

1 ▶ With **Slide 5** displayed, click the picture of *Sophia Ackerman*. Hold down Shift, and then click the pictures of *Joseph Mercado* and *Michael Lewis* so that all three pictures are selected.

2 ▶ On the **SMARTART TOOLS FORMAT tab**, in the **Shapes group**, click **Larger** two times to increase the size of the three pictures.

3 ▶ With the three pictures selected, on the **SMARTART TOOLS FORMAT tab**, in the **Shapes group**, click **Change Shape**. Under **Rectangles**, click the second shape—**Rounded Rectangle**.

4 ▶ Click anywhere on the slide to cancel the selection, and then compare your screen with Figure 2.51.

FIGURE 2.51

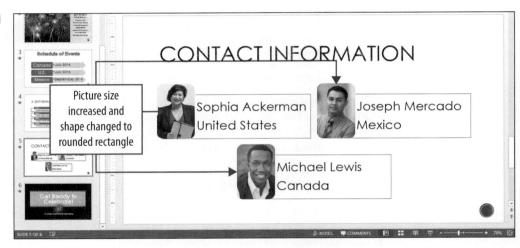

5 ▶ Save 💾 your presentation.

Activity 2.32 | Changing the SmartArt Layout

1 ▶ Display **Slide 3**, and then click anywhere in the SmartArt graphic. On the **SMARTART TOOLS DESIGN tab**, in the **Layouts group**, click **More** ▾, and then click **More Layouts**. In the **Choose a SmartArt Graphic** dialog box, click **List**. Scroll up or down as necessary to locate and then click **Vertical Block List**. Compare your screen with Figure 2.52.

FIGURE 2.52

2 ▶ Click **OK**, and then Save 💾 the presentation.

Activity 2.33 | Changing the Color and Style of a SmartArt Graphic

SmartArt Styles are combinations of formatting effects that you can apply to SmartArt graphics.

1 With **Slide 3** displayed, if necessary, select the SmartArt. On the **SMARTART TOOLS DESIGN tab**, in the **SmartArt Styles group**, click **Change Colors**. In the color gallery, under **Colorful**, click the second style—**Colorful Range - Accent Colors 2 to 3**—to change the colors.

2 On the **DESIGN tab**, in the **SmartArt Styles group**, click **More** ⊡ to display the **SmartArt Styles gallery**. Under **3-D**, click the third style, **Cartoon**. Compare your slide with Figure 2.53.

FIGURE 2.53

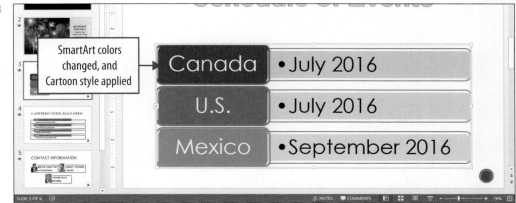

3 Save ⊟ the presentation.

Activity 2.34 | Converting a SmartArt to Text

1 Display **Slide 4**, and then click anywhere in the SmartArt graphic. On the **SMARTART TOOLS DESIGN tab**, in the **Reset group**, click **Convert**, and then click **Convert to Text** to convert the SmartArt graphic back to a bulleted list. Compare your screen with Figure 2.54.

FIGURE 2.54

2 Insert a **Header & Footer** on the **Notes and Handouts**. Include the **Date and time updated automatically**, the **Page number**, and a **Footer** with the text **Lastname_Firstname_2B_Celebrations**

3 Display the document properties. As the **Tags** type **independence day, celebrations** and as the **Subject** type your course and section number. Be sure your name displays as the author, and then **Save** your file.

4 View the slide show from the beginning, and then make any necessary adjustments. **Save** 🖫 your presentation. Print **Handouts 6 Slides Horizontal**, or submit your presentation electronically as directed by your instructor.

5 **Close** PowerPoint.

END | You have completed Project 2B

Objective | Create an Advertisement Presentation in PowerPoint Online

Activity | Creating an Advertisement Presentation in PowerPoint Online

In this activity, you will use PowerPoint Online to format a presentation similar to the one you created in Project 2B.

1 From the desktop, start Internet Explorer. Navigate to **http://onedrive.com**, and then sign in to your Microsoft account. Open your **GO! Web Projects** folder—or create and then open this folder if necessary.

2 On the OneDrive menu bar, click **Upload**, and then navigate to your student data files and select **p02_2B_Web**. Click **Open**. When the upload is complete, right click **p02_2B_Web**, and then click **Rename**. Using your own name, as the file name type **Lastname_Firstname_PPT_2B_Web** and then press Enter. Click your file, and then click **EDIT PRESENTATION**. Click **Edit in PowerPoint Online**.

3 Display **Slide 3**. In the content placeholder, click the first button—**Insert a SmartArt Graphic** 🖼. On the **SMARTART TOOLS DESIGN tab**, in the **Layouts group**, click the second layout—**Horizontal Bullet List** to change the SmartArt style.

4 Click in the upper left orange rectangle and notice that the content placeholder displays a bulleted list. Click the first bullet point—it may align with the left edge of the placeholder. Type **Canada** and then click in the indented bullet point below the text you typed. Type **July 2016** and then press Delete to remove the second bullet point.

5 Click the second solid bullet, and then type **U.S.** Click the indented bullet point below the text you typed. Type **July 2016** and then press Delete. Using the technique you practiced, in the third set of bullet points, type **Mexico** and **September 2016**

6 Compare your screen with Figure A.

7 Click outside the content placeholder to display the SmartArt graphic.

8 Select the SmartArt graphic, and then on the **SMARTART TOOLS DESIGN tab**, in the **SmartArt Styles group**, click **Change Colors**. Under **Colorful**, click the first style— **Colorful – Accent Colors**. In the **SmartArt Styles group**, click the small down arrow to display more styles, and then in the second row, click the third style—**Cartoon**.

FIGURE A

(GO! with Office Online (formerly Web Apps) continues on the next page)

9 ▶ Display **Slide 5**. In the content placeholder, click the first button—**Insert a SmartArt Graphic** . On the **SMARTART TOOLS DESIGN tab**, in the **Layouts group**, click the **More Layouts arrow**, and then in the third row, click the eighth layout—**Grouped List** to change the SmartArt style.

10 ▶ Click in the upper left shape. To the right of the first solid bullet, type **Sophia Ackerman** and then click in the indented bullet point below the text you typed. Type **United States** and then press Delete to remove the second bullet point.

11 ▶ Click to the right of the second solid bullet, and then type **Joseph Mercado** Click in the indented bullet point below the text you typed. Type **Mexico** and then press Delete. Using the technique you practiced, in the

third set of bullet points, type **Michael Lewis** and **Canada**

12 ▶ Click outside the content placeholder to display the SmartArt graphic.

13 ▶ Select the SmartArt graphic, and then on the **SMARTART TOOLS DESIGN tab**, in the **SmartArt Styles group**, click **Change Colors**. Under **Colorful**, click the first style— **Colorful – Accent Colors**. In the **SmartArt Styles group**, click the **More Styles arrow**, and then in the second row, click the third style—**Cartoon**.

14 ▶ Click in a blank area of the slide and then compare your screen with Figure B.

15 ▶ Submit your file as instructed. Sign out of your OneDrive and then close Internet Explorer.

FIGURE B

Office 365 combines tools for collaboration and productivity and delivers them to multiple users in an organization by using *cloud computing*—applications and services that are accessed over the Internet with multiple devices. For example, one cloud service with which you might be familiar is *OneDrive*, a free web-based application with which you can save, store, organize, and share files online. This cloud service is available for anyone who has a free Microsoft account.

Another cloud service from Microsoft is *Office Web Apps*. These are the online companions to the desktop versions of Microsoft Office Word, Excel, PowerPoint, and OneNote that enable you to create, access, share, and perform light editing on Microsoft Office documents from any device that connects to the Internet and uses a supported *web browser*. A web browser is software, such as Internet Explorer, Firefox, Safari, or Chrome, that displays web pages.

For an organization, cloud computing enables the addition of services without investing in additional hardware and software. For you as a team member, you can use your web browser to access, edit, store, and share files. You do not need to have a full version of Office installed on your computer to do this. You have all the tools and security that large organizations have!

When you use Office 365, your email and storage servers are hosted by Microsoft. Your organization gets business-class security from Microsoft—a large, well-established company. Sophisticated security and data management features are built into Office 365 so that you can control *permissions*—access rights that define the ability of an individual or group to view or make changes to documents—and provide secure email and communications.

Activity | Using Lync to Collaborate by Using a Video Call

This group project relates to the **Bell Orchid Hotels**. If your instructor assigns this project to your class, you can expect to use **Lync** in **Office 365** to collaborate on the following tasks for this chapter:

- If you are in the **Accounting Group**, you and your teammates will conduct a video call to discuss and agree on the format of the drawing objects, slide transitions, comments, and graphics in your Loan Presentation.

- If you are in the **Engineering Group**, you and your teammates will conduct a video call to discuss and agree on the format of the drawing objects, slide transitions, comments, and graphics in your Safety Presentation.

- If you are in the **Food and Beverage Group**, you and your teammates will conduct a video call to discuss and agree on the format of the drawing objects, slide transitions, comments, and graphics in your New Menu Item Presentation.

- If you are in the **Human Resources Group**, you and your teammates will conduct a video call to discuss and agree on the format of the drawing objects, slide transitions, comments, and graphics in your New Employees Presentation.

- If you are in the **Operations Group**, you and your teammates will conduct a video call to discuss and agree on the format of the drawing objects, slide transitions, comments, and graphics in your Front Desk Clerk Training Presentation.

- If you are in the **Sales and Marketing Group**, you and your teammates will conduct a video call to discuss and agree on the format of the drawing objects, slide transitions, comments, and graphics in your Marketing Plan Presentation.

FIGURE A

END OF CHAPTER

SUMMARY

Use numbered and bulleted lists in a presentation to focus attention on specific items. The theme that you select includes default styles for bullets, but you can change the shape and color of the symbols.

Use pictures to illustrate an idea. The Online Pictures feature enables you to search Office.com for images that emphasize important points. Using good keywords is critical to a successful search to find a great picture!

Objects are easily modified in PowerPoint. Removing the picture background and cropping eliminate unnecessary picture parts. Smart guides and alignment options are used to position pictures and shapes.

Use SmartArt graphics to present information and to illustrate processes, hierarchies, cycles, lists, and relationships. SmartArt graphics may include text and pictures, and can be formatted with styles and color combinations for maximum impact.

GO! LEARN IT ONLINE

Review the concepts and key terms in this chapter by completing these online challenges, which you can find at **www.pearsonhighered.com/go**.

Matching and Multiple Choice: Answer matching and multiple choice questions to test what you learned in this chapter. MyITLab®

Crossword Puzzle: Spell out the words that match the numbered clues, and put them in the puzzle squares.

Flipboard: Flip through the definitions of the key terms in this chapter and match them with the correct term.

GO! FOR JOB SUCCESS

Video: Business Lunch Interpersonal Communications

Your instructor may assign this video to your class, and then ask you to think about, or discuss with your classmates, these questions:

FotolEdhar / Fotolia

In what specific ways did Sara and Jordan demonstrate improper interpersonal communication during their lunch with Karen?

As a manager, did Chris follow the rules of interpersonal communication with his client? Explain your answer.

In what ways did Sara, Jordan, and Theo demonstrate proper or improper *nonverbal* communication skills?

END OF CHAPTER

REVIEW AND ASSESSMENT GUIDE FOR POWERPOINT CHAPTER 2

Your instructor may assign one or more of these projects to help you review the chapter and assess your mastery and understanding of the chapter.

	Review and Assessment Guide for PowerPoint Chapter 2		
Project	**Apply Skills from These Chapter Objectives**	**Project Type**	**Project Location**
2C	Objectives 1-4 from Project 2A	**2C Skills Review** A guided review of the skills from Project 2A.	On the following pages
2D	Objectives 5-6 from Project 2B	**2D Skills Review** A guided review of the skills from Project 2B.	On the following pages
2E	Objectives 1-4 from Project 2A	**2E Mastery (Grader Project)** A demonstration of your mastery of the skills in Project 2A with extensive decision making.	In MyITLab and on the following pages
2F	Objectives 5-6 from Project 2B	**2F Mastery (Grader Project)** A demonstration of your mastery of the skills in Project 2B with extensive decision making.	In MyITLab and on the following pages
2G	Objectives 1-6 from Projects 2A and 2B	**2G Mastery (Grader Project)** A demonstration of your mastery of the skills in Projects 2A and 2B with extensive decision making.	In MyITLab and on the following pages
2H	Combination of Objectives from Projects 2A and 2B	**2H GO! Fix It** A demonstration of your mastery of the skills in Projects 2A and 2B by creating a correct result from a document that contains errors you must find.	Online
2I	Combination of Objectives from Projects 2A and 2B	**2I GO! Make It** A demonstration of your mastery of the skills in Projects 2A and 2B by creating a result from a supplied picture.	Online
2J	Combination of Objectives from Projects 2A and 2B	**2J GO! Solve It** A demonstration of your mastery of the skills in Projects 2A and 2B, your decision-making skills, and your critical thinking skills. A task-specific rubric helps you self-assess your result.	Online
2K	Combination of Objectives from Projects 2A and 2B	**2K GO! Solve It** A demonstration of your mastery of the skills in Projects 2A and 2B, your decision-making skills, and your critical thinking skills. A task-specific rubric helps you self-assess your result.	On the following pages
2L	Combination of Objectives from Projects 2A and 2B	**2L GO! Think** A demonstration of your understanding of the Chapter concepts applied in a manner that you would outside of college. An analytic rubric helps you and your instructor grade the quality of your work by comparing it to the work an expert in the discipline would create.	On the following pages
2M	Combination of Objectives from Projects 2A and 2B	**2M GO! Think** A demonstration of your understanding of the Chapter concepts applied in a manner that you would outside of college. An analytic rubric helps you and your instructor grade the quality of your work by comparing it to the work an expert in the discipline would create.	Online
2N	Combination of Objectives from Projects 2A and 2B	**2N You and GO!** A demonstration of your understanding of the Chapter concepts applied in a manner that you would in a personal situation. An analytic rubric helps you and your instructor grade the quality of your work.	Online
2O	Combination of Objectives from Projects 2A and 2B	**2O Cumulative Group Project for PowerPoint Chapter 2** A demonstration of your understanding of concepts and your ability to work collaboratively in a group role-playing assessment, requiring both collaboration and self-management.	Online

GLOSSARY

GLOSSARY OF CHAPTER KEY TERMS

Background Removal A feature that removes unwanted portions of a picture so that the picture does not appear as a self-contained rectangle.

Clip A single media file, such as art, sound, animation, or a movie.

Crop A command that removes unwanted or unnecessary areas of a picture.

Crop handles Handles used to remove unwanted areas of a picture.

Crop pointer The pointer used to crop areas of a picture.

Crosshair pointer The pointer used to draw a shape.

Eyedropper A tool that captures the exact color from an object on your screen and then applies the color to any shape, picture, or text.

Fill color The inside color of text or of an object.

RGB A color model in which the colors red, green, and blue are added together to form another color.

Ruler guides Dotted red vertical and horizontal lines that display in the rulers indicating the pointer's position.

Shape A slide object such as a line, arrow, box, callout, or banner.

Smart Guides Dashed lines that display on your slide when you are moving an object to assist you with alignment.

SmartArt graphic A visual representation of information that you create by choosing from among various layouts to communicate your message or ideas effectively.

SmartArt Styles Combinations of formatting effects that you can apply to SmartArt graphics.

Text Box An object with which you can position text anywhere on a slide.

Text effects Formats applied to text that include shadows, reflections, glows, bevels, and 3-D rotations.

WordArt A gallery of text styles with which you can create decorative effects, such as shadowed or mirrored text.

CHAPTER REVIEW

Skills Review | Project 2C Concerts

Apply 2A skills from these Objectives:

1 Format Numbered and Bulleted Lists
2 Insert Online Pictures
3 Insert Text Boxes and Shapes
4 Format Objects

In the following Skills Review, you will format a presentation that describes annual Concerts in the Park events at several Sensation Park Entertainment Group amusement parks. Your completed presentation will look similar to Figure 2.55.

PROJECT FILES

For Project 2C, you will need the following file:

p02C_Concerts

You will save your presentation as:

Lastname_Firstname_2C_Concerts

PROJECT RESULTS

FIGURE 2.55

(Project 2C Concerts continues on the next page)

CHAPTER REVIEW

1 Start PowerPoint. From the student data files that accompany this textbook, locate and open **p02C_ Concerts**. On the **FILE tab**, click **Save As**, navigate to your PowerPoint Chapter 2 folder, and then using your own name, save the file as **Lastname_Firstname_2C_Concerts**

a. If necessary, display the Rulers. With **Slide 1** displayed, on the **INSERT tab**, in the **Illustrations group**, click **Shapes**, and then under **Basic Shapes**, in the second row, click the fifth shape—**Frame**.

b. Move the pointer to align the ruler guides with the **left half of the horizontal ruler at 3 inches** and with the **upper half of the vertical ruler at 2.5 inches**, and then click to insert the Frame.

c. On the **FORMAT tab**, in the **Size group**, click in the **Shape Height** box to select the number, and then type **1.7** Click in the **Shape Width** box. Replace the selected number with **5.5** and then press Enter to resize the shape.

d. With the frame selected, type **Sensation Park Entertainment Group** and then change the **Font Size** to **28**. On the **FORMAT tab** in the **Shape Styles group**, click **Shape Fill**, and then under **Theme Colors**, in the fourth column, click the first color— **Gray-25%, Text 2**.

2 On the **INSERT tab**, in the **Images group**, click **Online Pictures**. In the **Office.com Search** box, type **sheet music close up** and then press Enter.

a. Click the picture of the two lines of music on a music sheet, and then click **Insert**. If you cannot find the image, choose another picture.

b. On the **FORMAT tab**, in the **Size group**, click in the **Shape Height** box. Replace the selected number with **2.5** and then press Enter to resize the image.

c. Drag the picture down and to the right until intersecting red dashed Smart Guides display, indicating that the picture is center aligned with the title and its top edge aligns with the bottom edge of the title placeholder.

d. With the picture selected, on the **FORMAT tab**, in the **Size group**, click the **Crop arrow**, and then point to **Crop to Shape**. Under **Basic Shapes**, click the first shape—**Oval**. In the **Picture Styles group**, click **Picture Effects**, point to **Soft Edges**, and then click **25 Point**.

e. With the picture selected, hold down Shift, and then click the **frame shape** and the **title placeholder** so that all three objects are selected. Under **DRAWING TOOLS**, on the **FORMAT tab**, in the **Arrange group**, click **Align**, and then click **Align to Slide**. Click **Align** again, and then click **Align Center**. **Save** the presentation.

3 Display **Slide 2**. On the right side of the slide, in the content placeholder, click **Online Pictures**. In the **Search Office.com** box, type **drum kit** and then press Enter. Insert the picture of the drum set on a white background. If the picture is not available, choose another image.

a. On the **FORMAT tab**, in the **Picture Styles group**, click **Picture Effects**, point to **Soft Edges**, and then click **50 Point**.

b. Click in the placeholder containing the text *Every Friday in June and July*. On the **HOME tab**, in the **Paragraph group**, click **Bullets** to remove the bullet symbol from the title.

c. Select the text *Every Friday in June and July*. On the **HOME tab**, in the **Font group**, click the **Font Color button arrow**. Below the gallery, click **Eyedropper**, and then move the eyedropper pointer so that it is pointing to the bright gold area of the drum on the right side of the picture. Click one time to apply the color to the selected text. Apply **Bold** and **Italic** and change the **Font Size** to **28**.

4 Display **Slide 3**, and then select the third and fourth bullet points—*Seating is limited* and *Reserved seating is available*.

a. On the **HOME tab**, in the **Paragraph group**, click the **Bullets button arrow**, and then click **Bullets and Numbering**. In the second row, click the first style—**Hollow Square Bullets**. Replace the number in the **Size** box with **90** and then click the **Color arrow**. Under **Recent Colors**, apply the color chosen using the eyedropper on Slide 2—**Tan**. Click **OK**.

b. Display **Slide 4**, and then click the bulleted list placeholder. Click the dashed border so that the border displays as a solid line, and then on the **HOME tab**, in the **Paragraph group**, click **Numbering** to change the bullet symbols to numbers.

(Project 2C Concerts continues on the next page)

c. On the left side of the slide, select the title text, and then on the mini toolbar, click the **Font Color button arrow**. Under **Recent Colors**, click **Tan**.

5 ▶ Display **Slide 5**. On the **INSERT tab**, in the **Images group**, click **Online Pictures**. In the **Office.com search** box, type **electric guitar** and then press Enter. Insert the picture of the black electric guitar on the white, blue, and black background. If you cannot locate the picture, choose another image.

a. Change the picture **Height to 4.75** and then drag the picture so that its upper left corner aligns with the upper left corner of the purple area on the slide. On the **FORMAT tab**, in the **Picture Styles group**, click **Picture Effects**, and then point to **Soft Edges**. Click **2.5 Point**.

b. Press Ctrl + D and then drag the duplicated picture to the right about 1 inch. Press Ctrl + D to insert a third picture.

c. Point to the third guitar picture that you inserted and then drag to the right so that its upper right corner aligns with the upper right corner of the purple area on the slide.

d. Hold down Shift and then click the first two guitar pictures so that all three pictures are selected. On the **FORMAT tab**, in the **Arrange group**, click **Align**, and then click **Align to Slide**. Click **Align** again, and then click **Align Middle**.

e. With the three pictures selected, click **Align**, and then click **Align Selected Objects**. Click **Align** again, and then click **Distribute Horizontally**.

6 ▶ With **Slide 5** displayed, on the **INSERT tab**, in the **Text group**, click **Text Box**. Move the pointer to align the ruler guides with the **left half of the horizontal ruler at 2 inches** and with the **lower half of the vertical ruler at 2.5 inches**, and then click to insert the text box.

a. Type **Concerts Begin on June 21!** Select the text and then change the **Font Size** to **32**. On the **FORMAT tab**, in the **Arrange group**, click **Align**, and then click **Align Center**.

b. Insert a **Header & Footer** on the **Notes and Handouts tab**. Include the **Date and time updated automatically**, the **Page number**, and a **Footer** with the text **Lastname_Firstname_2C_Concerts**

c. Display the document properties. As the **Tags,** type **concerts** and as the **Subject,** type your course and section number. Be sure your name displays as the author, and then **Save** your file.

d. View the slide show from the beginning. Print **Handouts 6 Slides Horizontal**, or submit your presentation electronically as directed by your instructor. **Close** the presentation.

END | You have completed Project 2C

CHAPTER REVIEW

Apply **2B** skills from these Objectives:

5 Remove Picture Backgrounds and Insert WordArt

6 Create and Format a SmartArt Graphic

Skills Review Project 2D Corporate Events

In the following Skills Review, you will format a presentation by inserting and formatting WordArt and SmartArt graphics. Your completed presentation will look similar to Figure 2.56.

PROJECT FILES

For Project 2D, you will need the following file:

p02D_Corporate_Events

You will save your presentation as:

Lastname_Firstname_2D_Corporate_Events

PROJECT RESULTS

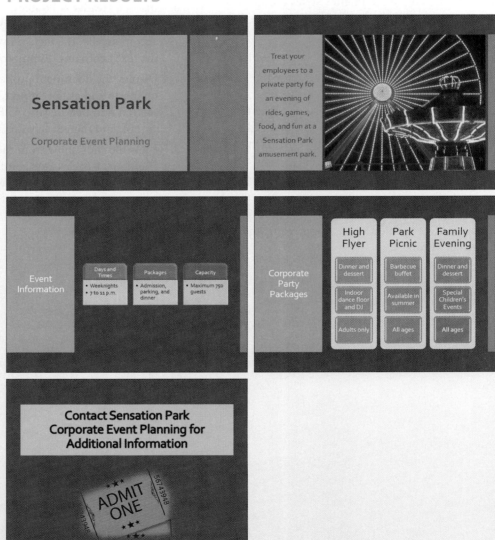

FIGURE 2.56

(Project 2D Corporate Events continues on the next page)

1 Start PowerPoint. From the student data files that accompany this textbook, locate and open **p02D_Corporate_Events**. **Save** the presentation in your **PowerPoint Chapter 2** folder as **Lastname_Firstname_2D_Corporate_Events**

a. With **Slide 1** displayed, select the text **Corporate Event Planning**. On the **FORMAT tab**, in the **WordArt Styles group**, click **More**. In the second row, click the last style—**Fill – Brown, Accent 3, Sharp Bevel**. Click outside the placeholder.

b. On the **INSERT tab**, in the **Text group**, click **WordArt**. In the **WordArt gallery**, in the third row, click the last style—**Fill - Brown, Background 2, Inner Shadow**. With the text *Your text here* selected, type **Sensation Park**

c. With the WordArt selected, hold down Shift, and then click the subtitle. On the **FORMAT tab**, in the **Arrange group**, click **Align**, and then click **Align Selected Objects**. Click **Align** again, and then click **Align Left**.

2 Display **Slide 3**. In the center of the content placeholder, click **Insert a SmartArt Graphic** to open the **Choose a SmartArt Graphic** dialog box. On the left, click **List**, and then scroll as necessary and locate and click **Horizontal Bullet List**. Click **OK**.

a. In the SmartArt graphic, in the first gold rectangle, click *Text*. Type **Days and Times** and then click in the rectangle below the text you typed. Type **Weeknights** and then click in the second bullet point. Type **7 to 11 p.m.**

b. In the second gold rectangle, type **Packages** and then click in the rectangle below the text you typed. Type **Admission, parking, and dinner** and then delete the second text bullet point in the rectangle.

c. In the third gold rectangle, type **Capacity** and then click in the rectangle below the text you typed. Type **Maximum 750 guests** and then delete the second text bullet point in the rectangle.

d. On the **SMARTART TOOLS DESIGN tab**, in the **SmartArt Styles group**, click **Change Colors**, and then under **Colorful**, click the last style **Colorful Range - Accent Colors 5 to 6**. In the **SmartArt Styles group**, click **More**, and then under **3-D**, in the first row, click the fourth style—**Powder**.

e. Click in the **Days and Times** rectangle, hold down Shift, and then click the **Packages** and **Capacity**

rectangles. On the **SMARTART TOOLS FORMAT tab**, in the **Shapes group**, click **Change Shape**. Under **Rectangles**, click the fourth shape—**Snip Same Side Corner Rectangle**.

3 Display **Slide 4**, and then click anywhere in the bulleted list. On the **HOME tab**, in the **Paragraph group**, click **Convert to SmartArt**. At the bottom of the gallery, click **More SmartArt Graphics**. On the left side of the **Choose a SmartArt Graphic** dialog box, click **List**. Locate and click **Grouped List**, and then click **OK** to convert the list to a SmartArt graphic.

a. Under **Family Evening**, click in the **Dinner and dessert** shape, and then on the **SMARTART TOOLS DESIGN tab**, in the **Create Graphic group**, click **Add Shape**. In the inserted shape, type **Special Children's Events**

b. With the *Special Children's Events* shape selected, add another shape, and then type **All ages**

c. On the **SMARTART TOOLS DESIGN tab**, in the **SmartArt Styles group**, click **Change Colors**. In the **Color** gallery, under **Colorful**, click the last style—**Colorful Range - Accent Colors 5 to 6**.

d. On the **DESIGN tab**, in the **SmartArt Styles group**, click **More** to display the **SmartArt Styles gallery**. Under **3-D**, in the first row, click the third style—**Cartoon**.

4 Display **Slide 5**. Select the picture of the admission tickets, and then on the **FORMAT tab**, in the **Adjust group**, click **Remove Background**. In the **Close group**, click **Keep Changes**.

a. With the picture selected, on the **FORMAT tab**, in the **Picture Styles group**, click **Picture Effects**. Point to **Soft Edges**, and then click **25 Point**.

b. Insert a **Header & Footer** on the **Notes and Handouts**. Include the **Date and time updated automatically**, a **Page number**, and a **Footer** with the text **Lastname_Firstname_2D_Corporate_Events**

c. Display the document properties. As the **Tags** type **corporate events** and as the **Subject** type your course and section number. Be sure your name displays as the author, and then **Save** your file.

d. View the slide show from the beginning. Print **Handouts 6 Slides Horizontal**, or submit your presentation electronically as directed by your instructor. **Close** the presentation.

END | You have completed Project 2D

CONTENT-BASED ASSESSMENTS

In the following Mastering PowerPoint project, you will format a presentation describing new roller coasters under construction at several Sensation Park Entertainment Group amusement parks. Your completed presentation will look similar to Figure 2.57.

Apply 2A skills from these Objectives:

1 Format Numbered and Bulleted Lists

2 Insert Online Pictures

3 Insert Text Boxes and Shapes

4 Format Objects

PROJECT FILES

For Project 2E, you will need the following file:

p02E_Coasters

You will save your presentation as:

Lastname_Firstname_2E_Coasters

PROJECT RESULTS

FIGURE 2.57

(Project 2E Coasters continues on the next page)

1 Start PowerPoint. From the student data files that accompany this textbook, locate and open **p02E_Coasters**. In your **PowerPoint Chapter 2** folder, **Save** the file as **Lastname_Firstname_2E_Coasters**

2 On **Slide 2**, remove the bullet symbol from the paragraph, and then **Center** the paragraph. With the content placeholder selected, display the **Shape Styles** gallery, and then in the fourth row, apply the sixth style—**Subtle Effect – Blue-Gray, Accent 5**. Apply the **Art Deco** beveled shape effect to the placeholder.

3 On **Slide 3**, apply **Numbering** to the first-level bullet points—*Intensity, Hang Time,* and *Last Chance.* Under each of the numbered items, change all of the circle bullet symbols to **Star Bullets**, and then change the bullet color to **Aqua, Accent 1, Lighter 40%**—in the fifth column, the fourth color.

4 On **Slide 3**, select the title. Change the **Font Color** using the **Eyedropper**. With the eyedropper pointer, click anywhere in the thick, light yellow stripe on the roller coaster car at the right side of the picture to apply the light yellow color to the title. If necessary, use the Zoom slider to zoom in on the picture. On **Slides 1** and **2**, apply the same light yellow color to the slide title on each slide.

5 Display **Slide 3**, and then apply an **Aqua, 5 pt glow, Accent color 2** picture effect to the picture.

6 Display **Slide 4**. Insert an **Online Picture** by searching for **roller coaster** and then insert the close-up picture of the roller coaster with the red cars and the people raising their hands in the air. If you cannot locate the picture, choose another image. **Crop** the picture by dragging the bottom-center crop handle up so that the crop handle is positioned on the **lower half of the vertical ruler at 1 inch**.

7 Align the upper left corner of the picture with the top left corner of the slide, and then change the **Height** to **4.5** Modify the picture effect by applying a **50 Point Soft Edges** effect.

8 Duplicate the picture, and then use the **Align to Slide** option to align the pictures with the left edge of the slide and to distribute the pictures vertically.

9 Insert a **Text Box** aligned with the **horizontal ruler at 0 inches** and with the **lower half of the vertical ruler at 1 inch**. In the text box, type **Starting Summer 2016!** Change the **Font Size** to **28**. Change the **Shape Fill** to the last color in the last column—**Blue, Accent 6, Darker 50%**.

10 Select the title and the text box, and then, using the **Align Selected Objects** option, apply **Align Right** alignment. Apply the **Box** transition to all of the slides in the presentation, and then view the slide show from the beginning.

11 Insert a **Header & Footer** on the **Notes and Handouts**. Include the **Date and time updated automatically**, the **Page number**, and a **Footer** with the text **Lastname_Firstname_2E_Coasters**

12 Display the document properties. As the **Tags** type **coasters** and as the **Subject** type your course and section number. Be sure your name displays as the author, and then **Save** your file.

13 **Save** your presentation. Submit your presentation electronically or print **Handouts 4 Slides Horizontal** as directed by your instructor. **Close** PowerPoint.

END | You have completed Project 2E

In the following Mastering PowerPoint project, you will format a presentation describing new attractions at several of the Sensation Park Entertainment Group amusement parks. Your completed presentation will look similar to Figure 2.58.

Apply 2B skills from these Objectives:

5 Remove Picture Backgrounds and Insert WordArt

6 Create and Format a SmartArt Graphic

PROJECT FILES

For Project 2F, you will need the following file:

p02F_Attractions

You will save your presentation as:

Lastname_Firstname_2F_Attractions

PROJECT RESULTS

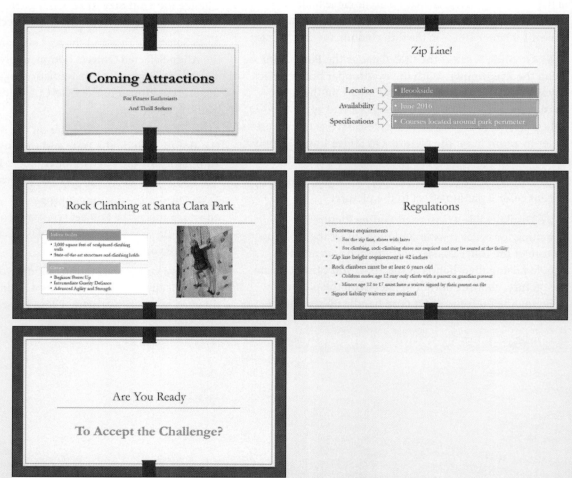

FIGURE 2.58

(Project 2F Attractions continues on the next page)

CONTENT-BASED ASSESSMENTS

1 Start PowerPoint. From the student data files that accompany this textbook, open **p02F_Attractions**, and then **Save** the file in your **PowerPoint Chapter 2** folder as **Lastname_Firstname_2F_Attractions**

2 On **Slide 1**, select the title and display the **WordArt Styles** gallery. In the third row, apply the first WordArt style—**Fill – Black, Text 1, Outline – Background 1, Hard Shadow – Background 1**. Change the **Text Outline** by applying, in the fourth column, the fourth color—**Dark Green, Text 2, Lighter 40%**.

3 On **Slide 2**, in the content placeholder, insert a **List** type **SmartArt** graphic using **Vertical Bracket List**. In the upper-left Text placeholder, type **Location** and then in the bullet point to the right of *Location*, type **Brookside** In the lower text placeholder, type **Availability** and then in the rectangle to the right of *Availability*, type **June 2016**

4 Click the *Availability* placeholder, and then add a shape after the placeholder. In the new placeholder, type **Specifications** and then add a bullet. Type **Courses located around park perimeter**

5 Change the SmartArt color to **Colorful Range - Accent Colors 4 to 5**, and then apply the **3-D Cartoon** style. Select the three bracket shapes, and then change the shapes to the **Right Arrow** shape. On the **FORMAT tab**, in the **Shapes group**, click the **Smaller** button two times to decrease the size of the arrows.

6 On **Slide 3**, convert the bulleted list to a **SmartArt** graphic by applying the **Vertical Box List** graphic. Change the SmartArt color to **Colorful Range - Accent Colors 4 to 5**, and then apply the **Polished** 3-D SmartArt style.

7 On **Slide 5**, insert a **WordArt**—in the first row, the last style—**Fill – Dark Teal, Accent 4, Soft Bevel**. Replace the WordArt text with **To Accept the Challenge?** Change the **Font Size** to **48**.

8 Hold down Shift and then drag the WordArt down so that its upper edge is positioned on the **lower half of the vertical ruler at 1**.

9 Apply the **Peel Off** transition to all the slides, and then view the slide show from the beginning.

10 **Insert** a **Header & Footer** on the **Notes and Handouts**. Include the **Date and time updated automatically**, the **Page number**, and a **Footer** with the text **Lastname_Firstname_2F_Attractions**

11 Display the document properties. As the **Tags** type **zip line, rock wall** and as the **Subject,** type your course and section number. Be sure your name displays as the author, and then **Save** your file.

12 **Save** your presentation. Submit your presentation electronically or print **Handouts 6 Slides Horizontal** as directed by your instructor. **Close** the presentation and exit PowerPoint.

END | You have completed Project 2F

CONTENT-BASED ASSESSMENTS

Mastering PowerPoint Project 2G Orientation

Apply 2A and 2B skills from these Objectives:

1 Format Numbered and Bulleted Lists
2 Insert Online Pictures
3 Insert Text Boxes and Shapes
4 Format Objects
5 Remove Picture Backgrounds and Insert WordArt
6 Create and Format a SmartArt Graphic

In the following Mastering PowerPoint project, you will edit an existing presentation that is shown to Sensation Park Entertainment Group employees on their first day of a three-day orientation. Your completed presentation will look similar to Figure 2.59.

PROJECT FILES

For Project 2G, you will need the following file:

p02G_Orientation

You will save your presentation as:

Lastname_Firstname_2G_Orientation

PROJECT RESULTS

FIGURE 2.59

(Project 2G Orientation continues on the next page)

1 Start PowerPoint, and then from your student data files, open the file **p02G_Orientation**. In your **PowerPoint Chapter 2** folder, **Save** the file as **Lastname_Firstname_2G_Orientation**

2 On **Slide 1**, format the subtitle—*New Employee Orientation*—with a **WordArt Style** using the second style in the first row—**Fill - Orange, Accent 1, Shadow**. Change the **Text Fill** to **Dark Red, Accent 2, Darker 50%**.

3 Select the picture and then **Crop** the image from the left side so that the center-left crop handle aligns with the **left half of the horizontal ruler at 5 inches**. Size the picture Height to **3.5** and then apply an **Orange, 8 pt glow, Accent color 1** picture effect to the image. Use the **Align Selected Objects** command to apply **Align Middle** to the title and the picture.

4 On **Slide 2**, remove the bullet symbol from the paragraph, and then change the **Shape Fill** to **Tan, Background 2, Darker 50%**, and the **Shape Outline** to **Black, Text 1**.

5 On **Slide 3**, convert the bulleted list to the **Hierarchy** type **SmartArt** graphic—**Hierarchy List**. Change the color to **Colorful Range - Accent Colors 3 to 4**, and then apply the **3-D Inset** style.

6 On **Slide 4**, change the two bulleted lists to **Numbering**. On **Slide 5**, change the bullet symbols to **Filled Square Bullets**, change the **Color** to **Tan, Background 2, Darker 50%**, and then change the **Size** to **100**

7 On **Slide 5**, in the placeholder on the right, insert an **Online Picture** by searching for **fire alarm** and then insert a picture of a fire alarm with a background. If the option

is available, remove the background from the picture, and then apply the **Brown, 18 pt glow, Accent color 3** picture effect.

8 On **Slide 5**, insert a **Text Box** below the content placeholder on the left side of the slide. In the text box, type **All employees will be tested on park safety procedures!** Using the **Align to Slide** option **Align Center** the text box and apply **Align Bottom**.

9 On **Slide 6**, from the **Shapes** gallery, under **Basic Shapes**, insert a **Diamond** of any size anywhere on the slide. Resize the diamond so that its **Shape Height** is **6** and its **Shape Width** is **8**

10 Using the **Align to Slide** option, apply the **Align Center**, and **Align Middle** alignment commands to the diamond shape. Apply the **Moderate Effect - Brown, Accent 3** shape style, and then in the diamond, type **Sensation Park Entertainment Group Welcomes You!** Change the **Font Size** to **28**, and then apply the **Art Deco Bevel** shape effect to the diamond shape.

11 Insert a **Header & Footer** on the **Notes and Handouts**. Include the **Date and time updated automatically**, the **Page number**, and a **Footer** with the text **Lastname_Firstname_2G_Orientation** Apply to all.

12 Display the document properties. As the **Tags** type **orientation** and as the **Subject** type your course and section number. Be sure your name displays as the author, and then **Save** your file.

13 **Save** your presentation. Submit your presentation electronically or print **Handouts 6 Slides Horizontal** as directed by your instructor. **Close** PowerPoint.

END | You have completed Project 2G

CONTENT-BASED ASSESSMENTS

GO! Fix It	Project 2H Summer Jobs	Online

GO! Make It	Project 2I Renovation Plans	Online

GO! Solve It	Project 2J Business Summary	Online

GO! Solve It	Project 2K Hotel	

PROJECT FILES

For Project 2K, you will need the following file:

p02K_Hotel

You will save your presentation as:

Lastname_Firstname_2K_Hotel

Open the file p02K_Hotel and save it as **Lastname_Firstname_2K_Hotel** Complete the presentation by inserting an online picture on the first slide and applying appropriate picture effects. On Slide 2, format the bullet point as a single paragraph and apply a shape style, and then on Slide 3, convert the bulleted list to an appropriate SmartArt graphic. Change the SmartArt color and apply a style. On Slide 4, insert and attractively position a WordArt with the text Save the Date! Insert a header and footer that includes the date and time updated automatically, the file name in the footer, and the page number. Add your name, your course name and section number, and the tags **hotel, accommodations** to the Properties area. Save your presentation. Print or submit as directed by your instructor.

Performance Level

		Exemplary	Proficient	Developing
Performance Criteria	**Insert and format an appropriate online picture**	An appropriate online picture was inserted and formatted in the presentation.	An online picture was inserted but was not appropriate for the presentation or was not formatted.	An online picture was not inserted.
	Insert and format appropriate SmartArt graphic	Appropriate SmartArt graphic was inserted and formatted in the presentation.	SmartArt graphic was inserted but was not appropriate for the presentation or was not formatted.	SmartArt graphic was not inserted.
	Insert and format appropriate WordArt	Appropriate WordArt was inserted and formatted in the presentation.	WordArt was inserted but was not appropriate for the presentation or was not formatted.	WordArt was not inserted.
	Remove bullet point and apply appropriate shape style	Bullet point was removed and an appropriate shape style was applied.	Either the bullet point was not removed or the shape style was not applied.	Bullet point was not removed and a shape style was not applied.

END | You have completed Project 2K

OUTCOMES-BASED ASSESSMENTS

RUBRIC

The following outcomes-based assessments are open-ended assessments. That is, there is no specific correct result; your result will depend on your approach to the information provided. Make Professional Quality your goal. Use the following scoring rubric to guide you in how to approach the problem and then to evaluate how well your approach solves the problem.

The *criteria*—Software Mastery, Content, Format and Layout, and Process—represent the knowledge and skills you have gained that you can apply to solving the problem. The *levels of performance*—Professional Quality, Approaching Professional Quality, or Needs Quality Improvements—help you and your instructor evaluate your result.

	Your completed project is of Professional Quality if you:	Your completed project is Approaching Professional Quality if you:	Your completed project Needs Quality Improvements if you:
1-Software Mastery	Choose and apply the most appropriate skills, tools, and features and identify efficient methods to solve the problem.	Choose and apply some appropriate skills, tools, and features, but not in the most efficient manner.	Choose inappropriate skills, tools, or features, or are inefficient in solving the problem.
2-Content	Construct a solution that is clear and well organized, contains content that is accurate, appropriate to the audience and purpose, and is complete. Provide a solution that contains no errors in spelling, grammar, or style.	Construct a solution in which some components are unclear, poorly organized, inconsistent, or incomplete. Misjudge the needs of the audience. Have some errors in spelling, grammar, or style, but the errors do not detract from comprehension.	Construct a solution that is unclear, incomplete, or poorly organized; contains some inaccurate or inappropriate content; and contains many errors in spelling, grammar, or style. Do not solve the problem.
3-Format & Layout	Format and arrange all elements to communicate information and ideas, clarify function, illustrate relationships, and indicate relative importance.	Apply appropriate format and layout features to some elements, but not others. Overuse features, causing minor distraction.	Apply format and layout that does not communicate information or ideas clearly. Do not use format and layout features to clarify function, illustrate relationships, or indicate relative importance. Use available features excessively, causing distraction.
4-Process	Use an organized approach that integrates planning, development, self-assessment, revision, and reflection.	Demonstrate an organized approach in some areas, but not others; or, use an insufficient process of organization throughout.	Do not use an organized approach to solve the problem.

OUTCOMES-BASED ASSESSMENTS

Apply a combination of the **2A** and **2B** skills.

Build from
Scratch

GO! Think   Project 2L Interactive Ride

PROJECT FILES

For Project 2L, you will need the following file:

New blank PowerPoint presentation

You will save your presentation as:

Lastname_Firstname_2L_Interactive_Ride

As part of its mission to combine fun with the discovery of math and science, Sensation Park Entertainment Group is opening a new, interactive roller coaster at its South Lake Tahoe location. Sensation Park's newest coaster is designed for maximum thrill and minimum risk. In a special interactive exhibit located next to the coaster, riders can learn about the physics behind this powerful coaster and even try their hand at building a coaster.

Guests will begin by setting the height of the first hill, which determines the coaster's maximum potential energy to complete its journey. Next they will set the exit path, and build additional hills, loops, and corkscrews. When completed, riders can submit their coaster for a safety inspection to find out whether the ride passes or fails.

In either case, riders can also take a virtual tour of the ride they created to see the maximum speed achieved, the amount of negative G-forces applied, the length of the track, and the overall thrill factor. They can also see how their coaster compares with other Sensation Park coasters, and they can email the coaster simulation to their friends.

Using the preceding information, create a presentation that Marketing Director, Annette Chosek, will present at a travel fair describing the new attraction. The presentation should include four to six slides with at least one SmartArt graphic and one online picture. Apply an appropriate theme and use slide layouts that will effectively present the content, and use text boxes, shapes, and WordArt styles if appropriate. Apply font formatting and slide transitions, and modify text alignment and line spacing as necessary. Save the file as **Lastname_Firstname_2L_Interactive_Ride** and then insert a header and footer that includes the date and time updated automatically, the file name in the footer, and the page number. Add your name, your course name and section number, and the tags **roller coaster, new rides** to the Properties area. Print or submit as directed by your instructor.

END | You have completed Project 2L

Build from
Scratch

GO! Think   Project 2M Research   Online

Build from
Scratch

You and GO!   Project 2N Theme Park   Online

GO! Cumulative Group Project   Project 2O Bell Orchid Hotels
Online

Enhancing a Presentation with Animation, Video, Tables, and Charts

PROJECT 3A	OUTCOMES
	Customize a presentation with animation and video.

OBJECTIVES

1. Customize Slide Backgrounds and Themes
2. Animate a Slide Show
3. Insert a Video

PROJECT 3B	OUTCOMES
	Create a presentation that includes data in tables and charts.

OBJECTIVES

4. Create and Modify Tables
5. Create and Modify Charts

forcpan / Fotolia

In This Chapter

In this chapter, you will learn how to customize a presentation by modifying the theme, formatting the slide background, and applying animation to slide elements. Additionally, you will learn how to enhance your presentations by inserting tables and charts that help your audience understand numeric data and trends just as pictures and diagrams help illustrate a concept. The data that you present should determine whether a table or a chart would most appropriately display your information. Styles applied to your tables and charts unify these slide elements by complementing your presentation theme.

The projects in this chapter relate to the city of **Pacifica Bay**, a coastal city south of San Francisco. The city's access to major transportation provides both residents and businesses an opportunity to compete in the global marketplace. The city's mission is to create a more beautiful and more economically viable community for its residents. Each year the city welcomes a large number of tourists who enjoy exploring the rocky coastline and seeing the famous landmarks in San Francisco. The city encourages best environmental practices and partners with cities in other countries to promote sound government at the local level.

Informational Presentation

PROJECT ACTIVITIES

In Activities 3.01 through 3.17, you will edit and format a presentation that Carol Lehman, Director of Pacifica Bay Parks and Recreation, is creating to inform residents about the benefits of using the city's parks and trails. Your completed presentation will look similar to Figure 3.1.

PROJECT FILES

For Project 3A, you will need the following files:

p03A_Hills
p03A_Trails
p03A_Video

You will save your presentation as:

Lastname_Firstname_3A_Trails

PROJECT RESULTS

FIGURE 3.1 Project 3A Informational Presentation

Video P3-1

You have practiced customizing presentations by applying themes with unified design elements, backgrounds, and colors that provide a consistent look in your presentation. Additional ways to customize a slide include changing theme fonts and colors, applying a background style, modifying the background color, or inserting a picture on the slide background.

NOTE | **If You Are Using a Touchscreen**

- Tap an item to click it.
- Press and hold for a few seconds to right-click; release when the information or commands display.
- Touch the screen with two or more fingers and then pinch together to zoom in or stretch your fingers apart to zoom out.
- Slide your finger on the screen to scroll—slide left to scroll right and slide right to scroll left.
- Slide to rearrange—similar to dragging with a mouse.
- Swipe from edge: from right to display charms; from left to expose open apps, snap apps, or close apps; from top or bottom to show commands or close an app.
- Swipe to select—slide an item a short distance with a quick movement—to select an item and bring up commands, if any.

Activity 3.01 | Changing Theme Colors

Recall that the presentation theme is a coordinated, predefined set of colors, fonts, lines, and fill effects. In this activity, you will open a presentation in which the Retrospect theme is applied, and then you will change the *theme colors*—a set of coordinating colors that are applied to the backgrounds, objects, and text in a presentation.

1 From the student data files that accompany this textbook, locate and open **p03A_Trails**. Display the **Save As** dialog box, create a **New Folder** with the name **PowerPoint Chapter 3** and then using your own name, **Save** the file in the folder you created as **Lastname_Firstname_3A_Trails**

2 Click the **DESIGN tab**, and then in the **Variants group**, click **More** ⬇. Point to **Colors** to display the sets of theme colors. Point to several sets and notice the color changes on **Slide 1**.

3 Click **Green** to change the presentation colors, and then compare your screen with Figure 3.2.

Changing the colors does not change the overall design of the presentation. In this presentation, the *Retrospect* presentation theme is still applied to the presentation. By modifying the theme colors, you retain the design of the *Retrospect* theme but apply colors that coordinate with the pictures in the presentation, and that are available as text, accent, and background colors.

FIGURE 3.2

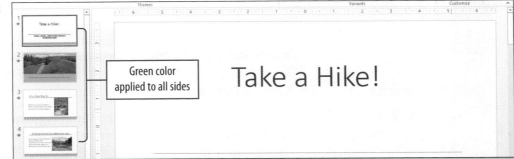

4 Save 🖫 your presentation.

In addition to theme colors, every presentation theme includes *theme fonts* that determine the font to apply to two types of slide text—headings and body. The ***Headings font*** is applied to slide titles and the ***Body font*** is applied to all other text. When you apply a new theme font to the presentation, the text on every slide is updated with the new heading and body fonts.

1 With **Slide 1** displayed, click anywhere in the title placeholder. Click the **HOME tab**, and then in the **Font group**, click the **Font button arrow**. Notice that at the top of the **Font** list, under **Theme Fonts**, Calibri Light (Headings) and Calibri (Body) display. Compare your screen with Figure 3.3.

FIGURE 3.3

2 Click anywhere on the slide to close the Font list. Click the **DESIGN tab**, and then in the **Variants group**, click **More**. Point to **Fonts**.

This list displays the name of each theme and the pair of fonts in the theme. The first and larger font in each pair is the Headings font and the second and smaller font in each pair is the Body font.

3 Point to several of the themes and watch as Live Preview changes the title and subtitle font. Scroll to the bottom of the **Fonts** list, and then click **Trebuchet MS**. Compare your screen with Figure 3.4, and then **Save** your presentation.

FIGURE 3.4

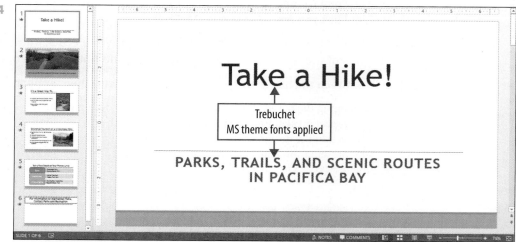

1 With **Slide 1** displayed, on the **DESIGN tab**, in the **Variants group**, click **More**. Point to **Background Styles**, and then compare your screen with Figure 3.5.

A ***background style*** is a predefined slide background fill variation that combines theme colors in different intensities or patterns.

FIGURE 3.5

> **2** Point to each of the background styles to view the style on **Slide 1**. Then, in the first row, click **Style 2**. Compare your screen with Figure 3.6.

The background style is applied to all the slides in the presentation.

FIGURE 3.6

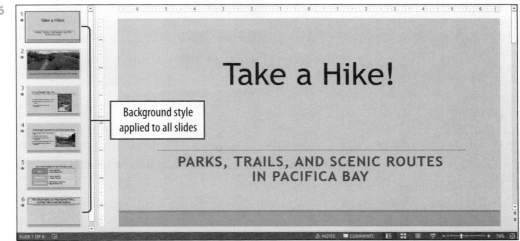

> **3** Display **Slide 5**. On the **DESIGN tab**, in the **Variants group**, click **More** ⮟. Point to **Background Styles**, and then in the third row, *right-click* the third style—**Style 11**—to display the shortcut menu. On the shortcut menu, click **Apply to Selected Slides** to apply the style to Slide 5.

Use this technique to apply a background style to individual slides.

> **4** **Save** 🖫 your presentation.

Activity 3.04 | Hiding Background Graphics

Many of the PowerPoint 2013 themes contain graphic elements that display on the slide background. In the Retrospect theme applied to this presentation, the background includes a rectangle shape and line. Sometimes the background graphics interfere with or clash with the slide content. When this happens, you can hide the background graphics.

> **1** Display **Slide 2**, and notice the bright green rectangle and line at the bottom of the slide.

You cannot delete these objects because they are a part of the slide background; however, you can hide them.

2 On the **DESIGN tab**, in the **Customize group**, click **Format Background** to display the **Format Background** pane.

In the Format Background pane, you can customize a slide background by changing the formatting options.

3 In the **Format Background** pane, be sure that under **Fill**, the fill options display, and if necessary, click Fill to display the options. Under **Fill**, select the **Hide Background Graphics** check box. Compare your slide with Figure 3.7.

The background objects—the rectangle and line below the picture—no longer display.

FIGURE 3.7

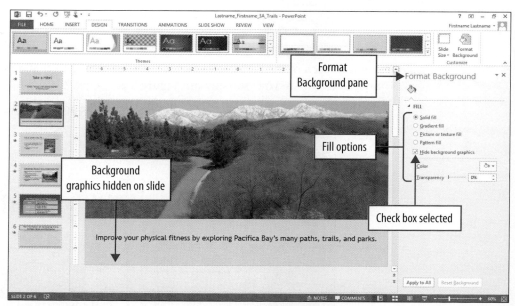

4 Close ☒ the **Format Background** pane, and then **Save** 🖫 your presentation.

More Knowledge | **Removing Background Objects from All Slides in a Presentation**

To remove the background objects from all of the slides in a presentation, in the Format Background pane, select the Hide background graphics check box, and then at the bottom of the Format Background pane, click Apply to All.

Activity 3.05 | **Applying a Background Fill Color to a Slide**

In addition to applying predefined background styles, you can apply a fill color to one or all of the slides in your presentation.

1 Display **Slide 1**. On the **DESIGN tab**, in the **Customize group**, click **Format Background**.

2 In the **Format Background** pane, under **Fill**, verify that **Solid fill** is selected, and select it if it is not. To the right of **Color**, click **Fill Color** 🖾. Under **Theme Colors**, in the third column, click the second color—**Tan, Background 2, Darker 10%**. Compare your screen with Figure 3.8.

The solid fill color is applied to the slide background.

FIGURE 3.8

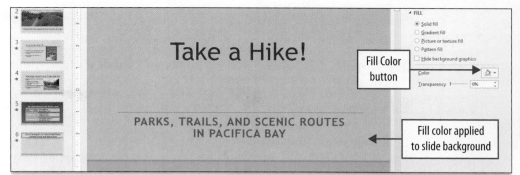

Fill Color
button

Fill color applied
to slide background

3 Leave the **Format Background** pane open for the next Activity. **Save** 🖫 your presentation.

<table>
<tr><td>***More* Knowledge**</td><td>**Applying a Fill Color to All the Slides in a Presentation**</td></tr>
</table>

To apply a fill color to all of the slides in a presentation, in the Format Background pane, select the fill color that you want to apply, and then at the bottom of the Format Background pane, click Apply to All.

Activity 3.06 | **Applying a Background Texture**

1 Display **Slide 2**, and then in the slide thumbnails, hold down ⇧Shift and click **Slide 4** to select **Slides 2**, **3**, and **4**.

Recall that you can select contiguous slides in this manner.

2 In the **Format Background** pane, under **Fill**, click **Picture or texture fill**.

A background picture or fill that is part of the Retrospect theme may display on the slide background of the three selected slides.

3 Under **Insert picture from**, to the right of **Texture**, click **Texture** 🖾 ▾. In the **Texture gallery**, in the third row, point to the fourth texture—**Recycled Paper**. Compare your screen with Figure 3.9.

FIGURE 3.9

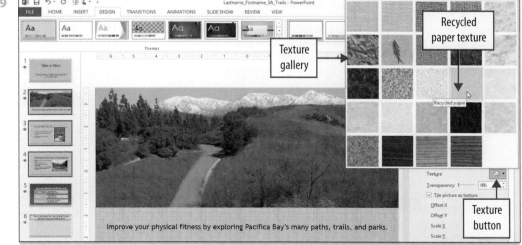

Texture
gallery

Recycled
paper texture

Texture
button

4 Click **Recycled Paper** to apply the textured background to the three selected slides.

5 Leave the **Format Background** pane open for the next Activity, and then **Save** 🖫 your presentation.

You can insert a picture on a slide background so that the image fills the entire slide.

1 Display **Slide 6**. In the **Format Background** pane, select the **Hide background graphics** check box.

2 Under **Fill**, click the **Picture or texture fill** option button. Under **Insert picture from**, click **File**. Navigate to your student data files, click **p03A_Hills**, and then click **Insert**. Compare your slide with Figure 3.10, and notice that the picture displays as the background of Slide 6.

> When a picture is applied to a slide background using the Format Background option, the picture is not treated as an object. The picture fills the entire background and you cannot move it or size it.

FIGURE 3.10

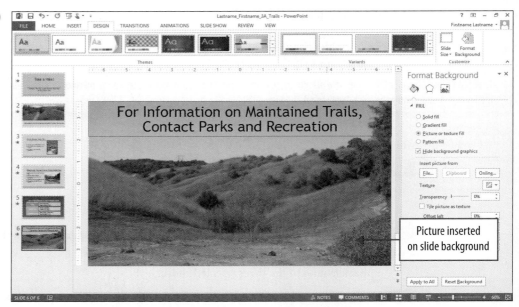

Picture inserted on slide background

3 In the **Format Background** pane, to the right of **Transparency**, notice that *0%* displays, indicating that the picture is inserted in full color. Click in the **Transparency box**, and then replace the number with **50**

> The transparency setting lightens the picture on the slide background. You can use the transparency option when there are other objects on the slide that do not display well against the slide background.

BY TOUCH Drag the Transparency slider to the left or right with your finger to adjust the transparency of the figure.

4 Replace the number in the **Transparency box** with **10%**.

> The 10% transparency setting provides good contrast for the title while still displaying the picture in a vibrant color.

5 Click in the title placeholder. On the **FORMAT tab**, in the **Shape Styles group**, click **More**. In the fourth row, click the second style—**Subtle Effect – Green, Accent 1**. Click anywhere on the slide outside of the title placeholder. Compare your screen with Figure 3.11.

> Adequate contrast between the slide background and slide text is important because it improves slide readability. Use combinations of transparency and text placeholder styles and fills to improve contrast.

FIGURE 3.11

6 Leave the **Format Background** pane open for the next Activity, and then **Save** 💾 your presentation.

Activity 3.08 | Resetting a Slide Background

1 Display **Slide 5**. At the bottom of the **Format Background** pane, click **Reset Background**, and then compare your slide with Figure 3.12.

After making changes to a slide background, you may decide that the original formatting is the best choice for displaying the text and graphics on a slide. The Reset Background feature restores the theme and color theme formatting to a slide.

FIGURE 3.12

2 **Close** ☒ the **Format Background** pane, and then **Save** 💾 your presentation.

Video P3-2

Animation is a visual or sound effect added to an object or text on a slide. Animation can focus the audience's attention, providing the speaker with an opportunity to emphasize important points using the slide element as an effective visual aid.

Activity 3.09 | Applying Animation Entrance Effects and Effect Options

Entrance effects are animations that bring a slide element onto the screen. You can modify an entrance effect by using the animation Effect Options command.

> 1 ▸ Display **Slide 3**, and then click anywhere in the bulleted list placeholder. On the **ANIMATIONS tab**, in the **Animation group**, click **More** ⬇, and then compare your screen with Figure 3.13.
>
> Recall that an entrance effect is animation that brings an object or text onto the screen. An *emphasis effect* is animation that emphasizes an object or text that is already displayed. An *exit effect* is animation that moves an object or text off the screen.

FIGURE 3.13

> 2 ▸ Under **Entrance**, click **Split**, and then notice the animation applied to the list. Compare your screen with Figure 3.14.
>
> The numbers *1*, *2*, and *3* display to the left of the bulleted list placeholder, indicating the order in which the bullet points will be animated during the slide show.

FIGURE 3.14

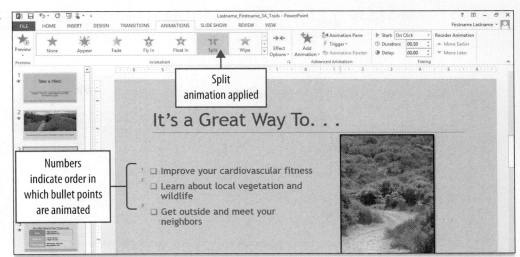

3 Select the bulleted list placeholder. In the **Animation group**, click **Effect Options**, and then compare your screen with Figure 3.15.

The Effect Options control the direction and sequence in which the animation displays. Additional options may be available with other entrance effects.

FIGURE 3.15

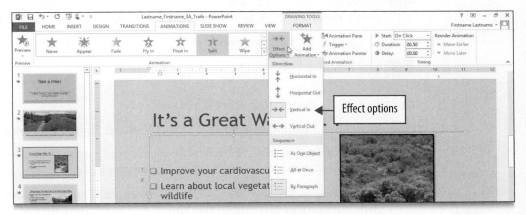

4 Click **Vertical Out** and notice the direction from which the animation is applied.

5 Select the picture. In the **Animation group**, click **More** ⬇, and then below the gallery, click **More Entrance Effects**. In the lower left corner of the **Change Entrance Effect** dialog box, verify that the **Preview Effect** check box is selected. Compare your screen with Figure 3.16.

The Change Entrance Effect dialog box displays additional entrance effects grouped in four categories: Basic, Subtle, Moderate, and Exciting.

FIGURE 3.16

6 Under **Basic**, click **Dissolve In**, and then watch as Live Preview displays the picture with the selected entrance effect. Click **OK**.

The number *4* displays next to the picture, indicating that it is fourth in the slide animation sequence.

7 Select the title. On the **ANIMATIONS tab**, in the **Animation group**, click **More** ⊽, and then under **Entrance**, click **Split** to apply the animation to the title.

The number *5* displays next to the title, indicating that it is fifth in the slide animation sequence.

8 Save 🖫 the presentation.

Activity 3.10 | Reordering Animation

1 With **Slide 3** displayed, on the **ANIMATIONS tab**, in the **Preview group**, click **Preview**.

The list displays first, followed by the picture, and then the title. The order in which animation is applied is the order in which objects display during the slide show.

2 Select the title. On the **ANIMATIONS tab**, in the **Timing group**, under **Reorder Animation**, click the **Move Earlier** button two times, and then compare your screen with Figure 3.17.

To the left of the title placeholder, the number *1* displays. You can use the Reorder Animation buttons to change the order in which text and objects are animated during the slide show.

FIGURE 3.17

Activity 3.11 | Setting Animation Start Options

Timing options control when animated items display in the animation sequence.

1 With the title selected, on the **ANIMATIONS tab**, in the **Timing group**, click the **Start button arrow** to display three options—*On Click*, *With Previous*, and *After Previous*. Compare your screen with Figure 3.18.

The **On Click** option begins the animation sequence for the selected slide element when the mouse button is clicked or the Spacebar is pressed. The **With Previous** option begins the animation sequence at the same time as the previous animation or slide transition. The **After Previous** option begins the animation sequence for the selected slide element immediately after the completion of the previous animation or slide transition.

FIGURE 3.18

2 Click **After Previous**, and then notice that next to the title, the number *1* is changed to *0*, indicating that the animation will begin immediately after the slide transition; the presenter does not need to click the mouse button or press Spacebar to display the title.

3 Select the picture, and then in the **Timing group**, click the **Start arrow**. Click **With Previous** and notice that the number is changed to *3*, indicating that the animation will begin at the same time as the third bullet point in the bulleted list.

4 On the **ANIMATIONS tab**, in the **Preview group**, click **Preview** and notice that the title displays first, and that the picture displays at the same time as the third bullet point.

5 Display **Slide 1**, and then click in the title placeholder. On the **ANIMATIONS tab**, in the **Animation group**, click the **Entrance** effect **Fly In**, and then click the **Effect Options button**. Click **From Top**. In the **Timing group**, click the **Start arrow**, and then click **After Previous**.

The number *0* displays to the left of the title indicating that the animation will begin immediately after the slide transition.

6 Save your presentation.

Activity 3.12 | Setting Animation Duration and Delay Timing Options

1 On **Slide 1**, if necessary, select the title. In the **Timing group**, click the **Duration arrows** as necessary so that *00.75* displays in the **Duration** box. Compare your screen with Figure 3.19.

Duration controls the speed of the animation. You can set the duration of an animation by typing a value in the Duration box, or you can use the spin box arrows to increase and decrease the duration in 0.25-second increments. When you decrease the duration, the animation speed increases. When you increase the duration, the animation is slowed.

FIGURE 3.19

2 Select the subtitle, and then in the **Animation group**, apply the **Fly In** entrance effect. In the **Timing group**, click the **Start arrow**, and then click **After Previous**. In the **Timing group**, select the value in the **Delay** box, type **00.50** and then press Enter. Compare your screen with Figure 3.20.

> You can use Delay to begin a selected animation after a specified amount of time has elapsed. Here, the animation is delayed by one-half of a second after the completion of the previous animation—the title animation. You can type a value in the Delay or Duration boxes, or you can use the up and down arrows to change the timing.

FIGURE 3.20

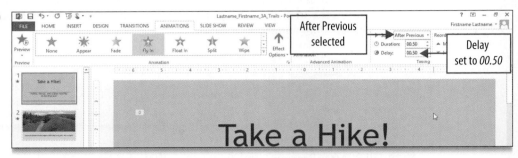

3 View the slide show from the beginning and notice the animation on Slides 1 and 3. When the black slide displays, press Esc to return to Normal view, and then **Save** 🖫 your presentation.

Activity 3.13 | Using Animation Painter and Removing Animation

Animation Painter is a feature that copies animation settings from one object to another.

1 Display **Slide 3**, and then click anywhere in the bulleted list. On the **ANIMATIONS tab**, in the **Advanced Animation group**, click **Animation Painter**. Display **Slide 4**, and then point anywhere in the bulleted list placeholder to display the Animation Painter pointer 🖈▲. Compare your screen with Figure 3.21.

FIGURE 3.21

2 Click the bulleted list to copy the animation settings from the list on **Slide 3** to the list on **Slide 4**.

3 Display **Slide 3**, and then select the picture. Using the technique that you just practiced, use **Animation Painter** to copy the animation from the picture on **Slide 3** to the picture on **Slide 4**. With **Slide 4** displayed, compare your screen with Figure 3.22.

> The numbers displayed to the left of the bulleted list and the picture indicate that animation is applied to the objects.

FIGURE 3.22

> **Animation applied to bulleted list and picture**

Ch... on a Wilderness Hike

- Over 25 miles in the 10, city-maintained trails
- Restroom facilities available
- Wildlife abounds so be aware of surroundings
- Maintained trails can be slippery and hot
- Bring adequate sun protection and hydration

4 Display **Slide 3**, and then click in the title placeholder. On the **ANIMATIONS tab**, in the **Animation group**, click **More**. At the top of the gallery, click **None** to remove the animation from the title placeholder. Compare your screen with Figure 3.23, and then **Save** your presentation.

FIGURE 3.23

> **None selected**

It's a Great Way To. . .

Objective 3 | Insert a Video

Video P3-3

You can insert, size, and move videos in a PowerPoint presentation, and you can format videos by applying styles and effects. Video editing features in PowerPoint 2013 enable you to trim parts of a video and to compress the video to make the presentation easier to share.

Activity 3.14 | Inserting a Video and Using Media Controls

1 Display **Slide 1**. On the **INSERT tab**, in the **Media group**, click **Video**, and then click **Video on My PC**. In the **Insert Video** dialog box, navigate to your student data files, and then click **p03A_Video**. Click **Insert**, and then compare your screen with Figure 3.24.

The video displays in the center of the slide, and media controls display in the control panel below the video. VIDEO TOOLS for FORMAT and PLAYBACK display on the Ribbon.

FIGURE 3.24

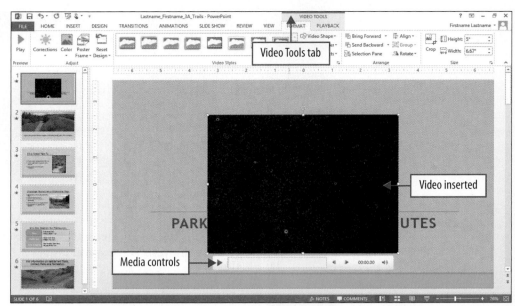

Video Tools tab

Video inserted

Media controls

2 Below the video, in the media controls, click **Play/Pause** ▶ to view the video and notice that as the video plays, the media controls display the time that has elapsed since the start of the video.

3 View the slide show from the beginning. On **Slide 1**, after the subtitle displays, point to the video to display the 🖑 pointer, and then compare your screen with Figure 3.25.

> When you point to the video during the slide show, the media controls display.

FIGURE 3.25

Pointer

Media controls

4 With the 🖑 pointer displayed, click the mouse button to view the video. Move the pointer away from the video and notice that the media controls no longer display. When the video is finished, press Esc to exit the slide show.

5 Save 🖫 your presentation.

Activity 3.15 | Sizing and Aligning a Video

1 With the video selected, on the **FORMAT tab**, in the **Size group**, click in the **Height** box. Type **2** and then press Enter. Notice that the video width adjusts proportionately.

2 On the **FORMAT tab**, in the **Arrange group**, click **Align**, and then click **Align Center**. Click **Align** again, and then click **Align Middle**. Compare your screen with Figure 3.26.

> The video is centered horizontally and vertically on the slide.

FIGURE 3.26

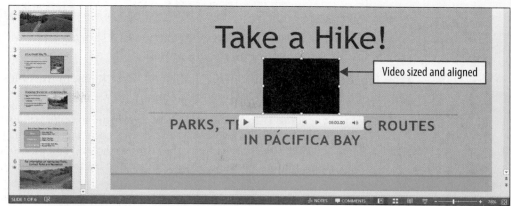

Caption: Video sized and aligned

3 Save your presentation.

Activity 3.16 | Changing the Style and Shape of a Video

You can apply styles and effects to a video and change the video shape and border. You can also recolor a video so that it coordinates with the presentation theme.

1 With **Slide 1** displayed, if necessary, select the video. On the **FORMAT tab**, in the **Video Styles group**, click **More** to display the **Video Styles** gallery.

2 Using the ScreenTips to view the style name, under **Subtle**, in the second row, click the last style—**Drop Shadow Rectangle**. Compare your screen with Figure 3.27.

FIGURE 3.27

Caption: Drop shadow applied to video

3 In the **Video Styles group**, click **Video Shape**, and then under **Rectangles**, click the second shape—**Rounded Rectangle**. Compare your screen with Figure 3.28.

You can format a video with any combination of styles, shapes, and effects.

FIGURE 3.28

Caption: Rounded Rectangle shape applied

You can *trim*—delete parts of a video to make it shorter—and you can compress a video file to reduce the file size of your PowerPoint presentation.

1 If necessary, select the video. On the **PLAYBACK tab**, in the **Editing group**, click **Trim Video**, and then compare your screen with Figure 3.29.

At the top of the Trim Video dialog box, the file name and the video duration display. Below the video, a timeline displays with start and end markers indicating the video start and end time. Start Time and End Time boxes display the current start and end of the video. The Previous Frame and Next Frame buttons move the video forward and backward one frame at a time.

FIGURE 3.29

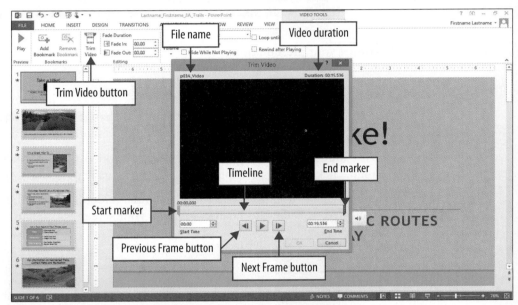

2 In the **End Time** box, replace the number with **00:16.865**. Compare your screen with Figure 3.30.

The blue section of the timeline indicates the portion of the video that will play during the slide show. The gray section indicates the portion of the video that is trimmed. The image in the Trim Video dialog box displays the last frame in the video based on the trim setting.

FIGURE 3.30

⟳ BY TOUCH   Drag the red ending marker with your finger until its ScreenTip displays the ending time that you want.

3 ▶ Click **OK** to apply the trim settings.

4 ▶ Click **FILE**, and then on the **Info tab**, click **Compress Media**. Read the description of each video quality option, and then click **Low Quality**. Compare your screen with Figure 3.31.

The Compress Media dialog box displays the slide number on which the selected video is inserted, the video file name, the original size of the video file, and when compression is complete, the amount that the file size was reduced.

FIGURE 3.31

5 ▶ In the **Compress Media** dialog box, click **Close**, and then on the left, click **Save**.

6 ▶ If necessary, select the video. On the **PLAYBACK tab**, in the **Video Options group**, click the **Start arrow**, and then click **Automatically** so that during the slide show, the video will begin automatically. Compare your screen with Figure 3.32.

FIGURE 3.32

7 ▶ Click the **SLIDE SHOW tab**, in the **Start Slide Show group**, click the **From Beginning** button, and then view the slide show. Notice that on Slide 1, the video begins playing immediately after the subtitle displays. After you view the video, click the mouse button to advance to the next slide and then continue to view the presentation. Press (Esc) when the black slide displays.

8 ▶ Insert a **Header & Footer** on the **Notes and Handouts**. Include the **Date and time** updated automatically, the **Page Number**, and a **Footer**. In the **Footer** box, using your own name, type **Lastname_Firstname_3A_Trails** and then click **Apply to All**.

9 ▶ Display the document properties. As the **Tags**, type **walking trails** and as the **Subject**, type your course and section number. Be sure your name displays as the author, and then **Save** your file.

10 ▶ Print **Handouts 6 Slides Horizontal**, or submit your presentation electronically as directed by your instructor.

11 ▶ **Close** the presentation.

END | You have completed Project 3A

GO! with Office Online (formerly Web Apps)

> **ALERT!** | **Working with Web-Based Applications and Services**
>
> Computer programs and services on the web receive continuous updates and improvements, so the steps to complete this web-based activity may differ from the ones shown. You can often look at the screens and the information presented to determine how to complete the activity.

Activity | Creating an Informational Presentation in PowerPoint Online

In this activity, you will use PowerPoint Online to create a presentation similar to the one you created in Project 3A.

1 From the desktop, start Internet Explorer. Navigate to **http://onedrive.com**, and then sign in to your Microsoft account. Open your **GO! Web Projects** folder—or create and then open this folder if necessary.

2 On the OneDrive menu bar, click **Upload**, and then navigate to your student data files and select **p03_3A_Web**. Click **Open**. When the upload is complete, right-click **p03_3A_Web**, and then click **Rename**. Using your own name, as the file name, type **Lastname_Firstname_PPT_3A_Web** and then press [Enter]. Click your file, and then click **EDIT PRESENTATION**. Click **Edit in PowerPoint Online**.

3 On the **DESIGN tab**, in the **Variants group**, click **Variant 2** to apply the green variant to the entire presentation.

4 On **Slide 1**, double-click in the title placeholder, and then drag to select the title text—*Take a Hike!* On the **HOME tab**, in the **Font Group**, click the **Font arrow**, and then click **Candara**.

5 Display **Slide 2**, and then at the bottom of the slide, point to the text placeholder and then click its outside

border. On the **FORMAT tab**, in the **Shape Styles group**, click the **Quick Styles arrow**, and then in the fourth row, click the second style—**Subtle Effect – Lime, Accent 1**. Change the **Font Size** to **48**.

6 With the placeholder selected, point to the center-left sizing handle, and then drag as far to the left as possible without exceeding the left edge of the slide. Repeat this process on the right side of the slide, and then click outside of the placeholder. Compare your screen with Figure A.

7 Display **Slide 3**, and then click the bulleted list. On the **ANIMATIONS tab**, in the **Animation group**, click **Fly In**. Click **Effect Options**, and then click **From Right**. Click the picture, and then in the **Animation group**, click **Appear**. Click the title, and then in the **Animation group**, click **Fly In**. Click **Effect Options**, and then click **From Top**.

8 With **Slide 3** displayed and the title selected, in the **Timing group**, under **Reorder Animation**, click **Move Earlier** several times until Move Earlier displays in gray, indicating that it will display first.

FIGURE A

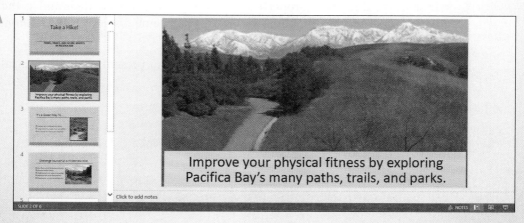

(GO! with Office Online (formerly Web Apps) continues on the next page)

9 Display **Slide 4**, and then click the title. On the **ANIMATIONS tab**, in the **Animation group**, click **Fly In**. Click **Effect Options**, and then click **From Top**. Click the bulleted list, and then in the **Animation group**, click **Fly In**. Click **Effect Options**, and then click **From Right**. Click the **Picture**, and then in the **Animation group**, click **Appear**.

10 Display **Slide 6**, and then click in the title. On the **ANIMATIONS tab**, in the **Animation group**, click **Fly In**. Click **Effect Options**, and then click **From Top**.

11 On the **TRANSITIONS tab**, in the **Transition to This slide group**, click **Push**. Click **Effect Options**, and then click **From Left**. Click **Apply to All**.

12 On the **VIEW tab**, click **Slide Show**, and then view the presentation. If a security warning displays, click Allow once. Click the mouse button to advance through the slides.

13 Submit your file as instructed. Sign out of your OneDrive and then close Internet Explorer.

FIGURE B

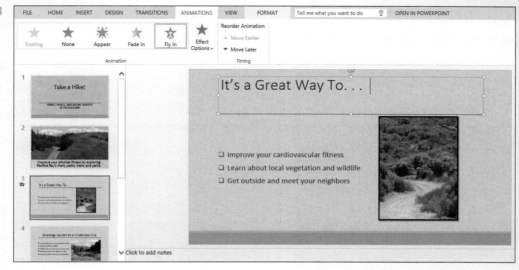

Summary and Analysis Presentation

PROJECT ACTIVITIES

In Activities 3.18 through 3.29, you will add a table and two charts to a presentation that Mindy Walker, Director of Parks and Recreation, is creating to inform the City Council about enrollment trends in Pacifica Bay recreation programs. Your completed presentation will look similar to Figure 3.33.

PROJECT FILES

For Project 3B, you will need the following file:
p03B_Enrollment

You will save your presentation as:
Lastname_Firstname_3B_Enrollment

PROJECT RESULTS

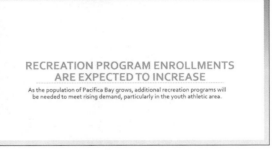

FIGURE 3.33 Project 3B Summary and Analysis Presentation

Video P3-4

A *table* is a format for information that organizes and presents text and data in columns and rows. The intersection of a column and row is referred to as a *cell* and is the location in which you type text in a table.

Activity 3.18 | Creating a Table

There are several ways to insert a table in a PowerPoint slide. For example, you can insert a slide with a Content Layout and then click the Insert Table button. Or, click the Insert tab and then click Table.

1 Start PowerPoint. From your student data files, open **p03B_Enrollment**, and then **Save** the presentation in your **PowerPoint Chapter 3** folder as **Lastname_Firstname_3B_Enrollment**

2 Display **Slide 2**. In the content placeholder, click **Insert Table** to display the **Insert Table** dialog box. In the **Number of columns** box, type **3** and then press Tab. In the **Number of rows** box, type **2** and then compare your screen with Figure 3.34.

Here you enter the number of columns and rows that you want the table to contain.

FIGURE 3.34

3 Click **OK** to create a table with three columns and two rows. Notice that the insertion point is blinking in the upper left cell of the table.

The table extends from the left side of the content placeholder to the right side, and the three columns are equal in width. By default, a style is applied to the table.

4 With the insertion point positioned in the first cell of the table, type **Athletics** and then press Tab.

Pressing Tab moves the insertion point to the next cell in the same row.

ALERT! **Did You Press Enter Instead of Tab?**

In a table, pressing Enter creates another line in the same cell. If you press Enter by mistake, you can remove the extra line by pressing Backspace.

---

5 With the insertion point positioned in the second cell of the first row, type **Leisure** and then press Tab. Type **Arts** and then press Tab to move the insertion point to the first cell in the second row. Compare your table with Figure 3.35.

FIGURE 3.35

6. With the insertion point positioned in the first cell of the second row, type **Team sports** and then press Tab. Type **Personal development classes** and then press Tab. Type **Music and dance classes**

7. Save your presentation.

Activity 3.19 | Inserting Rows and Columns in a Table

You can modify the layout of a table by inserting or deleting rows and columns.

1. With the insertion point positioned in the last cell of the table, press Tab and notice that a new blank row is inserted.

When the insertion point is positioned in the last cell of a table, pressing Tab inserts a new blank row at the bottom of the table.

2. In the first cell of the third row, type **Youth** and then press Tab. Type **Older adults** and then press Tab. Type **Young adults** and then compare your table with Figure 3.36.

FIGURE 3.36

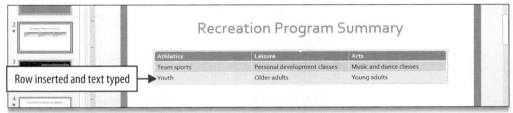

ALERT!   **Did You Add an Extra Row to the Table?**

Recall that when the insertion point is positioned in the last cell of the table, pressing Tab inserts a new blank row. If you inadvertently inserted a blank row in the table, on the Quick Access Toolbar, click Undo.

---

3. Click in any cell in the first column, and then click the **LAYOUT tab**. In the **Rows & Columns group**, click **Insert Left**.

A new first column displays and the width of the columns adjust so that all four columns are the same width.

4. In the *second* row, click in the first cell, and then type **Largest Enrollments**

5. In the third row, click in the first cell, and then type **Primary Market** Compare your table with Figure 3.37.

FIGURE 3.37

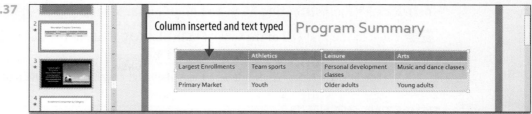

6 With the insertion point positioned in the third row, on the **LAYOUT tab**, in the **Rows & Columns group**, click **Insert Above** to insert a new third row. In the first cell of the new row, type **Average Enrollment** and then press (Tab). Type the remaining three entries, pressing (Tab) to move from cell to cell: **85% of capacity** and **62% of capacity** and **78% of capacity**

More Knowledge | **Deleting Rows and Columns**

To delete a row or column from a table, click in the row or column that you want to delete. Click the LAYOUT tab, and then in the Rows & Columns group, click Delete. In the displayed list, click Delete Columns or Delete Rows.

---

7 **Save** 🖫 your presentation.

Activity 3.20 | Sizing a Table

A selected table is surrounded by sizing handles and can be resized in the same manner in which a shape or picture is resized.

1 Point to the bottom, center sizing handle to display the ⬍ pointer. Compare your screen with Figure 3.38.

FIGURE 3.38

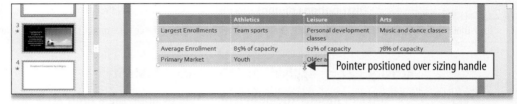

2 Drag down until the ruler guide is positioned on the **lower half of the vertical ruler at 2 inches**. Compare your screen with Figure 3.39.

> A dim border and the red dotted ruler guides display, indicating the size of the table.

FIGURE 3.39

3 Release the mouse button to size the table, and then **Save** 🖫 your presentation.

🔄 **ANOTHER WAY** On the LAYOUT tab, in the Table Size group, type an exact measurement in the Height or Width boxes.

Activity 3.21 | Distributing Rows and Aligning Table Text

1 Click in the first cell of the table. On the **LAYOUT tab**, in the **Cell Size group**, click **Distribute Rows**. Compare your table with Figure 3.40.

> The Distribute Rows command adjusts the height of the rows in the table so that they are equal.

FIGURE 3.40

Distribute Rows button

Distributed rows are equal in height

Recreation Program Summary

2 On the **LAYOUT tab**, in the **Table group**, click **Select**, and then click **Select Table**. In the **Alignment group**, click **Center** ☰, and then click **Center Vertically** ☷.

> All of the table text is centered horizontally and vertically within the cells.

3 **Save** 🖫 your presentation.

More Knowledge | **Distributing Columns**

To distribute columns, click anywhere in the table, and then on the LAYOUT tab, in the Cell Size group, click Distribute Columns.

Activity 3.22 | Applying and Modifying a Table Style

You can modify the design of a table by applying a *table style*. A table style formats the entire table so that it is consistent with the presentation theme. There are color categories within the table styles—Best Match for Document, Light, Medium, and Dark.

1 Click in any cell in the table. Under the **TABLE TOOLS**, click the **DESIGN tab**, and then in the **Table Styles group**, click **More** ⤓. In the displayed **Table Style**s gallery, point to several of the styles to view the Live Preview of the style.

2 Under **Light**, in the third row, click the fourth style—**Light Style 3 – Accent 3**—to apply the style to the table.

3 On the **TABLE TOOLS DESIGN tab**, in the **Table Style Options group**, clear the **Banded Rows** check box, and then select the **Banded Columns** check box. Compare your screen with Figure 3.41.

> The check boxes in the Table Style Options group control where Table Style formatting is applied.

FIGURE 3.41

4 Save the presentation.

Activity 3.23 | Applying Table Effects and Font Formatting

1 Move the pointer outside of the table so that it is positioned to the left of the first row in the table to display the → pointer, as shown in Figure 3.42.

FIGURE 3.42

2 With the → pointer pointing to the first row in the table, click the mouse button to select the entire row so that you can apply formatting to the selection. Move the pointer into the selected row, and then right-click to display the mini toolbar and shortcut menu. On the mini toolbar, change the **Font Size** to **28**.

3 With the first row still selected, on the **TABLE TOOLS DESIGN tab**, in the **Table Styles group**, click **Effects**. Point to **Cell Bevel**, and then under **Bevel**, click the first bevel—**Circle**.

4 Position the pointer above the first column to display the ↓ pointer, and then right-click to select the first column and display the mini toolbar and shortcut menu. Apply **Bold**.

5 Click in a blank area of the slide, and then compare your slide with Figure 3.43. **Save** the presentation.

FIGURE 3.43

Objective 5 | Create and Modify Charts

Video P3-5

A ***chart*** is a graphic representation of numeric data. Commonly used chart types include bar and column charts, pie charts, and line charts. A chart that you create in PowerPoint is stored in an Excel worksheet that is incorporated into the PowerPoint file.

Activity 3.24 | Inserting a Column Chart

A ***column chart*** is useful for illustrating comparisons among related numbers. In this activity, you will create a column chart that compares enrollment in each category of recreation activities by season.

1 Display **Slide 4**. In the content placeholder, click **Insert Chart** [icon] to display the **Insert Chart** dialog box. Compare your screen with Figure 3.44.

Along the left side of the dialog box, the types of charts that you can insert in your presentation display. Along the top of the dialog box, subtypes of the selected chart type display. By default, Column is selected and a Clustered Column chart displays in the preview area on the right side of the dialog box.

FIGURE 3.44

2 Along the top of the dialog box, point to each column chart to view the ScreenTip. Then, with the **Clustered Column** chart selected, click **OK**. Compare your screen with Figure 3.45.

> The PowerPoint window displays a column chart in the content placeholder. Above the chart, a *Chart in Microsoft PowerPoint* worksheet window displays with cells, columns, and rows. A cell is identified by the intersecting column letter and row number, forming the *cell reference*.

> The worksheet contains sample data from which the chart on the PowerPoint slide is generated. The column headings—*Series 1*, *Series 2*, and *Series 3* display in the chart *legend* and the row headings—*Category 1*, *Category 2*, *Category 3*, and *Category 4*—display as *category labels*. The legend identifies the patterns or colors that are assigned to the data series in the chart. The category labels display along the bottom of the chart to identify the categories of data.

FIGURE 3.45

Activity 3.25 | Entering Chart Data

1 In the *Chart in Microsoft PowerPoint* worksheet window, click in cell **B1**, which contains the text *Series 1*. Type **Athletics** and then press Tab to move to cell **C1**.

> Below the chart, the chart legend is updated to reflect the change in the Excel worksheet.

2 In cell **C1**, which contains the text *Series 2*, type **Leisure** and then press Tab to move to cell **D1**. Type **Arts** and then press Tab. Notice that cell **A2**, which contains the text *Category 1*, is selected. Compare your screen with Figure 3.46.

> The outlined cells define the area in which you are entering data. When you press Tab in the rightmost cell, the first cell in the next row becomes active.

FIGURE 3.46

3 Beginning in cell **A2**, type the following data (starting with *Spring*), pressing ⟨Tab⟩ to move from cell to cell. Notice that as you enter the data, the chart columns resize to display the entered amounts.

	ATHLETICS	LEISURE	ARTS
Spring	895	630	720
Summer	1250	350	820
Fall	1490	585	690
Winter	1130	750	

4 In cell **D5**, which contains the value 5, type **710** and then press ⟨Enter⟩.

Pressing ⟨Enter⟩ in the last cell of the outlined area maintains the existing data range.

ALERT! **Did You Press ⟨Tab⟩ After the Last Entry?**

If you pressed ⟨Tab⟩ after entering the data in cell D5, you expanded the chart range. In the Excel window, click Undo.

---

5 Compare your worksheet and your chart with Figure 3.47. Correct any typing errors by clicking in the cell that you want to change, and then retype the data.

Each of the 12 cells containing the numeric data that you entered is a ***data point***—a value that originates in a worksheet cell. Each data point is represented in the chart by a ***data marker***—a column, bar, area, dot, pie slice, or other symbol in a chart that represents a single data point. Related data points form a ***data series***; for example, there is a data series for *Athletics*, *Leisure*, and *Arts*. Each data series has a unique color or pattern represented in the chart legend. A placeholder for the chart title displays above the chart.

To the right of the chart, three buttons display. The ***Chart Elements button*** enables you to add, remove, or change chart elements such as the title, legend, gridlines, and data labels. The ***Chart Styles button*** enables you to set a style and color scheme for your chart. The ***Chart Filters button*** enables you to change which data displays in the chart.

FIGURE 3.47

6 In the upper right corner of the *Chart in Microsoft PowerPoint* worksheet window, click **Close** ✕. **Save** 🖫 the presentation.

When you save the presentation, the worksheet data is saved with it.

Activity 3.26 | Applying a Chart Style and Modifying Chart Elements

A *chart style* is set of predefined formats applied to a chart, including colors, backgrounds, and effects. *Chart elements* are the various components of a chart, including the chart title, axis titles, data series, legend, chart area, and plot area.

1 Be sure the chart is selected; click the outer edge of the chart if necessary to select it. On the **CHART TOOLS DESIGN tab**, in the **Chart Styles group**, click **More** to display the **Chart Styles** gallery.

2 In the **Chart Styles** gallery, point to each style to Live Preview the style. Notice that as you point to a chart style, a ScreenTip indicates the chart style number. Click **Style 5**. Compare your screen with Figure 3.48.

This style includes lightly shaded column data markers. Horizontal gridlines display behind the columns.

FIGURE 3.48

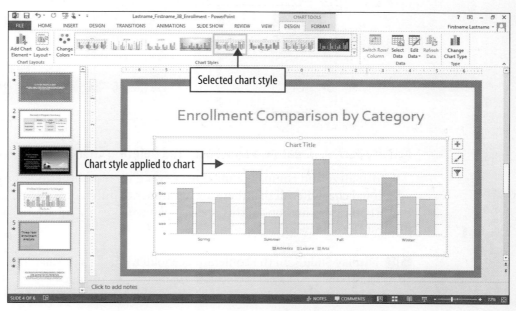

3 To the right of the chart, click **Chart Elements** ⊞, and then compare your screen with Figure 3.49.

A list of chart elements displays to the left of the chart. Here, you can select the chart elements that you wish to display in your chart. In this slide, the slide title describes the chart. Thus, chart title is not necessary.

FIGURE 3.49

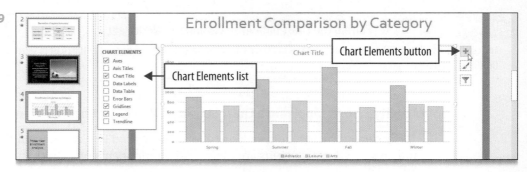

4 Under **Chart Elements**, click **Chart Title** to clear the check box and remove the chart title placeholder from the chart. Click **Chart Elements** ➕ to close the Chart Elements list.

5 Click in a blank area of the slide, and then compare your screen with Figure 3.50. **Save** 🖫 your presentation.

FIGURE 3.50

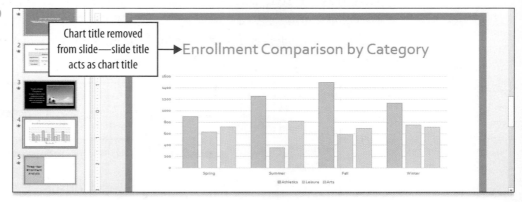

Activity 3.27 | Creating a Line Chart and Deleting Chart Data

To analyze and compare annual data over a three-year period, the presentation requires an additional chart. Recall that there are a number of different types of charts that you can insert in a PowerPoint presentation. In this activity, you will create a *line chart*, which is commonly used to illustrate trends over time.

1 Display **Slide 5**. In the content placeholder, click **Insert Chart** 📊. On the left side of the **Insert Chart** dialog box, click **Line**, and then on the right, click the fourth chart—**Line with Markers**. Click **OK**.

2 In the worksheet, click in cell **B1**, which contains the text *Series 1*. Type **Youth** and then press Tab. Type **Adult** and then press Tab. Type **Senior** and then press Tab.

3 Beginning in cell **A2**, type the following data, pressing Tab to move from cell to cell. If you make any typing errors, click in the cell that you want to change, and then retype the data.

	YOUTH	ADULT	SENIOR
2015	3822	1588	2240
2016	4675	1833	2534
2017	4535	1925	2897

4 In the worksheet, position the pointer over **row heading 5** so that the ➡ pointer displays. Compare your screen with Figure 3.51.

FIGURE 3.51

5 With the ➡ pointer displayed, *right-click* to select the row and display the shortcut menu. On the shortcut menu, click **Delete** to delete the extra row from the worksheet, and then compare your screen with Figure 3.52.

The data in the worksheet contains four columns and four rows, and the outline area defining the chart data range is resized. You must delete columns and rows from the sample worksheet data that you do not want to include in the chart. You can add additional rows and columns by typing column and row headings and then entering additional data. When data is typed in cells adjacent to the chart range, the range is resized to include the new data.

FIGURE 3.52

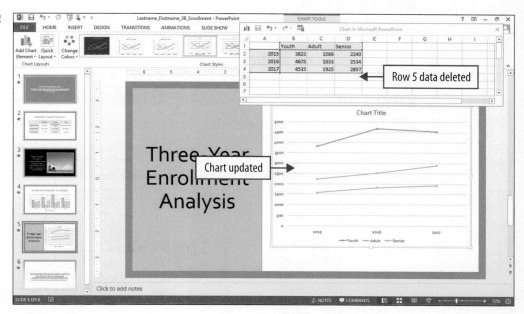

Activity 3.28 | Formatting a Line Chart

1 **Close** ☒ the worksheet window. To the right of the chart, click **Chart Styles** 🖌. Compare your screen with Figure 3.53.

The Chart Style gallery displays on the left side of the chart and the Style tab is active. The chart styles display in a vertical gallery.

FIGURE 3.53

2 In the **Chart Style** gallery, be sure that **Style** is selected. Scroll the list, and point to various styles to view the ScreenTips and the effect of the style on the chart. Click **Style 6** and then click anywhere outside of the chart to close the Chart Style gallery.

> The styles that display when you click the Chart Styles button are the same as those that display in the Chart Styles gallery on the ribbon. Apply chart styles using the technique that you prefer.

3 In the chart, click the text **Chart Title**, and then type **By Age Category**

4 Click in a blank area of the slide, and then compare your screen with Figure 3.54. **Save** 🖫 your presentation.

FIGURE 3.54

Activity 3.29 | Animating a Chart

1 Display **Slide 4**, and then click anywhere in the column chart to select it. On the **ANIMATIONS tab**, in the **Animation group**, click **More** 🖃, and then under **Entrance**, click **Split**.

2 In the **Animation group**, click **Effect Options**, and then under **Sequence**, click **By Series**. Compare your screen with Figure 3.55.

> The By Series option displays the chart one data series at a time, and the numbers 1, 2, 3, and 4 to the left of the chart indicate the four parts of the chart animation sequence. The chart animation sequence includes the background, followed by the Athletics data series for each season, and then the Leisure series, and then the Arts series.

FIGURE 3.55

3 View the slide show from the beginning. On **Slide 4**, notice the chart animation sequence.

4 Insert a **Header & Footer** on the **Notes and Handouts**. Include the **Date and time** updated automatically, the **Page Number**, and a **Footer**. In the Footer box, using your own name, type **Lastname_Firstname_3B_Enrollment** and then click **Apply to All**.

5 Display the document properties. As the **Tags**, type **recreation enrollment** and as the **Subject**, type your course and section number. Be sure your name displays as the author, and then **Save** your file.

6 Print **Handouts 6 Slides Horizontal**, or submit your presentation electronically as directed by your instructor.

7 **Close** the presentation.

END | You have completed Project 3B

GO! with Office Online (formerly Web Apps)

Objective | Create a Summary and Analysis Presentation in PowerPoint Online

> **ALERT!** **Working with Web-Based Applications and Services**
>
> Computer programs and services on the web receive continuous updates and improvements, so the steps to complete this web-based activity may differ from the ones shown. You can often look at the screens and the information presented to determine how to complete the activity.

Activity | Creating a Summary and Analysis Presentation in PowerPoint Online

In this activity, you will use PowerPoint Online to create a presentation similar to the one you created in Project 3B.

1 From the desktop, start Internet Explorer. Navigate to **http://onedrive.com**, and then sign in to your Microsoft account. Open your **GO! Web Projects** folder—or create and then open this folder if necessary.

2 On the OneDrive menu bar, click **Upload**, and then navigate to your student data files and select **p03_3B_Web**. Click **Open**. When the upload is complete, right-click **p03_3B_Web**, and then click **Rename**. Using your own name, as the file name, type **Lastname_Firstname_PPT_3B_Web** and then press Enter. Click your file, and then click **EDIT PRESENTATION**. Click **Edit in PowerPoint Online**.

3 Display **Slide 3**. In the text placeholder on the left side of the slide, type **The largest enrollment numbers in Pacifica Bay recreation programs continue to be in the athletic area, particularly in the youth soccer program.** Click outside of the placeholder to enter the text.

4 On the right side of the slide, click **Insert Picture**. From your student data files, insert **p03B_Web_Picture**.

5 With the picture selected, on the **FORMAT tab**, in the **Picture Styles group**, click the third style—**Metal Frame**.

6 Click in a blank area of the slide, and then compare your screen with Figure A.

7 Display **Slide 4**, and then select the title. On the **ANIMATIONS tab**, in the **Animation group**, click **Fly In**. Click **Effect Options**, and then click **From Top**. In the **Timing group**, click **Move Earlier** several times until the Move Earlier text displays in gray.

8 Display **Slide 5**, and then click in the title placeholder. Type **Three-Year Enrollment Analysis** and then click outside of the placeholder to enter the text.

FIGURE A

(GO! with Office Online (formerly Web Apps) continues on the next page)

9 On **Slide 5**, select the chart. On the **ANIMATIONS tab**, in the **Animation group**, click **Fade In**.

10 Compare your screen with Figure B.

11 Display **Slide 6**. In the title placeholder, type **Recreation Program Enrollments Are Expected to Increase** and then click outside of the placeholder to enter the text.

12 On the **VIEW tab**, click **Slide Show**, and then view the presentation. If a security warning displays, click Allow once. Click the mouse button to advance through the slides.

13 Submit your file as instructed. Sign out of your OneDrive and then close Internet Explorer.

FIGURE B

Andrew Rodriguez / Fotolia; FotolEdhar/ Fotolia; apops/ Fotolia; Yuri Arcurs/ Fotolia

The advantage of using Office 365 is that your organization does not have to purchase and install server hardware and software for sophisticated business applications and does not need a full-time IT person or staff just to manage the technology your teams need.

By using Office 365, you are able to have business-class services for your employees without investing in expensive hardware, software, and personnel. However, at least one person in an organization must be designated as the *Office 365 Administrator*—the person who creates and manages the account, adds new users, sets up the services your organization wants to use, sets permission levels, and manages the SharePoint team sites. You can have more than one Administrator if you want to share these tasks with others.

Microsoft provides easy-to-use instructions and videos to get you started, and you might also have contact with a Microsoft representative. You will probably find, however, that subscribing to and setting up the account, adding users, and activating services is a straightforward process that requires little or no assistance.

After purchasing the required number of licenses, you will add each team member as a user that includes his or her email address.

The Admin Overview page, as shown in the Figure below, assists the Office 365 Administrator. On the left there are links to manage the users and domains in your Office 365 account. This is where you can add new users, delete users, set permission levels, enter and change passwords, and update the user properties and the licenses.

In the center, you can see the various services available to you in Office 365. In the site shown in the Figure, Outlook, Lync, SharePoint (team sites), and a public-facing website are all part of the services.

Activity | Using a Team Site to Collaborate

This group project relates to the **Bell Orchid Hotels**. If your instructor assigns this project to your class, you can expect to use a SharePoint team site in **Office 365** to collaborate on the following tasks for this chapter:

- If you are in the **Accounting Group**, you and your teammates will finalize the Loan Presentation and post the final presentation on the SharePoint team site.
- If you are in the **Engineering Group**, you and your teammates will finalize the Safety Presentation and post the final presentation on the SharePoint team site.
- If you are in the **Food and Beverage Group**, you and your teammates will finalize the New Menu Item presentation and post the final presentation on the SharePoint team site.
- If you are in the **Human Resources Group**, you and your teammates will finalize the New Employees Orientation presentation and post the final presentation on the SharePoint team site.
- If you are in the **Operations Group**, you and your teammates will finalize the Front Desk Clerk Training Presentation presentation and post the final presentation on the SharePoint team site.
- If you are in the **Sales and Marketing Group**, you and your teammates will finalize the Marketing Plan Presentation presentation and post the final presentation on the SharePoint team site.

(GO! with Microsoft Office 365 continues on the next page)

FIGURE A

Microsoft Office 365

Home Outlook Team Site | **Admin**

Admin
My profile | Sign out

Admin

Bell Orchid Hotels

Admin Overview

Management
Users
Domains

Subscriptions
Manage
Licenses
Purchase

Support
Overview
Service Health
Planned
Maintenance

Admin shortcuts

Reset user passwords | Add new users | Assign user licenses

Outlook

Manage Outlook and Exchange settings.
Settings | Distribution groups

Lync

Manage Lync instant messaging, audio and video calling, and online meetings.
Settings

Team sites and documents

Manage your team sites and document libraries with SharePoint.
Manage team sites | Change permissions | Add sites and templates

Website

Design and edit your public-facing website.
Edit website

Search help and community

Resources

Admin introduction for Office 365

Setting up email on mobile phones

Release notes

Downloads

Community

Ask a question in the forums

Check out our blog

Participate in the community

3
POWERPOINT

END OF CHAPTER

SUMMARY

There are many ways to modify a presentation theme and customize a presentation. You can apply background styles, insert pictures and textures on slide backgrounds, and change theme fonts and colors.

One way to enhance a presentation and engage an audience is by inserting interesting and informative video. Styles, shapes, and effects can be applied to videos. A video can be trimmed and compressed to make the file size smaller.

Use animation to focus audience attention on a particular slide element in order to draw attention to important points. Apply animation to slide elements in the order in which you want them to display.

Use tables to present information in an organized and attractive manner. Use charts to visually represent data. Apply styles to charts and tables to give your presentations a consistent and informative look.

GO! LEARN IT ONLINE

Review the concepts and key terms in this chapter by completing these online challenges, which you can find at **www.pearsonhighered.com/go.**

Matching and Multiple Choice:
Answer matching and multiple choice questions to test what you learned in this chapter. MyITLab®

Crossword Puzzle:
Spell out the words that match the numbered clues, and put them in the puzzle squares.

Flipboard:
Flip through the definitions of the key terms in this chapter and match them with the correct term.

GO! FOR JOB SUCCESS

Video: Making Ethical Choices
Your instructor may assign this video to your class, and then ask you to think about, or discuss with your classmates, these questions:

FotolEdhar / Fotolia

Which behaviors in this video do you think were unethical?

Is it unethical to "borrow" things from your employer? Why? What would you do if you saw this behavior going on?

What do you think an employer could do to prevent unethical behavior?

END OF CHAPTER

REVIEW AND ASSESSMENT GUIDE FOR POWERPOINT CHAPTER 3

Your instructor may assign one or more of these projects to help you review the chapter and assess your mastery and understanding of the chapter.

	Review and Assessment Guide for PowerPoint Chapter 3		
Project	**Apply Skills from These Chapter Objectives**	**Project Type**	**Project Location**
3C	Objectives 1-3 from Project 3A	**3C Skills Review** A guided review of the skills from Project 3A.	On the following pages
3D	Objectives 4-5 from Project 3B	**3D Skills Review** A guided review of the skills from Project 3B.	On the following pages
3E	Objectives 1-3 from Project 3A	**3E Mastery (Grader Project)** A demonstration of your mastery of the skills in Project 3A with extensive decision making.	In MyITLab and on the following pages
3F	Objectives 4-5 from Project 3B	**3F Mastery (Grader Project)** A demonstration of your mastery of the skills in Project 3B with extensive decision making.	In MyITLab and on the following pages
3G	Objectives 1-5 from Projects 3A and 3B	**3G Mastery (Grader Project)** A demonstration of your mastery of the skills in Projects 3A and 3B with extensive decision making.	In MyITLab and on the following pages
3H	Combination of Objectives from Projects 3A and 3B	**3H GO! Fix It** A demonstration of your mastery of the skills in Projects 3A and 3B by creating a correct result from a document that contains errors you must find.	Online
3I	Combination of Objectives from Projects 3A and 3B	**3I GO! Make It** A demonstration of your mastery of the skills in Projects 3A and 3B by creating a result from a supplied picture.	Online
3J	Combination of Objectives from Projects 3A and 3B	**3J GO! Solve It** A demonstration of your mastery of the skills in Projects 3A and 3B, your decision-making skills, and your critical thinking skills. A task-specific rubric helps you self-assess your result.	Online
3K	Combination of Objectives from Projects 3A and 3B	**3K GO! Solve It** A demonstration of your mastery of the skills in Projects 3A and 3B, your decision-making skills, and your critical thinking skills. A task-specific rubric helps you self-assess your result.	On the following pages
3L	Combination of Objectives from Projects 3A and 3B	**3L GO! Think** A demonstration of your understanding of the Chapter concepts applied in a manner that you would outside of college. An analytic rubric helps you and your instructor grade the quality of your work by comparing it to the work an expert in the discipline would create.	On the following pages
3M	Combination of Objectives from Projects 3A and 3B	**3M GO! Think** A demonstration of your understanding of the Chapter concepts applied in a manner that you would outside of college. An analytic rubric helps you and your instructor grade the quality of your work by comparing it to the work an expert in the discipline would create.	Online
3N	Combination of Objectives from Projects 3A and 3B	**3N You and GO!** A demonstration of your understanding of the Chapter concepts applied in a manner that you would in a personal situation. An analytic rubric helps you and your instructor grade the quality of your work.	Online
3O	Combination of Objectives from Projects 3A and 3B	**3O Cumulative Group Project for PowerPoint Chapter 3** A demonstration of your understanding of concepts and your ability to work collaboratively in a group role-playing assessment, requiring both collaboration and self-management.	Online
Capstone Project for PowerPoint Chapters 1-3	Combination of Objectives from Projects 1A, 1B, 2A, 2B, 3A, and 3B	A demonstration of your mastery of the skills in Chapters 1-3 with extensive decision making. **(Grader Project)**	In MyITLab and online

A comprehensive Book Capstone Project that covers all of the Word, Excel, Access, and PowerPoint chapters in this book is available online. Instructors can download the Book Capstone Project from the Instructor Resource Center.

GLOSSARY

GLOSSARY OF CHAPTER KEY TERMS

After Previous An animation option that begins the animation sequence for the selected slide element immediately after the completion of the previous animation or slide transition.

Animation A visual or sound effect added to an object or text on a slide.

Animation Painter A feature that copies animation settings from one object to another.

Background style A predefined slide background fill variation that combines theme colors in different intensities or patterns.

Body font A font that is applied to all slide text except slide titles.

Category labels Text that displays along the bottom of a chart to identify the categories of data.

Cell The intersection of a column and row in a table.

Cell reference The intersecting column letter and row number that identify a cell.

Chart A graphic representation of numeric data.

Chart elements The various components of a chart, including the chart title, axis titles, data series, legend, chart area, and plot area.

Chart Elements button A button that displays options for adding, removing, or changing chart elements.

Chart Filters button A button that displays options for changing the data displayed in a chart.

Chart style A set of predefined formats applied to a chart, including colors, backgrounds, and effects.

Chart Styles button A button that displays options for setting the style and color scheme for a chart.

Column chart A type of chart used for illustrating comparisons among related numbers.

Data marker A column, bar, area, dot, pie slice, or other symbol in a chart that represents a single data point.

Data point A chart value that originates in a worksheet cell.

Data series A group of related data points.

Emphasis effect Animation that emphasizes an object or text that is already displayed.

Entrance effect Animation that brings a slide element onto the screen.

Exit effect Animation that moves an object or text off the screen.

Headings font A font that is applied to all slide title text.

Legend A chart element that identifies the patterns or colors that are assigned to the data series in the chart.

Line chart A type of chart commonly used to illustrate trends over time.

On Click An animation option that begins the animation sequence for the selected slide element when the mouse button is clicked or the Spacebar is pressed.

Table A format for information that organizes and presents text and data in columns and rows.

Table style A format applied to a table that is consistent with the presentation theme.

Theme colors A set of coordinating colors that are applied to the backgrounds, objects, and text in a presentation.

Theme fonts The fonts applied to two types of slide text—headings and body.

Timing options Animation options that control when animated items display in the animation sequence.

Trim A command that deletes parts of a video to make it shorter.

With Previous An animation option that begins the animation sequence at the same time as the previous animation or slide transition.

CHAPTER REVIEW

Skills Review | Project 3C Park

Apply 3A skills from these Objectives:

1 Customize Slide Backgrounds and Themes

2 Animate a Slide Show

3 Insert a Video

In the following Skills Review, you will format a presentation by applying slide background styles, colors, pictures, and animation. Your completed presentation will look similar to Figure 3.56.

PROJECT FILES

For Project 3C, you will need the following files:

p03C_Park
p03C_Park_Scenery
p03C_Park_Video

You will save your presentation as:

Lastname_Firstname_3C_Park

PROJECT RESULTS

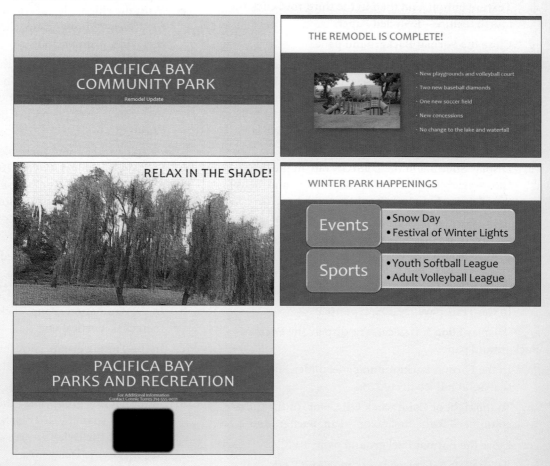

FIGURE 3.56

(Project 3C Park continues on the next page)

CHAPTER REVIEW

1 Start PowerPoint, from your student data files, open **p03C_Park**, and then **Save** the presentation in your **PowerPoint Chapter 3** folder as **Lastname_Firstname_3C_Park**

a. On the **DESIGN tab**, in the **Variants group**, click **More**, point to **Colors**, and then click **Orange Red** to change the theme colors.

b. On the **DESIGN tab**, in the **Variants group**, click **More**, point to **Fonts**, and then click **Candara** to change the theme fonts.

c. On the **DESIGN tab**, in the **Customize group**, click **Format Background**. In the **Format Background** pane, under **Fill**, click **Picture or texture fill**. Under **Insert picture from**, to the right of **Texture**, click the **Texture** button, and then in the third row, click the fourth texture—**Recycled Paper**.

d. **Close** the **Format Background** pane.

2 Display **Slide 2**. Hold down Ctrl and click **Slide 4** so that both **Slides 2** and **4** are selected. On the **DESIGN tab**, in the **Variants group**, click **More**, and then point to **Background Styles**. In the second row, *right-click* the third style—**Style 7**, and then on the shortcut menu, click **Apply to Selected Slides**.

a. Display **Slide 3**. On the **DESIGN tab**, in the **Customize group**, click **Format Background**. Select the **Hide Background Graphics** check box.

b. In the **Format Background** pane, under **Fill**, click the **Picture or texture fill** option button. Under **Insert picture from**, click **File**, and then navigate to your student data files. Click **p03C_Park_Scenery**, and then click **Insert**.

c. In the **Transparency** box, type **10%**

3 Display **Slide 5**. If necessary, display the **Format Background** pane.

a. In the **Format Background** pane, under **Fill**, verify that **Solid Fill** is selected.

b. To the right of **Color**, click **Fill Color**. In the third column, click the first color—**Tan, Background 2**.

c. **Close** the **Format Background** pane.

4 With **Slide 5** displayed, on the **INSERT tab**, in the **Media group**, click **Video**, and then click **Video on My PC**. Navigate to your student data files, and then click **p03C_Park_Video**. Click **Insert** to insert the video.

a. With the video selected, on the **FORMAT tab**, in the **Size group**, replace the value in the **Height** box with **2.5** and then press Enter.

b. On the **FORMAT tab**, in the **Arrange group**, click **Align**, and then click **Align Center**. Click **Align** again, and then click **Align Bottom** so that the video is centered and aligned with the lower edge of the slide.

c. With the video selected, on the **FORMAT tab**, in the **Video Styles** group, click **More**, and then under **Subtle**, click the third style—**Soft Edge Rectangle**.

d. In the **Video Styles group**, click **Video Shape**, and then under **Rectangles**, click the second shape—**Rounded Rectangle**.

e. With the video selected, on the **PLAYBACK tab**, in the **Video Options group**, click the **Start arrow**, and then click **Automatically**.

f. On the **PLAYBACK tab**, in the **Editing group**, click **Trim Video**. Select the number in the **End Time** box, and then type **00:14** and notice that the video ends with a picture of the park. Click **OK** to apply the trim settings.

5 Display **Slide 2**, and then select the text in the in the bulleted list placeholder. On the **HOME tab**, in the **Font group**, click the **Font Color button arrow**, and then in the second column, click the first color—**White, Text 1** so that the text displays with more contrast against the slide background.

a. With the bulleted list selected, on the **ANIMATIONS tab**, in the **Animation group**, click **More**, and then under **Entrance**, click **Split**.

b. In the **Animation group**, click **Effect Options**, and then click **Vertical Out**.

c. In the **Timing group**, click the **Start arrow**, and then click **After Previous** so that the list displays after the slide transition.

d. In the **Timing group**, click the **Duration up arrow** two times so that *01.00* displays in the **Duration** box. Click the **Delay up arrow** one time so that *00.25* displays in the **Delay** box.

(Project 3C Park continues on the next page)

CHAPTER REVIEW

6 Display **Slide 3**, and then click in the title placeholder. On the **ANIMATIONS tab**, in the **Animation group**, click **More**, and then under **Entrance**, click **Wipe**. In the **Timing group**, click the **Start arrow**, and then click **After Previous** so that the title displays immediately after the slide transition.

a. With the title selected, in the **Advanced Animation group**, click **Animation Painter**. Click **Slide 1**, and then click the subtitle—*Remodel Update*—to apply the animation effect to the subtitle.

b. On **Slide 1**, select the title. Notice that in the Animation group, the Bounce animation is applied. On the **ANIMATIONS tab**, in the **Animation group**, click **More**, and then click **None** to remove the animation from the title.

c. Insert a **Header & Footer** for the **Notes and Handouts**. Include the **Date and time updated automatically**, the **Page number**, and a **Footer** with the file name **Lastname_Firstname_3C_Park**

END | You have completed Project 3C

---

d. On the **SLIDE SHOW tab**, in the **Start Slide Show group**, click **From Beginning**, and then view your presentation, clicking the mouse button to advance through the slides. When the video on Slide 5 finishes, press Esc to return to the presentation.

7 Click the **FILE tab**, and then on the **Info tab**, click **Compress Media**. Click **Low Quality** to make the presentation size smaller and easier to submit. When the compression is complete, in the **Compress Media** dialog box, click **Close**.

a. Display the document properties. As the **Tags** type **park remodel** and as the **Subject** type your course and section number. Be sure your name displays as the author, and then **Save** your file.

b. Print **Handouts 6 Slides Horizontal**, or submit your presentation electronically as directed by your instructor. **Close** the presentation.

CHAPTER REVIEW

Skills Review Project 3D Budget

In the following Skills Review, you will format a presentation by inserting and formatting a table, a column chart, and a line chart. Your completed presentation will look similar to Figure 3.57.

PROJECT FILES

For Project 3D, you will need the following file:

p03D_Budget

You will save your presentation as:

Lastname_Firstname_3D_Budget

PROJECT RESULTS

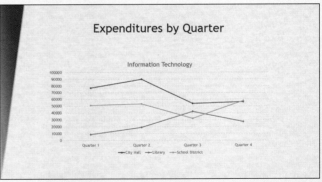

FIGURE 3.57

(Project 3D Budget continues on the next page)

1 Start PowerPoint, from your student data files, open **p03D_Budget**, and then **Save** the presentation in your **PowerPoint Chapter 3** folder as **Lastname_Firstname_3D_Budget**

a. Display **Slide 2**. In the content placeholder, click **Insert Table** to display the **Insert Table** dialog box. In the **Number of columns box**, type **3** and then press Tab. In the **Number of rows** box, type **2** and then click **OK** to create the table.

b. In the first row of the table, click in the second cell. Type **City Hall** and then press Tab. Type **School District** and then press Tab to move the insertion point to the first cell in the second row.

c. With the insertion point positioned in the first cell of the second row, type **Network Upgrade** and then press Tab. Type **75% complete** and then press Tab. Type **50% complete** and then press Tab to insert a new blank row. In the first cell of the third row, type **Software Training** and then press Tab. Type **50% complete** and then press Tab. Type **20% complete**

d. With the insertion point positioned in the last column, on the **LAYOUT tab**, in the **Rows & Columns group**, click **Insert Left** to insert a new column. Click in the top cell of the inserted column, and then type **Library** In the second and third rows of the inserted column, type **85% complete** and **65% complete**

e. With the insertion point positioned in the third row, on the **LAYOUT tab**, in the **Rows & Columns group**, click **Insert Above**. Click in the first cell of the row you inserted, type **Software Testing** and then press Tab. Type the remaining three entries in the row as follows: **Complete** and **Complete** and **40% complete**

2 At the center of the lower border surrounding the table, point to the sizing handle, and make the table larger by dragging down until the lower edge of the table aligns **on the lower half of the vertical ruler at 2 inches.**

a. Click in the first cell of the table. On the **LAYOUT tab**, in the **Cell Size group**, click **Distribute Rows**.

b. On the **LAYOUT tab**, in the **Table group**, click **Select**, and then click **Select Table**. In the **Alignment group**, click **Center**, and then click **Center Vertically**.

c. Click in any cell in the table. Under **TABLE TOOLS**, click the **DESIGN tab**, and then in the **Table Styles group**, click **More**. Under **Medium**, in the third row, click the second style—**Medium Style 3 – Accent 1**—to apply the style to the table.

d. Move the pointer outside of the table so that is positioned to the left of the first row in the table to display the ➡ pointer, and then click one time to select the entire row. On the **DESIGN tab**, in the **Table Styles group**, click **Effects**. Point to **Cell Bevel**, and then under **Bevel**, click the first bevel—**Circle**. Change the **Font Size** of the text in the first row to **24**.

3 Display **Slide 3**. In the content placeholder, click **Insert Chart** to display the **Insert Chart** dialog box. With the *Clustered* **Column** chart selected, click **OK**.

a. In the worksheet window, click in cell **B1**, which contains the text *Series 1*. Type **City Hall** and then press Tab to move to cell **C1**.

b. In cell **C1**, which contains the text *Series 2*, type **Library** and then press Tab to move to cell **D1**, which contains the text *Series 3*. Type **School District** and then press Tab.

c. Beginning in cell **A2**, type the following data, pressing Tab to move from cell to cell.

	City Hall	Library	School District
Budget	235650	110500	185635
Actual	275895	95760	192570

d. In the worksheet window, position the pointer over **row heading 4** so that the ➡ pointer displays. Then, drag down to select both **rows 4** and **5**. *Right-click* in one of the selected the rows to display the shortcut menu. On the shortcut menu, click **Delete**. **Close** the worksheet window.

e. With the chart selected, under **CHART TOOLS**, on the **DESIGN tab**, in the **Chart Styles group**, click **More**. In the **Chart Styles** gallery, in the second row, click **Style 13** to apply the style to the chart.

f. To the right of the chart, click **Chart Elements** ➕, and then *clear* the **Chart Title** box to remove it from the chart.

(Project 3D Budget continues on the next page)

CHAPTER REVIEW

g. With the chart selected, click the **ANIMATIONS tab**, and then in the **Animation group**, click **More**. Under **Entrance**, click **Split**. In the **Animation group**, click **Effect Options**, and then under **Sequence**, click **By Series**.

4 Display **Slide 4**. In the content placeholder, click **Insert Chart**. On the left side of the **Insert Chart** dialog box, click **Line**, and then under **Line**, click the fourth chart—**Line with Markers**. Click **OK**.

a. In the worksheet, click in cell **B1**, which contains the text *Series 1*. Type **City Hall** and then press Tab. Type **Library** and then press Tab. Type **School District** and then press Tab.

b. Beginning in cell **A2**, type the following data, pressing Tab to move from cell to cell. After you finish entering the data, close the worksheet window.

	City Hall	Library	School District
Quarter 1	76575	8265	50665
Quarter 2	89670	18675	52830
Quarter 3	53620	41730	31560
Quarter 4	56030	27090	57515

END | You have completed Project 3D

c. Click in the **Chart Title**, and then type **Information Technology**

d. Insert a **Header & Footer** for the **Notes and Handouts**. Include the **Date and time updated automatically**, the **Page number**, and a **Footer** with the file name **Lastname_Firstname_3D_Budget**

e. Display the document properties. As the **Tags** type **technology budget** and as the **Subject** type your course and section number. Be sure your name displays as the author, and then **Save** your file.

f. Print **Handouts 4 Slides Horizontal**, or submit your presentation electronically as directed by your instructor. **Close** the presentation.

CONTENT-BASED ASSESSMENTS

Mastering PowerPoint Project 3E Gardens

In the following Mastering PowerPoint project, you will format a presentation created by the Pacifica Bay Public Relations department that describes the City of Pacifica Bay Botanical Gardens. Your completed presentation will look similar to Figure 3.58.

Apply 3A skills from these Objectives:

1 Customize Slide Backgrounds and Themes
2 Animate a Slide Show
3 Insert a Video

PROJECT FILES

For Project 3E, you will need the following files:

p03E_Garden
p03E_Flower
p03E_Video

You will save your presentation as:

Lastname_Firstname_3E_Garden

PROJECT RESULTS

FIGURE 3.58

(Project 3E Gardens continues on the next page)

CONTENT-BASED ASSESSMENTS

1 Start PowerPoint. From the student data files that accompany this textbook, locate and open **p03E_ Garden**. Save the presentation in your **PowerPoint Chapter 3** folder as **Lastname_Firstname_3E_Garden**

2 Change the **Colors** for the presentation to **Violet**, and the **Fonts** to **Cambria**. On **Slide 1**, format the background by changing the **Color** of the Solid fill to **Gray – 25%, Text 2, Darker 90%**—in the fourth column, the last color.

3 Select **Slides 2** and **3**, and then format the background of the two selected slides with the **Green marble** texture.

4 On **Slide 2**, select the paragraph on the right side of the slide, and then apply the **Split** entrance effect. Change the **Effect Options** to **Horizontal Out**. Change the **Start** setting to **After Previous**, and then change the **Duration** to **01.00**.

5 Use **Animation Painter** to apply the same animation from the paragraph on **Slide 2** to the bulleted list on **Slide 3**. Then, on **Slide 3,** remove the animation from the title.

6 On **Slide 4,** hide the background graphics, and then format the background with a picture from your student data files—**p03E_Flower**. Change the **Transparency** to **50%**

7 Format the title placeholder with a **Shape Fill** color—in the fifth column, the last color—**Lavender, Accent 1, Darker 50%**.

8 From your student data files, insert the video **p03E_Video**. Change the **Video Height** to **6.25** and then using the **Align to Slide** option, apply the **Align Center** and **Align Bottom** options. Format the video by applying, from the **Video Styles** gallery, an **Intense** style—**Bevel Rectangle**.

9 Change the video **Start** setting to **Automatically**, and then trim the video to **00:14** Compress the video using the **Low Quality** setting.

10 Insert a **Header & Footer** on the **Notes and Handouts**. Include the **Date and time updated automatically**, the **Page number**, and a **Footer** with the text **Lastname_Firstname_3E_Garden**

11 Display the document properties. As the **Tags** type **botanical garden** and as the **Subject** type your course and section number. Be sure your name displays as the author, and then **Save** your file.

12 View the slide show from the beginning, and then print **Handouts 4 Slides Horizontal**, or submi t your presentation electronically as directed by your instructor. **Close** the presentation.

END | You have completed Project 3E

CONTENT-BASED ASSESSMENTS

In the following Mastering PowerPoint project, you will format several of the slides in a presentation that the City Manager is developing for an upcoming City Council meeting. Your completed presentation will look similar to Figure 3.59.

Apply 3B skills from these Objectives:

4 Create and Modify Tables

5 Create and Modify Charts

PROJECT FILES

For Project 3F, you will need the following file:

p03F_Report

You will save your presentation as:

Lastname_Firstname_3F_Report

PROJECT RESULTS

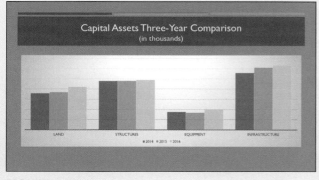

FIGURE 3.59

(Project 3F Report continues on the next page)

CONTENT-BASED ASSESSMENTS

1 Start PowerPoint. From your student data files, open **p03F_Report**, and then **Save** the presentation in your **PowerPoint Chapter 3** folder as **Lastname_Firstname_3F_Report**

2 On **Slide 3**, in the content placeholder, insert a **Line with Markers** chart. In the worksheet, in cell **B1**, type **Taxes** and then enter the following data:

	Taxes	City Fees	Capital Grants
Quarter 1	7480	4154	2650
Quarter 2	6380	3092	3785
Quarter 3	6695	3260	4150
Quarter 4	8370	4190	3970

3 **Close** the worksheet window. Apply **Chart Style 7**, and then apply the **Wipe** entrance effect to the chart. Including the parentheses, change the **Chart Title** to **(In Thousands)**

4 On **Slide 4**, in the content placeholder, insert a **Table** with **2 columns** and **5 rows**, and then type the text in the table below

Item	Description
Flood Control	Main Street storm drain replacement
City Buildings	Infrastructure upgrades
Street Improvements	Rio Avenue asphalt, signage, and street lighting
City Parks	Monterey Park installation of two baseball diamonds

5 Resize the table so that its lower edge extends to **3 inches on the lower half of the vertical ruler**. Align the table text so that it is centered horizontally and vertically

within the cells. Apply table style **Medium Style 3 - Accent 2**, and then to the first row, apply a **Cell Bevel** using the **Circle** effect. Change the **Font Size** of the text in the first row to **24**.

6 On **Slide 5**, in the content placeholder, insert a **Clustered Column** chart. In the worksheet, in cell **B1**, type **2014** and then enter the following data:

	2014	2015	2016
Land	71534	72823	83653
Structures	95746	95920	97812
Equipment	35042	33465	39767
Infrastructure	111586	121860	125873

7 **Close** the worksheet window. Apply **Chart Style 4** to the chart, and then display the **CHART ELEMENTS** list. Clear the **Data Labels** check box so that the data labels do not display at the top of each column. Apply the **Wipe** entrance effect to the chart. Change the **Effect Options** so that the animation is applied **By Series**. Change the **Timing** so that the animation starts **After Previous**. Remove the **Chart Title** element.

8 Insert a **Header & Footer** on the **Notes and Handouts**. Include the **Date and time updated automatically**, the **Page number**, and a **Footer** with the text **Lastname_Firstname_3F_Report**

9 Display the document properties. As the **Tags**, type **city council report** and as the **Subject**, type your course and section number. Be sure your name displays as the author, and then **Save** your file.

10 View the slide show from the beginning, and then print **Handouts 6 Slides Horizontal**, or submit your presentation electronically as directed by your instructor. **Close** the presentation.

END | You have completed Project 3F

CONTENT-BASED ASSESSMENTS

Mastering PowerPoint | Project 3G Travel

In the following Mastering PowerPoint project, you will format a presentation that the Pacifica Bay Travel and Tourism Director will show at a conference for travel agents in California. Your completed presentation will look similar to Figure 3.60.

Apply 3A and 3B skills from these Objectives:

1. Customize Slide Backgrounds and Themes
2. Animate a Slide Show
3. Insert a Video
4. Create and Modify Tables
5. Create and Modify Charts

PROJECT FILES

For Project 3G, you will need the following files:

p03G_Travel
p03G_Video
p03G_Background

You will save your presentation as:

Lastname_Firstname_3G_Travel

PROJECT RESULTS

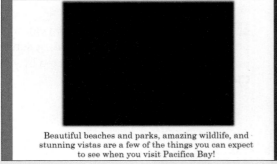

FIGURE 3.60

(Project 3G Travel continues on the next page)

Project 3G: Travel | PowerPoint   **881**

CONTENT-BASED ASSESSMENTS

1 Start PowerPoint. From the student data files that accompany this textbook, locate and open **p03G_ Travel**. Save the presentation in your **PowerPoint Chapter 3** folder as **Lastname_Firstname_3G_Travel**

2 Change the **Colors** for the presentation to **Blue Warm**. On **Slide 1**, format the background with the **Water droplets Texture**, and then change the **Transparency** to **50%**

3 Select **Slides 2 through 4**, and then format the background of the selected slides with a **Solid fill** using the color **Teal, Accent 5, Lighter 60%**—in the second to last column, the third color.

4 On **Slide 2**, hide the background graphics, and then insert a **Table** with **3 columns** and **4 rows**. Apply table style **Medium Style 3 - Accent 3**, and then type the information in the table below.

Trip Type	Day One	Day Two
Adventure Seeker	Kayak and Snorkel	Nature Preserve Hike
Family-Friendly	Pacifica Bay Zoo	Beach Day and Horseback Riding
Arts & Culture	Pacifica Bay Art Museum	Artisan Walk

5 Resize the table so that its lower edge extends to **3 inches on the lower half of the vertical ruler**, and then distribute the table rows. Align the table text so that it is centered horizontally and vertically within the cells, and then change the **Font Size** of the first row of the table text to **24**. Apply a **Circle** style **Cell Bevel** to the first row.

6 On **Slide 3**, animate the picture using the **Wipe** entrance effect starting **After Previous**. Change the **Duration** to **01:00**. Apply the **Split** entrance effect to the bulleted list placeholder, and then change the **Effect Options** to **Vertical Out**.

7 On **Slide 4**, insert a **Clustered Column** chart. In the worksheet, in cell **B1** type **2014** and then enter the following data:

	2014	2015	2016
Spring	75600	72300	81460
Summer	105300	128730	143600
Fall	35900	58300	58320
Winter	41600	58430	67300

8 **Close** the worksheet window, apply **Chart Style 8** to the chart, and then remove the **Chart Title** element. Apply the **Wipe** entrance effect to the chart and change the **Effect Options** to **By Series**.

9 On **Slide 5**, apply the **Style 1** background style to this slide only. From your student data files, insert the video **p03G_Video**. Change the **Video Height** to **6** and use the **Align Center** and **Align Top** options to position the video. Apply the **Soft Edge Rectangle** video style.

10 On the **Playback tab**, change the **Video Options** to **Start** the video **Automatically**. **Trim** the video so that the **End Time** is **00:22** and then compress the media in **Low Quality**.

11 On **Slide 6**, hide the background graphics, and then format the slide background by inserting a picture from your student data files—**p03G_Background**. Set the **Transparency** to **0%**

12 Insert a **Header & Footer** on the **Notes and Handouts**. Include the **Date and time updated automatically**, the **Page number**, and a **Footer** with the text **Lastname_Firstname_3G_Travel**

13 Display the document properties. As the **Tags** type **travel, tourism** and as the **Subject** type your course and section number. Be sure your name displays as the author, and then **Save** your file.

14 View the slide show from the beginning, and then print **Handouts 6 Slides Horizontal**, or submit your presentation electronically as directed by your instructor. **Close** PowerPoint.

END | You have completed Project 3G

CONTENT-BASED ASSESSMENTS

Apply a combination of the 3A and 3B skills.

GO! Fix It	Project 3H Housing Developments	Online
GO! Make It	Project 3I Water Usage	Online
GO! Solve It	Project 3J Aquatic Center	Online
GO! Solve It	Project 3K Power	

PROJECT FILES

For Project 3K, you will need the following files:

p03K_Power
p03K_Tower

You will save your presentation as:

Lastname_Firstname_3K_Power

Open the file p03K_Power and save it as **Lastname_Firstname_3K_Power** Apply a theme and then format the slide background of the title slide with the picture found in your student data files—p03K_Tower. Format the title slide so that the title text displays attractively against the background. Format the background of at least one other slide using a background style, solid fill color, or texture. On Slide 3, insert a table with the following information:

Power Sources	Percent Used by City
Natural gas	32%
Hydroelectric	17%
Renewables	18%
Coal	23%
Nuclear	10%

On Slide 4, insert and format an appropriate chart to demonstrate the revenue collected from residential power sales over the past three years. Revenue in 2014 was 35.5 million dollars, in 2015 revenue was 42.6 million dollars, and in 2016 revenue was 48.2 million dollars. Apply appropriate animation and and insert an appropriate header and footer. Add your name, your course name and section number, and the tags **power sources, revenue** to the Properties. Save and then print or submit the presentation as directed by your instructor.

(Project 3K Power continues on the next page)

CONTENT-BASED ASSESSMENTS

Performance Level

Performance Elements	Exemplary	Proficient	Developing
	You consistently applied the relevant skills	You sometimes, but not always, applied the relevant skills.	You rarely or never applied the relevant skills.
Format two slide backgrounds with pictures and styles	Two slide backgrounds were formatted attractively and text displayed with good contrast against backgrounds.	Slide backgrounds were formatted but text did not display well, or only one slide background was formatted.	Slide backgrounds were not formatted with pictures or styles.
Insert and format appropriate table and chart	Appropriate table and chart were inserted and formatted and the entered data was accurate.	A table and a chart were inserted but were not appropriate for the presentation or either a table or a chart was omitted.	Table and chart were not inserted.
Apply appropriate animation	Appropriate animation was applied to the presentation.	Animation was applied but was not appropriate for the presentation.	Animation was not applied.

END | You have completed Project 3K

OUTCOMES-BASED ASSESSMENTS

RUBRIC

The following outcomes-based assessments are open-ended assessments. That is, there is no specific correct result; your result will depend on your approach to the information provided. Make Professional Quality your goal. Use the following scoring rubric to guide you in how to approach the problem and then to evaluate how well your approach solves the problem.

The *criteria*—Software Mastery, Content, Format and Layout, and Process—represent the knowledge and skills you have gained that you can apply to solving the problem. The *levels of performance*—Professional Quality, Approaching Professional Quality, or Needs Quality Improvements—help you and your instructor evaluate your result.

	Your completed project is of Professional Quality if you:	Your completed project is Approaching Professional Quality if you:	Your completed project Needs Quality Improvements if you:
1-Software Mastery	Choose and apply the most appropriate skills, tools, and features and identify efficient methods to solve the problem.	Choose and apply some appropriate skills, tools, and features, but not in the most efficient manner.	Choose inappropriate skills, tools, or features, or are inefficient in solving the problem.
2-Content	Construct a solution that is clear and well organized, contains content that is accurate, appropriate to the audience and purpose, and is complete. Provide a solution that contains no errors in spelling, grammar, or style.	Construct a solution in which some components are unclear, poorly organized, inconsistent, or incomplete. Misjudge the needs of the audience. Have some errors in spelling, grammar, or style, but the errors do not detract from comprehension.	Construct a solution that is unclear, incomplete, or poorly organized; contains some inaccurate or inappropriate content; and contains many errors in spelling, grammar, or style. Do not solve the problem.
3-Format & Layout	Format and arrange all elements to communicate information and ideas, clarify function, illustrate relationships, and indicate relative importance.	Apply appropriate format and layout features to some elements, but not others. Overuse features, causing minor distraction.	Apply format and layout that does not communicate information or ideas clearly. Do not use format and layout features to clarify function, illustrate relationships, or indicate relative importance. Use available features excessively, causing distraction.
4-Process	Use an organized approach that integrates planning, development, self-assessment, revision, and reflection.	Demonstrate an organized approach in some areas, but not others; or, use an insufficient process of organization throughout.	Do not use an organized approach to solve the problem.

OUTCOMES-BASED ASSESSMENTS

Apply a combination of the 3A and 3B skills.

Build from Scratch

GO! Think | Project 3L Animal Sanctuary

PROJECT FILES

For Project 3L, you will need the following file:

New blank PowerPoint presentation

You will save your presentation as:

Lastname_Firstname_3L_Animal_Sanctuary

The Pacifica Bay Animal Sanctuary, a non-profit organization, provides shelter and care for animals in need, including dogs, cats, hamsters, and guinea pigs. The Sanctuary, which celebrates its tenth anniversary in July, has cared for more than 12,000 animals since it opened and is a state-of-the-art facility. Funding for the Sanctuary comes in the form of business sponsorships, individual donations, and pet adoption fees. The following table indicates revenue generated by the Sanctuary during the past three years.

	Fees	Donations	Sponsorships
2014	125,085	215,380	175,684
2015	110,680	256,785	156,842
2016	132,455	314,682	212,648

In addition to shelter services, the Sanctuary offers community service and training programs, veterinarian services, and vaccine clinics. Examples of these services include Canine Obedience classes, microchipping ($25 fee), and the Healthy Pet Hotline (free). Canine Obedience classes are for puppies and adult dogs to improve obedience, socialization, and behavior. Classes last two, three, or four months and cost $150 to $250.

Using the preceding information, create the first five slides of a presentation that the director of the Pacifica Bay Animal Sanctuary will show at an upcoming pet fair. Apply an appropriate theme and use slide layouts that will effectively present the content. Include a line chart with the revenue data, a table with the community service programs information, and at least one slide formatted with a dog or cat on the slide background. Apply styles to the table and chart, and apply animation and slide transitions to the slides. Use the techniques that you practiced in this chapter so that your presentation is professional and attractive. Save the file as **Lastname_Firstname_3L_Animal_Sanctuary** and then insert a header and footer that includes the date and time updated automatically, the file name in the footer, and the page number. Add your name, your course name and section number, and the keywords **animals, pets** to the properties. Save and then print or submit the presentation as directed by your instructor.

END | You have completed Project 3L

Build from Scratch

GO! Think | Project 3M Water Sources   Online

You and GO! | Project 3N Recreation Programs   Online

Build from Scratch

GO! Cumulative Group Project | Project 3O Bell Orchid Hotels
Online

Build from Scratch

Integrating Word, Excel, Access, and PowerPoint

PROJECT 1A

OUTCOMES
Create an Excel workbook that includes data exported from Access and data copied from Word and PowerPoint.

PROJECT 1B

OUTCOMES
Link Excel data to a Word document and complete a mail merge in Word using Access data.

OBJECTIVES

1. Export Access Data to Excel
2. Create an Excel Worksheet from a Word Table
3. Copy and Paste an Excel Chart into Other Programs
4. Copy and Paste an Object from PowerPoint into Excel

OBJECTIVES

5. Link Excel Data to a Word Document
6. Modify Linked Data and Update Links
7. Create a Table in Word from Access Data
8. Use Access Data to Complete a Mail Merge in Word

EpicStockMedia / Fotolia

In This Chapter

All applications in a software suite, for example Microsoft Office, are designed to work well with one another. You can input data or create objects, such as a chart or table, in one application and then export the data to another application without retyping the data or recreating the object. It is important to identify the appropriate software within the suite to produce solutions that best utilize the functions of the various applications. In this chapter, you will copy and paste data and objects between applications. You will link, modify, and update data and use mail merge to create individualized documents.

The projects in this chapter relate to **Ultimate Action Sports Gear**, one of the country's leading retailers of sports equipment and outdoor recreational merchandise. The company has a growing online business in addition to large retail stores in Colorado, New Mexico, Oregon, and Washington. Major merchandise categories include fishing, camping, golf, rock climbing, winter sports, action sports, aquatic sports, team sports, racquet sports, fitness and athletic apparel, and footwear. The company's inventory is constantly updated to provide customers with the newest products in the action sports industry.

PROJECT ACTIVITIES

In Activities 1.01 through 1.12, you will export Access data into an Excel workbook, and then you will copy and paste Word data into the Excel workbook. In Excel, you will create a chart based on the data, and then copy the chart into a PowerPoint presentation. Your completed documents will look similar to Figure 1.1.

PROJECT FILES

For Project 1A, you will need the following files:

New blank Excel workbook
i01A_Store_Locations
i01A_State_Sales
i01A_Sales_Presentation

You will save your files as:

Lastname_Firstname_1A_Sales_Chart
Lastname_Firstname_1A_Store_Locations
Lastname_Firstname_1A_State_Sales
Lastname_Firstname_1A_Sales_Presentation

PROJECT RESULTS

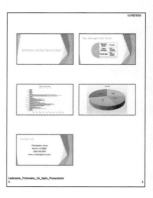

FIGURE 1.1 Project 1A State Sales

- Tap an item to click it.
- Press and hold for a few seconds to right-click; release when the information or command displays.
- Touch the screen with two or more fingers and then pinch together to zoom in or stretch your fingers apart to zoom out.
- Slide your finger on the screen to scroll—slide left to scroll right and slide right to scroll left.
- Slide to rearrange—similar to dragging with a mouse.
- Swipe from edge: from right to display charms; from left to expose open apps, snap apps, or close apps; from top or bottom to show commands or close an app.
- Swipe to select—slide an item a short distance with a quick movement to select an item and bring up commands, if any.

Objective 1 | Export Access Data to Excel

Access includes a tool to export data from an Access database into an Excel workbook. When you export Access data, you create a copy of the data in Excel.

Activity 1.01 | Exporting Access Data to Excel

In the following activity, you will export Access data into an Excel workbook.

1 **Start** Access. Near the bottom left of the screen, click **Open Other Files**, and then under **Places**, double-click **Computer**. In the **Open** dialog box, navigate to your student data files, and then open the Access database **i01A_Store_Locations**. Click the **FILE tab**, and then click **Save As**. On the **Save As** screen, with **Save Database As** selected, click **Save As**.

2 In the **Save As** dialog box, navigate to the location where you are saving your files. Click **New folder**, type **Integrated Projects** and then press Enter. In the **File name** box, type **Lastname_Firstname_1A_Store_Locations** and then press Enter. On the **Message Bar** that displays a SECURITY WARNING, click **Enable Content**.

3 In the **navigation pane**, double-click the **Managers** table. At the bottom of the table, select *Firstname*, and then type your own firstname. Press Tab to select *Lastname*, type your own lastname, and then press Enter.

4 In the **navigation pane**, double-click the query **Store Locations by Manager**, and then be sure that your name displays. Compare your screen with Figure 1.2.

FIGURE 1.2

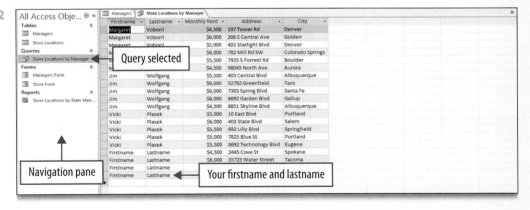

5 On the **EXTERNAL DATA tab**, in the **Export group**, click **Excel**. In the **Export - Excel Spreadsheet** dialog box, click **Browse**. Navigate to your **Integrated Projects** folder, type the file name **Lastname_Firstname_1A_Sales_Chart** and then click **Save**.

6 ▶ In the **Export - Excel Spreadsheet** dialog box, be sure that the **File format** is **Excel Workbook** (***.xlsx**). Select the **Export data with formatting and layout** check box, and then compare your screen with Figure 1.3.

FIGURE 1.3

7 ▶ In the **Export – Excel Spreadsheet** dialog box, click **OK**. In the dialog box, be sure that the **Save export steps** check box is not selected, and then click **Close**.

8 ▶ **Close** ☒ Access.

9 ▶ **Start** Excel. Near the bottom left of the screen, click **Open Other Workbooks**, and then under **Places**, double-click **Computer**. In the **Open** dialog box, navigate to your **Integrated Projects** folder, and then open the Excel workbook **Lastname_Firstname_1A_Sales_Chart**.

> Notice that the Excel worksheet name is changed to the exported Access query name—*Store Locations by Manager*.

Activity 1.02 | Creating and Sorting an Excel Table

To easily manage and analyze a group of related data, you can convert a range of cells to an Excel table. An Excel table typically contains data in a series of rows and columns; the Excel table can be managed independently from the data in other rows and columns in the worksheet. In the following activity, you will change a range of data into an Excel table, and then sort the data.

1 ▶ Click cell **A1**. On the **INSERT tab**, in the **Tables group**, click **Table**. In the **Create Table** dialog box, under **Where is the data for your table?**, be sure that the range is **=$A$1:$E$21** and that the **My table has headers** check box is selected. Compare your screen with Figure 1.4.

FIGURE 1.4

2 ▶ In the **Create Table** dialog box, click **OK**.

3 ▶ Click in cell **E1**, click the **City arrow**, and then click **Sort A to Z** to sort the entire table. Compare your screen with Figure 1.5.

> The rows display in a different order based on column E—the City column—so that city names display in ascending order.

> After a column is sorted in ascending or descending order, a small arrow displays to the right of *City* to indicate the sort order.

FIGURE 1.5

4 ▸ **Save** 🖫 your Excel workbook.

Activity 1.03 | Inserting a Total Row in an Excel Table

To quickly total the data in the columns of an Excel table, display a total row at the end of the table, and then use the functions that are provided for each cell in the total row.

1 ▸ With cell *E1* selected, on the **DESIGN tab**, in the **Table Style Options group**, select the **Total Row** check box. Click cell **E22**, and then compare your screen with Figure 1.6.

Cell E22 displays the number 20. The Total Row counts the number of cells containing text in column E. The header row is not included in the Total Row calculations.

FIGURE 1.6

2 ▸ To the right of cell *E22*, click the **arrow**, and then click **None**.

Because the cells in column E contain text, a calculation is not required.

3 ▸ Click cell **C22**. To the right of cell *C22*, click the **arrow**, and then click **Sum**. Compare your screen with Figure 1.7.

The Total Monthly Rent for all locations displays in cell C22.

FIGURE 1.7

17	Firstname			nding Way	Seattle
18	Firstname			e St	Spokane
19	Vicki			Blvd	Springfield
20	Firstname	Lastname	$6,000.00	35725 Water Street	Tacoma
21	Jim	Wolfgang	$6,000.00	52792 Greenfield	Taos
22	Total		$108,000.00		
23					
24					
25					

Total displays in cell C22

Cell E22 is blank

4 ▸ **Save** 🖫 your Excel workbook.

Objective 2 | Create an Excel Worksheet from a Word Table

There are times when you might want to use data stored in one file in a different file without having to reenter the data.

Activity 1.04 | Formatting a Word Table

1 ▸ **Start** Word. Navigate to your student data files, and then open the document **i01A_State_Sales**. Press F12 to display the **Save As** dialog box. Navigate to your **Integrated Projects** folder, and then **Save** the document as **Lastname_Firstname_1A_State_Sales**

2 ▸ On the **INSERT tab**, in the **Header & Footer group**, click **Footer**. At the bottom of the **Footer** gallery, click **Edit Footer**. On the ribbon, under **HEADER & FOOTER TOOLS**, on the **DESIGN tab**, in the **Insert group**, click **Document Info**, and then click **File Name**. In the **Close group**, click **Close Header and Footer**. Display the ruler and formatting marks, if necessary.

3 ▸ Scroll down to display the table. Click the first cell in the table, and then compare your screen with Figure 1.8.

> When the entire table or a table element is selected, the TABLE TOOLS tabs—DESIGN and LAYOUT—display.

FIGURE 1.8

Insertion point in first cell

TABLE TOOLS DESIGN and LAYOUT tabs

4 ▸ Under **TABLE TOOLS**, on the **DESIGN tab**, in the **Table Styles group**, click **More** ⊤. In the **Table Styles** gallery, scroll down, and then under **List Tables**, in the third row, click the last style—**List Table 3 - Accent 6**.

5 ▸ On the **LAYOUT tab**, in the **Cell Size group**, click **AutoFit**, and then click **AutoFit Contents**. In the **Table group**, click **Properties**. In the **Table Properties** dialog box, on the **Table tab**, under **Alignment**, click **Center**. Compare your screen with Figure 1.9.

FIGURE 1.9

6 > In the **Table Properties** dialog box, click **OK** to center the table horizontally on the page.

7 > **Save** 🖫 your Word document.

Activity 1.05 | Copying and Pasting a Word Table into an Excel Workbook

After entering data in a Word document, you may realize that you can manipulate the data better in another program, such as Excel. Instead of starting over and retyping the data, you can copy the data from the Word document, and then paste the data into an Excel workbook.

> **N O T E** **Working with Multiple Open Windows**
>
> In this chapter, you will work with a number of different files and will have a number of different windows open. When you have completed the work in one file, save the file, and then minimize the window. When you need to use the file again, click the appropriate program icon on the taskbar to maximize that window.

1 > Be sure that Word is the active window. On the **LAYOUT tab**, in the **Table group**, click **Select**, and then click **Select Table**. On the **HOME tab** in the **Clipboard group**, click **Copy** 🖹.

The entire table is selected and copied.

2 > On the taskbar, click the **Excel** icon 🗷 to make the Excel window active.

3 > At the bottom of the worksheet, click **New sheet** ⊕ to insert a new blank worksheet. Right-click the **Sheet1** worksheet tab, and then click **Rename**. Type **Sales** and then press Enter. Compare your screen with Figure 1.10.

FIGURE 1.10

4 > On the **PAGE LAYOUT tab**, in the **Themes group**, click **Themes**, and then under **Office**, click **Office**.

5 > Click cell **A4** to make it the active cell. On the **HOME tab**, in the **Clipboard group**, click **Paste**. Compare your screen with Figure 1.11.

The Word data is pasted into the Excel worksheet, starting in cell A4—the active cell.

The pound sign (#) will display if a column is not wide enough to display an entire number.

FIGURE 1.11

6 ▸ Click cell **A4**. On the **HOME tab**, in the **Cells group**, click **Format**, and then click **Column Width**. In the **Column Width** dialog box, type **16** and then click **OK**.

7 ▸ Select the range **B4:E4**. In the **Cells group**, click **Format**, and then click **Column Width**. In the **Column Width** dialog box, type **12** and then click **OK**.

Due to the increased column widths, all data displays in the worksheet.

8 ▸ Select the range **A4:A16**. In the **Cells group**, click **Format**, and then click **Row Height**. In the **Row Height** dialog box, type **17** and then click **OK**. Click in an empty cell, and then compare your screen with Figure 1.12.

FIGURE 1.12

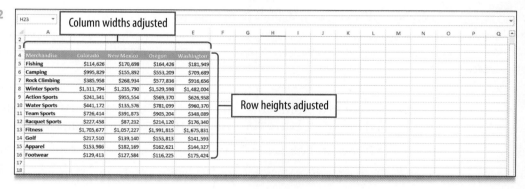

9 ▸ In cell **A1**, type **Ultimate Action Sports Gear** and then press Enter. In cell **A2**, type **Sales by State** and then press Enter. Select the range **A1:F1**, and then on the **HOME tab**, in the **Alignment group**, click **Merge & Center**. In the **Styles group**, click **Cell Styles**, and then click **Accent6**. In the **Font group**, click the **Font Size button arrow** ⎣11 ▾⎦, and then click **16**.

10 ▸ Select the range **A2:F2**. Click **Merge & Center**, apply the cell style **60% - Accent6**, and then change the **Font Size** to **14**. Compare your screen with Figure 1.13.

FIGURE 1.13

11 ▸ **Save** 🖫 your Excel workbook.

One of Excel's most powerful features is the capability to perform mathematical calculations. In the following activity, you will use the SUM function to add numbers.

1 Click cell **F4**, type **Total Sales** and then press Enter.

2 Be sure that **F5** is the active cell. On the **HOME tab**, in the **Editing group**, click **AutoSum**, and then on the **Formula Bar**, click **Enter** ✓ to confirm the entry and keep cell **F5** as the active cell. Using the technique you previously practiced, change the width of column **F** to **13**

ALERT! **The Formula Bar May Not Display**

If the Formula Bar does not display, on the VIEW tab, in the Show group, select the Formula Bar check box.

---

3 In cell **F5**, point to the fill handle until the ➕ pointer displays, hold down the left mouse button, and then drag down to cell **F16**. Release the mouse button. In the **Font group**, click **Increase Font Size** 🅰, and then compare your screen with Figure 1.14.

FIGURE 1.14

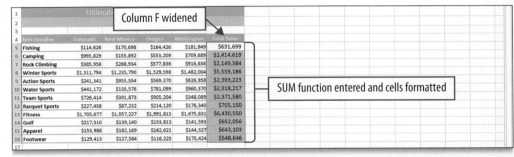

4 Click cell **A17**, type **Total** and then press Tab.

5 With cell **B17** selected, in the **Editing group**, click **AutoSum**, and then on the **Formula Bar**, click **Enter** ✓. Using the technique you just practiced, use the fill handle to copy the formula to cells **C17:F17**.

6 Select the range **A5:E16**. In the **Font group**, click the **Border button arrow** ▦ ▾, and then click **No Border**. Select the range **B17:F17**. In the **Styles group**, click **Cell Styles**, and then under **Titles and Headings**, click **Total**. In the **Font group**, click **Increase Font Size** 🅰. Click in an empty cell, and then compare your screen with Figure 1.15.

FIGURE 1.15

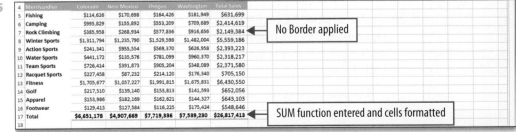

7 **Save** 💾 your Excel workbook.

A chart displays numerical data in a visual format. You can copy an Excel chart, and then paste it in files created with other applications.

Activity 1.07 | Creating and Formatting a Bar Chart in Excel

In the following activity, you will create and format a bar chart showing a comparison of merchandise sales by state.

1 Select the range **A4:E16**. On the **INSERT tab**, in the **Charts group**, click **Insert Bar Chart arrow** ⬛▾, and then under **3-D Bar**, click the first chart—**3-D Clustered Bar**. Under **CHART TOOLS**, on the **DESIGN tab**, in the **Location group**, click **Move Chart**. In the **Move Chart** dialog box, click the **New sheet** option button, type **Merchandise Chart** and then click **OK**. Compare your screen with Figure 1.16.

A 3-D bar chart is created and moved to a new chart sheet named Merchandise Chart.

FIGURE 1.16

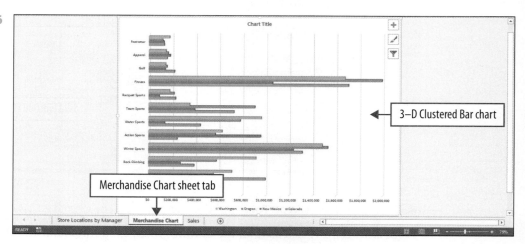

2 In the chart, select the text *Chart Title*, and then type **Retail Sales by State** Click in a blank area of the chart to deselect the chart title.

3 To the right of the chart, click **Chart Styles** 🖌. In the **STYLE** gallery, scroll down, and then click **Style 10**.

4 To the right of the chart, click **Chart Elements** ➕. Under **CHART ELEMENTS**, point to **Legend**, click the **Legend arrow**, and then click **Top**.

5 Under **CHART ELEMENTS**, point to **Axes**, click the **Axes arrow**, and then click **More Options**. In the **Format Axis** pane, under **AXIS OPTIONS**, click **Size & Properties** 🔳. Under **ALIGNMENT**, in the **Custom angle** box, type **30** and then press Enter. Compare your screen with Figure 1.17.

The numbers on the horizontal axis display at an angle of 30 degrees.

FIGURE 1.17

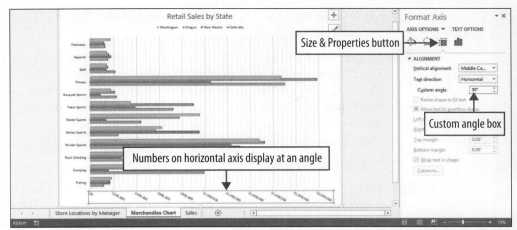

Size & Properties button

Custom angle box

Numbers on horizontal axis display at an angle

6 ▸ **Close** ☒ the **Format Axis** pane.

7 ▸ **Save** 🖫 your Excel workbook.

Activity 1.08 │ Creating and Formatting a Pie Chart in Excel

In the following activity, you will create a pie chart to show each state's percentage of total sales.

1 ▸ Click the **Sales** worksheet tab. Select the range **B4:E4**, press and hold Ctrl, and then select the range **B17:E17**.

The range B4:E4 and the range B17:E17 are selected. Recall that holding down Ctrl enables you to select nonadjacent cells.

2 ▸ On the **INSERT tab**, in the **Charts group**, click **Insert Pie or Doughnut Chart arrow** 🍩▾, and then under **3-D Pie**, click **3-D Pie**. On the ribbon, under **CHART TOOLS**, on the **DESIGN tab**, in the **Location group**, click **Move Chart**. In the **Move Chart** dialog box, click the **New sheet** option button, type **State Sales Chart** and then click **OK**.

3 ▸ To the right of the chart, click **Chart Styles** ✎. In the **STYLE** gallery, scroll down, and then click **Style 5**. Press Esc to close the gallery. Compare your screen with Figure 1.18.

FIGURE 1.18

3–D Pie chart with Style 5 applied

State Sales Chart sheet tab

4 ▸ In the chart, select the text *Chart Title*, type **State Sales** and then click in a blank area of the chart.

5 Click **Chart Elements** ➕, and then under **CHART ELEMENTS**, click **Legend** to remove the legend from the chart.

6 Under **CHART ELEMENTS**, select the **Data Labels** check box. Point to **Data Labels**, click the **Data Labels arrow**, and then click **More Options**. In the **Format Data Labels** pane, under **Label Contains**, select the **Category Name** check box, clear the **Value** check box, and then select the **Percentage** check box. Under **Label Position**, click the **Center** option button. With the data labels selected, on the **HOME tab**, change the **Font Size** `11 ▾` to **16**. Click in a blank area of the chart to deselect the data labels.

> The pane changes to the *Format Chart Area* pane.

7 In the **Format Chart Area** pane, under **CHART OPTIONS**, click **Fill & Line** ◇. Click **FILL**, and then click the **Gradient fill** option button. Click the **Preset gradients arrow**, and then in the first row, click the third gradient—**Light Gradient – Accent 3**. **Close** ✖ the **Format Chart Area** pane, and then compare your screen with Figure 1.19.

FIGURE 1.19

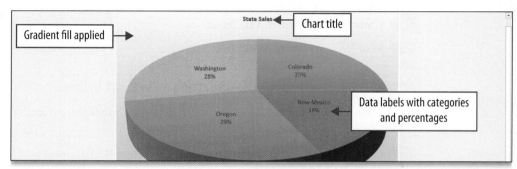

8 Press and hold `Ctrl`, and then click the **Merchandise Chart** sheet tab.

> Both chart sheets are selected.

9 On the **PAGE LAYOUT tab**, in the **Page Setup group**, click the **Dialog Box Launcher** 🖳. In the **Page Setup** dialog box, click the **Header/Footer tab**, and then click **Custom Footer**. In the **Footer** dialog box, be sure that the insertion point is in the *Left section*, and then click **Insert File Name** 📑. Compare your screen with Figure 1.20.

> In the Left section box, the file name is inserted—*& [File]* displays.

FIGURE 1.20

10 In the **Footer** dialog box, click **OK**, and then in the **Page Setup** dialog box, click **OK**.

> The file name is inserted in the footer of both chart sheets.

11 Click the **Sales** worksheet tab to make it the active worksheet and to deselect the chart sheets. Press and hold `Ctrl`, and then click the **Store Locations by Manager** worksheet tab.

12 On the **PAGE LAYOUT tab**, in the **Page Setup group**, click the **Dialog Box Launcher** 🔲. In the **Page Setup** dialog box, click the **Header/Footer tab**, and then click **Custom Footer**. In the **Footer** dialog box, with the insertion point in the *Left section*, click **Insert File Name** 🔲. Click **OK** two times to close the dialog boxes.

> You must insert footers in worksheets separately from inserting them in chart sheets. In this case, the file name is inserted in the footer of both worksheets.

13 Press Ctrl + Home to display the top of the worksheet. Right-click the **Sales** sheet tab, and then click **Ungroup Sheets**.

14 **Save** 🔲 your Excel workbook.

Activity 1.09 | Copying and Pasting an Excel Chart into Word

1 On the **HOME tab**, in the **Clipboard group**, click the **Dialog Box Launcher** 🔲 to display the Clipboard pane. In the **Clipboard** pane, click **Clear All**. Click the **State Sales Chart** sheet tab, and then click the border of the pie chart to select the chart. On the **HOME tab** in the **Clipboard group**, click **Copy** 🔲. Compare your screen with Figure 1.21.

FIGURE 1.21

2 Click the **Merchandise Chart** sheet tab, and then if necessary, click the border of the bar chart to select the chart. In the **Clipboard group**, click **Copy** 🔲.

3 At the bottom of the screen, on the taskbar, click the **Word icon** 🔲. Press Ctrl + End to move the insertion point to the end of the document.

4 Press Ctrl + Enter.

> A new blank Page 2 is inserted.

5 With the insertion point at the top of **Page 2**, type **In the chart below, our state sales managers can view their sales results.** Press Enter.

6 On the **HOME tab**, in the **Clipboard group**, click the **Dialog Box Launcher** 🔲 to display the Clipboard pane, as shown in Figure 1.22.

FIGURE 1.22

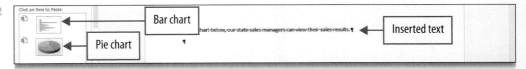

7 In the **Clipboard** pane, click the **bar chart**.

> The bar chart is pasted into the Word document.

8 **Close** ❌ the **Clipboard** pane, and then press Ctrl + Home.

9 ▸ Click the **FILE tab**, and then in the lower right portion of the screen, at the bottom of the **Properties** list, click **Show All Properties**. In the **Tags** box, type **memo, state sales chart** and in the **Subject** box, type your course name and section number. Be sure your name displays as the author; edit if necessary.

10 ▸ **Save** 🖫 your Word document, and then **Close** ✕ Word.

Activity 1.10 | Pasting an Excel Chart in PowerPoint

1 ▸ Start PowerPoint. Navigate to the student data files, and then open the presentation **i01A_Sales_Presentation**. Press F12 to display the **Save As** dialog box. Navigate to your **Integrated Projects** folder, and then **Save** the presentation as **Lastname_Firstname_1A_Sales_Presentation**

2 ▸ On the **INSERT tab**, in the **Text group**, click **Header & Footer**. In the **Header and Footer** dialog box, click the **Notes and Handouts tab**. Select the **Footer** check box, click in the **Footer** box, and then type **Lastname_Firstname_1A_Sales_Presentation** and then compare your screen with Figure 1.23.

FIGURE 1.23

3 ▸ Click **Apply to All**.

4 ▸ In the **Slides** pane, click **Slide 2**. On the **HOME tab**, in the **Slides group**, click the **New Slide button arrow**, and then from the **Slides** gallery, click **Blank**. On the **DESIGN tab**, in the **Customize group**, click **Format Background**. In the **Format Background** pane, under **FILL**, select the **Hide background graphics** check box. Compare your screen with Figure 1.24.

A new blank Slide 3 is inserted into the presentation, and the background graphics do not display.

FIGURE 1.24

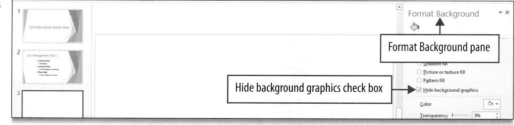

5 ▸ **Close** ✕ the **Format Background** pane. On the **HOME tab**, in the **Clipboard group**, click the **Dialog Box Launcher** ✕. In the **Clipboard** pane, click the bar chart.

The bar chart is pasted into Slide 3 of the presentation.

6 ▸ On the **HOME tab**, in the **Slides group**, click the **New Slide button arrow**, and then from the **Slides** gallery, click **Blank**. Using the technique you practiced, select the **Hide background graphics** check box. In the **Clipboard** pane, click the pie chart. Compare your screen with Figure 1.25.

FIGURE 1.25

Bar chart in Slide 3

Pie chart in Slide 4

7 ▶ **Close** ☒ the **Clipboard** pane, and then **Save** ☐ the presentation.

Objective 4 | Copy and Paste an Object from PowerPoint into Excel

In PowerPoint, bullet points can be converted into a SmartArt graphic to illustrate your message visually. After you create a SmartArt graphic in PowerPoint, you can copy the graphic and paste it into a file created with another program. This can save you time because there is no need to recreate the graphic.

Activity 1.11 | Inserting a SmartArt Graphic

1 ▶ Click **Slide 2** to make it the active slide. Click in the placeholder containing the names of the managers. On the **HOME tab**, in the **Paragraph group**, click **Convert to SmartArt**. In the **SmartArt** gallery, in the first row, click the fourth layout—**Target List**. If the Text Pane displays to the left of the SmartArt placeholder, click Close ☒.

2 ▶ On the ribbon, under **SMARTART TOOLS**, on the **DESIGN tab**, in the **SmartArt Styles group**, click **More** ⊽. In the **SmartArt Styles** gallery, under **3-D**, in the first row, click the third style—**Cartoon**.

3 ▶ With the **SmartArt** graphic selected, on the **ANIMATIONS tab**, in the **Animation group**, click **More** ⊽. In the **Animation** gallery, under **Entrance**, click **Wheel**. Click in a blank area of the slide to deselect the SmartArt graphic, and then compare your screen with Figure 1.26.

The number 1 displays to the left of the SmartArt graphic, which indicates that an animation effect is applied to the object.

FIGURE 1.26

Animation effect indicator

Bullet points converted to SmartArt graphic and Cartoon style applied

4 ▶ On the **SLIDE SHOW tab**, in the **Start Slide Show group**, click **From Beginning** to view the presentation. Press [Enter] to view the second slide.

5 Continue to press [Enter] to view the remaining slides, and then press [Enter] to return to **Normal** view.

6 Save 🖫 the presentation.

Activity 1.12 | Copying and Pasting a SmartArt Graphic

After you create an object in one file, you can copy the object and paste it in a file created with a different program. In this activity, you will copy the SmartArt graphic in the PowerPoint presentation, and then paste it in an Excel workbook.

1 Click the border of the SmartArt graphic.

> By clicking the border of an object, you select the entire object, not just a part of the object.

2 On the **HOME tab**, in the **Clipboard group**, click **Copy** 🖹.

3 On the taskbar, click the **Excel icon** 🗷.

4 In **Excel**, click the **Sales** worksheet tab, and then click cell **A20**. On the **HOME tab**, in the **Clipboard group**, click **Paste**.

> The SmartArt graphic is pasted into the Sales worksheet. The top left corner of the graphic is in cell A20.

5 Scroll down to view the entire graphic. On the ribbon, under **SMARTART TOOLS**, on the **FORMAT tab**, click **Size**, if necessary. Click in the **Shape Height** box, and then type **3.5** Click in the **Shape Width** box, type **5.5** and then press [Enter].

6 Right-click the right border of the SmartArt graphic, and then above the shortcut menu, click **Color**. In the **Color** gallery, under **Colorful**, click the fourth color—**Colorful Range – Accent Colors 4 to 5**. Compare your screen with Figure 1.27.

FIGURE 1.27

7 In the **Clipboard** pane, click **Clear All**, and then **Close** ✖ the **Clipboard** pane.

8 Click the **FILE tab**, and then at the right, at the bottom of the **Properties** list, click **Show All Properties**. In the **Tags** box, type **charts, SmartArt** In the **Subject** box, type your course name and section number. Be sure your name displays as the author; edit if necessary.

9 Save 🖫 the Excel workbook, and then **Close** ✖ Excel.

10 In the PowerPoint file, click the **FILE tab**, and then at the right, at the bottom of the **Properties** list, click **Show All Properties**. In the **Tags** box, type **company info, charts, SmartArt** In the **Subject** box, type your course name and section number. Be sure your name displays as the author; edit if necessary.

11 Save 🖫 the presentation, and then **Close** ✖ PowerPoint.

12 Submit your printed or electronic files as directed by your instructor.

> **END | You have completed Project 1A**

Taos Welcome

PROJECT ACTIVITIES

In Activities 1.13 through 1.19, you will link and update Excel data in a Word document. Because Microsoft Office programs work together, you can quickly create individualized documents in Word using data stored in a different application. You will use Word's mail merge feature and data stored in an Access database to create individualized memos. Your completed files will look similar to Figure 1.28.

PROJECT FILES

For Project 1B, you will need the following files:

i01B_Welcome_Memo
i01B_Taos_Inventory
i01B_All_Associates

You will save your files as:

Lastname_Firstname_1B_Welcome_Memo
Lastname_Firstname_1B_Taos_Memo
Lastname_Firstname_1B_Taos_Inventory
Lastname_Firstname_1B_All_Associates
Lastname_Firstname_1B_Store_Location

PROJECT RESULTS

FIGURE 1.28 Project 1B Taos Welcome

Use the linking tools in Office to connect the data in an Excel worksheet to a Word document. When you link an Excel workbook to a Word document, changes you make to data in the Excel workbook will be updated in the linked Word document. Information about the link is saved with the Word document. By default, when you open the Word document, Word checks all linked files and prompts you to apply any changes.

Activity 1.13 │ Using Paste Special to Link Files

In this activity, you will insert Excel data into a Word document. By selecting options in the Paste Special dialog box, you can link your Word document to the data in the Excel workbook.

1 ▶ Start Word. Navigate to the student data files and then open the document **i01B_Welcome_Memo**. Press F12, and then **Save** the document in your **Integrated Projects** folder as **Lastname_Firstname_1B_Welcome_Memo** If necessary, display the ruler and formatting marks.

2 ▶ **Start** Excel. Navigate to the student data files, and then open the Excel workbook **i01B_Taos_Inventory**. Press F12, and then **Save** the workbook in your **Integrated Projects** folder as **Lastname_Firstname_1B_Taos_Inventory**

3 ▶ On the **PAGE LAYOUT tab**, in the **Page Setup group**, click the **Dialog Box Launcher**. In the **Page Setup** dialog box, click the **Header/Footer tab**, and then click **Custom Footer**. In the **Footer** dialog box, with the insertion point in the *Left section*, click **Insert File Name**—& [File] displays. Click **OK** two times to close the dialog boxes.

4 ▶ Press Ctrl + Home to display the top of the worksheet, and then **Save** the Excel workbook.

5 ▶ Select the range **A3:B22**. On the **Home tab**, in the **Clipboard group**, click **Copy**. Compare your screen with Figure 1.29.

FIGURE 1.29

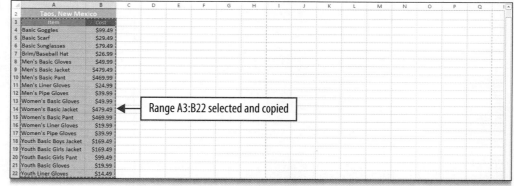

Range A3:B22 selected and copied

6 ▶ On the taskbar, click the **Word** icon. In the Word document, below the paragraph that begins *I am pleased to welcome you*, click in the blank paragraph.

7 ▶ On the **HOME tab**, in the **Clipboard group**, click the **Paste button arrow**, and then click **Paste Special**. In the **Paste Special** dialog box, click the **Paste link** option button, and then under **As**, click **Microsoft Excel Worksheet Object**. Compare your screen to Figure 1.30.

FIGURE 1.30

Paste Special dialog box

Paste link option button selected

Microsoft Excel Worksheet Object selected

8 In the **Paste Special** dialog box, click **OK**.

The linked data from Excel is pasted into the Word document.

9 With the pasted object selected, on the **HOME tab**, in the **Paragraph group**, click **Center** ☰.

10 **Save** 🖫 your Word document.

11 Click the **FILE tab**, and then click **Close** to close the document but leave Word open.

NOTE   **Updating Links**

From this point forward, when you reopen a Word document that has a link to an external file, a Security Notice will automatically display. The notice will inform you that the file contains links and you have the option of updating the links or not updating them. If you trust the source of the file, you can update links. If you do not know where a file originated, you should cancel the update and investigate where the file came from before continuing.

---

12 In Word, navigate to your **Integrated Projects** folder, and then open the file **Lastname_Firstname_1B_Welcome_Memo**. A message box displays, as shown in Figure 1.31.

The message box informs you that the Word document is linked to another file, and it asks whether you want to update the data in the document.

FIGURE 1.31

Message box

13 In the message box, click **Yes**.

The linked information is updated.

Objective 6 | Modify Linked Data and Update Links

It is common to make changes to your data in saved files. You can modify the data in the source file and all linked data to that source file is updated to reflect the changes.

Activity 1.14 | Updating Linked Data

In the following activity, you will edit data in the linked Excel workbook, and then be sure that the updated data displays in the Word document.

1 Double-click the pasted data in the Word document to display the source file—the linked Excel workbook.

Excel becomes the active window.

2 If necessary, maximize the Excel worksheet, and then press [Esc] to cancel the copy. Click cell **B9**, type **389.99** and then press [Enter]. Click cell **B14**, type **379.99** and then press [Enter]. Compare your screen with Figure 1.32.

FIGURE 1.32

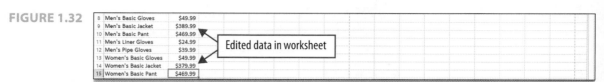

3 Save 🖫 the Excel workbook.

4 On the taskbar, click the **Word** icon 📃. Compare your screen to Figure 1.33.

The changes made in the Excel workbook are reflected in the linked Word document.

ALERT! **What If the Data Is Not Updated?**

If you do not see the new numbers in the Word document, click one time in the data to select it, and then press [F9] to update the Excel data.

FIGURE 1.33

5 Save 🖫 the Word document.

6 On the taskbar, click the **Excel** icon 📊 to display the workbook.

7 Click the **FILE tab**, and then at the right, at the bottom of the **Properties** list, click **Show All Properties**. In the **Tags** box, type **edited data, linked** In the **Subject** box, type your course name and section number. Be sure your name displays as the author; edit if necessary.

8 Save 🖫 your changes, and then **Close** [✕] Excel.

Objective 7 | Create a Table in Word from Access Data

You can export data from an Access file to another file—for example, an Excel worksheet, a Word document, or another database. Exporting is similar to copying and pasting. In Access, you can export large amounts of data by selecting the name of the object that contains the data you want to export. Exporting data eliminates the need to retype information; and, as a result, the possibility of data entry errors is reduced.

Activity 1.15 | Exporting an Access Table to an RTF File

1 **Start** Access. Navigate to the student data files and then open the Access database **i01B_All_Associates**. Click the **FILE tab**, click **Save As**, and then with **Save Database As** selected, click **Save As**.

2 In the **Save As** dialog box, navigate to your **Integrated Projects** folder, and then **Save** the database as **Lastname_Firstname_1B_All_Associates** On the **Message Bar** that displays a Security Warning, click **Enable Content**.

3 In the **navigation pane**, click the **Store Location** table to select it. On the **EXTERNAL DATA tab**, in the **Export group**, click **More**, and then click **Word**.

The Export – RTF File dialog box displays.

4 In the **Export – RTF File** dialog box, click **Browse**, and then navigate to your **Integrated Projects** folder. In the **File name** box, type **Lastname_Firstname_1B_Store_Location** and then click **Save**. Compare your screen with Figure 1.34.

The Access table is saved as a rich text format file. Rich text format is a universal file format, using the .rtf file extension, which can be read by many word processing programs.

FIGURE 1.34

5 In the **Export – RTF File** dialog box, click **OK**. In the dialog box asking if you want to save these export steps, be sure the **Save export steps** check box is not selected. Click **Close**.

Activity 1.16 | Inserting Access Data into a Word Document

1 On the taskbar, click the **Word** icon. Press Ctrl + End to move to the end of the document.

2 On the **INSERT tab**, in the **Text group**, click the **Object button arrow**, and then click **Text from File**. In the **Insert File** dialog box, navigate to your **Integrated Projects** folder, click the file name **Lastname_Firstname_1B_Store_Location**, and then click **Insert**. Compare your screen with Figure 1.35.

FIGURE 1.35

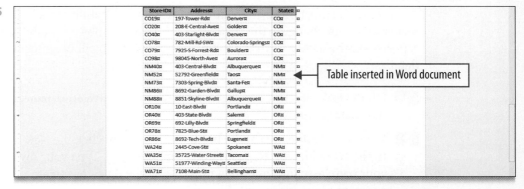

3 In the inserted table, click in the first cell, **Store ID,** to make the cell the active cell. On the ribbon, under **TABLE TOOLS**, on the **DESIGN tab**, in the **Table Styles group**, click **More**. In the **Table Styles** gallery, scroll down, and then under **List Tables**, in the third row, click the third style—click **List Table 3 - Accent 2**.

4 In the cell **Store ID**, right-click, on the mini toolbar, click **Delete**, and then click **Delete Columns** to delete the Store ID column.

5 On the **LAYOUT tab**, in the **Cell Size group**, click **AutoFit**, and then click **AutoFit Contents**.

The columns are automatically resized to fit the contents of the cells.

6 In the **Table group**, click **Properties**, and then on the **Table tab**, under **Alignment**, click **Center**. Click **OK**, and then compare your screen with Figure 1.36.

The table is centered horizontally on the page.

FIGURE 1.36

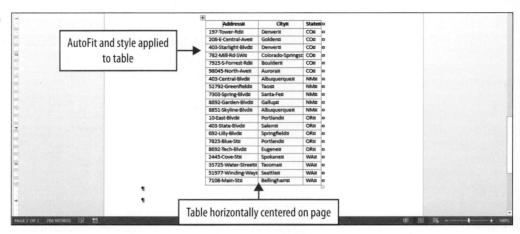

7 Save 🖫 the Word document.

Objective 8 | Use Access Data to Complete a Mail Merge in Word

If you already have information in an existing data source—for example, an Access database—you do not need to enter the data again during the mail merge process. You can filter data to quickly find a portion of the total records available. Filtered data displays only the records that meet the conditions you specify and hides the records that do not meet the conditions.

Activity 1.17 | Adding Records to an Access Table

One of the most powerful features of Access is the ability to add, edit, or delete existing records without changing the structure of the existing objects—tables, queries, forms, and reports—in the database. In the following activity, you will use a form to add a record to a database.

1 On the taskbar, click the **Access** icon 🅰. In the **navigation pane**, double-click the **Sales Associates Form**.

2 In the navigation area at the bottom of the form, click the **New (blank) record** button ▶✱. In the **ID** field, type **10-60531** and then press Tab. Type your own firstname, press Tab, type your own lastname, and then press Tab. Type **Sales Associate** press Tab, type **NM52** and then compare your screen with Figure 1.37.

FIGURE 1.37

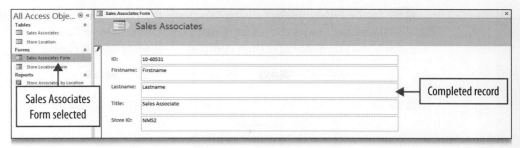

3 Press [Tab] to accept your record.

4 In the **navigation pane**, double-click the report **Store Associates by Location**. Scroll through the report and be sure that your name displays under **NM** for the **Taos** location.

5 **Close** [**✕**] Access.

Access automatically saves records that have been added to a database; there is no need to save the file before closing Access.

Activity 1.18 | Starting Mail Merge in Word

Mail Merge can be used to add placeholders for inserting a data field into a document to make each document unique. In the following activity, you will start the mail merge process in Word and filter the Access records.

1 On the taskbar, click the Word icon [W] to make the Word document active.

2 Press [Ctrl] + [Home]. On the **MAILINGS tab**, in the **Start Mail Merge group**, click the **Select Recipients** button, and then click **Use an Existing List**.

3 In the **Select Data Source** dialog box, navigate to your **Integrated Projects** folder, select the **Lastname_Firstname_1B_All_Associates** database, and then click **Open** to display the **Select Table** dialog box. Compare your screen with Figure 1.38.

The Access database contains more than one table. You need to select which table will be used for the mail merge.

FIGURE 1.38

4 In the **Select Table** dialog box, be sure that **Sales Associates** is selected, and then click **OK**.

5 In the **Start Mail Merge group**, click **Edit Recipient List**.

You can add or edit fields in the Mail Merge Recipients dialog box.

6 In the **Mail Merge Recipients** dialog box, under **Refine recipient list**, click **Filter**.

7 In the **Filter and Sort** dialog box, with the **Filter Records tab** selected, click the **Field arrow**, and then click **Store ID**. Under **Comparison**, be sure that **Equal to** is selected. In the **Compare to** box, type **NM52** and then compare your screen with Figure 1.39.

You can filter on any of the fields.

FIGURE 1.39

8 At the bottom of the **Filter and Sort** dialog box, click **OK**.

The three Taos records—including your record—display.

9 In the **Mail Merge Recipients** dialog box, click **OK**.

Activity 1.19 | Inserting Merge Fields

You can add merge fields as placeholders in the Word document for the information that will be inserted from the Access database. In the mail merge process, you combine a data source and a main document to create a new Word document—for example, a document that contains individualized memos, letter, or mailing labels.

1 Near the top of the document, in the heading *TO*, click to position the insertion point to the left of the paragraph mark.

2 On the **MAILINGS tab**, in the **Write & Insert Fields group**, click the **Insert Merge Field button arrow**, and then click **Firstname**. Compare your screen with Figure 1.40.

The Firstname field is inserted in the memo.

A merge field is surrounded by double angle brackets (<< >>). These formatting marks help distinguish the merge fields in the main document and do not display in the final document—after the merge process is completed.

FIGURE 1.40

3 Press [Spacebar]. Click the **Insert Merge Field button arrow**, and then click **Lastname**.

This is the location in the memo where the sales associate names will be inserted.

4 In the **Preview Results group**, click **Preview Results**. In the **Preview Results group**, click **Next Record** ▶ two times to preview the three memos.

> The memo—the main document—displays with changes based on each record in the filtered data source—in this case, the sales associate's name.

5 In the **Preview Results** group, click **Preview Results**, to turn off the feature. Notice the merge fields display in the document.

6 In the **Finish group**, click **Finish & Merge**, and then click **Edit Individual Documents**. In the **Merge to New Document** dialog box, be sure that the **All** option button is selected, and then click **OK**. Compare your screen with Figure 1.41.

> A new Word document—Letters1—displays. The six-page document contains three individualized memos and is no longer connected to the Access database. The firstname and lastname in the first record displays on Page 1.

FIGURE 1.41

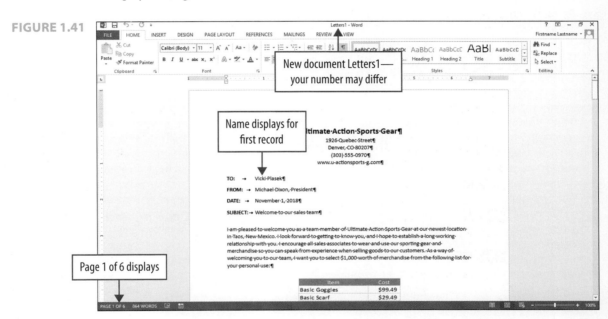

7 Press F12. **Save** the new merged document in your **Integrated Projects** folder with the file name **Lastname_Firstname_1B_Taos_Memo**

8 Right-click in the footer area, and then click **Edit Footer**. Under **HEADER & FOOTER TOOLS**, on the **DESIGN tab**, in the **Insert group**, click **Document Info**, and then click **File Name**. In the **Close group**, click **Close Header and Footer**.

9 Click the **FILE tab**, and then at the right, at the bottom of the **Properties** list, click **Show All Properties**. In the **Tags** box, type **linked table, merged** In the **Subject** box, type your course name and section number. Be sure your name displays as the author; edit if necessary.

10 **Save** 🖫 your changes, and then **Close** ❌ the **Lastname_Firstname_1B_Taos_Memo**.

11 In the **Lastname_Firstname_1B_Welcome_Memo**, right-click in the footer area, and then click **Edit Footer**. Under **HEADER & FOOTER TOOLS**, on the **DESIGN tab**, in the **Insert group**, click **Document Info**, and then click **File Name**. In the **Close group**, click **Close Header and Footer**.

12 Click the **FILE tab**, and then at the right, at the bottom of the **Properties** list, click **Show All Properties**. In the **Tags** box, type **linked table, merge fields** In the **Subject** box, type your course name and section number. Be sure your name displays as the author; edit if necessary.

13 Save 🖫 your changes, and then **Close** ☒ Word.

14 Submit your printed or electronic files as directed by your instructor.

END | You have completed Project 1B

Glossary

.jpg An image file format, commonly pronounced *JPEG*, that stands for Joint Photographic Experts Group; this is a common file type used by digital cameras and computers to store digital pictures; JPEG is popular because it can store a high-quality picture in a relatively small file.

.png An image file format, commonly pronounced *PING*, that stands for Portable Network Graphic; this is an image file type that can be transferred over the Internet.

3-D The shortened term for *three-dimensional*, which refers to an image that appears to have all three spatial dimensions—length, width, and depth.

Absolute cell reference A cell reference that refers to cells by their fixed position in a worksheet; an absolute cell reference remains the same when the formula is copied.

Accounting Number Format The Excel number format that applies a thousand comma separator where appropriate, inserts a fixed U.S. dollar sign aligned at the left edge of the cell, applies two decimal places, and leaves a small amount of space at the right edge of the cell to accommodate a parenthesis for negative numbers.

Action Center Located in the notification area, a central place to view alerts and take actions related to things that need your attention.

Active cell The cell, surrounded by a black border, ready to receive data or be affected by the next Excel command.

Address bar (Internet Explorer) The area at the top of the Internet Explorer window that displays, and where you can type, a URL—Uniform Resource Locator—which is an address that uniquely identifies a location on the Internet.

Address bar (Windows File Explorer) The bar at the top of a folder window with which you can navigate to a different folder or library, or go back to a previous one; displays your current location in the folder structure as a series of links separated by arrows.

Administrator account A user account that lets you make changes that will affect other users of the computer; the most powerful of the three types of accounts because it permits the most control over the computer.

After Previous An animation option that begins the animation sequence for the selected slide element immediately after the completion of the previous animation or slide transition.

Aggregate functions Calculations such as Min, Max, Avg, and Sum that are performed on a group of records.

Alignment The placement of text or objects relative to the left and right margins.

Alignment guides Green vertical or horizontal lines that display when you are moving or sizing an object to assist you with object placement.

American Psychological Association (APA) One of two commonly used style guides for formatting research papers.

AND condition A compound criteria used to display records that match all parts of the specified criteria.

AND condition A condition in which records display only where all of the values are present in the selected fields.

Animation A visual or sound effect added to an object or text on a slide.

Animation Painter A feature that copies animation settings from one object to another.

App The term that commonly refers to computer programs that run from the device software on a smartphone or a tablet computer—for example, iOS, Android, or Windows Phone—or computer programs that run from the browser software on a desktop PC or laptop PC—for example Internet Explorer, Safari, Firefox, or Chrome. App is the shortened version of the word *application*.

App bar An area at the bottom of every Windows Store app containing various controls pertaining to the app.

App for Office A webpage that works within one of the Office applications, such as Excel, and that you download from the Office Store.

App switcher The thumbnail view of open apps that displays when you move your mouse down from the Back tip in the upper left corner; to switch to an app that is still open, you can click any of the thumbnails.

Append To add on to the end of an object; for example, to add records to the end of an existing table.

Application A set of instructions that a computer uses to accomplish a task; also called a program.

Apps for Office 2013 and SharePoint 2013 A collection of downloadable apps that enable you to create and view information within your familiar Office programs.

Arguments The values that an Excel function uses to perform calculations or operations.

Arithmetic operators The symbols +, −, *, /, %, and ^ used to denote addition, subtraction (or negation), multiplication, division, percentage, and exponentiation in an Excel formula.

Artistic effects Formats applied to images that make pictures resemble sketches or paintings.

Ascending order A sorting order that arranges text alphabetically (A to Z) and numbers from the lowest number to the highest number.

Aspect ratio The ratio of the width of a display to the height of the display.

Auto Fill An Excel feature that generates and extends values into adjacent cells based on the values of selected cells.

AutoCalculate A feature that displays three calculations in the status bar by default—Average, Count, and Sum—when you select a range of numerical data.

AutoComplete A feature that speeds your typing and lessens the likelihood of errors; if the first few characters you type in a cell match an existing entry in the column, Excel fills in the remaining characters for you.

AutoCorrect A feature that corrects common typing and spelling errors as you type, for example changing *teh* to *the*.

AutoFit An Excel feature that adjusts the width of a column to fit the cell content of the widest cell in the column.

AutoNumber data type A data type that describes a unique sequential or random number assigned by Access as each record is entered and that is useful for data that has no distinct field that can be considered unique.

AutoSum A button that provided quick access to the SUM function.

AVERAGE function An Excel function that adds a group of values, and then divides the result by the number of values in the group.

Axis A line that serves as a frame of reference for measurement and which borders the chart plot area.

Back tip The upper left corner of the screen that when pointed to displays a thumbnail image of the last screen you were on; you can use it to *go back* to your previous screen.

Background Removal A feature that removes unwanted portions of a picture so that the picture does not appear as a self-contained rectangle.

Background style A predefined slide background fill variation that combines theme colors in different intensities or patterns.

Backstage tabs The area along the left side of Backstage view with tabs to display screens with related groups of commands.

Backstage view A centralized space for file management tasks; for example, opening, saving, printing, publishing, or sharing a file. A navigation pane displays along the left side with tabs that group file-related tasks together.

Badge An icon that displays on the Lock screen, below the time, day, and date, that represents the status of your Internet connection, your battery if you are using a tablet or laptop, or any other Lock screen apps you might have selected.

Base The starting point when you divide the amount of increase by it to calculate the rate of increase.

Best Fit An Access command that adjusts the width of a column to accommodate the column's longest entry.

Between ... And operator A comparison operator that looks for values within a range.

Bevel A shape effect that uses shading and shadows to make the edges of a shape appear to be curved or angled.

Bibliography A list of cited works in a report or research paper; also referred to as Works Cited, Sources, or References, depending upon the report style.

Black slide A slide that displays after the last slide in a presentation indicating that the presentation is over.

Blank desktop database A database that has no data and has no database tools—you must create the data and tools as you need them; the database is stored on your computer or other storage device.

Body The text of a letter.

Body font A font that is applied to all slide text except slide titles.

Booting the computer The process of turning on a computer when the computer has been completely shut down.

Bound control A control that retrieves its data from an underlying table or query; a text box control is an example of a bound control.

Bound A term used to describe objects and controls that are based on data that is stored in tables.

Brightness The relative lightness of a picture.

Bulleted list A list of items with each item introduced by a symbol such as a small circle or check mark, and which is useful when the items in the list can be displayed in any order.

Bullets Text symbols such as small circles or check marks that precede each item in a bulleted list.

Calculated control A control that contains an expression, often a formula or function, that most often summarizes a field that contains numerical data.

Calculated field A field that stores the value of a mathematical operation.

Caption A property setting that displays a name for a field in a table, query, form, or report other than that listed as the field name.

Cascade Delete Related Records A cascade option that enables you to delete a record in a table on the *one* side of the relationship and also delete all of the related records in related tables.

Cascade options Relationship options that enable you to update records in related tables when referential integrity is enforced.

Cascade Update Related Fields A cascade option that enables you to change the data in the primary key field in the table on the *one* side of the relationship and update that change to any fields storing that same data in related tables.

Category axis The area along the bottom of a chart that identifies the categories of data; also referred to as the x-axis.

Category labels The labels that display along the bottom of a chart to identify the categories of data; Excel uses the row titles as the category names.

Cell The intersection of a column and a row.

Cell address Another name for a cell reference.

Cell content Anything typed into a cell.

Cell reference The identification of a specific cell by its intersecting column letter and row number.

Cell style A defined set of formatting characteristics, such as font, font size, font color, cell borders, and cell shading.

Center alignment The alignment of text or objects that is centered horizontally between the left and right margins.

Charms A set of buttons that display when you point or swipe in from the right side of the screen that you can use in every app—whether a Windows Store app or a desktop app—and that enable you to search, share, access devices, or adjust your PC settings.

Chart The graphic representation of data in a worksheet; data presented as a chart is usually easier to understand than a table of numbers.

Chart area The entire chart and all of its elements.

Chart elements The various components of a chart, including the chart title, axis titles, data series, legend, chart area, and plot area.

Chart Elements button A button that enables you to add, remove, or change chart elements such as the title, legend, gridlines, and data labels.

Chart Filters button A button that displays options for changing the data displayed in a chart.

Chart layout The combination of chart elements that can be displayed in a chart such as a title, legend, labels for the columns, and the table of charted cells.

Chart sheet A workbook sheet that contains only a chart.

Chart style The overall visual look of a chart in terms of its graphic effects, colors, and backgrounds; for example, you can have flat or beveled columns, colors that are solid or transparent, and backgrounds that are dark or light.

Chart Styles button A button that displays options for setting the style and color scheme for a chart.

Chart Styles gallery A group of predesigned chart styles that you can apply to an Excel chart.

Chart types Various chart formats used in a way that is meaningful to the reader; common examples are column charts, pie charts, and line charts.

Citation A note inserted into the text of a research paper that refers the reader to a source in the bibliography.

Click The action of pressing and releasing the left button on a mouse pointing device one time.

Clip A single media file such as art, sound, animation, or a movie.

Clip art Downloadable predefined graphics available online from Office.com and other sites.

Clipboard A temporary storage area that holds text or graphics that you select and then cut or copy.

Clipboard A temporary storage area for information that you have copied or moved from one place and plan to use somewhere else.

Cloud computing Refers to applications and services that are accessed over the Internet, rather than to applications that are installed on your local computer.

Cloud storage Online storage of data so that you can access your data from different places and devices.

Collaborate To work with others as a team in an intellectual endeavor to complete a shared task or to achieve a shared goal.

Collaboration The action of working together with others as a team in an intellectual endeavor to complete a shared task or achieve a shared goal.

Column A vertical group of cells in a worksheet.

Column break indicator A dotted line containing the words *Column Break* that displays at the bottom of the column.

Column chart A chart in which the data is arranged in columns and which is useful for showing data changes over a period of time or for illustrating comparisons among items.

Column heading The letter that displays at the top of a vertical group of cells in a worksheet; beginning with the first letter of the alphabet, a unique letter or combination of letters identifies each column.

Comma Style The Excel number format that inserts thousand comma separators where appropriate and applies two decimal places; Comma Style also leaves space at the right to accommodate a parenthesis when negative numbers are present.

Commands An instruction to a computer program that causes an action to be carried out.

Common dialog boxes The set of dialog boxes that includes Open, Save, and Save As, which are provided by the Windows programming interface, and which display and operate in all of the Office programs in the same manner.

Common field A field in two or more tables that stores the same data.

Comparison operators Symbols that are used to evaluate data in the field to determine whether it is the same (=), greater than (>), less than (<), or in between a range of values as specified by the criteria.

Complimentary closing A parting farewell in a business letter.

Compound criteria Multiple conditions in a query or filter.

Compressed file A file that has been reduced in size and that takes up less storage space and can be transferred to other computers faster than uncompressed files.

Compressed folder A folder that has been reduced in size and thus takes up less storage space and can be transferred to other computers quickly; also called a *zipped* folder.

Conditional format A format that changes the appearance of a cell—for example, by adding cell shading or font color—based on a condition; if the condition is true, the cell is formatted based on that condition, and if the condition is false, the cell is *not* formatted.

Constant value Numbers, text, dates, or times of day that you type into a cell.

Content control In a template, an area indicated by placeholder text that can be used to add text, pictures, dates, or lists.

Context menus Menus that display commands and options relevant to the selected text or object; also called *shortcut menus*.

Context sensitive A command associated with the currently selected or active object; often activated by right-clicking a screen item.

Context-sensitive commands Commands that display on a shortcut menu that relate to the object or text that you right-clicked.

Contextual tabs Tabs that are added to the ribbon automatically when a specific object, such as a picture, is selected, and that contain commands relevant to the selected object.

Contiguous slides Slides that are adjacent to each other in a presentation.

Contrast The difference between the darkest and lightest area of a picture.

Control An object on a form or report that displays data or text, performs actions, and lets you view and work with information.

Control layout The grouped arrangement of controls on a form or report; for example, the Stacked layout.

Copy A command that duplicates a selection and places it on the Clipboard.

COUNTIF function A statistical function that counts the number of cells within a range that meet the given condition and that has two arguments—the range of cells to check and the criteria.

Cover letter A document that you send with your resume to provide additional information about your skills and experience.

Criteria (Access) Conditions in a query that identify the specific records you are looking for.

Criteria (Excel) Conditions that you specify in a logical function.

Crop A command that removes unwanted or unnecessary areas of a picture.

Crop handles Handles used to remove unwanted areas of a picture.

Crop pointer The pointer used to crop areas of a picture.

Crosshair pointer The pointer used to draw a shape.

Crosstab query A query that uses an aggregate function for data that can be grouped by two types of information and displays the data in a compact, spreadsheet-like format with column headings and row headings.

Currency data type An Access data type that describes monetary values and numeric data that can be used in mathematical calculations involving values with one to four decimal places.

Custom web app A database that you can publish and share with others over the Internet.

Cut A command that removes a selection and places it on the Clipboard.

Dashboard A descriptive term for the Windows 8 Start screen that provides a one-screen view of links to information and programs that matter most to the signed-in user.

Data Facts about people, events, things, or ideas.

Data bar A cell format consisting of a shaded bar that provides a visual cue to the reader about the value of a cell relative to other cells; the length of the bar represents the value in the cell—a longer bar represents a higher value and a shorter bar represents s lower value.

Data entry The action of entering the data into a record in a database table or form.

Data management The process of managing your files and folders in an organized manner so that you can find information when you need it.

Data marker A column, bar, area, dot, pie slice, or other symbol in a chart that represents a single data point; related data points form a data series.

Data point A value that originates in a worksheet cell and that is represented in a chart by a data marker.

Data series Related data points represented by data markers; each data series has a unique color or pattern represented in the chart legend.

Data source (Access) The table or tables from which a form, query, or report retrieves its data.

Data source (Word) A document that contains a list of variable information, such as names and addresses, that is merged with a main document to create customized form letters or labels.

Data type The characteristic that defines the kind of data that can be stored in a field, such as numbers, text, or dates.

Data (Excel) Text or numbers in a cell.

Data (Windows) All the files—documents, workbooks, pictures, songs, and so on—that you create and store during the day-to-day use of your computer.

Database An organized collection of facts about people, events, things, or ideas related to a specific topic or purpose.

Database management system (DBMS) Database software that controls how related collections of data are stored, organized, retrieved, and secured; also known as a DBMS.

Database template A preformatted database that contains prebuilt tables, queries, forms, and reports that perform a specific task, such as tracking events.

Datasheet view The Access view that displays data organized in columns and rows similar to an Excel worksheet.

Date & Time A command with which you can automatically insert the current date and time into a document in a variety of formats.

Date control A control on a form or report that inserts the current date each time the form or report is opened.

Dateline The first line in a business letter that contains the current date and which is positioned just below the letterhead if a letterhead is used.

DBMS An acronym for database management system.

Default The term that refers to the current selection or setting that is automatically used by a computer program unless you specify otherwise.

Descending order A sorting order that arranges text in reverse alphabetical order (Z to A) and numbers from the highest number to the lowest number.

Deselect The action of canceling the selection of an object or block of text by clicking outside of the selection.

Design grid The lower area of the query window that displays the design of the query.

Design view An Access view that displays the detailed structure of a table, query, form, or report. For forms and reports, may be the view in which some tasks must be performed, and only the controls, and not the data, display in this view.

Desktop The area in Windows 8 where you use desktop apps and that serves as a surface for your work, like the top of an actual desk.

Desktop app The term that commonly refers to a computer program that is installed on your computer and requires a computer operating system like Microsoft Windows or Apple OS to run.

Desktop background Displays the colors and graphics of your desktop; you can change the desktop background to look the way you want it.

Desktop shortcuts Desktop icons that link to any item accessible on your computer or on a network, such as a program, file, folder, disk drive, printer, or another computer.

Destination table The table to which you import or append data.

Detail section The section of a form or report that displays the records from the underlying table or query.

Detail sheets The worksheets that contain the details of the information summarized on a summary sheet.

Details pane Displays the most common properties associated with the selected file.

Details view The file list view in File Explorer that displays a list of files or folders and their most common properties.

Dialog box A small window that displays options for completing a task.

Dialog Box Launcher A small icon that displays to the right of some group names on the ribbon, and which opens a related dialog box or pane providing additional options and commands related to that group.

Displayed value The data that displays in a cell.

Document properties Details about a file that describe or identify it, including the title, author name, subject, and keywords that identify the document's topic or contents; also known as *metadata*.

Dot leader A series of dots preceding a tab that guides the eye across the line.

Double-click The action of pressing the left mouse button twice in rapid succession while holding the mouse still.

Drag The action of moving something from one location on the screen to another while holding down the left mouse button; the action of dragging includes releasing the mouse button at the desired time or location.

Drag and drop The action of moving a selection by dragging it to a new location.

Drawing objects Graphic objects, such as shapes, diagrams, lines, or circles.

Drive An area of storage that is formatted with a file system compatible with your operating system and is identified by a drive letter.

Edit The process of making changes to text or graphics in an Office file.

Editing (PowerPoint) The process of modifying a presentation by adding and deleting slides or by changing the contents of individual slides.

Ellipsis A set of three dots indicating incompleteness; an ellipsis following a command name indicates that a dialog box will display if you click the command.

Em dash A punctuation symbol used to indicate an explanation or emphasis.

Embed code A code that creates a link to a video, picture, or other type of rich media content.

Emphasis effect Animation that emphasizes an object or text that is already displayed.

Enclosures Additional documents included with a business letter.

Endnote In a research paper, a note placed at the end of a document or chapter.

Enhanced ScreenTip A ScreenTip that displays more descriptive text than a normal ScreenTip.

Enterprise fund A municipal government fund that reports income and expenditures related to municipal services for which a fee is charged in exchange for goods or services.

Entrance effect Animation that brings a slide element onto the screen.

Excel pointer An Excel window element with which you can display the location of the pointer.

Excel table A series of rows and columns that contains related data that is managed independently from the data in other rows and columns in the worksheet.

Exit effect Animation that moves an object or text off the screen.

Expand Formula Bar button An Excel window element with which you can Increase the height of the Formula Bar to display lengthy cell content.

Expand horizontal scroll bar button An Excel window element with which you can increase the width of the horizontal scroll bar.

Explode The action of pulling out one or more pie slices from a pie chart for emphasis.

Export The process of copying data from one file into another file, such as an Access table into an Excel spreadsheet.

Expression A formula.

Extract The action of decompressing—pulling out—files from a compressed form.

Eyedropper A tool that captures the exact color from an object on your screen and then applies it to any shape, picture, or text.

Field (Access) A single piece of information that is stored in every record; represented by a column in a database table.

Field list A list of field names in a table.

Field properties Characteristics of a field that control how the field displays and how data can be entered in the field.

Fields (Word) In a mail merge, the column headings in the data source.

File A collection of information that is stored on a computer under a single name, for example a text document, a picture, or a program.

File Explorer The program within Windows 8 that displays the contents of libraries, folders, and files on your computer, and which also enables you to perform tasks related to your files and folders such as copying, moving, and renaming. File Explorer is at work anytime you are viewing the contents of a library, a folder, or a file.

File list Displays the contents of the current folder or library; if you type text into the Search box, only the folders and files that match your search will display here—including files in subfolders.

File properties Information about a file such as its author, the date the file was last changed, and any descriptive tags.

Fill color The inside color of text or of an object.

Fill handle The small black square in the lower right corner of a selected cell.

Fill The inside color of an object.

Filter The process of displaying only a portion of the data based on matching a specific value to show only the data that meets the criteria that you specify.

Filter by Form An Access command that filters the records in a form based on one or more fields, or based on more than one value in the field.

Filter by Selection An Access command that displays only the records that contain the value in the selected field and hides the records that do not contain the value.

Filtering The process of displaying only a portion of the total records (a subset) based on matching specific values to provide a quick answer to a question.

Find and replace A command that searches the cells in a worksheet—or in a selected range—for matches and then replaces each match with a replacement value of your choice.

First principle of good database design A principle of good database design stating that data is organized in tables so that there is no redundant data.

Flash Fill Recognizes a pattern in your data, and then automatically fills in values when you enter examples of the output that you want. Use it to split data from two or more cells or to combine data from two cells.

Flat database A simple database file that is not related or linked to any other collection of data.

Flip A command that creates a reverse image of a picture or object.

Floating object A graphic that can be moved independently of the surrounding text characters.

Folder A container in which you store files.

Folder structure The hierarchy of folders in Windows 8.

Folder window In Windows, a window that displays the contents of the current folder, library, or device, and contains helpful parts so that you can navigate the Windows file structure.

Font A set of characters with the same design and shape.

Font styles Formatting emphasis such as bold, italic, and underline.

Footer Text that displays at the bottom of every slide or that prints at the bottom of a sheet of slide handouts or notes pages.

Footnote In a research paper, a note placed at the bottom of the page.

Foreign key The field that is included in the related table so the field can be joined with the primary key in another table for the purpose of creating a relationship.

Form An Access object you can use to enter new records into a table, edit or delete existing records in a table, or display existing records.

Form Footer Information at the bottom of the screen in Form view or Layout view that is printed after the last detail section on the last page of a printout.

Form Header Information such as a form's title that displays at the top of the screen in Form view or Layout view and is printed at the top of the first page when records are printed as forms.

Form tool An Access tool that creates a form with a single mouse click, which includes all of the fields from the underlying data source (table or query).

Form view The Access view in which you can view, modify, delete, or add to the records in a table; but you cannot change the layout or design of the form.

Form Wizard An Access tool that walks you step by step through the creation of a form and that gives you more flexibility in the design, layout, and number of fields in a form.

Format Changing the appearance of cells and worksheet elements to make a worksheet attractive and easy to read.

Formatting The process of establishing the overall appearance of text, graphics, and pages in an Office file—for example, in a Word document.

Formatting marks Characters that display on the screen, but do not print, indicating where the Enter key, the Spacebar, and the Tab key were pressed; also called *nonprinting characters*.

Formula An equation that performs mathematical calculations on values in a worksheet.

Formula AutoComplete An Excel feature that, after typing an = (equal sign) and the beginning letter or letters of a function name, displays a list of function names that match the typed letter(s), and from which you can insert the function by pointing to its name and pressing the Tab key or double-clicking.

Formula Bar An element in the Excel window that displays the value or formula contained in the active cell; here you can also enter or edit values or formulas.

Free/Busy information In the Outlook calendar, one of four indicators—Busy, Free, Tentative, or Out of Office—associated with your availability for a specific date and time.

Free-form snip When using Snipping Tool, the type of snip that lets you draw an irregular line, such as a circle, around an area of the screen.

Freeze Panes A command that enables you to select one or more rows or columns and freeze (lock) them into place; the locked rows and columns become separate panes.

Full-screen snip When using Snipping Tool, the type of snip that captures the entire screen.

Function A predefined formula—a formula that Excel has already built for you—that performs calculations by using specific values in a particular order or structure.

Fund A sum of money set aside for a specific purpose.

Gallery An Office feature that displays a list of potential results instead of just the command name.

General format The default format that Excel applies to numbers; this format has no specific characteristics—whatever you type in the cell will display, with the exception that trailing zeros to the right of a decimal point will not display.

General fund The term used to describe money set aside for the normal operating activities of a government entity such as a city.

Goal Seek A what-if analysis tool that finds the input needed in one cell to arrive at the desired result in another cell.

Gradient fill A fill effect in which one color fades into another.

Graphical user interface The system by which you interact with your computer and which uses graphics such as an image of a file folder or wastebasket that you click to activate the item represented.

Graphics Pictures, charts, or drawing objects.

Group Footer Information printed at the end of each group of records; used to display summary information for the group.

Group Header Information printed at the beginning of each new group of records; for example, the group name.

Group, Sort, and Total pane A pane that displays at the bottom of the screen in which you can control how information is sorted and grouped in a report; provides the most flexibility for adding or modifying groups, sort orders, or totals options on a report.

Groups On the Office ribbon, the sets of related commands that you might need for a specific type of task.

GUI The acronym for a graphical user interface, pronounced *GOO-ee*.

Hanging indent An indent style in which the first line of a paragraph extends to the left of the remaining lines and that is commonly used for bibliographic entries.

Hard disk drive The primary storage device located inside your computer and where most of your files and programs are typically stored; usually labeled as drive C.

Header Text that prints at the top of each sheet of slide handouts or notes pages.

Headings font A font that is applied to all slide title text.

Hierarchy An arrangement where items are ranked and where each level is lower in rank than the item above it.

Icons Small images that represent commands, files, applications, or other windows.

IF function A function that uses a logical test to check whether a condition is met, and then returns one value if true, and another value if false.

Immersive The term that describes the Windows 8 style screens, meaning they have no borders, no menus, and they behave differently from traditional Windows desktop programs because there is no taskbar, an app cannot be minimized like a desktop program, nor can an app be dragged around as a smaller window; the idea is that you are immersed in the app with no screen distractions.

Import The process of copying data from another file, such as a Word table or an Excel workbook, into a separate file, such as an Access database.

Info tab The tab in Backstage view that displays information about the current file.

Information Data that is organized in a useful manner.

Inline Object An object or graphic inserted in a document that acts like a character in a sentence.

Innermost sort field When sorting on multiple fields in Datasheet view, the field that will be used for the second level of sorting.

Insertion point A blinking vertical line that indicates where text or graphics will be inserted.

Inside address The name and address of the person receiving the letter and positioned below the date line.

Interactive media Computer interaction that responds to your actions; for example by presenting text, graphics, animation, video, audio, or games. Also referred to as rich media.

Internet Explorer The web browser program developed by Microsoft that is included with Windows 8.

Is Not Null A criteria that searches for fields that are not empty.

Is Null A criteria that searches for fields that are empty.

Join line In the Relationships window, the line joining two tables that visually indicates the common fields and the type of relationship.

JPEG An acronym for Joint Photographic Experts Group, and which is a common file type used by digital cameras and computers to store digital pictures; JPEG is popular because it can store a high-quality picture in a relatively small file. A JPEG file has a .jpg file extension.

Jump List A list that displays when you right-click a button on the taskbar, and which displays locations (in the upper portion) and tasks (in the lower portion) from a program's taskbar button.

Justified alignment An arrangement of text in which the text aligns evenly on both the left and right margins.

Keyboard shortcut A combination of two or more keyboard keys, used to perform a task that would otherwise require a mouse.

KeyTip The letter that displays on a command in the ribbon and that indicates the key you can press to activate the command when keyboard control of the ribbon is activated.

Keywords Custom file properties in the form of words that you associate with a document to give an indication of the document's content; used to help find and organize files. Also called *tags*.

Label Another name for a text value, and which usually provides information about number values.

Label control A control on a form or report that contains descriptive information, usually a field name or title.

Landscape orientation A page orientation in which the paper is wider than it is tall.

Layout The arrangement of elements, such as title and subtitle text, lists, pictures, tables, charts, shapes, and movies, on a slide.

Layout Options Picture formatting options that control the manner in which text wraps around a picture or other object.

Layout Options button A button that displays when an object is selected and that has commands to choose how the object interacts with surrounding text.

Layout selector A small symbol that displays in the upper left corner of a selected control layout in a form or report that is displayed in Layout view or Design view; used to move or format an entire group of controls.

Layout view The Access view in which you can make changes to a form or report while the object is running—the data from the underlying data source displays.

Leader character Characters that form a solid, dotted, or dashed line that fills the space preceding a tab stop.

Left alignment The cell format in which characters align at the left edge of the cell; this is the default for text entries and is an example of formatting information stored in a cell.

Legend A chart element that identifies the patterns or colors that are assigned to the categories in the chart.

Lettered column headings The area along the top edge of a worksheet that identifies each column with a unique letter or combination of letters.

Letterhead The personal or company information that displays at the top of a letter.

Library A collection of items, such as files and folders, assembled from various locations.

Line break indicator A non-printing character in the shape of a bent arrow that indicates a manual line break.

Line chart A chart type that displays trends over time; time displays along the bottom axis and the data point values are connected with a line.

Line spacing The distance between lines of text in a paragraph.

Link A connection to data in another file.

List level An outline level in a presentation represented by a bullet symbol and identified in a slide by the indentation and the size of the text.

Live Layout A feature that reflows text as you move or size an object so that you can view the placement of surrounding text.

Live Preview A technology that shows the result of applying an editing or formatting change as you point to possible results—*before* you actually apply it.

Live tiles Tiles on the Windows 8 Start screen that are constantly updated with fresh information relevant to the signed-in user; for example, the number of new email messages, new sports scores of interest, or new updates to social networks such as Facebook or Twitter.

Local account A user account in which the information associated with each user is local to a single Windows 8 computer.

Location Any disk drive, folder, or other place in which you can store files and folders.

Lock screen The first screen that displays after turning on a Windows 8 device, which displays the time, day, and date, and one or more icons representing the status of the device's Internet connection, battery status on a tablet or laptop, and any Lock screen apps that are installed such as email notifications.

Lock screen apps Apps that display on a Windows 8 Lock screen and that show quick status and notifications, even if the screen is locked, and include Calendar, Mail, Messaging, and Weather.

Logical functions A group of functions that test for specific conditions and that typically use conditional tests to determine whether specified conditions are true or false.

Logical operators Operators that are used to evaluate data to determine if a condition is met (true) or not met (false). With two criteria, AND requires that both conditions be met and OR requires that either condition be met for a record to display in the query results.

Logical test Any value or expression that can be evaluated as being true or false.

Mail merge A feature that joins a main document and a data source to create customized letters or labels.

Main document In a mail merge, the document that contains the text or formatting that remains constant.

Major unit The value in a chart's value axis that determines the spacing between tick marks and between the gridlines in the plot area.

Manual column break An artificial end to a column to balance columns or to provide space for the insertion of other objects.

Manual line break A break that moves text to the right of the insertion point to a new line while keeping the text in the same paragraph.

Manual page break The action of forcing a page to end and placing subsequent text at the top of the next page.

Margins The space between the text and the top, bottom, left, and right edges of the paper.

MAX function An Excel function that determines the largest value in a selected range of values.

MEDIAN function An Excel function that finds the middle value that has as many values above it in the group as are below it; it differs from AVERAGE in that the result is not affected as much by a single value that is greatly different from the others.

Menu bar A group of menus.

Menu A list of commands within a category.

Merge & Center A command that joins selected cells in an Excel worksheet into one larger cell and centers the contents in the merged cell.

Message Bar The area directly below the ribbon that displays information such as security alerts when there is potentially unsafe, active content in an Office document that you open.

Metadata Details about a file that describe or identify it, including the title, author name, subject, and keywords that identify the document's topic or contents; also known as *document properties*.

Microsoft account A user account that allows you to set up one Windows 8 computer and then synchronize all the same settings from that computer to any other device you have that uses Windows 8.

Microsoft Design Language The design principles in Windows 8 that include tiles with white text on deeply colored backgrounds, consistent fonts, simpler navigation, and the use of the entire screen; the idea is that you are immersed in the app with no screen distractions.

Microsoft Office 365 A set of secure online services that enable people in an organization to communicate and collaborate by using any Internet-connected device—a computer, a tablet, or a mobile phone.

MIN function An Excel function that determines the smallest value in a selected range of values.

Mini toolbar A small toolbar containing frequently used formatting commands that displays as a result of selecting text or objects.

Modern Language Association (MLA) One of two commonly used style guides for formatting research papers.

Mouse pointer Any symbol that displays on your screen in response to moving your mouse.

MRU Acronym for *most recently used*, which refers to the state of some commands that retain the characteristic most recently applied; for example, the Font Color button retains the most recently used color until a new color is chosen.

Multiple-items form A form that enables you to display or enter multiple records in a table.

Name Box An element of the Excel window that displays the name of the selected cell, table, chart, or object.

Nameplate The banner on the front page of a newsletter that identifies the publication.

Navigate The process of exploring within the organizing structure of Windows.

Navigate (File Explorer): Explore within the file organizing structure of Windows 8.

Navigation area An area at the bottom of the Access window that indicates the number of records in the table and contains controls in the form of arrows that you click to navigate among the records.

Navigation pane In a folder window, the area on the left in which you can navigate to, open, and display favorites, libraries, folders, saved searches, and an expandable list of drives.

Newsletter A periodical that communicates news and information to a specific group.

No Paragraph Style The built-in paragraph style—available from the Paragraph Spacing command—that inserts *no* extra space before or after a paragraph and uses line spacing of 1.

Noncontiguous slides Slides that are not adjacent to each other in a presentation.

Nonprinting characters Characters that display on the screen, but do not print, indicating where the Enter key, the Spacebar, and the Tab key were pressed; also called *formatting marks*.

Normal template The template that serves as a basis for all Word documents.

Normal view A screen view that maximizes the number of cells visible on your screen and keeps the column letters and row numbers close to the columns and rows.

Normalization The process of applying design rules and principles to ensure that your database performs as expected.

Note In a research paper, information that expands on the topic, but that does not fit well in the document text.

Notes page A printout that contains the slide image on the top half of the page and notes that you have created on the Notes pane in the lower half of the page.

Notes pane An area of the Normal view window that displays below the Slide pane with space to type notes regarding the active slide.

Notification area Displays notification icons and the system clock; sometimes referred to as the *system tray*.

Notification bar In Internet Explorer 10, a bar at the bottom of your screen that displays information about pending downloads, security issues, add-ons, and other issues related to the operation of your computer.

NOW function An Excel function that retrieves the date and time from your computer's calendar and clock and inserts the information into the selected cell.

Number data type An Access data type that describes numbers that might be used in calculations.

Number format A specific way in which Excel displays numbers in a cell.

Number values Constant values consisting of only numbers.

Numbered list A list that uses consecutive numbers or letters to introduce each item in a list.

Numbered row headings The area along the left edge of a worksheet that identifies each row with a unique number.

Object A text box, picture, table, or shape that you can select and then move and resize.

Object anchor The symbol that indicates to which paragraph an object is attached.

Object tab In the object window, a tab that identifies the object and which enables you to make the open object active.

Object window An area of the Access window that displays open objects, such as tables, queries, forms, or reports; by default, each object displays on its own tab.

Objects (Access) The basic parts of a database that you create to store your data and to work with your data; for example, tables, queries, forms, and reports.

Office 365 Administrator In Office 365, the person who creates and manages the account, adds new users, sets up the services your organization wants to use, sets permission levels, and manages the SharePoint team sites.

Office Online (formerly Web Apps) The free online companions to Microsoft Word, Excel, PowerPoint, Access, and OneNote.

Office Presentation Service A Word feature to present your Word document to others who can watch in a web browser.

On Click An animation option that begins the animation sequence for the selected slide element when the mouse button is clicked or the [Spacebar] is pressed.

One-click Row/Column Insertion A Word table feature with which you can insert a new row or column by pointing to the desired location and then clicking.

One-to-many relationship A relationship between two tables where one record in the first table corresponds to many records in the second table—the most common type of relationship in Access.

OneDrive (formerly SkyDrive) A free file storage and file sharing service provided by Microsoft when you sign up for a Microsoft account.

Open dialog box A dialog box from which you can navigate to, and then open on your screen, an existing file that was created in that same program.

Operating system A specific type of computer program that manages the other programs on a computer—including computer devices such as desktop computers, laptop computers, smartphones, tablet computers, and game consoles.

Operators The symbols with which you can specify the type of calculation you want to perform in an Excel formula.

Option button In a dialog box, a round button that enables you to make one choice among two or more options.

Options dialog box A dialog box within each Office application where you can select program settings and other options and preferences.

OR condition A compound criteria used to display records that match at least one of the specified criteria.

Order of operations The mathematical rules for performing multiple calculations within a formula.

Outermost sort field When sorting on multiple fields in Datasheet view, the field that will be used for the first level of sorting.

Outline View A PowerPoint view that displays the presentation outline to the left of the Slide pane.

Page break indicator A dotted line with the text *Page Break* that indicates where a manual page break was inserted.

Page Footer Information printed at the bottom of every page in a report; most often includes the page number.

Page Header Information printed at the top of every page in a report.

Page Layout view A screen view in which you can use the rulers to measure the width and height of data, set margins for printing, hide or display the numbered row headings and the lettered column headings, and change the page orientation; this view is useful for preparing your worksheet for printing.

Page number control A control on a form or report that inserts the page numbers when displayed in Print Preview or when printed.

Paint A program that comes with Windows 8 with which you can create and edit drawings and display and edit stored photos.

Pane (Excel) A portion of a worksheet window bounded by and separated from other portions by vertical and horizontal bars.

Pane A separate area of a window.

Paragraph symbol The symbol ¶ that represents the end of a paragraph.

Parameter A value that can be changed.

Parameter query A query that prompts you for criteria before running the query.

Parent folder In the file organizing structure of File Explorer, the location where the folder you are viewing is saved—one level up in the hierarchy.

Parenthetical references References that include the last name of the author or authors, and the page number in the referenced source.

Paste area The target destination for data that has been cut or copied using the Office Clipboard.

Paste Options gallery A gallery of buttons that provides a Live Preview of all the Paste options available in the current context.

Paste The action of placing cell contents that have been copied or moved to the Clipboard into another location.

Path A sequence of folders (directories) that leads to a specific file or folder.

PC settings The area from which you can control almost everything about how Windows 8 looks and works; you can change colors and backgrounds, the picture on your Lock screen, or your account picture, manage other users (if you are the administrator), connect devices like printers, or set up a network.

PDF The acronym for Portable Document Format, which is a file format that creates an image that preserves the look of your file; this is a popular format for sending documents electronically because the document will display on most computers.

PDF Reflow The ability to import PDF files into Word so that you can transform a PDF back into a fully editable Word document.

Percent for new value = base percent + percent of increase The formula for calculating a percentage by which a value increases by adding the base percentage—usually 100%—to the percent increase.

Percentage rate of increase The percent by which one number increases over another number.

Personal folder A folder created for each user account on a Windows 8 computer, labeled with the account holder's name, and which contains the subfolders *Documents*, *Pictures*, *Music*, and *Videos*.

Picture element A point of light measured in dots per square inch on a screen; 64 pixels equals 8.43 characters, which is the average number of characters that will fit in a cell in an Excel worksheet using the default font.

Picture styles Frames, shapes, shadows, borders, and other special effects that can be added to an image to create an overall visual style for the image.

Pie chart A chart that shows the relationship of each part to a whole.

PING An acronym for Portable Network Graphic, and which is a common file type that can be transferred over the Internet. A PING file has a .png file extension.

Pixel The abbreviated name for a picture element.

Placeholder A box on a slide with dotted or dashed borders that holds title and body text or other content such as charts, tables, and pictures.

Placeholder text The text in a content control that indicates the type of information to be entered in a specific location.

Plot area The area bounded by the axes of a chart, including all the data series.

Point The action of moving your mouse pointer over something on your screen.

Point and click method The technique of constructing a formula by pointing to and then clicking cells; this method is convenient when the referenced cells are not adjacent to one another.

Point to The action of moving the mouse pointer over a specific area.

Pointer Any symbol that displays on your screen in response to moving your mouse and with which you can select objects and commands.

Pointing device A mouse, touchpad, or other device that controls the pointer position on the screen.

Points A measurement of the size of a font; there are 72 points in an inch.

Populate The action of filling a database table with records.

Portable Document Format A file format that creates an image that preserves the look of your file, but that cannot be easily changed; a popular format for sending documents electronically, because the document will display on most computers.

Portrait orientation A page orientation in which the paper is taller than it is wide.

Primary key The field in a table that uniquely identifies a record; for example, a Student ID number at a college.

Print Preview A view of a document as it will appear when you print it.

Print Titles An Excel command that enables you to specify rows and columns to repeat on each printed page.

Program A set of instructions that a computer uses to accomplish a task; also called an application.

Progress bar In a dialog box or taskbar button, a bar that indicates visually the progress of a task such as a download or file transfer.

Property Sheet A list of characteristics—properties—for fields or controls on a form or report in which you can make precise changes to each property associated with the field or control.

Protected View A security feature in Office 2013 that protects your computer from malicious files by opening them in a restricted environment until you enable them; you might encounter this feature if you open a file from an email or download files from the Internet.

pt The abbreviation for *point*; for example, when referring to a font size.

Query A database object that retrieves specific data from one or more database objects—either tables or other queries—and then, in a single datasheet, displays only the data you specify.

Quick Access Toolbar In an Office program window, the small row of buttons in the upper left corner of the screen from which you can perform frequently used commands.

Quick Analysis Tool A tool that displays in the lower right corner of a selected range with which you can analyze your data by using Excel tools such as charts, color-coding, and formulas.

Range Two or more selected cells on a worksheet that are adjacent or nonadjacent; because the range is treated as a single unit, you can make the same changes or combination of changes to more than one cell at a time.

Range finder An Excel feature that outlines cells in color to indicate which cells are used in a formula; useful for verifying which cells are referenced in a formula.

Rate = amount of increase/base The mathematical formula to calculate a rate of increase.

Read Mode A view in Word that optimizes the Word screen for the times when you are reading Word documents on the screen and not creating or editing them.

Read-Only A property assigned to a file that prevents the file from being modified or deleted; it indicates that you cannot save any changes to the displayed document unless you first save it with a new name.

Reading view A view in PowerPoint that displays a presentation in a manner similar to a slide show but in which the taskbar, title bar, and status bar remain available in the presentation window.

Recolor A feature that enables you to change all colors in the picture to shades of a single color.

Recommended Charts An Excel feature that displays a customized set of charts that, according to Excel's calculations, will best fit your data based on the range of data that you select.

Record All of the categories of data pertaining to one person, place, event, thing, or idea; represented by a row in a database table.

Record selector bar The vertical bar at the left edge of a record when it is displayed in a form that is used to select an entire record.

Record selector box The small box at the left of a record in Datasheet view that, when clicked, selects the entire record.

Record source The tables or queries that provide the underlying data for a form or report.

Rectangular snip When using Snipping Tool, the type of snip that lets you draw a precise box by dragging the mouse pointer around an area of the screen to form a rectangle.

Recycle Bin A folder that stores anything that you delete from your computer, and from which anything stored can be retrieved until the contents are permanently deleted by activating the Empty Recycle Bin command.

Redundant In a database, information that is duplicated in a manner that indicates poor database design.

Referential integrity A set of rules that Access uses to ensure that the data between related tables is valid.

Relational database A sophisticated type of database that has multiple collections of data within the file that are related to one another.

Relationship An association that you establish between two tables based on common fields.

Relative cell reference In a formula, the address of a cell based on the relative positions of the cell that contains the formula and the cell referred to in the formula.

Removable storage device A portable device on which you can store files, such as a USB flash drive, a flash memory card, or an external hard drive, commonly used to transfer information from one computer to another.

Report A database object that summarizes the fields and records from a query or table in an easy-to-read format suitable for printing.

Report Footer Information printed at the bottom of the last page of a report.

Report Header Information printed on the first page of a report; used for logos, titles, and dates.

Report tool An Access tool that creates a report with one mouse click and displays all of the fields and records from the record source that you select.

Report Wizard An Access tool that walks you step by step through the creation of a report and that gives you more flexibility in the design, layout, and number of fields in a report.

Resources A term used to refer collectively to the parts of your computer such as the central processing unit (CPU), memory, and any attached devices such as a printer.

RGB A color model in which the colors red, green, and blue are added together to form another color.

Ribbon The area at the top of a folder window in File Explorer that groups common tasks such as copying and moving, creating new folders, emailing and zipping items, and changing views on related tabs.

Rich media Computer interaction that responds to your actions; for example by presenting text, graphics, animation, video, audio, or games. Also referred to as interactive media.

Rich Text Format (RTF) A standard file format that contains text and some formatting such as underline, bold, italic, font sizes, and colors; RTF documents can be opened in many word processing programs and text editors.

Right alignment An arrangement of text in which the text aligns at the right margin, leaving the left margin uneven.

Right-click The action of clicking the right mouse button one time.

Roam The ability to set up one computer, for example a desktop computer, and then synchronize—roam—all the same settings to a laptop, to a tablet PC, to a Windows phone, or to any other device to which one signs in with the same Microsoft account.

Rotation handle A symbol with which you can rotate a graphic to any angle; displays above the top center sizing handle.

Rounding A procedure in which you determine which digit at the right of the number will be the last digit displayed and then increase it by one if the next digit to its right is 5, 6, 7, 8, or 9.

Row A horizontal group of cells in a worksheet.

Row heading The numbers along the left side of an Excel worksheet that designate the row numbers.

Ruler guides Dotted red vertical and horizontal lines that display in the rulers indicating the pointer's position.

Run The process in which Access looks at the records in the table(s) included in the query design, finds the records that match the specified criteria, and then displays the records in a datasheet; only the fields included in the query design display.

Salutation The greeting line of a business letter.

Sans serif font A font design with no lines or extensions on the ends of characters.

Scale A command that resizes a picture to a percentage of its size.

Scale to Fit Excel commands that enable you to stretch or shrink the width, height, or both, of printed output to fit a maximum number of pages.

Scaling The process of shrinking the width and/or height of printed output to fit a maximum number of pages.

Screen capture An image file that contains the contents of a computer screen.

Screenshot An image of an active window on your computer that you can paste into a document.

ScreenTip A small box that that displays useful information when you perform various mouse actions such as pointing to screen elements or dragging.

Scroll arrow An arrow at the top and bottom, or left and right, of a scroll bar that when clicked, moves the window in small increments.

Scroll bar A bar that displays on the bottom or right side of a window when the contents of a window are not completely visible; used to move the window up, down, left, or right to bring the contents into view.

Scroll box The box in the vertical and horizontal scroll bars that can be dragged to reposition the contents of a window or pane on the screen.

Second principle of good database design A principle stating that appropriate database techniques are used to ensure the accuracy and consistency of data as it is entered into the table.

Section A portion of a document that can be formatted differently from the rest of the document.

Section bar In Design view, a gray bar in a form or report that identifies and separates one section from another; used to select the section and to change the size of the section.

Section break A double dotted line that indicates the end of one section and the beginning of another section.

Section header A type of slide layout that changes the look and flow of a presentation by providing text placeholders that do not contain bullet points.

Secure environment A system that uses controlled servers to ensure the security and privacy of email, to control the storage and use of information and to protect against the loss of confidential data.

Select To specify, by highlighting, a block of data or text on the screen with the intent of performing some action on the selection.

Select All box A box in the upper left corner of the worksheet grid that, when clicked, selects all the cells in a worksheet.

Select query A type of Access query that retrieves (selects) data from one or more tables or queries, displaying the selected data in a datasheet; also known as a simple select query.

Selecting Highlighting, by dragging with your mouse, areas of text or data or graphics, so that the selection can be edited, formatted, copied, or moved.

Series A group of things that come one after another in succession; for example, January, February, March, and so on.

Serif font A font design that includes small line extensions on the ends of the letters to guide the eye in reading from left to right.

Server A computer that provides services on a network such as an email server or a file server.

Shape A slide object such as a line, arrow, box, callout, or banner.

Shapes Lines, arrows, stars, banners, ovals, rectangles, and other basic shapes with which you can illustrate an idea, a process, or a workflow.

SharePoint Collaboration software with which people in an organization can set up team sites to share information, manage documents, and publish reports for others to see.

Sheet tab scrolling buttons Buttons to the left of the sheet tabs used to display Excel sheet tabs that are not in view; used when there are more sheet tabs than will display in the space provided.

Sheet tabs The labels along the lower border of the Excel window that identify each worksheet.

Short Text data type An Access data type that describes text, a combination of text and numbers, or numbers that are not used in calculations, such as a Postal Code.

Shortcut menu A menu that displays commands and options relevant to the selected text or object; also called a *context menu*.

Show Formulas A command that displays the formula in each cell instead of the resulting value.

Shut down Turning off your computer in a manner that closes all open programs and files, closes your network connections, stops the hard disk, and discontinues the use of electrical power.

Simple select query Another name for a select query.

Single spacing The common name for line spacing in which there is *no* extra space before or after a paragraph and that uses line spacing of 1.

Single-record form A form that enables you to display or enter one record at a time in a table.

Sizing handles Small squares surrounding a picture that indicate that the picture is selected.

Sizing handles Small squares that indicate a picture or object is selected.

SkyDrive see OneDrive

Skype A Microsoft product with which you can make voice calls, make video calls, transfer files, or send messages—including instant message and text messages—over the Internet.

Sleep Turning off your computer in a manner that automatically saves your work, stops the fan, and uses a small amount of electrical power to maintain your work in memory.

Slide A presentation page that can contain text, pictures, tables, charts, and other multimedia or graphic objects.

Slide handout Printed images of slides on a sheet of paper.

Slide pane A PowerPoint screen element that displays a large image of the active slide.

Slide Sorter view A presentation view that displays thumbnails of all of the slides in a presentation.

Slide transitions Motion effects that occur in Slide Show view when you move from one slide to the next during a presentation.

Small caps A font effect that changes lowercase letters to uppercase letters, but with the height of lowercase letters.

Smart guides Dashed lines that display on your slide when you are moving an object to assist you with alignment.

SmartArt A designer-quality visual representation of your information that you can create by choosing from among many different layouts to effectively communicate your message or ideas.

SmartArt graphic A visual representation of information that you create by choosing from among various layouts to communicate your message or ideas effectively.

SmartArt Styles Combinations of formatting effects that you can apply to SmartArt graphics.

Snap (desktop apps): A Windows 8 desktop feature that automatically resizes windows when you move—*snap*—them to the edge of the screen.

Snip The image captured using Snipping Tool.

Snipping Tool A program included with Windows 8 with which you can capture an image of all or part of a computer screen, and then annotate, save, copy, or share the image via email.

Sort The process of arranging data in a specific order based on the value in each field.

Sorting The process of arranging data in a specific order based on the value in a field.

Source file When importing a file, refers to the file being imported.

Sparkline A tiny chart in the background of a cell that gives a visual trend summary alongside your data; makes a pattern more obvious.

Speakers icon Displays the status of the computer's speakers (if any).

Spin box A small box with an upward- and downward-pointing arrow that lets you move rapidly through a set of values by clicking.

Split Splits the window into multiple resizable panes that contain views of your worksheet. This is useful to view multiple distant parts of your worksheet at one time.

Split button A button divided into two parts and in which clicking the main part of the button performs a command and clicking the arrow opens a menu with choices.

Spreadsheet Another name for a worksheet.

Stacked layout A control layout format that is similar to a paper form, with label controls placed to the left of each text box control; the controls are grouped together for easy editing.

Start screen The first screen that displays after signing in to a Windows 8 device, which displays square and rectangular boxes—referred to as tiles—from which one can access apps, websites, programs, and tools for using the computer by clicking or tapping them.

Start search The search feature in Windows 8 in which, from the Start screen, you can begin to type and by default, Windows 8 searches for apps; you can adjust the search to search for files or settings.

Start tip The thumbnail that displays when you point to the lower left corner of your screen.

Statistical functions Excel functions, including the AVERAGE, MEDIAN, MIN, and MAX functions, which are useful to analyze a group of measurements.

Status bar The area along the lower edge of the Excel window that displays, on the left side, the current cell mode, page number, and worksheet information; on the right side, when numerical data is selected, common calculations such as Sum and Average display.

Structure In Access, the underlying design of a table, including field names, data types, descriptions, and field properties.

Style (PowerPoint) A collection of formatting options that you can apply to a picture, text, or an object.

Style (Word) A group of formatting commands, such as font, font size, font color, paragraph alignment, and line spacing that can be applied to a paragraph with one command.

Style guide A manual that contains standards for the design and writing of documents.

Subdatasheet A format for displaying related records when you click the plus sign (+) next to a record in a table on the *one* side of the relationship.

Subfolder A folder within a folder.

Subject line The optional line following the inside address in a business letter that states the purpose of the letter.

Subset A portion of the total records available.

SUM function A predefined formula that adds all the numbers in a selected range of cells.

Summary sheet A worksheet where totals from other worksheets are displayed and summarized.

Suppress A Word feature that hides header and footer information, including the page number, on the first page of a document.

Switch Row/Column A charting command to swap the data over the axis—data being charted on the vertical axis will move to the horizontal axis and vice versa

Switcher Another name for *app switcher*.

Synchronization The process of updating computer files that are in two or more locations according to specific rules—also called *syncing*.

Syncing The process of updating computer files that are in two or more locations according to specific rules—also called *synchronization*.

Synonyms Words with the same or similar meaning.

System tray Another name for the notification area on the taskbar.

Tab order The order in which the insertion point moves from one field to another in a form when you press the Tab key.

Tab stop A specific location on a line of text, marked on the Word ruler, to which you can move the insertion point by pressing the Tab key, and which is used to align and indent text.

Table A format for information that organizes and presents text and data in columns and rows.

Table area The upper area of the query window that displays field lists for the tables that are used in a query.

Table style A format applied to a table that is consistent with the presentation theme.

Tables and Related Views An arrangement in the Navigation Pane that groups objects by the table to which they are related.

Tabs (ribbon) On the Office ribbon, the name of each activity area.

Tags Custom file properties in the form of words that you associate with a document to give an indication of the document's content; used to help find and organize files. Also called *keywords*.

Taskbar The area of the desktop that contains program buttons, and buttons for all open programs; by default, it is located at the bottom of the desktop, but you can move it.

Team A group of workers tasked with working together to solve a problem, make a decision, or create a work product.

Template An existing document that you use as a starting point for a new document; it opens a copy of itself, unnamed, and then you use the structure—and possibly some content, such as headings—as the starting point for new a document.

Text alignment The horizontal placement of text within a placeholder.

Text box An object with which you can position text anywhere on a slide.

Text box control A bound control on a form or report that displays the data from the underlying table or query.

Text control A content control that accepts only a text entry.

Text effects Decorative formats, such as shadowed or mirrored text, text glow, 3-D effects, and colors that make text stand out.

Text string A sequence of characters.

Text values Constant values consisting of only text, and which usually provides information about number values; also referred to as labels.

Text wrapping The manner in which text displays around an object.

Theme A predesigned set of colors, fonts, lines, and fill effects that look good together and that can be applied to all of the objects in the database or to individual objects in the database.

Theme colors A set of coordinating colors that are applied to the backgrounds, objects, and text in a presentation.

Theme fonts The fonts to apply to two types of slide text—headings and body.

Thesaurus A research tool that provides a list of synonyms.

Thumbnail A reduced image of a graphic.

Tiles Square and rectangular boxes on the Windows 8 Start screen from which one can access apps, websites, programs, and tools for using the computer by simply clicking or tapping them.

Timing options Animation options that control when animated items display in the animation sequence.

Title bar The bar at the top edge of the program window that indicates the name of the current file and the program name.

Title slide A slide layout—most commonly the first slide in a presentation—that provides an introduction to the presentation topic.

Toggle button A button that can be turned on by clicking it once, and then turned off by clicking it again.

Toolbar In a folder window, a row of buttons with which you can perform common tasks, such as changing the view of your files and folders or burning files to a CD.

Trim A command that deletes parts of a video to make it shorter.

Triple-click The action of clicking the left mouse button three times in rapid succession.

Truncated Refers to data that is cut off or shortened because the field or column is not wide enough to display all of the data or the field size is too small to contain all of the data.

Trust Center An area of Access where you can view the security and privacy settings for your Access installation.

Trusted Documents A security feature in Office that remembers which files you have already enabled; you might encounter this feature if you open a file from an email or download files from the Internet.

Unbound control A control that does not have a source of data, such as the title in a form or report.

Underlying formula The formula entered in a cell and visible only on the Formula Bar.

Underlying value The data that displays in the Formula Bar.

Uniform Resource Locator An address that uniquely identifies a location on the Internet.

URL The acronym for Uniform Resource Locator, which is an address that uniquely identifies a location on the Internet.

USB flash drive A small data storage device that plugs into a computer USB port.

User account A collection of information that tells Windows 8 what files and folders the account holder can access, what changes the account holder can make to the computer system, and what the account holder's personal preferences are.

Value Another name for a constant value.

Value after increase = base x percent for new value The formula for calculating the value after an increase by multiplying the original value—the base—by the percent for new value (see the *Percent for new value* formula).

Value axis A numerical scale on the left side of a chart that shows the range of numbers for the data points; also referred to as the Y-axis.

Variant A variation on the presentation theme style and color.

Volatile A term used to describe an Excel function that is subject to change each time the workbook is reopened; for example the NOW function updates itself to the current date and time each time the workbook is opened.

Wallpaper Another term for the desktop background.

Web browser Software with which you display webpages and navigate the Internet.

What-if analysis The process of changing the values in cells to see how those changes affect the outcome of formulas in a worksheet.

Wildcard character In a query, a character that serves as a placeholder for one or more unknown characters in criteria; an asterisk (*) represents one or more unknown characters, and a question mark (?) represents a single unknown character.

Window A rectangular area on a computer screen in which programs and content appear, and which can be moved, resized, minimized, or closed.

Window snip When using Snipping Tool, the type of snip that captures the entire displayed window.

Windows 8 An operating system developed by Microsoft Corporation designed to work with mobile computing devices of all types and also with traditional PCs.

Windows Reader app A Windows Store app with which you can open a PDF or XPS file, zoom, find words or phrases, take notes, save changes, and then print or share the file.

Windows Store apps Apps built for specific purposes; for example, to view photos, read sports information, organize a list of contacts, or read updates to social networks like Facebook and Twitter.

With Previous An animation option that begins the animation sequence at the same time as the previous animation or slide transition

Wizard A feature in Microsoft Office that walks you step by step through a process.

WordArt A gallery of text styles with which you can create decorative effects, such as shadowed or mirrored text

Wordwrap The feature that moves text from the right edge of a paragraph to the beginning of the next line as necessary to fit within the margins.

Workbook An Excel file that contains one or more worksheets.

Workbook-level buttons Buttons at the far right of the Ribbon tabs that minimize or restore a displayed workbook.

Works Cited In the MLA style, a list of cited works placed at the end of a research paper or report.

Worksheet The primary document that you use in Excel to work with and store data, and which is formatted as a pattern of uniformly spaced horizontal and vertical lines.

Worksheet grid area A part of the Excel window that displays the columns and rows that intersect to form the worksheet's cells.

Writer's identification The name and title of the author of a letter, placed near the bottom of the letter under the complimentary closing—also referred to as the *writer's signature block*.

Writer's signature block The name and title of the author of a letter, placed near the bottom of the letter, under the complimentary closing—also referred to as the *writer's identification*.

X-axis Another name for the horizontal (category) axis.

XML Paper Specification A Microsoft file format that creates an image of your document and that opens in the XPS viewer.

XPS The acronym for XML Paper Specification—a Microsoft file format that creates an image of your document and that opens in the XPS viewer.

Y-axis Another name for the vertical (value) axis.

Zipped folder A folder that has been reduced in size and thus takes up less storage space and can be transferred to other computers quickly; also called a *compressed* folder.

Zoom The action of increasing or decreasing the size of the viewing area on the screen.

Index

Layout view (Access) (*Continued*)
   control layout, 658–659
   formatting controls, 660–661
   grouping controls, 656–657
   modifying reports, 669–671
layouts (slides), 720
   SmartArt graphics, 806
leader characters, 152
left alignment
   definition, 310
   paragraphs, 142
legends
   definition, 323, 434
   removing from pie charts, 435–437
less than comparison operator, 379
libraries
   definition, 10
   displaying, 32–37
   Documents
     address bar, 33
     Back button, 33
     column headings, 33
     copying files from removable storage
       devices to, 44–45
     File list, 33
     Forward button, 33
     Library Tools contextual tab, 33
     Minimize button, 33
     Navigation pane, 33
     Recent button, 33
     ribbon, 34
     Search box, 34
     Up button, 33
   navigation pane, 11
Library Tools contextual tab, Documents library, 33
line breaks, manually adding, 267–268
line charts, 455–462
   formatting
     axis fonts, 460–462
     chart area, 459–460
     plot area gridlines, 460–462
   formulating axes, 457–459
   inserting multiple rows, 455–456
   presentations
     creating, 860–861
     formatting, 861–862
line spacing, 143–144
   default settings, 124
   formatting presentations, 745–746
linking files, 904–905
   updating links, 905–906
links, definition, 498
list levels
   definition, 722
   increasing/decreasing, 722–723
lists (Word), modifying
   bulleted, 147
   customizing bullets, 149–150
   numbered lists, 148–149
Live Layout, picture resizing, 128–129
Live Preview, definition, 82

live tiles, 7
local accounts, 4
locations, 10, 83
Lock screen, definition, 5
logical functions, definition, 378
logical operators, definition, 594
logical tests, definition, 379
Lync, Microsoft Office 365, 409, 465, 811

M

Mail Merge (Word), starting, 909–910
Mail Merge Recipients dialog box, 909
Mail Merge Wizard, 269–271
mail merges, 268–274
mailing labels, newsletters, 268–274
main documents, 268
many-to-many relationships, 570
margins
   alignment guides, 98
   defaults, 124
   setting, 141–142
mathematical operations, constructing formulas for, 337–340
MAX function, 375–376
   queries, 602–604
Maximize button, 77
media controls, inserting video in presentations, 843–844
MEDIAN function, 374–375
Medium citation, 245
menu bar, definition, 14
menus
   context, definition, 79
   definition, 14
   shortcut, definition, 79
Merge & Center command, formatting cells, 318
merge fields, inserting into documents, 910–912
Message Bar, definition, 564
metadata, definition, 84
Microsoft accounts, 26
   creating, 112–113
   signing in to, 94
Microsoft Clip Art collection, 96
Microsoft Design Language, 17
Microsoft Office 365, 754–755
   collaborating on team sites, 866–867
   Lync, 409, 465, 811
   Outlook Calendar, 612
   Outlook Meeting tool, 349, 534–535, 754
   signing in to accounts, 94
Microsoft Office Help, Excel, 110–111
Microsoft Office Online. *See* **Office Online**
Microsoft templates, 210–212
MIN function, 375–376
   queries, 602–604
mini toolbar, definition, 79
Minimize button, 77
   Documents library, 33

misspelled words, checking spelling, 79–80
MLA Handbook for Writes of Research Papers, **248**
Modern Language Association (MLA), 239
modifying. *See also* **editing**
   charts, presentations, 856–863, 859–860
   controls, 676–677
   data types, 495
   forms
     Design view, 661–663
     Layout view, 656–661
   query design, 577–578
   reports, 515–517
     design, 674–679
     Layout view, 669–671
   table column widths, 505–506
   table styles (in presentations), 854–255
   tables (in presentations), 851–856
   workbook theme colors, 344–346
   worksheet tab color, 393–394
   worksheet views, 387
More Commands dialog box, 95
most recently used. *See* **MRU**
mouse pointer, definition, 7
moving
   controls, modifying forms, 658–659
   data (Excel), 376–377
   files, 48–49
     snapping two windows, 50–51
   moving between Start screen and Desktop, 23–24
   slides, 741–742
     in Slide Sorter view, 747–748
     multiple slides in Slide Sorter view, 748
     objects with arrow keys, 783
   worksheet columns, 372–373
MRU (most recently used), 103
multiple 1.08 spacing, 144
multiple fields, sorting records in tables, 573–574
multiple slides, moving in Slide Sorter view, 748
multiple totals (Excel cells), 401
multiple windows, 893
multiple-items forms, 522–524
   building tables by entering records in, 522–524
   definition, 522

N

Name Box, 310–311
naming. *See also* **renaming**
   fields, 493–495
   files, 84–87
     with new names, 92–93
   folders, 45–46
   tabs, 12
   workbooks, 307
navigating, 10
   definition, 393
   keyboard keys, 99–100

keyboard shortcuts, 105
workbooks, 307–309, 393–394
navigation pane, 11, 250
  definition, 74, 493
  displaying folder structures, 37–38
  Documents library, 33
  Favorites, desktop shortcuts, 42
  Open dialog box, 40
  organizing Access objects, 525–526
Network area, 8
Network notification icon, 8
newsletters
  mailing labels, 268–274
  multiple-column, 256–265
  special formatting, 265–268
noncontiguous slides, definition, 748
nonprinting characters, 123
  definition, 77
Normal view, 717
  definition, 307
  editing presentations, 720–724
    adding speaker's notes, 723
    displaying slides, 723–724
    inserting slides, 720–722
    list levels, 722–723
normalization, 490
notes
  adding to presentations, 723
  printing presentations, 733–734
notes pages, 730
Notes pane (PowerPoint), 723
Notification bar, 31
  definition, 74
NOW function, 382
Number data type, definition, 527
number formats, definition, 314
number values (cell content), definition, 309
numbered lists, 147–149
  formatting in presentations, 777–779
numbers
  adding, SUM function, 895
  entering data in worksheets, 314
numeric criteria, specifying in queries, 588–593

O

Object button, 124
Object button arrows, 124
Object dialog box, 124
object window, definition, 493
objects
  aligning, 792–793
  alignment guides, 98
  applying themes to, 657
  databases, 490
    headers/footers, 508
    organizing in navigation pane, 525–526
  duplicating, 792
  grouped, 794–795
  Layout Options, 97
  moving with arrow keys, 783
  renaming, 667–668

Office 365 Administrators, 465, 684
Office Online (formerly Office Web Apps), 84
Office Presentation Service, 191–192
Office Web Apps. *See* **Office Online**
On Click option, 841
One-click Row/Column Insertion, 186
one-to-many relationships, definition, 565
one-to-many table relationships, creating, 589–591
one-to-one relationships, 570
OneDrive (formerly SkyDrive), 10, 811
  definition, 83
  saving spreadsheets to, 664–665
  uploading Word files to, 682–683
OneNote, 445–446
online pictures, inserting in presentations, 780–785
online presentations, 751
Open dialog box, 39, 92
opening
  databases, 563–564, 643–644, 667–668
    existing databases, 588–589
  files, 38–42
    existing files, 92–93
opening screen elements (Access), 491
operating systems
  definition, 3
  functions, 17
operators, definition, 337
option buttons, definition, 81
OR condition, 595
  definition, 652
order of operations, definition, 448
organizing Access objects in Navigation Pane, 525–526
orientation, 100–101
outcomes-based assessments
  Access, 559–560, 639–640, 711–712
  Excel, 367–368, 429, 483–484
  PowerPoint, 772–774, 827–828, 885–886
  Windows 8, 67–70
  Word, 176–178, 235–236, 300–302
outermost sort fields, definition, 573
Outline view, 740–741
outlines
  displaying presentations, 740–741
  editing presentations, 740–741
Outlook Calendar, Microsoft Office 365, 612
Outlook Meeting tool, Microsoft Office 365, 349, 534–535, 754
overview presentation, creating with PowerPoint Online, 735–736

P

Page Footer, definition, 678
Page Header, definition, 678
page layout
  changing orientation, 100–101
  zoom level, 100–101
page number controls, definition, 678
page orientation, 100–101

worksheets, 328–330
Page Width command, 101
Paint, 38
panes, definition, 74, 382
paragraph symbol, definition, 78
paragraphs (Word)
  borders, 267–268
  default settings, 124
  layout
    aligning text, 142–143
    line space, 143–144
    margin setting, 141–142
    space addition before and after, 146
    text indention, 145
parameter queries, creating, 607–609
parameter query prompts, 609
parent folder, 33
parentheses
  percentage rate of increase, 448–450
  using in formulas, 450
parenthetical references, 245
Paste command, 47, 106
Paste Options gallery, 106–107, 397–398
Paste Special, 452–454
Paste Special dialog box, linking files, 904–905
pasting
  definition, 105
  Excel charts into PowerPoint, 900–901
  Excel charts into Word, 899–900
  SmartArt graphics into workbooks, 901–902
  tables (Word) into workbooks, 893–894
paths, definition, 12, 75
PC settings, 26–28
PDF Reflow, 251–253
PDFs (Portable Document Format), 89
  creating (PowerPoint Online), 736
  creating from Word Online, 139
  exporting queries to, Access Web App, 585–586
  printing single forms, 514
  printing single forms in, 649
percent for new value, definition, 451
Percent Style, formatting cells, 341–342
percentages
  calculating, 451
    formulas (cell content), 340
    rate of increase, 448–450
  rate of increase, definition, 448
permanent positions, 207
permissions, definition, 811
personal folders, 45
personalizing Start screen, 42–44
Picture Effects, 791
picture elements (pixels), definition, 312
PICTURE TOOLS, 97–99, 726
pictures. *See also* **graphics; images**
  alignment guides, 98
  applying styles, 130
  coloring, 263–264
  cropping, 261–263
  documents
    artistic effects, 130–131

definition, 320
summary sheets, 402
speaker's notes (presentations)
adding, 723
printing, 733–734
Speakers icon, 8
specifying criteria, queries, 580–584
**specifying numeric criteria in queries,
588–593**
spell check, worksheets, 334–335
spelling
checking, 79–80
documents, 206–209
Spelling pane, checking spelling, 79–80
spin boxes, 128
split button, definition, 14, 106, 720
Split command, 387
**splitting worksheet windows into panes,
387**
spreadsheets. *See* **worksheets**
Stacked layout format, definition, 657
Start charm, 25
Start screen
displaying, 19
moving between Desktop and, 23–24
personalizing, 42–44
Windows 8, 7
Start search
finding desktop apps, 75–77
searching for apps, 9
starting desktop apps, 75–77
Start tip, definition, 23
starting
desktop apps with Start search, 75–77
Mail Merges (Word), 909–910
programs, 38–42
Statistical functions, definition, 371
**statistics, calculating in queries,
602–605**
status bar, 77
storage
cloud, 10, 83
devices, creating folders on, 10–12
files, 42
hard disk drives, 10
locations, 83
OneDrive, 10, 83
structure, changing in tables, 500–510
adding a second table to a database,
503–505
adjusting column widths, 505–506
deleting a table field, 500–501
field size/descriptions, 501–502
printing tables, 506–510
viewing the primary key, 502–503
structure (field design), definition, 493
style guides, 239
styles
applying to pictures, 726
definition, 82, 726
font, formatting text, 101–103
videos in presentations, 845

subdatasheets
definition, 570
displaying records, 569–570
subsets
definition, 649
records, 574
SUM function, 373–374, 895
constructing formulas, 315–316
queries, 602–604
**summary and analysis presentations,
creating (PowerPoint Online), 864–865**
summary sheets, definition, 402
suppressed first page numbers, 241
Switch/Row Column command, 322
switcher. *See* **app switcher**
symbols
arithmetic operators, 337
bulleted lists, 149
font formatting, 266–267
synchronization, definition, 83
syncing, definition, 83
system tray, definition, 8

T

tab color, worksheets, 393–394
Tab order, definition, 646
tab stops
modifying, 152–153
setting, 150–151
table relationships
creating, 564–571
*displaying subdatasheet records,
569–570*
*printing and saving relationship reports,
569*
*selecting tables and common fields,
564–567*
setting relationship options, 567–568
testing cascade options, 570–571
one-to-many, creating, 589–591
viewing, 667–668
Table tool, creating tables, 526–527
tables
filtering, Excel Online, 390–391
functions, Excel Online, 390–391
importing spreadsheets as, 588–589
sorting, Excel Online, 390–391
tables (Access)
adding records to, 495–497, 646–647,
908–909
building by entering records in multiple-
items forms, 522–524
changing structure, 500–510
*adding a second table to a database,
503–505*
adjusting column widths, 505–506
deleting a table field, 500–501
field size/descriptions, 501–502
printing tables, 506–510
viewing the primary key, 502–503
creating, Table tool, 526–527

creating in databases, 490–500
adding additional records to tables, 497
adding records to tables, 495–497
*assigning data types and field names,
493–495*
blank desktop databases, 490–492
*importing data from Excel workbooks,
497–500*
*renaming fields and changing data
types, 495*
creating queries based on more than one
table, 596–597
definition, 489
deleting records from, 648
entering records in, 527–529
exporting to Excel spreadsheets, Access
Web App, 518–519, 532–533
exporting to RTF files, 906–907
importing Excel workbook data into,
497–500
printing, 506–510, 529–531
relationships, viewing, 643–644
renaming, 564, 643–644
renaming/deleting, 497
sorting records, 572–574
tables (Excel)
converting to a range of data, 386
creating, 383–384, 890–891
filtering, 385–386, 390–391
inserting rows into, 891–892
sorting, 384–385, 390–391, 890–891
tables (PowerPoint)
creating, 851–856
modifying, 851–856, 854–255
styles, definition, 854
tables (Word)
copying/pasting into workbooks, 893–894
converting into text, 192
converting text into, 190
creating, 181
borders, 189–190
formatting, 185–190
merging cells, 187
Spacing After, 188–189
typing text into, 182–184
formatting, 892–893
gridlines, 190
inserting into document, 205–206
presenting online, 191–192
Tables and Related Views category, 525
tabs, 77, 95
Backstage, definition, 84
contextual, 12
definition, 87
Info, definition, 84
names, 12
tags, 36
definition, 88
Taskbar, 8
pinning programs to, 9
taskbar, definition, 73
taskbar button, progress bar, 32